Thanks to everyone's support, the *Naruto* anime will also celebrate its tenth anniversary next year. I am eternally indebted to everyone on the animation staff! And I also have nothing but words of gratitude to all you readers who have continuously supported *Naruto!* ...No, really, I'm dead serious!!

岸本斉史

—Masashi Kishimoto, 2011

Author/artist Masashi Kishimoto was born in 1974 in rural Okayama Prefecture, Japan. After spending time in art college, he won the Hop Step Award for new manga artists with his manga **Karakuri** (Mechanism). Kishimoto decided to base his next story on traditional Japanese culture. His first version of **Naruto**, drawn in 1997, was a one-shot story about fox spirits; his final version, which debuted in **Weekly Shonen Jump** in 1999, quickly became the most popular ninja manga in Japan.

NARUTO

3-in-1 Edition
Volume 20
SHONEN JUMP Manga Omnibus Edition
A compilation of the graphic novel volumes 58–60

STORY AND ART BY MASASHI KISHIMOTO

Translation/Mari Morimoto
English Adaptation/Joel Enos
Touch-up Art & Lettering/Inori Fukuda Trant, Sabrina Heep
Design/Sam Elzway (Original Series and Omnibus Edition)
Editor/Megan Bates (Manga Edition)
Managing Editor/Erica Yee (Omnibus Edition)

Printed in the U.S.A.

Published by VIZ Media, LLC
P.O. Box 77010
San Francisco, CA 94107

10 9 8 7 6 5 4 3 2 1
Omnibus edition first printing, October 2017

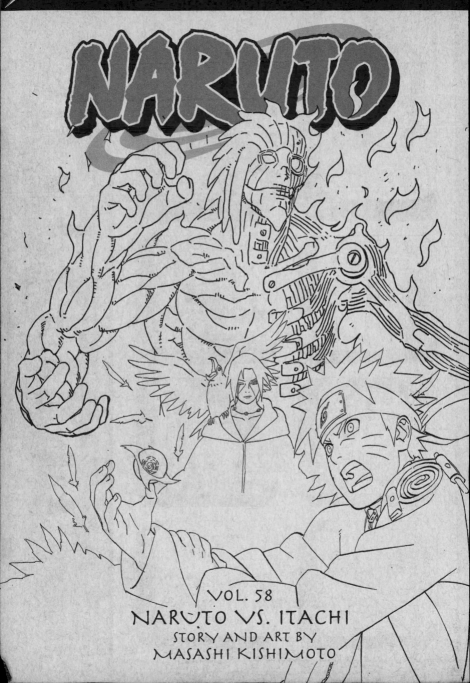

SHONEN JUMP MANGA EDITION

NARUTO

VOL. 58

NARUTO VS. ITACHI

STORY AND ART BY
MASASHI KISHIMOTO

CHARACTERS

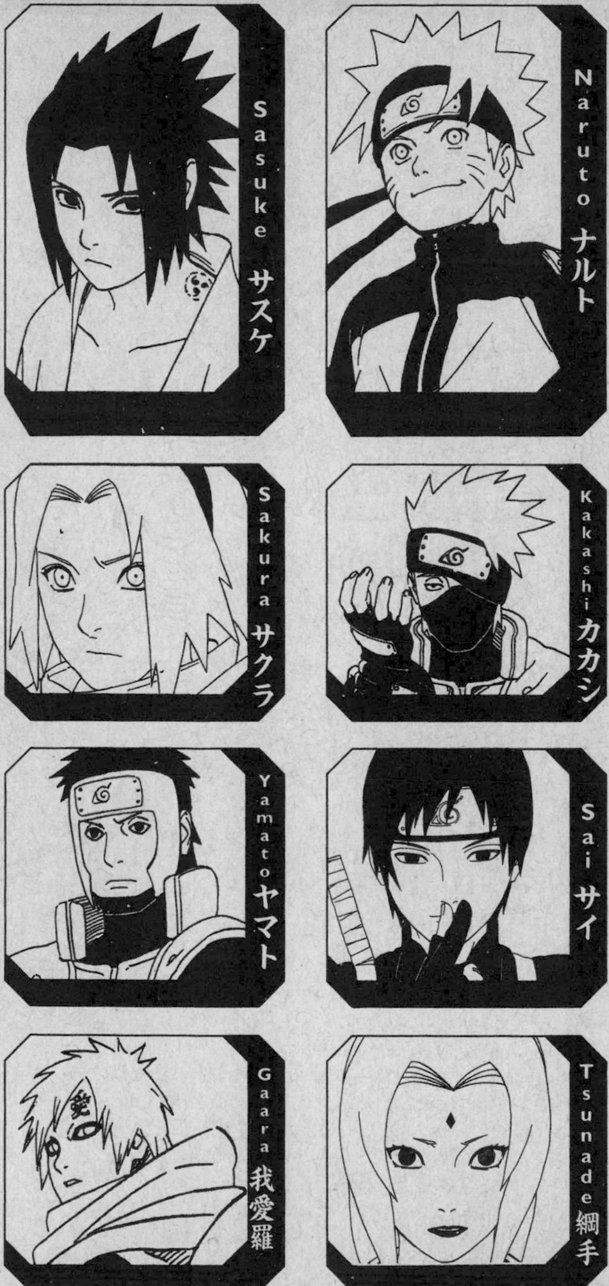
Naruto ナルト
Sasuke サスケ
Kakashi カカシ
Sakura サクラ
Sai サイ
Yamato ヤマト
Tsunade 綱手
Gaara 我愛羅

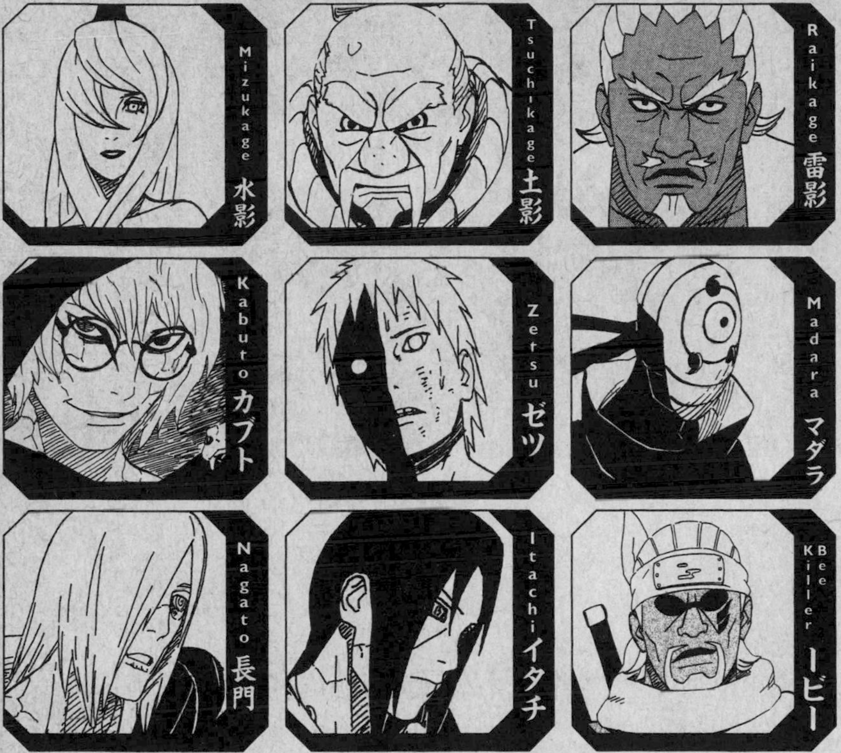
Raikage 雷影
Tsuchikage 土影
Mizukage 水影
Madara マダラ
Zetsu ゼツ
Kabuto カブト
Killer Bee ービー
Itachi イタチ
Nagato 長門

THE STORY SO FAR...

Naruto, the biggest troublemaker at the Ninja Academy in the Village of Konohagakure, finally becomes a ninja along with his classmates Sasuke and Sakura. They grow and mature through countless trials and battles. However, Sasuke, unable to give up his quest for vengeance, leaves Konohagakure to seek out power from the renegade ninja Orochimaru.

Two years pass. Naruto grows up and engages in fierce battles against the Tailed Beast-targeting Akatsuki. Elsewhere, after winning the heroic battle against Itachi and learning his older brother's true intentions, Sasuke allies with the Akatsuki and sets out to destroy Konoha.

Upon Madara's declaration of war, the Five Kage put together an Allied Shinobi Force. The Fourth Great Ninja War against the Akatsuki begins. After Naruto learns that the war was launched with him as the target, he and Bee break out of the training grounds. They then dissuade Tsunade and Raikage, who had come to stop them, and rush towards the battlefield!!

NARUTO

VOL. 58
NARUTO VS. ITACHI

CONTENTS

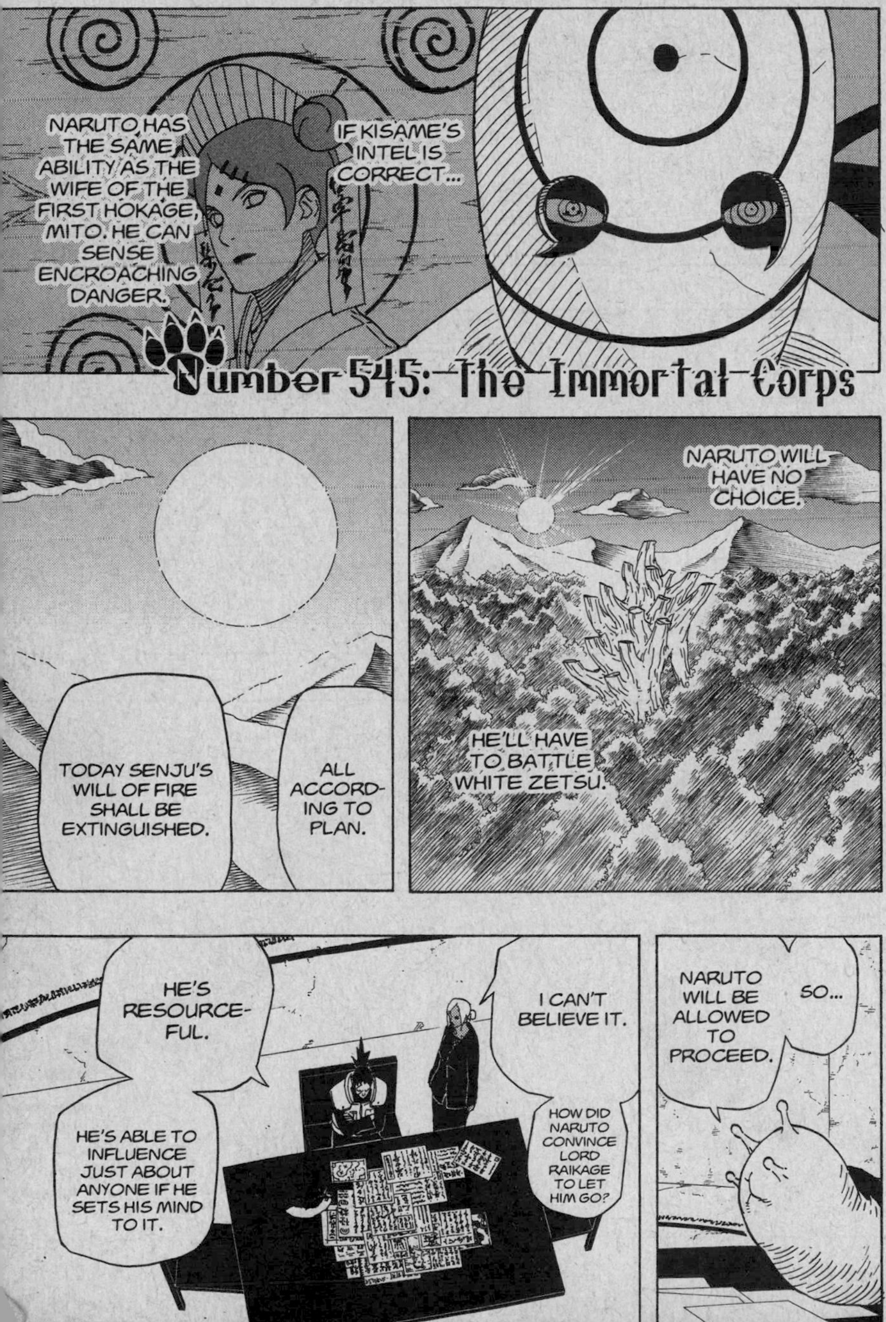

IF KISAME'S INTEL IS CORRECT...
NARUTO HAS THE SAME ABILITY AS THE WIFE OF THE FIRST HOKAGE, MITO. HE CAN SENSE ENCROACHING DANGER.
Number 545: The Immortal Corps
NARUTO WILL HAVE NO CHOICE.
HE'LL HAVE TO BATTLE WHITE ZETSU.
ALL ACCORD-ING TO PLAN.
TODAY SENJU'S WILL OF FIRE SHALL BE EXTINGUISHED.
SO...
NARUTO WILL BE ALLOWED TO PROCEED.
I CAN'T BELIEVE IT.
HOW DID NARUTO CONVINCE LORD RAIKAGE TO LET HIM GO?
HE'S RESOURCE-FUL.
HE'S ABLE TO INFLUENCE JUST ABOUT ANYONE IF HE SETS HIS MIND TO IT.

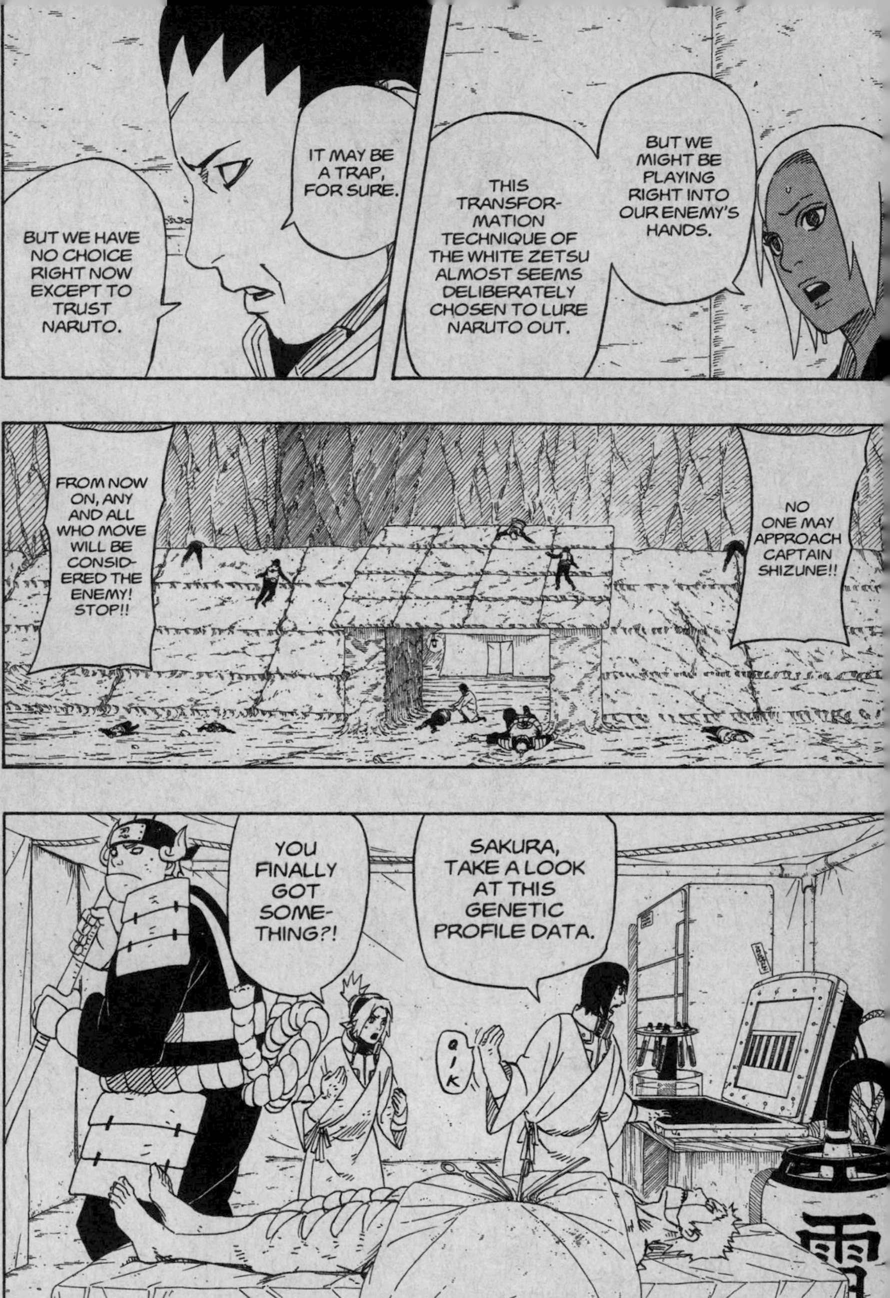
BUT WE MIGHT BE PLAYING RIGHT INTO OUR ENEMY'S HANDS.
THIS TRANSFORMATION TECHNIQUE OF THE WHITE ZETSU ALMOST SEEMS DELIBERATELY CHOSEN TO LURE NARUTO OUT.
IT MAY BE A TRAP, FOR SURE.
BUT WE HAVE NO CHOICE RIGHT NOW EXCEPT TO TRUST NARUTO.
NO ONE MAY APPROACH CAPTAIN SHIZUNE!!
FROM NOW ON, ANY AND ALL WHO MOVE WILL BE CONSIDERED THE ENEMY! STOP!!
SAKURA, TAKE A LOOK AT THIS GENETIC PROFILE DATA.
QIK
YOU FINALLY GOT SOMETHING?!

READ THIS WAY

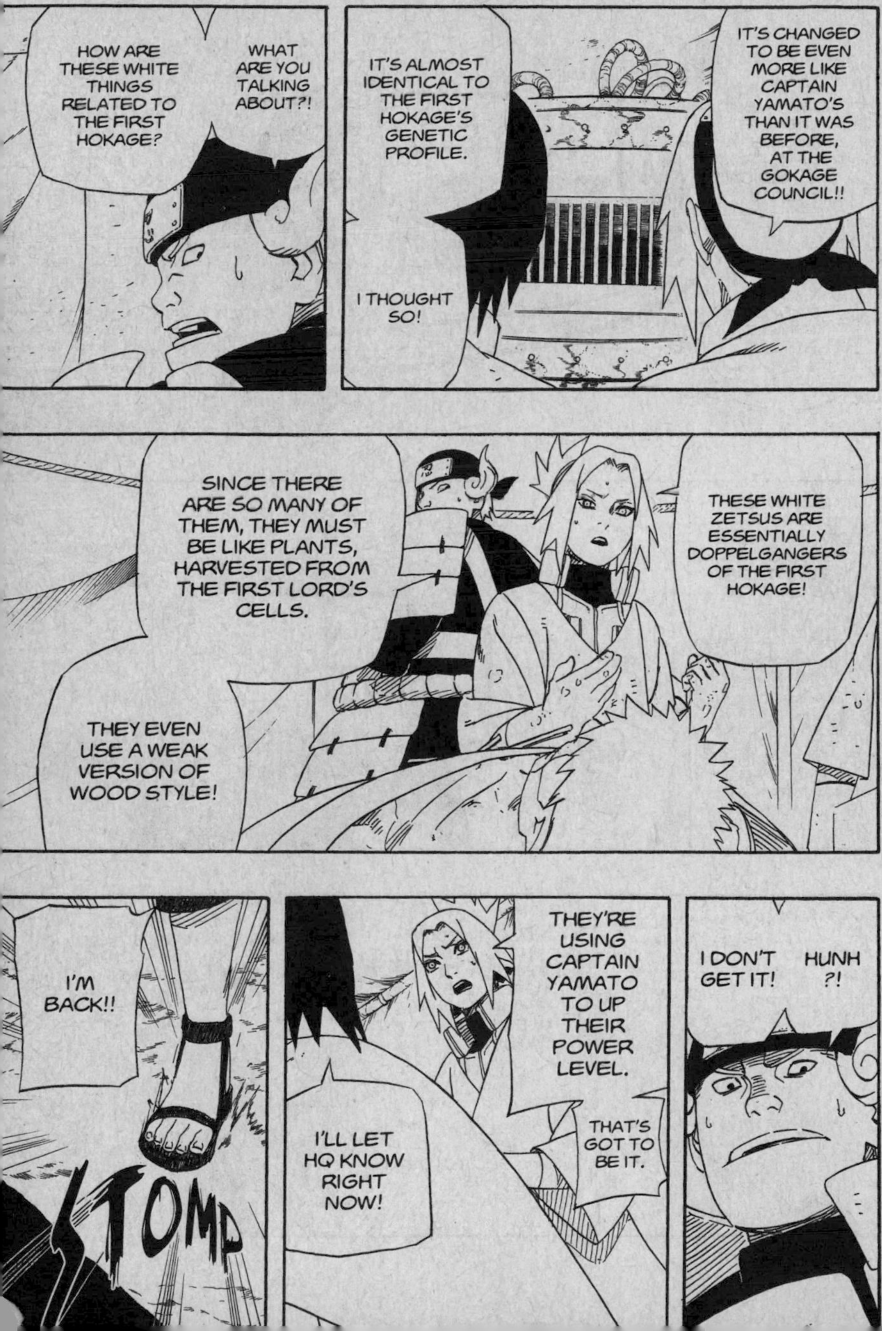
IT'S CHANGED TO BE EVEN MORE LIKE CAPTAIN YAMATO'S THAN IT WAS BEFORE, AT THE GOKAGE COUNCIL!!
IT'S ALMOST IDENTICAL TO THE FIRST HOKAGE'S GENETIC PROFILE.
I THOUGHT SO!
WHAT ARE YOU TALKING ABOUT?!
HOW ARE THESE WHITE THINGS RELATED TO THE FIRST HOKAGE?
THESE WHITE ZETSUS ARE ESSENTIALLY DOPPELGANGERS OF THE FIRST HOKAGE!
SINCE THERE ARE SO MANY OF THEM, THEY MUST BE LIKE PLANTS, HARVESTED FROM THE FIRST LORD'S CELLS.
THEY EVEN USE A WEAK VERSION OF WOOD STYLE!
HUNH ?!
I DON'T GET IT!
THEY'RE USING CAPTAIN YAMATO TO UP THEIR POWER LEVEL.
THAT'S GOT TO BE IT.
I'LL LET HQ KNOW RIGHT NOW!
I'M BACK!!
STOMP

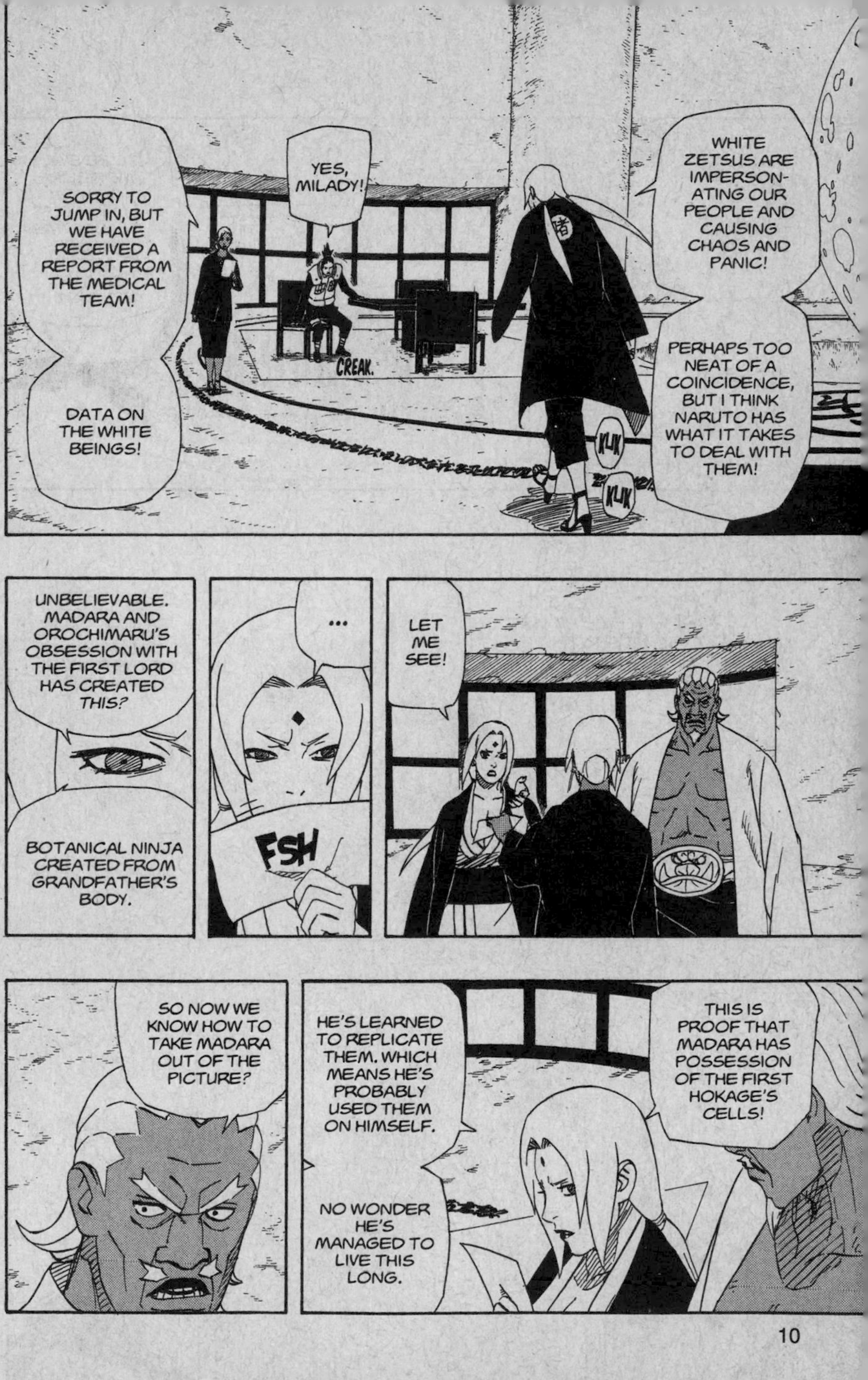
WHITE ZETSUS ARE IMPERSONATING OUR PEOPLE AND CAUSING CHAOS AND PANIC!
PERHAPS TOO NEAT OF A COINCIDENCE, BUT I THINK NARUTO HAS WHAT IT TAKES TO DEAL WITH THEM!
KLIK
KLIK
YES, MILADY!
CREAK.
SORRY TO JUMP IN, BUT WE HAVE RECEIVED A REPORT FROM THE MEDICAL TEAM!
DATA ON THE WHITE BEINGS!
LET ME SEE!
...
FSH
UNBELIEVABLE. MADARA AND OROCHIMARU'S OBSESSION WITH THE FIRST LORD HAS CREATED THIS?
BOTANICAL NINJA CREATED FROM GRANDFATHER'S BODY.
THIS IS PROOF THAT MADARA HAS POSSESSION OF THE FIRST HOKAGE'S CELLS!
HE'S LEARNED TO REPLICATE THEM. WHICH MEANS HE'S PROBABLY USED THEM ON HIMSELF.
NO WONDER HE'S MANAGED TO LIVE THIS LONG.
SO NOW WE KNOW HOW TO TAKE MADARA OUT OF THE PICTURE?

READ THIS WAY

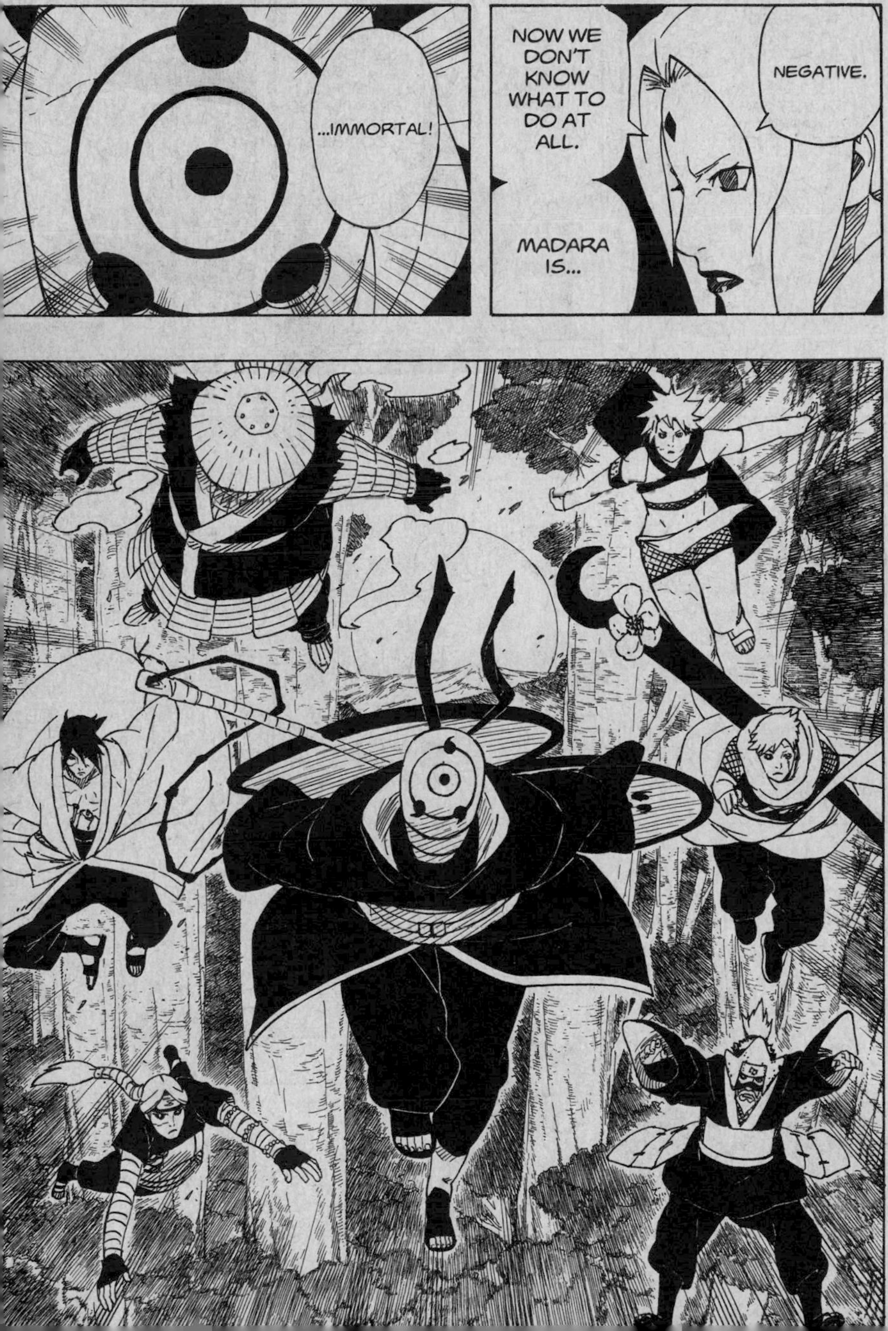
NEGATIVE.
NOW WE DON'T KNOW WHAT TO DO AT ALL.
MADARA IS...
...IMMORTAL!

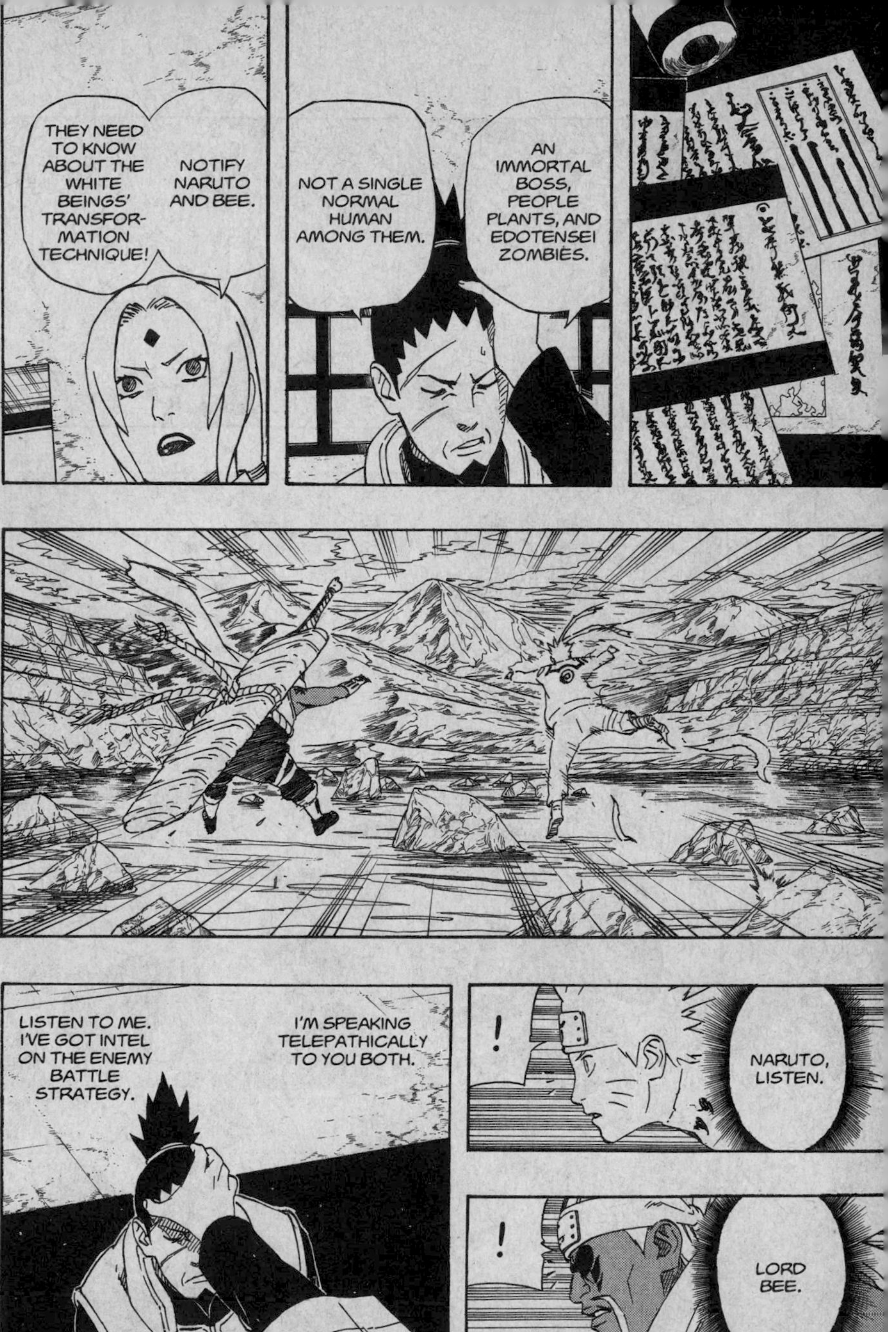
AN IMMORTAL BOSS, PEOPLE PLANTS, AND EDOTENSEI ZOMBIES.
NOT A SINGLE NORMAL HUMAN AMONG THEM.
NOTIFY NARUTO AND BEE.
THEY NEED TO KNOW ABOUT THE WHITE BEINGS' TRANSFORMATION TECHNIQUE!
!
NARUTO, LISTEN.
!
LORD BEE.
I'M SPEAKING TELEPATHICALLY TO YOU BOTH.
LISTEN TO ME. I'VE GOT INTEL ON THE ENEMY BATTLE STRATEGY.

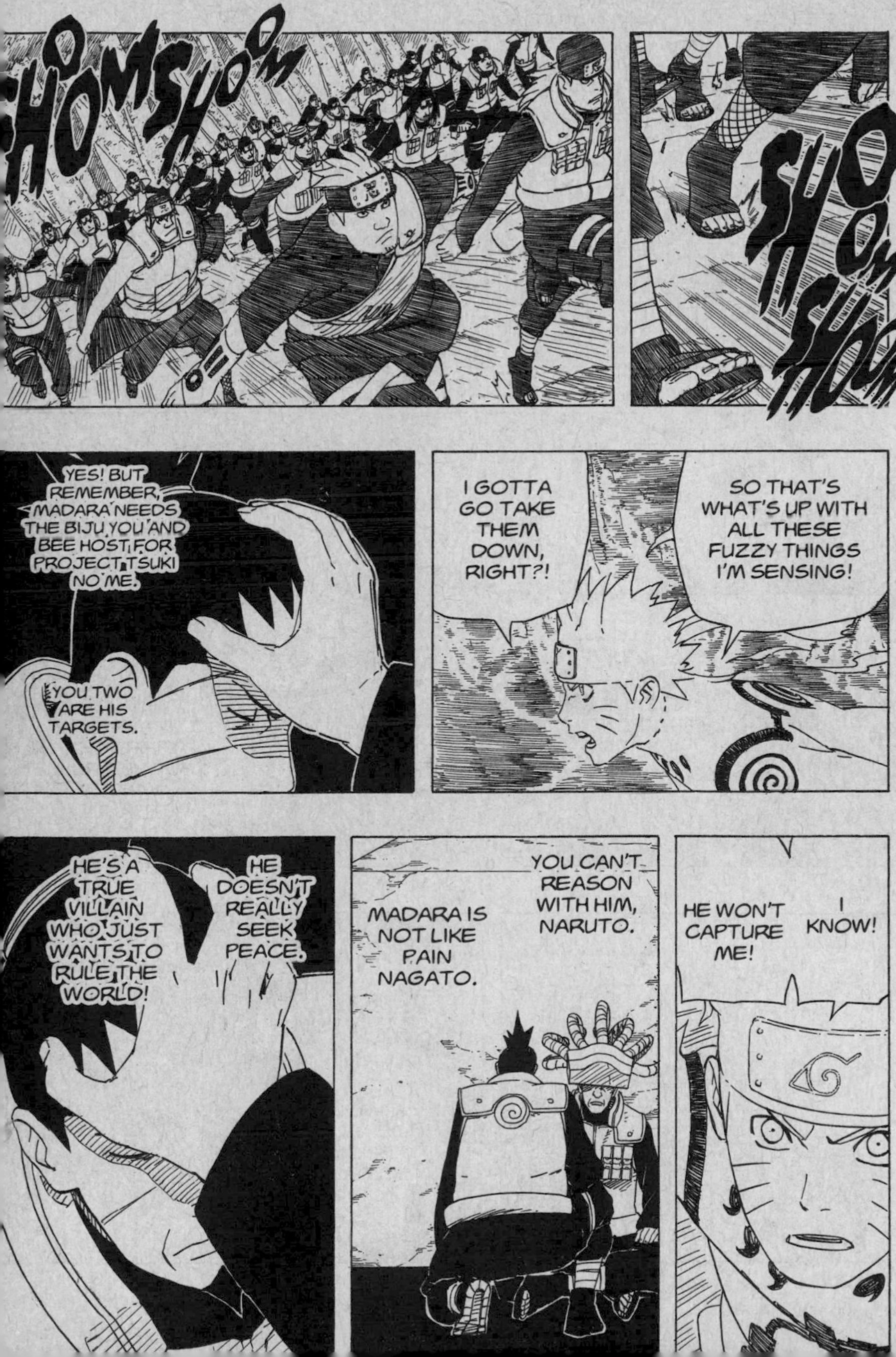
SHOOM SHOOM
SHOOM SHOOM
SO THAT'S WHAT'S UP WITH ALL THESE FUZZY THINGS I'M SENSING!
I GOTTA GO TAKE THEM DOWN, RIGHT?!
YES! BUT REMEMBER, MADARA NEEDS THE BIJU YOU AND BEE HOST FOR PROJECT TSUKI NO ME.
YOU TWO ARE HIS TARGETS.
I KNOW!
HE WON'T CAPTURE ME!
YOU CAN'T REASON WITH HIM, NARUTO.
MADARA IS NOT LIKE PAIN NAGATO.
HE DOESN'T REALLY SEEK PEACE.
HE'S A TRUE VILLAIN WHO JUST WANTS TO RULE THE WORLD!

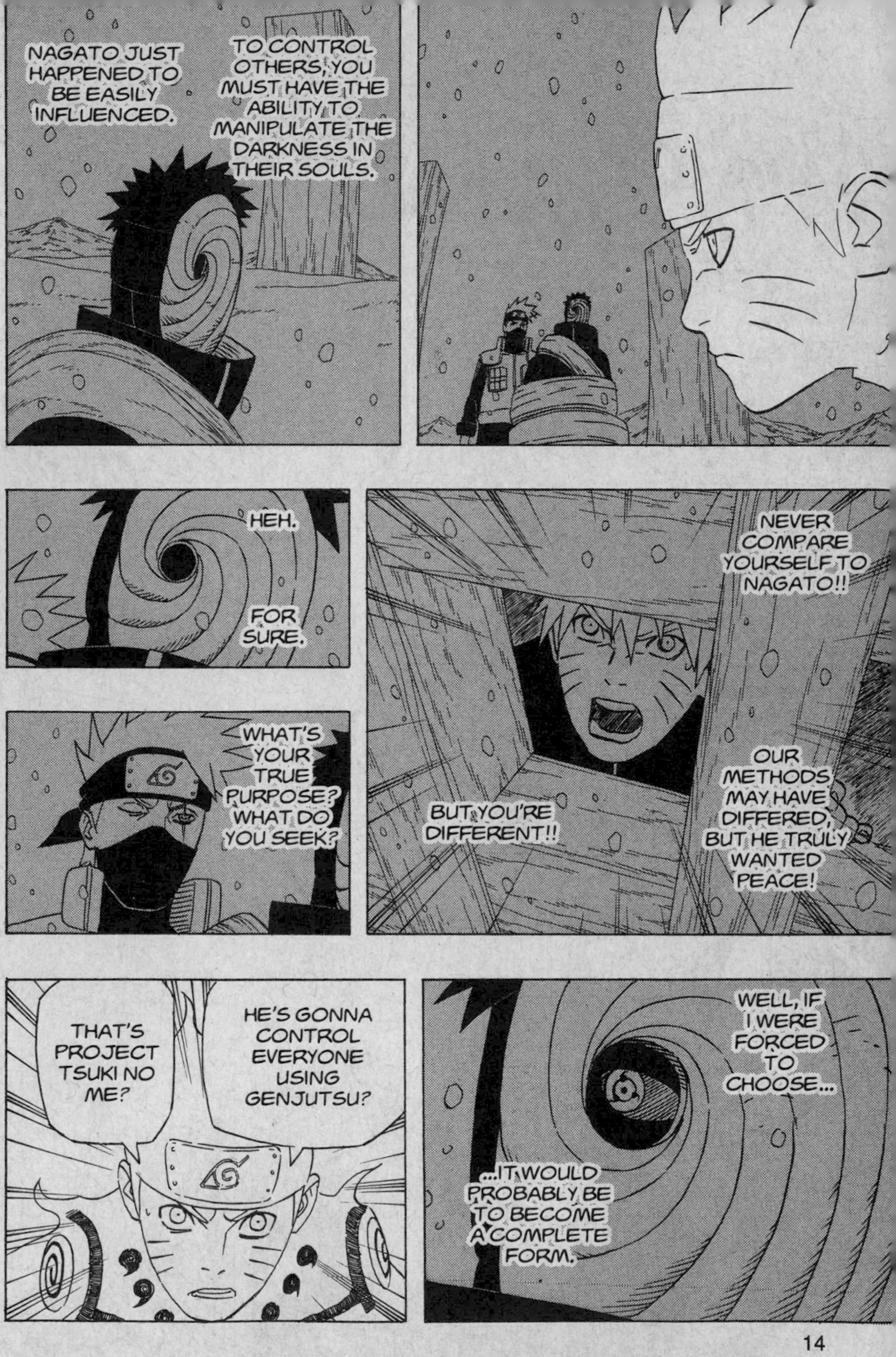
TO CONTROL OTHERS, YOU MUST HAVE THE ABILITY TO MANIPULATE THE DARKNESS IN THEIR SOULS.
NAGATO JUST HAPPENED TO BE EASILY INFLUENCED.
NEVER COMPARE YOURSELF TO NAGATO!!
OUR METHODS MAY HAVE DIFFERED, BUT HE TRULY WANTED PEACE!
BUT YOU'RE DIFFERENT!!
HEH.
FOR SURE.
WHAT'S YOUR TRUE PURPOSE? WHAT DO YOU SEEK?
WELL, IF I WERE FORCED TO CHOOSE...
...IT WOULD PROBABLY BE TO BECOME A COMPLETE FORM.
HE'S GONNA CONTROL EVERYONE USING GENJUTSU?
THAT'S PROJECT TSUKI NO ME?

READ THIS WAY

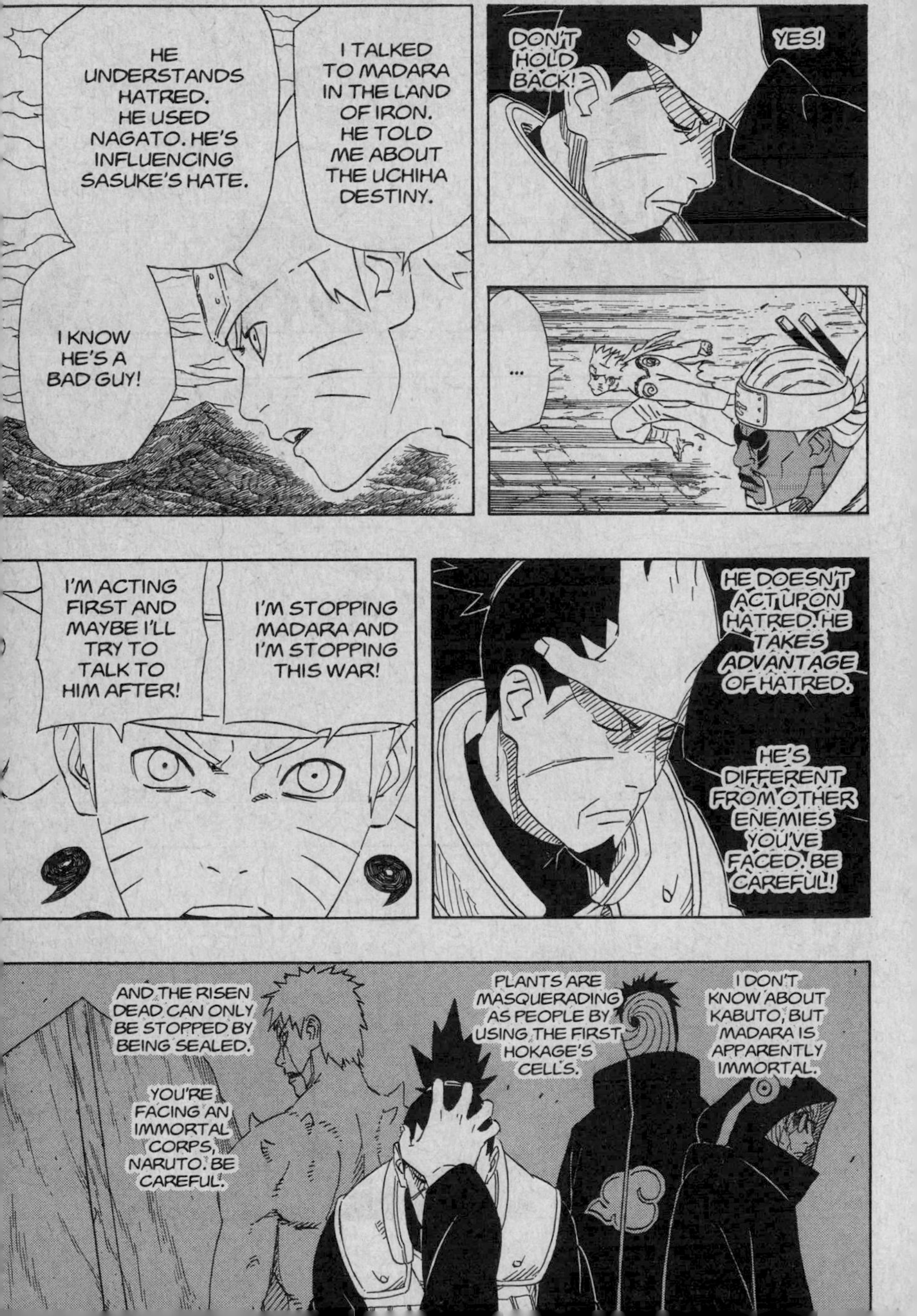
YES!
DON'T HOLD BACK!
...
I TALKED TO MADARA IN THE LAND OF IRON. HE TOLD ME ABOUT THE UCHIHA DESTINY.
HE UNDERSTANDS HATRED. HE USED NAGATO. HE'S INFLUENCING SASUKE'S HATE.
I KNOW HE'S A BAD GUY!
HE DOESN'T ACT UPON HATRED. HE TAKES ADVANTAGE OF HATRED.
HE'S DIFFERENT FROM OTHER ENEMIES YOU'VE FACED. BE CAREFUL!
I'M STOPPING MADARA AND I'M STOPPING THIS WAR!
I'M ACTING FIRST AND MAYBE I'LL TRY TO TALK TO HIM AFTER!
I DON'T KNOW ABOUT KABUTO, BUT MADARA IS APPARENTLY IMMORTAL.
PLANTS ARE MASQUERADING AS PEOPLE BY USING THE FIRST HOKAGE'S CELLS.
AND THE RISEN DEAD CAN ONLY BE STOPPED BY BEING SEALED.
YOU'RE FACING AN IMMORTAL CORPS, NARUTO. BE CAREFUL.

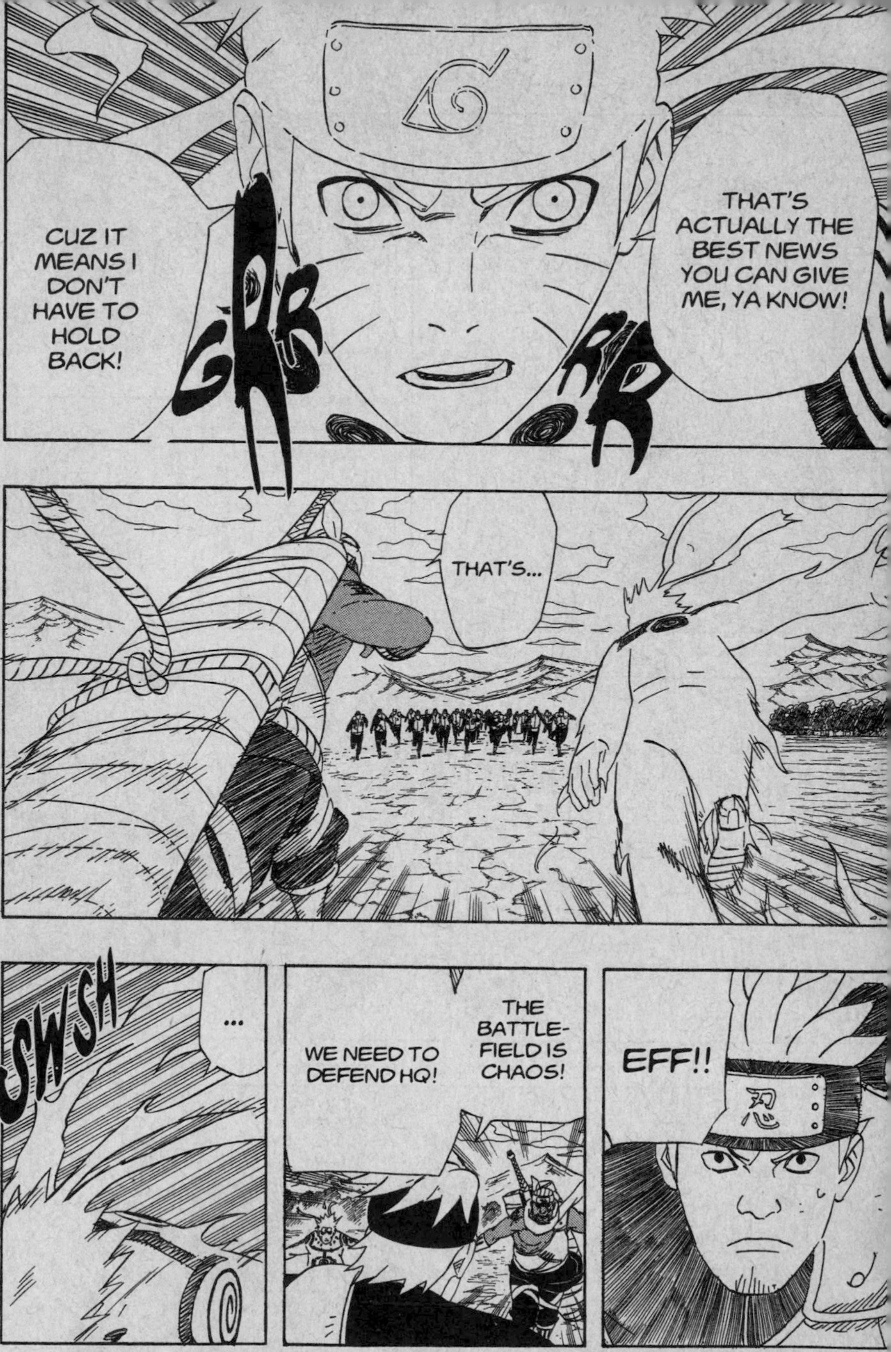
THAT'S ACTUALLY THE BEST NEWS YOU CAN GIVE ME, YA KNOW!
CUZ IT MEANS I DON'T HAVE TO HOLD BACK!
THAT'S...
EFF!!
THE BATTLE-FIELD IS CHAOS!
WE NEED TO DEFEND HQ!
...
SWSH

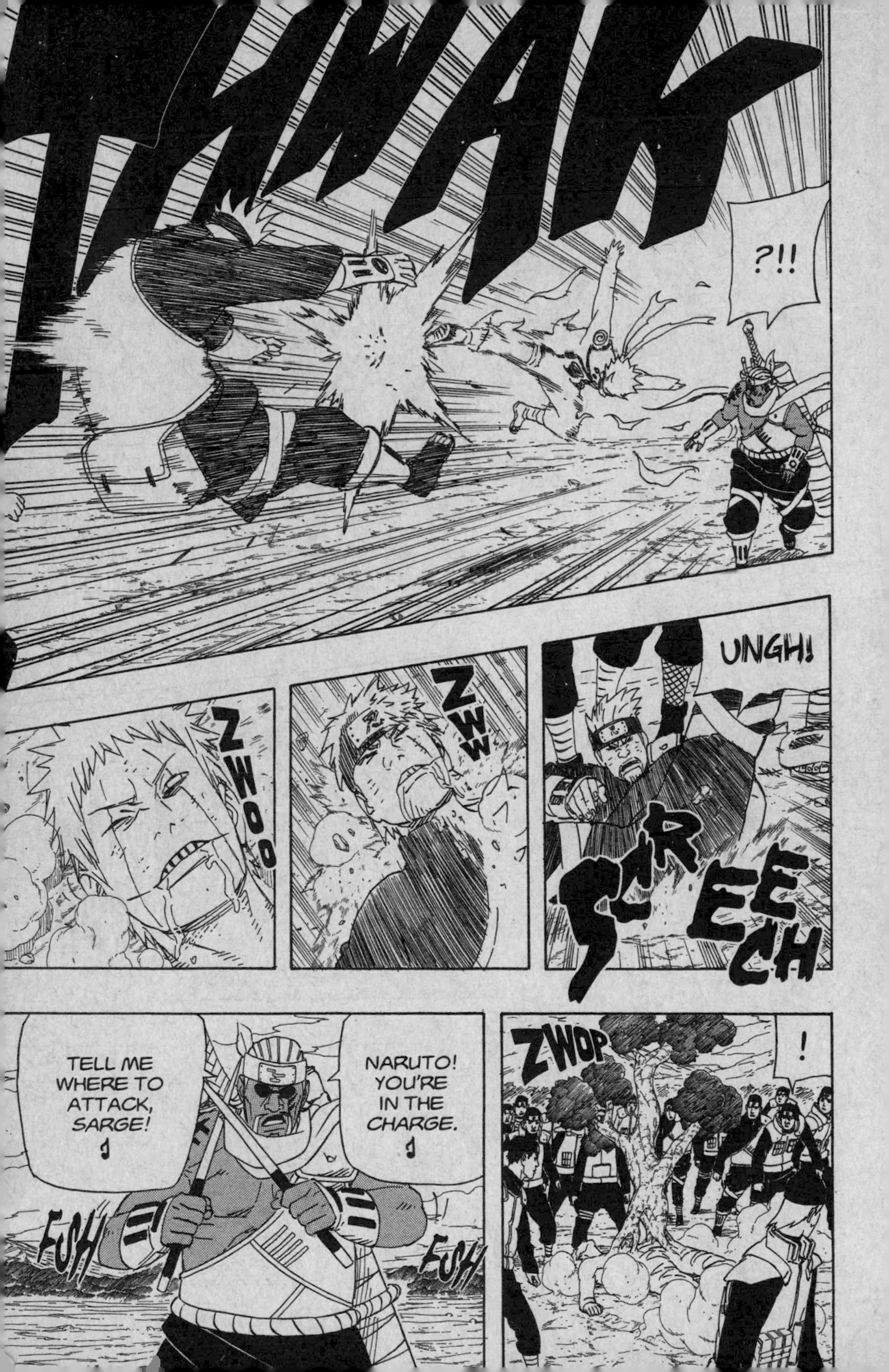
THWAK
?!!
UNGH!
SCREECH
ZWW
ZWOO
ZWOP
!
NARUTO! YOU'RE IN THE CHARGE. ♪
TELL ME WHERE TO ATTACK, SARGE! ♪
FSH
FSH

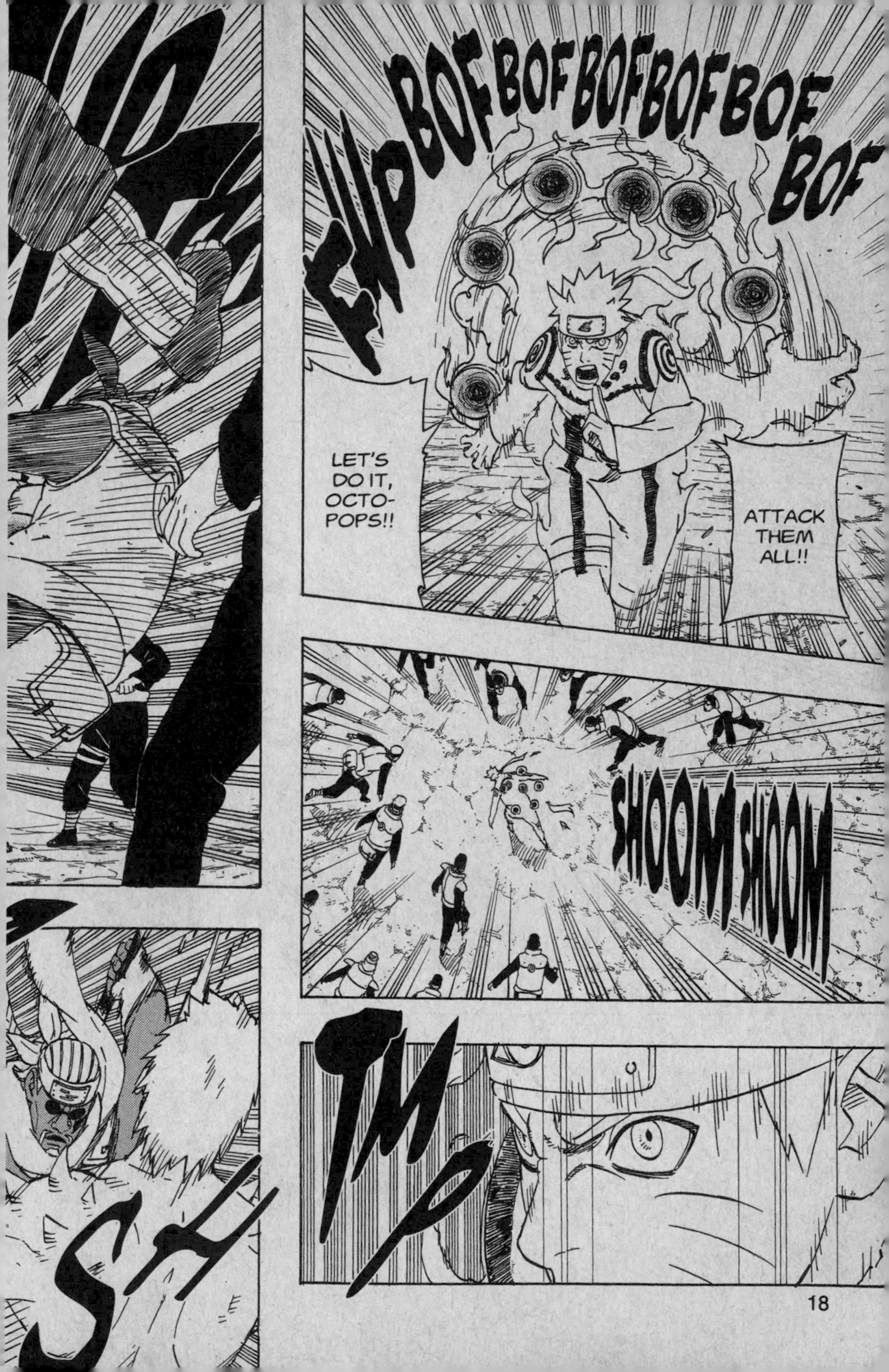
FWP BOF BOF BOF BOF BOF BOF
ATTACK THEM ALL!!
LET'S DO IT, OCTO-POPS!!
SHOOM SHOOM
TMP
SH

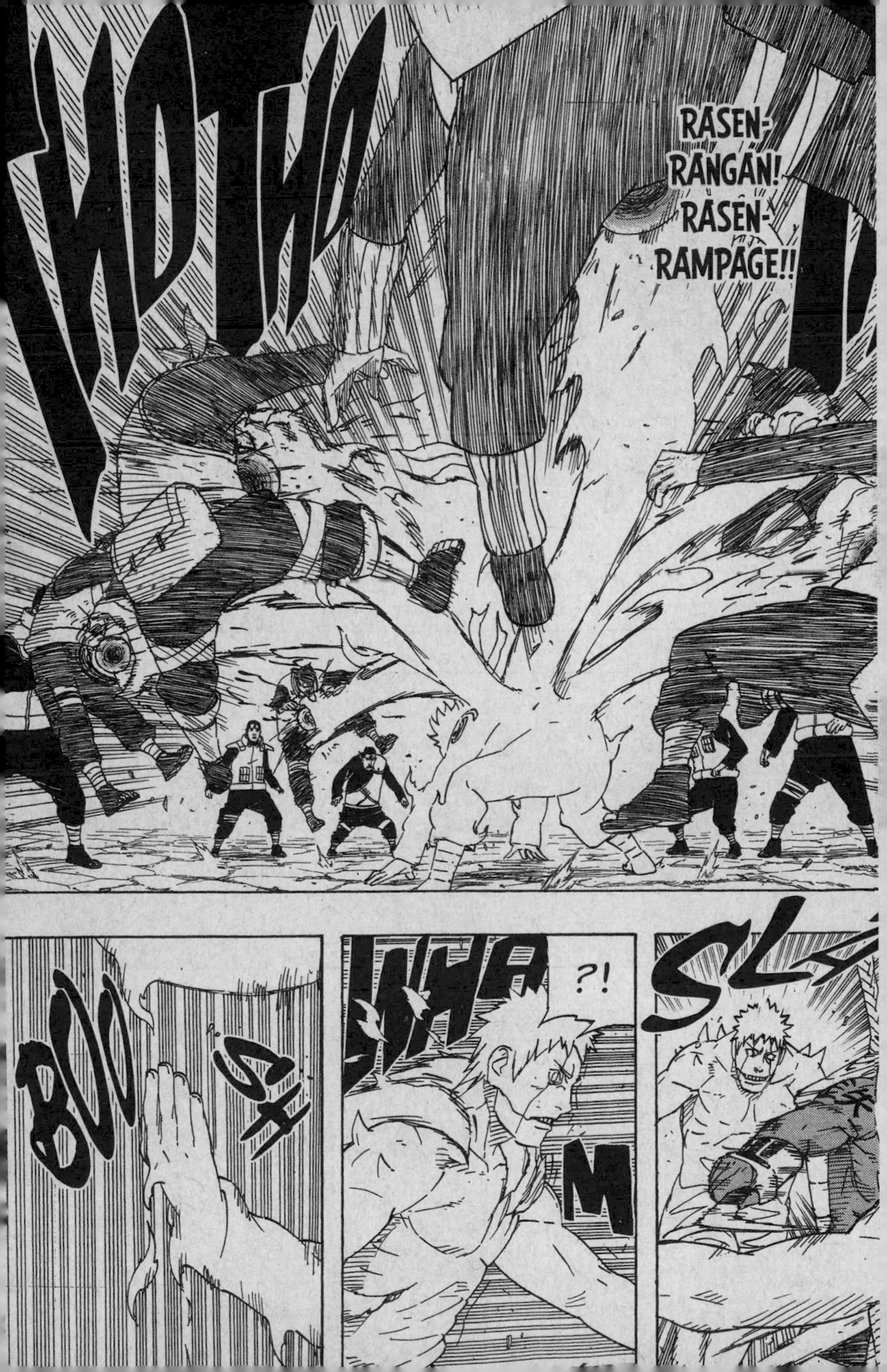
RASEN-RANGAN! RASEN-RAMPAGE!!
?!

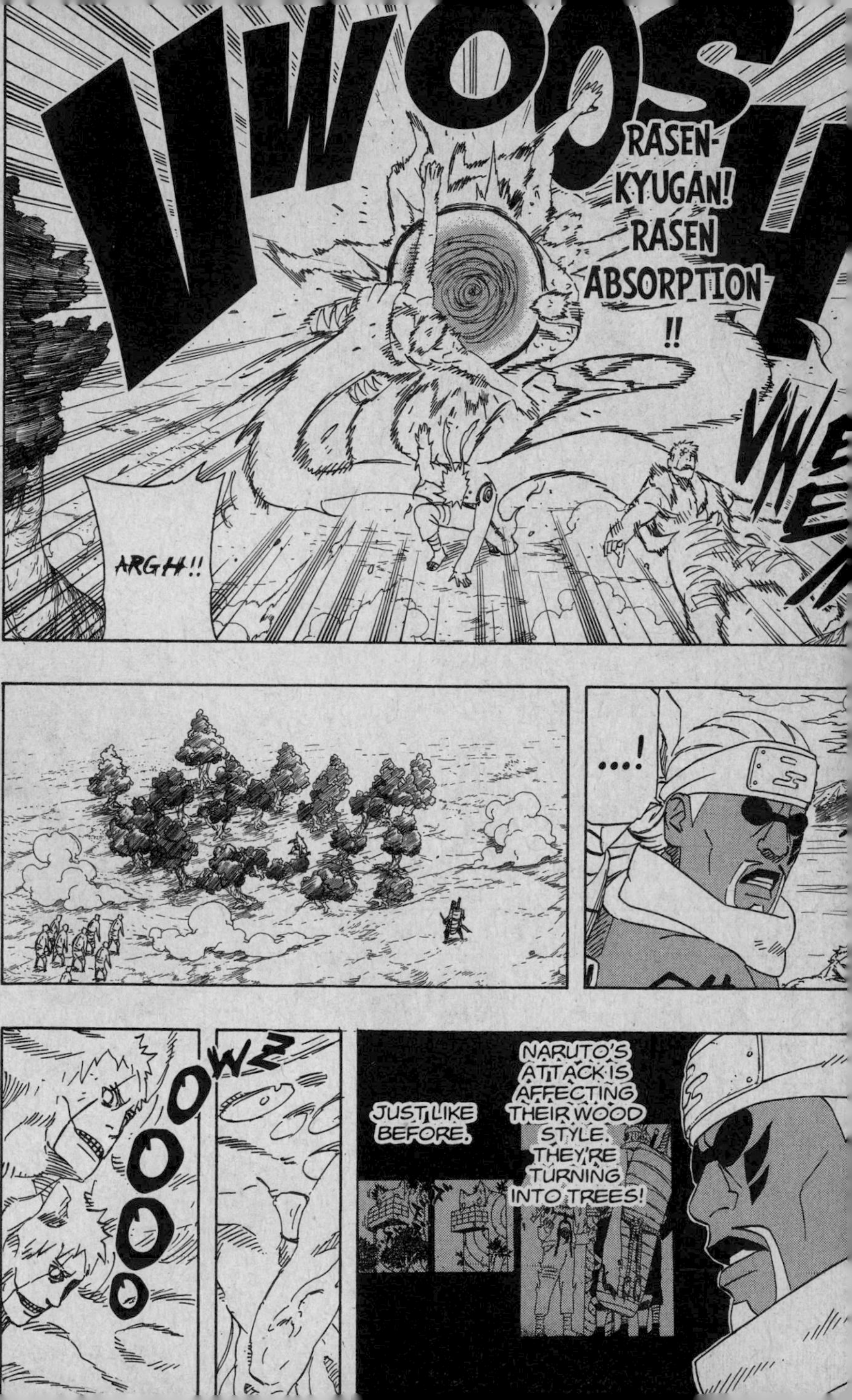
RASEN-KYUGAN! RASEN ABSORPTION !!
ARGH!!
...!
NARUTO'S ATTACK IS AFFECTING THEIR WOOD STYLE. THEY'RE TURNING INTO TREES!
JUST LIKE BEFORE.

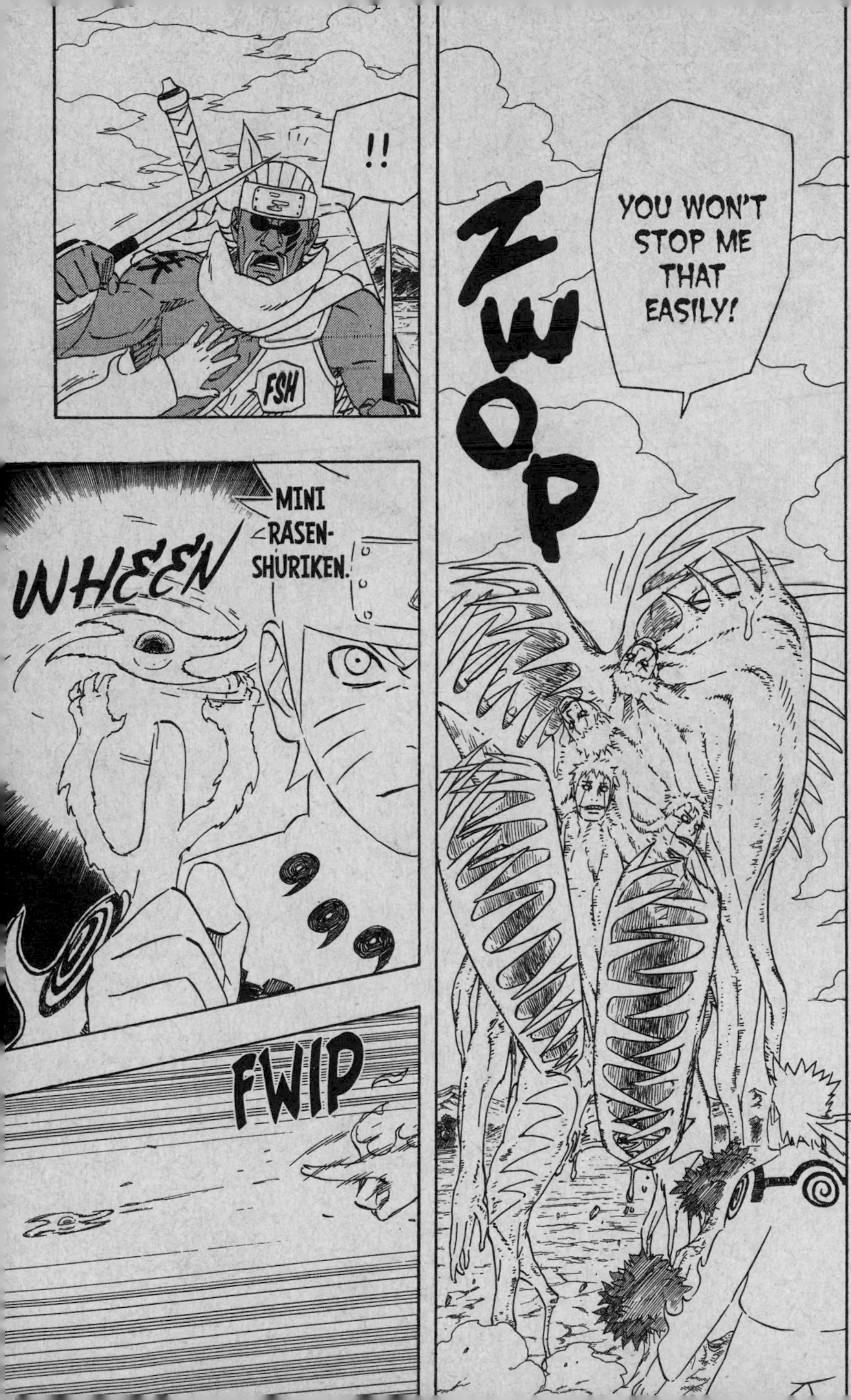
ZWOP
YOU WON'T STOP ME THAT EASILY!
!!
FSH
MINI RASEN-SHURIKEN.
WHEEN
FWIP

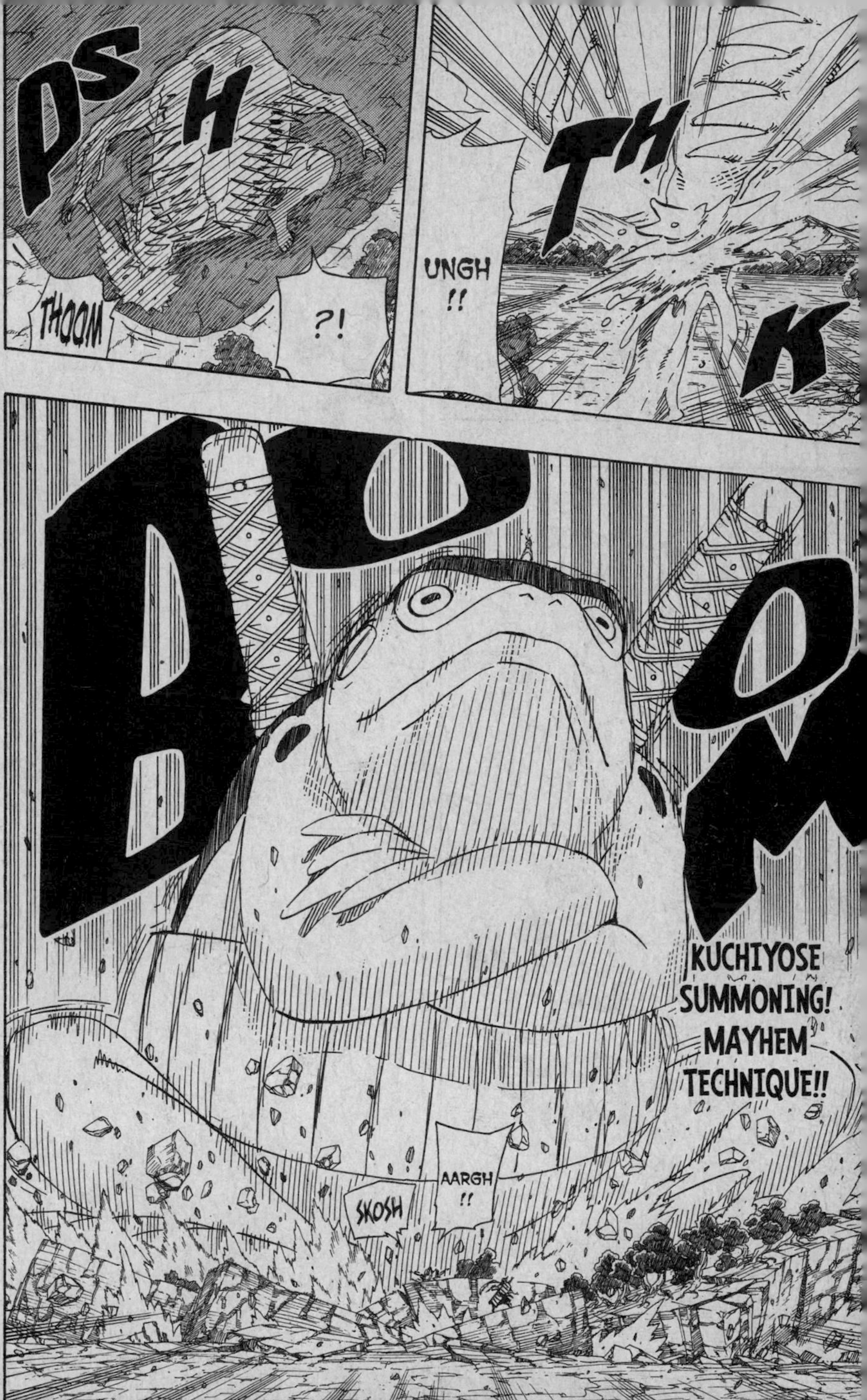

Th
UNGH !!
K
PSH
?!
THOOM
KUCHIYOSE SUMMONING! MAYHEM TECHNIQUE!!
AARGH !!
SKOSH

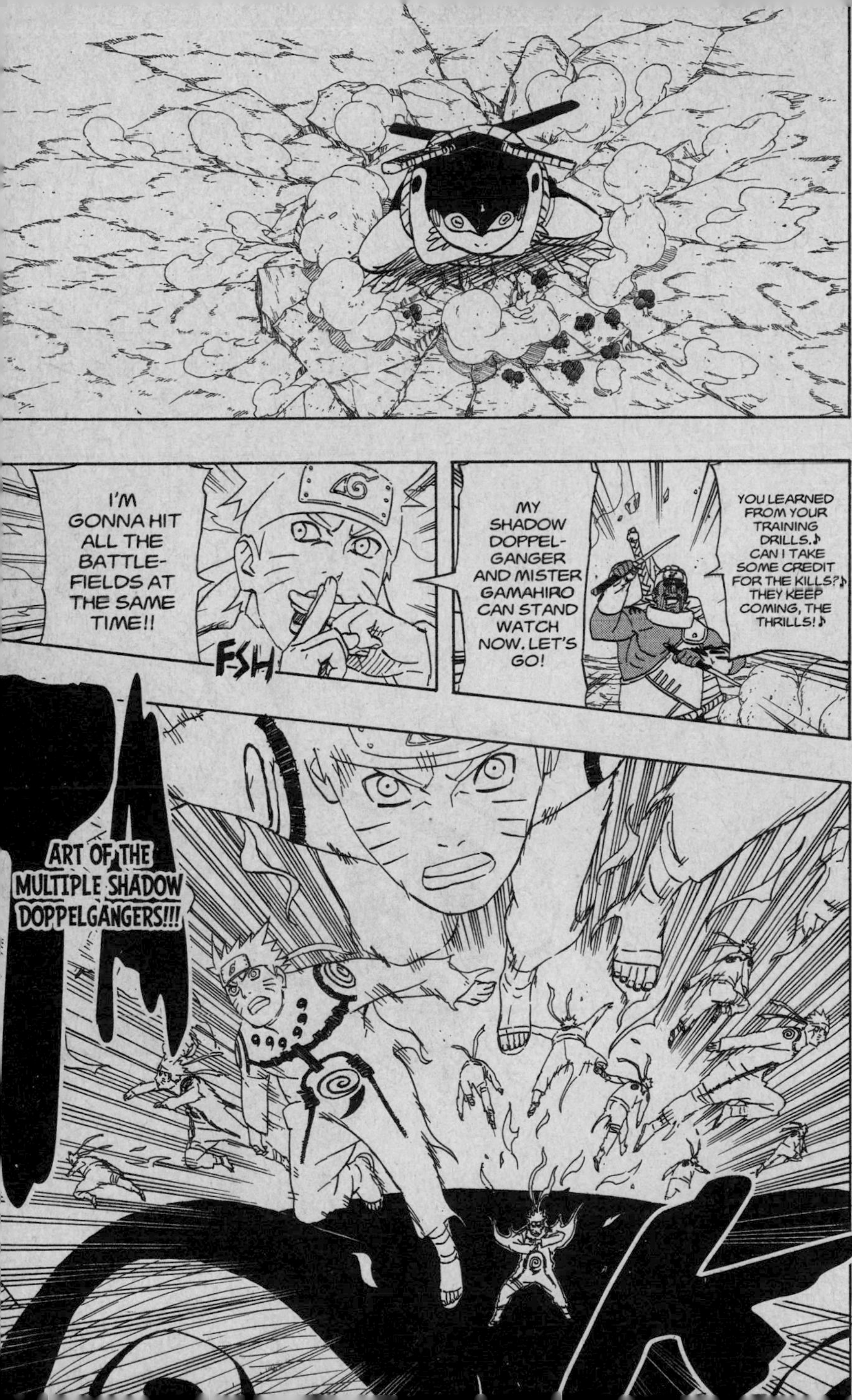
YOU LEARNED FROM YOUR TRAINING DRILLS.♪ CAN I TAKE SOME CREDIT FOR THE KILLS?♪ THEY KEEP COMING, THE THRILLS!♪
MY SHADOW DOPPEL-GANGER AND MISTER GAMAHIRO CAN STAND WATCH NOW. LET'S GO!
I'M GONNA HIT ALL THE BATTLE-FIELDS AT THE SAME TIME!!
FSH
ART OF THE MULTIPLE SHADOW DOPPELGANGERS!!!

Number 546: Kage Showdown!!

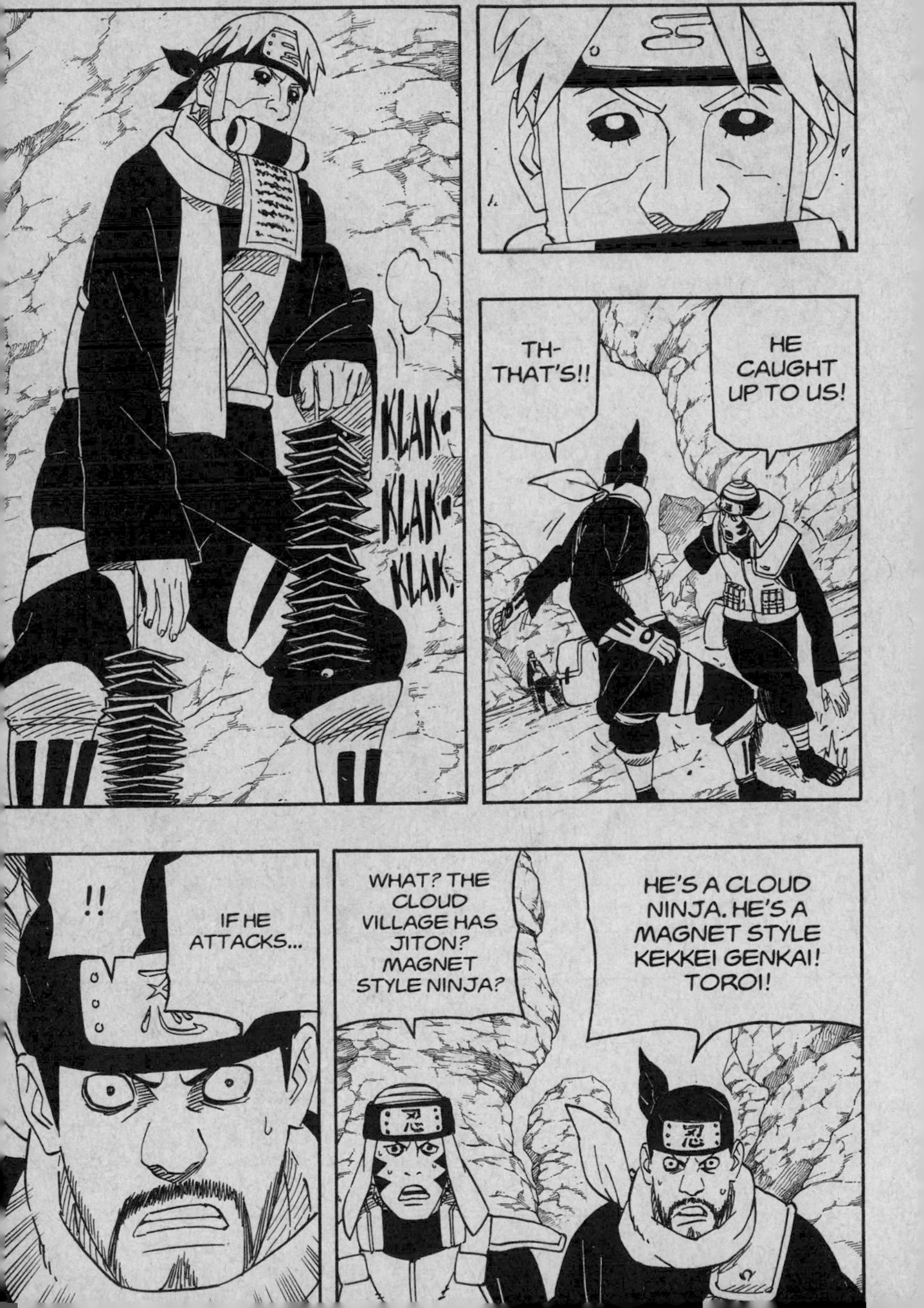
HE CAUGHT UP TO US!
TH- THAT'S!!
KLAK- KLAK- KLAK.
HE'S A CLOUD NINJA. HE'S A MAGNET STYLE KEKKEI GENKAI! TOROI!
WHAT? THE CLOUD VILLAGE HAS JITON? MAGNET STYLE NINJA?
!!
IF HE ATTACKS...

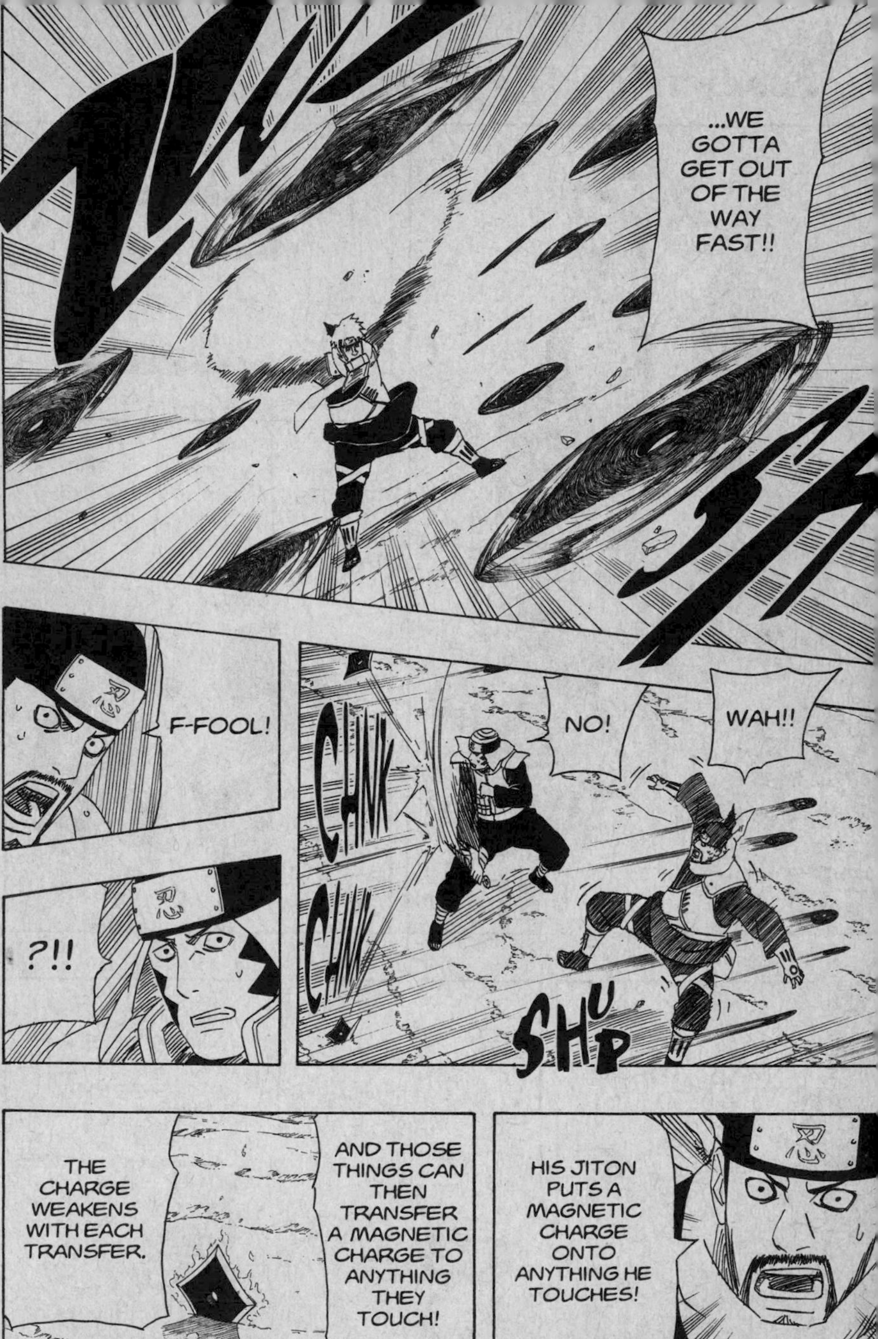
...WE GOTTA GET OUT OF THE WAY FAST!!
WAH!!
NO!
CHINK
CHINK
SHUP
F-FOOL!
?!!
HIS JITON PUTS A MAGNETIC CHARGE ONTO ANYTHING HE TOUCHES!
AND THOSE THINGS CAN THEN TRANSFER A MAGNETIC CHARGE TO ANYTHING THEY TOUCH!
THE CHARGE WEAKENS WITH EACH TRANSFER.

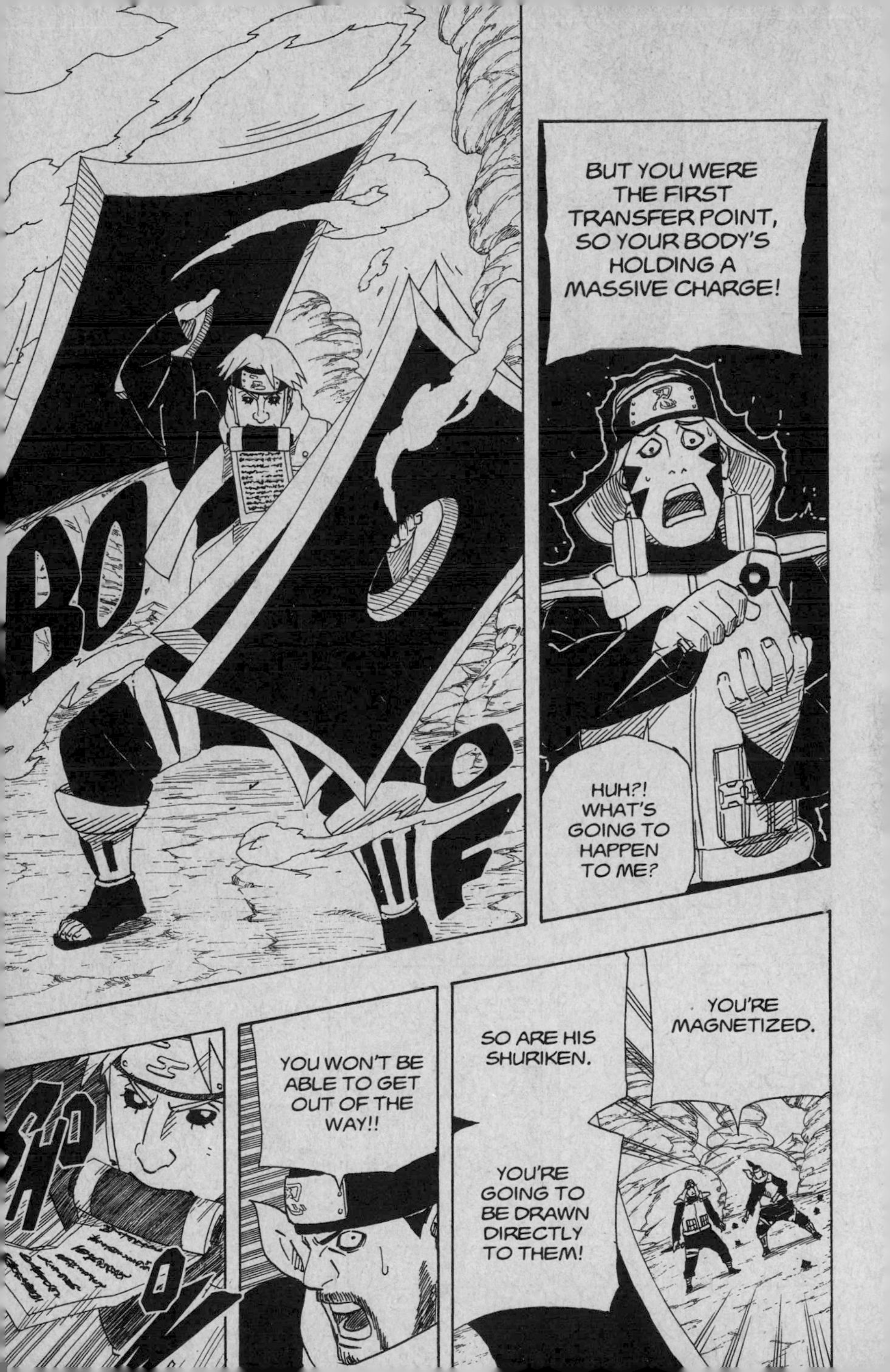
BUT YOU WERE THE FIRST TRANSFER POINT, SO YOUR BODY'S HOLDING A MASSIVE CHARGE!
HUH?! WHAT'S GOING TO HAPPEN TO ME?
BOOF
YOU'RE MAGNETIZED.
SO ARE HIS SHURIKEN.
YOU'RE GOING TO BE DRAWN DIRECTLY TO THEM!
YOU WON'T BE ABLE TO GET OUT OF THE WAY!!

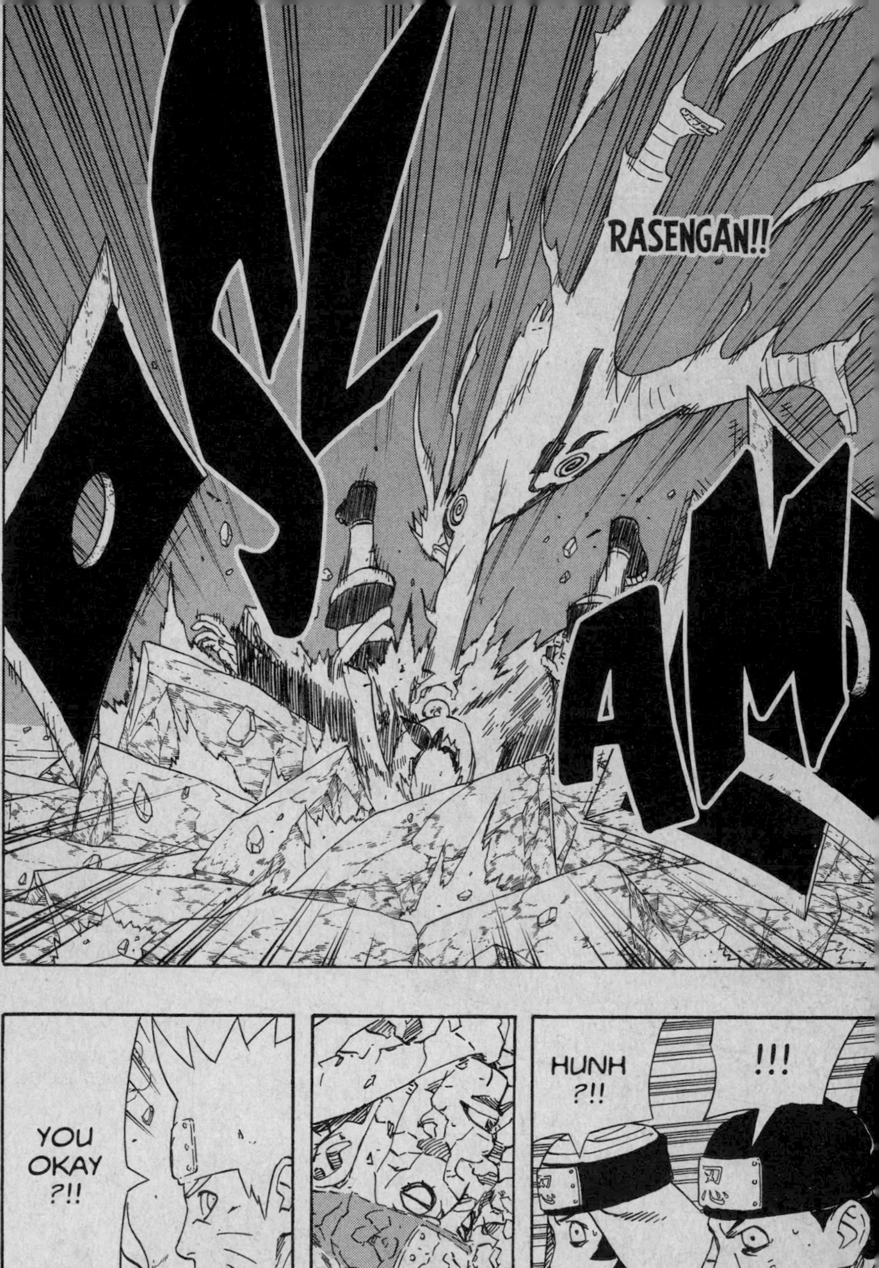
RASENGAN!!
!!!
HUNH ?!!
YOU OKAY ?!!

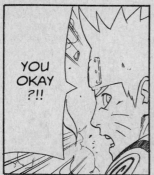

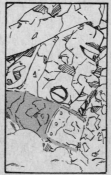

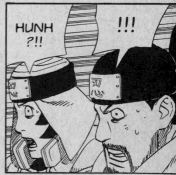

READ THIS WAY

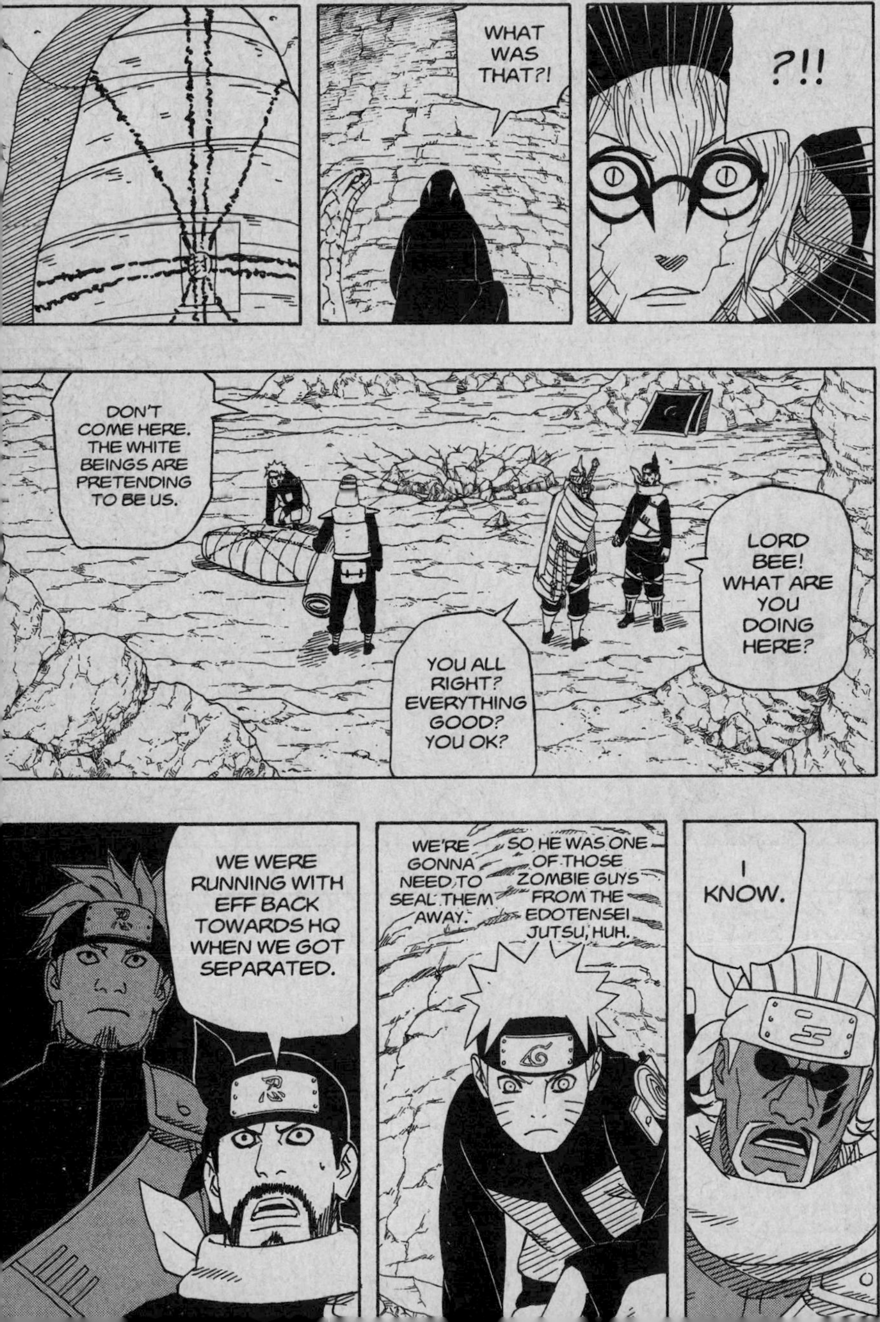
?!!
WHAT WAS THAT?!
LORD BEE! WHAT ARE YOU DOING HERE?
YOU ALL RIGHT? EVERYTHING GOOD? YOU OK?
DON'T COME HERE. THE WHITE BEINGS ARE PRETENDING TO BE US.
I KNOW.
SO HE WAS ONE OF THOSE ZOMBIE GUYS FROM THE EDOTENSEI JUTSU, HUH.
WE'RE GONNA NEED TO SEAL THEM AWAY.
WE WERE RUNNING WITH EFF BACK TOWARDS HQ WHEN WE GOT SEPARATED.

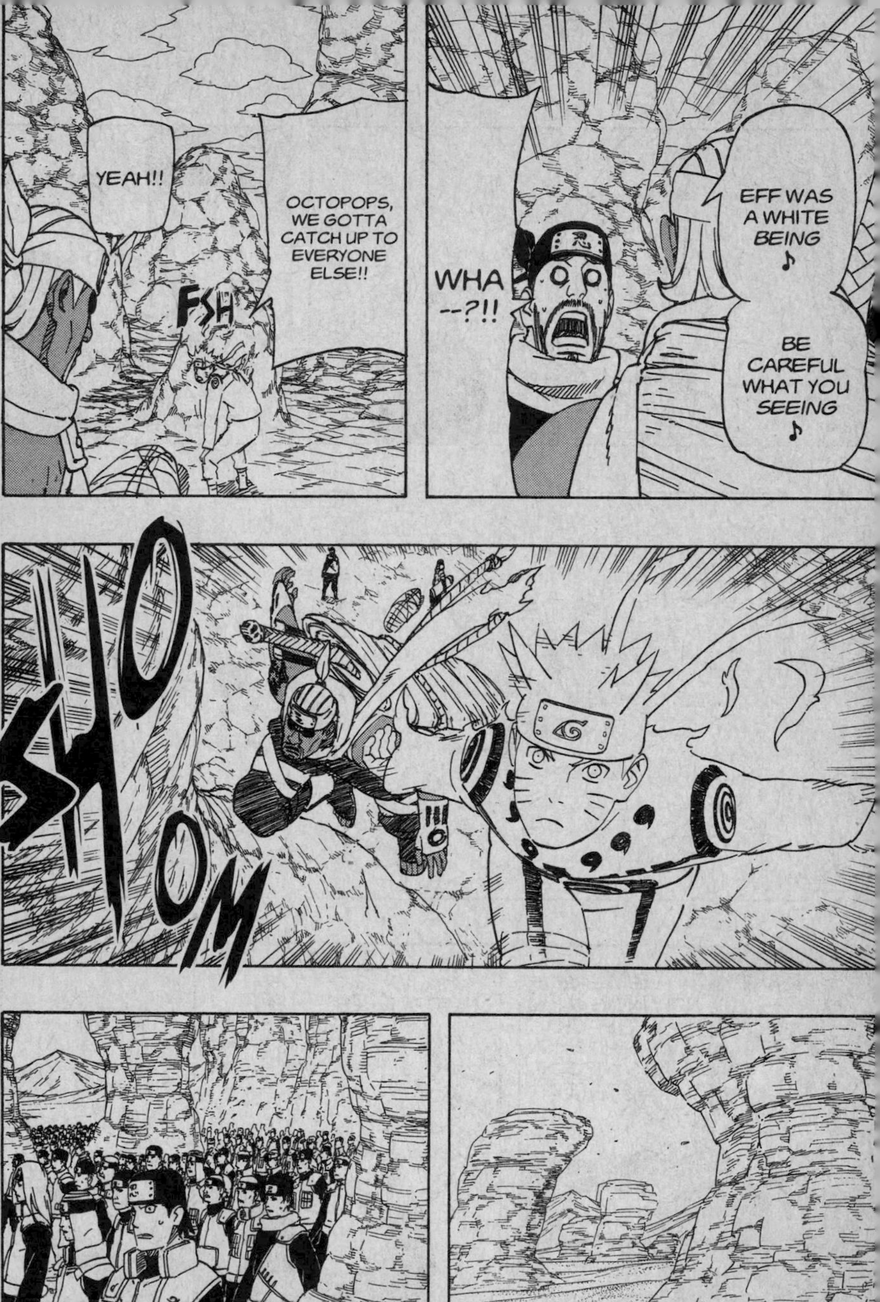
EFF WAS A WHITE BEING ♪
BE CAREFUL WHAT YOU SEEING ♪
WHA--?!!
OCTOPOPS, WE GOTTA CATCH UP TO EVERYONE ELSE!!
YEAH!!
FSH
SHOOM

READ THIS WAY

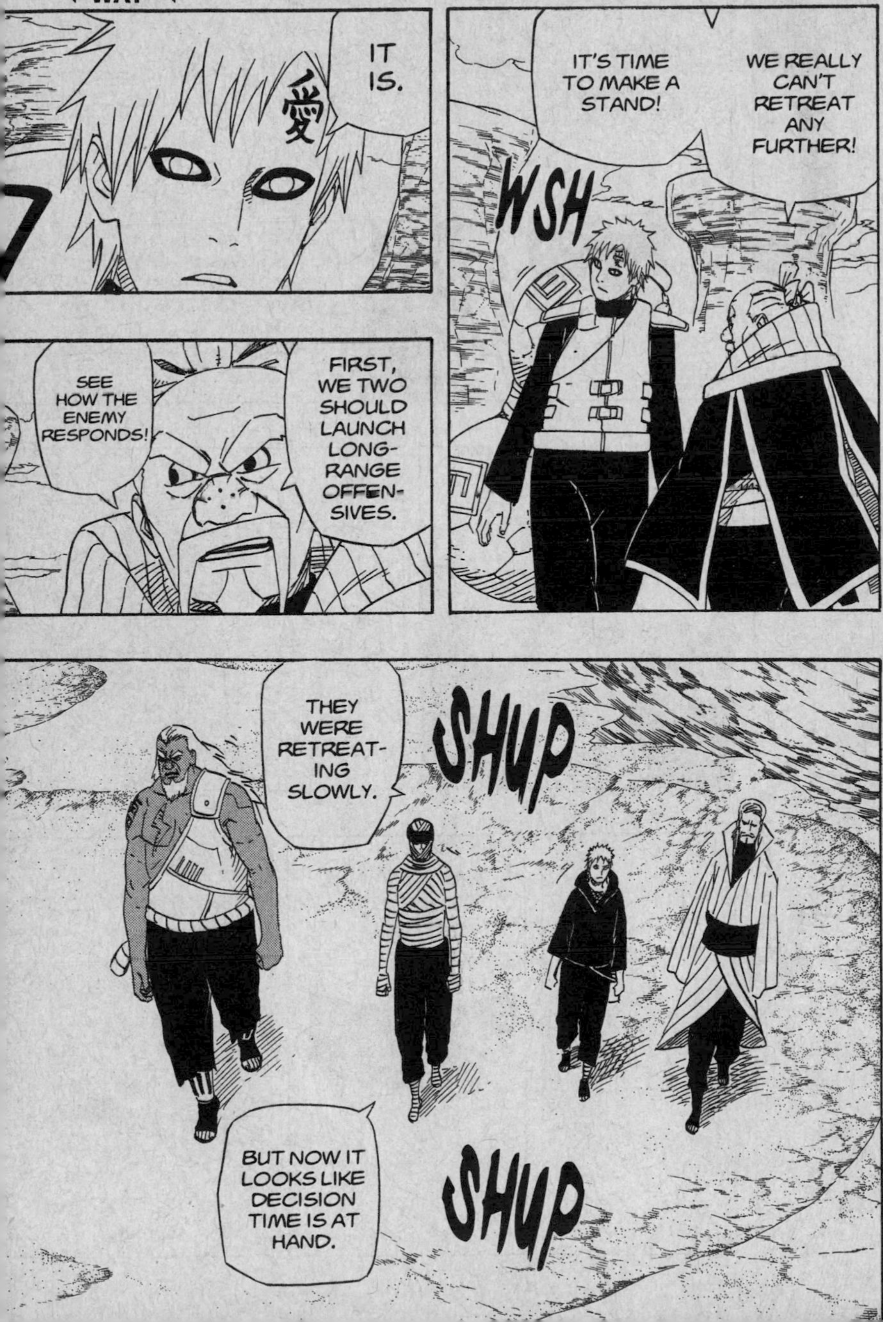
WE REALLY CAN'T RETREAT ANY FURTHER!
IT'S TIME TO MAKE A STAND!
WSH
IT IS.
FIRST, WE TWO SHOULD LAUNCH LONG-RANGE OFFENSIVES.
SEE HOW THE ENEMY RESPONDS!
SHUP
THEY WERE RETREATING SLOWLY.
SHUP
BUT NOW IT LOOKS LIKE DECISION TIME IS AT HAND.

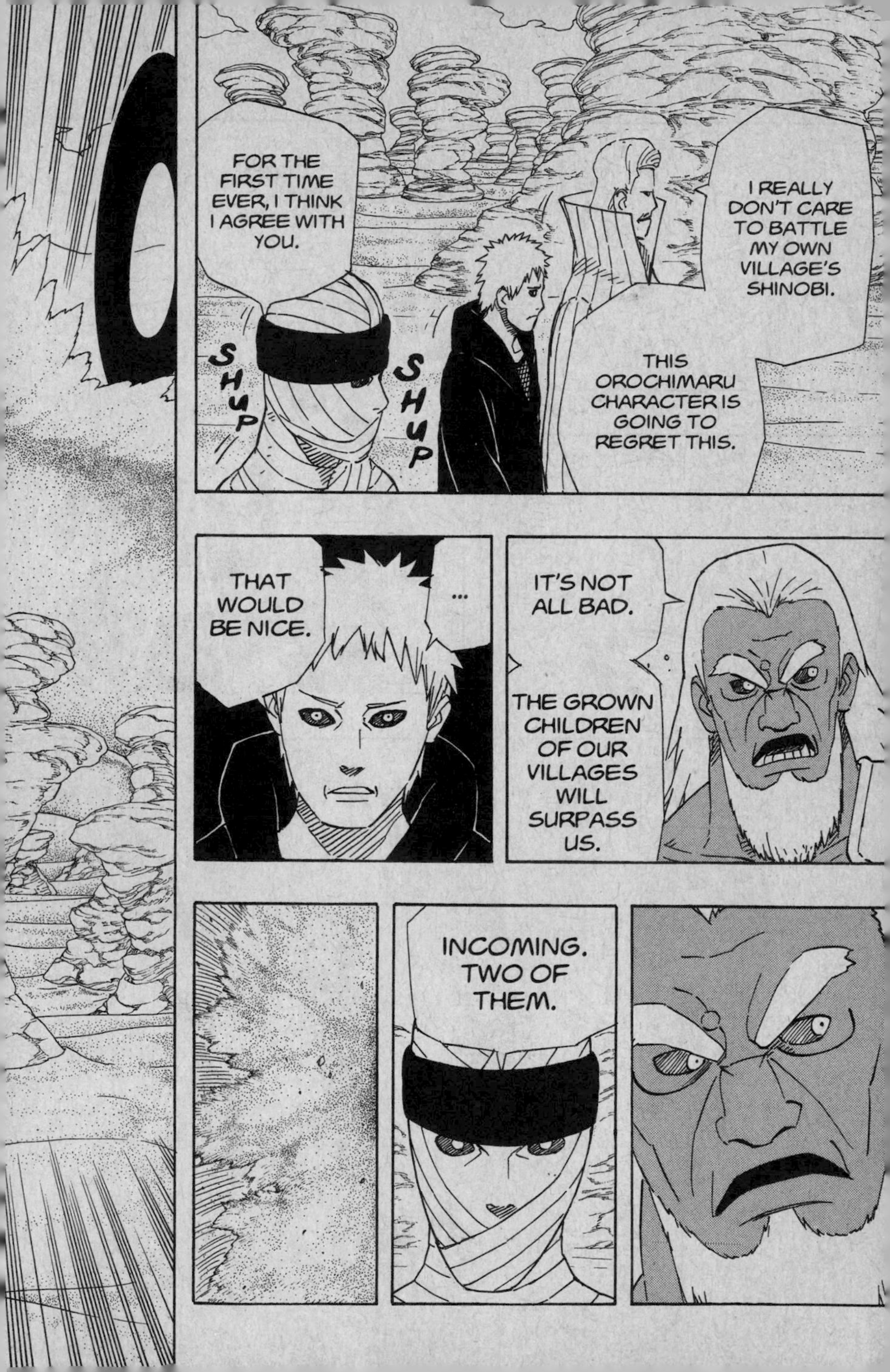
I REALLY DON'T CARE TO BATTLE MY OWN VILLAGE'S SHINOBI.
FOR THE FIRST TIME EVER, I THINK I AGREE WITH YOU.
THIS OROCHIMARU CHARACTER IS GOING TO REGRET THIS.
SHUP
SHUP
IT'S NOT ALL BAD.
THE GROWN CHILDREN OF OUR VILLAGES WILL SURPASS US.
...
THAT WOULD BE NICE.
INCOMING. TWO OF THEM.

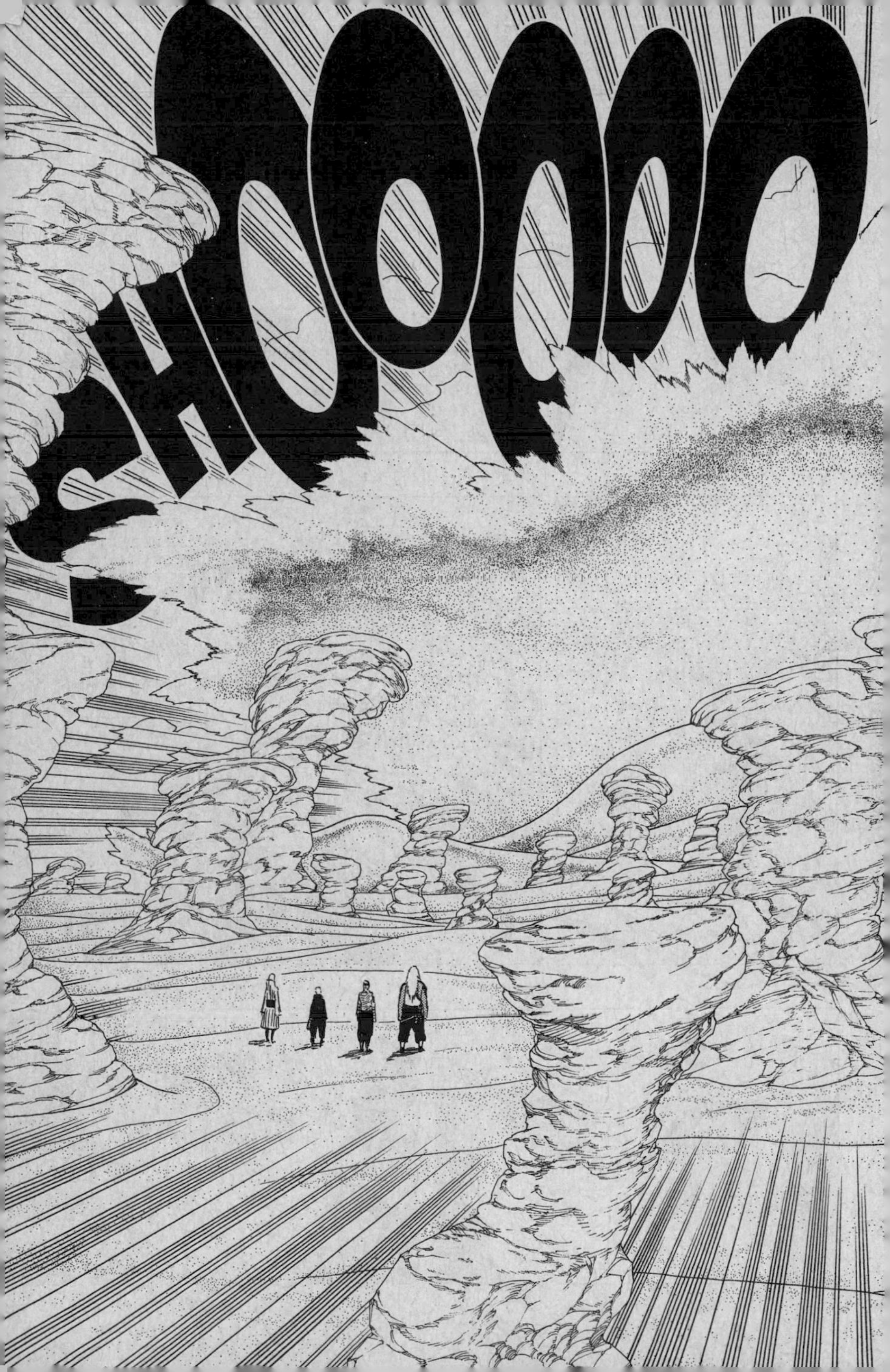
SHOOOOO

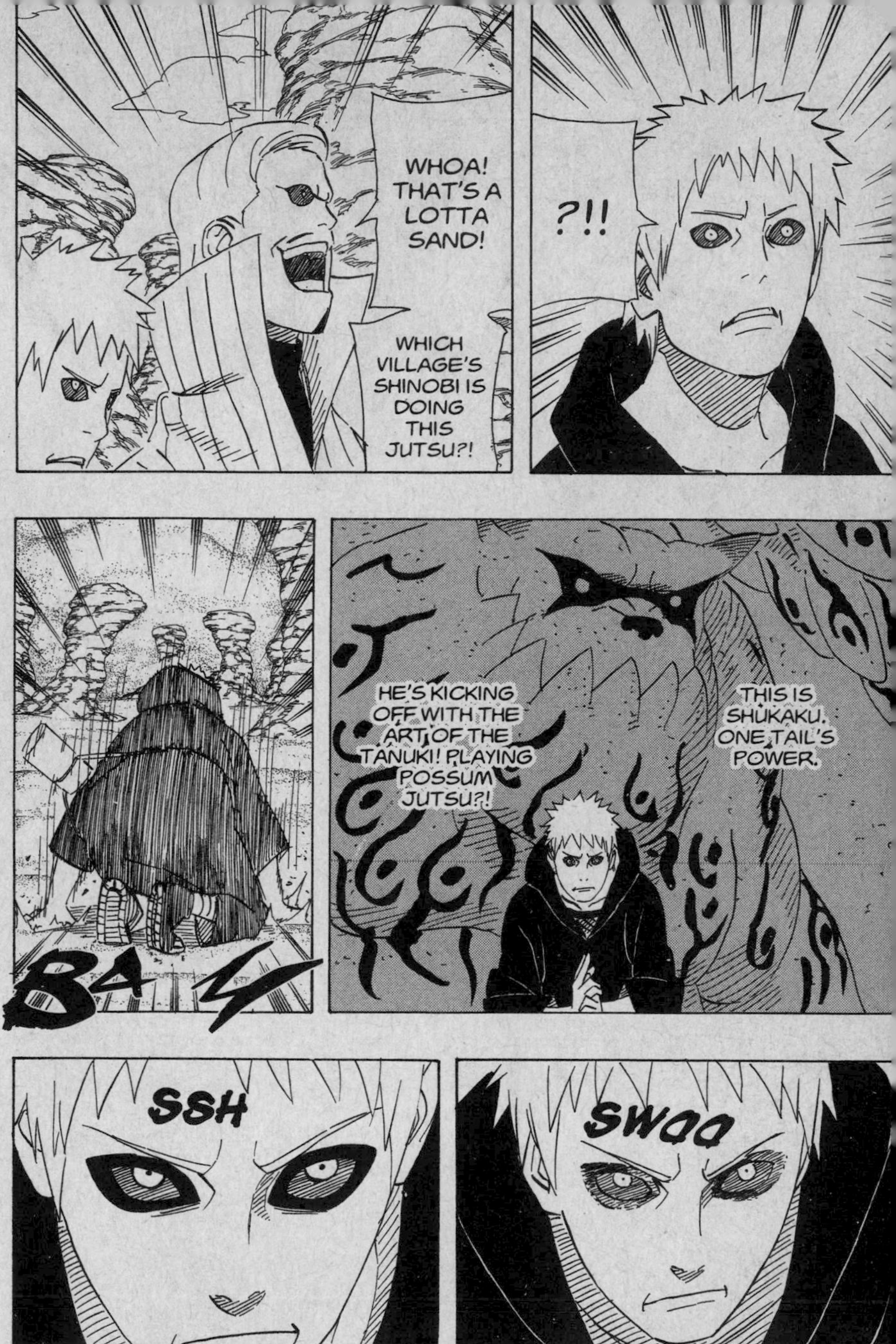
?!!
WHOA! THAT'S A LOTTA SAND!
WHICH VILLAGE'S SHINOBI IS DOING THIS JUTSU?!
THIS IS SHUKAKU. ONE TAIL'S POWER.
HE'S KICKING OFF WITH THE ART OF THE TANUKI! PLAYING POSSUM JUTSU?!
BAM
SWOO
SSH

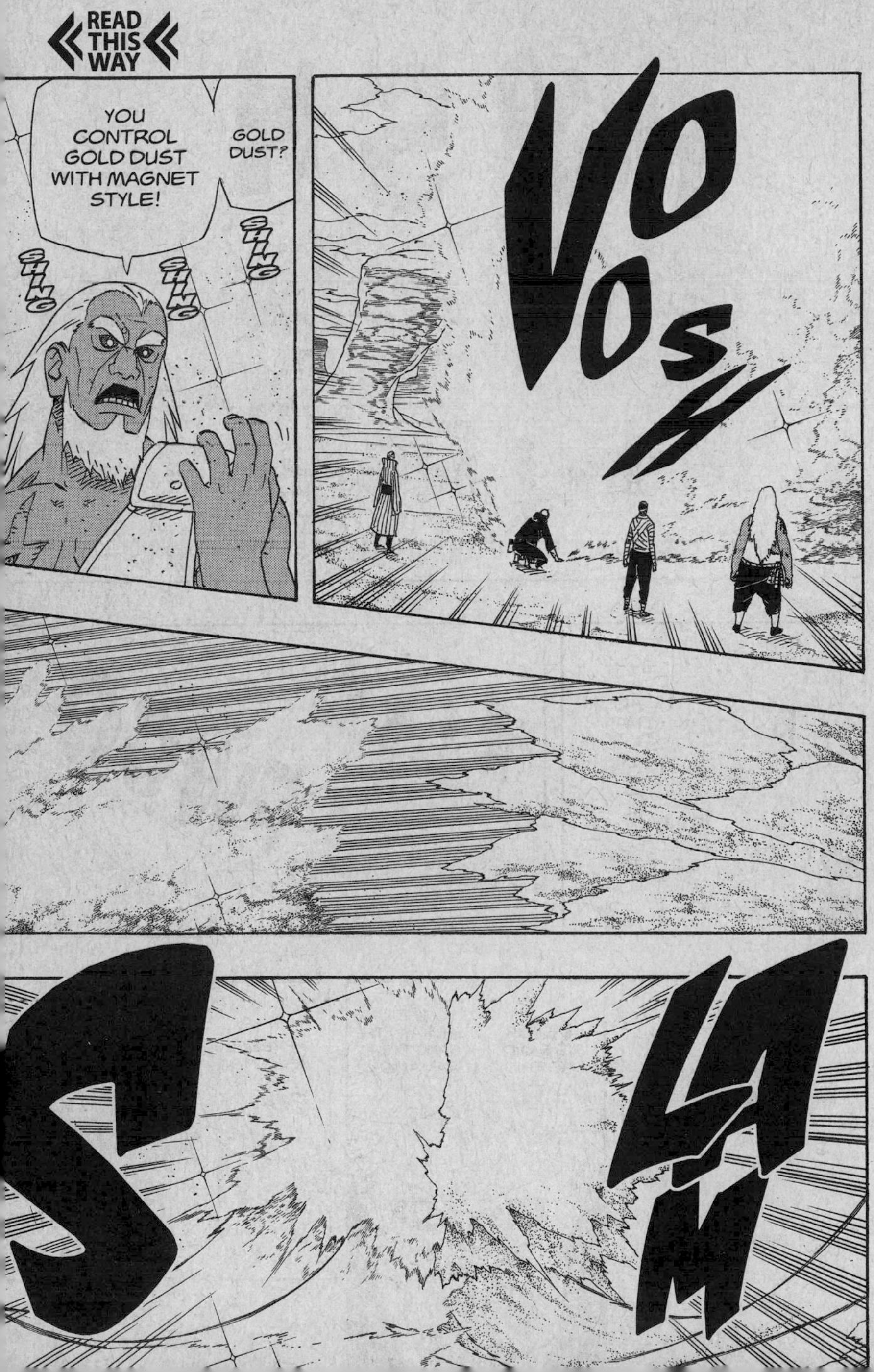
READ THIS WAY
VOOSH
GOLD DUST?
YOU CONTROL GOLD DUST WITH MAGNET STYLE!
SHING
SHING
SHING
SLAM

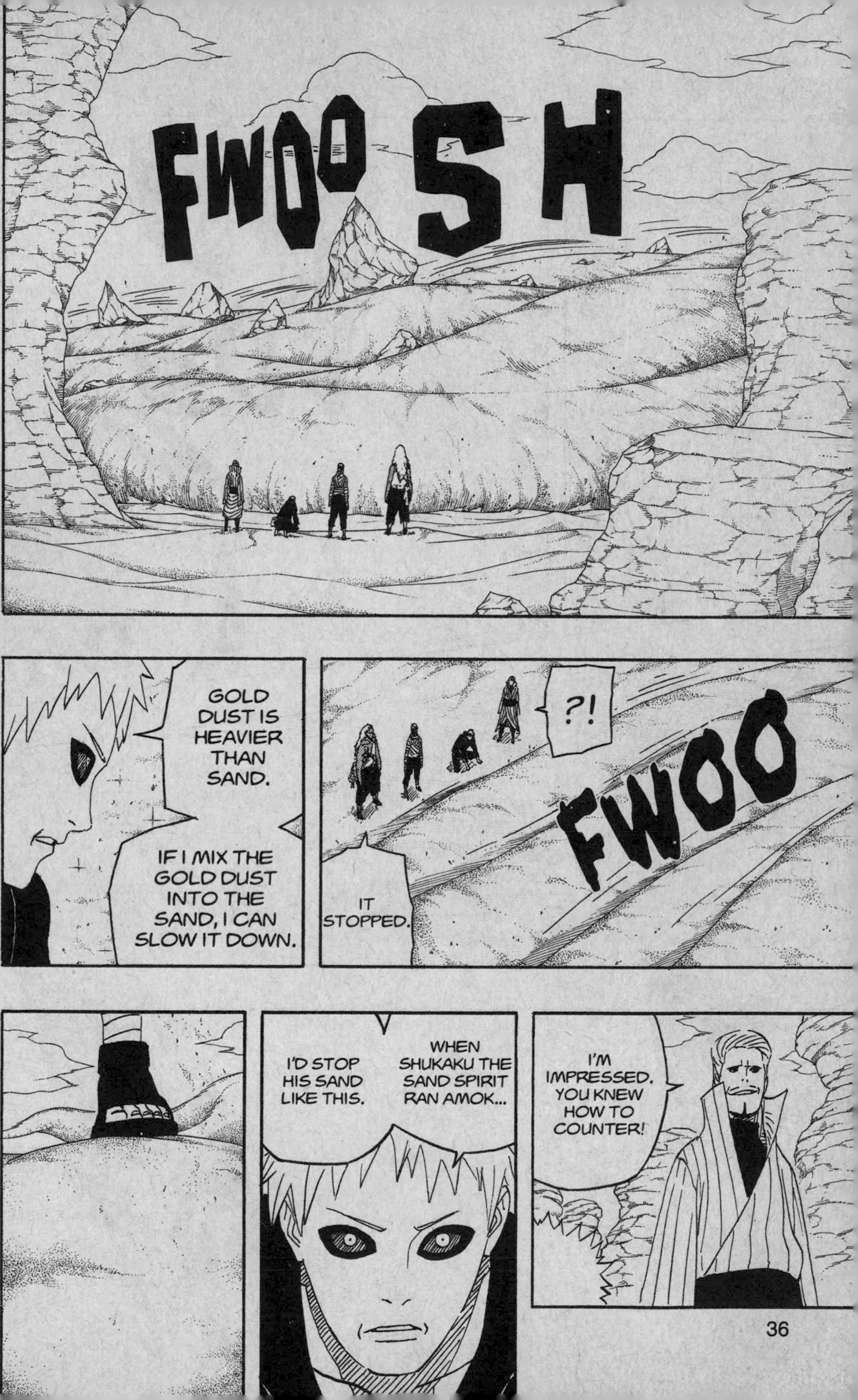
FWOOSH
?!
FWOO
IT STOPPED.
GOLD DUST IS HEAVIER THAN SAND.
IF I MIX THE GOLD DUST INTO THE SAND, I CAN SLOW IT DOWN.
I'M IMPRESSED. YOU KNEW HOW TO COUNTER!
WHEN SHUKAKU THE SAND SPIRIT RAN AMOK...
I'D STOP HIS SAND LIKE THIS.

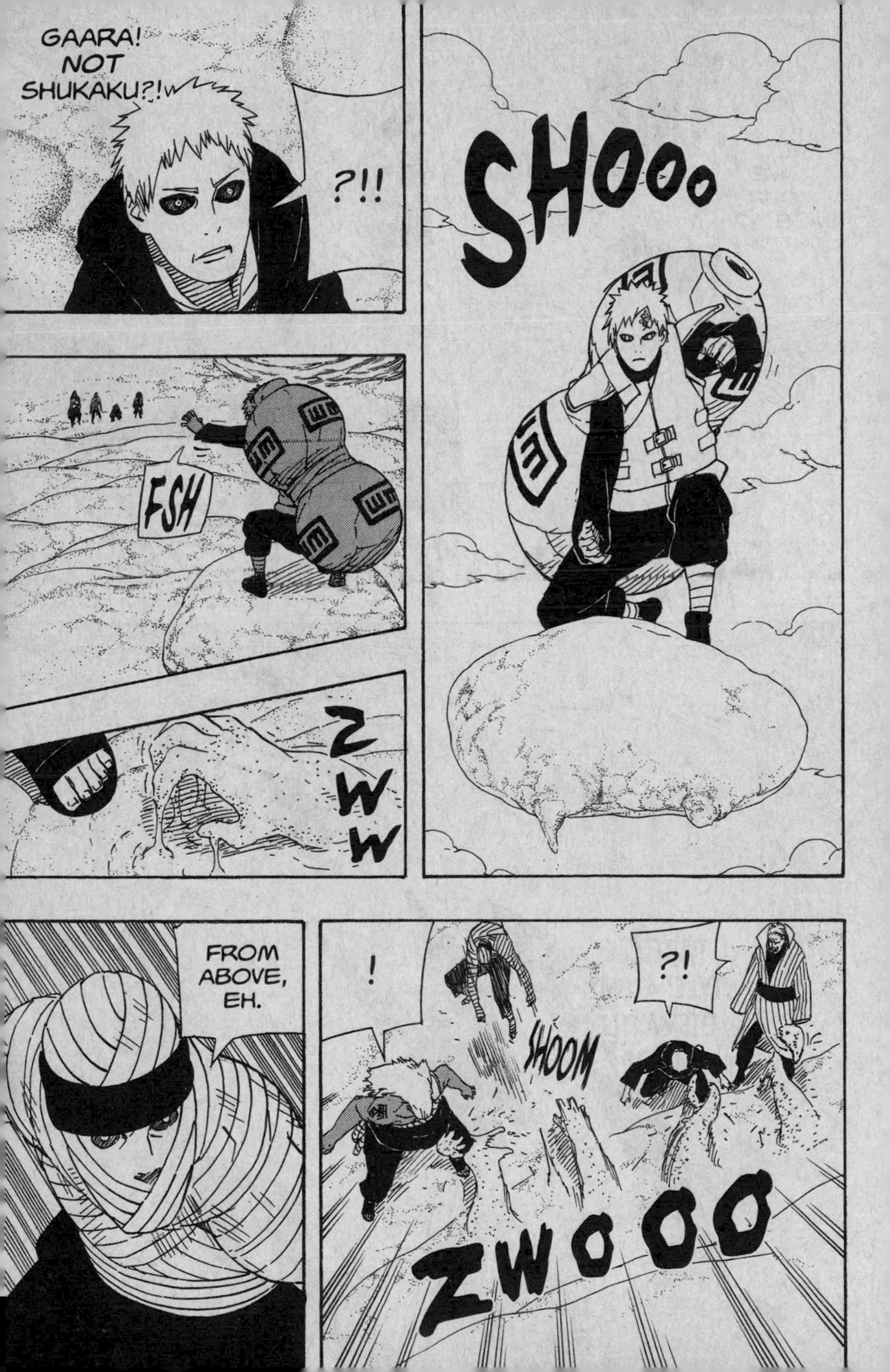
SHOOo
GAARA! NOT SHUKAKU?!
?!!
FSH
ZWW
?!
!
SHOOM
ZWOOO
FROM ABOVE, EH.

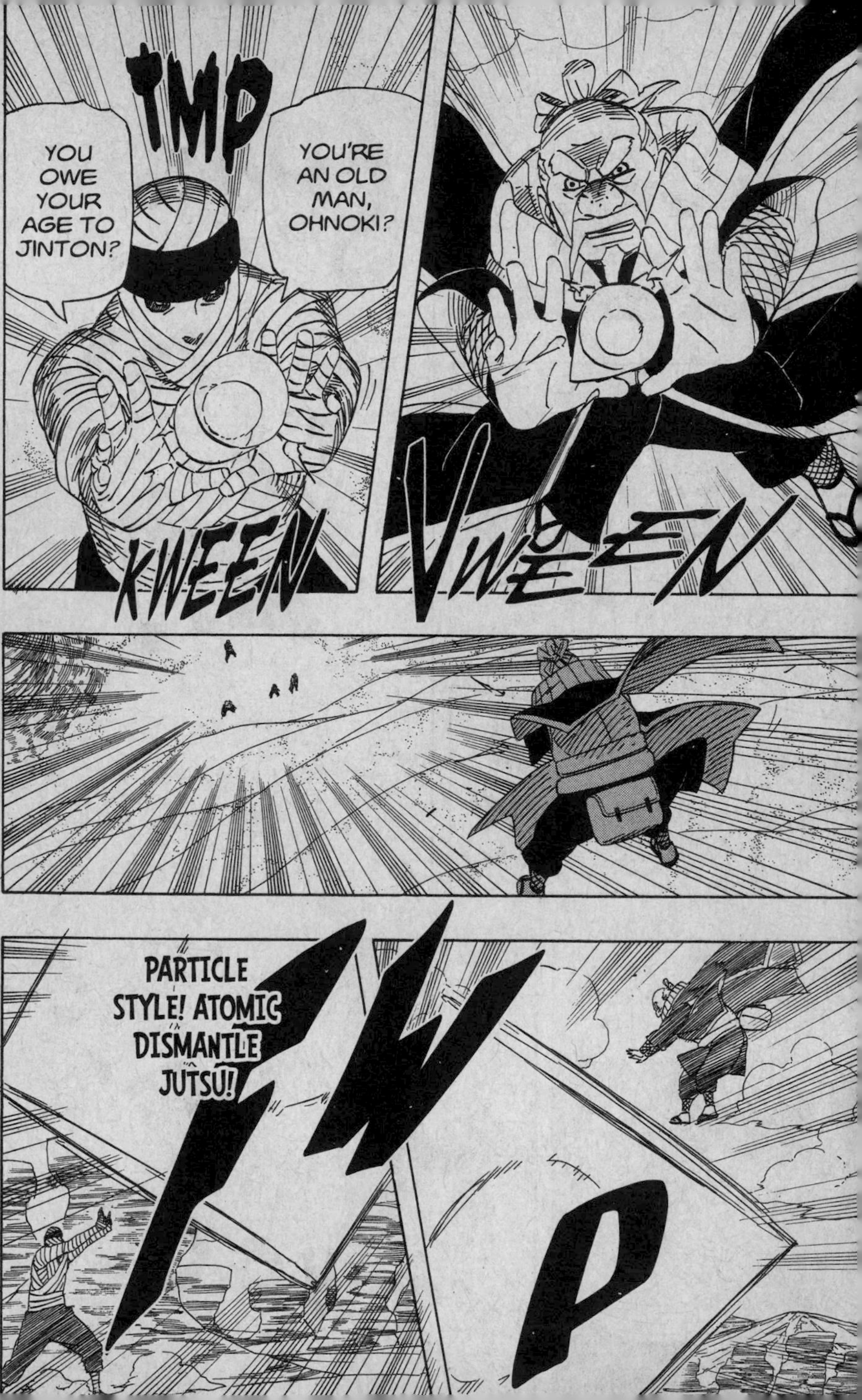
VWEEN
TMP
YOU'RE AN OLD MAN, OHNOKI?
YOU OWE YOUR AGE TO JINTON?
KWEEN
PARTICLE STYLE! ATOMIC DISMANTLE JUTSU!

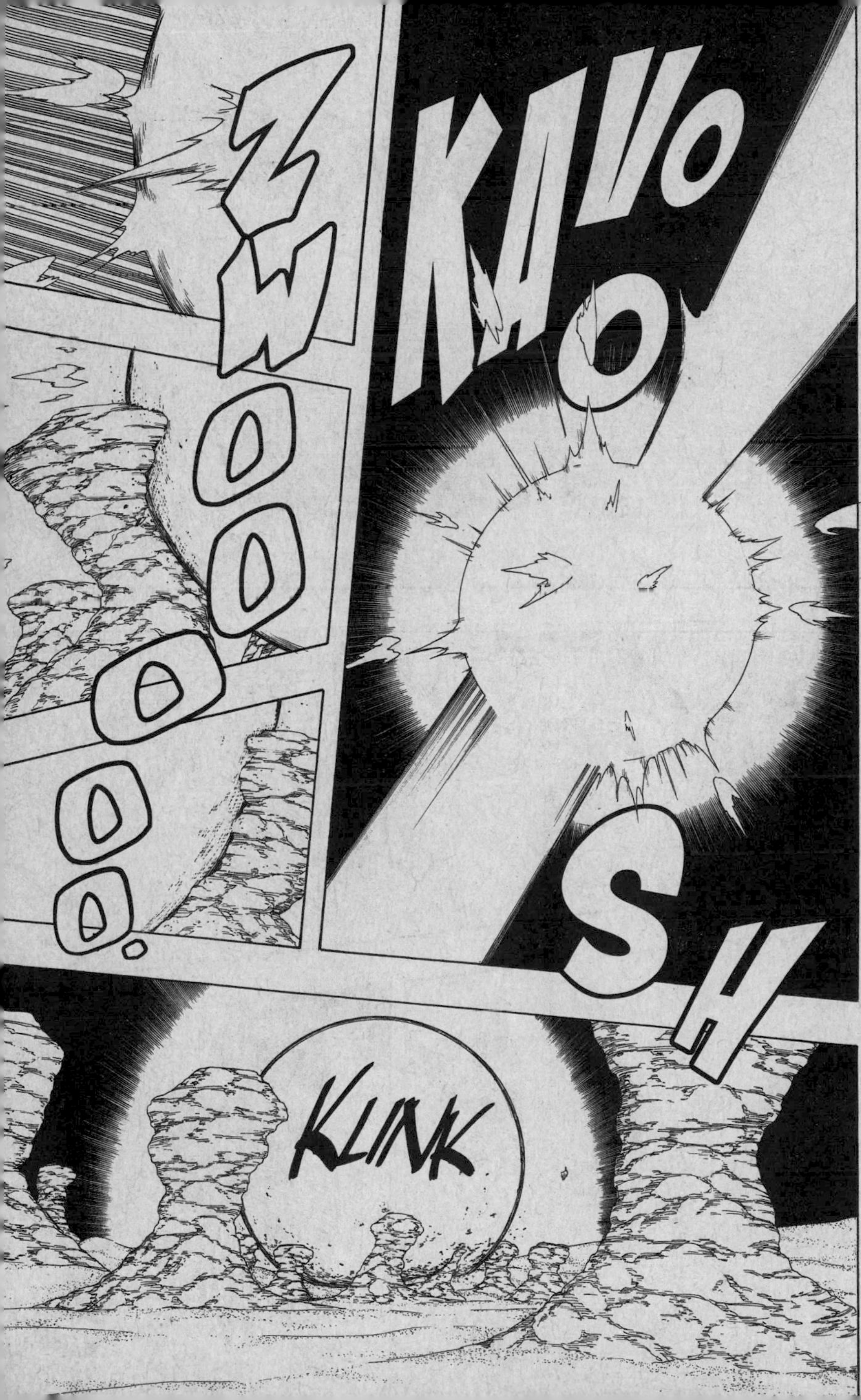
KAVOOSH
ZWOOOOO.
KLINK

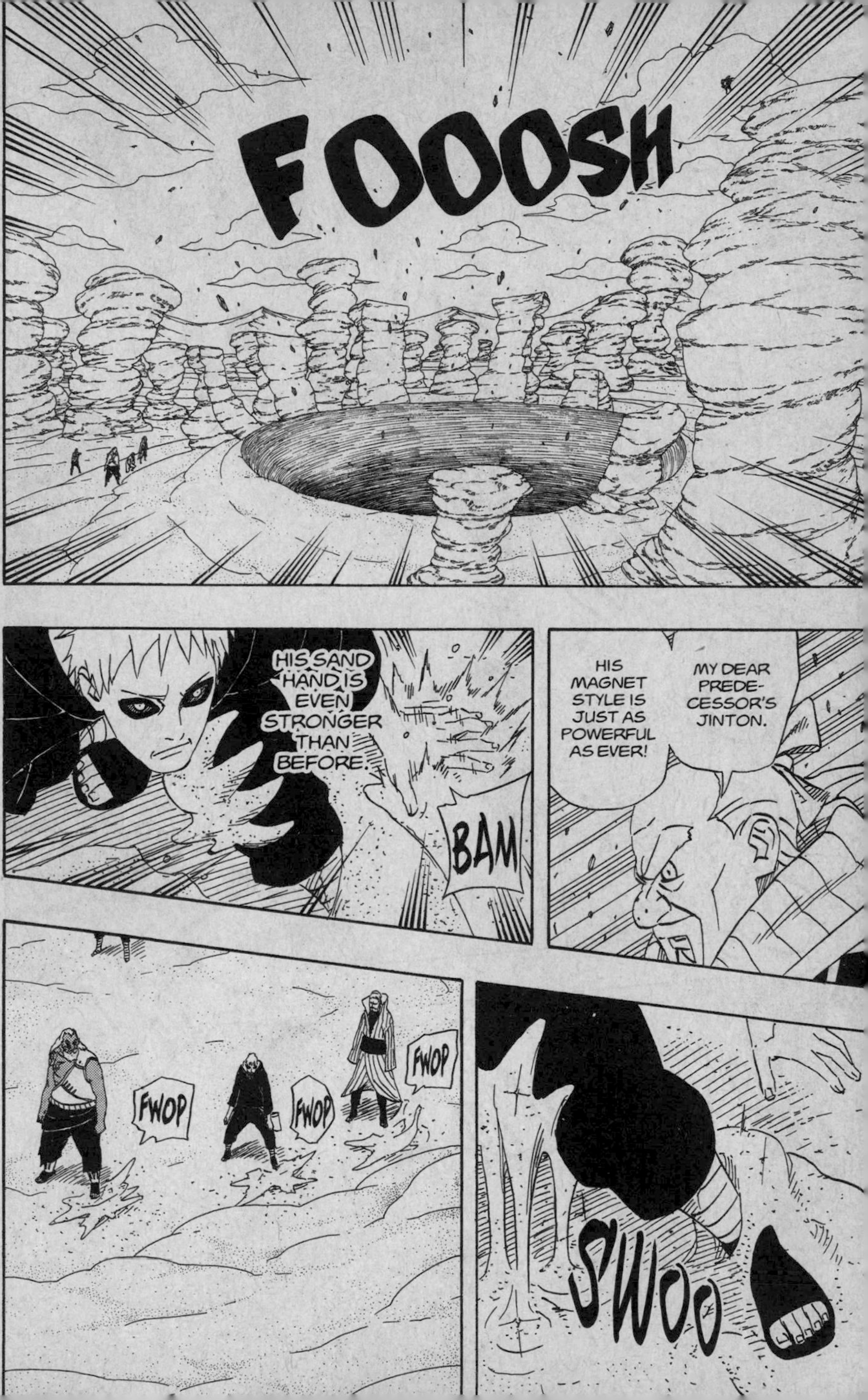
FOOOSH
MY DEAR PREDE-CESSOR'S JINTON.
HIS MAGNET STYLE IS JUST AS POWERFUL AS EVER!
HIS SAND HAND IS EVEN STRONGER THAN BEFORE.
BAM
SWOO
FWOP
FWOP
FWOP

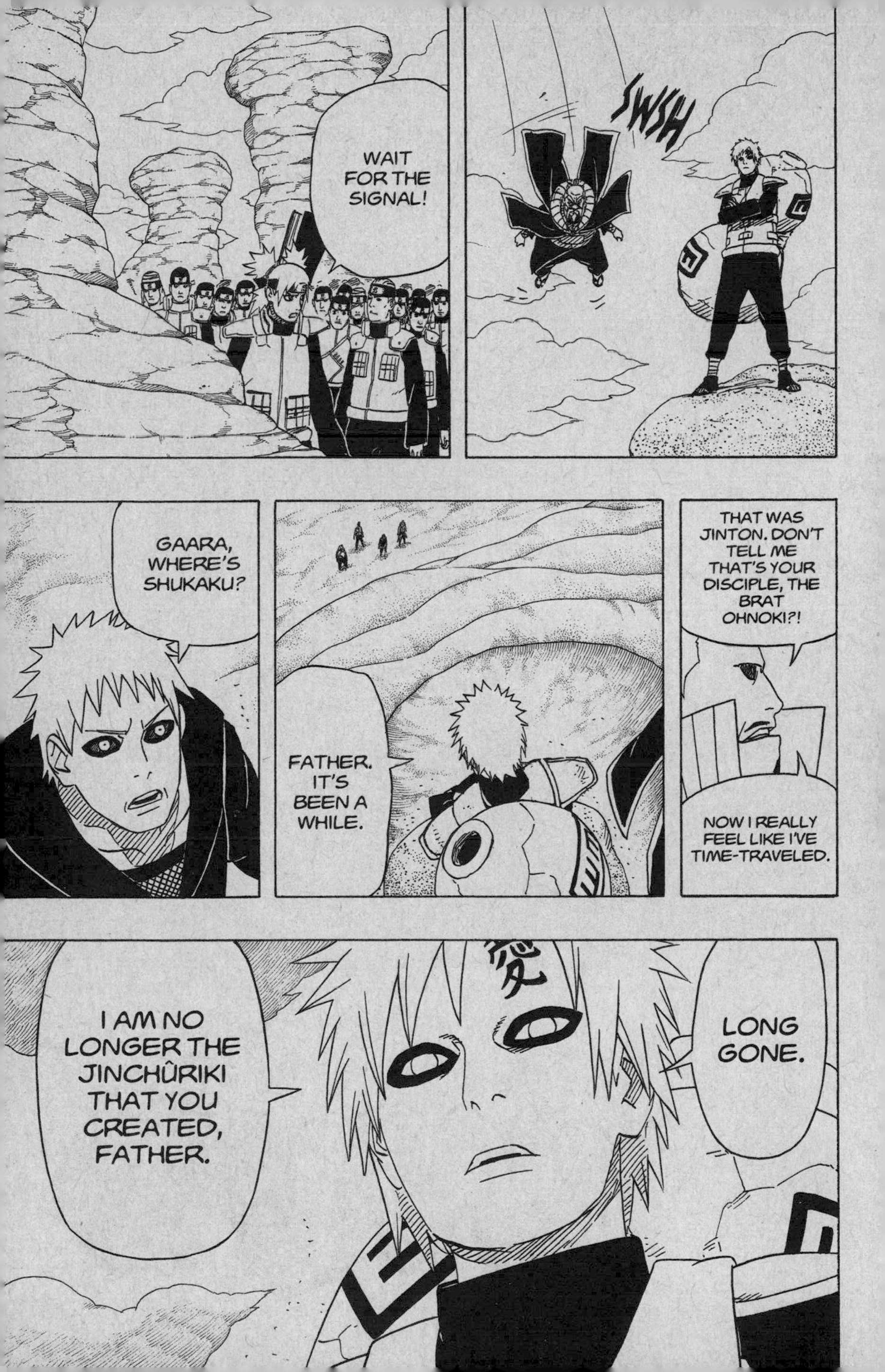
SWSH
WAIT FOR THE SIGNAL!
THAT WAS JINTON. DON'T TELL ME THAT'S YOUR DISCIPLE, THE BRAT OHNOKI?!
NOW I REALLY FEEL LIKE I'VE TIME-TRAVELED.
FATHER. IT'S BEEN A WHILE.
GAARA, WHERE'S SHUKAKU?
LONG GONE.
I AM NO LONGER THE JINCHÛRIKI THAT YOU CREATED, FATHER.

NARUTO

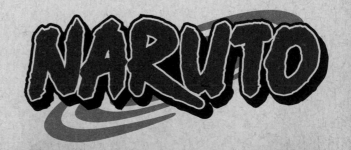

Number 547: Valued Treasures!!

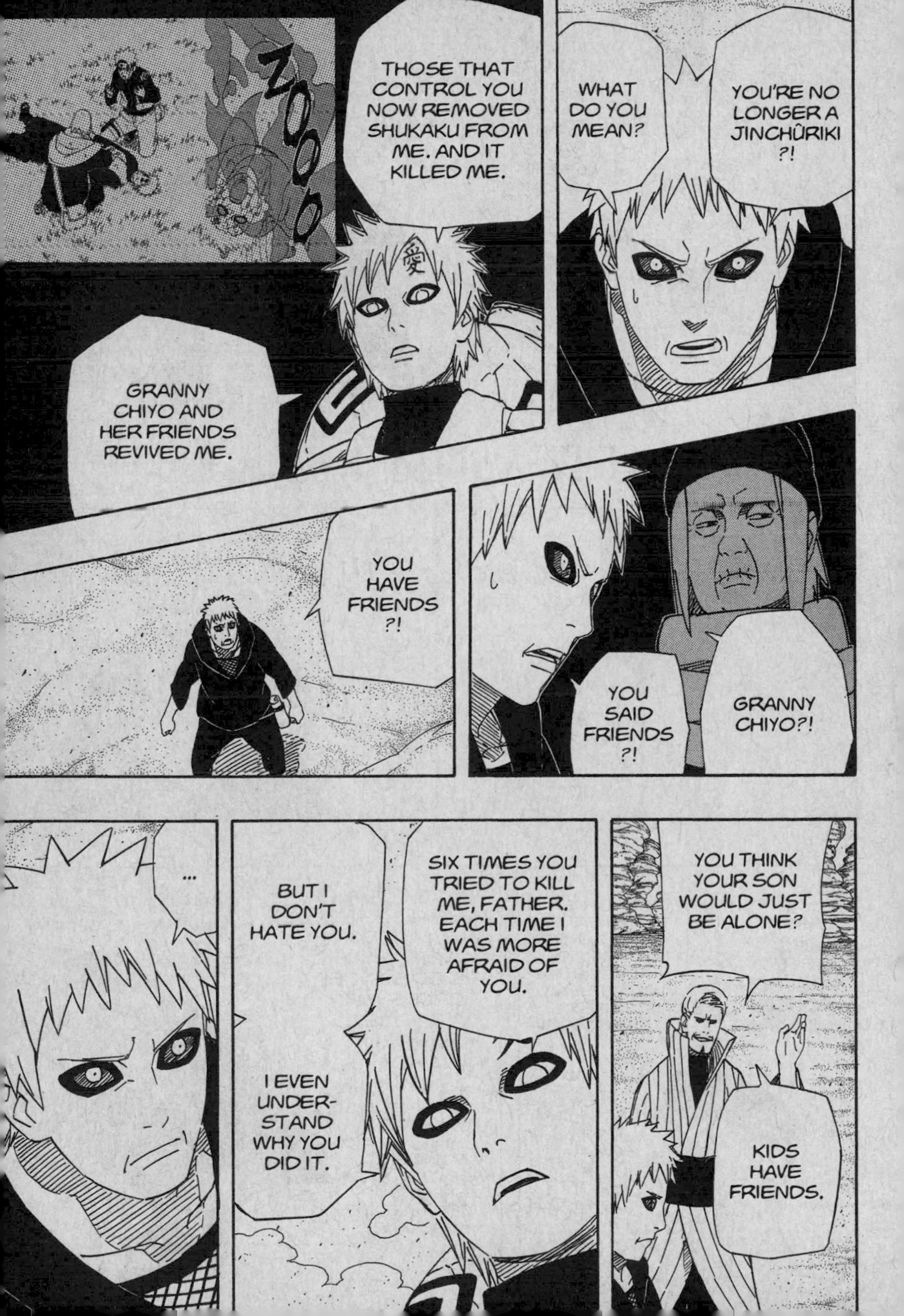
YOU'RE NO LONGER A JINCHÛRIKI ?!
WHAT DO YOU MEAN?
ZOOO
THOSE THAT CONTROL YOU NOW REMOVED SHUKAKU FROM ME. AND IT KILLED ME.
GRANNY CHIYO AND HER FRIENDS REVIVED ME.
GRANNY CHIYO?!
YOU SAID FRIENDS ?!
YOU HAVE FRIENDS ?!
YOU THINK YOUR SON WOULD JUST BE ALONE?
KIDS HAVE FRIENDS.
SIX TIMES YOU TRIED TO KILL ME, FATHER. EACH TIME I WAS MORE AFRAID OF YOU.
BUT I DON'T HATE YOU.
I EVEN UNDER-STAND WHY YOU DID IT.
...

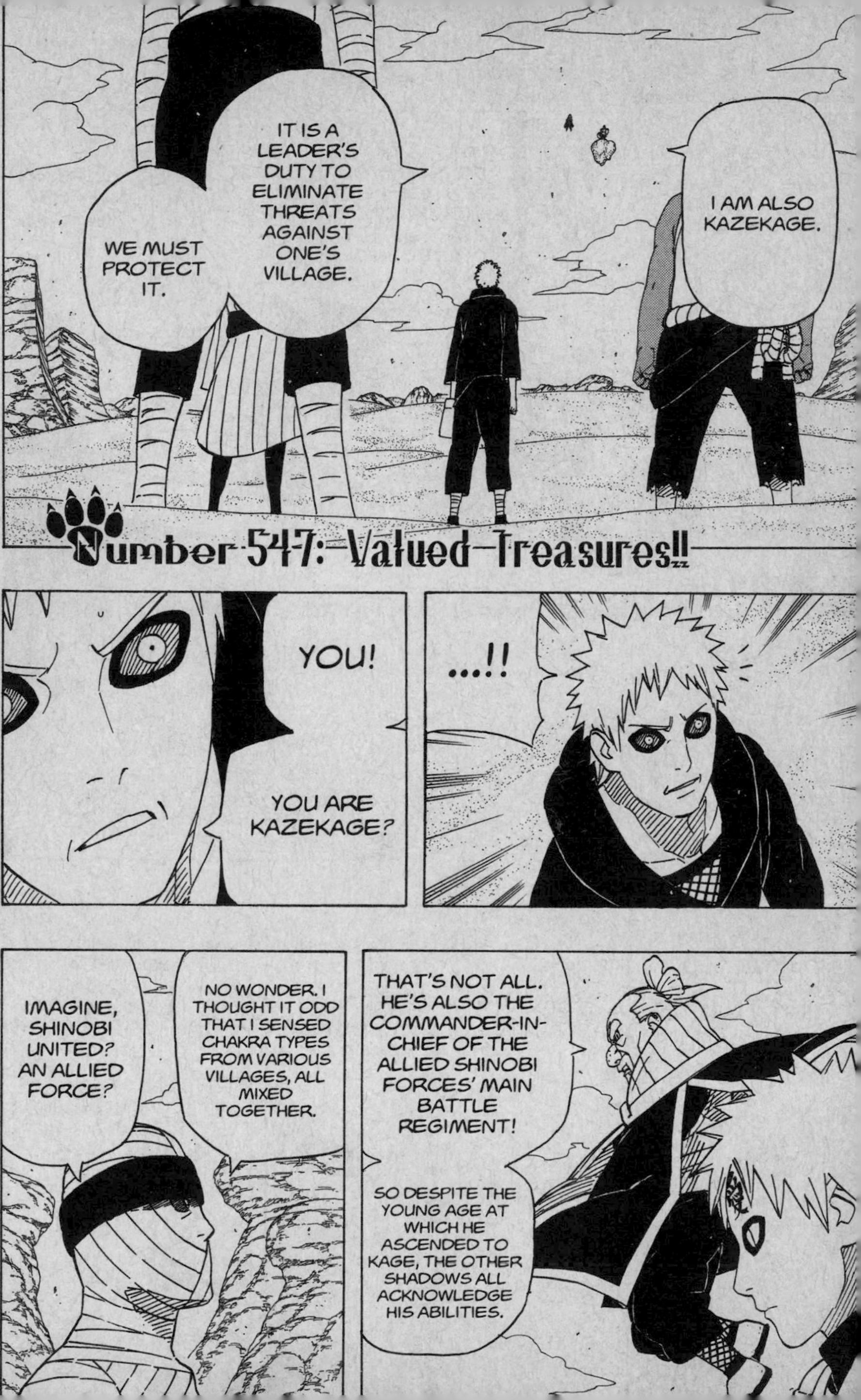
I AM ALSO KAZEKAGE.
IT IS A LEADER'S DUTY TO ELIMINATE THREATS AGAINST ONE'S VILLAGE.
WE MUST PROTECT IT.
Number 547: Valued Treasures!!
...!!
YOU!
YOU ARE KAZEKAGE?
THAT'S NOT ALL. HE'S ALSO THE COMMANDER-IN-CHIEF OF THE ALLIED SHINOBI FORCES' MAIN BATTLE REGIMENT!
SO DESPITE THE YOUNG AGE AT WHICH HE ASCENDED TO KAGE, THE OTHER SHADOWS ALL ACKNOWLEDGE HIS ABILITIES.
NO WONDER. I THOUGHT IT ODD THAT I SENSED CHAKRA TYPES FROM VARIOUS VILLAGES, ALL MIXED TOGETHER.
IMAGINE, SHINOBI UNITED? AN ALLIED FORCE?

READ THIS WAY

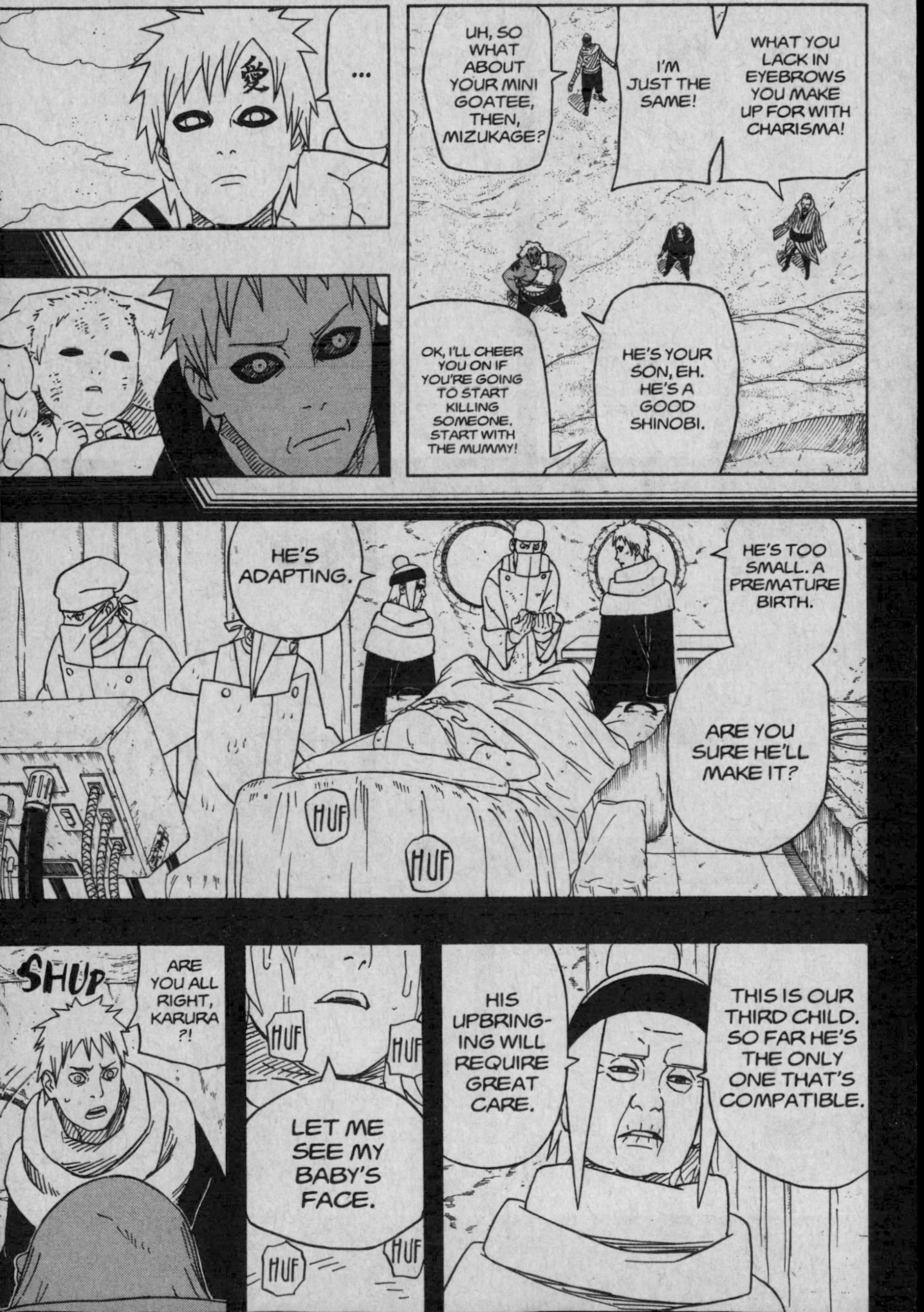
WHAT YOU LACK IN EYEBROWS YOU MAKE UP FOR WITH CHARISMA!
I'M JUST THE SAME!
UH, SO WHAT ABOUT YOUR MINI GOATEE, THEN, MIZUKAGE?
HE'S YOUR SON, EH. HE'S A GOOD SHINOBI.
OK, I'LL CHEER YOU ON IF YOU'RE GOING TO START KILLING SOMEONE. START WITH THE MUMMY!
...
HE'S TOO SMALL. A PREMATURE BIRTH.
ARE YOU SURE HE'LL MAKE IT?
HE'S ADAPTING.
HUF
HUF
THIS IS OUR THIRD CHILD. SO FAR HE'S THE ONLY ONE THAT'S COMPATIBLE.
HIS UPBRING-ING WILL REQUIRE GREAT CARE.
HUF
HUF
LET ME SEE MY BABY'S FACE.
HUF
HUF
ARE YOU ALL RIGHT, KARURA?!
SHUP

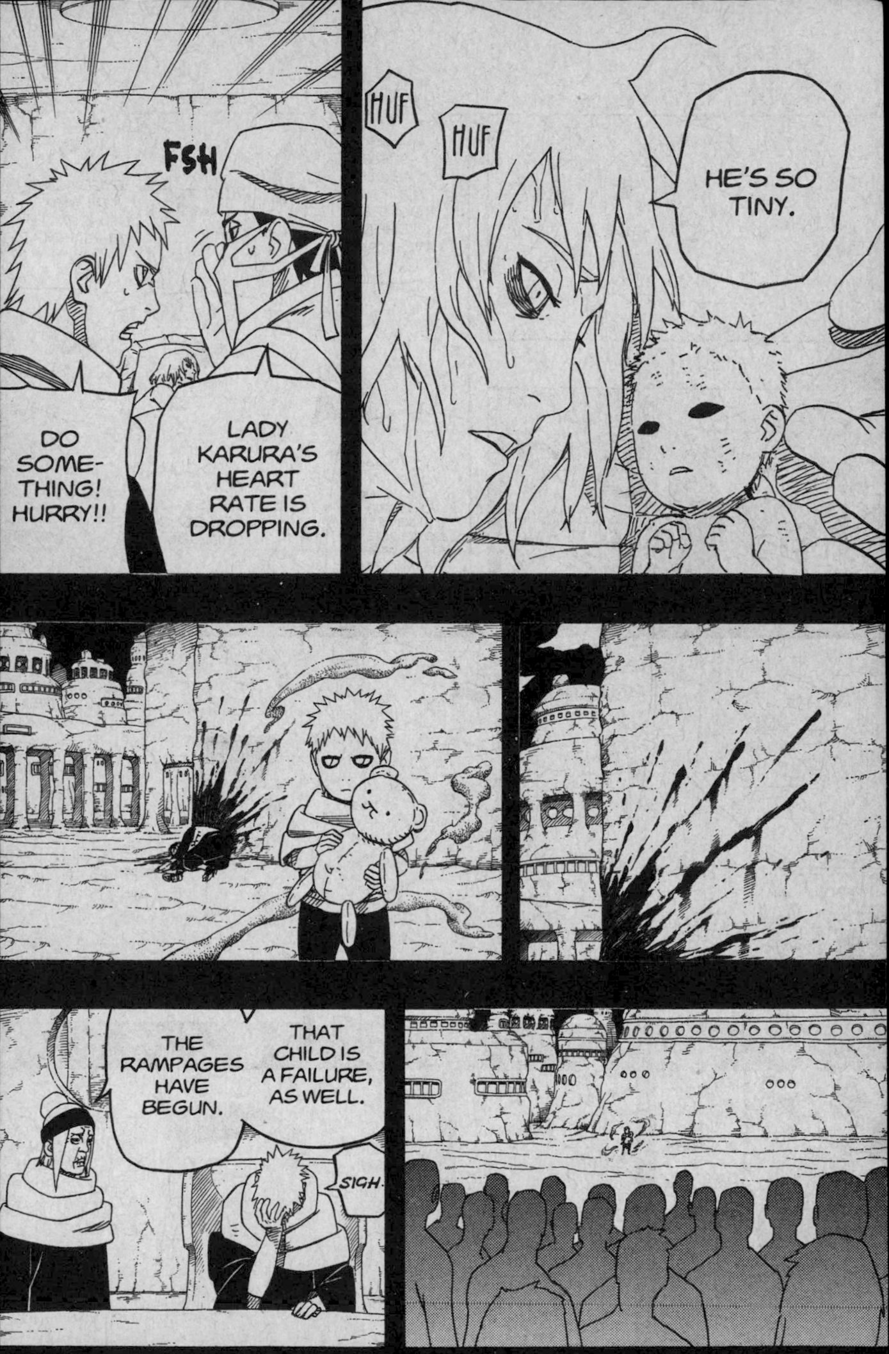
HUF
HUF
HE'S SO TINY.
FSH
LADY KARURA'S HEART RATE IS DROPPING.
DO SOME-THING! HURRY!!
THAT CHILD IS A FAILURE, AS WELL.
THE RAMPAGES HAVE BEGUN.
SIGH.

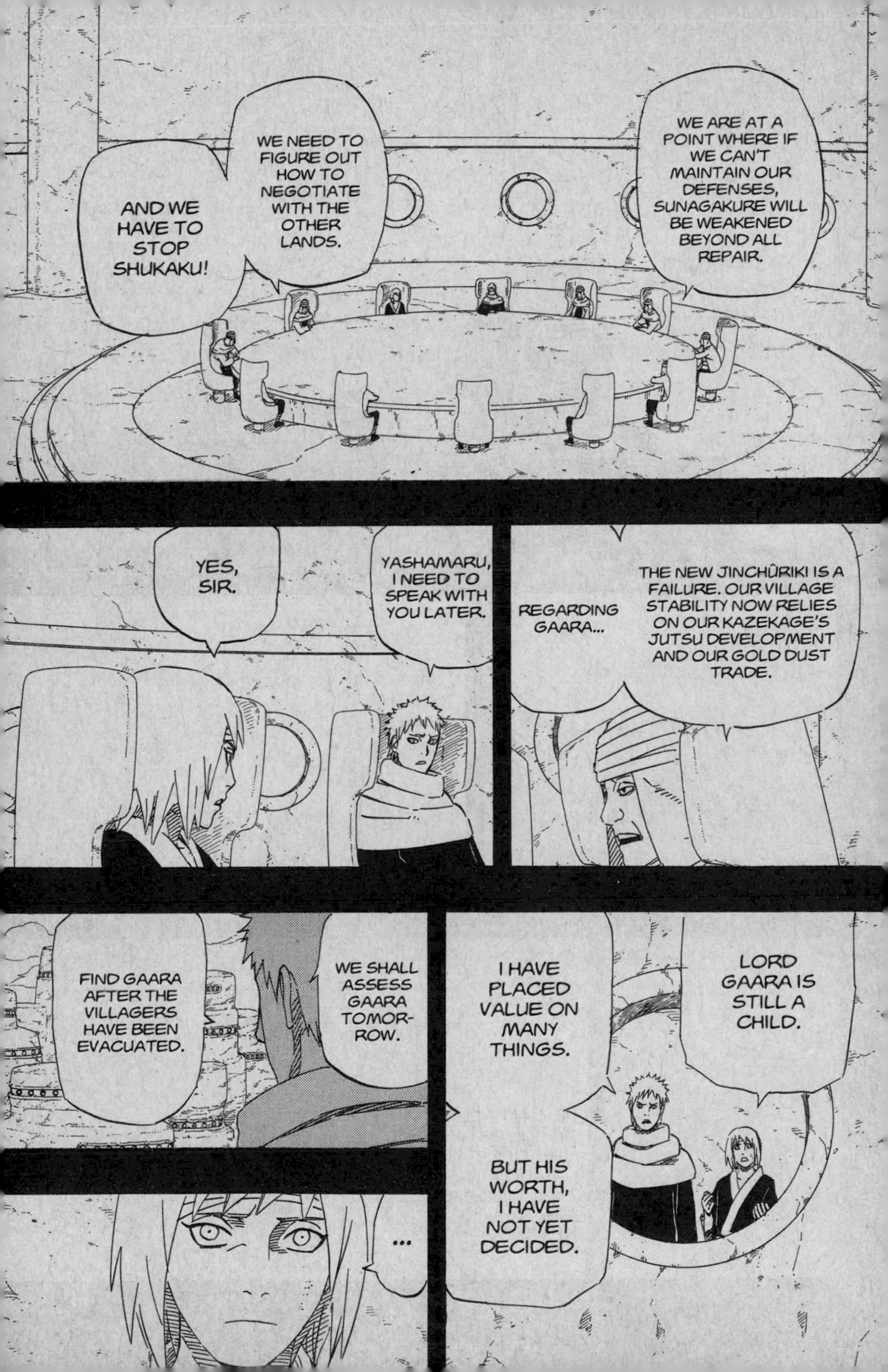
WE ARE AT A POINT WHERE IF WE CAN'T MAINTAIN OUR DEFENSES, SUNAGAKURE WILL BE WEAKENED BEYOND ALL REPAIR.
WE NEED TO FIGURE OUT HOW TO NEGOTIATE WITH THE OTHER LANDS.
AND WE HAVE TO STOP SHUKAKU!
THE NEW JINCHÛRIKI IS A FAILURE. OUR VILLAGE STABILITY NOW RELIES ON OUR KAZEKAGE'S JUTSU DEVELOPMENT AND OUR GOLD DUST TRADE.
REGARDING GAARA...
YASHAMARU, I NEED TO SPEAK WITH YOU LATER.
YES, SIR.
LORD GAARA IS STILL A CHILD.
I HAVE PLACED VALUE ON MANY THINGS.
BUT HIS WORTH, I HAVE NOT YET DECIDED.
WE SHALL ASSESS GAARA TOMOR-ROW.
FIND GAARA AFTER THE VILLAGERS HAVE BEEN EVACUATED.
...

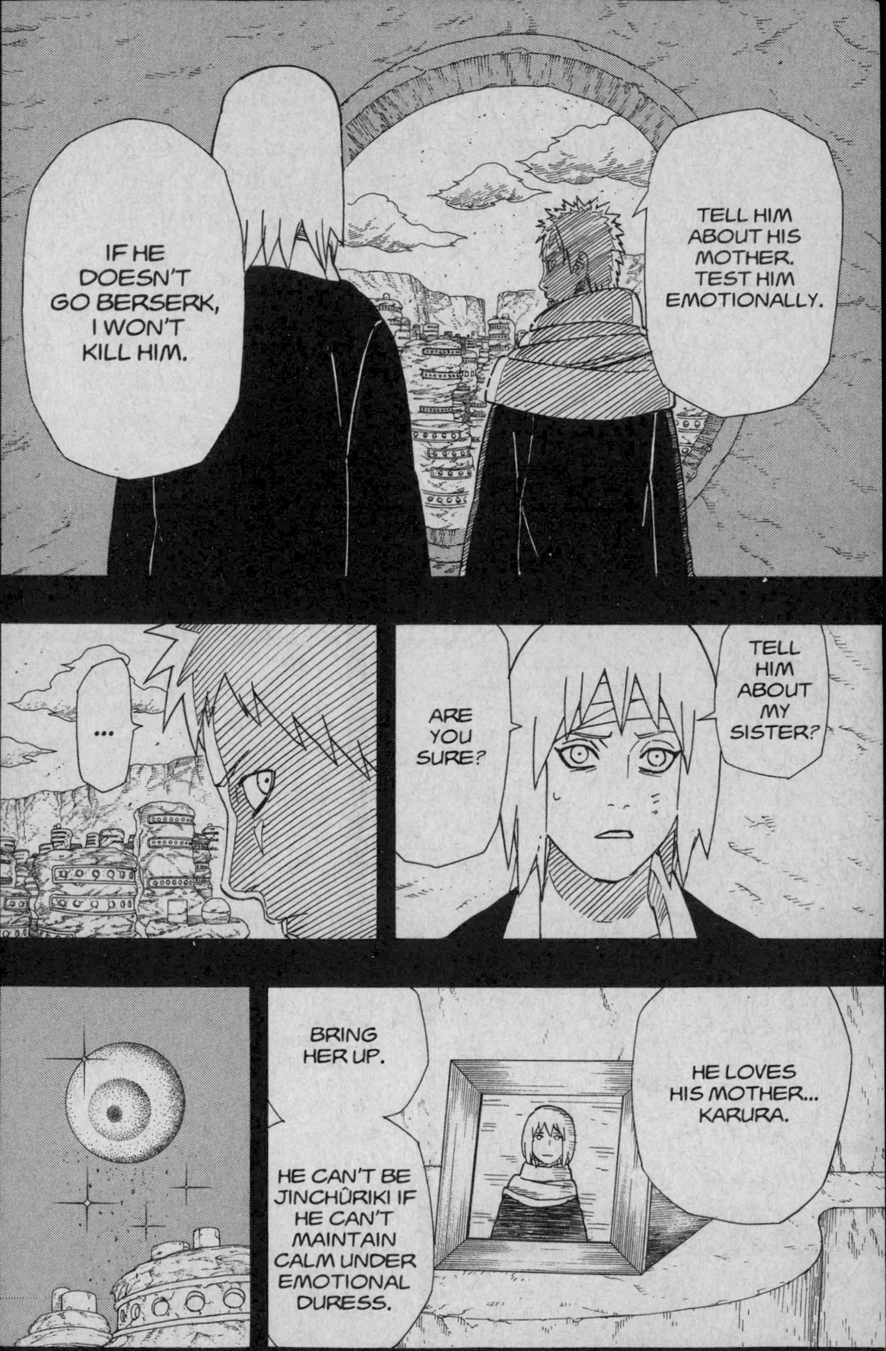
TELL HIM ABOUT HIS MOTHER. TEST HIM EMOTIONALLY.
IF HE DOESN'T GO BERSERK, I WON'T KILL HIM.
TELL HIM ABOUT MY SISTER?
ARE YOU SURE?
...
HE LOVES HIS MOTHER... KARURA.
BRING HER UP.
HE CAN'T BE JINCHÛRIKI IF HE CAN'T MAINTAIN CALM UNDER EMOTIONAL DURESS.

READ THIS WAY

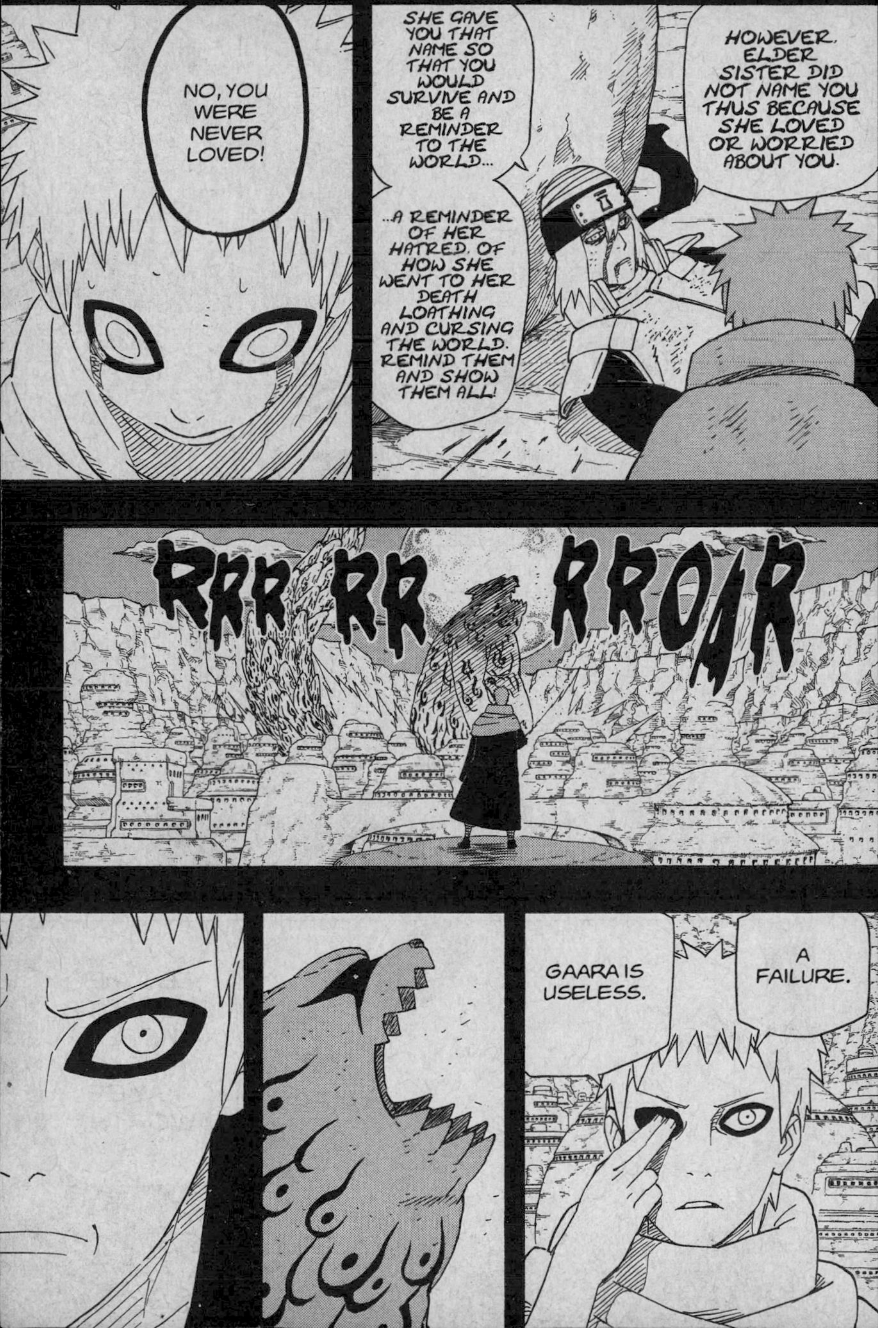
HOWEVER, ELDER SISTER DID NOT NAME YOU THUS BECAUSE SHE LOVED OR WORRIED ABOUT YOU.
SHE GAVE YOU THAT NAME SO THAT YOU WOULD SURVIVE AND BE A REMINDER TO THE WORLD...
...A REMINDER OF HER HATRED, OF HOW SHE WENT TO HER DEATH LOATHING AND CURSING THE WORLD. REMIND THEM AND SHOW THEM ALL!
NO, YOU WERE NEVER LOVED!
RRR RR RROAR
A FAILURE.
GAARA IS USELESS.

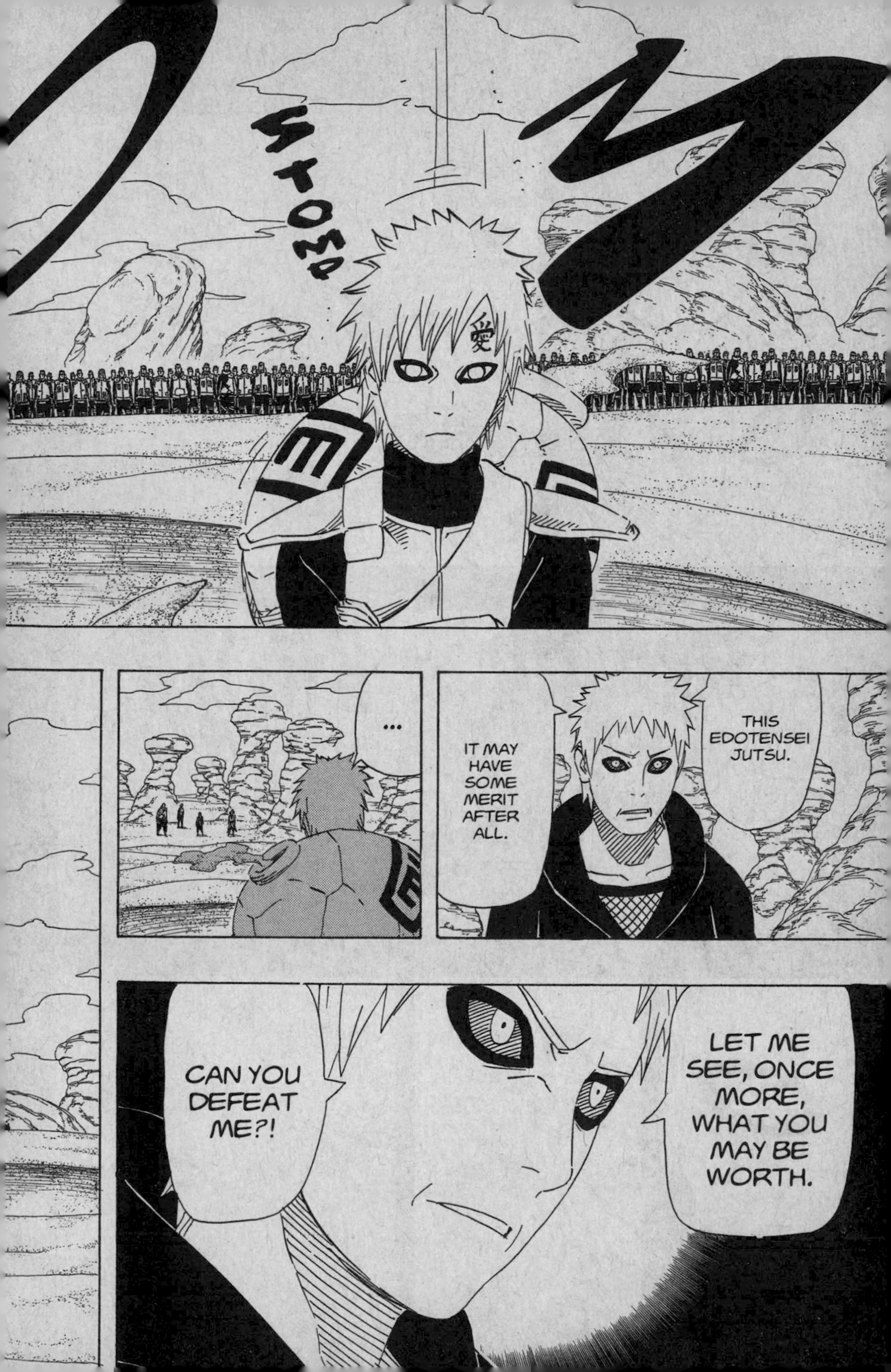
STOMP
THIS EDOTENSEI JUTSU.
IT MAY HAVE SOME MERIT AFTER ALL.
...
LET ME SEE, ONCE MORE, WHAT YOU MAY BE WORTH.
CAN YOU DEFEAT ME?!

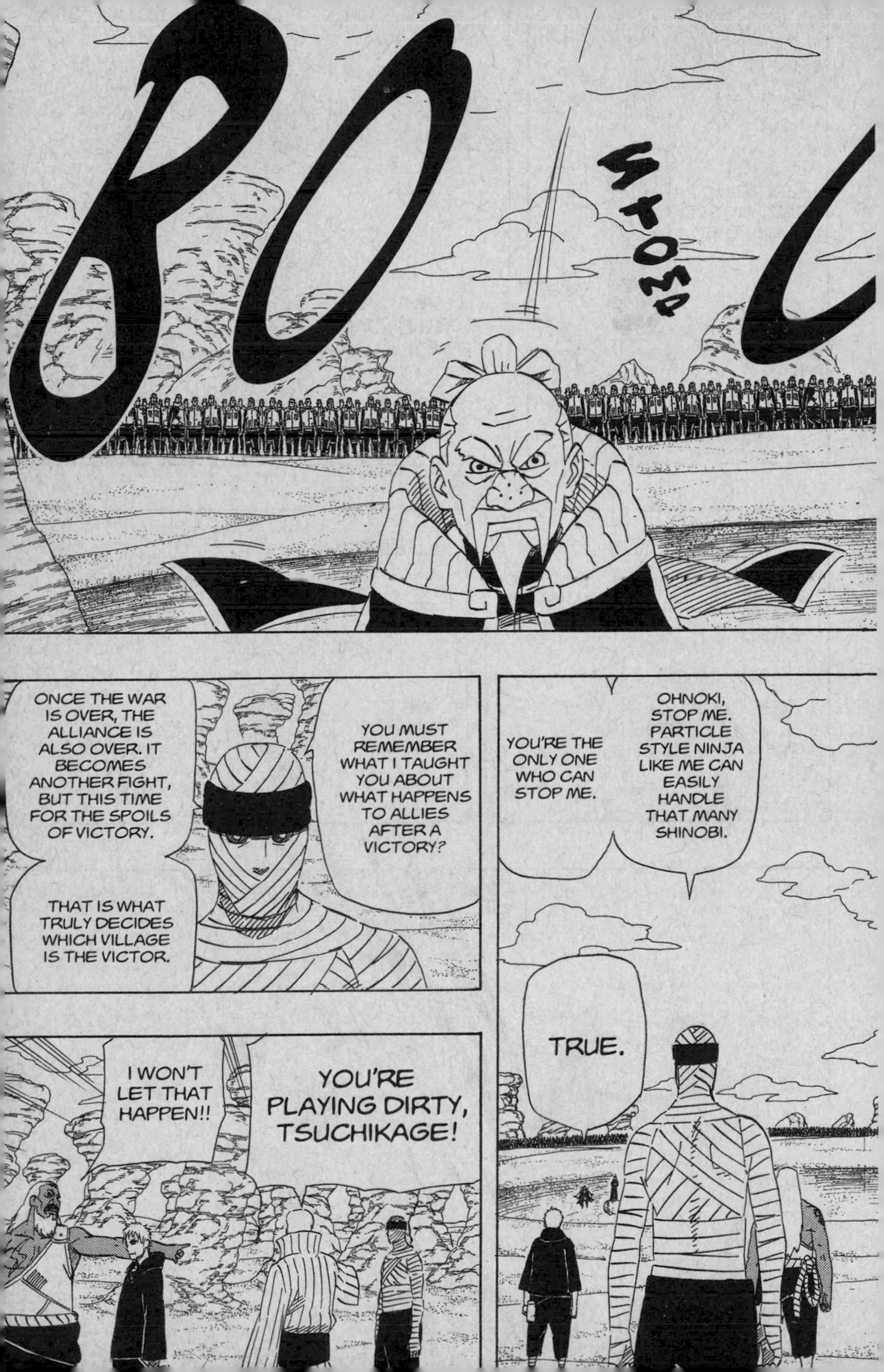
STOMP
OHNOKI, STOP ME. PARTICLE STYLE NINJA LIKE ME CAN EASILY HANDLE THAT MANY SHINOBI.
YOU'RE THE ONLY ONE WHO CAN STOP ME.
YOU MUST REMEMBER WHAT I TAUGHT YOU ABOUT WHAT HAPPENS TO ALLIES AFTER A VICTORY?
ONCE THE WAR IS OVER, THE ALLIANCE IS ALSO OVER. IT BECOMES ANOTHER FIGHT, BUT THIS TIME FOR THE SPOILS OF VICTORY.
THAT IS WHAT TRULY DECIDES WHICH VILLAGE IS THE VICTOR.
TRUE.
YOU'RE PLAYING DIRTY, TSUCHIKAGE!
I WON'T LET THAT HAPPEN!!

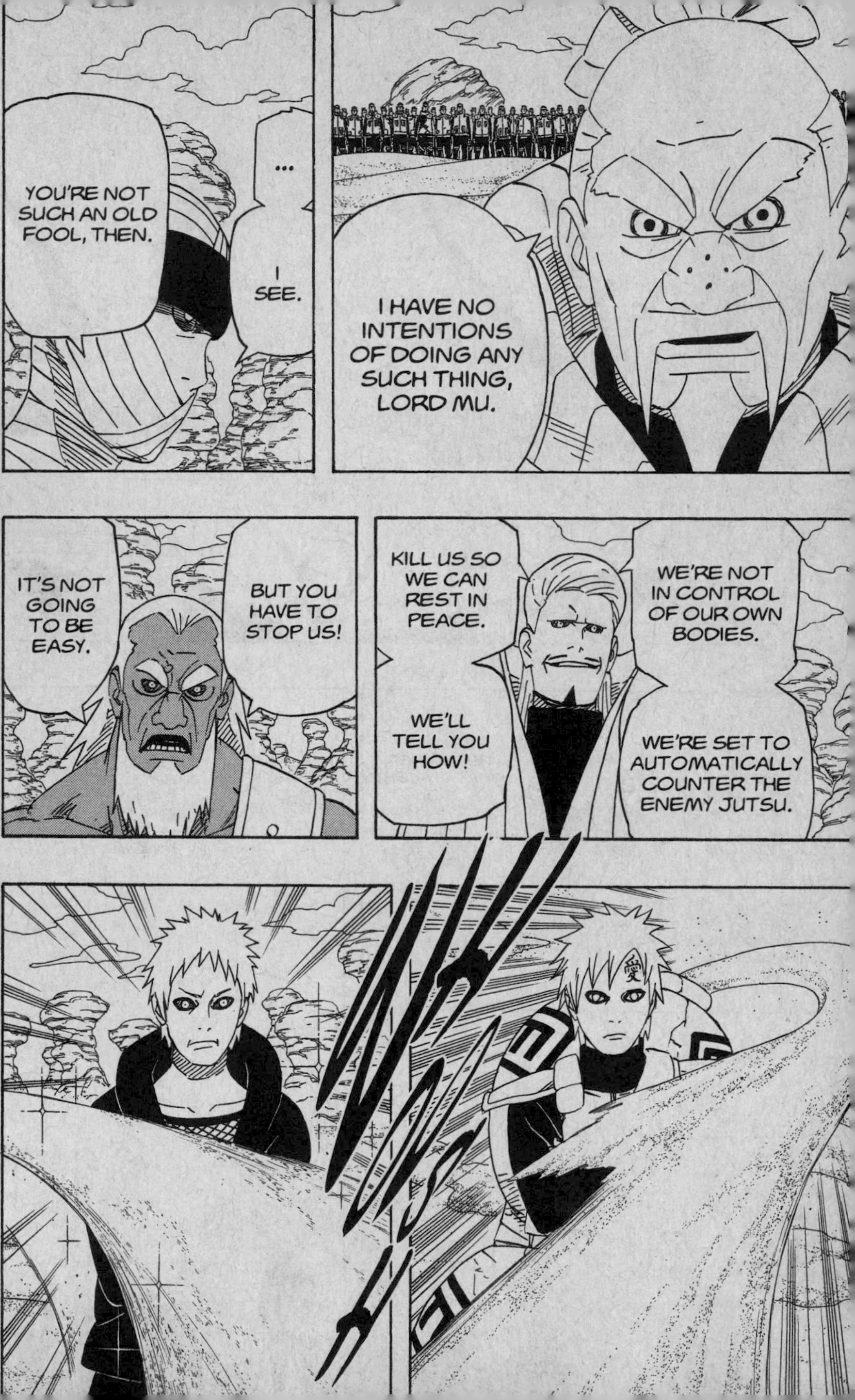
I HAVE NO INTENTIONS OF DOING ANY SUCH THING, LORD MU.
...
I SEE.
YOU'RE NOT SUCH AN OLD FOOL, THEN.
WE'RE NOT IN CONTROL OF OUR OWN BODIES.
WE'RE SET TO AUTOMATICALLY COUNTER THE ENEMY JUTSU.
KILL US SO WE CAN REST IN PEACE.
WE'LL TELL YOU HOW!
BUT YOU HAVE TO STOP US!
IT'S NOT GOING TO BE EASY.

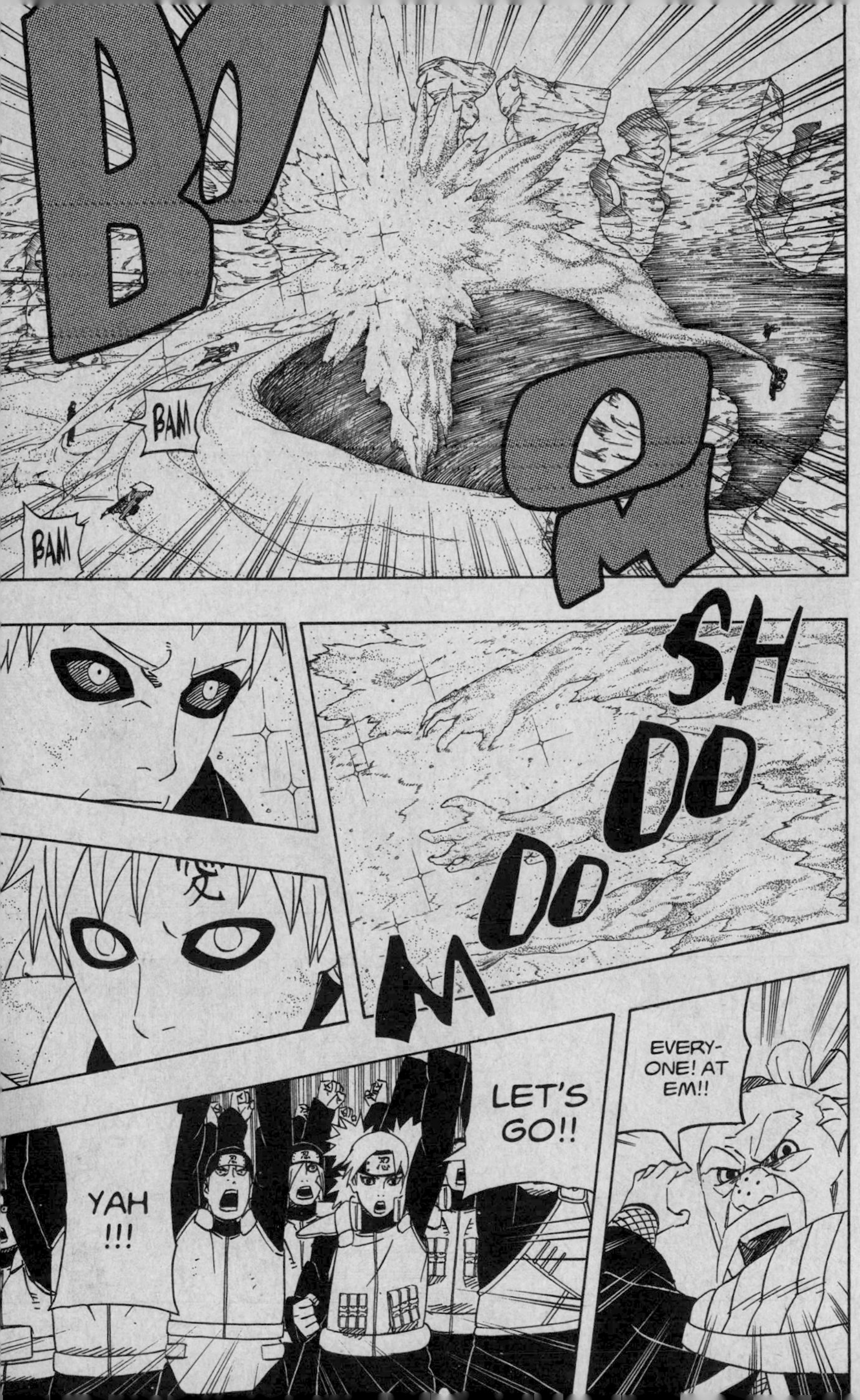
BOOOM
BAM
BAM
SHDODOM
EVERY-ONE! AT EM!!
LET'S GO!!
YAH!!!

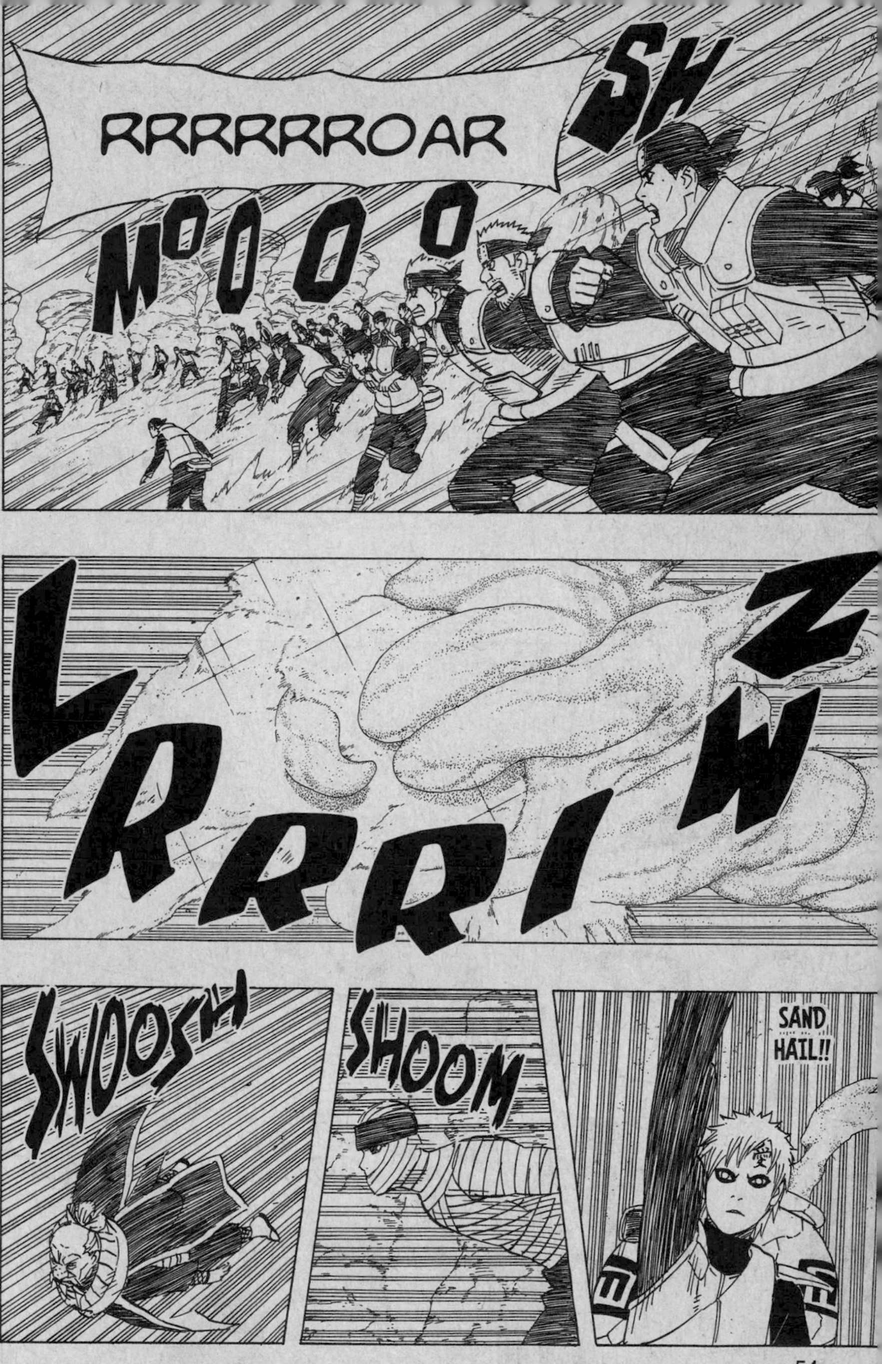
RRRRRROAR
SAND HAIL!!
SHOOM
SWOOSH

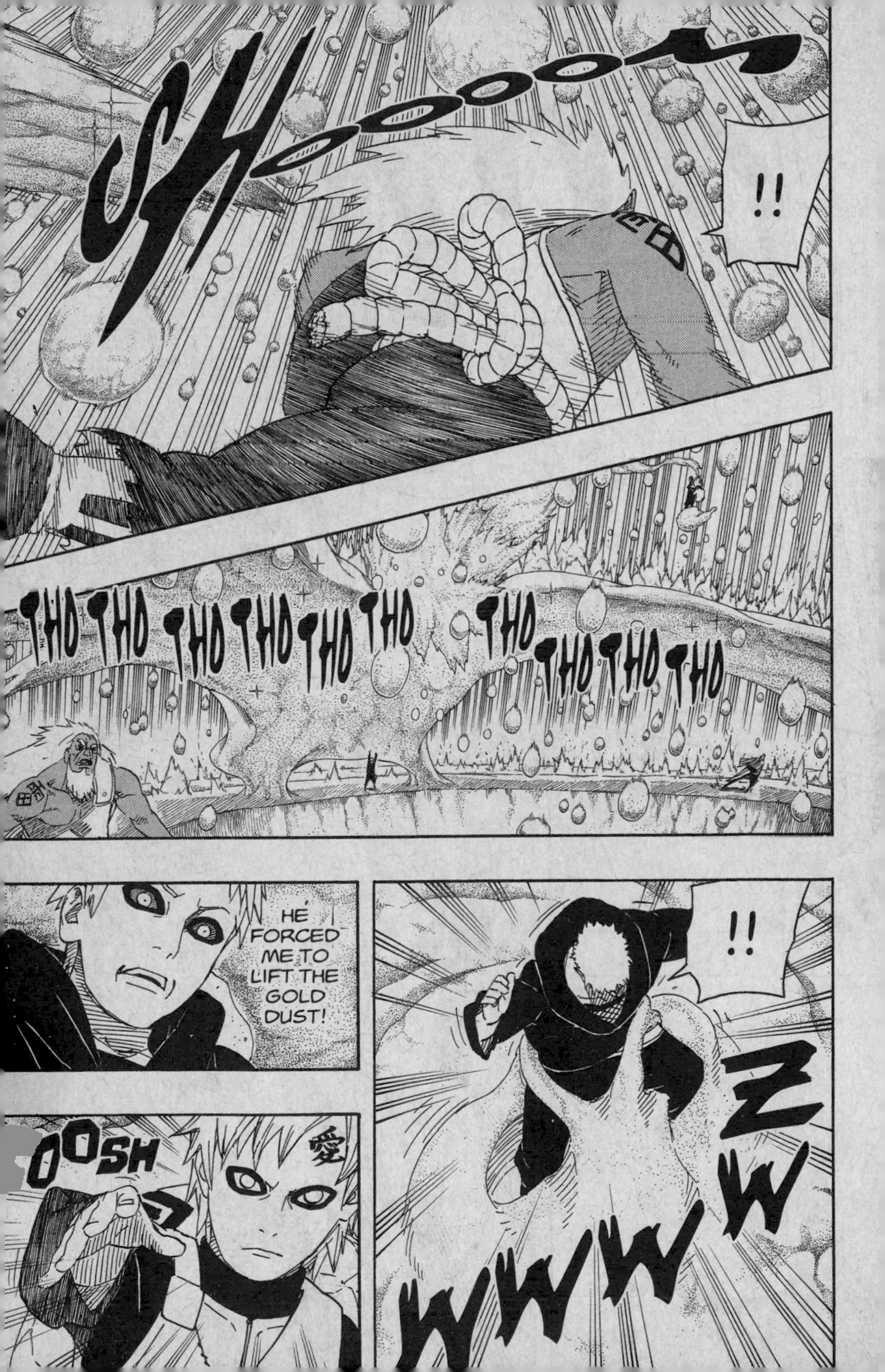
SHOOOOOM
!!
THO THO THO THO THO THO THO THO THO THO
!!
ZWWWWWW
HE FORCED ME TO LIFT THE GOLD DUST!
OOSH

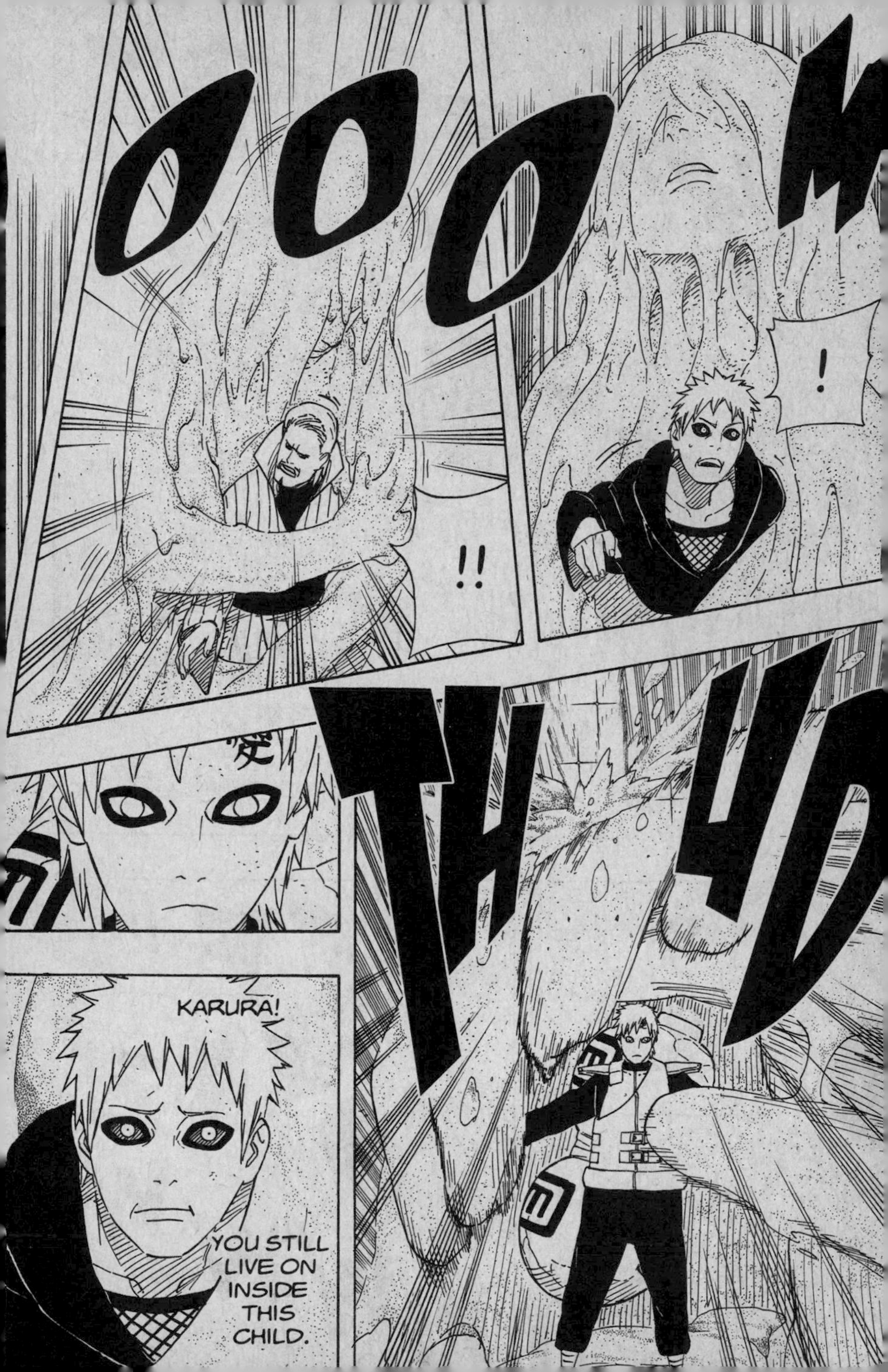
OOOM
!
!!
THUD
KARURA!
YOU STILL LIVE ON INSIDE THIS CHILD.

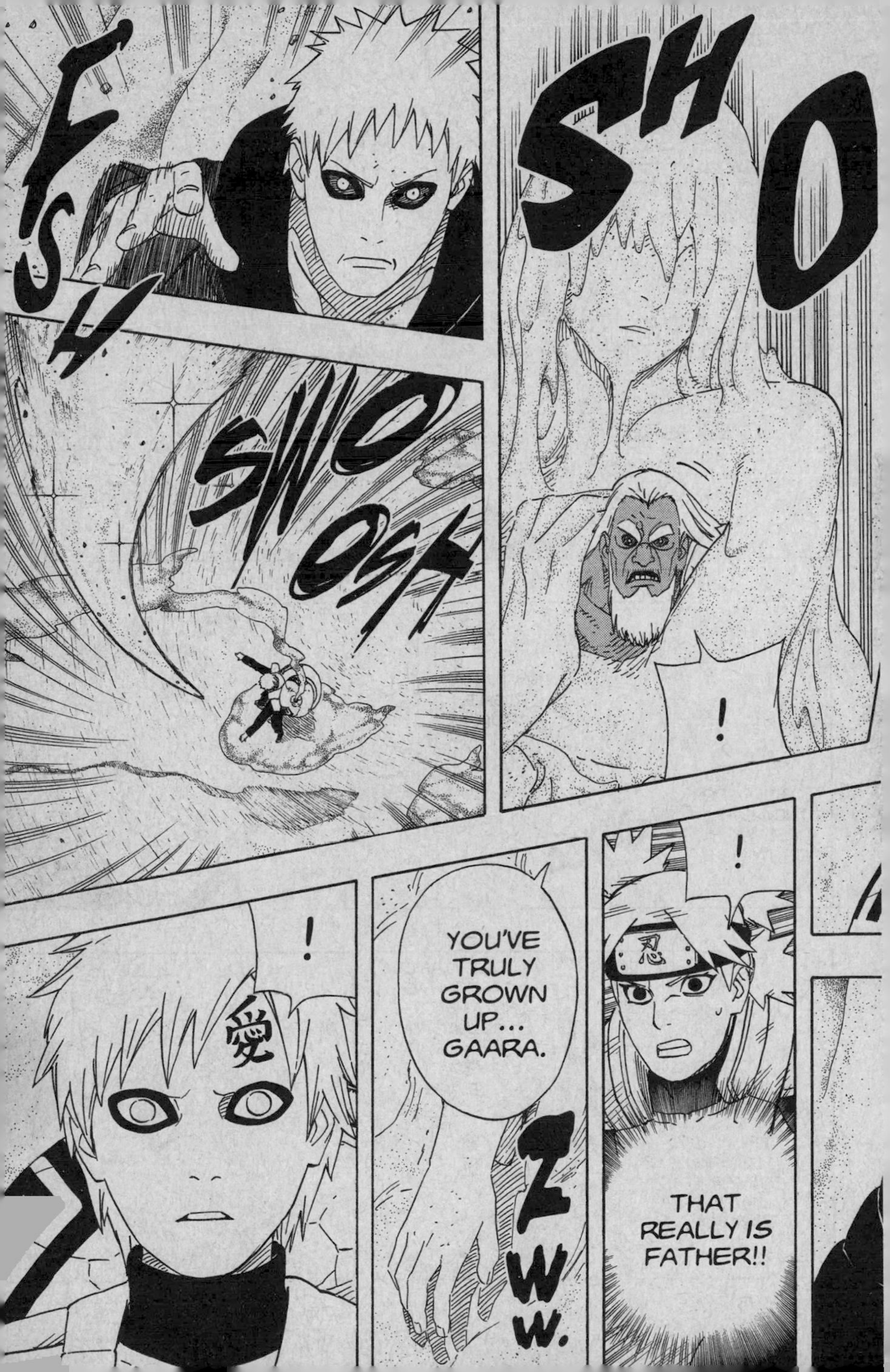
SHO
!
FSH
SWOOSH
!
THAT REALLY IS FATHER!!
YOU'VE TRULY GROWN UP... GAARA.
ZWW.
!

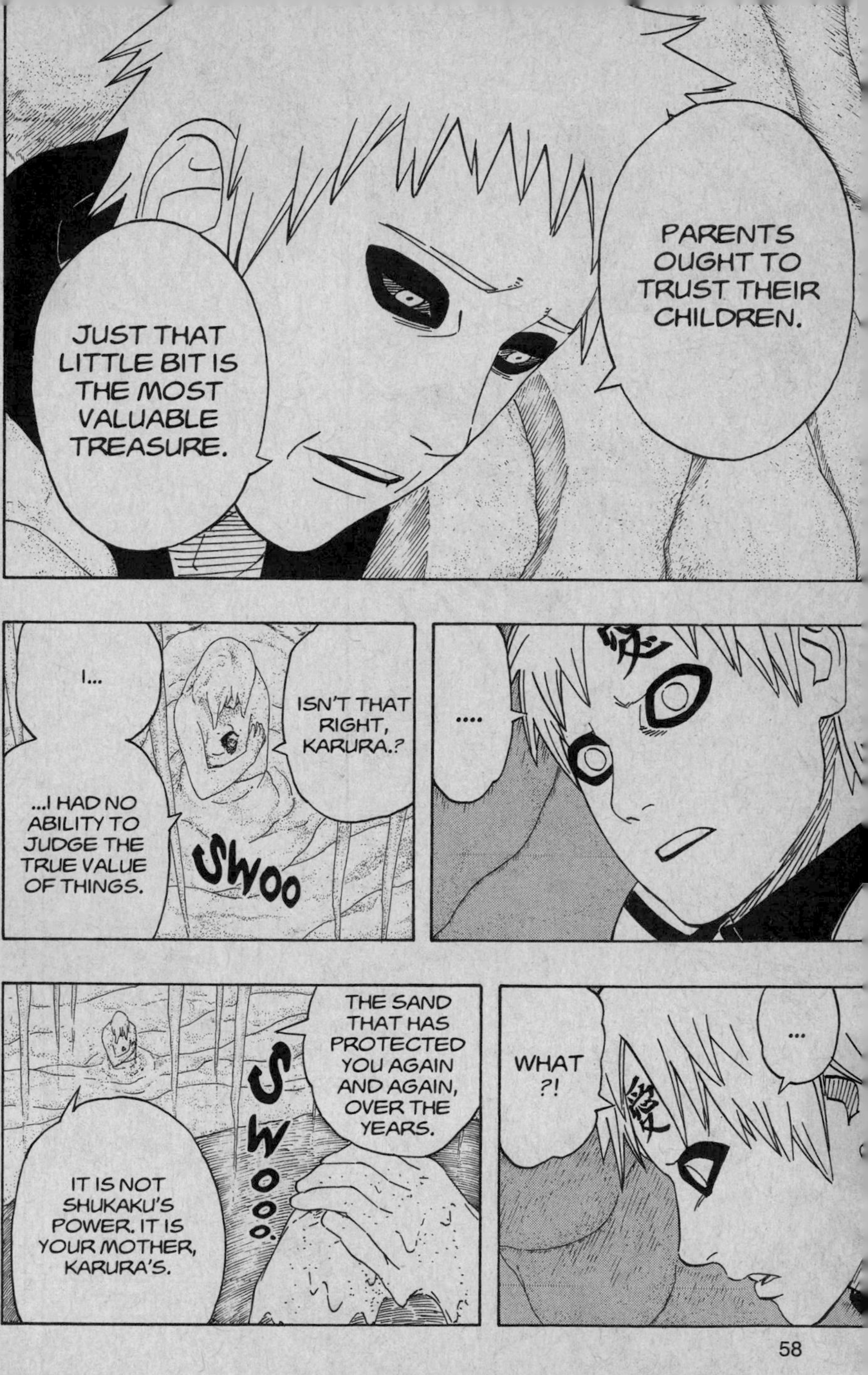
PARENTS OUGHT TO TRUST THEIR CHILDREN.
JUST THAT LITTLE BIT IS THE MOST VALUABLE TREASURE.
....
ISN'T THAT RIGHT, KARURA.?
I...
...I HAD NO ABILITY TO JUDGE THE TRUE VALUE OF THINGS.
SWOO
...
WHAT ?!
THE SAND THAT HAS PROTECTED YOU AGAIN AND AGAIN, OVER THE YEARS.
SWOOOO
IT IS NOT SHUKAKU'S POWER. IT IS YOUR MOTHER, KARURA'S.

READ THIS WAY

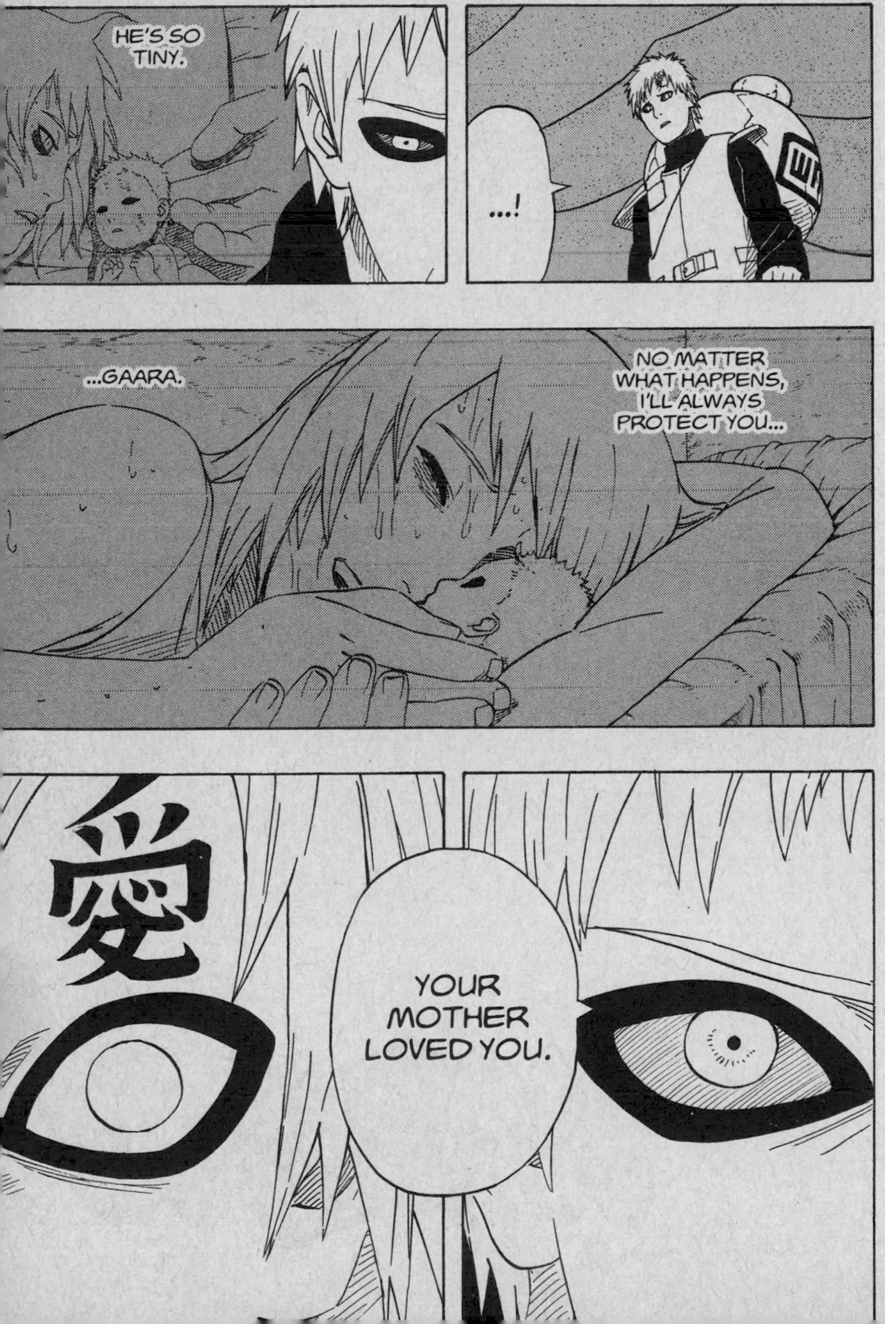
...!
HE'S SO TINY.
NO MATTER WHAT HAPPENS, I'LL ALWAYS PROTECT YOU...
...GAARA.
YOUR MOTHER LOVED YOU.
愛

NARUTO

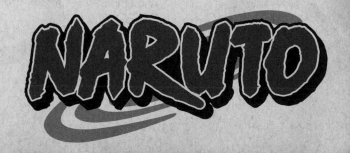

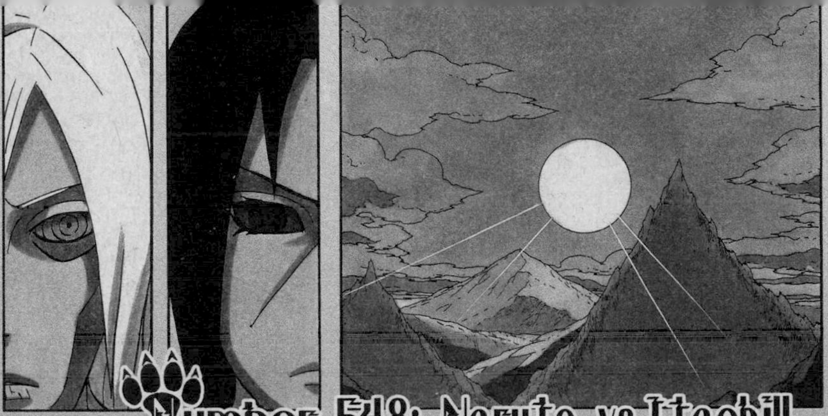

Number 548: Naruto vs. Itachi!!

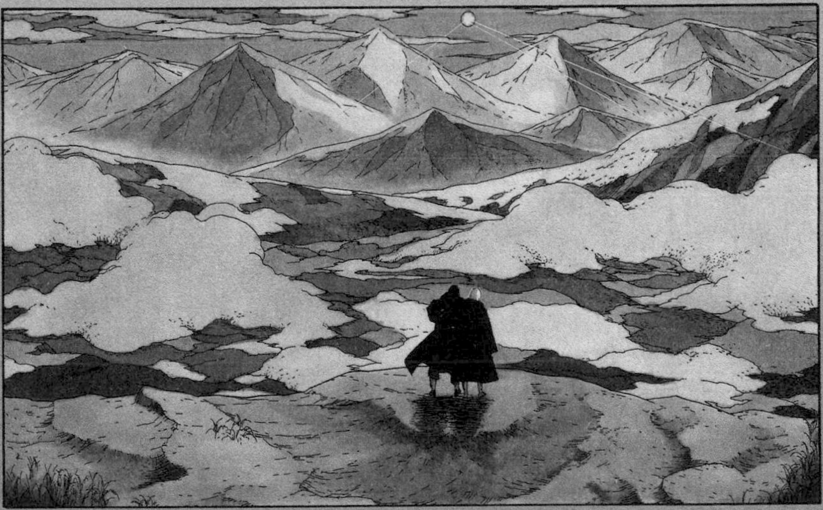

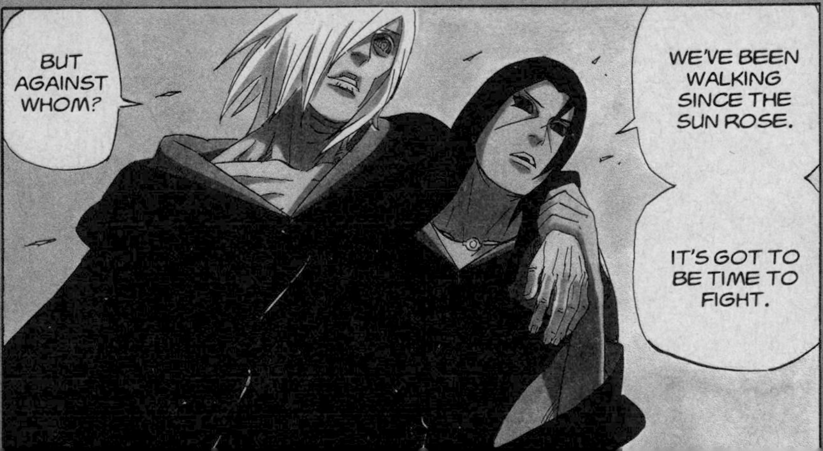
WE'VE BEEN WALKING SINCE THE SUN ROSE.
IT'S GOT TO BE TIME TO FIGHT.
BUT AGAINST WHOM?

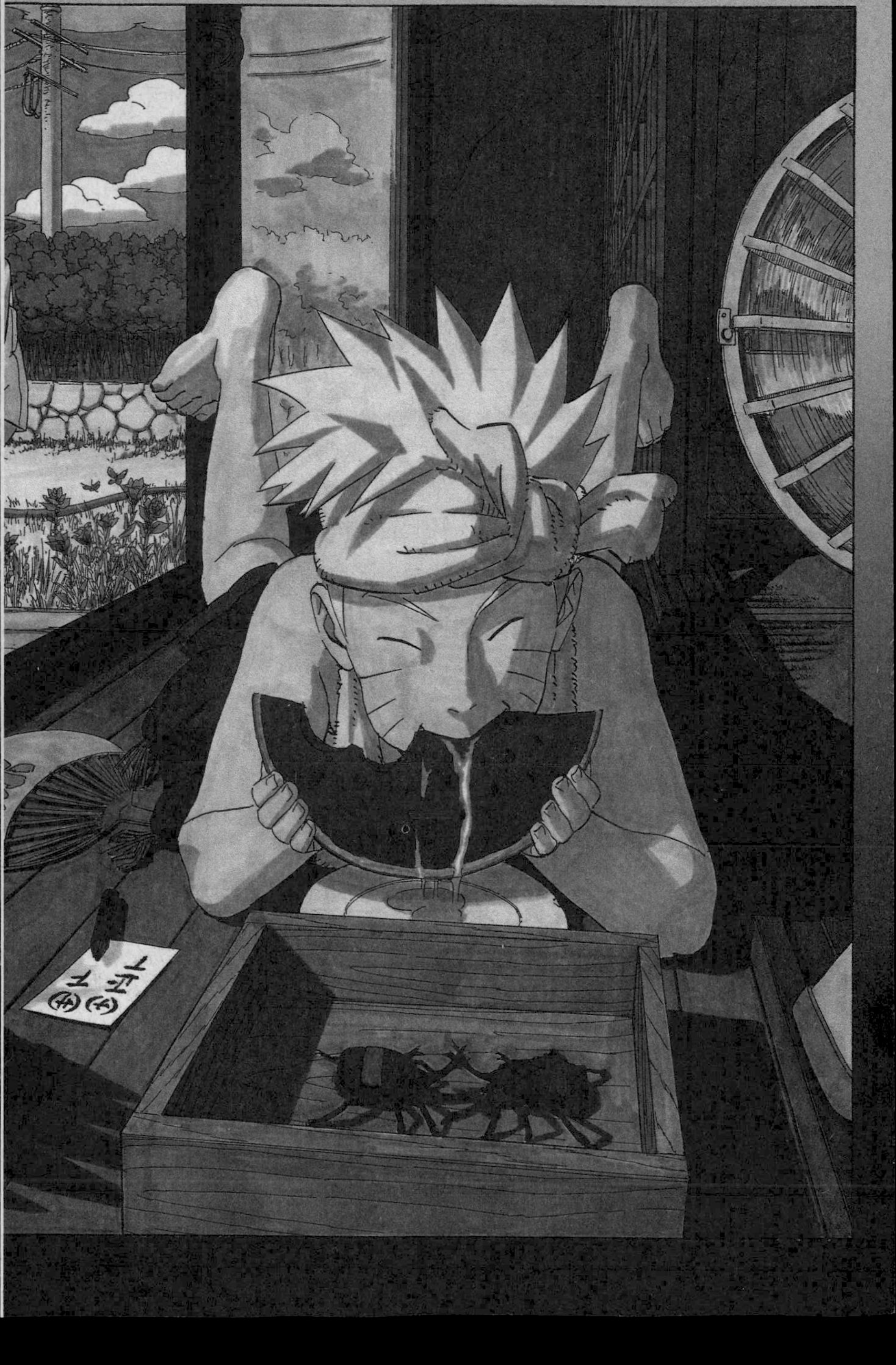

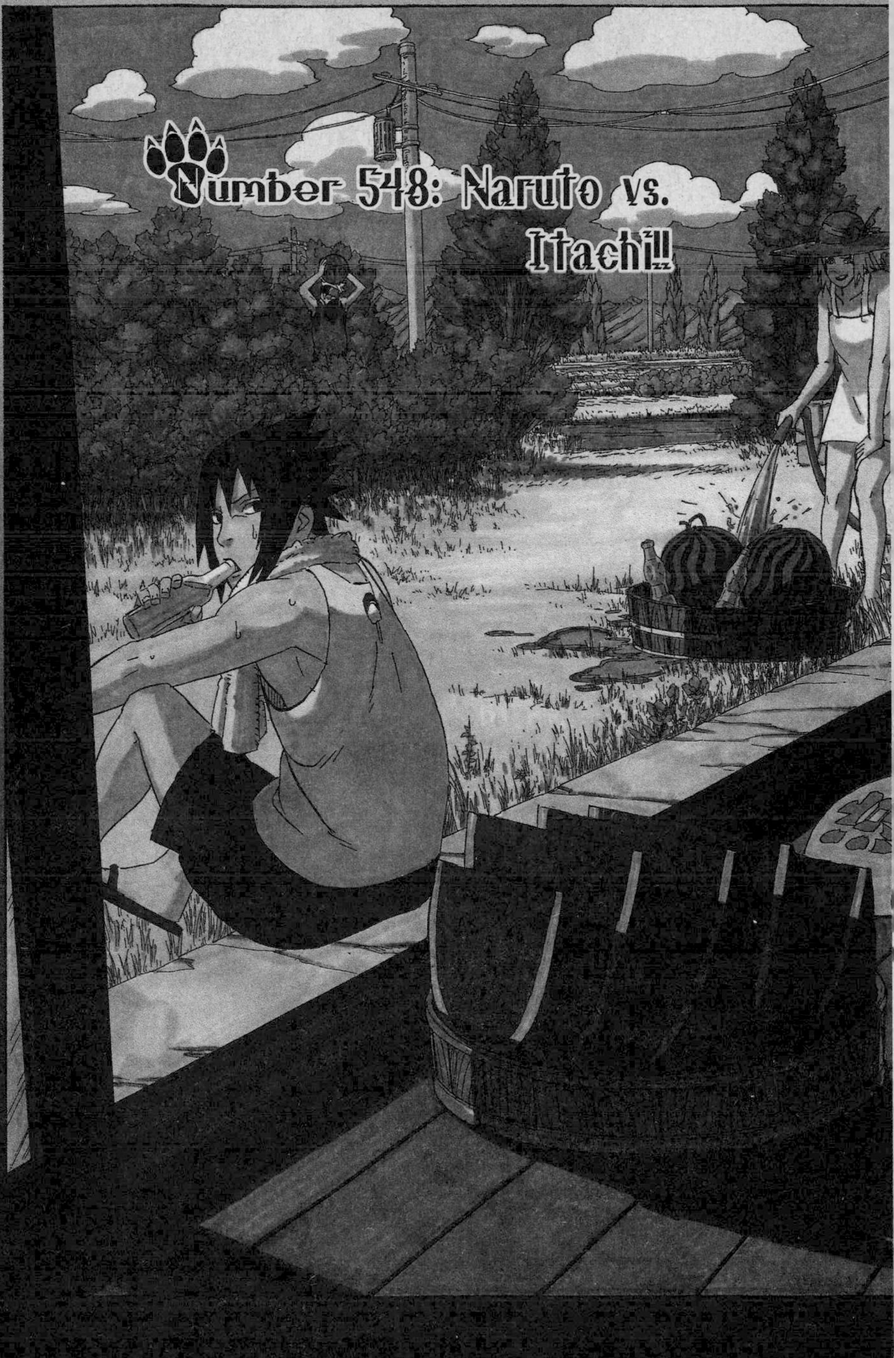
Number 548: Naruto vs. Itachi!!

NARUTO

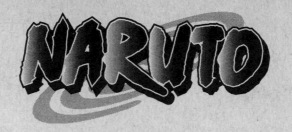

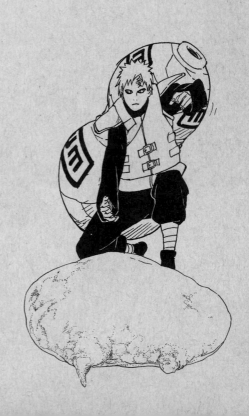

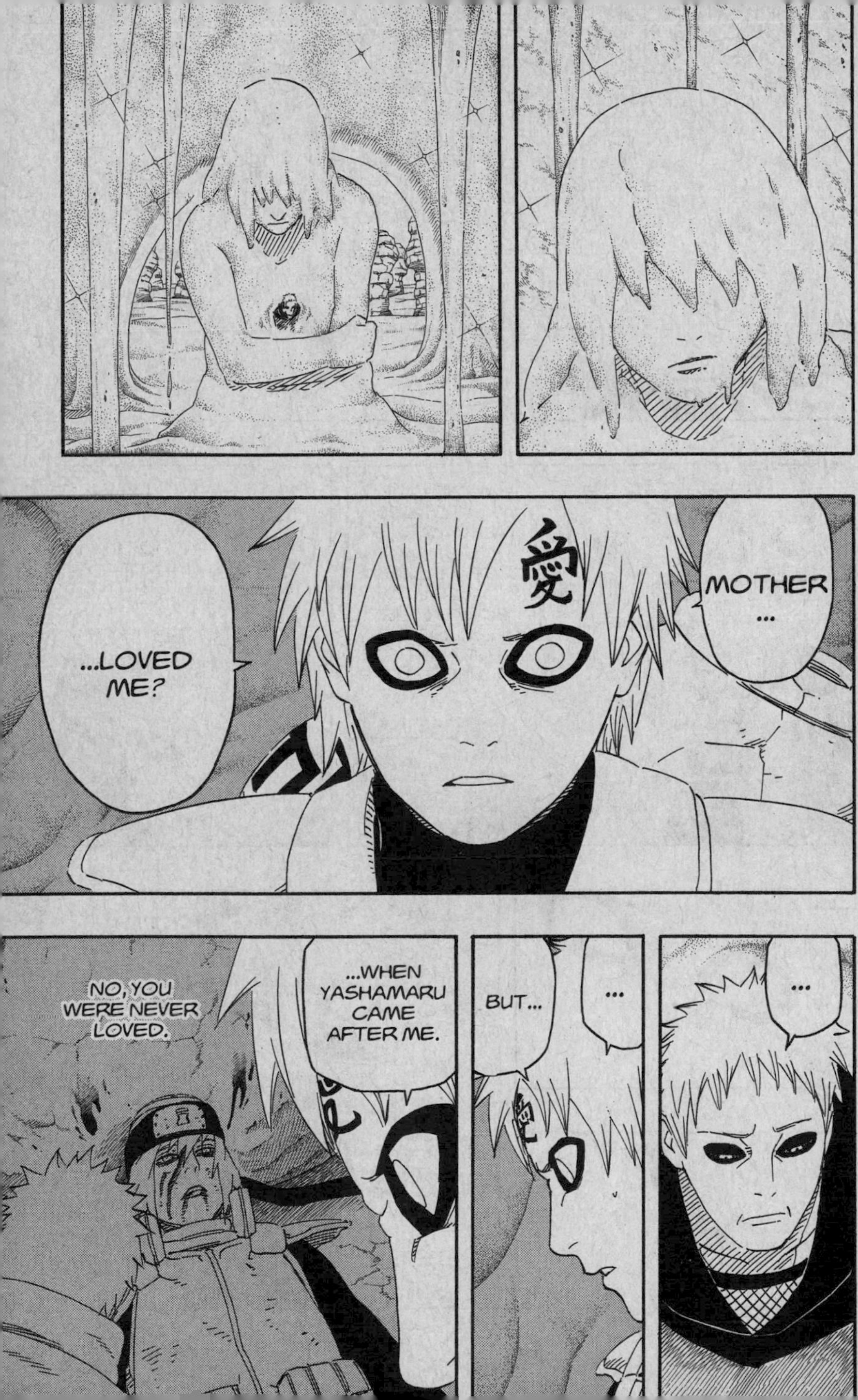
MOTHER ...
...LOVED ME?
...
...
BUT...
...WHEN YASHAMARU CAME AFTER ME.
NO, YOU WERE NEVER LOVED.

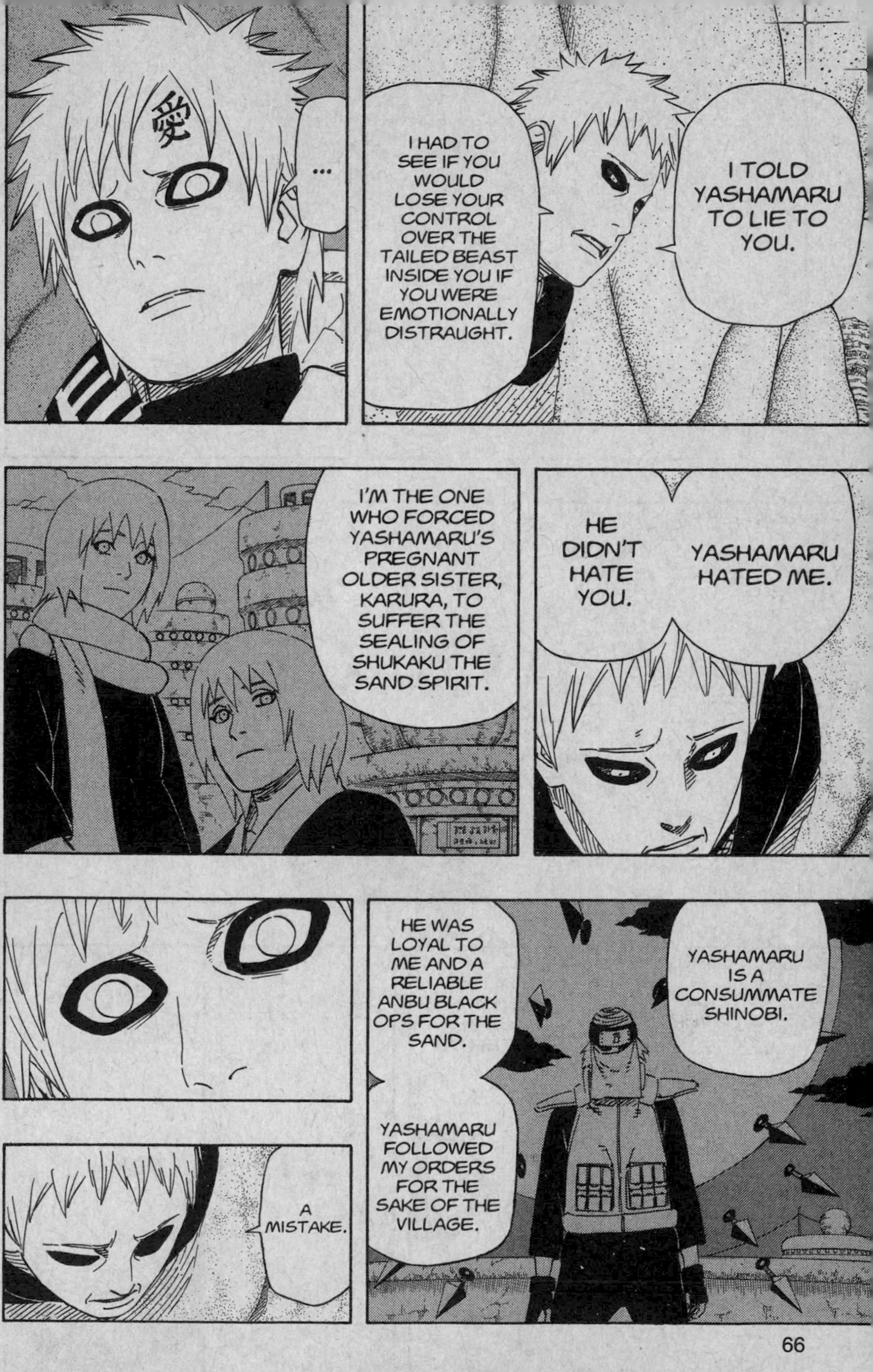
I TOLD YASHAMARU TO LIE TO YOU.
I HAD TO SEE IF YOU WOULD LOSE YOUR CONTROL OVER THE TAILED BEAST INSIDE YOU IF YOU WERE EMOTIONALLY DISTRAUGHT.
...
YASHAMARU HATED ME.
HE DIDN'T HATE YOU.
I'M THE ONE WHO FORCED YASHAMARU'S PREGNANT OLDER SISTER, KARURA, TO SUFFER THE SEALING OF SHUKAKU THE SAND SPIRIT.
YASHAMARU IS A CONSUMMATE SHINOBI.
HE WAS LOYAL TO ME AND A RELIABLE ANBU BLACK OPS FOR THE SAND.
YASHAMARU FOLLOWED MY ORDERS FOR THE SAKE OF THE VILLAGE.
A MISTAKE.

READ THIS WAY

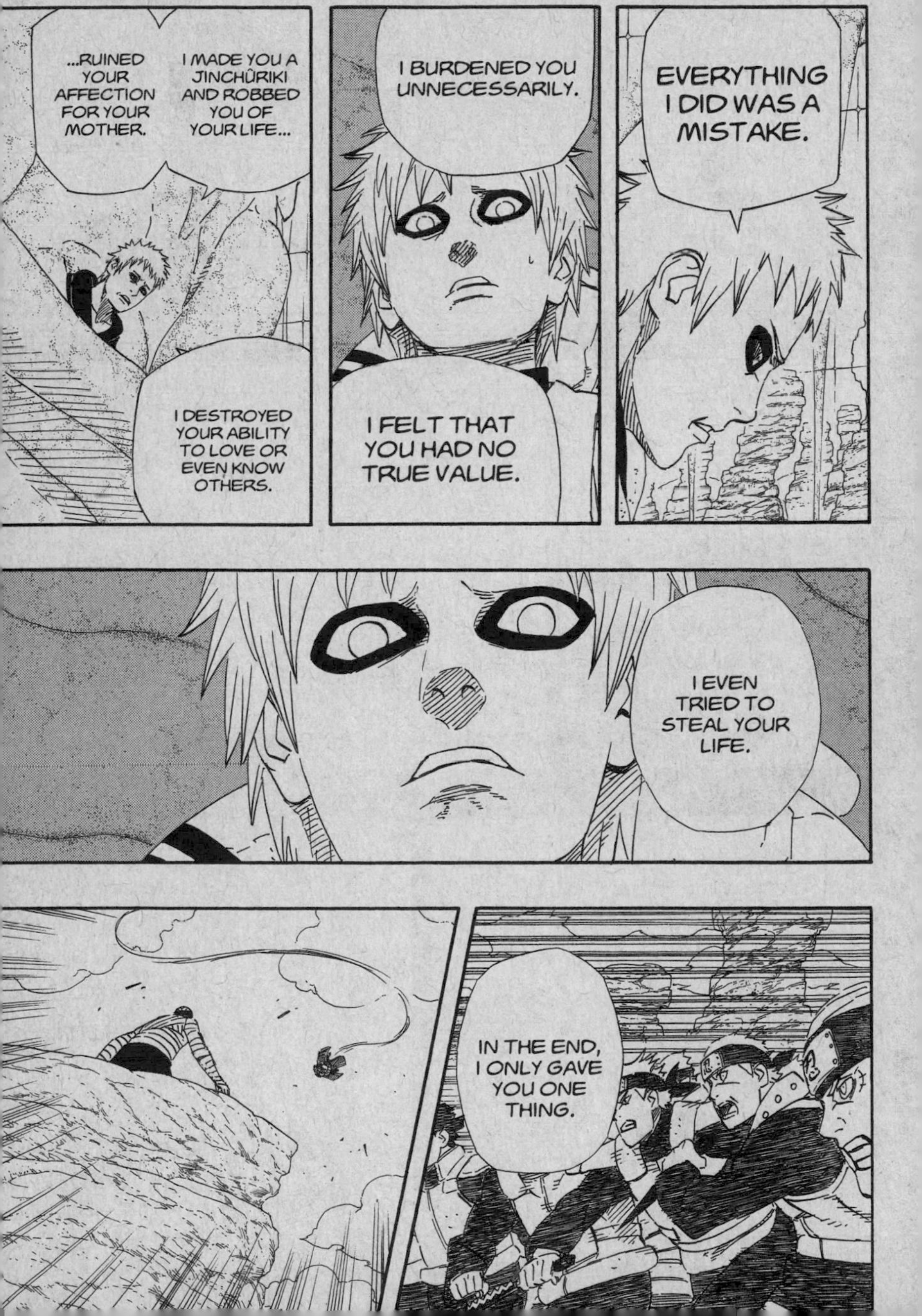
EVERYTHING I DID WAS A MISTAKE.
I BURDENED YOU UNNECESSARILY.
I FELT THAT YOU HAD NO TRUE VALUE.
I MADE YOU A JINCHŪRIKI AND ROBBED YOU OF YOUR LIFE...
...RUINED YOUR AFFECTION FOR YOUR MOTHER.
I DESTROYED YOUR ABILITY TO LOVE OR EVEN KNOW OTHERS.
I EVEN TRIED TO STEAL YOUR LIFE.
IN THE END, I ONLY GAVE YOU ONE THING.

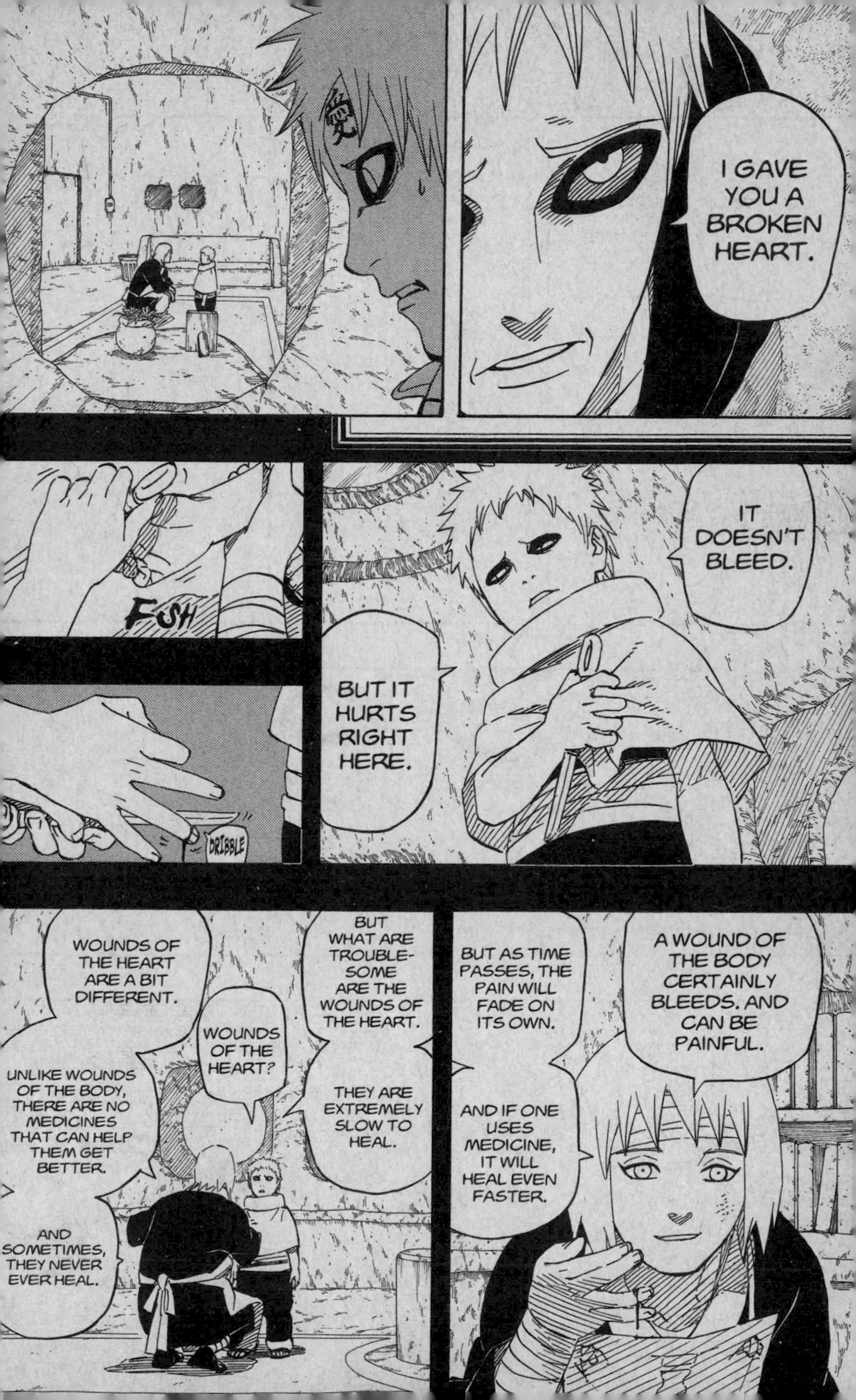
I GAVE YOU A BROKEN HEART.
IT DOESN'T BLEED.
BUT IT HURTS RIGHT HERE.
FSH
DRIBBLE
A WOUND OF THE BODY CERTAINLY BLEEDS. AND CAN BE PAINFUL.
BUT AS TIME PASSES, THE PAIN WILL FADE ON ITS OWN.
AND IF ONE USES MEDICINE, IT WILL HEAL EVEN FASTER.
BUT WHAT ARE TROUBLE-SOME ARE THE WOUNDS OF THE HEART.
THEY ARE EXTREMELY SLOW TO HEAL.
WOUNDS OF THE HEART?
WOUNDS OF THE HEART ARE A BIT DIFFERENT.
UNLIKE WOUNDS OF THE BODY, THERE ARE NO MEDICINES THAT CAN HELP THEM GET BETTER.
AND SOMETIMES, THEY NEVER EVER HEAL.

READ THIS WAY

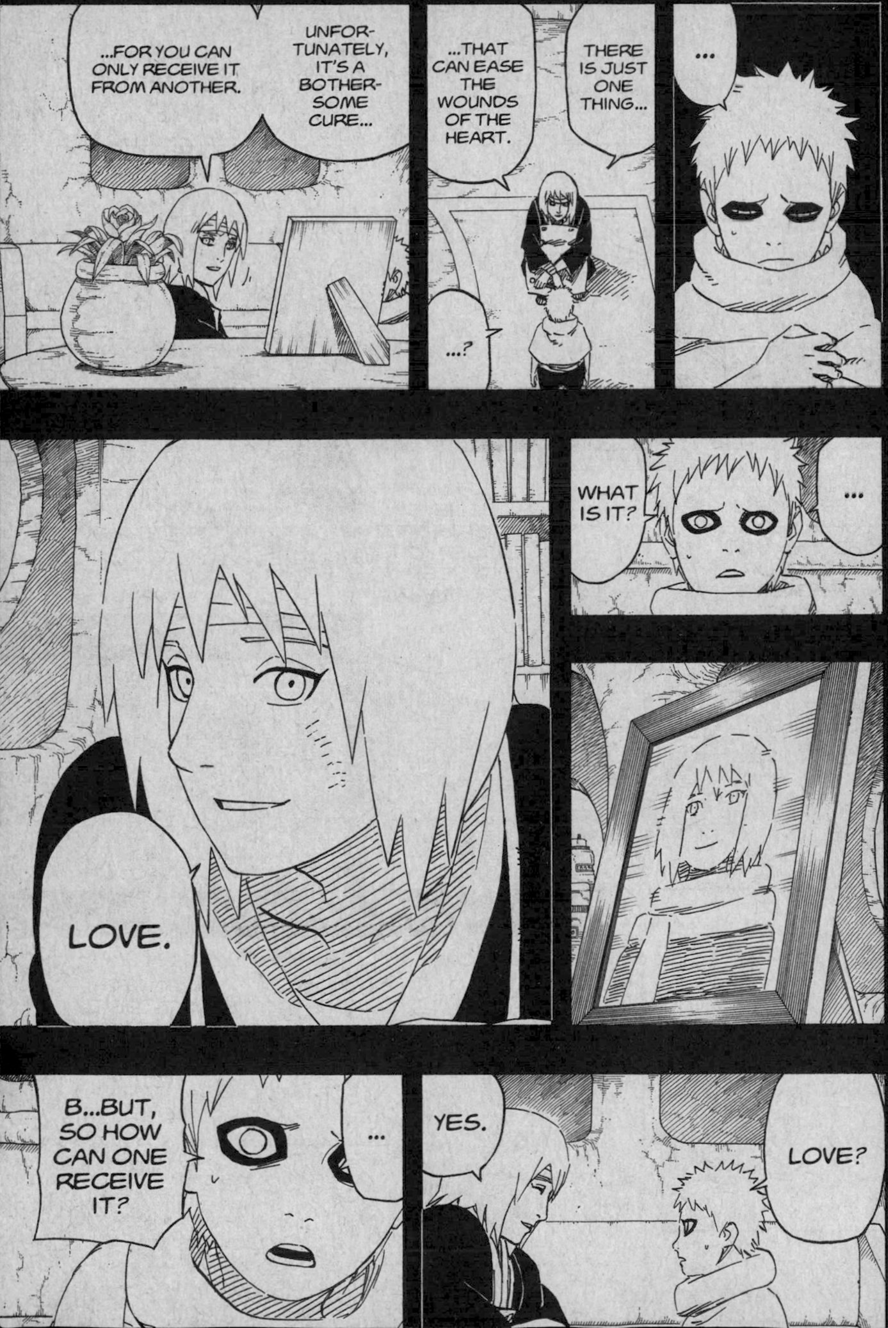
...
THERE IS JUST ONE THING...
...THAT CAN EASE THE WOUNDS OF THE HEART.
...?
UNFORTUNATELY, IT'S A BOTHERSOME CURE...
...FOR YOU CAN ONLY RECEIVE IT FROM ANOTHER.
...
WHAT IS IT?
LOVE.
LOVE?
YES.
...
B...BUT, SO HOW CAN ONE RECEIVE IT?

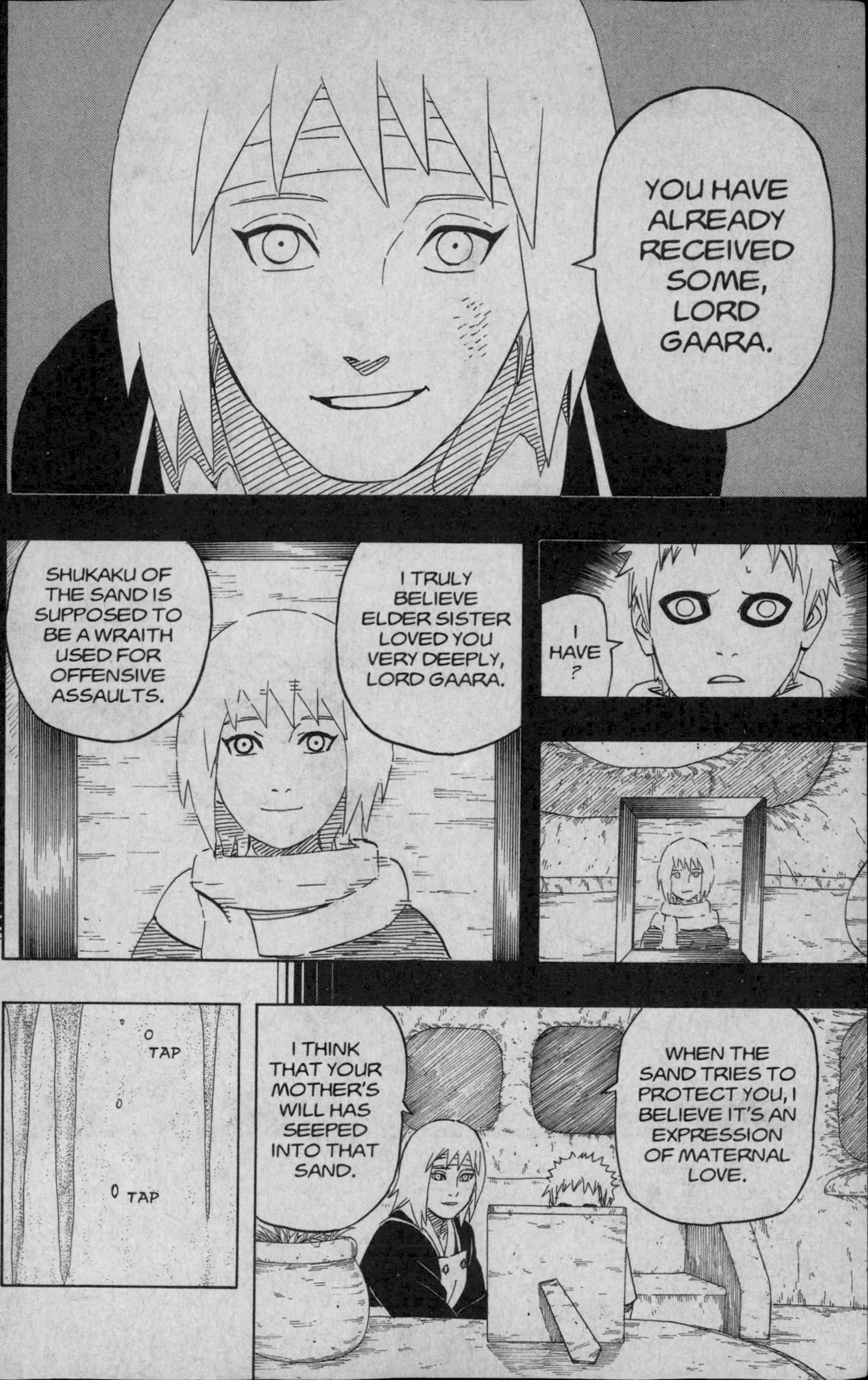
YOU HAVE ALREADY RECEIVED SOME, LORD GAARA.
I HAVE?
I TRULY BELIEVE ELDER SISTER LOVED YOU VERY DEEPLY, LORD GAARA.
SHUKAKU OF THE SAND IS SUPPOSED TO BE A WRAITH USED FOR OFFENSIVE ASSAULTS.
WHEN THE SAND TRIES TO PROTECT YOU, I BELIEVE IT'S AN EXPRESSION OF MATERNAL LOVE.
I THINK THAT YOUR MOTHER'S WILL HAS SEEPED INTO THAT SAND.
TAP
TAP

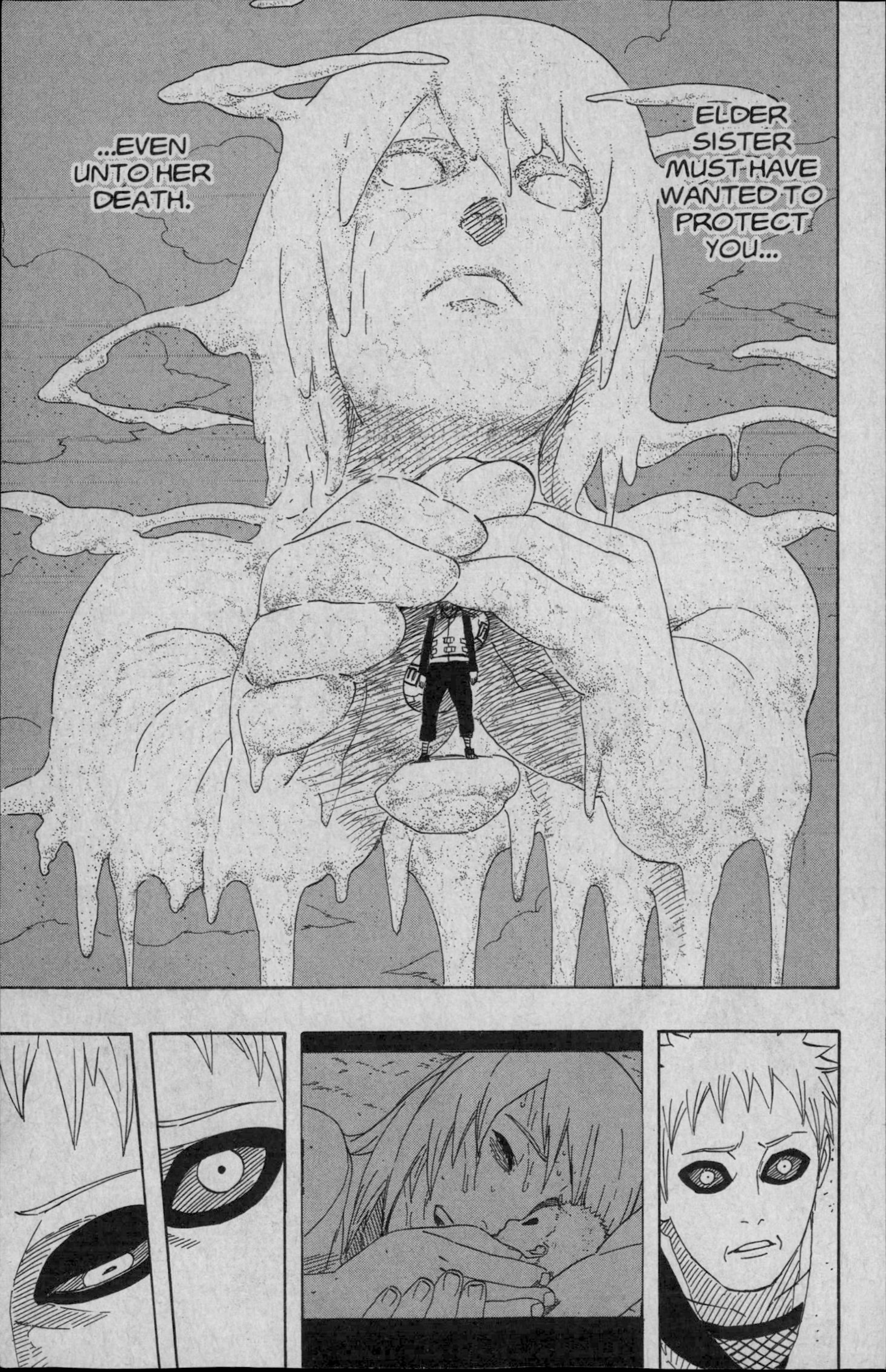
ELDER SISTER MUST HAVE WANTED TO PROTECT YOU...
...EVEN UNTO HER DEATH.

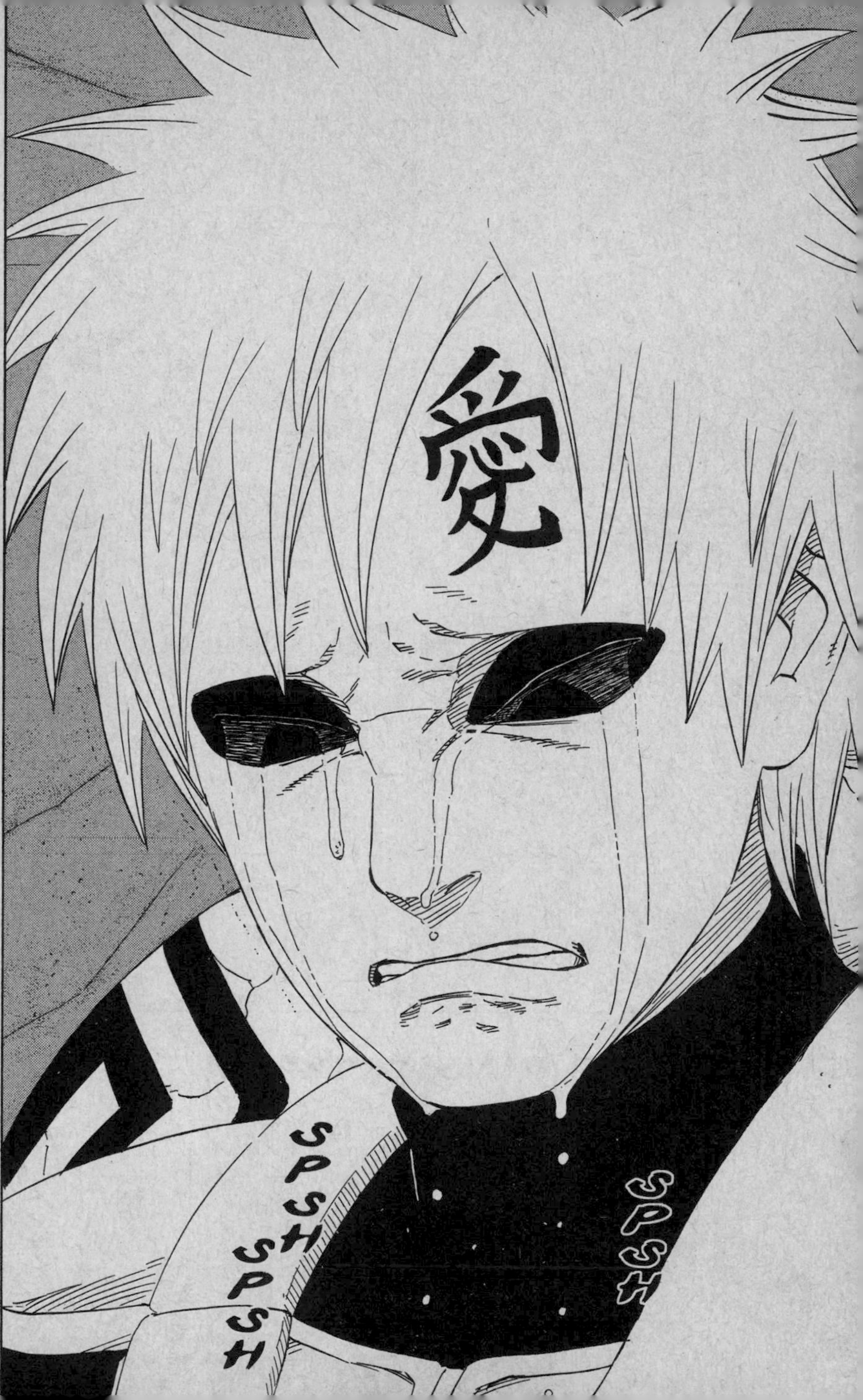
愛
SPSH
SPSH SPSH SPSH

READ THIS WAY

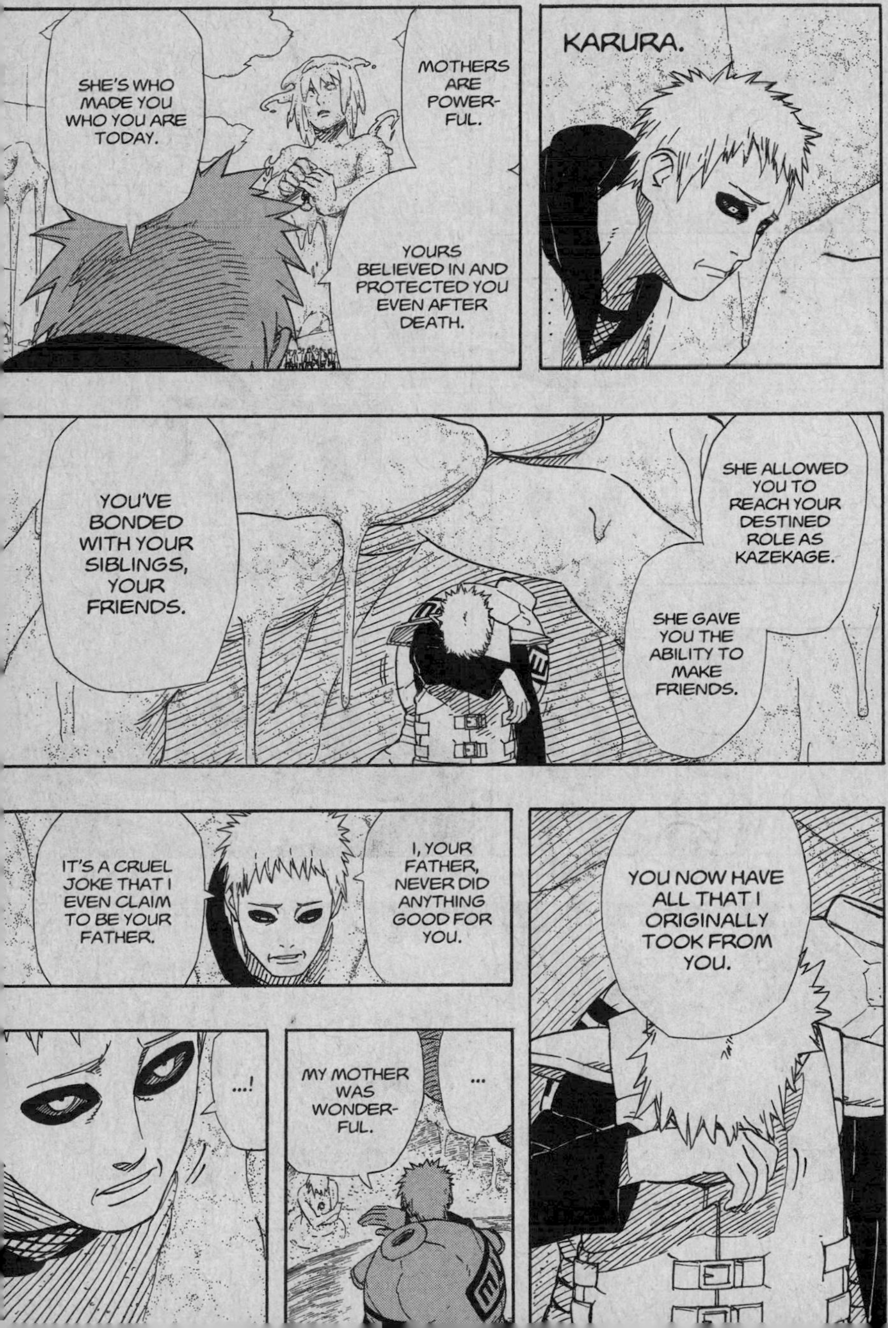
KARURA.
MOTHERS ARE POWERFUL.
YOURS BELIEVED IN AND PROTECTED YOU EVEN AFTER DEATH.
SHE'S WHO MADE YOU WHO YOU ARE TODAY.
SHE ALLOWED YOU TO REACH YOUR DESTINED ROLE AS KAZEKAGE.
SHE GAVE YOU THE ABILITY TO MAKE FRIENDS.
YOU'VE BONDED WITH YOUR SIBLINGS, YOUR FRIENDS.
YOU NOW HAVE ALL THAT I ORIGINALLY TOOK FROM YOU.
I, YOUR FATHER, NEVER DID ANYTHING GOOD FOR YOU.
IT'S A CRUEL JOKE THAT I EVEN CLAIM TO BE YOUR FATHER.
...
MY MOTHER WAS WONDERFUL.
...!

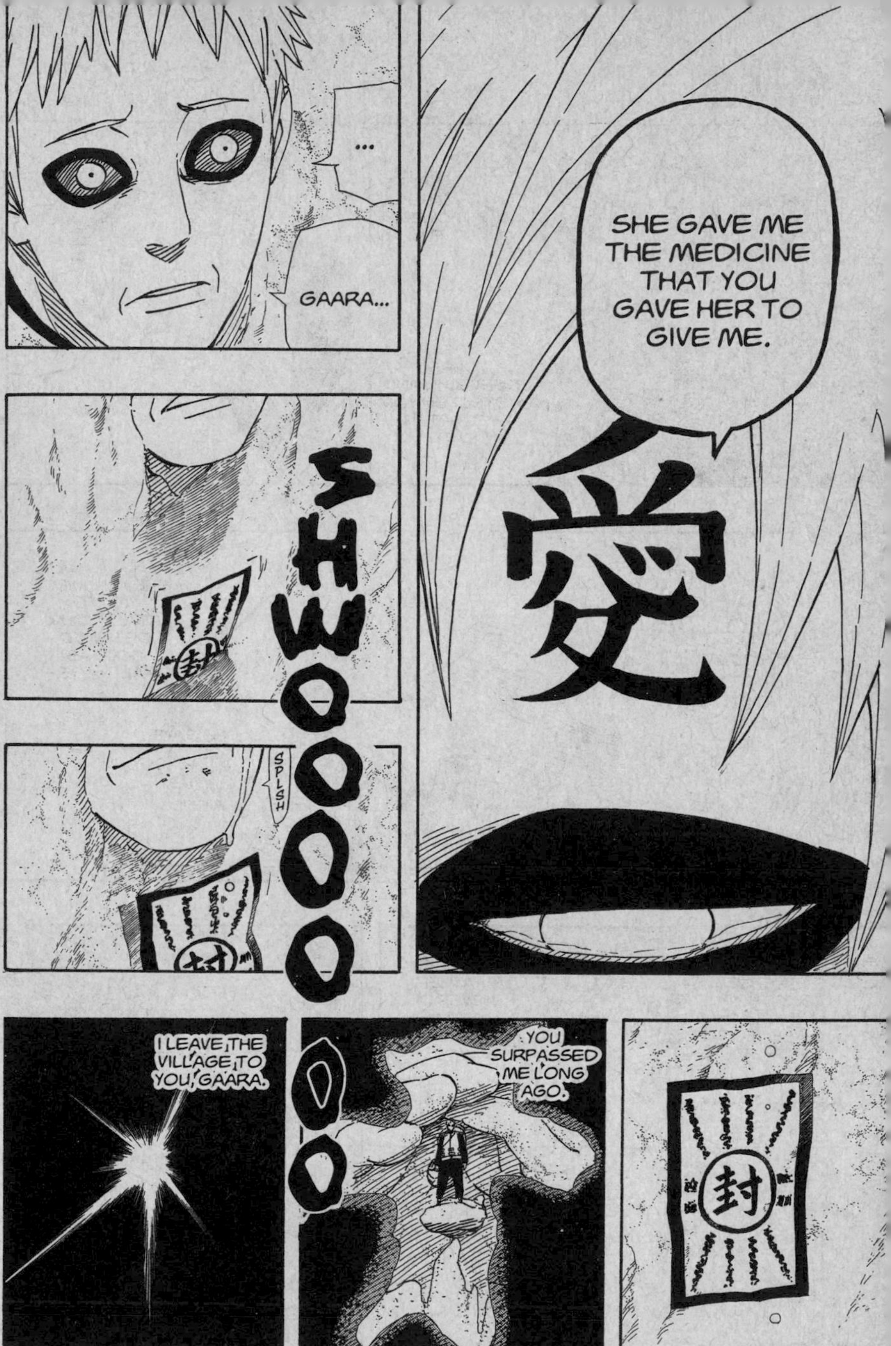
SHE GAVE ME THE MEDICINE THAT YOU GAVE HER TO GIVE ME.
...
GAARA...
SHWOOOOOOO
SPLSH
YOU SURPASSED ME LONG AGO.
I LEAVE THE VILLAGE TO YOU, GAARA.

READ THIS WAY

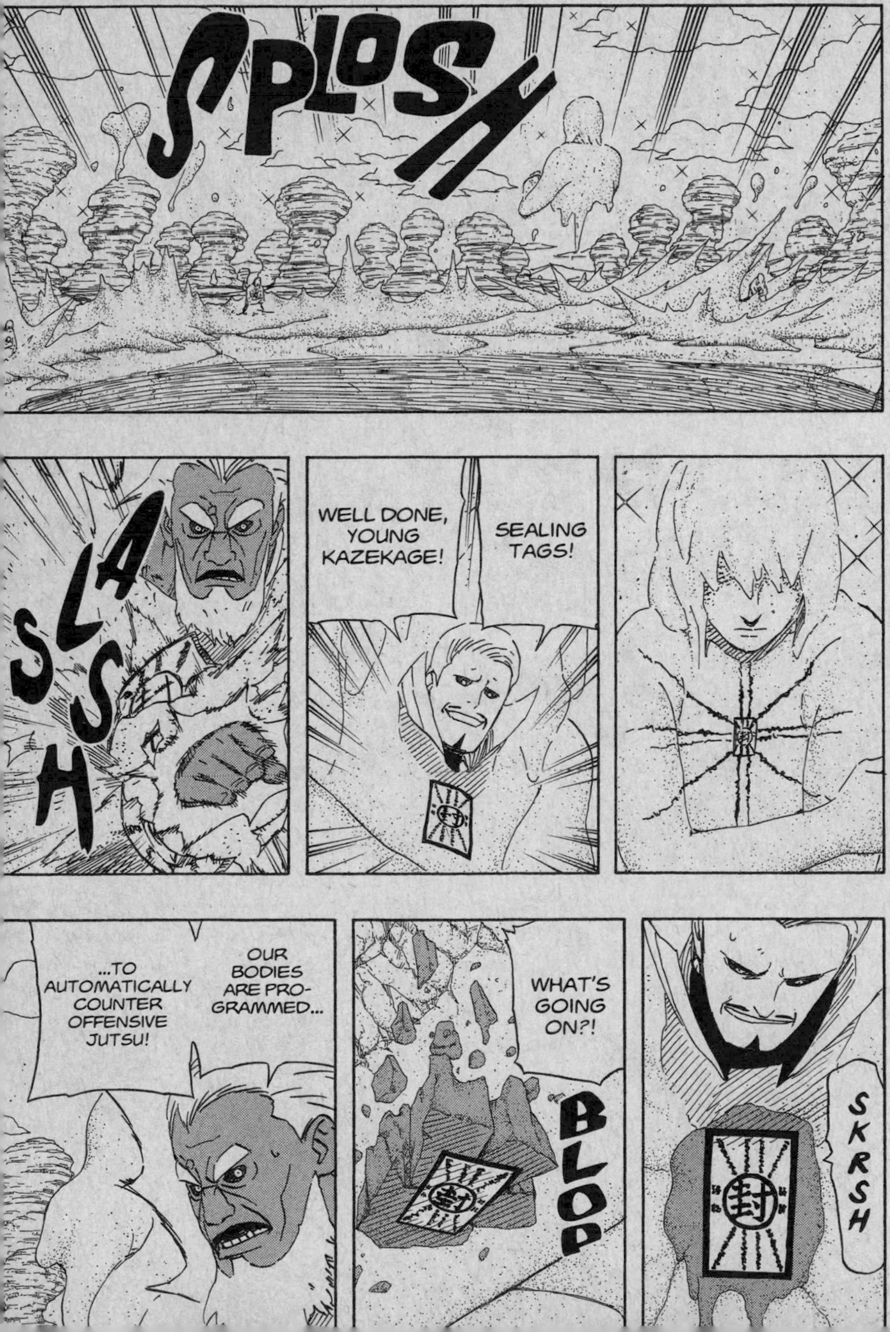
SPLOSH
SEALING TAGS!
WELL DONE, YOUNG KAZEKAGE!
SLASH
SKRSH
WHAT'S GOING ON?!
BLOP
OUR BODIES ARE PRO-GRAMMED...
...TO AUTOMATICALLY COUNTER OFFENSIVE JUTSU!

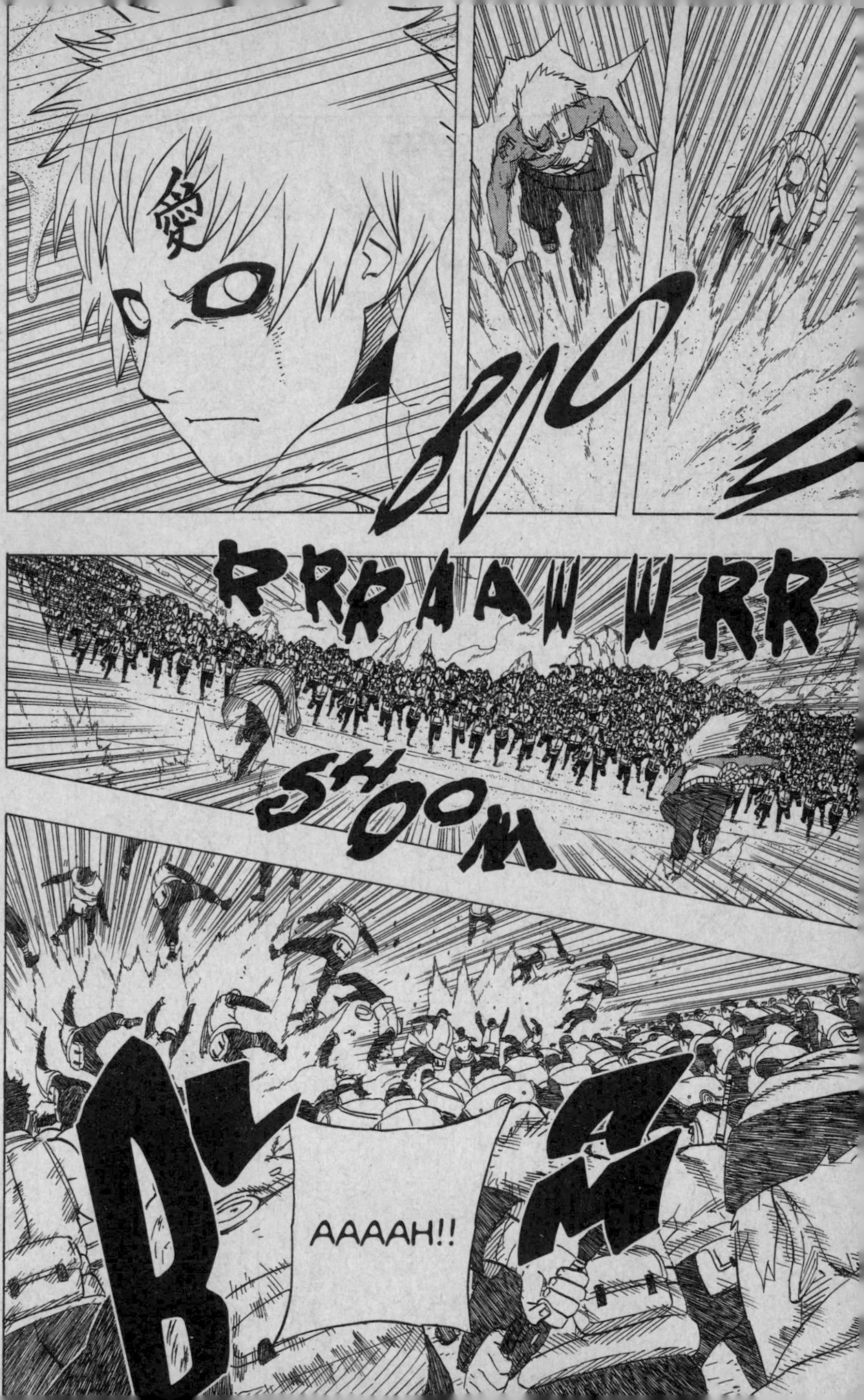
RRRAAW WRR
SHOOM
BLAM
AAAAH!!

READ THIS WAY

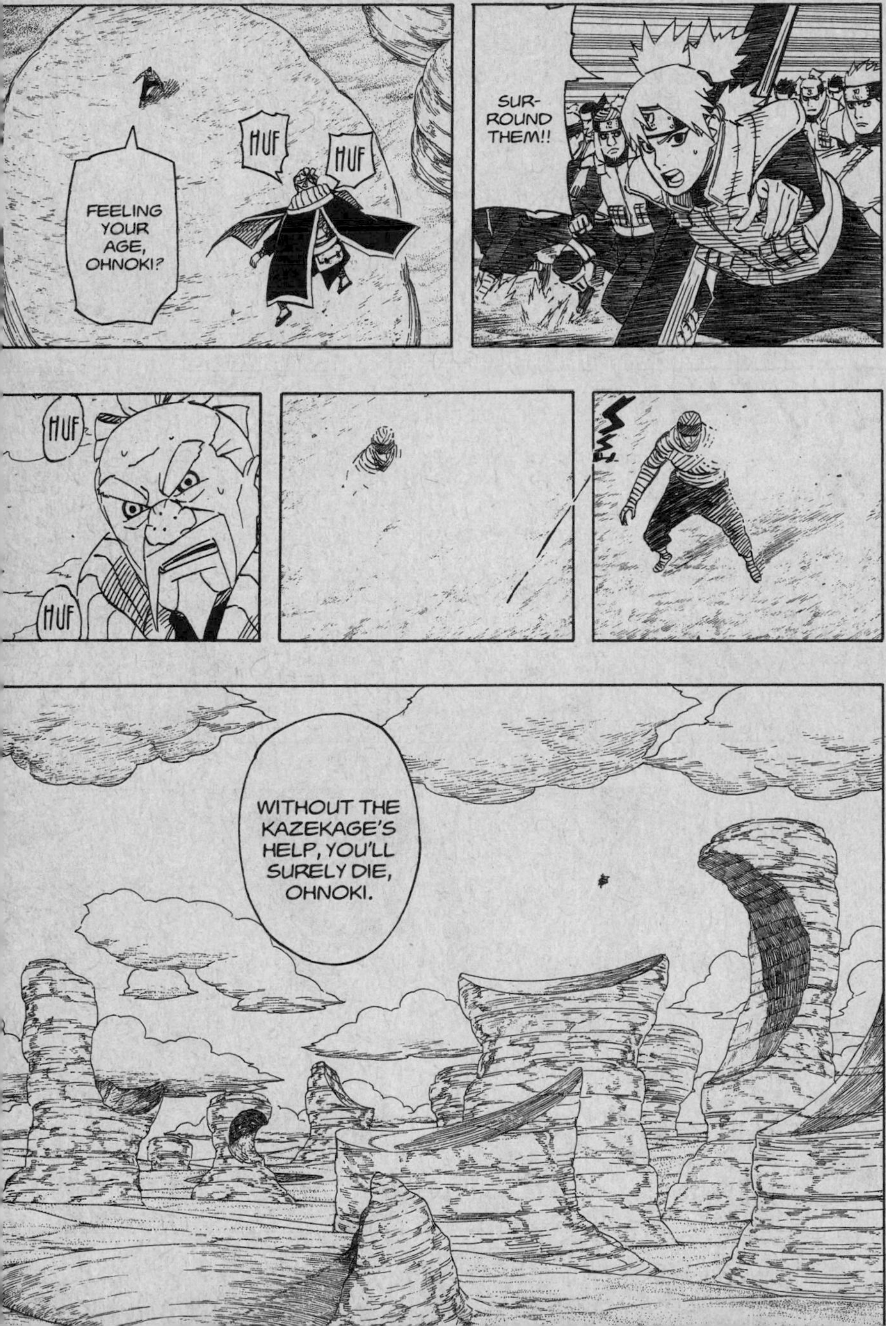
SUR-ROUND THEM!!
HUF
HUF
FEELING YOUR AGE, OHNOKI?
HUF
HUF
WITHOUT THE KAZEKAGE'S HELP, YOU'LL SURELY DIE, OHNOKI.

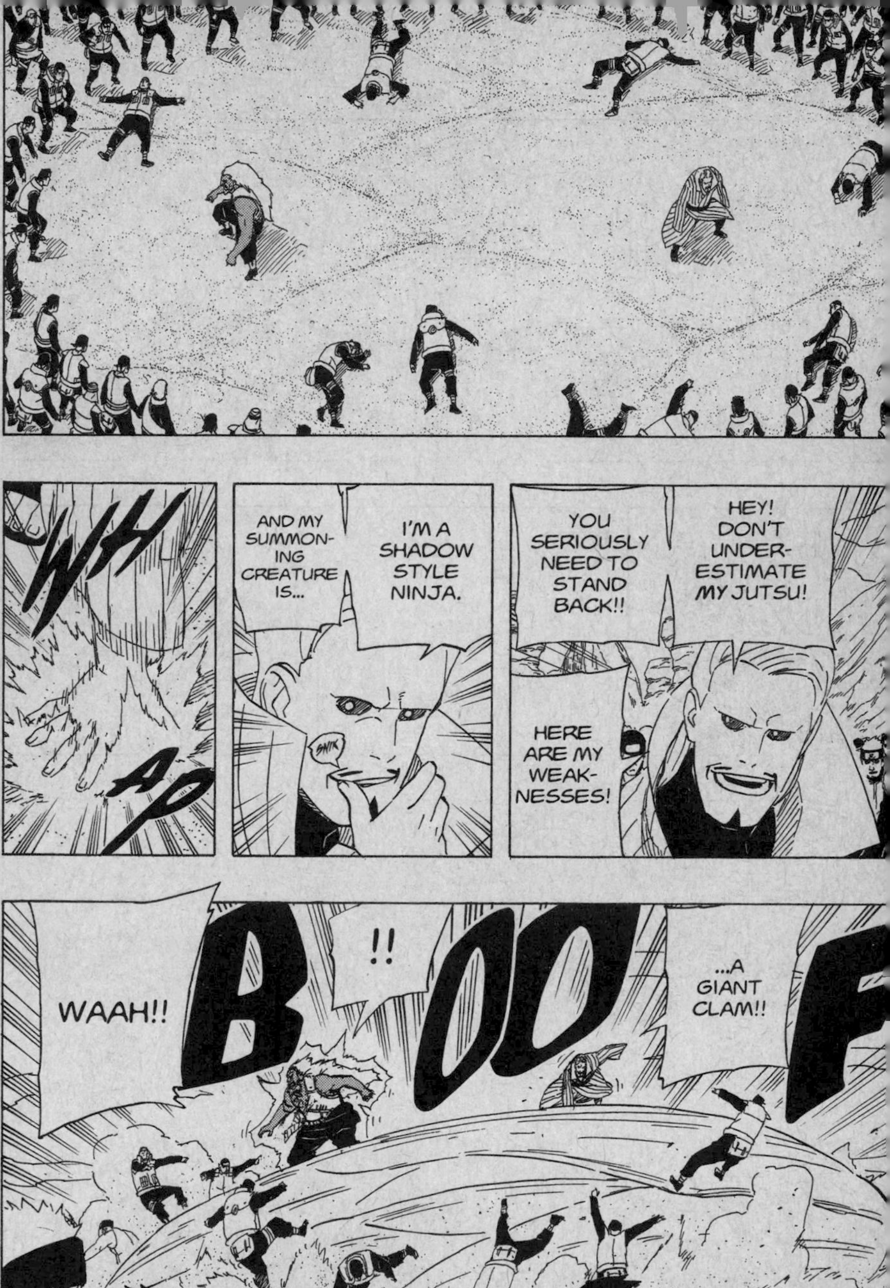
HEY! DON'T UNDER-ESTIMATE MY JUTSU!
YOU SERIOUSLY NEED TO STAND BACK!!
HERE ARE MY WEAK-NESSES!
I'M A SHADOW STYLE NINJA.
AND MY SUMMON-ING CREATURE IS...
SNIK
WHAP
...A GIANT CLAM!!
BOOF
!!
WAAH!!

READ THIS WAY

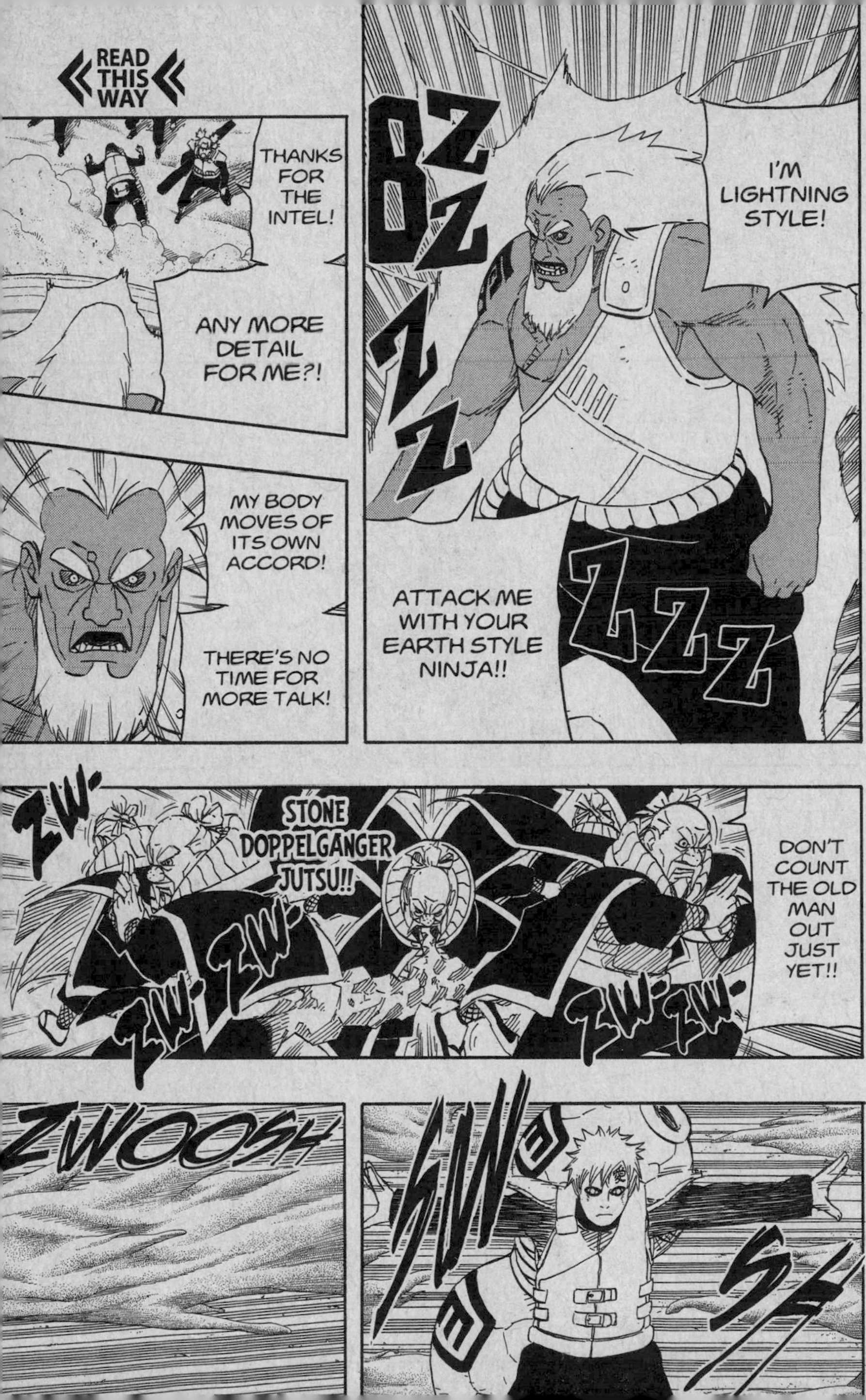
I'M LIGHTNING STYLE!
BZZZZ
ATTACK ME WITH YOUR EARTH STYLE NINJA!!
ZZZ
THANKS FOR THE INTEL!
ANY MORE DETAIL FOR ME?!
MY BODY MOVES OF ITS OWN ACCORD!
THERE'S NO TIME FOR MORE TALK!
DON'T COUNT THE OLD MAN OUT JUST YET!!
ZW-ZW-
STONE DOPPELGANGER JUTSU!!
ZW-ZW-
ZW-
SHWA
SH
ZWOOSH

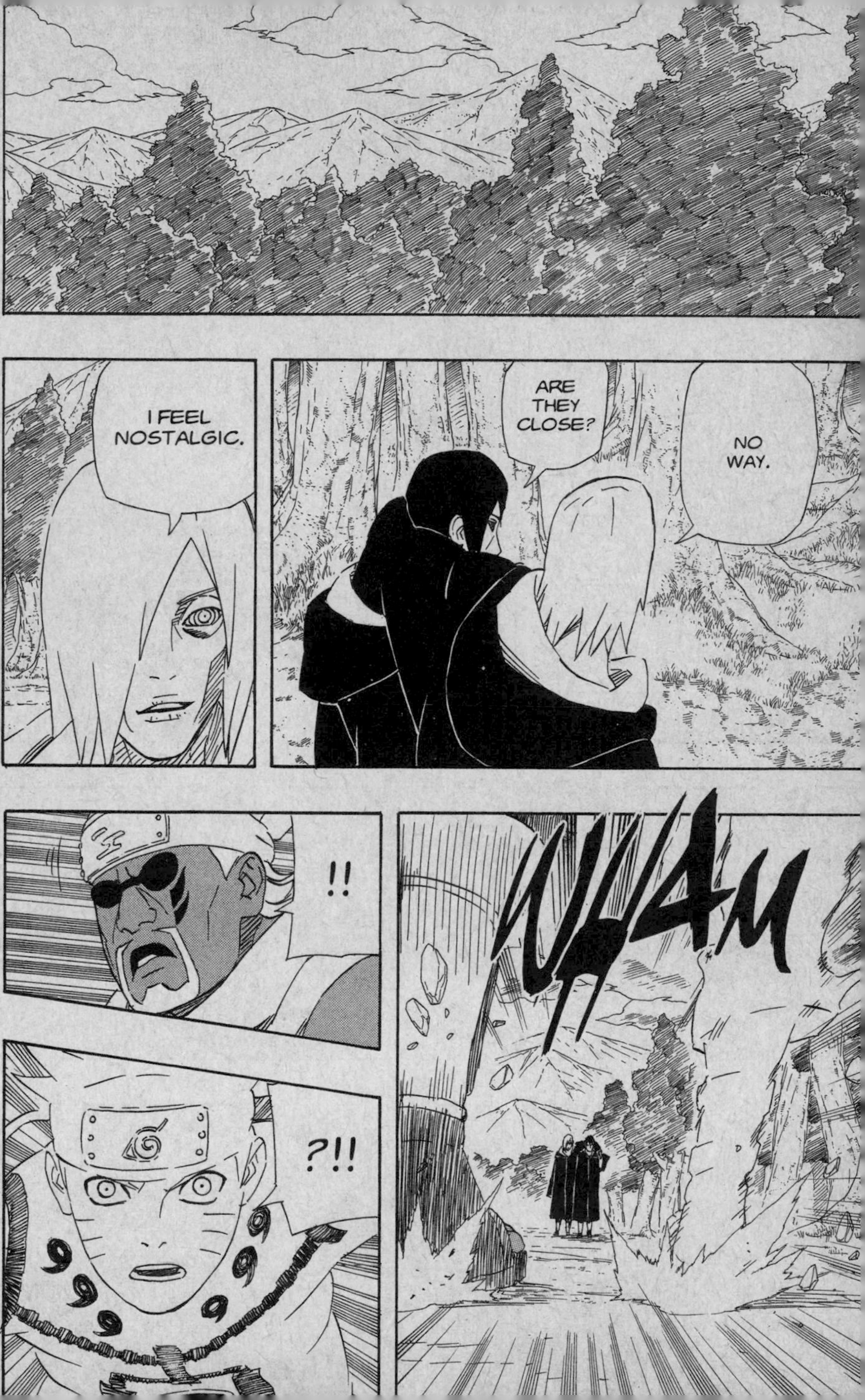
NO WAY.
ARE THEY CLOSE?
I FEEL NOSTALGIC.
WHAM
!!
?!!

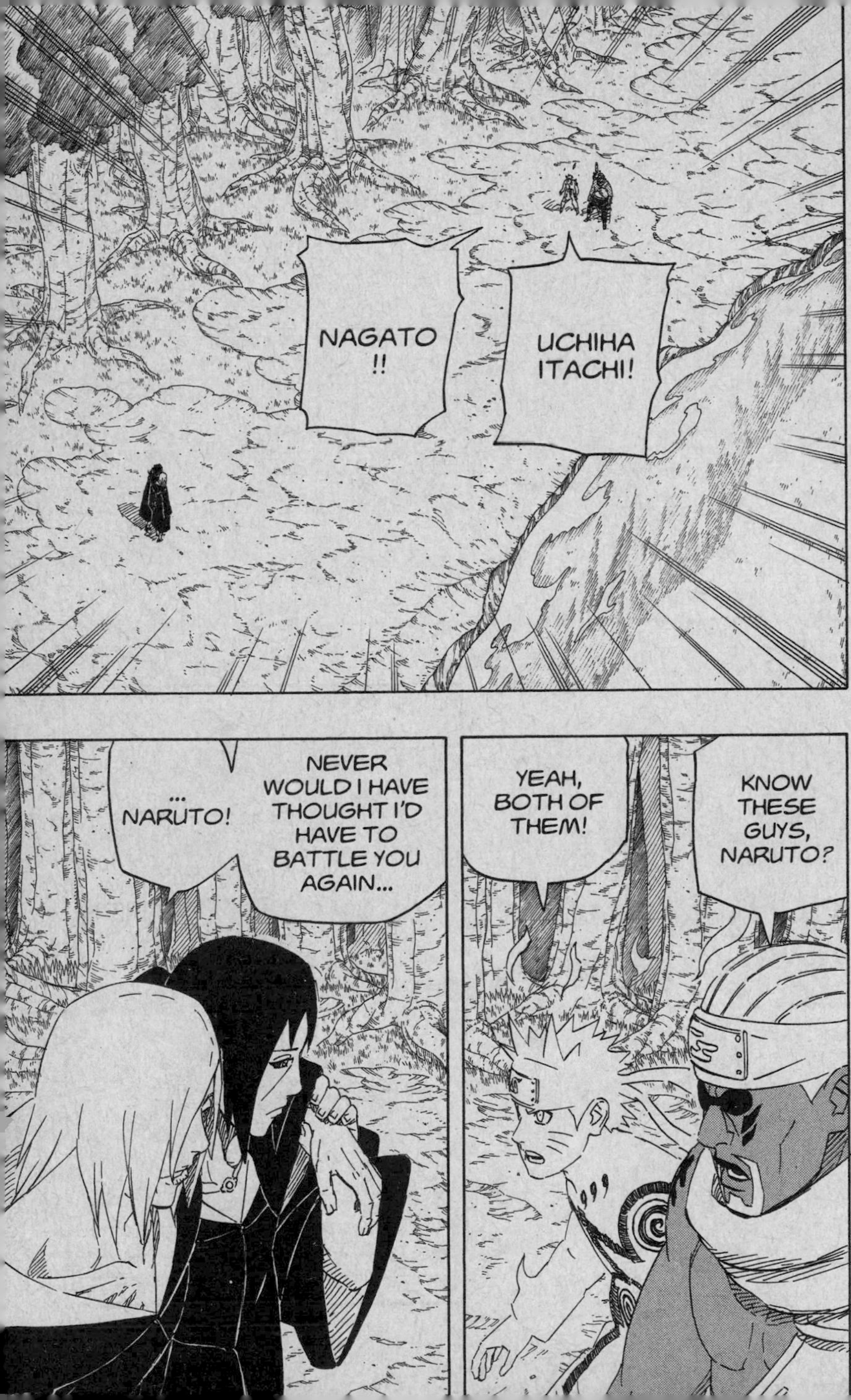
UCHIHA ITACHI!
NAGATO !!
KNOW THESE GUYS, NARUTO?
YEAH, BOTH OF THEM!
NEVER WOULD I HAVE THOUGHT I'D HAVE TO BATTLE YOU AGAIN...
... NARUTO!

Number 549: Itachi's Question!!

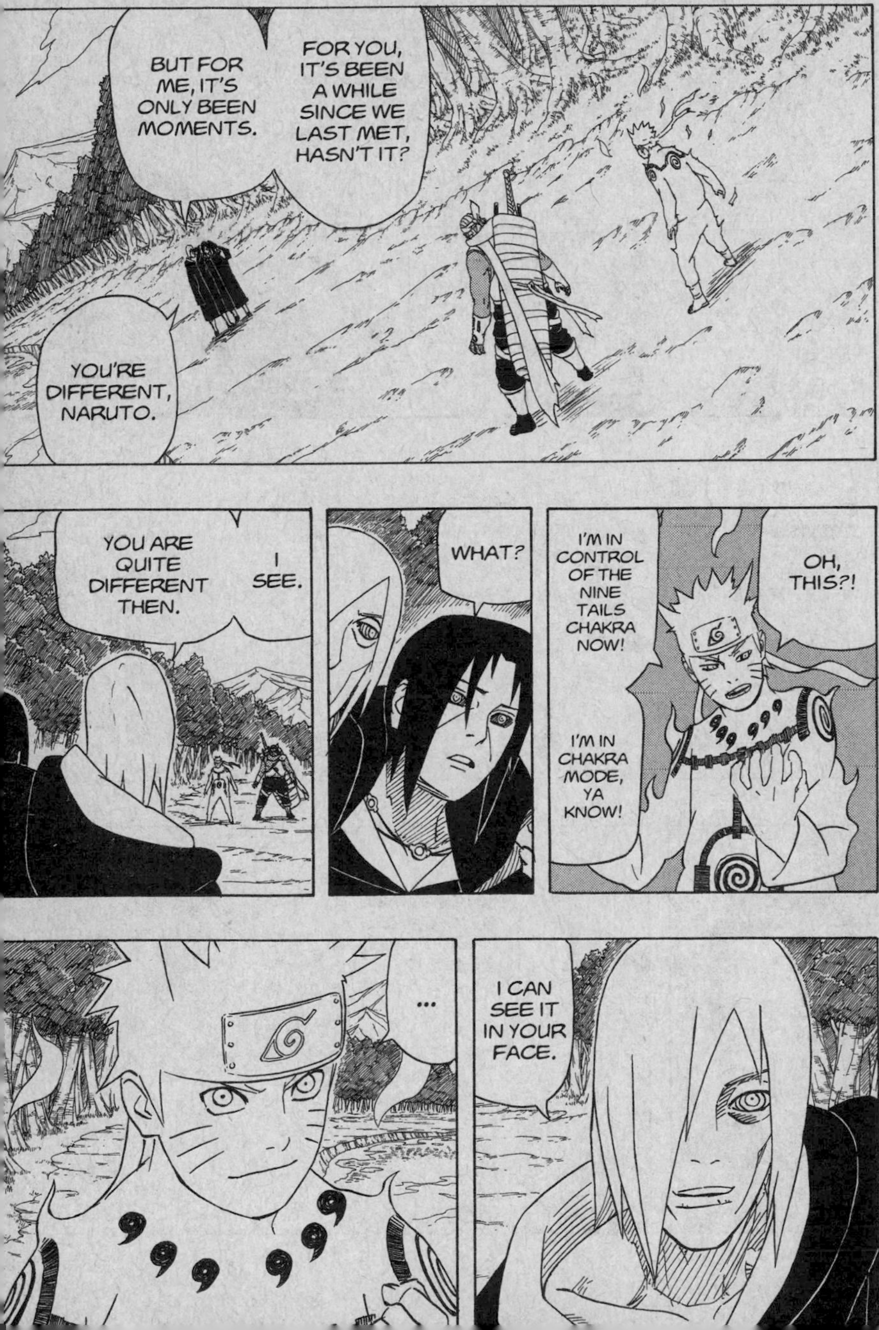

FOR YOU, IT'S BEEN A WHILE SINCE WE LAST MET, HASN'T IT?
BUT FOR ME, IT'S ONLY BEEN MOMENTS.
YOU'RE DIFFERENT, NARUTO.
OH, THIS?!
I'M IN CONTROL OF THE NINE TAILS CHAKRA NOW!
I'M IN CHAKRA MODE, YA KNOW!
WHAT?
I SEE.
YOU ARE QUITE DIFFERENT THEN.
I CAN SEE IT IN YOUR FACE.
...

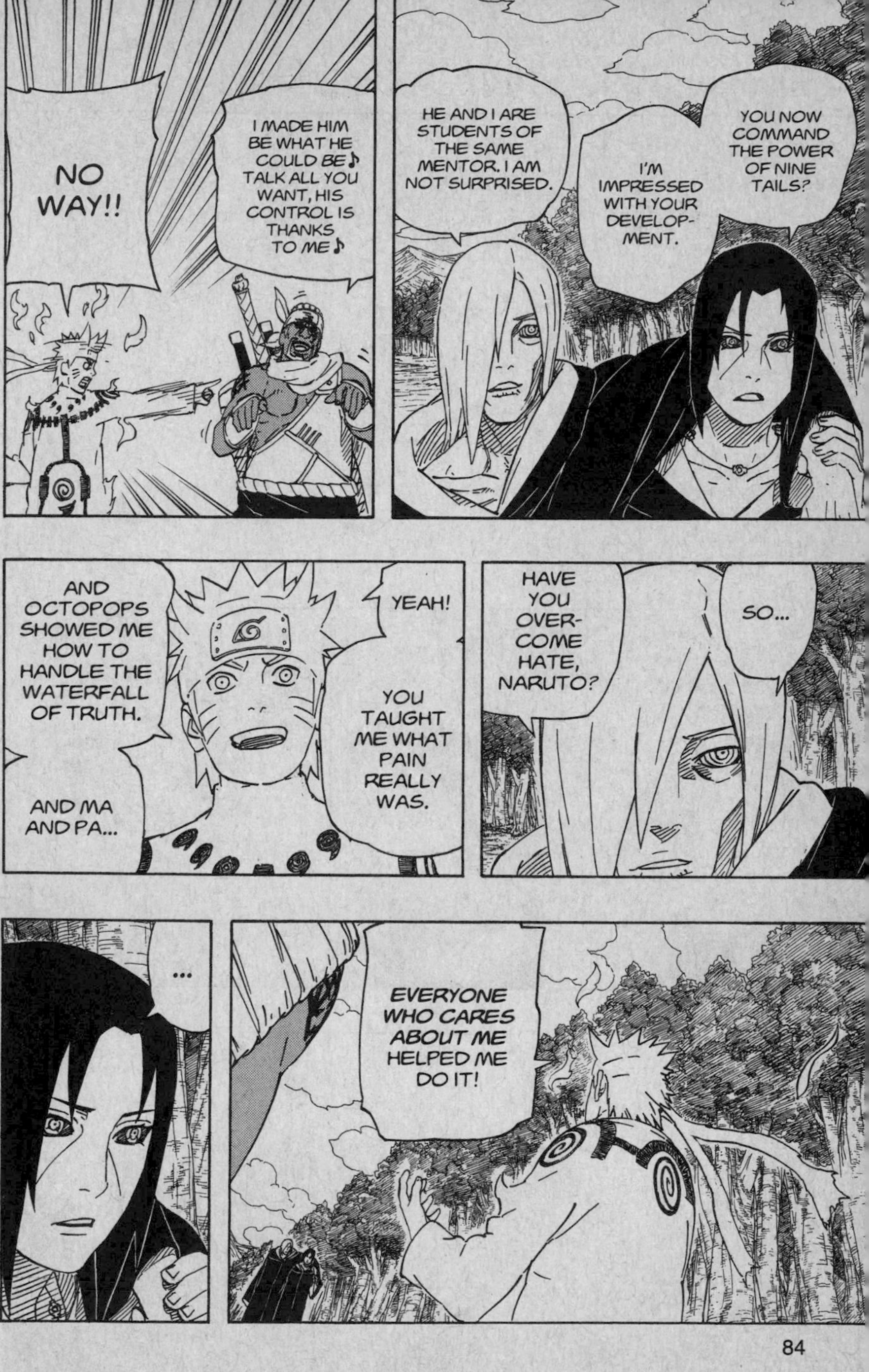
YOU NOW COMMAND THE POWER OF NINE TAILS?
I'M IMPRESSED WITH YOUR DEVELOPMENT.
HE AND I ARE STUDENTS OF THE SAME MENTOR. I AM NOT SURPRISED.
I MADE HIM BE WHAT HE COULD BE♪ TALK ALL YOU WANT, HIS CONTROL IS THANKS TO ME♪
NO WAY!!
SO...
HAVE YOU OVERCOME HATE, NARUTO?
YEAH!
YOU TAUGHT ME WHAT PAIN REALLY WAS.
AND OCTOPOPS SHOWED ME HOW TO HANDLE THE WATERFALL OF TRUTH.
AND MA AND PA...
EVERYONE WHO CARES ABOUT ME HELPED ME DO IT!
...

READ THIS WAY

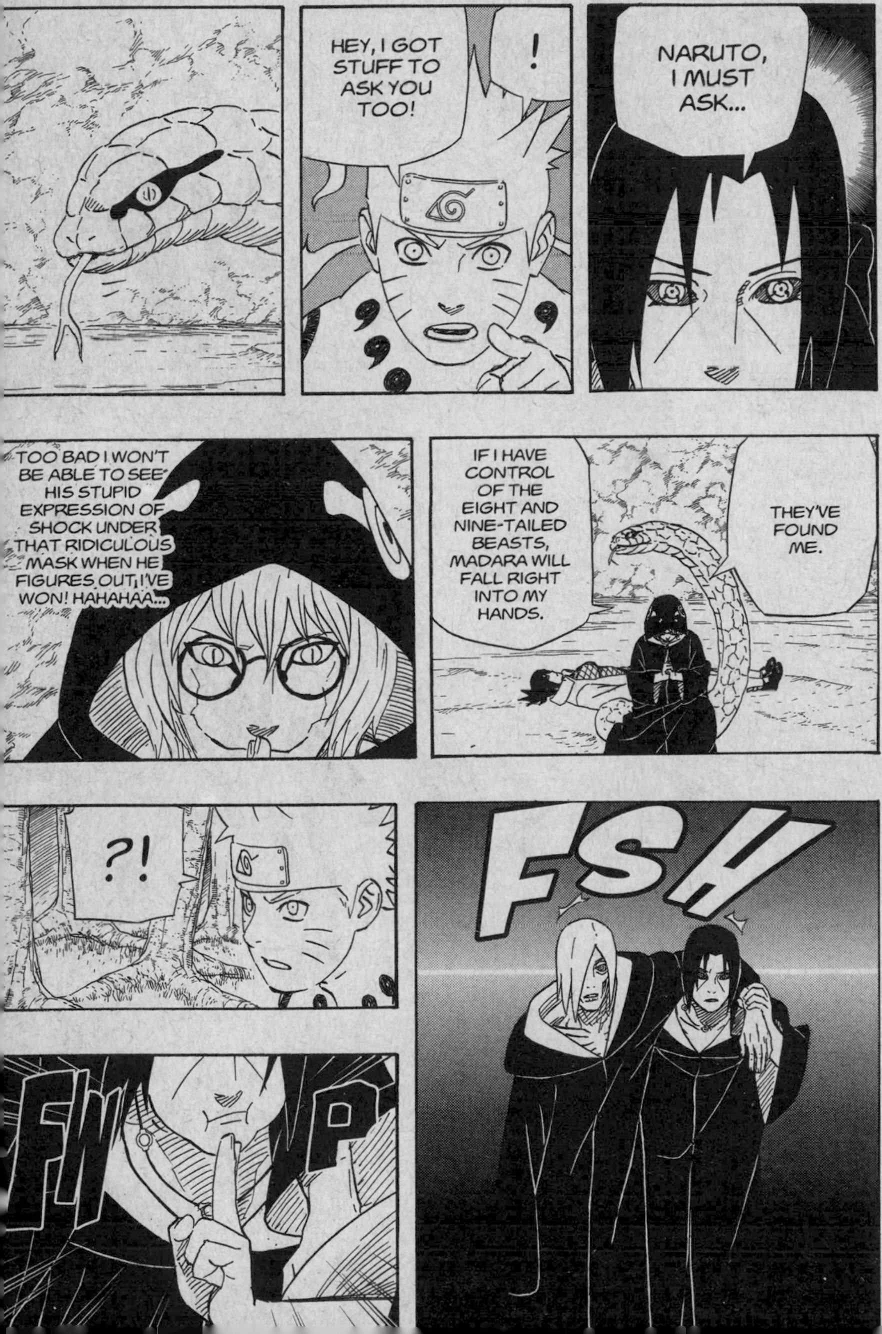
NARUTO, I MUST ASK...
!
HEY, I GOT STUFF TO ASK YOU TOO!
THEY'VE FOUND ME.
IF I HAVE CONTROL OF THE EIGHT AND NINE-TAILED BEASTS, MADARA WILL FALL RIGHT INTO MY HANDS.
TOO BAD I WON'T BE ABLE TO SEE HIS STUPID EXPRESSION OF SHOCK UNDER THAT RIDICULOUS MASK WHEN HE FIGURES OUT I'VE WON! HAHAHAA...
FSH
?!
FWP

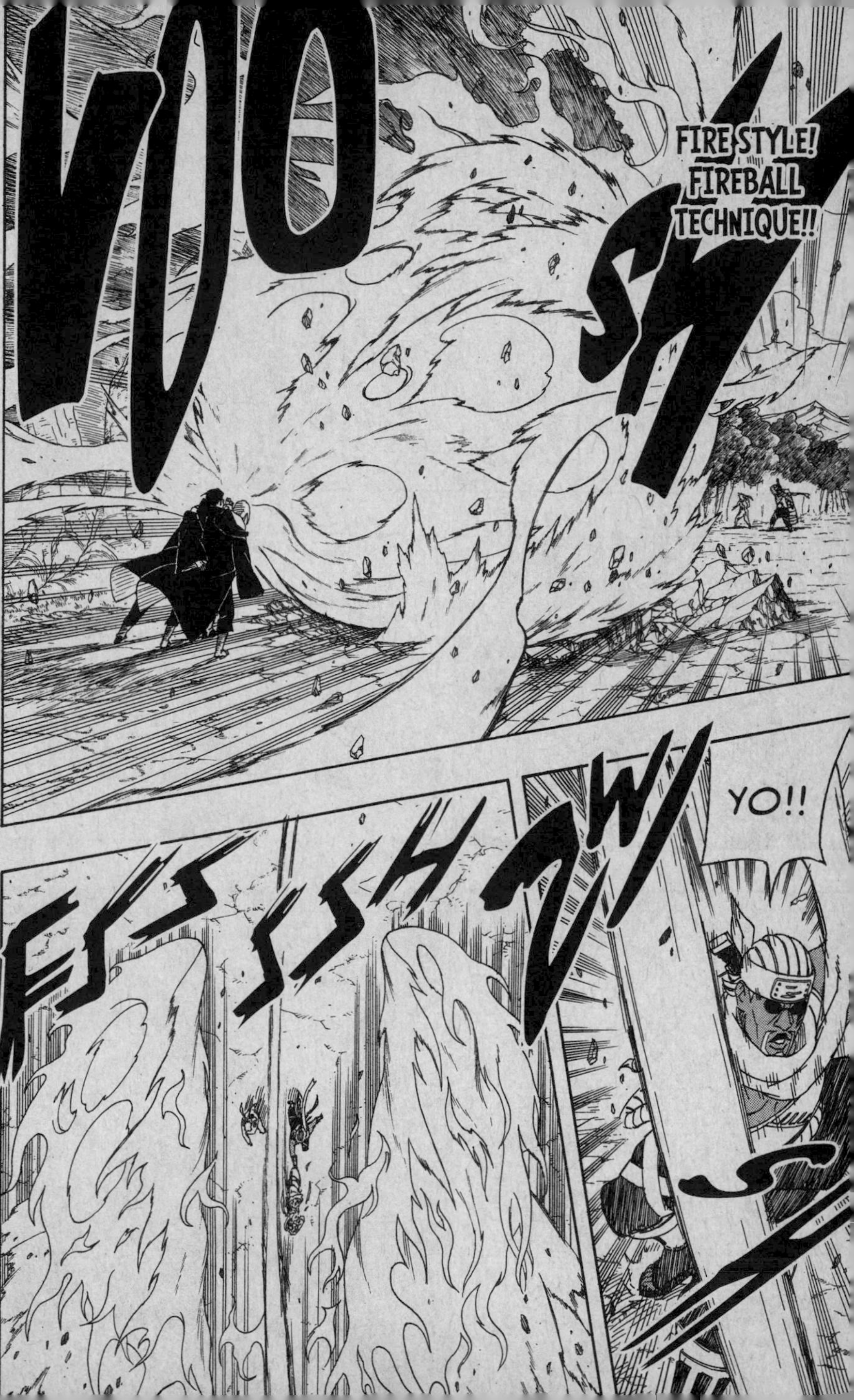
FIRE STYLE! FIREBALL TECHNIQUE!!
YO!!

READ THIS WAY

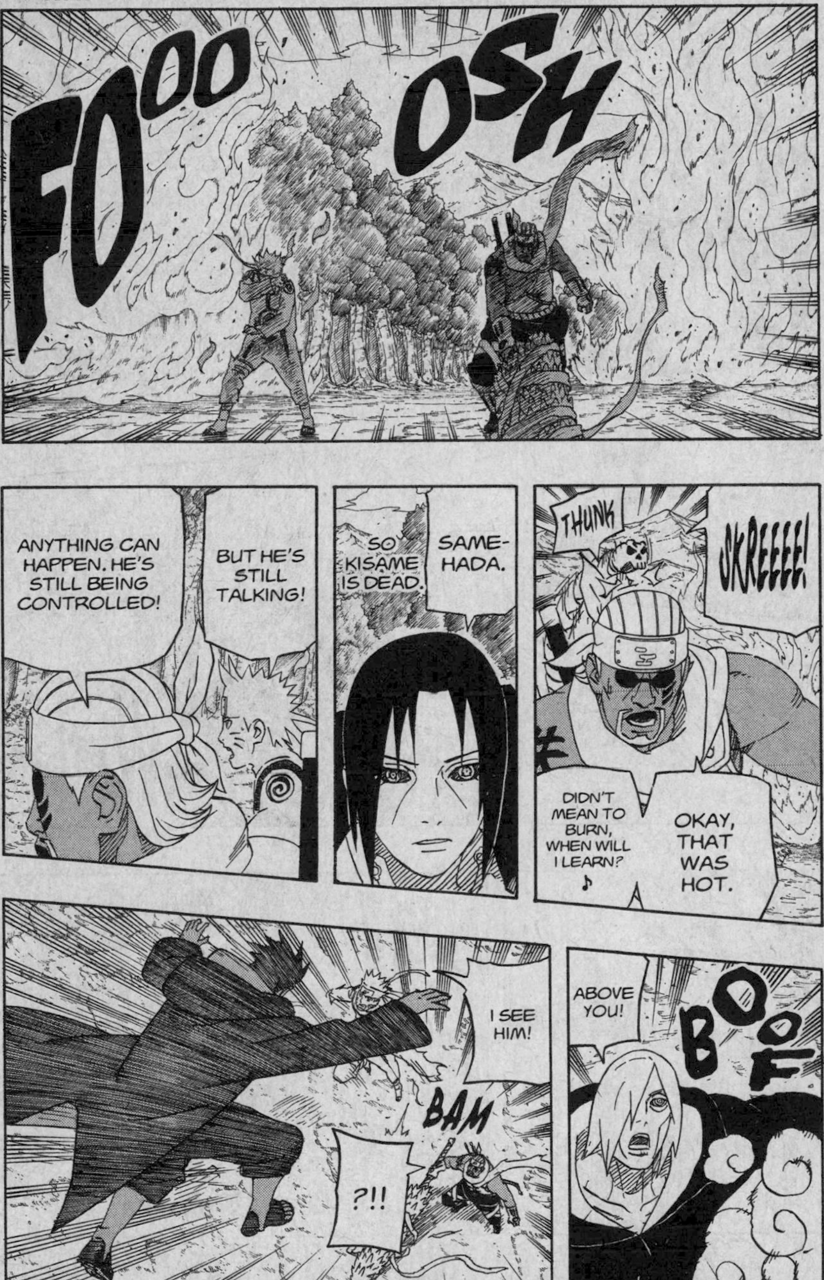
FOOOOSH
THUNK
SKREEEE!
OKAY, THAT WAS HOT.
DIDN'T MEAN TO BURN, WHEN WILL I LEARN? ♪
SAME-HADA.
SO KISAME IS DEAD.
BUT HE'S STILL TALKING!
ANYTHING CAN HAPPEN. HE'S STILL BEING CONTROLLED!
ABOVE YOU!
BOOF
I SEE HIM!
BAM
?!!

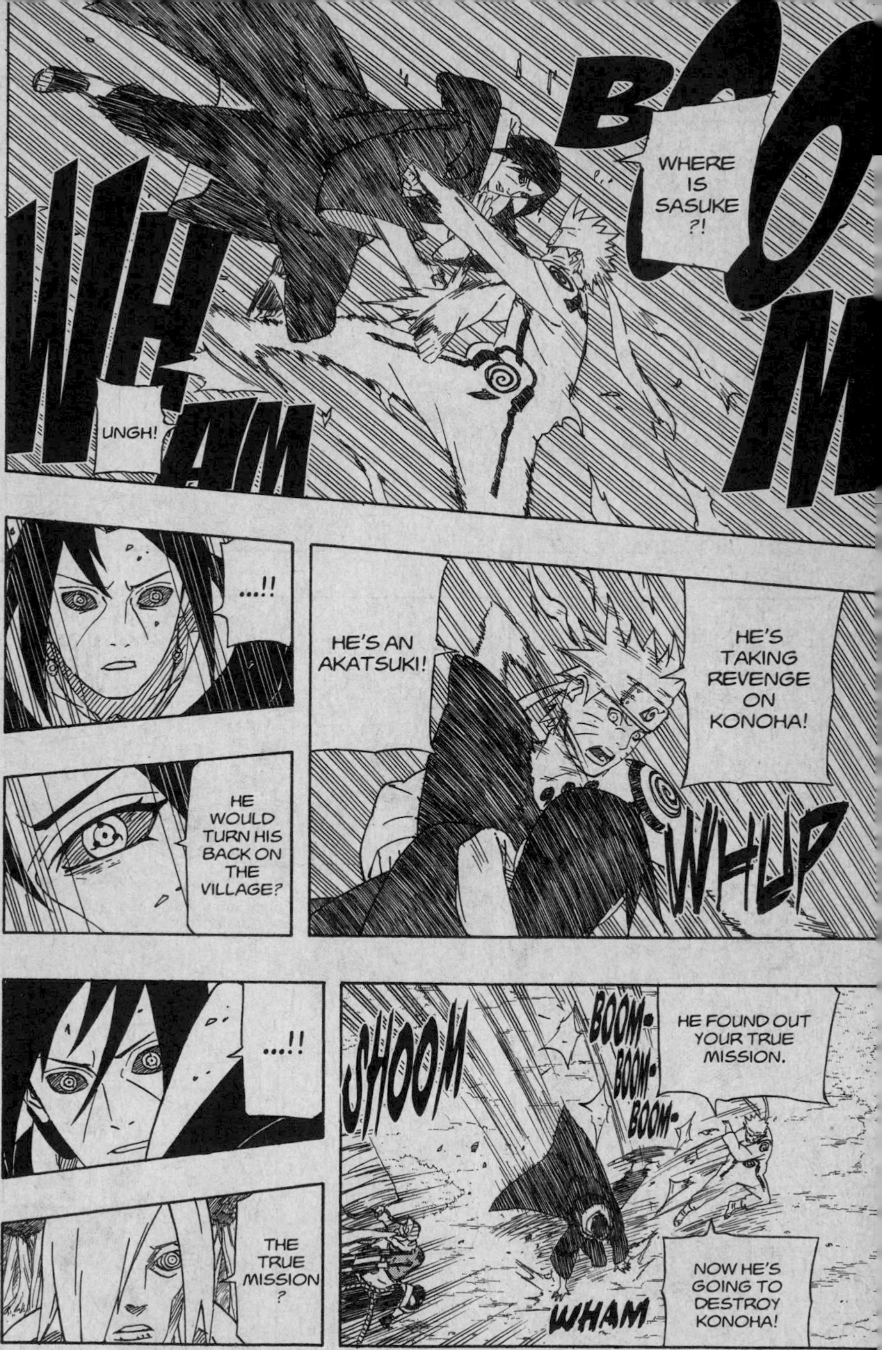
BOOM
WHERE IS SASUKE ?!
WHAM
UNGH!
HE'S TAKING REVENGE ON KONOHA!
HE'S AN AKATSUKI!
WHUP
...!!
HE WOULD TURN HIS BACK ON THE VILLAGE?
HE FOUND OUT YOUR TRUE MISSION.
BOOM-BOOM-BOOM-
SHOOM
NOW HE'S GOING TO DESTROY KONOHA!
WHAM
...!!
THE TRUE MISSION ?

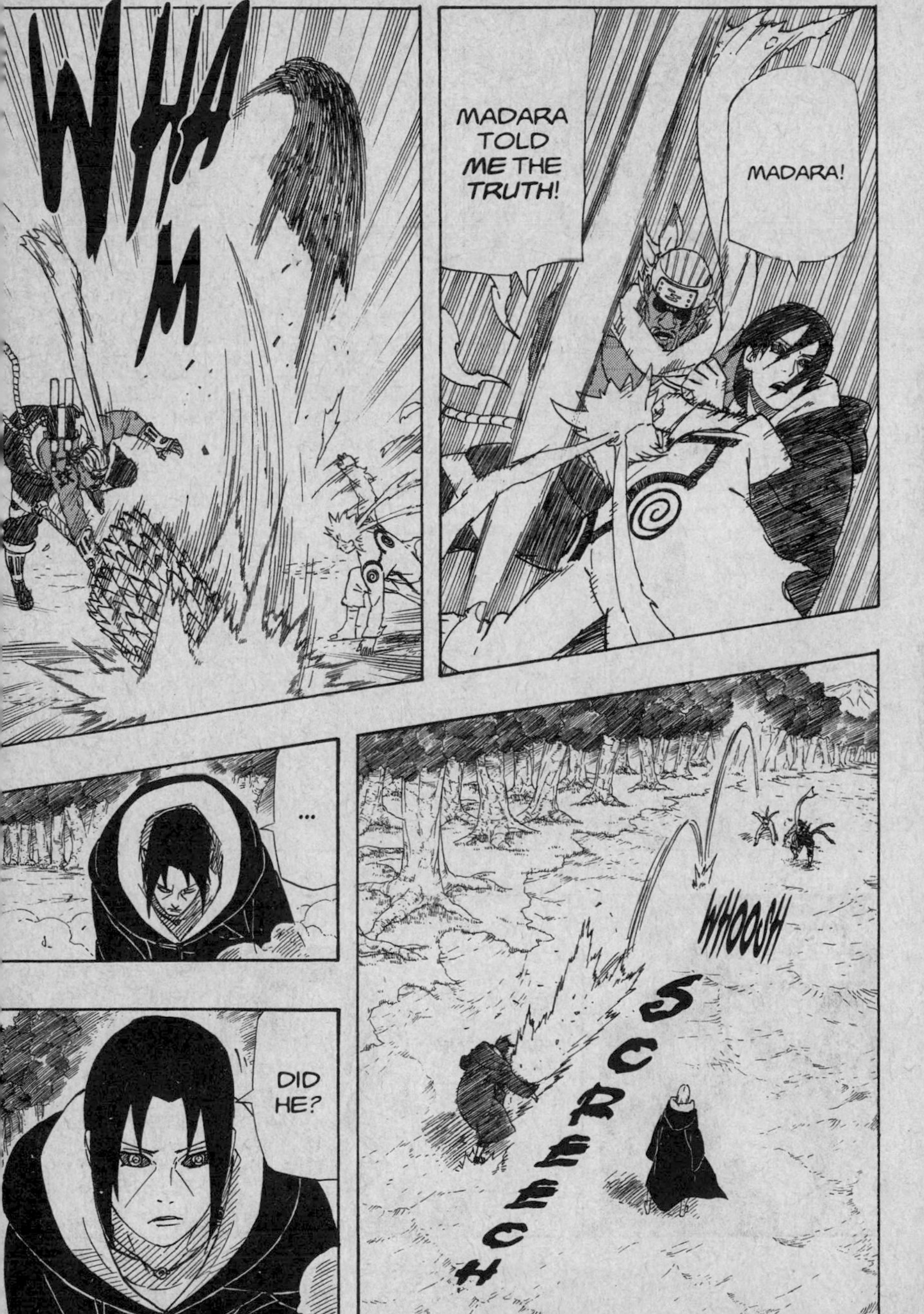
MADARA!
MADARA TOLD ME THE TRUTH!
WHAMM
WHOOSH
SCREECH
...
DID HE?

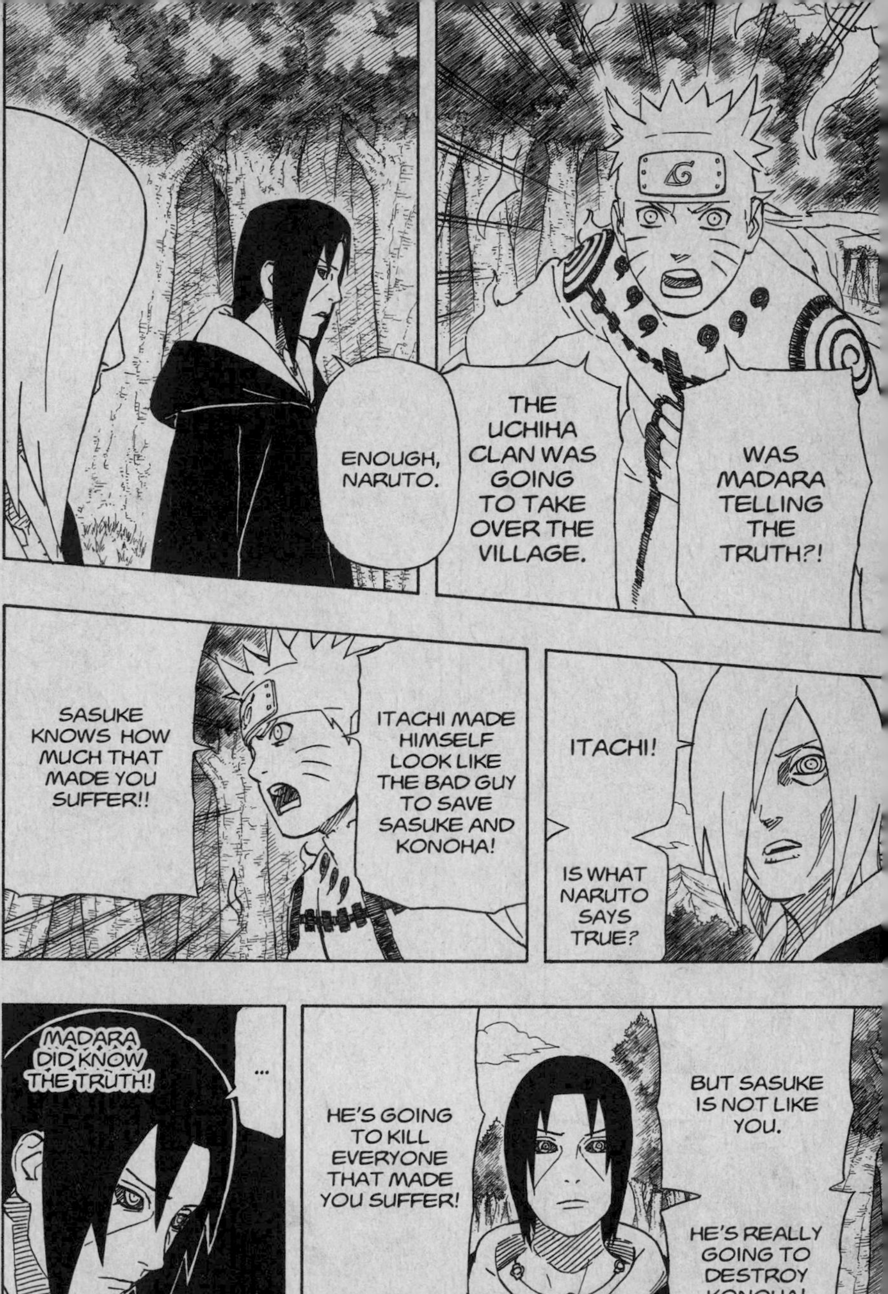

WAS MADARA TELLING THE TRUTH?!
THE UCHIHA CLAN WAS GOING TO TAKE OVER THE VILLAGE.
ENOUGH, NARUTO.
ITACHI!
IS WHAT NARUTO SAYS TRUE?
ITACHI MADE HIMSELF LOOK LIKE THE BAD GUY TO SAVE SASUKE AND KONOHA!
SASUKE KNOWS HOW MUCH THAT MADE YOU SUFFER!!
BUT SASUKE IS NOT LIKE YOU.
HE'S REALLY GOING TO DESTROY KONOHA!
HE'S GOING TO KILL EVERYONE THAT MADE YOU SUFFER!
...
MADARA DID KNOW THE TRUTH!

READ THIS WAY

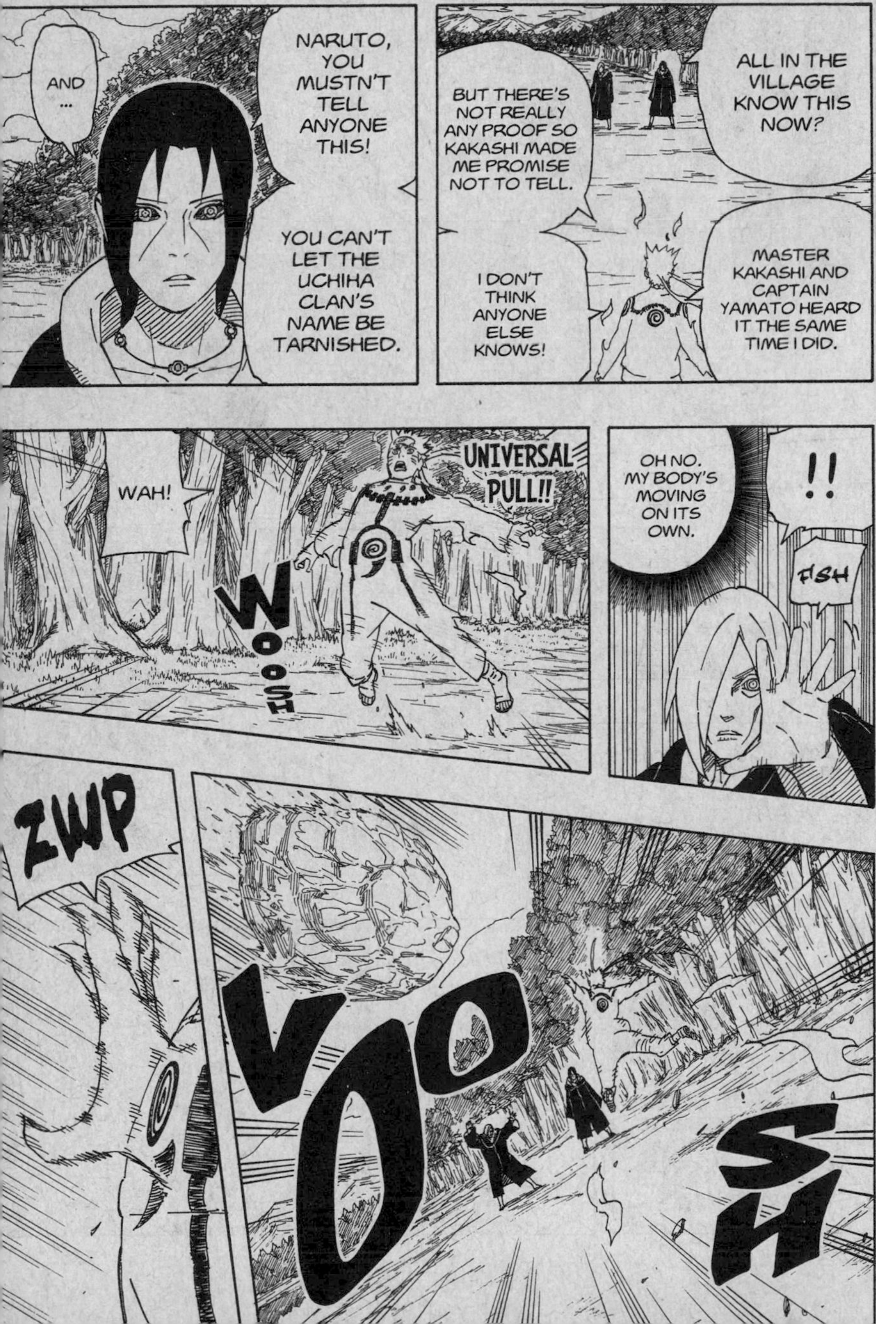
ALL IN THE VILLAGE KNOW THIS NOW?
MASTER KAKASHI AND CAPTAIN YAMATO HEARD IT THE SAME TIME I DID.
BUT THERE'S NOT REALLY ANY PROOF SO KAKASHI MADE ME PROMISE NOT TO TELL.
I DON'T THINK ANYONE ELSE KNOWS!
NARUTO, YOU MUSTN'T TELL ANYONE THIS!
YOU CAN'T LET THE UCHIHA CLAN'S NAME BE TARNISHED.
AND ...
!!
OH NO. MY BODY'S MOVING ON ITS OWN.
FISH
UNIVERSAL PULL!!
WAH!
WOOSH
VOOSH
ZWP

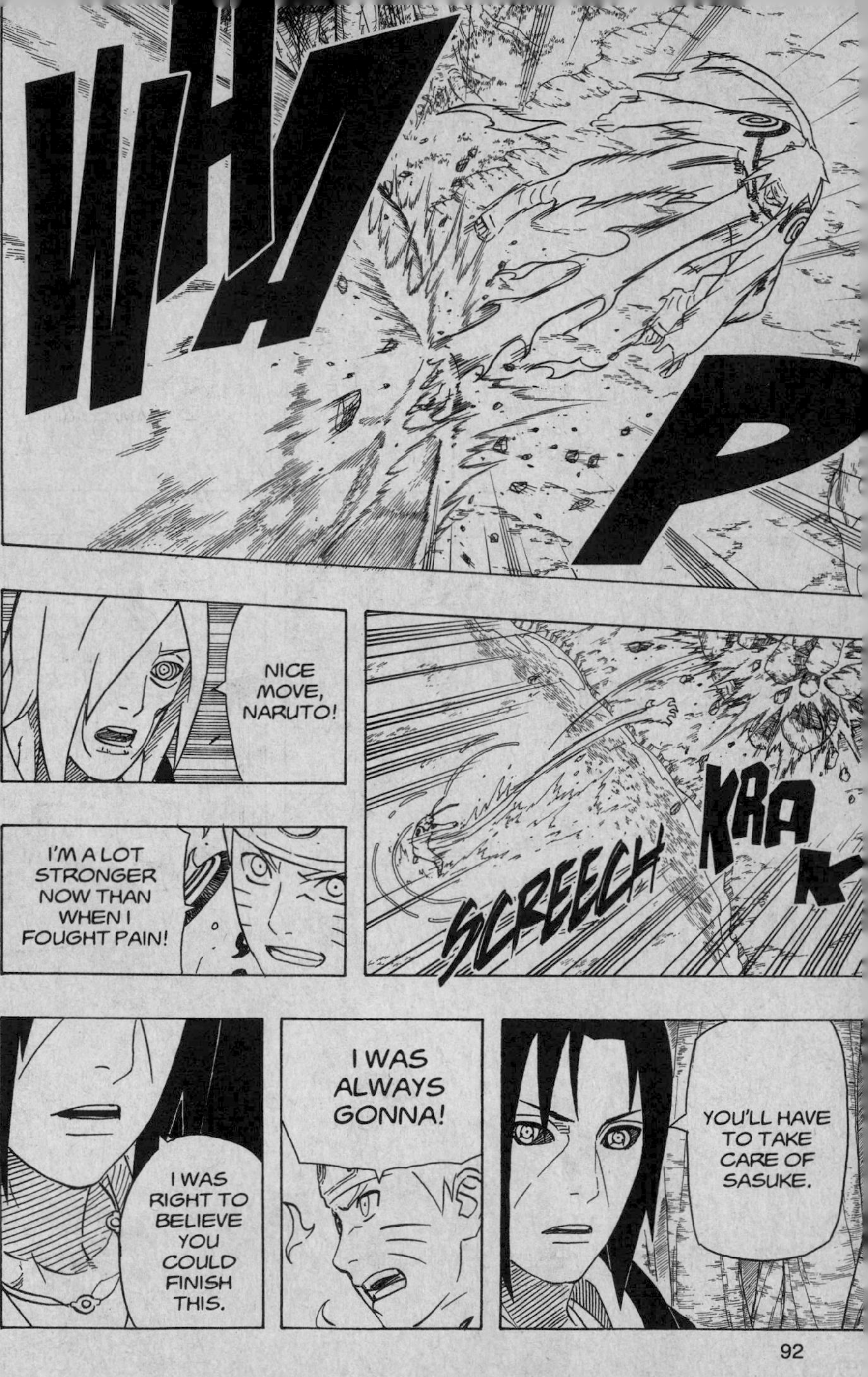
WHAP
KRAK
SCREECH
NICE MOVE, NARUTO!
I'M A LOT STRONGER NOW THAN WHEN I FOUGHT PAIN!
YOU'LL HAVE TO TAKE CARE OF SASUKE.
I WAS ALWAYS GONNA!
I WAS RIGHT TO BELIEVE YOU COULD FINISH THIS.

READ THIS WAY

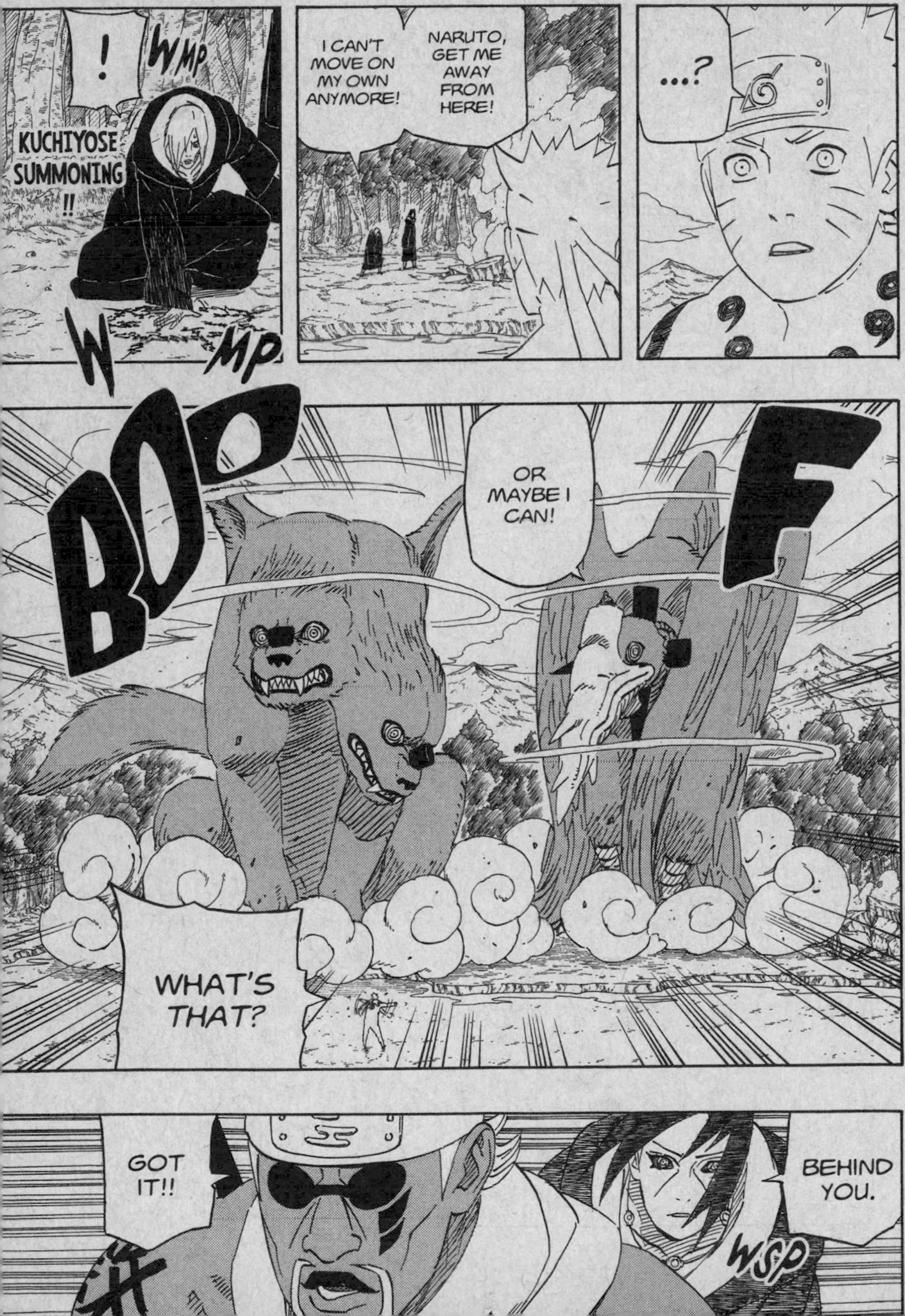
...?
NARUTO, GET ME AWAY FROM HERE!
I CAN'T MOVE ON MY OWN ANYMORE!
!
WMP
KUCHIYOSE SUMMONING!!
WMP
OR MAYBE I CAN!
BOOF
WHAT'S THAT?
BEHIND YOU.
WSP
GOT IT!!

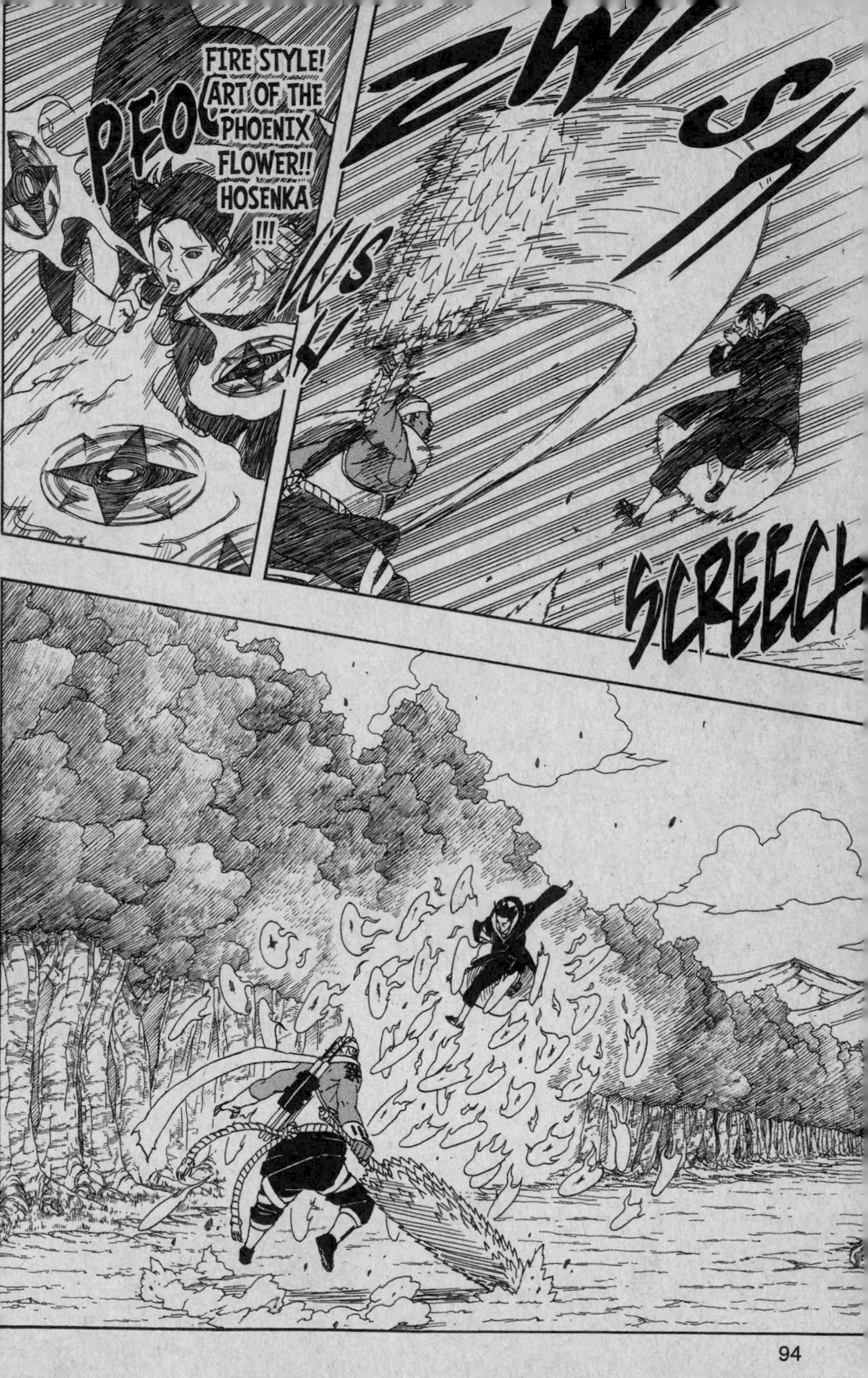
ZWISH
WUSH
SCREECH
PFO
FIRE STYLE! ART OF THE PHOENIX FLOWER!! HOSENKA !!!

READ THIS WAY

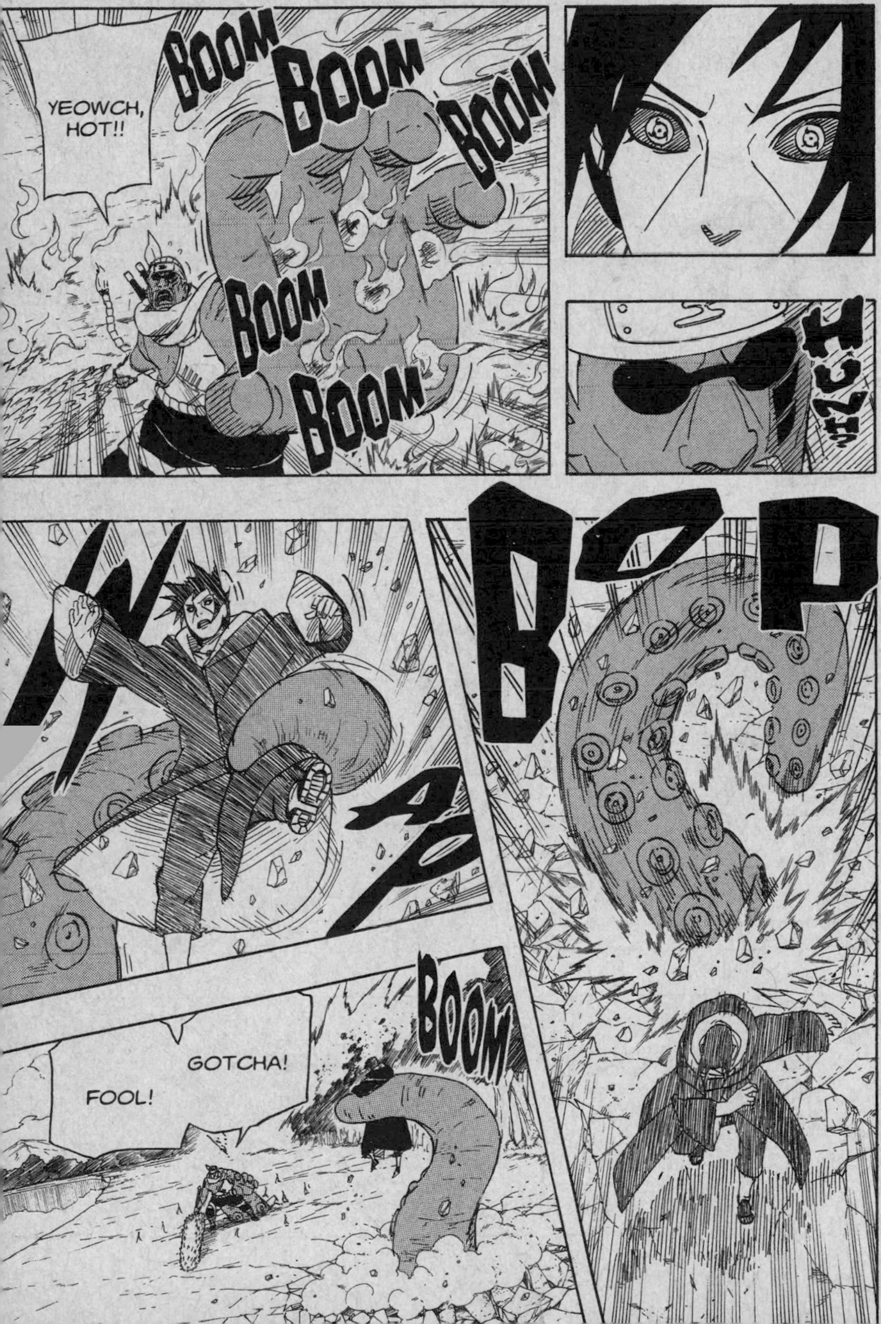
HUNH?!
BOOM
BOOM
BOOM
BOOM
BOOM
YEOWCH, HOT!!
BOP
WHAP
BOOM
GOTCHA!
FOOL!

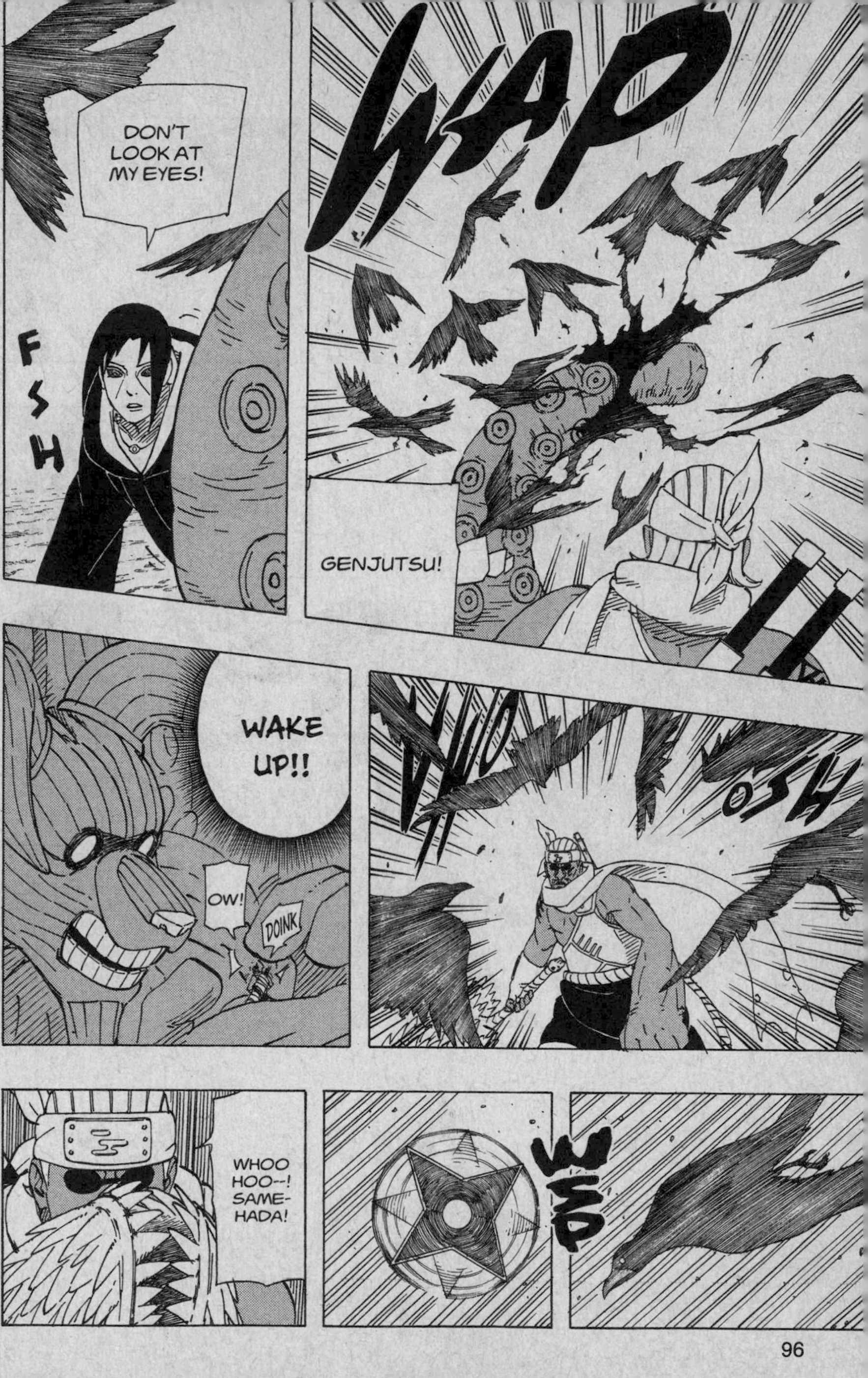
WAP
GENJUTSU!
DON'T LOOK AT MY EYES!
FSH
WHOOSH
WAKE UP!!
OW!
DOINK
WSP
WHOO HOO--! SAME-HADA!

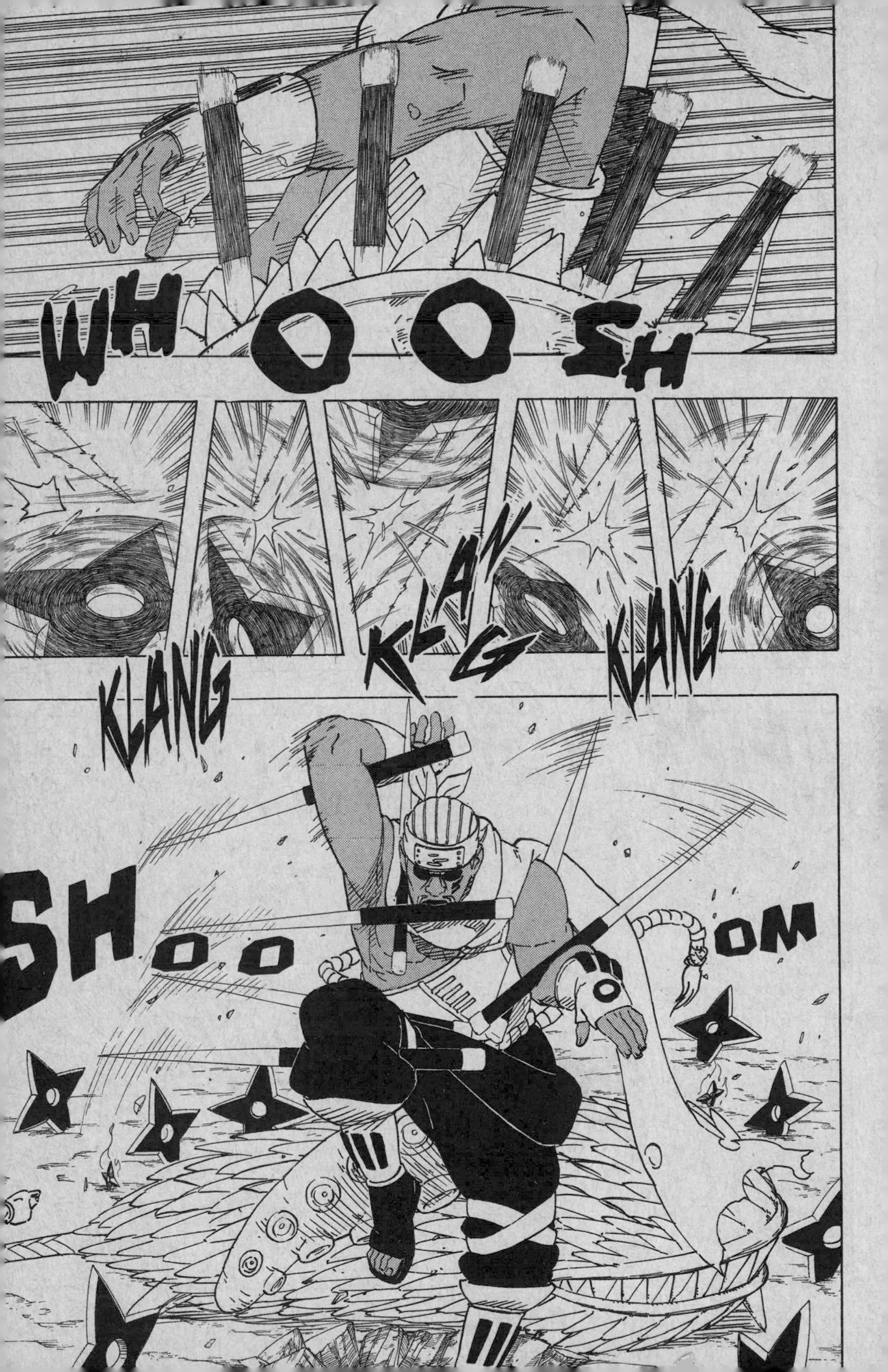
WHOOSH
KLANG
KLANG
KLANG
SHOOOM

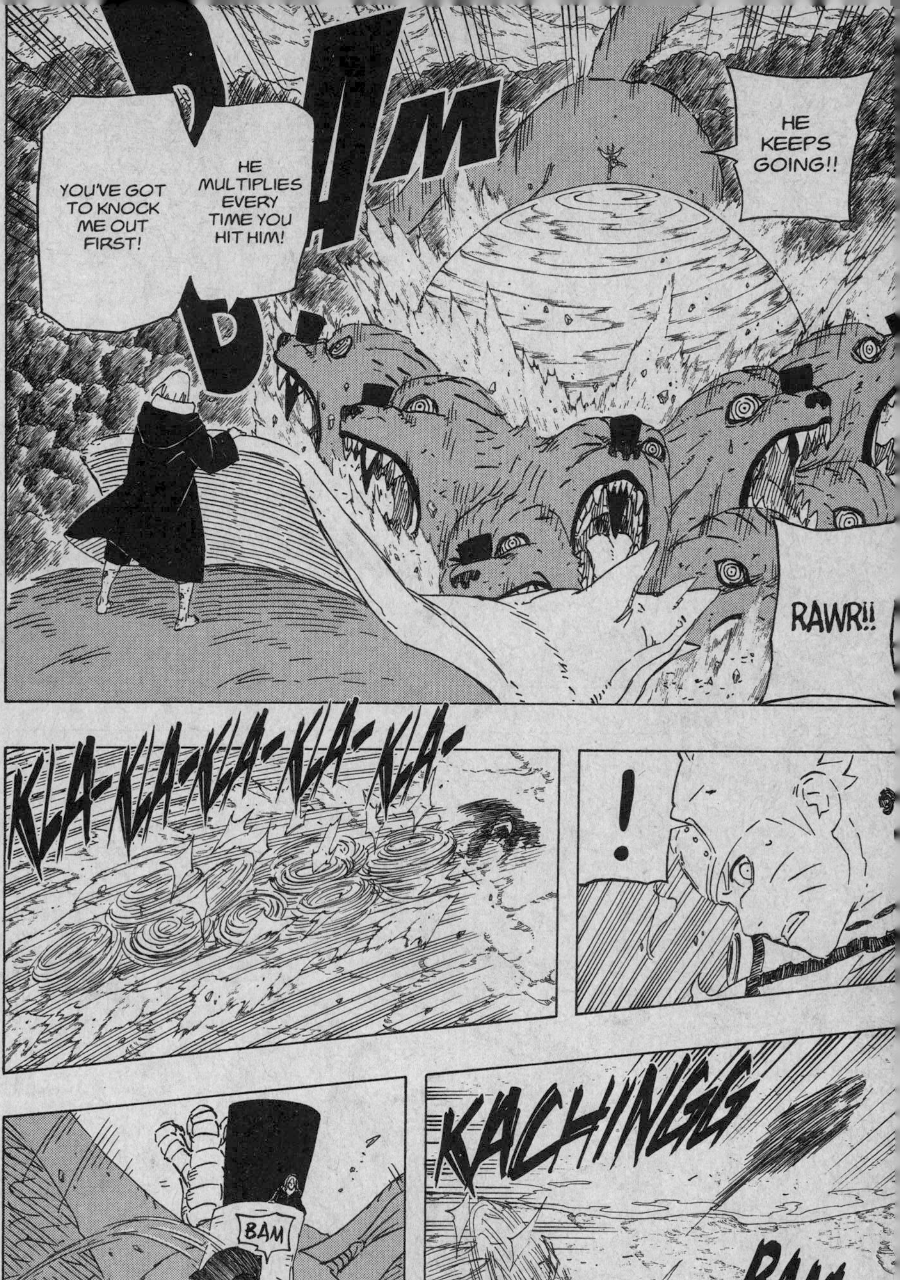
HE KEEPS GOING!!
HE MULTIPLIES EVERY TIME YOU HIT HIM!
YOU'VE GOT TO KNOCK ME OUT FIRST!
RAWR!!
!
KLA-KLA-KLA-KLA-KLA-KLA-
KACHINGG
BAM
BAM

READ THIS WAY

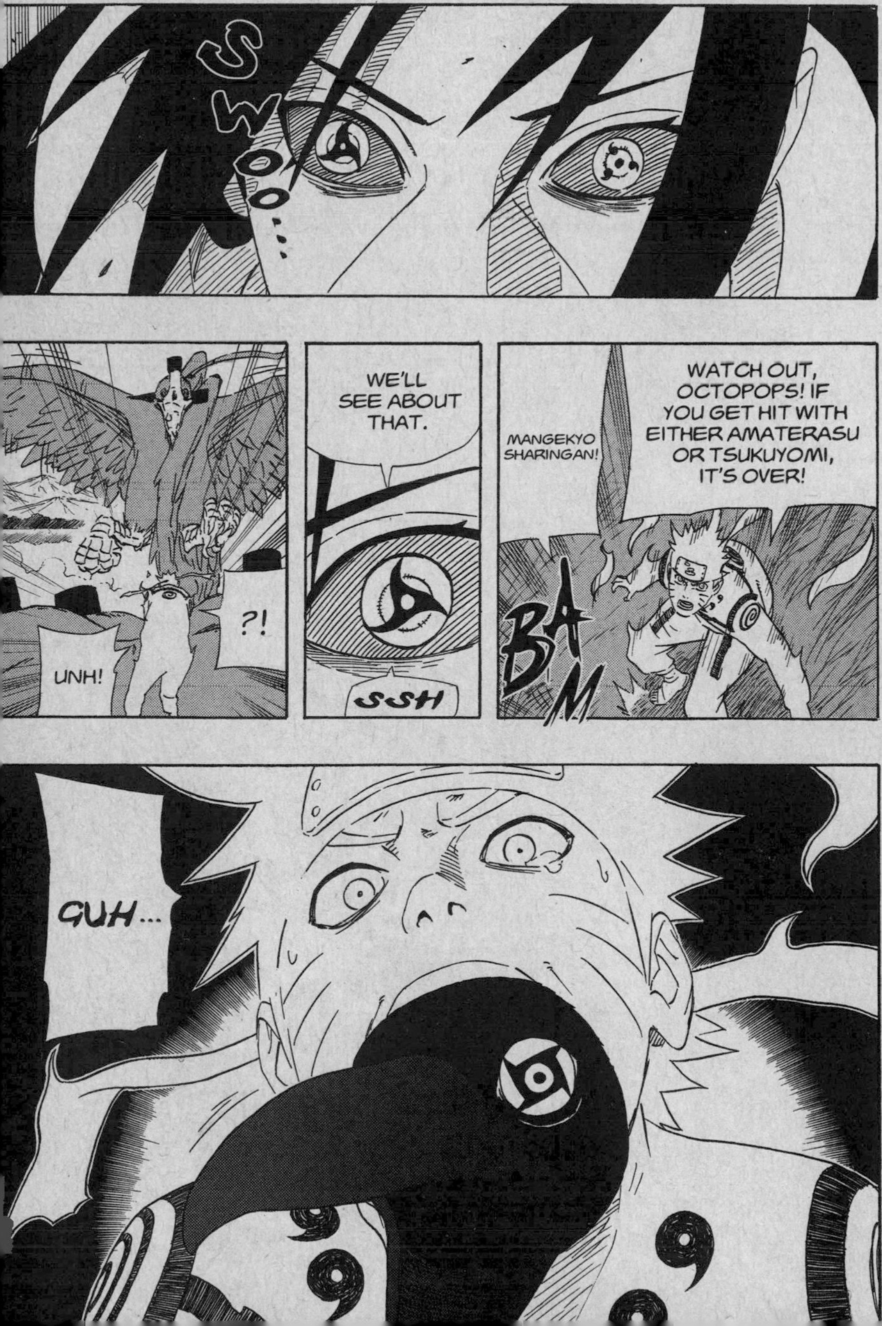
SWOOO...
WATCH OUT, OCTOPOPS! IF YOU GET HIT WITH EITHER AMATERASU OR TSUKUYOMI, IT'S OVER!
MANGEKYO SHARINGAN!
BAM
WE'LL SEE ABOUT THAT.
SSH
?!
UNH!
GUH...

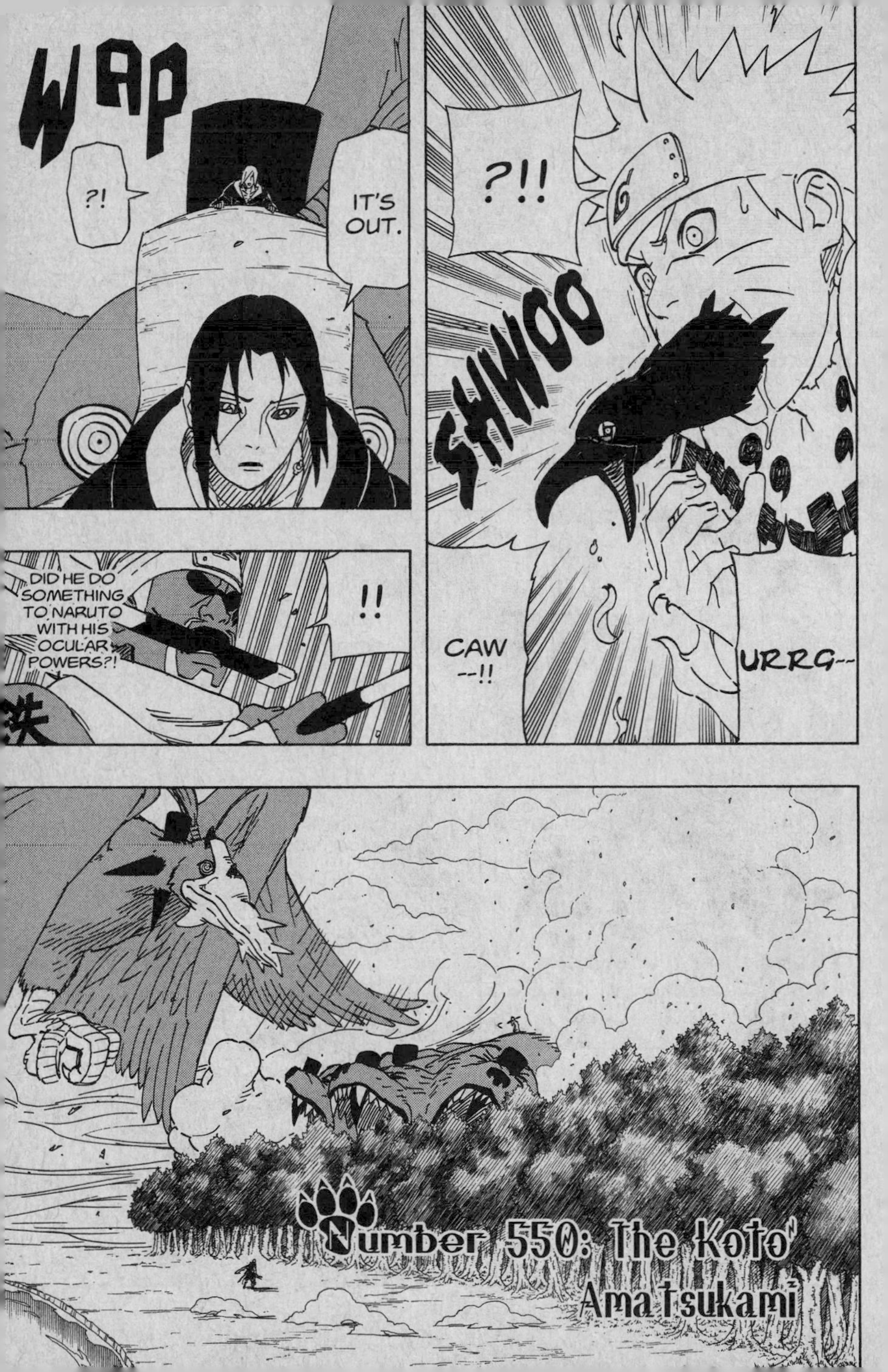
?!!
SHWOO
URRG--
CAW --!!
WAP
?!
IT'S OUT.
!!
DID HE DO SOMETHING TO NARUTO WITH HIS OCULAR POWERS?!
Number 550: The Koto Amatsukami

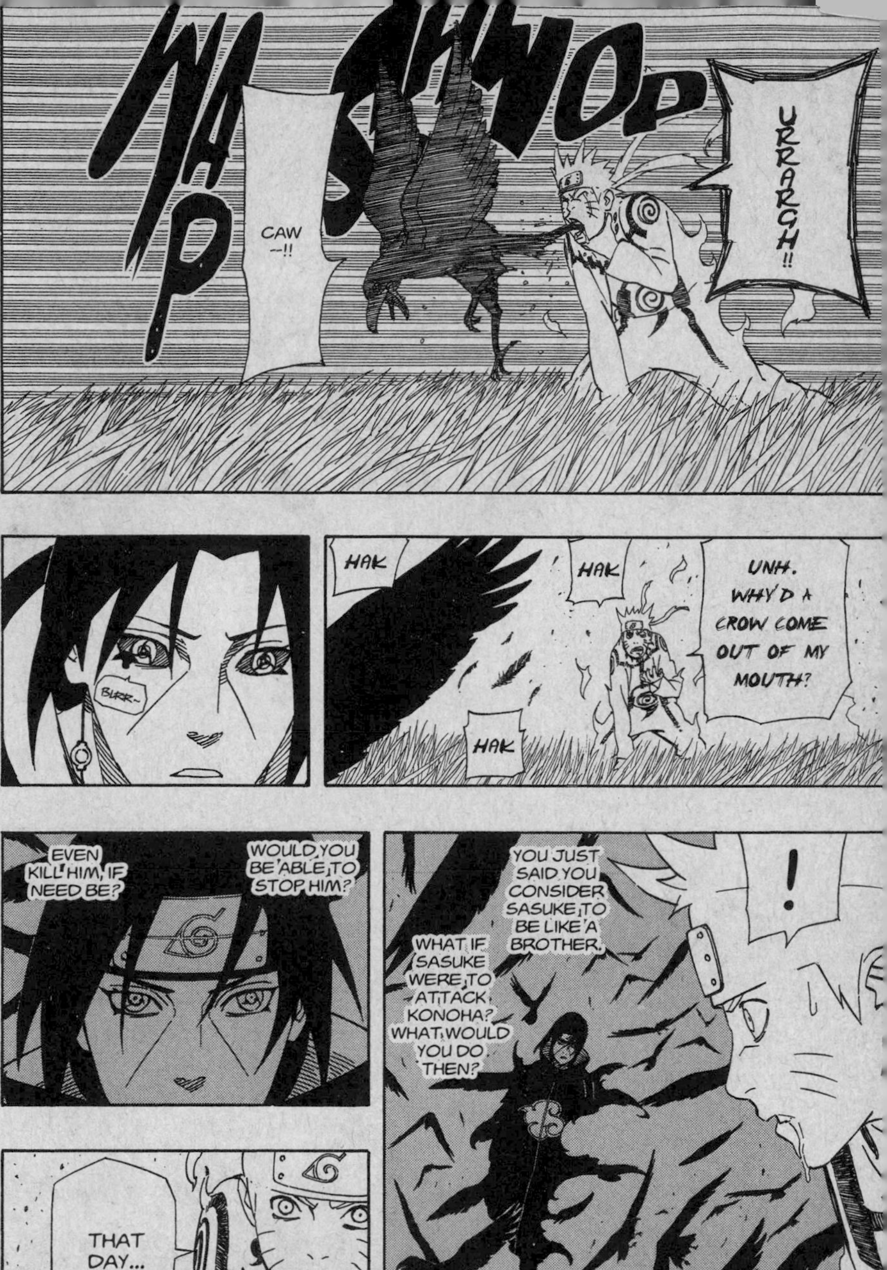
URRARGH!!
CAW --!!
HAK
HAK
UNH. WHY'D A CROW COME OUT OF MY MOUTH?
HAK
!
YOU JUST SAID YOU CONSIDER SASUKE TO BE LIKE A BROTHER.
WHAT IF SASUKE WERE TO ATTACK KONOHA? WHAT WOULD YOU DO THEN?
WOULD YOU BE ABLE TO STOP HIM?
EVEN KILL HIM, IF NEED BE?
THAT DAY...

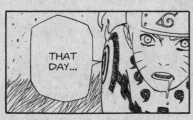

READ THIS WAY

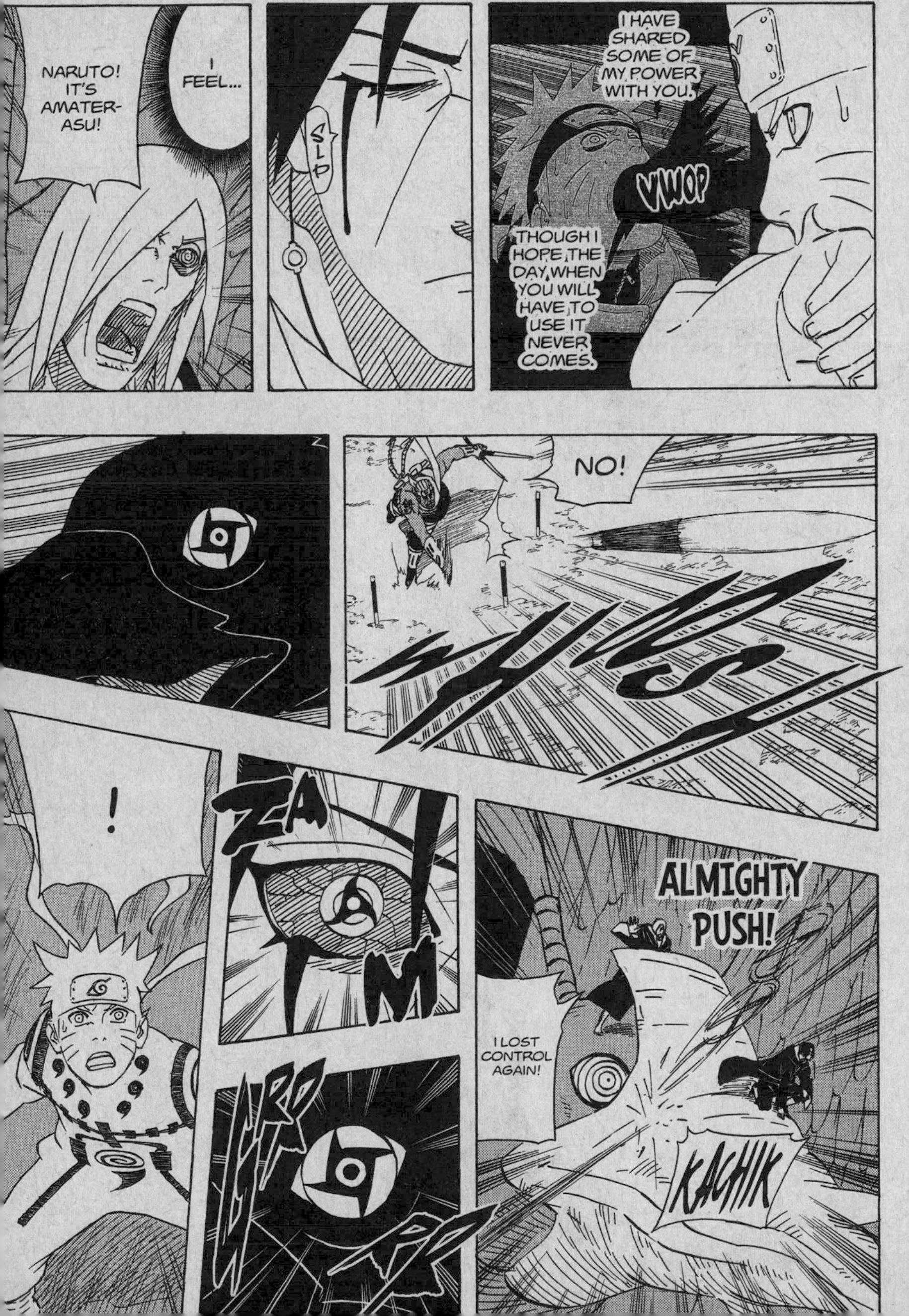

I HAVE SHARED SOME OF MY POWER WITH YOU.
VWOP
THOUGH I HOPE THE DAY WHEN YOU WILL HAVE TO USE IT NEVER COMES.
SLP
I FEEL...
NARUTO! IT'S AMATER-ASU!
NO!
WHOOSH
ALMIGHTY PUSH!
I LOST CONTROL AGAIN!
KACHIK
ZAM
!

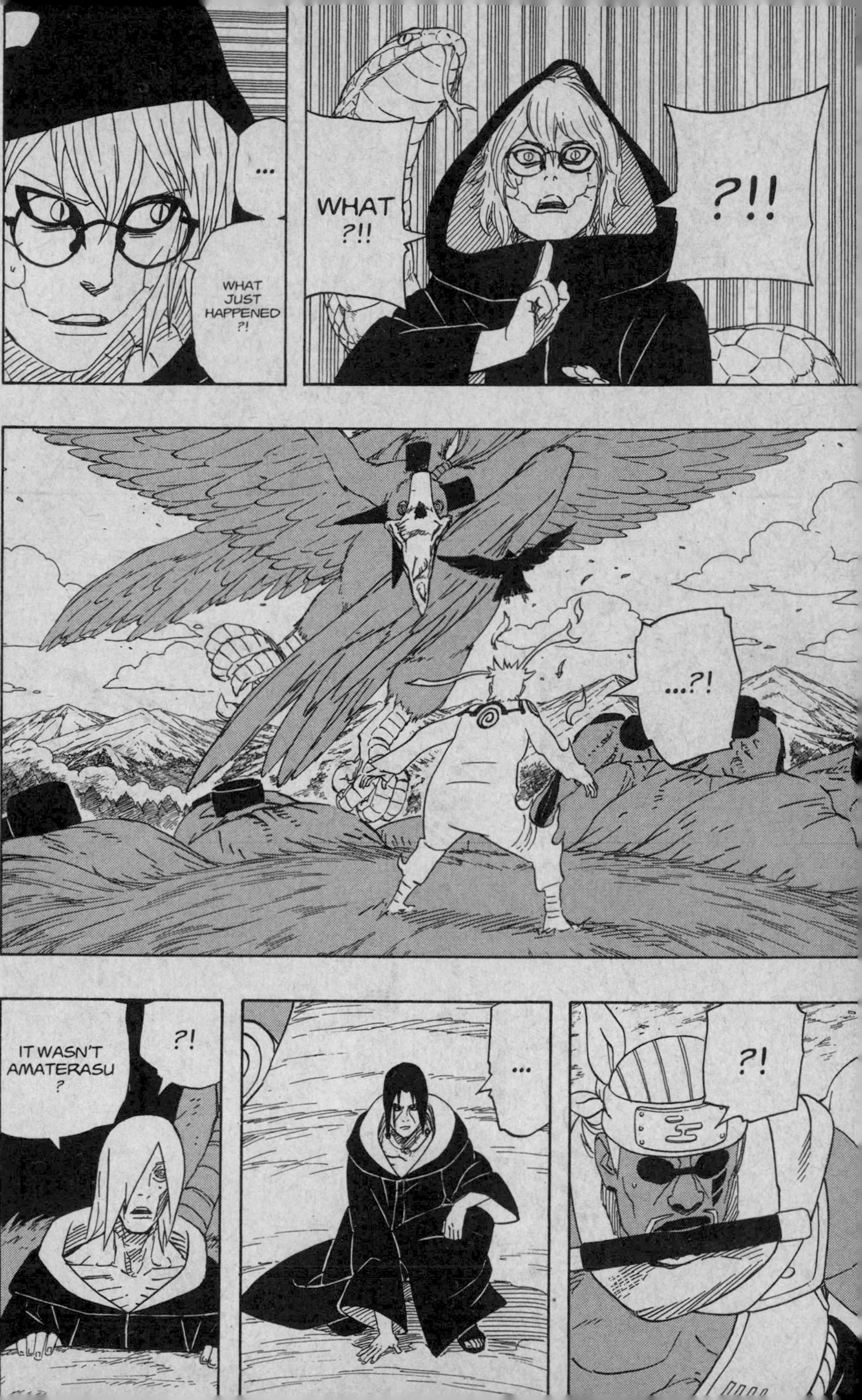
?!!
WHAT ?!!
...
WHAT JUST HAPPENED ?!
...?!
?!
...
?!
IT WASN'T AMATERASU ?

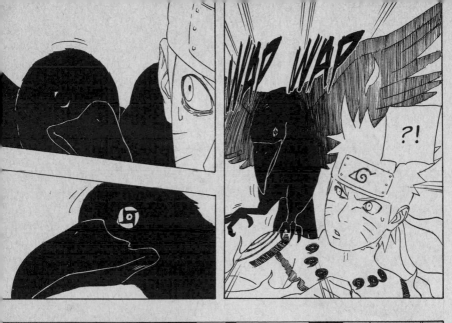

?!

SO THIS IS IT?

?!

AMATERASU!!

WHAT'S GOING ON?

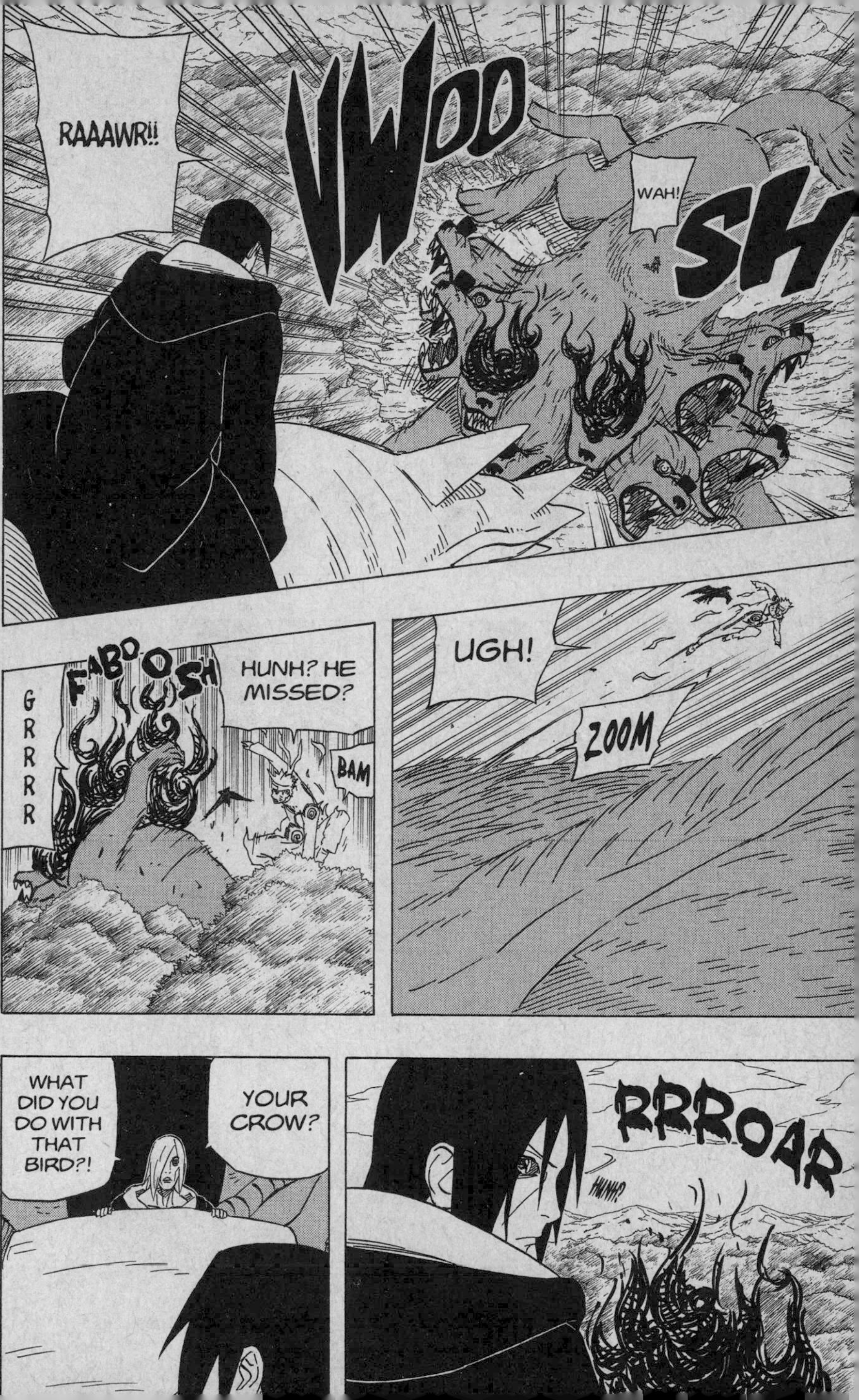
WAH!
VWOOSH
RAAAWR!!
UGH!
ZOOM
HUNH? HE MISSED?
BAM
FABOOSH
GRRRR
RRROAR
HUNH?
YOUR CROW?
WHAT DID YOU DO WITH THAT BIRD?!

READ THIS WAY

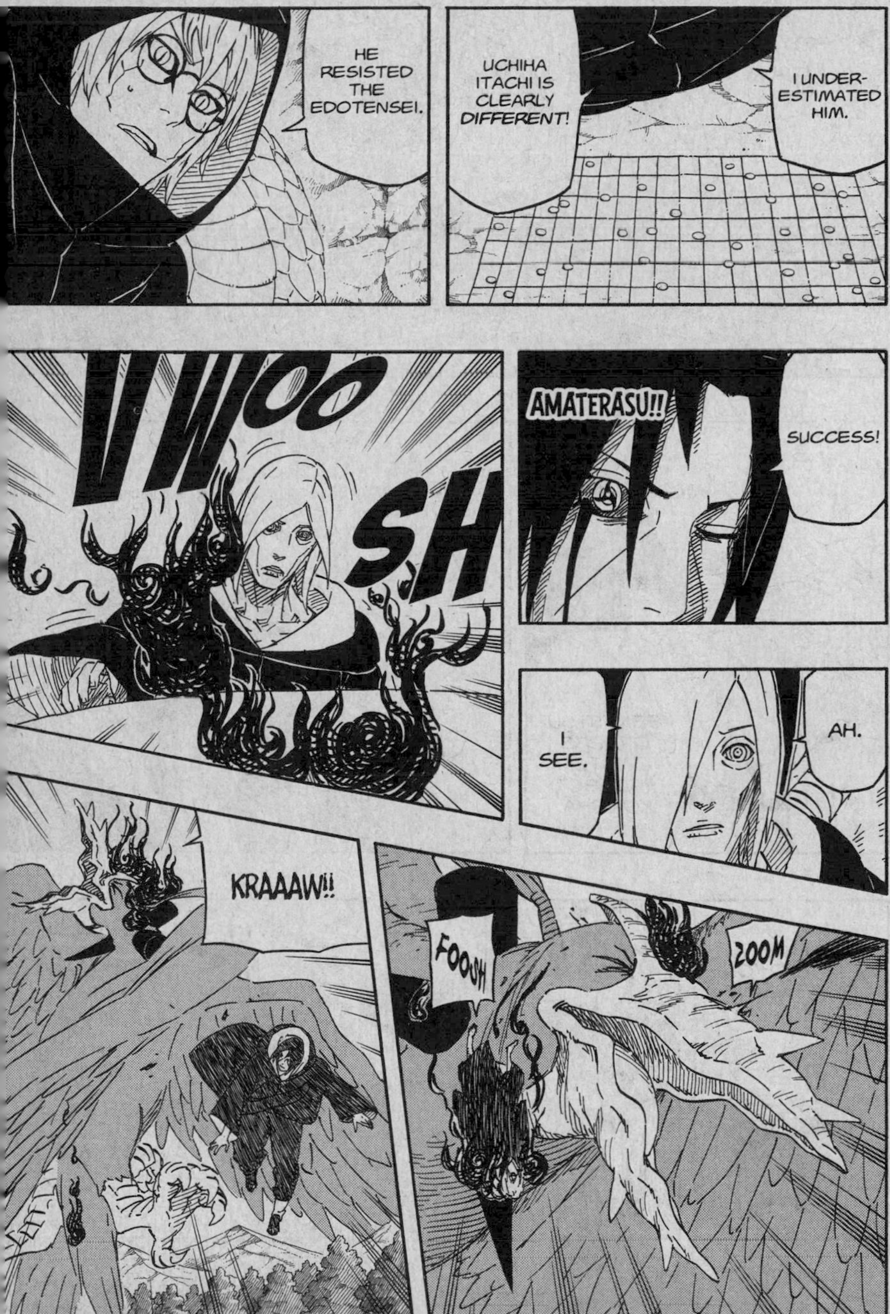

I UNDER-ESTIMATED HIM.
UCHIHA ITACHI IS CLEARLY DIFFERENT!
HE RESISTED THE EDOTENSEI.
SUCCESS!
AMATERASU!!
AH.
I SEE.
VWOOSH
ZOOM
FOOSH
KRAAAW!!

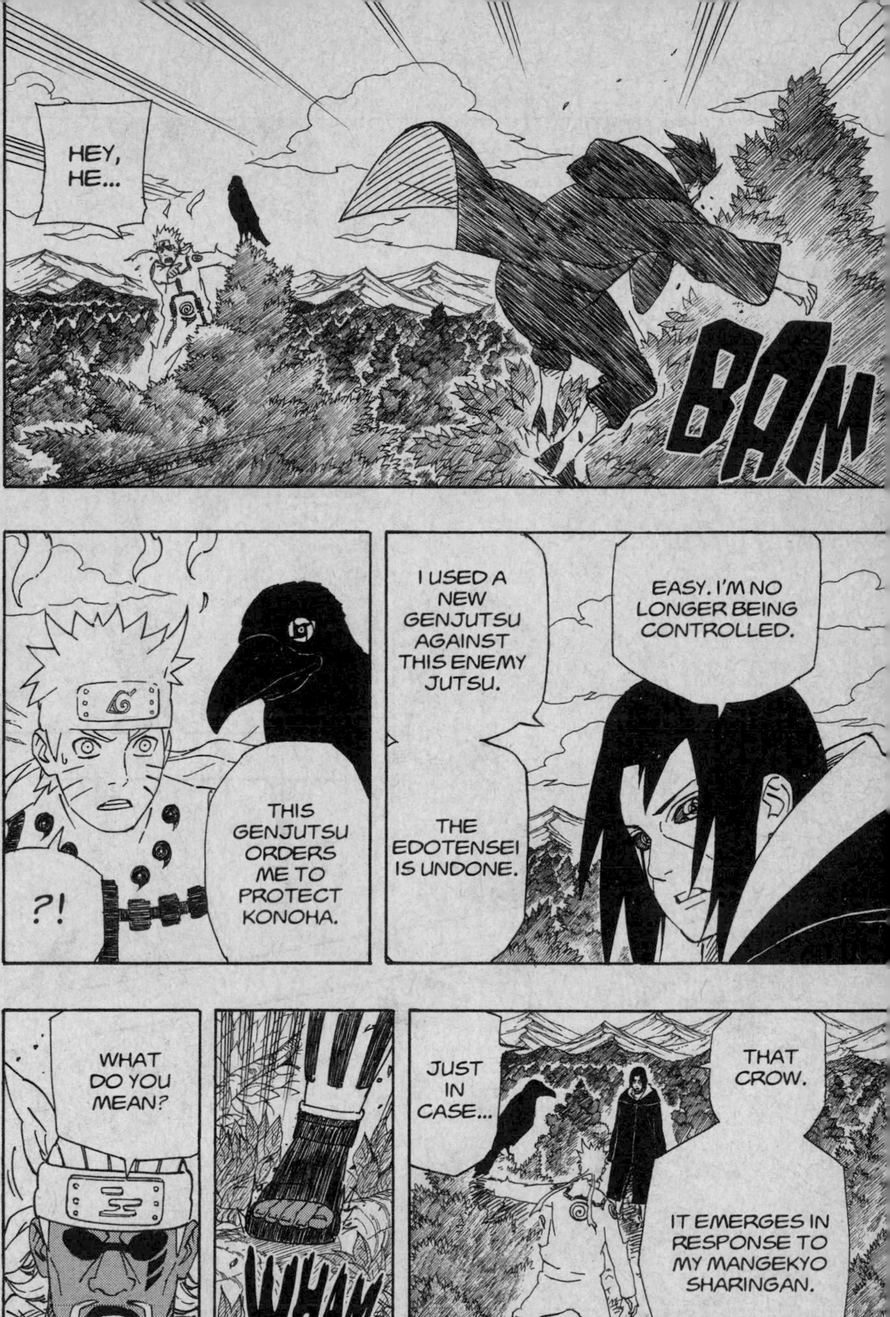
HEY, HE...
BAM
EASY. I'M NO LONGER BEING CONTROLLED.
I USED A NEW GENJUTSU AGAINST THIS ENEMY JUTSU.
THE EDOTENSEI IS UNDONE.
THIS GENJUTSU ORDERS ME TO PROTECT KONOHA.
?!
THAT CROW.
JUST IN CASE...
IT EMERGES IN RESPONSE TO MY MANGEKYO SHARINGAN.
WHAM
WHAT DO YOU MEAN?

READ THIS WAY

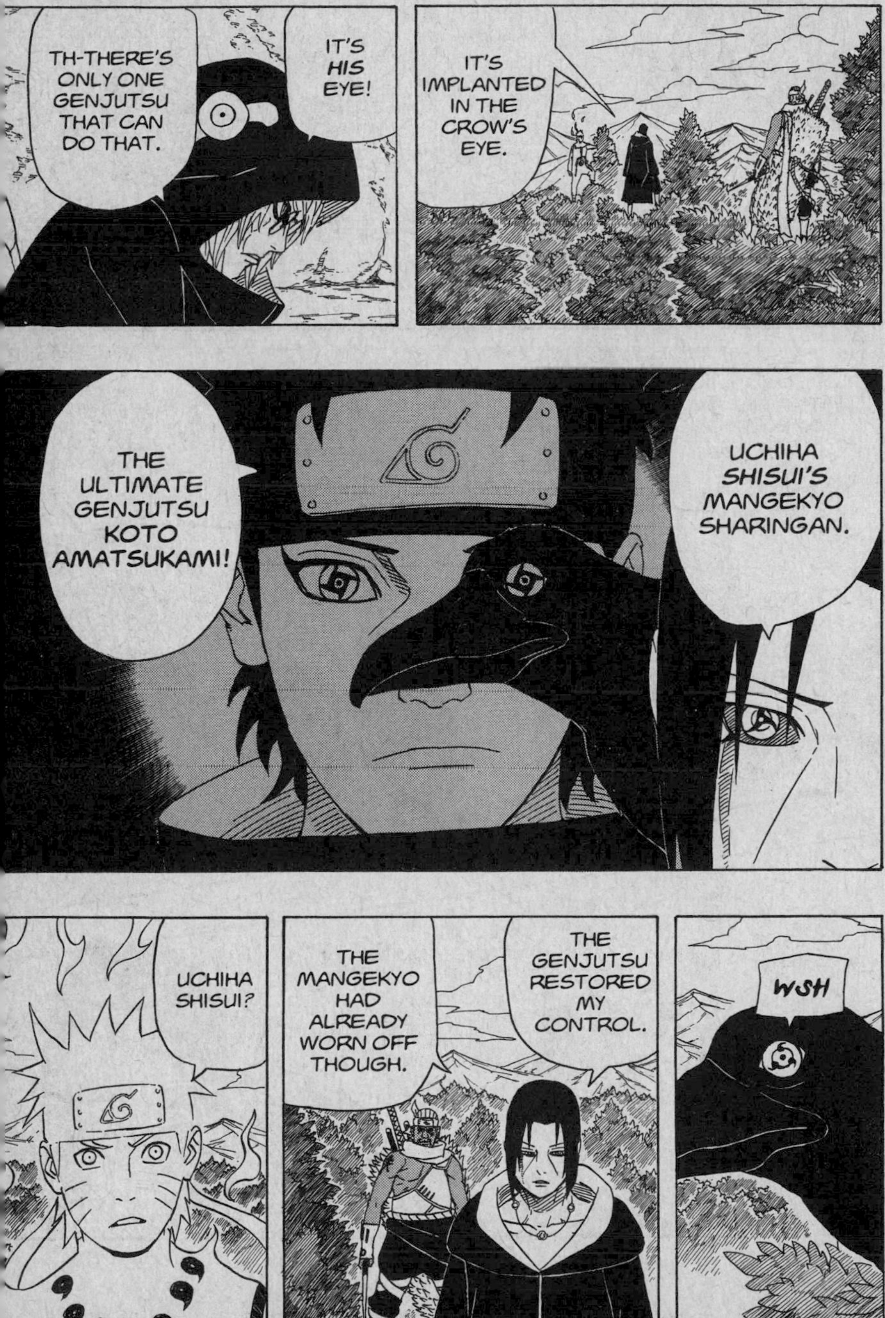
IT'S IMPLANTED IN THE CROW'S EYE.
IT'S HIS EYE!
TH-THERE'S ONLY ONE GENJUTSU THAT CAN DO THAT.
UCHIHA SHISUI'S MANGEKYO SHARINGAN.
THE ULTIMATE GENJUTSU KOTO AMATSUKAMI!
WSH
THE GENJUTSU RESTORED MY CONTROL.
THE MANGEKYO HAD ALREADY WORN OFF THOUGH.
UCHIHA SHISUI?

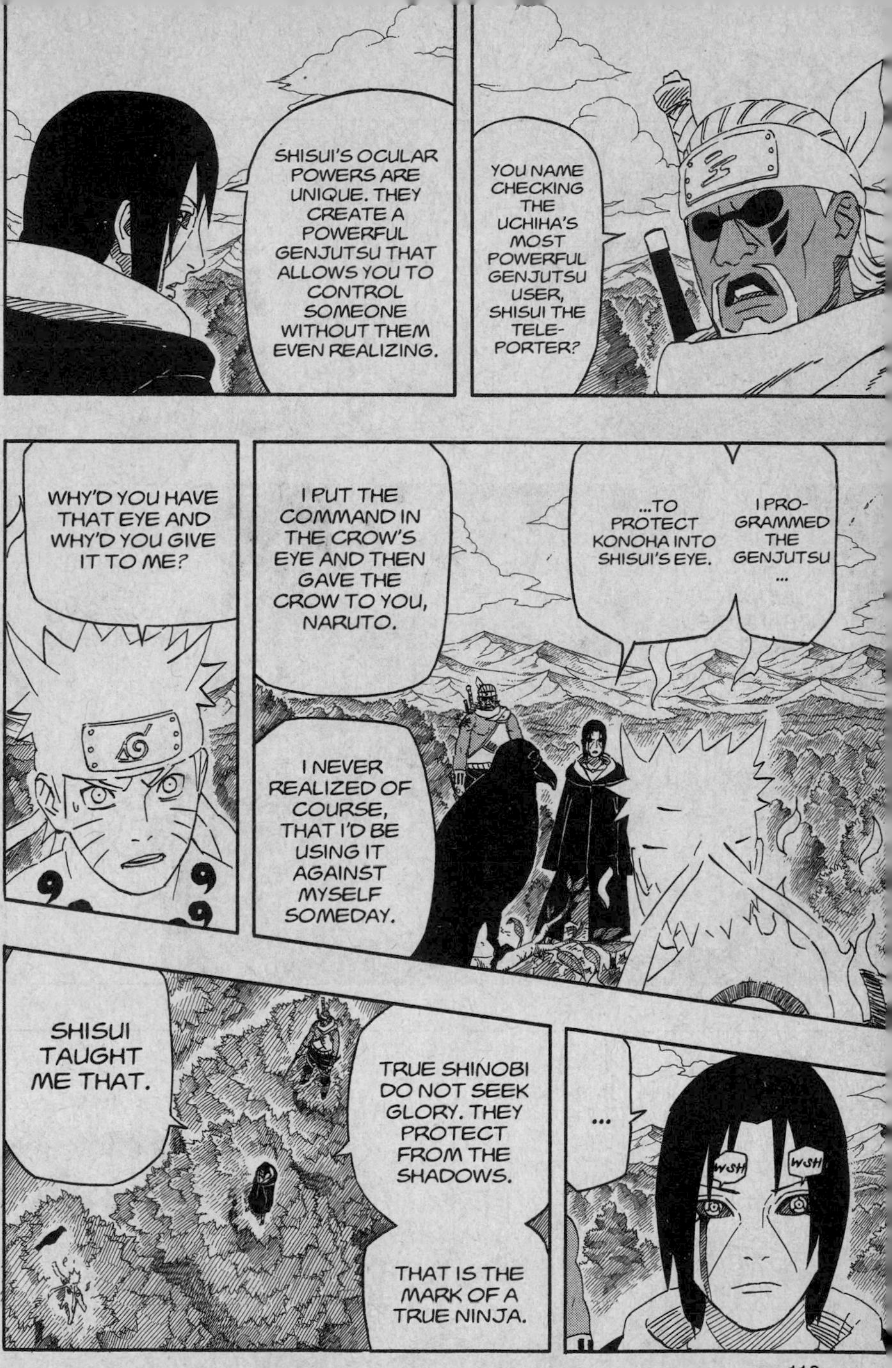
YOU NAME CHECKING THE UCHIHA'S MOST POWERFUL GENJUTSU USER, SHISUI THE TELE-PORTER?
SHISUI'S OCULAR POWERS ARE UNIQUE. THEY CREATE A POWERFUL GENJUTSU THAT ALLOWS YOU TO CONTROL SOMEONE WITHOUT THEM EVEN REALIZING.
I PRO-GRAMMED THE GENJUTSU ...
...TO PROTECT KONOHA INTO SHISUI'S EYE.
I PUT THE COMMAND IN THE CROW'S EYE AND THEN GAVE THE CROW TO YOU, NARUTO.
I NEVER REALIZED OF COURSE, THAT I'D BE USING IT AGAINST MYSELF SOMEDAY.
WHY'D YOU HAVE THAT EYE AND WHY'D YOU GIVE IT TO ME?
...
WSH
WSH
TRUE SHINOBI DO NOT SEEK GLORY. THEY PROTECT FROM THE SHADOWS.
THAT IS THE MARK OF A TRUE NINJA.
SHISUI TAUGHT ME THAT.

READ THIS WAY

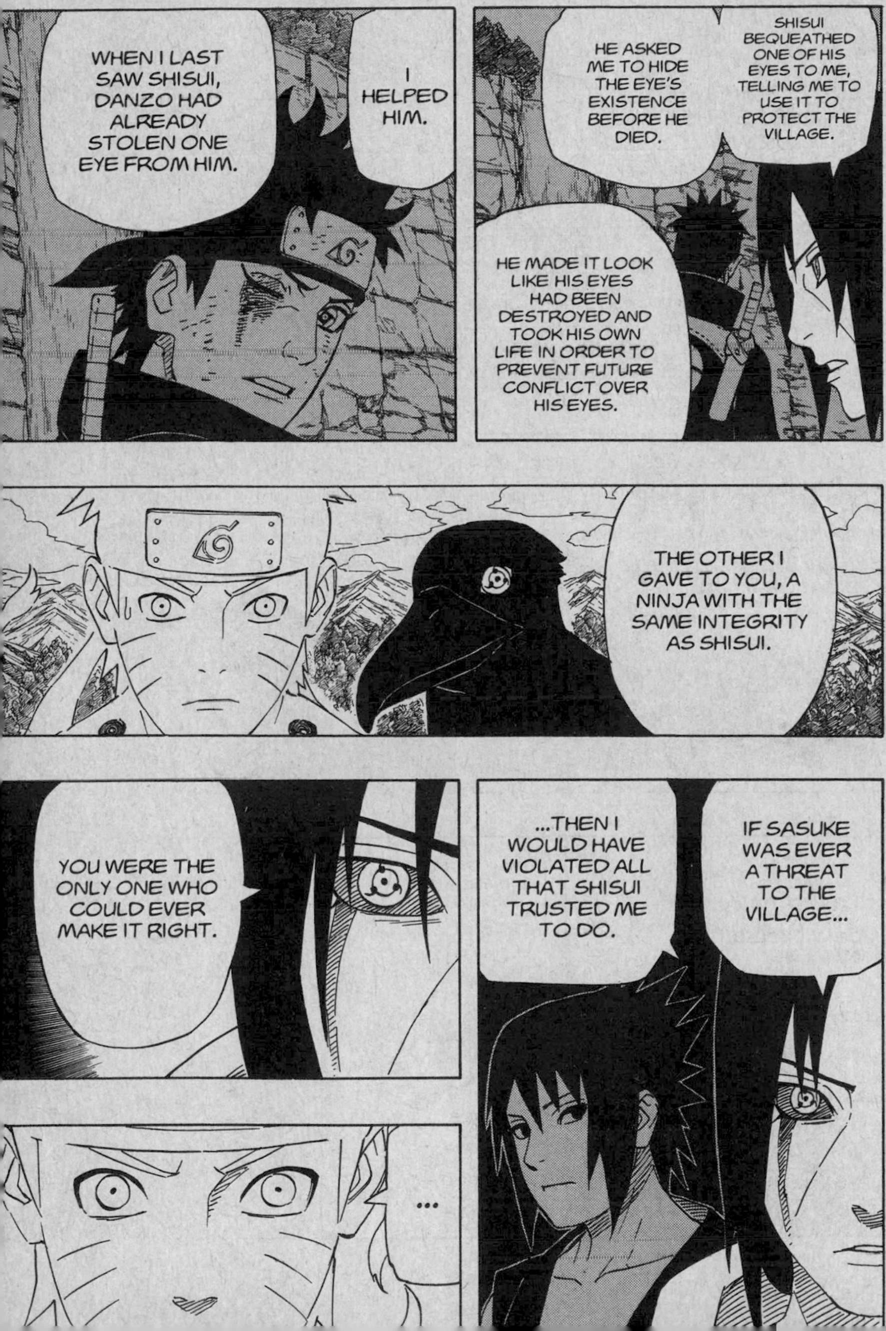
SHISUI BEQUEATHED ONE OF HIS EYES TO ME, TELLING ME TO USE IT TO PROTECT THE VILLAGE.
HE ASKED ME TO HIDE THE EYE'S EXISTENCE BEFORE HE DIED.
HE MADE IT LOOK LIKE HIS EYES HAD BEEN DESTROYED AND TOOK HIS OWN LIFE IN ORDER TO PREVENT FUTURE CONFLICT OVER HIS EYES.
I HELPED HIM.
WHEN I LAST SAW SHISUI, DANZO HAD ALREADY STOLEN ONE EYE FROM HIM.
THE OTHER I GAVE TO YOU, A NINJA WITH THE SAME INTEGRITY AS SHISUI.
IF SASUKE WAS EVER A THREAT TO THE VILLAGE...
...THEN I WOULD HAVE VIOLATED ALL THAT SHISUI TRUSTED ME TO DO.
YOU WERE THE ONLY ONE WHO COULD EVER MAKE IT RIGHT.
...

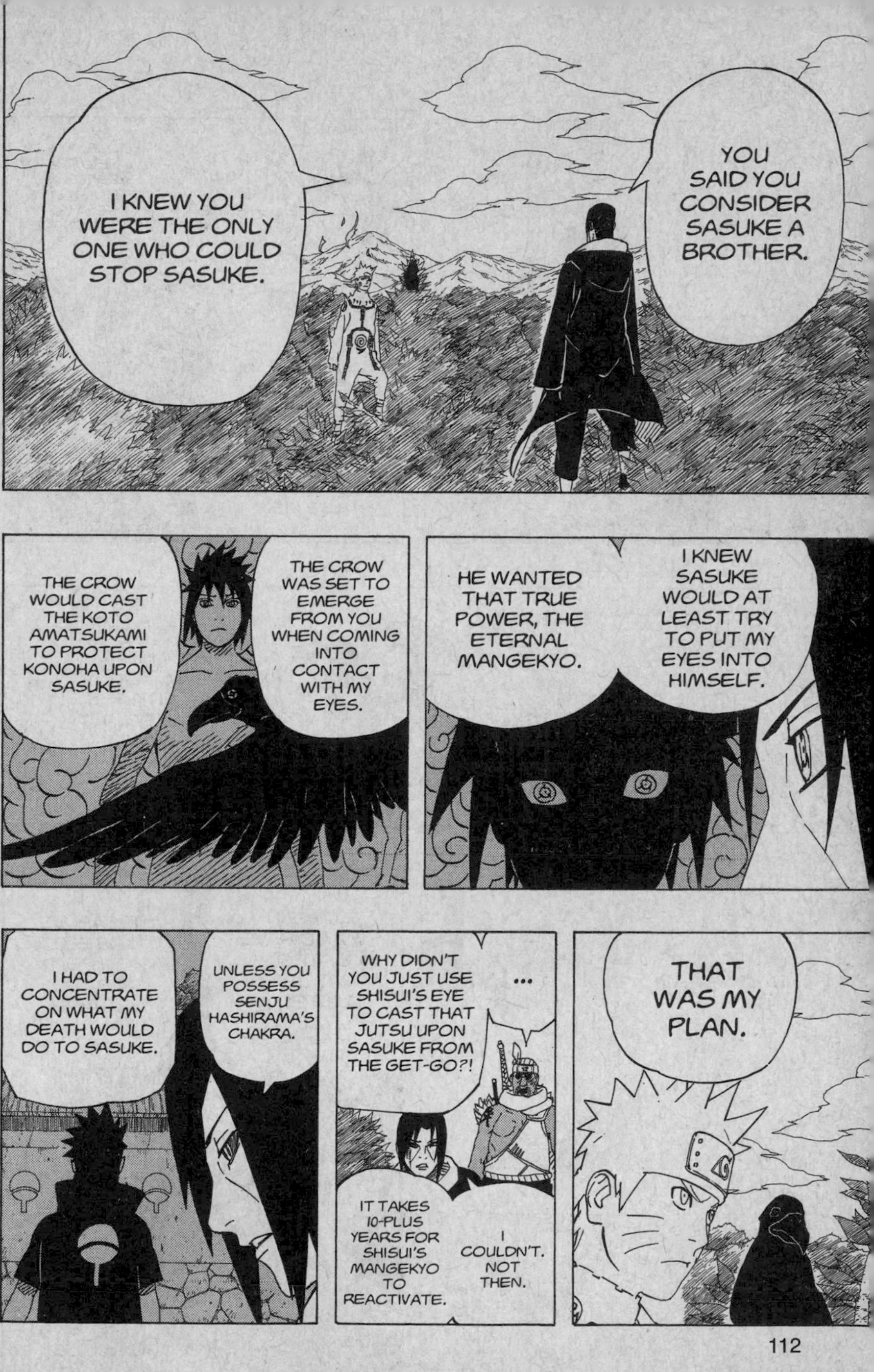
YOU SAID YOU CONSIDER SASUKE A BROTHER.
I KNEW YOU WERE THE ONLY ONE WHO COULD STOP SASUKE.
I KNEW SASUKE WOULD AT LEAST TRY TO PUT MY EYES INTO HIMSELF.
HE WANTED THAT TRUE POWER, THE ETERNAL MANGEKYO.
THE CROW WAS SET TO EMERGE FROM YOU WHEN COMING INTO CONTACT WITH MY EYES.
THE CROW WOULD CAST THE KOTO AMATSUKAMI TO PROTECT KONOHA UPON SASUKE.
THAT WAS MY PLAN.
WHY DIDN'T YOU JUST USE SHISUI'S EYE TO CAST THAT JUTSU UPON SASUKE FROM THE GET-GO?!
...
I COULDN'T. NOT THEN.
IT TAKES 10-PLUS YEARS FOR SHISUI'S MANGEKYO TO REACTIVATE.
UNLESS YOU POSSESS SENJU HASHIRAMA'S CHAKRA.
I HAD TO CONCENTRATE ON WHAT MY DEATH WOULD DO TO SASUKE.

READ THIS WAY

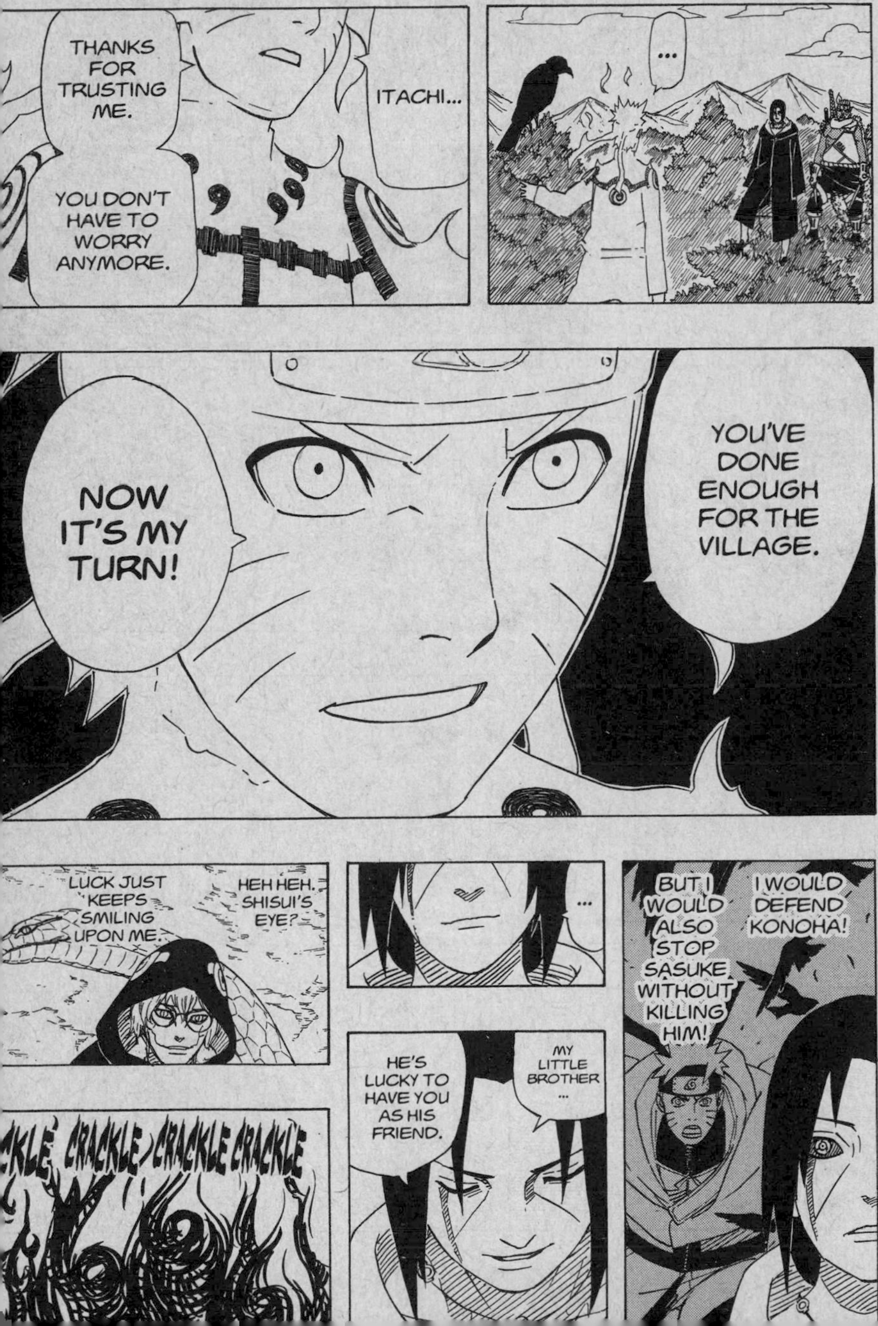
...
ITACHI...
THANKS FOR TRUSTING ME.
YOU DON'T HAVE TO WORRY ANYMORE.
YOU'VE DONE ENOUGH FOR THE VILLAGE.
NOW IT'S MY TURN!
I WOULD DEFEND KONOHA!
BUT I WOULD ALSO STOP SASUKE WITHOUT KILLING HIM!
...
MY LITTLE BROTHER ...
HE'S LUCKY TO HAVE YOU AS HIS FRIEND.
HEH HEH. SHISUI'S EYE?
LUCK JUST KEEPS SMILING UPON ME.
CRACKLE CRACKLE CRACKLE

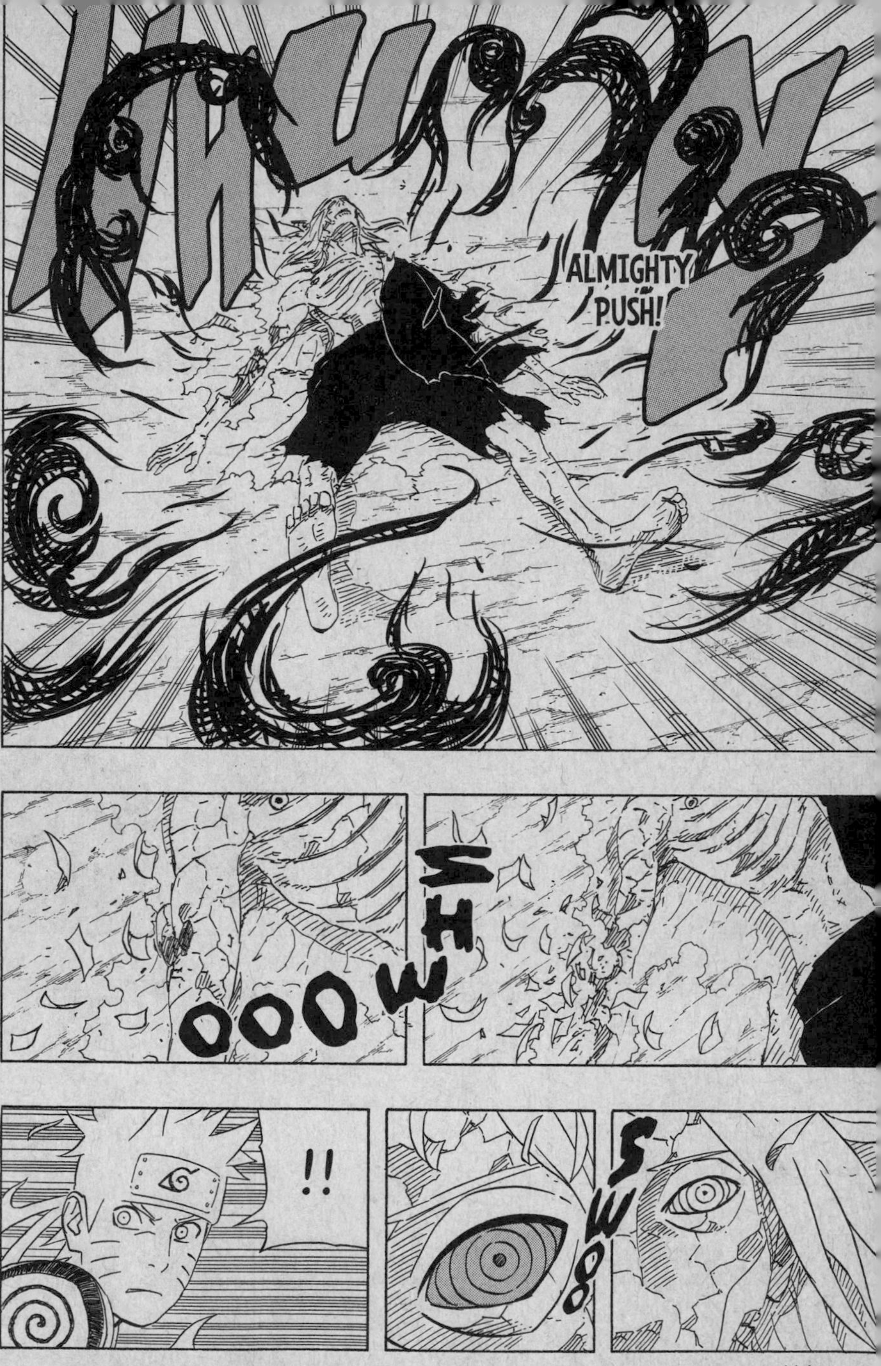
ALMIGHTY PUSH!
!!

READ THIS WAY

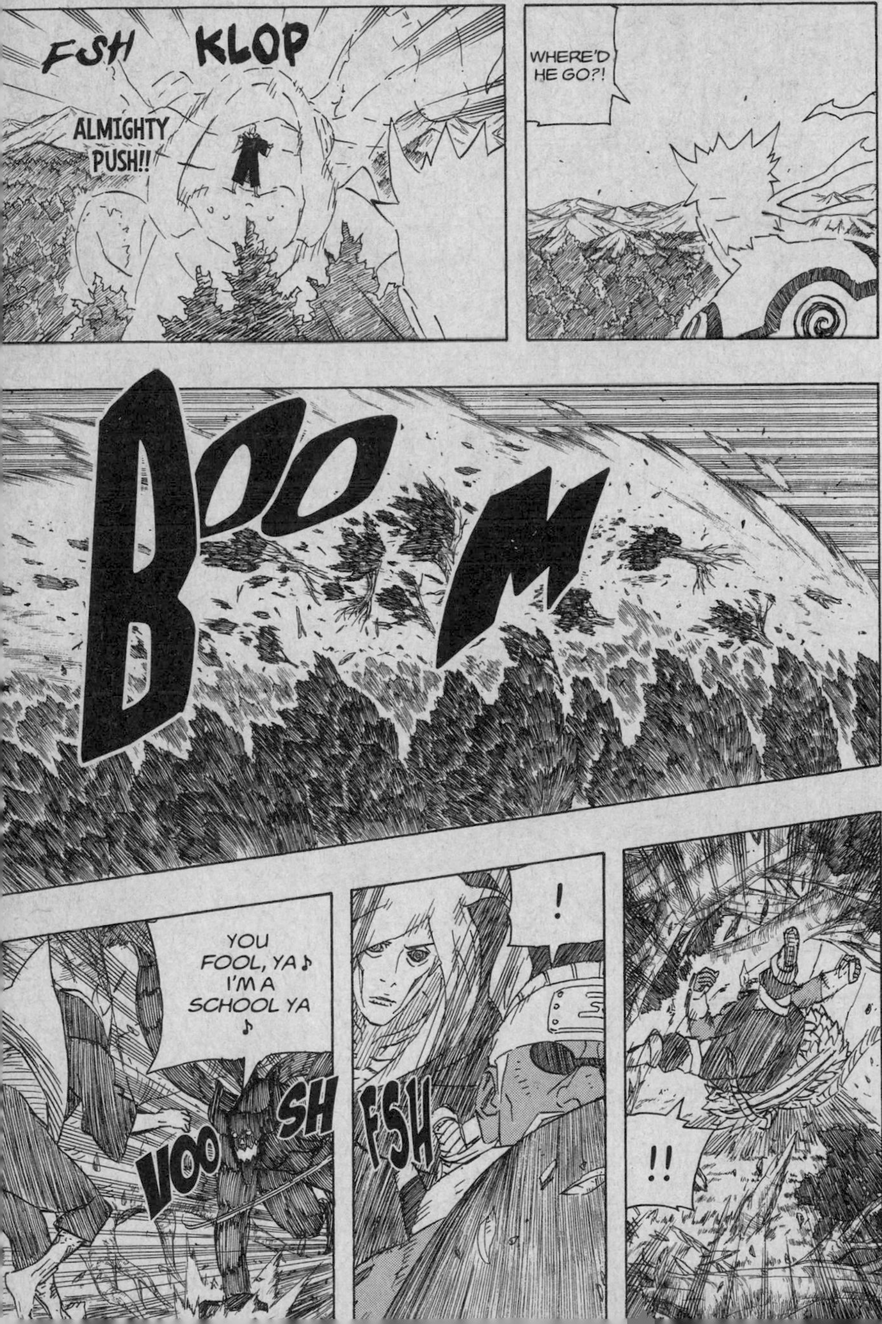
WHERE'D HE GO?!
KLOP
FSH
ALMIGHTY PUSH!!
BOOM
!!
!
FSH
YOU FOOL, YA♪ I'M A SCHOOL YA ♪
WOOSH

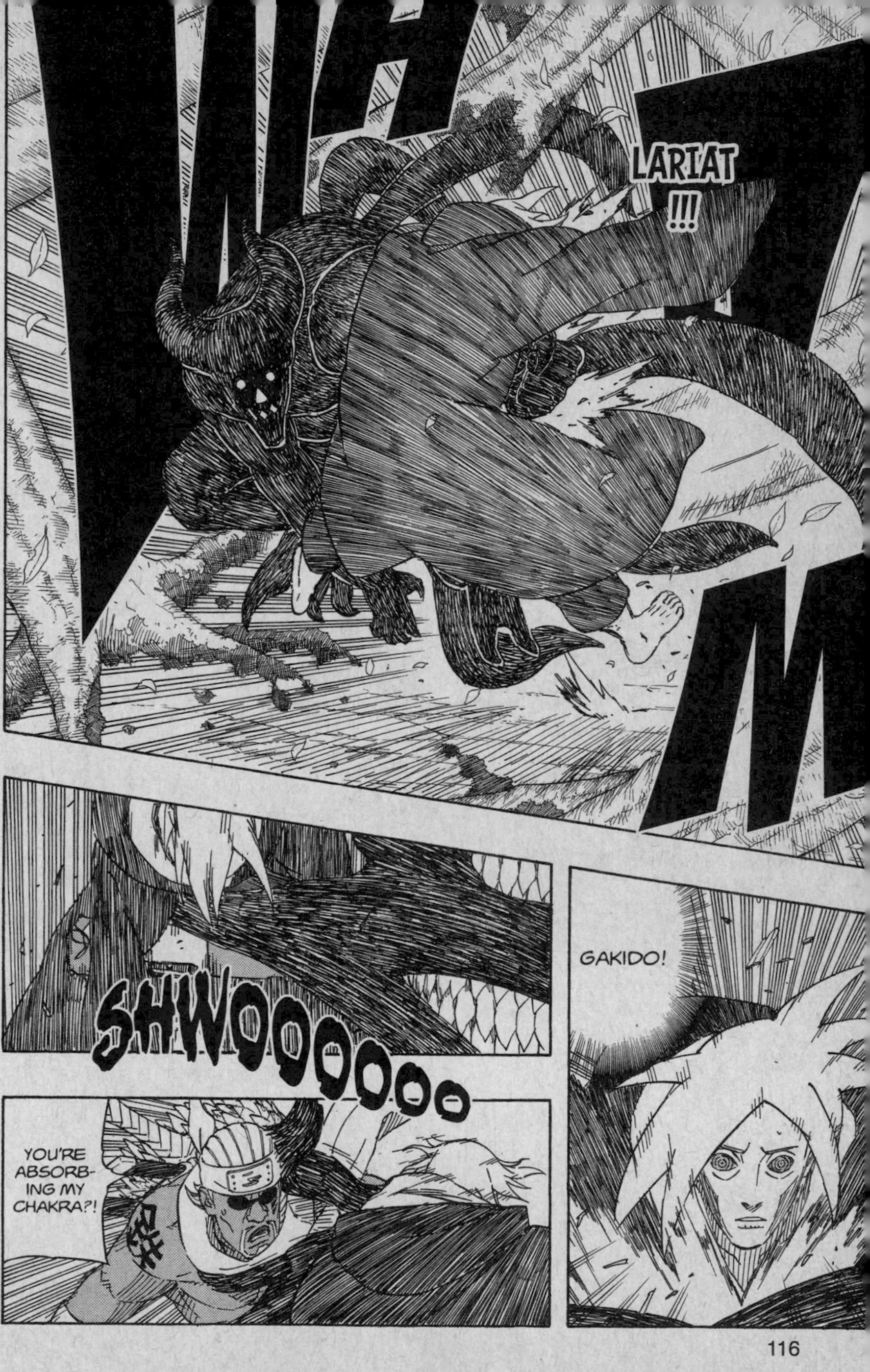
LARIAT !!!
GAKIDO!
SHWOOOOOO
YOU'RE ABSORBING MY CHAKRA?!

READ THIS WAY

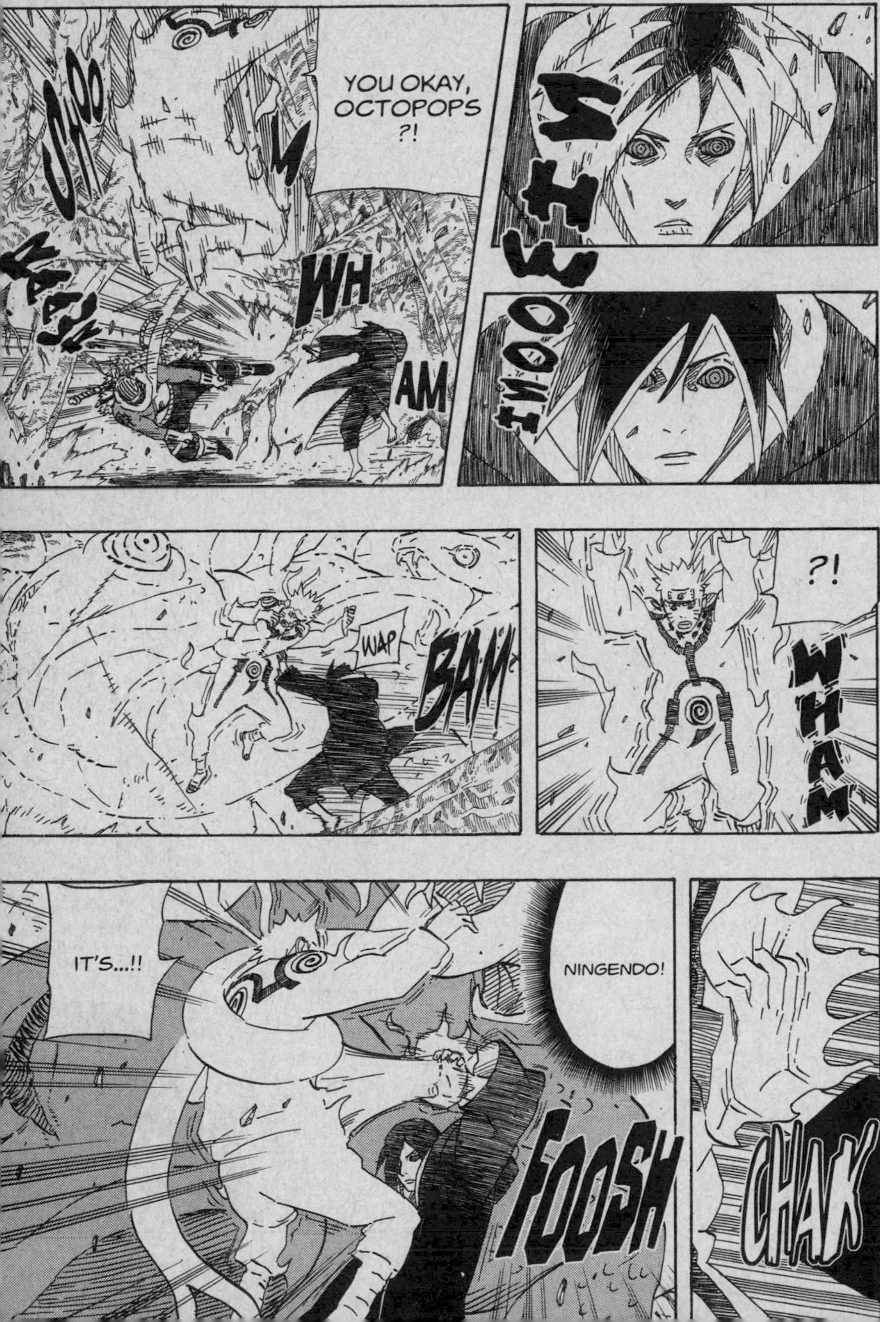
YOU OKAY, OCTOPOPS ?!
WHAM
?!
WHAM
WAP
BAM
CHAK
IT'S...!!
NINGENDO!
FOOSH

Number 551: Stop Nagato!!

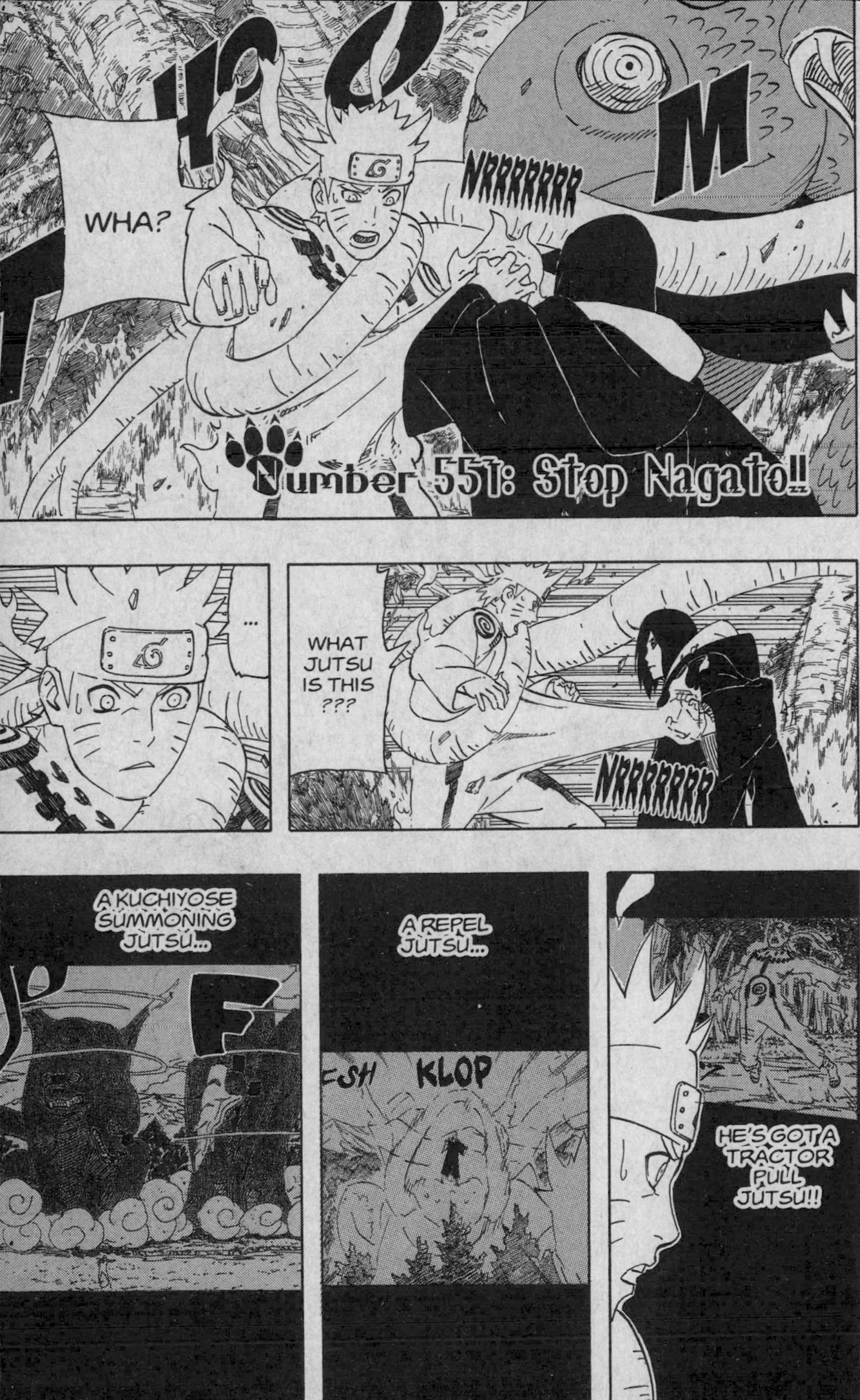
HOOM
NRRRRRRR
WHA?
WHAT JUTSU IS THIS ???
NRRRRRRR
...
HE'S GOT A TRACTOR PULL JUTSU!!
A REPEL JUTSU...
KLOP
FSH
A KUCHIYOSE SUMMONING JUTSU...

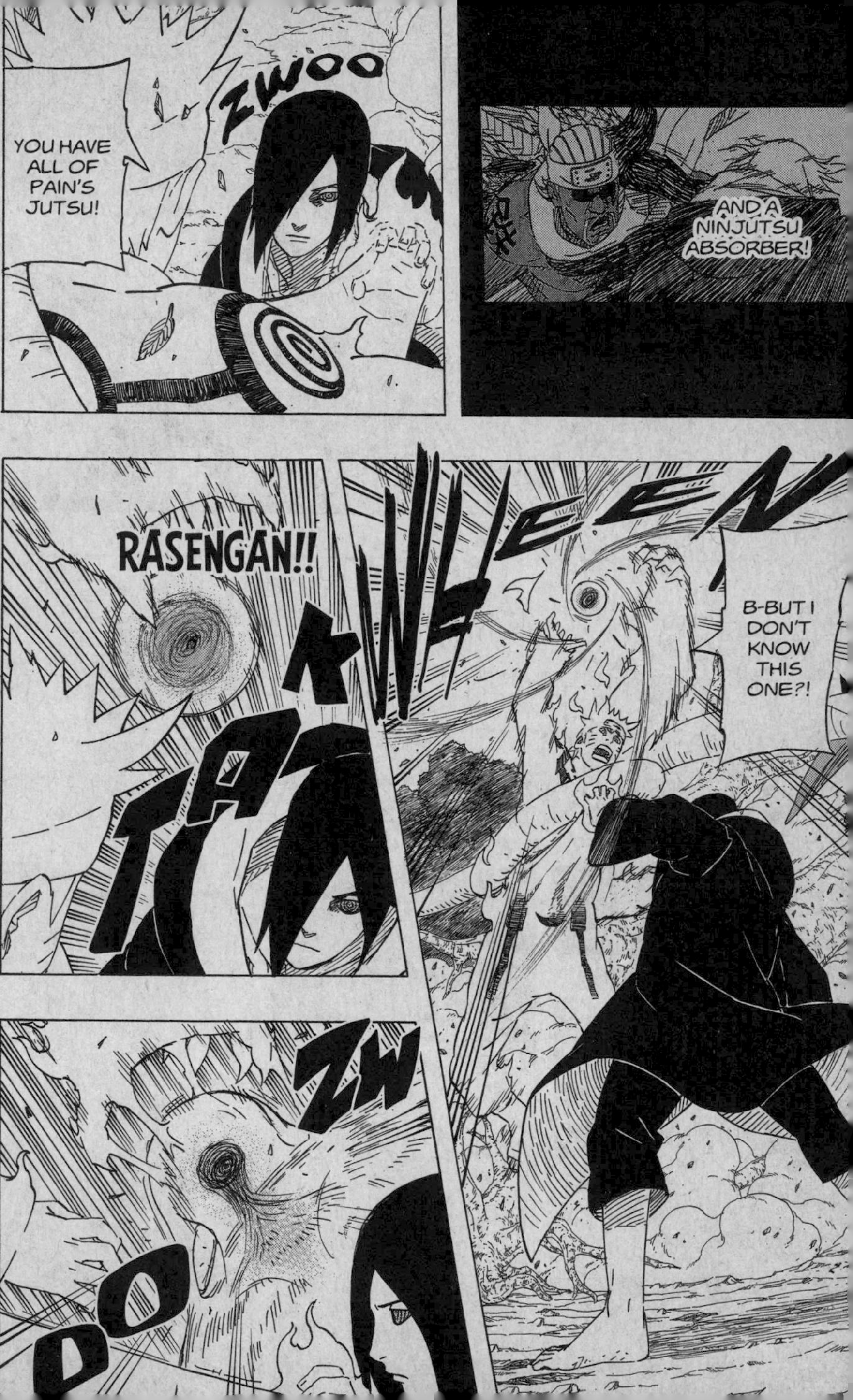
AND A NINJUTSU ABSORBER!
ZWOO
YOU HAVE ALL OF PAIN'S JUTSU!
WHEEEN
B-BUT I DON'T KNOW THIS ONE?!
RASENGAN!!
TA
ZW
DO

READ THIS WAY

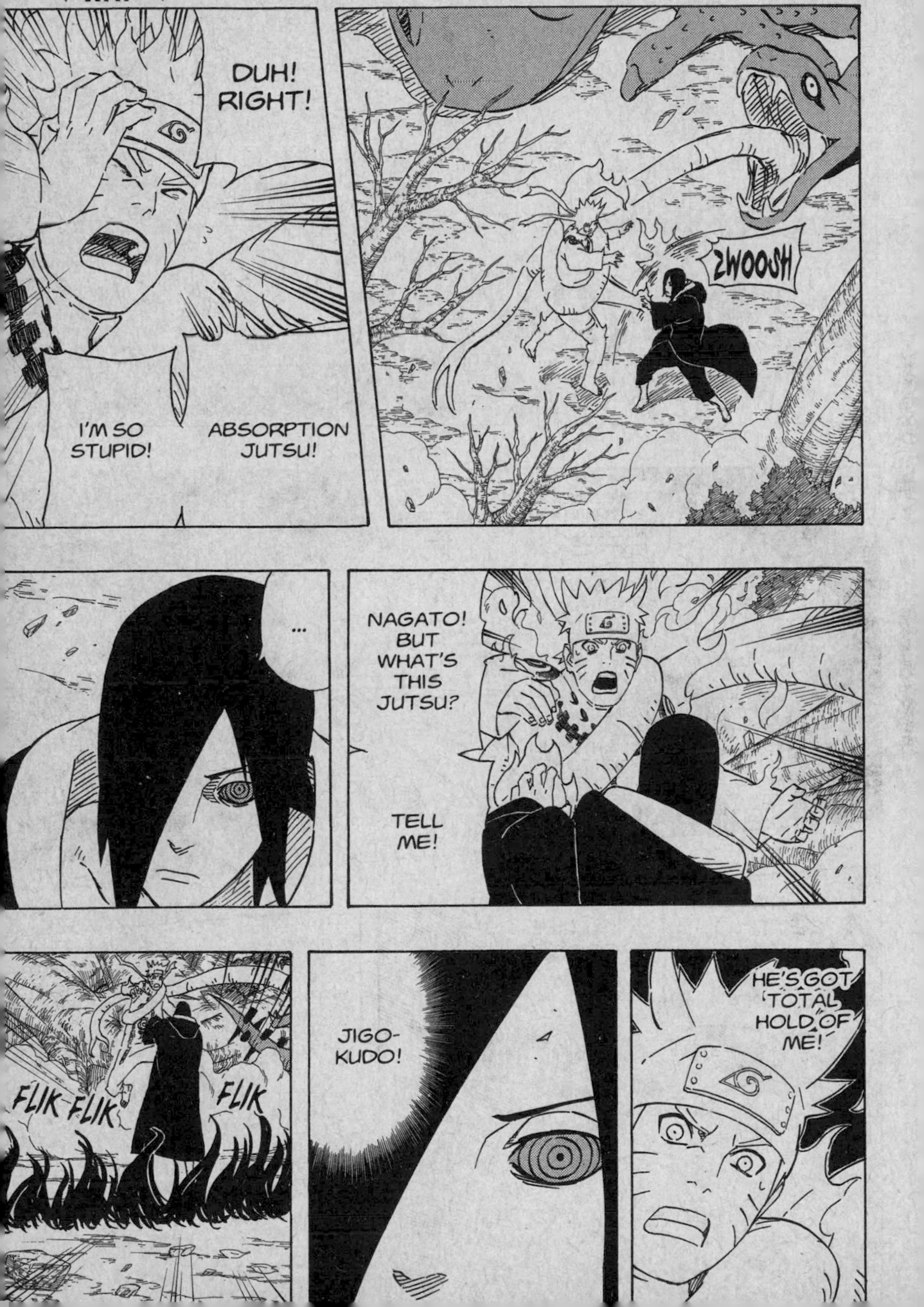
ZWOOSH
DUH! RIGHT!
ABSORPTION JUTSU!
I'M SO STUPID!
NAGATO! BUT WHAT'S THIS JUTSU?
TELL ME!
...
HE'S GOT TOTAL HOLD OF ME!
JIGO-KUDO!
FLIK
FLIK FLIK

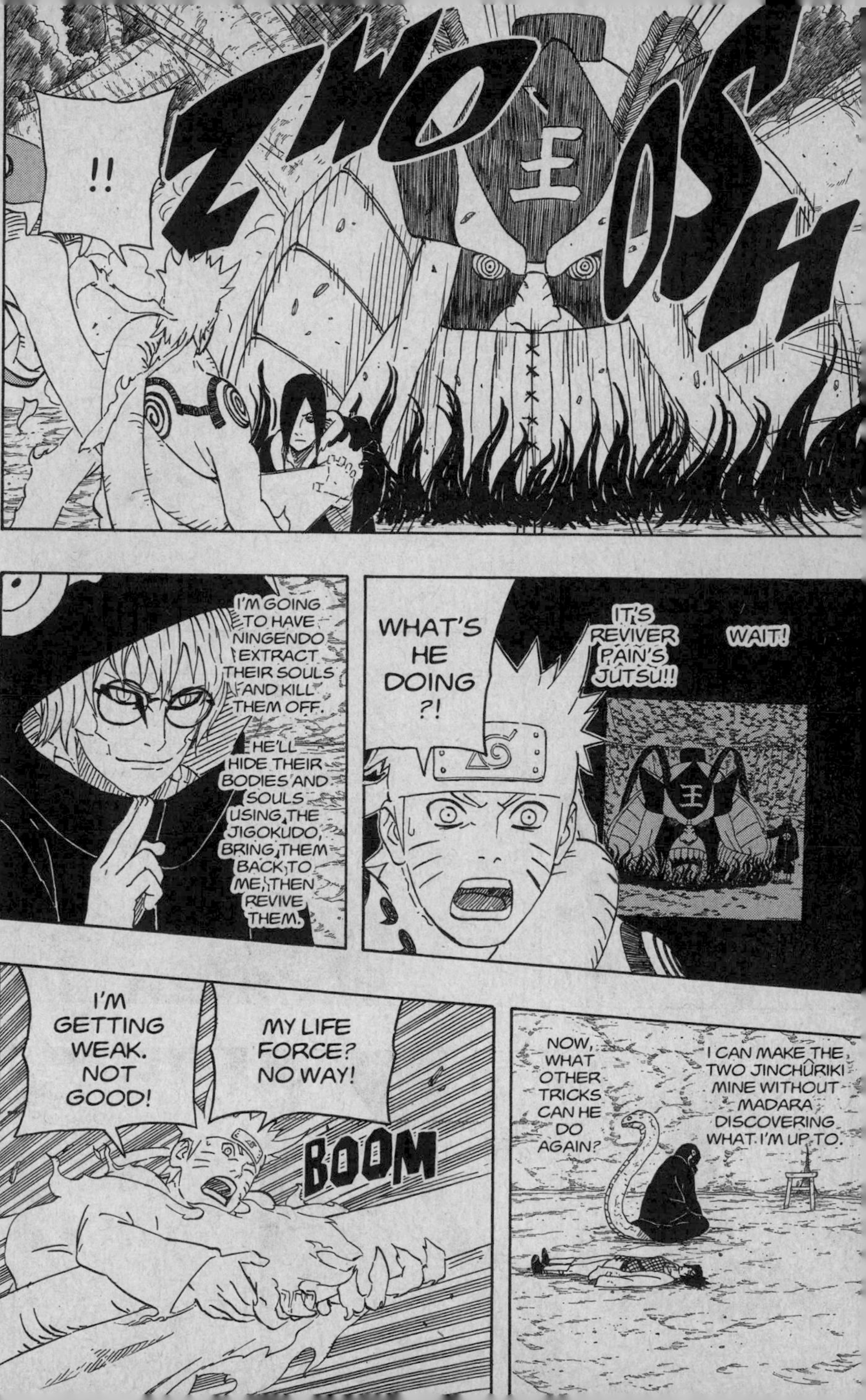
ZWOOSH
!!
WAIT!
IT'S REVIVER PAIN'S JUTSU!!
WHAT'S HE DOING ?!
I'M GOING TO HAVE NINGENDO EXTRACT THEIR SOULS AND KILL THEM OFF.
HE'LL HIDE THEIR BODIES AND SOULS USING THE JIGOKUDO, BRING THEM BACK TO ME, THEN REVIVE THEM.
I CAN MAKE THE TWO JINCHÛRIKI MINE WITHOUT MADARA DISCOVERING WHAT I'M UP TO.
NOW, WHAT OTHER TRICKS CAN HE DO AGAIN?
MY LIFE FORCE? NO WAY!
I'M GETTING WEAK. NOT GOOD!
BOOM

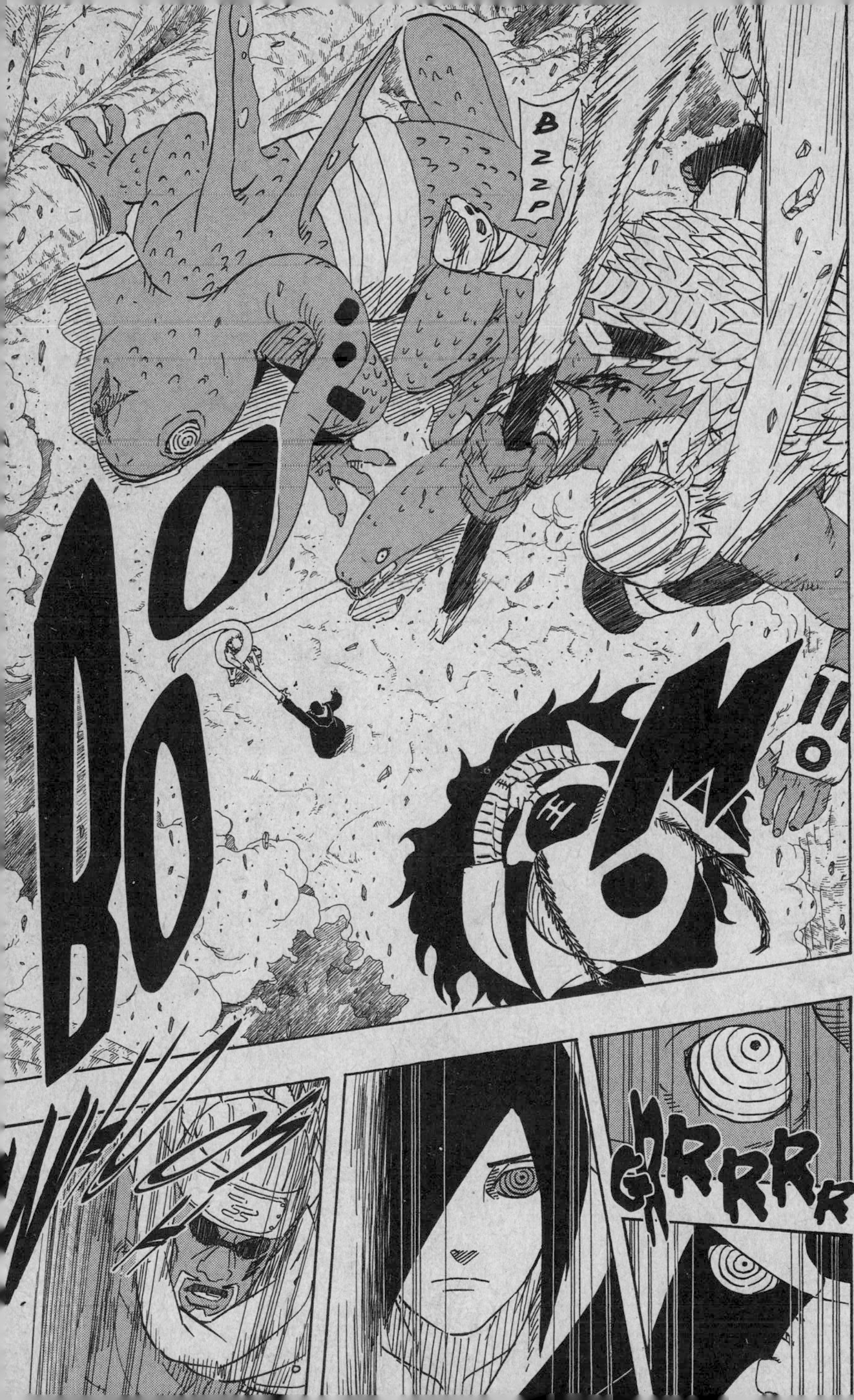
BZZP
BOOM
GRRRR

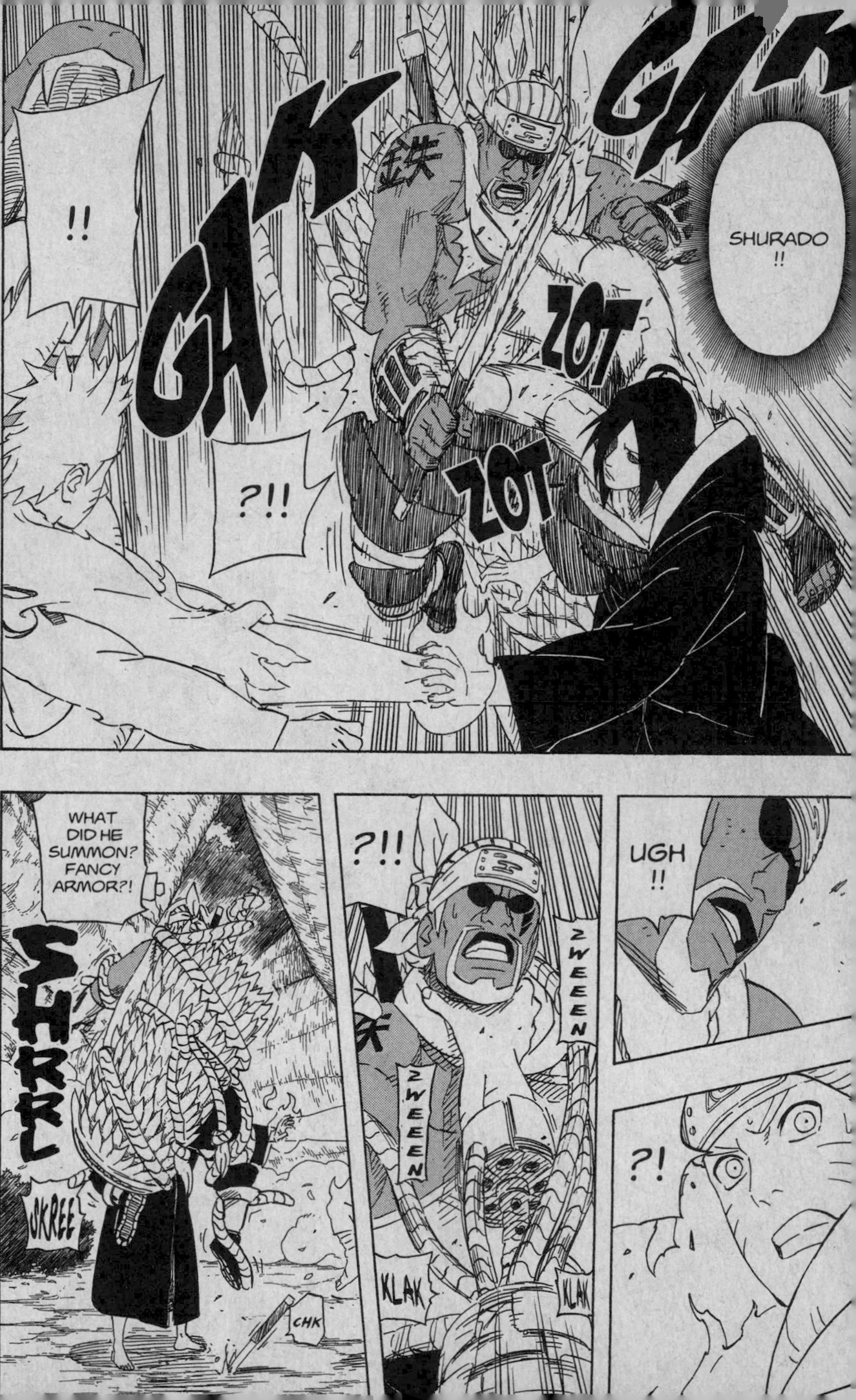

GAK
SHURADO !!
GAK
!!
ZOT
ZOT
?!!
UGH !!
?!
?!!
ZWEEEN
ZWEEEN
KLAK
KLAK
WHAT DID HE SUMMON? FANCY ARMOR?!
SHRRL
SKREE
CHK

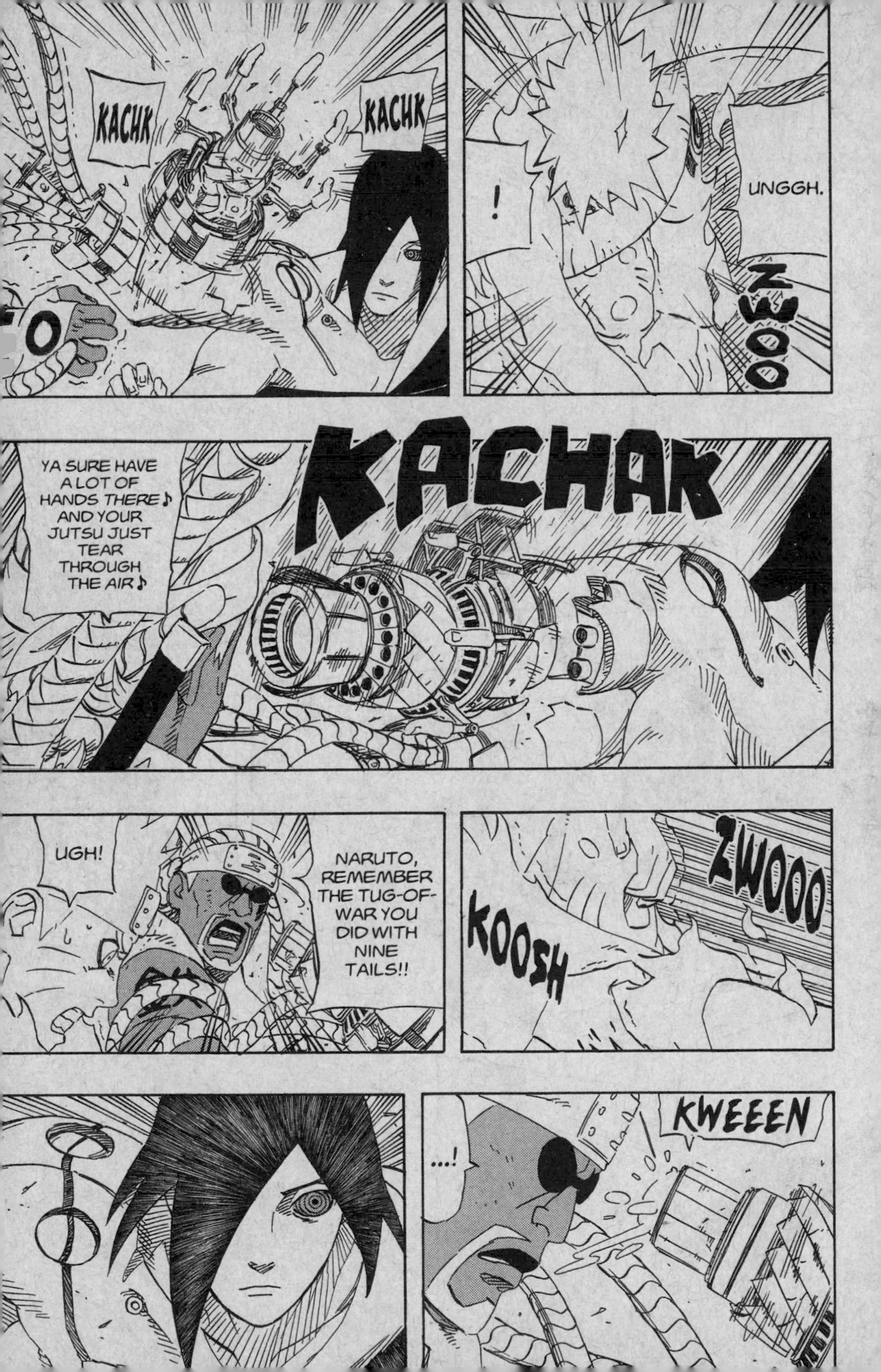
UNGGH.
!
ZWOO
KACHK
KACHK
KACHAK
YA SURE HAVE A LOT OF HANDS THERE♪ AND YOUR JUTSU JUST TEAR THROUGH THE AIR♪
ZWOOO
KOOSH
NARUTO, REMEMBER THE TUG-OF-WAR YOU DID WITH NINE TAILS!!
UGH!
KWEEEN
...!

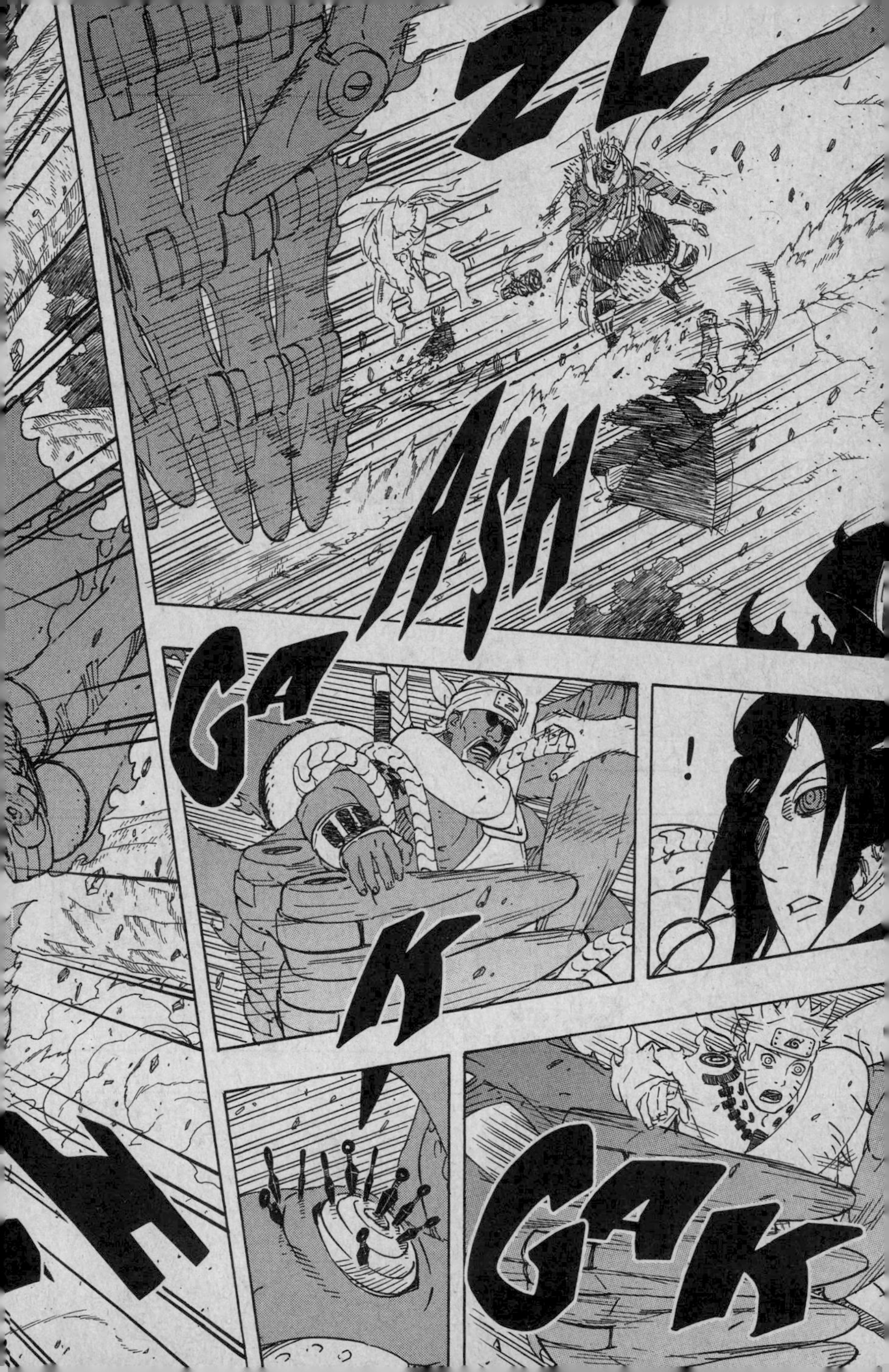
ASH
!
GAK
GAK

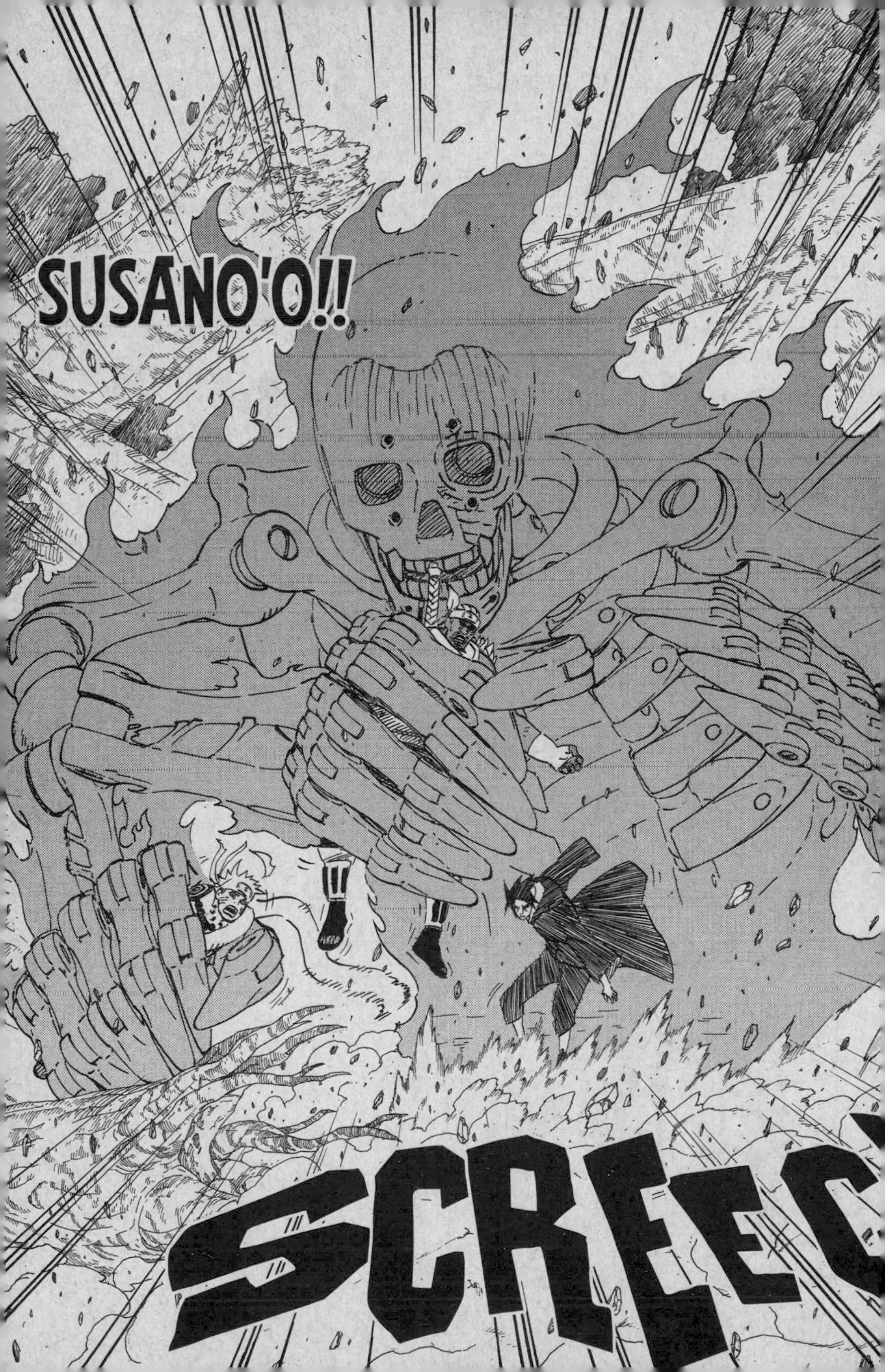
SUSANO'O!!
SCREEC

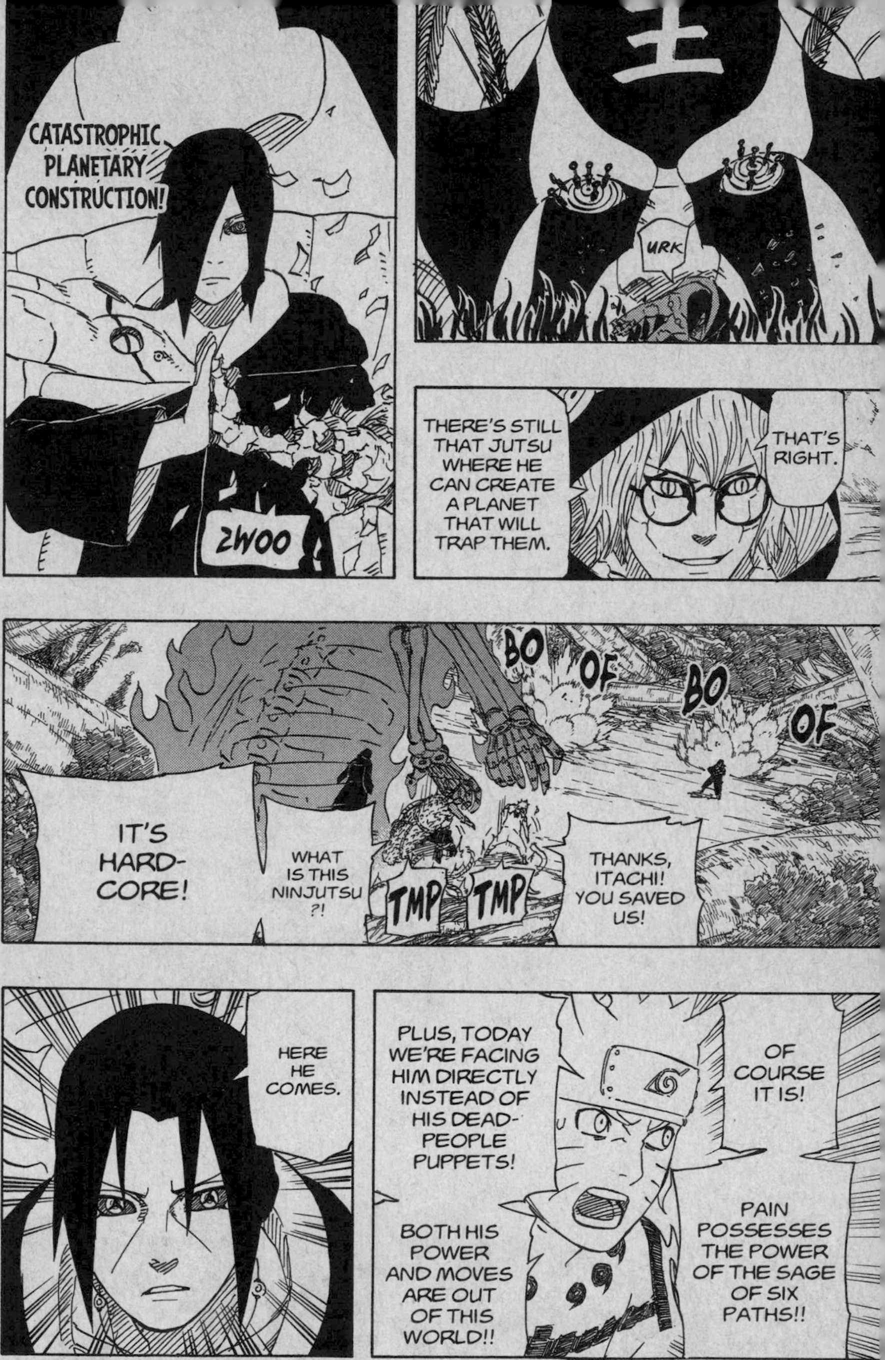
URK
THAT'S RIGHT.
THERE'S STILL THAT JUTSU WHERE HE CAN CREATE A PLANET THAT WILL TRAP THEM.
CATASTROPHIC PLANETARY CONSTRUCTION!
ZWOO
BO OF BO OF
THANKS, ITACHI! YOU SAVED US!
TMP TMP
WHAT IS THIS NINJUTSU ?!
IT'S HARD-CORE!
OF COURSE IT IS!
PLUS, TODAY WE'RE FACING HIM DIRECTLY INSTEAD OF HIS DEAD-PEOPLE PUPPETS!
PAIN POSSESSES THE POWER OF THE SAGE OF SIX PATHS!!
BOTH HIS POWER AND MOVES ARE OUT OF THIS WORLD!!
HERE HE COMES.

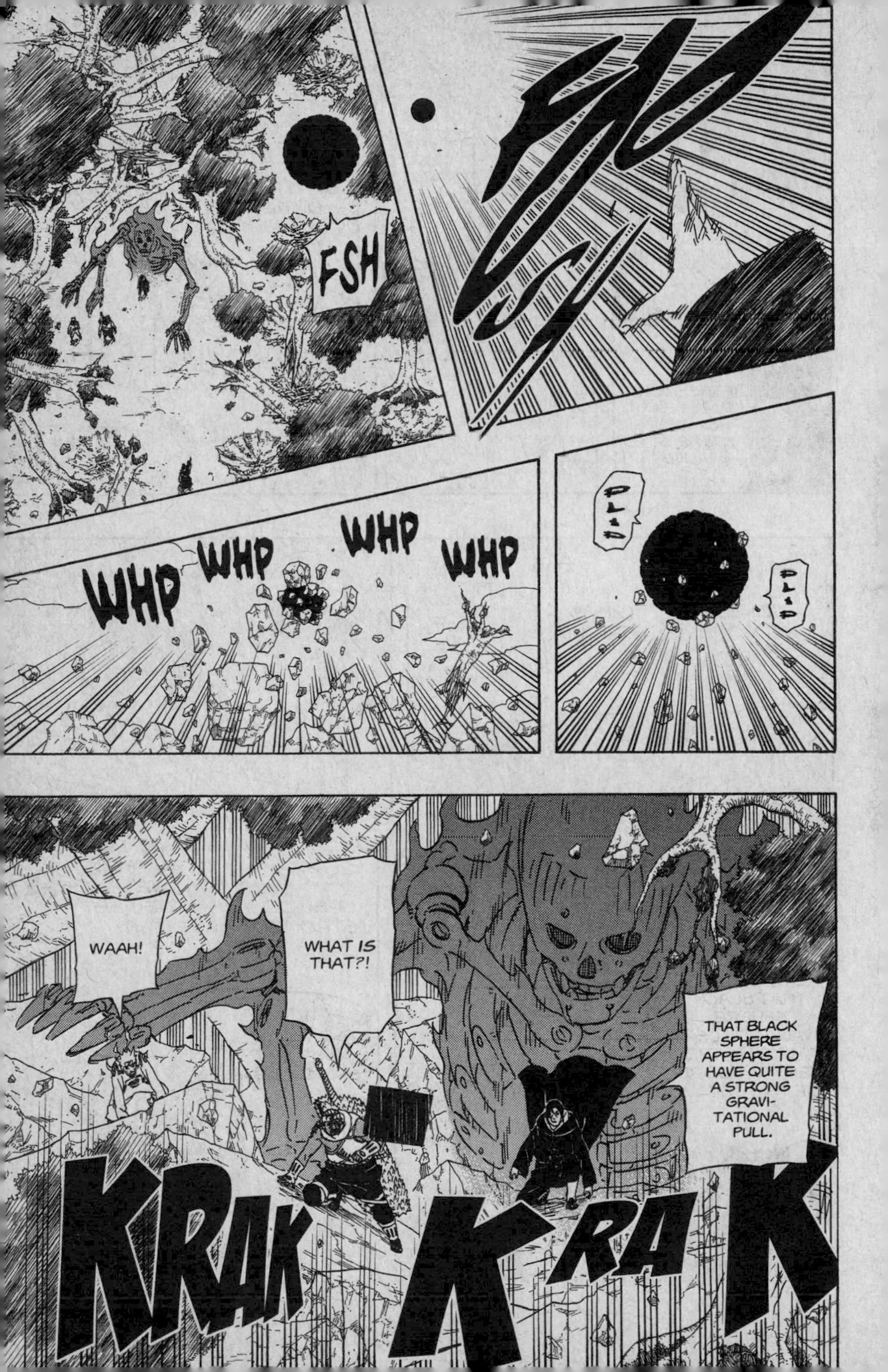
FSH
PLIP
PLIP
WHP
WHP
WHP
WHP
THAT BLACK SPHERE APPEARS TO HAVE QUITE A STRONG GRAVI-TATIONAL PULL.
WHAT IS THAT?!
WAAH!
KRAK
KRAK

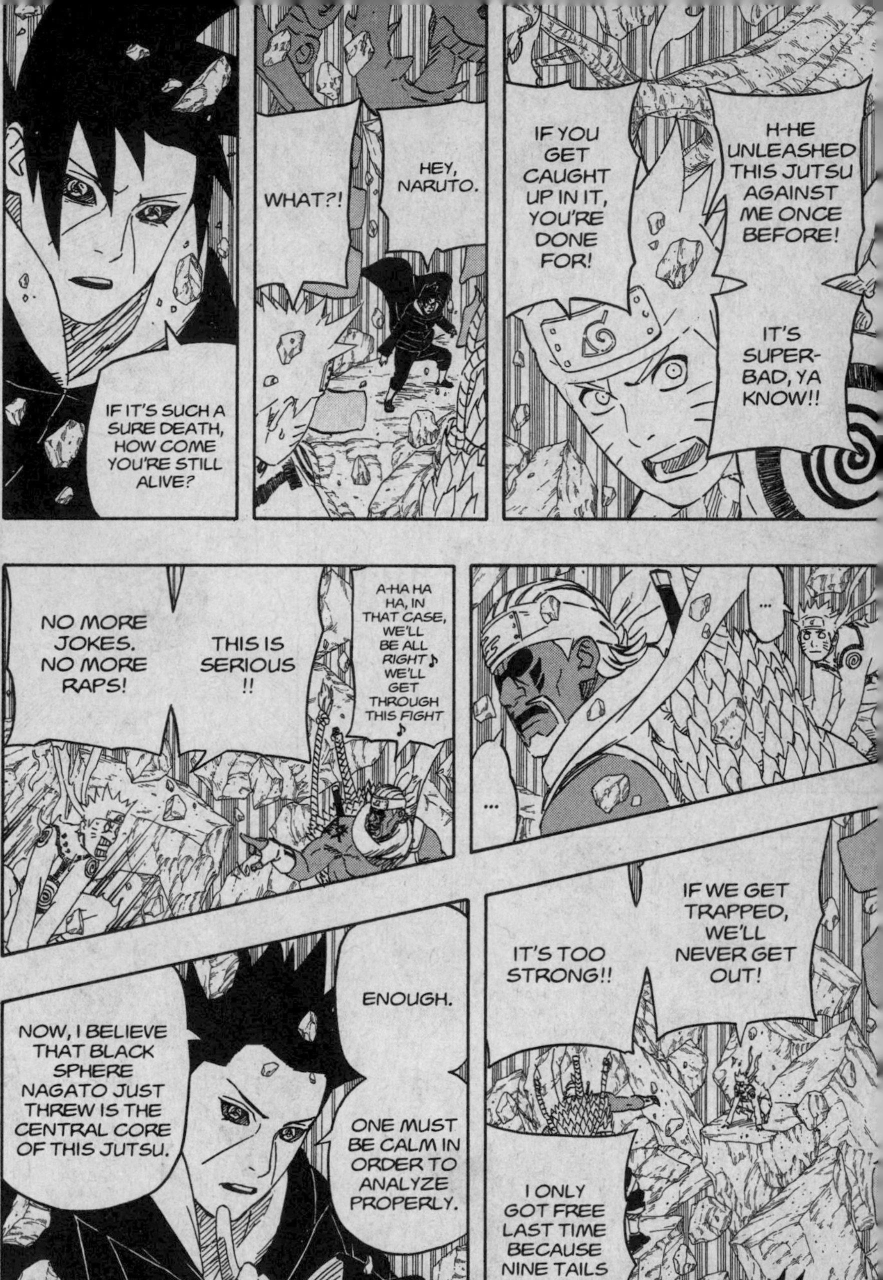
H-HE UNLEASHED THIS JUTSU AGAINST ME ONCE BEFORE!
IF YOU GET CAUGHT UP IN IT, YOU'RE DONE FOR!
IT'S SUPER-BAD, YA KNOW!!
HEY, NARUTO.
WHAT?!
IF IT'S SUCH A SURE DEATH, HOW COME YOU'RE STILL ALIVE?
...
...
A-HA HA HA, IN THAT CASE, WE'LL BE ALL RIGHT ♪ WE'LL GET THROUGH THIS FIGHT ♪
THIS IS SERIOUS!!
NO MORE JOKES. NO MORE RAPS!
IF WE GET TRAPPED, WE'LL NEVER GET OUT!
IT'S TOO STRONG!!
I ONLY GOT FREE LAST TIME BECAUSE NINE TAILS RAMPAGED!
ENOUGH.
ONE MUST BE CALM IN ORDER TO ANALYZE PROPERLY.
NOW, I BELIEVE THAT BLACK SPHERE NAGATO JUST THREW IS THE CENTRAL CORE OF THIS JUTSU.

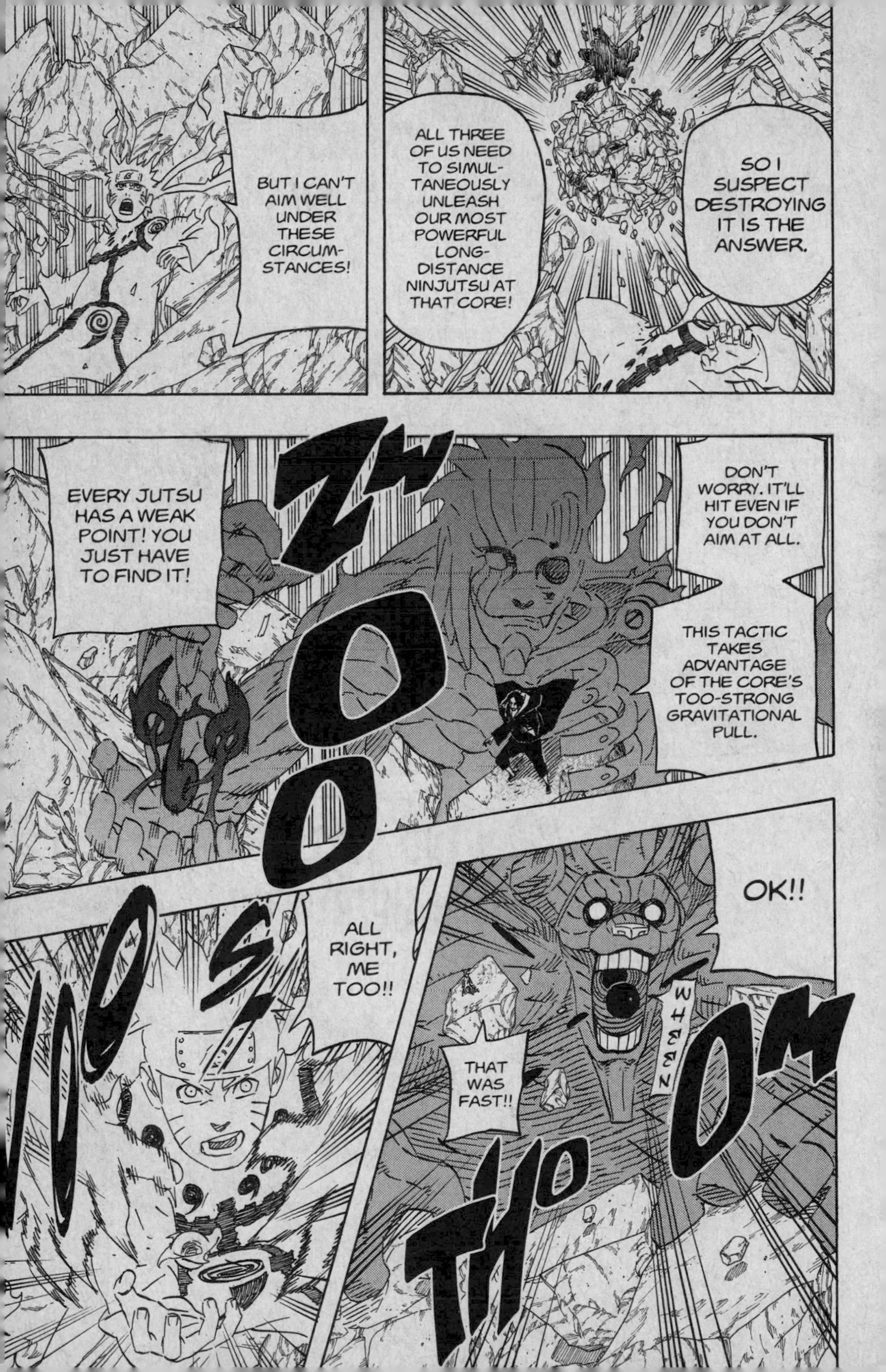
SO I SUSPECT DESTROYING IT IS THE ANSWER.
ALL THREE OF US NEED TO SIMULTANEOUSLY UNLEASH OUR MOST POWERFUL LONG-DISTANCE NINJUTSU AT THAT CORE!
BUT I CAN'T AIM WELL UNDER THESE CIRCUMSTANCES!
DON'T WORRY. IT'LL HIT EVEN IF YOU DON'T AIM AT ALL.
THIS TACTIC TAKES ADVANTAGE OF THE CORE'S TOO-STRONG GRAVITATIONAL PULL.
EVERY JUTSU HAS A WEAK POINT! YOU JUST HAVE TO FIND IT!
OK!!
THAT WAS FAST!!
THOOM
ALL RIGHT, ME TOO!!

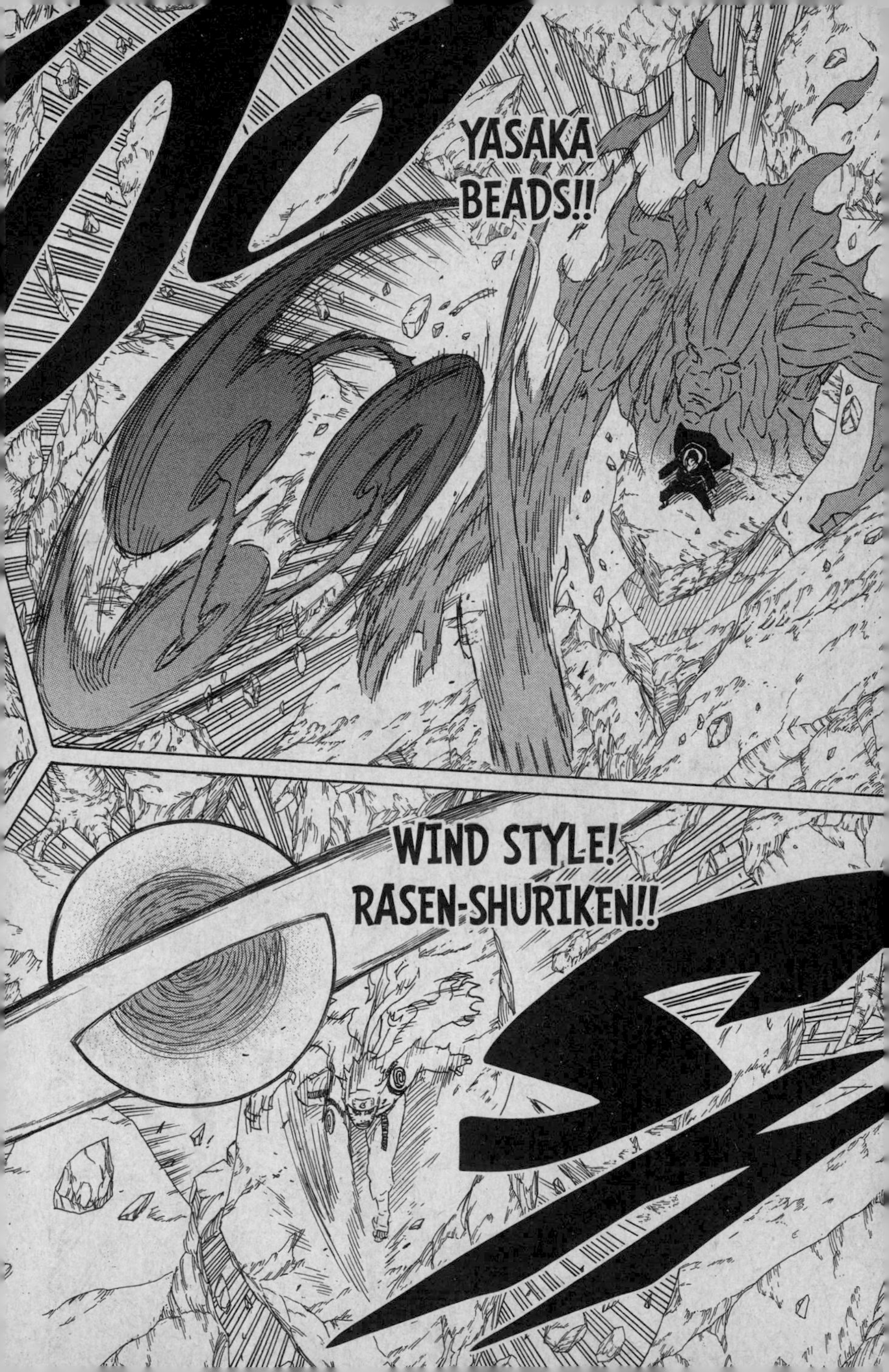
YASAKA BEADS!!
WIND STYLE! RASEN-SHURIKEN!!

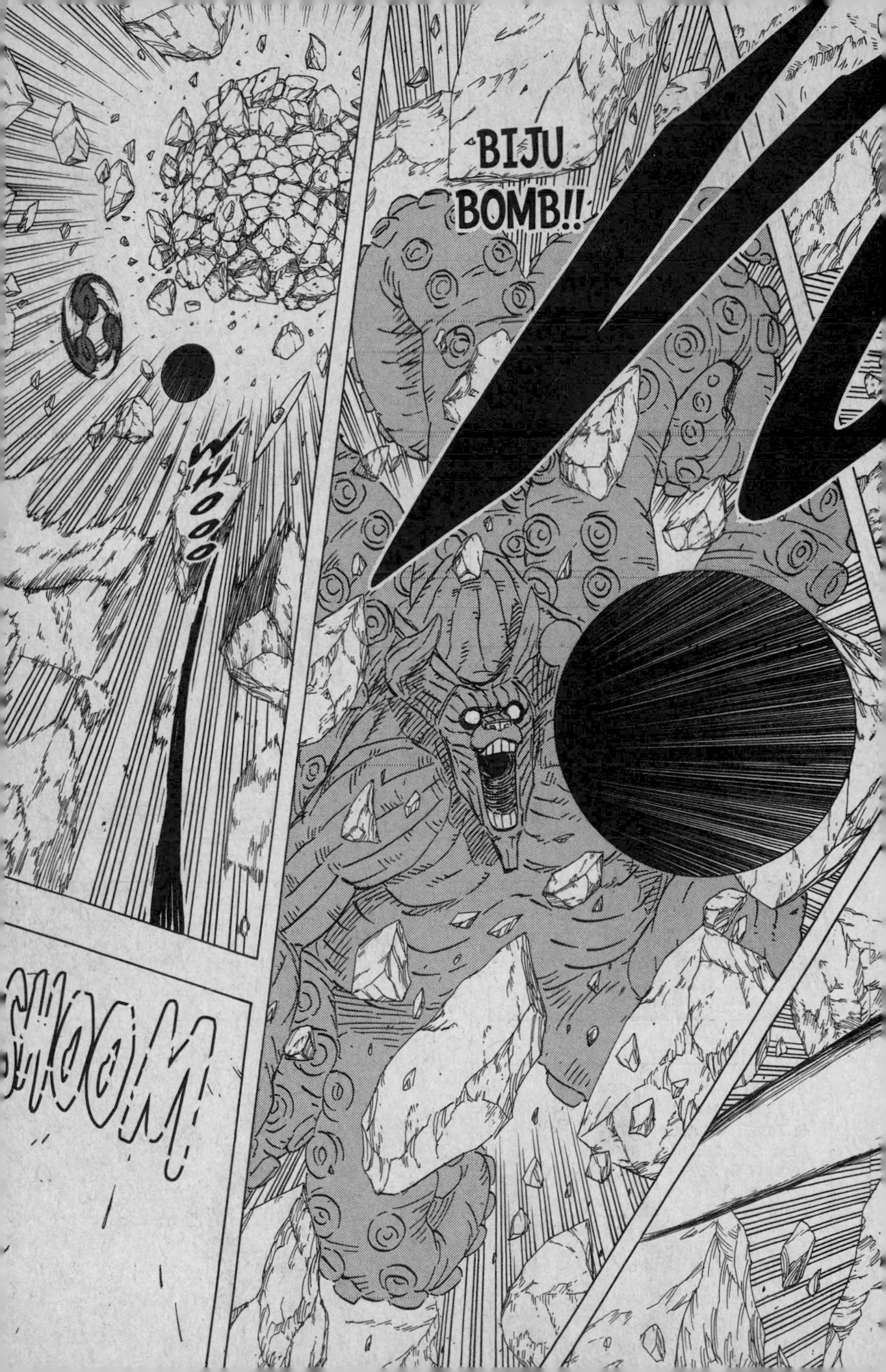
BIJU BOMB!!
WHOOOO
SHOOM

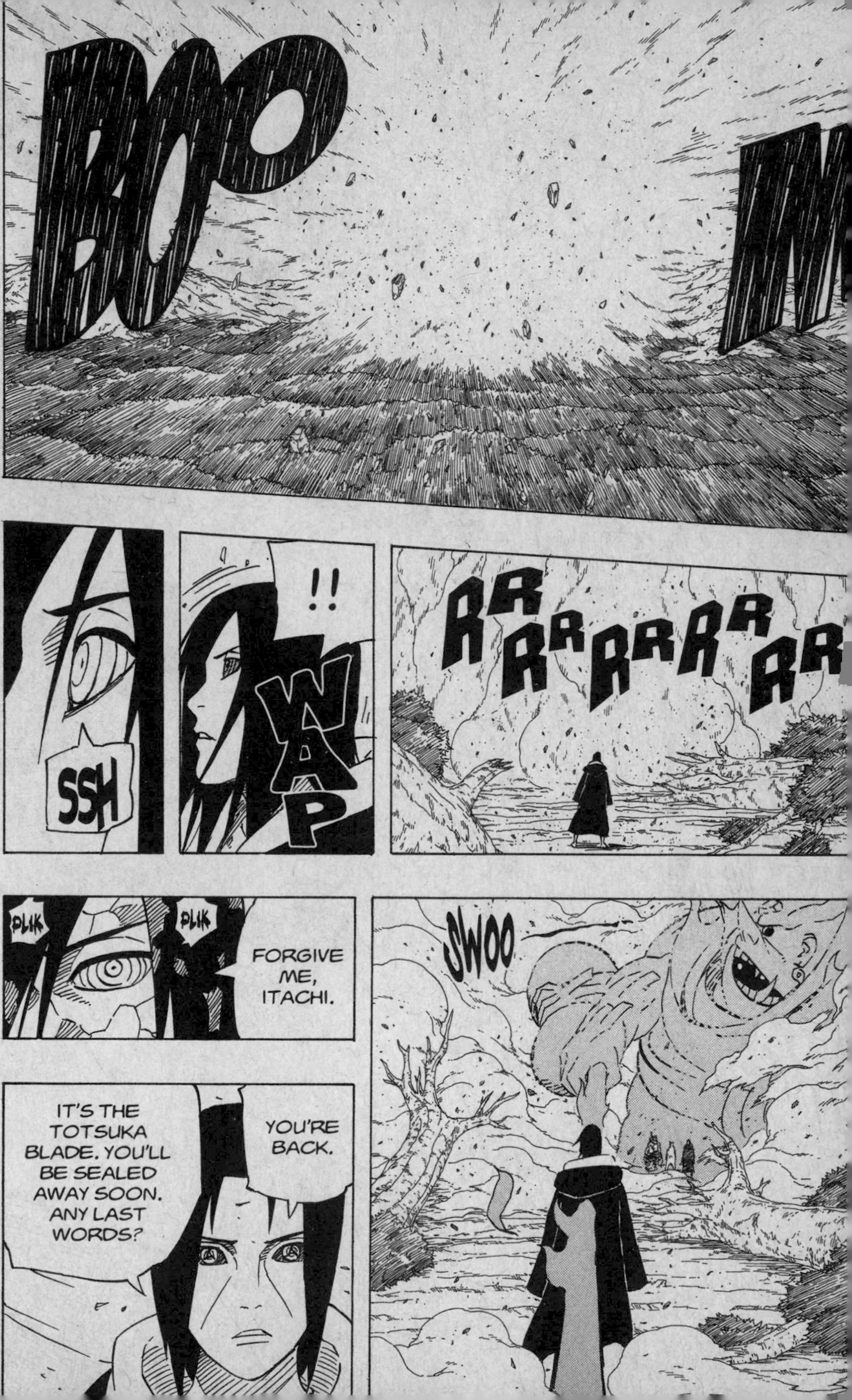
BOOM
RRRRRRRRRRR
!!
WAP
SSH
SWOO
PLIK
PLIK
FORGIVE ME, ITACHI.
YOU'RE BACK.
IT'S THE TOTSUKA BLADE. YOU'LL BE SEALED AWAY SOON. ANY LAST WORDS?

READ THIS WAY

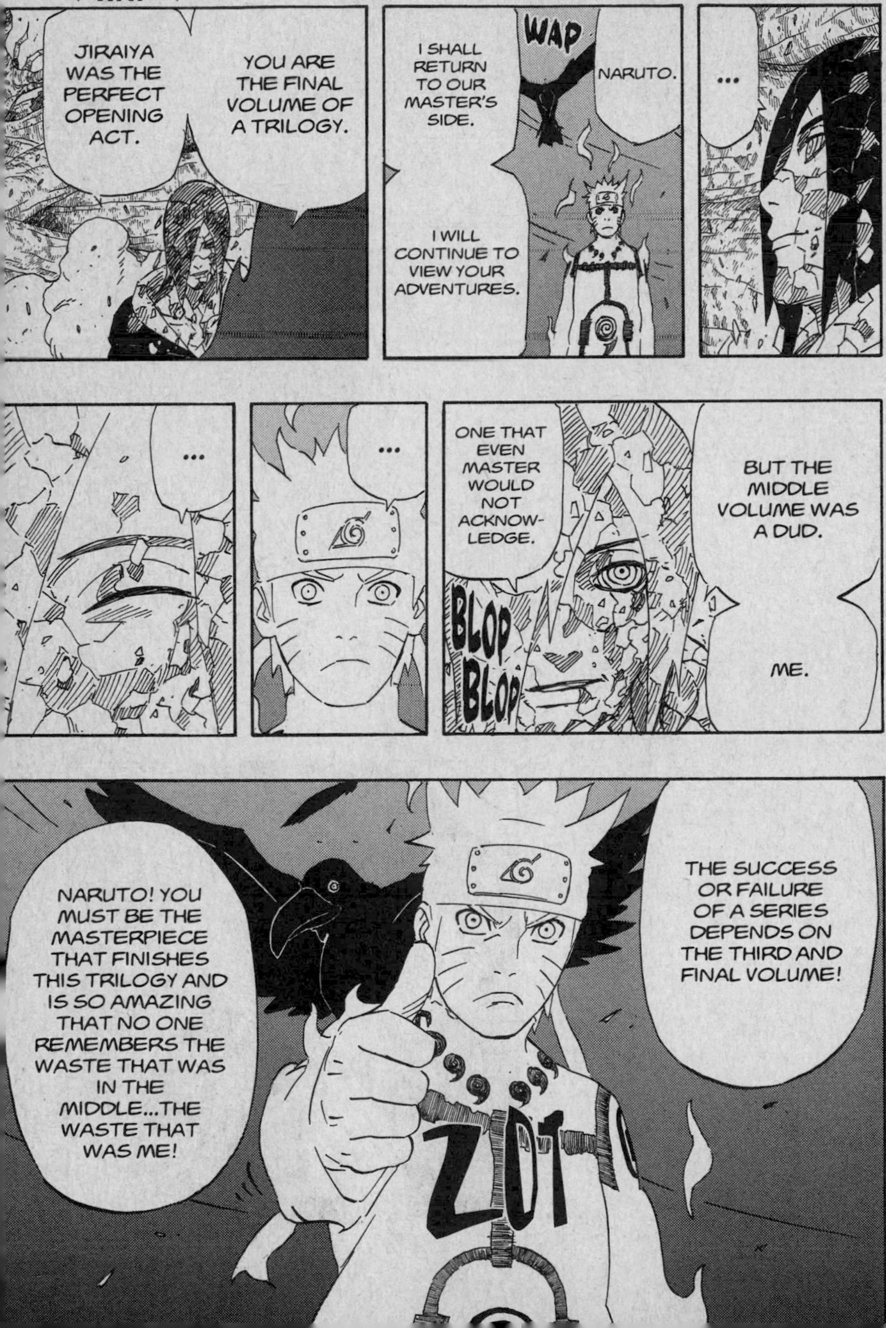
...
NARUTO.
I SHALL RETURN TO OUR MASTER'S SIDE.
WAP
I WILL CONTINUE TO VIEW YOUR ADVENTURES.
JIRAIYA WAS THE PERFECT OPENING ACT.
YOU ARE THE FINAL VOLUME OF A TRILOGY.
BUT THE MIDDLE VOLUME WAS A DUD.
ONE THAT EVEN MASTER WOULD NOT ACKNOWLEDGE.
BLOP BLOP
ME.
...
...
THE SUCCESS OR FAILURE OF A SERIES DEPENDS ON THE THIRD AND FINAL VOLUME!
NARUTO! YOU MUST BE THE MASTERPIECE THAT FINISHES THIS TRILOGY AND IS SO AMAZING THAT NO ONE REMEMBERS THE WASTE THAT WAS IN THE MIDDLE...THE WASTE THAT WAS ME!
ZOT

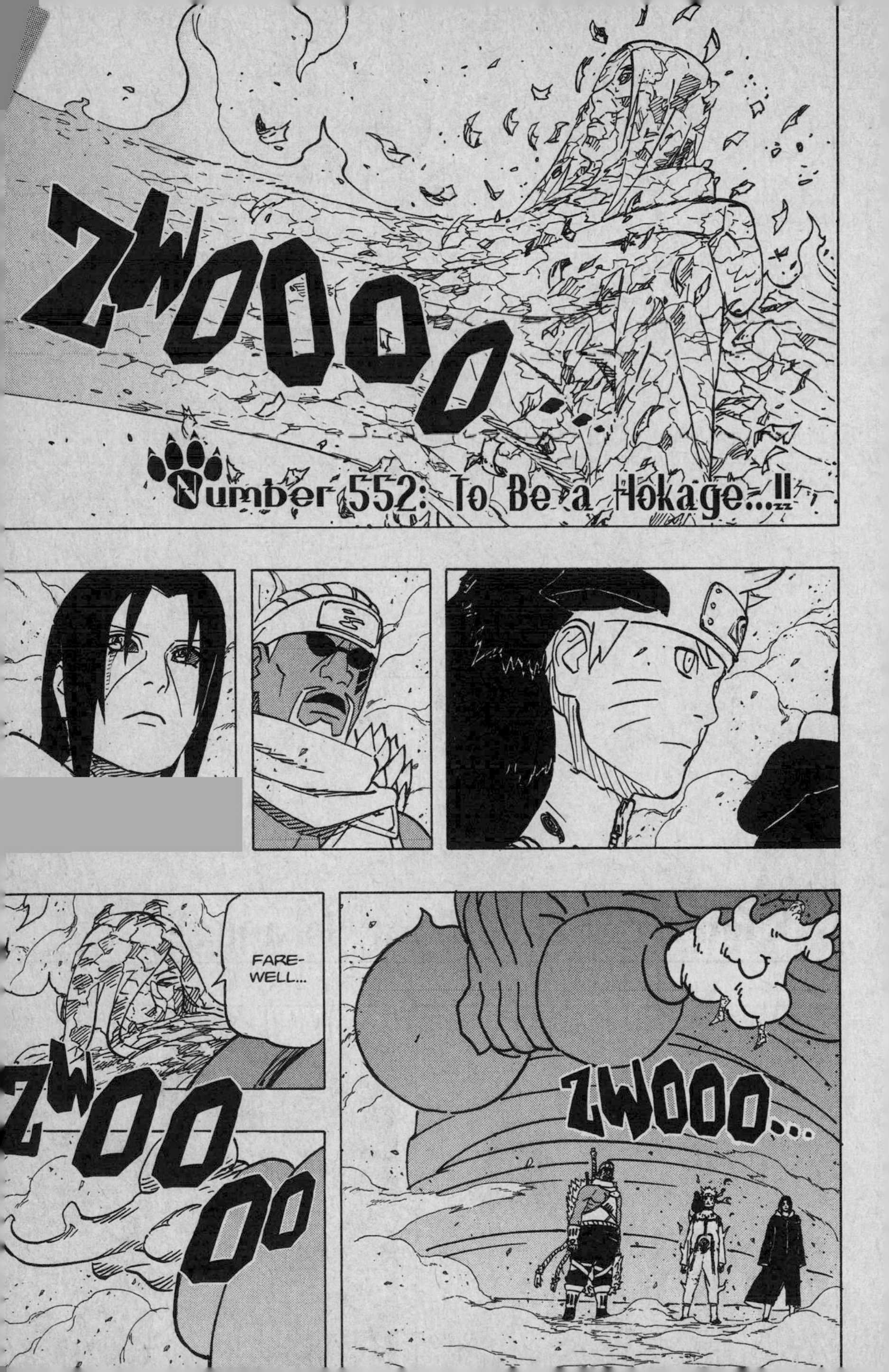
ZWOOOO...
Number 552: To Be a Hokage...!!
ZWOOO...
FARE-WELL...
ZWOOOOO

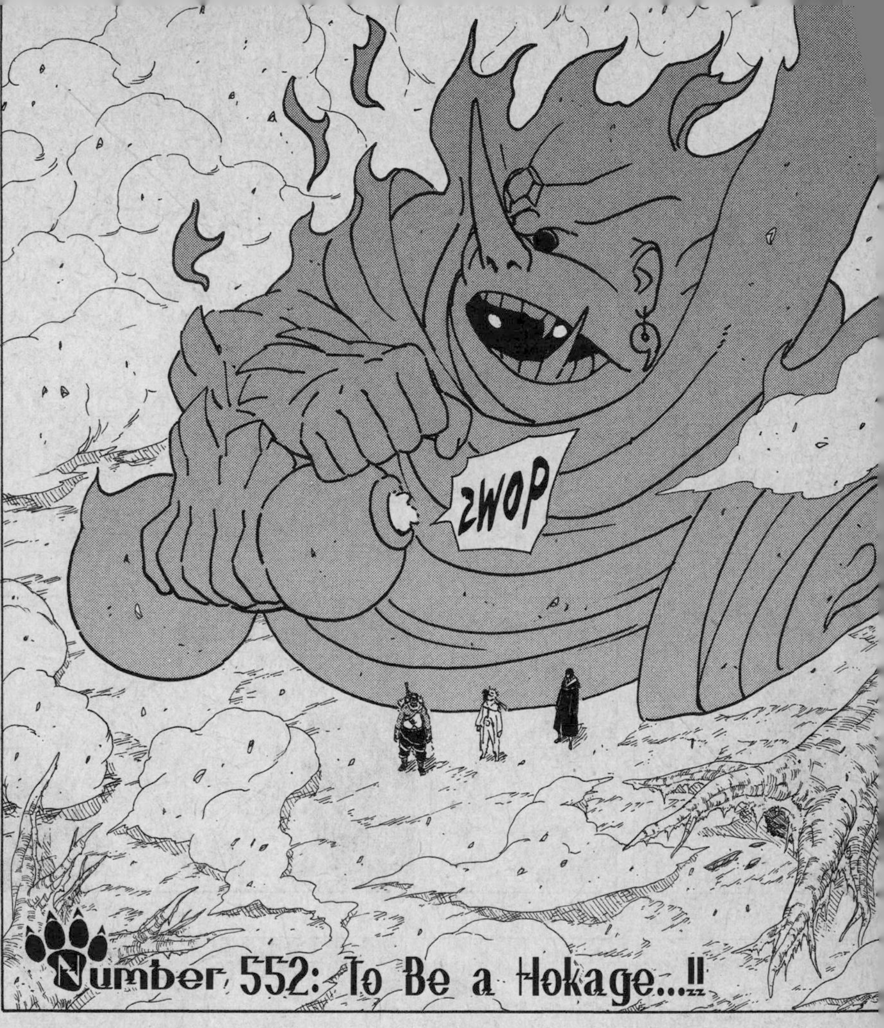
ZWOP

Number 552: To Be a Hokage...!!

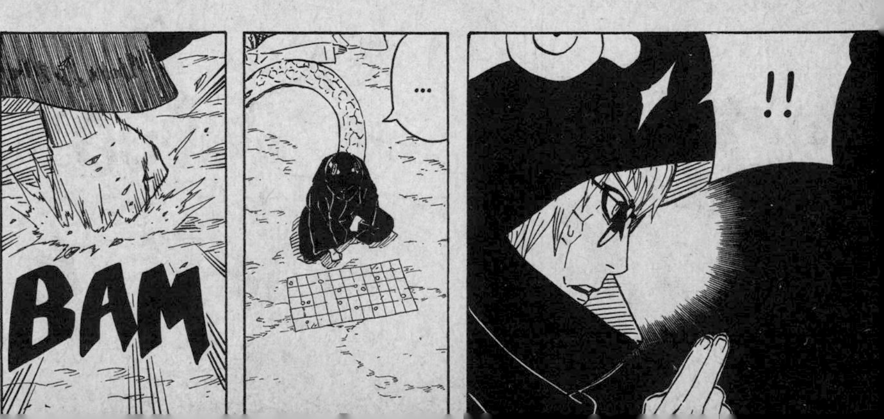
!!
...
BAM

READ THIS WAY

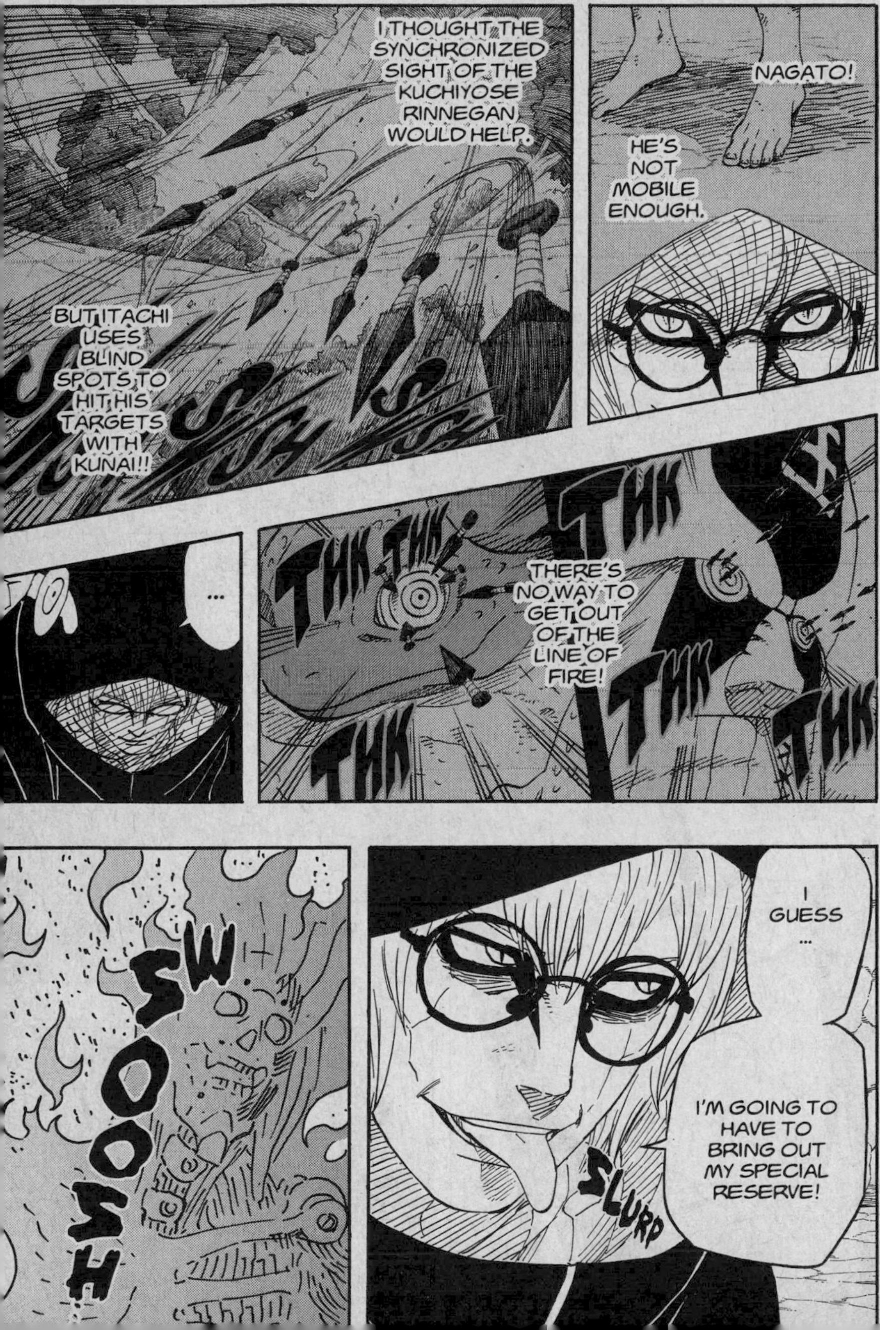
NAGATO!
HE'S NOT MOBILE ENOUGH.
I THOUGHT THE SYNCHRONIZED SIGHT OF THE KUCHIYOSE RINNEGAN WOULD HELP.
BUT ITACHI USES BLIND SPOTS TO HIT HIS TARGETS WITH KUNAI!!
THK
THK
THK
THK
THK
THK
THERE'S NO WAY TO GET OUT OF THE LINE OF FIRE!
...
I GUESS ...
I'M GOING TO HAVE TO BRING OUT MY SPECIAL RESERVE!
SLURP
SWOOOSH

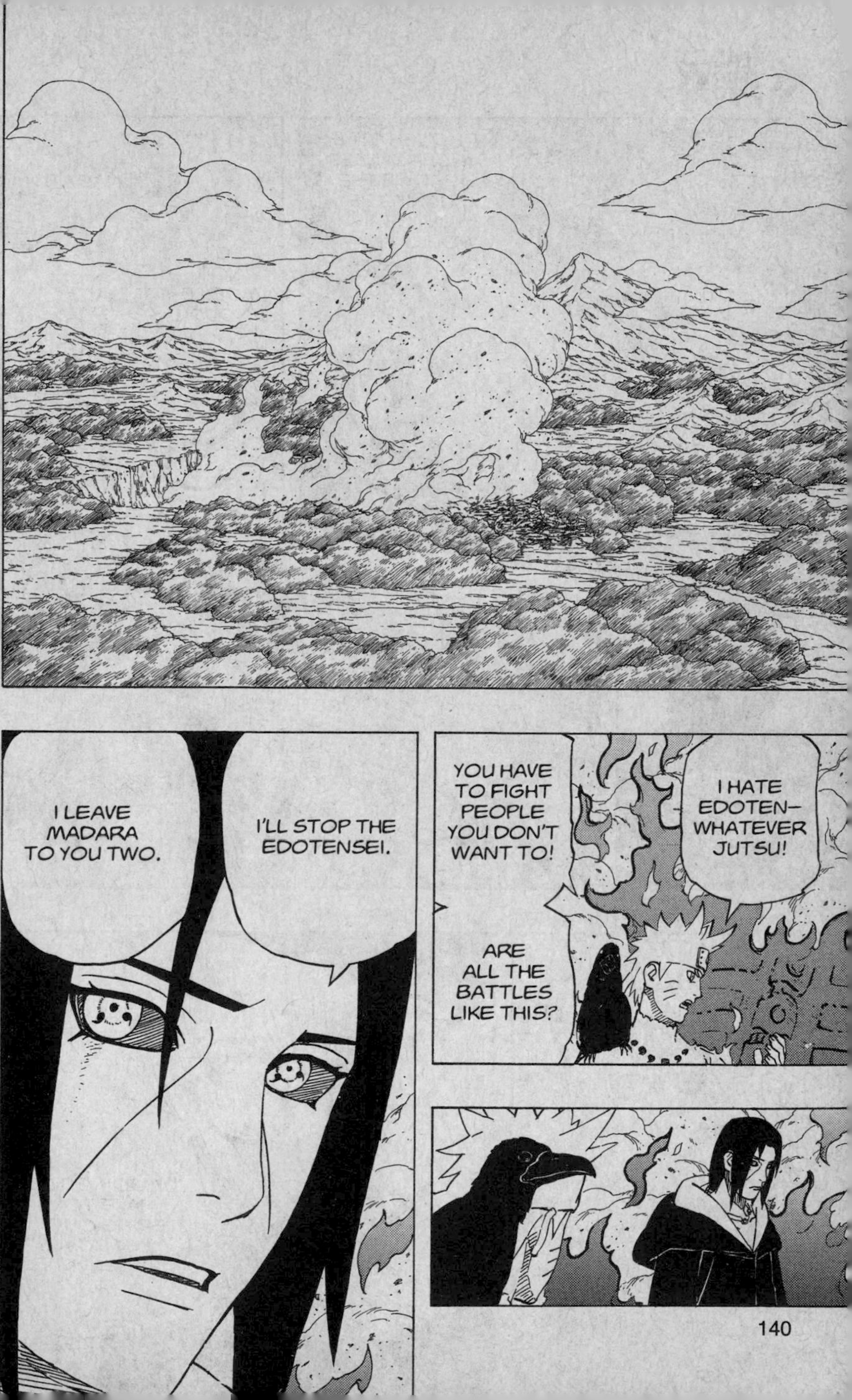
I HATE EDOTEN-WHATEVER JUTSU!
YOU HAVE TO FIGHT PEOPLE YOU DON'T WANT TO!
ARE ALL THE BATTLES LIKE THIS?
I'LL STOP THE EDOTENSEI.
I LEAVE MADARA TO YOU TWO.

READ THIS WAY

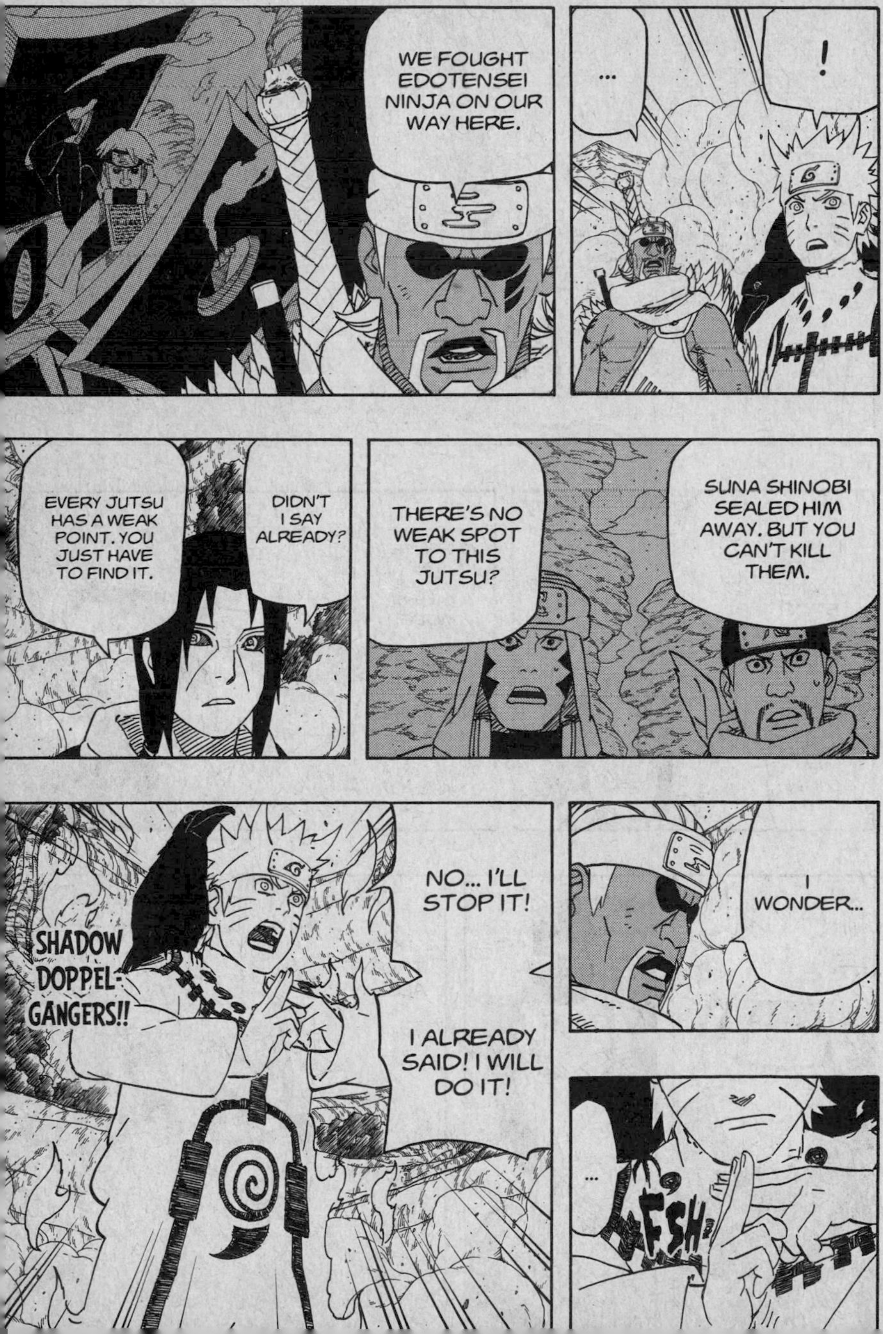
!
...
WE FOUGHT EDOTENSEI NINJA ON OUR WAY HERE.
SUNA SHINOBI SEALED HIM AWAY. BUT YOU CAN'T KILL THEM.
THERE'S NO WEAK SPOT TO THIS JUTSU?
DIDN'T I SAY ALREADY?
EVERY JUTSU HAS A WEAK POINT. YOU JUST HAVE TO FIND IT.
I WONDER...
...
FSH
NO... I'LL STOP IT!
I ALREADY SAID! I WILL DO IT!
SHADOW DOPPELGANGERS!!

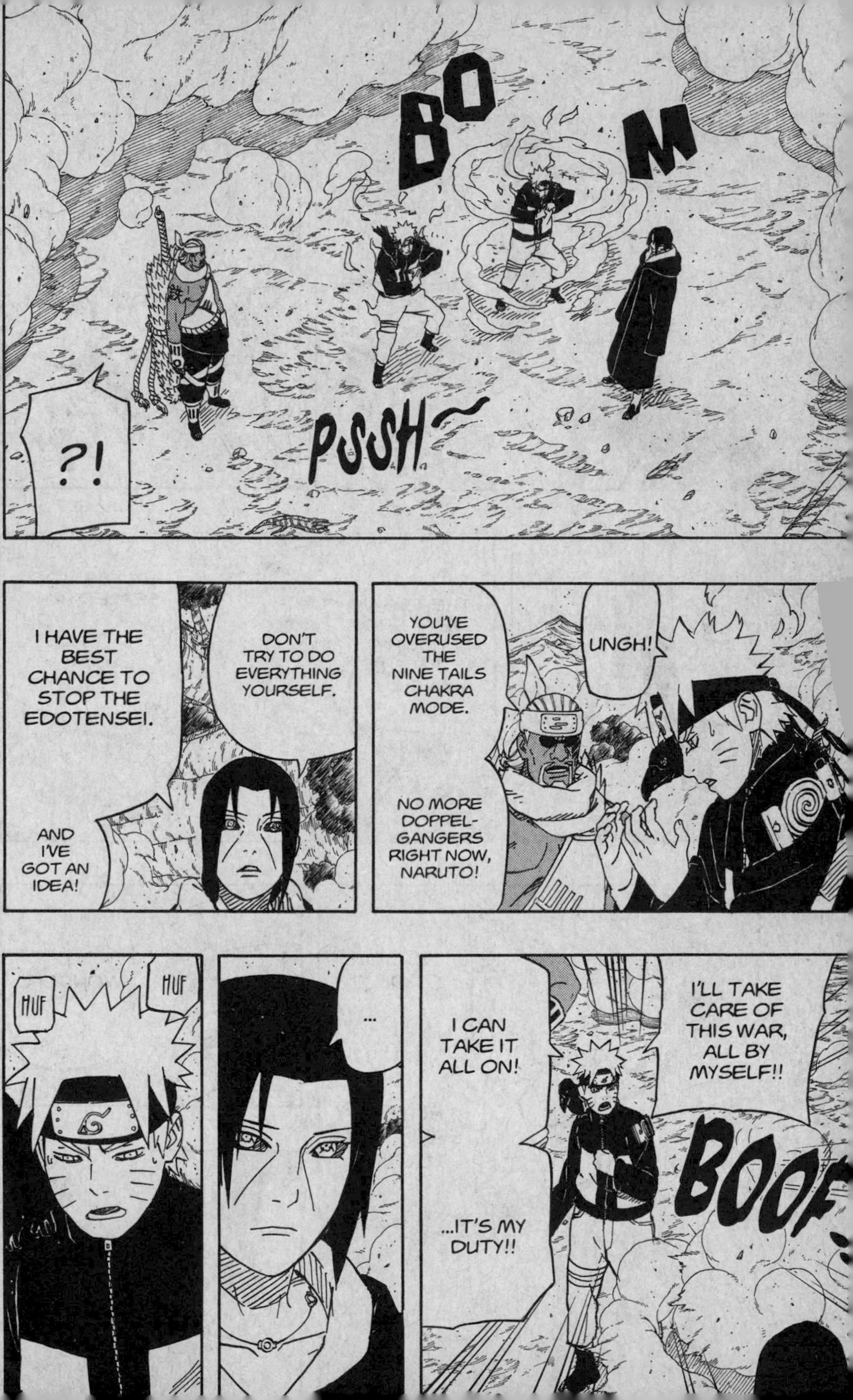
BOOM
PSSH~
?!
UNGH!
YOU'VE OVERUSED THE NINE TAILS CHAKRA MODE.
NO MORE DOPPEL-GANGERS RIGHT NOW, NARUTO!
DON'T TRY TO DO EVERYTHING YOURSELF.
I HAVE THE BEST CHANCE TO STOP THE EDOTENSEI.
AND I'VE GOT AN IDEA!
BOOF
I'LL TAKE CARE OF THIS WAR, ALL BY MYSELF!!
I CAN TAKE IT ALL ON!
...IT'S MY DUTY!!
...
HUF
HUF

READ THIS WAY

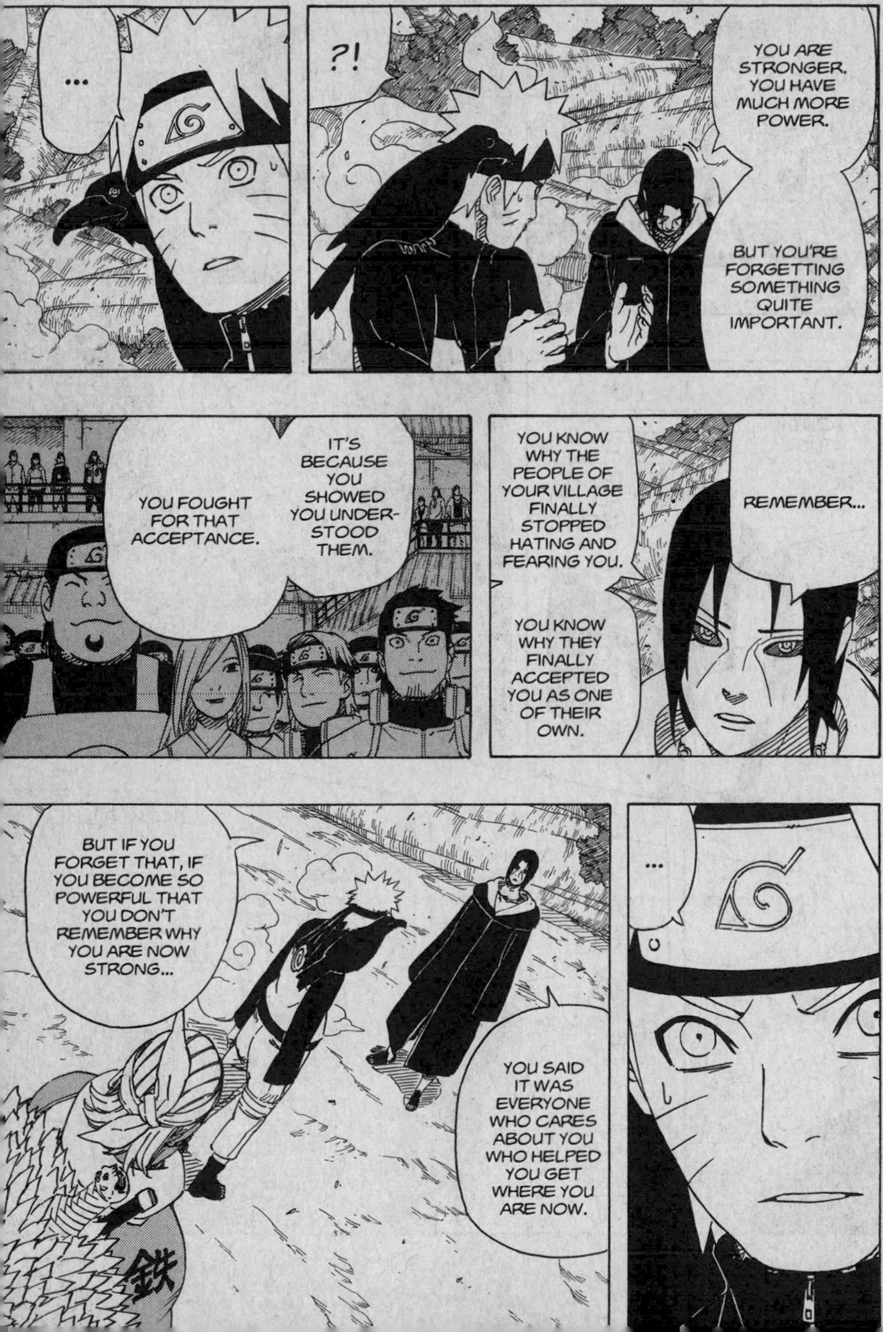
YOU ARE STRONGER. YOU HAVE MUCH MORE POWER.
?!
BUT YOU'RE FORGETTING SOMETHING QUITE IMPORTANT.
...
REMEMBER...
YOU KNOW WHY THE PEOPLE OF YOUR VILLAGE FINALLY STOPPED HATING AND FEARING YOU.
YOU KNOW WHY THEY FINALLY ACCEPTED YOU AS ONE OF THEIR OWN.
IT'S BECAUSE YOU SHOWED YOU UNDER-STOOD THEM.
YOU FOUGHT FOR THAT ACCEPTANCE.
...
YOU SAID IT WAS EVERYONE WHO CARES ABOUT YOU WHO HELPED YOU GET WHERE YOU ARE NOW.
BUT IF YOU FORGET THAT, IF YOU BECOME SO POWERFUL THAT YOU DON'T REMEMBER WHY YOU ARE NOW STRONG...

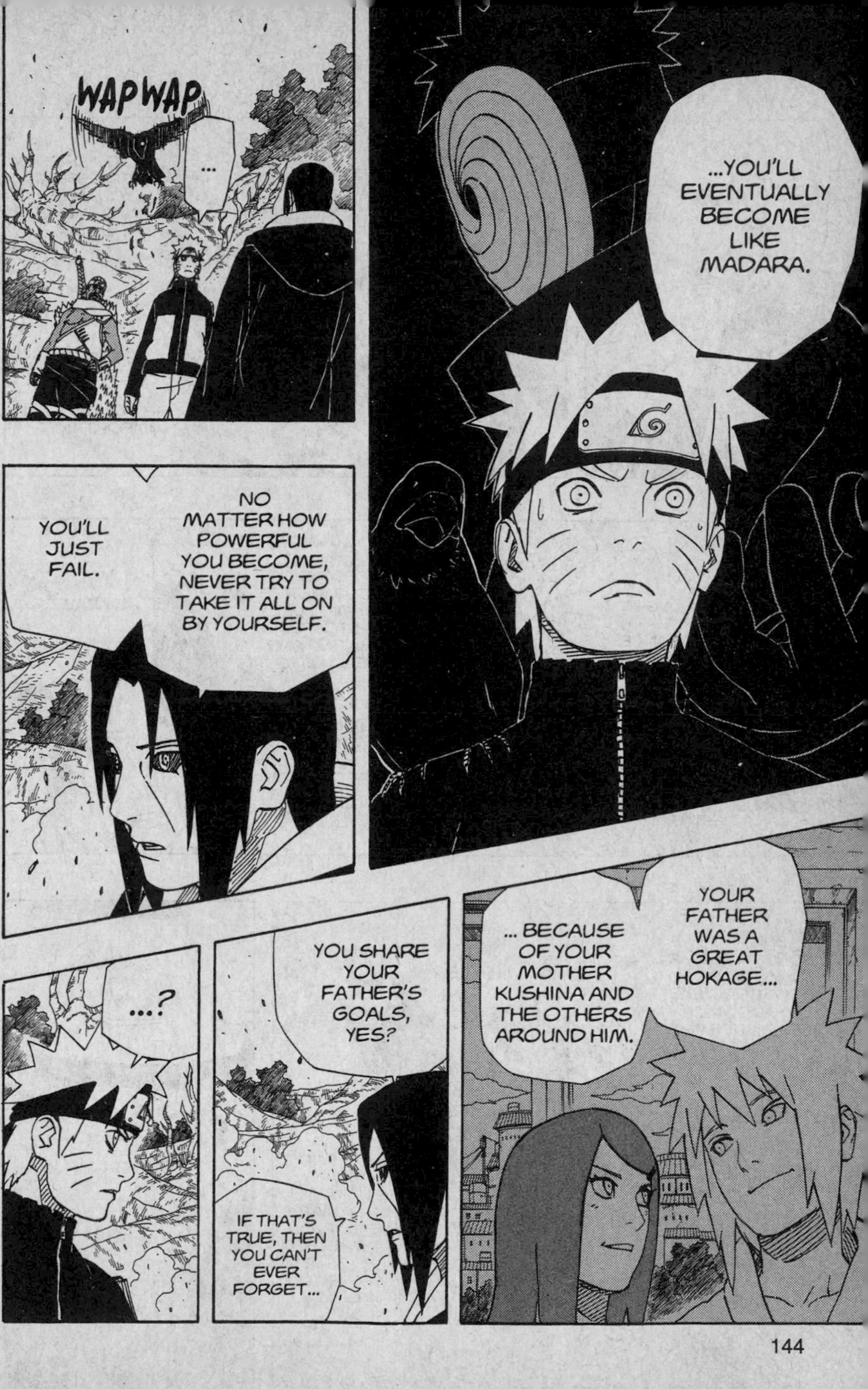
WAP WAP
...
NO MATTER HOW POWERFUL YOU BECOME, NEVER TRY TO TAKE IT ALL ON BY YOURSELF.
YOU'LL JUST FAIL.
...YOU'LL EVENTUALLY BECOME LIKE MADARA.
YOUR FATHER WAS A GREAT HOKAGE...
... BECAUSE OF YOUR MOTHER KUSHINA AND THE OTHERS AROUND HIM.
YOU SHARE YOUR FATHER'S GOALS, YES?
IF THAT'S TRUE, THEN YOU CAN'T EVER FORGET...
...?

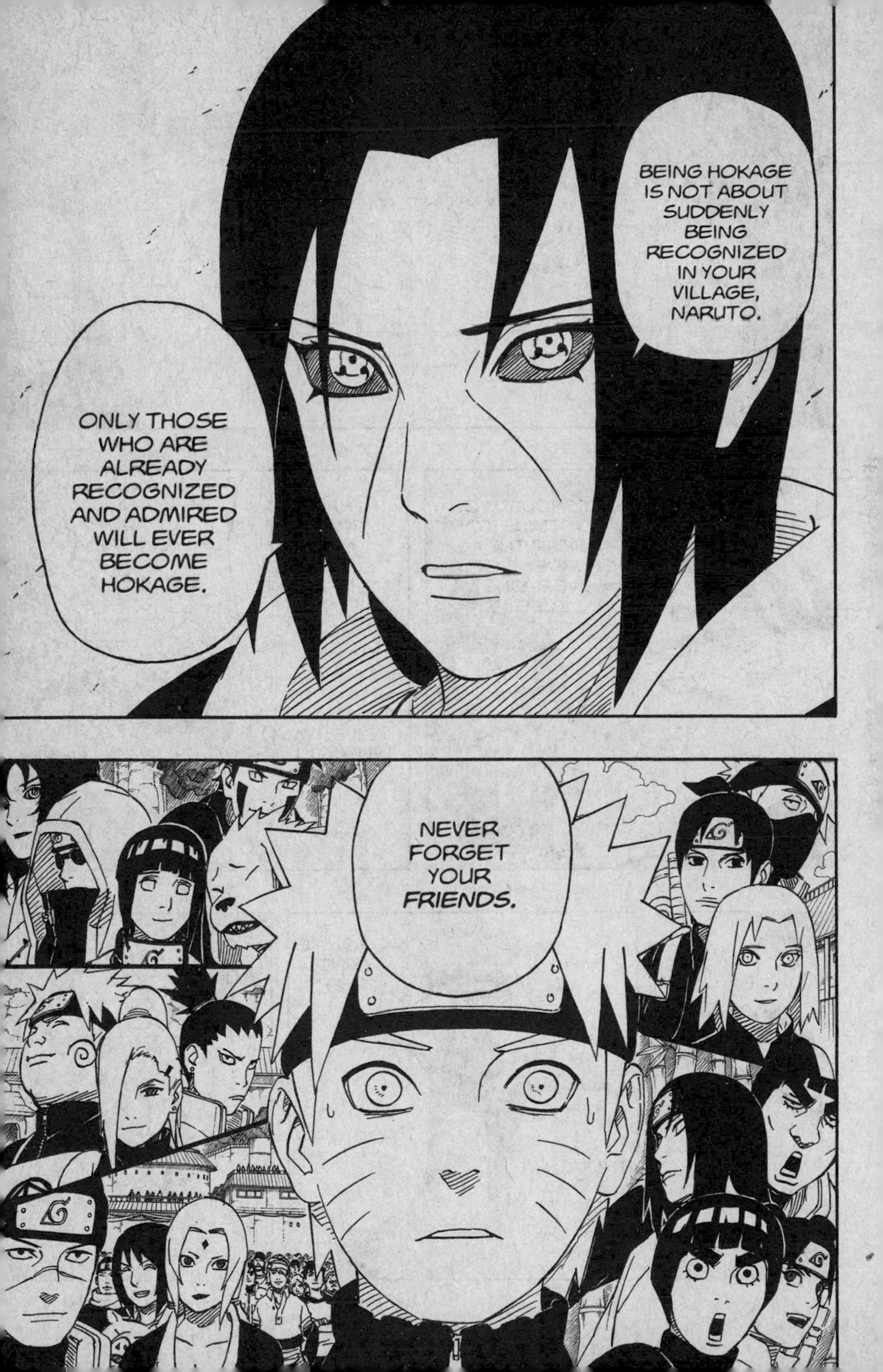
BEING HOKAGE IS NOT ABOUT SUDDENLY BEING RECOGNIZED IN YOUR VILLAGE, NARUTO.
ONLY THOSE WHO ARE ALREADY RECOGNIZED AND ADMIRED WILL EVER BECOME HOKAGE.
NEVER FORGET YOUR FRIENDS.

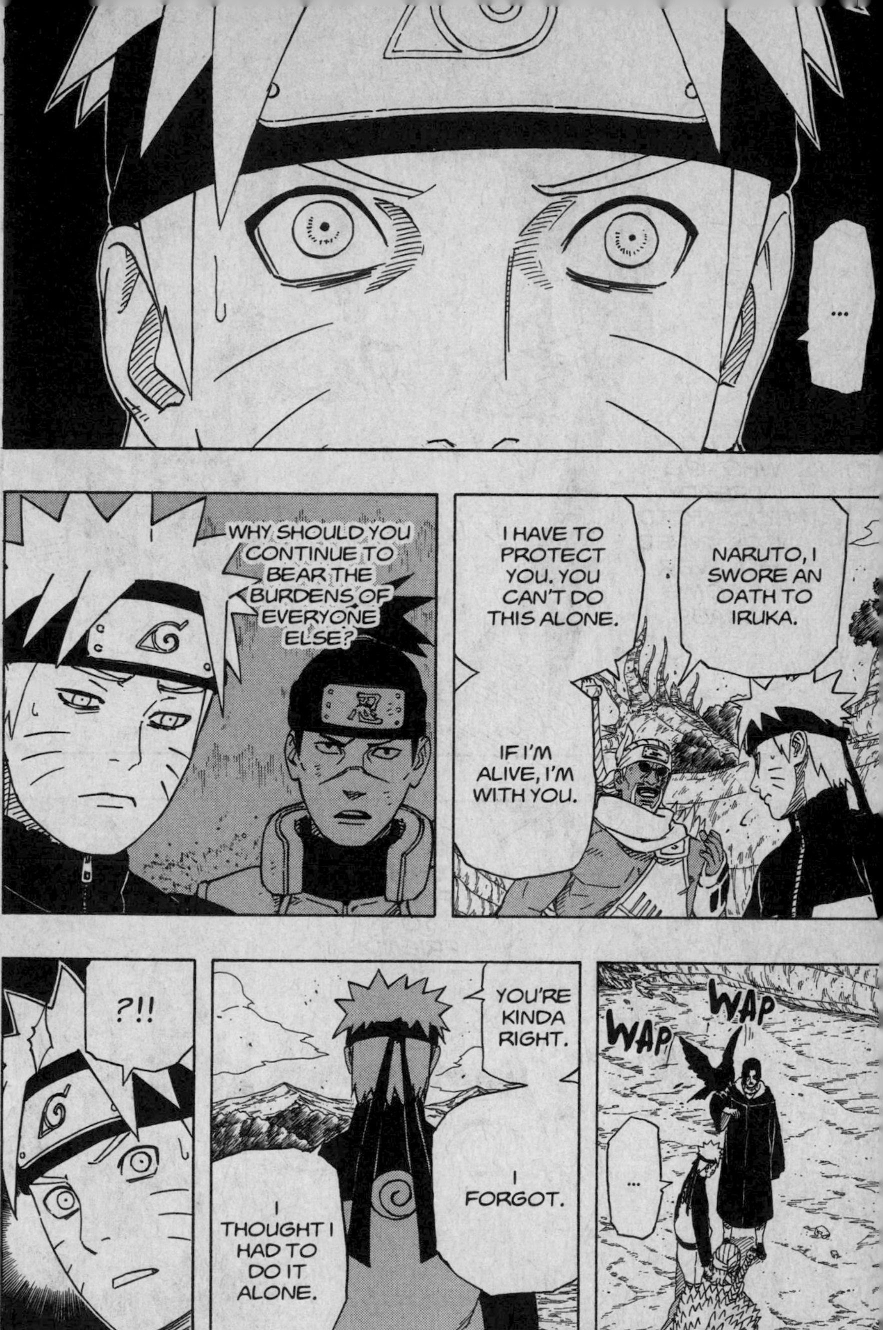
...
NARUTO, I SWORE AN OATH TO IRUKA.
I HAVE TO PROTECT YOU. YOU CAN'T DO THIS ALONE.
IF I'M ALIVE, I'M WITH YOU.
WHY SHOULD YOU CONTINUE TO BEAR THE BURDENS OF EVERYONE ELSE?
WAP
WAP
...
YOU'RE KINDA RIGHT.
I FORGOT.
I THOUGHT I HAD TO DO IT ALONE.
?!!

READ THIS WAY

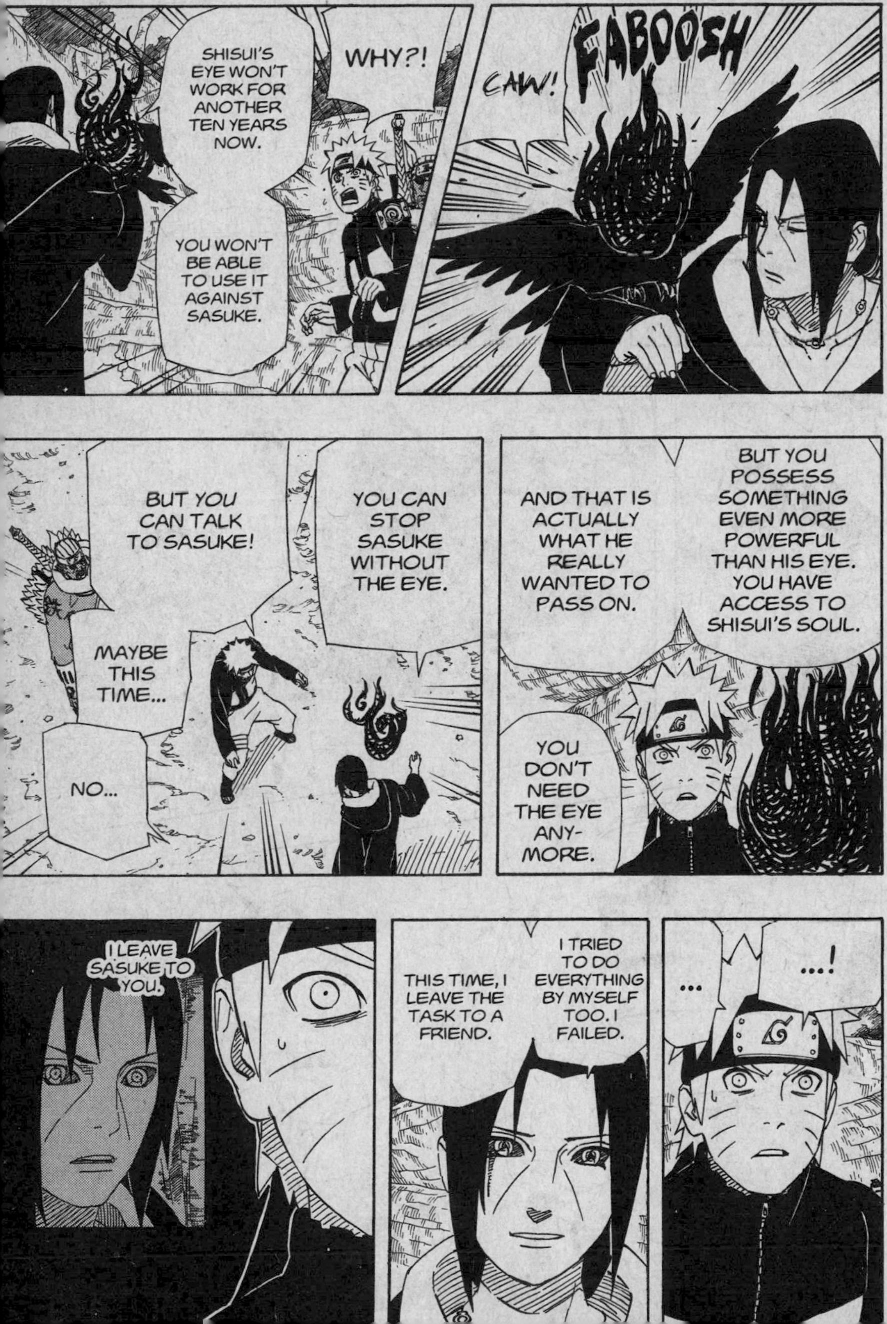
FABOOSH
CAW!
WHY?!
SHISUI'S EYE WON'T WORK FOR ANOTHER TEN YEARS NOW.
YOU WON'T BE ABLE TO USE IT AGAINST SASUKE.
BUT YOU POSSESS SOMETHING EVEN MORE POWERFUL THAN HIS EYE. YOU HAVE ACCESS TO SHISUI'S SOUL.
AND THAT IS ACTUALLY WHAT HE REALLY WANTED TO PASS ON.
YOU DON'T NEED THE EYE ANY-MORE.
YOU CAN STOP SASUKE WITHOUT THE EYE.
BUT YOU CAN TALK TO SASUKE!
MAYBE THIS TIME...
NO...
...!
...
I TRIED TO DO EVERYTHING BY MYSELF TOO. I FAILED.
THIS TIME, I LEAVE THE TASK TO A FRIEND.
I LEAVE SASUKE TO YOU.

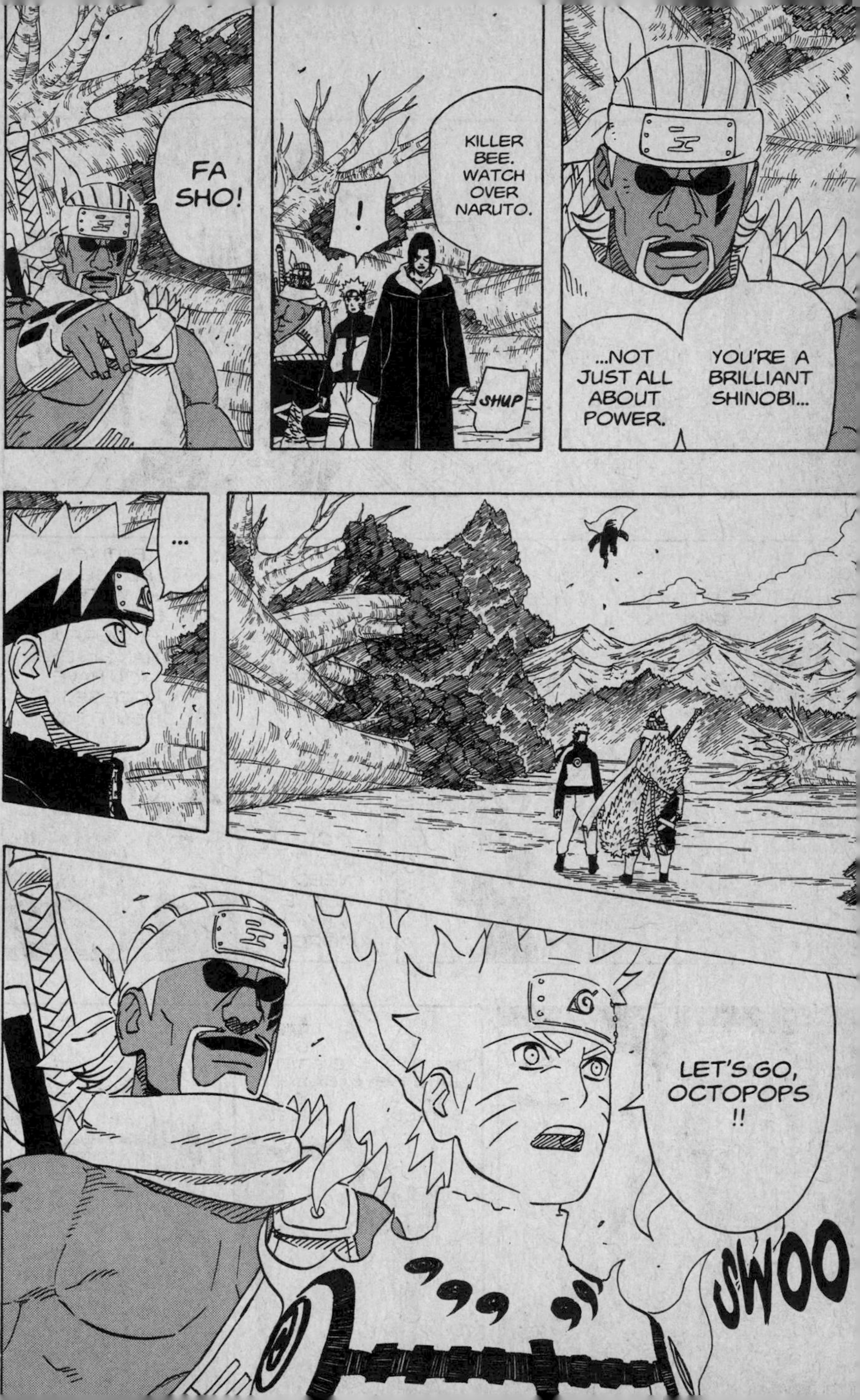
YOU'RE A BRILLIANT SHINOBI...
...NOT JUST ALL ABOUT POWER.
KILLER BEE. WATCH OVER NARUTO.
!
SHUP
FA SHO!
...
LET'S GO, OCTOPOPS !!
SWOO

READ THIS WAY

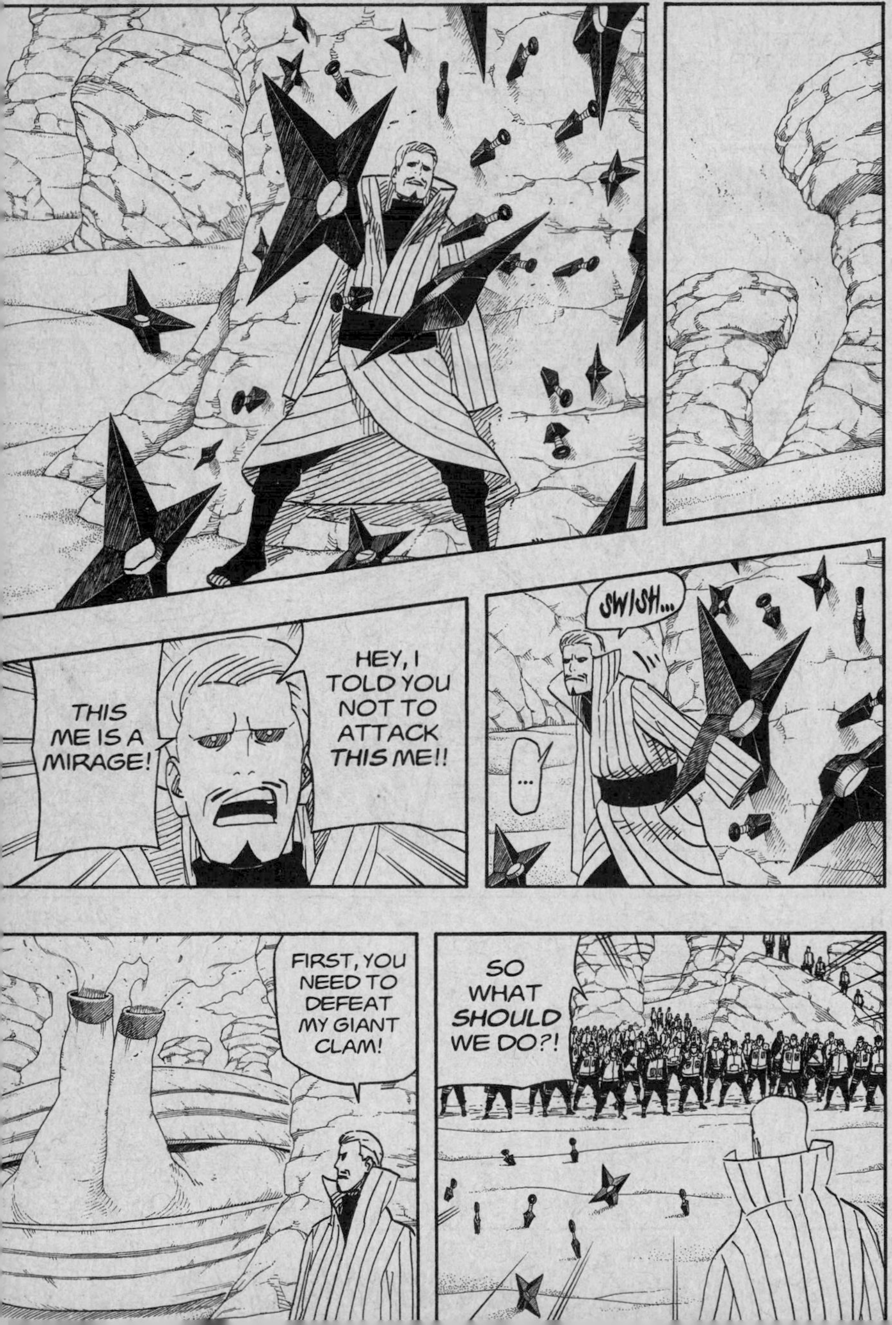
SWISH...
...
HEY, I TOLD YOU NOT TO ATTACK THIS ME!!
THIS ME IS A MIRAGE!
SO WHAT SHOULD WE DO?!
FIRST, YOU NEED TO DEFEAT MY GIANT CLAM!

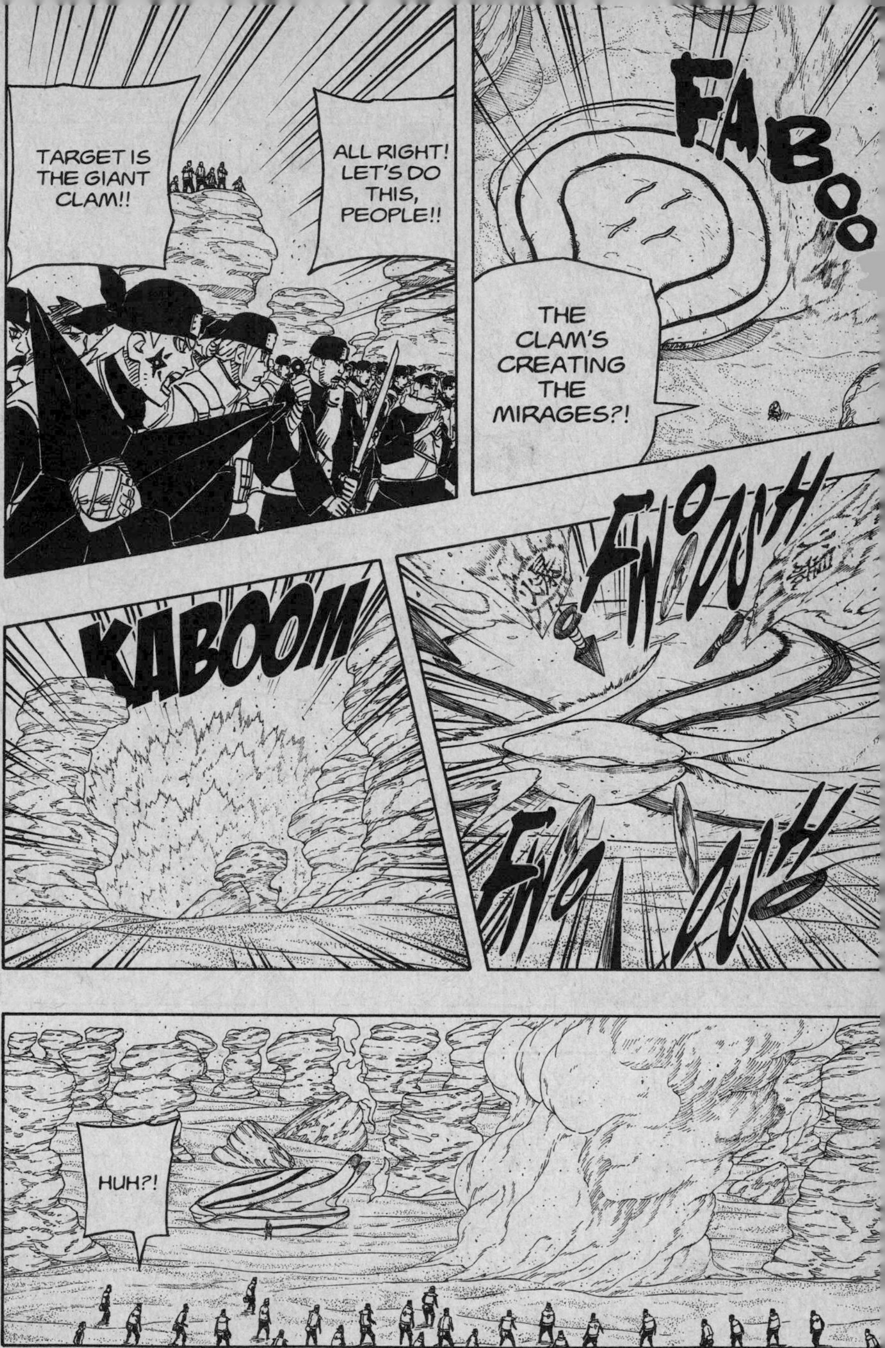
FABOO
THE CLAM'S CREATING THE MIRAGES?!
ALL RIGHT! LET'S DO THIS, PEOPLE!!
TARGET IS THE GIANT CLAM!!
FWOOSH
FWOOSH
KABOOM
HUH?!

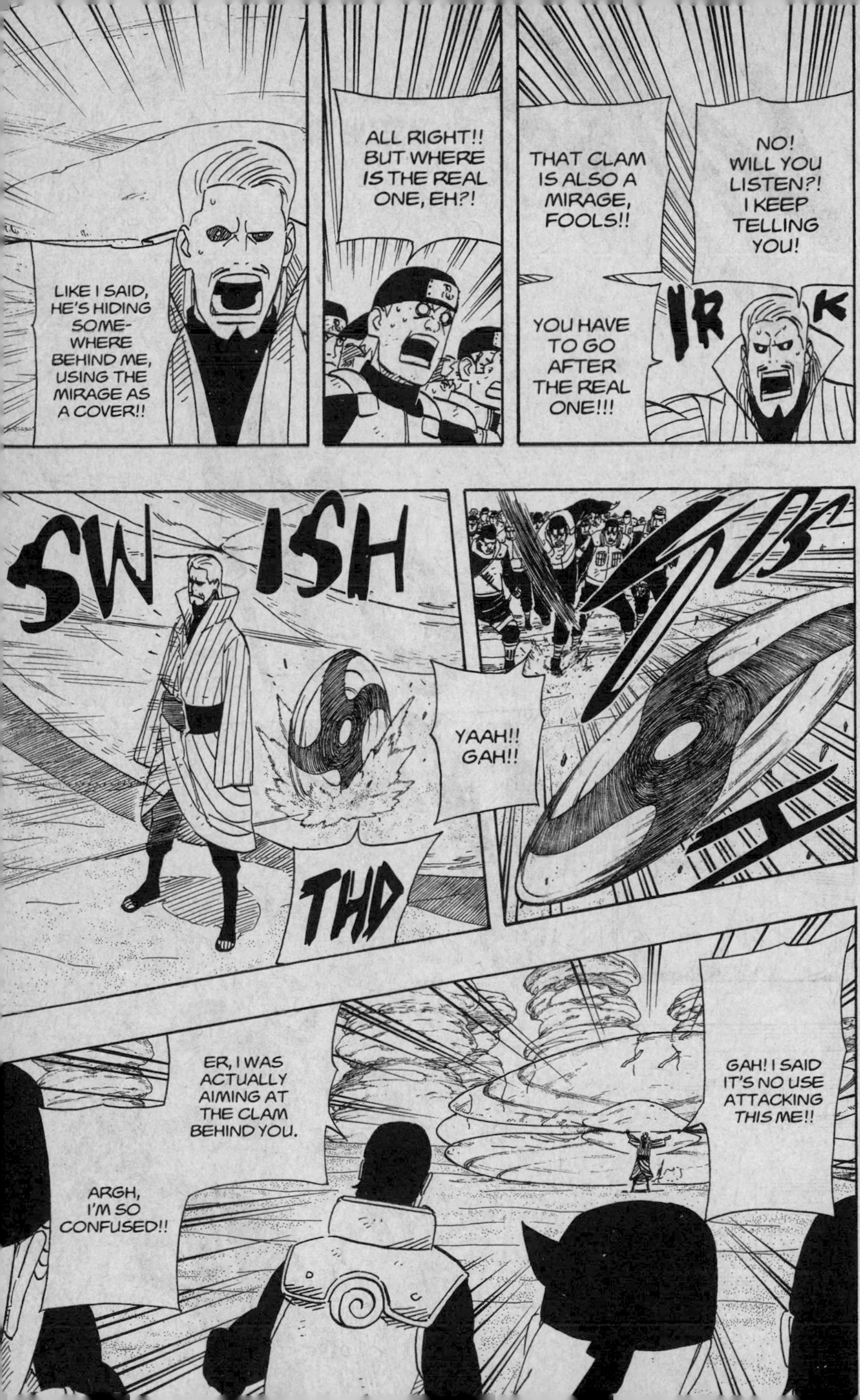
NO! WILL YOU LISTEN?! I KEEP TELLING YOU!
THAT CLAM IS ALSO A MIRAGE, FOOLS!!
IRK
YOU HAVE TO GO AFTER THE REAL ONE!!!
ALL RIGHT!! BUT WHERE IS THE REAL ONE, EH?!
LIKE I SAID, HE'S HIDING SOME-WHERE BEHIND ME, USING THE MIRAGE AS A COVER!!
YAAH!! GAH!!
SWISH
THD
GAH! I SAID IT'S NO USE ATTACKING THIS ME!!
ER, I WAS ACTUALLY AIMING AT THE CLAM BEHIND YOU.
ARGH, I'M SO CONFUSED!!

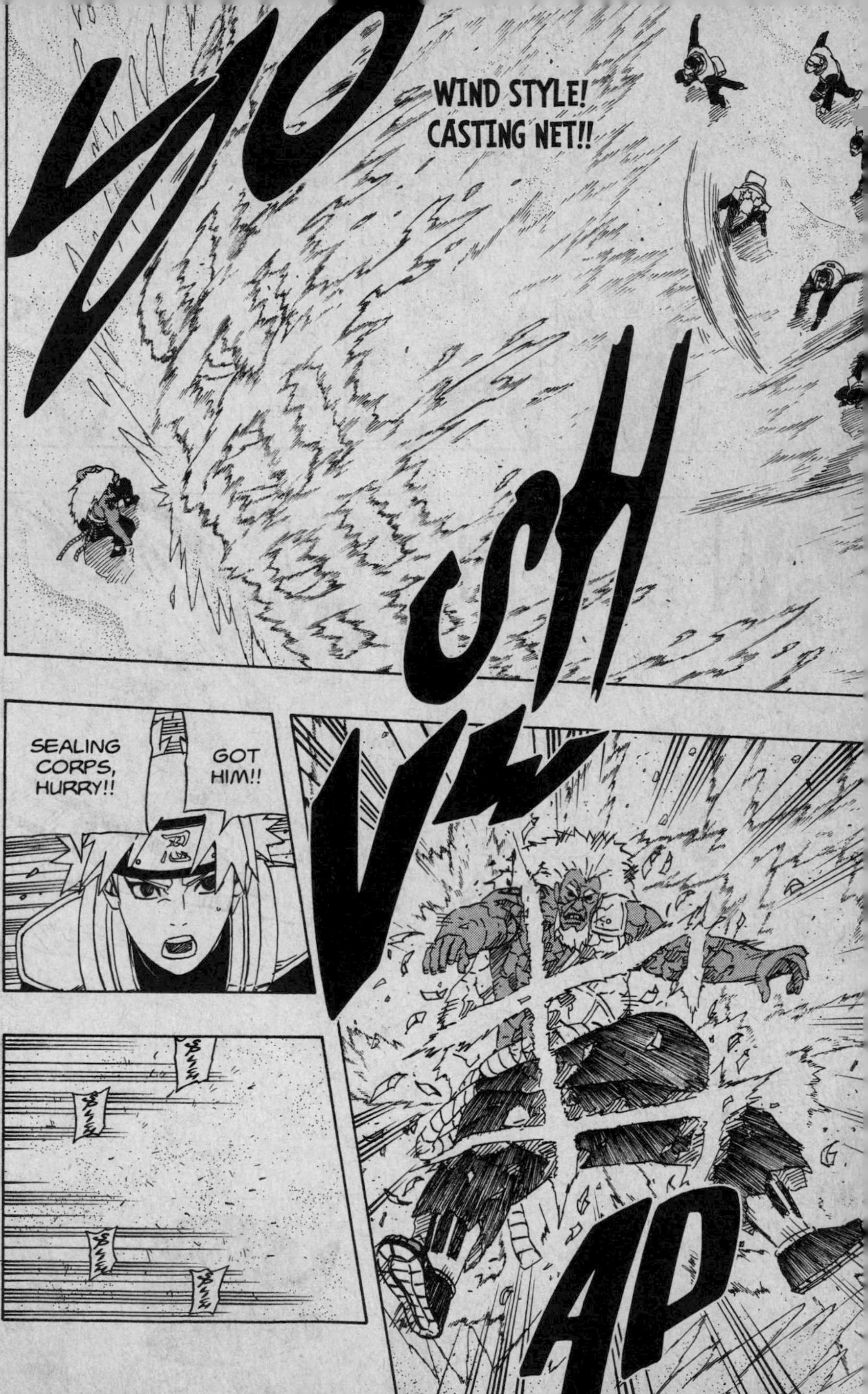
WIND STYLE!
CASTING NET!!
GOT HIM!!
SEALING CORPS, HURRY!!

READ THIS WAY

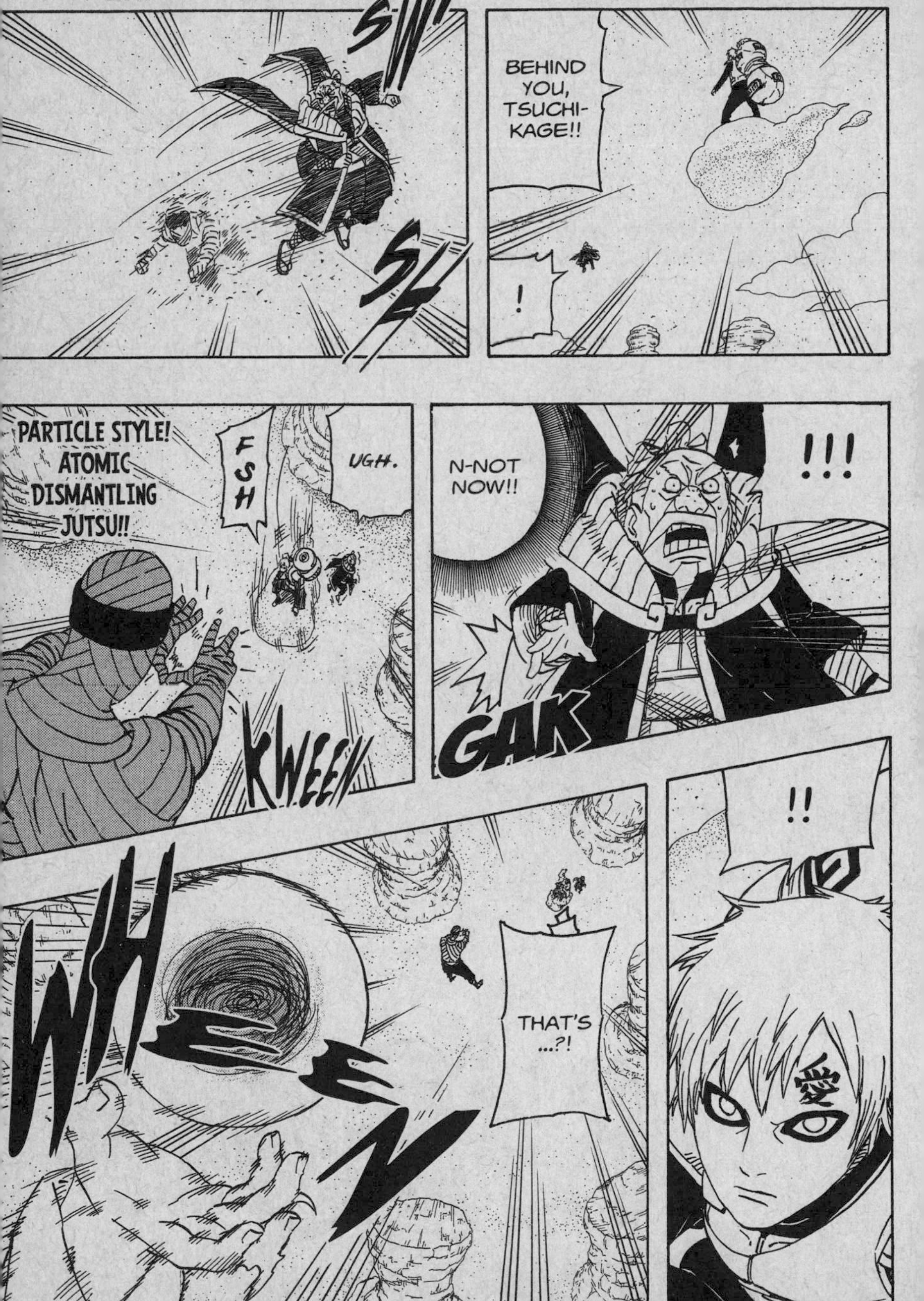

BEHIND YOU, TSUCHIKAGE!!
!
N-NOT NOW!!
!!!
GAK
PARTICLE STYLE! ATOMIC DISMANTLING JUTSU!!
FSH
UGH.
KWEEN
!!
THAT'S ...?!
WHEEN

NARUTO

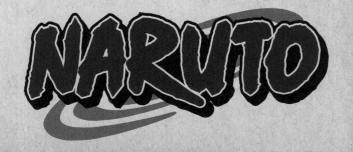

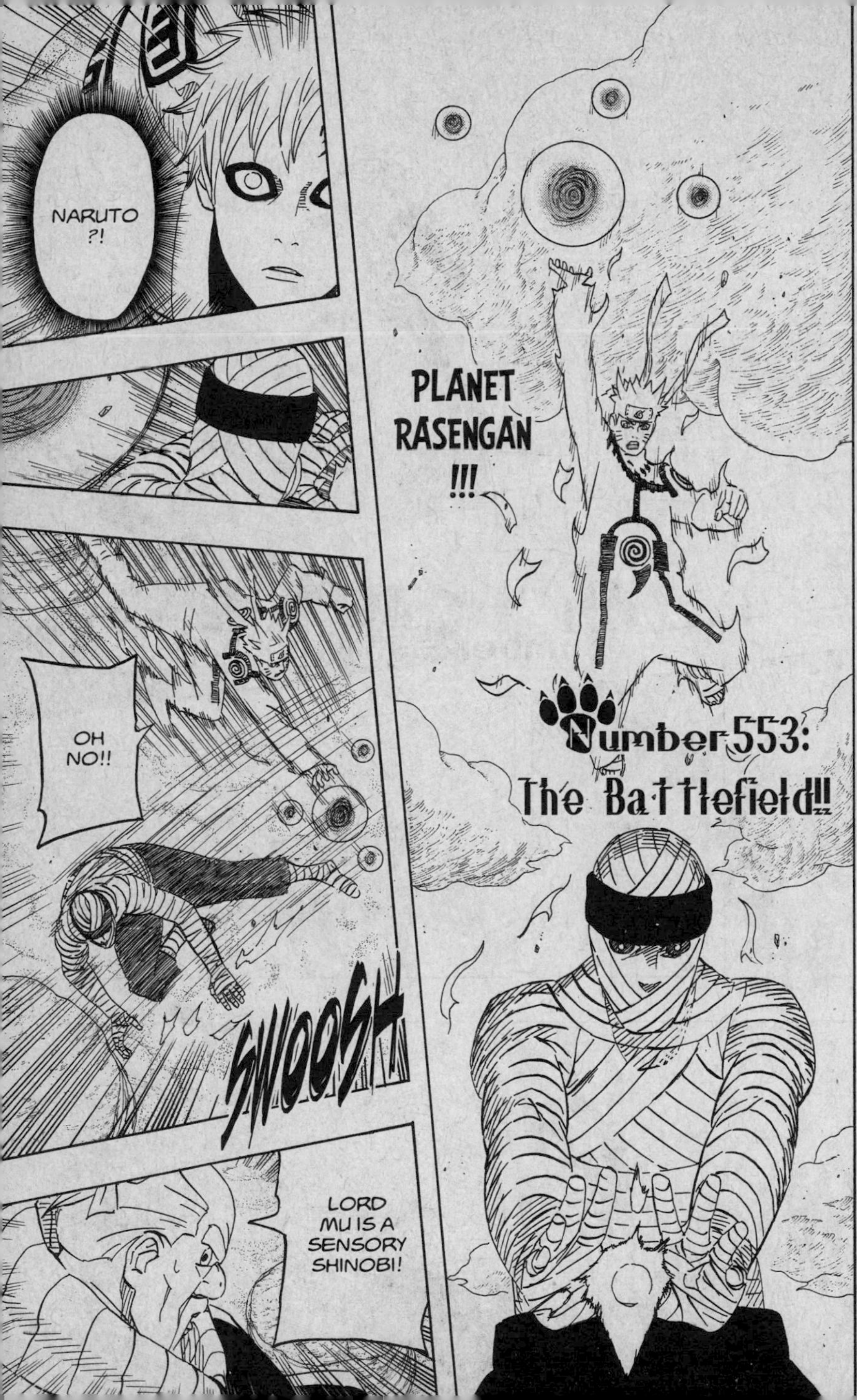
PLANET RASENGAN!!!
Number 553: The Battlefield!!
NARUTO ?!
OH NO!!
SWOOSH
LORD MU IS A SENSORY SHINOBI!

Number 553: The Battlefield!!

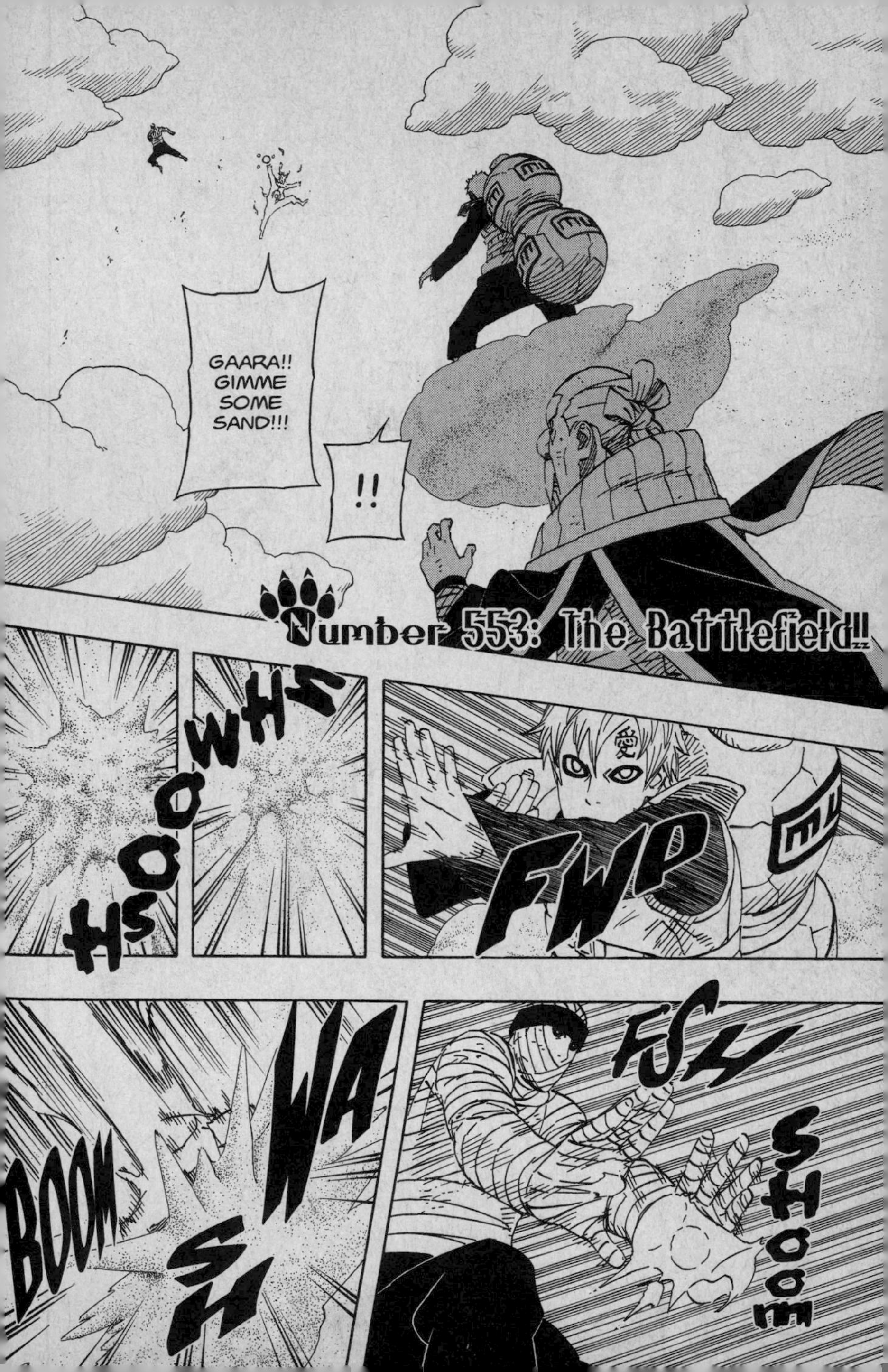

GAARA!! GIMME SOME SAND!!!
!!
FWP
SHOOSH
FSH
SHOOM
WASHSH
BOOM

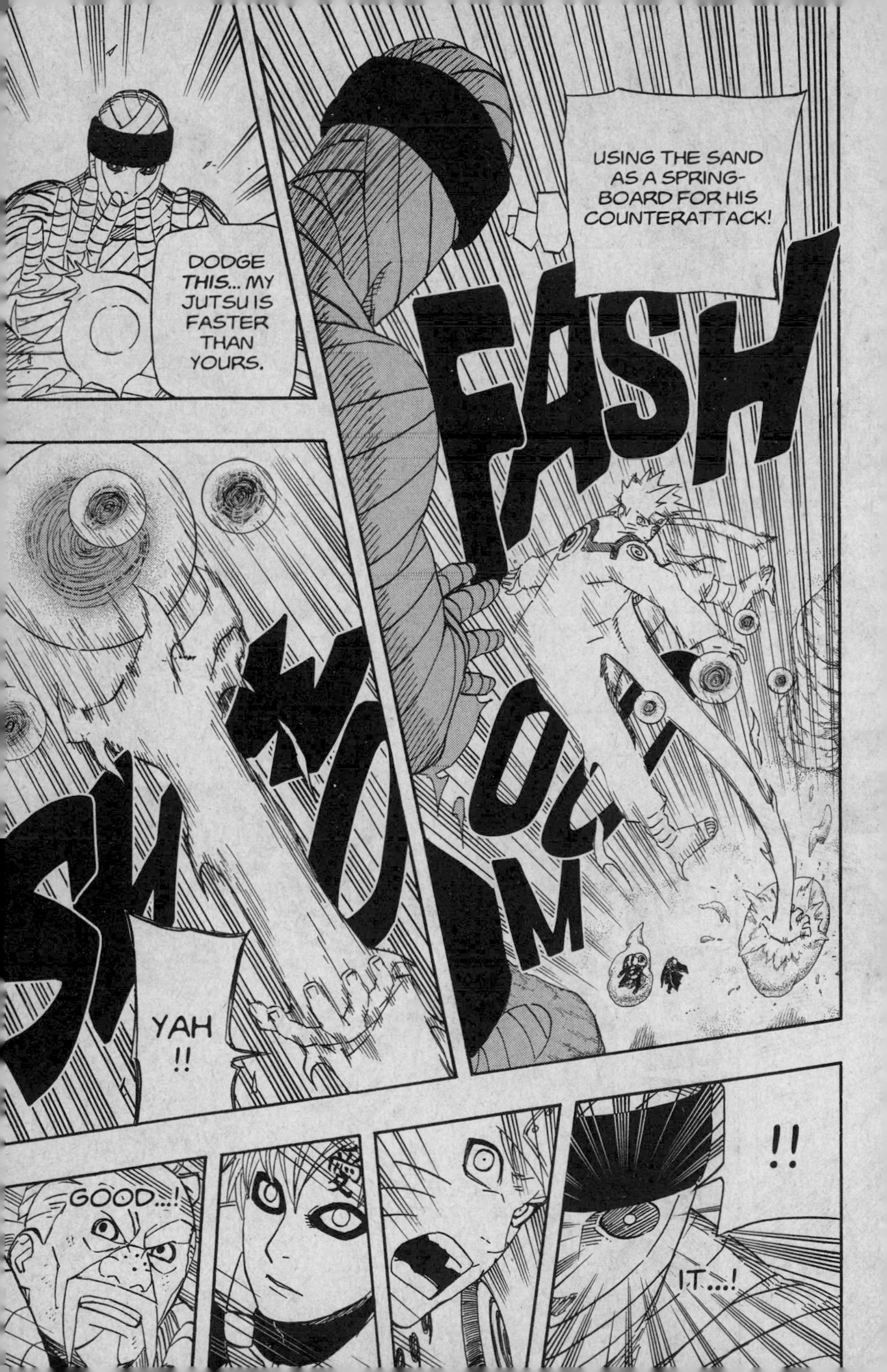

USING THE SAND AS A SPRING-BOARD FOR HIS COUNTERATTACK!
FASH
WOOM
DODGE THIS... MY JUTSU IS FASTER THAN YOURS.
SH
YAH!!
!!
IT...!
GOOD...!

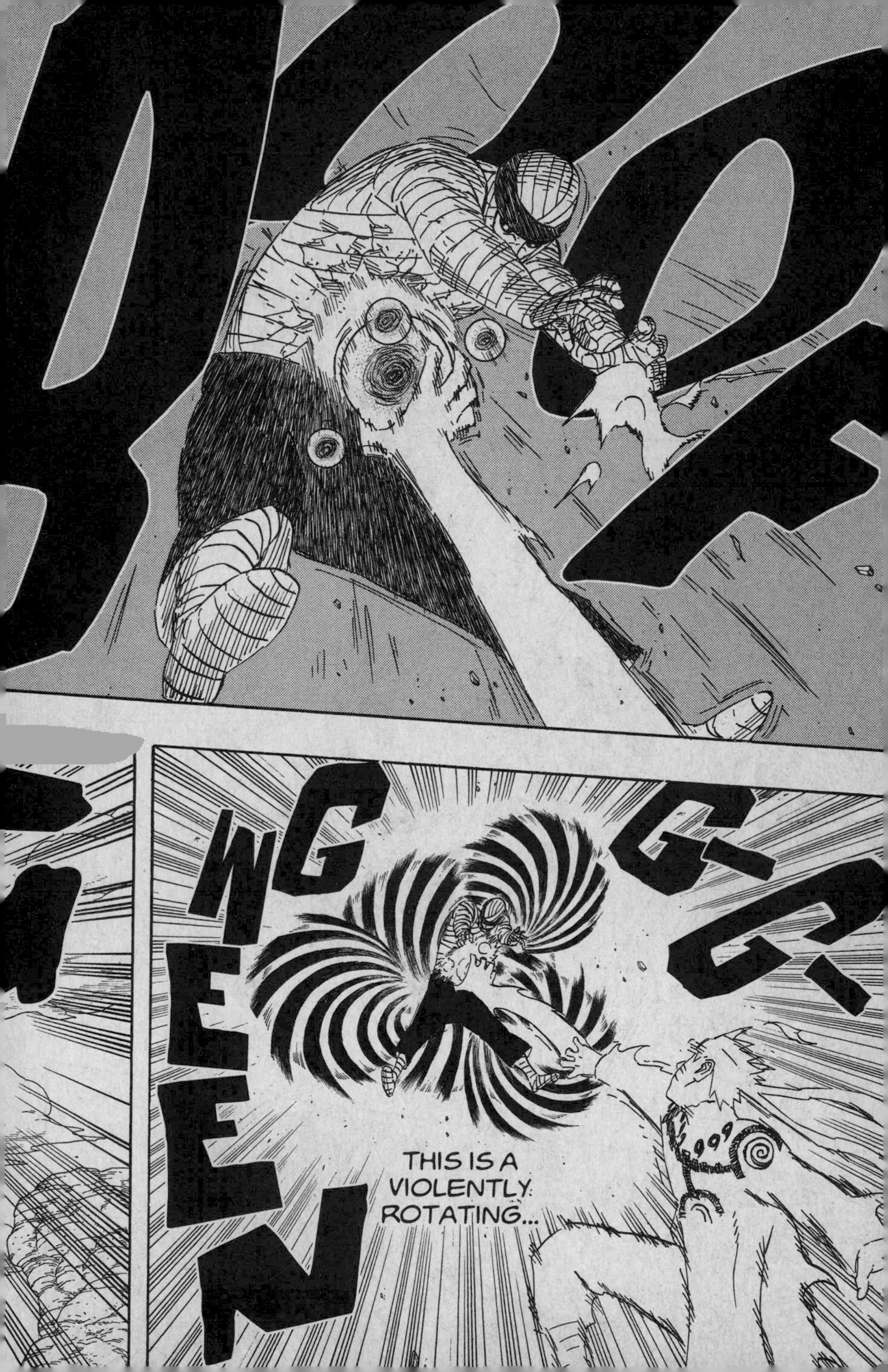
THIS IS A VIOLENTLY ROTATING...

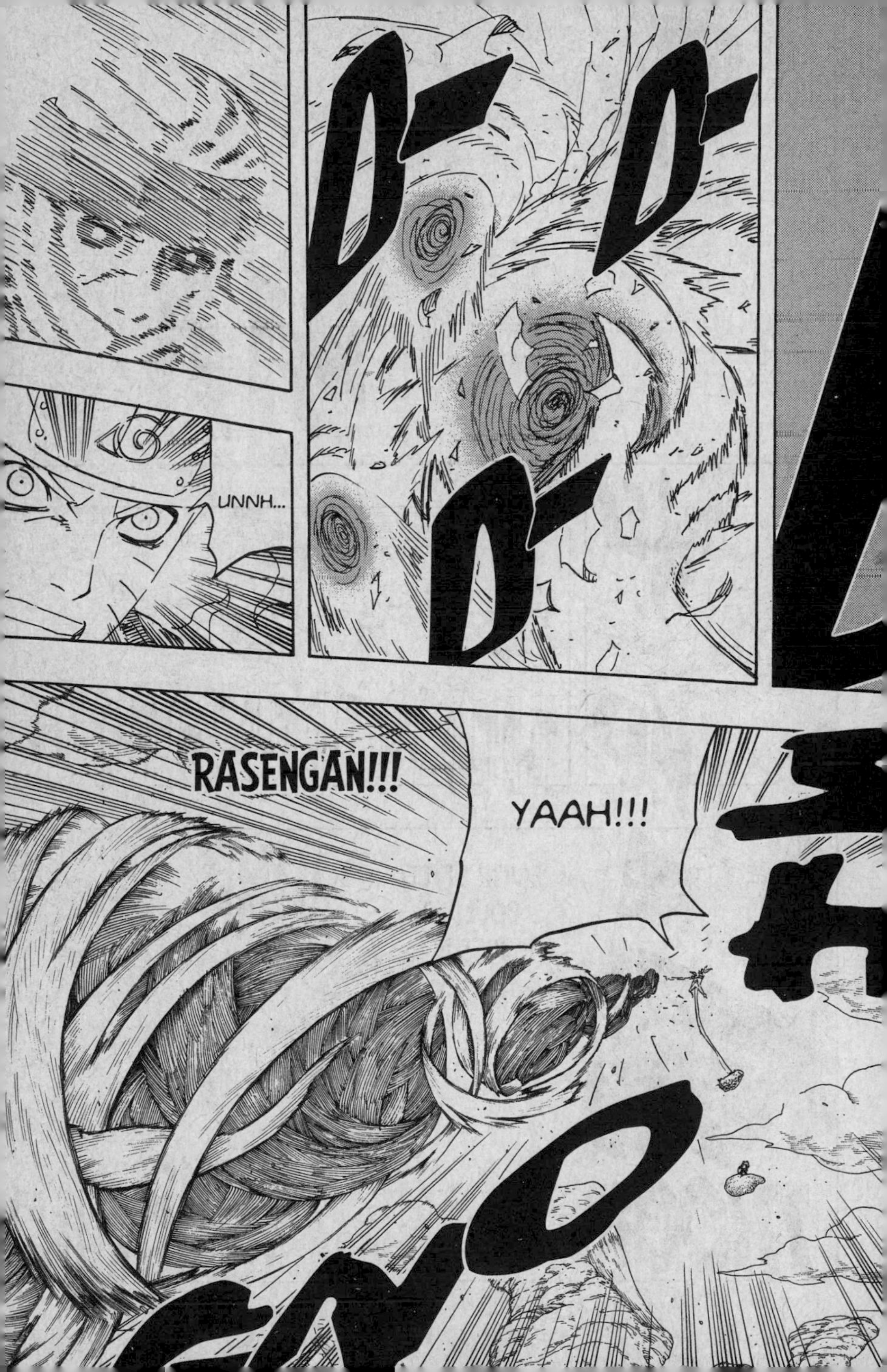
UNNH...
YAAH!!!
RASENGAN!!!

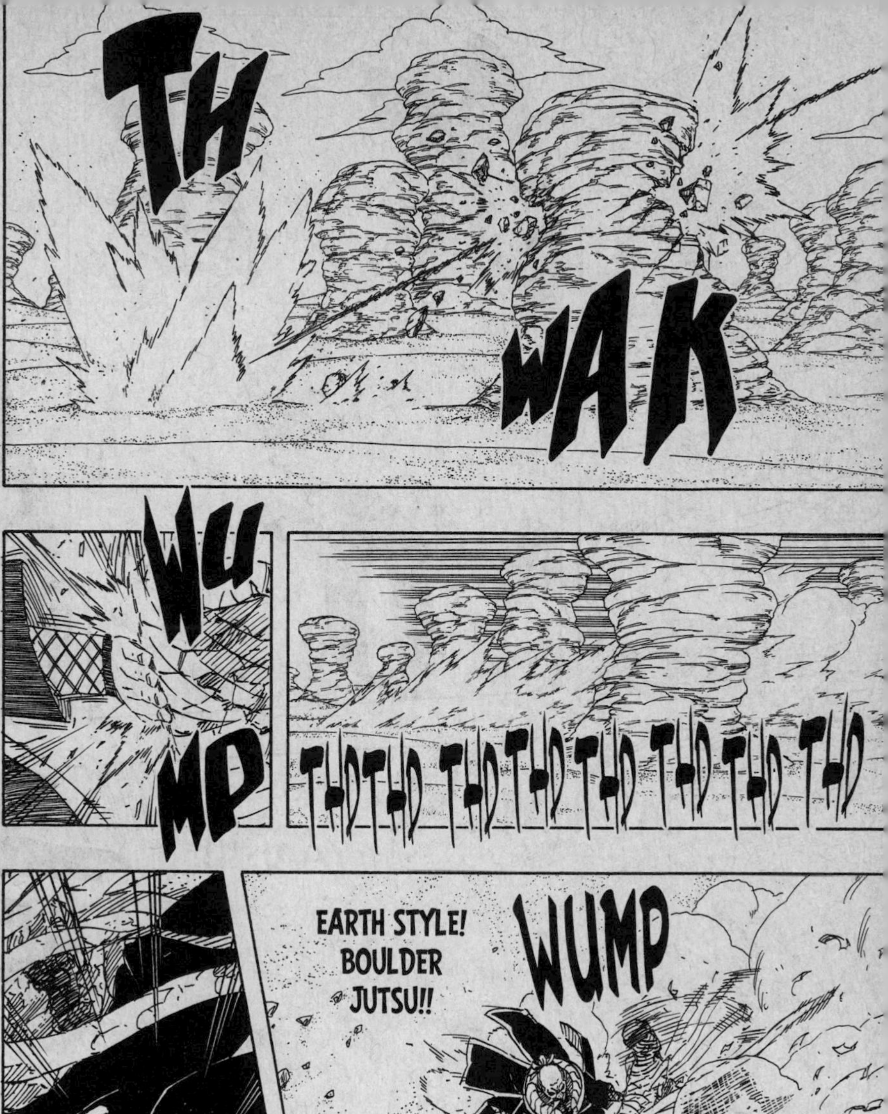
THWAK
THD THD THD THD THD THD THD THD
WUMP
EARTH STYLE! BOULDER JUTSU!!
WUMP
WUMP WUMP
THOOM

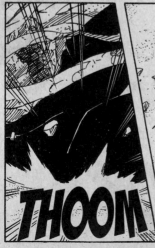

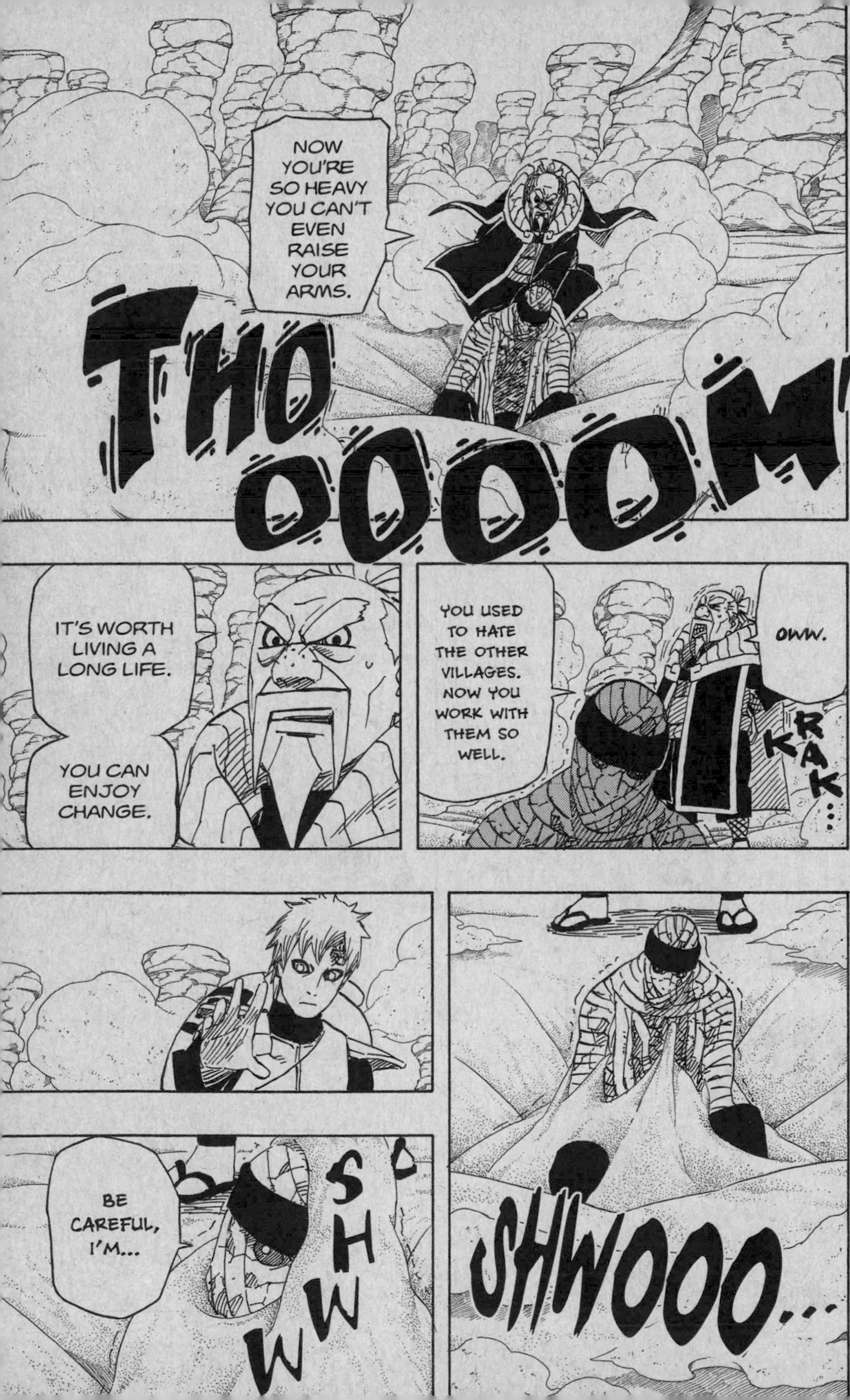
NOW YOU'RE SO HEAVY YOU CAN'T EVEN RAISE YOUR ARMS.
THOOOOOM
OWW.
KRAK...
YOU USED TO HATE THE OTHER VILLAGES. NOW YOU WORK WITH THEM SO WELL.
IT'S WORTH LIVING A LONG LIFE.
YOU CAN ENJOY CHANGE.
SHWOOO...
BE CAREFUL, I'M...
SHWW

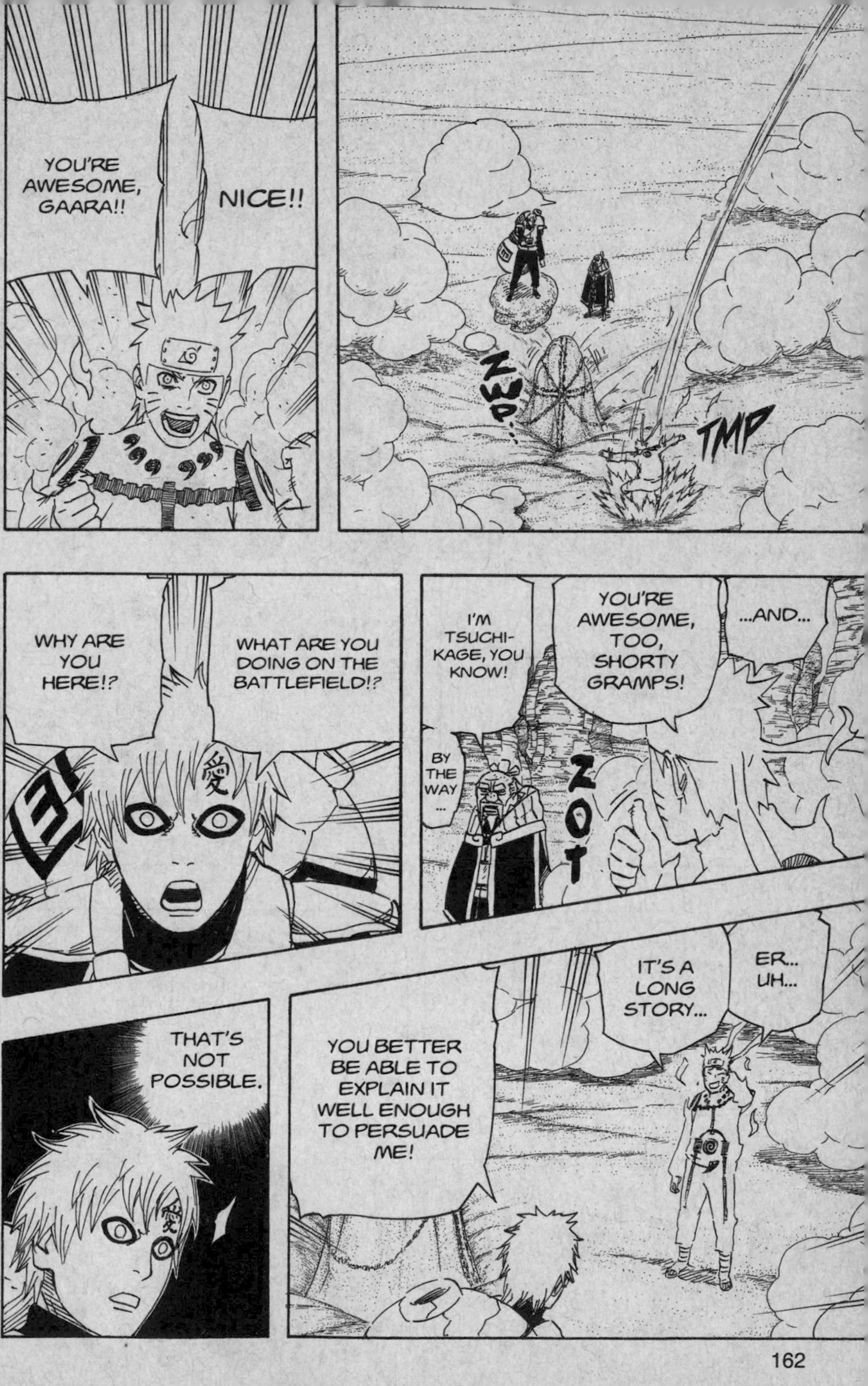
TMP
ZWP...
NICE!!
YOU'RE AWESOME, GAARA!!
...AND...
YOU'RE AWESOME, TOO, SHORTY GRAMPS!
I'M TSUCHIKAGE, YOU KNOW!
ZOT
BY THE WAY...
WHAT ARE YOU DOING ON THE BATTLEFIELD!?
WHY ARE YOU HERE!?
ER... UH...
IT'S A LONG STORY...
YOU BETTER BE ABLE TO EXPLAIN IT WELL ENOUGH TO PERSUADE ME!
THAT'S NOT POSSIBLE.

READ THIS WAY

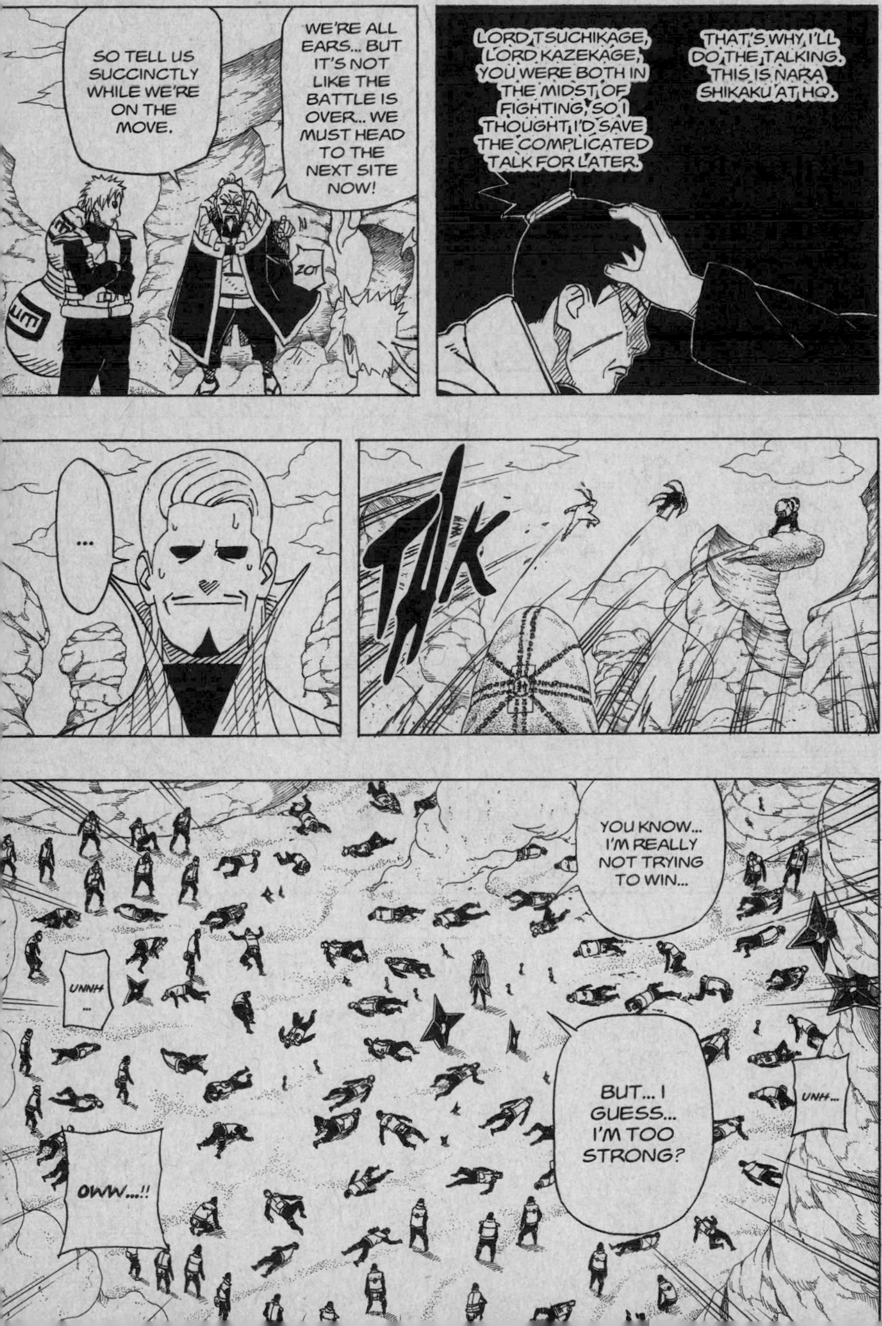
THAT'S WHY I'LL DO THE TALKING. THIS IS NARA SHIKAKU AT HQ.
LORD TSUCHIKAGE, LORD KAZEKAGE, YOU WERE BOTH IN THE MIDST OF FIGHTING, SO I THOUGHT I'D SAVE THE COMPLICATED TALK FOR LATER.
WE'RE ALL EARS... BUT IT'S NOT LIKE THE BATTLE IS OVER... WE MUST HEAD TO THE NEXT SITE NOW!
ZOT
SO TELL US SUCCINCTLY WHILE WE'RE ON THE MOVE.
TAK
...
YOU KNOW... I'M REALLY NOT TRYING TO WIN...
BUT... I GUESS... I'M TOO STRONG?
UNH...
UNNH...
OWW...!!

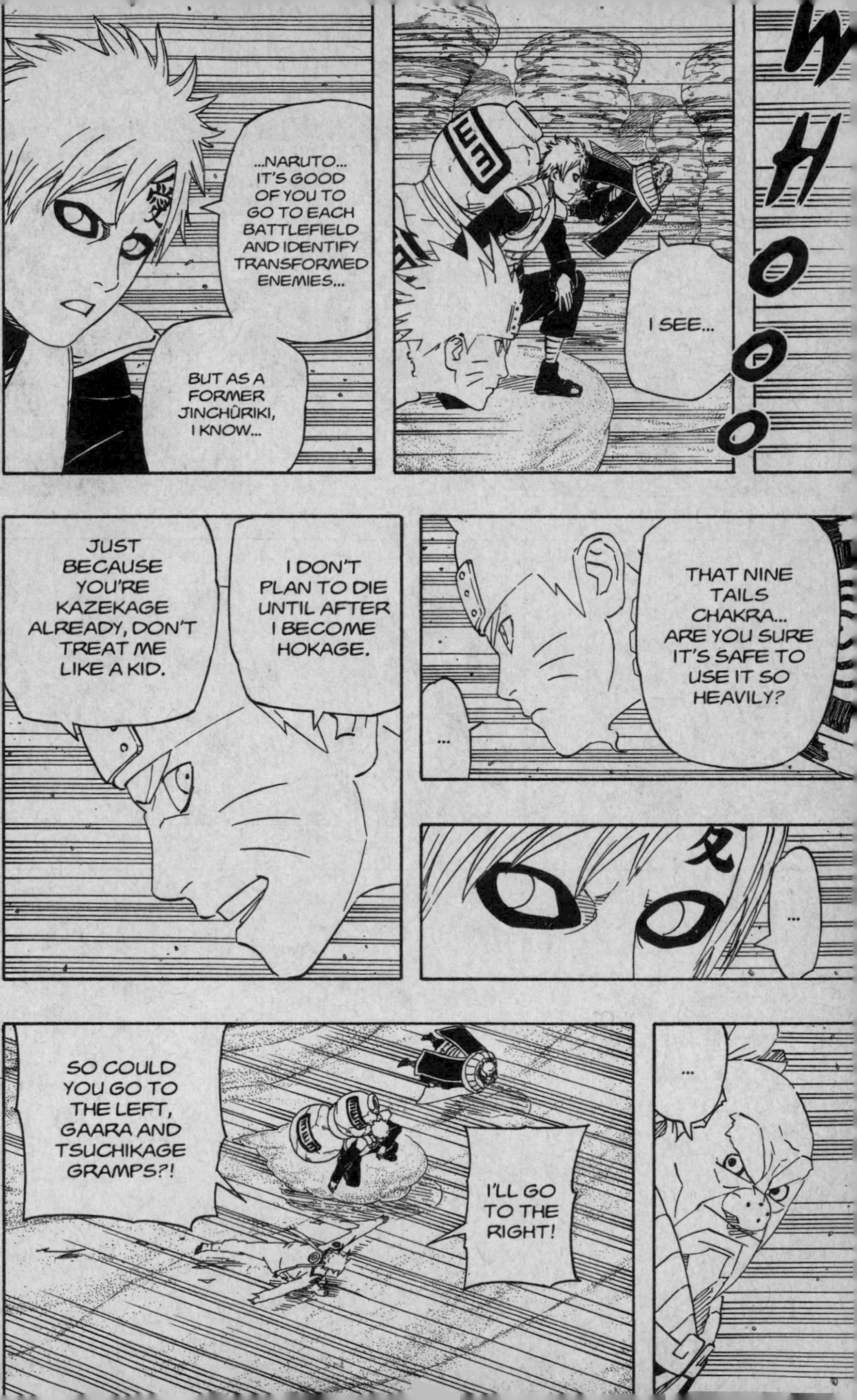
WHOOOOO
I SEE...
...NARUTO... IT'S GOOD OF YOU TO GO TO EACH BATTLEFIELD AND IDENTIFY TRANSFORMED ENEMIES...
BUT AS A FORMER JINCHÛRIKI, I KNOW...
THAT NINE TAILS CHAKRA... ARE YOU SURE IT'S SAFE TO USE IT SO HEAVILY?
...
...
I DON'T PLAN TO DIE UNTIL AFTER I BECOME HOKAGE.
JUST BECAUSE YOU'RE KAZEKAGE ALREADY, DON'T TREAT ME LIKE A KID.
...
SO COULD YOU GO TO THE LEFT, GAARA AND TSUCHIKAGE GRAMPS?!
I'LL GO TO THE RIGHT!

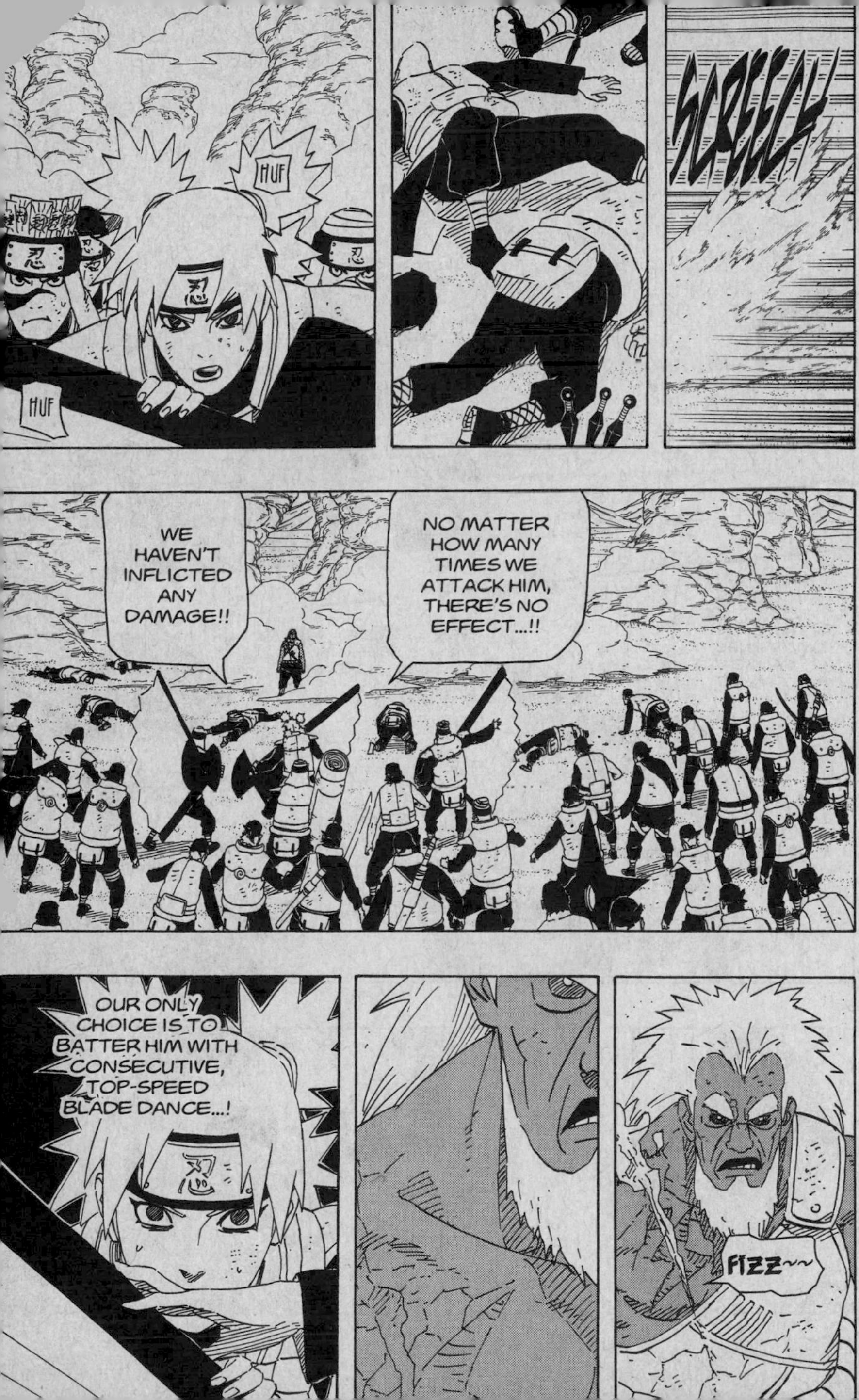
SCREECH
HUF
HUF
NO MATTER HOW MANY TIMES WE ATTACK HIM, THERE'S NO EFFECT...!!
WE HAVEN'T INFLICTED ANY DAMAGE!!
FIZZ~~
OUR ONLY CHOICE IS TO BATTER HIM WITH CONSECUTIVE, TOP-SPEED BLADE DANCE...!

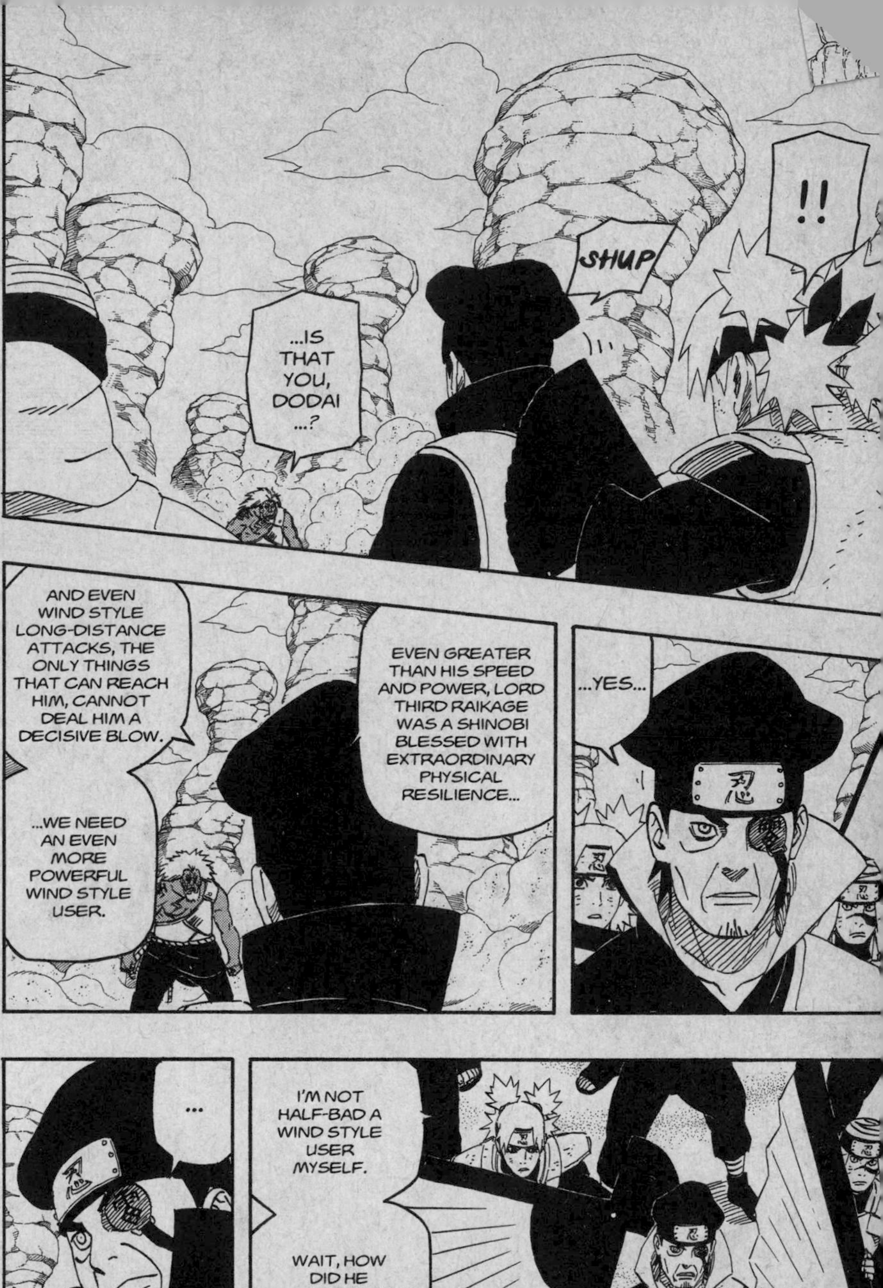
!!
SHUP
...IS THAT YOU, DODAI ...?
...YES...
EVEN GREATER THAN HIS SPEED AND POWER, LORD THIRD RAIKAGE WAS A SHINOBI BLESSED WITH EXTRAORDINARY PHYSICAL RESILIENCE...
AND EVEN WIND STYLE LONG-DISTANCE ATTACKS, THE ONLY THINGS THAT CAN REACH HIM, CANNOT DEAL HIM A DECISIVE BLOW.
...WE NEED AN EVEN MORE POWERFUL WIND STYLE USER.
I'M NOT HALF-BAD A WIND STYLE USER MYSELF.
WAIT, HOW DID HE ACTUALLY DIE?
...

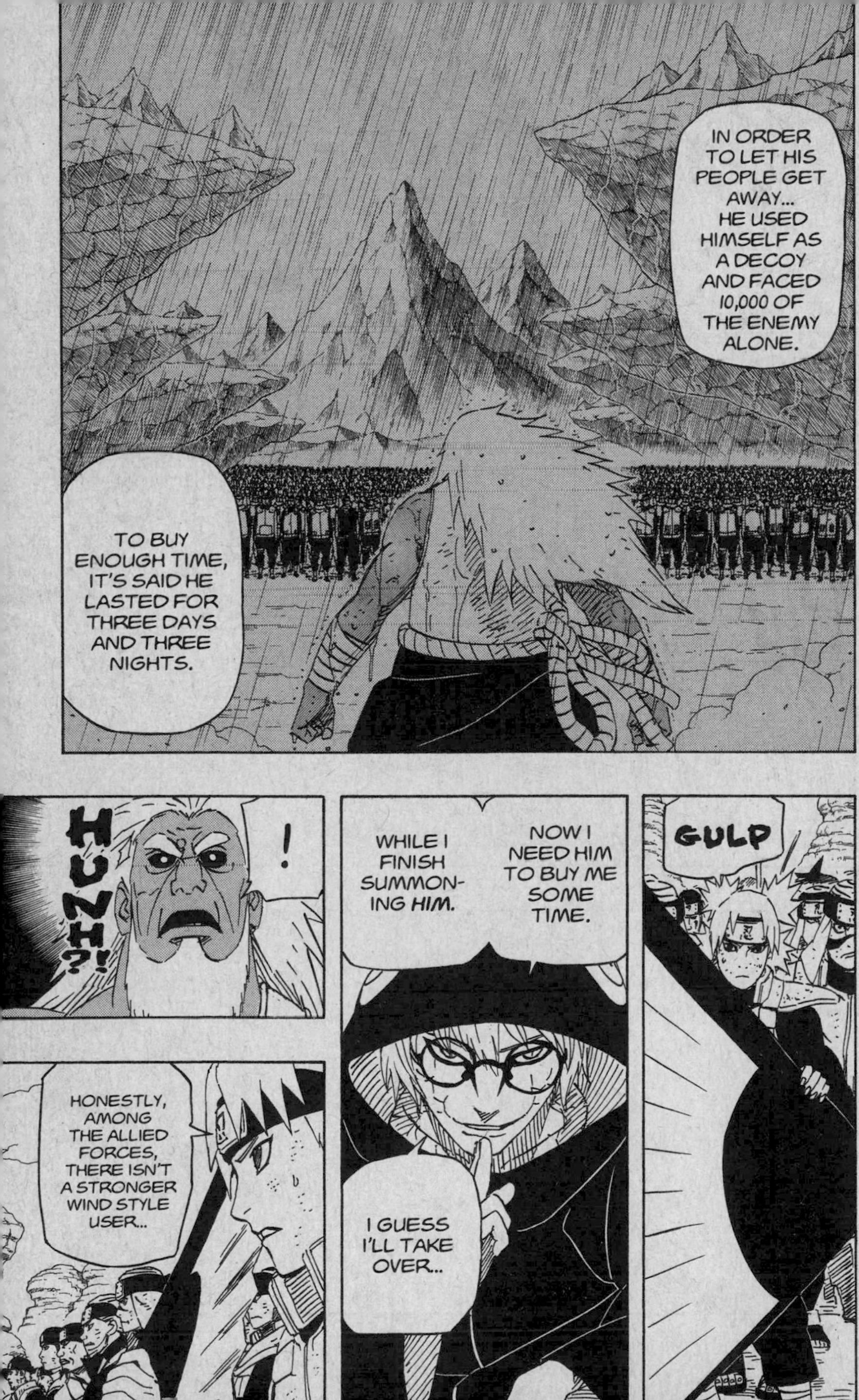
IN ORDER TO LET HIS PEOPLE GET AWAY... HE USED HIMSELF AS A DECOY AND FACED 10,000 OF THE ENEMY ALONE.
TO BUY ENOUGH TIME, IT'S SAID HE LASTED FOR THREE DAYS AND THREE NIGHTS.
GULP
NOW I NEED HIM TO BUY ME SOME TIME.
WHILE I FINISH SUMMONING HIM.
I GUESS I'LL TAKE OVER...
!
HUNH?!
HONESTLY, AMONG THE ALLIED FORCES, THERE ISN'T A STRONGER WIND STYLE USER...

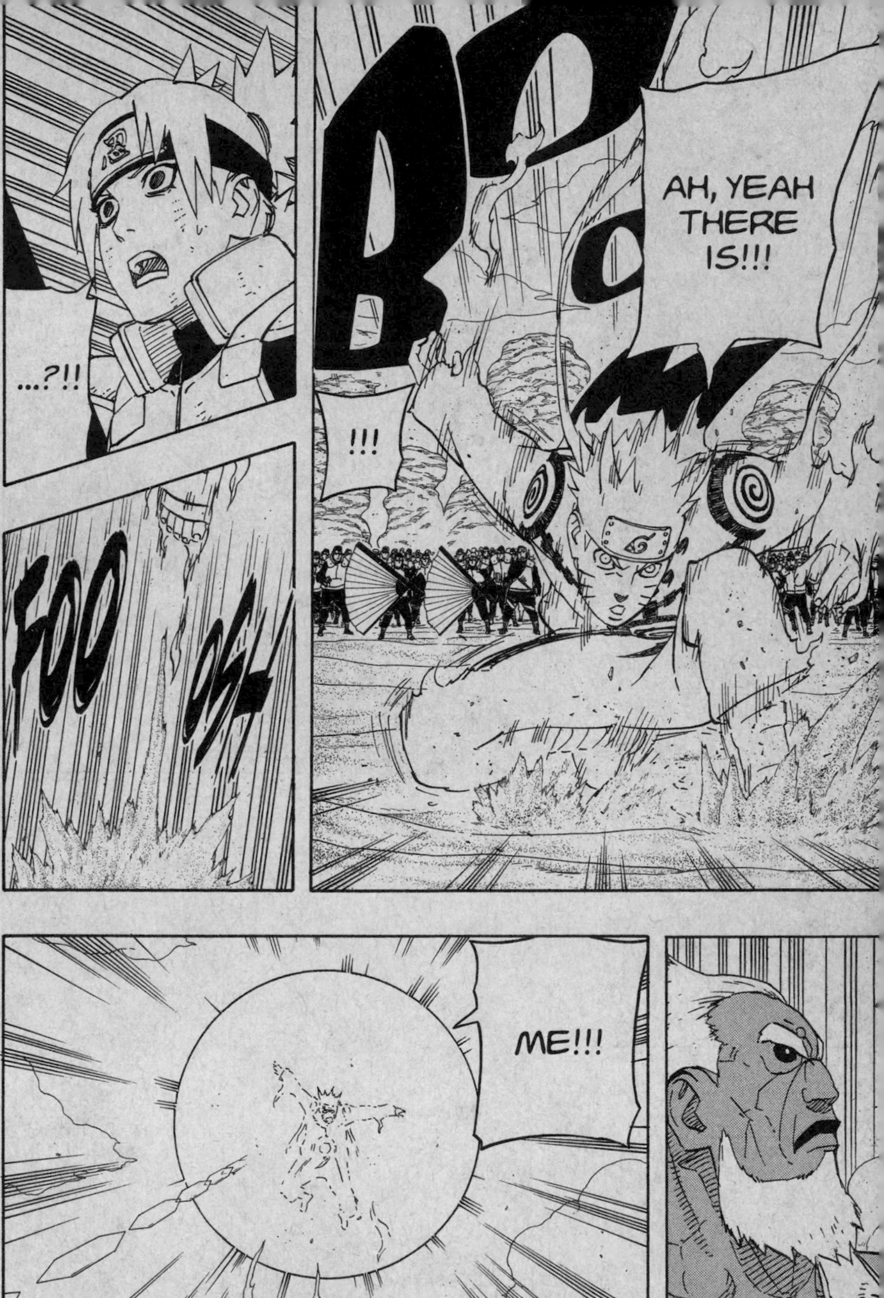
BOOM
AH, YEAH THERE IS!!!
!!!
...?!!
FOOOSH
ME!!!

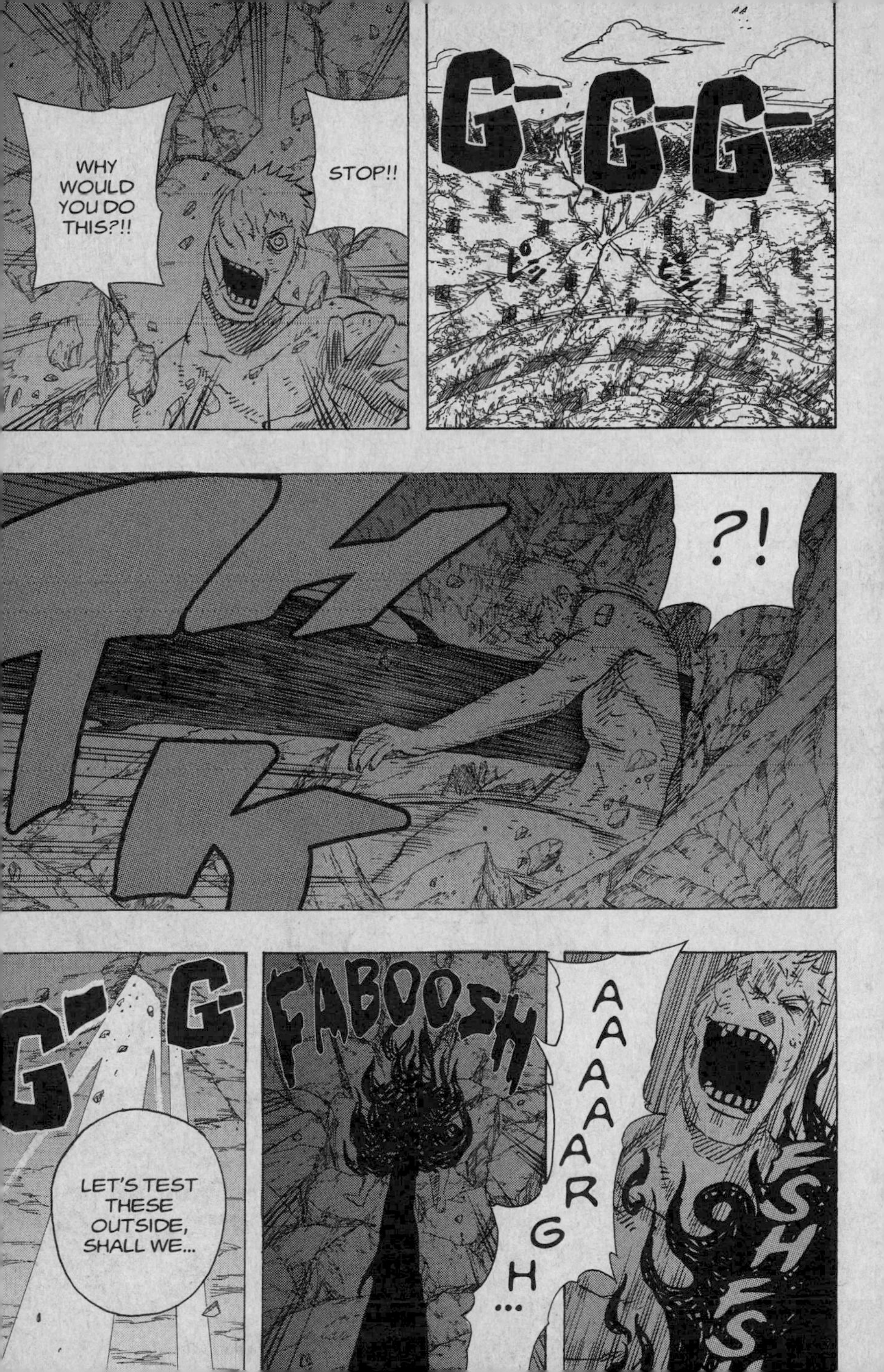
G-G-G-
STOP!!
WHY WOULD YOU DO THIS?!!
?!
THK
AAAAARGH...
FSH FSH
FABOOSH
G-G-
LET'S TEST THESE OUTSIDE, SHALL WE...

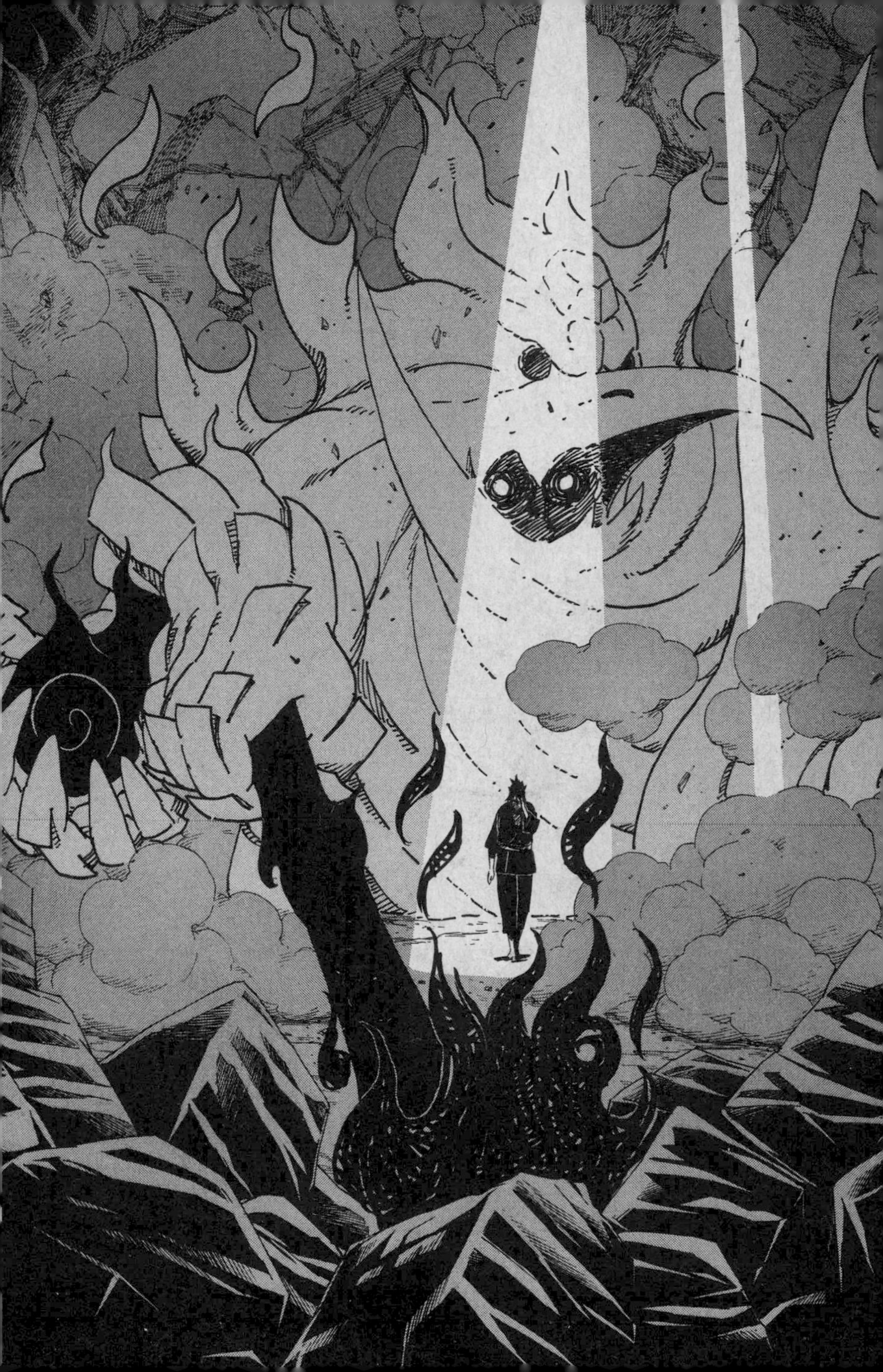

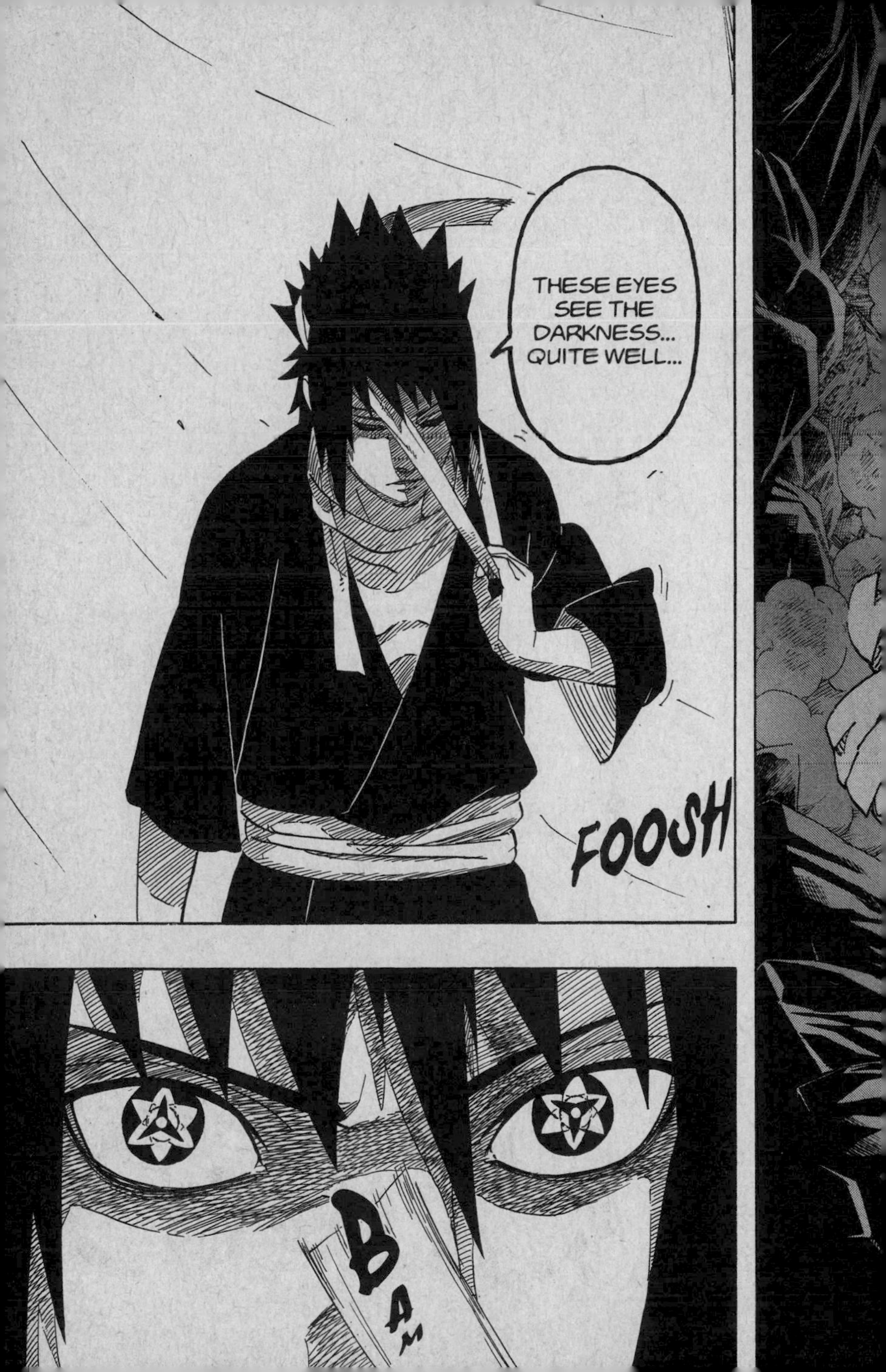
THESE EYES SEE THE DARKNESS... QUITE WELL...
FOOSH
BAM

NARUTO

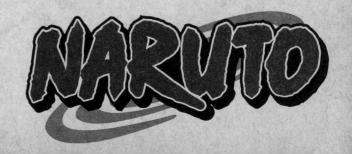

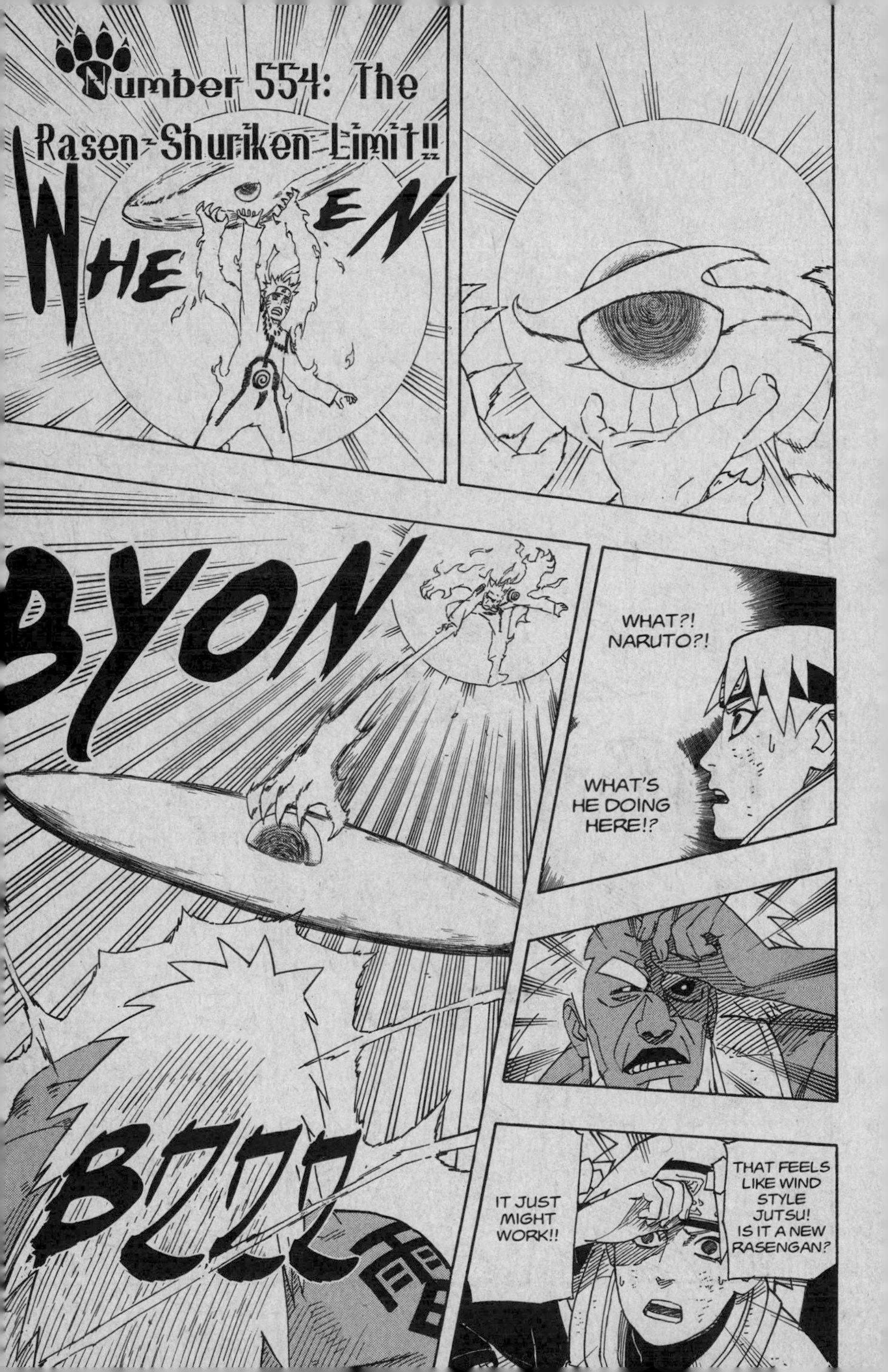
Number 554: The Rasen-Shuriken Limit!!
WHEEN
WHAT?! NARUTO?!
WHAT'S HE DOING HERE!?
THAT FEELS LIKE WIND STYLE JUTSU! IS IT A NEW RASENGAN?
IT JUST MIGHT WORK!!
BYON
BZZZ

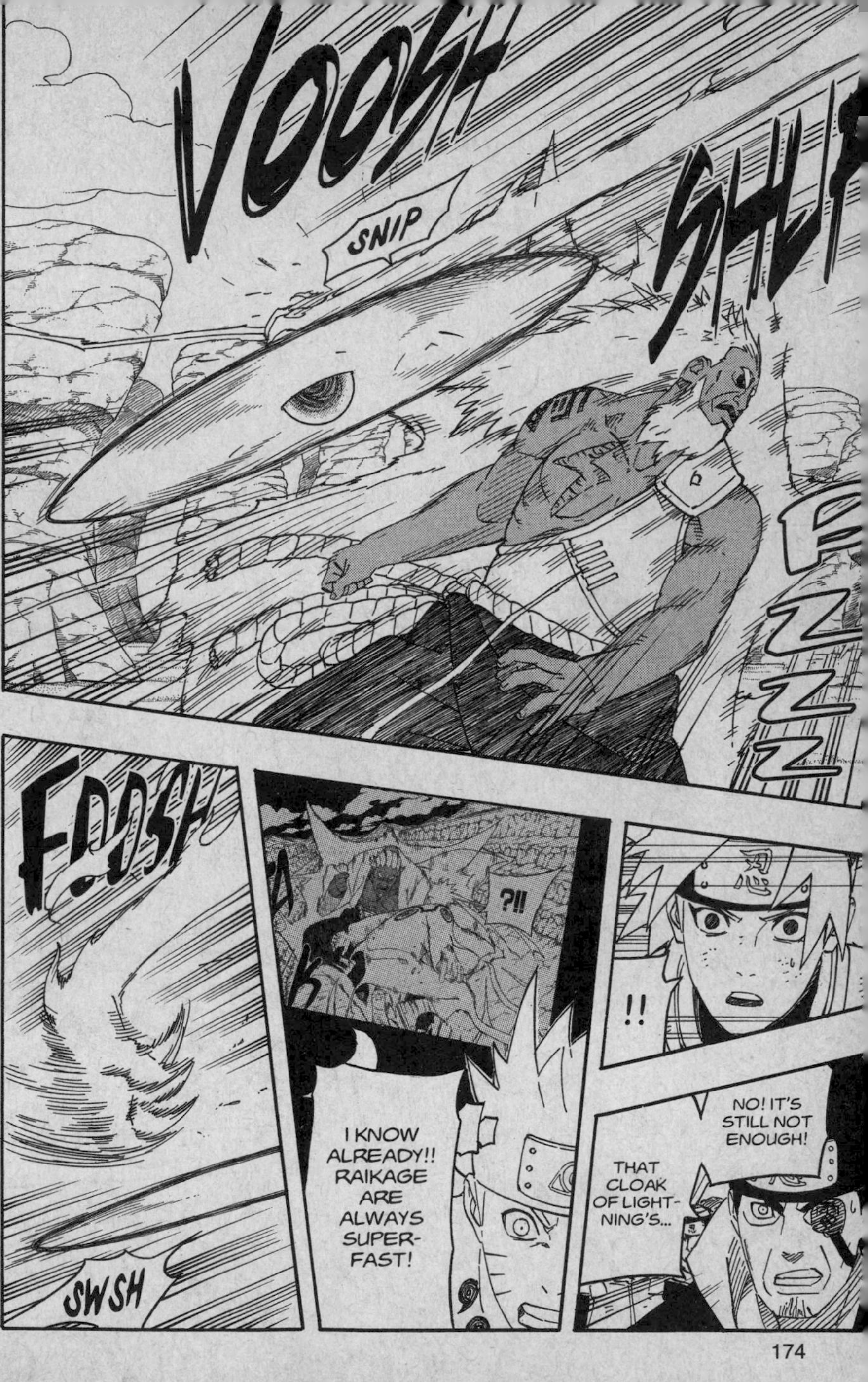
VOOSH
SNIP
SHUF
FZZZZ
!!
?!!
NO! IT'S STILL NOT ENOUGH!
THAT CLOAK OF LIGHTNING'S...
I KNOW ALREADY!! RAIKAGE ARE ALWAYS SUPER-FAST!
FOOSH
SWSH

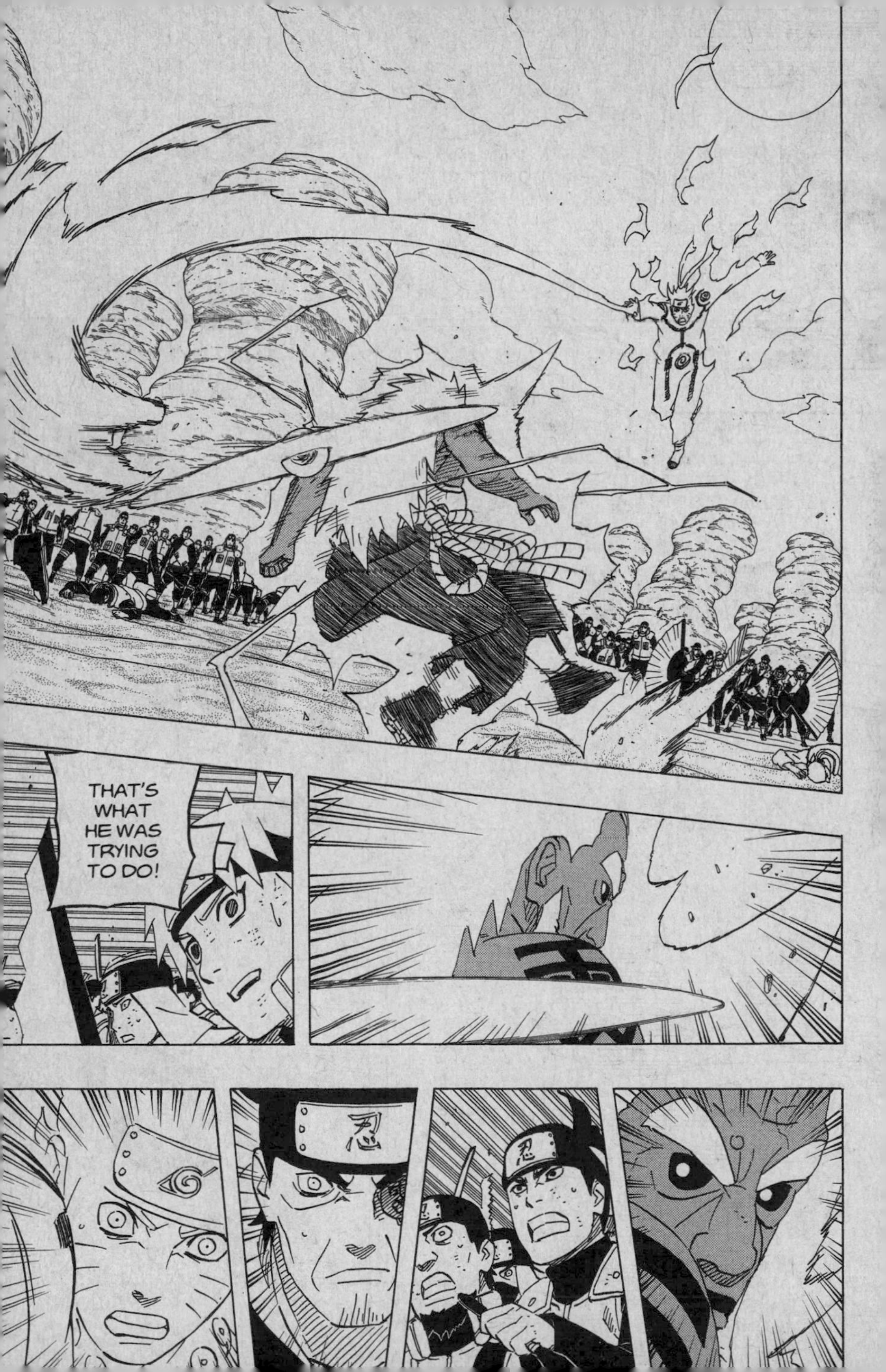
THAT'S WHAT HE WAS TRYING TO DO!

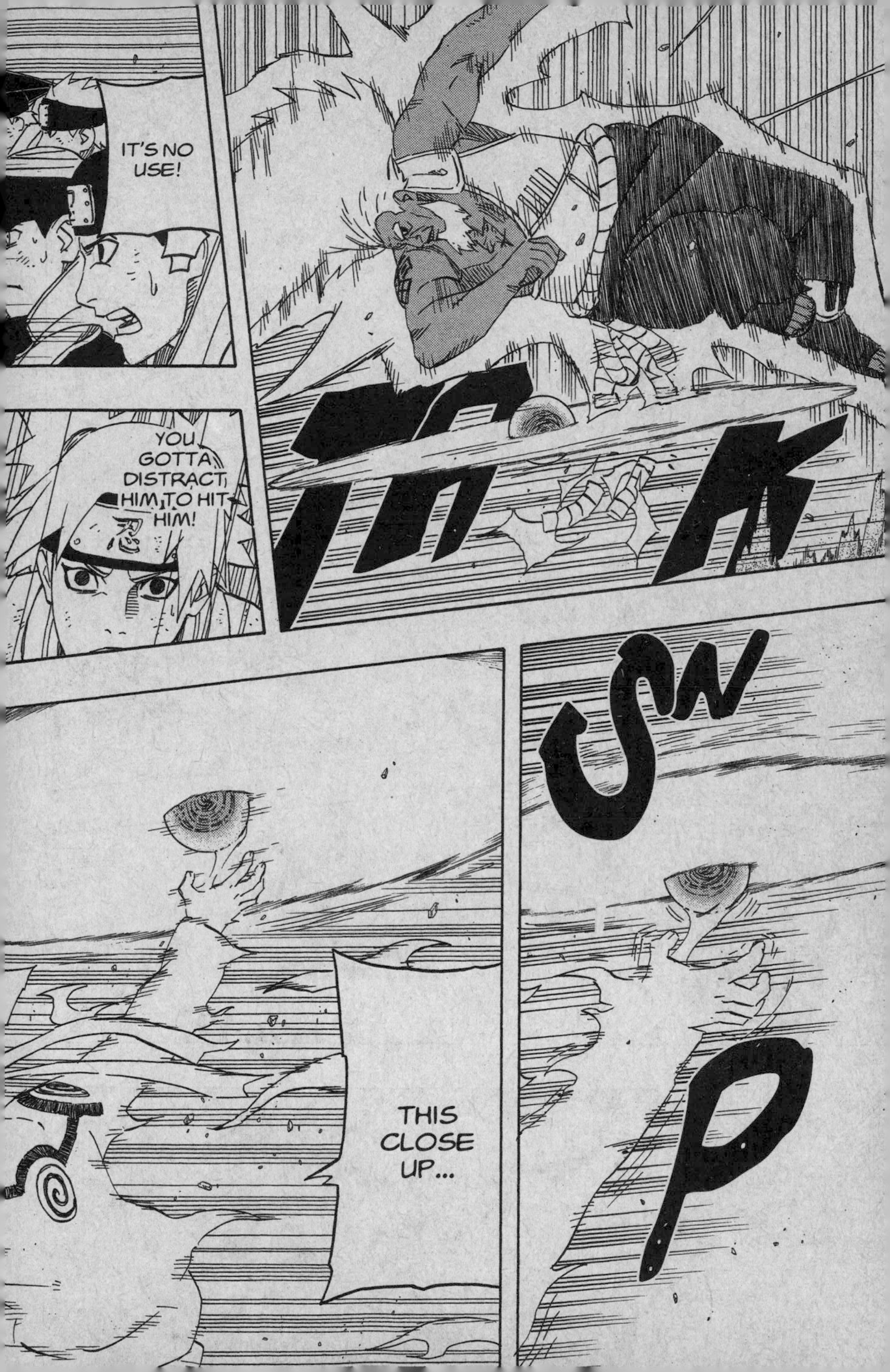
IT'S NO USE!
YOU GOTTA DISTRACT HIM TO HIT HIM!
THIS CLOSE UP...

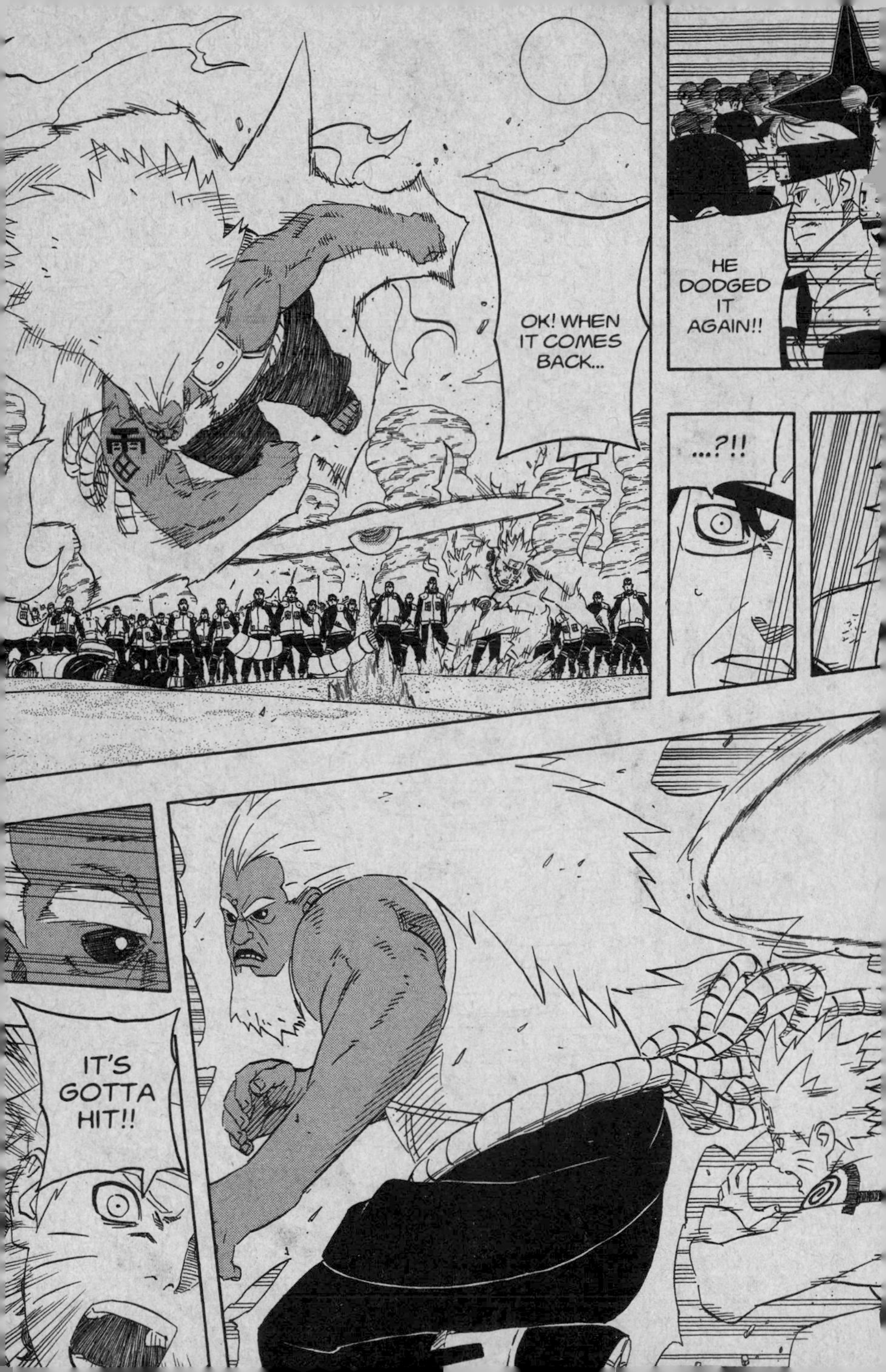
HE DODGED IT AGAIN!!
...?!!
OK! WHEN IT COMES BACK...
IT'S GOTTA HIT!!

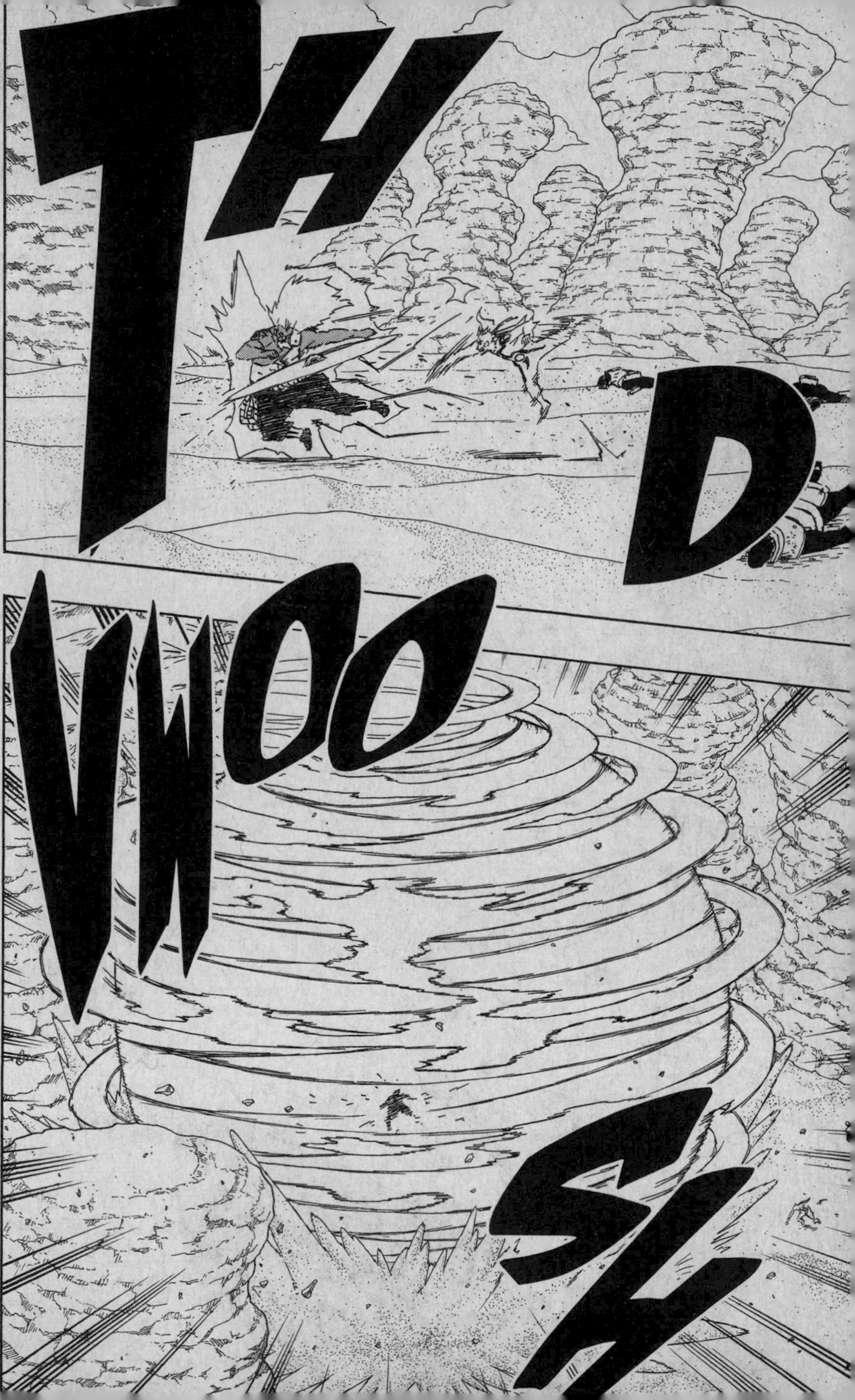
THD
VWOOSH

READ THIS WAY

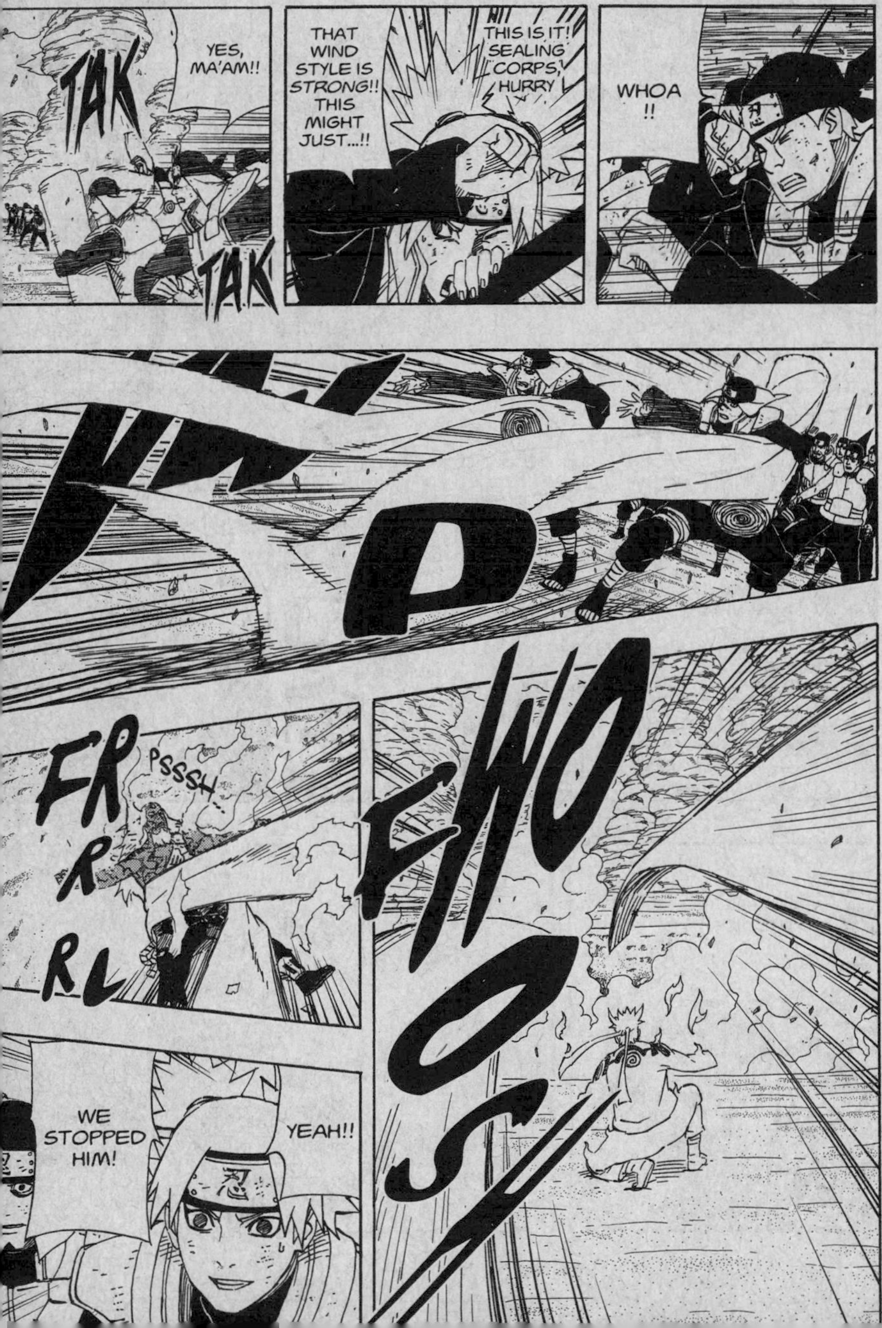
WHOA !!
THIS IS IT! SEALING CORPS, HURRY
THAT WIND STYLE IS STRONG!! THIS MIGHT JUST...!!
YES, MA'AM!!
TAK
TAK
FRRRL
PSSSH...
YEAH!!
WE STOPPED HIM!

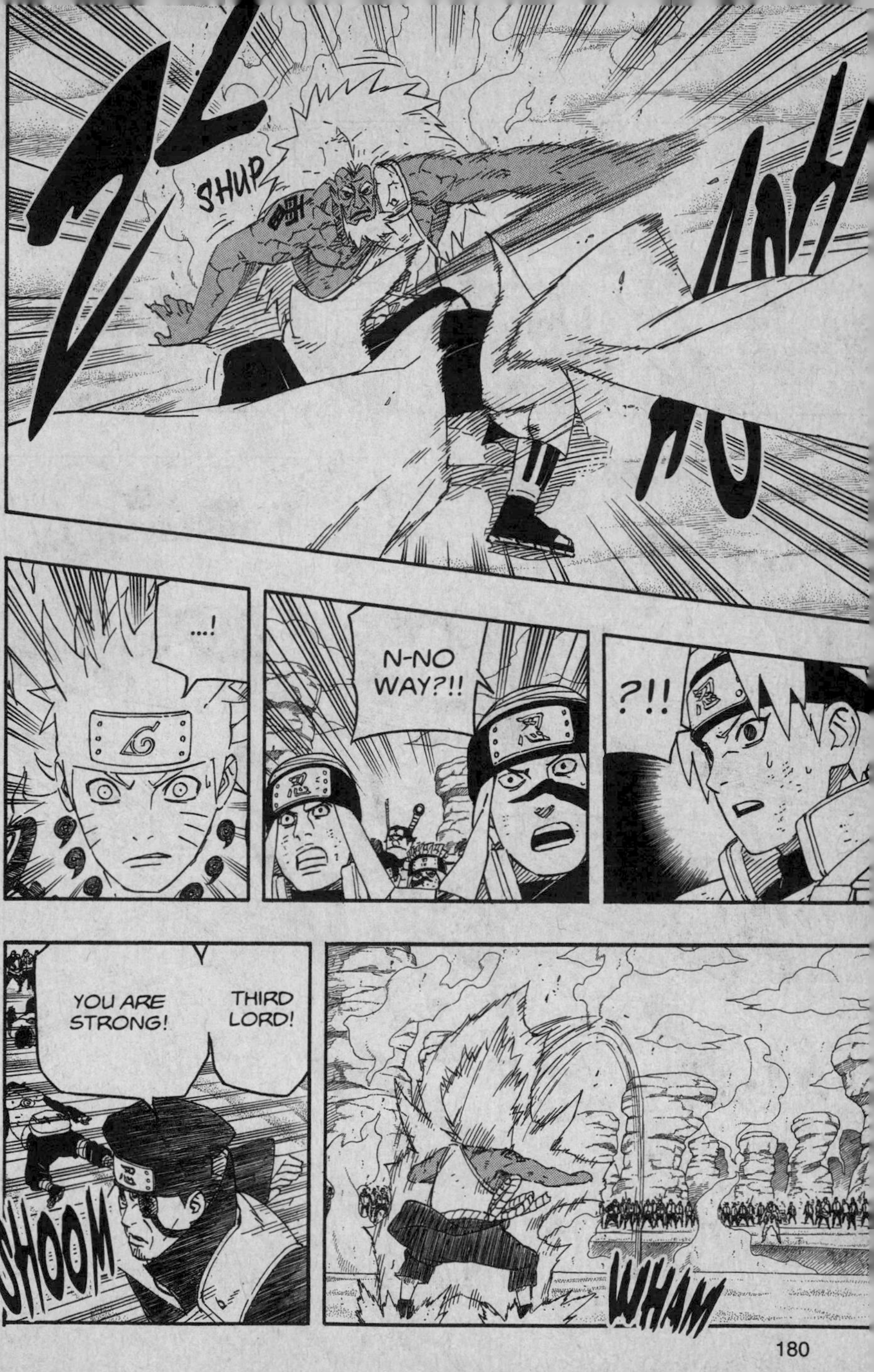
SHUP
?!!
N-NO WAY?!!
...!
WHAM
THIRD LORD!
YOU ARE STRONG!
SHOOM

READ THIS WAY

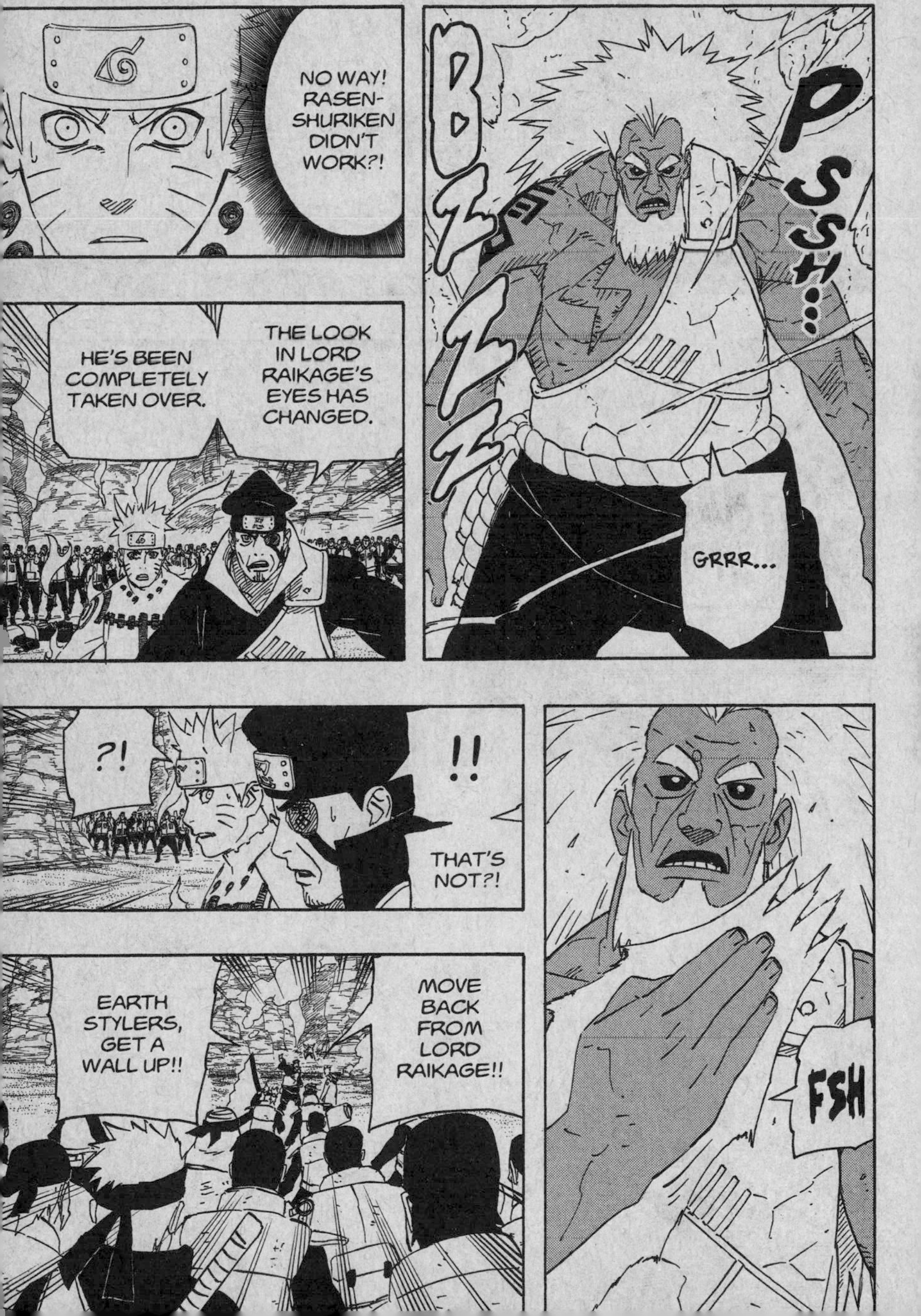
PSSH...
GRRR...
NO WAY! RASEN-SHURIKEN DIDN'T WORK?!
THE LOOK IN LORD RAIKAGE'S EYES HAS CHANGED.
HE'S BEEN COMPLETELY TAKEN OVER.
FSH
!!
THAT'S NOT?!
?!
MOVE BACK FROM LORD RAIKAGE!!
EARTH STYLERS, GET A WALL UP!!

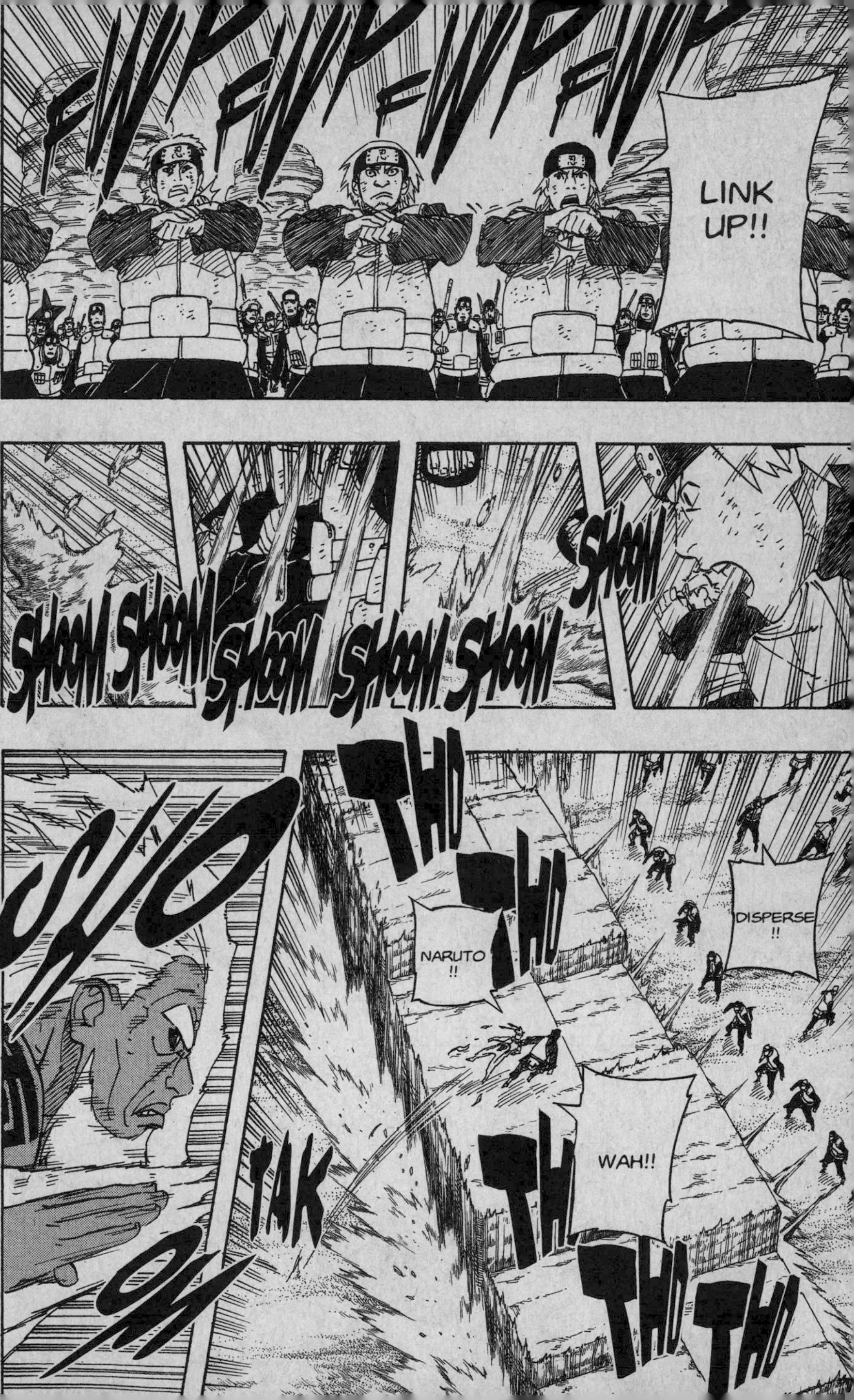

FWP FWP FWP FWP FWP FWP
LINK UP!!
SHOOM
SHOOM SHOOM SHOOM SHOOM SHOOM
DISPERSE!!
THD
NARUTO!!
THD THD
WAH!!
THD THD THD
TAK
SHOOM

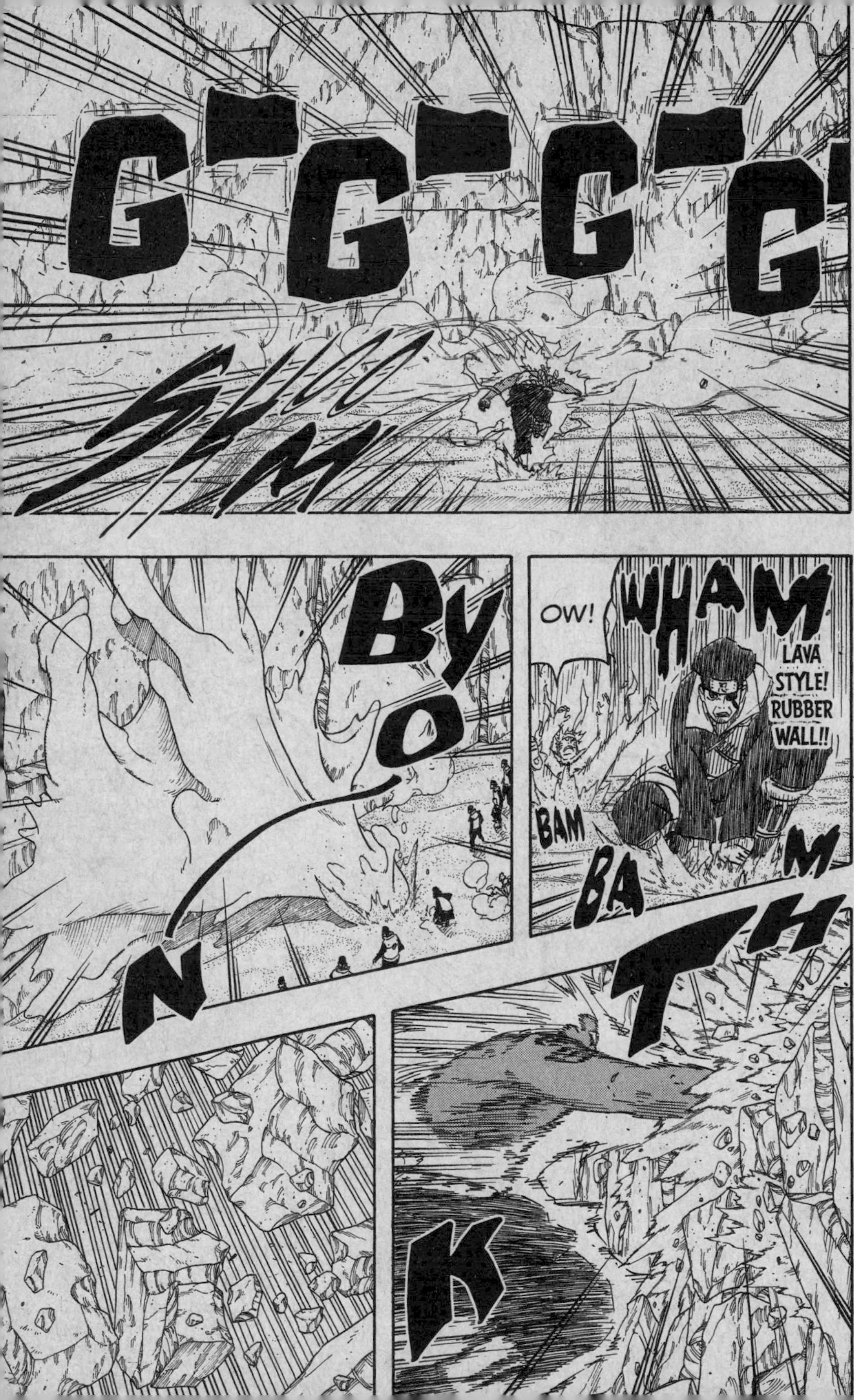
GGGG
SHUOOM
OW!
WHAM
LAVA STYLE! RUBBER WALL!!
BAM
BAM
BYON
TH
K

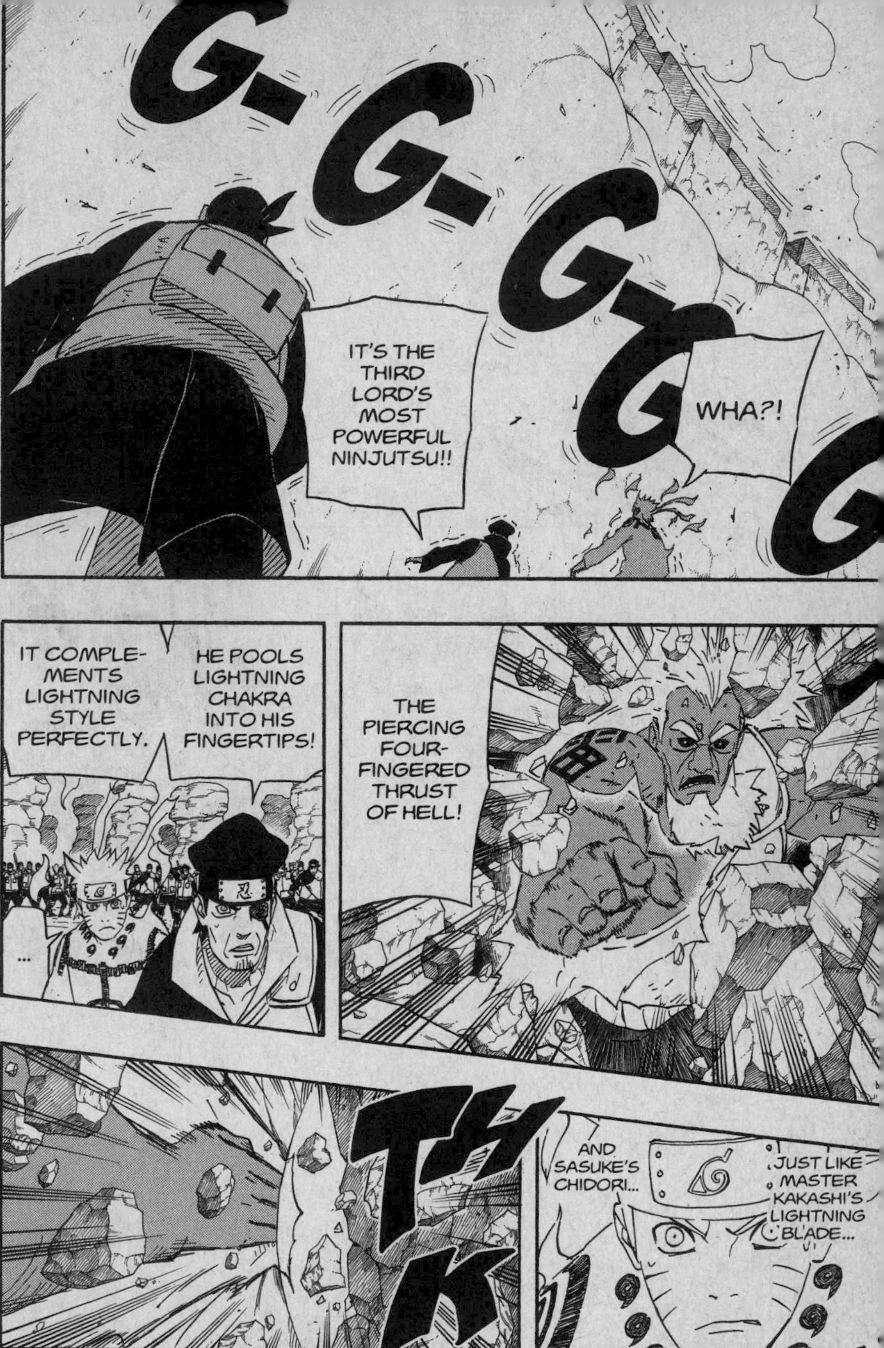
G-G-G-G-G-G
WHA?!
IT'S THE THIRD LORD'S MOST POWERFUL NINJUTSU!!
THE PIERCING FOUR-FINGERED THRUST OF HELL!
HE POOLS LIGHTNING CHAKRA INTO HIS FINGERTIPS!
IT COMPLEMENTS LIGHTNING STYLE PERFECTLY.
...
JUST LIKE MASTER KAKASHI'S LIGHTNING BLADE...
AND SASUKE'S CHIDORI...
TZK

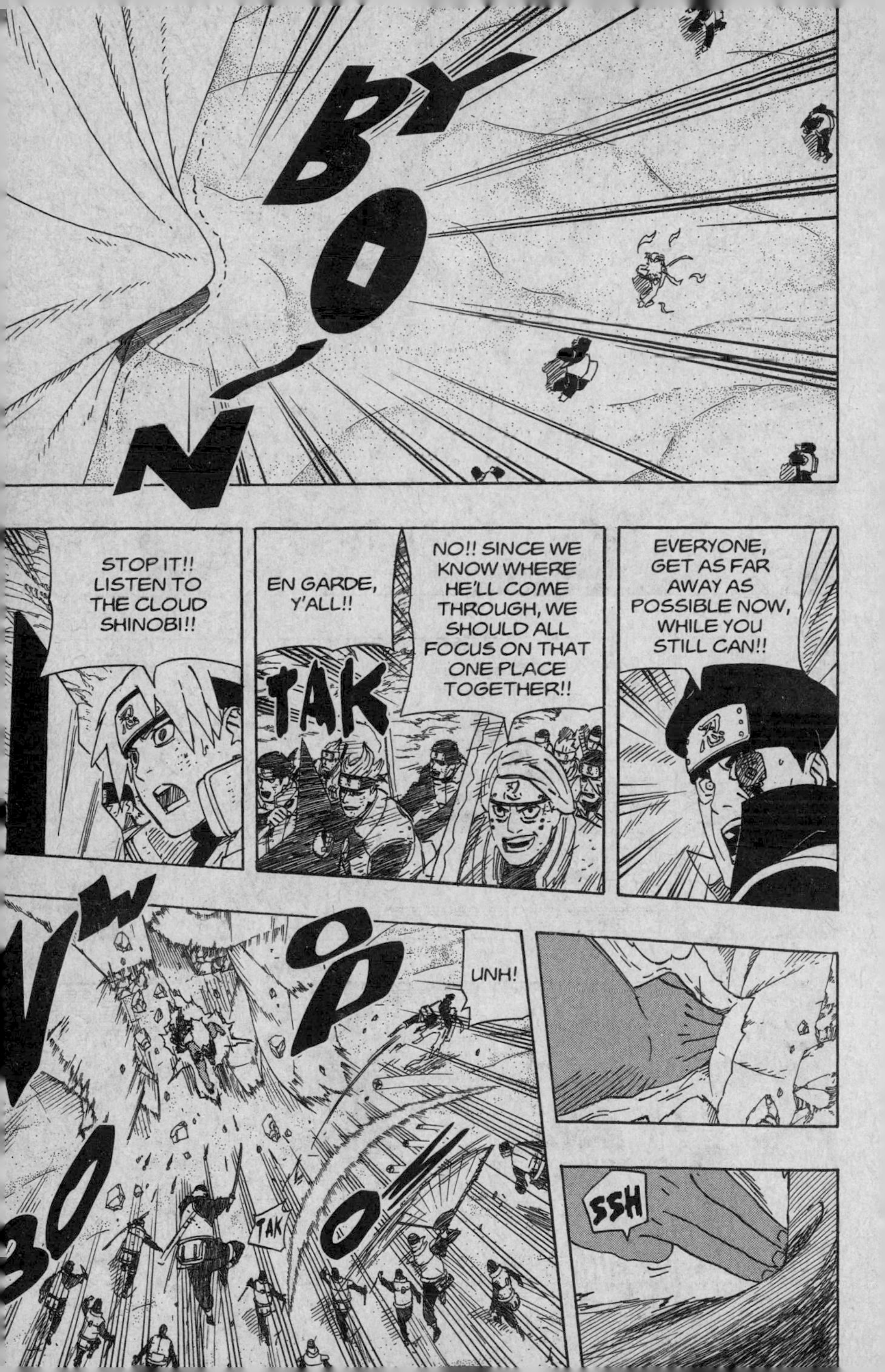
EVERYONE, GET AS FAR AWAY AS POSSIBLE NOW, WHILE YOU STILL CAN!!
NO!! SINCE WE KNOW WHERE HE'LL COME THROUGH, WE SHOULD ALL FOCUS ON THAT ONE PLACE TOGETHER!!
EN GARDE, Y'ALL!!
TAK
STOP IT!! LISTEN TO THE CLOUD SHINOBI!!
SSH
UNH!
TAK

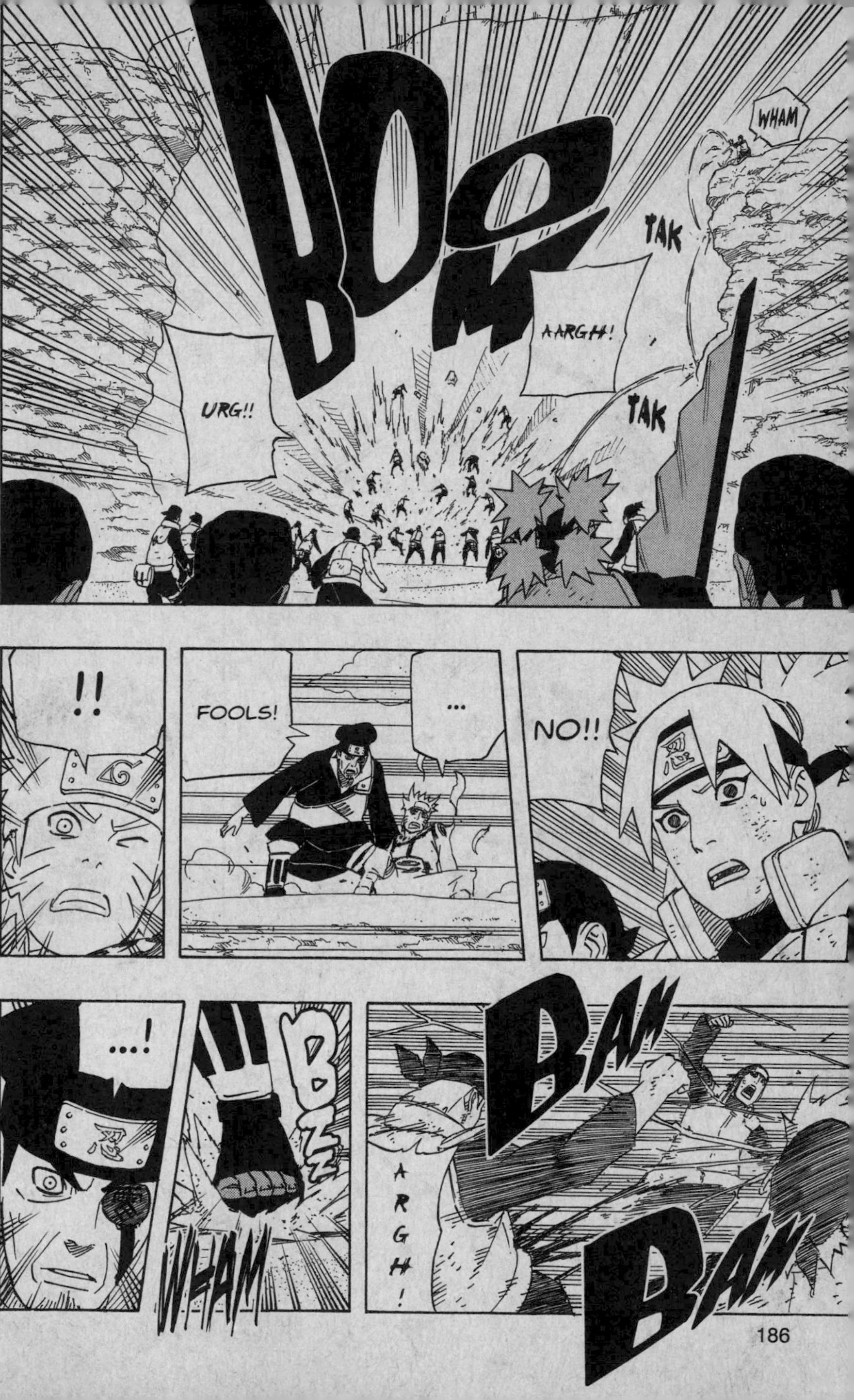
WHAM
TAK
AARGH!
BOOM
TAK
URG!!
NO!!
...
FOOLS!
!!
BAM
BAM
ARGH!
BONK
WHAM
...!

READ THIS WAY

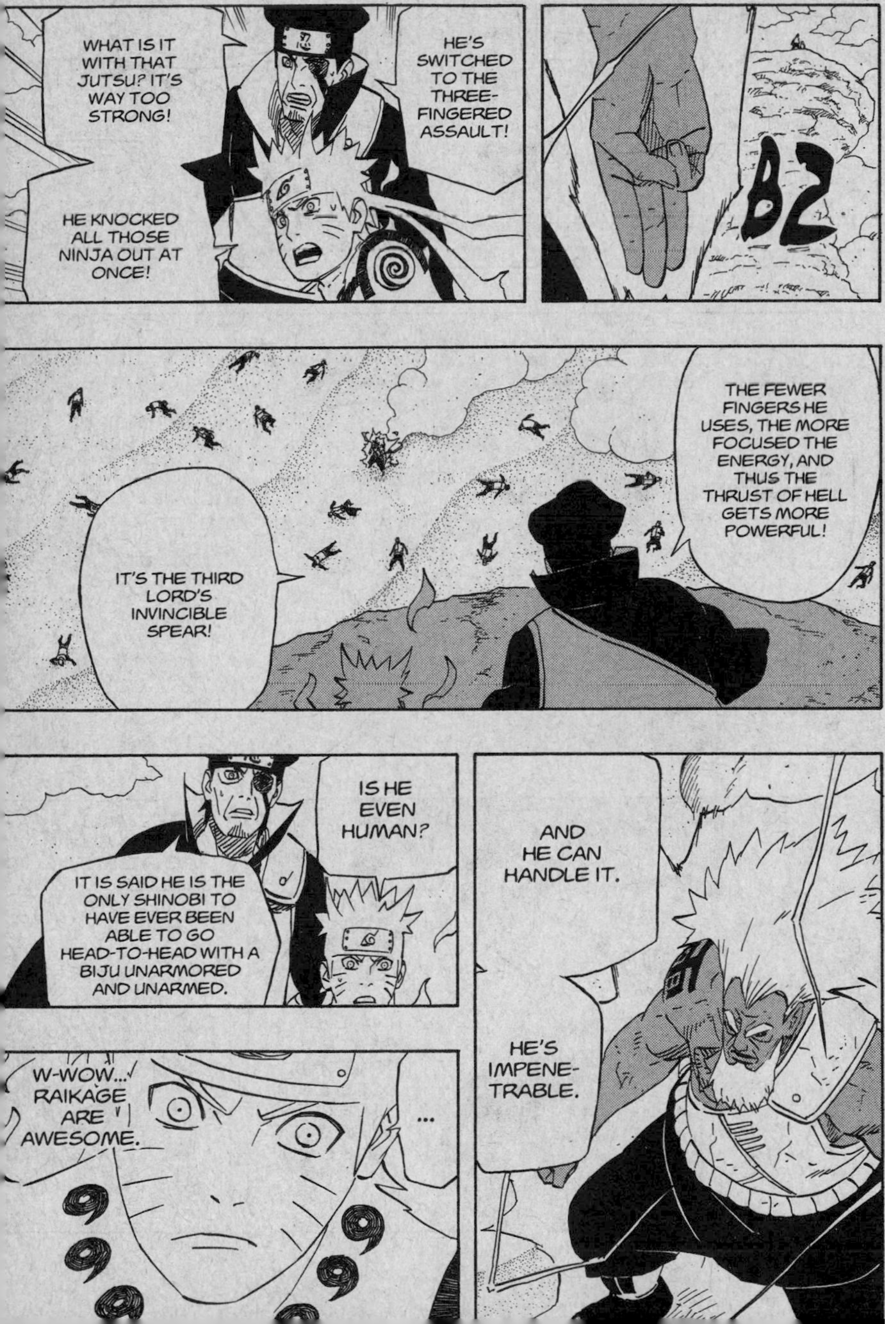
B2
HE'S SWITCHED TO THE THREE-FINGERED ASSAULT!
WHAT IS IT WITH THAT JUTSU? IT'S WAY TOO STRONG!
HE KNOCKED ALL THOSE NINJA OUT AT ONCE!
THE FEWER FINGERS HE USES, THE MORE FOCUSED THE ENERGY, AND THUS THE THRUST OF HELL GETS MORE POWERFUL!
IT'S THE THIRD LORD'S INVINCIBLE SPEAR!
AND HE CAN HANDLE IT.
HE'S IMPENE-TRABLE.
IS HE EVEN HUMAN?
IT IS SAID HE IS THE ONLY SHINOBI TO HAVE EVER BEEN ABLE TO GO HEAD-TO-HEAD WITH A BIJU UNARMORED AND UNARMED.
...
W-WOW... RAIKAGE ARE AWESOME.

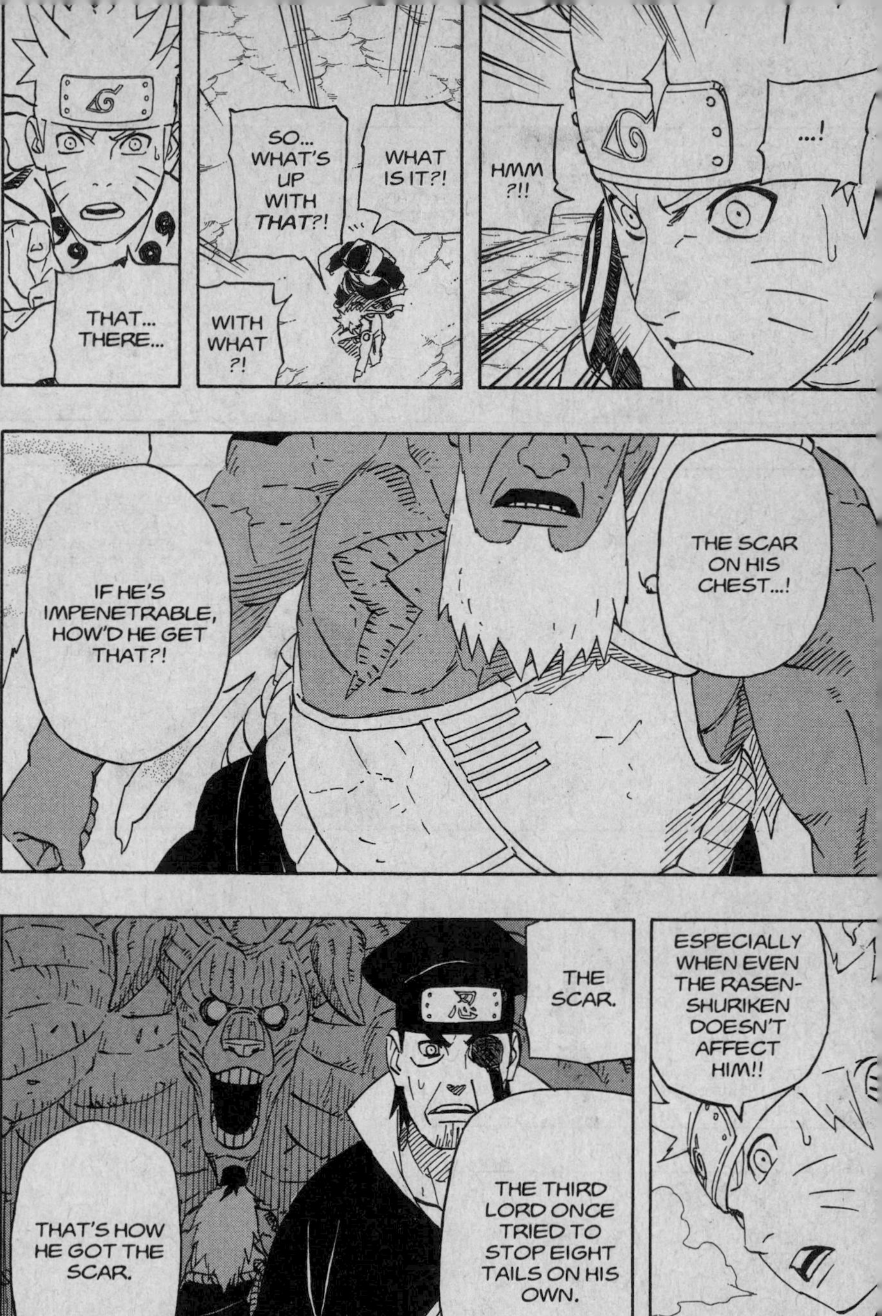
...!
HMM ?!!
WHAT IS IT?!
SO... WHAT'S UP WITH THAT?!
WITH WHAT ?!
THAT... THERE...
THE SCAR ON HIS CHEST...!
IF HE'S IMPENETRABLE, HOW'D HE GET THAT?!
ESPECIALLY WHEN EVEN THE RASEN-SHURIKEN DOESN'T AFFECT HIM!!
THE SCAR.
THE THIRD LORD ONCE TRIED TO STOP EIGHT TAILS ON HIS OWN.
THAT'S HOW HE GOT THE SCAR.

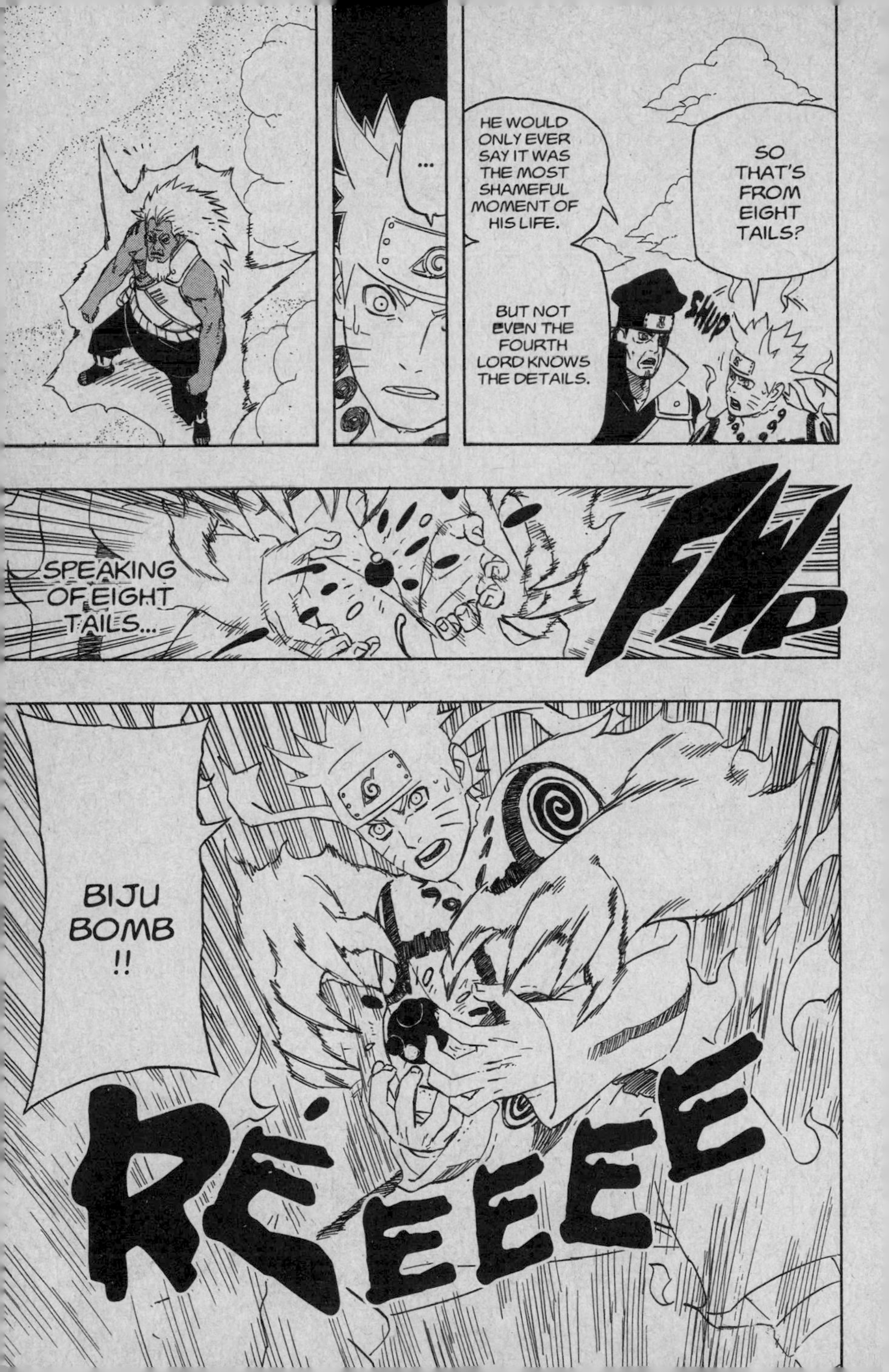
SO THAT'S FROM EIGHT TAILS?
HE WOULD ONLY EVER SAY IT WAS THE MOST SHAMEFUL MOMENT OF HIS LIFE.
SHUP
BUT NOT EVEN THE FOURTH LORD KNOWS THE DETAILS.
...
FWP
SPEAKING OF EIGHT TAILS...
BIJU BOMB !!
REEEEE

NARUTO

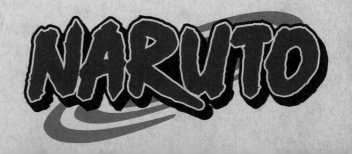

Number 555: Paradox

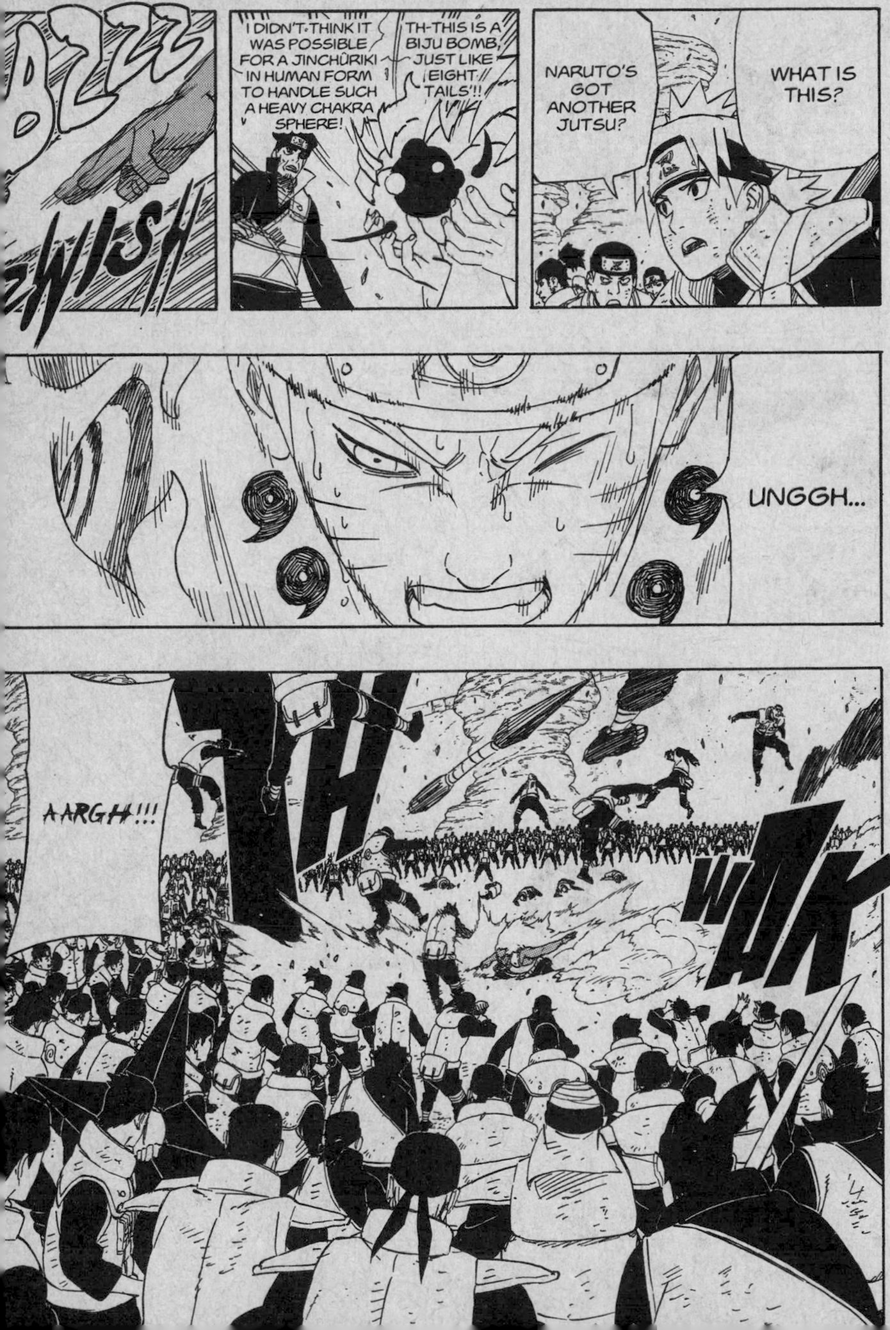

WHAT IS THIS?
NARUTO'S GOT ANOTHER JUTSU?
TH-THIS IS A BIJU BOMB, JUST LIKE EIGHT TAILS'!!
I DIDN'T THINK IT WAS POSSIBLE FOR A JINCHŪRIKI IN HUMAN FORM TO HANDLE SUCH A HEAVY CHAKRA SPHERE!
BZZZZ
ZWISH
UNGGH...
WHAK
TH
AARGH!!!

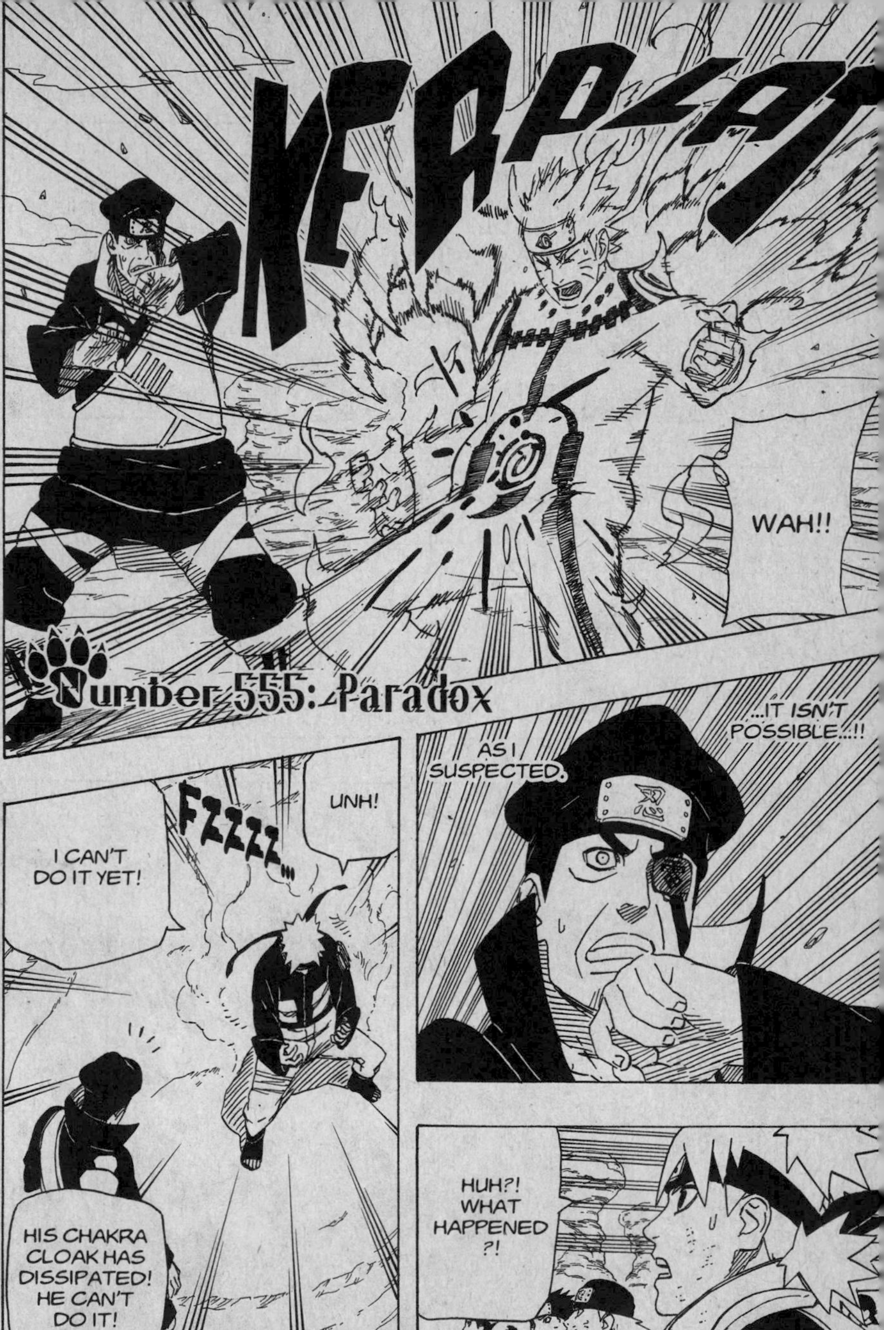
WAH!!
Number 555: Paradox
...IT ISN'T POSSIBLE...!!
AS I SUSPECTED.
HUH?! WHAT HAPPENED ?!
UNH!
FZZZZ...
I CAN'T DO IT YET!
HIS CHAKRA CLOAK HAS DISSIPATED! HE CAN'T DO IT!

READ THIS WAY

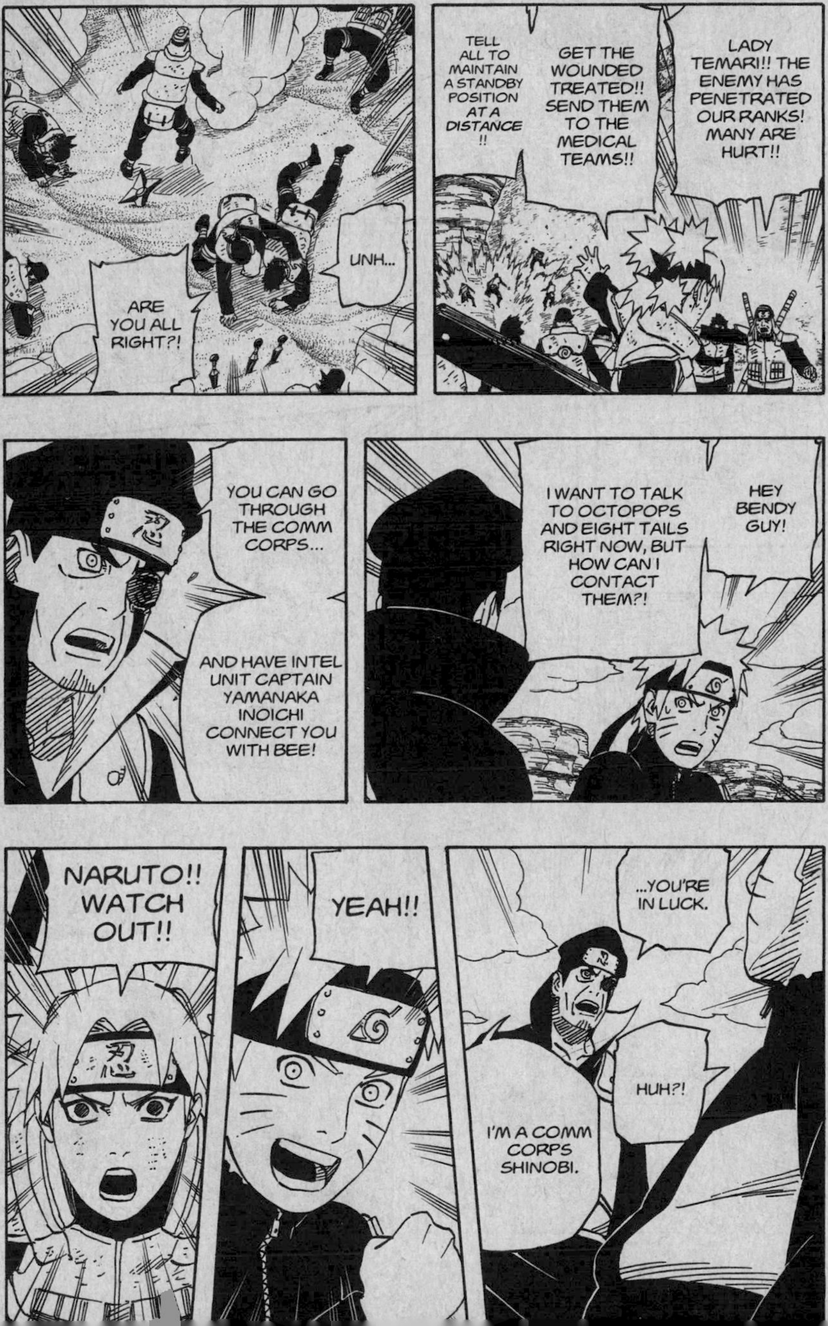
LADY TEMARI!! THE ENEMY HAS PENETRATED OUR RANKS! MANY ARE HURT!!
GET THE WOUNDED TREATED!! SEND THEM TO THE MEDICAL TEAMS!!
TELL ALL TO MAINTAIN A STANDBY POSITION AT A DISTANCE!!
UNH...
ARE YOU ALL RIGHT?!
HEY BENDY GUY!
I WANT TO TALK TO OCTOPOPS AND EIGHT TAILS RIGHT NOW, BUT HOW CAN I CONTACT THEM?!
YOU CAN GO THROUGH THE COMM CORPS...
AND HAVE INTEL UNIT CAPTAIN YAMANAKA INOICHI CONNECT YOU WITH BEE!
...YOU'RE IN LUCK.
HUH?!
I'M A COMM CORPS SHINOBI.
YEAH!!
NARUTO!! WATCH OUT!!

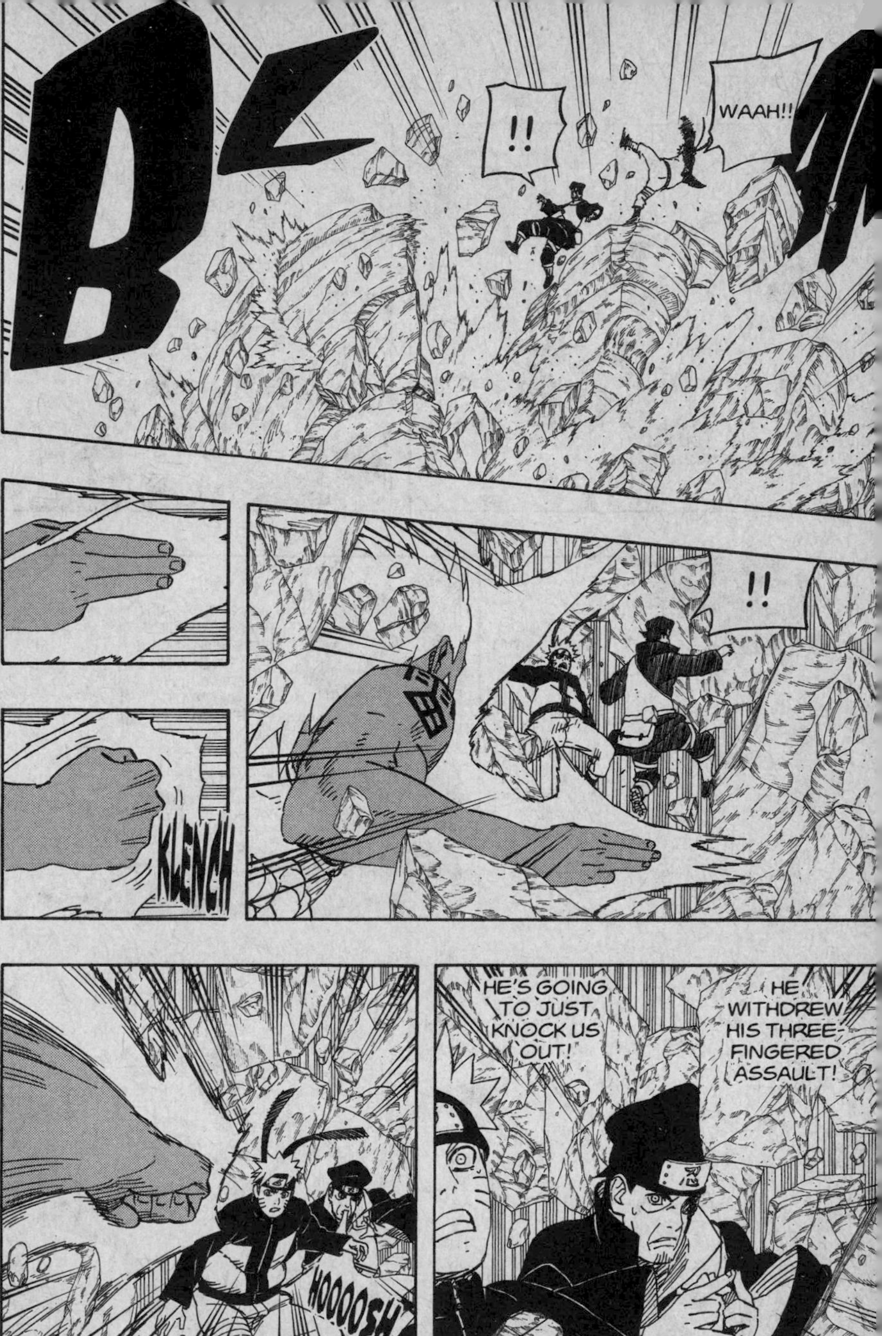
WAAH!!
!!
!!
KLENCH
HE WITHDREW HIS THREE-FINGERED ASSAULT!
HE'S GOING TO JUST KNOCK US OUT!
HOOOOSH

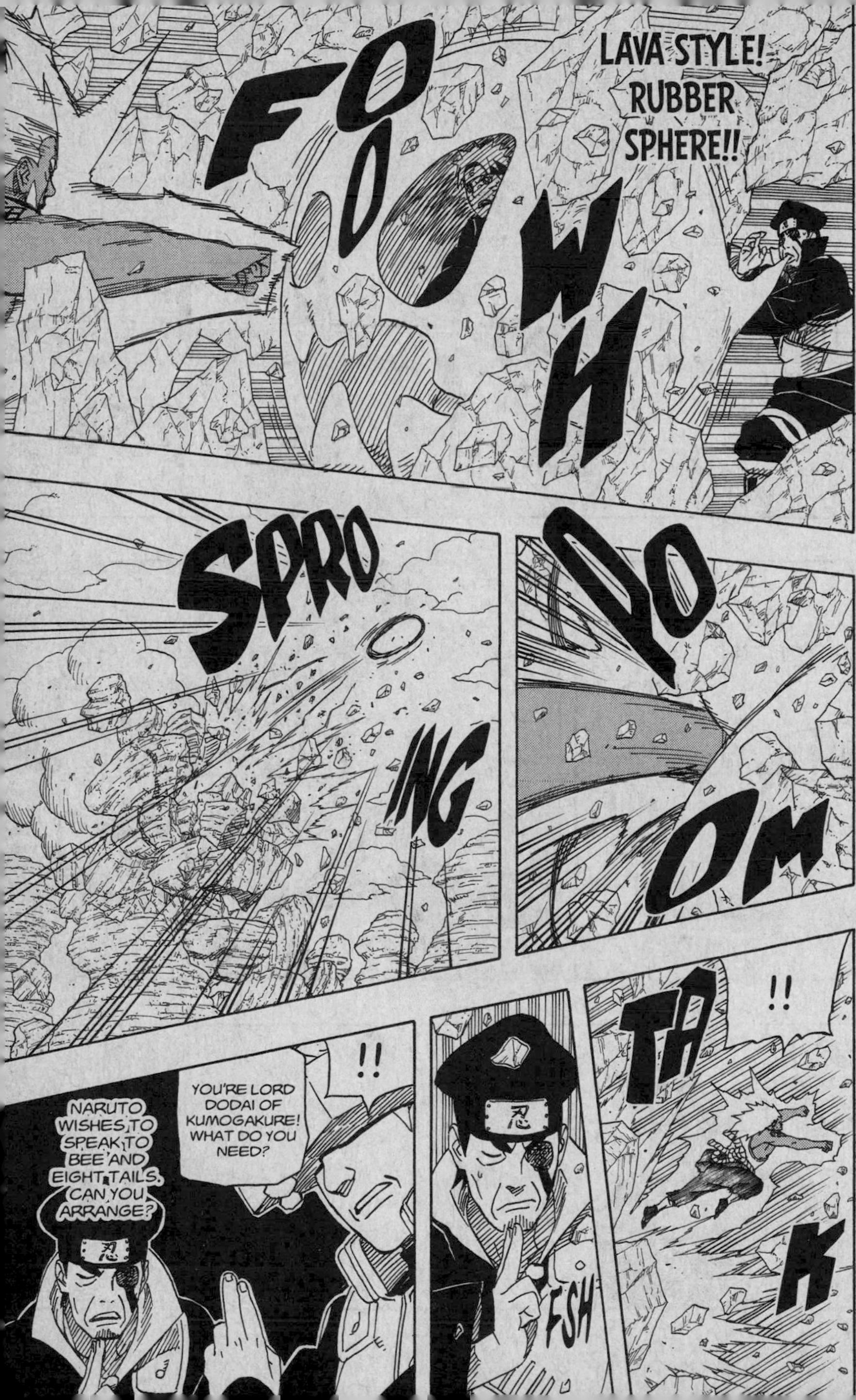
LAVA STYLE! RUBBER SPHERE!!
FOOWHH
DOOM
SPROING
!!
THK
!!
YOU'RE LORD DODAI OF KUMOGAKURE! WHAT DO YOU NEED?
FSH
NARUTO WISHES TO SPEAK TO BEE AND EIGHT TAILS. CAN YOU ARRANGE?

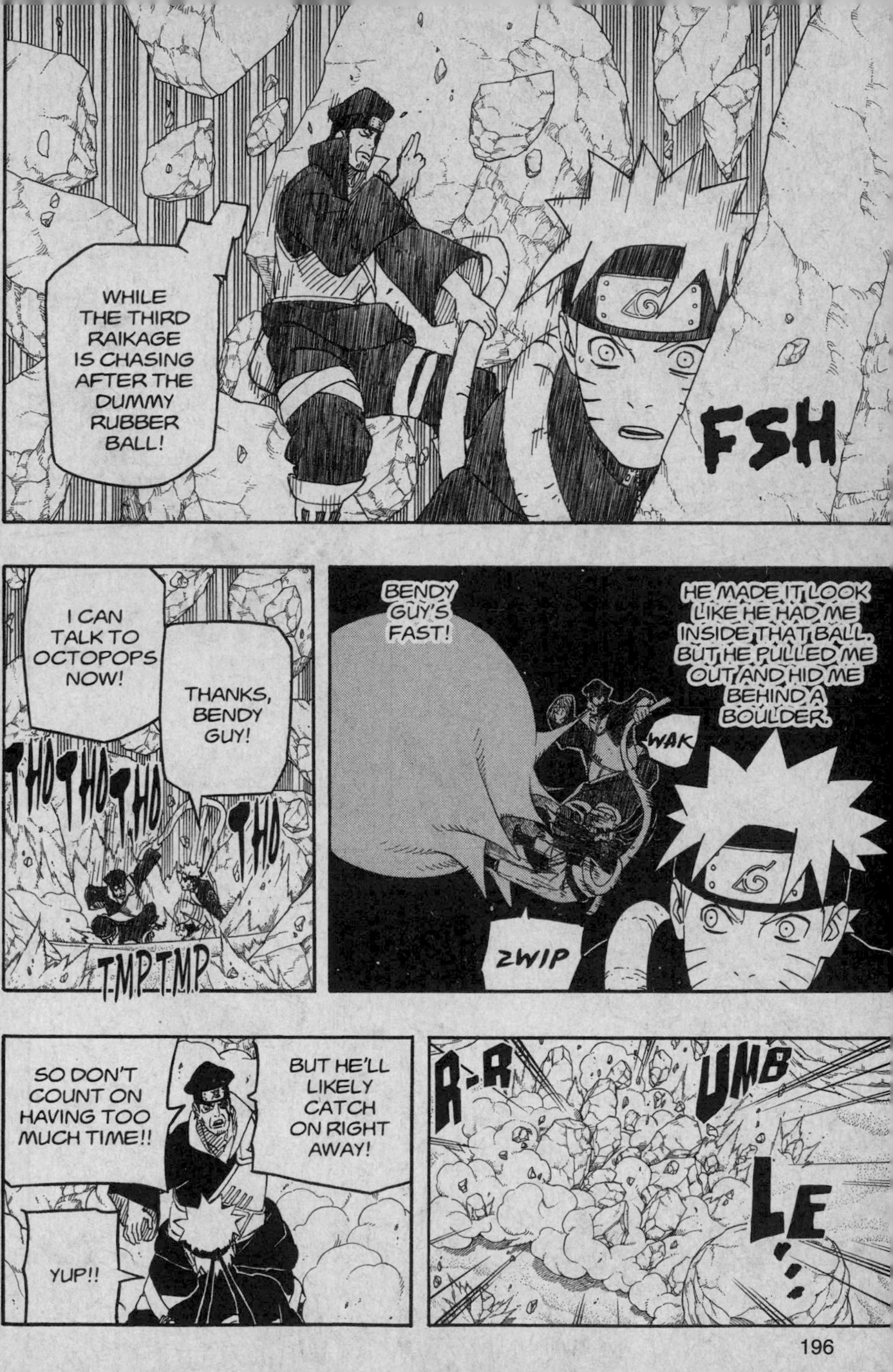
WHILE THE THIRD RAIKAGE IS CHASING AFTER THE DUMMY RUBBER BALL!
FSH
HE MADE IT LOOK LIKE HE HAD ME INSIDE THAT BALL, BUT HE PULLED ME OUT AND HID ME BEHIND A BOULDER.
BENDY GUY'S FAST!
WAK
ZWIP
THANKS, BENDY GUY!
I CAN TALK TO OCTOPOPS NOW!
THO THO THO THO
T.M.P T.M.P
R-RUMBLE
BUT HE'LL LIKELY CATCH ON RIGHT AWAY!
SO DON'T COUNT ON HAVING TOO MUCH TIME!!
YUP!!

READ THIS WAY

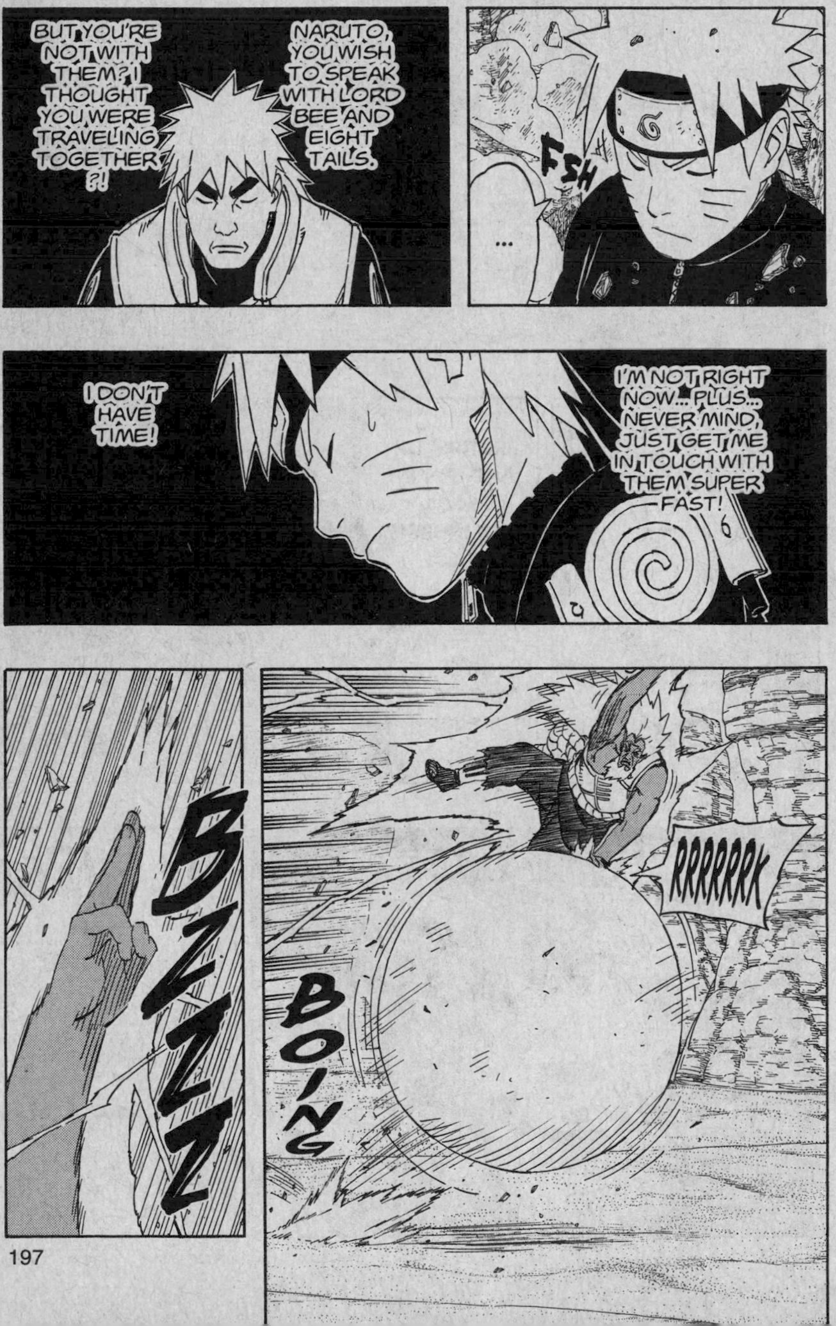
FSH
...
NARUTO, YOU WISH TO SPEAK WITH LORD BEE AND EIGHT TAILS.
BUT YOU'RE NOT WITH THEM?! I THOUGHT YOU WERE TRAVELING TOGETHER?!
I'M NOT RIGHT NOW... PLUS... NEVER MIND, JUST GET ME IN TOUCH WITH THEM SUPER FAST!
I DON'T HAVE TIME!
RRRRRK
BOING
BZZZZ

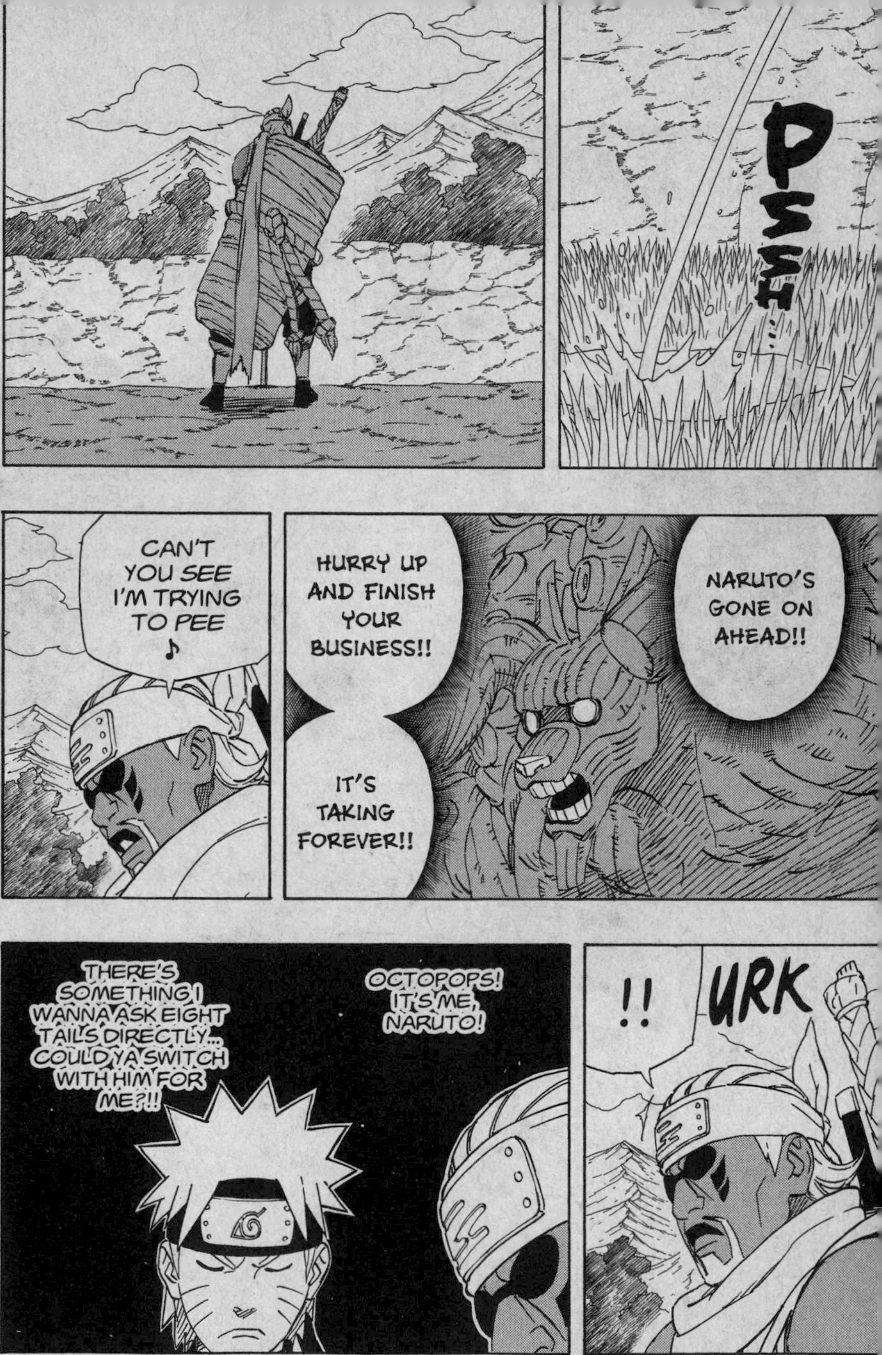
PSSH...
NARUTO'S GONE ON AHEAD!!
HURRY UP AND FINISH YOUR BUSINESS!!
IT'S TAKING FOREVER!!
CAN'T YOU SEE I'M TRYING TO PEE ♪
URK
!!
OCTOPOPS! IT'S ME, NARUTO!
THERE'S SOMETHING I WANNA ASK EIGHT TAILS DIRECTLY... COULD YA SWITCH WITH HIM FOR ME?!!

READ THIS WAY

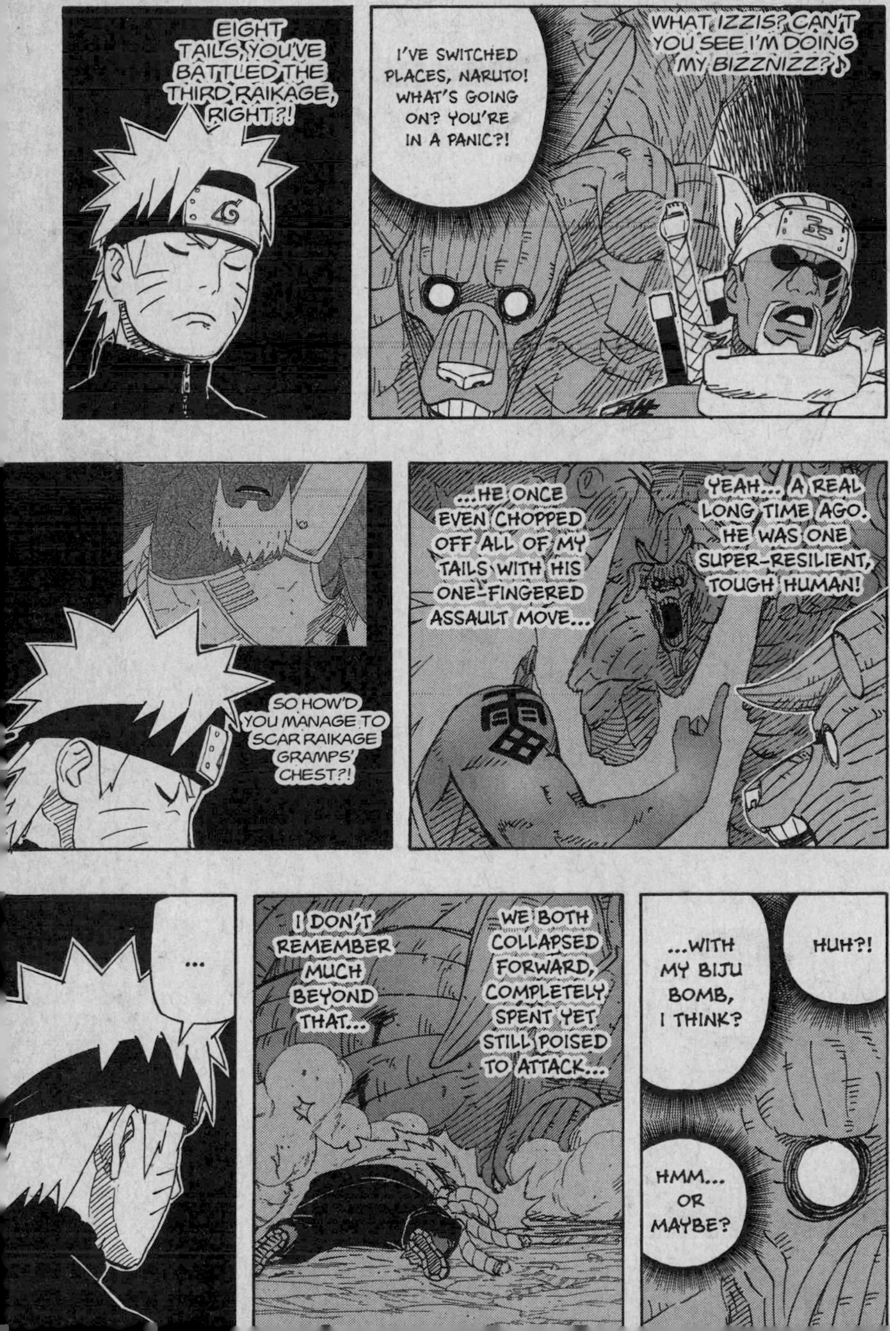
WHAT IZZIS? CAN'T YOU SEE I'M DOING MY BIZZNIZZ? ♪
I'VE SWITCHED PLACES, NARUTO! WHAT'S GOING ON? YOU'RE IN A PANIC?!
EIGHT TAILS, YOU'VE BATTLED THE THIRD RAIKAGE, RIGHT?!
YEAH... A REAL LONG TIME AGO. HE WAS ONE SUPER-RESILIENT, TOUGH HUMAN!
...HE ONCE EVEN CHOPPED OFF ALL OF MY TAILS WITH HIS ONE-FINGERED ASSAULT MOVE...
SO HOW'D YOU MANAGE TO SCAR RAIKAGE GRAMPS' CHEST?!
HUH?!
...WITH MY BIJU BOMB, I THINK?
HMM... OR MAYBE?
WE BOTH COLLAPSED FORWARD, COMPLETELY SPENT YET STILL POISED TO ATTACK...
I DON'T REMEMBER MUCH BEYOND THAT...
...

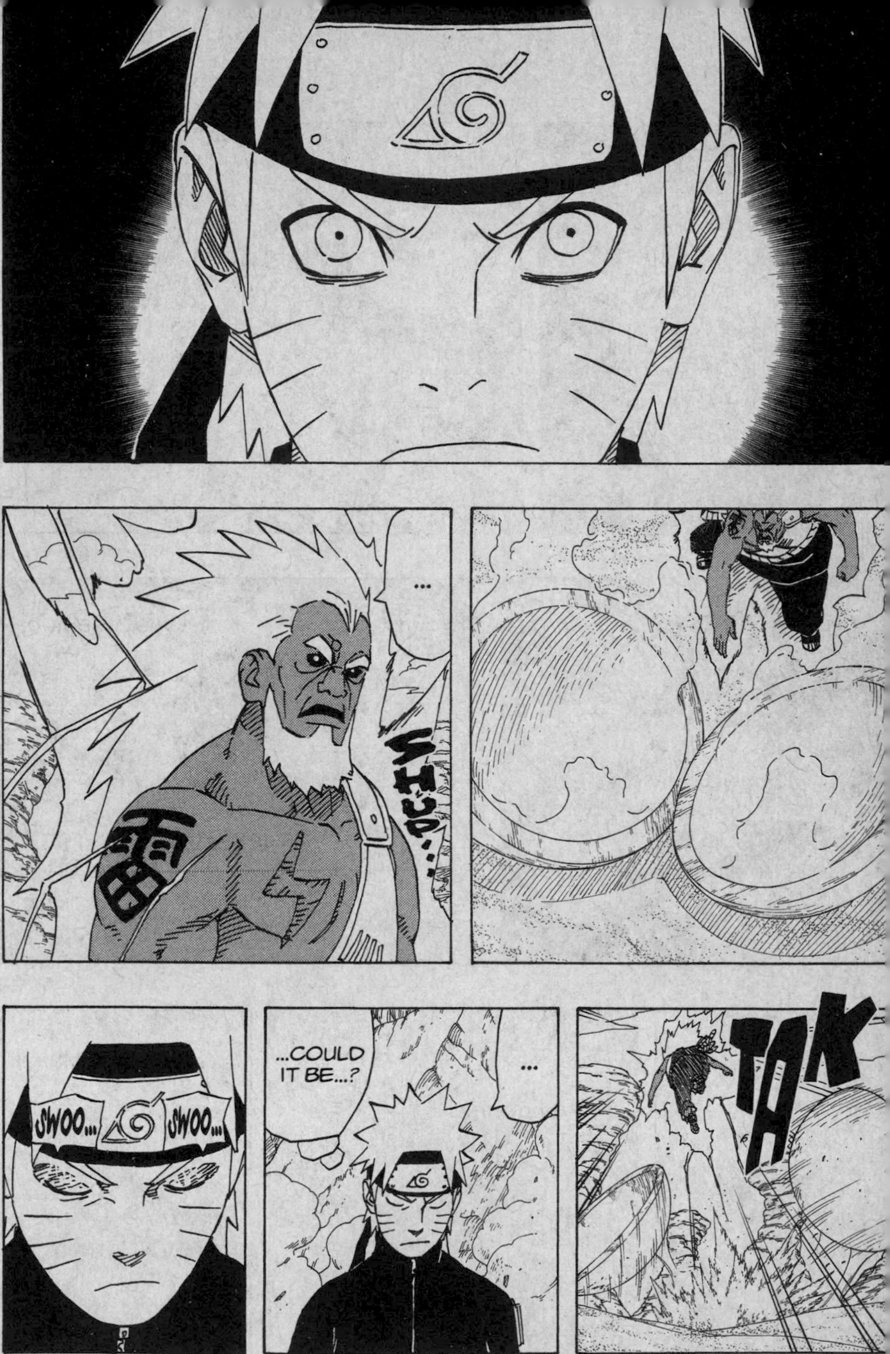
...
SHUP...
TAK
TA
...
...COULD IT BE...?
SWOO... SWOO...

READ THIS WAY

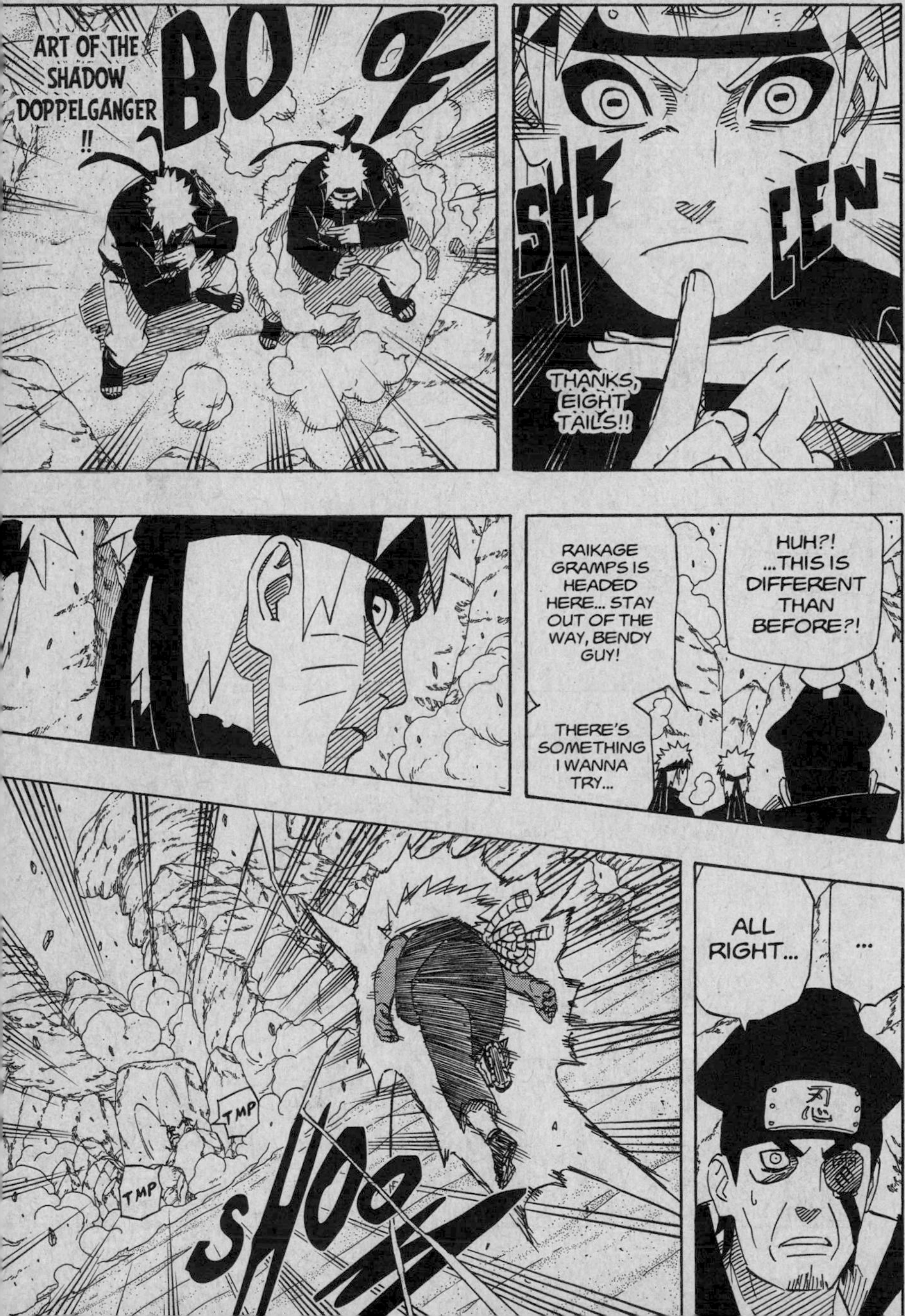
SHK
EEN
THANKS, EIGHT TAILS!!
ART OF THE SHADOW DOPPELGANGER!!
BOOF
HUH?! ...THIS IS DIFFERENT THAN BEFORE?!
RAIKAGE GRAMPS IS HEADED HERE... STAY OUT OF THE WAY, BENDY GUY!
THERE'S SOMETHING I WANNA TRY...
...
ALL RIGHT...
TMP
TMP
SHOO

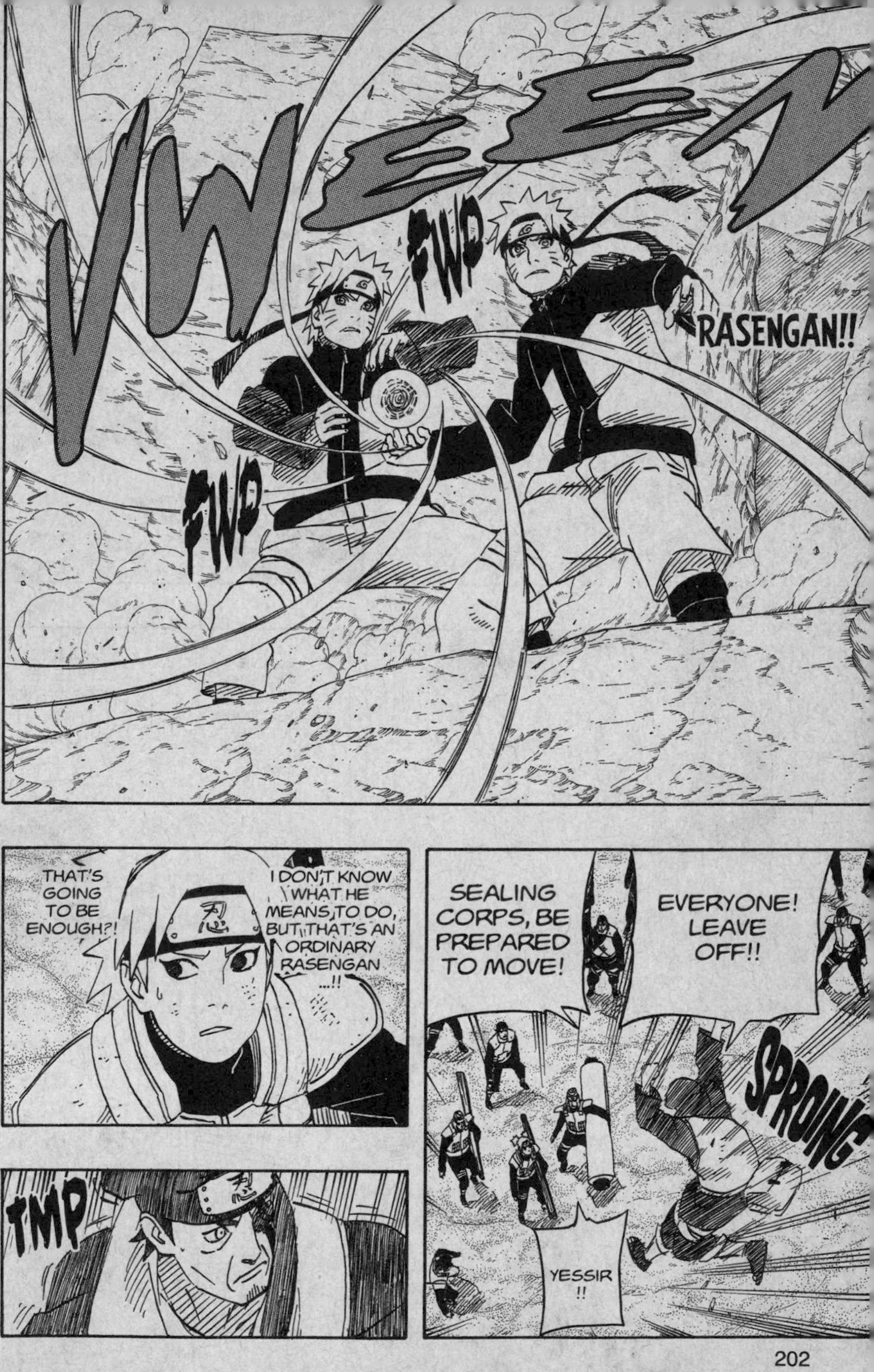

VWEEEN
RASENGAN!!
FWP
FWP
EVERYONE! LEAVE OFF!!
SEALING CORPS, BE PREPARED TO MOVE!
SPROING
YESSIR !!
I DON'T KNOW WHAT HE MEANS TO DO, BUT THAT'S AN ORDINARY RASENGAN ...!!
THAT'S GOING TO BE ENOUGH?!
TMP

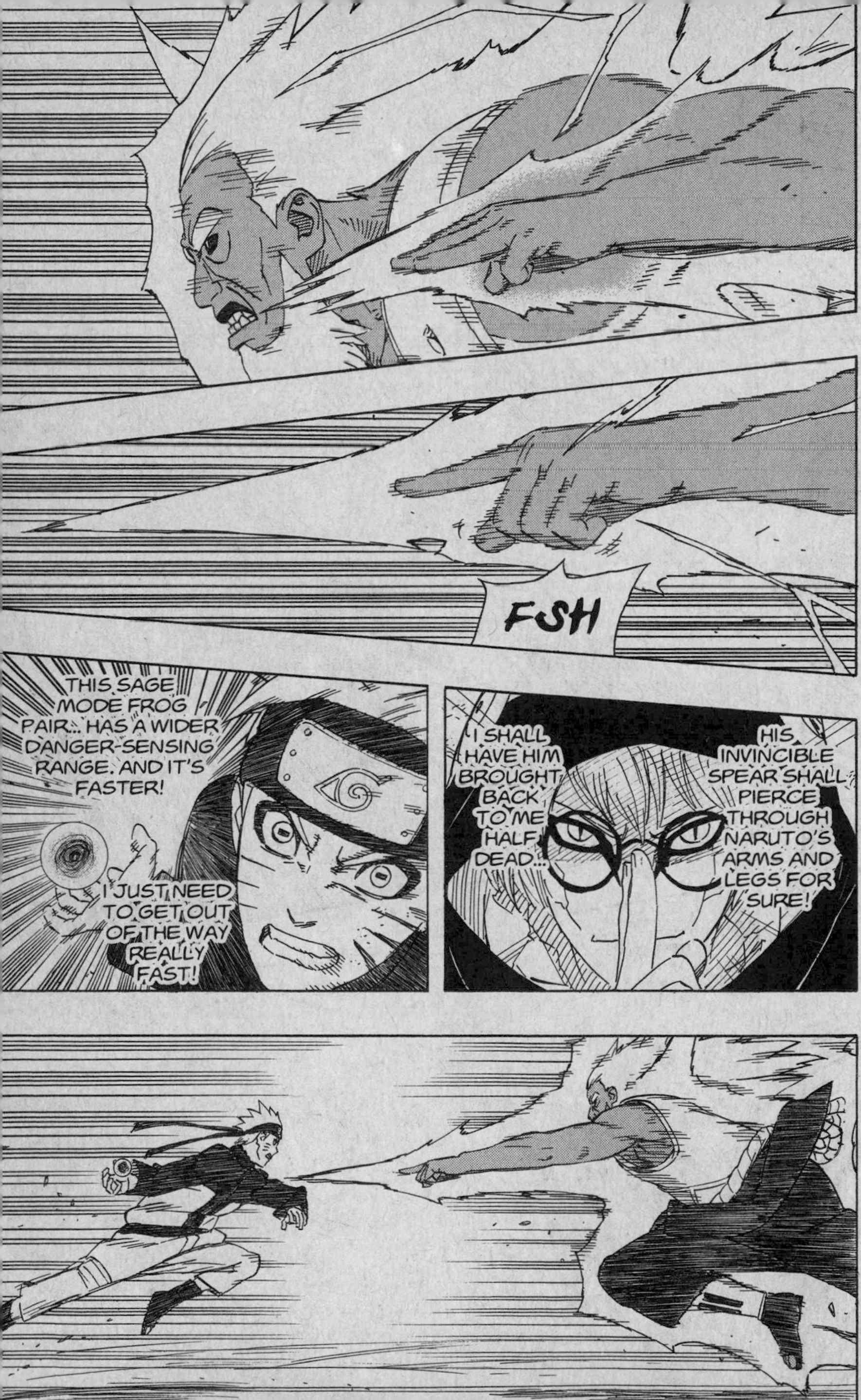
FSH
HIS INVINCIBLE SPEAR SHALL PIERCE THROUGH NARUTO'S ARMS AND LEGS FOR SURE!
I SHALL HAVE HIM BROUGHT BACK TO ME HALF DEAD...
THIS SAGE MODE FROG PAIR... HAS A WIDER DANGER-SENSING RANGE. AND IT'S FASTER!
I JUST NEED TO GET OUT OF THE WAY REALLY FAST!

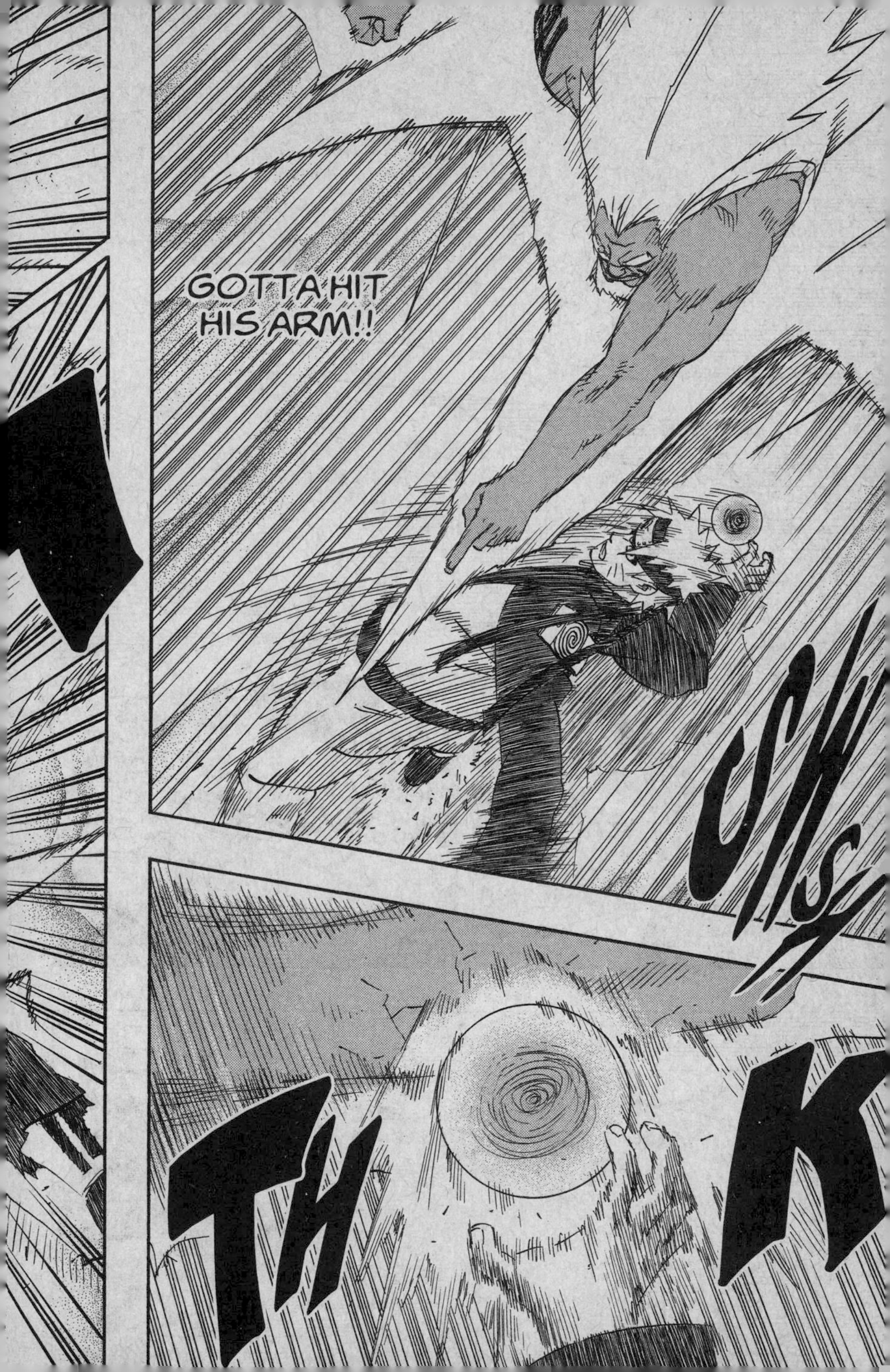
GOTTA HIT HIS ARM!!

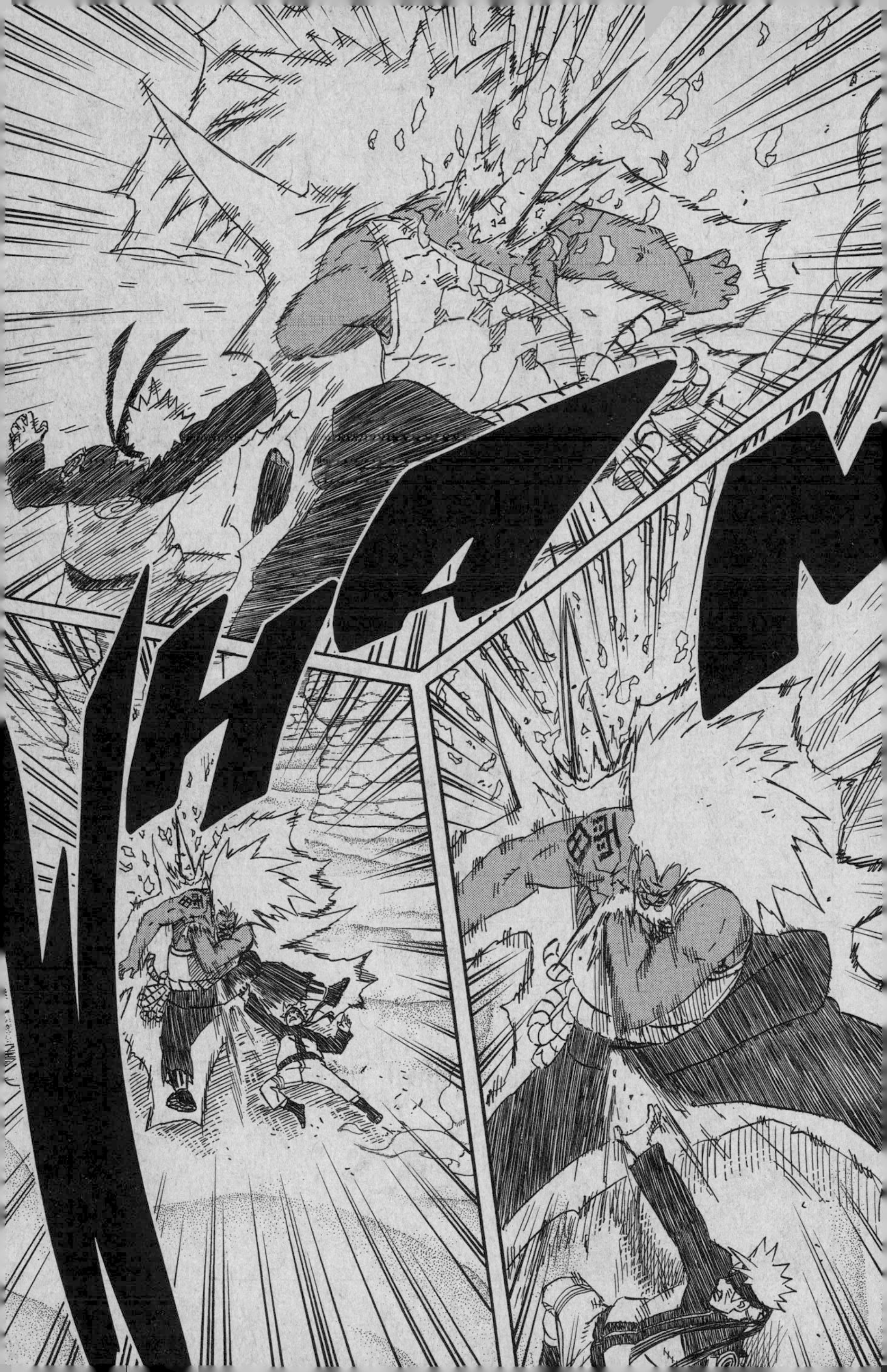
WHAM

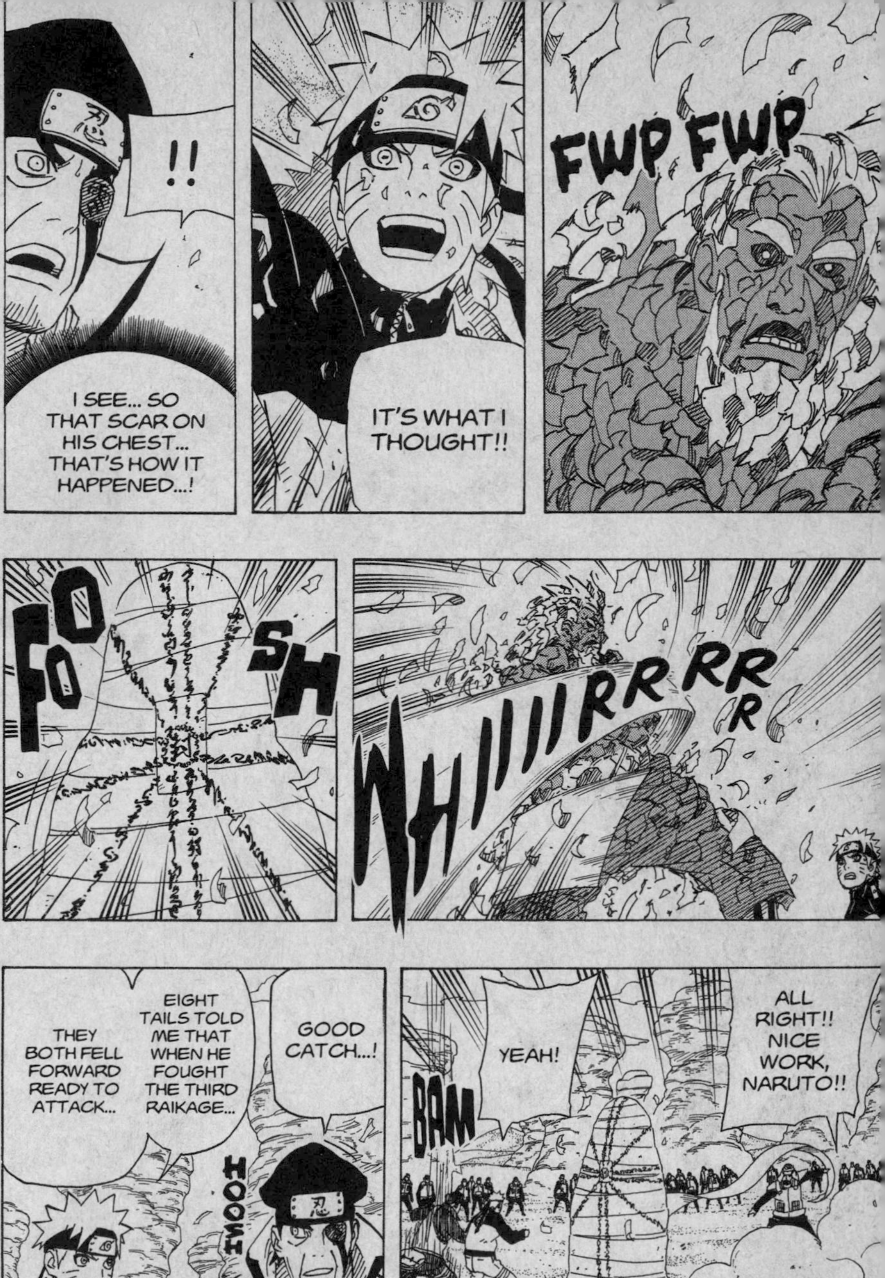
FWP FWP
IT'S WHAT I THOUGHT!!
!!
I SEE... SO THAT SCAR ON HIS CHEST... THAT'S HOW IT HAPPENED...!
WHIIIIIRRRRR
FOOSH
ALL RIGHT!! NICE WORK, NARUTO!!
YEAH!
BAM
GOOD CATCH...!
EIGHT TAILS TOLD ME THAT WHEN HE FOUGHT THE THIRD RAIKAGE...
THEY BOTH FELL FORWARD READY TO ATTACK...
HOOSH

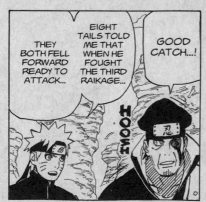

READ THIS WAY

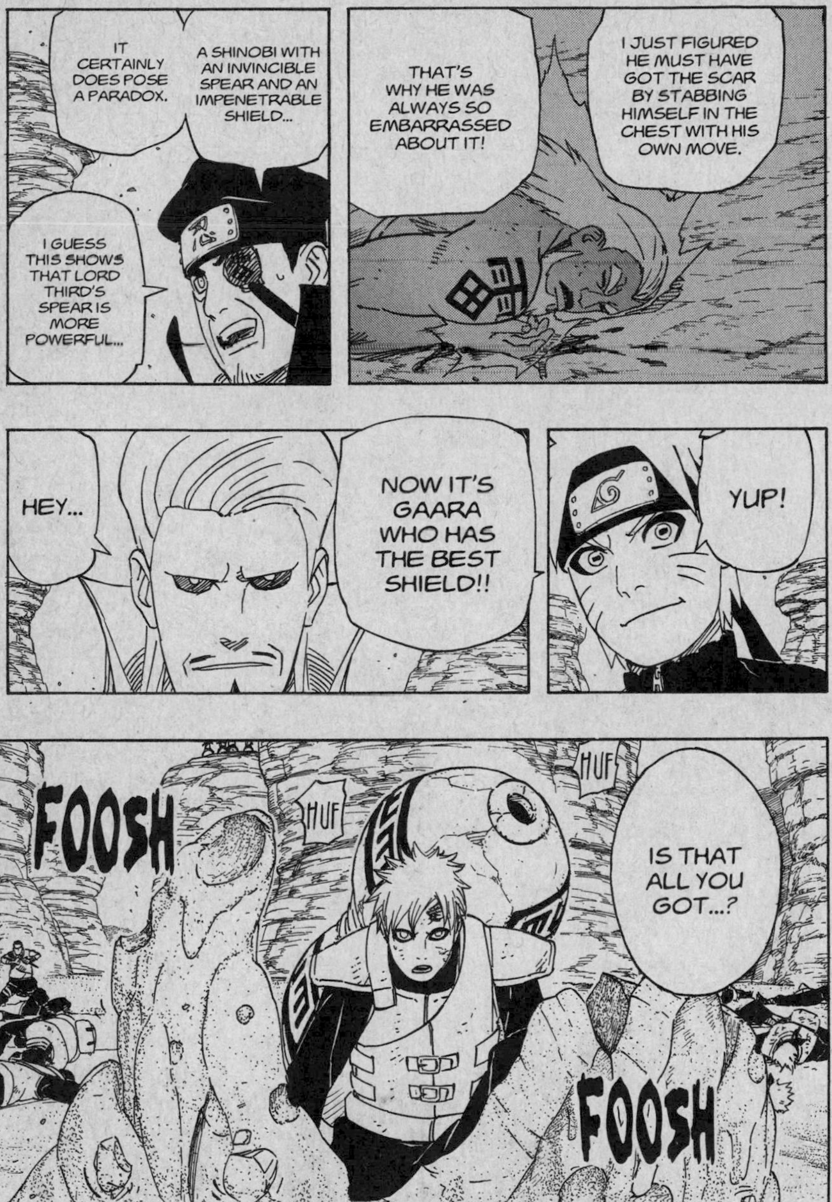

I JUST FIGURED HE MUST HAVE GOT THE SCAR BY STABBING HIMSELF IN THE CHEST WITH HIS OWN MOVE.
THAT'S WHY HE WAS ALWAYS SO EMBARRASSED ABOUT IT!
A SHINOBI WITH AN INVINCIBLE SPEAR AND AN IMPENETRABLE SHIELD...
IT CERTAINLY DOES POSE A PARADOX.
I GUESS THIS SHOWS THAT LORD THIRD'S SPEAR IS MORE POWERFUL...
YUP!
NOW IT'S GAARA WHO HAS THE BEST SHIELD!!
HEY...
HUF
IS THAT ALL YOU GOT...?
HUF
FOOSH
FOOSH

NARUTO

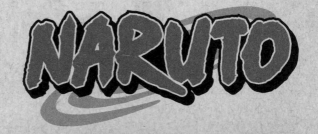

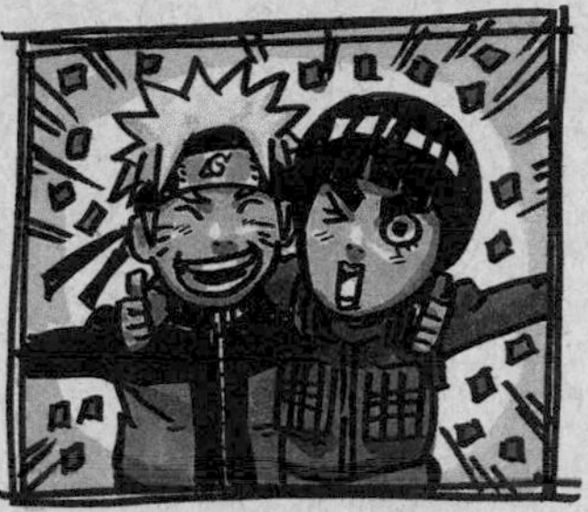

岸本斉史

Can you believe it?!
Rock Lee has become a main character!
Rock Lee & His Ninja Pals!!! (by Kenji Taira) is being simultaneously released with this volume*!! *Rock Lee* is fundamentally a youthful gag manga that revolves around Lee, but we're also aiming for a comedic touch and to dig further where all of you *Naruto* fans wished we'd gone before... A-ha ha!! In any case, congrats, Lee!!

—Masashi Kishimoto, 2012

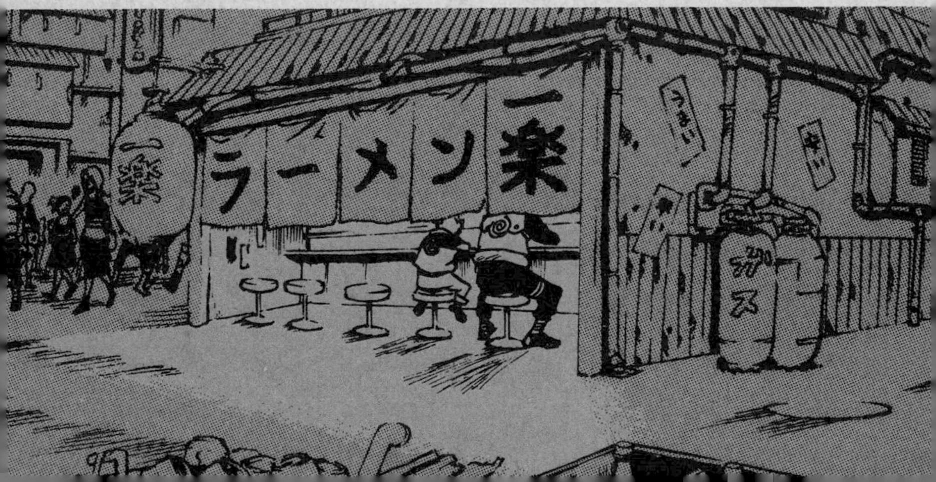
ラーメン一楽
一楽

NARUTO

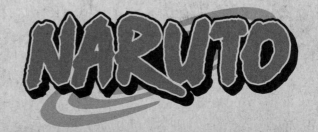

Sasuke サスケ

Naruto ナルト

Sakura サクラ

Kakashi カカシ

Yamato ヤマト

Sai サイ

Gaara 我愛羅

Tsunade 綱手

CHARACTERS

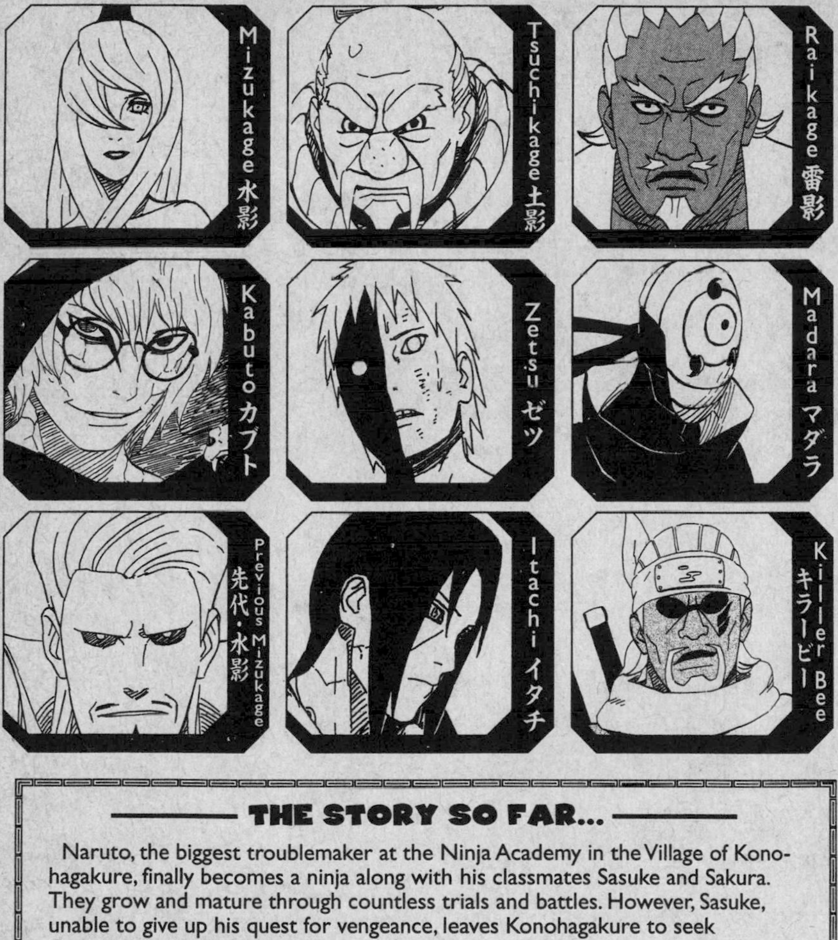
Raikage 雷影
Tsuchikage 土影
Mizukage 水影
Madara マダラ
Zetsu ゼツ
Kabuto カブト
Killer Bee キラービー
Itachi イタチ
Previous Mizukage 先代・水影

THE STORY SO FAR...

Naruto, the biggest troublemaker at the Ninja Academy in the Village of Konohagakure, finally becomes a ninja along with his classmates Sasuke and Sakura. They grow and mature through countless trials and battles. However, Sasuke, unable to give up his quest for vengeance, leaves Konohagakure to seek Orochimaru and his power.

Two years pass. Naruto grows up and engages in fierce battles against the Tailed Beast-targeting Akatsuki. Elsewhere, after winning the heroic battle against Itachi and learning his older brother's true intentions, Sasuke allies with the Akatsuki and sets out to destroy Konoha.

Upon Madara of the Akatsuki's declaration of war against the Ninja Alliance, the Five Kage put together an Allied Shinobi Force. The Fourth Great Ninja War against the Akatsuki begins. Upon breaking out of the training grounds and rushing forth to each battleground, Naruto helps his comrades successfully seal away the previous Raikage, who had been called up through Edotensei, a method of using dead ninja reanimated as soldiers. Now Gaara, leader of the Sand Village, and Ohnoki, leader of the Stone Village, battle the previous Mizukage, former leaders of the Mist Village!

NARUTO

VOL. 59
THE FIVE KAGE

CONTENTS

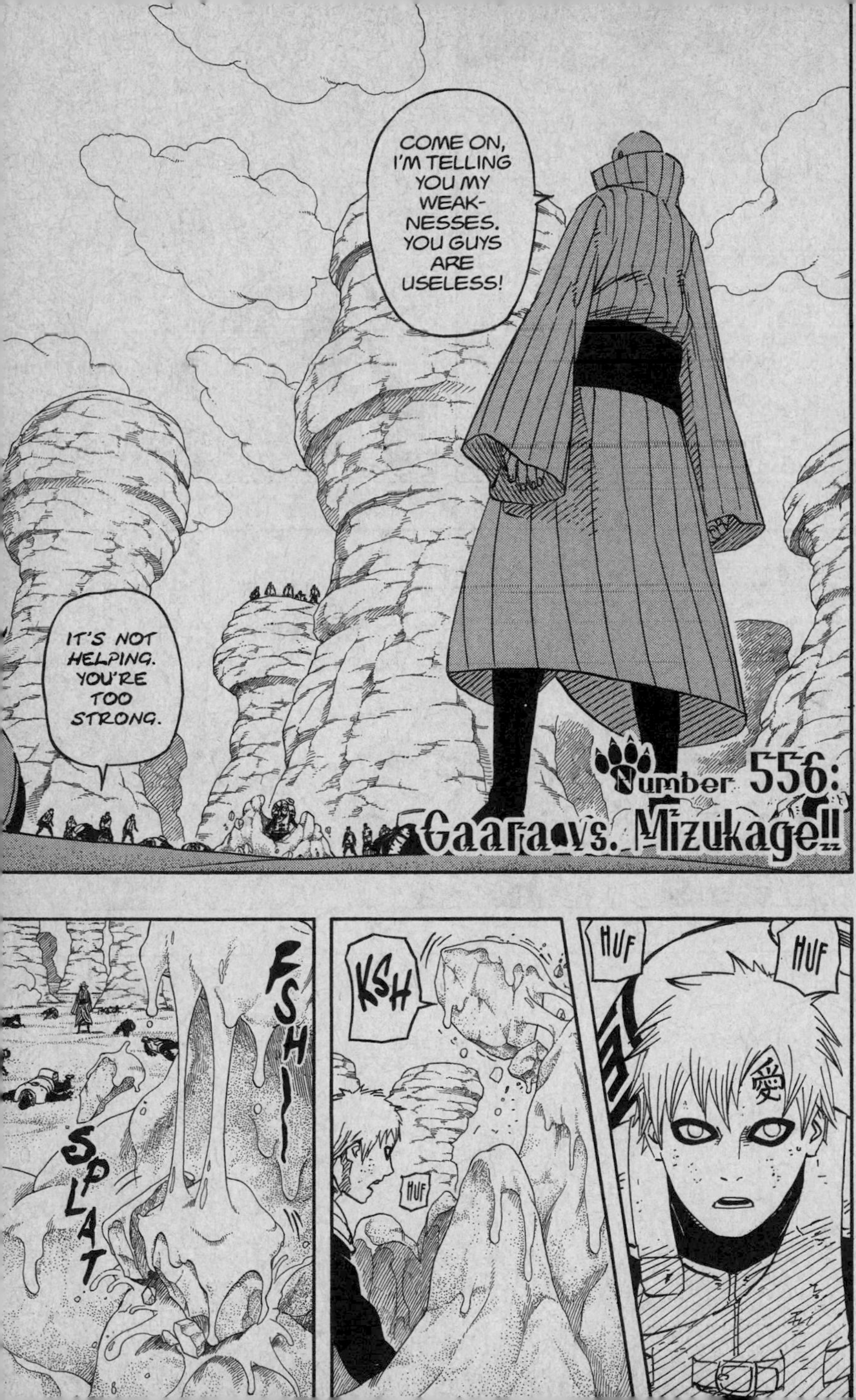
COME ON, I'M TELLING YOU MY WEAKNESSES. YOU GUYS ARE USELESS!
IT'S NOT HELPING. YOU'RE TOO STRONG.
Number 556: Gaara vs. Mizukage!!
HUF
HUF
KSH
HUF
FSH
SPLAT

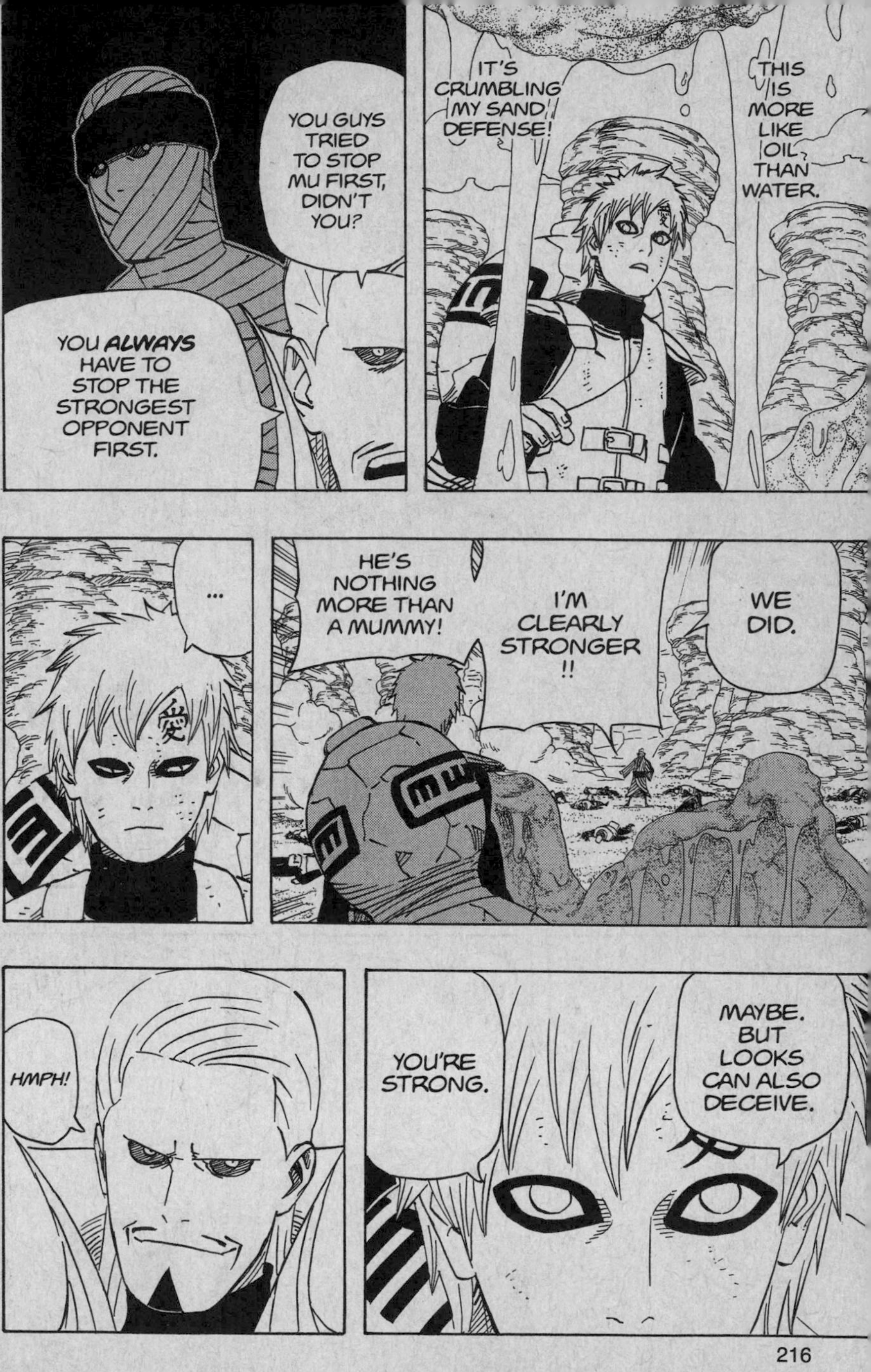
THIS IS MORE LIKE OIL THAN WATER.
IT'S CRUMBLING MY SAND DEFENSE!
YOU GUYS TRIED TO STOP MU FIRST, DIDN'T YOU?
YOU **ALWAYS** HAVE TO STOP THE STRONGEST OPPONENT FIRST.
WE DID.
I'M CLEARLY STRONGER !!
HE'S NOTHING MORE THAN A MUMMY!
...
MAYBE. BUT LOOKS CAN ALSO DECEIVE.
YOU'RE STRONG.
HMPH!

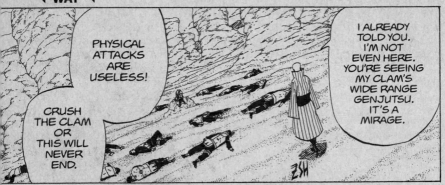

READ THIS WAY

I ALREADY TOLD YOU. I'M NOT EVEN HERE. YOU'RE SEEING MY CLAM'S WIDE RANGE GENJUTSU. IT'S A MIRAGE.
ZSH
PHYSICAL ATTACKS ARE USELESS!
CRUSH THE CLAM OR THIS WILL NEVER END.
!!
OH!!
AH, YES. YOU'RE USING THE SAND.
SHUP
I LIKE TO LET MY ACTIONS DO THE TALKING.
SHUP
SPLICH
SPLICH
SPLICH
SPLICH
SPLICH
SPLICH
SPLICH
SPLICH

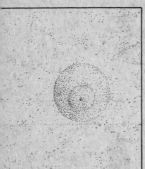

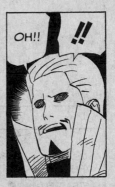

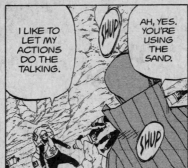

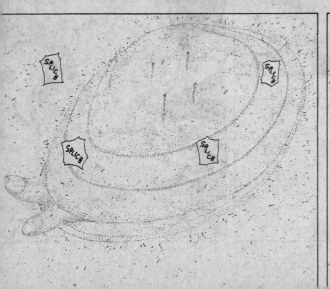

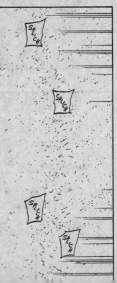

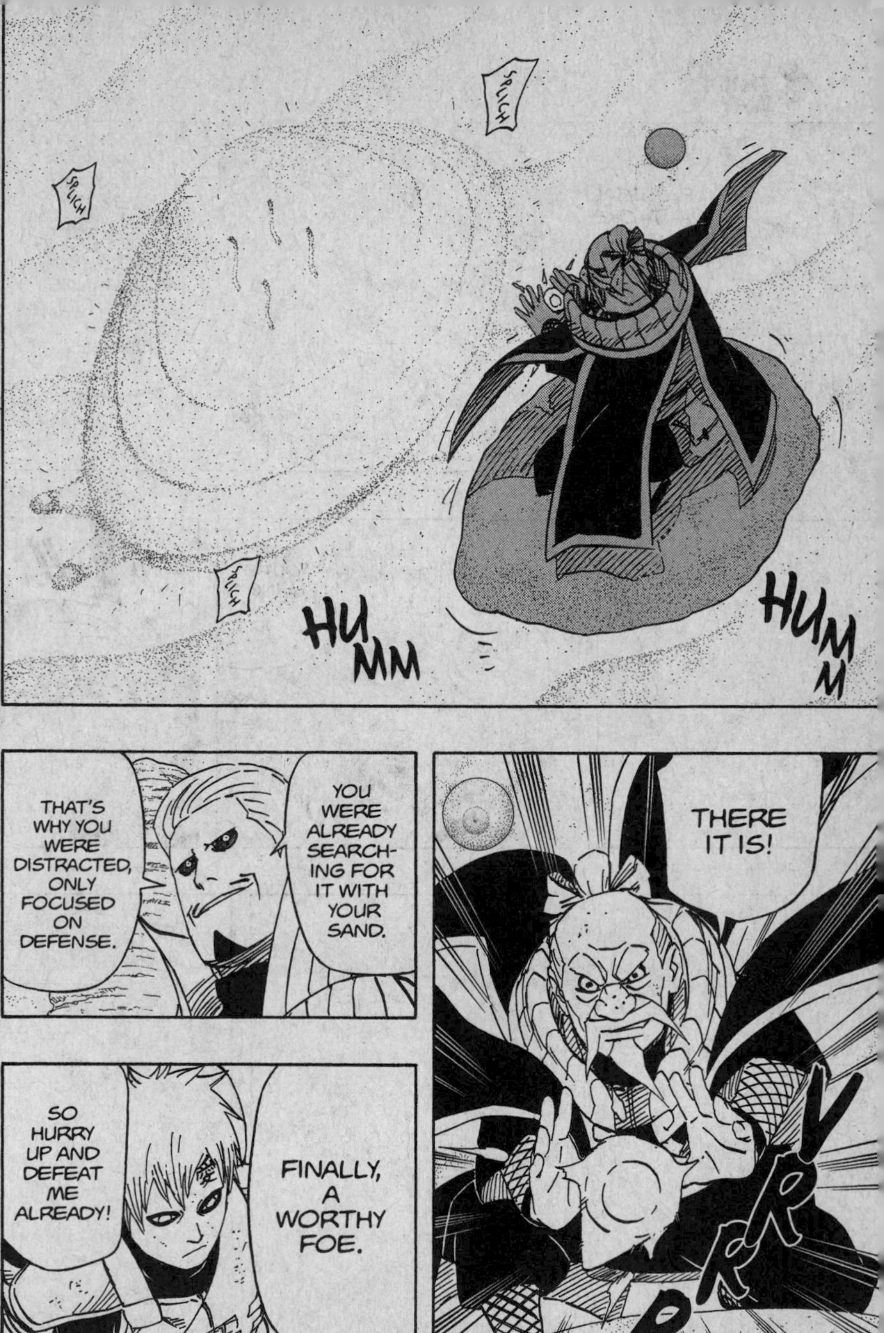
SPLICH
SPLICH
SPLICH
HUMMM
HUMM
THERE IT IS!
RRRRY
YOU WERE ALREADY SEARCHING FOR IT WITH YOUR SAND.
THAT'S WHY YOU WERE DISTRACTED, ONLY FOCUSED ON DEFENSE.
FINALLY, A WORTHY FOE.
SO HURRY UP AND DEFEAT ME ALREADY!

READ THIS WAY

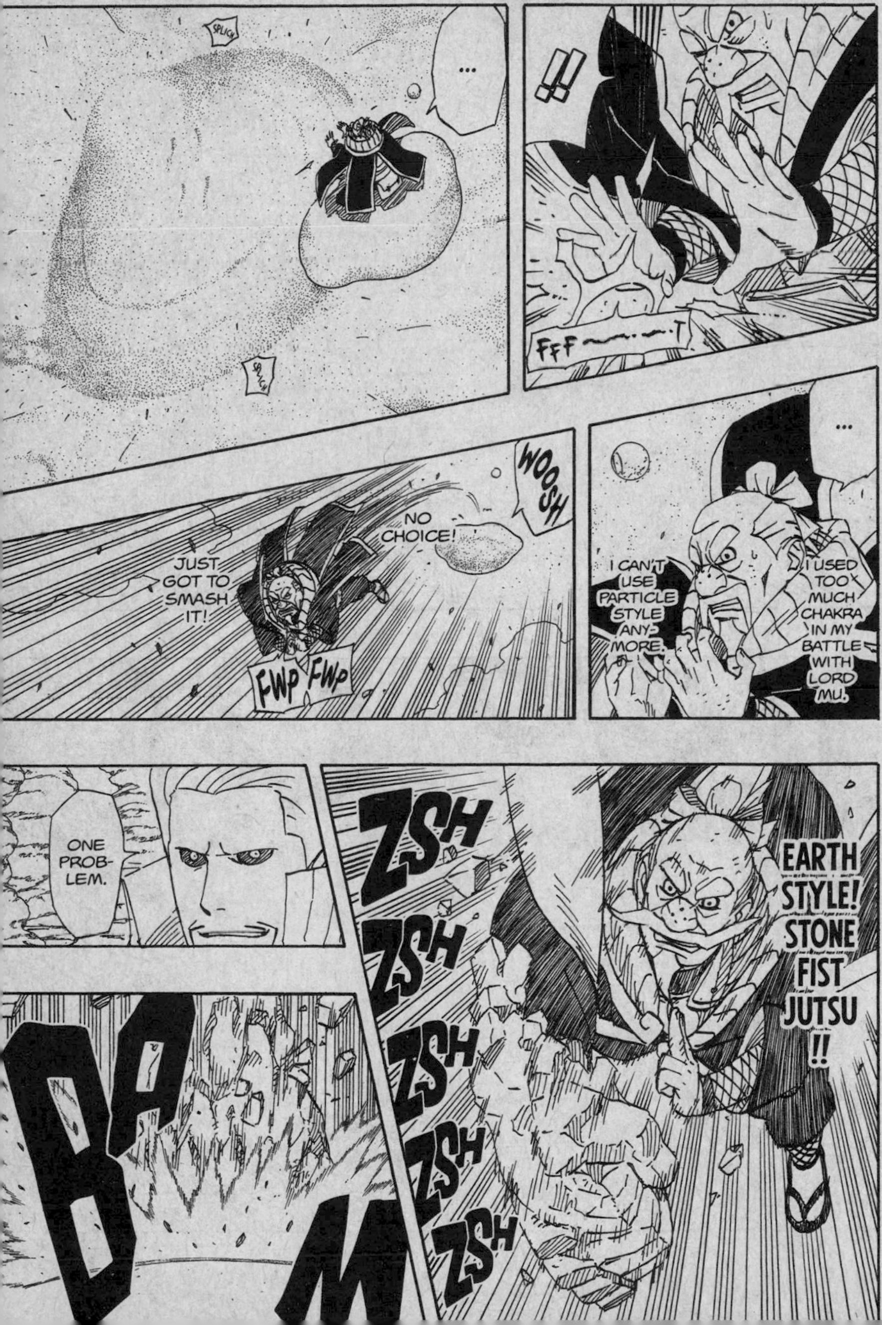
!!
FFF~~T
...
...
I USED TOO MUCH CHAKRA IN MY BATTLE WITH LORD MU.
I CAN'T USE PARTICLE STYLE ANYMORE.
WOOSH
NO CHOICE!
JUST GOT TO SMASH IT!
FWP FWP
ZSH ZSH ZSH ZSH ZSH ZSH
EARTH STYLE! STONE FIST JUTSU!!
ONE PROBLEM.
BAM

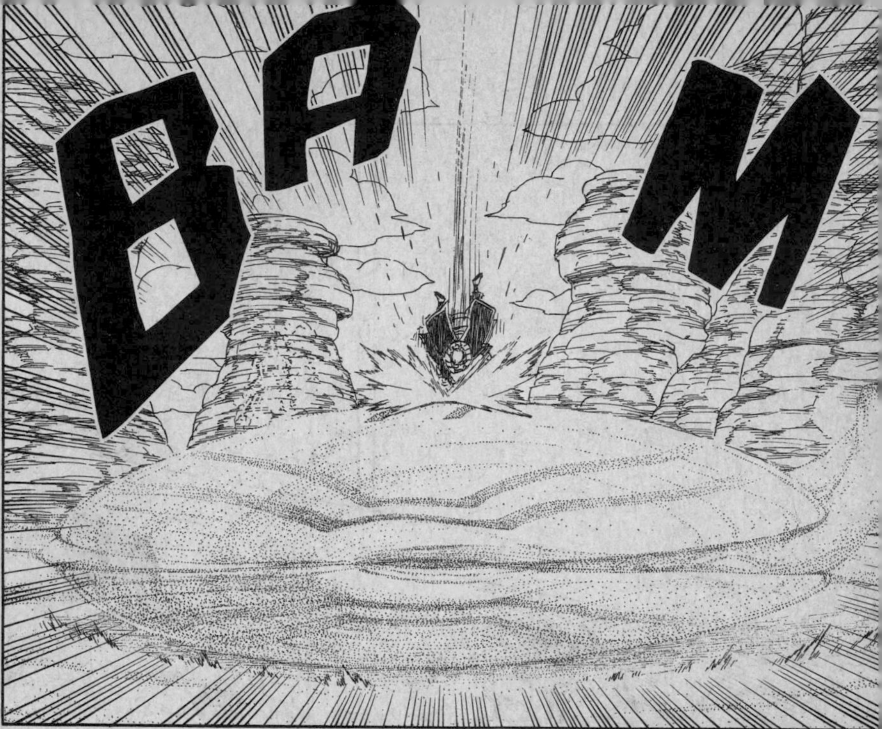
BAM

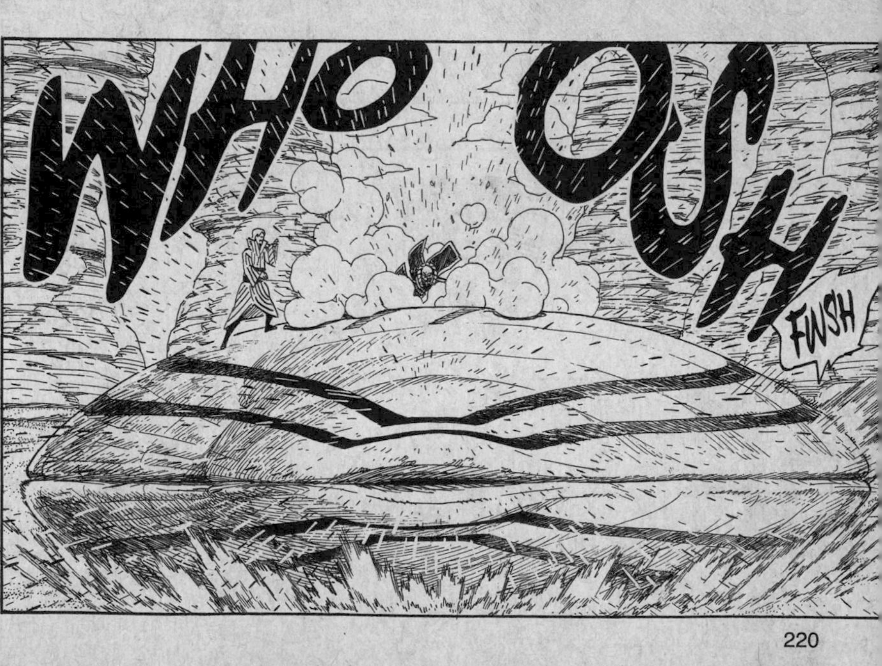
WHOOSH
FWSH

READ THIS WAY

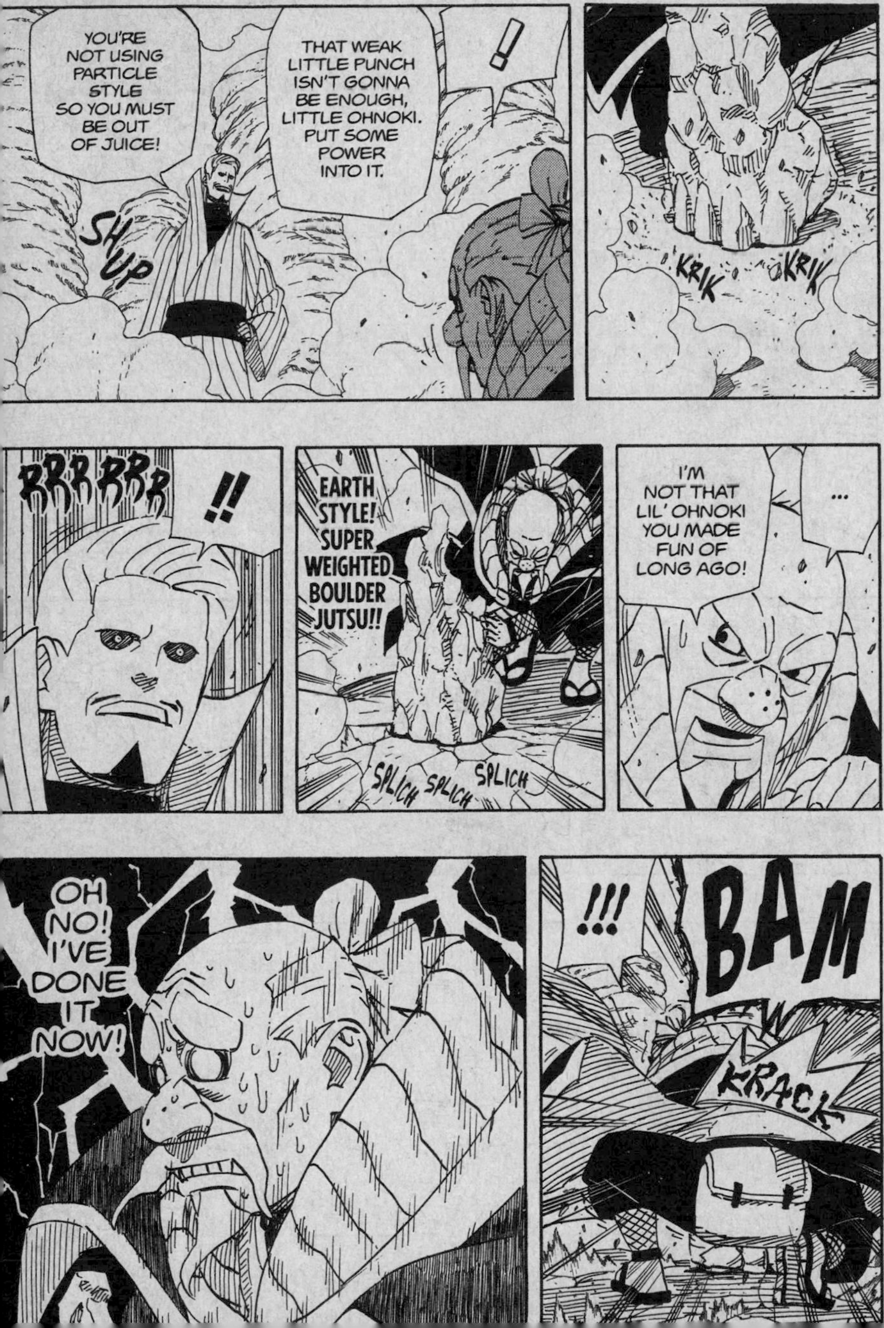

KRIK
KRIK
!
THAT WEAK LITTLE PUNCH ISN'T GONNA BE ENOUGH, LITTLE OHNOKI. PUT SOME POWER INTO IT.
YOU'RE NOT USING PARTICLE STYLE SO YOU MUST BE OUT OF JUICE!
SHUP
...
I'M NOT THAT LIL' OHNOKI YOU MADE FUN OF LONG AGO!
EARTH STYLE! SUPER WEIGHTED BOULDER JUTSU!!
SPLICH
SPLICH
SPLICH
!!
RRRRRR
BAM
!!!
KRACK
OH NO! I'VE DONE IT NOW!

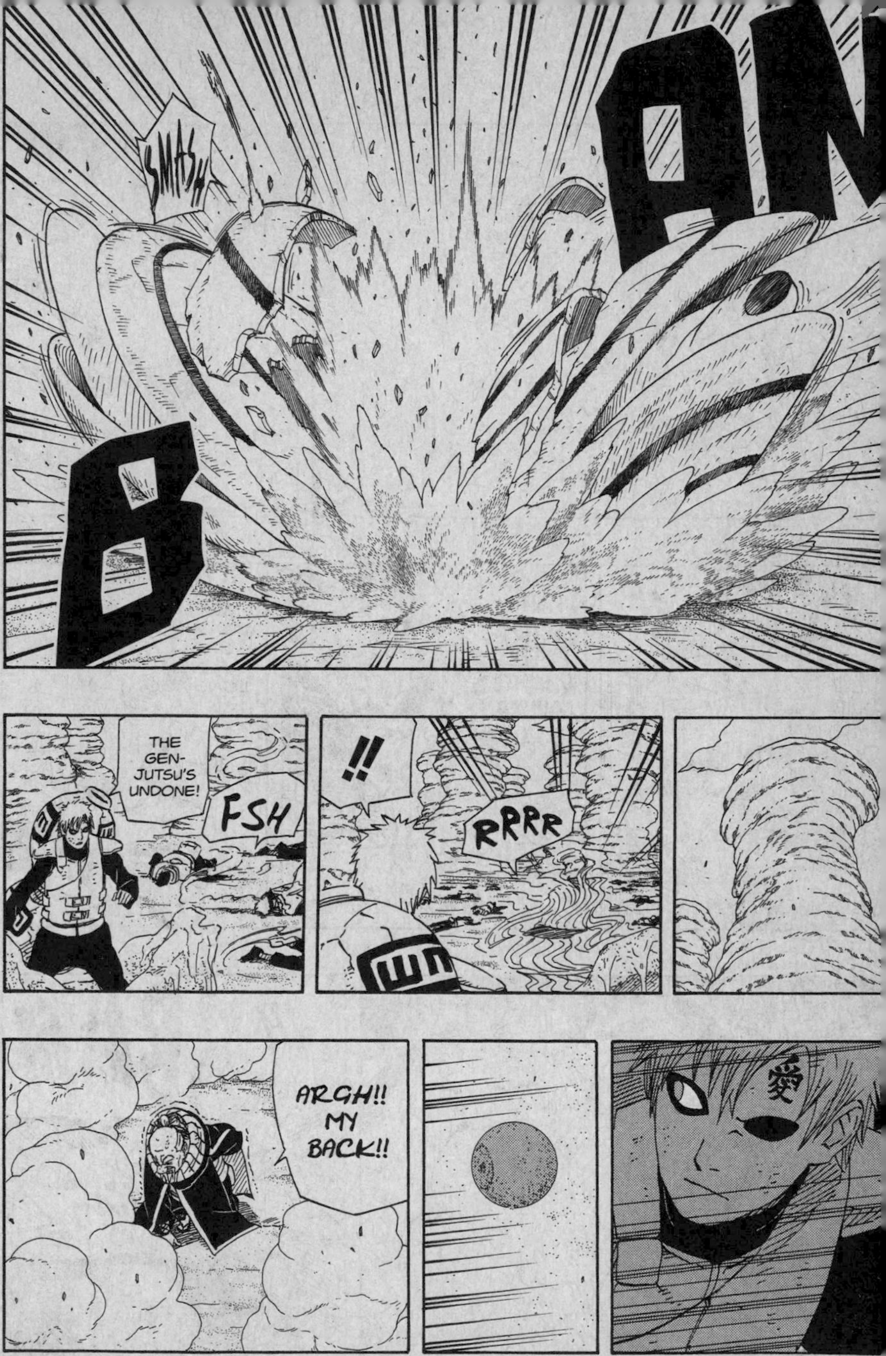
SMASH
!!
RRRR
THE GEN-JUTSU'S UNDONE!
FSH
ARGH!! MY BACK!!

READ THIS WAY

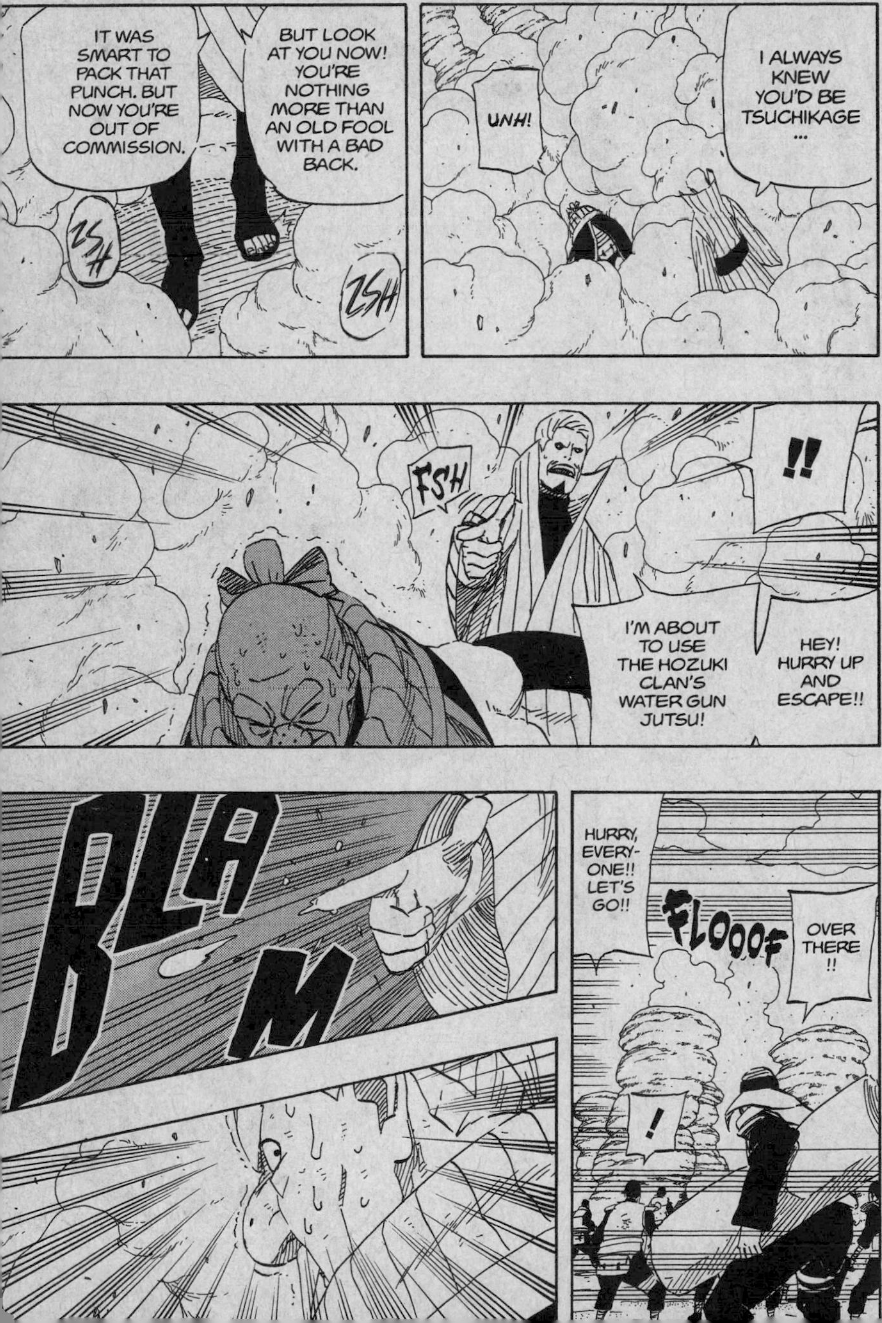

I ALWAYS KNEW YOU'D BE TSUCHIKAGE ...
UNH!
BUT LOOK AT YOU NOW! YOU'RE NOTHING MORE THAN AN OLD FOOL WITH A BAD BACK.
IT WAS SMART TO PACK THAT PUNCH. BUT NOW YOU'RE OUT OF COMMISSION.
ZSH
ZSH
!!
HEY! HURRY UP AND ESCAPE!!
I'M ABOUT TO USE THE HOZUKI CLAN'S WATER GUN JUTSU!
FSH
OVER THERE !!
HURRY, EVERY-ONE!! LET'S GO!!
FLOOOF
!
BLAM

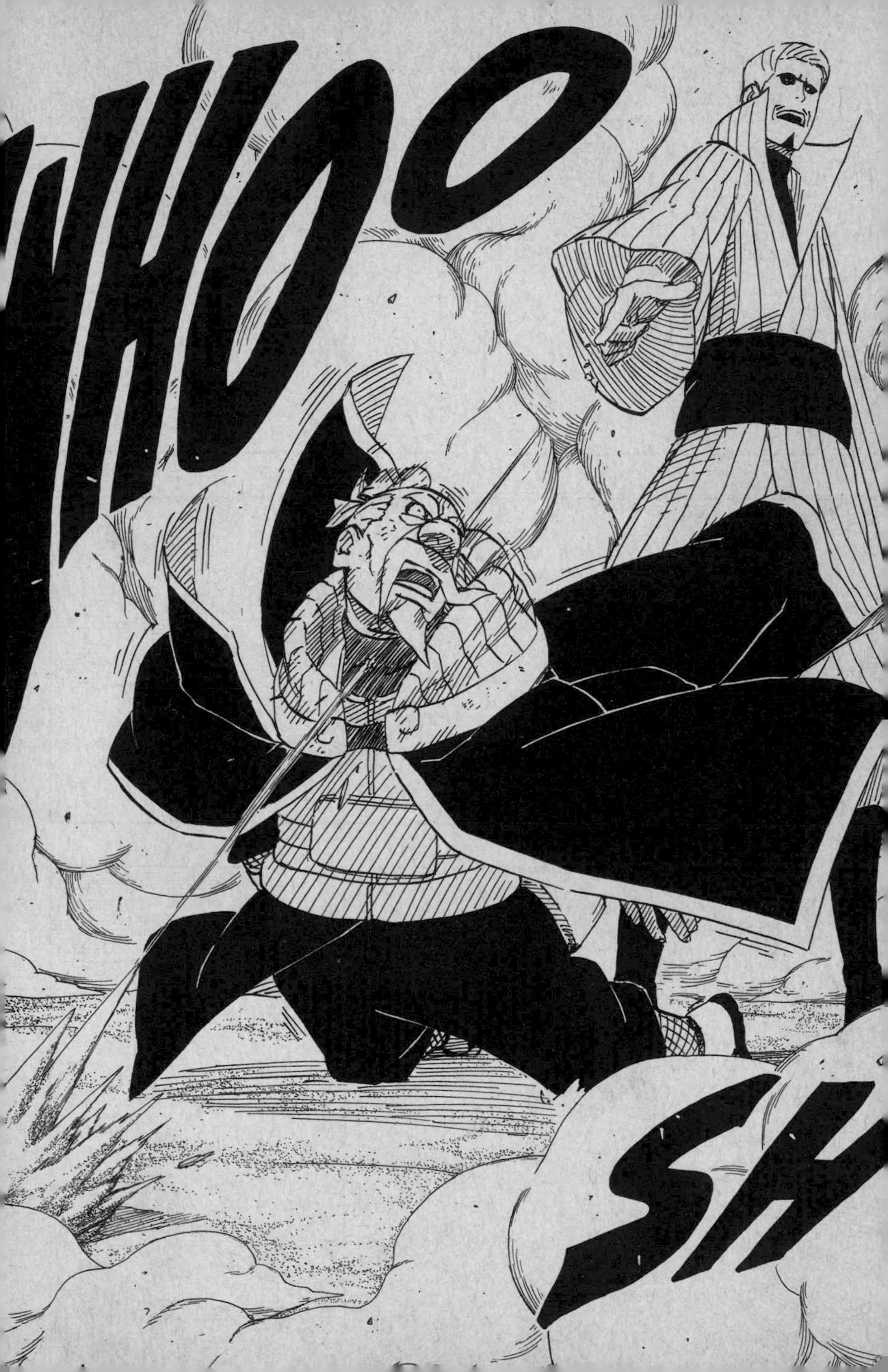
WHOO
SH

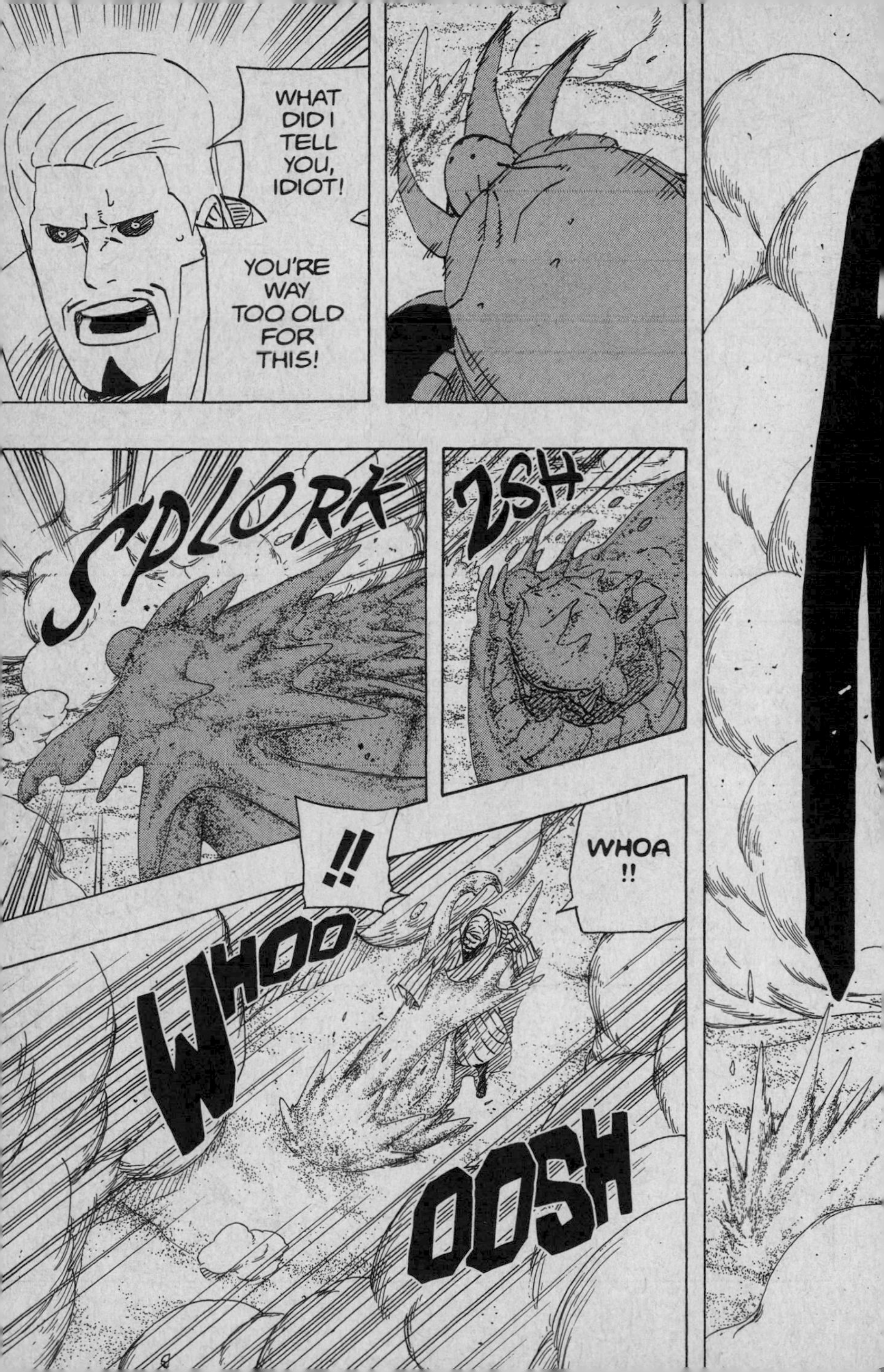
WHAT DID I TELL YOU, IDIOT!
YOU'RE WAY TOO OLD FOR THIS!
ZSH
SPLORK
WHOA !!
!!
WHOO
OOSH

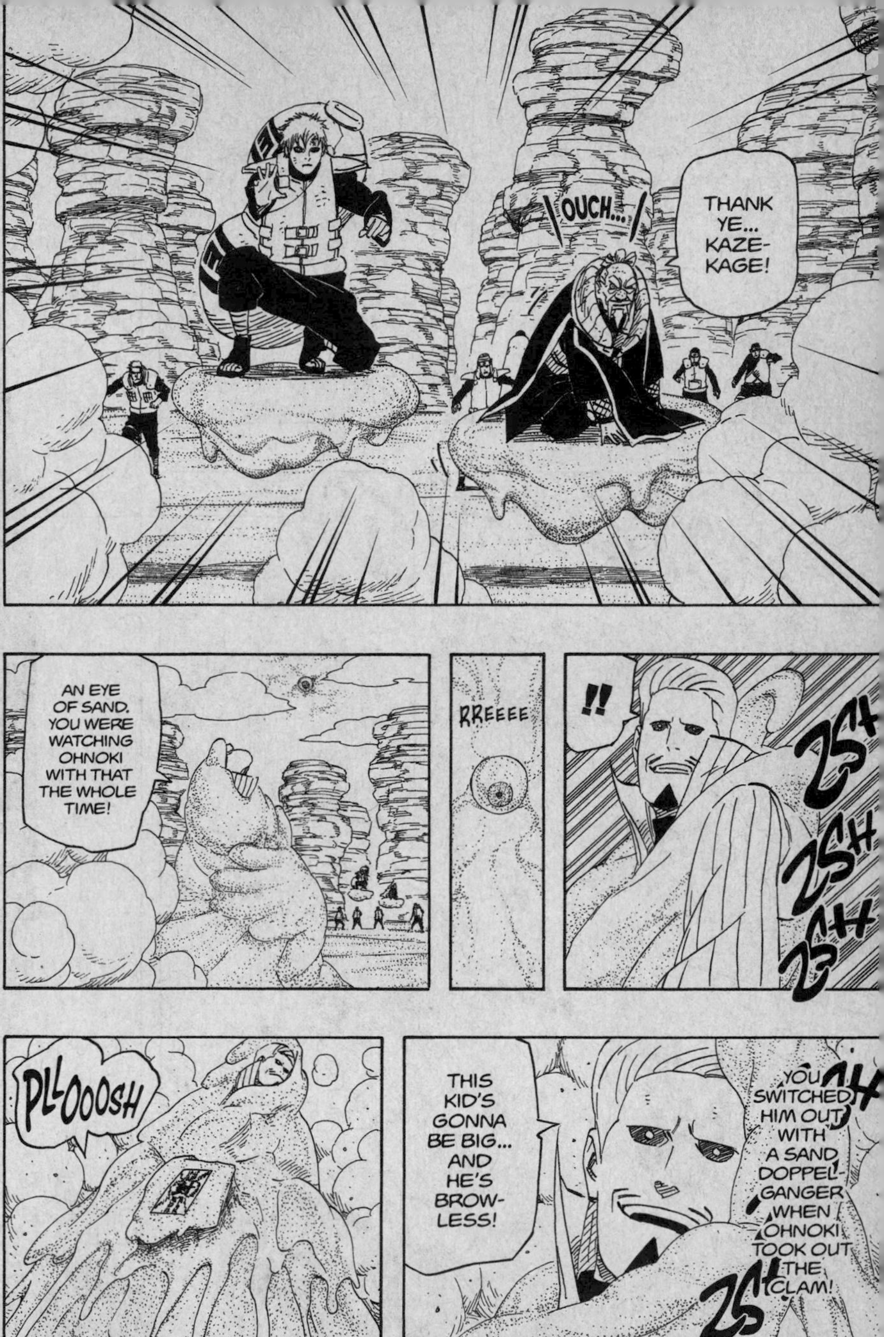
THANK YE... KAZE-KAGE!
OUCH...
!!
ZSH
ZSH
ZSH
RREEEE
AN EYE OF SAND. YOU WERE WATCHING OHNOKI WITH THAT THE WHOLE TIME!
YOU SWITCHED HIM OUT WITH A SAND DOPPEL-GANGER WHEN OHNOKI TOOK OUT THE CLAM!
ZSH
ZSH
THIS KID'S GONNA BE BIG... AND HE'S BROW-LESS!
PLLOOOSH

READ THIS WAY

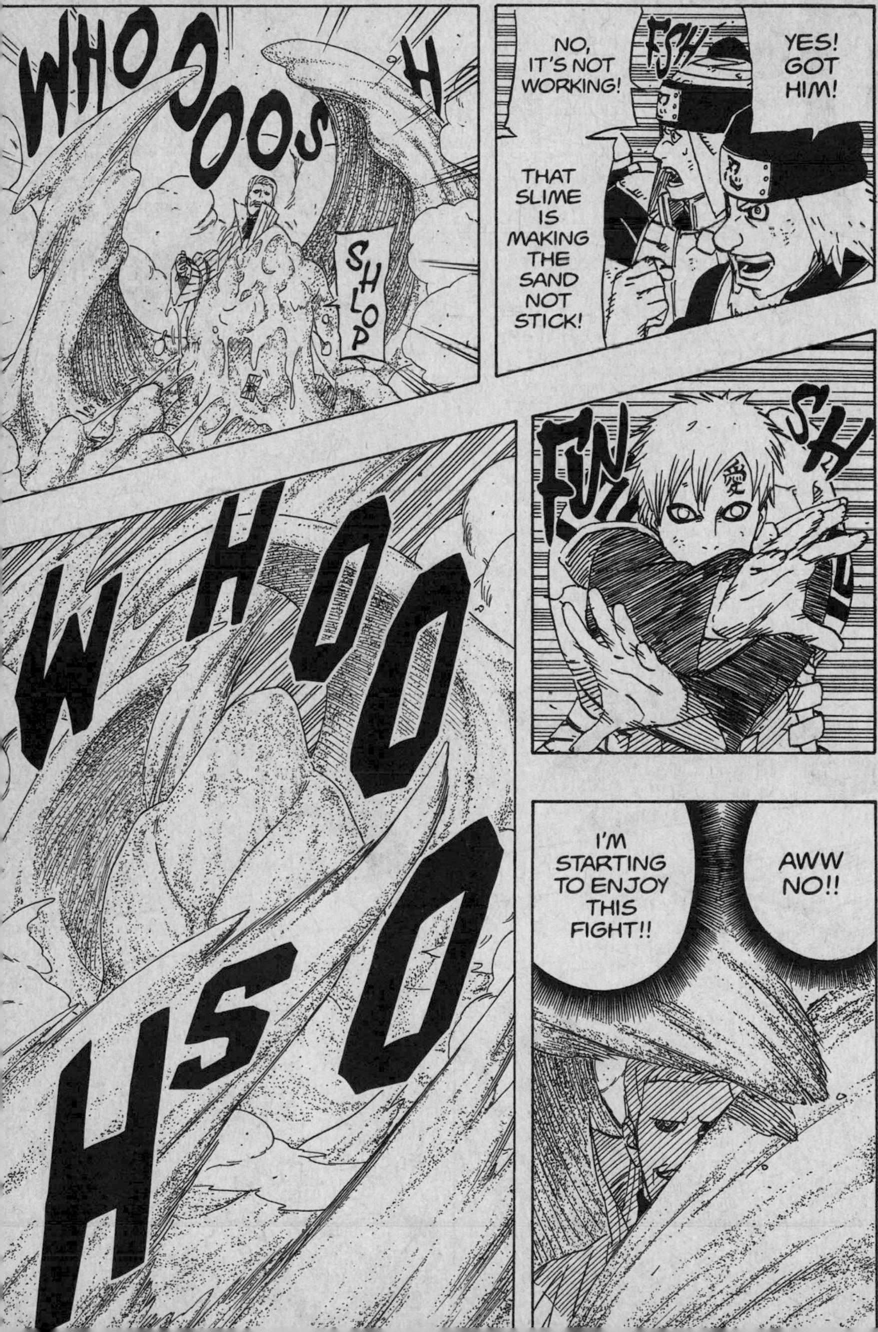
YES! GOT HIM!
FSH
NO, IT'S NOT WORKING!
THAT SLIME IS MAKING THE SAND NOT STICK!
WHOOOOSH
SHLOP
SH
FUN
AWW NO!!
I'M STARTING TO ENJOY THIS FIGHT!!
WHOOOSH

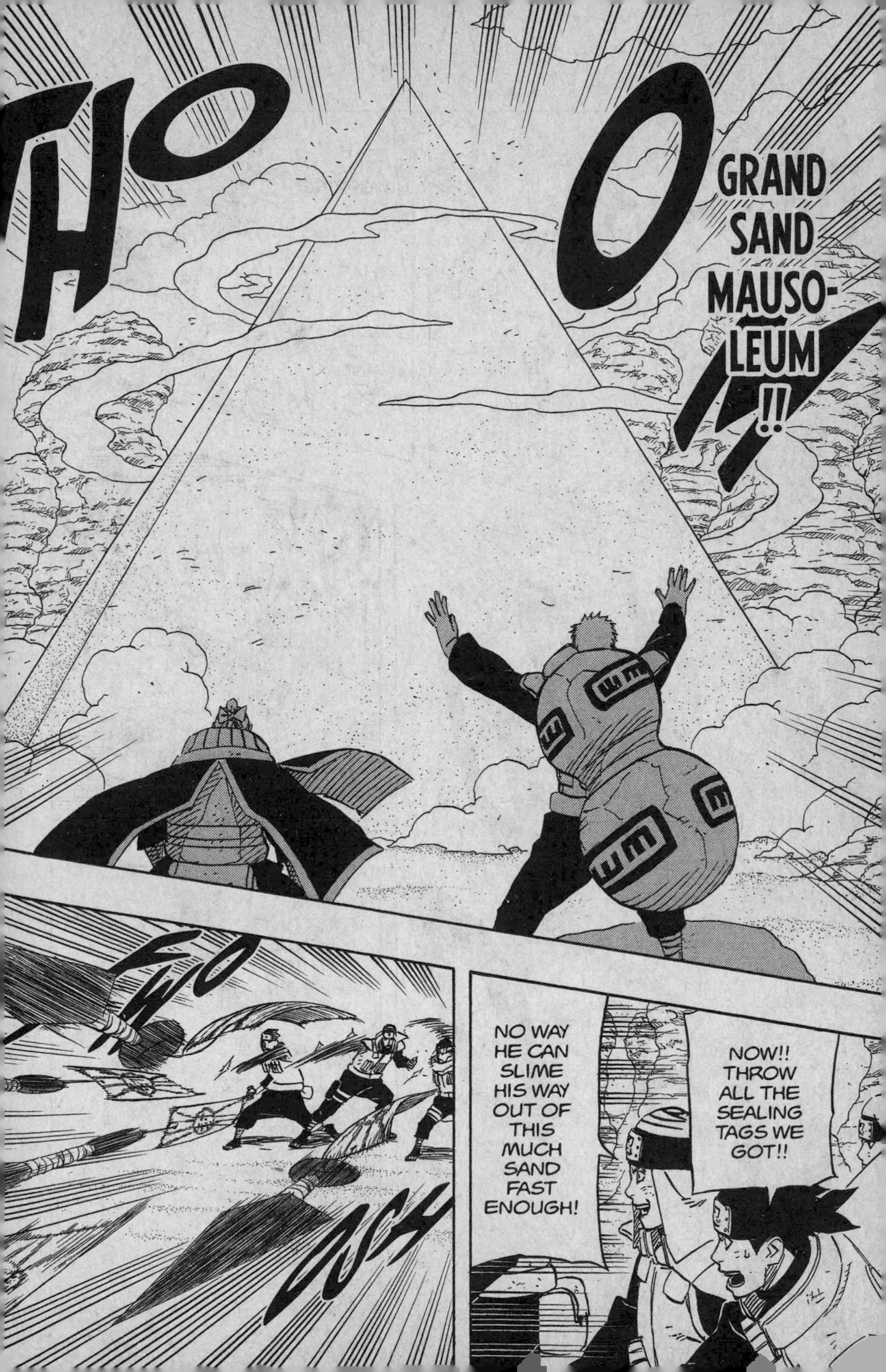
THOO
GRAND SAND MAUSO-LEUM!!
NOW!! THROW ALL THE SEALING TAGS WE GOT!!
NO WAY HE CAN SLIME HIS WAY OUT OF THIS MUCH SAND FAST ENOUGH!
FWO
OOSH

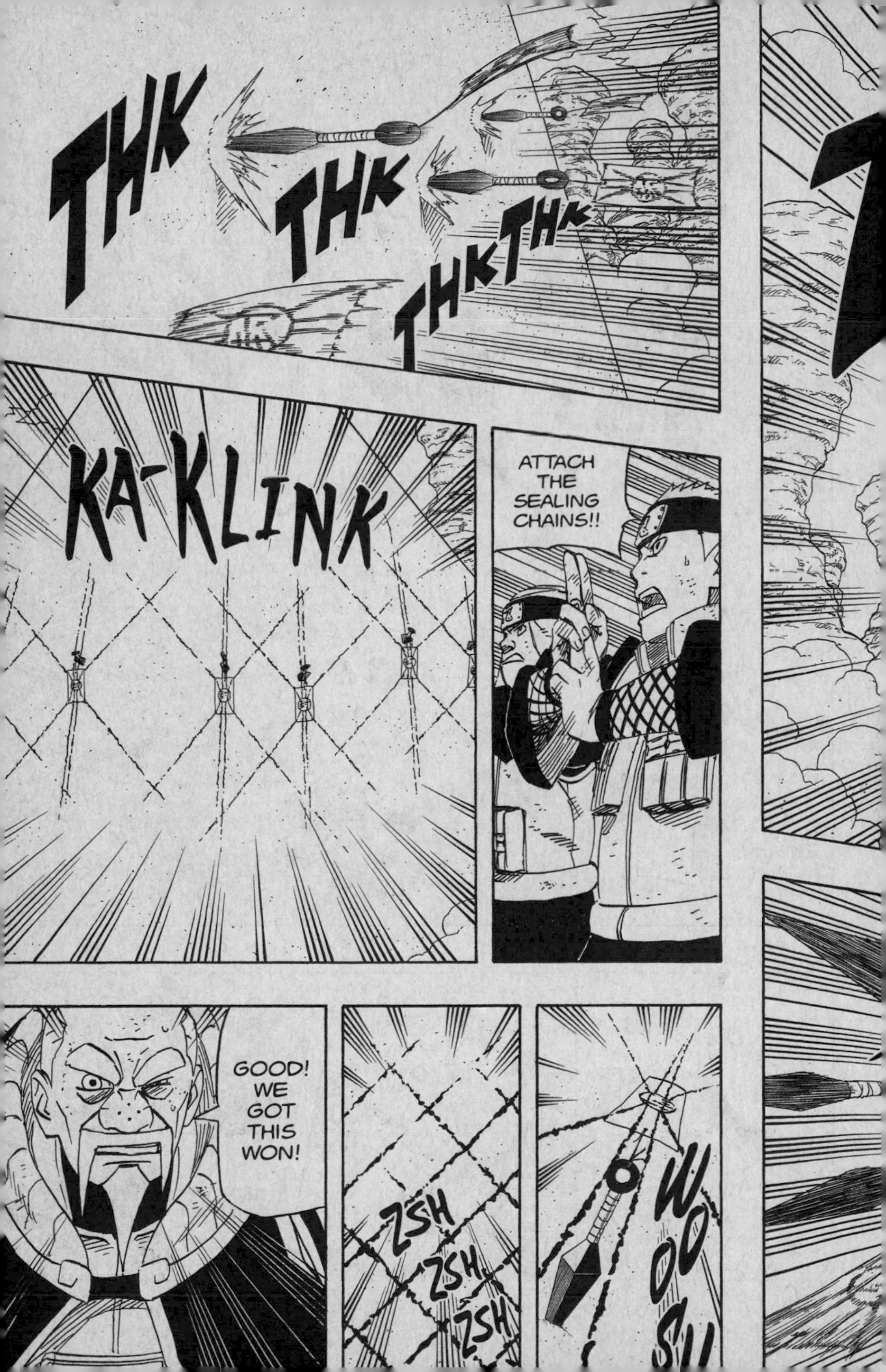
THK
THK
THKTHK
ATTACH THE SEALING CHAINS!!
KA-KLINK
ZSH
ZSH
ZSH
GOOD! WE GOT THIS WON!

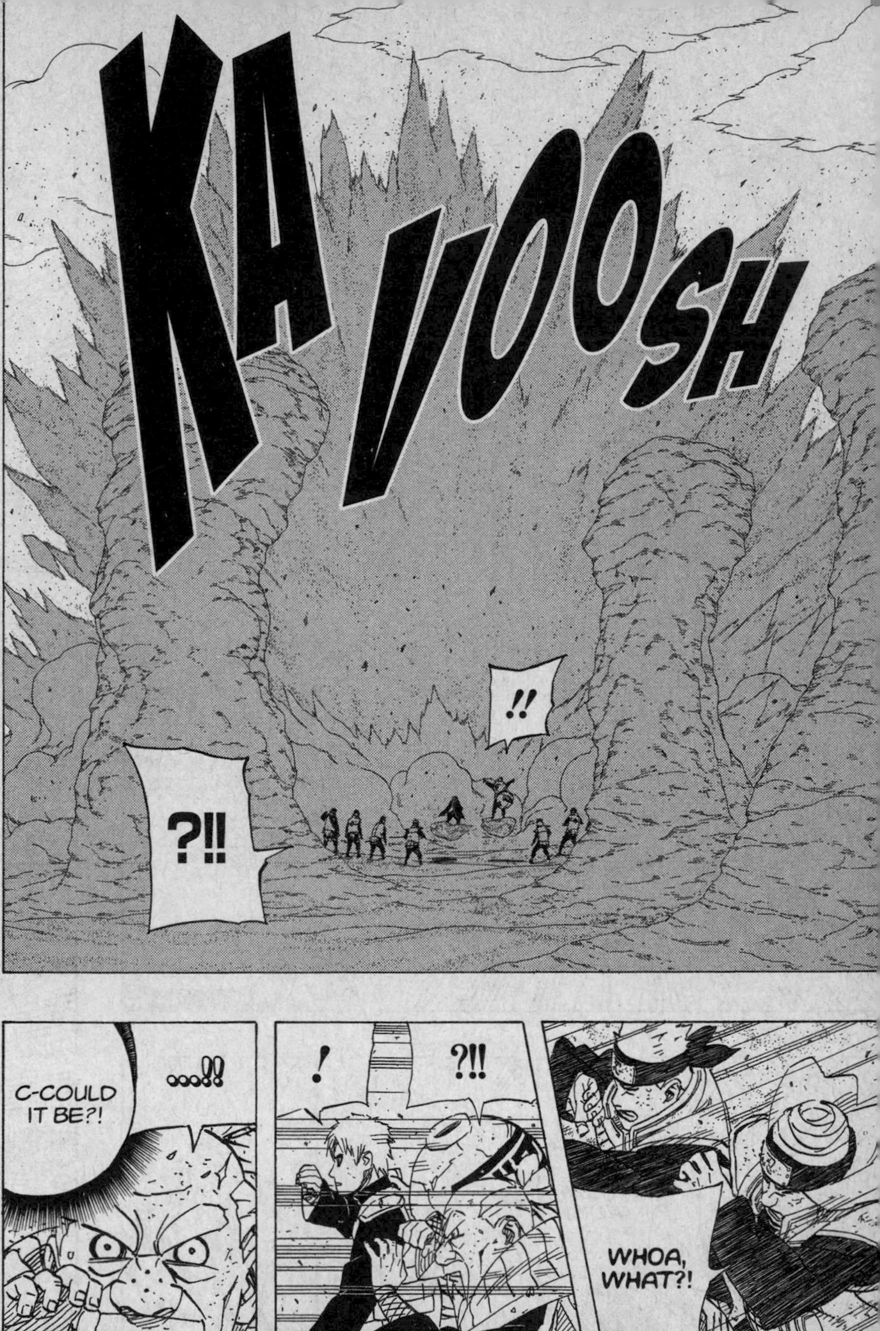
KA VOOSH
!!
?!!
WHOA, WHAT?!
?!!
!
...!!
C-COULD IT BE?!

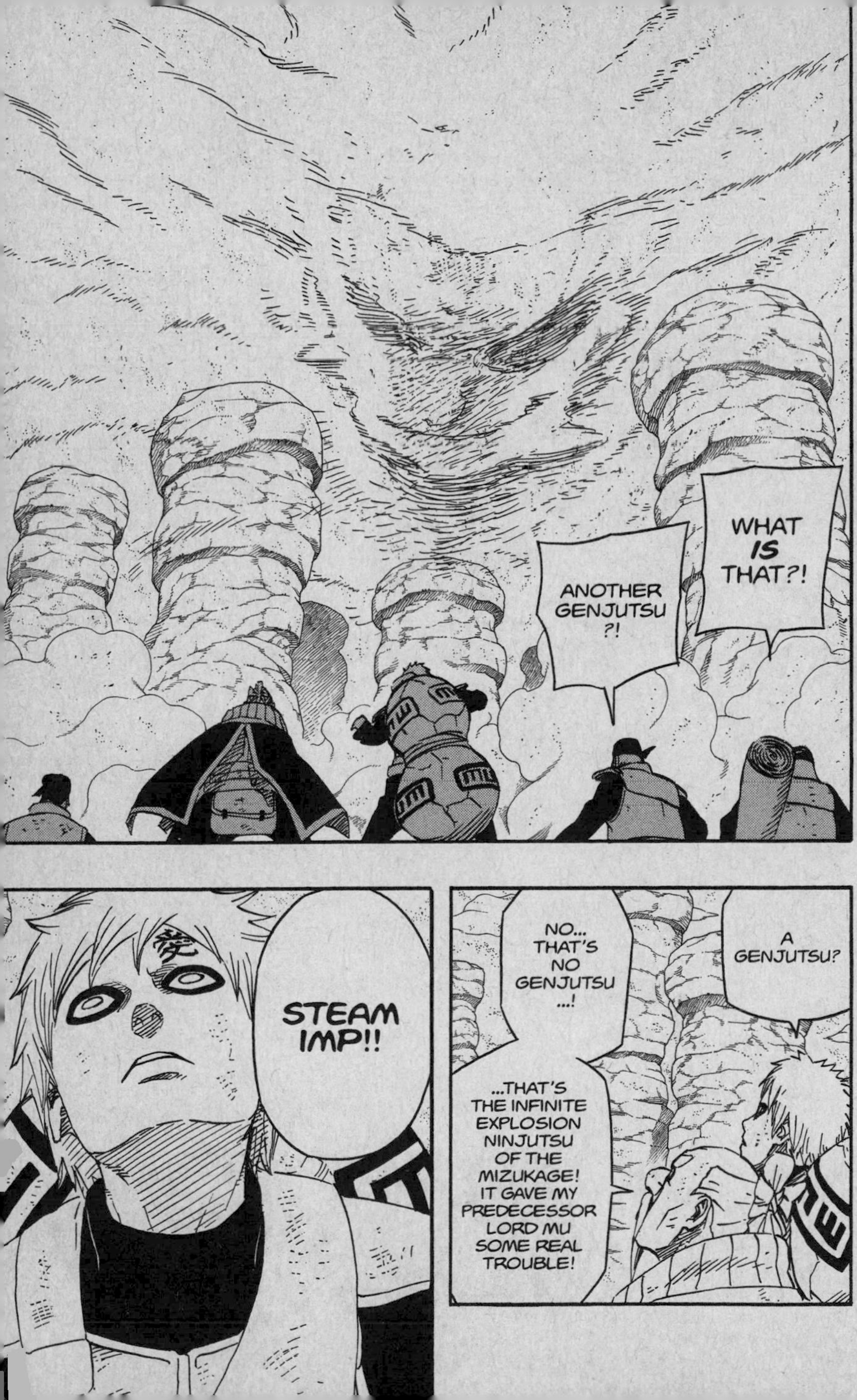
WHAT *IS* THAT?!
ANOTHER GENJUTSU?!
A GENJUTSU?
NO... THAT'S NO GENJUTSU ...!
...THAT'S THE INFINITE EXPLOSION NINJUTSU OF THE MIZUKAGE! IT GAVE MY PREDECESSOR LORD MU SOME REAL TROUBLE!
STEAM IMP!!

NARUTO

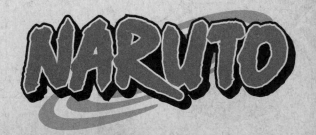

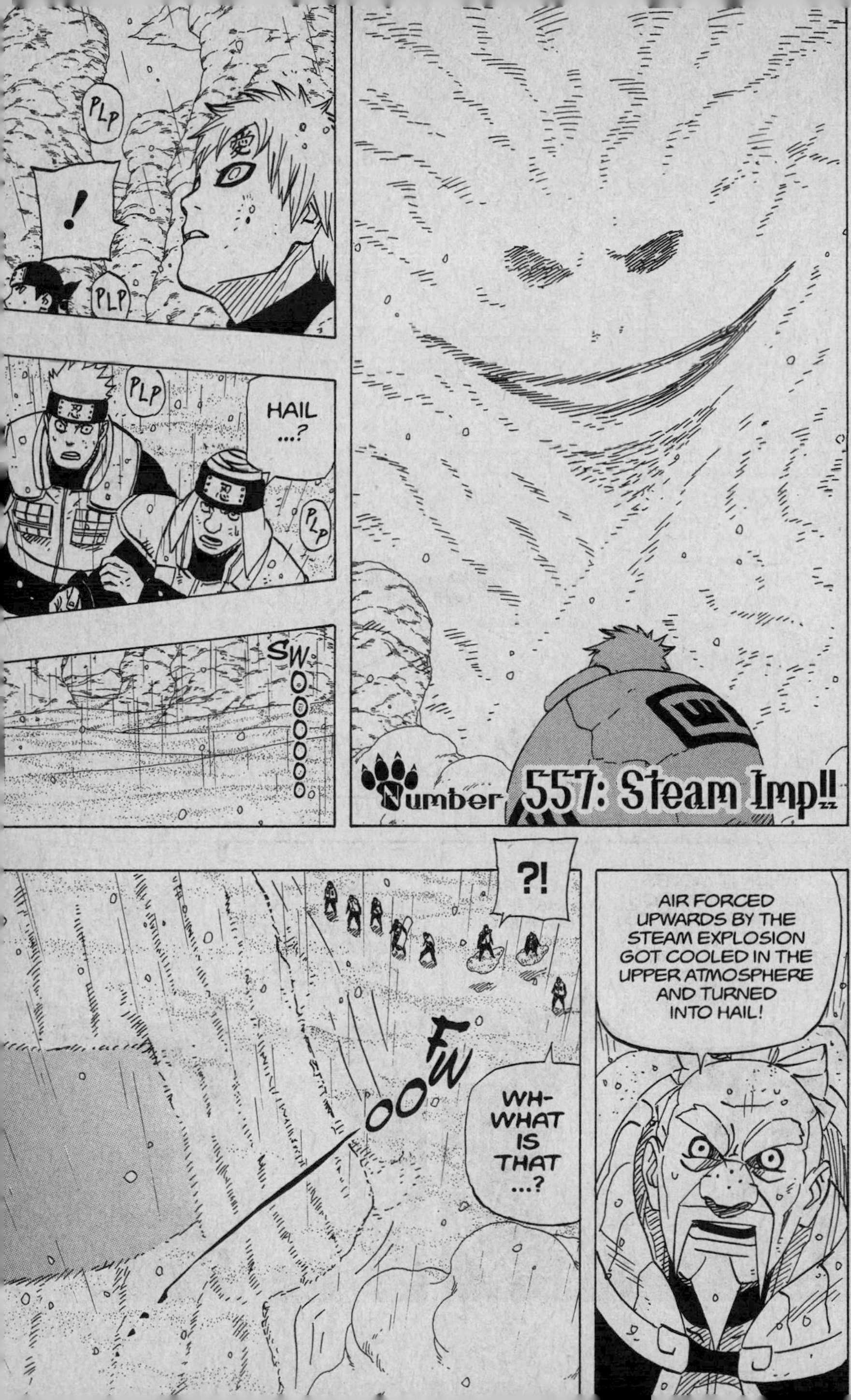
Number 557: Steam Imp!!
PLP
!
PLP
PLP
HAIL ...?
PLP
SWOOOOOOOO
AIR FORCED UPWARDS BY THE STEAM EXPLOSION GOT COOLED IN THE UPPER ATMOSPHERE AND TURNED INTO HAIL!
?!
FWOO
WH- WHAT IS THAT ...?

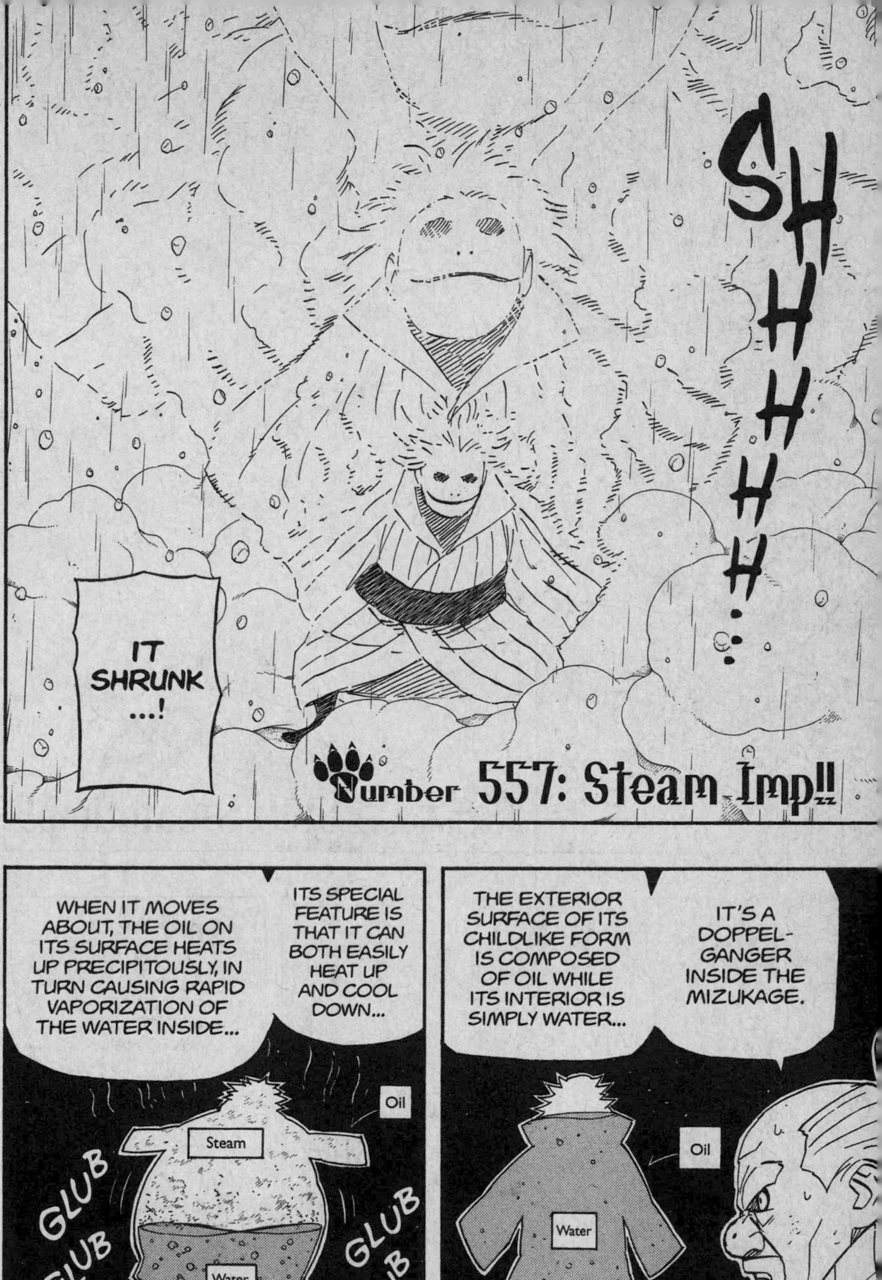

SHHHHHH...
IT SHRUNK ...!
Number 557: Steam Imp!!
IT'S A DOPPEL- GANGER INSIDE THE MIZUKAGE.
THE EXTERIOR SURFACE OF ITS CHILDLIKE FORM IS COMPOSED OF OIL WHILE ITS INTERIOR IS SIMPLY WATER...
Oil
Water
ITS SPECIAL FEATURE IS THAT IT CAN BOTH EASILY HEAT UP AND COOL DOWN...
WHEN IT MOVES ABOUT, THE OIL ON ITS SURFACE HEATS UP PRECIPITOUSLY, IN TURN CAUSING RAPID VAPORIZATION OF THE WATER INSIDE...
Oil
Steam
Water
GLUB GLUB
GLUB GLUB

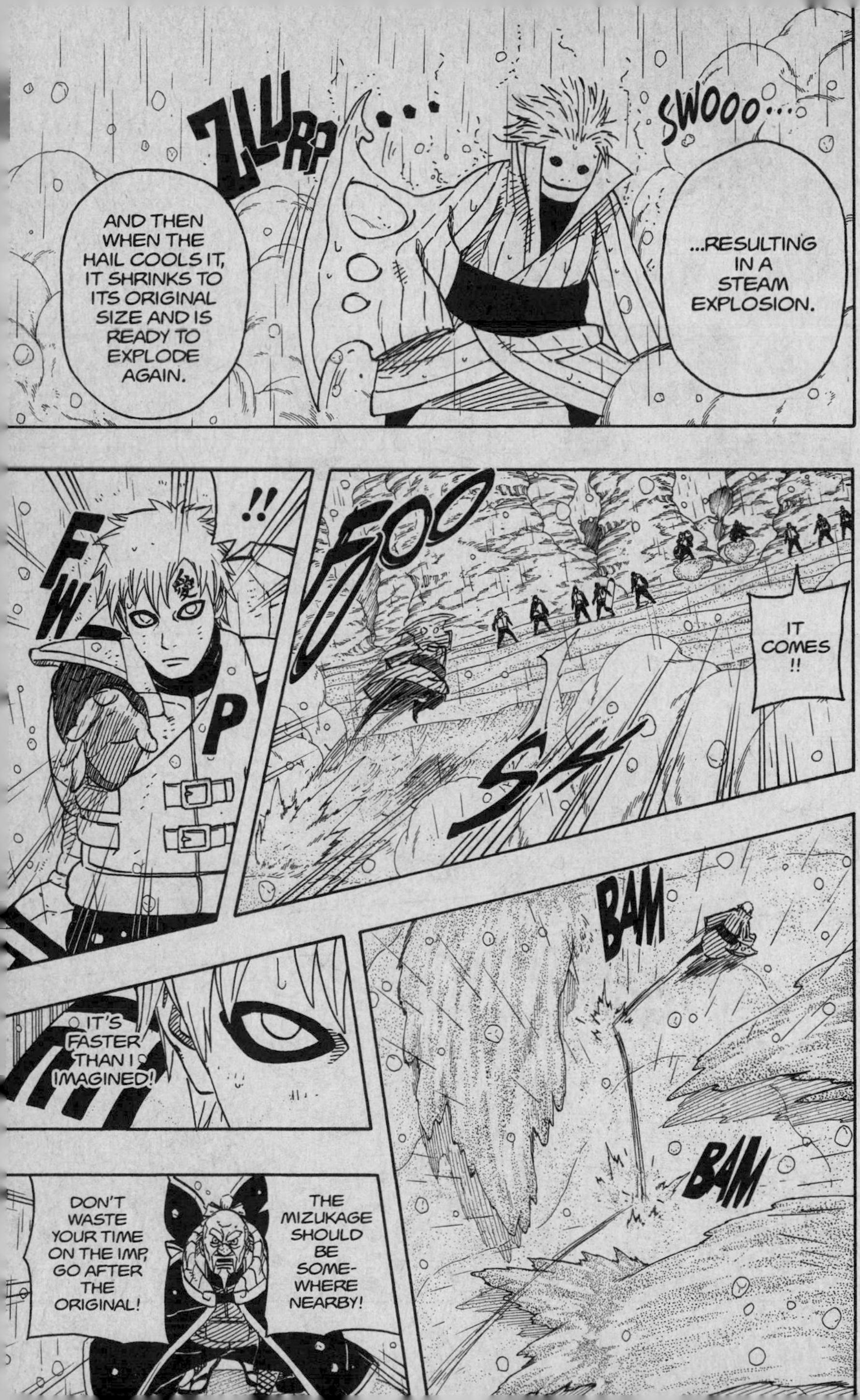
SWOOO...
...RESULTING IN A STEAM EXPLOSION.
ZLURP
AND THEN WHEN THE HAIL COOLS IT, IT SHRINKS TO ITS ORIGINAL SIZE AND IS READY TO EXPLODE AGAIN.
IT COMES !!
SHOO
SH
!!
FWP
BAM
BAM
IT'S FASTER THAN I IMAGINED!
THE MIZUKAGE SHOULD BE SOME-WHERE NEARBY!
DON'T WASTE YOUR TIME ON THE IMP, GO AFTER THE ORIGINAL!

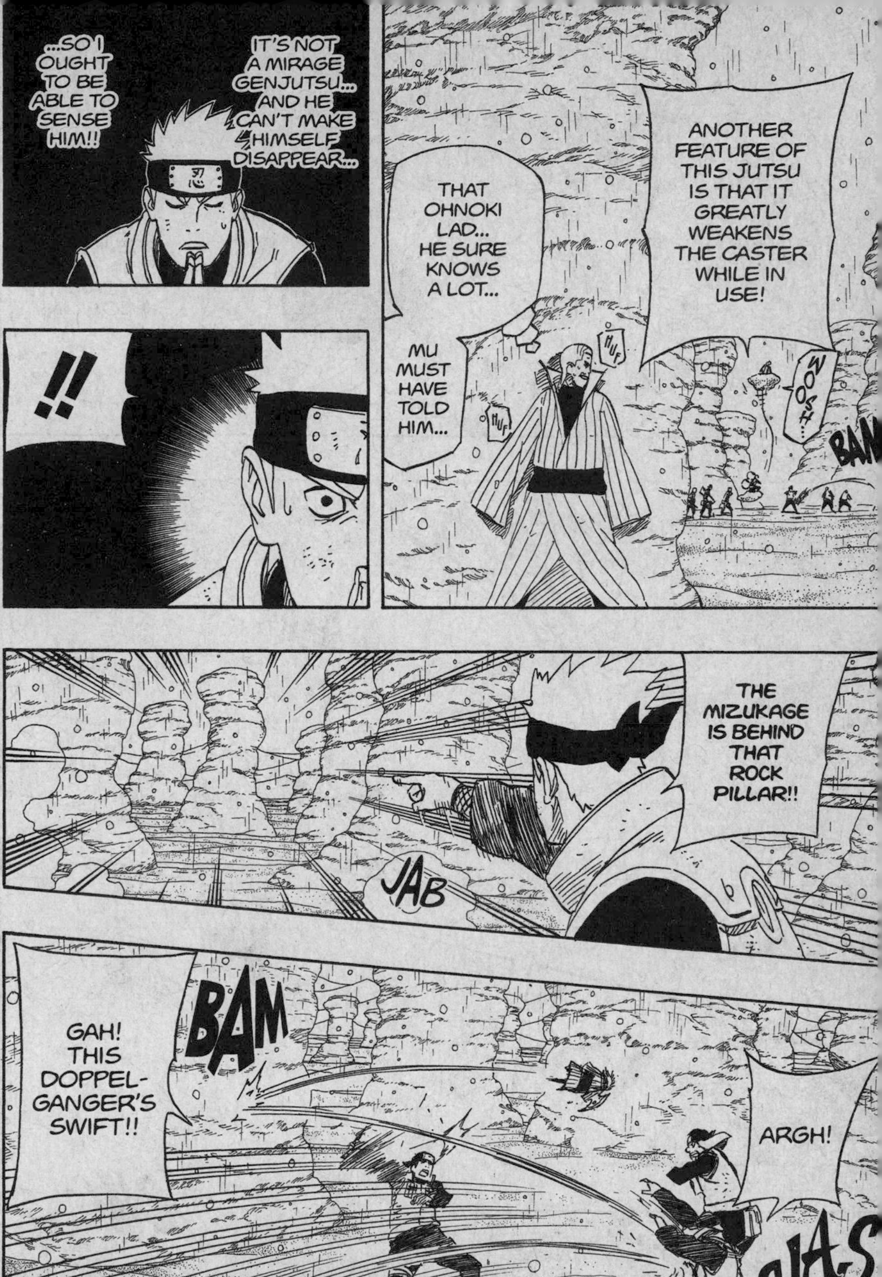
ANOTHER FEATURE OF THIS JUTSU IS THAT IT GREATLY WEAKENS THE CASTER WHILE IN USE!
THAT OHNOKI LAD... HE SURE KNOWS A LOT...
HUF
HUF
MU MUST HAVE TOLD HIM...
WOOSH...
BAM
IT'S NOT A MIRAGE GENJUTSU... AND HE CAN'T MAKE HIMSELF DISAPPEAR...
...SO I OUGHT TO BE ABLE TO SENSE HIM!!
!!
THE MIZUKAGE IS BEHIND THAT ROCK PILLAR!!
JAB
ARGH!
SLAS
BAM
GAH! THIS DOPPEL-GANGER'S SWIFT!!

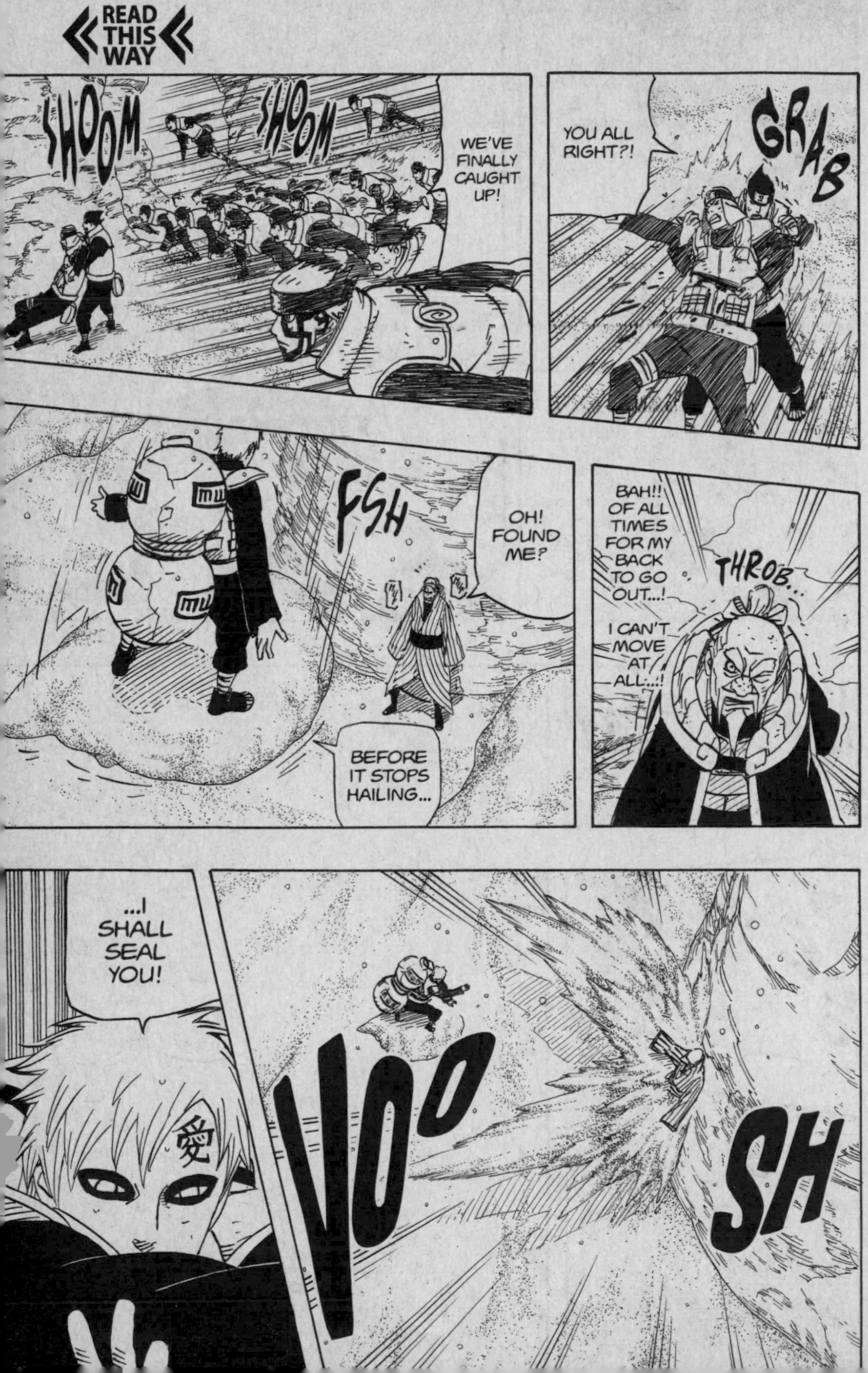
READ THIS WAY
YOU ALL RIGHT?!
GRAB
WE'VE FINALLY CAUGHT UP!
SHOOM
SHOOM
BAH!! OF ALL TIMES FOR MY BACK TO GO OUT...!
THROB...
I CAN'T MOVE AT ALL...!
OH! FOUND ME?
FSH
BEFORE IT STOPS HAILING...
VOOSH
...I SHALL SEAL YOU!

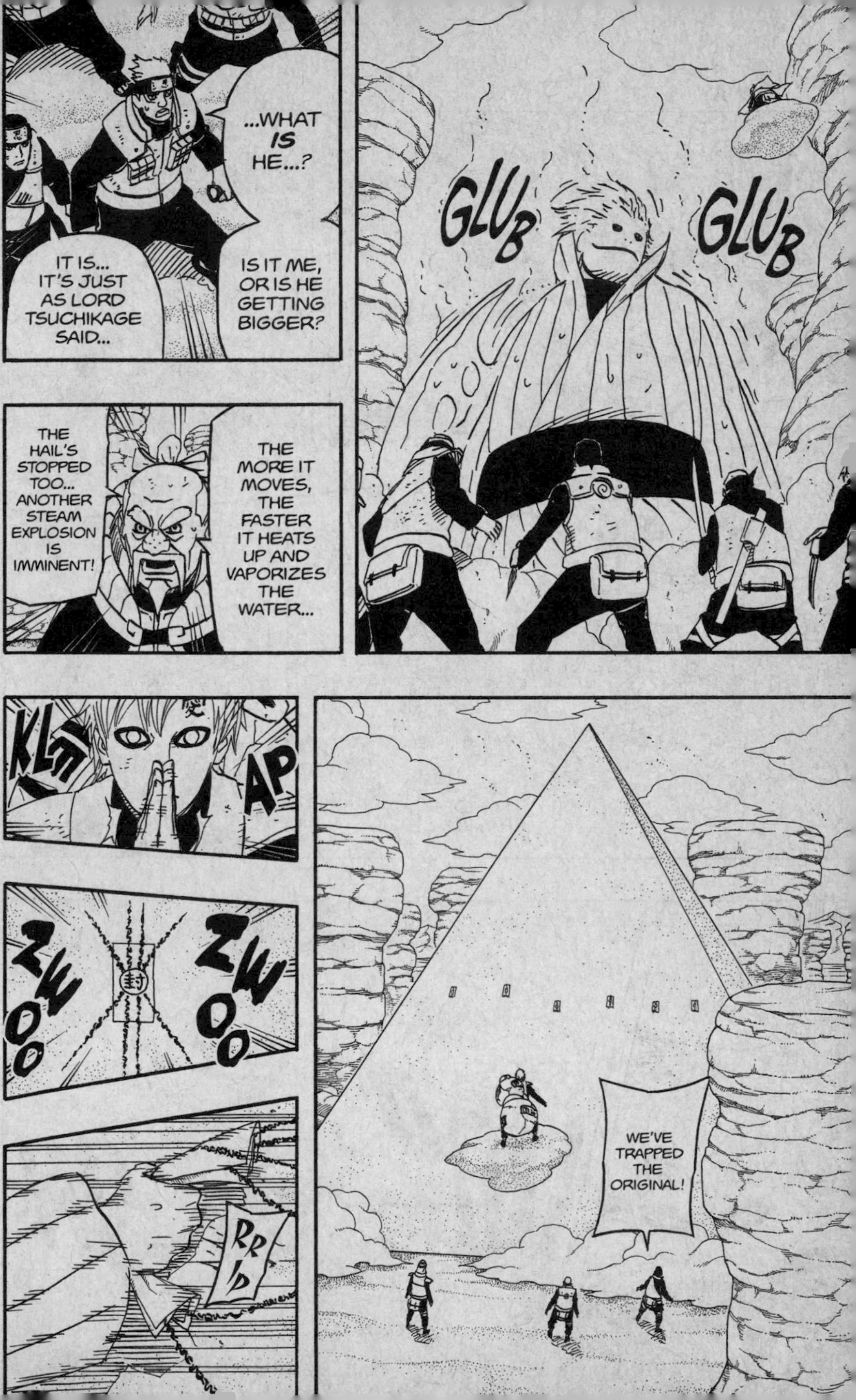
GLUB
GLUB
...WHAT IS HE...?
IS IT ME, OR IS HE GETTING BIGGER?
IT IS... IT'S JUST AS LORD TSUCHIKAGE SAID...
THE MORE IT MOVES, THE FASTER IT HEATS UP AND VAPORIZES THE WATER...
THE HAIL'S STOPPED TOO... ANOTHER STEAM EXPLOSION IS IMMINENT!
WE'VE TRAPPED THE ORIGINAL!
KLAP
ZWOO
ZWOO
RRIP

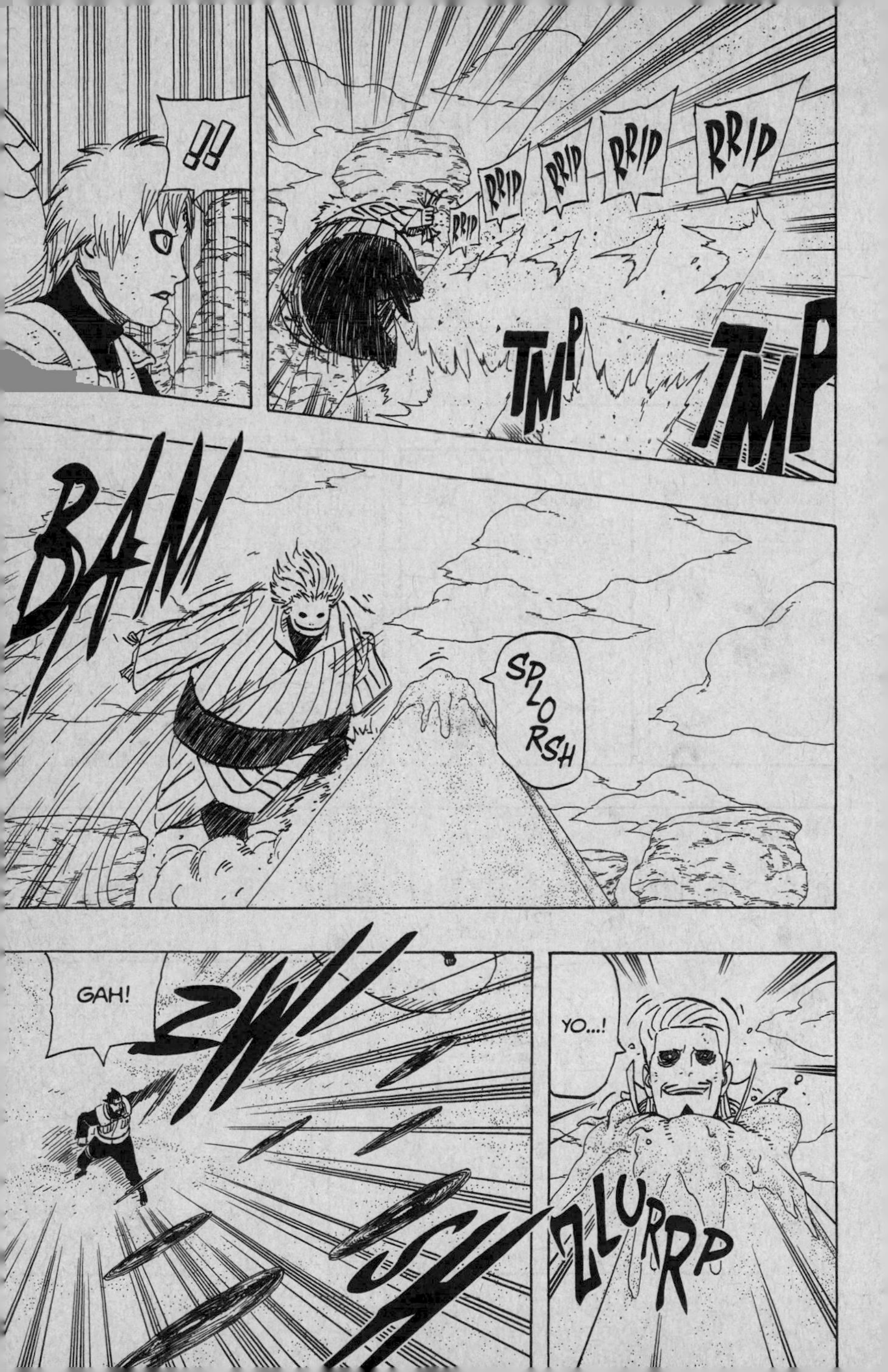

RRIP
RRIP
RRIP
RRIP
RRIP
TMP
TMP
!!
BAM
SPLORSH
YO...!
ZLURRP
GAH!
ZWI
SH

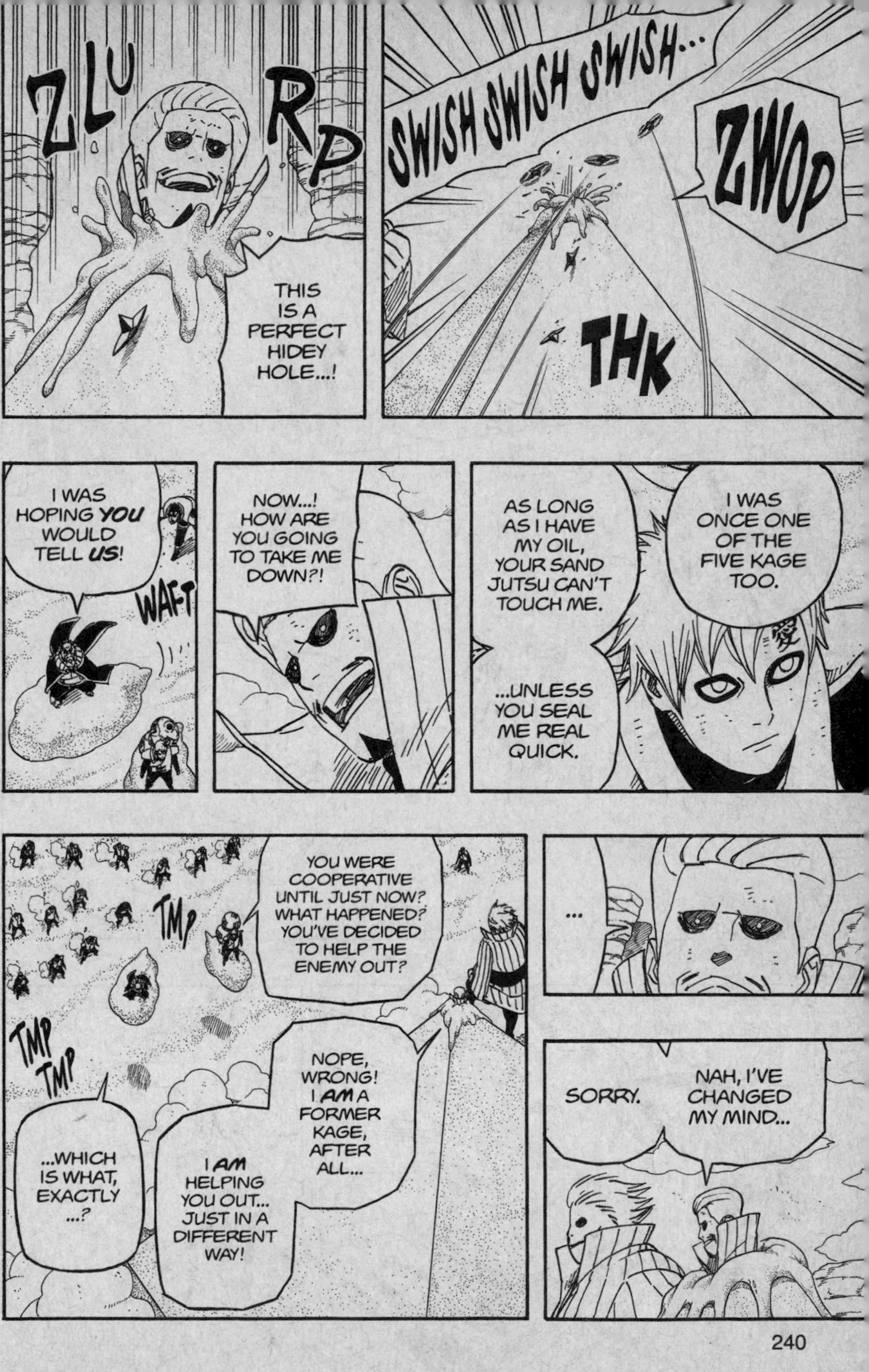
SWISH SWISH SWISH...
ZWOP
THK
ZLURP
THIS IS A PERFECT HIDEY HOLE...!
I WAS ONCE ONE OF THE FIVE KAGE TOO.
AS LONG AS I HAVE MY OIL, YOUR SAND JUTSU CAN'T TOUCH ME.
...UNLESS YOU SEAL ME REAL QUICK.
NOW...! HOW ARE YOU GOING TO TAKE ME DOWN?!
I WAS HOPING **YOU** WOULD TELL **US**!
WAFT
...
NAH, I'VE CHANGED MY MIND...
SORRY.
YOU WERE COOPERATIVE UNTIL JUST NOW? WHAT HAPPENED? YOU'VE DECIDED TO HELP THE ENEMY OUT?
TMP
NOPE, WRONG! I **AM** A FORMER KAGE, AFTER ALL...
I **AM** HELPING YOU OUT... JUST IN A DIFFERENT WAY!
...WHICH IS WHAT, EXACTLY ...?
TMP TMP

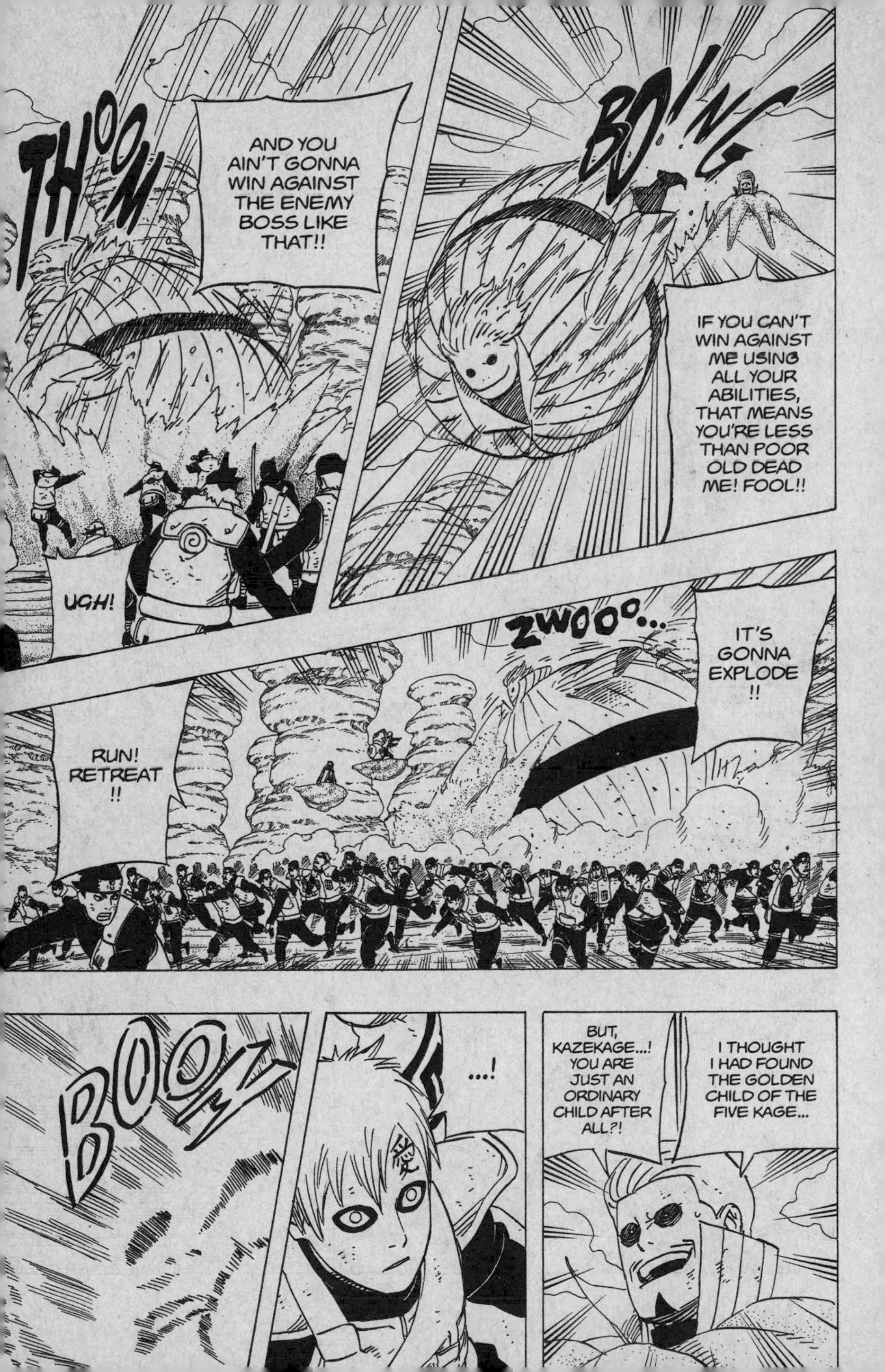
BOING
IF YOU CAN'T WIN AGAINST ME USING ALL YOUR ABILITIES, THAT MEANS YOU'RE LESS THAN POOR OLD DEAD ME! FOOL!!
THOOM
AND YOU AIN'T GONNA WIN AGAINST THE ENEMY BOSS LIKE THAT!!
UGH!
ZWOOO...
IT'S GONNA EXPLODE!!
RUN! RETREAT!!
I THOUGHT I HAD FOUND THE GOLDEN CHILD OF THE FIVE KAGE...
BUT, KAZEKAGE...! YOU ARE JUST AN ORDINARY CHILD AFTER ALL?!
...!
BOOM

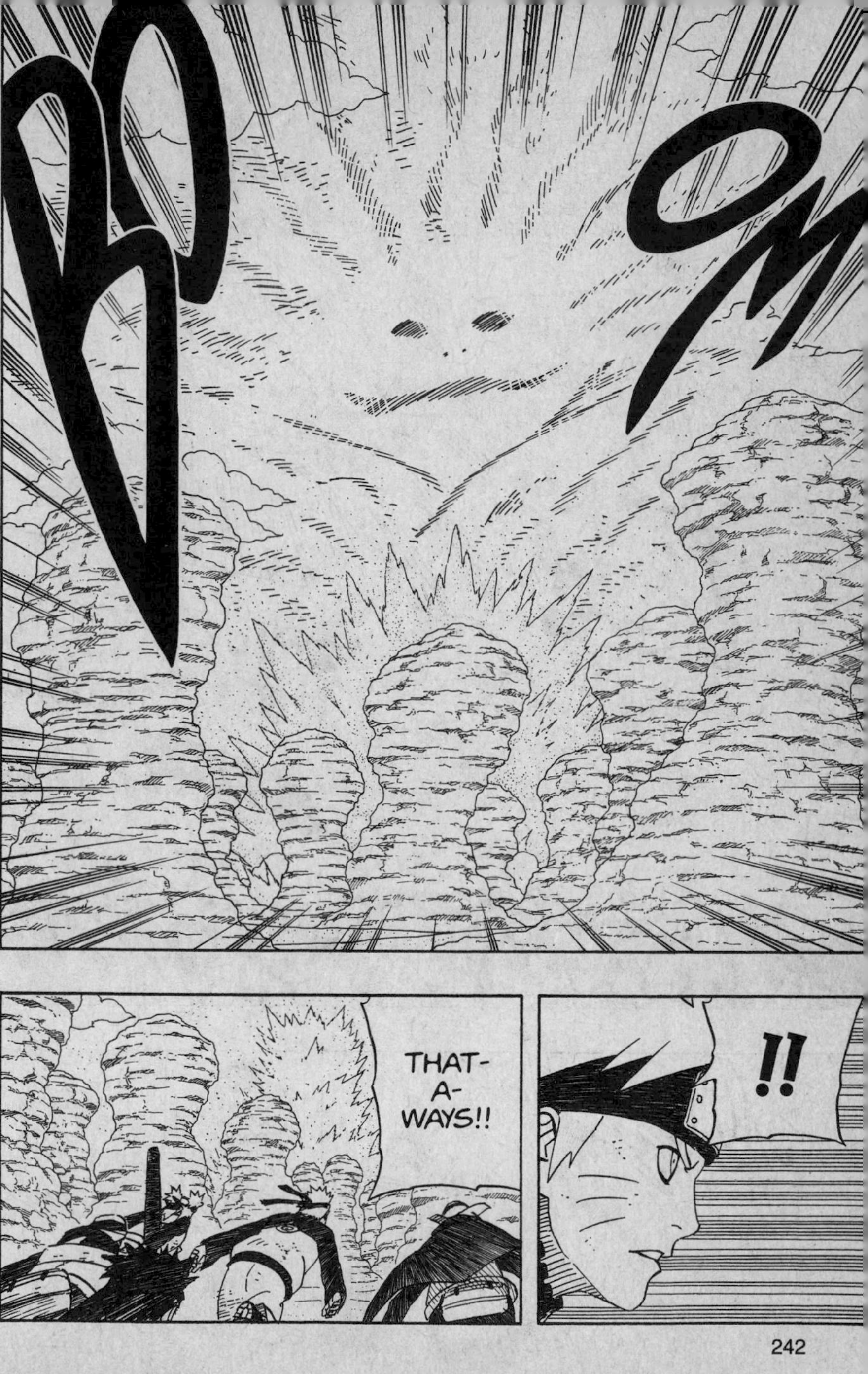
BOOM
!!
THAT-A-WAYS!!

READ THIS WAY

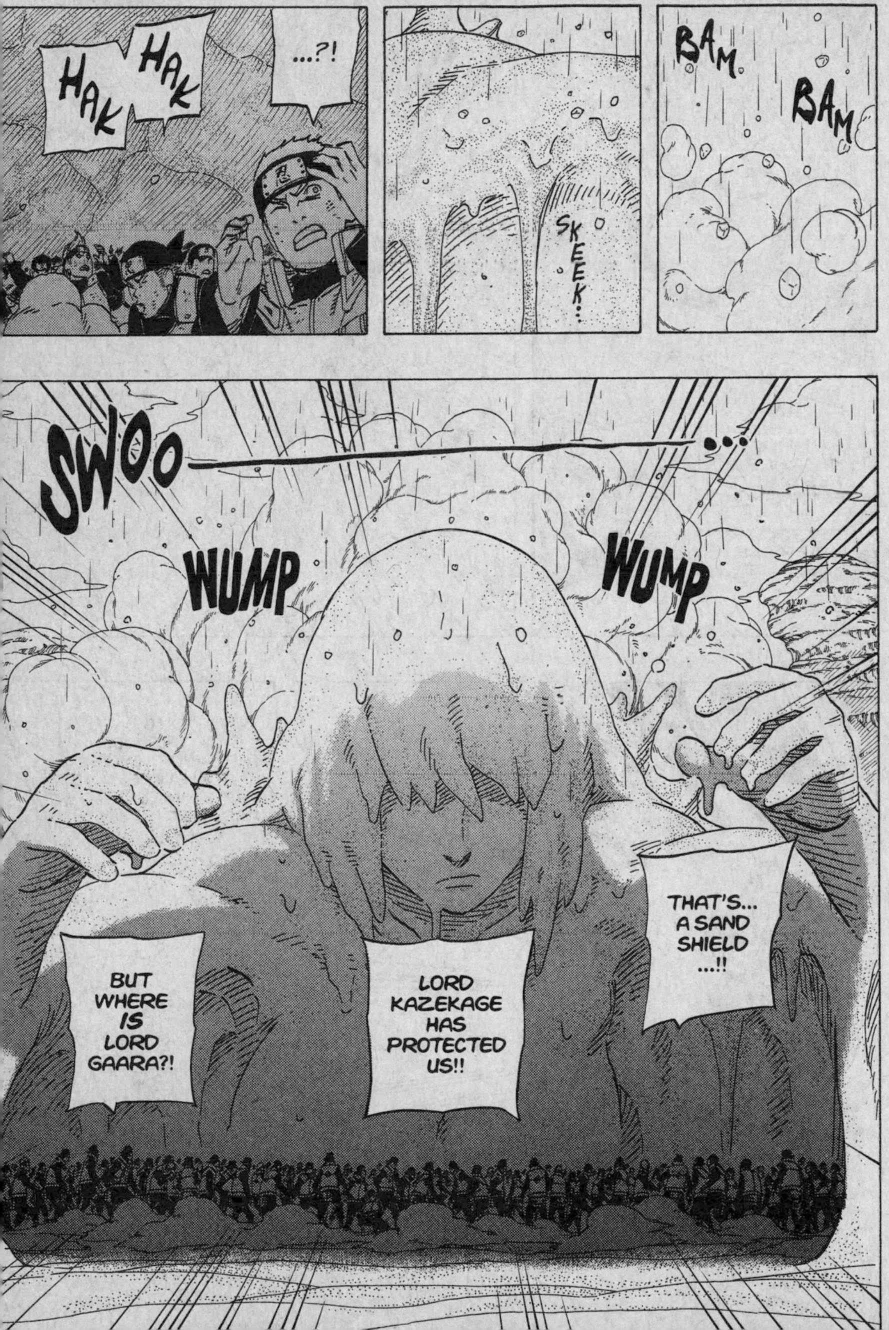
BAM BAM
SKEEK...
HAK HAK
...?!
SWOO—...
WUMP
WUMP
THAT'S... A SAND SHIELD ...!!
LORD KAZEKAGE HAS PROTECTED US!!
BUT WHERE IS LORD GAARA?!

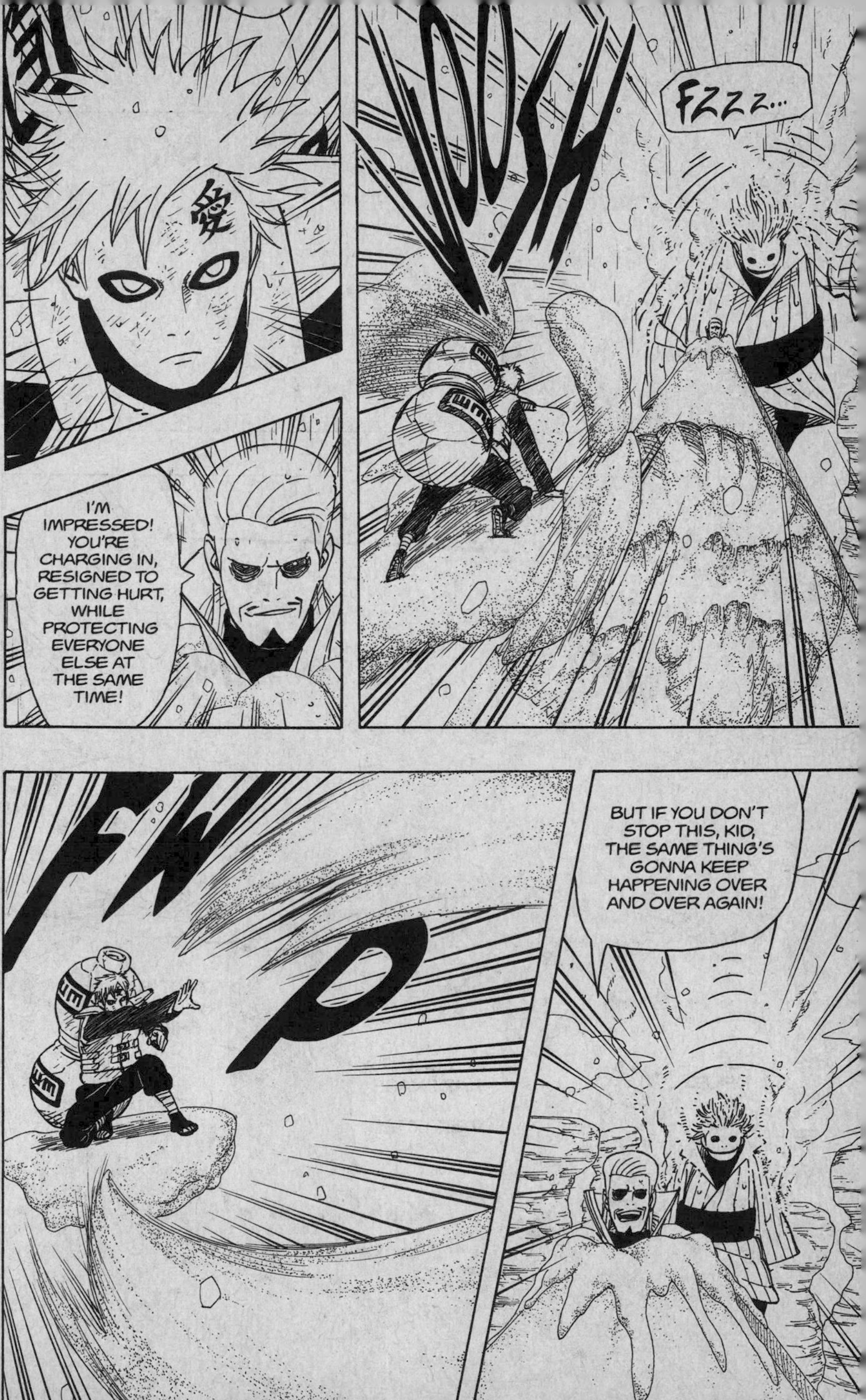
FZZZ...
WOOSH
I'M IMPRESSED! YOU'RE CHARGING IN, RESIGNED TO GETTING HURT, WHILE PROTECTING EVERYONE ELSE AT THE SAME TIME!
BUT IF YOU DON'T STOP THIS, KID, THE SAME THING'S GONNA KEEP HAPPENING OVER AND OVER AGAIN!
FWP

READ THIS WAY

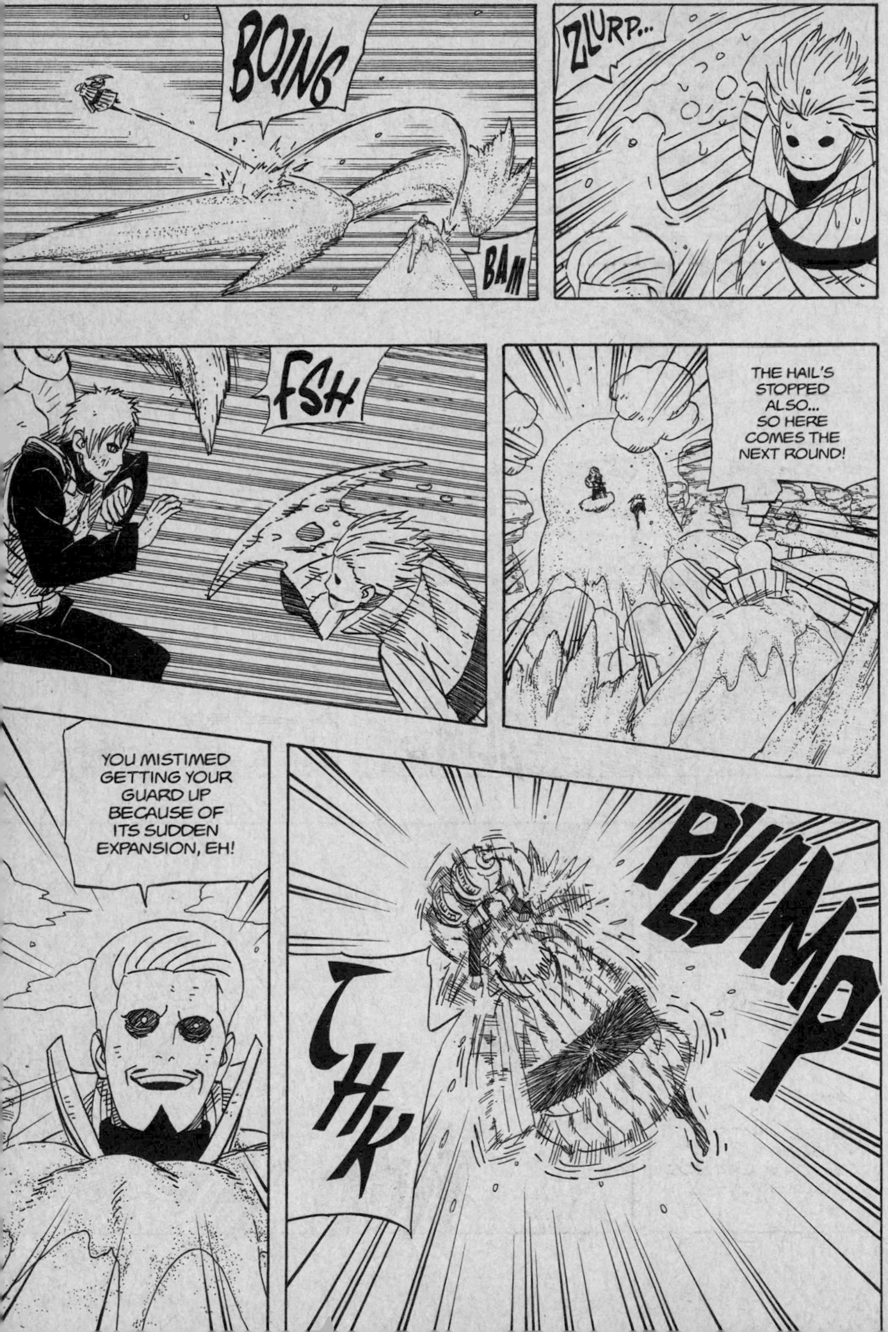

ZLURP...
BOING
BAM
THE HAIL'S STOPPED ALSO... SO HERE COMES THE NEXT ROUND!
FSH
PLUMP
CHK
YOU MISTIMED GETTING YOUR GUARD UP BECAUSE OF ITS SUDDEN EXPANSION, EH!

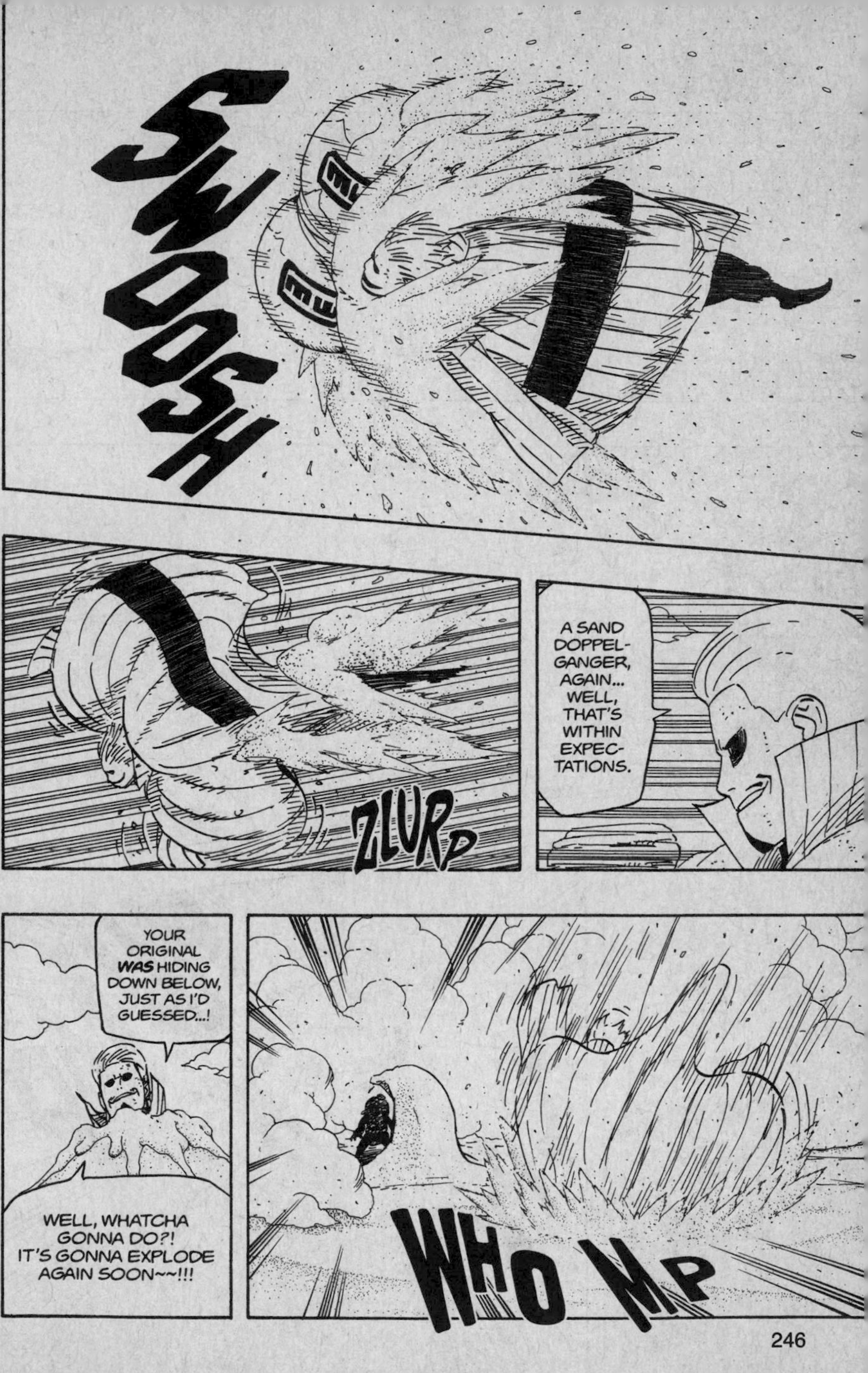
SWOOSH
A SAND DOPPEL-GANGER, AGAIN... WELL, THAT'S WITHIN EXPECTATIONS.
ZLURP
WHOMP
YOUR ORIGINAL ***WAS*** HIDING DOWN BELOW, JUST AS I'D GUESSED...!
WELL, WHATCHA GONNA DO?! IT'S GONNA EXPLODE AGAIN SOON~~!!!

READ THIS WAY

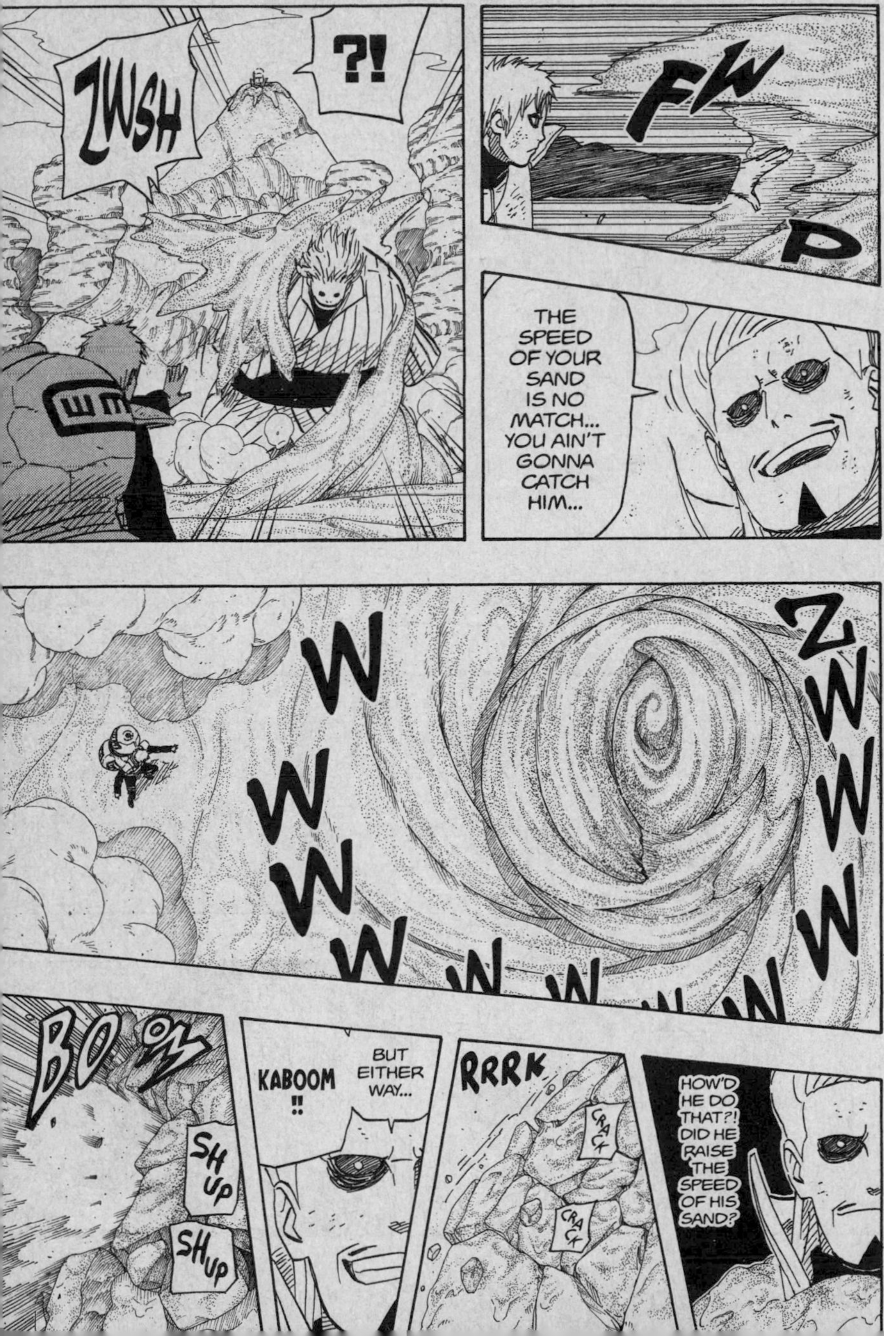

FWP
THE SPEED OF YOUR SAND IS NO MATCH... YOU AIN'T GONNA CATCH HIM...
?!
ZWSH
ZWWWWWWWWWW
HOW'D HE DO THAT?! DID HE RAISE THE SPEED OF HIS SAND?
RRRK
CRACK
CRACK
BUT EITHER WAY...
KABOOM!!
BOOM
SHUP
SHUP

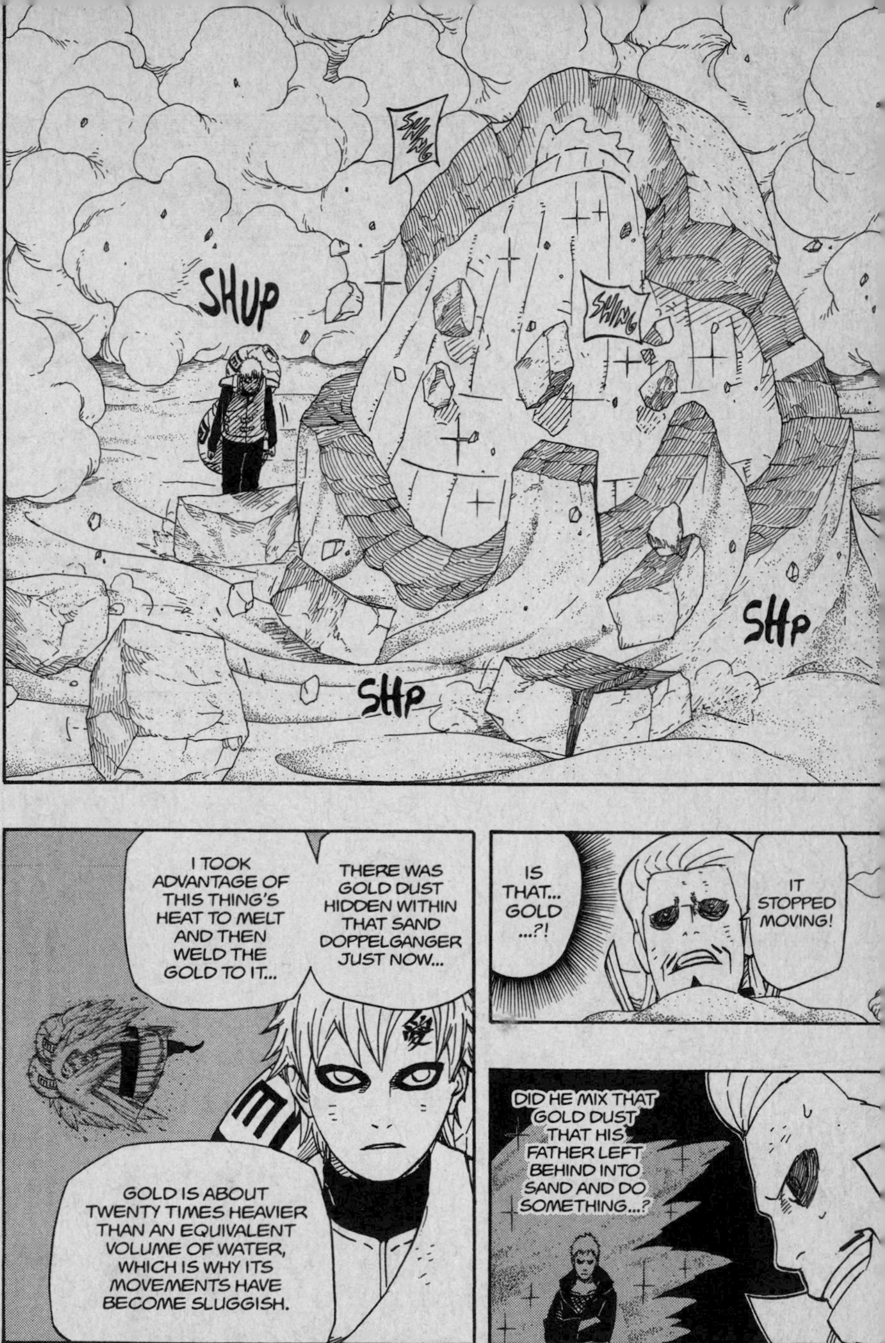
SHING
SHING
SHUP
SHP
SHP
IT STOPPED MOVING!
IS THAT... GOLD ...?!
DID HE MIX THAT GOLD DUST THAT HIS FATHER LEFT BEHIND INTO SAND AND DO SOMETHING...?
THERE WAS GOLD DUST HIDDEN WITHIN THAT SAND DOPPELGANGER JUST NOW...
I TOOK ADVANTAGE OF THIS THING'S HEAT TO MELT AND THEN WELD THE GOLD TO IT...
GOLD IS ABOUT TWENTY TIMES HEAVIER THAN AN EQUIVALENT VOLUME OF WATER, WHICH IS WHY ITS MOVEMENTS HAVE BECOME SLUGGISH.

READ THIS WAY

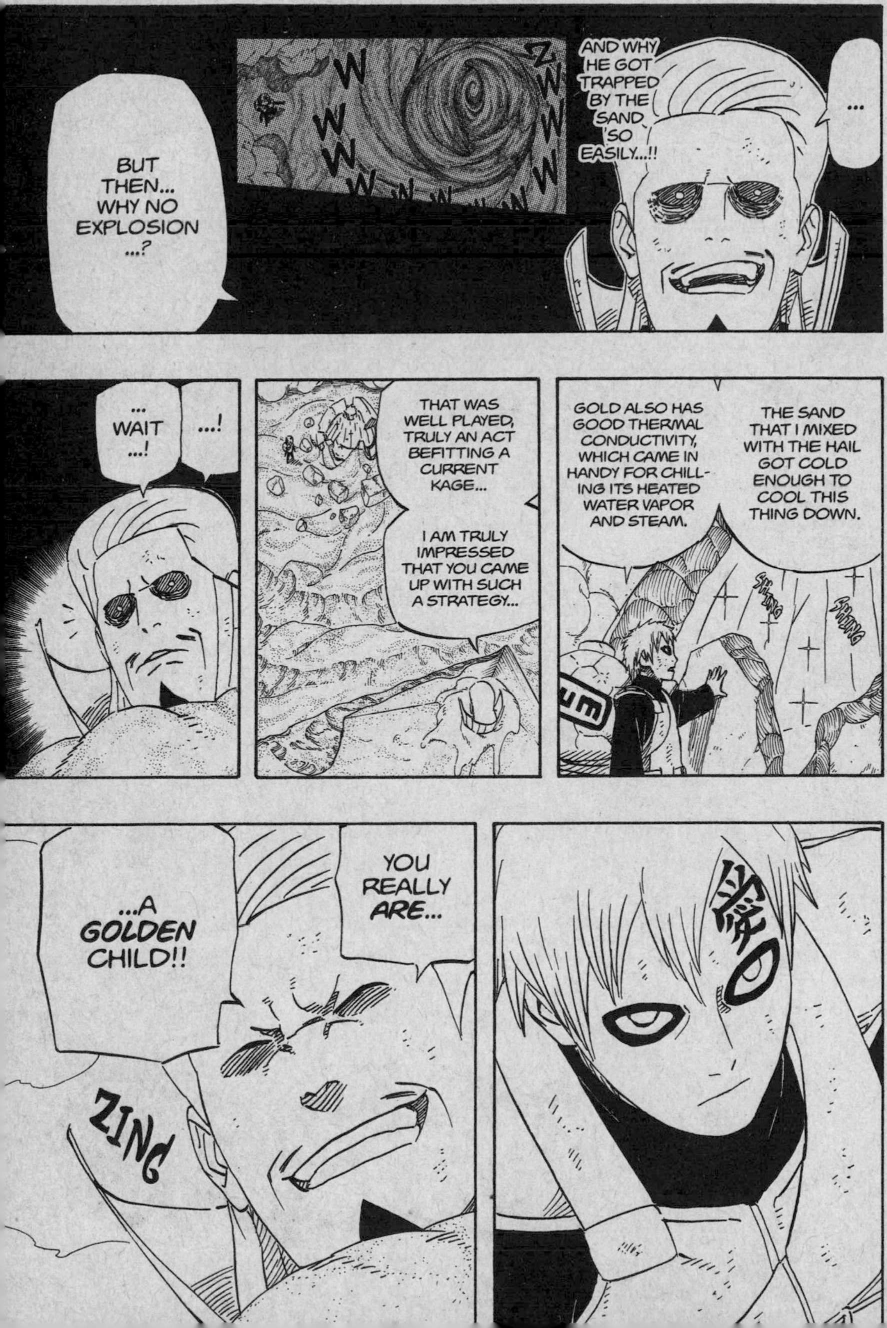
...
AND WHY HE GOT TRAPPED BY THE SAND SO EASILY...!!
ZWWWWWWWWWWWWW
BUT THEN... WHY NO EXPLOSION ...?
THE SAND THAT I MIXED WITH THE HAIL GOT COLD ENOUGH TO COOL THIS THING DOWN.
GOLD ALSO HAS GOOD THERMAL CONDUCTIVITY, WHICH CAME IN HANDY FOR CHILL-ING ITS HEATED WATER VAPOR AND STEAM.
SHING
SHING
THAT WAS WELL PLAYED, TRULY AN ACT BEFITTING A CURRENT KAGE...
I AM TRULY IMPRESSED THAT YOU CAME UP WITH SUCH A STRATEGY...
...!
... WAIT ...!
YOU REALLY ARE...
...A GOLDEN CHILD!!
ZING

NARUTO

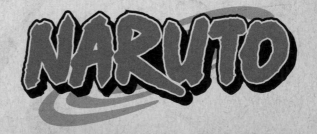

Number 558: Kabuto's Trump Card...!!

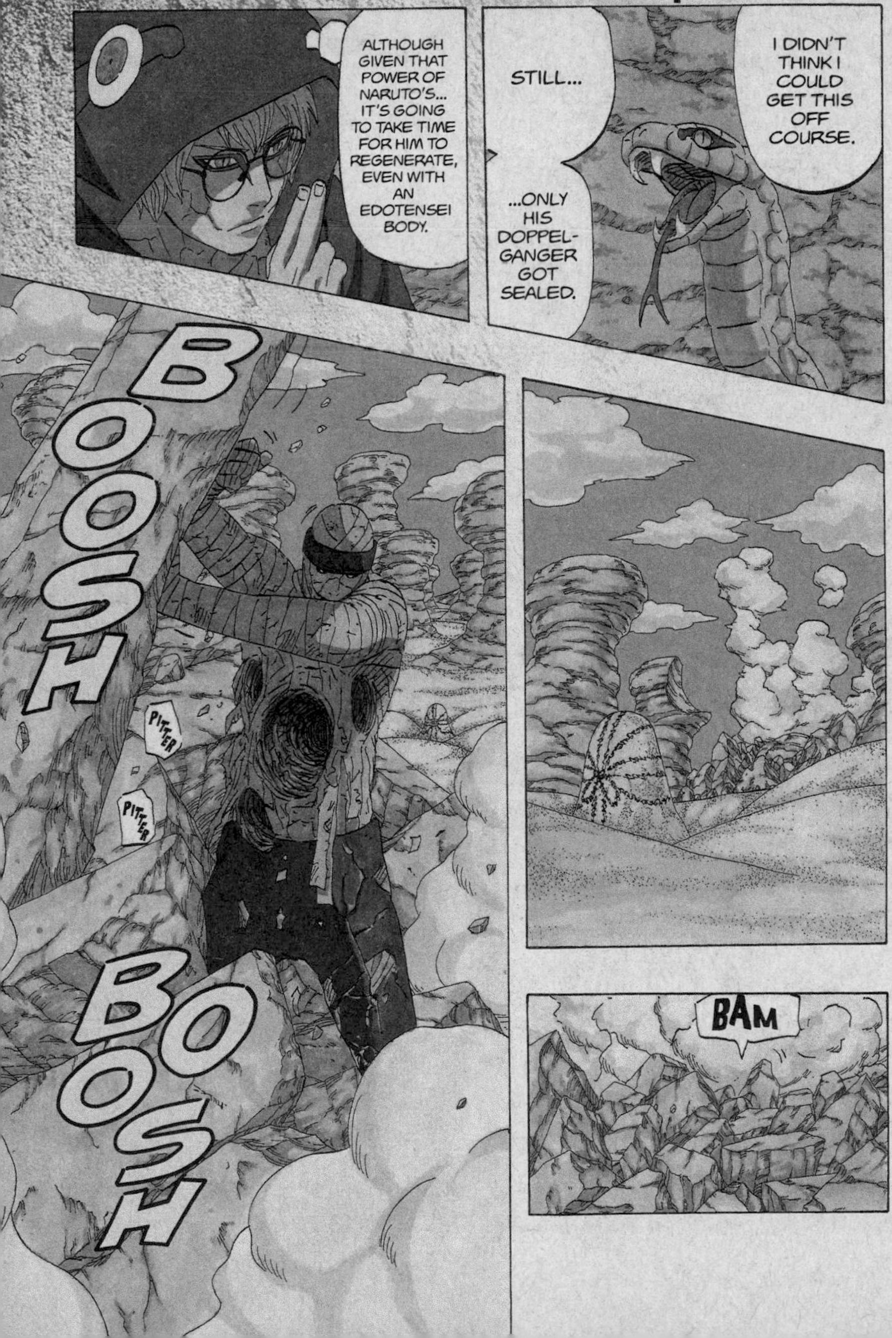
I DIDN'T THINK I COULD GET THIS OFF COURSE.
STILL...
...ONLY HIS DOPPEL-GANGER GOT SEALED.
ALTHOUGH GIVEN THAT POWER OF NARUTO'S... IT'S GOING TO TAKE TIME FOR HIM TO REGENERATE, EVEN WITH AN EDOTENSEI BODY.
BAM
BOOSH
PITTER
PITTER
BOOSH

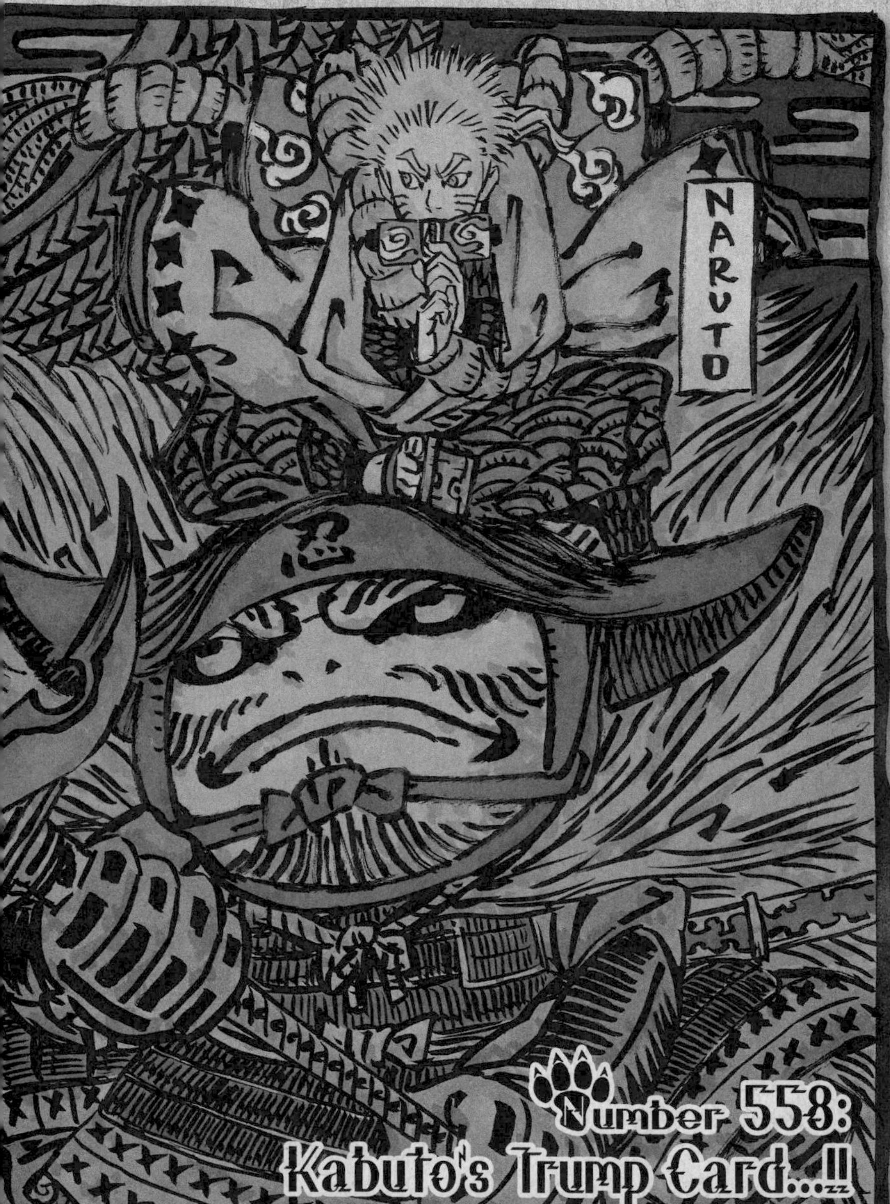
NARUTO
忍
Number 558:
Kabuto's Trump Card...!!

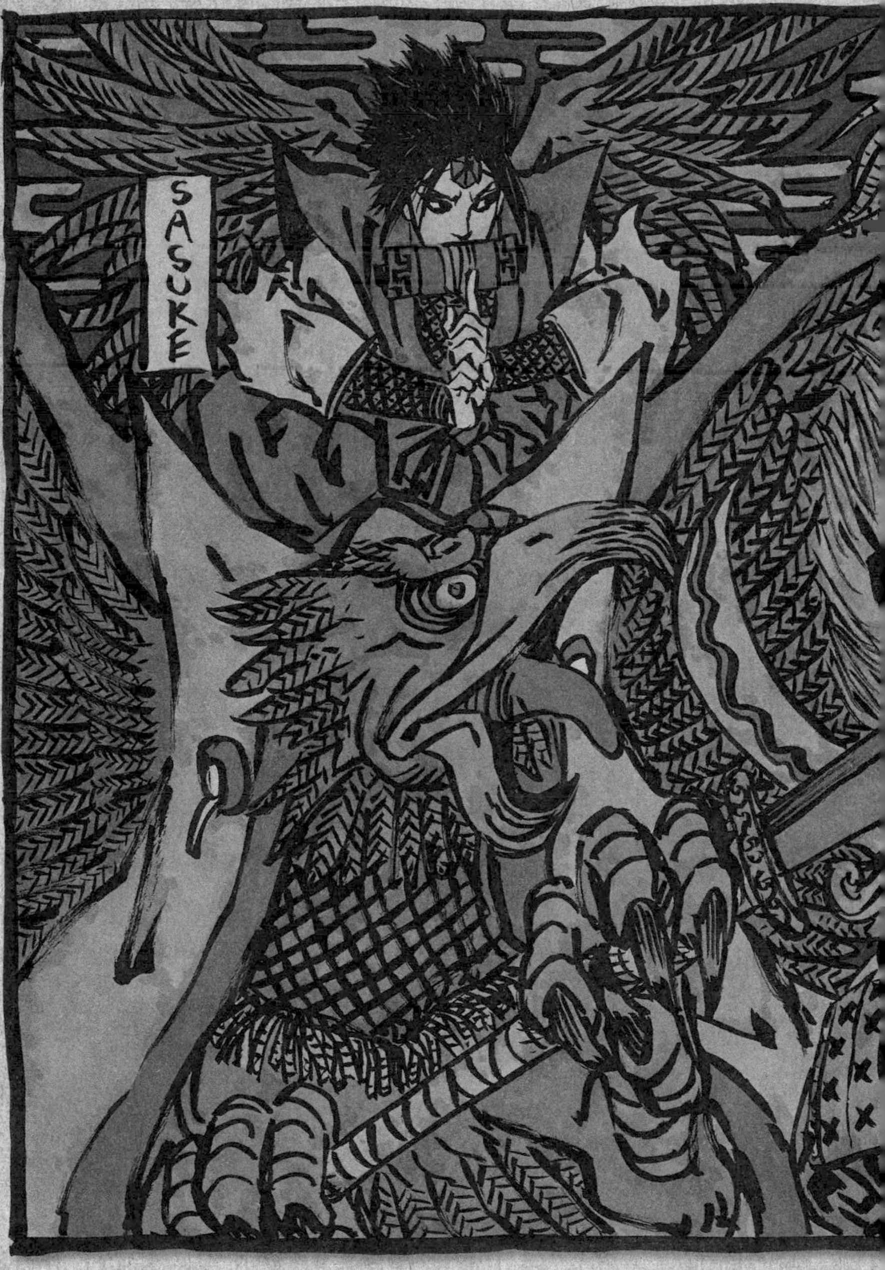
SASUKE

NARUTO

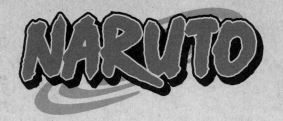

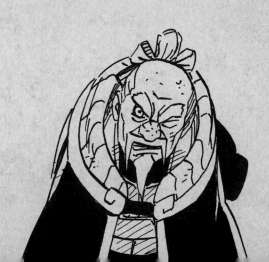

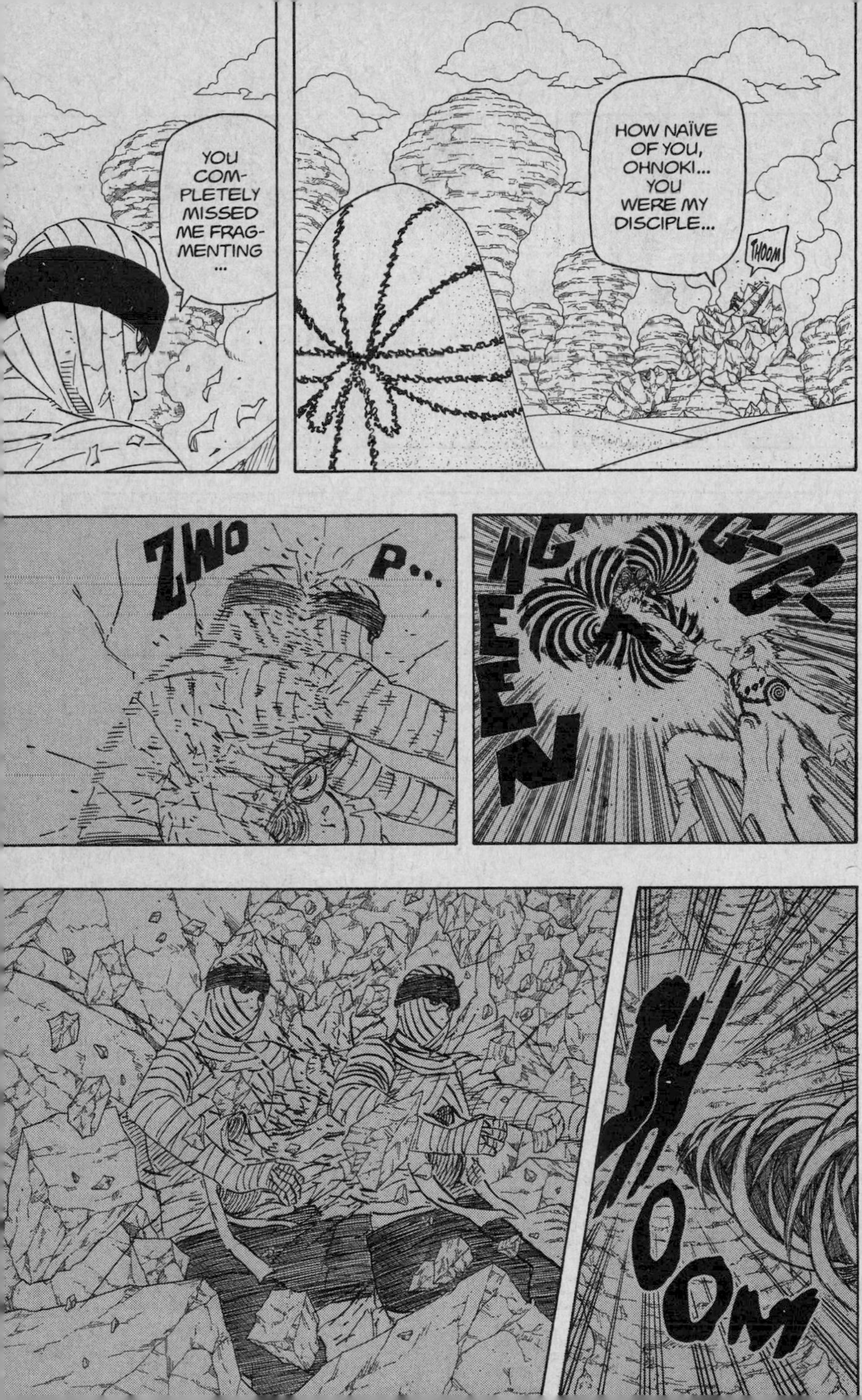
HOW NAÏVE OF YOU, OHNOKI... YOU WERE MY DISCIPLE...
THOOM
YOU COMPLETELY MISSED ME FRAGMENTING ...
G-G-
WGEEEN
ZWOP...
SHOOM

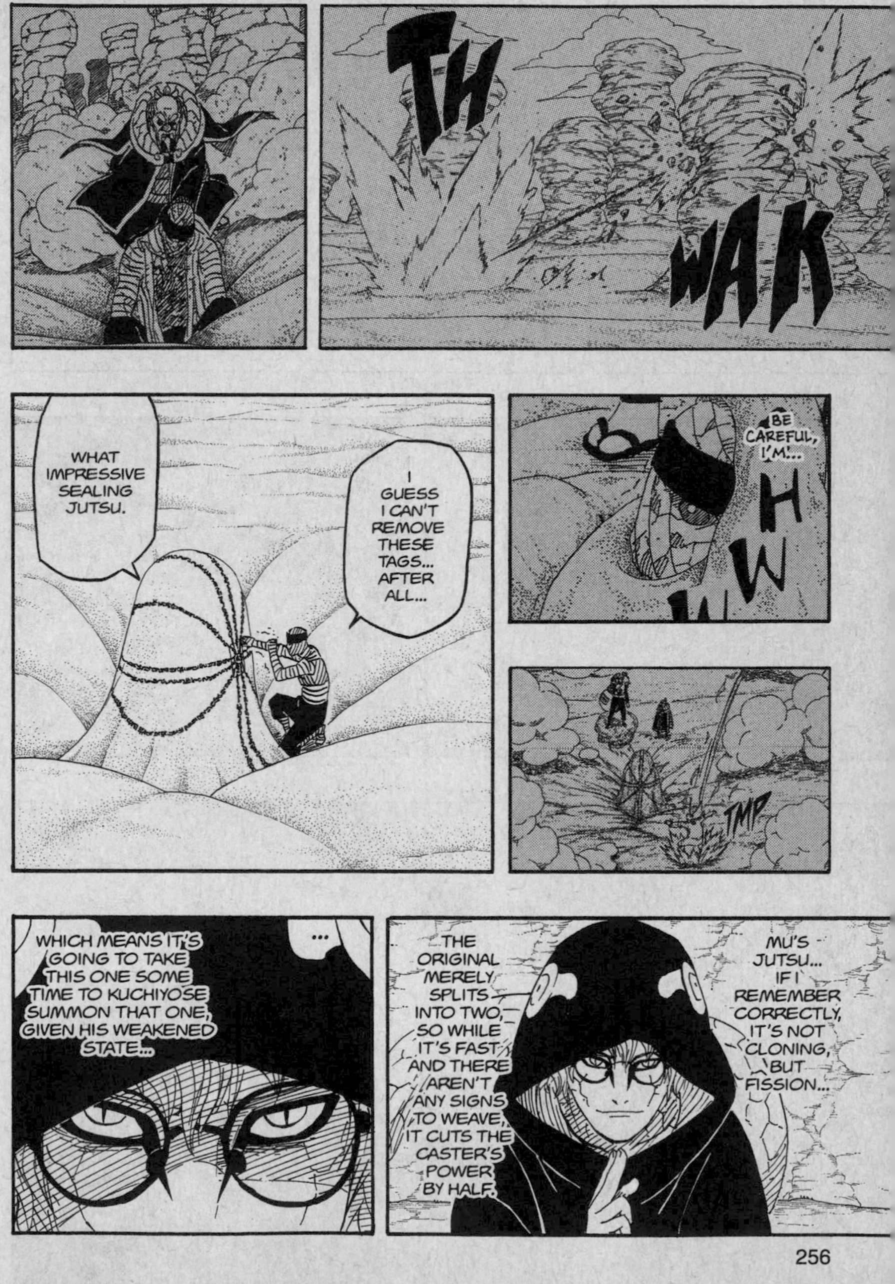
TH
WAK
BE CAREFUL, I'M...
HWW
TMP
I GUESS I CAN'T REMOVE THESE TAGS... AFTER ALL...
WHAT IMPRESSIVE SEALING JUTSU.
MU'S JUTSU... IF I REMEMBER CORRECTLY, IT'S NOT CLONING, BUT FISSION...
THE ORIGINAL MERELY SPLITS INTO TWO, SO WHILE IT'S FAST AND THERE AREN'T ANY SIGNS TO WEAVE, IT CUTS THE CASTER'S POWER BY HALF.
...
WHICH MEANS IT'S GOING TO TAKE THIS ONE SOME TIME TO KUCHIYOSE SUMMON THAT ONE, GIVEN HIS WEAKENED STATE...

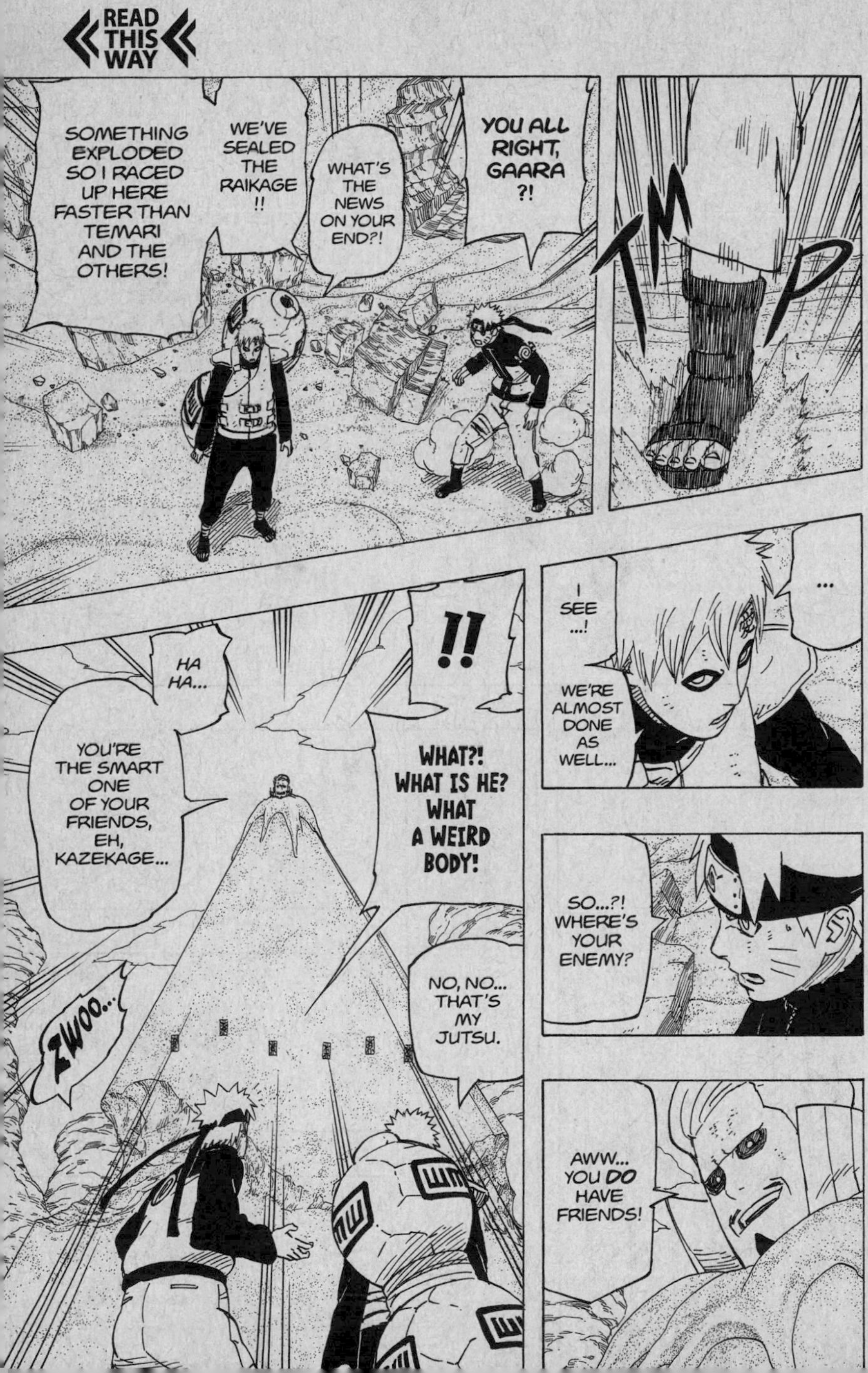
READ THIS WAY
TMP
YOU ALL RIGHT, GAARA ?!
WHAT'S THE NEWS ON YOUR END?!
WE'VE SEALED THE RAIKAGE !!
SOMETHING EXPLODED SO I RACED UP HERE FASTER THAN TEMARI AND THE OTHERS!
...
I SEE ...!
WE'RE ALMOST DONE AS WELL...
SO...?! WHERE'S YOUR ENEMY?
AWW... YOU DO HAVE FRIENDS!
!!
WHAT?! WHAT IS HE? WHAT A WEIRD BODY!
NO, NO... THAT'S MY JUTSU.
HA HA...
YOU'RE THE SMART ONE OF YOUR FRIENDS, EH, KAZEKAGE...
ZWOO...

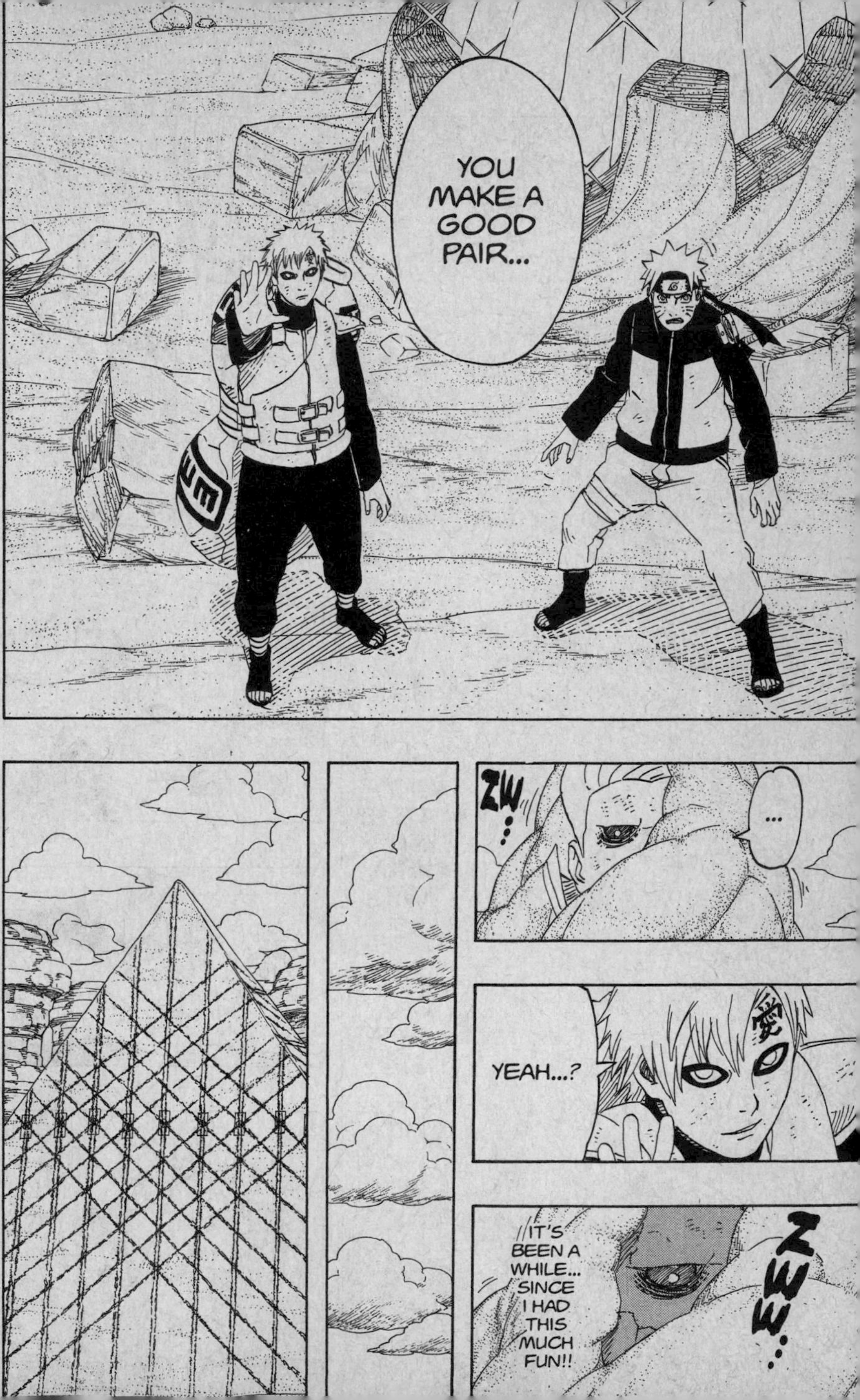
YOU MAKE A GOOD PAIR...
...
ZW..
YEAH...?
ZWW..
IT'S BEEN A WHILE... SINCE I HAD THIS MUCH FUN!!

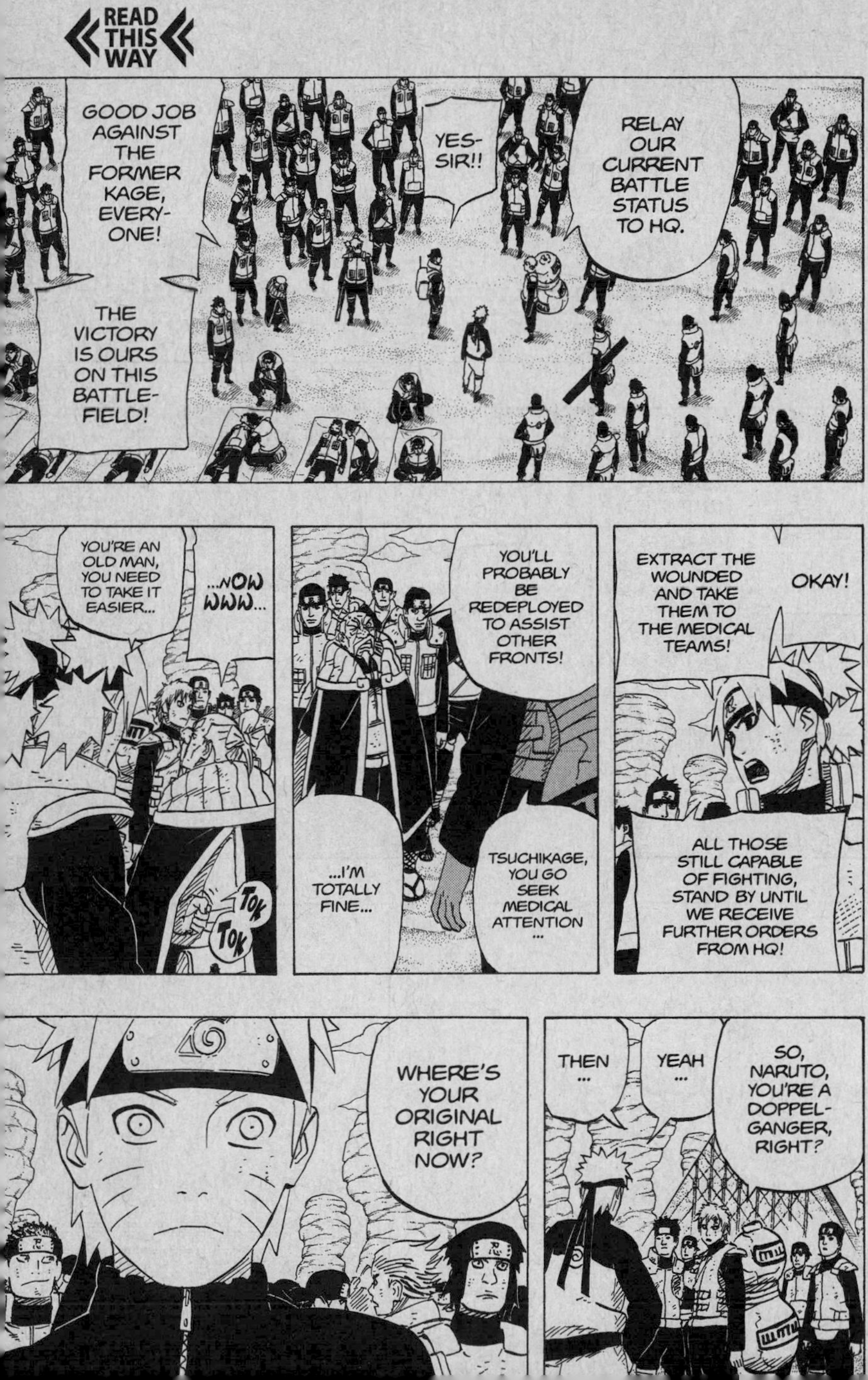
READ THIS WAY
RELAY OUR CURRENT BATTLE STATUS TO HQ.
YES-SIR!!
GOOD JOB AGAINST THE FORMER KAGE, EVERYONE!
THE VICTORY IS OURS ON THIS BATTLEFIELD!
EXTRACT THE WOUNDED AND TAKE THEM TO THE MEDICAL TEAMS!
OKAY!
ALL THOSE STILL CAPABLE OF FIGHTING, STAND BY UNTIL WE RECEIVE FURTHER ORDERS FROM HQ!
YOU'LL PROBABLY BE REDEPLOYED TO ASSIST OTHER FRONTS!
TSUCHIKAGE, YOU GO SEEK MEDICAL ATTENTION ...
...I'M TOTALLY FINE...
...NOW WWW...
YOU'RE AN OLD MAN, YOU NEED TO TAKE IT EASIER...
TOK TOK
SO, NARUTO, YOU'RE A DOPPEL-GANGER, RIGHT?
YEAH ...
THEN ...
WHERE'S YOUR ORIGINAL RIGHT NOW?

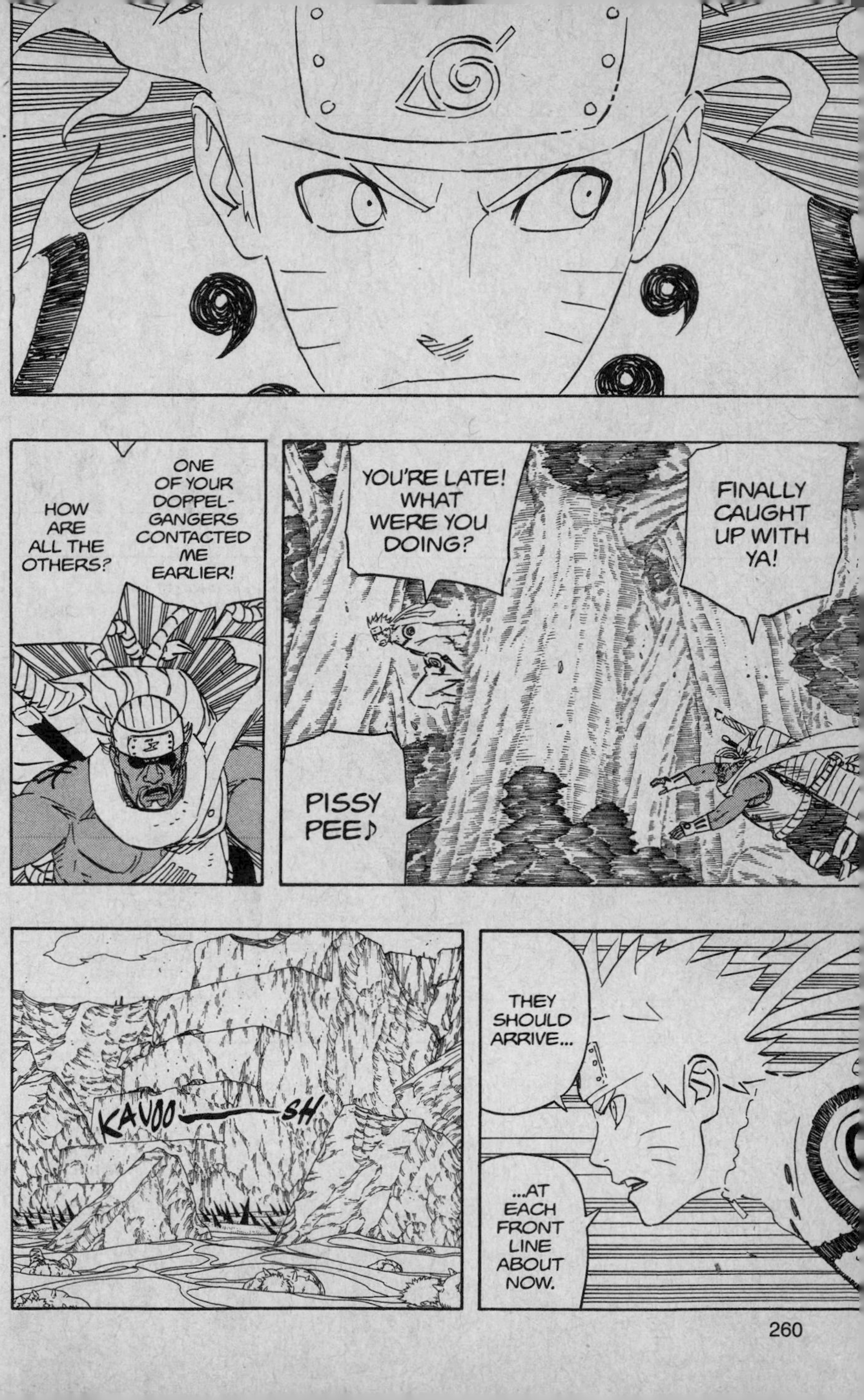
FINALLY CAUGHT UP WITH YA!
YOU'RE LATE! WHAT WERE YOU DOING?
PISSY PEE♪
ONE OF YOUR DOPPEL-GANGERS CONTACTED ME EARLIER!
HOW ARE ALL THE OTHERS?
THEY SHOULD ARRIVE...
...AT EACH FRONT LINE ABOUT NOW.
KAVOO——SH

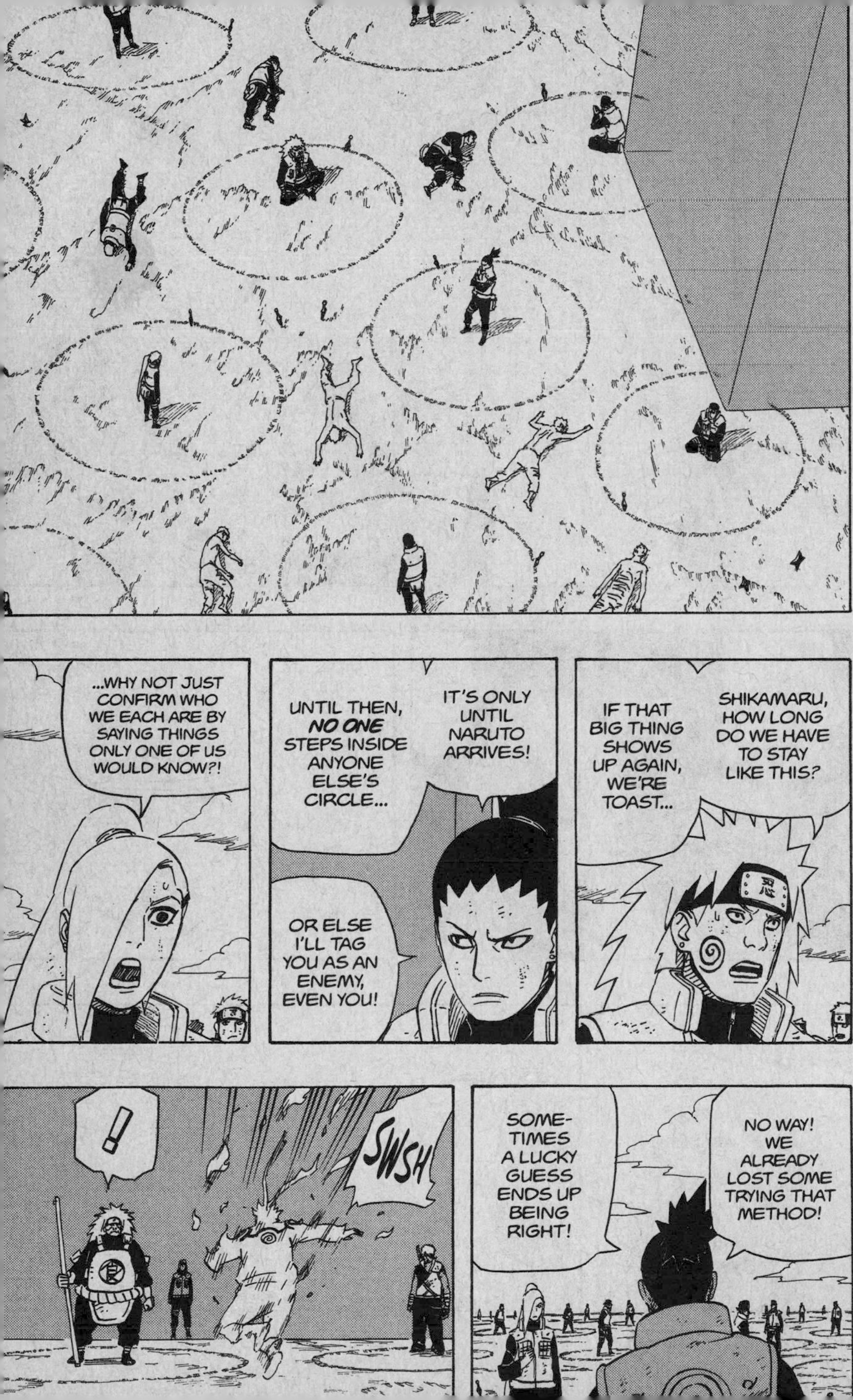
SHIKAMARU, HOW LONG DO WE HAVE TO STAY LIKE THIS?
IF THAT BIG THING SHOWS UP AGAIN, WE'RE TOAST...
IT'S ONLY UNTIL NARUTO ARRIVES!
UNTIL THEN, NO ONE STEPS INSIDE ANYONE ELSE'S CIRCLE...
OR ELSE I'LL TAG YOU AS AN ENEMY, EVEN YOU!
...WHY NOT JUST CONFIRM WHO WE EACH ARE BY SAYING THINGS ONLY ONE OF US WOULD KNOW?!
NO WAY! WE ALREADY LOST SOME TRYING THAT METHOD!
SOME-TIMES A LUCKY GUESS ENDS UP BEING RIGHT!
!
SWSH

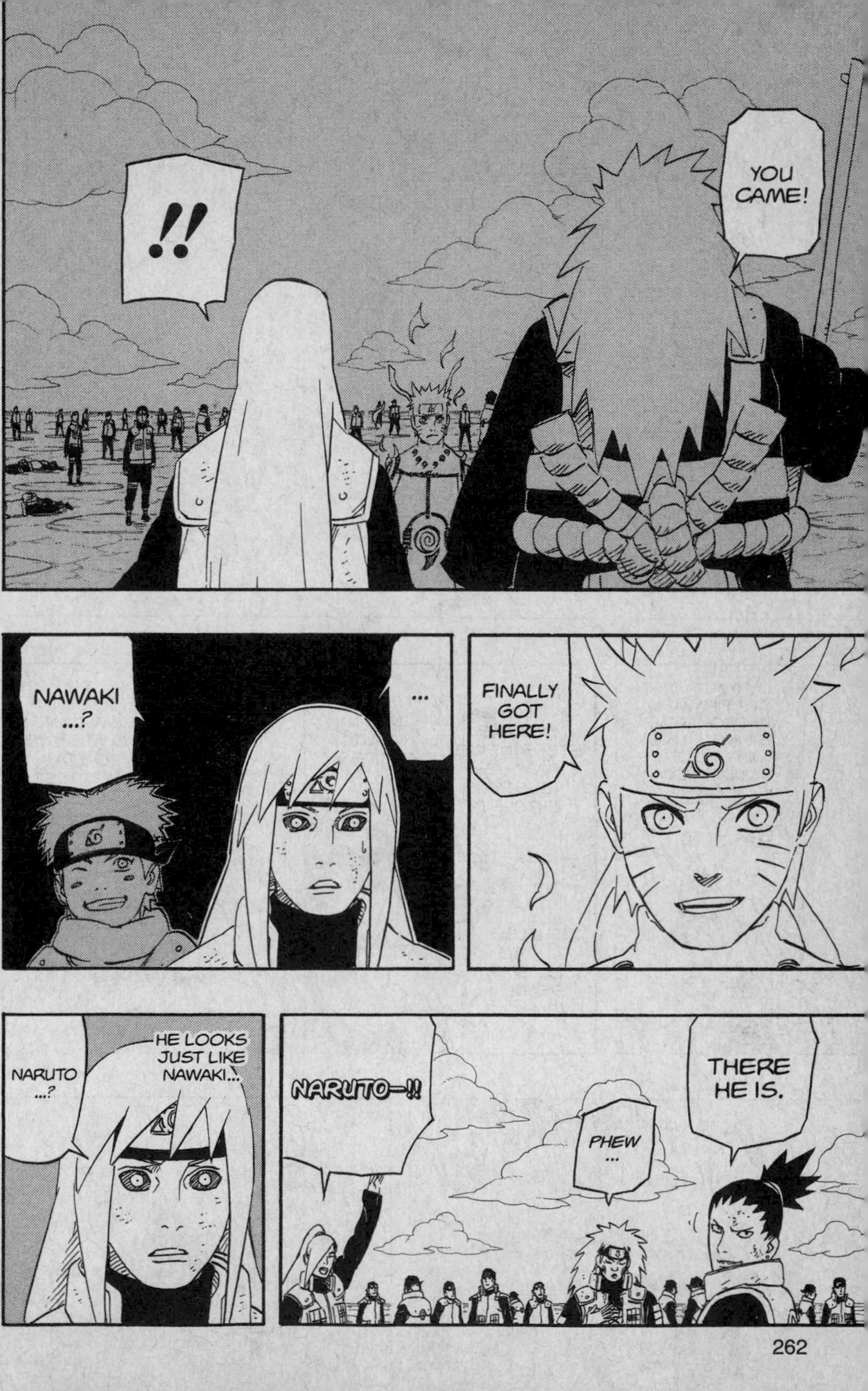
YOU CAME!
!!
FINALLY GOT HERE!
...
NAWAKI ...?
THERE HE IS.
PHEW ...
NARUTO—!!
HE LOOKS JUST LIKE NAWAKI...
NARUTO ...?

READ THIS WAY

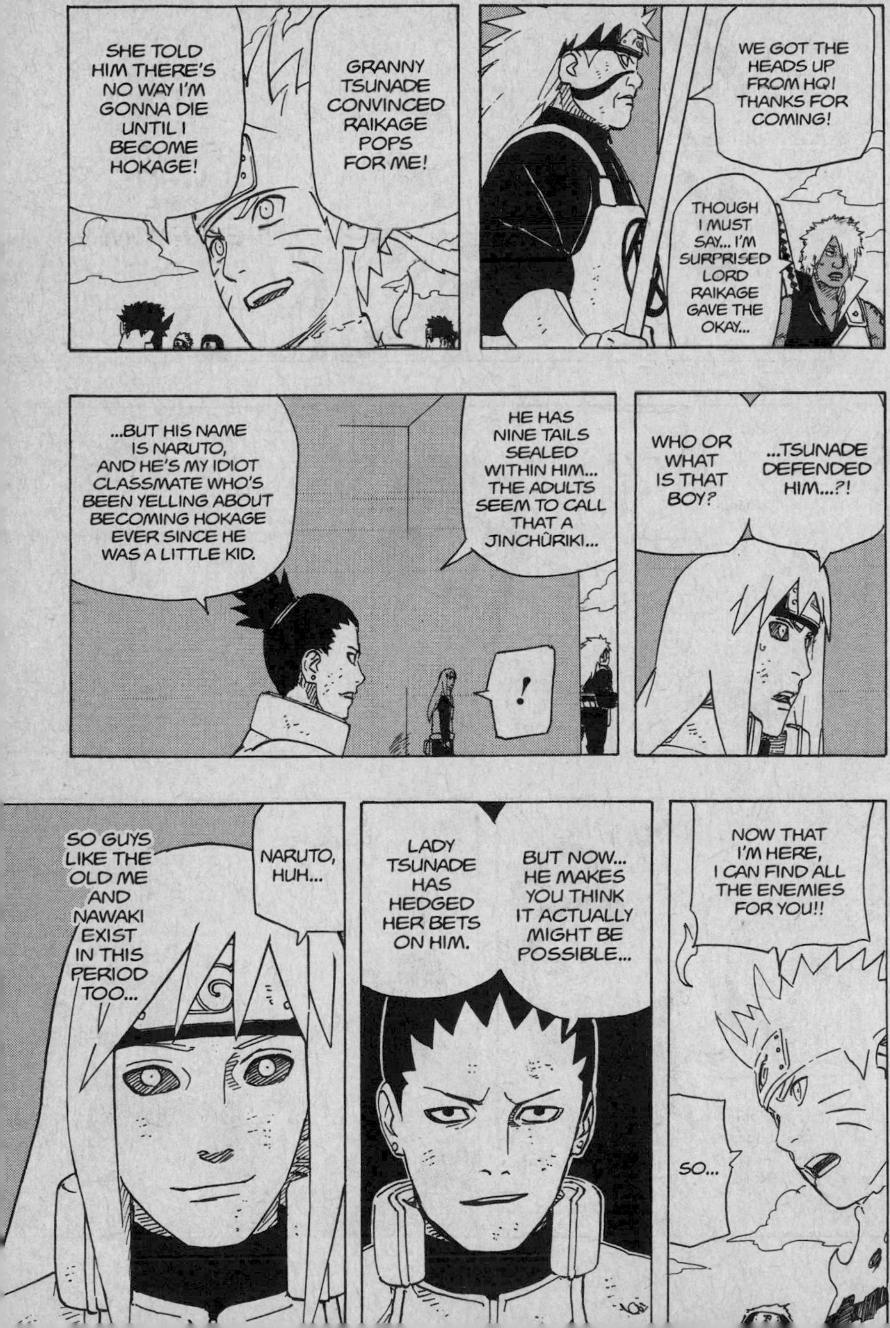
WE GOT THE HEADS UP FROM HQ! THANKS FOR COMING!
THOUGH I MUST SAY... I'M SURPRISED LORD RAIKAGE GAVE THE OKAY...
GRANNY TSUNADE CONVINCED RAIKAGE POPS FOR ME!
SHE TOLD HIM THERE'S NO WAY I'M GONNA DIE UNTIL I BECOME HOKAGE!
...TSUNADE DEFENDED HIM...?!
WHO OR WHAT IS THAT BOY?
HE HAS NINE TAILS SEALED WITHIN HIM... THE ADULTS SEEM TO CALL THAT A JINCHŪRIKI...
...BUT HIS NAME IS NARUTO, AND HE'S MY IDIOT CLASSMATE WHO'S BEEN YELLING ABOUT BECOMING HOKAGE EVER SINCE HE WAS A LITTLE KID.
!
NOW THAT I'M HERE, I CAN FIND ALL THE ENEMIES FOR YOU!!
SO...
BUT NOW... HE MAKES YOU THINK IT ACTUALLY MIGHT BE POSSIBLE...
LADY TSUNADE HAS HEDGED HER BETS ON HIM.
NARUTO, HUH...
SO GUYS LIKE THE OLD ME AND NAWAKI EXIST IN THIS PERIOD TOO...

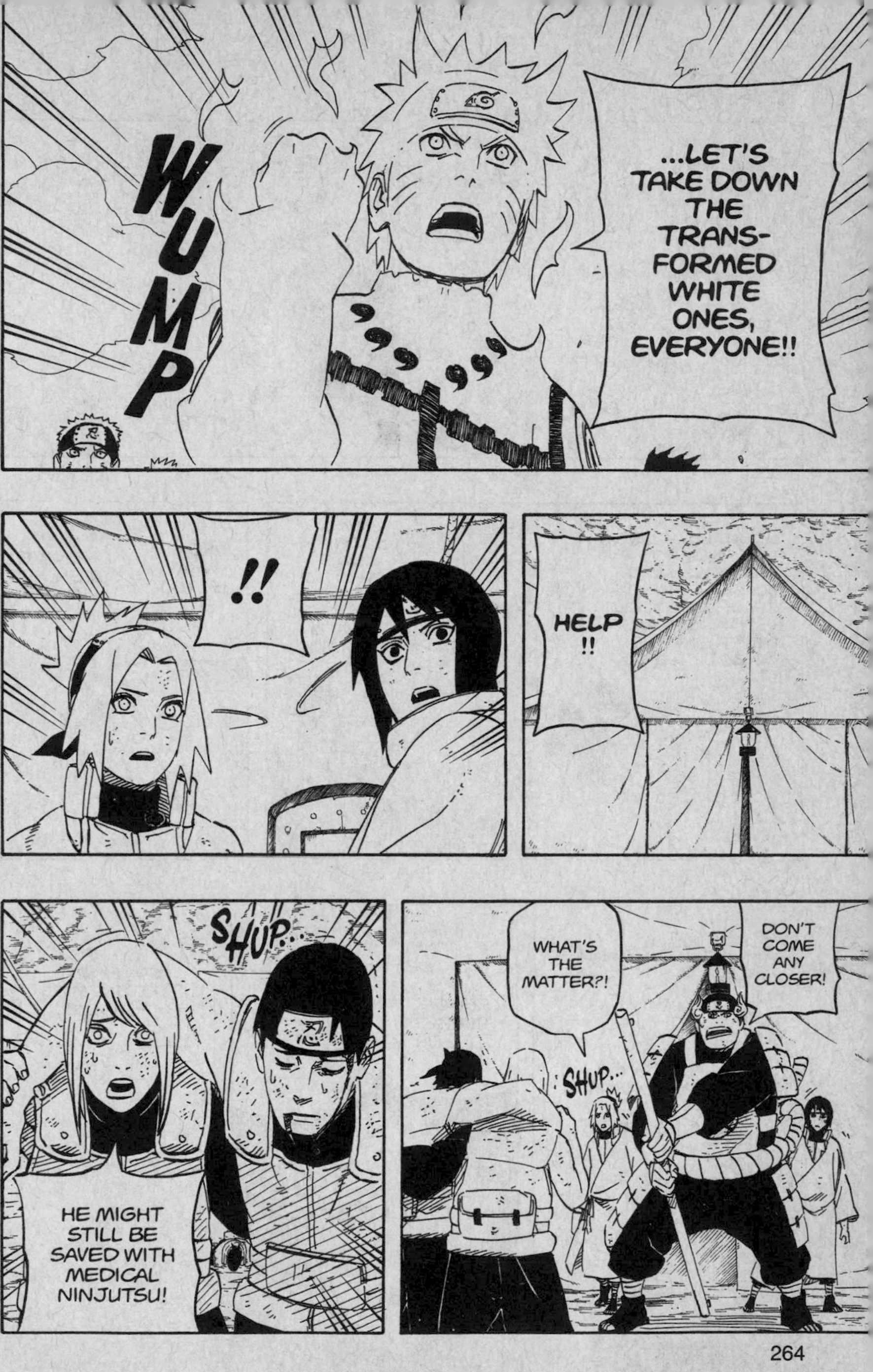
...LET'S TAKE DOWN THE TRANS-FORMED WHITE ONES, EVERYONE!!
WUMP
HELP!!
!!
DON'T COME ANY CLOSER!
WHAT'S THE MATTER?!
SHUP...
SHUP...
HE MIGHT STILL BE SAVED WITH MEDICAL NINJUTSU!

READ THIS WAY

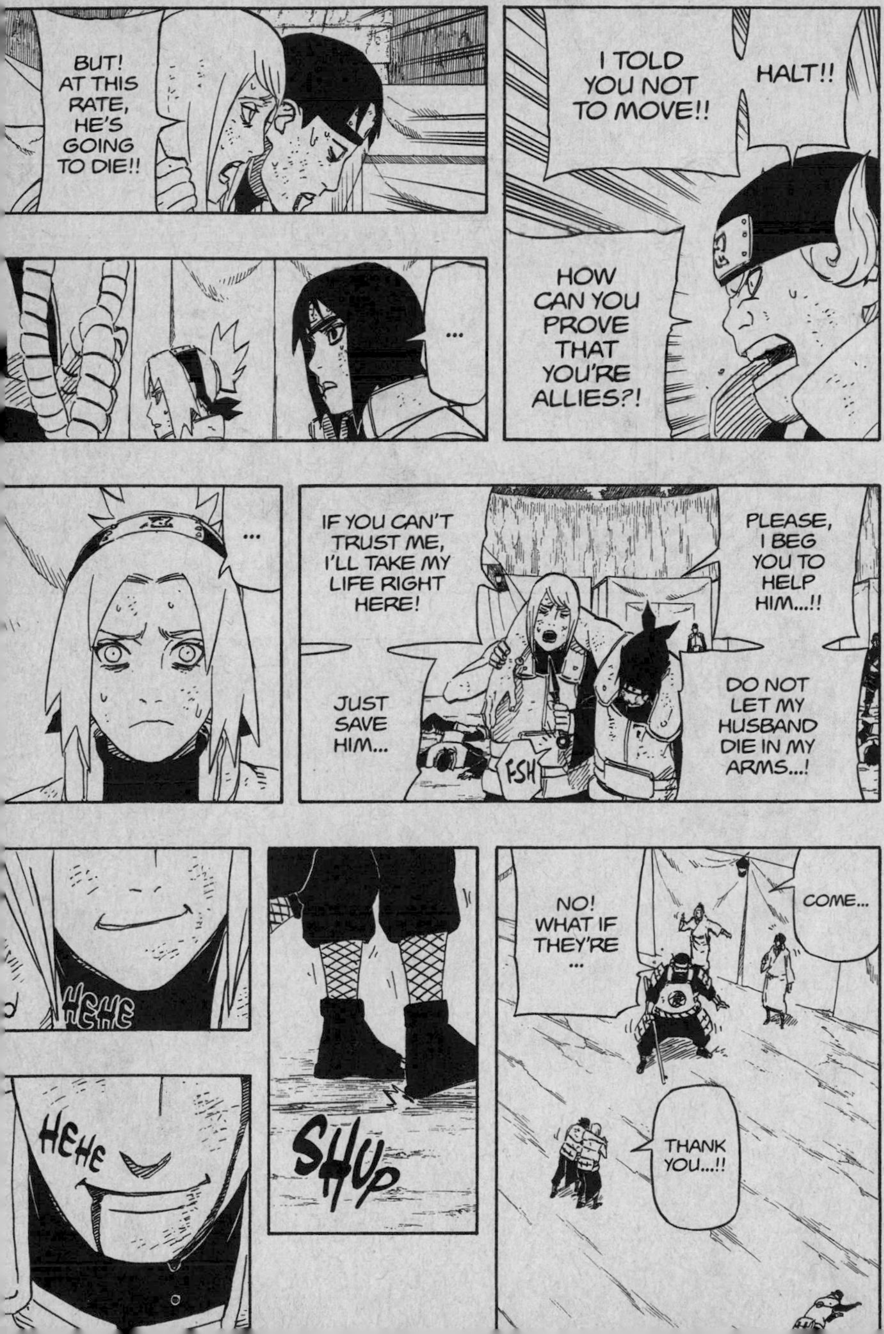

HALT!!
I TOLD YOU NOT TO MOVE!!
HOW CAN YOU PROVE THAT YOU'RE ALLIES?!
BUT! AT THIS RATE, HE'S GOING TO DIE!!
...
PLEASE, I BEG YOU TO HELP HIM...!!
IF YOU CAN'T TRUST ME, I'LL TAKE MY LIFE RIGHT HERE!
DO NOT LET MY HUSBAND DIE IN MY ARMS...!
JUST SAVE HIM...
FSH
...
COME...
NO! WHAT IF THEY'RE ...
THANK YOU...!!
SHUP
HEHE
HEHE

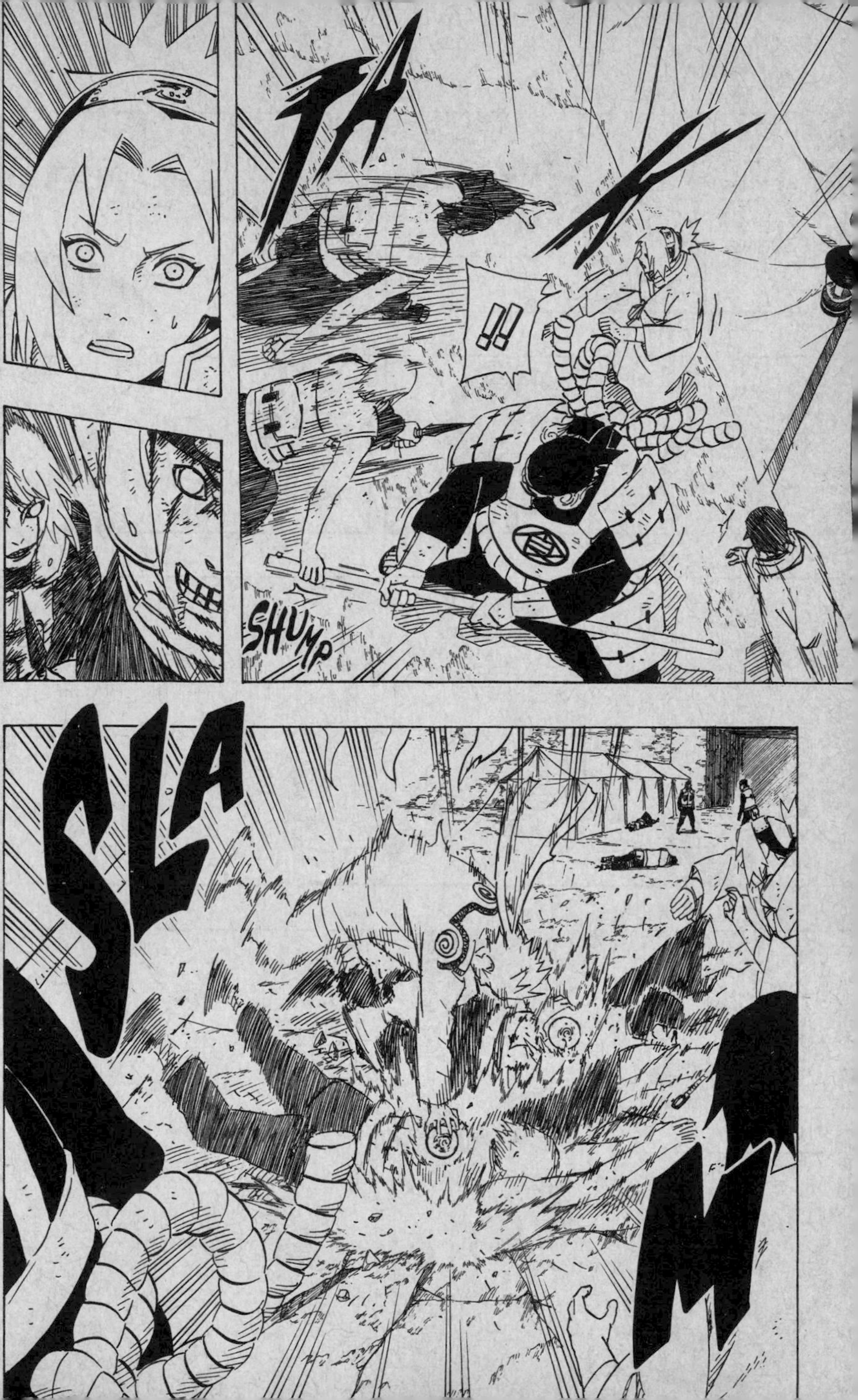
TAK
!!
SHUMP
SLAM

READ THIS WAY

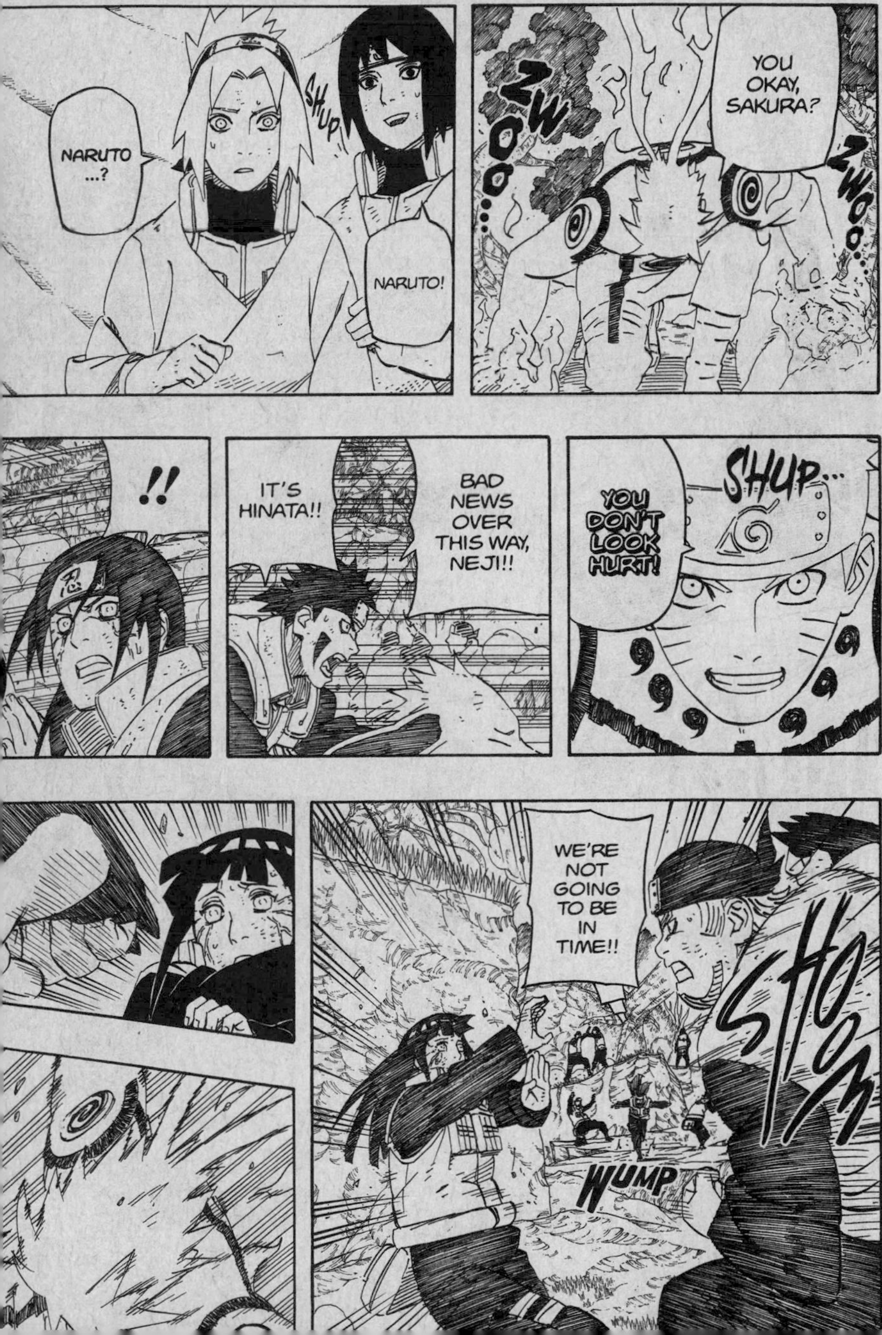
ZWOOO...
YOU OKAY, SAKURA?
ZWOOO...
SHUP
NARUTO ...?
NARUTO!
SHUP...
YOU DON'T LOOK HURT!
BAD NEWS OVER THIS WAY, NEJI!!
IT'S HINATA!!
!!
WE'RE NOT GOING TO BE IN TIME!!
SHOM
WUMP

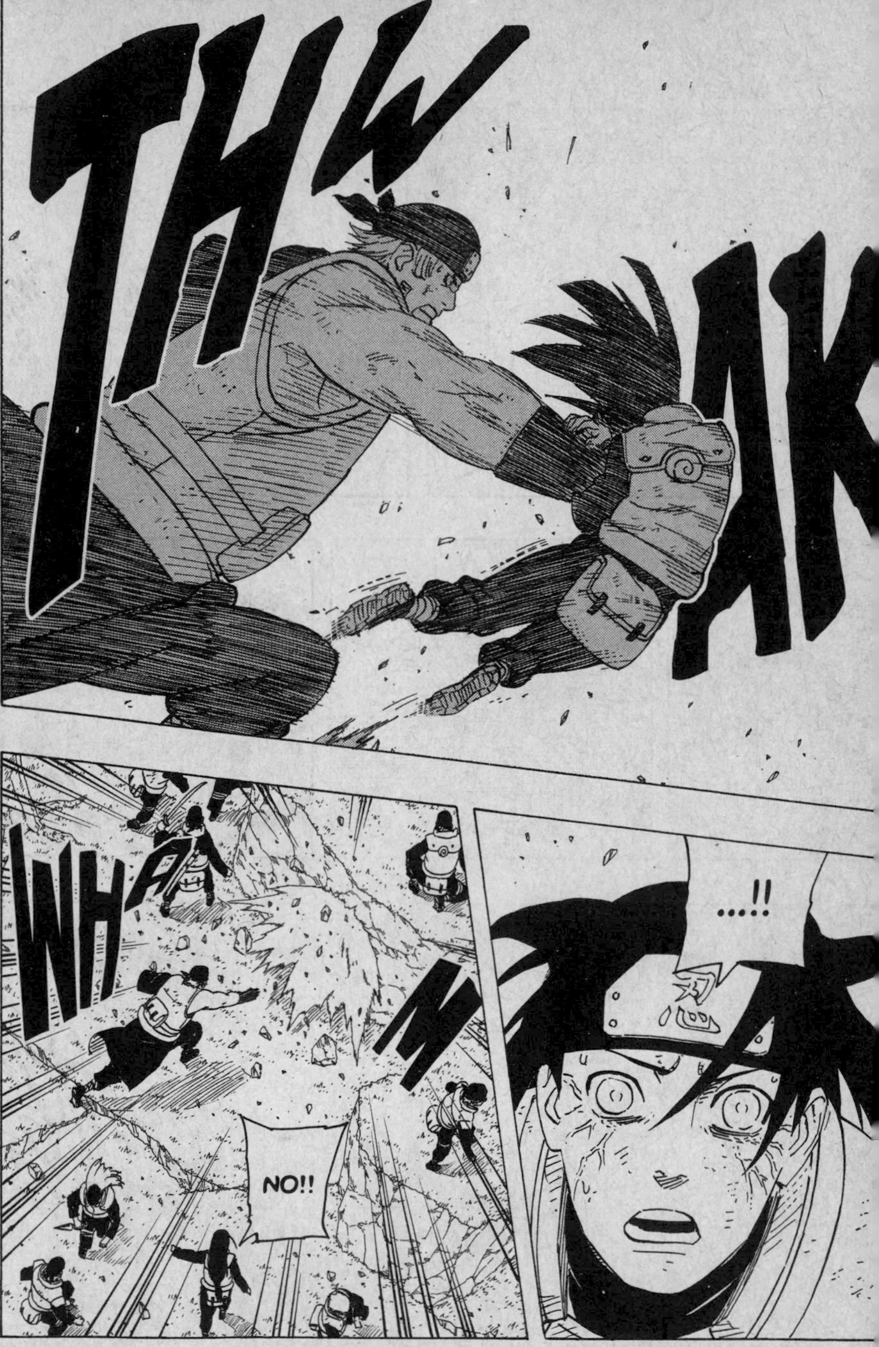
THWAK
...!!
WHAM
NO!!

READ THIS WAY

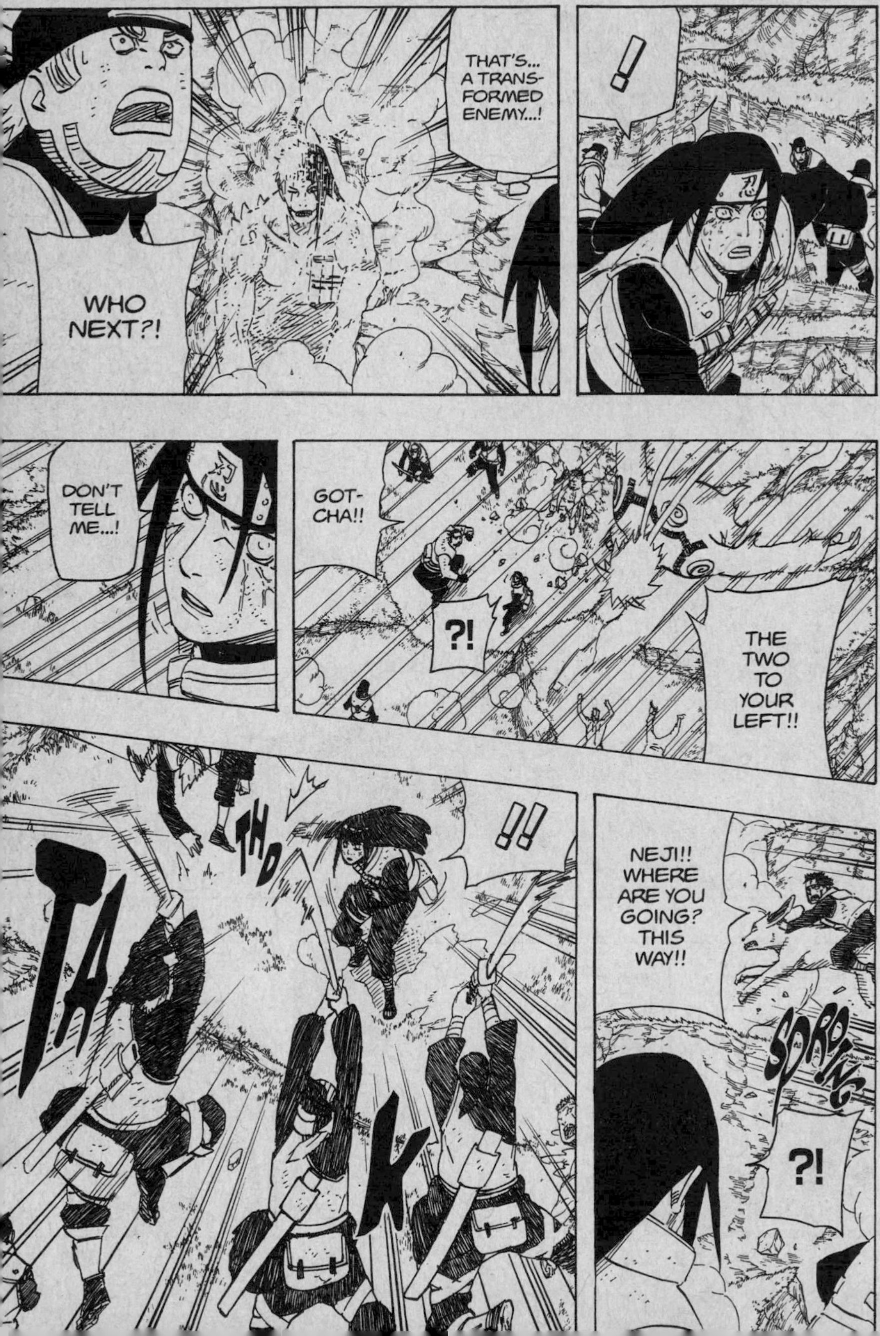
!
THAT'S... A TRANS-FORMED ENEMY...!
WHO NEXT?!
GOT-CHA!!
?!
THE TWO TO YOUR LEFT!!
DON'T TELL ME...!
NEJI!! WHERE ARE YOU GOING? THIS WAY!!
SPROING
?!
!!
THD
TACK

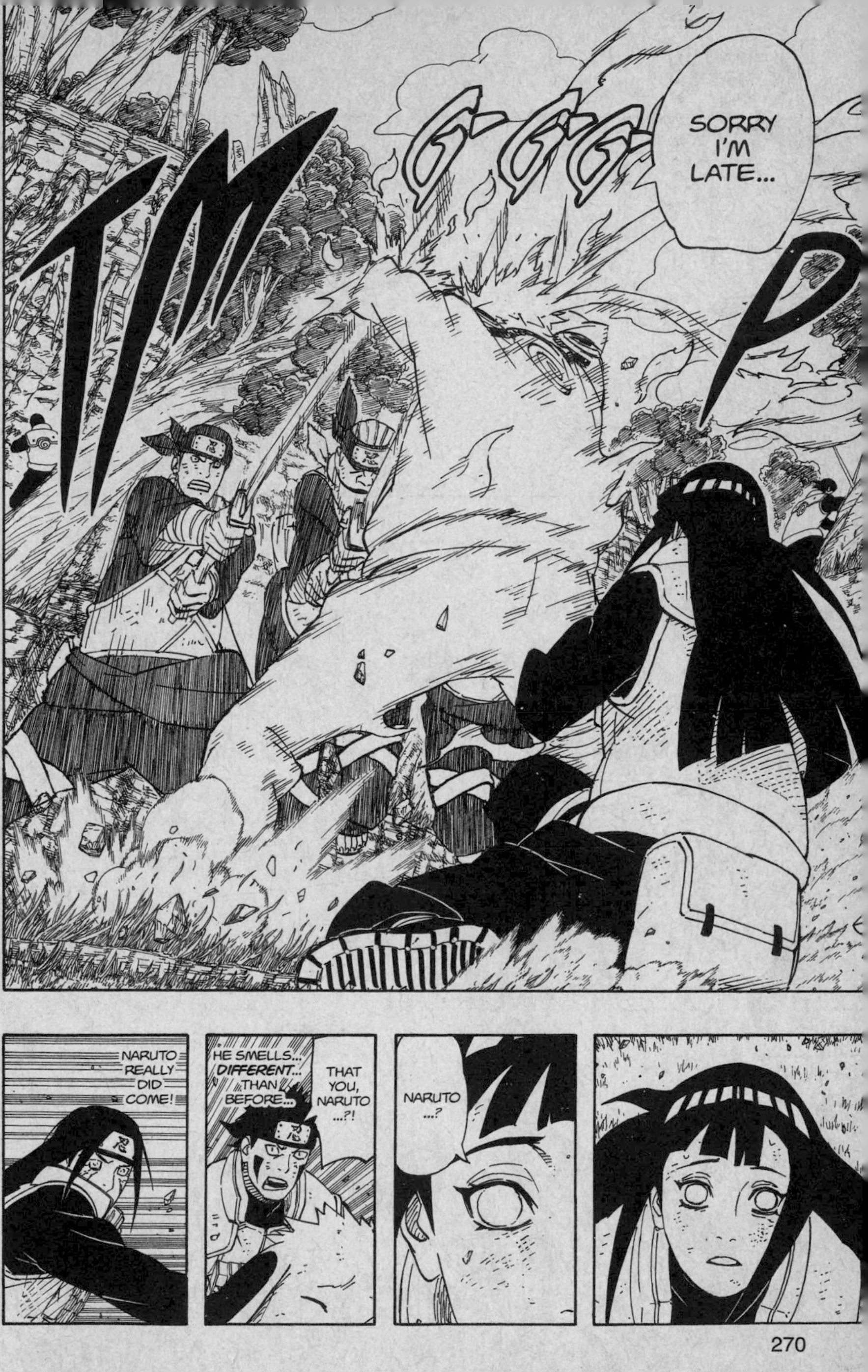
SORRY I'M LATE...
G-G-G
TMP
NARUTO ...?
THAT YOU, NARUTO ...?!
HE SMELLS... *DIFFERENT*... THAN BEFORE...
NARUTO REALLY DID COME!

READ THIS WAY

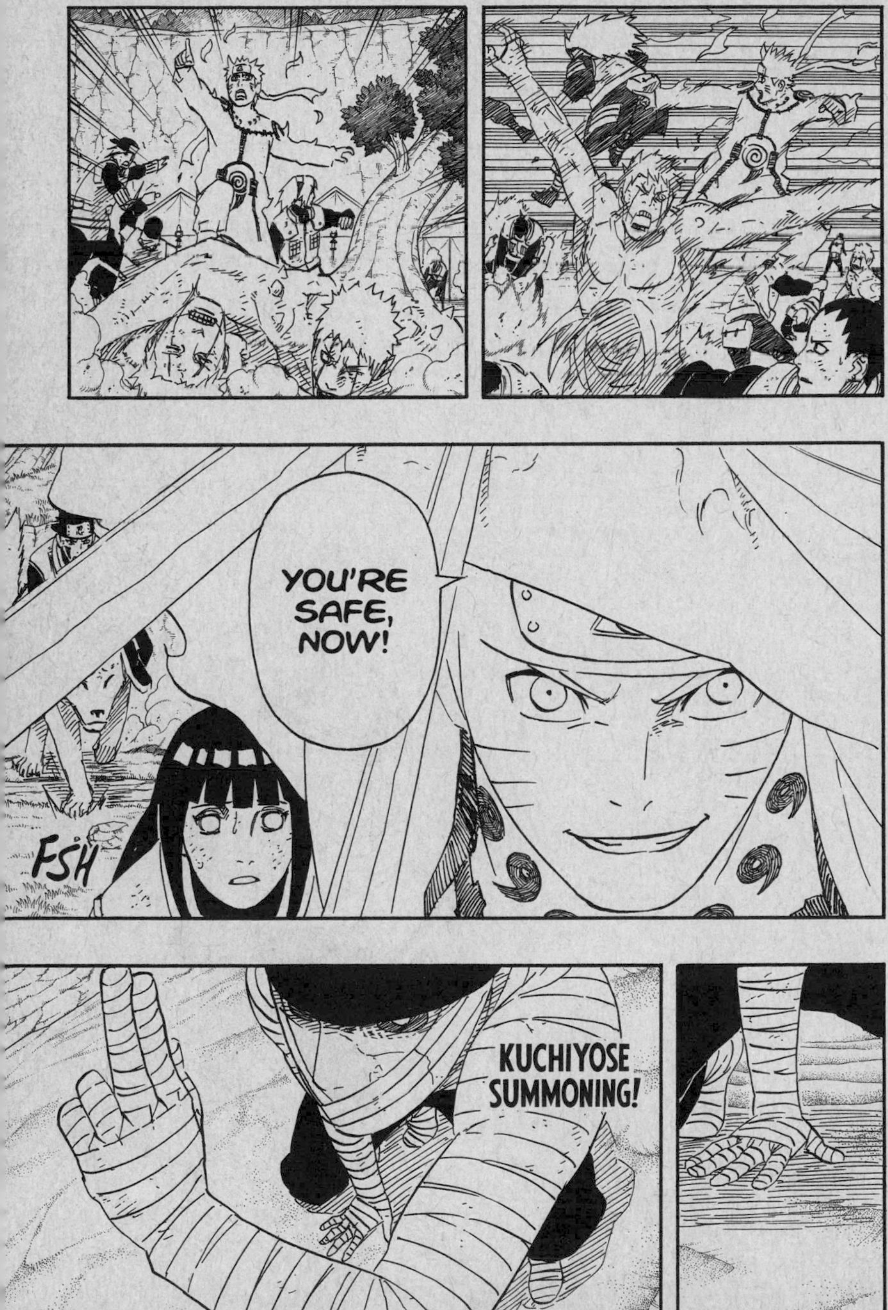
YOU'RE SAFE, NOW!
FSH
KUCHIYOSE SUMMONING!

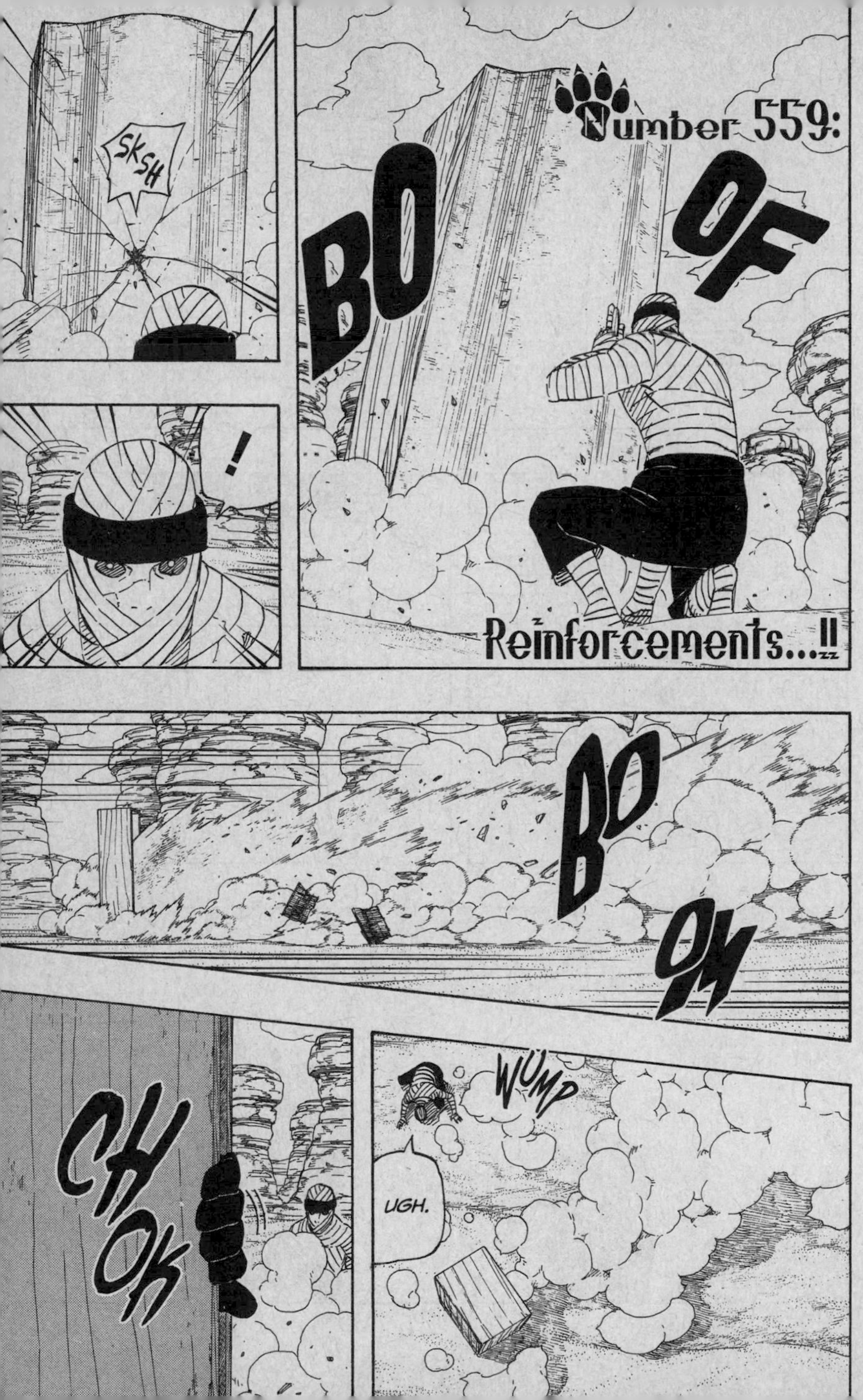
Number 559:
BOOF
Reinforcements...!!
SKSH
!
BOOOM
WUMP
UGH.
CHOK

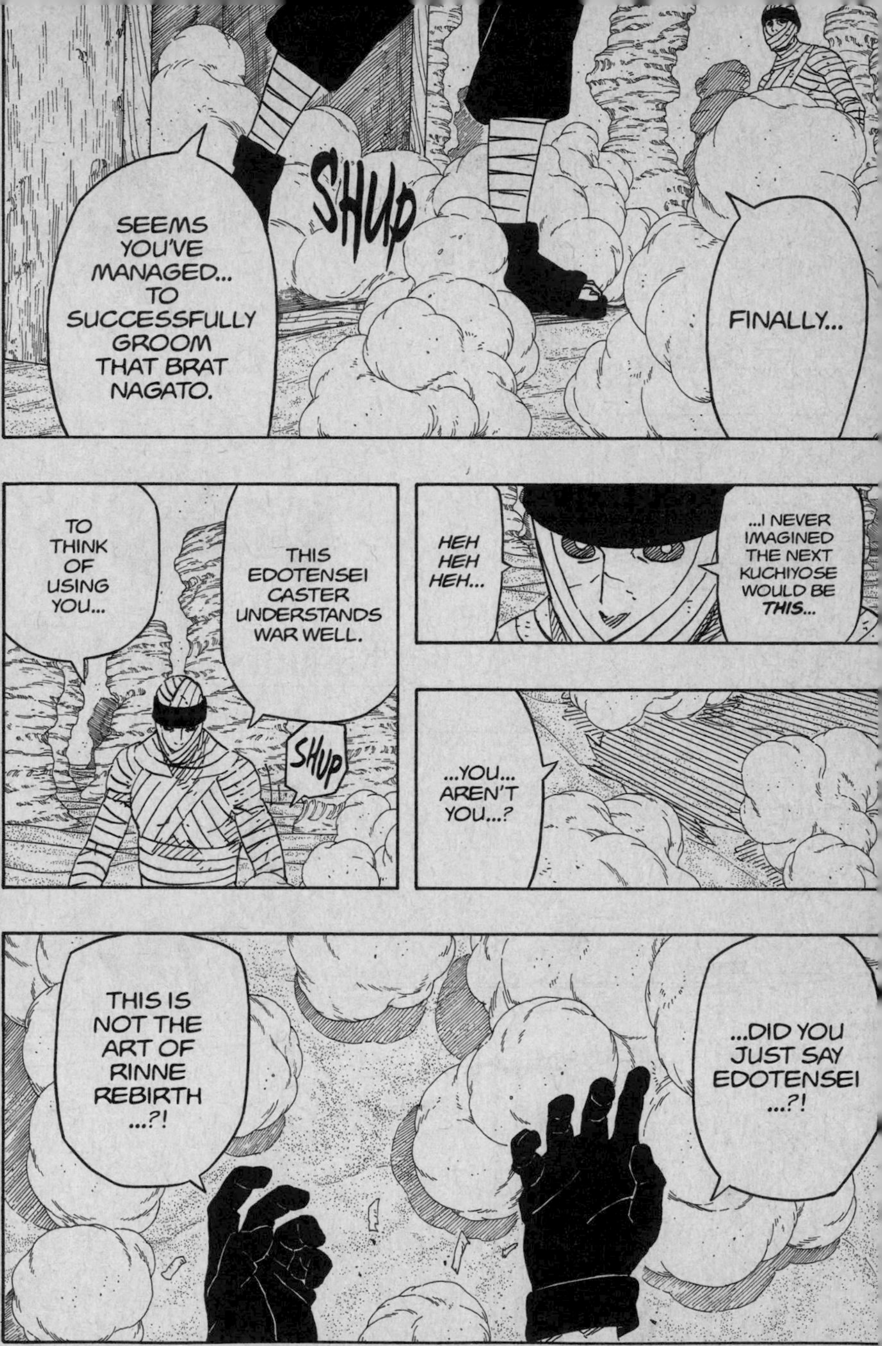
FINALLY...
SHUP
SEEMS YOU'VE MANAGED... TO SUCCESSFULLY GROOM THAT BRAT NAGATO.
...I NEVER IMAGINED THE NEXT KUCHIYOSE WOULD BE *THIS*...
HEH HEH HEH...
...YOU... AREN'T YOU...?
THIS EDOTENSEI CASTER UNDERSTANDS WAR WELL.
TO THINK OF USING YOU...
SHUP
...DID YOU JUST SAY EDOTENSEI ...?!
THIS IS NOT THE ART OF RINNE REBIRTH ...?!

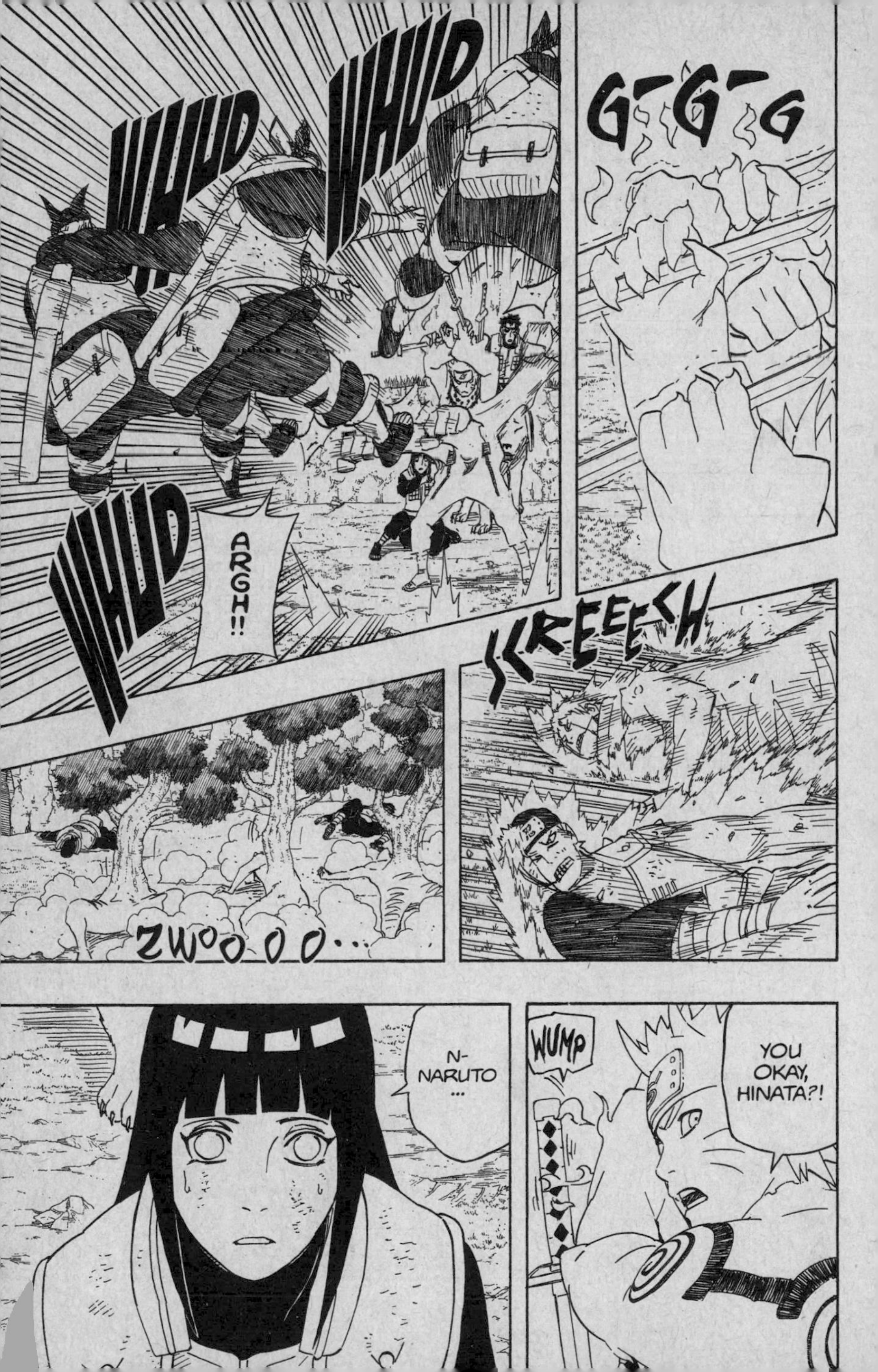
G-G-G
WHUD
WHUD
ARGH!!
WHUD
SKREEECH
ZWOOOO...
WUMP
YOU OKAY, HINATA?!
N-NARUTO...

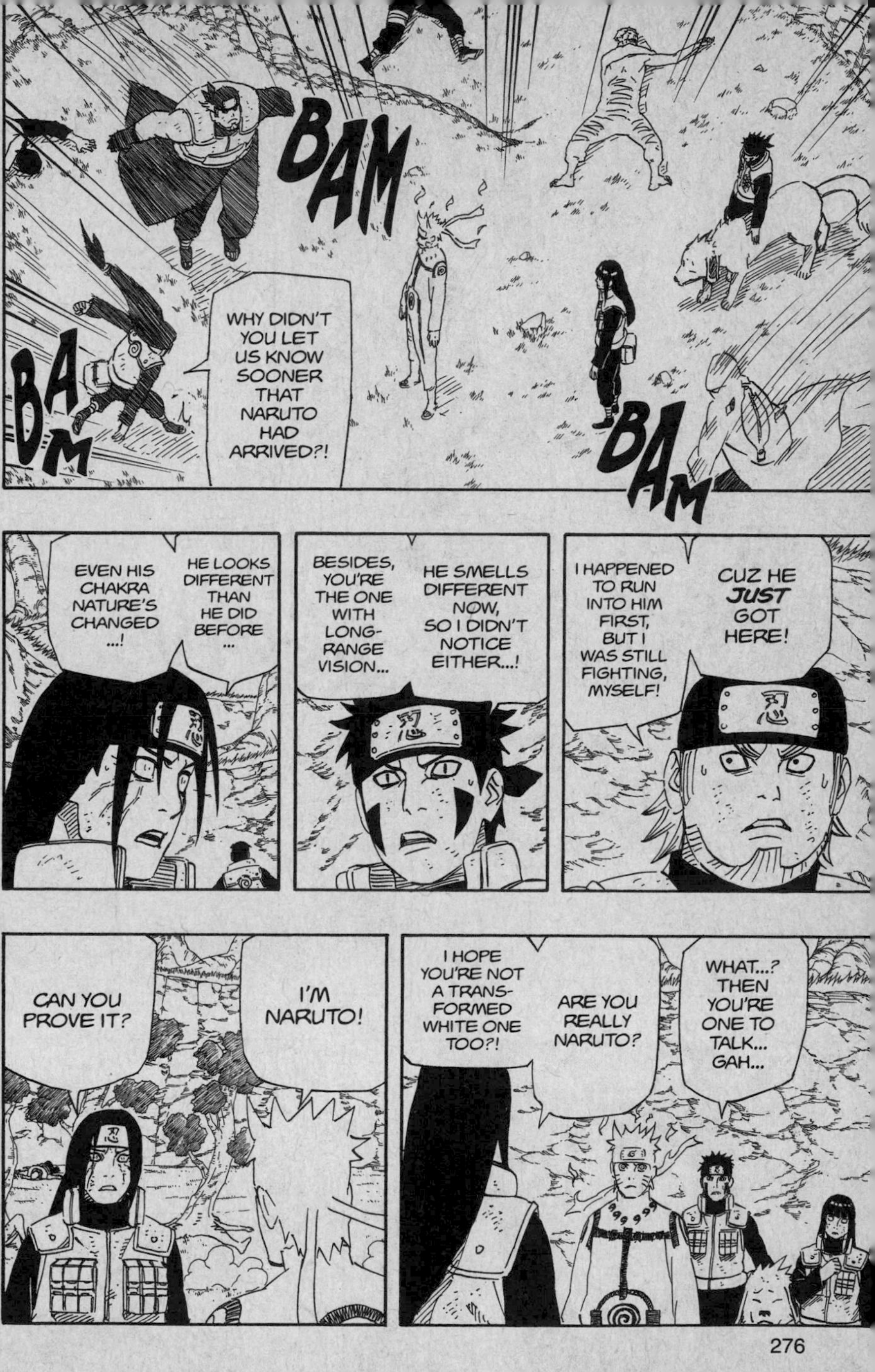
BAM
BAM
WHY DIDN'T YOU LET US KNOW SOONER THAT NARUTO HAD ARRIVED?!
BAM
CUZ HE JUST GOT HERE!
I HAPPENED TO RUN INTO HIM FIRST, BUT I WAS STILL FIGHTING, MYSELF!
HE SMELLS DIFFERENT NOW, SO I DIDN'T NOTICE EITHER...!
BESIDES, YOU'RE THE ONE WITH LONG-RANGE VISION...
HE LOOKS DIFFERENT THAN HE DID BEFORE...
EVEN HIS CHAKRA NATURE'S CHANGED...!
WHAT...? THEN YOU'RE ONE TO TALK... GAH...
ARE YOU REALLY NARUTO?
I HOPE YOU'RE NOT A TRANSFORMED WHITE ONE TOO?!
I'M NARUTO!
CAN YOU PROVE IT?

READ THIS WAY

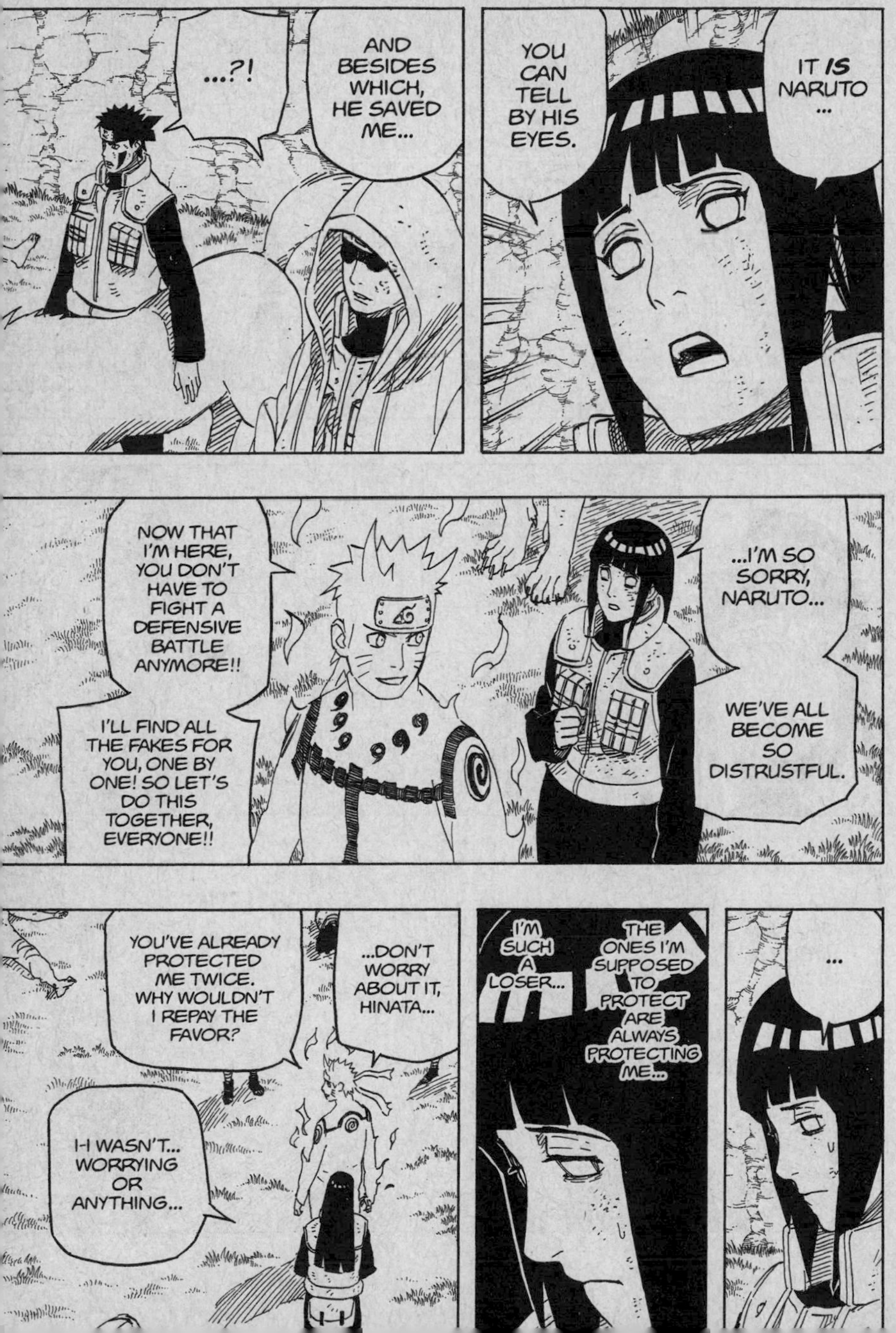
IT *IS* NARUTO ...
YOU CAN TELL BY HIS EYES.
AND BESIDES WHICH, HE SAVED ME...
...?!
...I'M SO SORRY, NARUTO...
WE'VE ALL BECOME SO DISTRUSTFUL.
NOW THAT I'M HERE, YOU DON'T HAVE TO FIGHT A DEFENSIVE BATTLE ANYMORE!!
I'LL FIND ALL THE FAKES FOR YOU, ONE BY ONE! SO LET'S DO THIS TOGETHER, EVERYONE!!
...
THE ONES I'M SUPPOSED TO PROTECT ARE ALWAYS PROTECTING ME...
I'M SUCH A LOSER...
...DON'T WORRY ABOUT IT, HINATA...
YOU'VE ALREADY PROTECTED ME TWICE. WHY WOULDN'T I REPAY THE FAVOR?
I-I WASN'T... WORRYING OR ANYTHING...

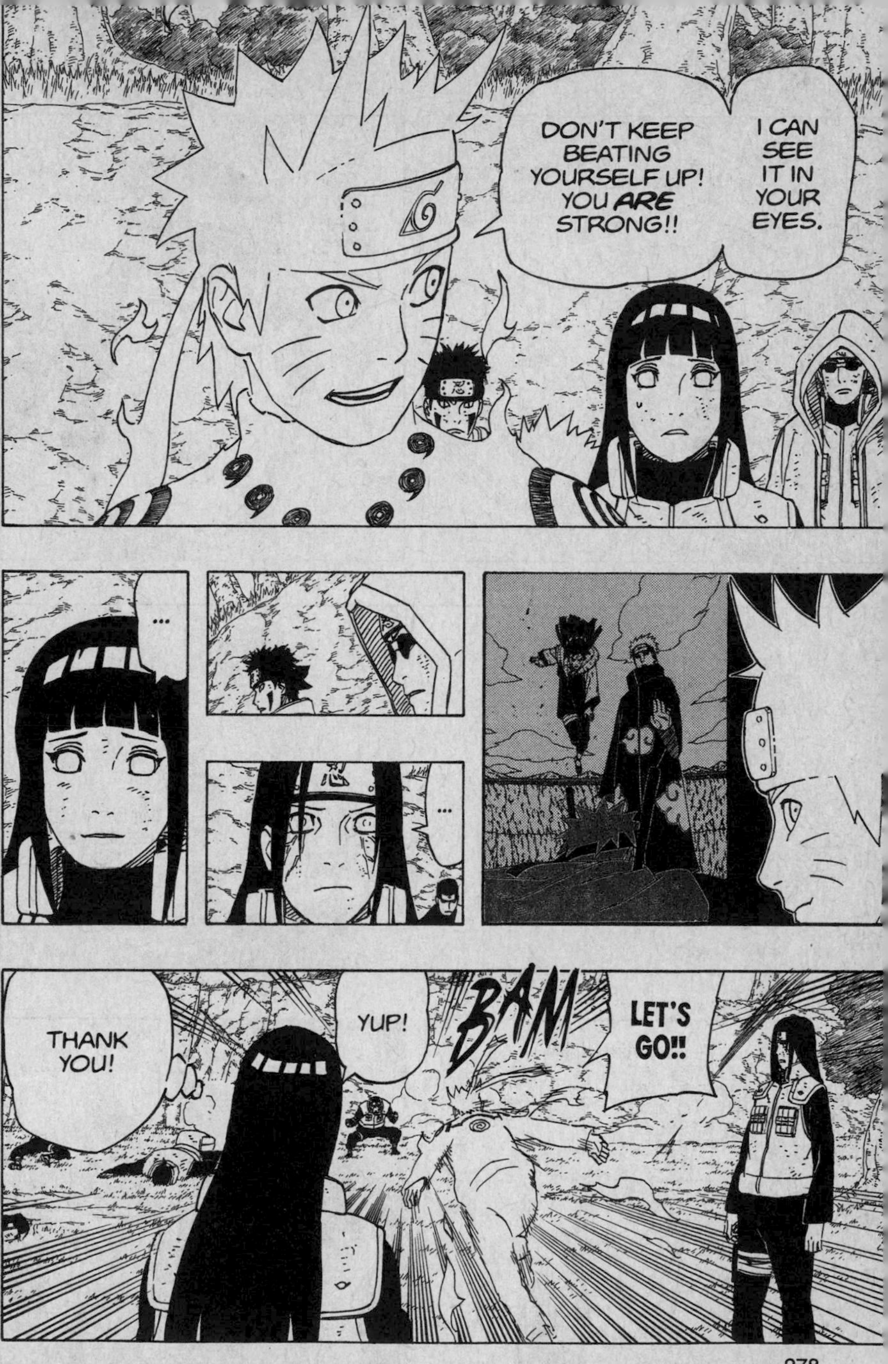
I CAN SEE IT IN YOUR EYES.
DON'T KEEP BEATING YOURSELF UP! YOU ARE STRONG!!
...
...
LET'S GO!!
BAM
YUP!
THANK YOU!

READ THIS WAY

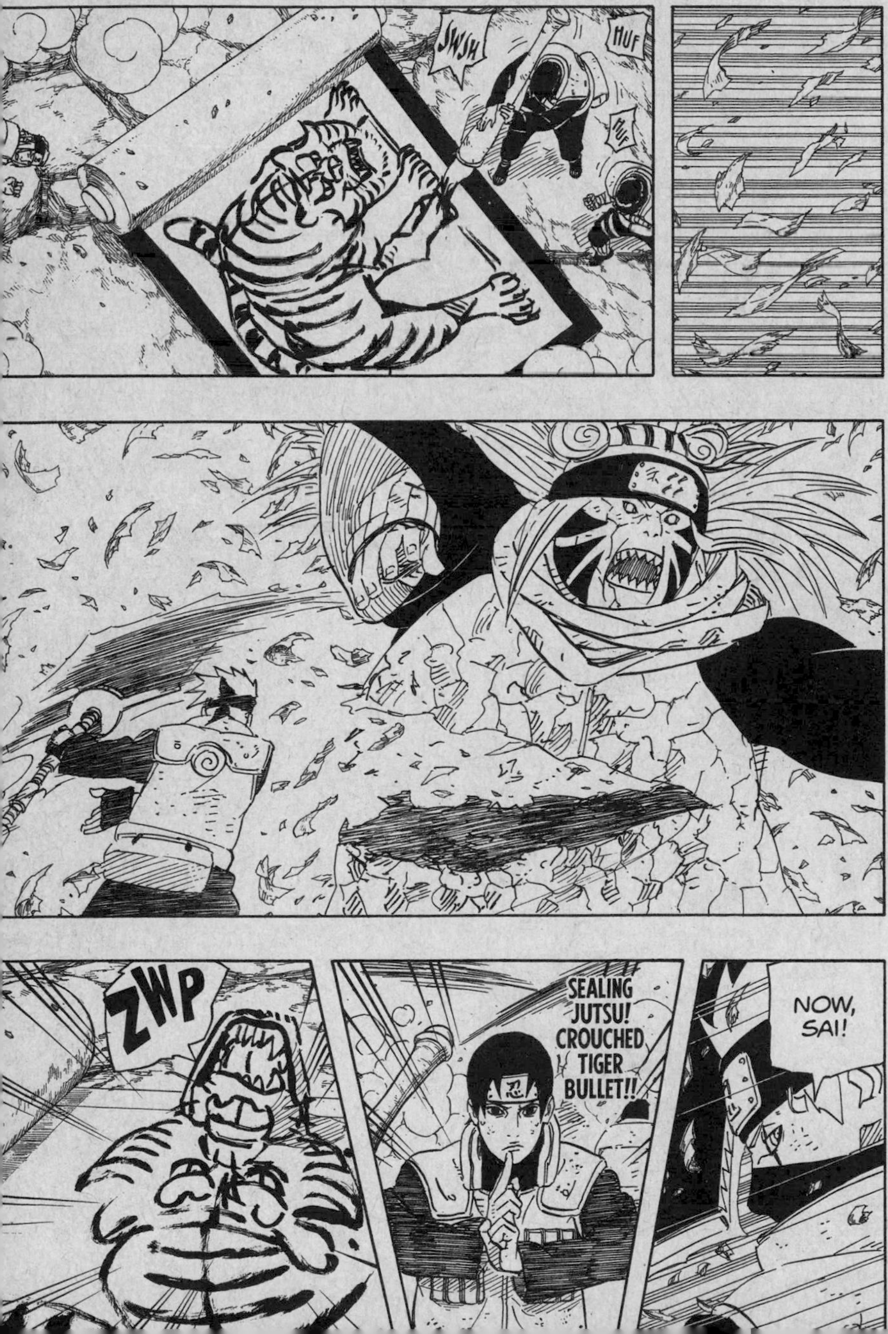
HUF
SWSH
HUF
NOW, SAI!
SEALING JUTSU! CROUCHED TIGER BULLET!!
ZWP

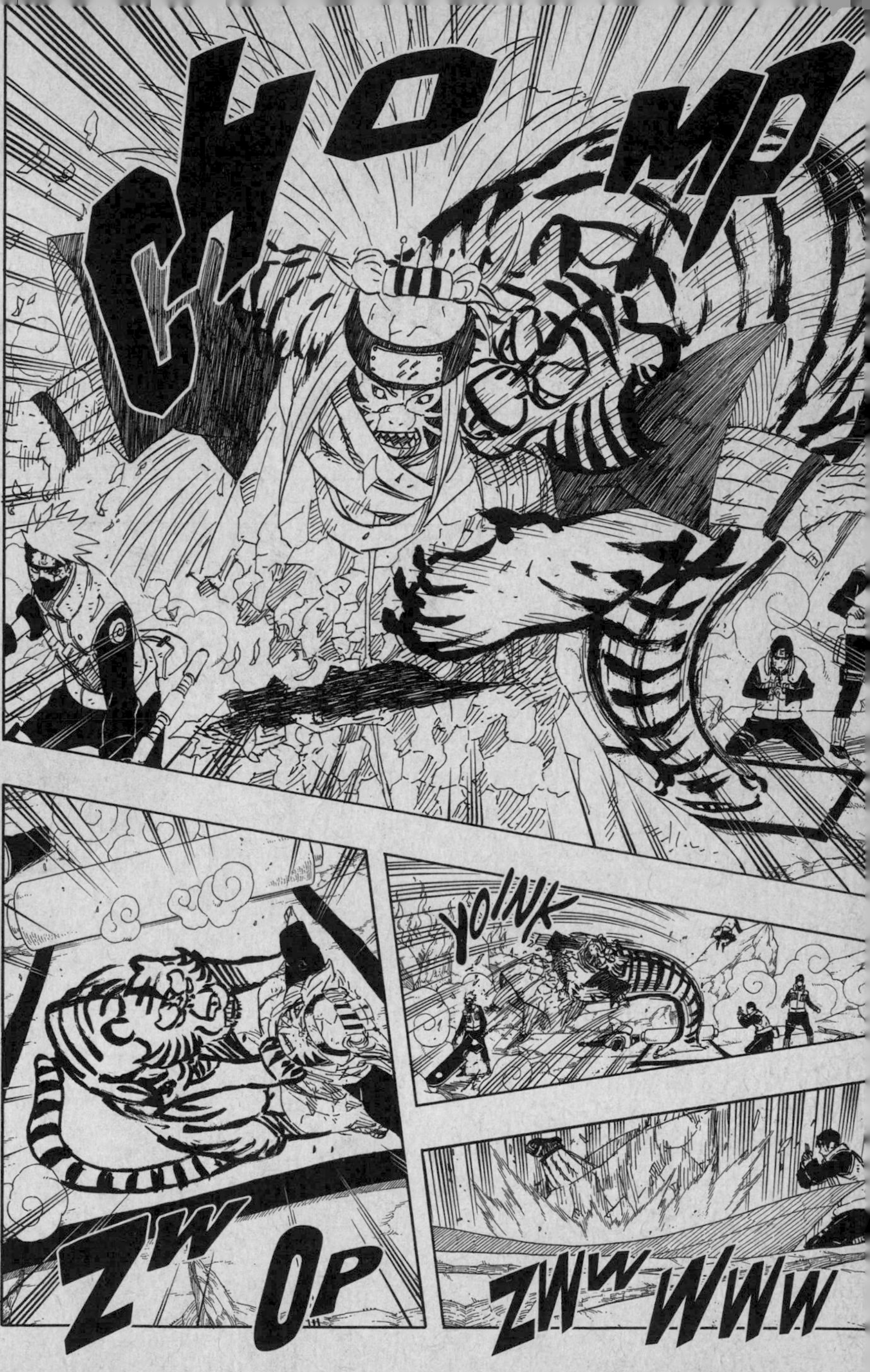
CHOMP
YOINK
ZWWWWW
ZWOP

READ THIS WAY

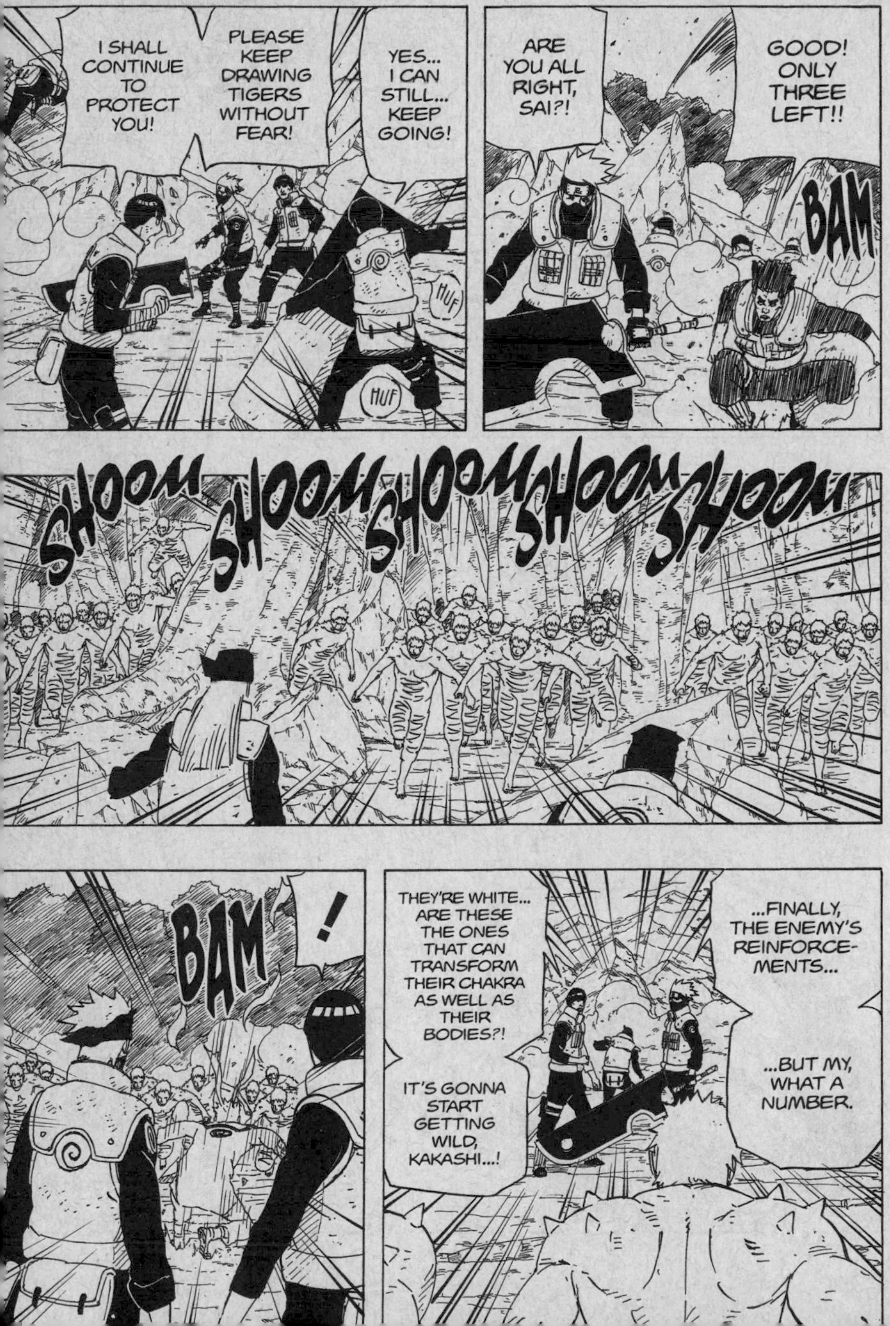
GOOD! ONLY THREE LEFT!!
ARE YOU ALL RIGHT, SAI?!
BAM
YES... I CAN STILL... KEEP GOING!
PLEASE KEEP DRAWING TIGERS WITHOUT FEAR!
I SHALL CONTINUE TO PROTECT YOU!
HUF
HUF
SHOOM
SHOOM
SHOOM
SHOOM
SHOOM
...FINALLY, THE ENEMY'S REINFORCE- MENTS...
...BUT MY, WHAT A NUMBER.
THEY'RE WHITE... ARE THESE THE ONES THAT CAN TRANSFORM THEIR CHAKRA AS WELL AS THEIR BODIES?!
IT'S GONNA START GETTING WILD, KAKASHI...!
!
BAM

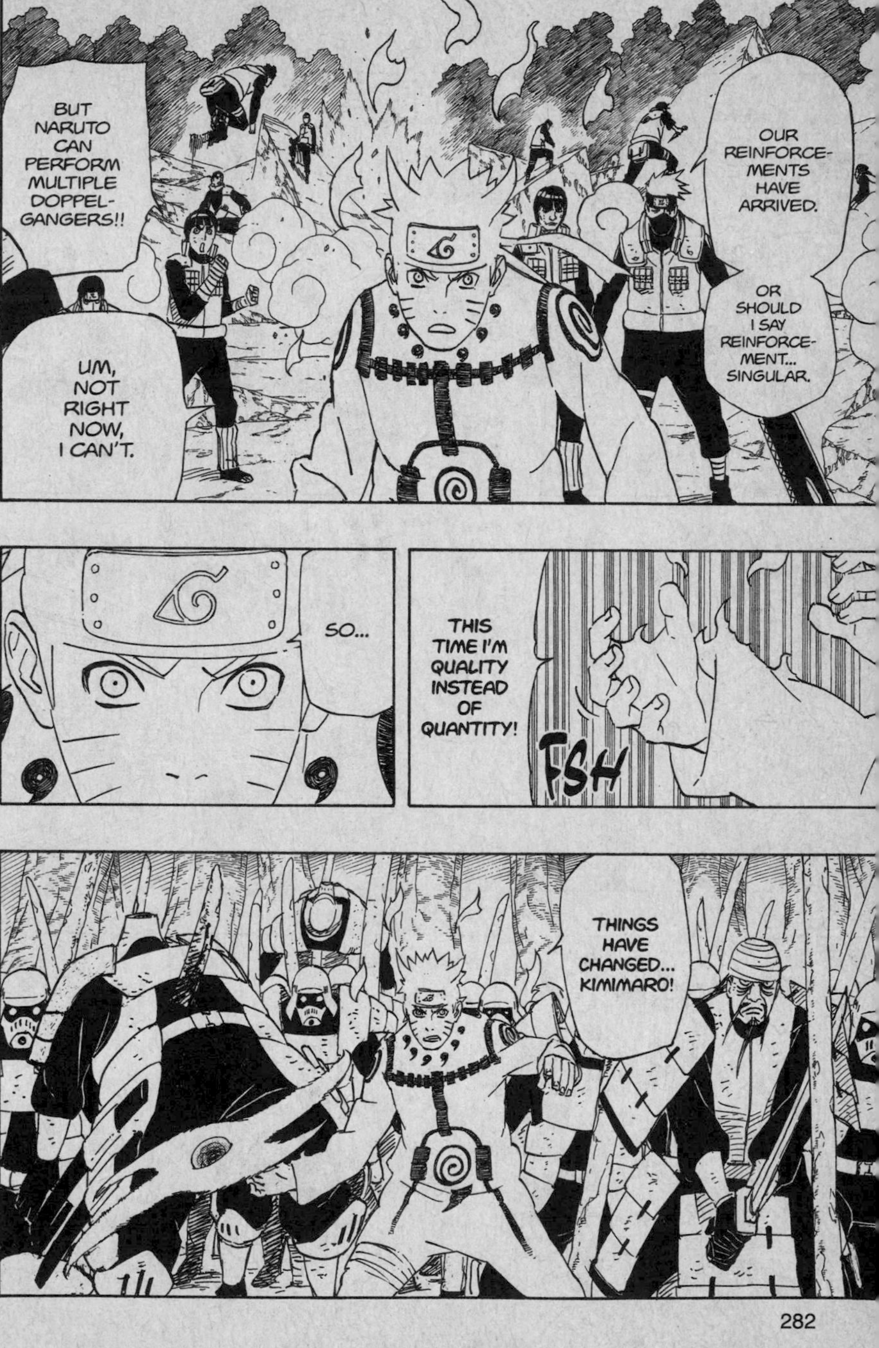
OUR REINFORCE-MENTS HAVE ARRIVED.
OR SHOULD I SAY REINFORCE-MENT... SINGULAR.
BUT NARUTO CAN PERFORM MULTIPLE DOPPEL-GANGERS!!
UM, NOT RIGHT NOW, I CAN'T.
THIS TIME I'M QUALITY INSTEAD OF QUANTITY!
FSH
SO...
THINGS HAVE CHANGED... KIMIMARO!

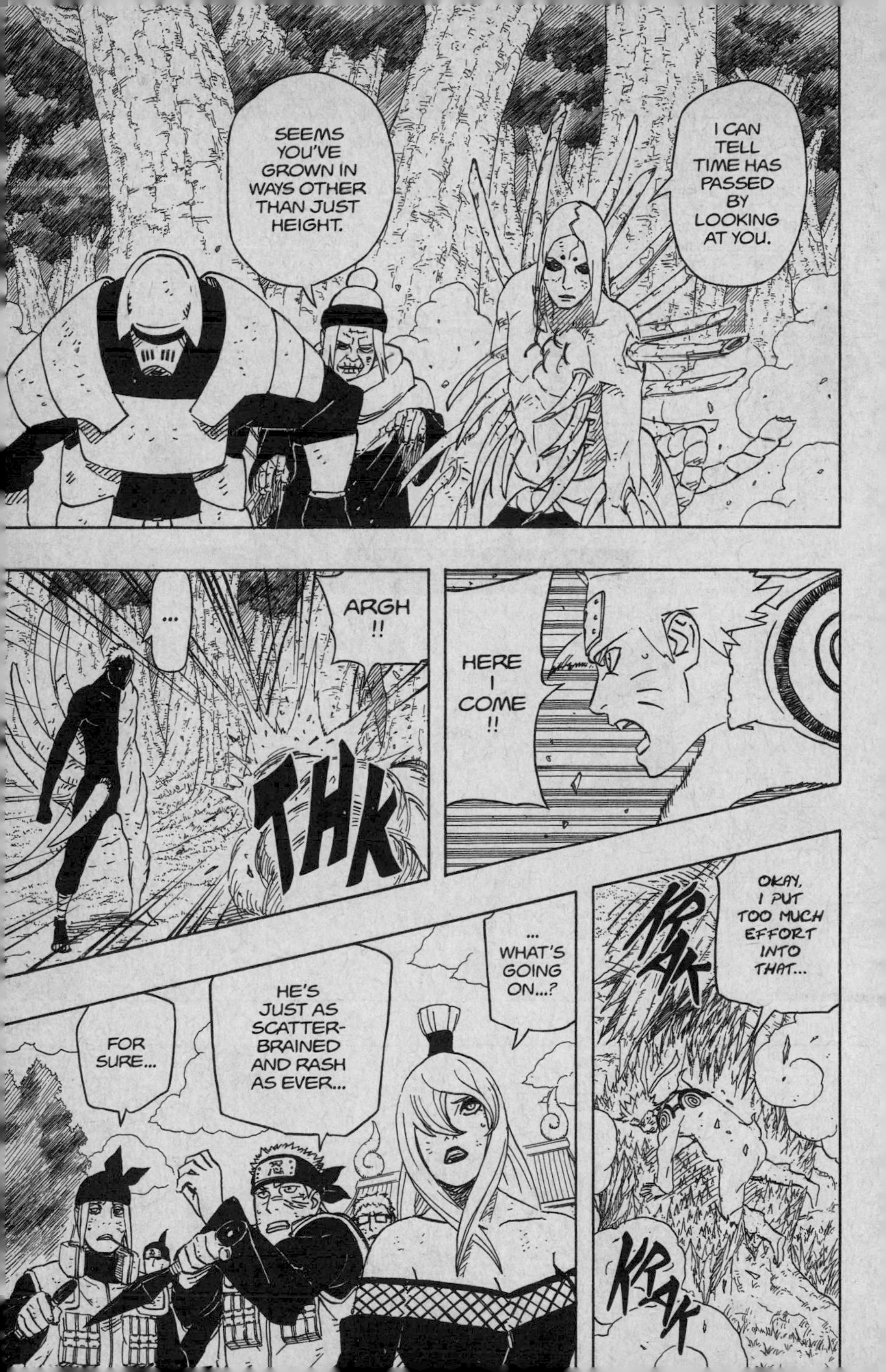
I CAN TELL TIME HAS PASSED BY LOOKING AT YOU.
SEEMS YOU'VE GROWN IN WAYS OTHER THAN JUST HEIGHT.
HERE I COME!!
ARGH!!
...
THK
KRAK
OKAY, I PUT TOO MUCH EFFORT INTO THAT...
KRAK
... WHAT'S GOING ON...?
HE'S JUST AS SCATTER-BRAINED AND RASH AS EVER...
FOR SURE...

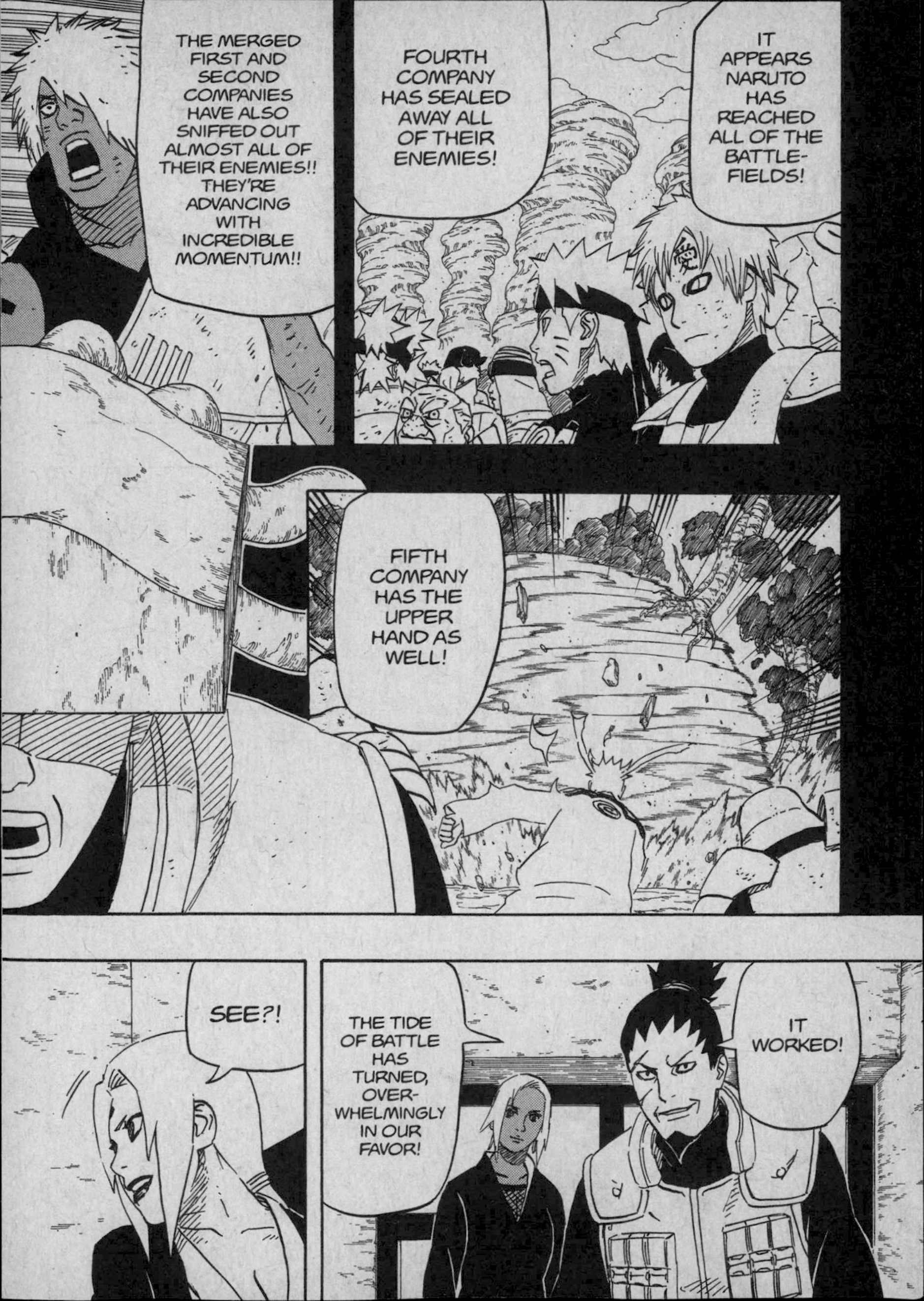
IT APPEARS NARUTO HAS REACHED ALL OF THE BATTLE-FIELDS!
FOURTH COMPANY HAS SEALED AWAY ALL OF THEIR ENEMIES!
THE MERGED FIRST AND SECOND COMPANIES HAVE ALSO SNIFFED OUT ALMOST ALL OF THEIR ENEMIES!! THEY'RE ADVANCING WITH INCREDIBLE MOMENTUM!!
FIFTH COMPANY HAS THE UPPER HAND AS WELL!
IT WORKED!
THE TIDE OF BATTLE HAS TURNED, OVER-WHELMINGLY IN OUR FAVOR!
SEE?!

READ THIS WAY

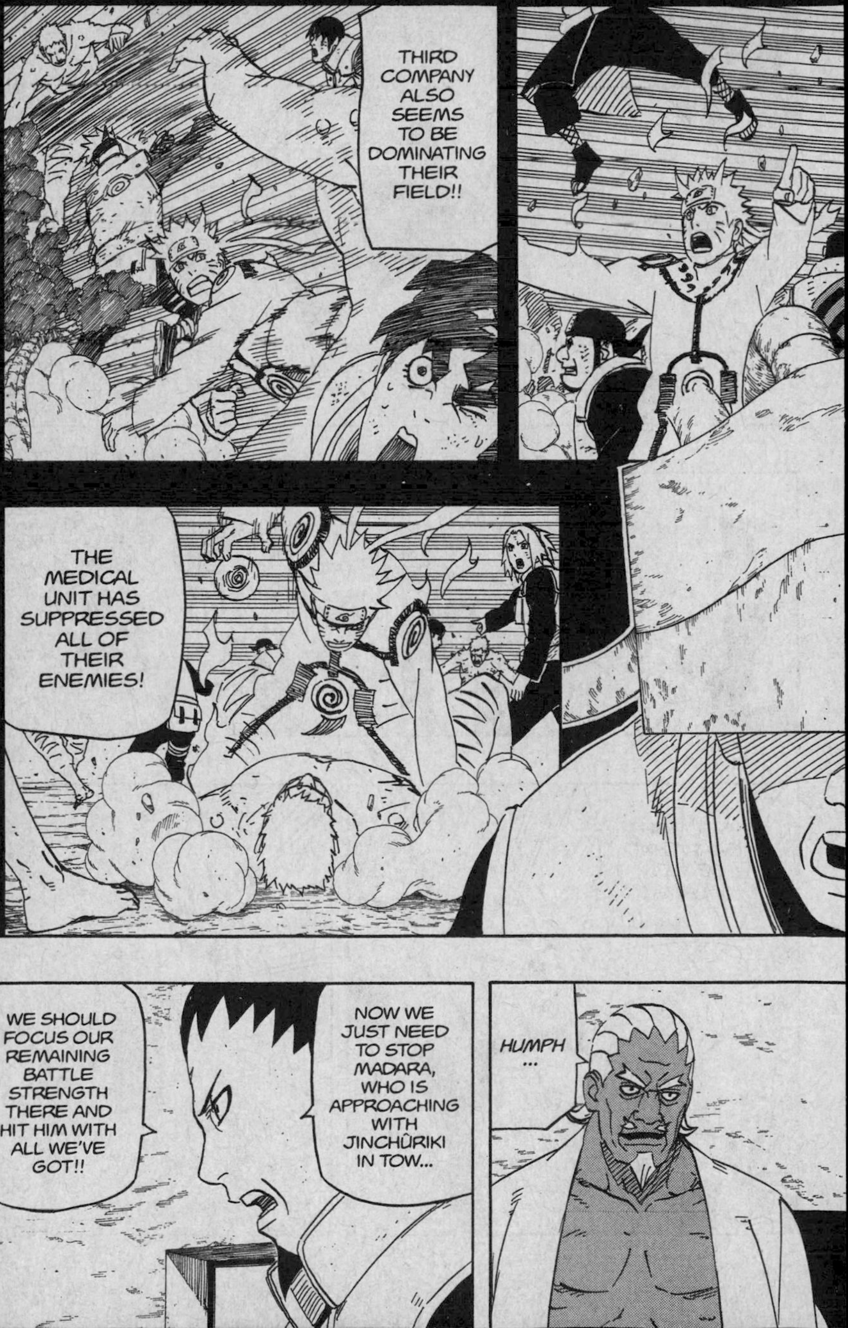
THIRD COMPANY ALSO SEEMS TO BE DOMINATING THEIR FIELD!!
THE MEDICAL UNIT HAS SUPPRESSED ALL OF THEIR ENEMIES!
HUMPH...
NOW WE JUST NEED TO STOP MADARA, WHO IS APPROACHING WITH JINCHÛRIKI IN TOW...
WE SHOULD FOCUS OUR REMAINING BATTLE STRENGTH THERE AND HIT HIM WITH ALL WE'VE GOT!!

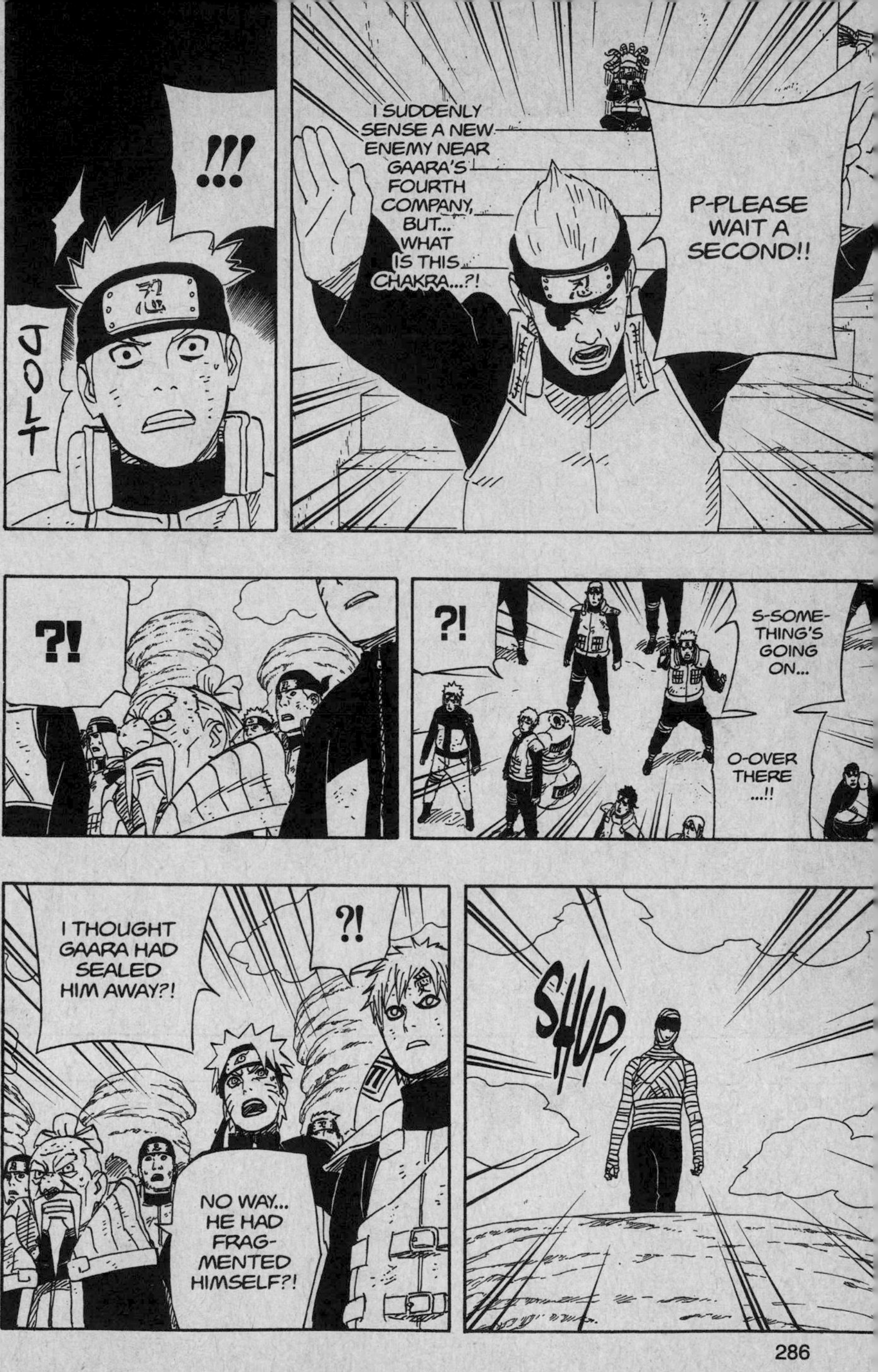
P-PLEASE WAIT A SECOND!!
I SUDDENLY SENSE A NEW ENEMY NEAR GAARA'S FOURTH COMPANY, BUT... WHAT IS THIS CHAKRA...?!
!!!
JOLT
S-SOMETHING'S GOING ON...
O-OVER THERE ...!!
?!
?!
SHUP
?!
I THOUGHT GAARA HAD SEALED HIM AWAY?!
NO WAY... HE HAD FRAGMENTED HIMSELF?!

READ THIS WAY

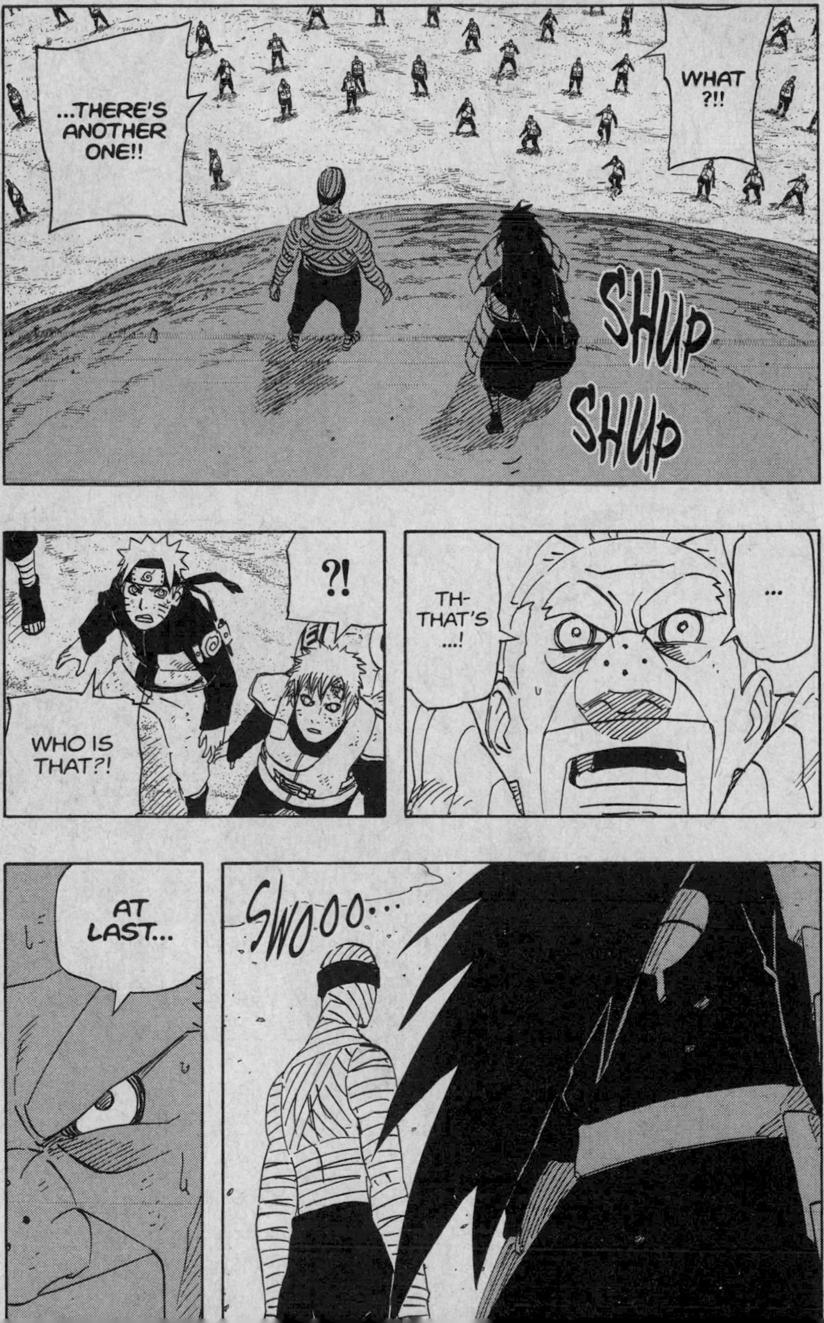
WHAT ?!!
...THERE'S ANOTHER ONE!!
SHUP SHUP
...
TH- THAT'S ....!
?!
WHO IS THAT?!
SWOO-O-O...
AT LAST...

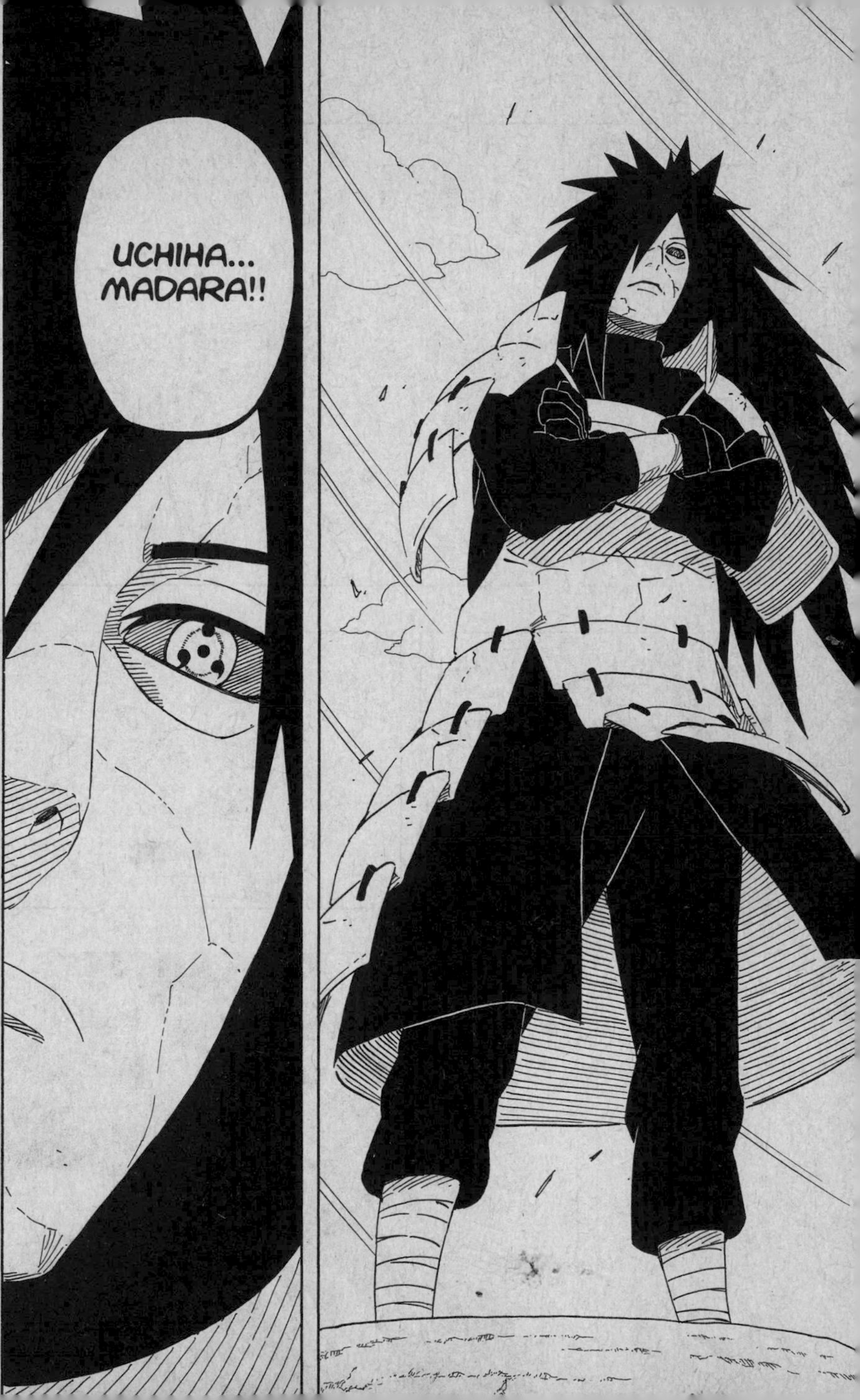
UCHIHA...
MADARA!!

READ THIS WAY

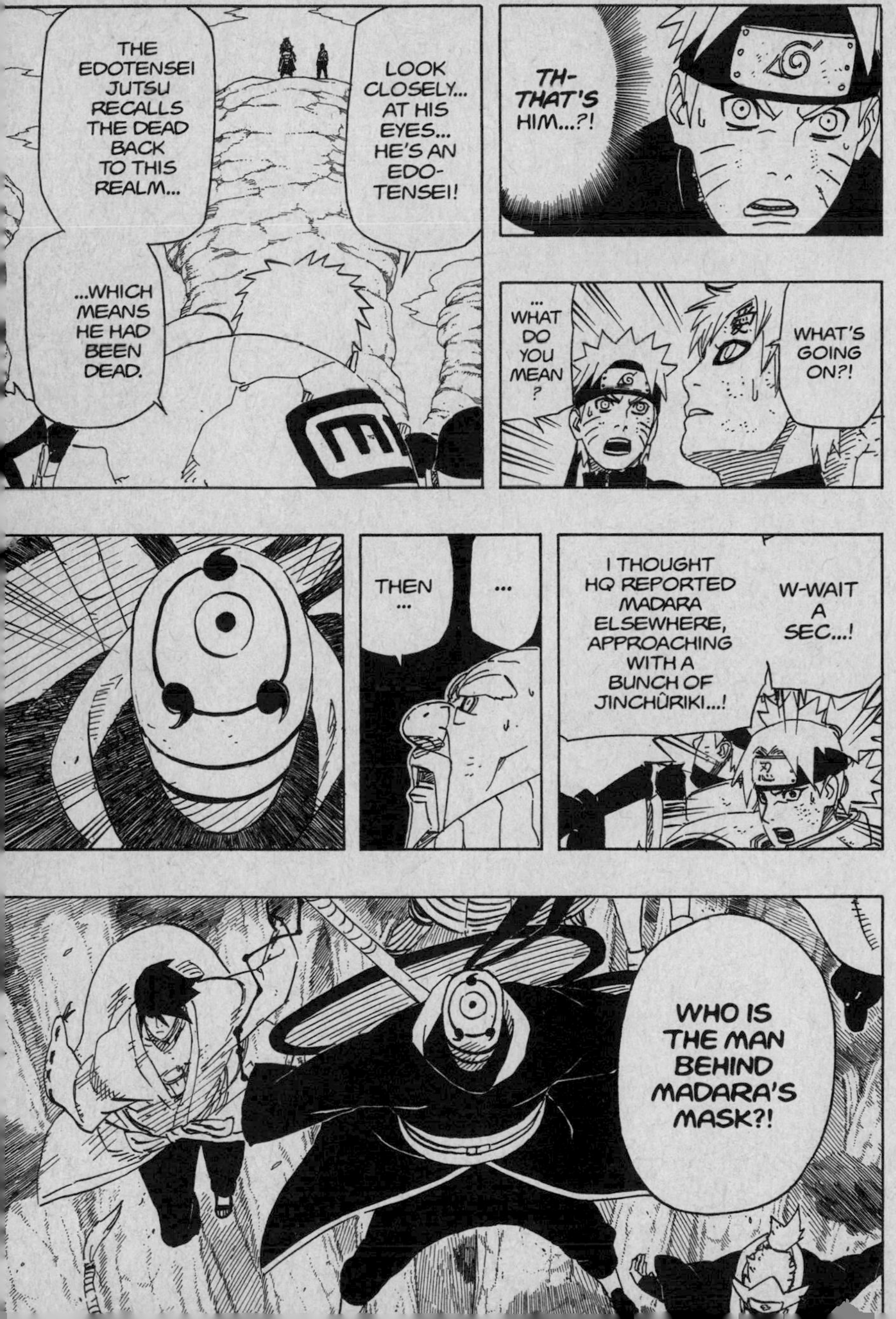
TH-THAT'S HIM...?!
WHAT'S GOING ON?!
...WHAT DO YOU MEAN?
LOOK CLOSELY... AT HIS EYES... HE'S AN EDO-TENSEI!
THE EDOTENSEI JUTSU RECALLS THE DEAD BACK TO THIS REALM...
...WHICH MEANS HE HAD BEEN DEAD.
W-WAIT A SEC...!
I THOUGHT HQ REPORTED MADARA ELSEWHERE, APPROACHING WITH A BUNCH OF JINCHÛRIKI...!
...
THEN ...
WHO IS THE MAN BEHIND MADARA'S MASK?!

Number 560: Uchiha Madara

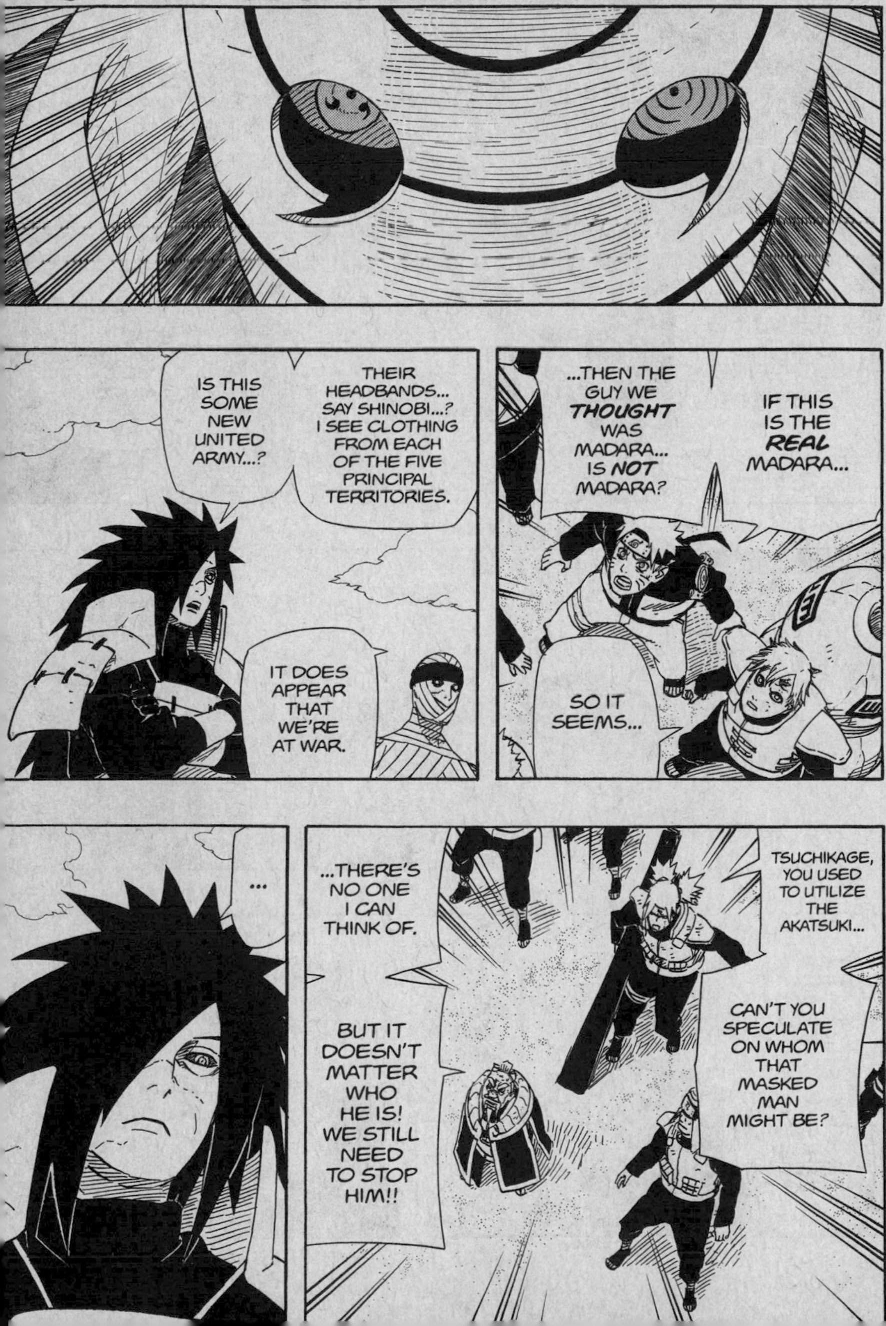
IF THIS IS THE *REAL* MADARA...
...THEN THE GUY WE *THOUGHT* WAS MADARA... IS *NOT* MADARA?
SO IT SEEMS...
THEIR HEADBANDS... SAY SHINOBI...? I SEE CLOTHING FROM EACH OF THE FIVE PRINCIPAL TERRITORIES.
IS THIS SOME NEW UNITED ARMY...?
IT DOES APPEAR THAT WE'RE AT WAR.
TSUCHIKAGE, YOU USED TO UTILIZE THE AKATSUKI...
CAN'T YOU SPECULATE ON WHOM THAT MASKED MAN MIGHT BE?
...THERE'S NO ONE I CAN THINK OF.
BUT IT DOESN'T MATTER WHO HE IS! WE STILL NEED TO STOP HIM!!
...

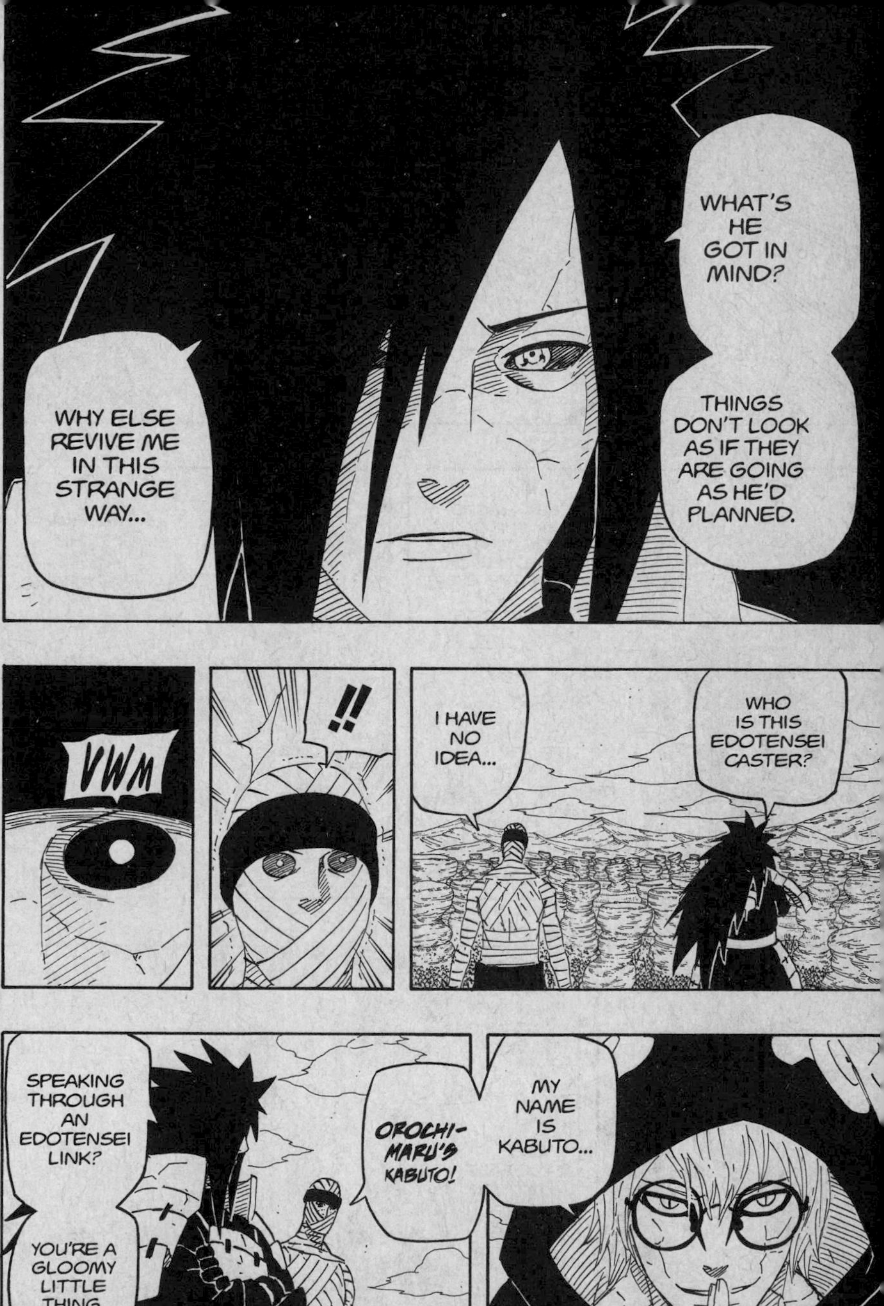
WHAT'S HE GOT IN MIND?
THINGS DON'T LOOK AS IF THEY ARE GOING AS HE'D PLANNED.
WHY ELSE REVIVE ME IN THIS STRANGE WAY...
WHO IS THIS EDOTENSEI CASTER?
I HAVE NO IDEA...
!!
VWM
MY NAME IS KABUTO...
OROCHI-MARU'S KABUTO!
SPEAKING THROUGH AN EDOTENSEI LINK?
YOU'RE A GLOOMY LITTLE THING.

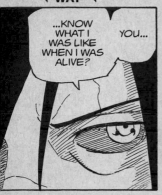

READ THIS WAY

YOUR EDOTENSEI IS QUITE SPECIAL.
I EVEN FIXED YOU UP A BIT. YOU'RE NOW EVEN GREATER THAN WHEN YOU WERE ALIVE.
WHEN I WAS ALIVE?
...
YOU...
...KNOW WHAT I WAS LIKE WHEN I WAS ALIVE?
NO...
WHICH IS WHY... I WOULD LOVE TO SEE YOU AND YOUR LEGENDARY UCHIHA POWER IN ACTION HERE...
VOO
OOSH
WUMP
ZWISH
WSH
TMP

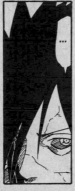

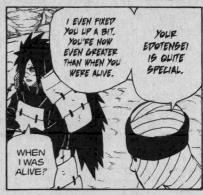

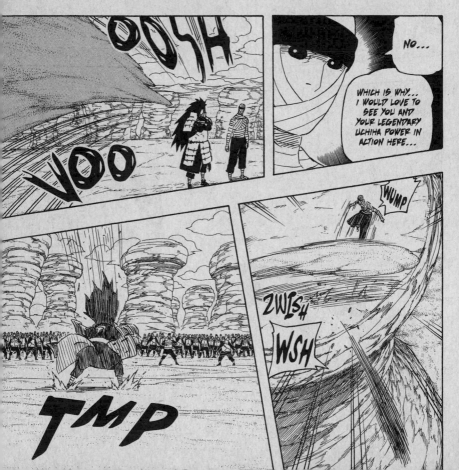

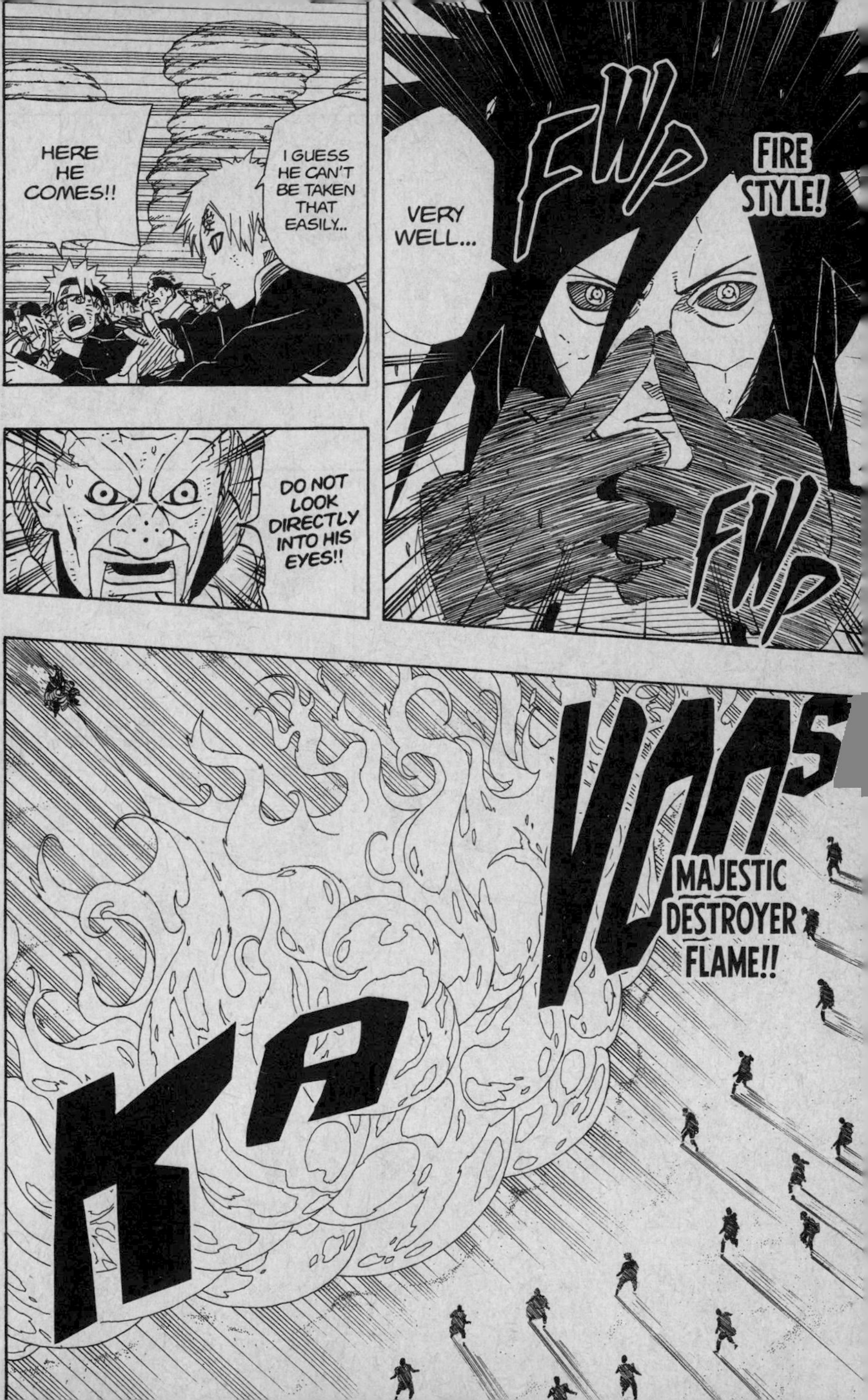
FWP
FIRE STYLE!
VERY WELL...
FWP
I GUESS HE CAN'T BE TAKEN THAT EASILY...
HERE HE COMES!!
DO NOT LOOK DIRECTLY INTO HIS EYES!!
MAJESTIC DESTROYER FLAME!!
KA

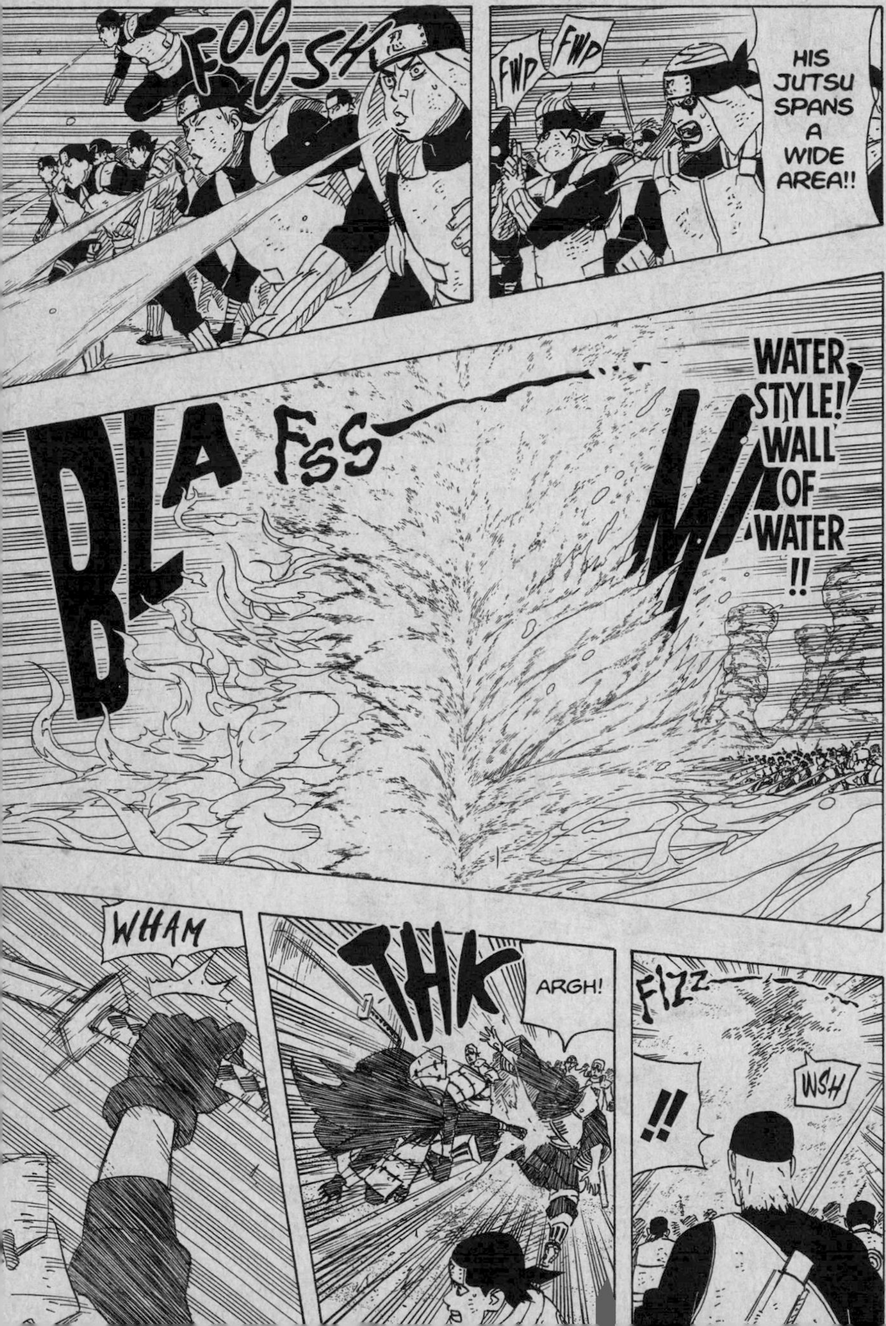
FWP
FWP
HIS JUTSU SPANS A WIDE AREA!!
FOOOOSH
WATER STYLE! WALL OF WATER!!
BLAM
FSS
FIZZ
WSH
!!
THK
ARGH!
WHAM

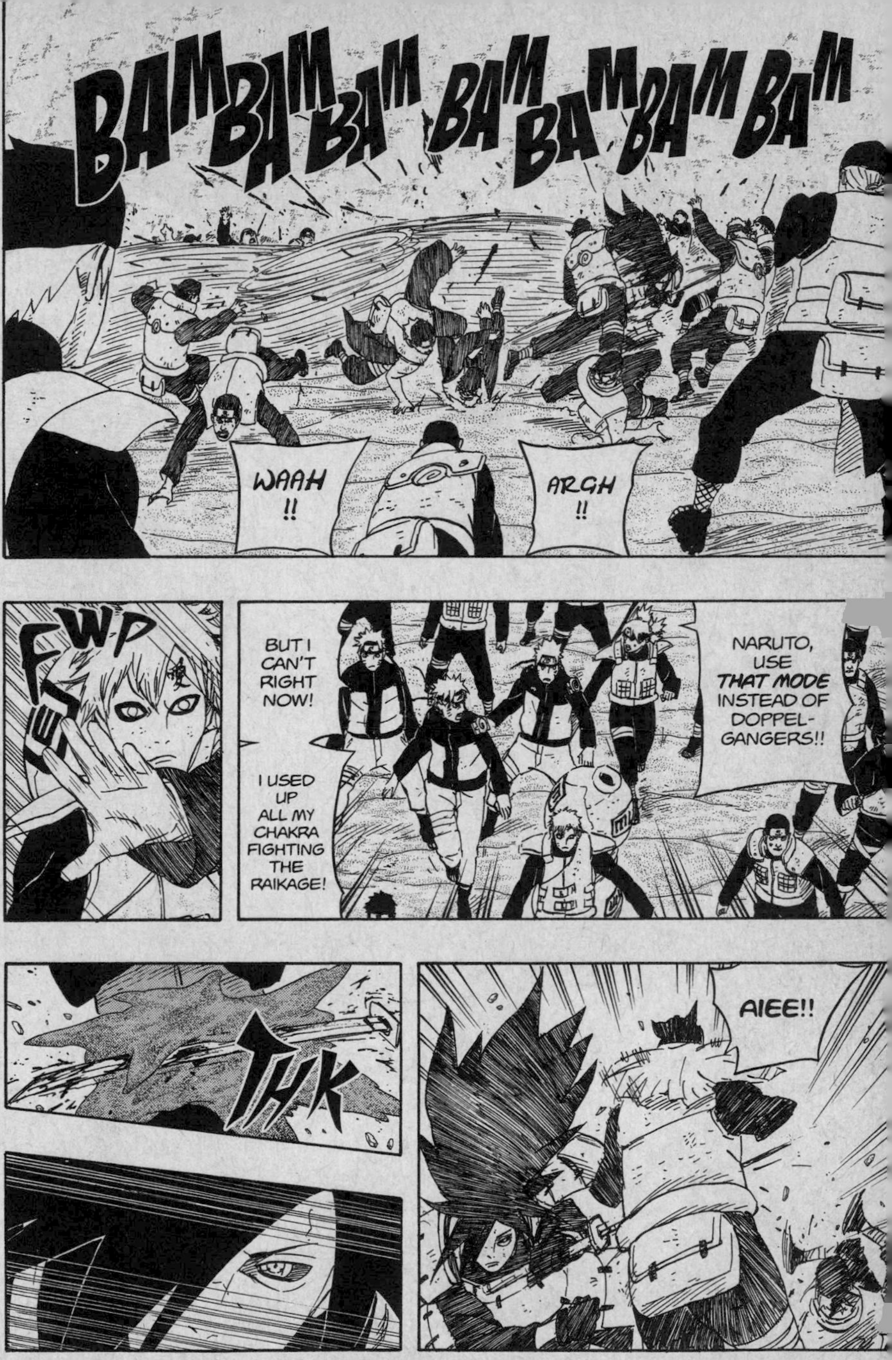
BAM BAM BAM BAM BAM BAM BAM
ARGH!!
WAAH!!
NARUTO, USE THAT MODE INSTEAD OF DOPPEL-GANGERS!!
BUT I CAN'T RIGHT NOW!
I USED UP ALL MY CHAKRA FIGHTING THE RAIKAGE!
FWP
AIEE!!
THK

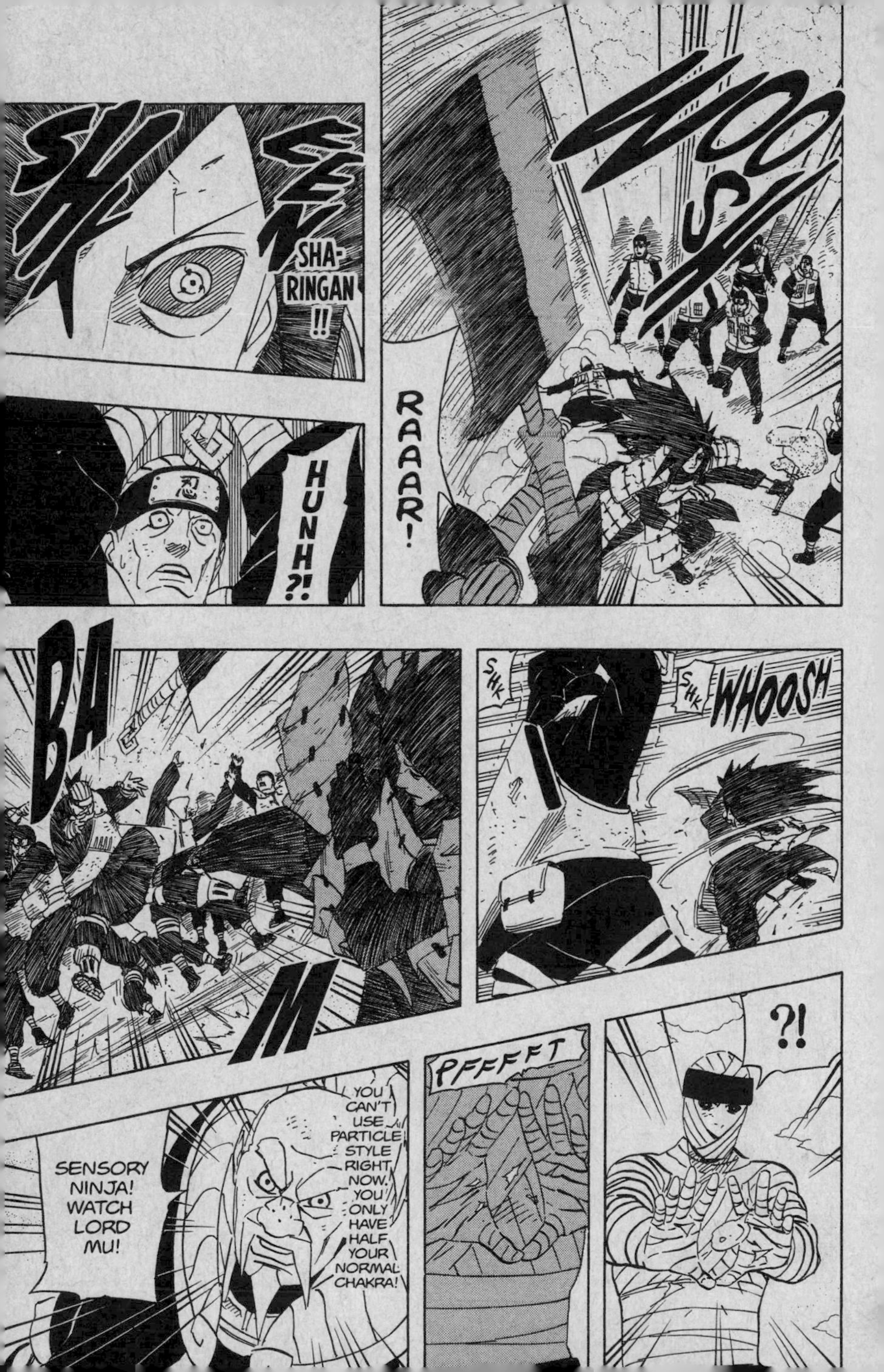
WHOOSH
RAAAAR!
SHA-RINGAN!!
HUNH?!
SHK
SHK
WHOOSH
BAM
?!
PFFFFT
YOU CAN'T USE PARTICLE STYLE RIGHT NOW. YOU ONLY HAVE HALF YOUR NORMAL CHAKRA!
SENSORY NINJA! WATCH LORD MU!

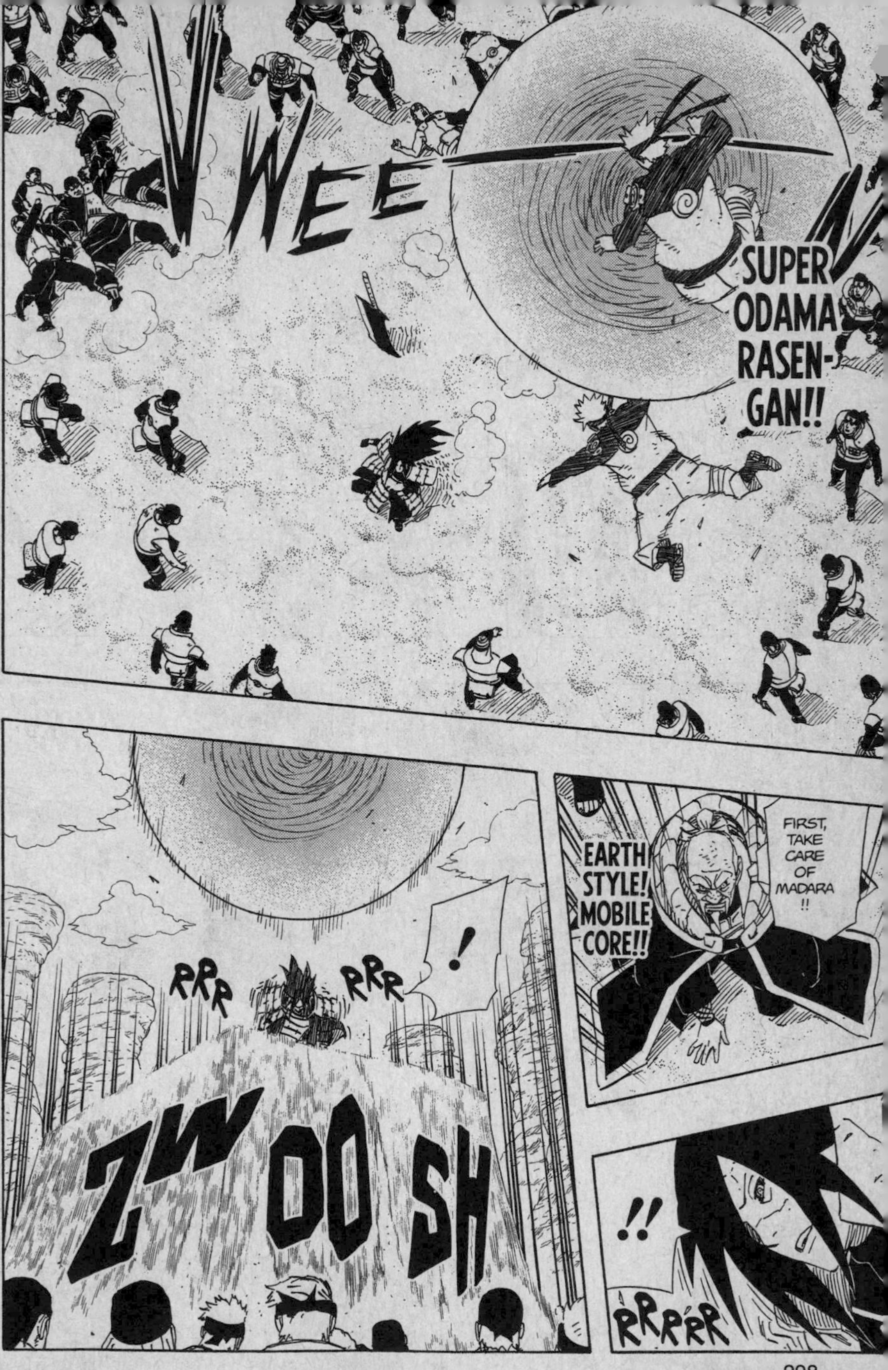
VWEEN
SUPER ODAMA RASEN-GAN!!
FIRST, TAKE CARE OF MADARA!!
EARTH STYLE! MOBILE CORE!!
!!
RRRRR
RRR
RRR
!
ZWOOSH

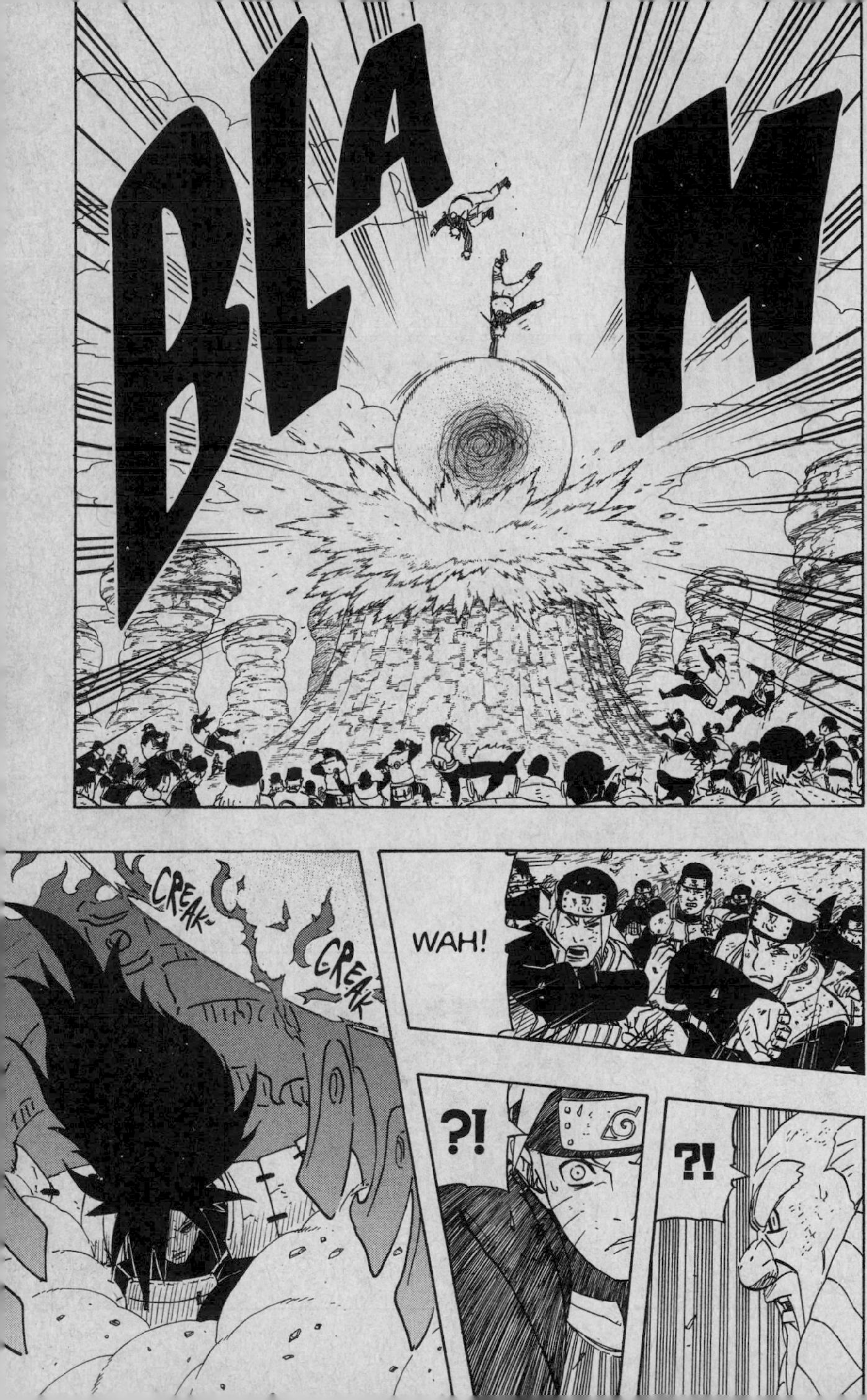
BLAM
WAH!
?!
?!
CREAK-
CREAK

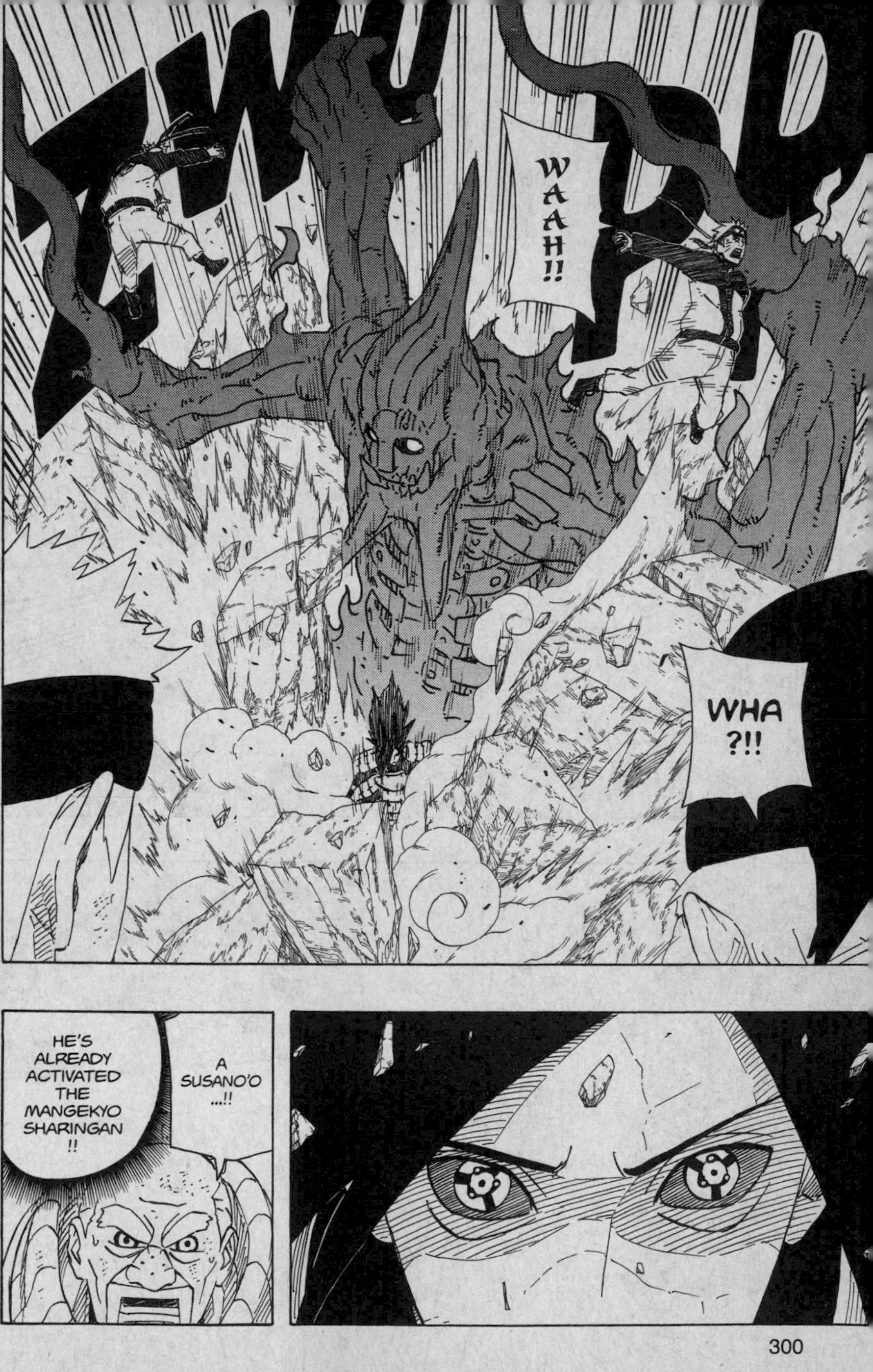
WAAH!!
WHA ?!!
A SUSANO'O ...!!
HE'S ALREADY ACTIVATED THE MANGEKYO SHARINGAN !!

READ THIS WAY

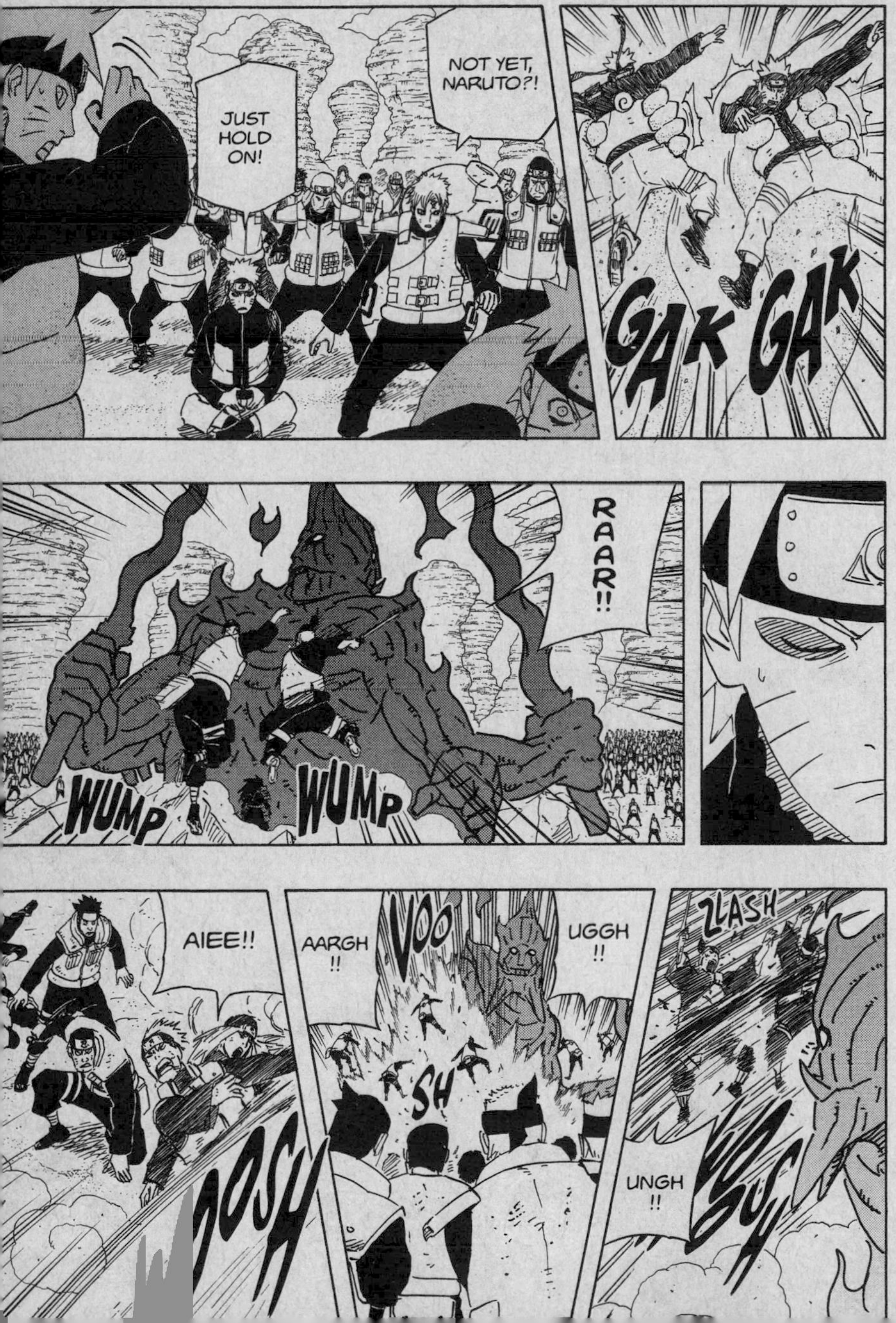
GAK GAK
NOT YET, NARUTO?!
JUST HOLD ON!
RAAR!!
WUMP
WUMP
ZLASH
UNGH!!
UGGH!!
VOO
AARGH!!
SH
AIEE!!

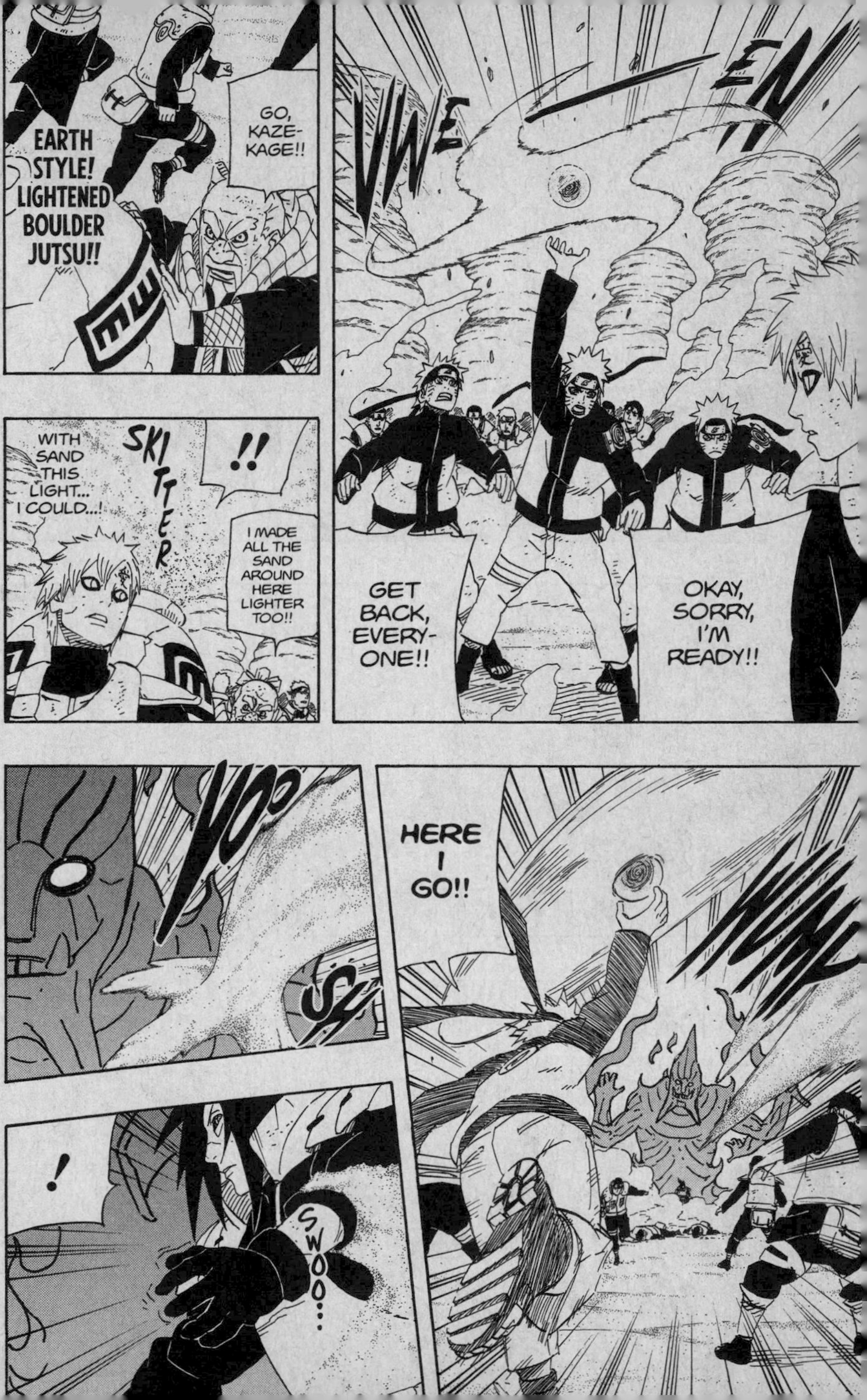
VWE
EN
OKAY, SORRY, I'M READY!!
GET BACK, EVERY-ONE!!
GO, KAZE-KAGE!!
EARTH STYLE! LIGHTENED BOULDER JUTSU!!
!!
I MADE ALL THE SAND AROUND HERE LIGHTER TOO!!
SKITTER
WITH SAND THIS LIGHT... I COULD...!
HERE I GO!!
YOO
SH
!
SWOO...

READ THIS WAY

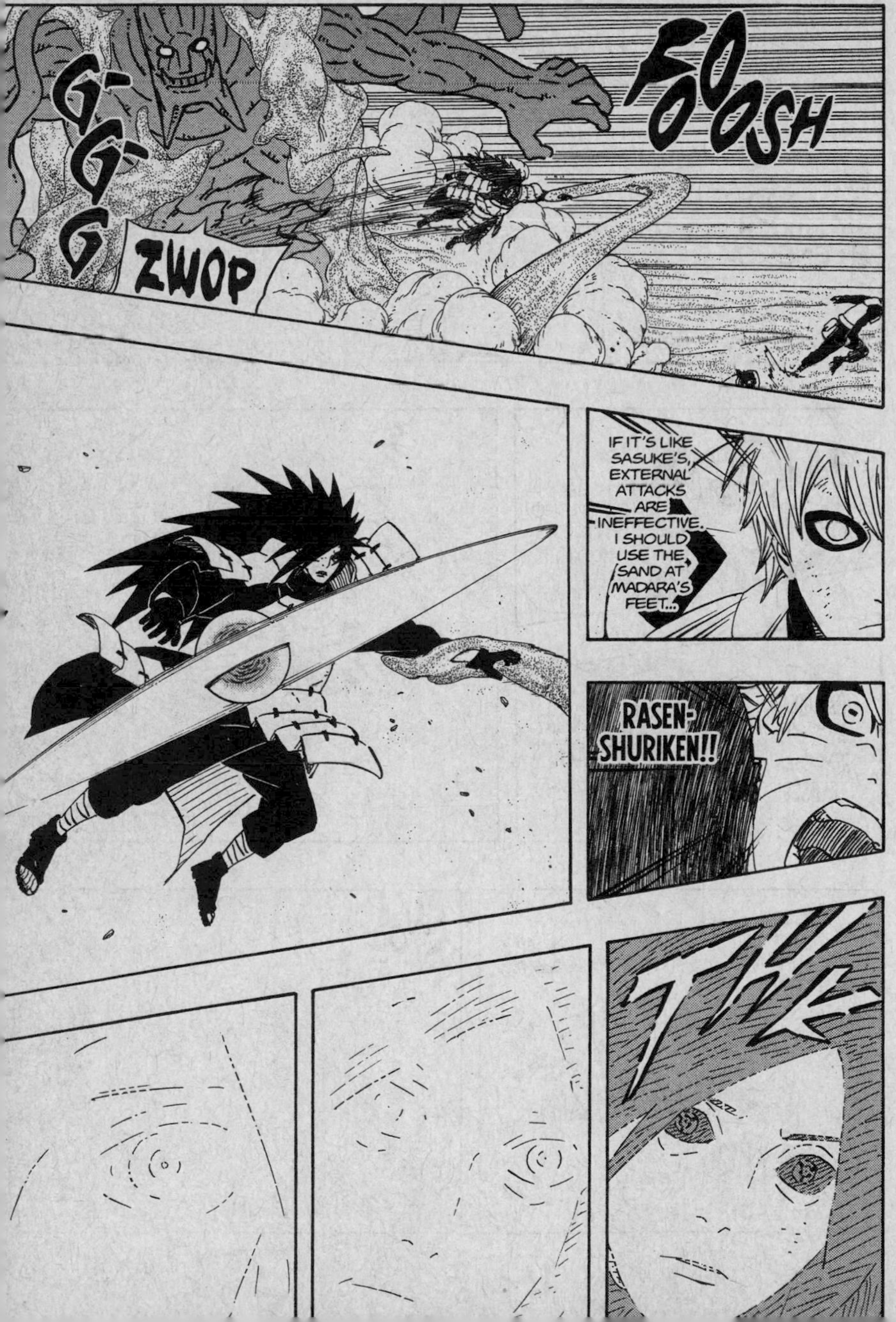
FOOOSH
G-G-G
ZWOP
IF IT'S LIKE SASUKE'S, EXTERNAL ATTACKS ARE INEFFECTIVE. I SHOULD USE THE SAND AT MADARA'S FEET...
RASEN-SHURIKEN!!
TH

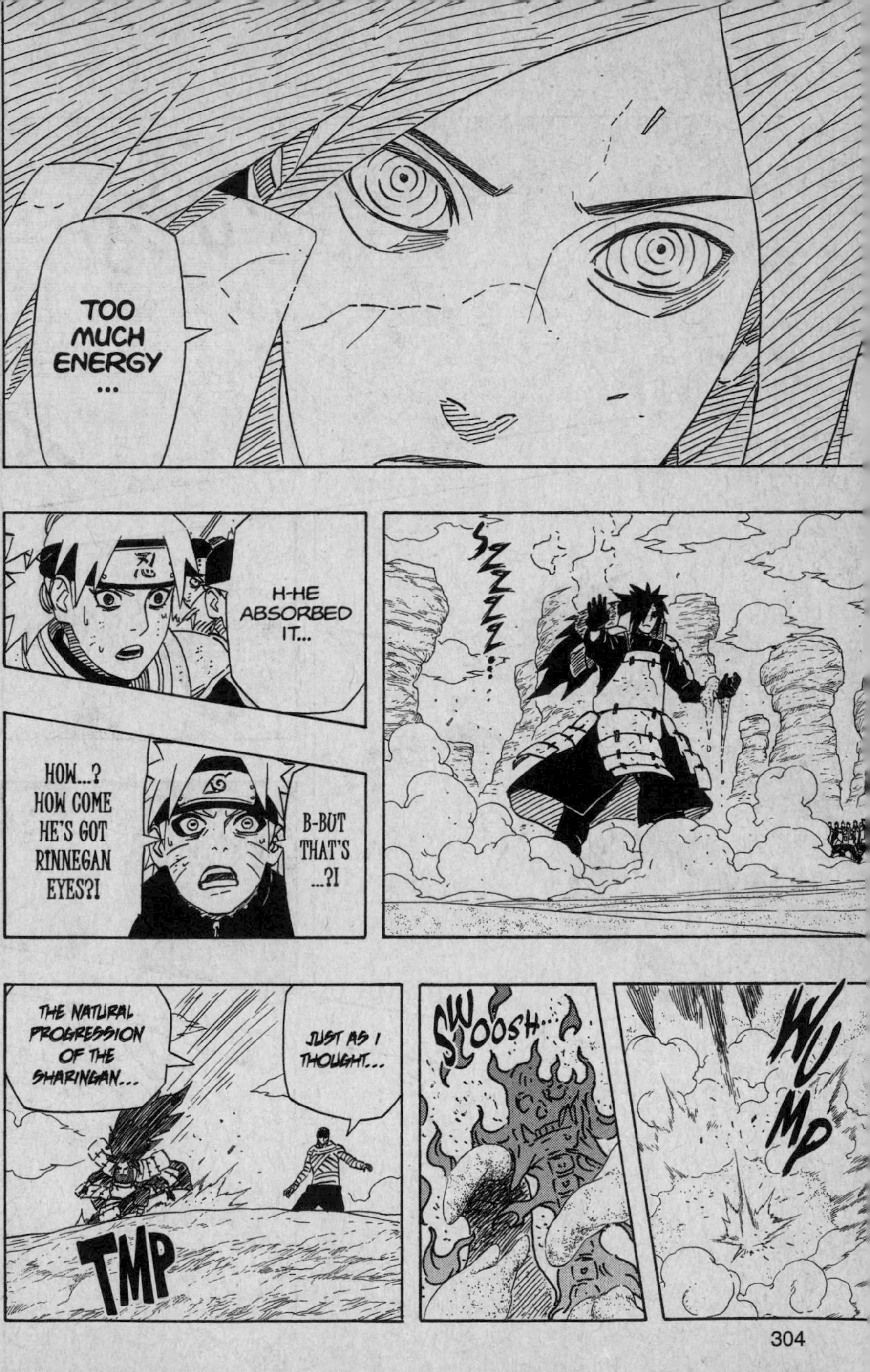
TOO MUCH ENERGY ...
SZZZZZ...
H-HE ABSORBED IT...
B-BUT THAT'S ...?!
HOW...? HOW COME HE'S GOT RINNEGAN EYES?!
WUMP
SWOOSH...
JUST AS I THOUGHT...
THE NATURAL PROGRESSION OF THE SHARINGAN...
TMP

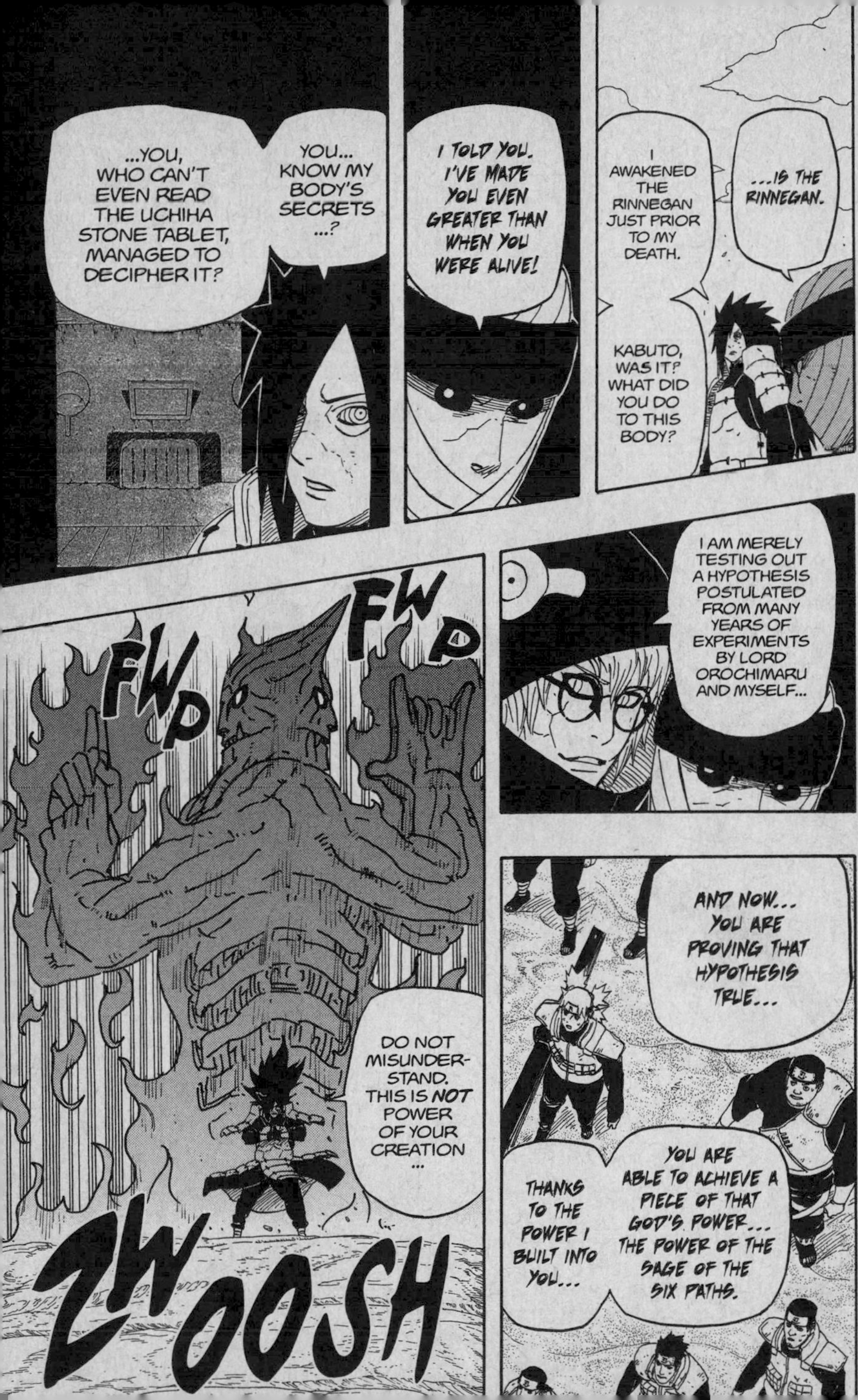
I AWAKENED THE RINNEGAN JUST PRIOR TO MY DEATH.
...IS THE RINNEGAN.
KABUTO, WAS IT? WHAT DID YOU DO TO THIS BODY?
I TOLD YOU. I'VE MADE YOU EVEN GREATER THAN WHEN YOU WERE ALIVE!
YOU... KNOW MY BODY'S SECRETS ...?
...YOU, WHO CAN'T EVEN READ THE UCHIHA STONE TABLET, MANAGED TO DECIPHER IT?
I AM MERELY TESTING OUT A HYPOTHESIS POSTULATED FROM MANY YEARS OF EXPERIMENTS BY LORD OROCHIMARU AND MYSELF...
AND NOW... YOU ARE PROVING THAT HYPOTHESIS TRUE...
YOU ARE ABLE TO ACHIEVE A PIECE OF THAT GOD'S POWER... THE POWER OF THE SAGE OF THE SIX PATHS.
THANKS TO THE POWER I BUILT INTO YOU...
FWP
FWP
DO NOT MISUNDERSTAND. THIS IS *NOT* POWER OF YOUR CREATION ...
ZWOOSH

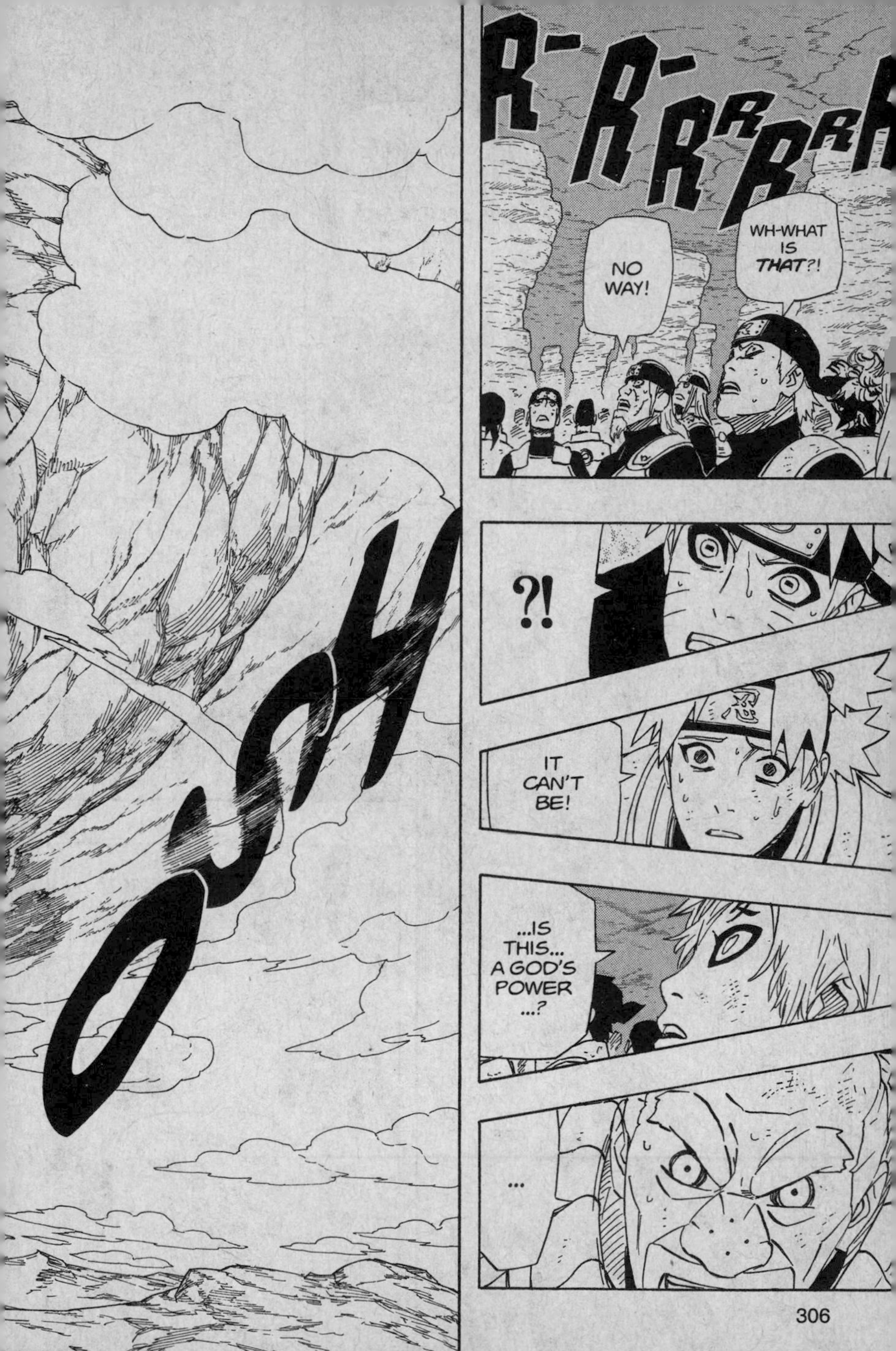
R-R-RRRRR
WH-WHAT IS *THAT*?!
NO WAY!
?!
IT CAN'T BE!
...IS THIS... A GOD'S POWER ...?
...
OOSH

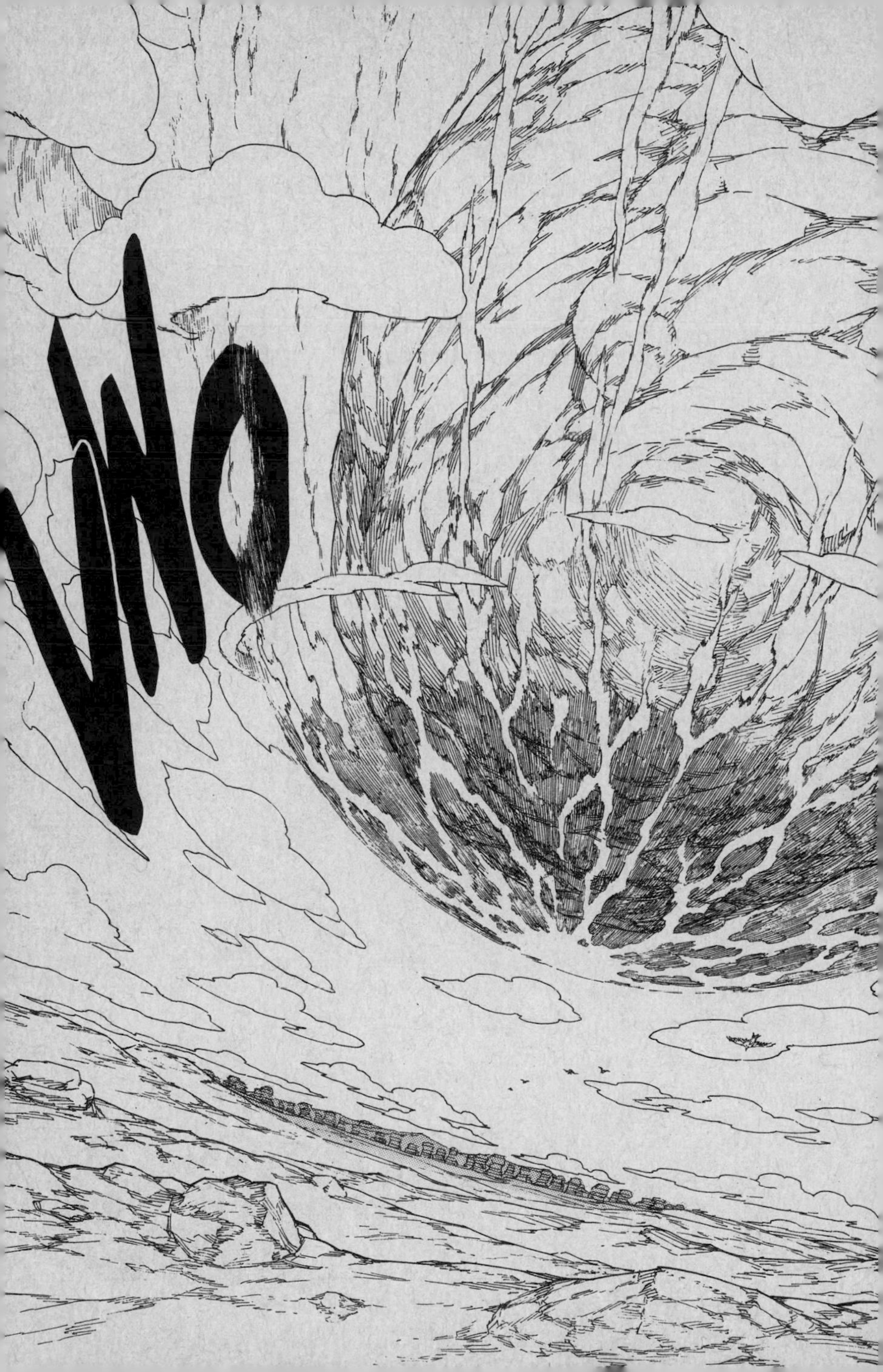

NARUTO

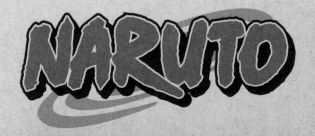

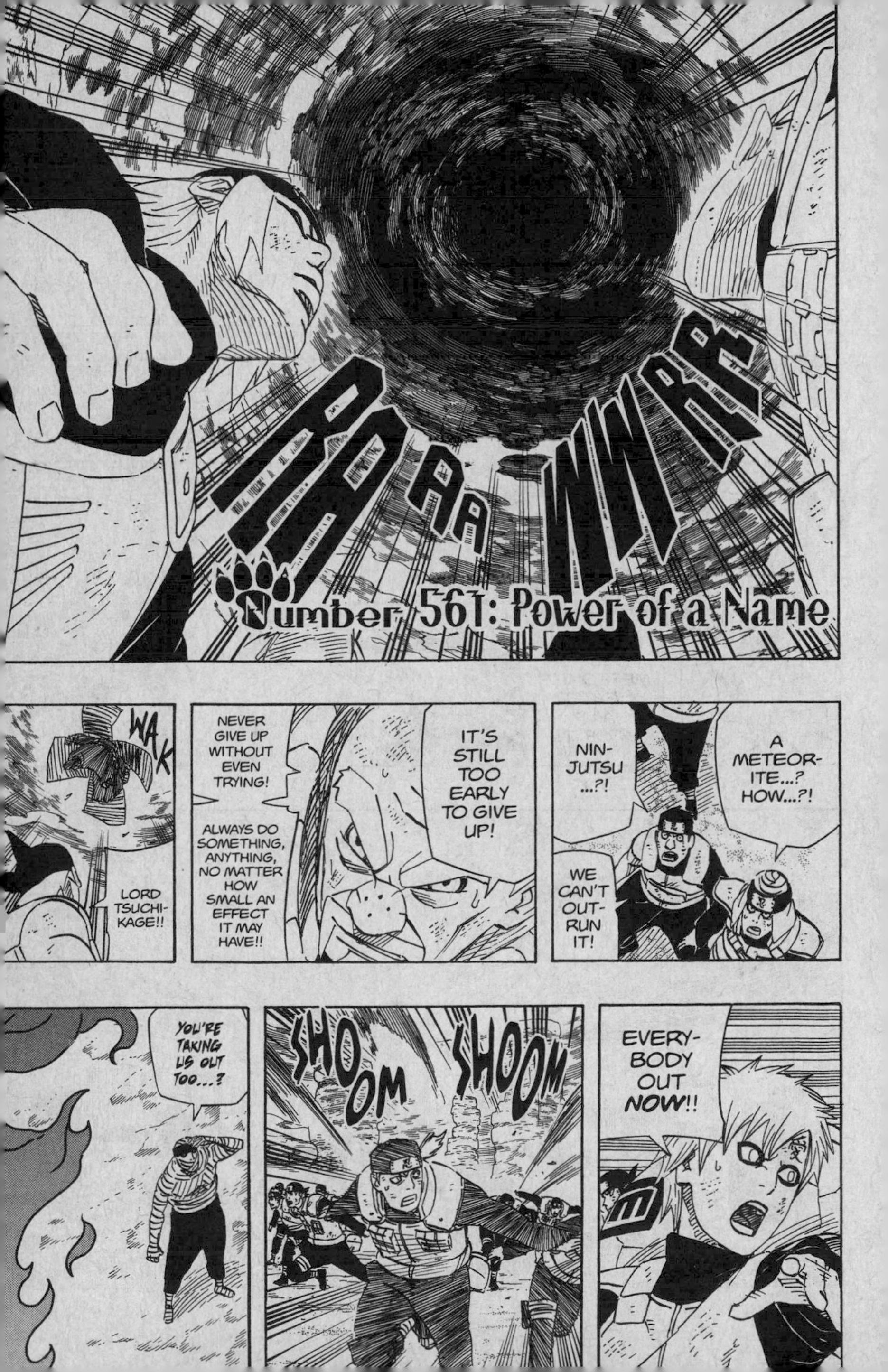
Number 561: Power of a Name
A METEORITE...? HOW...?!
NINJUTSU...?!
WE CAN'T OUTRUN IT!
IT'S STILL TOO EARLY TO GIVE UP!
NEVER GIVE UP WITHOUT EVEN TRYING!
ALWAYS DO SOMETHING, ANYTHING, NO MATTER HOW SMALL AN EFFECT IT MAY HAVE!!
WAK
LORD TSUCHIKAGE!!
EVERYBODY OUT NOW!!
SHOOM
SHOOM
YOU'RE TAKING US OUT TOO...?

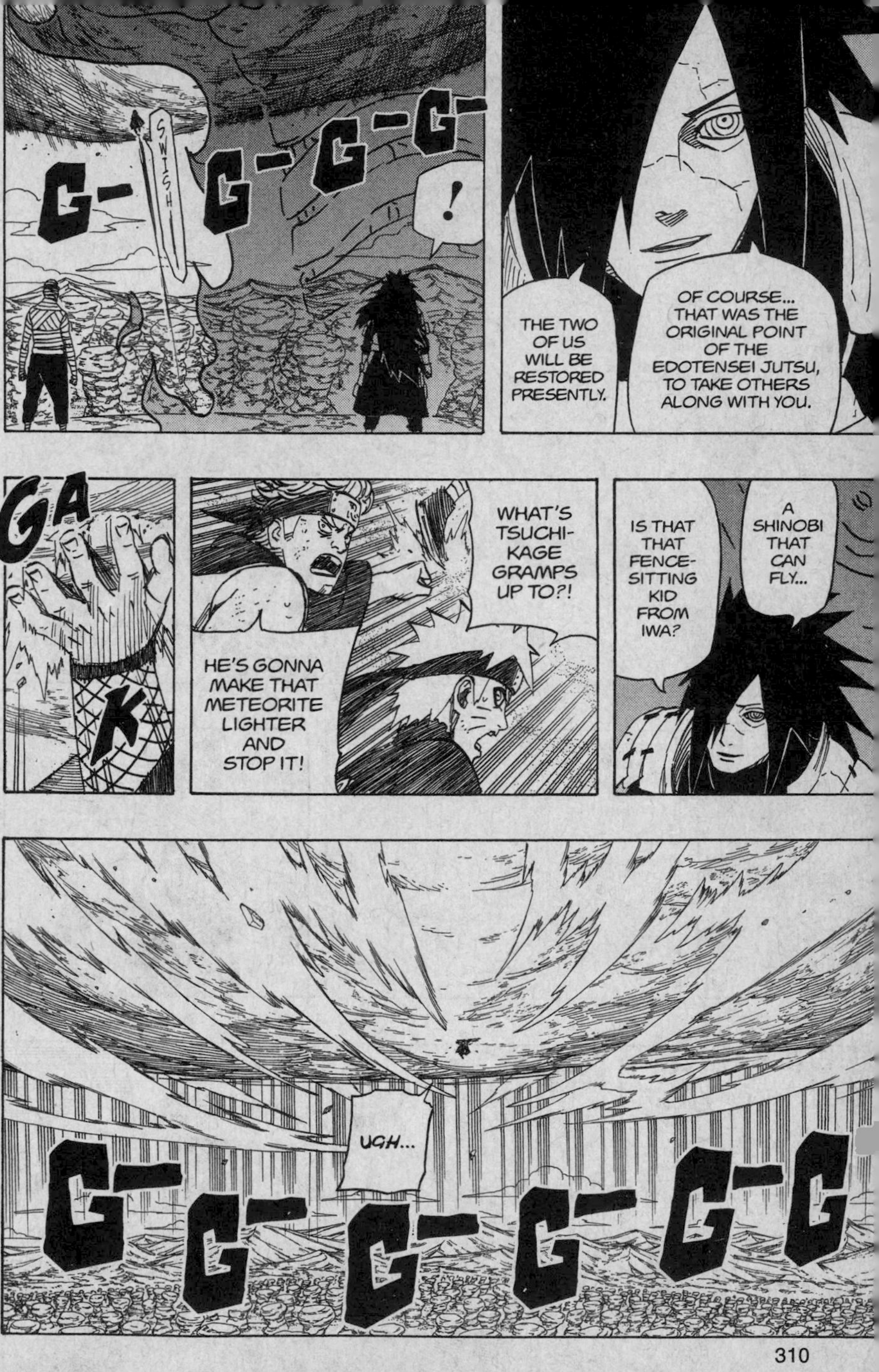
OF COURSE... THAT WAS THE ORIGINAL POINT OF THE EDOTENSEI JUTSU, TO TAKE OTHERS ALONG WITH YOU.
THE TWO OF US WILL BE RESTORED PRESENTLY.
!
G-G-G-
SWISH
G-
A SHINOBI THAT CAN FLY...
IS THAT THAT FENCE-SITTING KID FROM IWA?
WHAT'S TSUCHIKAGE GRAMPS UP TO?!
HE'S GONNA MAKE THAT METEORITE LIGHTER AND STOP IT!
GAK
UGH...
G-G-G-G-G-G

READ THIS WAY

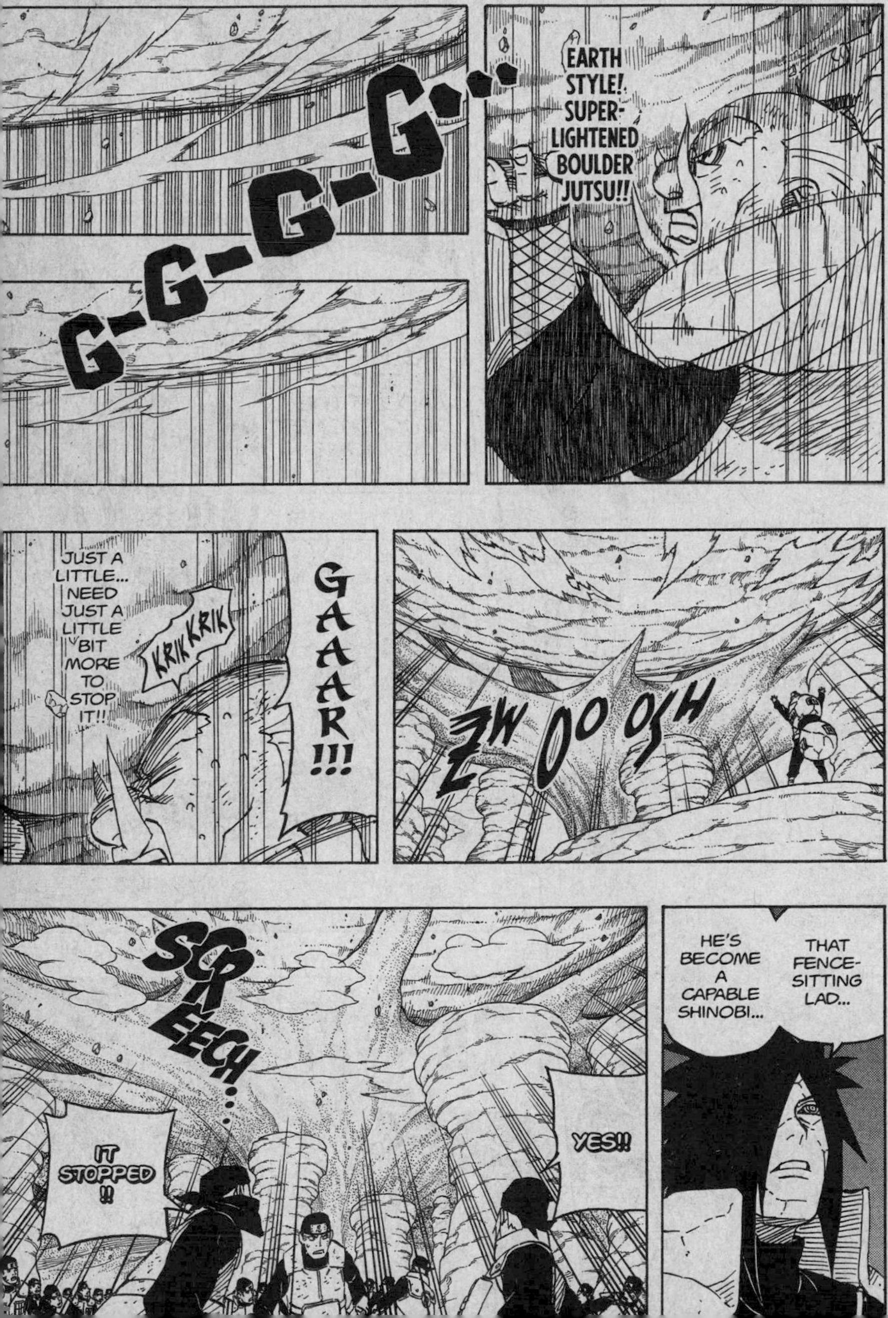
EARTH STYLE!! SUPER-LIGHTENED BOULDER JUTSU!!
G-G-G-G-G
ZWOOOSH
JUST A LITTLE... NEED JUST A LITTLE BIT MORE TO STOP IT!!
KRIK KRIK
GAAAR!!!
THAT FENCE-SITTING LAD...
HE'S BECOME A CAPABLE SHINOBI...
SCREECH...
YES!!
IT STOPPED!!

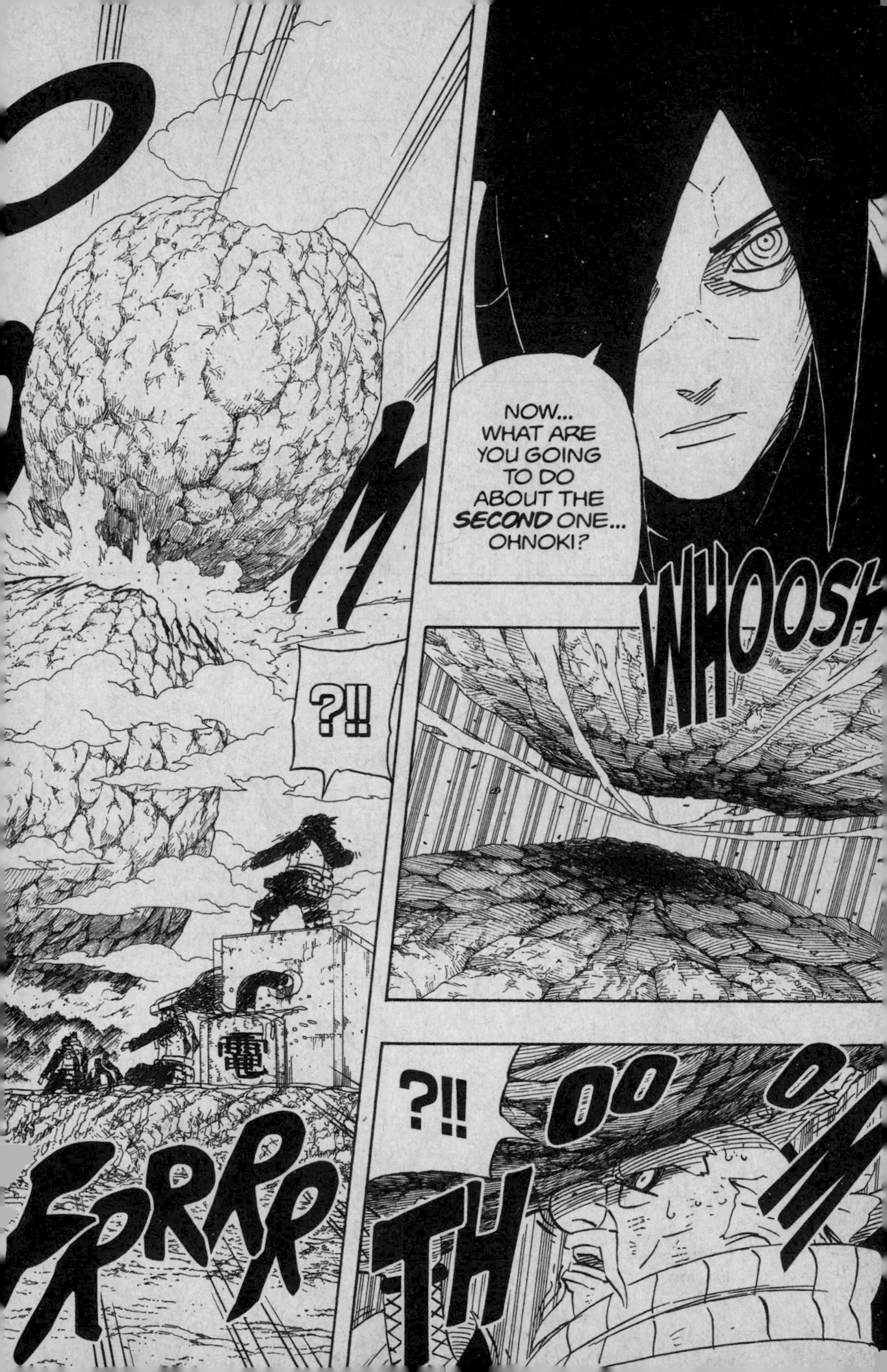
NOW... WHAT ARE YOU GOING TO DO ABOUT THE SECOND ONE... OHNOKI?
WHOOSH
?!!
?!!

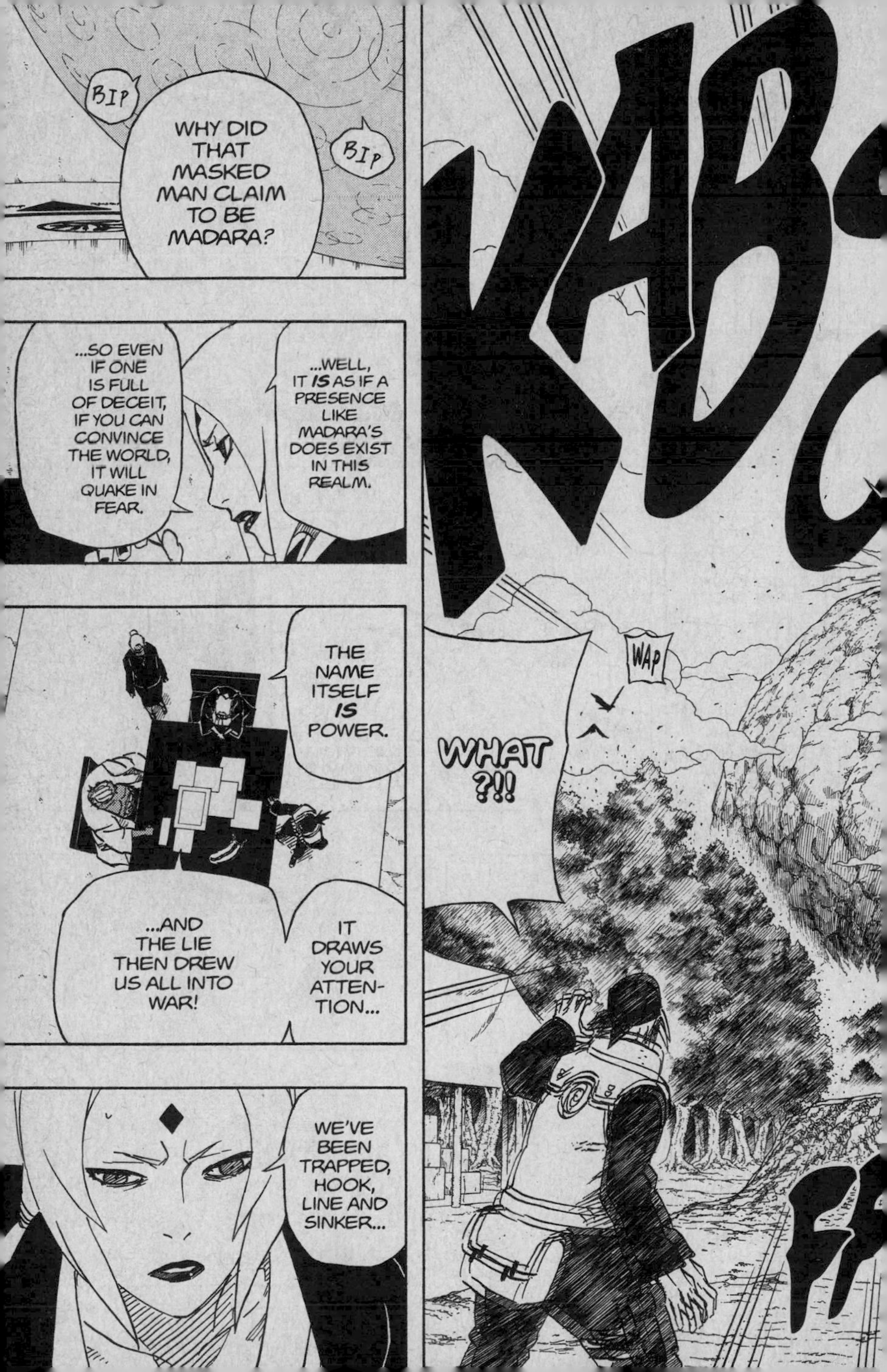
KAB
WAP
WHAT ?!!
BIP
WHY DID THAT MASKED MAN CLAIM TO BE MADARA?
BIP
...WELL, IT IS AS IF A PRESENCE LIKE MADARA'S DOES EXIST IN THIS REALM.
...SO EVEN IF ONE IS FULL OF DECEIT, IF YOU CAN CONVINCE THE WORLD, IT WILL QUAKE IN FEAR.
THE NAME ITSELF IS POWER.
IT DRAWS YOUR ATTENTION...
...AND THE LIE THEN DREW US ALL INTO WAR!
WE'VE BEEN TRAPPED, HOOK, LINE AND SINKER...

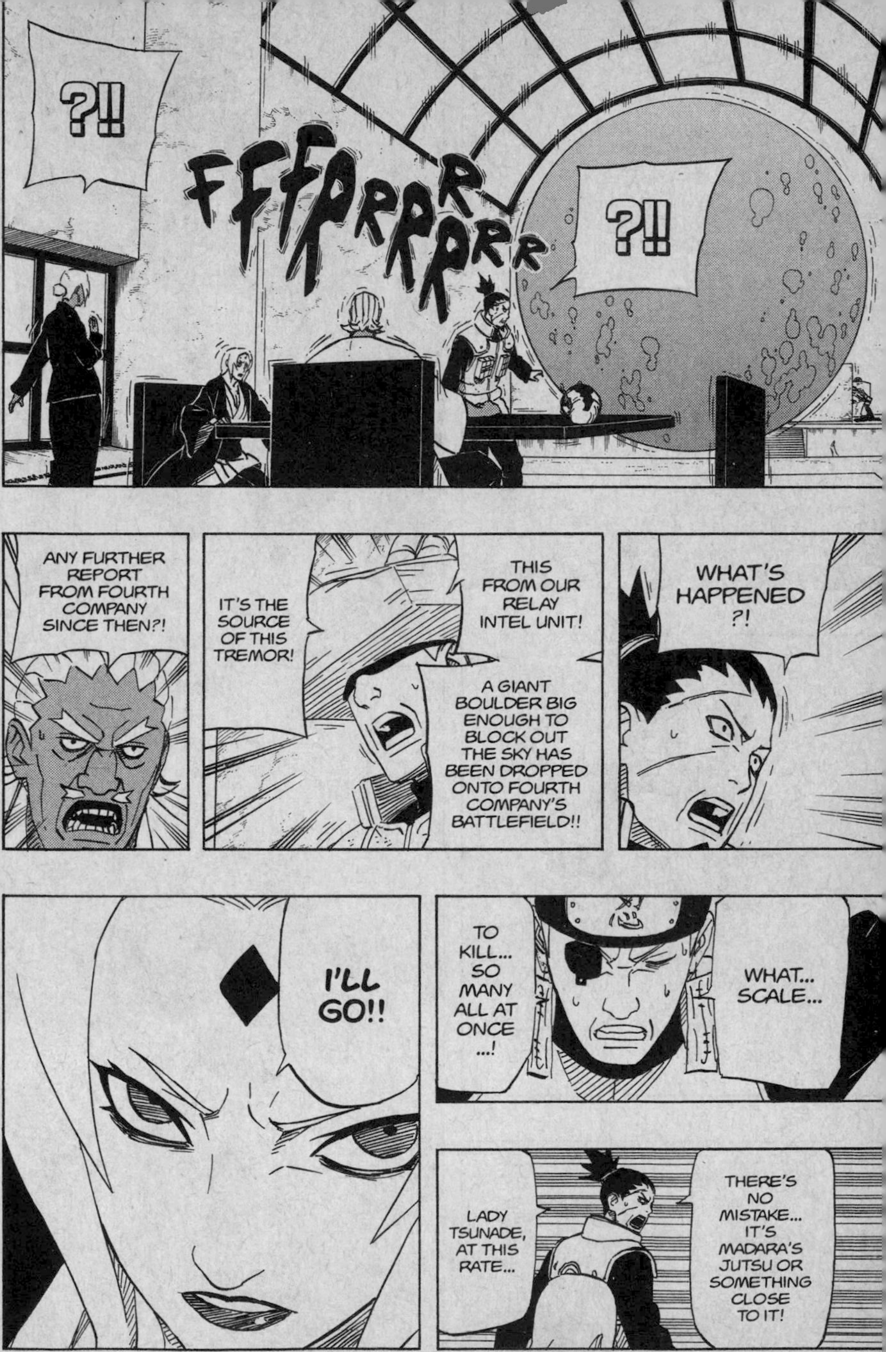
?!!
FFFRRRRRRRR
?!!
WHAT'S HAPPENED?!
THIS FROM OUR RELAY INTEL UNIT!
A GIANT BOULDER BIG ENOUGH TO BLOCK OUT THE SKY HAS BEEN DROPPED ONTO FOURTH COMPANY'S BATTLEFIELD!!
IT'S THE SOURCE OF THIS TREMOR!
ANY FURTHER REPORT FROM FOURTH COMPANY SINCE THEN?!
WHAT... SCALE...
TO KILL... SO MANY ALL AT ONCE...!
THERE'S NO MISTAKE... IT'S MADARA'S JUTSU OR SOMETHING CLOSE TO IT!
LADY TSUNADE, AT THIS RATE...
I'LL GO!!

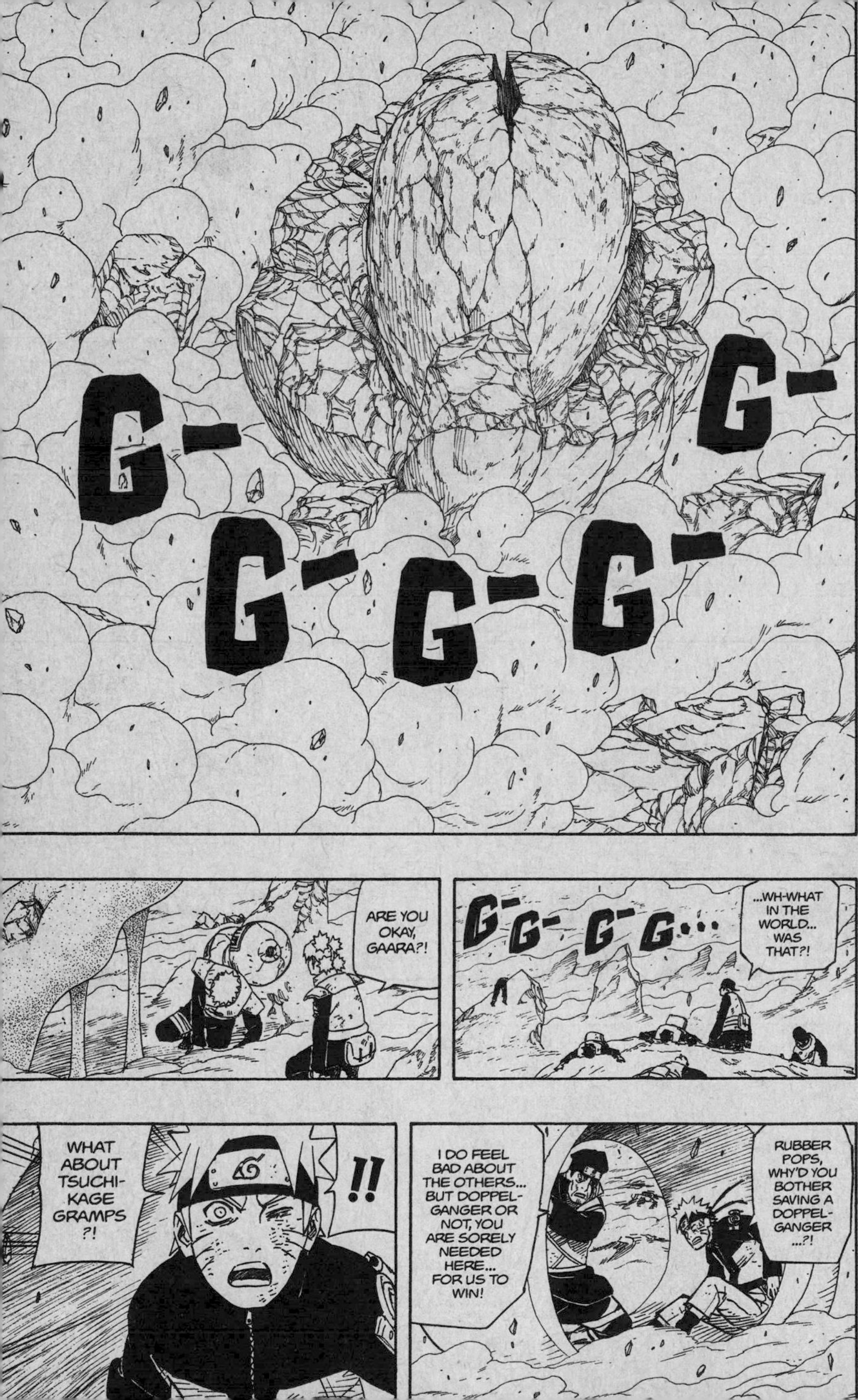
G- G- G- G- G-
G-G-G-G...
...WH-WHAT IN THE WORLD... WAS THAT?!
ARE YOU OKAY, GAARA?!
RUBBER POPS, WHY'D YOU BOTHER SAVING A DOPPEL-GANGER ...?!
I DO FEEL BAD ABOUT THE OTHERS... BUT DOPPEL-GANGER OR NOT, YOU ARE SORELY NEEDED HERE... FOR US TO WIN!
!!
WHAT ABOUT TSUCHI-KAGE GRAMPS ?!

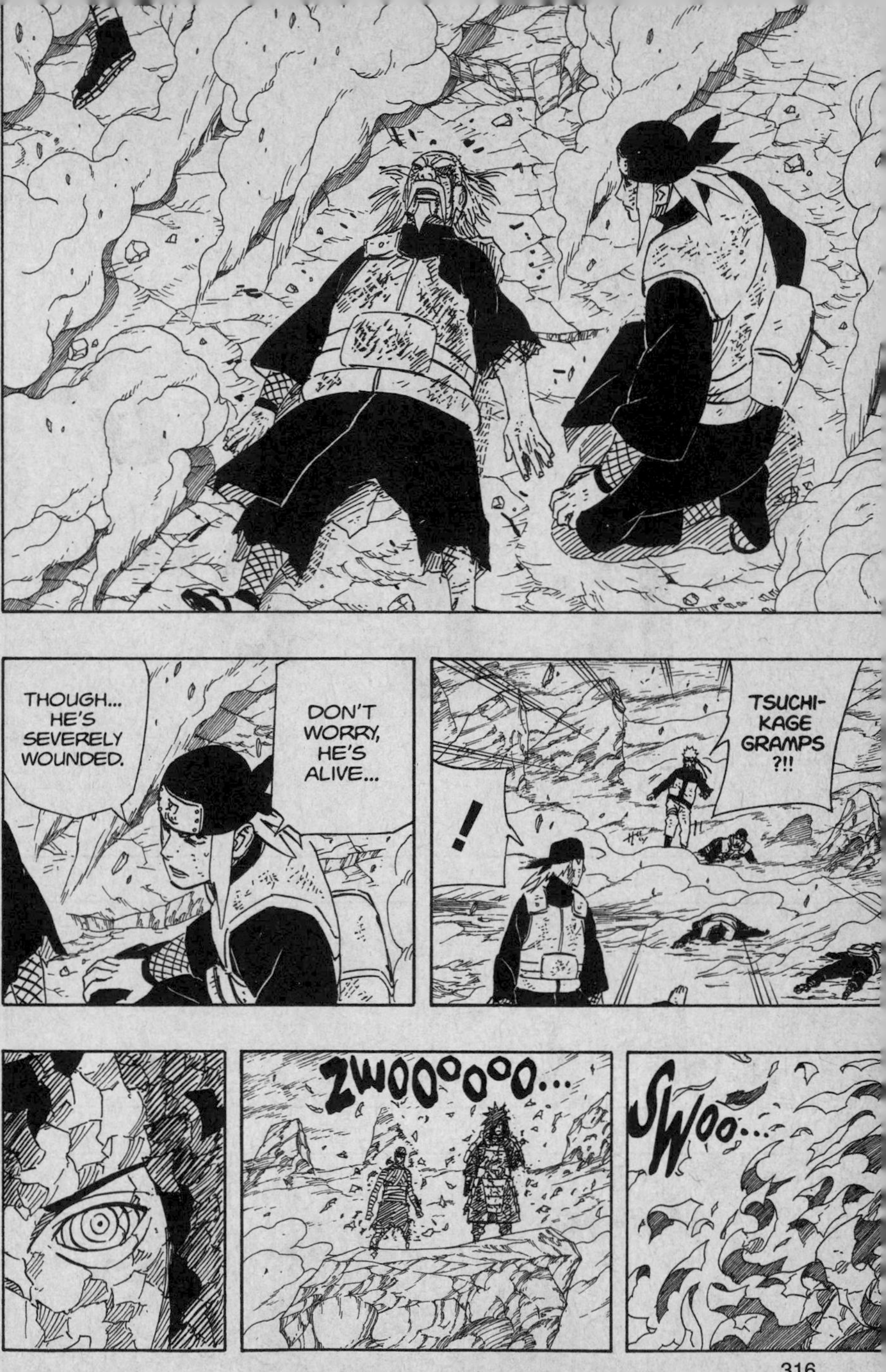
TSUCHI-KAGE GRAMPS ?!!
!
DON'T WORRY, HE'S ALIVE...
THOUGH... HE'S SEVERELY WOUNDED.
SWOO...
ZWOOOOOO...

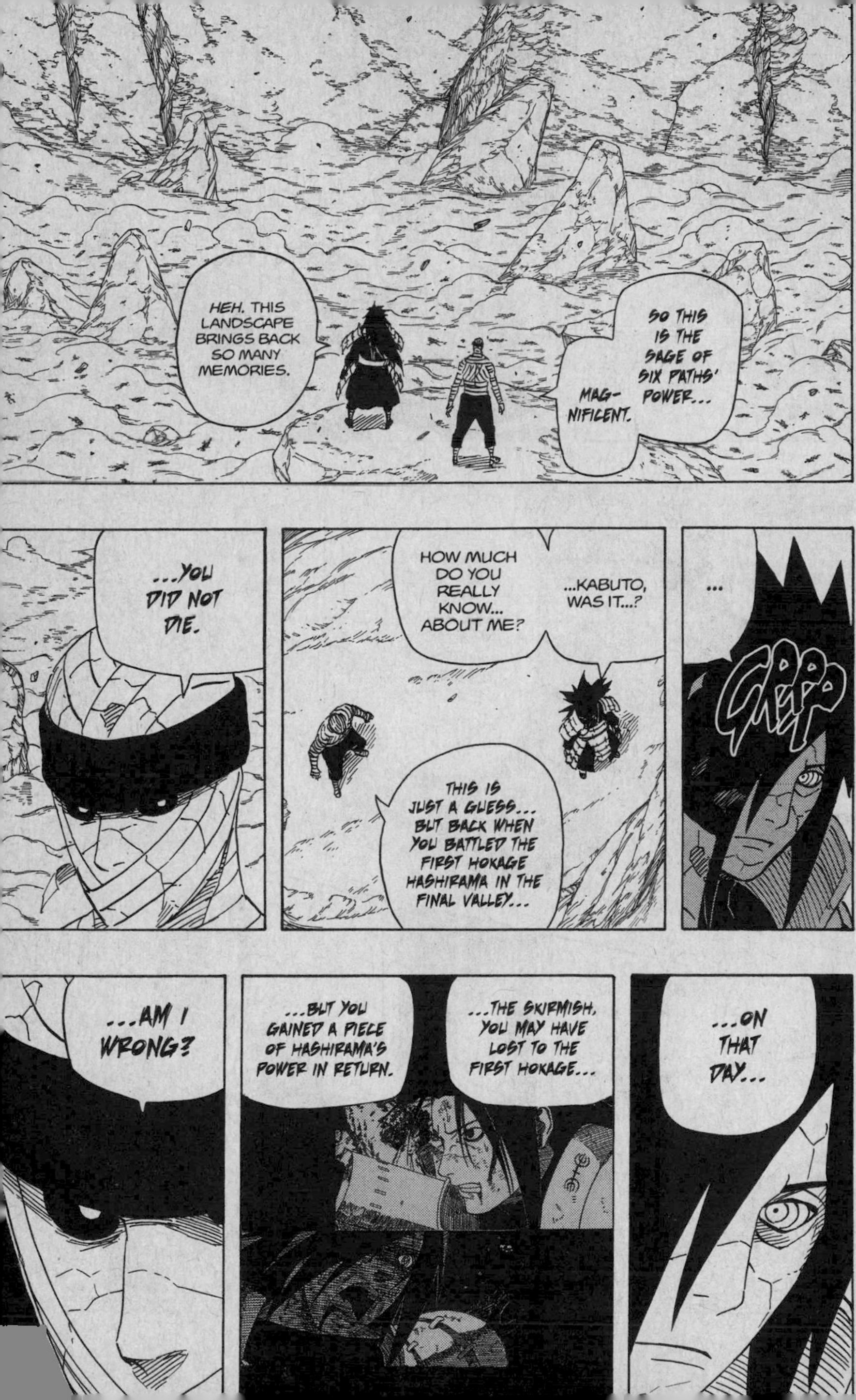
SO THIS IS THE SAGE OF SIX PATHS' POWER...
MAGNIFICENT.
HEH. THIS LANDSCAPE BRINGS BACK SO MANY MEMORIES.
...
...KABUTO, WAS IT...?
HOW MUCH DO YOU REALLY KNOW... ABOUT ME?
THIS IS JUST A GUESS... BUT BACK WHEN YOU BATTLED THE FIRST HOKAGE HASHIRAMA IN THE FINAL VALLEY...
...YOU DID NOT DIE.
...ON THAT DAY...
...THE SKIRMISH, YOU MAY HAVE LOST TO THE FIRST HOKAGE...
...BUT YOU GAINED A PIECE OF HASHIRAMA'S POWER IN RETURN.
...AM I WRONG?

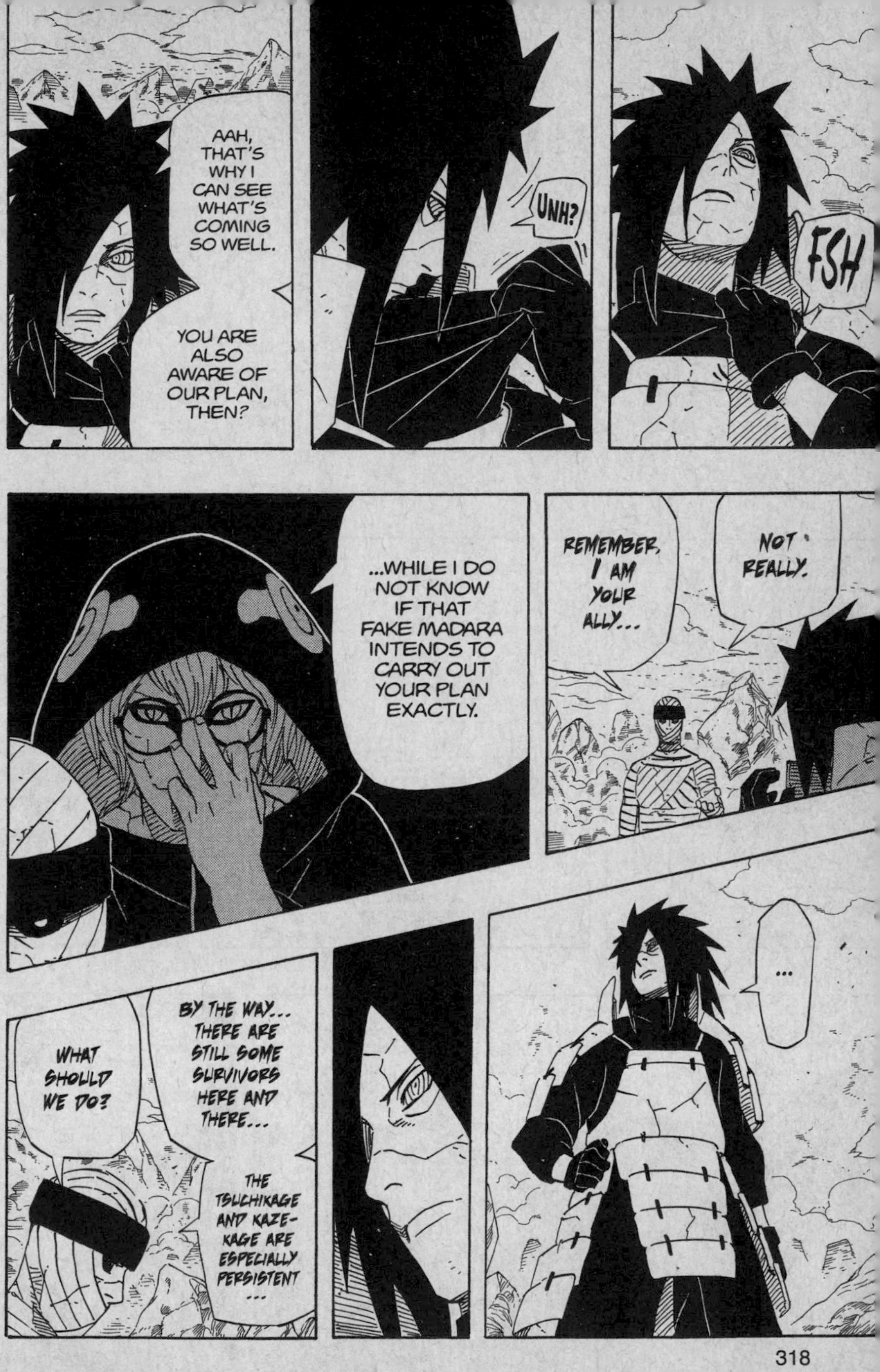
FSH
UNH?
AAH, THAT'S WHY I CAN SEE WHAT'S COMING SO WELL.
YOU ARE ALSO AWARE OF OUR PLAN, THEN?
NOT REALLY.
REMEMBER, I AM YOUR ALLY...
...WHILE I DO NOT KNOW IF THAT FAKE MADARA INTENDS TO CARRY OUT YOUR PLAN EXACTLY.
...
BY THE WAY... THERE ARE STILL SOME SURVIVORS HERE AND THERE...
THE TSUCHIKAGE AND KAZE-KAGE ARE ESPECIALLY PERSISTENT...
WHAT SHOULD WE DO?

READ THIS WAY

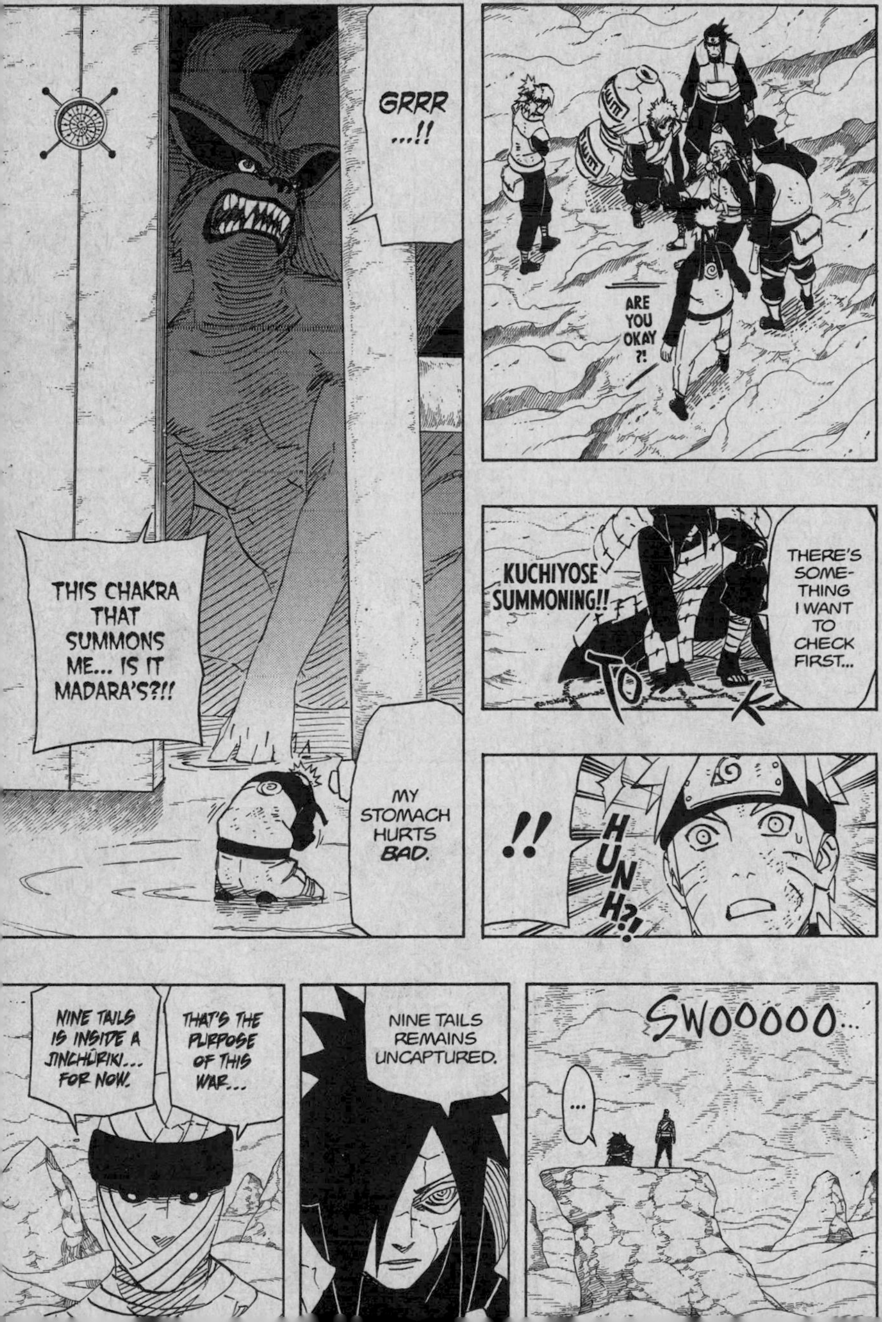
ARE YOU OKAY ?!
THERE'S SOMETHING I WANT TO CHECK FIRST...
KUCHIYOSE SUMMONING!!
TOK
!!
HUNH?!!
GRRR ...!!
THIS CHAKRA THAT SUMMONS ME... IS IT MADARA'S?!!
MY STOMACH HURTS BAD.
SWOOOOO...
...
NINE TAILS REMAINS UNCAPTURED.
THAT'S THE PURPOSE OF THIS WAR...
NINE TAILS IS INSIDE A JINCHŪRIKI... FOR NOW.

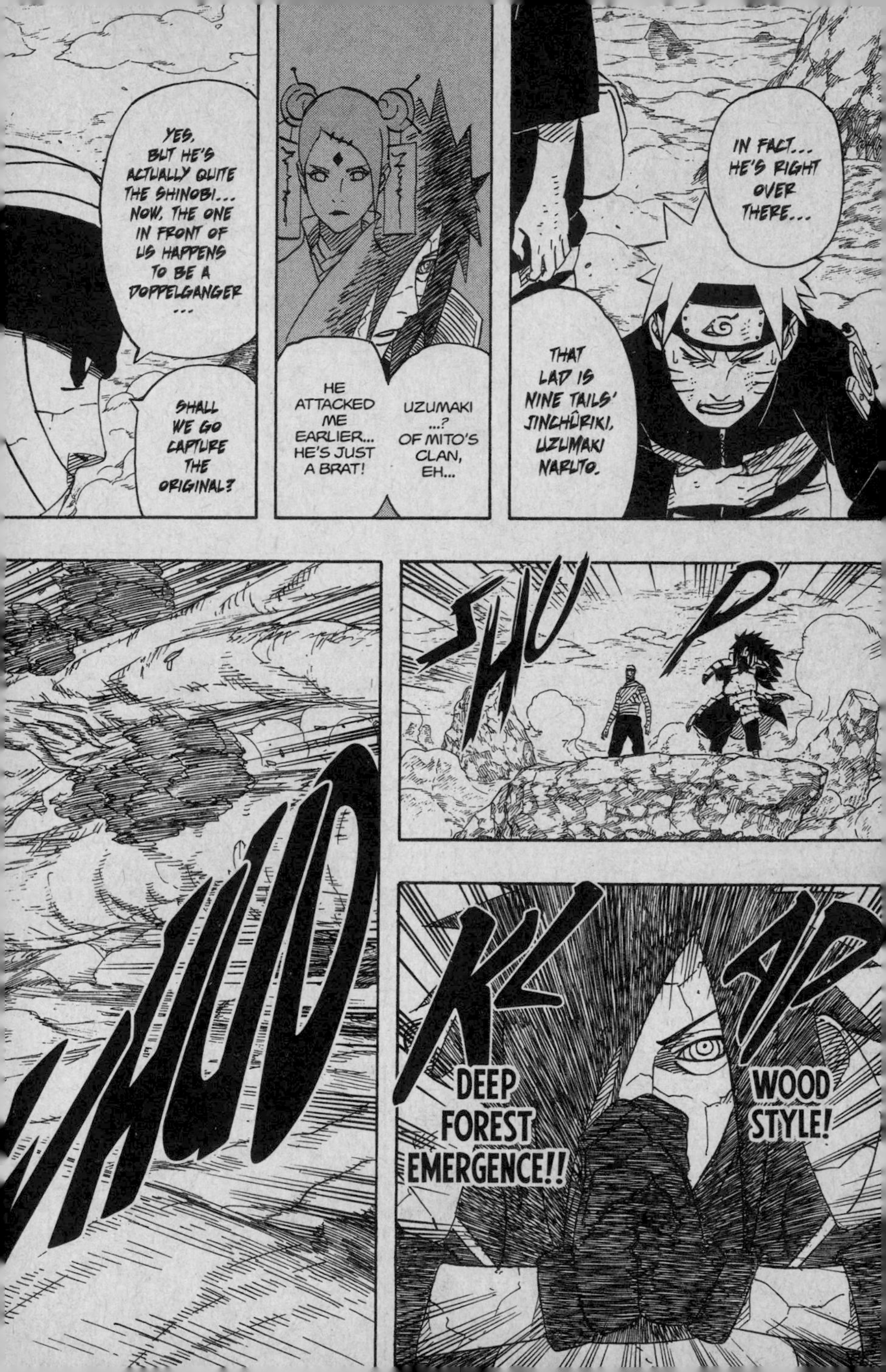
IN FACT... HE'S RIGHT OVER THERE...
THAT LAD IS NINE TAILS' JINCHÛRIKI, UZUMAKI NARUTO.
UZUMAKI ...? OF MITO'S CLAN, EH...
HE ATTACKED ME EARLIER... HE'S JUST A BRAT!
YES, BUT HE'S ACTUALLY QUITE THE SHINOBI... NOW, THE ONE IN FRONT OF US HAPPENS TO BE A DOPPELGANGER ...
SHALL WE GO CAPTURE THE ORIGINAL?
SHUP
WOOD STYLE!
DEEP FOREST EMERGENCE!!
WHUD

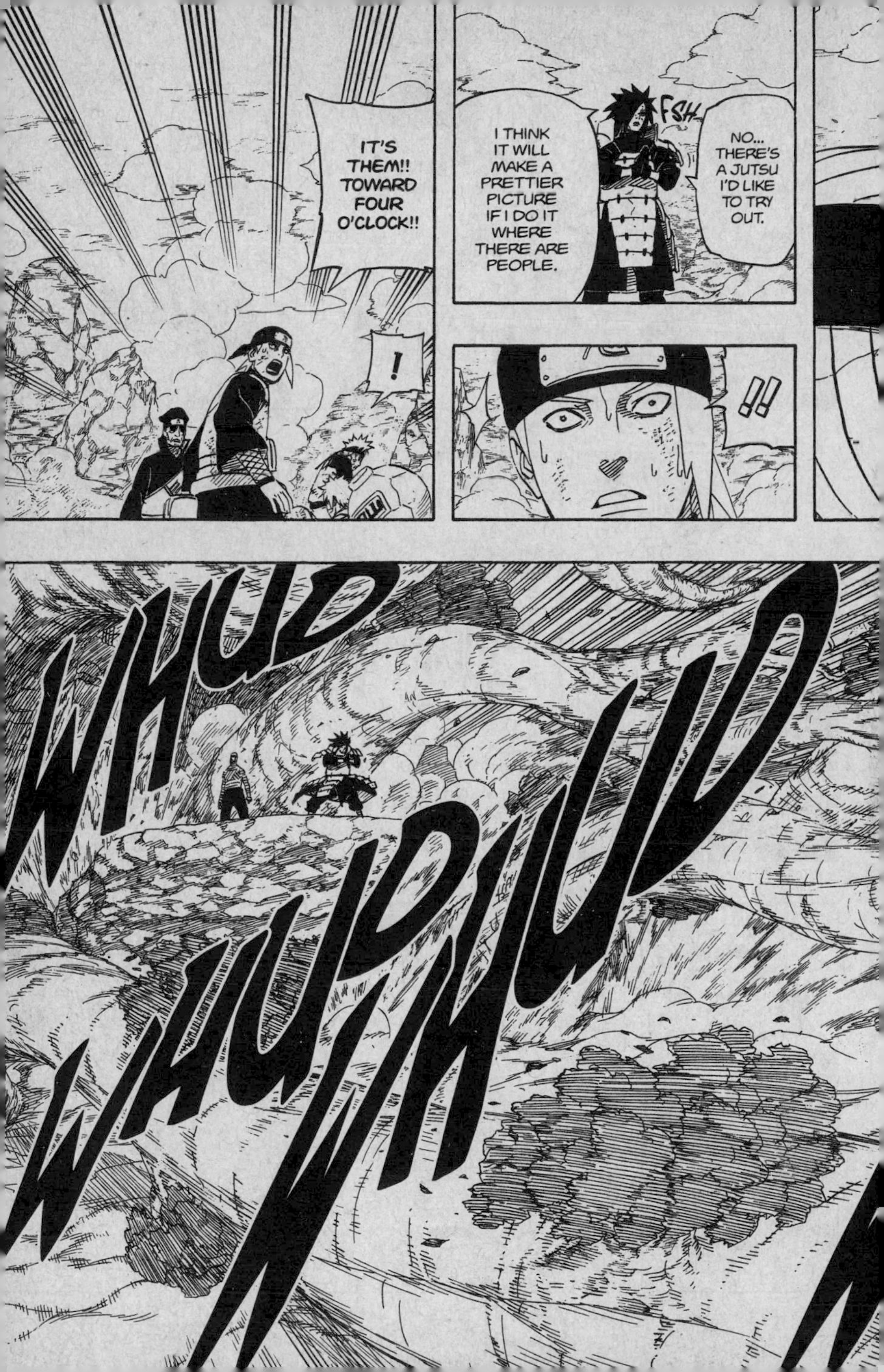
NO... THERE'S A JUTSU I'D LIKE TO TRY OUT.
FSH
I THINK IT WILL MAKE A PRETTIER PICTURE IF I DO IT WHERE THERE ARE PEOPLE.
!!
IT'S THEM!! TOWARD FOUR O'CLOCK!!
!

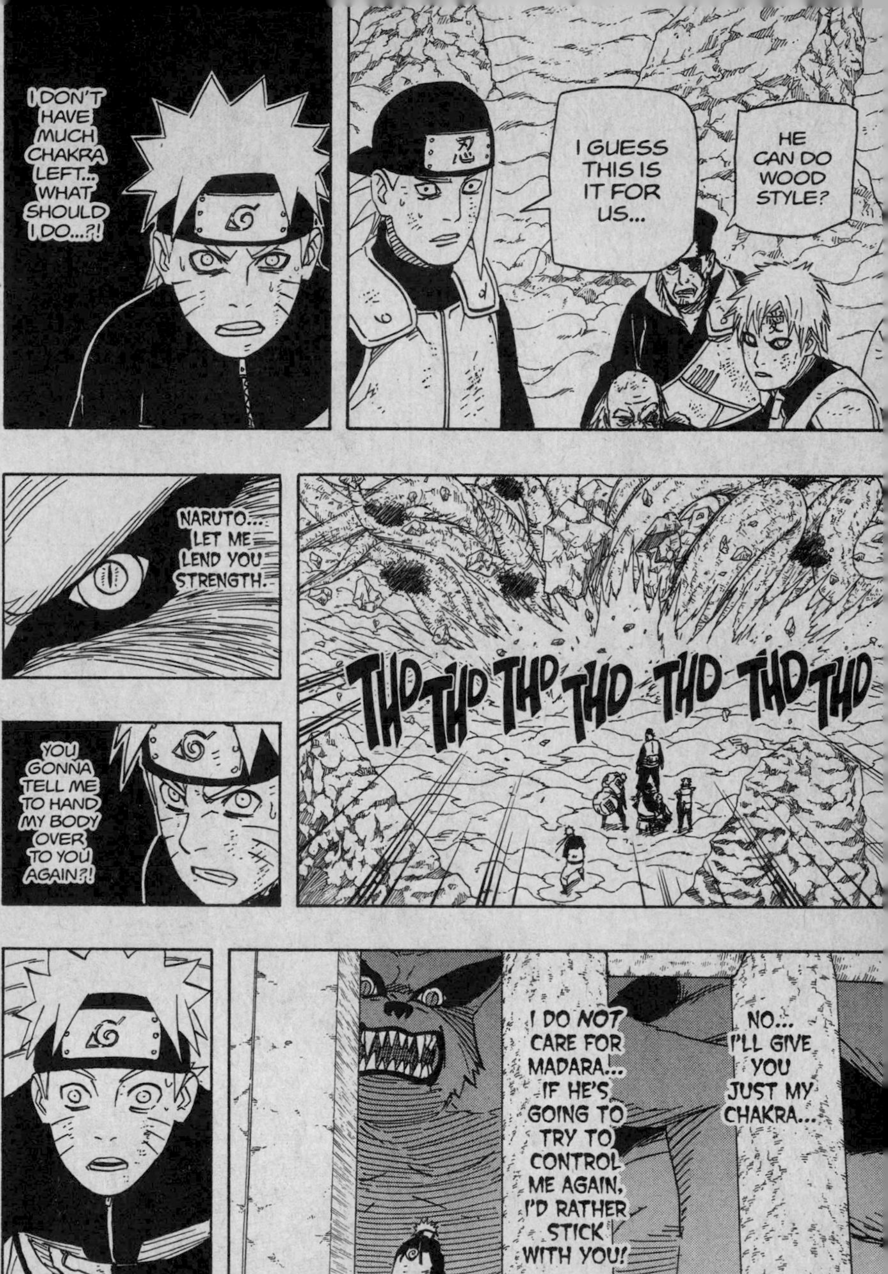
HE CAN DO WOOD STYLE?
I GUESS THIS IS IT FOR US...
I DON'T HAVE MUCH CHAKRA LEFT... WHAT SHOULD I DO...?!
THD THD THD THD THD THD THD
NARUTO... LET ME LEND YOU STRENGTH.
YOU GONNA TELL ME TO HAND MY BODY OVER TO YOU AGAIN?!
NO... I'LL GIVE YOU JUST MY CHAKRA...
I DO NOT CARE FOR MADARA... IF HE'S GOING TO TRY TO CONTROL ME AGAIN, I'D RATHER STICK WITH YOU!

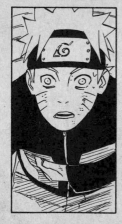

READ THIS WAY

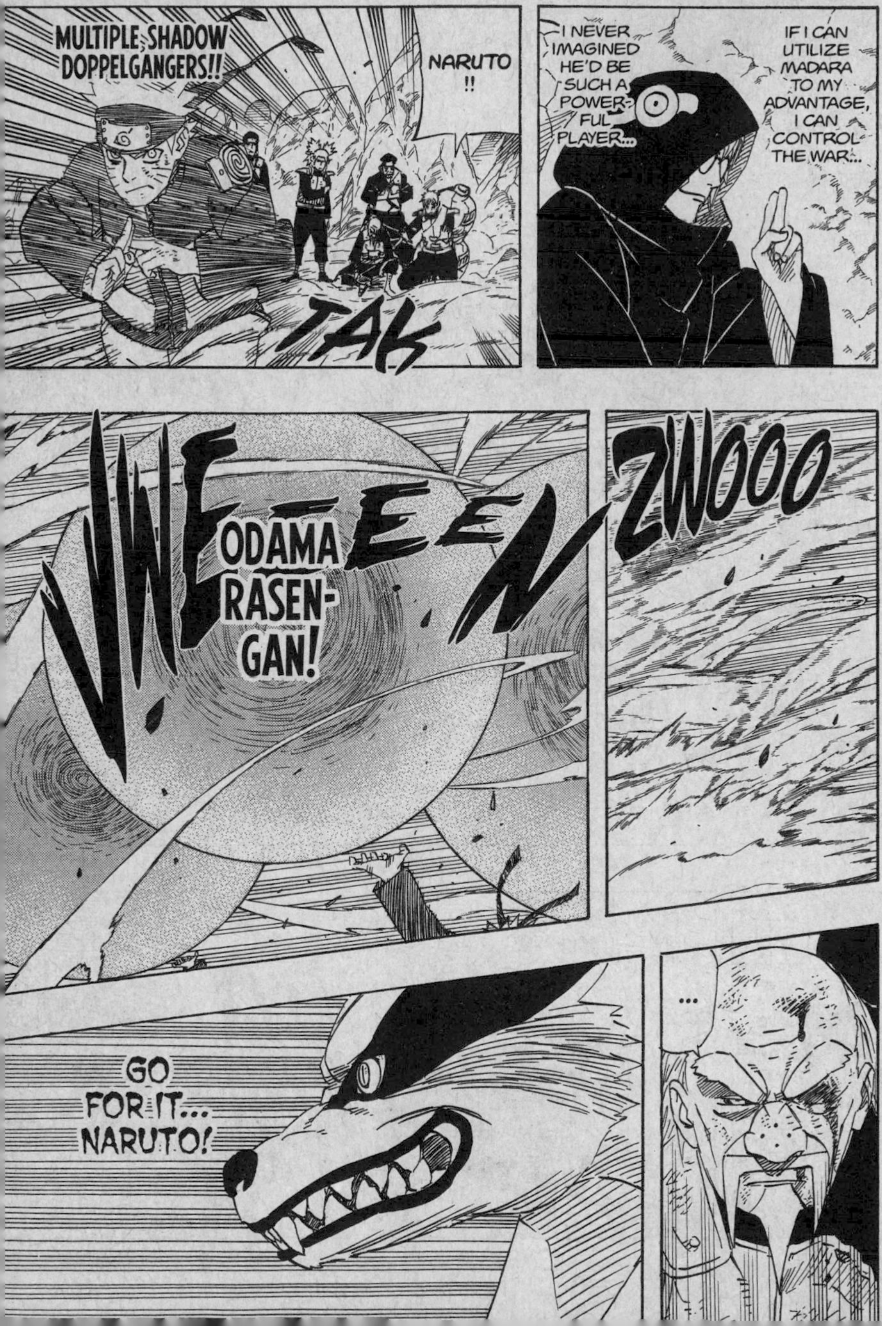

IF I CAN UTILIZE MADARA TO MY ADVANTAGE, I CAN CONTROL THE WAR...
I NEVER IMAGINED HE'D BE SUCH A POWER-FUL PLAYER...
NARUTO !!
MULTIPLE SHADOW DOPPELGANGERS!!
TAK
ZWOOO
VWEEEEN
ODAMA RASEN-GAN!
...
GO FOR IT... NARUTO!

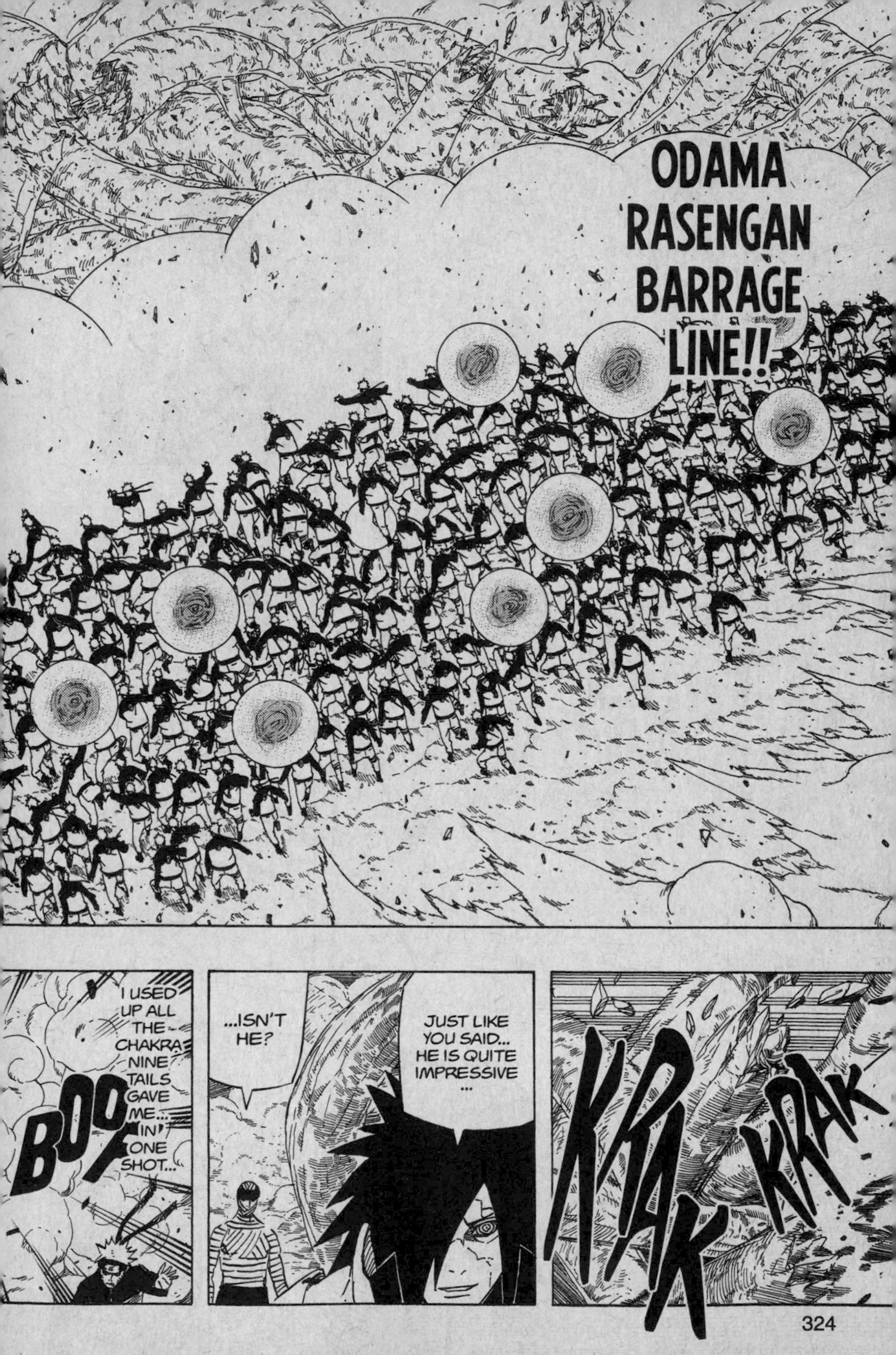
ODAMA RASENGAN BARRAGE LINE!!
KRAK
KRAK
JUST LIKE YOU SAID... HE IS QUITE IMPRESSIVE ...
...ISN'T HE?
I USED UP ALL THE CHAKRA NINE TAILS GAVE ME... IN ONE SHOT...
BOOF

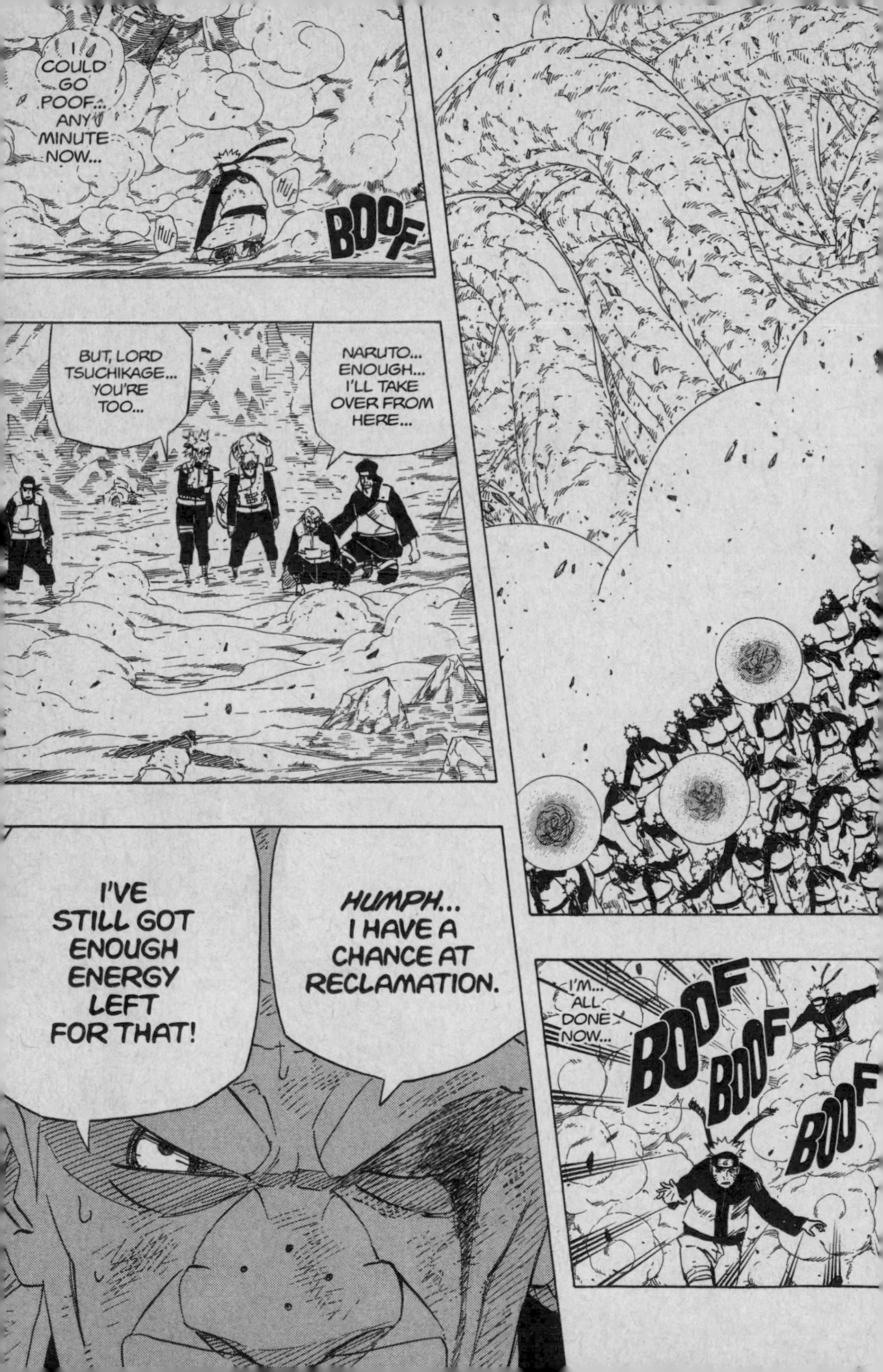
I'M... ALL DONE NOW...
BOOF
BOOF
BOOF
I COULD GO POOF... ANY MINUTE NOW...
HUF
HUF
BOOF
NARUTO... ENOUGH... I'LL TAKE OVER FROM HERE...
BUT, LORD TSUCHIKAGE... YOU'RE TOO...
HUMPH... I HAVE A CHANCE AT RECLAMATION.
I'VE STILL GOT ENOUGH ENERGY LEFT FOR THAT!

Number 562: Reclamation

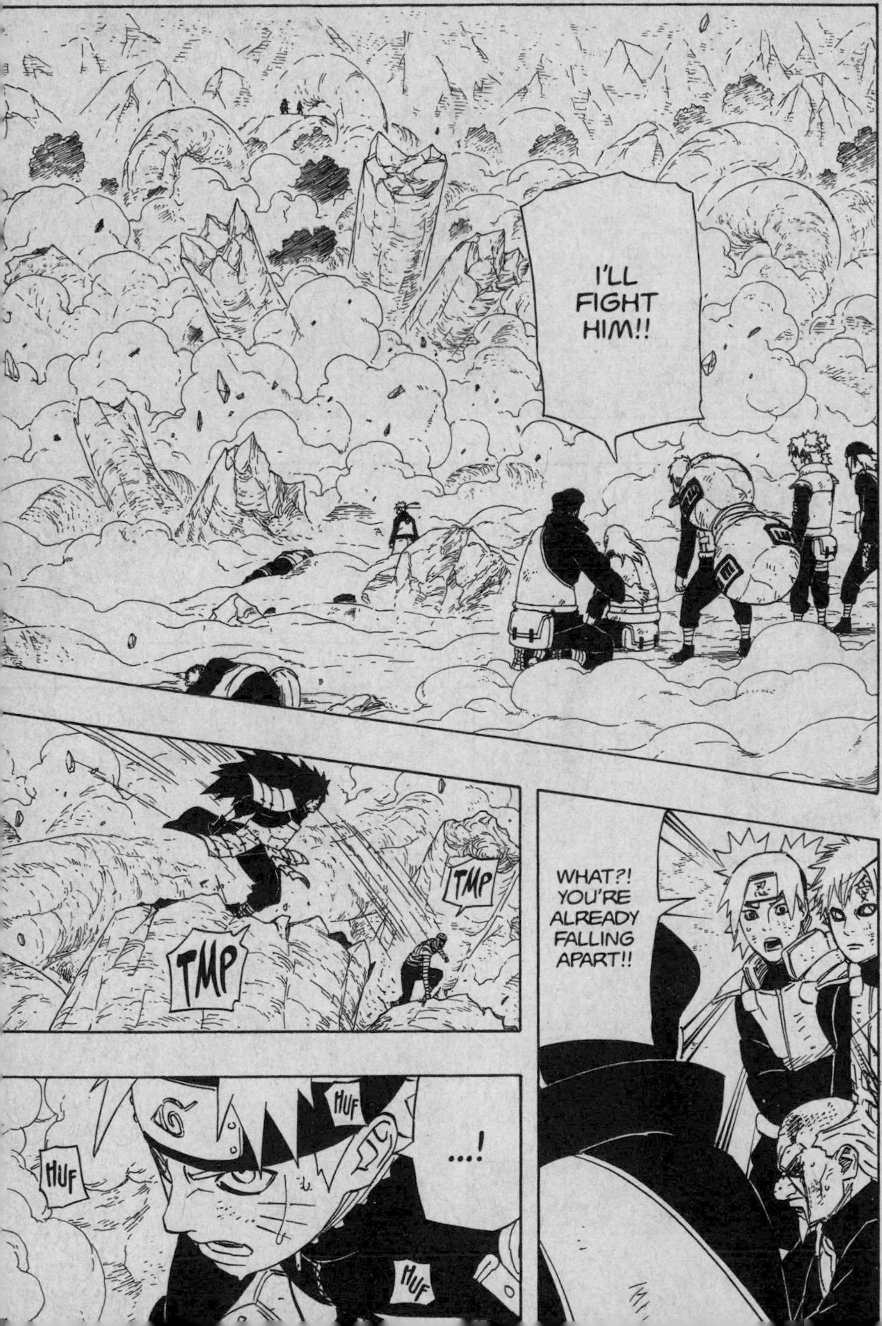
I'LL FIGHT HIM!!
WHAT?! YOU'RE ALREADY FALLING APART!!
TMP
TMP
HUF
HUF
...!
HUF

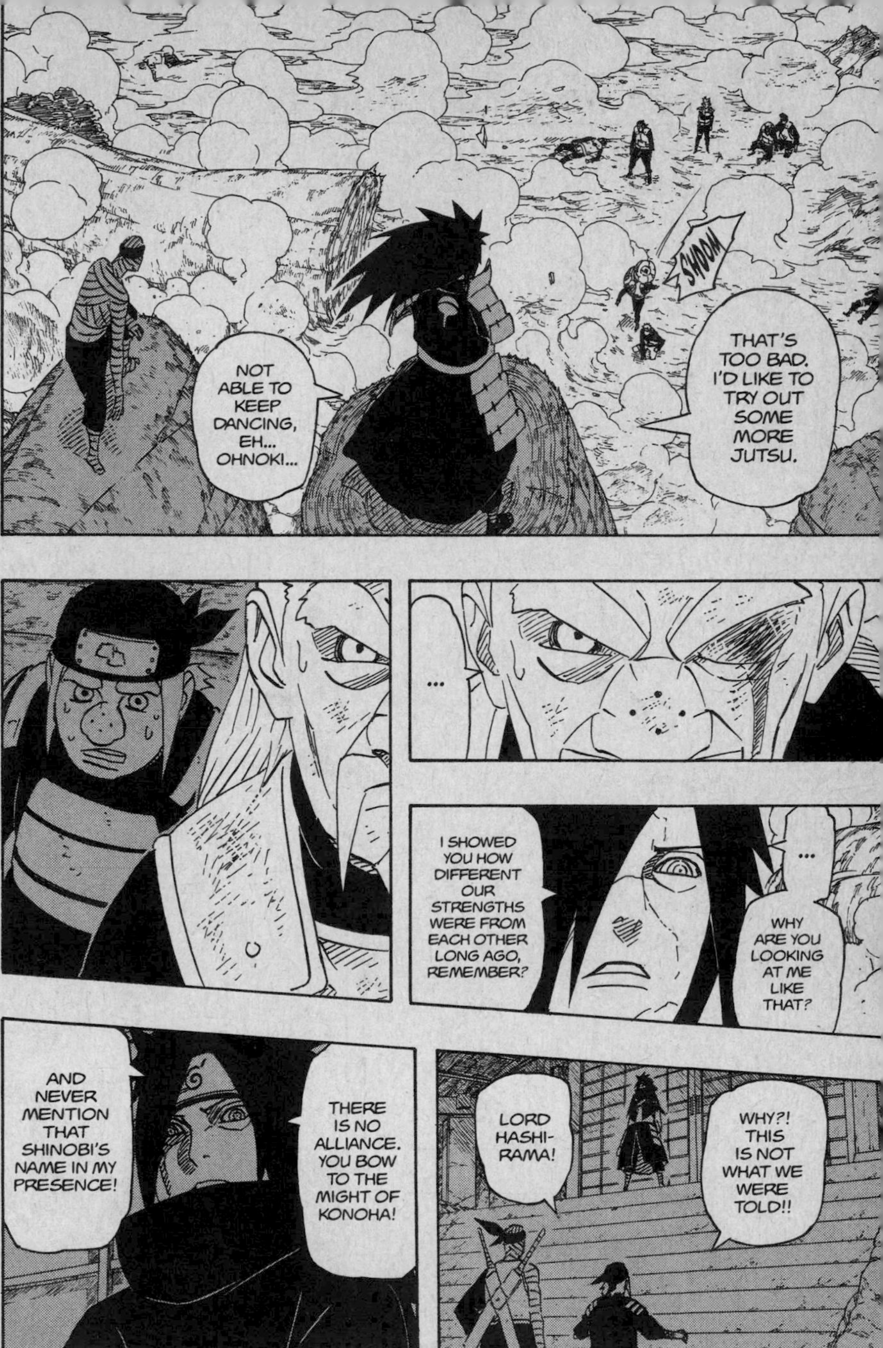
SHOOM
NOT ABLE TO KEEP DANCING, EH... OHNOKI...
THAT'S TOO BAD. I'D LIKE TO TRY OUT SOME MORE JUTSU.
...
...
WHY ARE YOU LOOKING AT ME LIKE THAT?
I SHOWED YOU HOW DIFFERENT OUR STRENGTHS WERE FROM EACH OTHER LONG AGO, REMEMBER?
WHY?! THIS IS NOT WHAT WE WERE TOLD!!
LORD HASHI-RAMA!
THERE IS NO ALLIANCE. YOU BOW TO THE MIGHT OF KONOHA!
AND NEVER MENTION THAT SHINOBI'S NAME IN MY PRESENCE!

READ THIS WAY

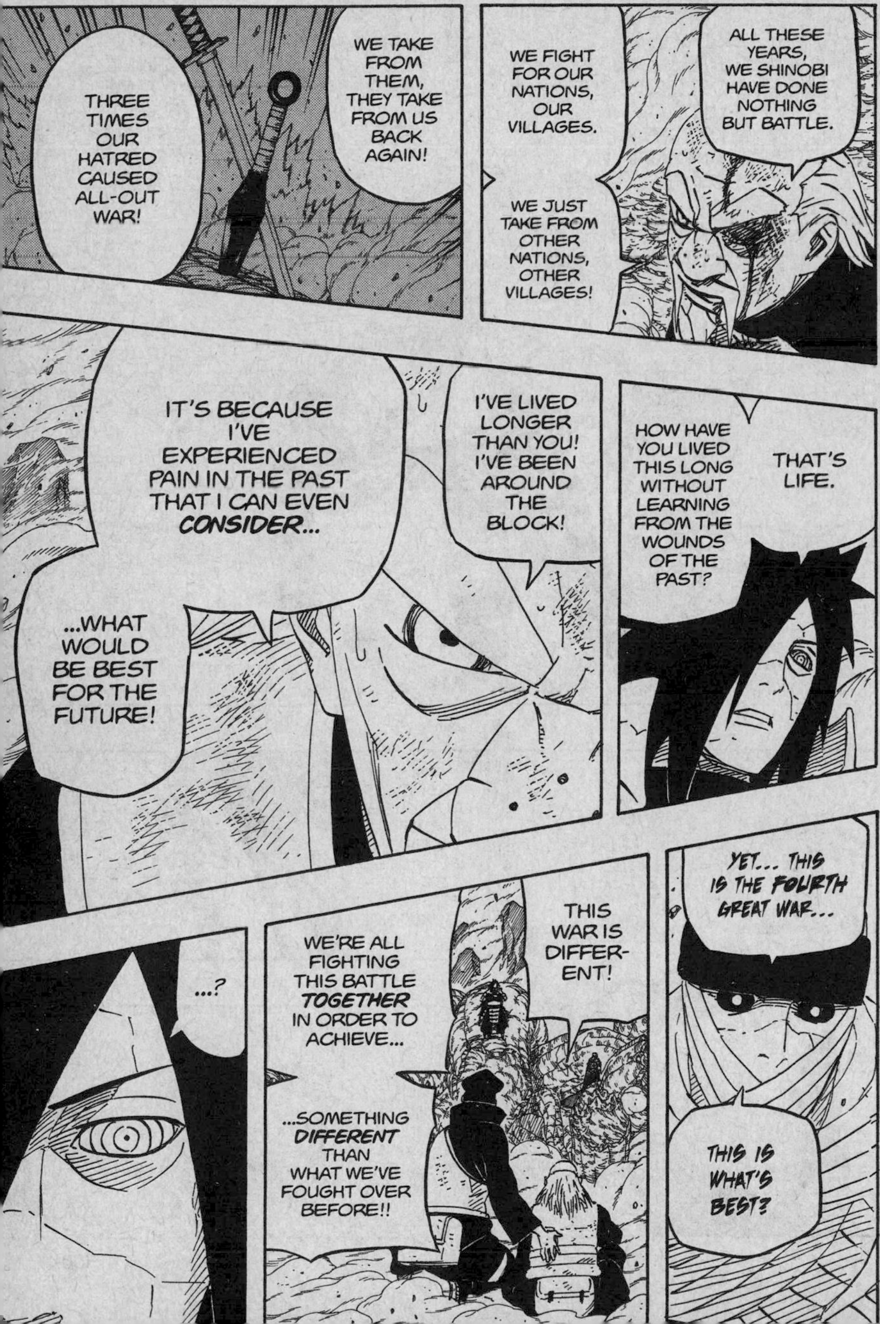
ALL THESE YEARS, WE SHINOBI HAVE DONE NOTHING BUT BATTLE.
WE FIGHT FOR OUR NATIONS, OUR VILLAGES.
WE JUST TAKE FROM OTHER NATIONS, OTHER VILLAGES!
WE TAKE FROM THEM, THEY TAKE FROM US BACK AGAIN!
THREE TIMES OUR HATRED CAUSED ALL-OUT WAR!
THAT'S LIFE.
HOW HAVE YOU LIVED THIS LONG WITHOUT LEARNING FROM THE WOUNDS OF THE PAST?
I'VE LIVED LONGER THAN YOU! I'VE BEEN AROUND THE BLOCK!
IT'S BECAUSE I'VE EXPERIENCED PAIN IN THE PAST THAT I CAN EVEN CONSIDER...
...WHAT WOULD BE BEST FOR THE FUTURE!
YET... THIS IS THE FOURTH GREAT WAR...
THIS IS WHAT'S BEST?
THIS WAR IS DIFFERENT!
WE'RE ALL FIGHTING THIS BATTLE TOGETHER IN ORDER TO ACHIEVE...
...SOMETHING DIFFERENT THAN WHAT WE'VE FOUGHT OVER BEFORE!!
...?

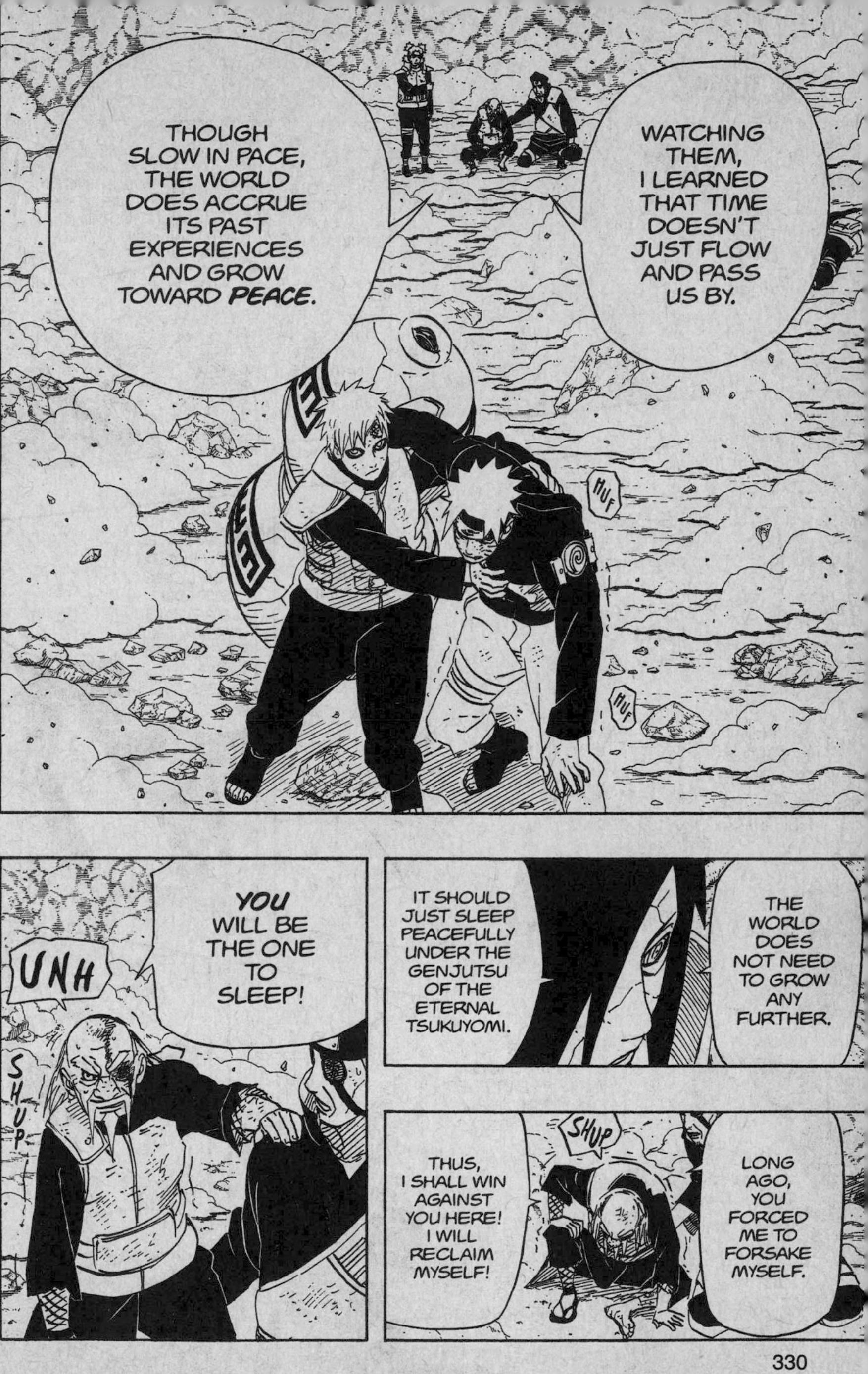
WATCHING THEM, I LEARNED THAT TIME DOESN'T JUST FLOW AND PASS US BY.
THOUGH SLOW IN PACE, THE WORLD DOES ACCRUE ITS PAST EXPERIENCES AND GROW TOWARD ***PEACE***.
HUF
HUF
THE WORLD DOES NOT NEED TO GROW ANY FURTHER.
IT SHOULD JUST SLEEP PEACEFULLY UNDER THE GENJUTSU OF THE ETERNAL TSUKUYOMI.
LONG AGO, YOU FORCED ME TO FORSAKE MYSELF.
SHUP
THUS, I SHALL WIN AGAINST YOU HERE! I WILL RECLAIM MYSELF!
YOU WILL BE THE ONE TO SLEEP!
UNH
SHUP

READ THIS WAY

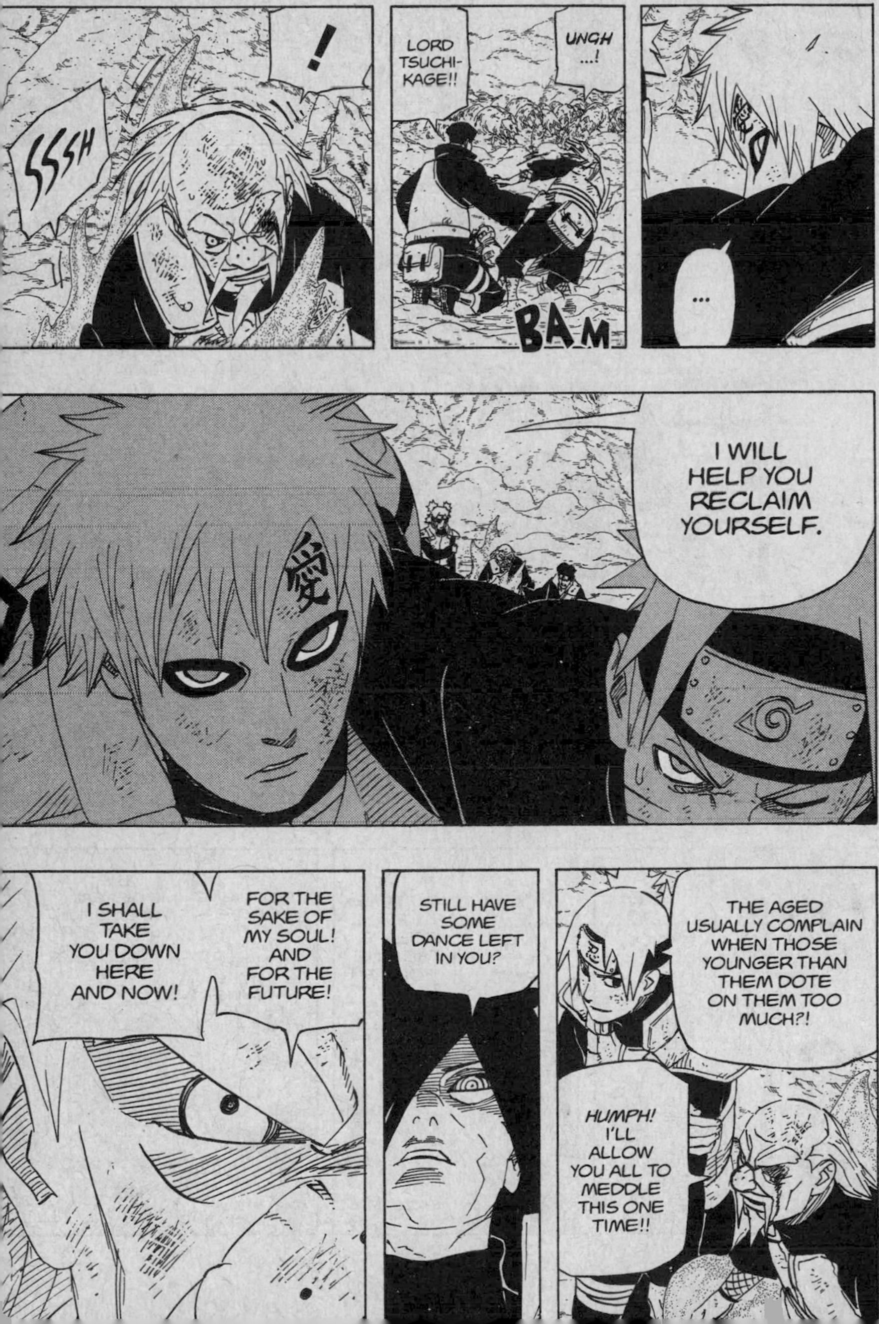
...
UNGH ...!
LORD TSUCHI-KAGE!!
BAM
!
SSSH
I WILL HELP YOU RECLAIM YOURSELF.
THE AGED USUALLY COMPLAIN WHEN THOSE YOUNGER THAN THEM DOTE ON THEM TOO MUCH?!
HUMPH! I'LL ALLOW YOU ALL TO MEDDLE THIS ONE TIME!!
STILL HAVE SOME DANCE LEFT IN YOU?
FOR THE SAKE OF MY SOUL! AND FOR THE FUTURE!
I SHALL TAKE YOU DOWN HERE AND NOW!

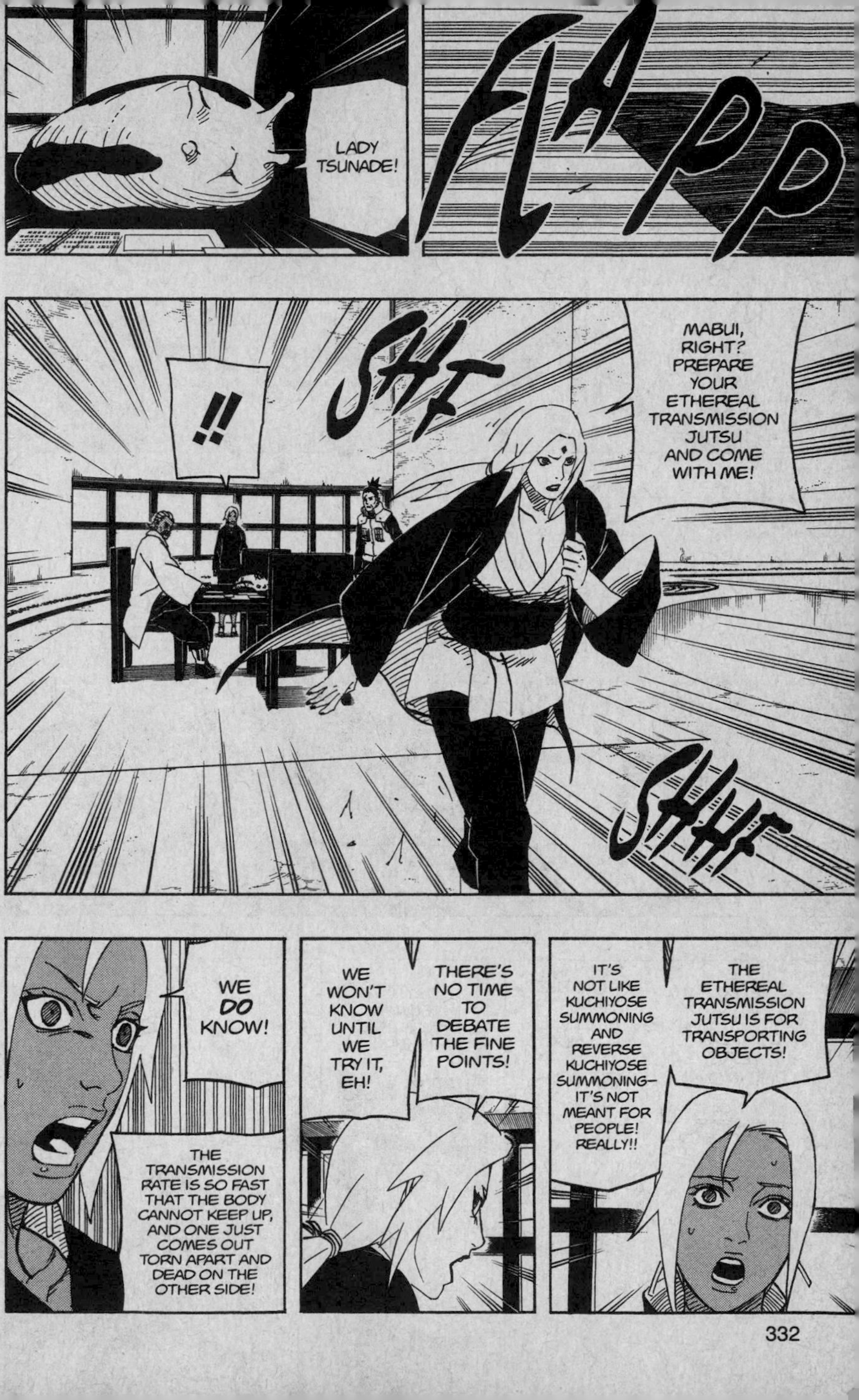
FLAPP
LADY TSUNADE!
MABUI, RIGHT? PREPARE YOUR ETHEREAL TRANSMISSION JUTSU AND COME WITH ME!
SHF
!!
SHHF
THE ETHEREAL TRANSMISSION JUTSU IS FOR TRANSPORTING OBJECTS!
IT'S NOT LIKE KUCHIYOSE SUMMONING AND REVERSE KUCHIYOSE SUMMONING— IT'S NOT MEANT FOR PEOPLE! REALLY!!
THERE'S NO TIME TO DEBATE THE FINE POINTS!
WE WON'T KNOW UNTIL WE TRY IT, EH!
WE DO KNOW!
THE TRANSMISSION RATE IS SO FAST THAT THE BODY CANNOT KEEP UP, AND ONE JUST COMES OUT TORN APART AND DEAD ON THE OTHER SIDE!

READ THIS WAY

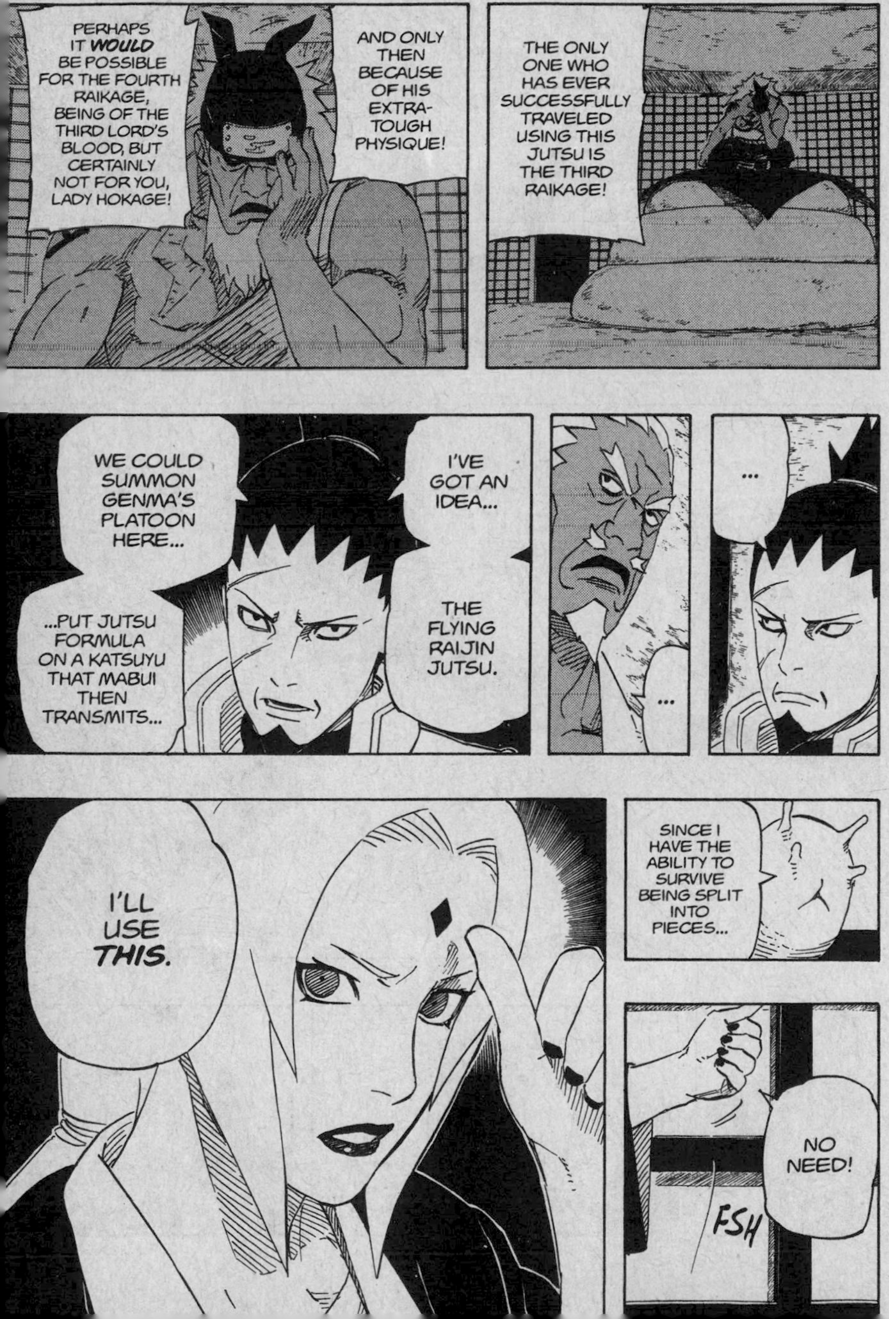

THE ONLY ONE WHO HAS EVER SUCCESSFULLY TRAVELED USING THIS JUTSU IS THE THIRD RAIKAGE!
AND ONLY THEN BECAUSE OF HIS EXTRA-TOUGH PHYSIQUE!
PERHAPS IT ***WOULD*** BE POSSIBLE FOR THE FOURTH RAIKAGE, BEING OF THE THIRD LORD'S BLOOD, BUT CERTAINLY NOT FOR YOU, LADY HOKAGE!
...
...
I'VE GOT AN IDEA...
THE FLYING RAIJIN JUTSU.
WE COULD SUMMON GENMA'S PLATOON HERE...
...PUT JUTSU FORMULA ON A KATSUYU THAT MABUI THEN TRANSMITS...
SINCE I HAVE THE ABILITY TO SURVIVE BEING SPLIT INTO PIECES...
NO NEED!
FSH
I'LL USE ***THIS.***

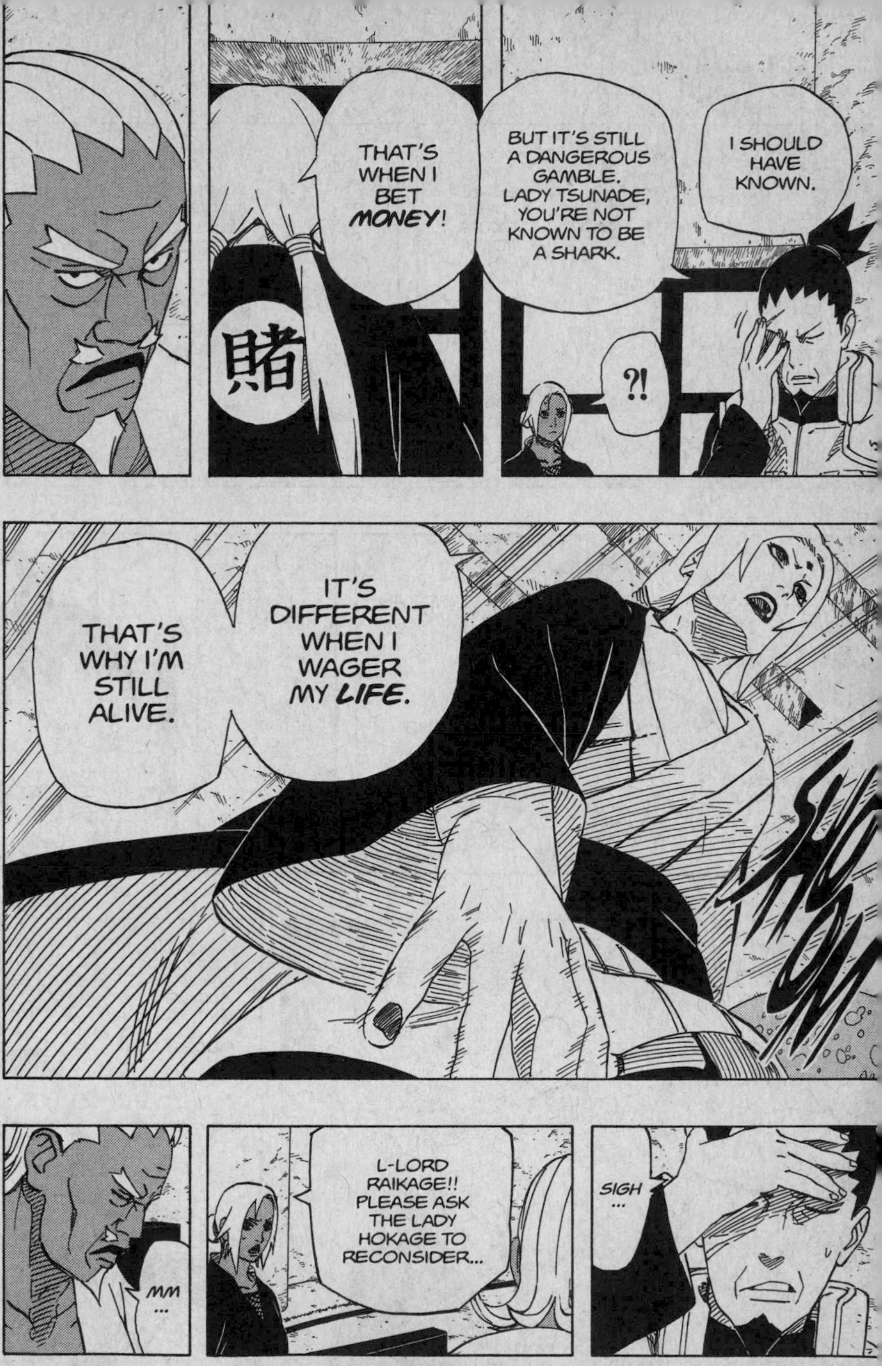
I SHOULD HAVE KNOWN.
BUT IT'S STILL A DANGEROUS GAMBLE. LADY TSUNADE, YOU'RE NOT KNOWN TO BE A SHARK.
?!
THAT'S WHEN I BET MONEY!
賭
IT'S DIFFERENT WHEN I WAGER MY LIFE.
THAT'S WHY I'M STILL ALIVE.
SIGH ...
L-LORD RAIKAGE!! PLEASE ASK THE LADY HOKAGE TO RECONSIDER...
MM ...

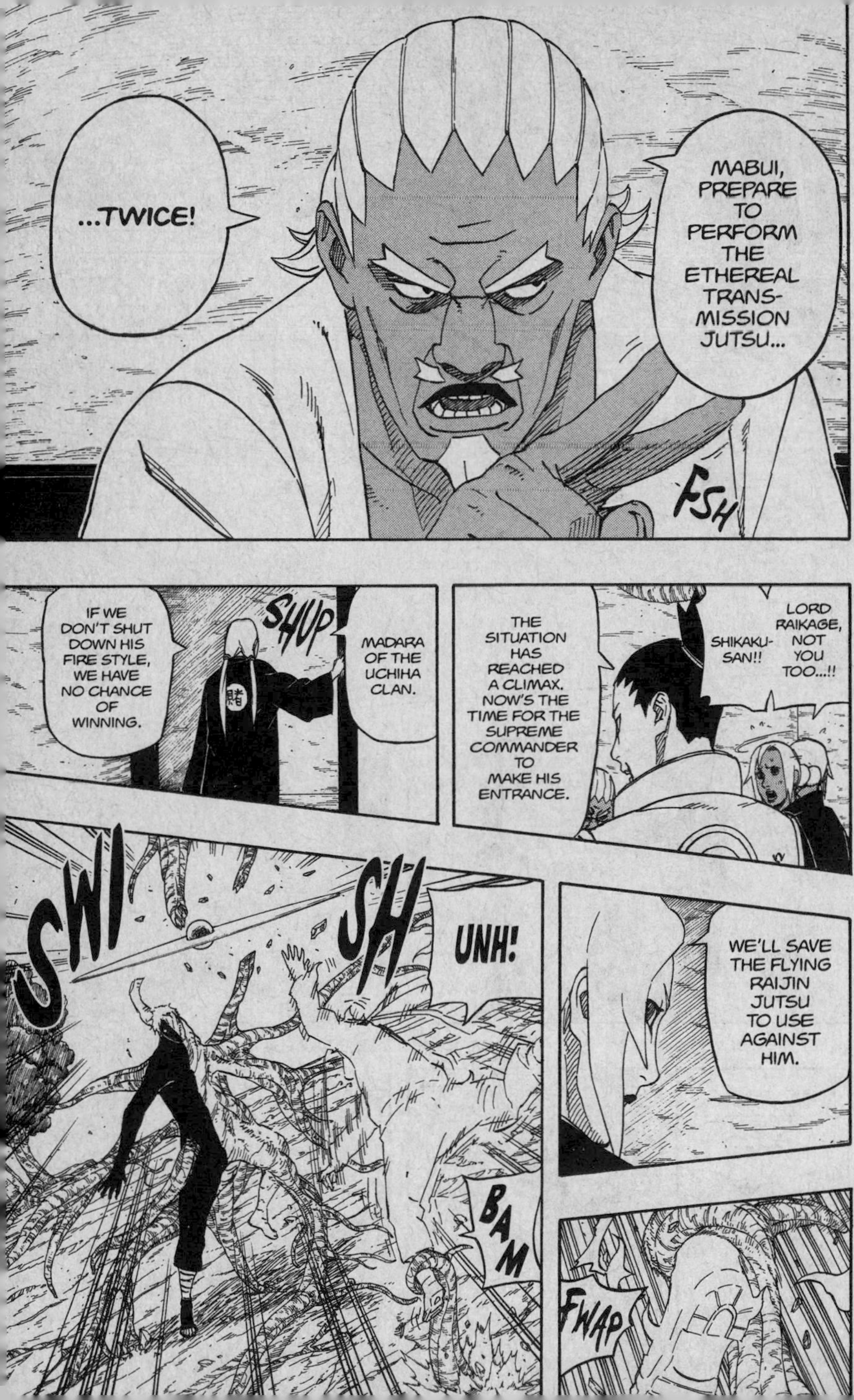
MABUI, PREPARE TO PERFORM THE ETHEREAL TRANS-MISSION JUTSU...
...TWICE!
FSH
LORD RAIKAGE, NOT YOU TOO...!!
SHIKAKU-SAN!!
THE SITUATION HAS REACHED A CLIMAX. NOW'S THE TIME FOR THE SUPREME COMMANDER TO MAKE HIS ENTRANCE.
MADARA OF THE UCHIHA CLAN.
SHUP
IF WE DON'T SHUT DOWN HIS FIRE STYLE, WE HAVE NO CHANCE OF WINNING.
WE'LL SAVE THE FLYING RAIJIN JUTSU TO USE AGAINST HIM.
FWAP
UNH!
SWISH
BAM

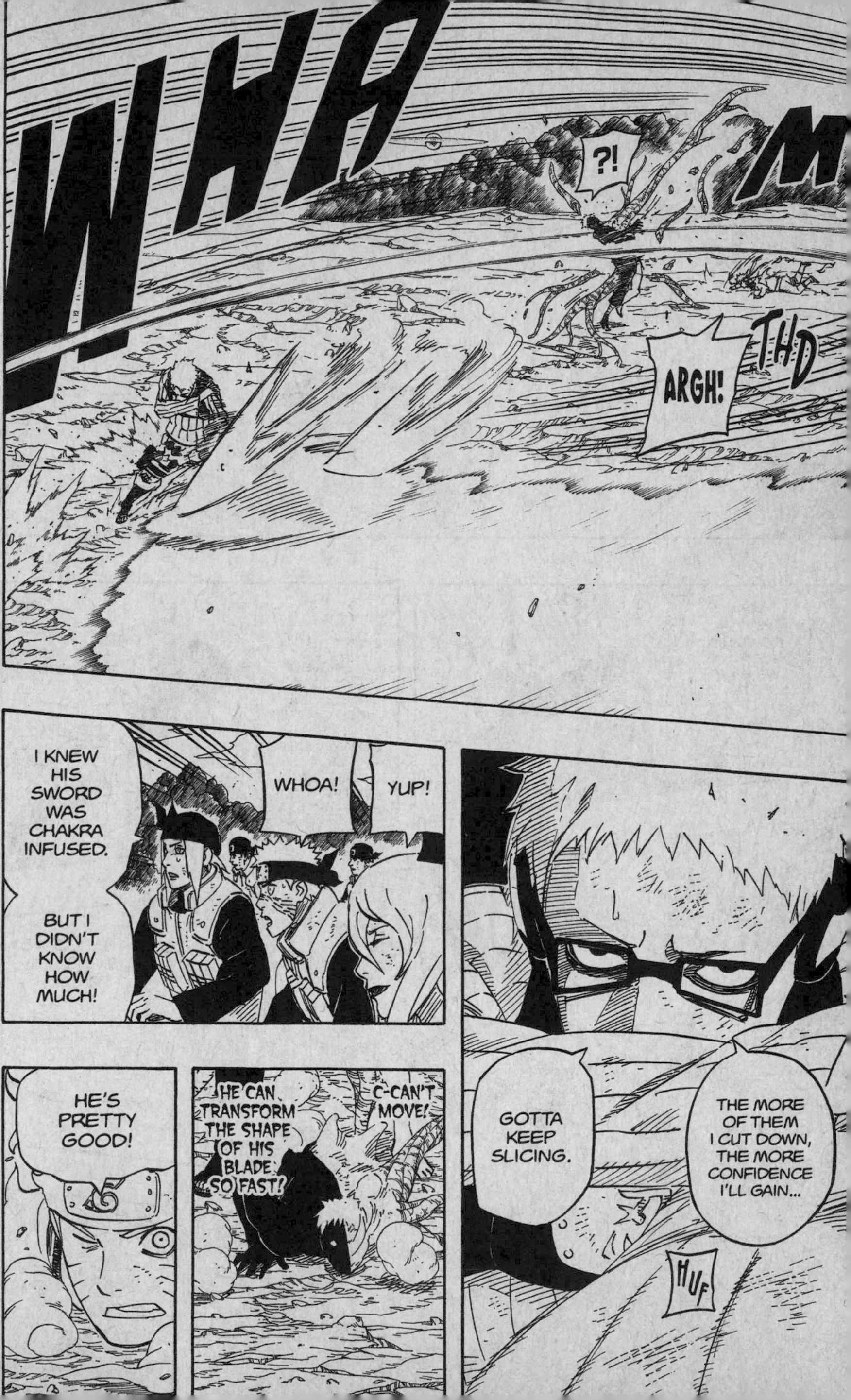
?!
ARGH!
THD
THE MORE OF THEM I CUT DOWN, THE MORE CONFIDENCE I'LL GAIN...
GOTTA KEEP SLICING.
HUF
YUP!
WHOA!
I KNEW HIS SWORD WAS CHAKRA INFUSED.
BUT I DIDN'T KNOW HOW MUCH!
C-CAN'T MOVE!
HE CAN TRANSFORM THE SHAPE OF HIS BLADE SO FAST!
HE'S PRETTY GOOD!

READ THIS WAY

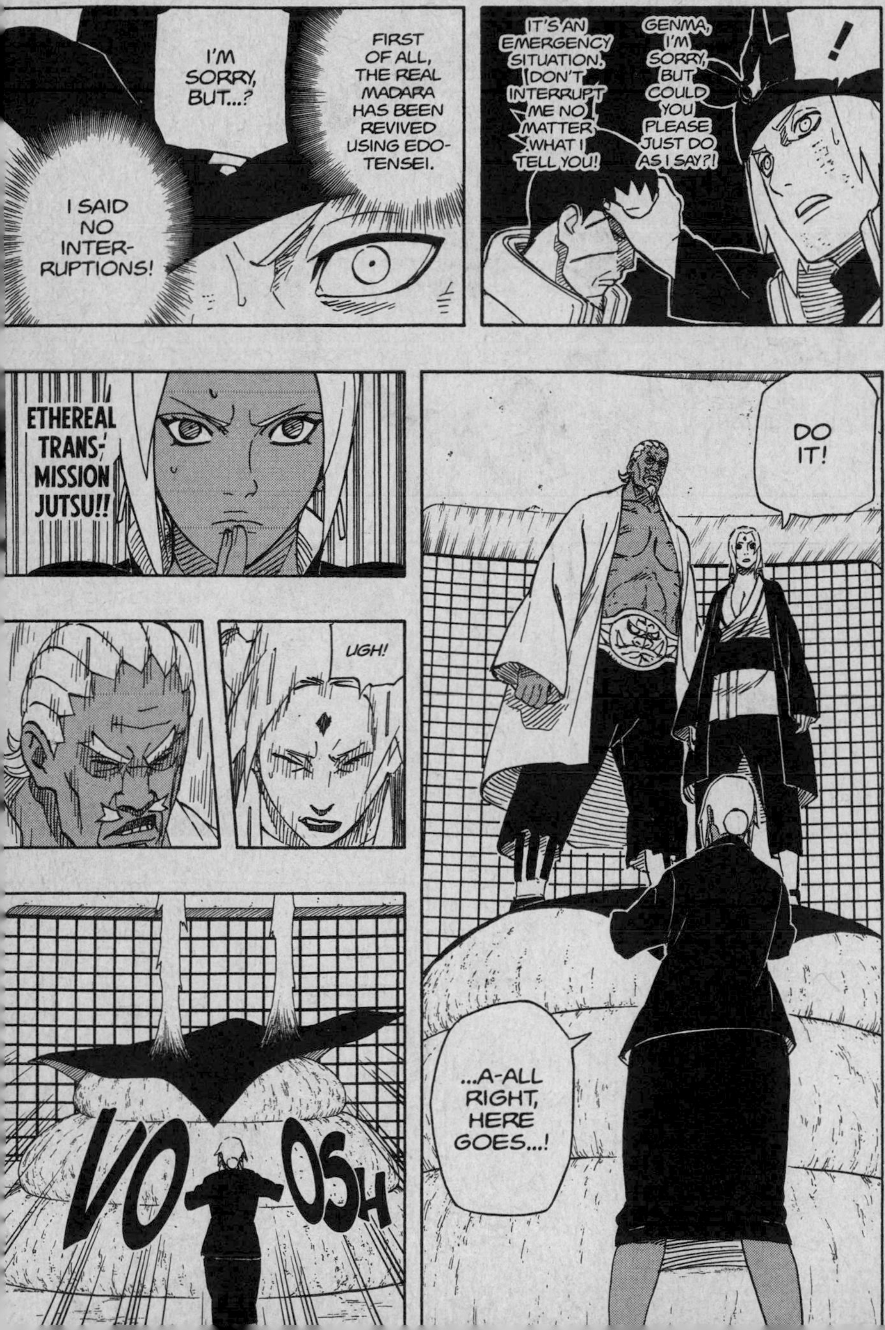
!
GENMA, I'M SORRY, BUT COULD YOU PLEASE JUST DO AS I SAY?!
IT'S AN EMERGENCY SITUATION. DON'T INTERRUPT ME NO MATTER WHAT I TELL YOU!
FIRST OF ALL, THE REAL MADARA HAS BEEN REVIVED USING EDO-TENSEI.
I'M SORRY, BUT...?
I SAID NO INTER-RUPTIONS!
DO IT!
...A-ALL RIGHT, HERE GOES...!
ETHEREAL TRANS-MISSION JUTSU!!
UGH!
VOOSH

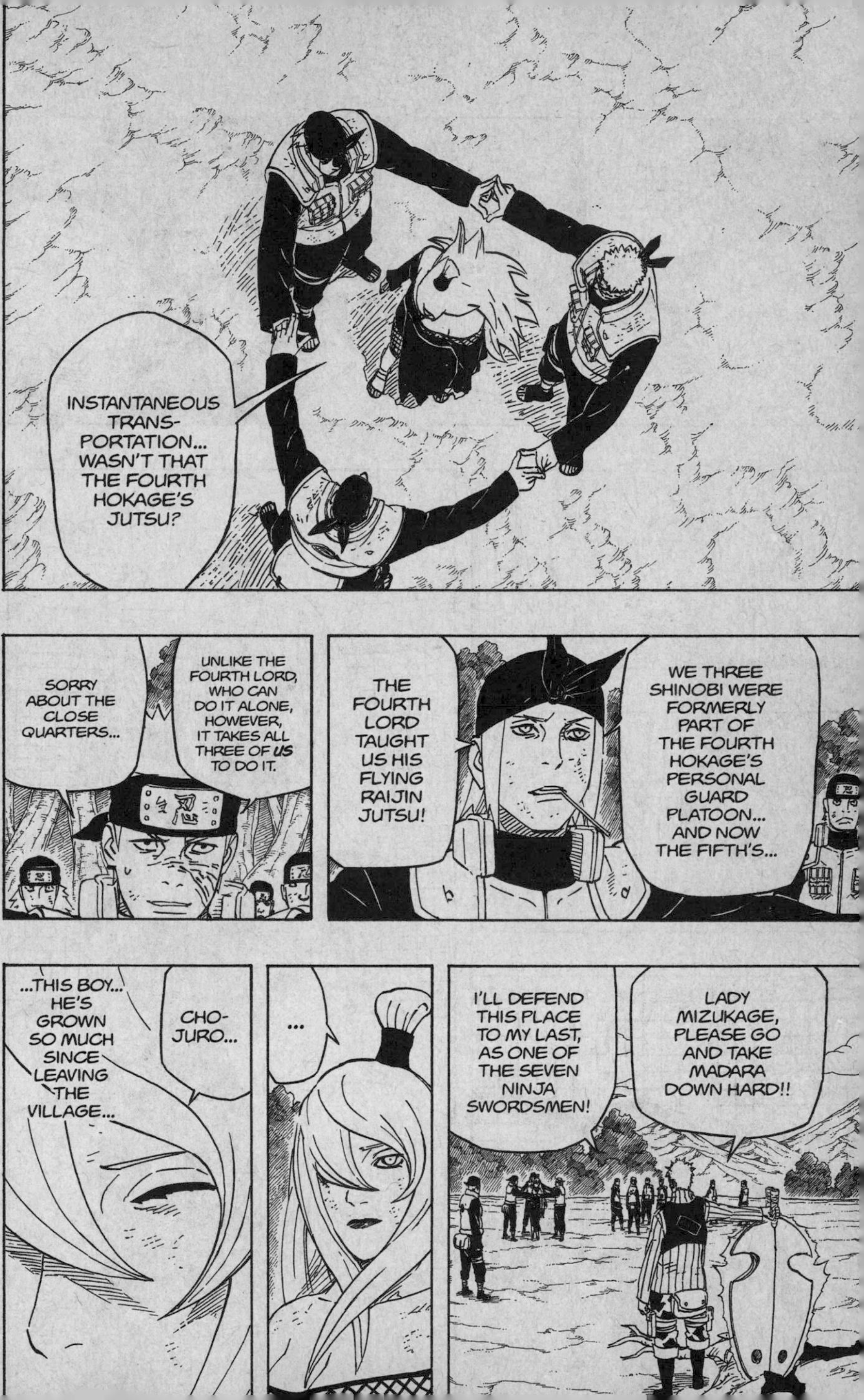
INSTANTANEOUS TRANS-PORTATION... WASN'T THAT THE FOURTH HOKAGE'S JUTSU?
WE THREE SHINOBI WERE FORMERLY PART OF THE FOURTH HOKAGE'S PERSONAL GUARD PLATOON... AND NOW THE FIFTH'S...
THE FOURTH LORD TAUGHT US HIS FLYING RAIJIN JUTSU!
UNLIKE THE FOURTH LORD, WHO CAN DO IT ALONE, HOWEVER, IT TAKES ALL THREE OF *US* TO DO IT.
SORRY ABOUT THE CLOSE QUARTERS...
LADY MIZUKAGE, PLEASE GO AND TAKE MADARA DOWN HARD!!
I'LL DEFEND THIS PLACE TO MY LAST, AS ONE OF THE SEVEN NINJA SWORDSMEN!
...
CHO-JURO...
...THIS BOY... HE'S GROWN SO MUCH SINCE LEAVING THE VILLAGE...

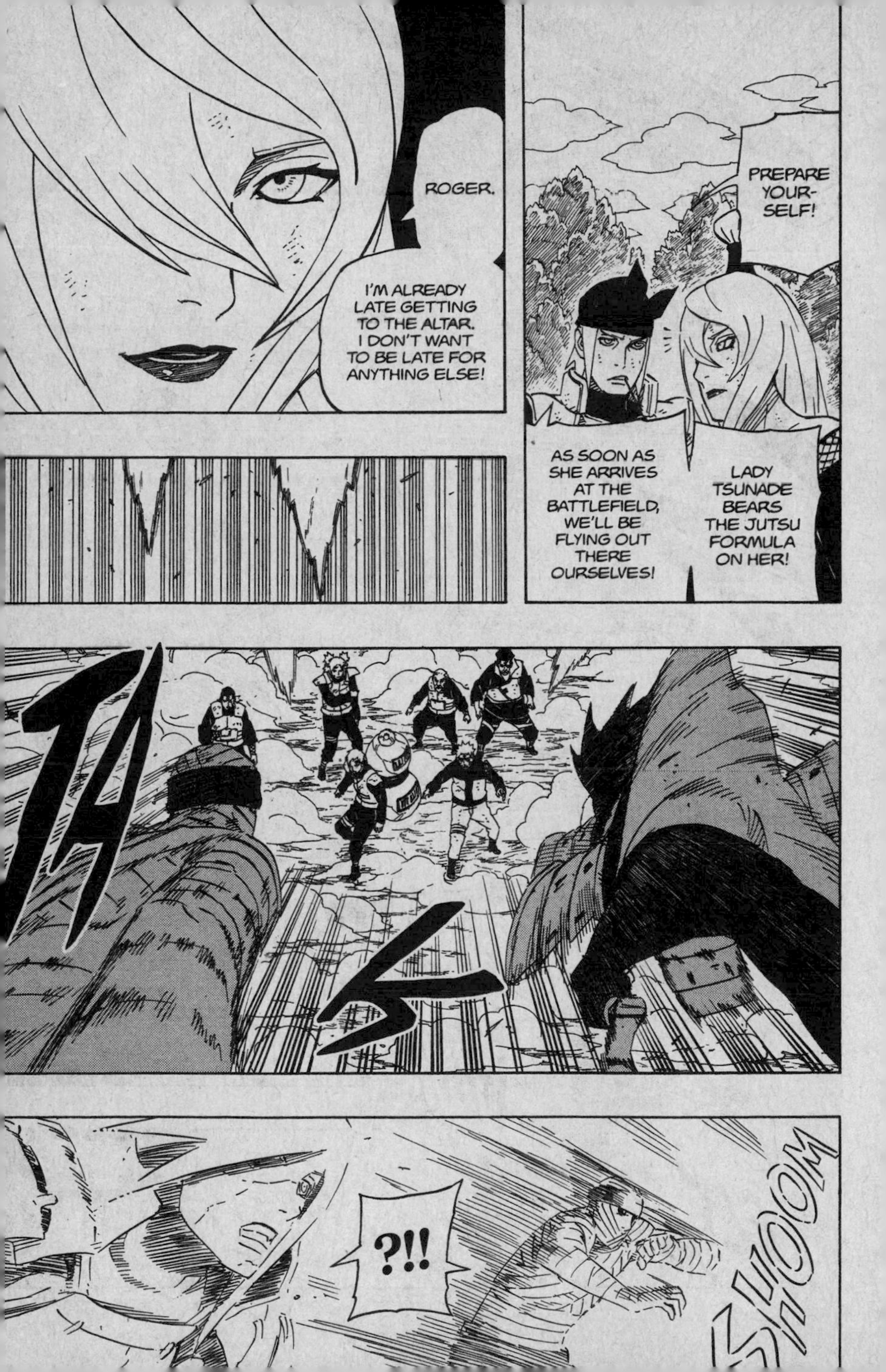
PREPARE YOURSELF!
LADY TSUNADE BEARS THE JUTSU FORMULA ON HER!
AS SOON AS SHE ARRIVES AT THE BATTLEFIELD, WE'LL BE FLYING OUT THERE OURSELVES!
ROGER.
I'M ALREADY LATE GETTING TO THE ALTAR. I DON'T WANT TO BE LATE FOR ANYTHING ELSE!
SHOOM
?!!

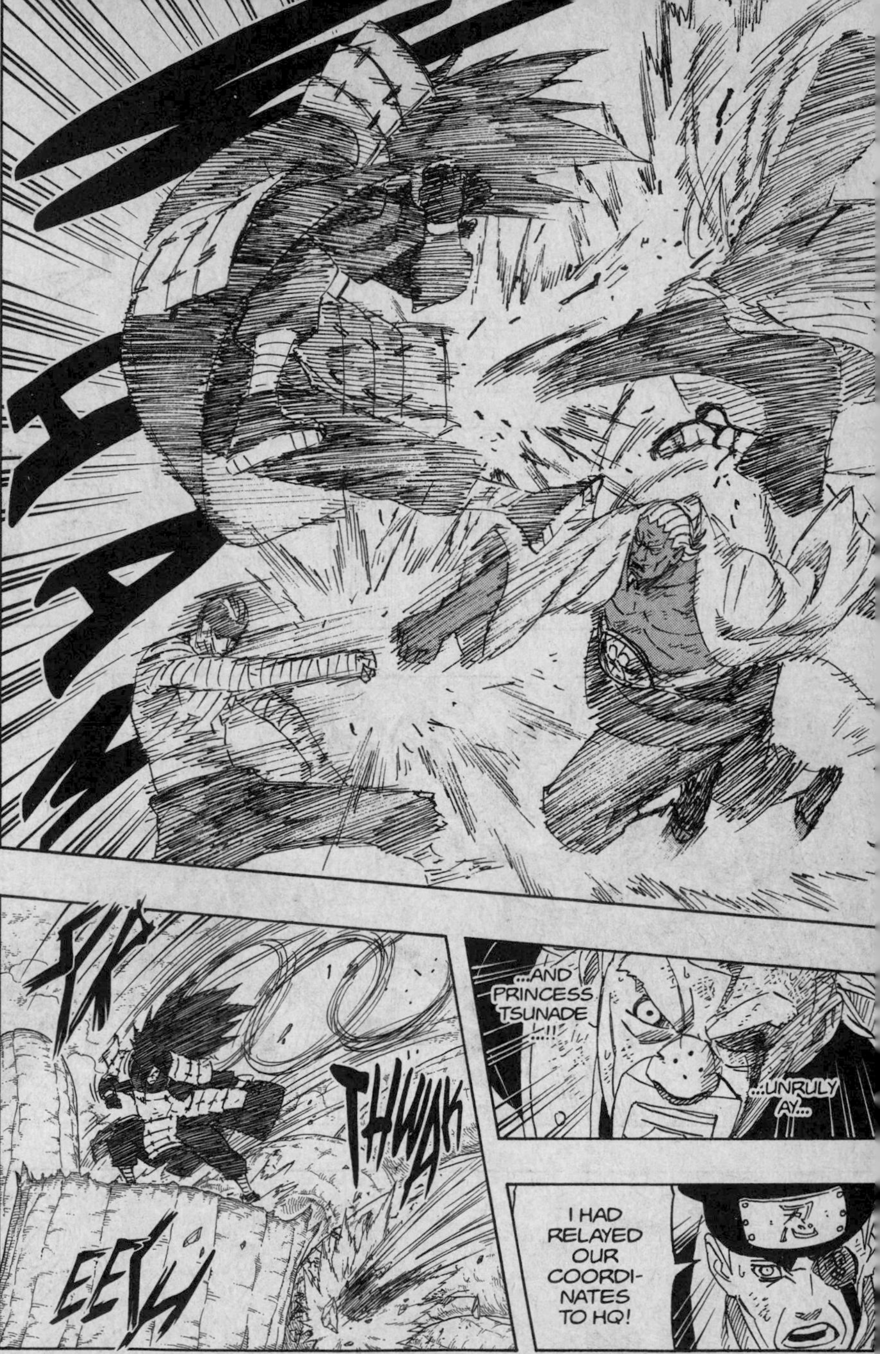
WHAM
...AND PRINCESS TSUNADE ...!!
...UNRULY AY...
I HAD RELAYED OUR COORDINATES TO HQ!
SK
THWAK

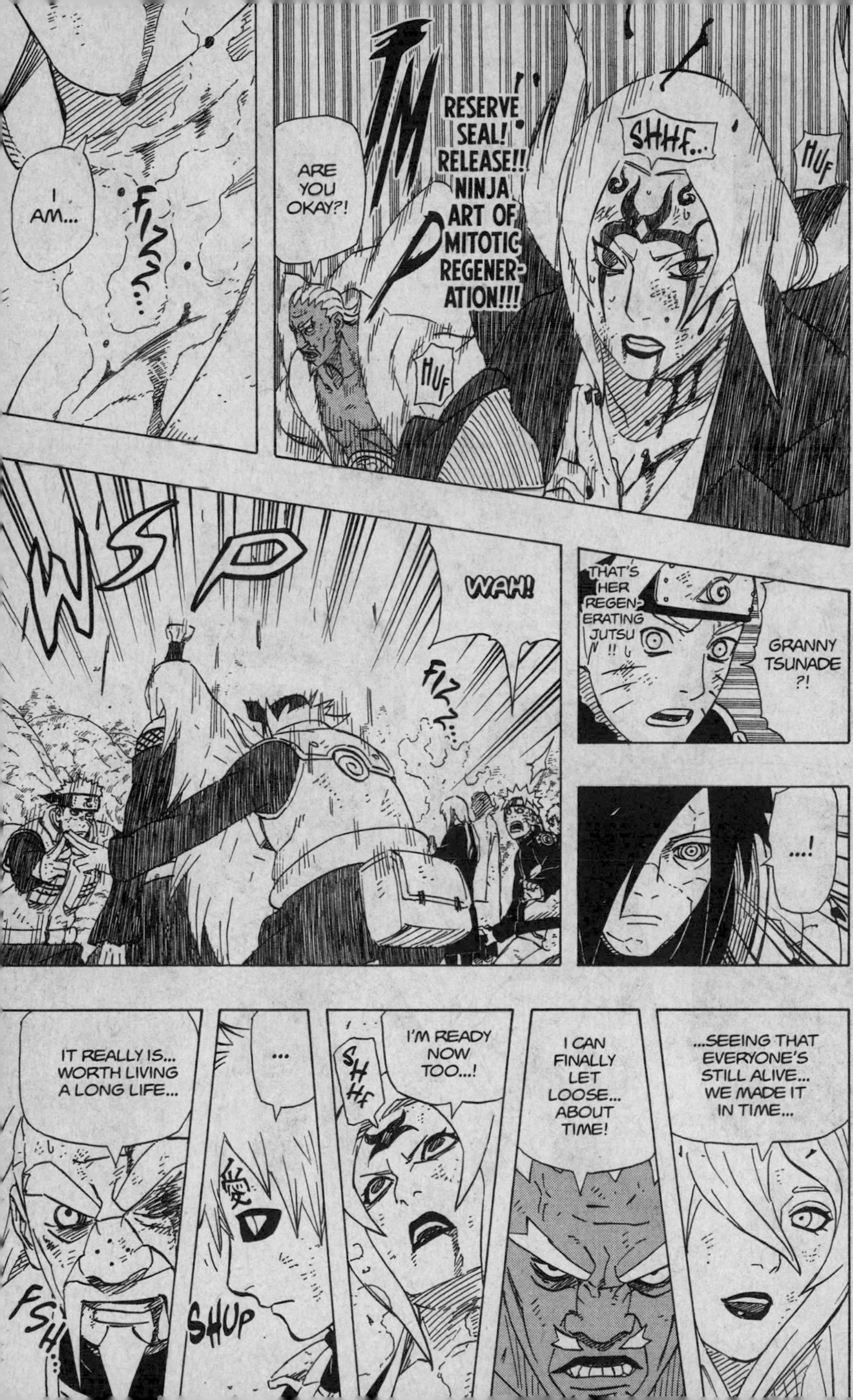
SHHF...
HUF
RESERVE SEAL! RELEASE!! NINJA ART OF MITOTIC REGENER-ATION!!!
ARE YOU OKAY?!
HUF
I AM...
FIZZZ...
GRANNY TSUNADE ?!
THAT'S HER REGEN-ERATING JUTSU !!
...!
WAH!
FIZZZ...
WSP
...SEEING THAT EVERYONE'S STILL ALIVE... WE MADE IT IN TIME...
I CAN FINALLY LET LOOSE... ABOUT TIME!
I'M READY NOW TOO...!
SHHF
...
SHUP
IT REALLY IS... WORTH LIVING A LONG LIFE...
FSH...

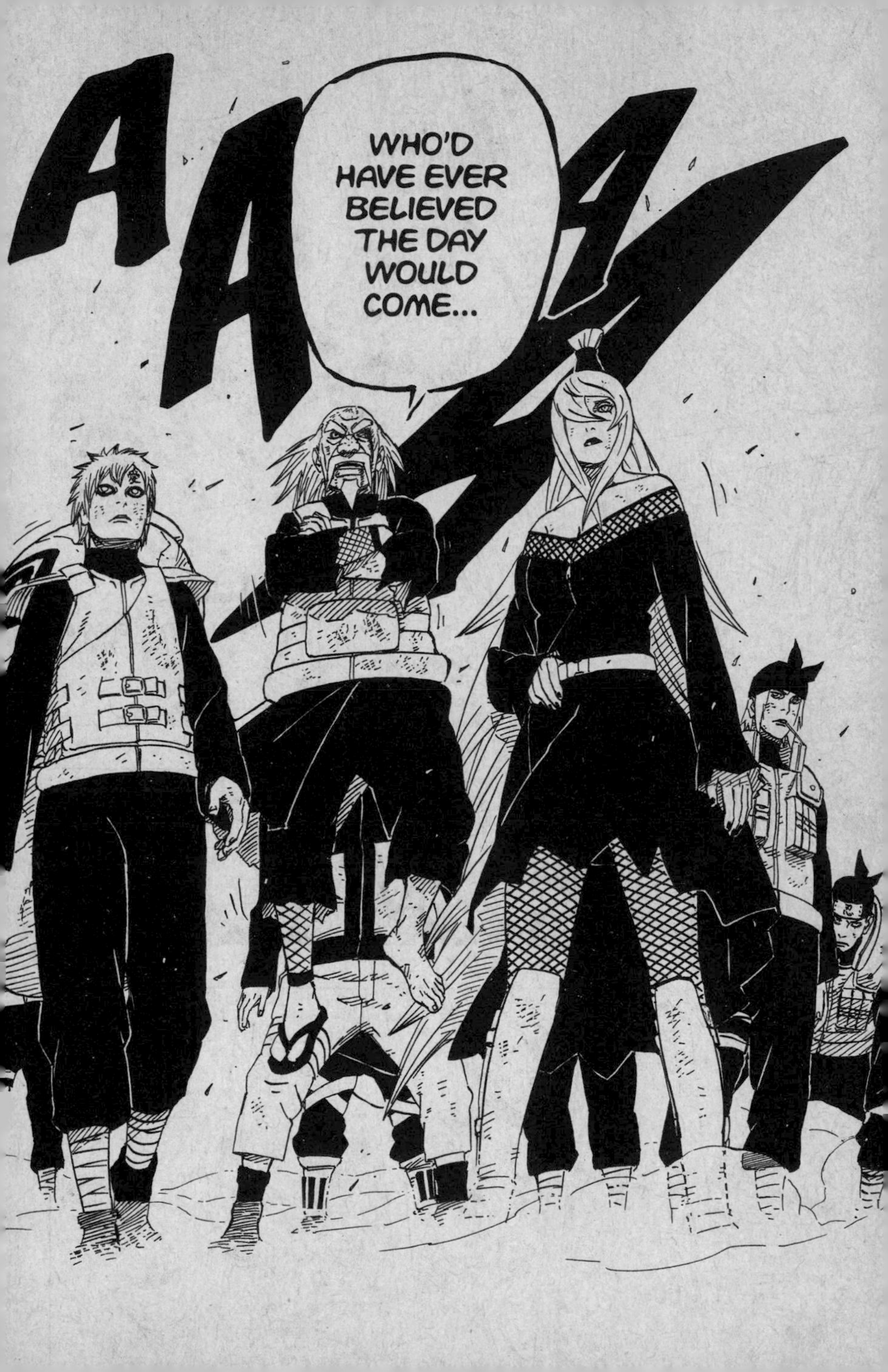
AAAA
WHO'D HAVE EVER BELIEVED THE DAY WOULD COME...

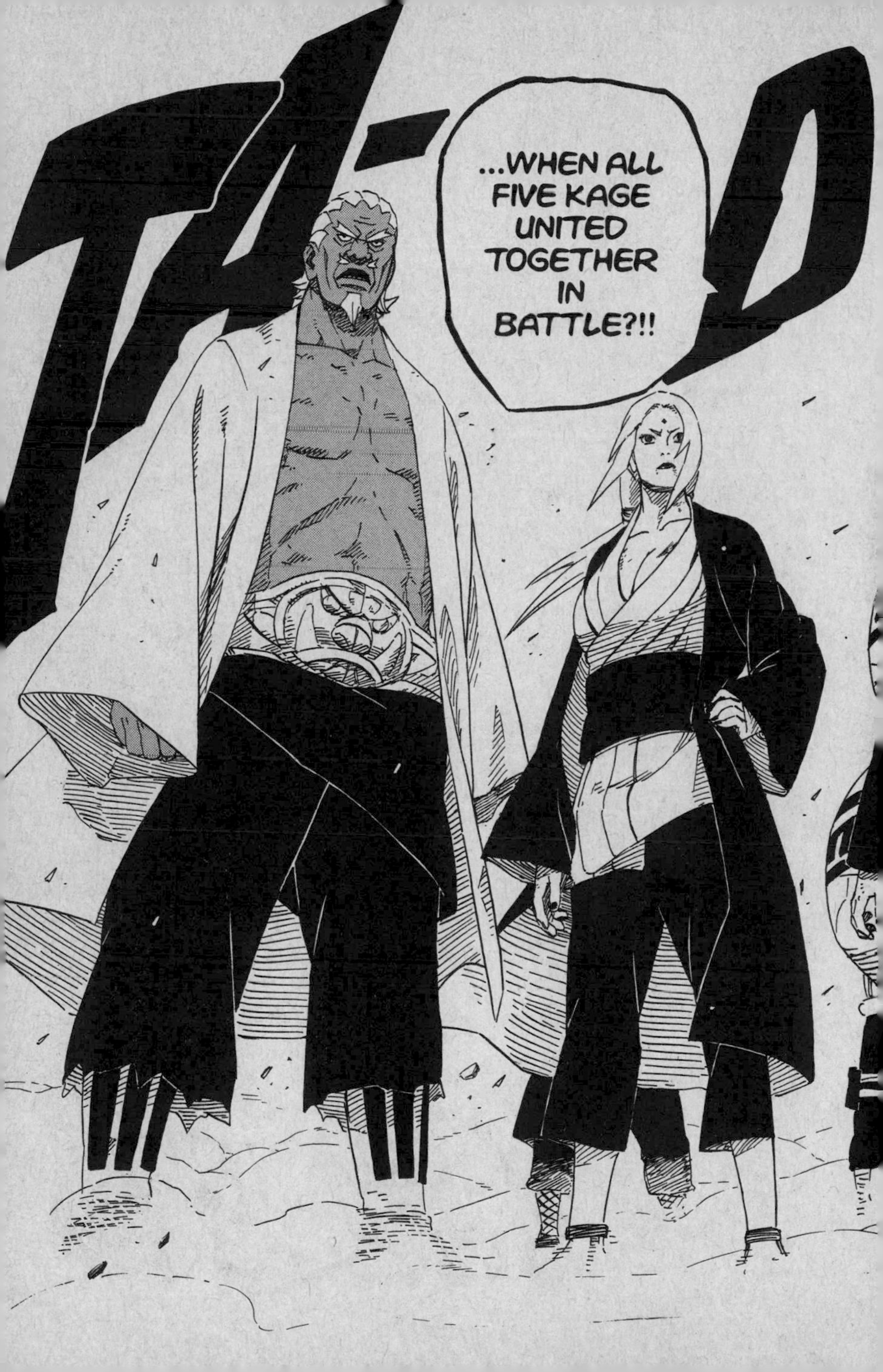
TA-D
...WHEN ALL FIVE KAGE UNITED TOGETHER IN BATTLE?!!

NARUTO

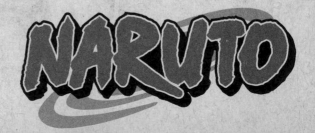

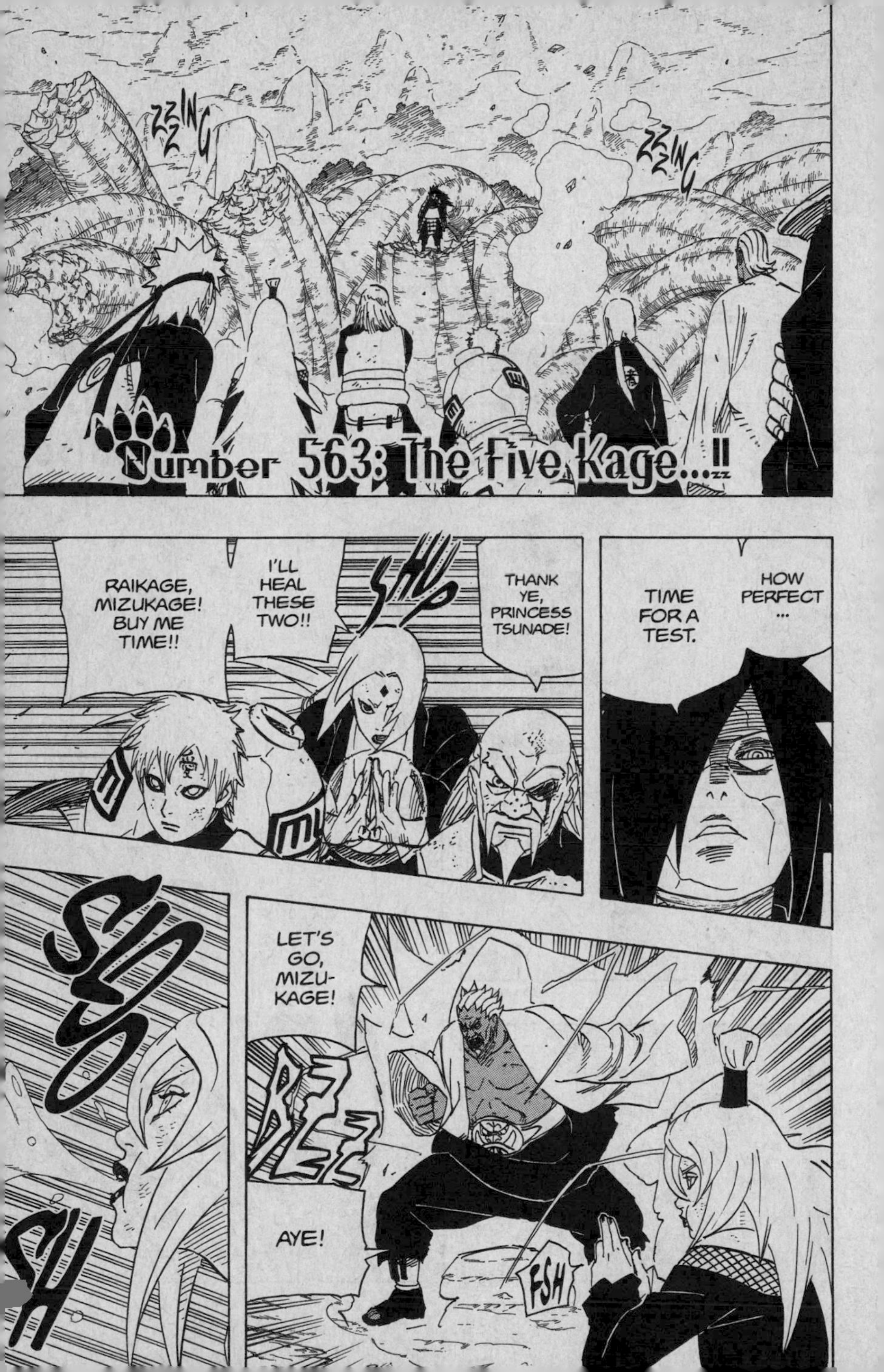
ZZZING
ZZZING
Number 563: The Five Kage...!!
HOW PERFECT ...
TIME FOR A TEST.
THANK YE, PRINCESS TSUNADE!
SHUP
I'LL HEAL THESE TWO!!
RAIKAGE, MIZUKAGE! BUY ME TIME!!
LET'S GO, MIZU-KAGE!
AYE!
FSH

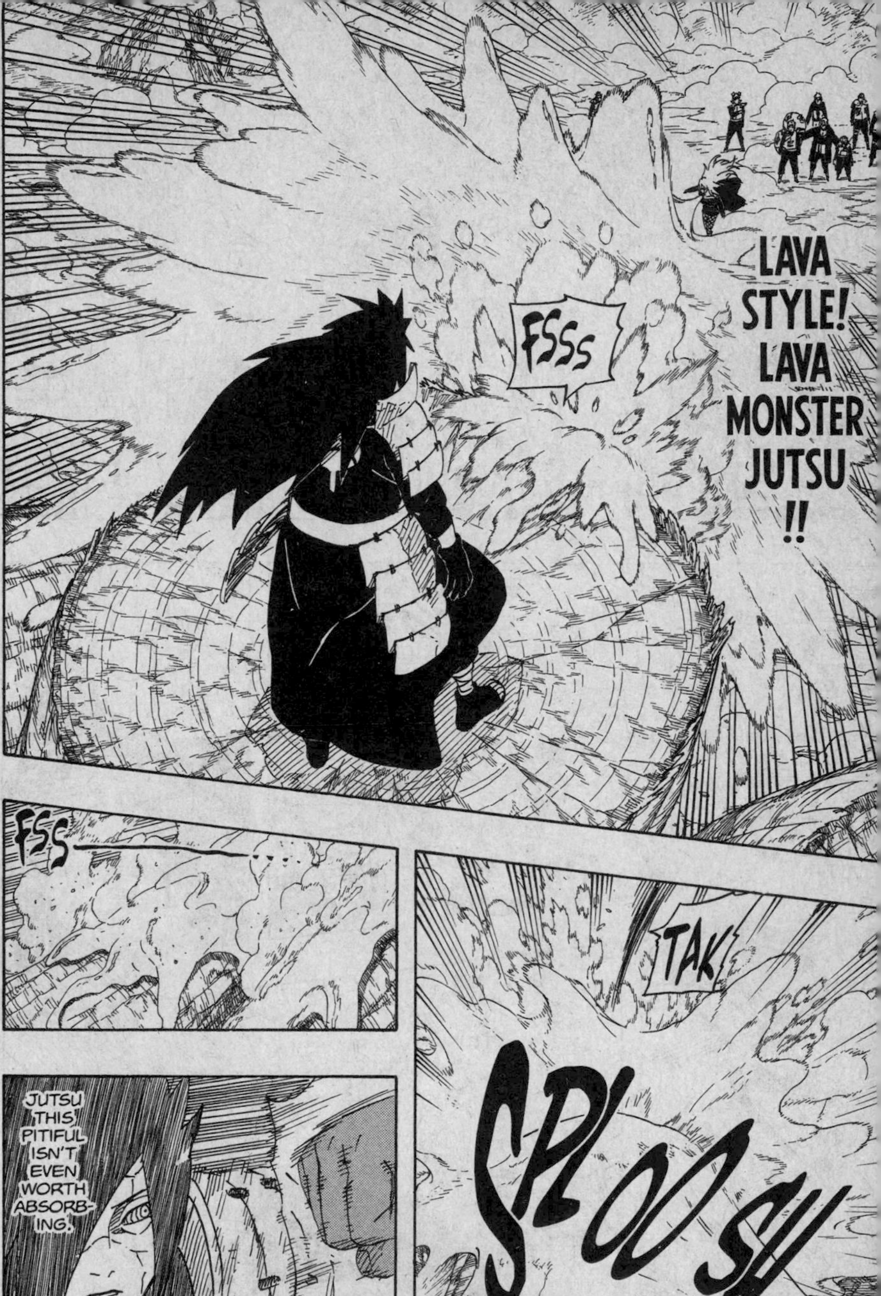
LAVA STYLE! LAVA MONSTER JUTSU!!
FSSS
TAK
SPLOOSH
FSS
JUTSU THIS PITIFUL ISN'T EVEN WORTH ABSORBING.

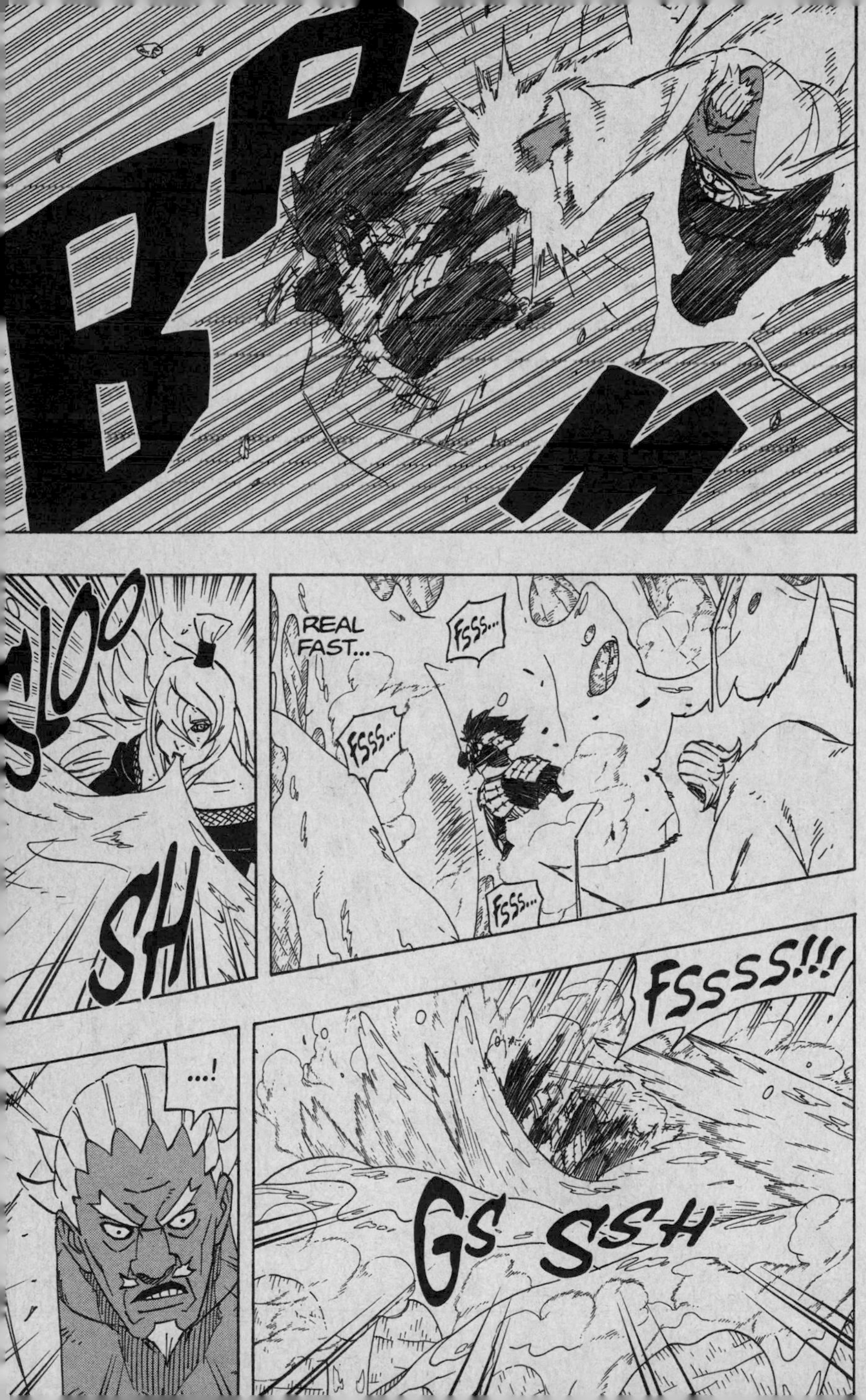
BAM
REAL FAST...
FSSS...
FSSS...
FSSS...
SLOO
SH
FSSSS!!!
GSSSH
...!

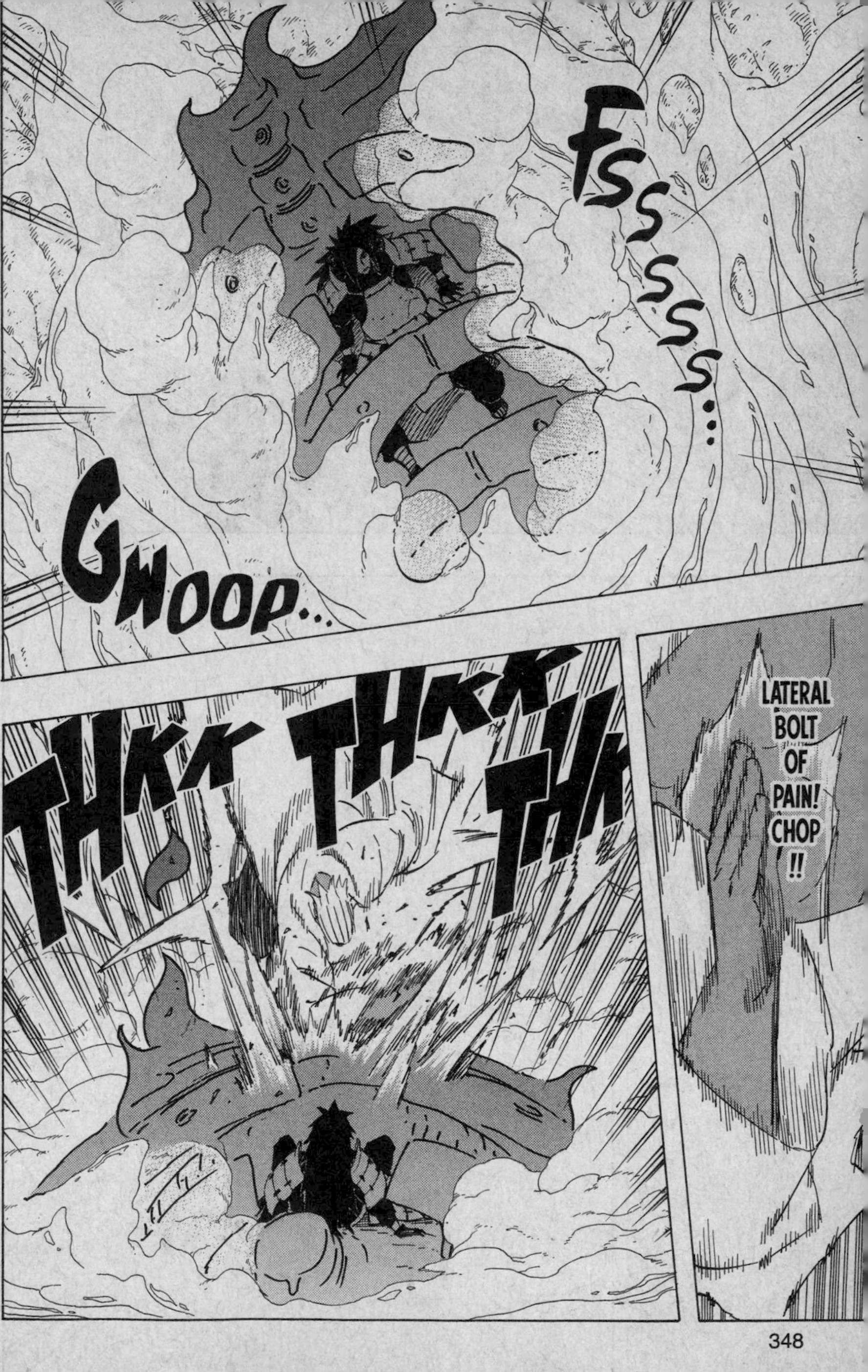
FSSSSSS...
GWOOP...
LATERAL BOLT OF PAIN! CHOP !!
THKK THKK THK

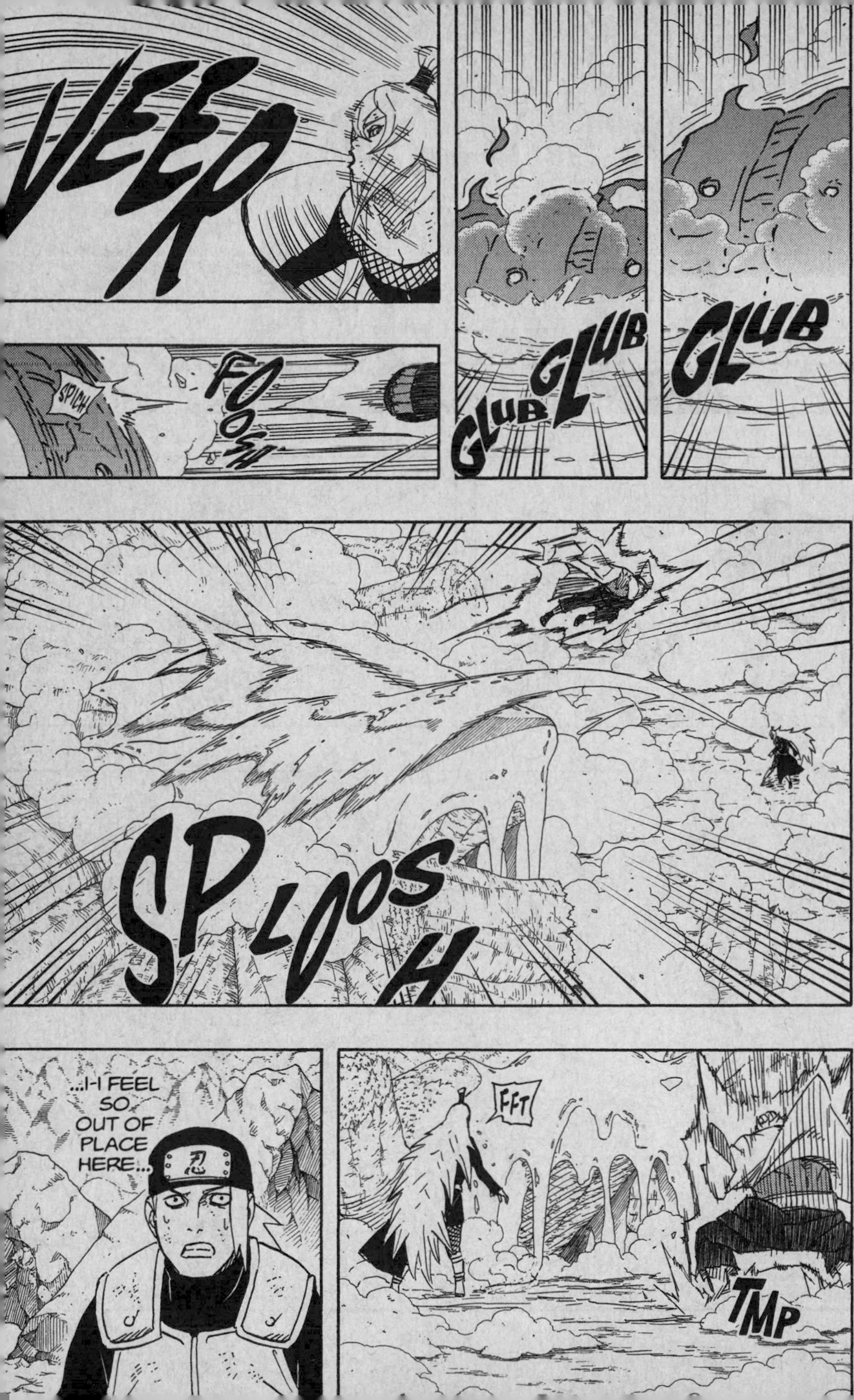
GLUB
GLUB GLUB
VEEP
SPICH
FOOSH
SPLOOSH
FFT
TMP
...I-I FEEL SO OUT OF PLACE HERE...

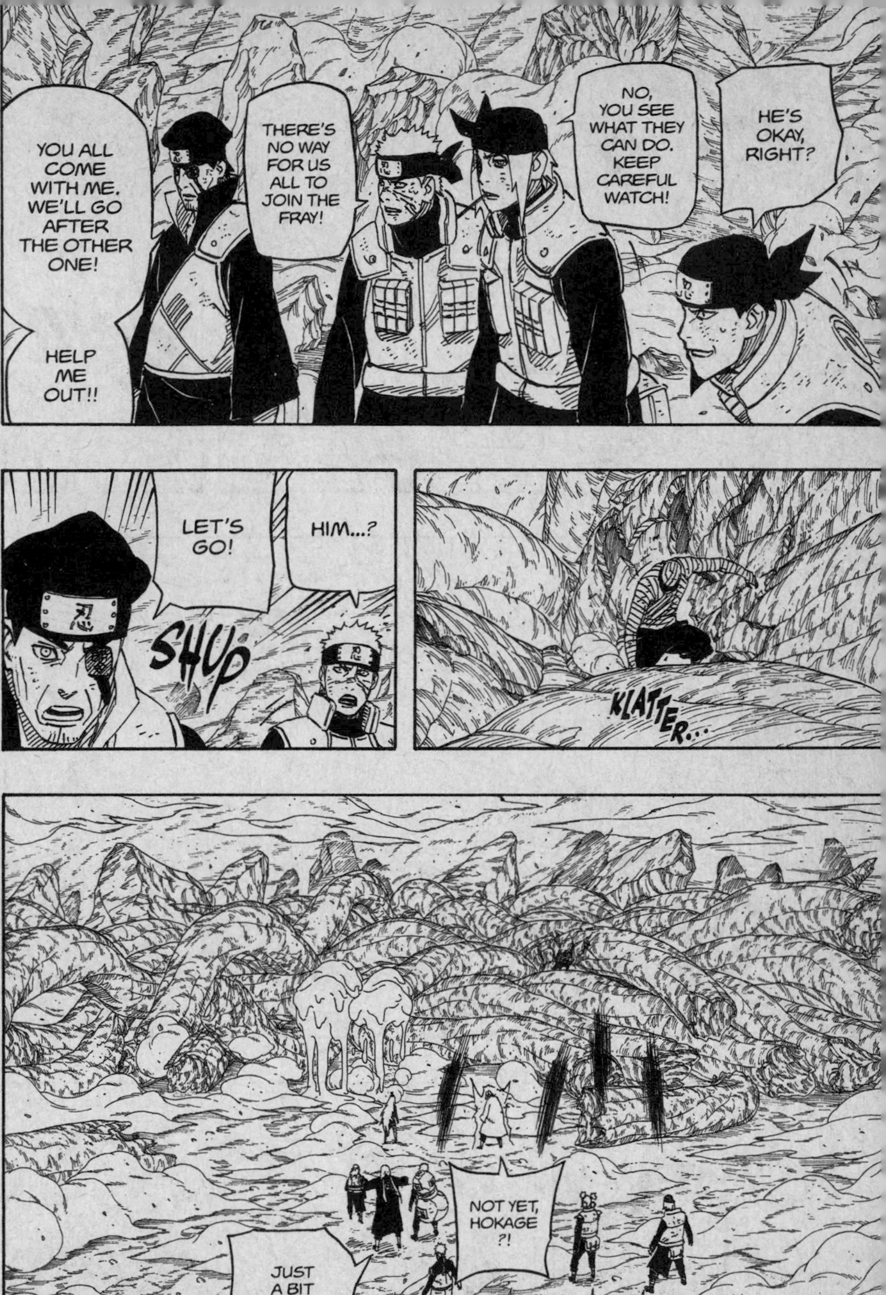
HE'S OKAY, RIGHT?
NO, YOU SEE WHAT THEY CAN DO. KEEP CAREFUL WATCH!
THERE'S NO WAY FOR US ALL TO JOIN THE FRAY!
YOU ALL COME WITH ME. WE'LL GO AFTER THE OTHER ONE!
HELP ME OUT!!
KLATTER...
HIM...?
LET'S GO!
SHUP
NOT YET, HOKAGE ?!
JUST A BIT LONGER...!

READ THIS WAY

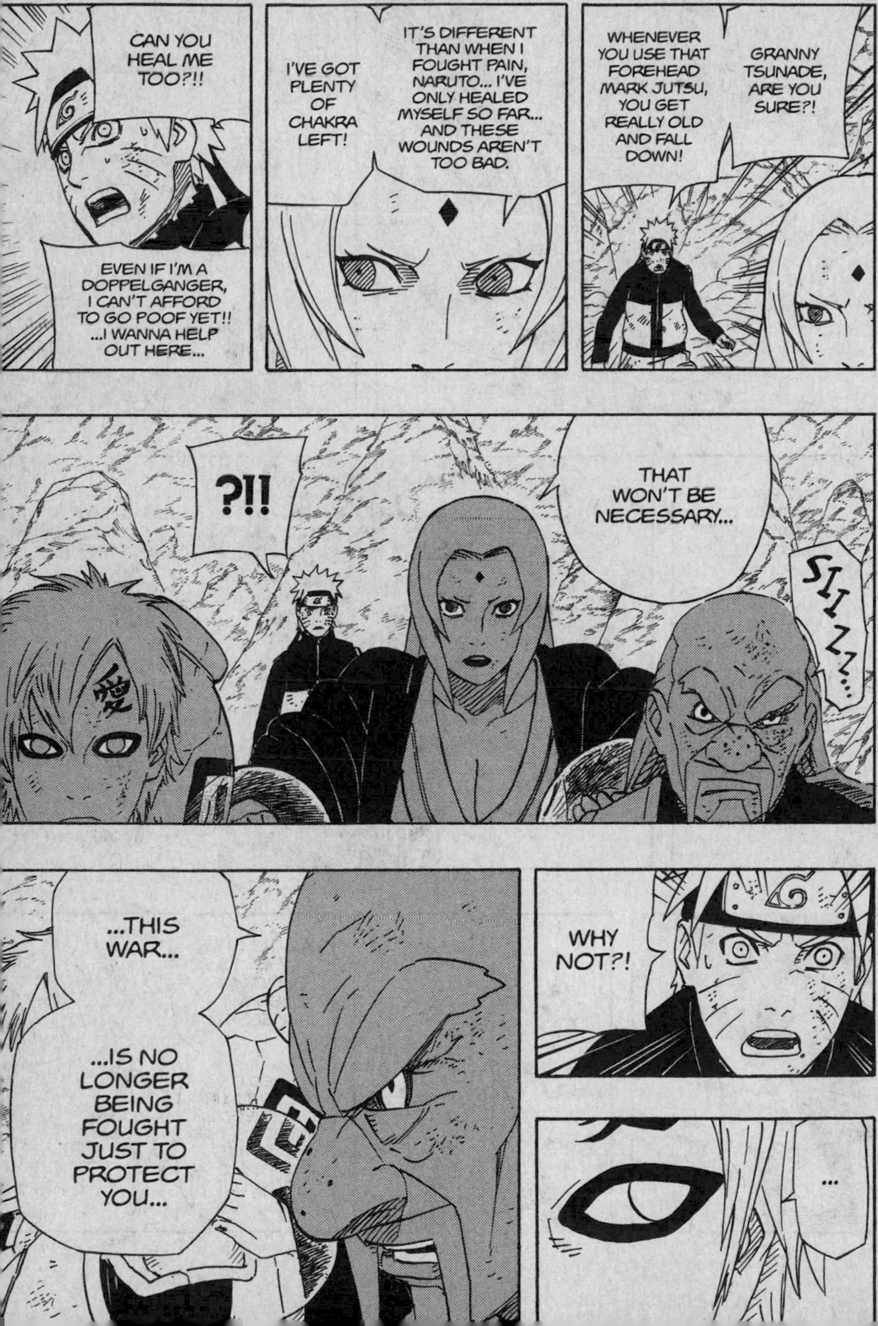
GRANNY TSUNADE, ARE YOU SURE?!
WHENEVER YOU USE THAT FOREHEAD MARK JUTSU, YOU GET REALLY OLD AND FALL DOWN!
IT'S DIFFERENT THAN WHEN I FOUGHT PAIN, NARUTO... I'VE ONLY HEALED MYSELF SO FAR... AND THESE WOUNDS AREN'T TOO BAD.
I'VE GOT PLENTY OF CHAKRA LEFT!
CAN YOU HEAL ME TOO?!!
EVEN IF I'M A DOPPELGANGER, I CAN'T AFFORD TO GO POOF YET!! ...I WANNA HELP OUT HERE...
THAT WON'T BE NECESSARY...
SIIZZZ...
?!!
WHY NOT?!
...
...THIS WAR...
...IS NO LONGER BEING FOUGHT JUST TO PROTECT YOU...

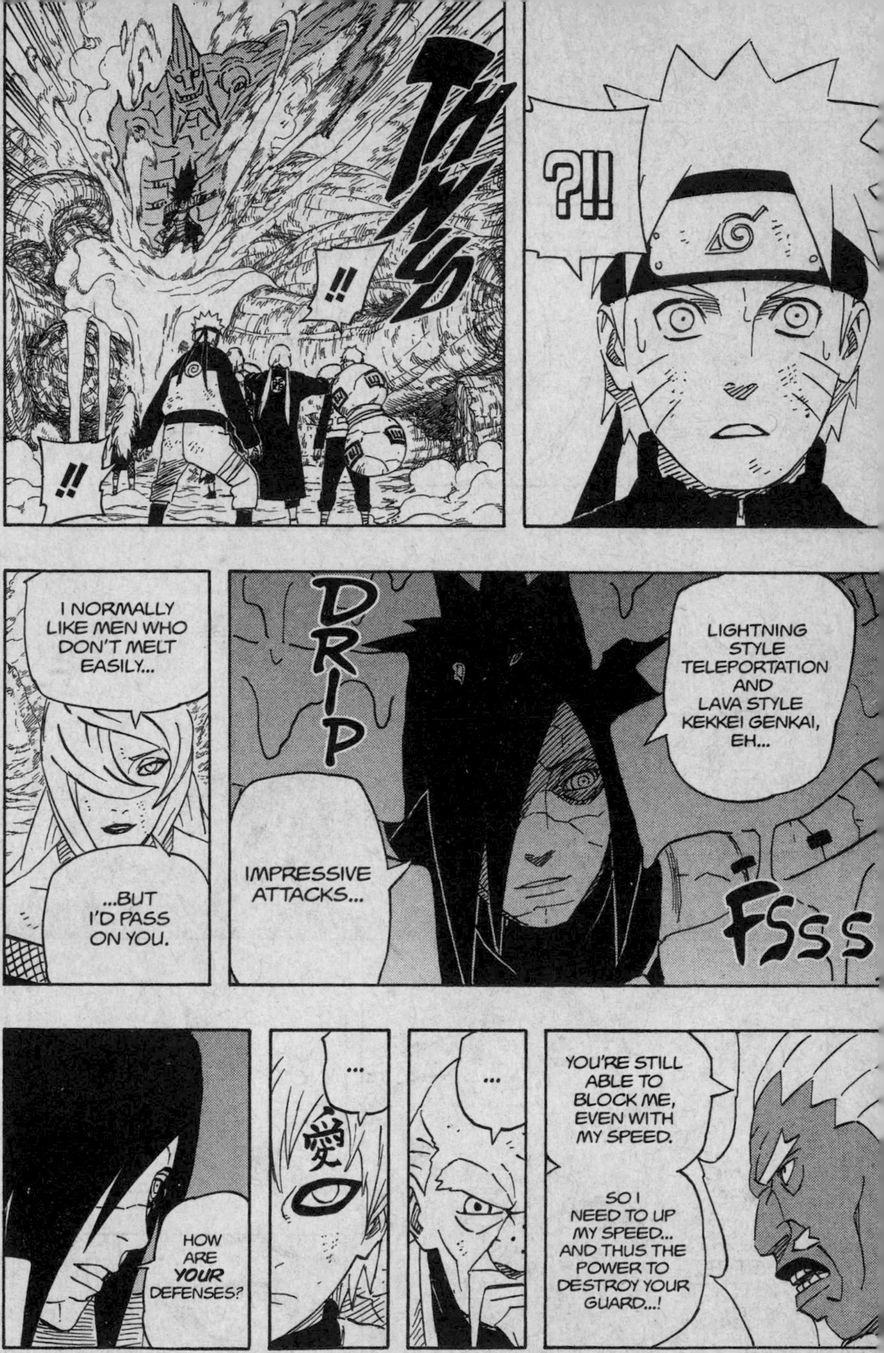
?!!
!!
!!
LIGHTNING STYLE TELEPORTATION AND LAVA STYLE KEKKEI GENKAI, EH...
FSSS
DRIP
IMPRESSIVE ATTACKS...
I NORMALLY LIKE MEN WHO DON'T MELT EASILY...
...BUT I'D PASS ON YOU.
YOU'RE STILL ABLE TO BLOCK ME, EVEN WITH MY SPEED.
SO I NEED TO UP MY SPEED... AND THUS THE POWER TO DESTROY YOUR GUARD...!
...
愛
...
HOW ARE ***YOUR*** DEFENSES?

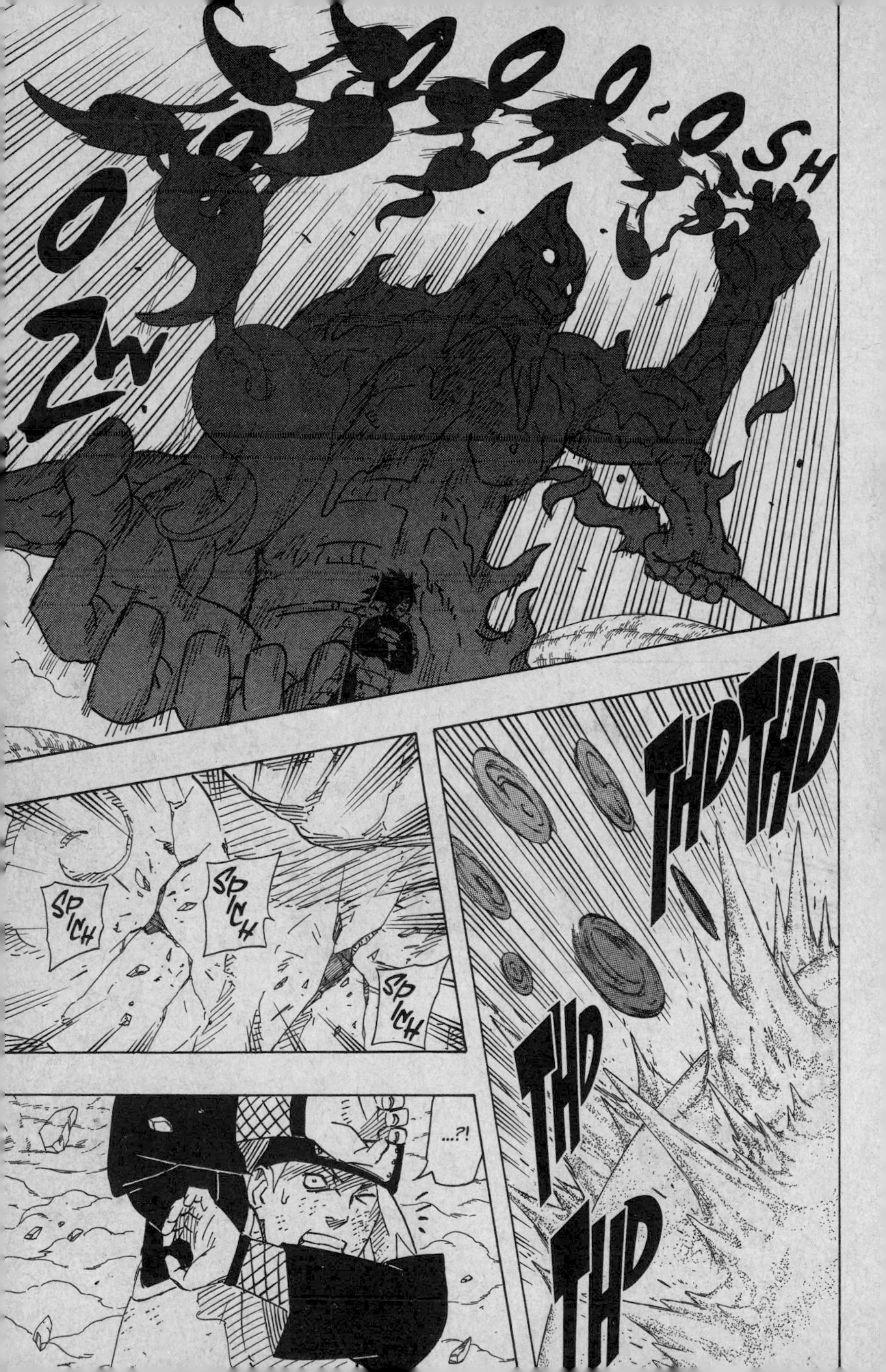
ZWOOOOOOOOOSH
THD THD
THD
THD
SPICH
SPICH
SPICH
...?!

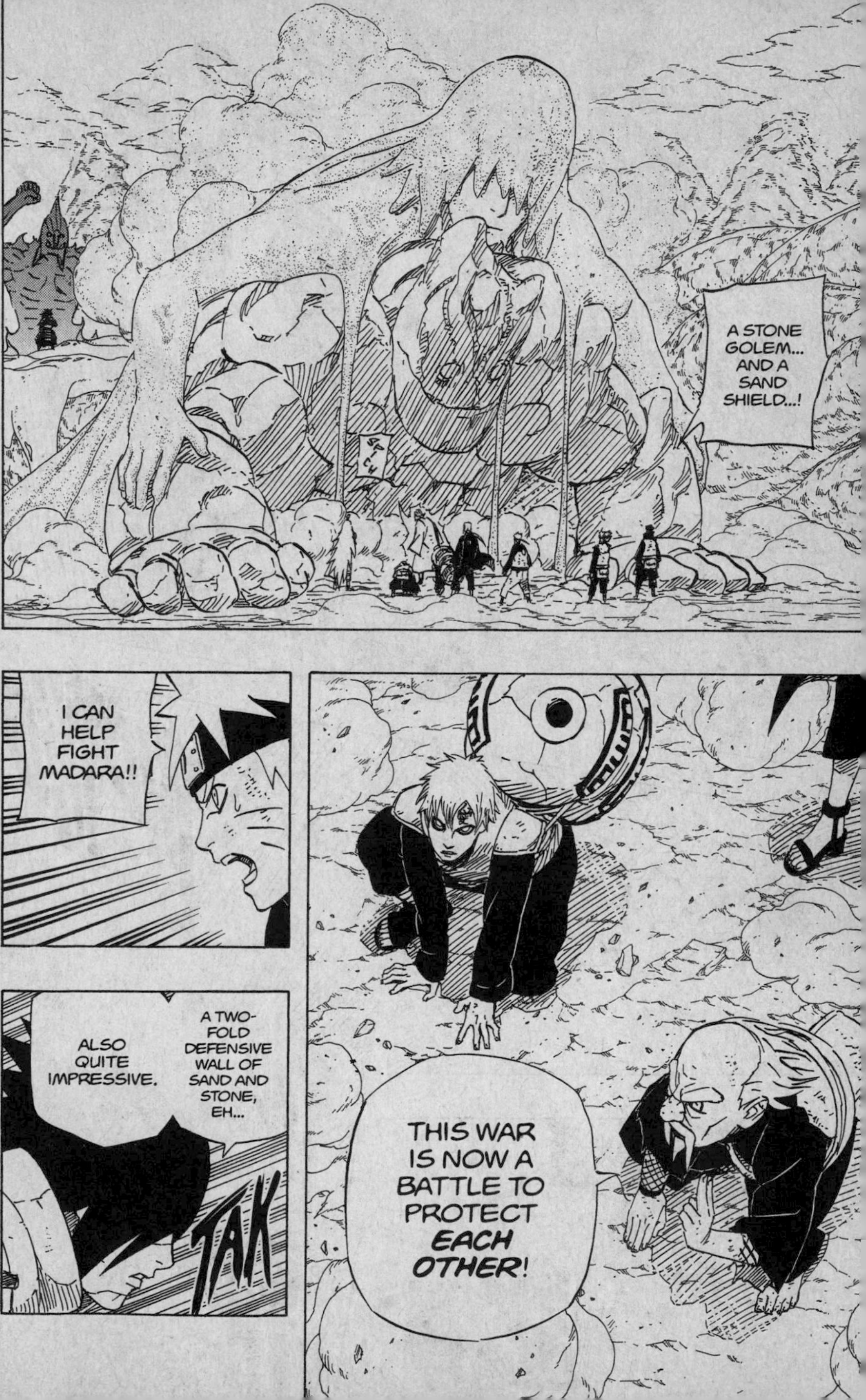
A STONE GOLEM... AND A SAND SHIELD...!
THIS WAR IS NOW A BATTLE TO PROTECT EACH OTHER!
I CAN HELP FIGHT MADARA!!
A TWO-FOLD DEFENSIVE WALL OF SAND AND STONE, EH...
ALSO QUITE IMPRESSIVE.
TAK

READ THIS WAY

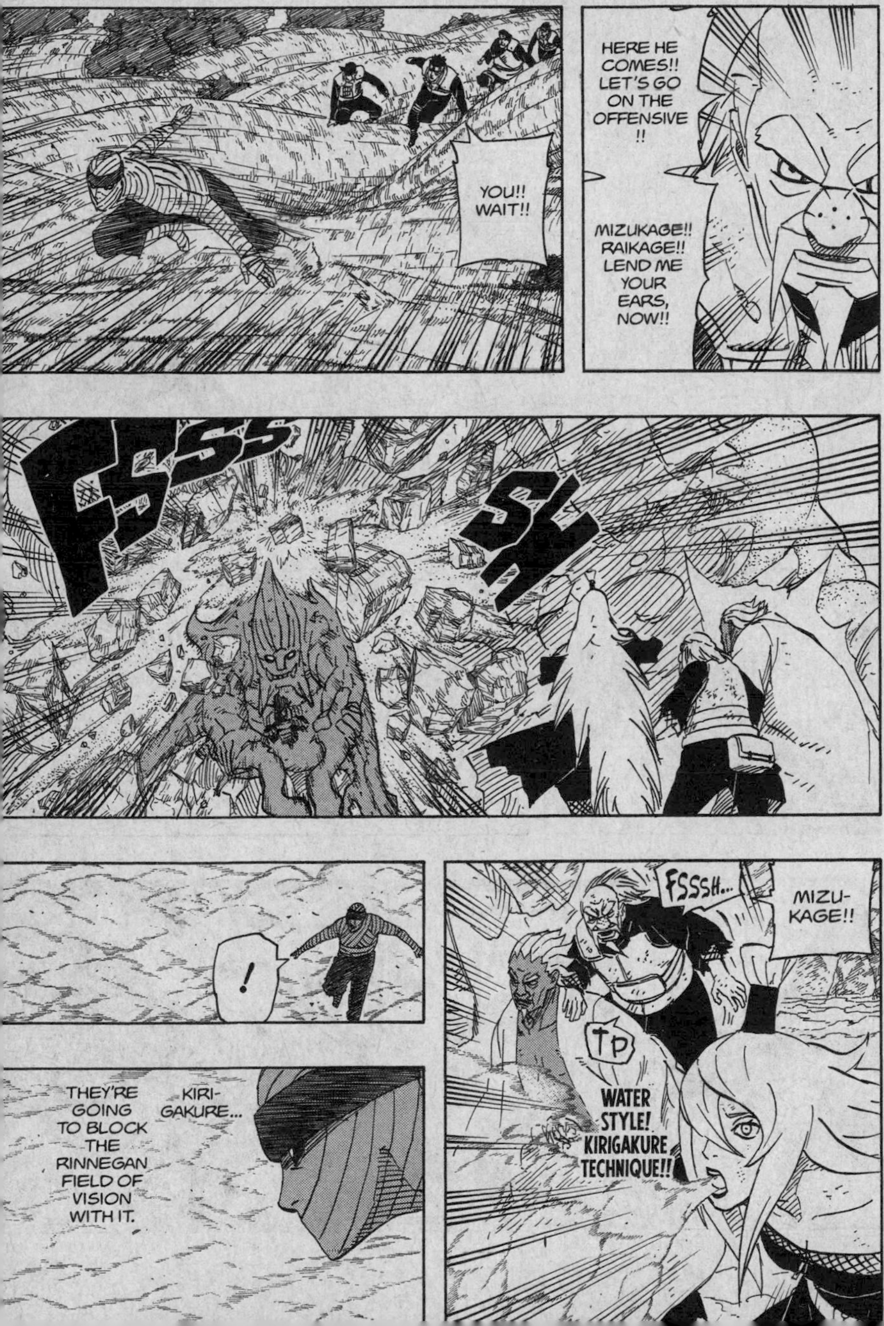
HERE HE COMES!! LET'S GO ON THE OFFENSIVE !!
MIZUKAGE!! RAIKAGE!! LEND ME YOUR EARS, NOW!!
YOU!! WAIT!!
FSSS
SH
MIZU-KAGE!!
FSSSH...
TP
WATER STYLE! KIRIGAKURE TECHNIQUE!!
!
KIRI-GAKURE...
THEY'RE GOING TO BLOCK THE RINNEGAN FIELD OF VISION WITH IT.

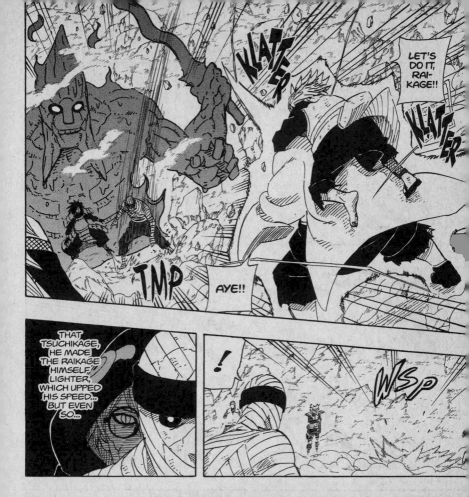

LET'S DO IT, RAI-KAGE!!

KLATTER

KLATTER

TMP

AYE!!

THAT TSUCHIKAGE, HE MADE THE RAIKAGE HIMSELF LIGHTER, WHICH UPPED HIS SPEED... BUT EVEN SO...

!

WSP

...IT'LL TURN OUT THE SAME AS BEFORE.

NO WORRY...

LOUSY PUNCH.

WHOOM

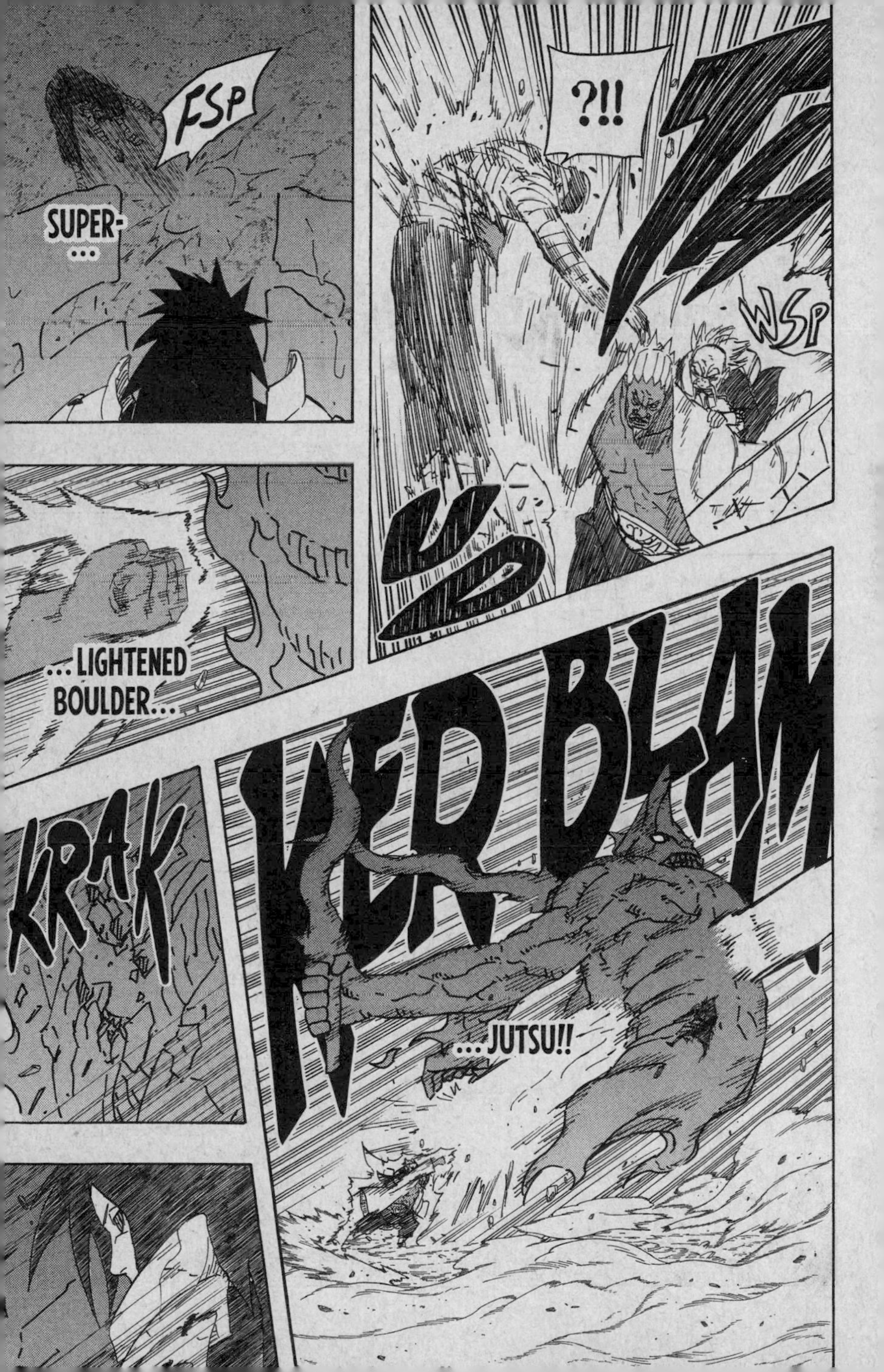

?!!
WSP
FSP
SUPER-
...
... LIGHTENED BOULDER...
... JUTSU!!
KRAK

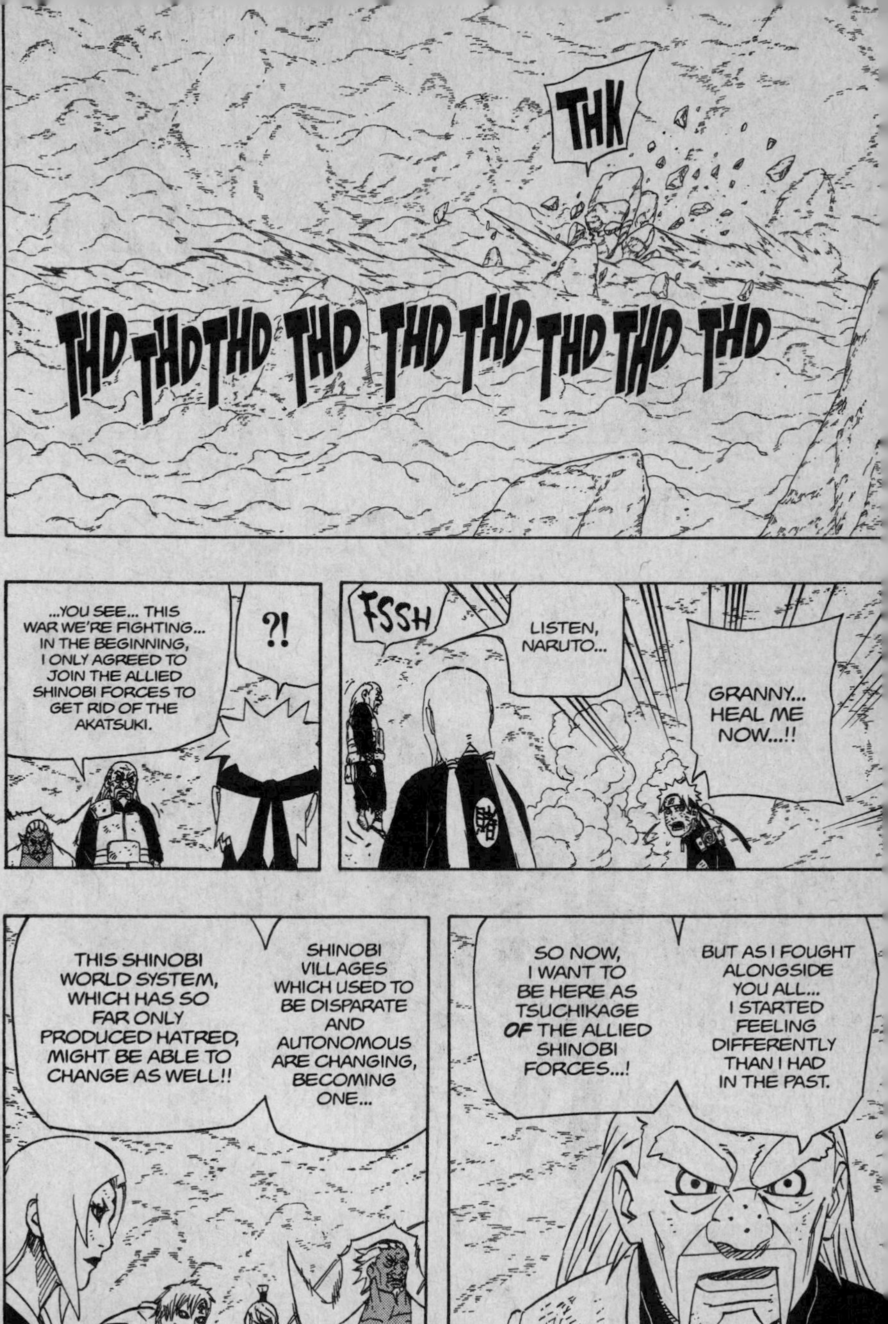
THK
THD THD THD THD THD THD THD THD THD
GRANNY... HEAL ME NOW...!!
LISTEN, NARUTO...
FSSH
?!
...YOU SEE... THIS WAR WE'RE FIGHTING... IN THE BEGINNING, I ONLY AGREED TO JOIN THE ALLIED SHINOBI FORCES TO GET RID OF THE AKATSUKI.
BUT AS I FOUGHT ALONGSIDE YOU ALL... I STARTED FEELING DIFFERENTLY THAN I HAD IN THE PAST.
SO NOW, I WANT TO BE HERE AS TSUCHIKAGE OF THE ALLIED SHINOBI FORCES...!
SHINOBI VILLAGES WHICH USED TO BE DISPARATE AND AUTONOMOUS ARE CHANGING, BECOMING ONE...
THIS SHINOBI WORLD SYSTEM, WHICH HAS SO FAR ONLY PRODUCED HATRED, MIGHT BE ABLE TO CHANGE AS WELL!!

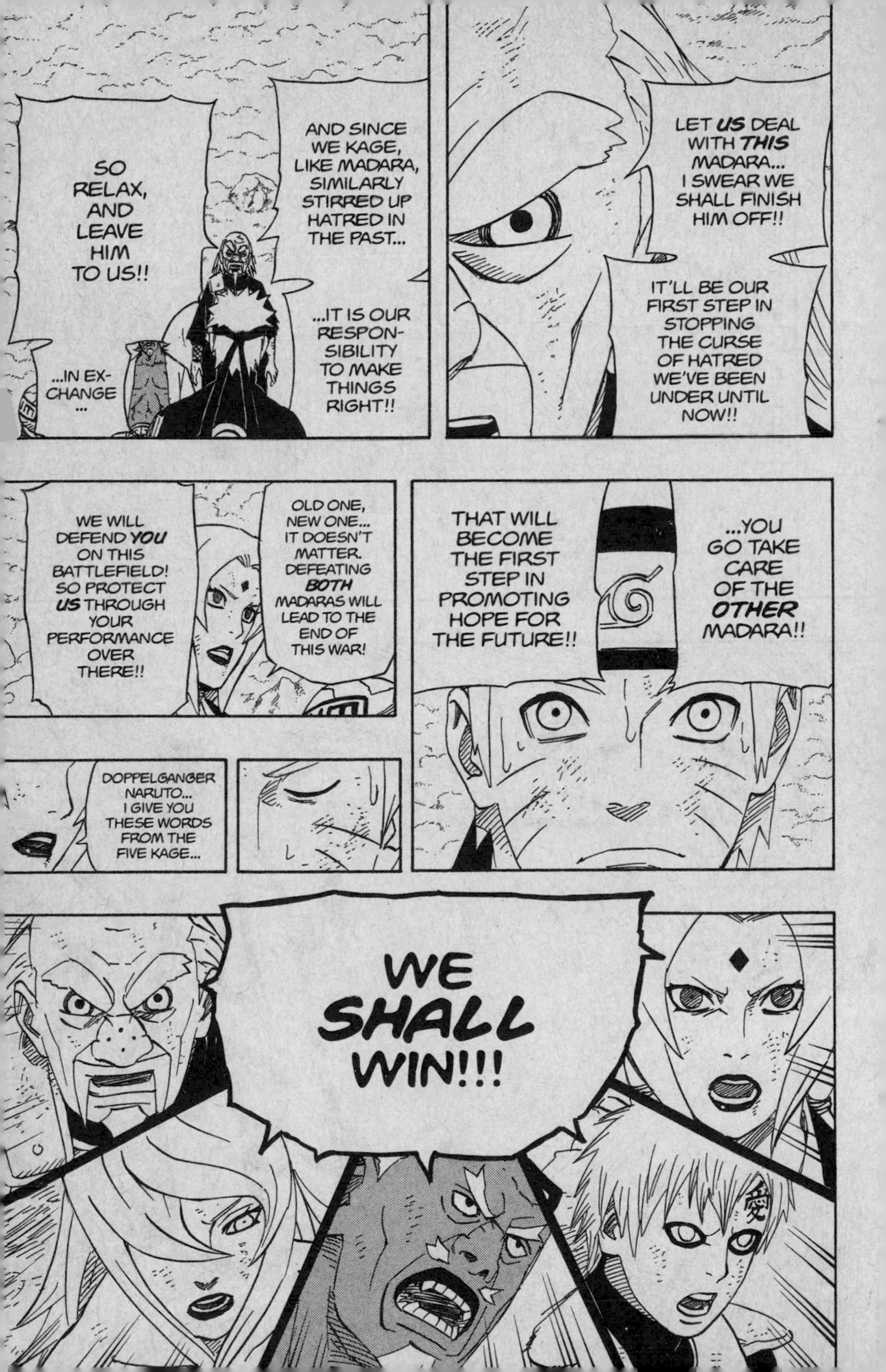

LET US DEAL WITH THIS MADARA... I SWEAR WE SHALL FINISH HIM OFF!!
IT'LL BE OUR FIRST STEP IN STOPPING THE CURSE OF HATRED WE'VE BEEN UNDER UNTIL NOW!!
AND SINCE WE KAGE, LIKE MADARA, SIMILARLY STIRRED UP HATRED IN THE PAST...
...IT IS OUR RESPON-SIBILITY TO MAKE THINGS RIGHT!!
SO RELAX, AND LEAVE HIM TO US!!
...IN EX-CHANGE...
...YOU GO TAKE CARE OF THE OTHER MADARA!!
THAT WILL BECOME THE FIRST STEP IN PROMOTING HOPE FOR THE FUTURE!!
OLD ONE, NEW ONE... IT DOESN'T MATTER. DEFEATING BOTH MADARAS WILL LEAD TO THE END OF THIS WAR!
WE WILL DEFEND YOU ON THIS BATTLEFIELD! SO PROTECT US THROUGH YOUR PERFORMANCE OVER THERE!!
DOPPELGANGER NARUTO... I GIVE YOU THESE WORDS FROM THE FIVE KAGE...
WE SHALL WIN!!!

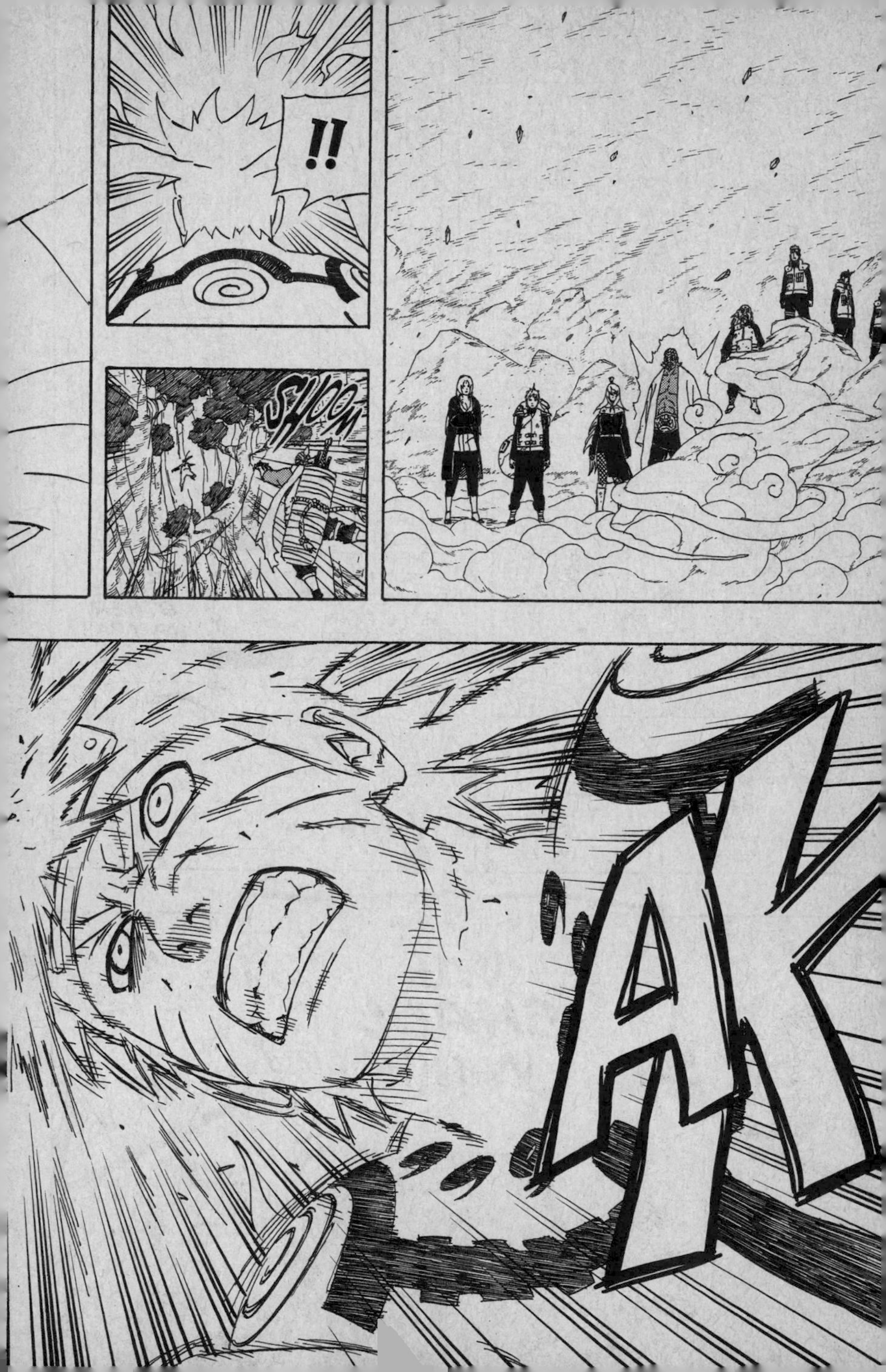
!!
SHOOM
AK

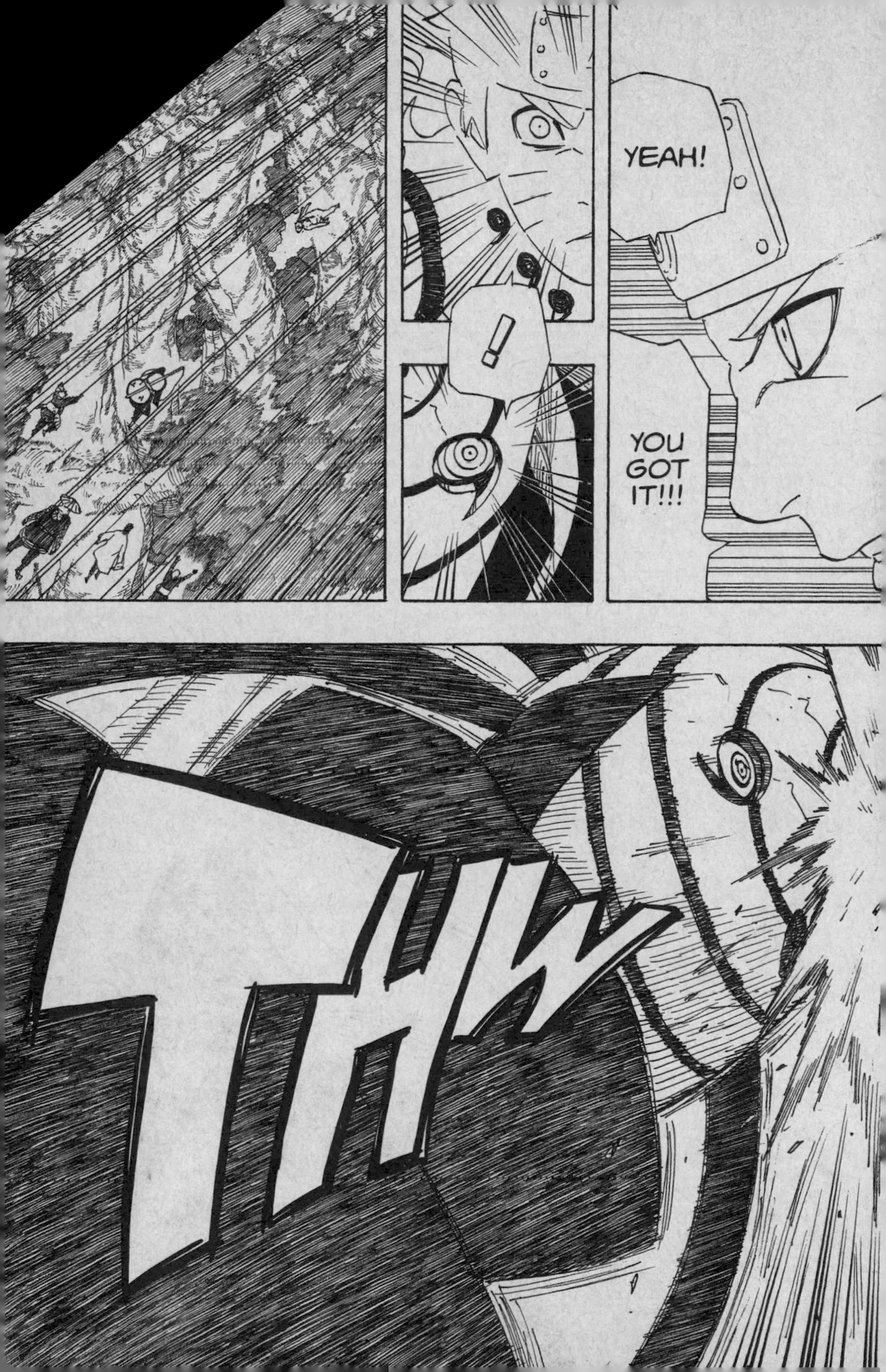
YEAH!
YOU GOT IT!!!
!
THW

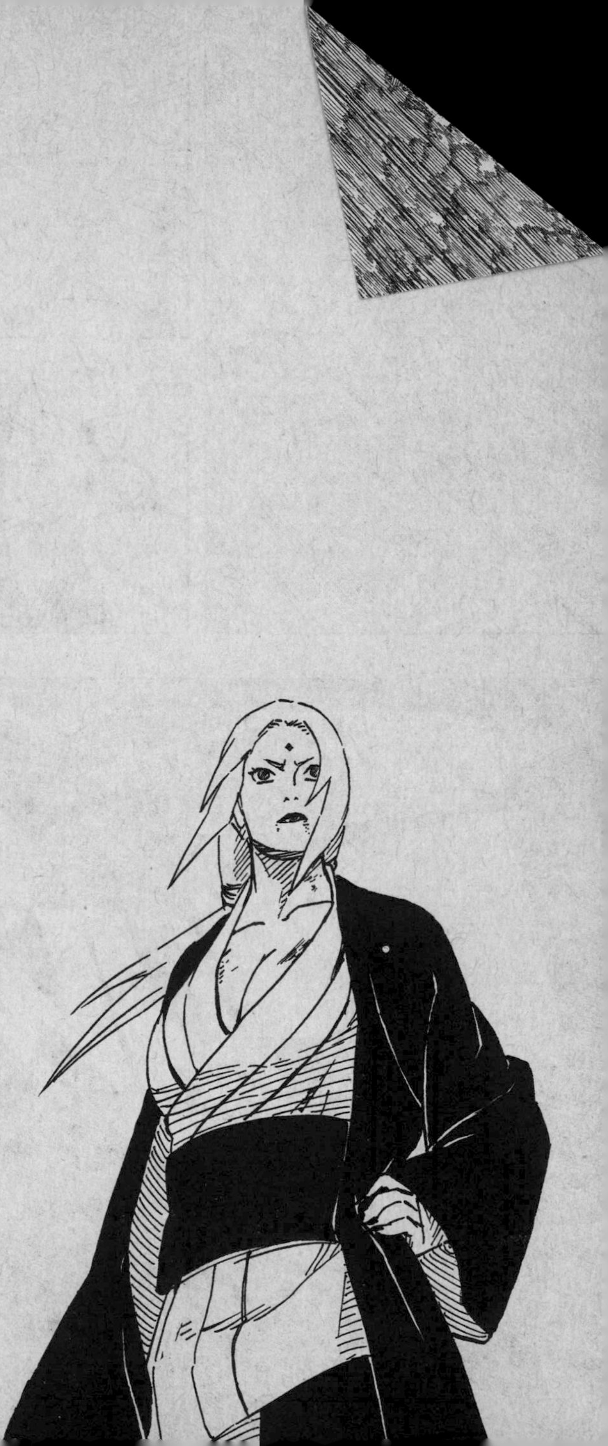

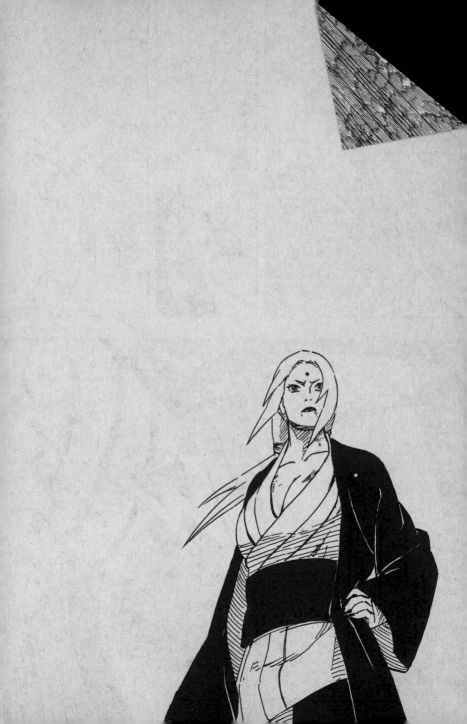

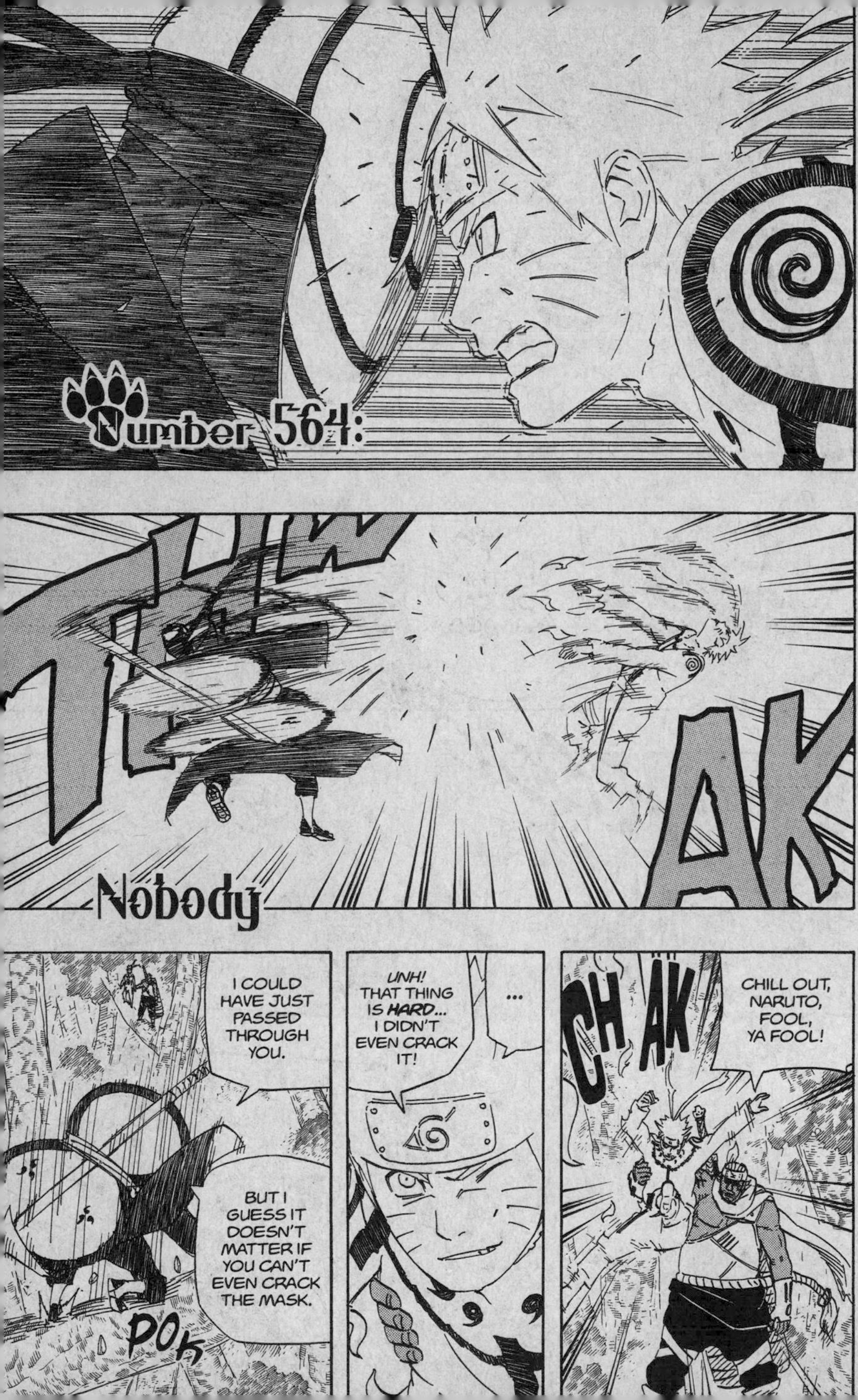
Number 564:
Nobody
THWAK
CHAK
CHILL OUT, NARUTO, FOOL, YA FOOL!
...
UNH! THAT THING IS *HARD*... I DIDN'T EVEN CRACK IT!
I COULD HAVE JUST PASSED THROUGH YOU.
BUT I GUESS IT DOESN'T MATTER IF YOU CAN'T EVEN CRACK THE MASK.
POK

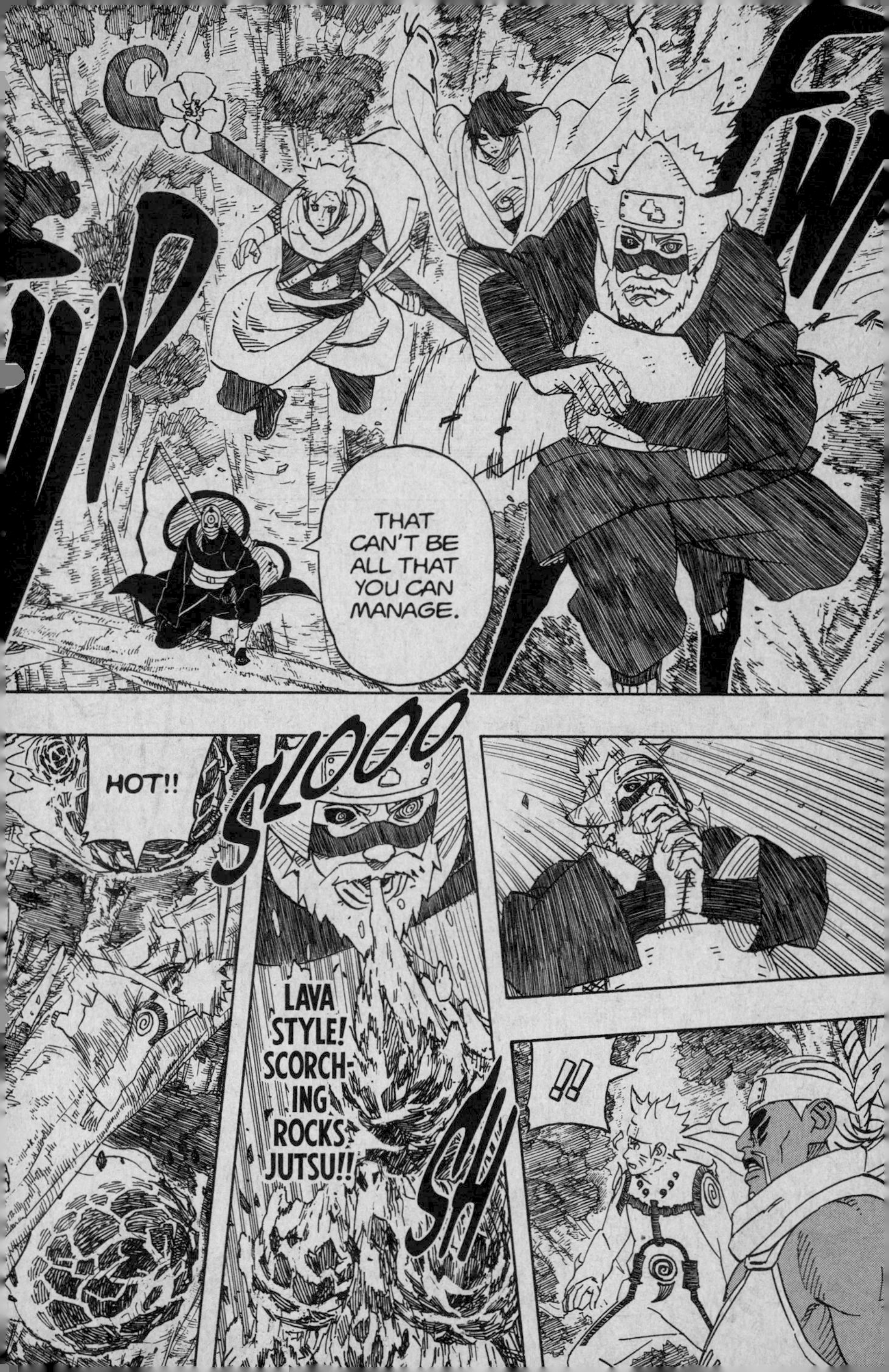
THAT CAN'T BE ALL THAT YOU CAN MANAGE.
!!
SZLOOO
LAVA STYLE! SCORCHING ROCKS JUTSU!!
SH
HOT!!

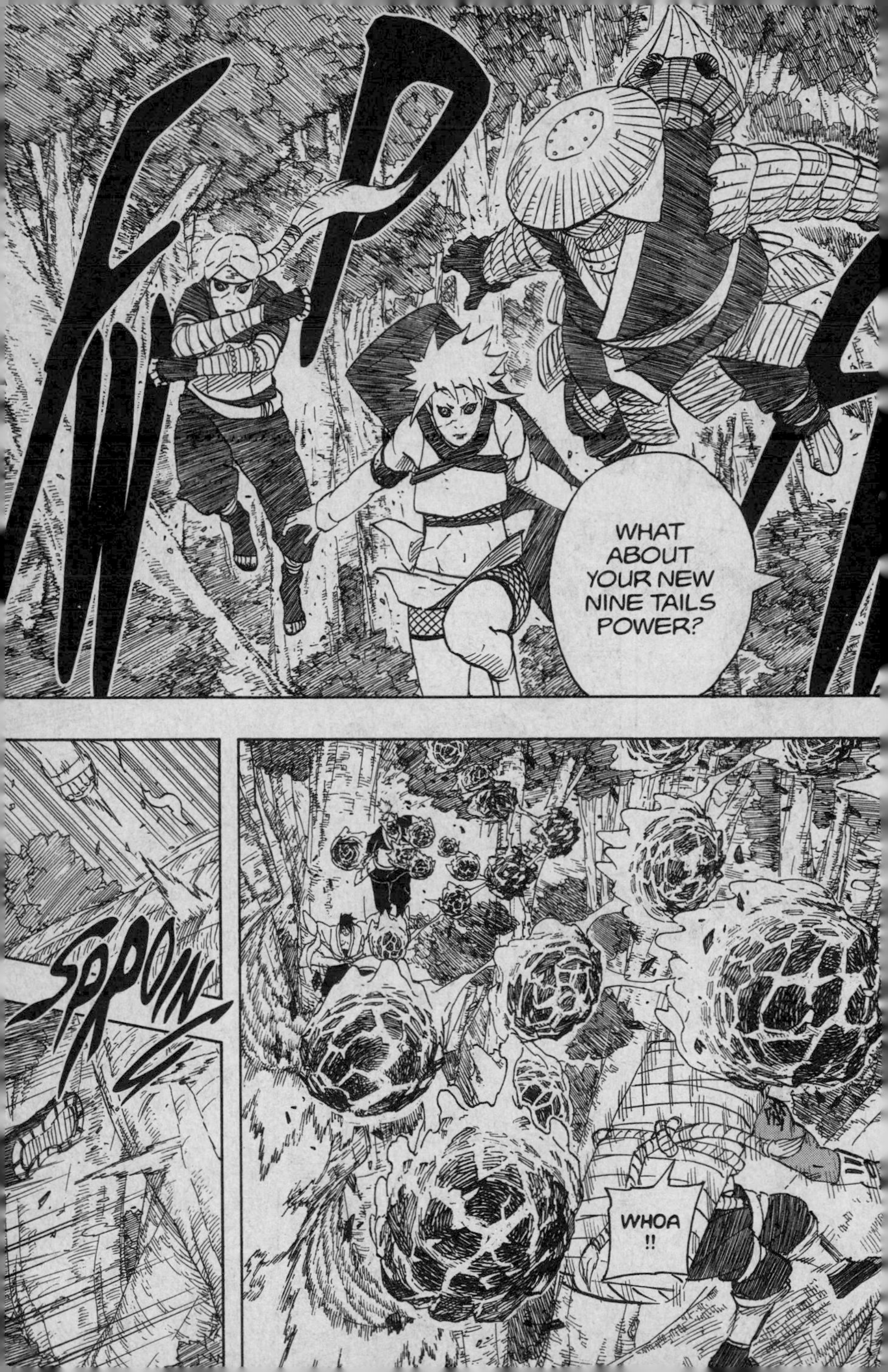
WHAT ABOUT YOUR NEW NINE TAILS POWER?
WHOA!!

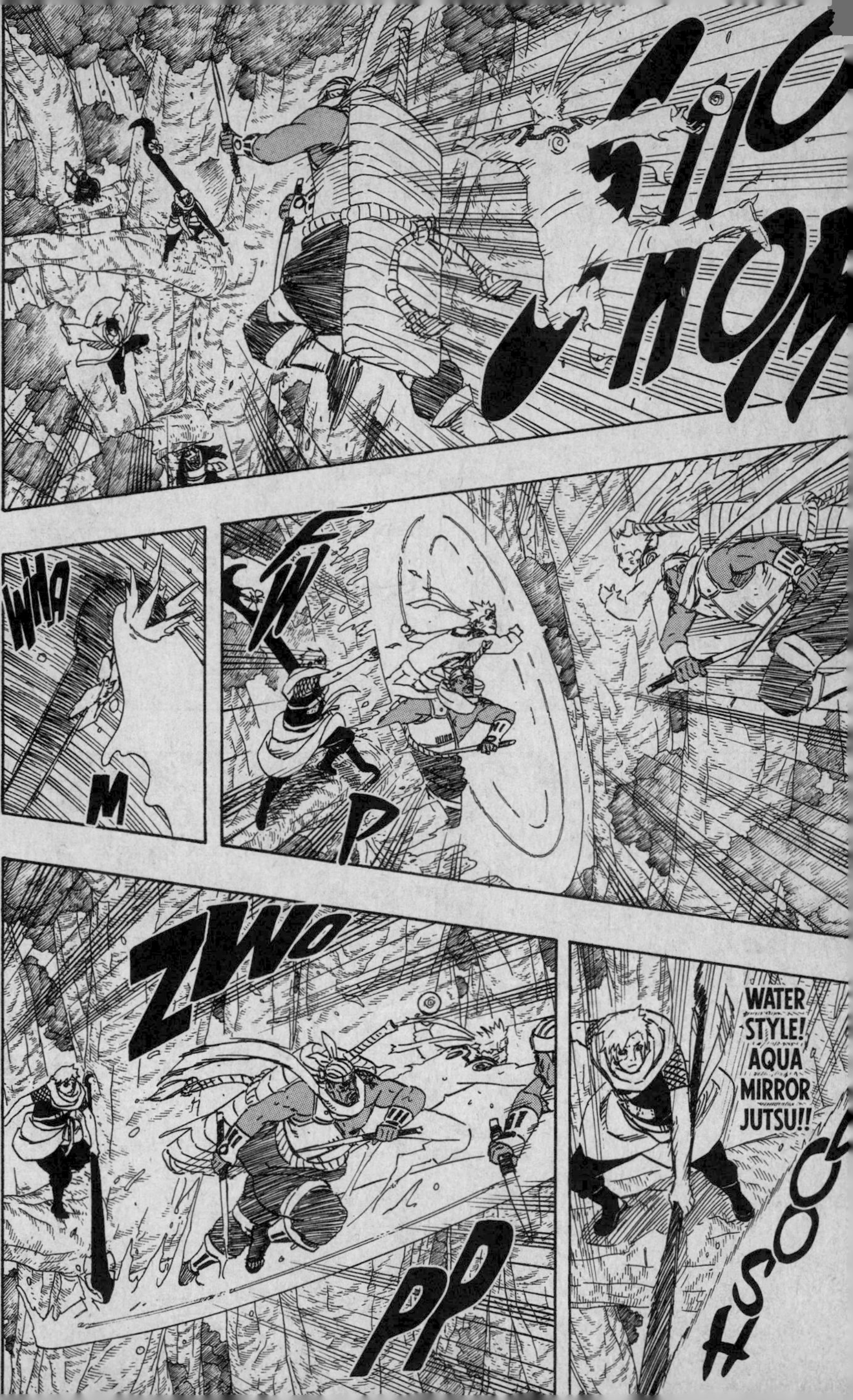
WHAM
WATER STYLE! AQUA MIRROR JUTSU!!

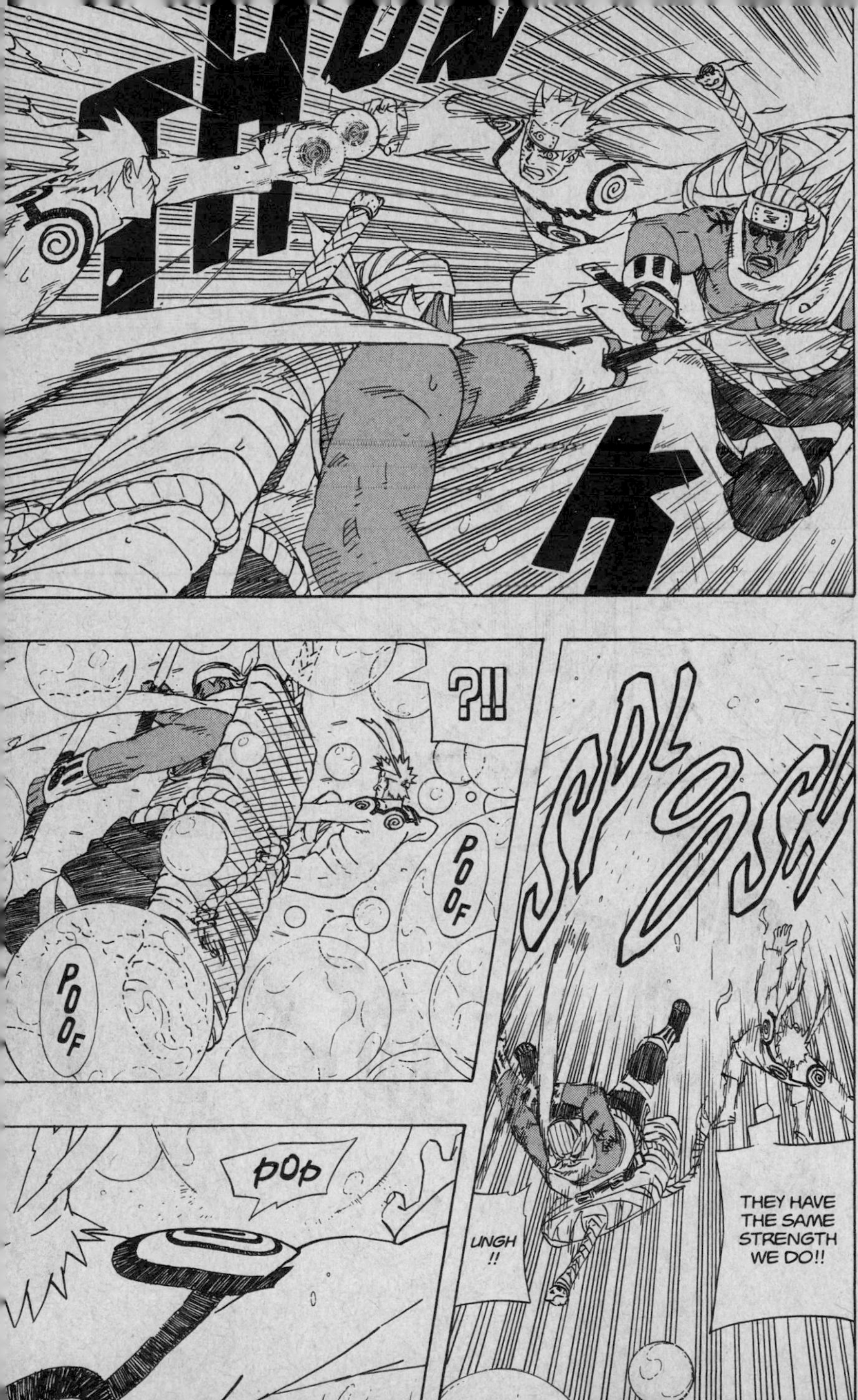
THUN
K
SPLOSCH
THEY HAVE THE SAME STRENGTH WE DO!!
UNGH !!
?!!
POOF
POOF
POP

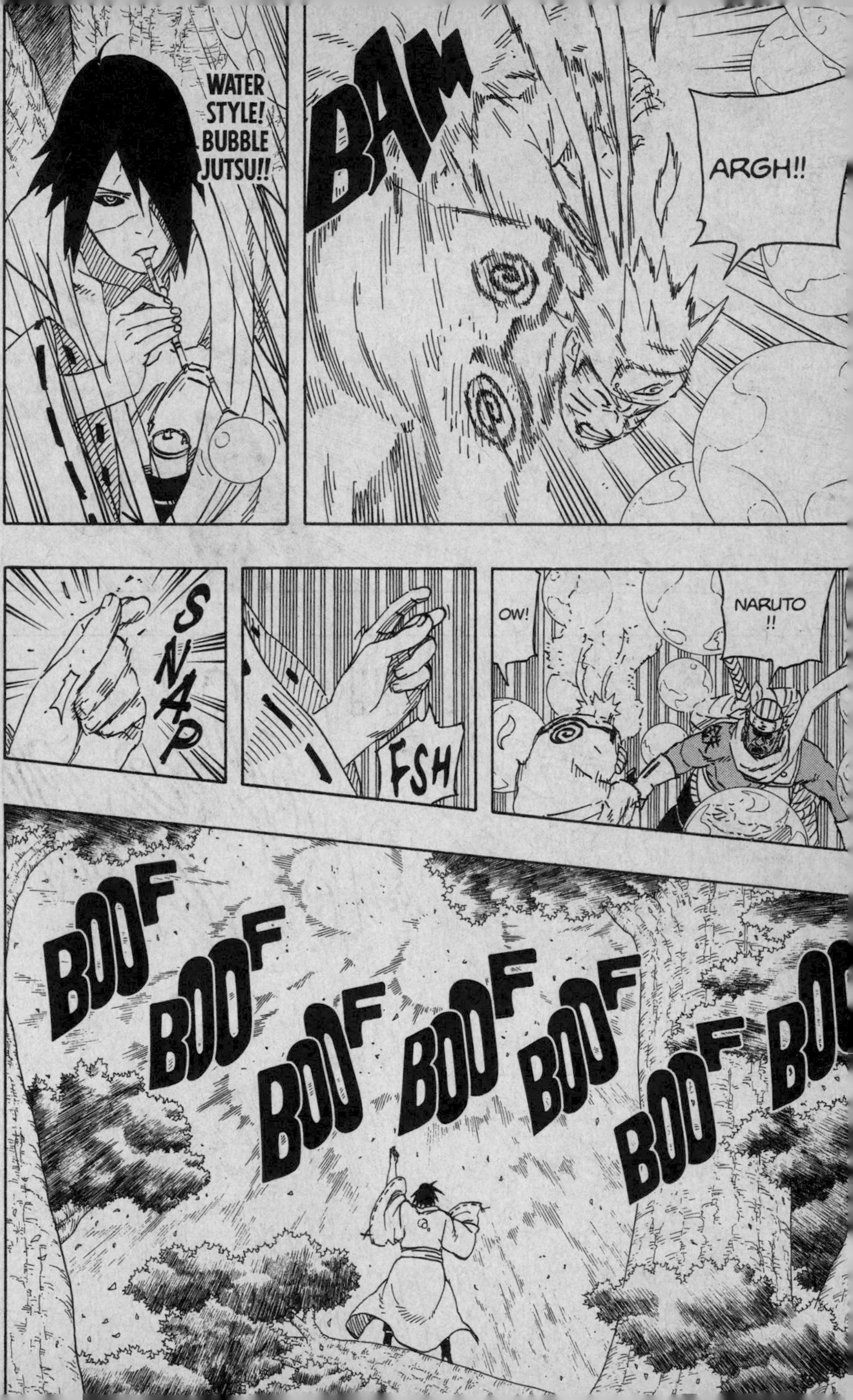
ARGH!!
BAM
WATER STYLE! BUBBLE JUTSU!!
NARUTO !!
OW!
FSH
SNAP
BOOF
BOOF
BOOF
BOOF
BOOF
BOOF
BOO

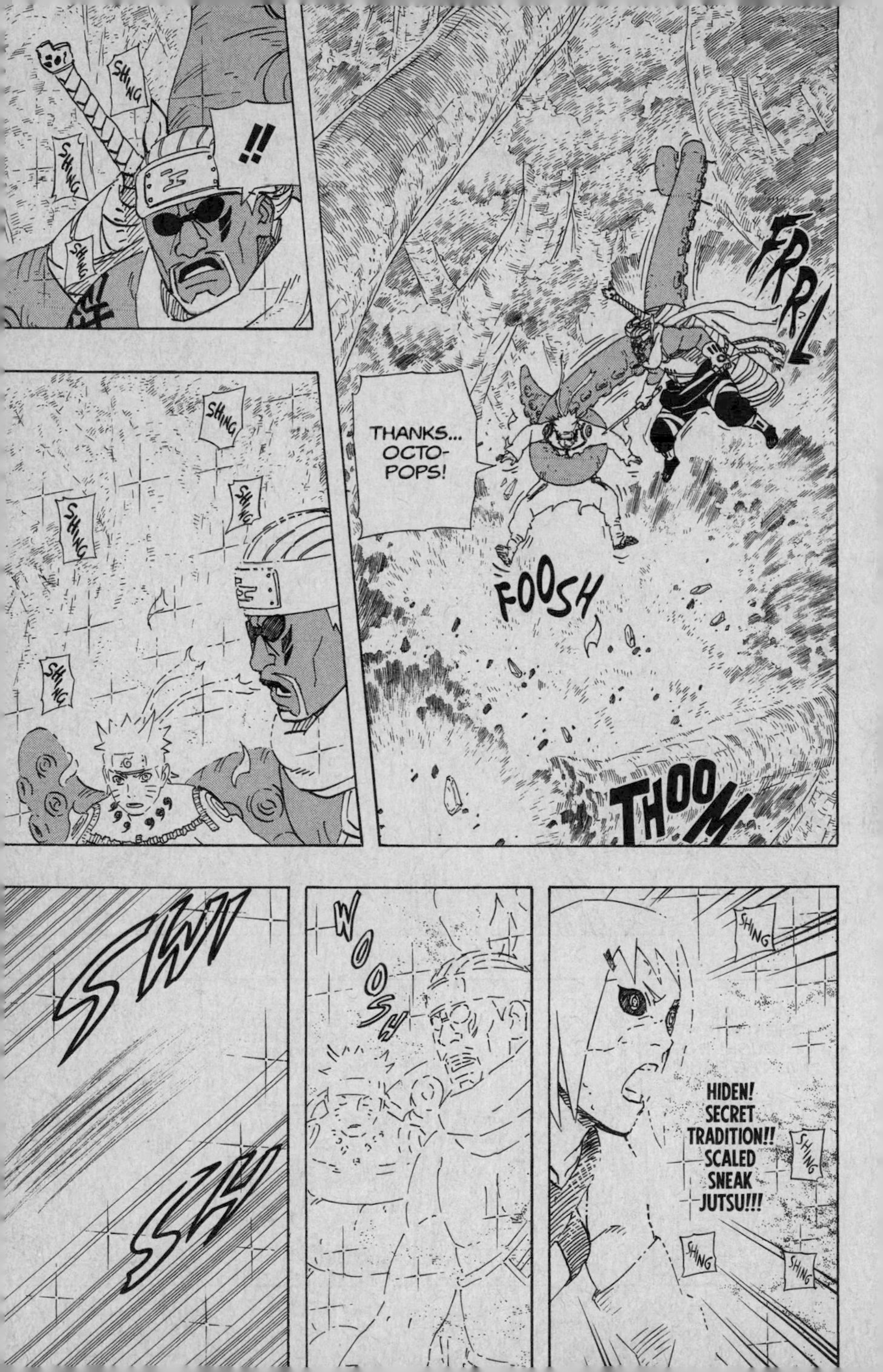
FRRL
THANKS... OCTO-POPS!
FOOSH
THOOM
!!
SHING
SHING
SHING
SHING
SHING
SHING
SHING
SHING
HIDEN! SECRET TRADITION!! SCALED SNEAK JUTSU!!!
SHING
SHING
SHING
WOOOSH
SWH
SSH

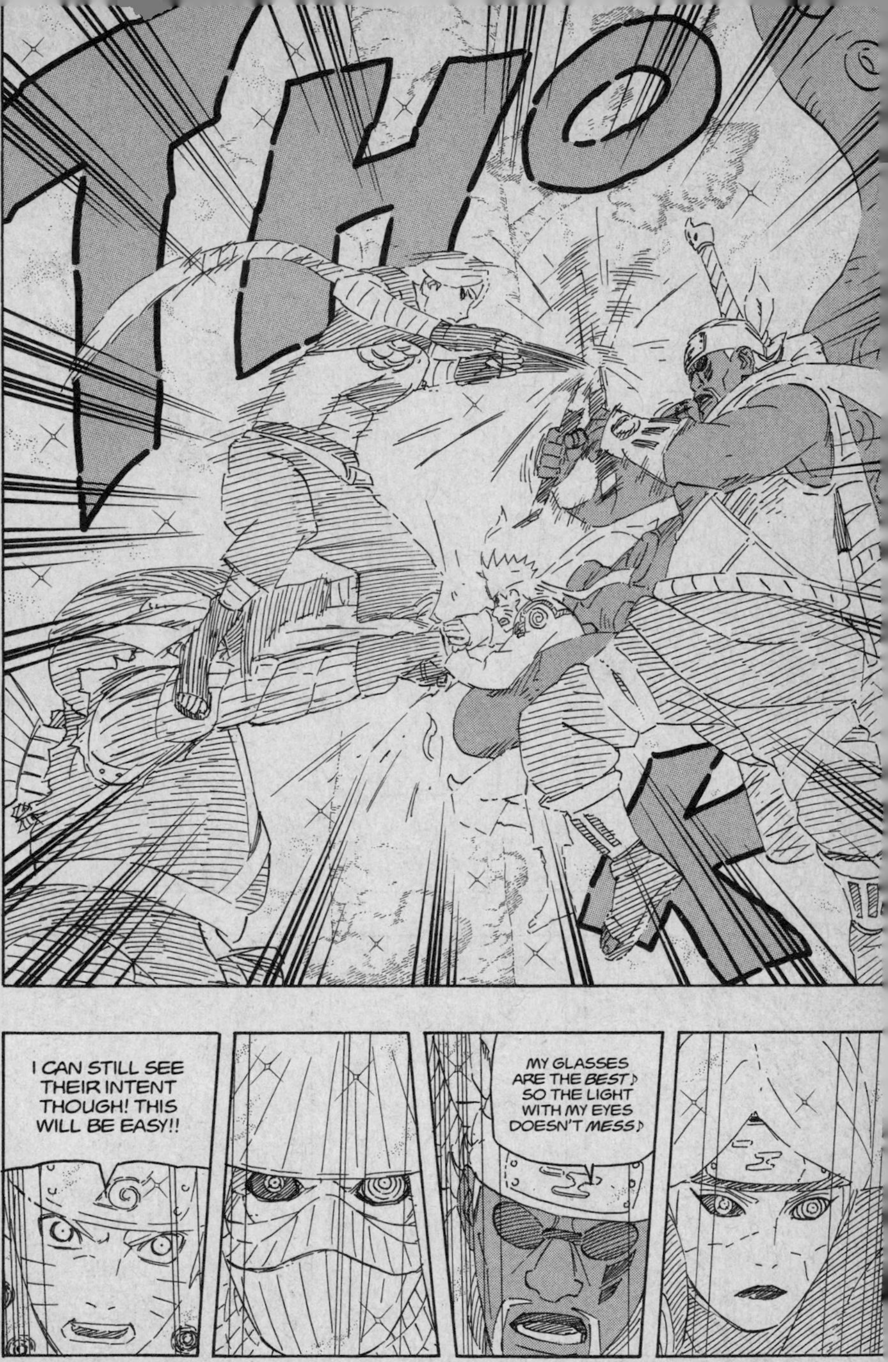
MY GLASSES ARE THE *BEST*♪ SO THE LIGHT WITH MY EYES DOESN'T *MESS*♪
I CAN STILL SEE THEIR INTENT THOUGH! THIS WILL BE EASY!!

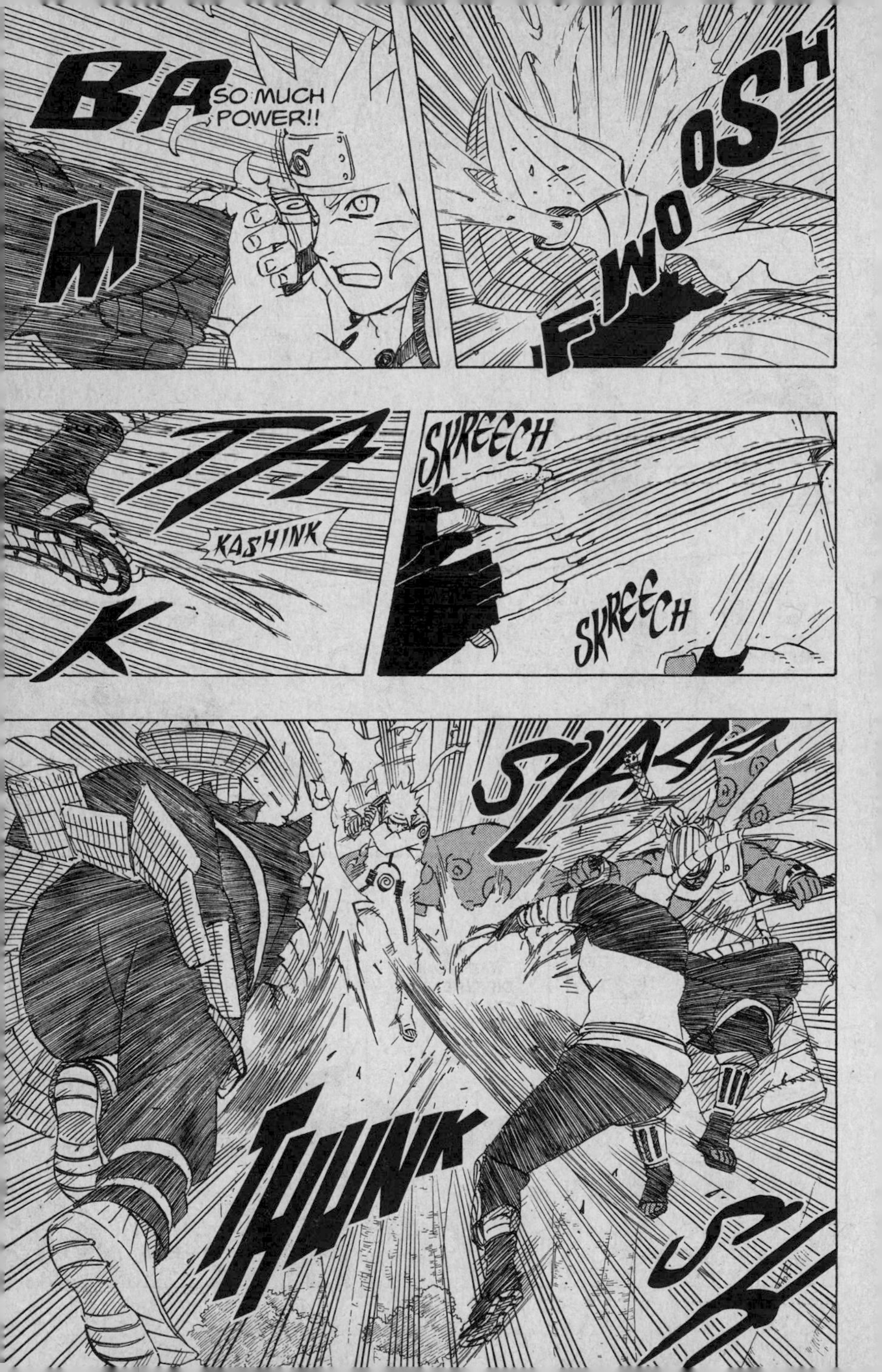
FWOOSH
BAM
SO MUCH POWER!!
SKREECH
SKREECH
TAK
KASHINK
SLAAA
THUNK
SH

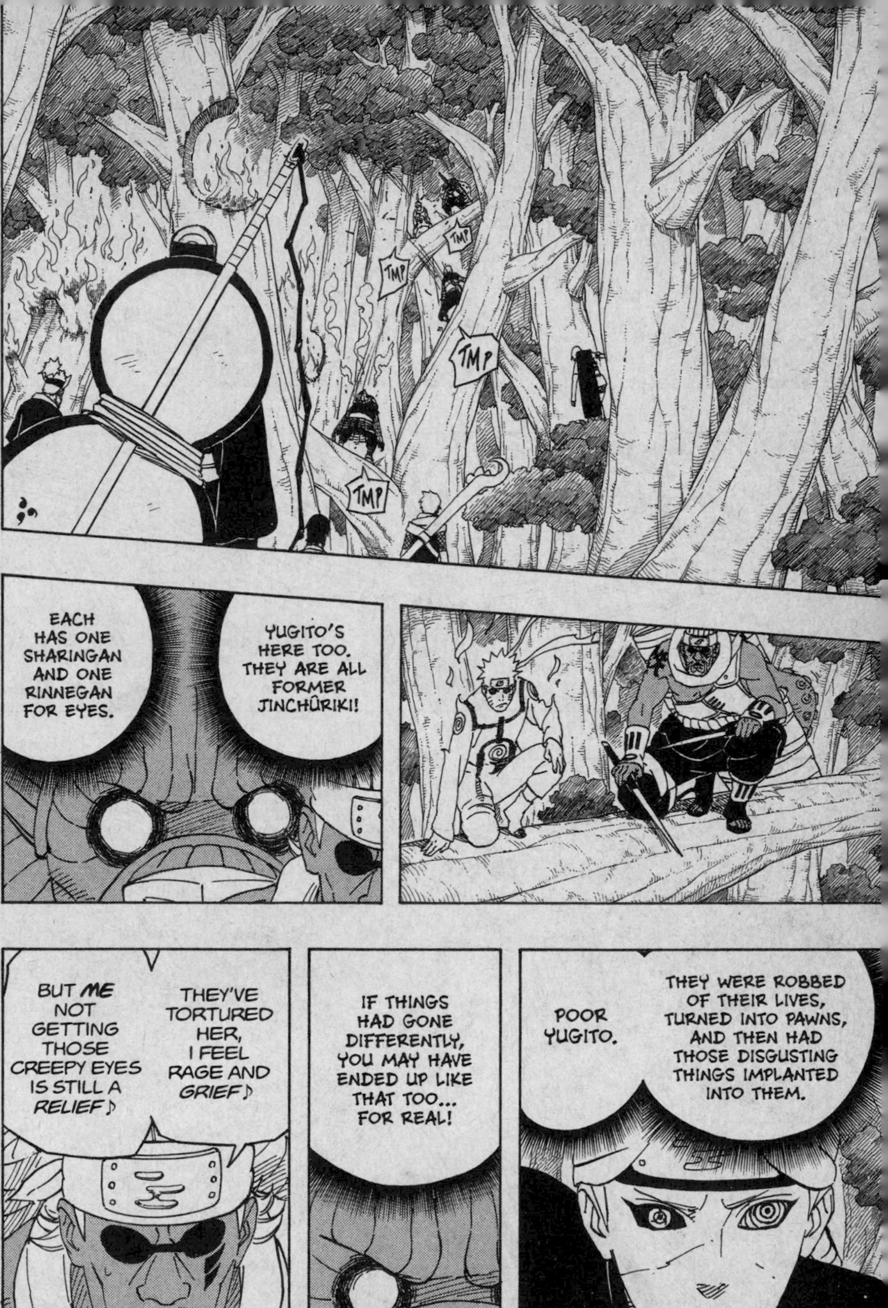
TMP
TMP
TMP
TMP
YUGITO'S HERE TOO. THEY ARE ALL FORMER JINCHŪRIKI!
EACH HAS ONE SHARINGAN AND ONE RINNEGAN FOR EYES.
THEY WERE ROBBED OF THEIR LIVES, TURNED INTO PAWNS, AND THEN HAD THOSE DISGUSTING THINGS IMPLANTED INTO THEM.
POOR YUGITO.
IF THINGS HAD GONE DIFFERENTLY, YOU MAY HAVE ENDED UP LIKE THAT TOO... FOR REAL!
THEY'VE TORTURED HER, I FEEL RAGE AND GRIEF♪
BUT ME NOT GETTING THOSE CREEPY EYES IS STILL A RELIEF♪

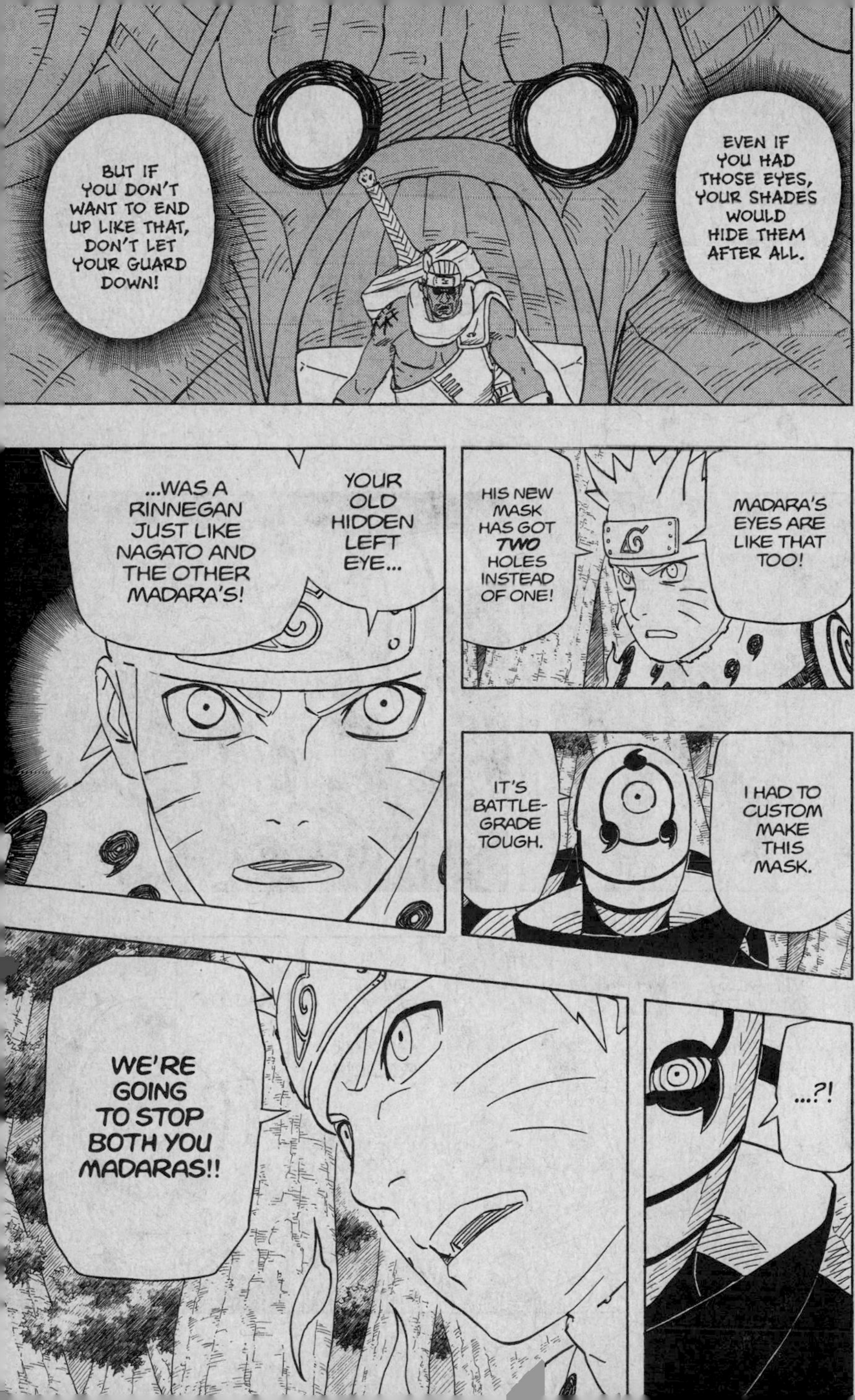
EVEN IF YOU HAD THOSE EYES, YOUR SHADES WOULD HIDE THEM AFTER ALL.
BUT IF YOU DON'T WANT TO END UP LIKE THAT, DON'T LET YOUR GUARD DOWN!
MADARA'S EYES ARE LIKE THAT TOO!
HIS NEW MASK HAS GOT *TWO* HOLES INSTEAD OF ONE!
I HAD TO CUSTOM MAKE THIS MASK.
IT'S BATTLE-GRADE TOUGH.
YOUR OLD HIDDEN LEFT EYE...
...WAS A RINNEGAN JUST LIKE NAGATO AND THE OTHER MADARA'S!
...?!
WE'RE GOING TO STOP BOTH YOU MADARAS!!

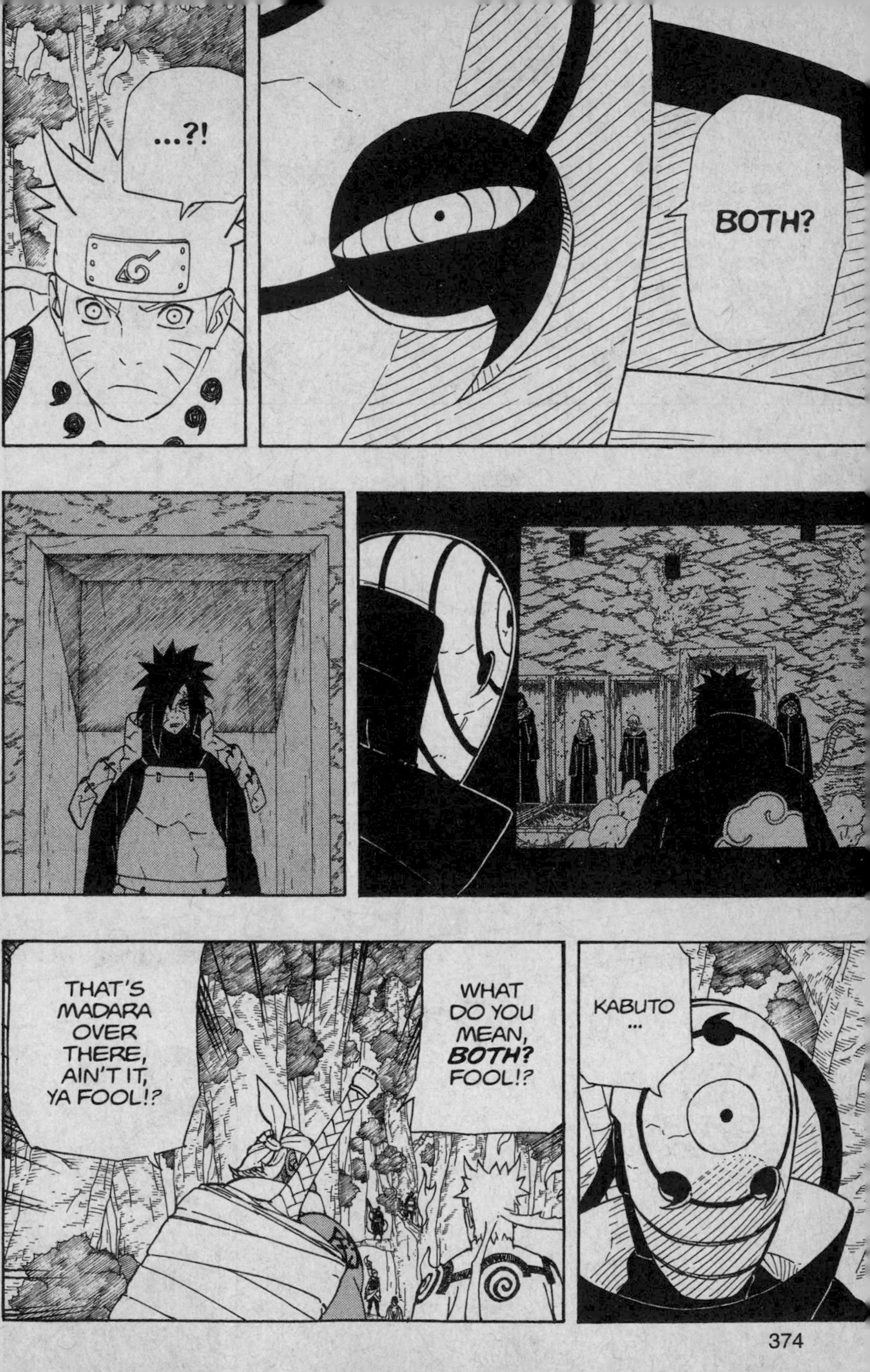
BOTH?
...?!
KABUTO ...
WHAT DO YOU MEAN, **BOTH?** FOOL!?
THAT'S MADARA OVER THERE, AIN'T IT, YA FOOL!?

READ THIS WAY

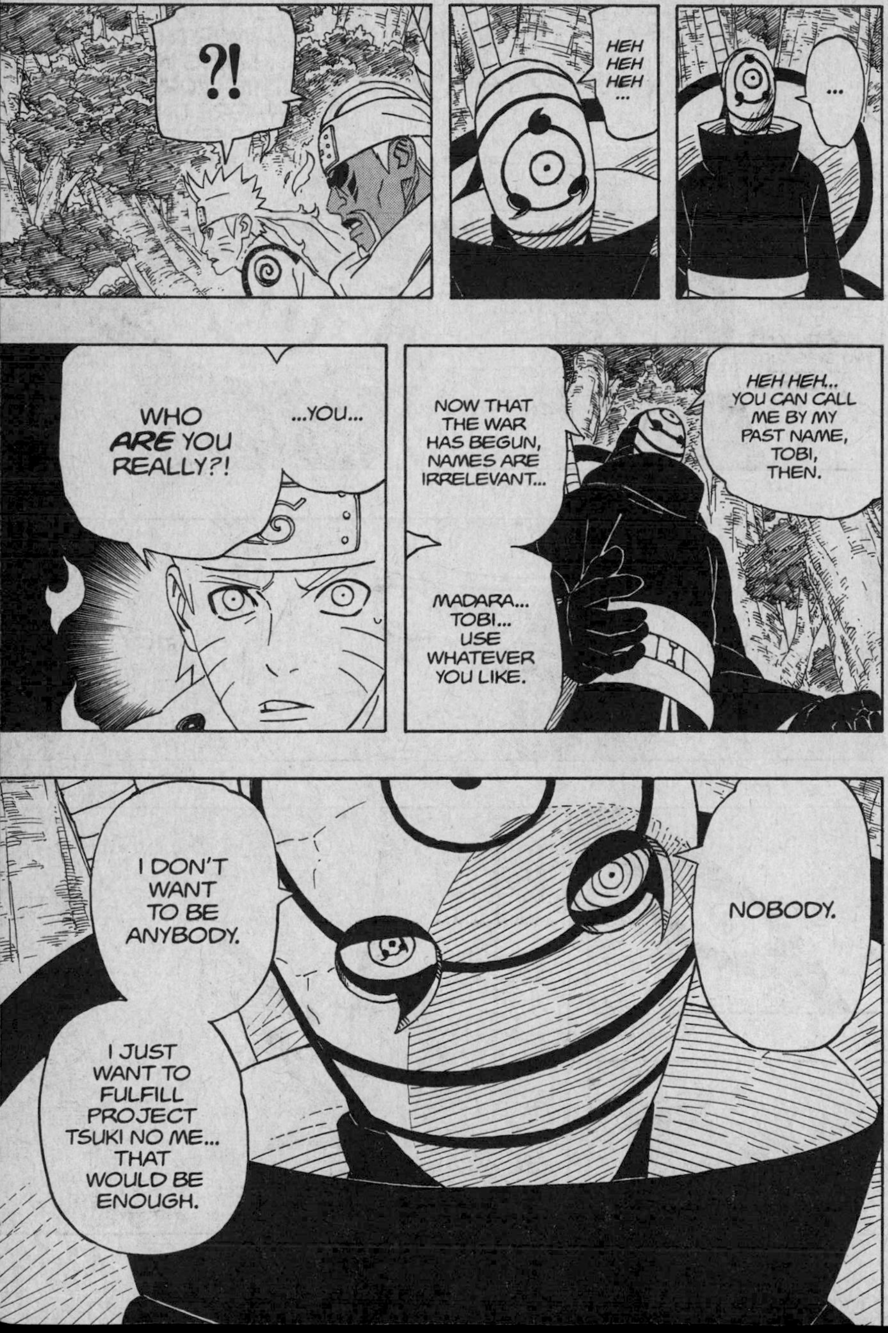
...
HEH HEH HEH ...
?!
HEH HEH... YOU CAN CALL ME BY MY PAST NAME, TOBI, THEN.
NOW THAT THE WAR HAS BEGUN, NAMES ARE IRRELEVANT...
MADARA... TOBI... USE WHATEVER YOU LIKE.
...YOU...
WHO *ARE* YOU REALLY?!
NOBODY.
I DON'T WANT TO BE ANYBODY.
I JUST WANT TO FULFILL PROJECT TSUKI NO ME... THAT WOULD BE ENOUGH.

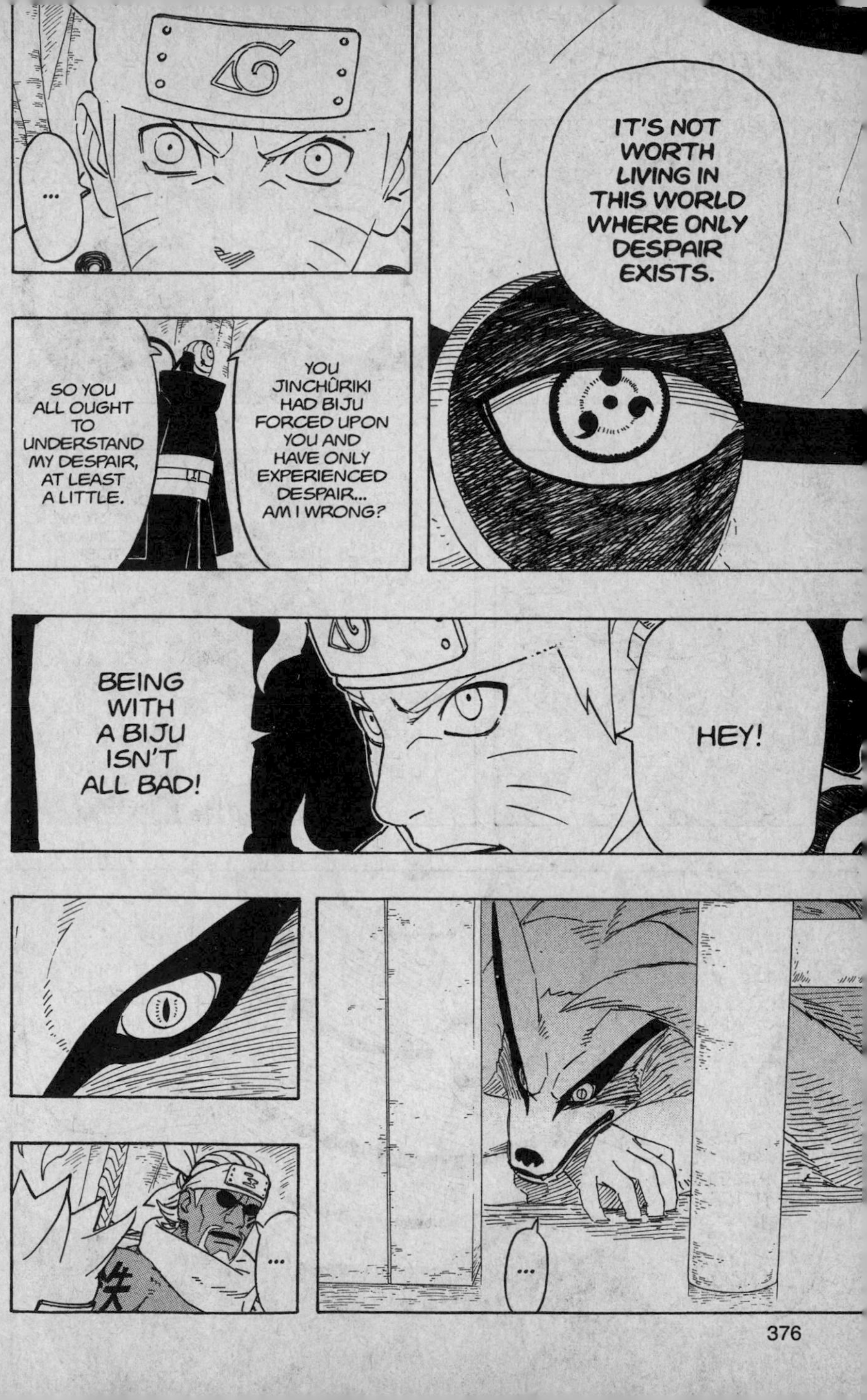
IT'S NOT WORTH LIVING IN THIS WORLD WHERE ONLY DESPAIR EXISTS.
...
YOU JINCHŪRIKI HAD BIJU FORCED UPON YOU AND HAVE ONLY EXPERIENCED DESPAIR... AM I WRONG?
SO YOU ALL OUGHT TO UNDERSTAND MY DESPAIR, AT LEAST A LITTLE.
HEY!
BEING WITH A BIJU ISN'T ALL BAD!
...
...

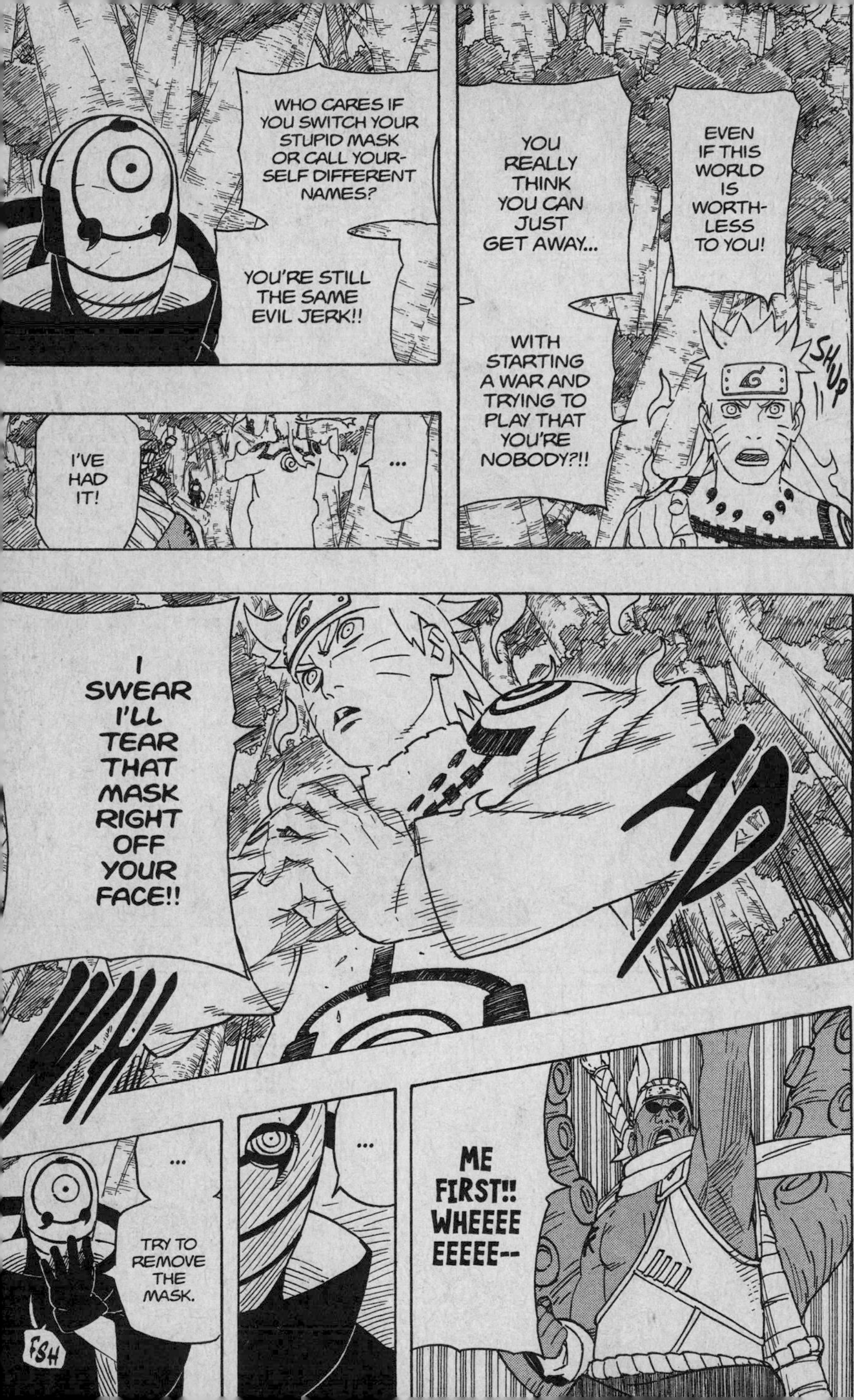
EVEN IF THIS WORLD IS WORTHLESS TO YOU!
YOU REALLY THINK YOU CAN JUST GET AWAY...
WITH STARTING A WAR AND TRYING TO PLAY THAT YOU'RE NOBODY?!!
SHUP
WHO CARES IF YOU SWITCH YOUR STUPID MASK OR CALL YOURSELF DIFFERENT NAMES?
YOU'RE STILL THE SAME EVIL JERK!!
...
I'VE HAD IT!
I SWEAR I'LL TEAR THAT MASK RIGHT OFF YOUR FACE!!
ME FIRST!! WHEEEE EEEEE--
...
...
TRY TO REMOVE THE MASK.
FSH

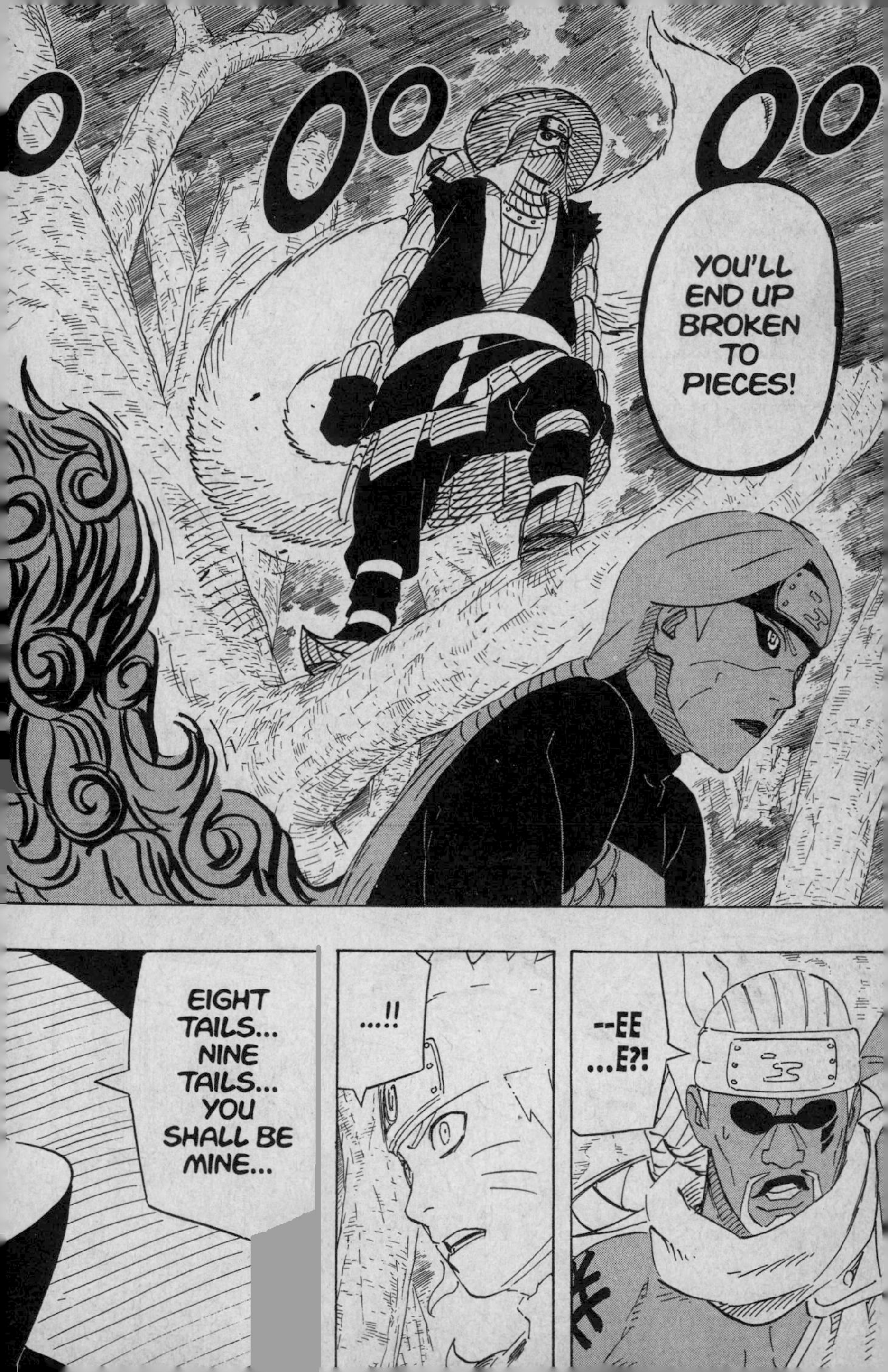

YOU'LL END UP BROKEN TO PIECES!
--EE ...E?!
...!!
EIGHT TAILS... NINE TAILS... YOU SHALL BE MINE...

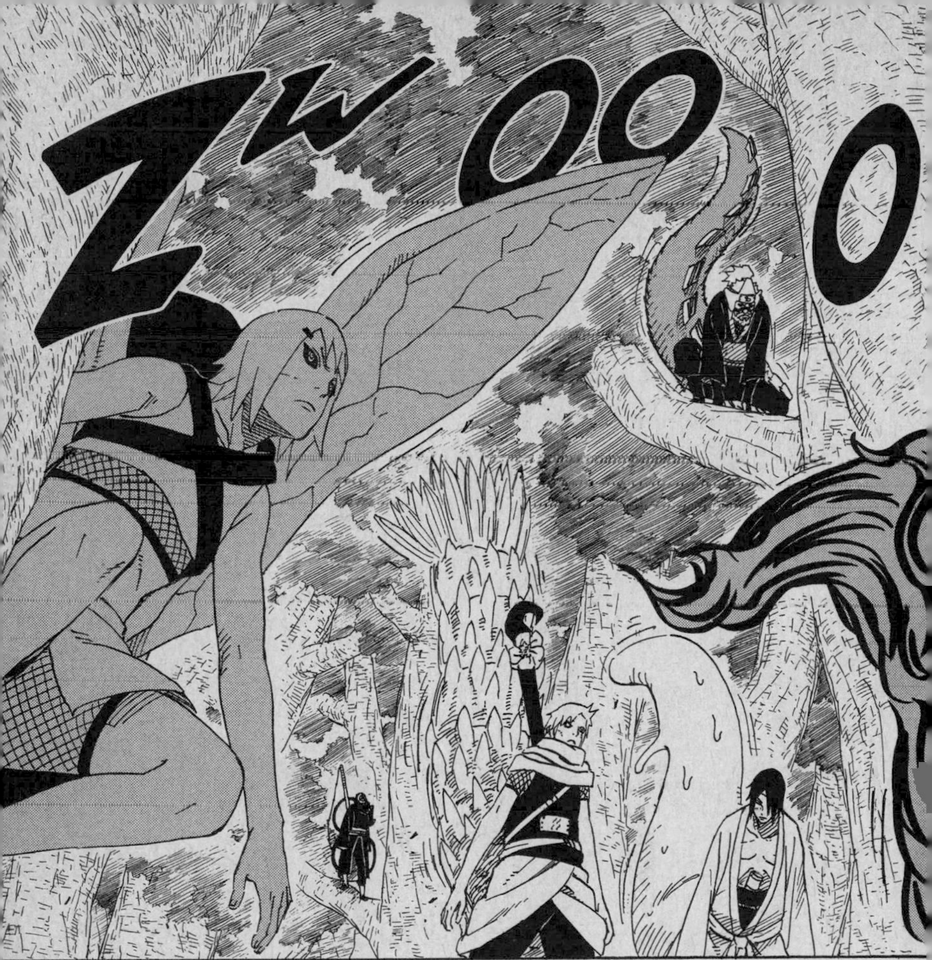
ZWOOOO
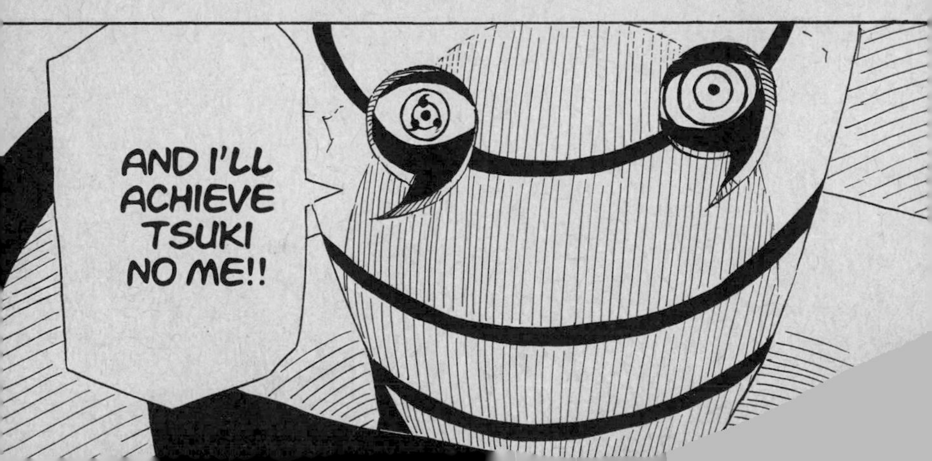
AND I'LL ACHIEVE TSUKI NO ME!!

NARUTO

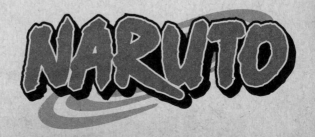

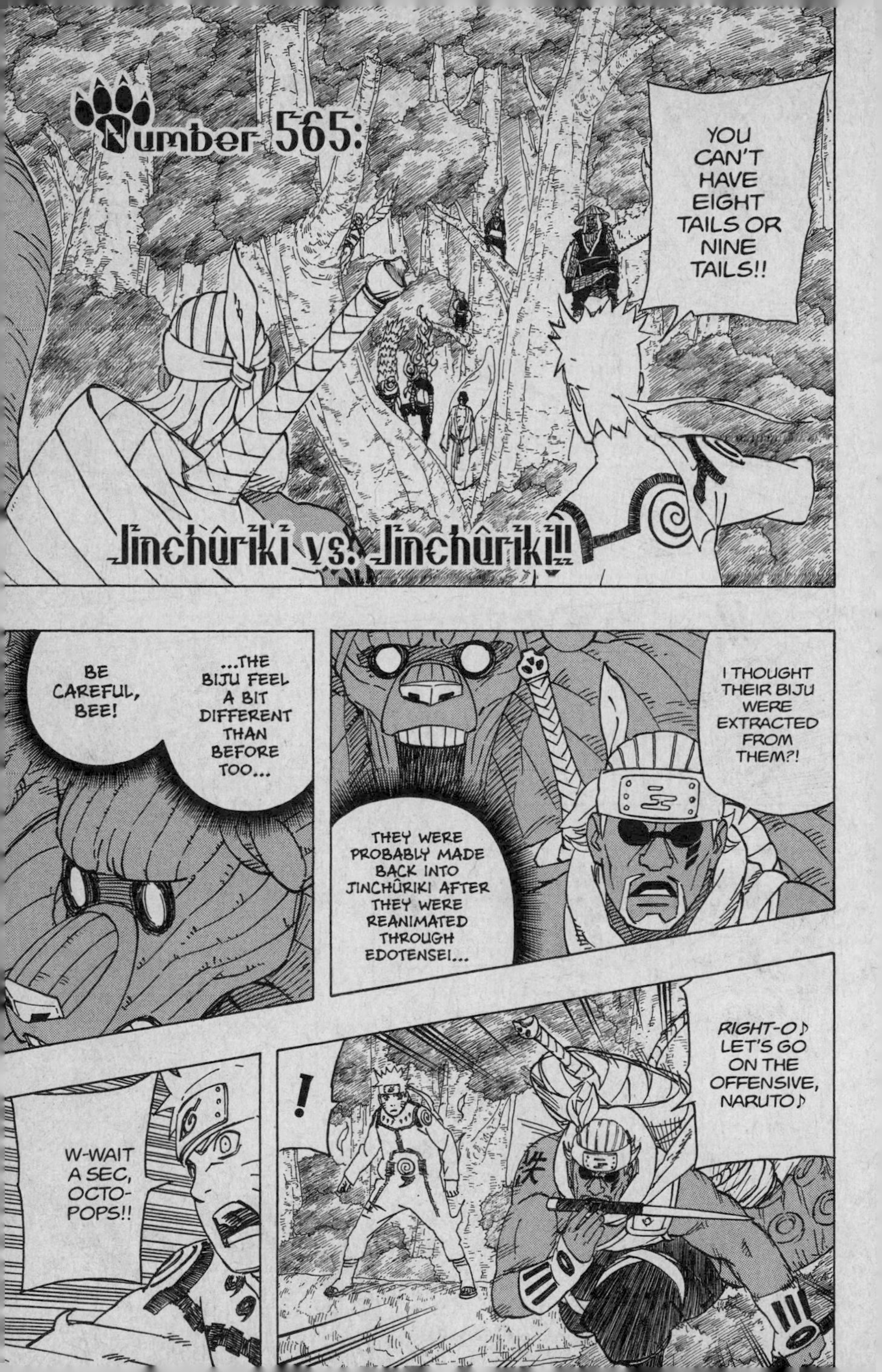

Number 565:
Jinchûriki vs. Jinchûriki!!
YOU CAN'T HAVE EIGHT TAILS OR NINE TAILS!!
I THOUGHT THEIR BIJU WERE EXTRACTED FROM THEM?!
THEY WERE PROBABLY MADE BACK INTO JINCHÛRIKI AFTER THEY WERE REANIMATED THROUGH EDOTENSEI...
...THE BIJU FEEL A BIT DIFFERENT THAN BEFORE TOO...
BE CAREFUL, BEE!
RIGHT-O♪ LET'S GO ON THE OFFENSIVE, NARUTO♪
!
W-WAIT A SEC, OCTO-POPS!!

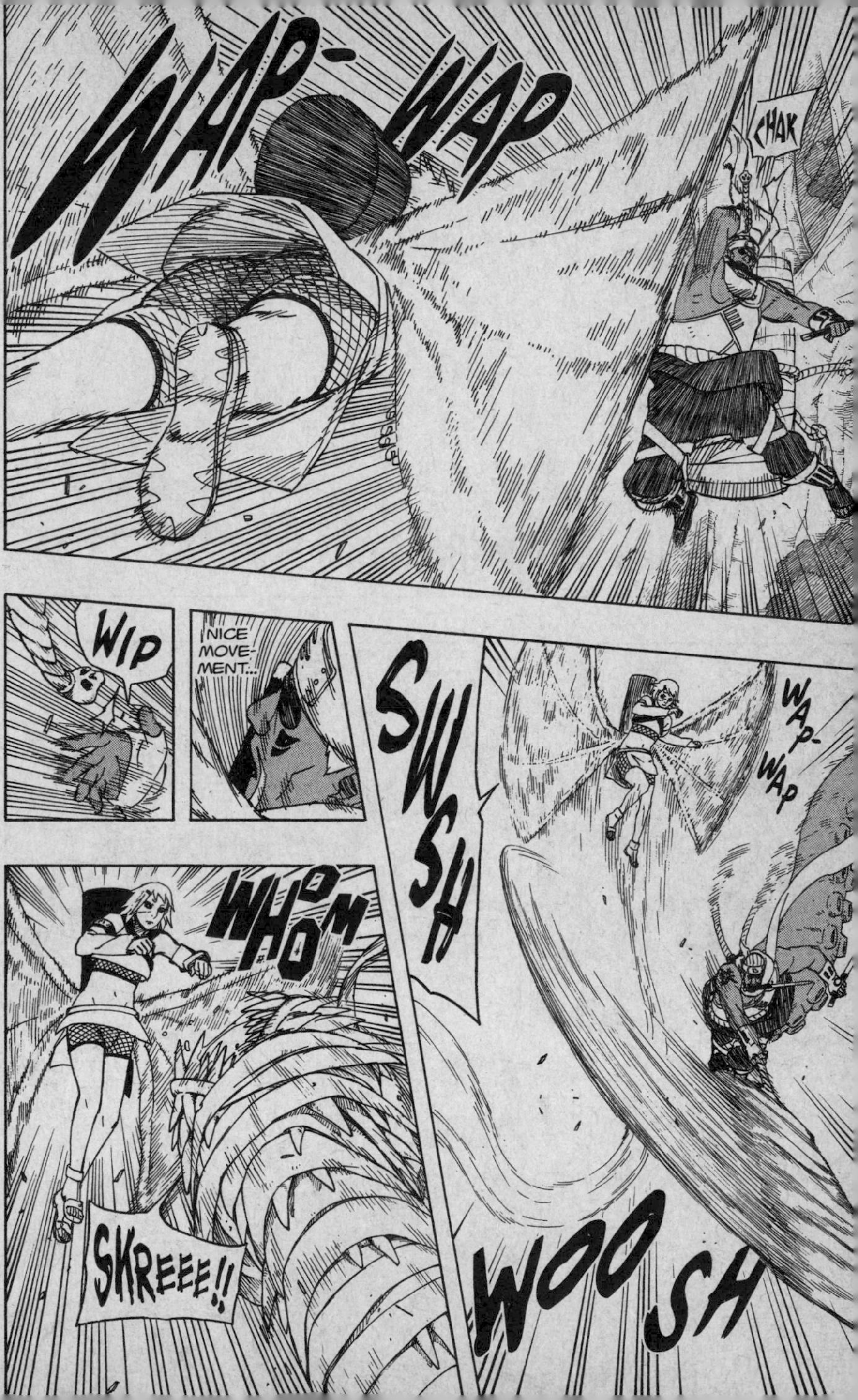
WAP-WAP
CHAK
SWISH
WAP-WAP
WOOSH
NICE MOVEMENT...
WIP
WHOOM
SKREEE!!

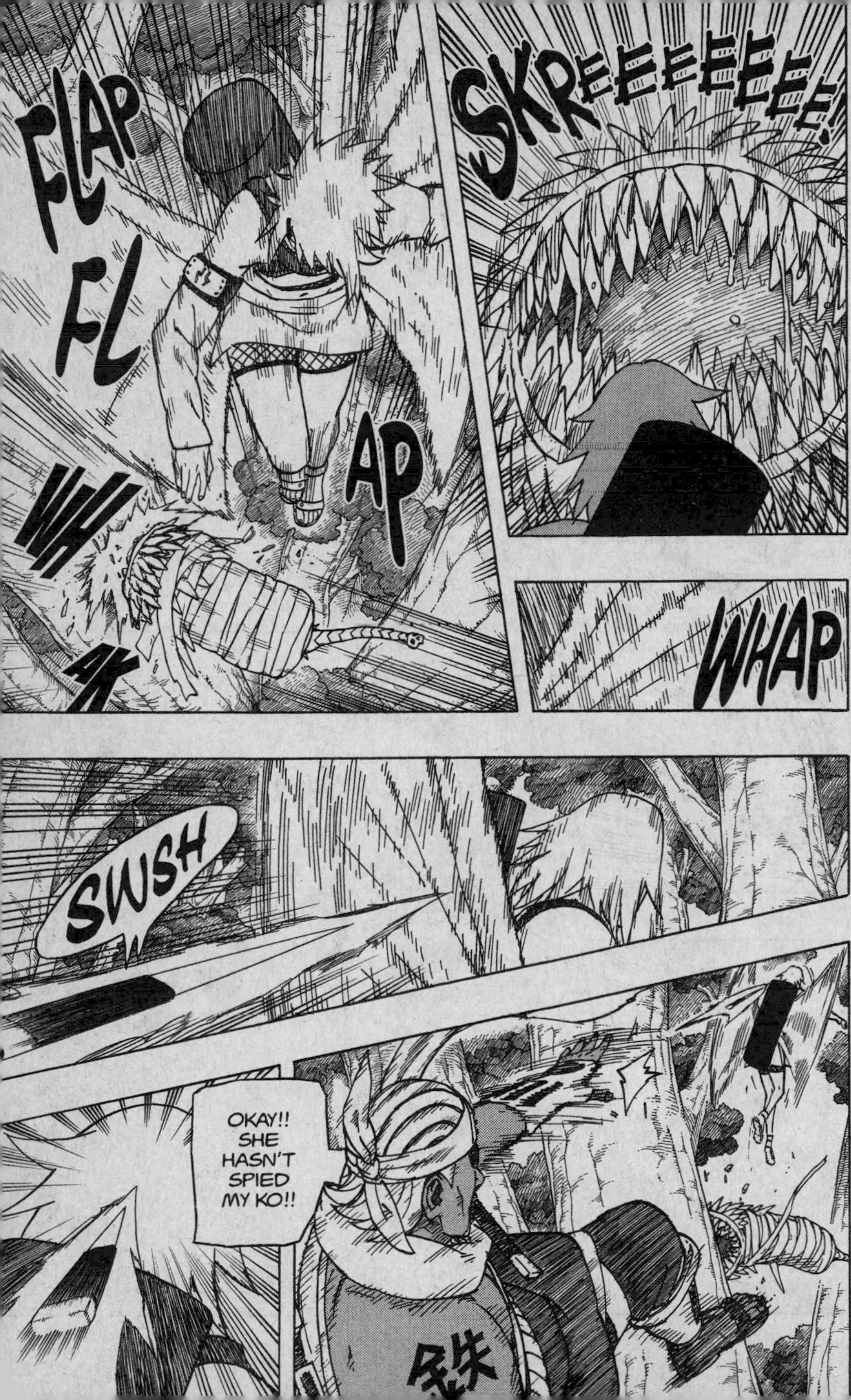
SKREEEEEEEEE!
WHAP
FLAP
FLAP
WHAK
SWSH
OKAY!! SHE HASN'T SPIED MY KO!!

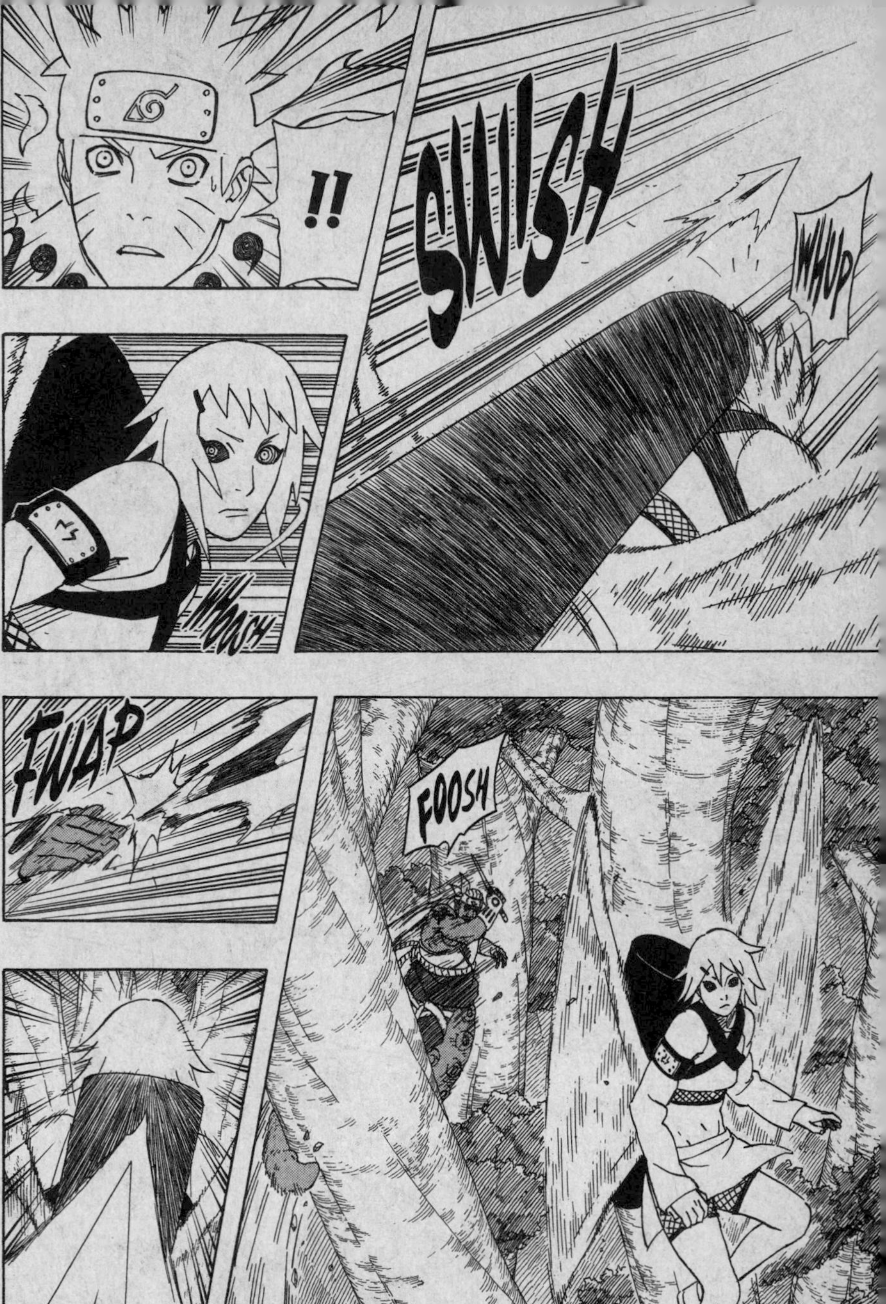
WHUP
SWISH
!!
WHOOSH
FOOSH
FWAP

READ THIS WAY

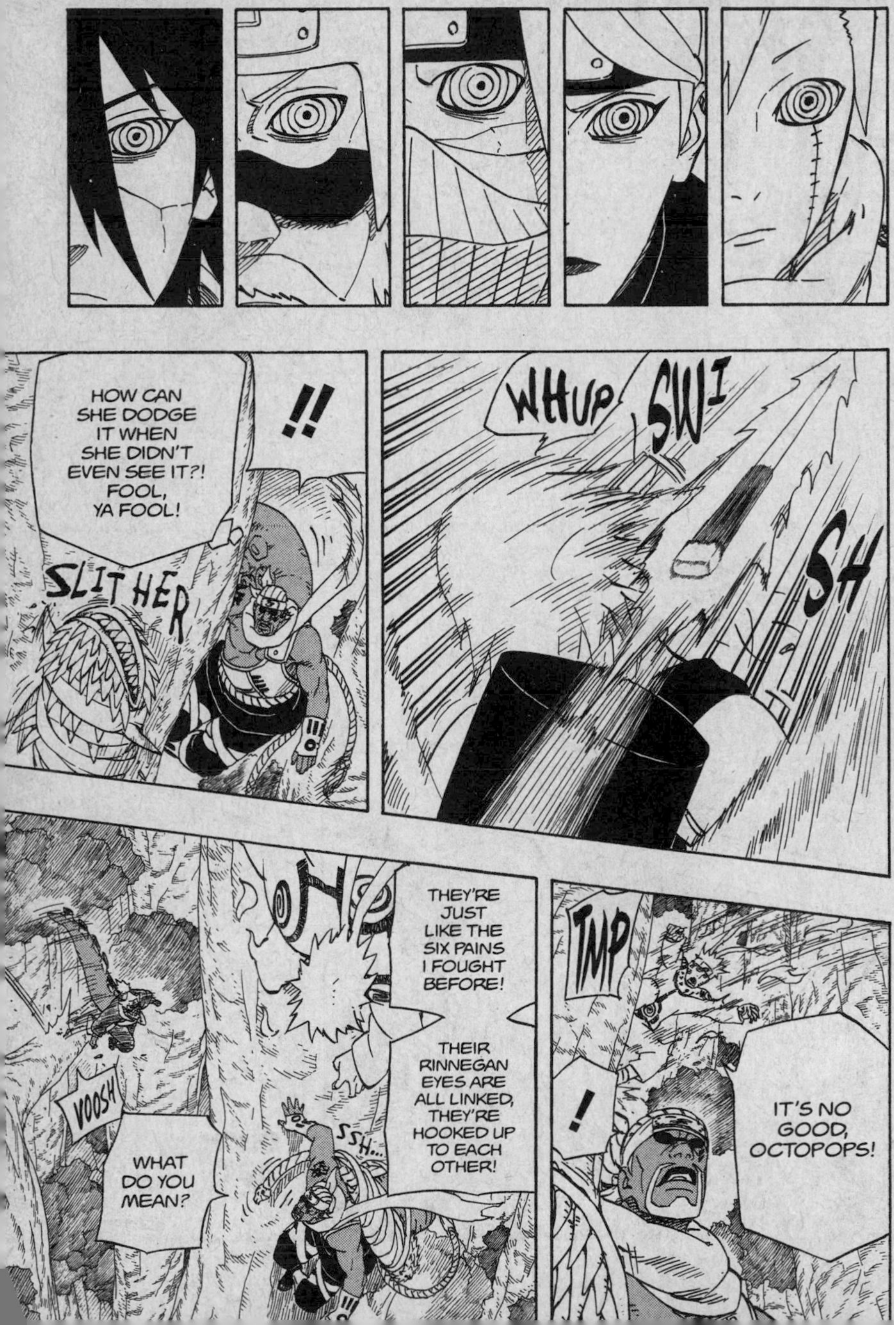
WHUP
SWI
SH
!!
HOW CAN SHE DODGE IT WHEN SHE DIDN'T EVEN SEE IT?! FOOL, YA FOOL!
SLITHER
TMP
!
IT'S NO GOOD, OCTOPOPS!
THEY'RE JUST LIKE THE SIX PAINS I FOUGHT BEFORE!
THEIR RINNEGAN EYES ARE ALL LINKED, THEY'RE HOOKED UP TO EACH OTHER!
SSH...
VOOSH
WHAT DO YOU MEAN?

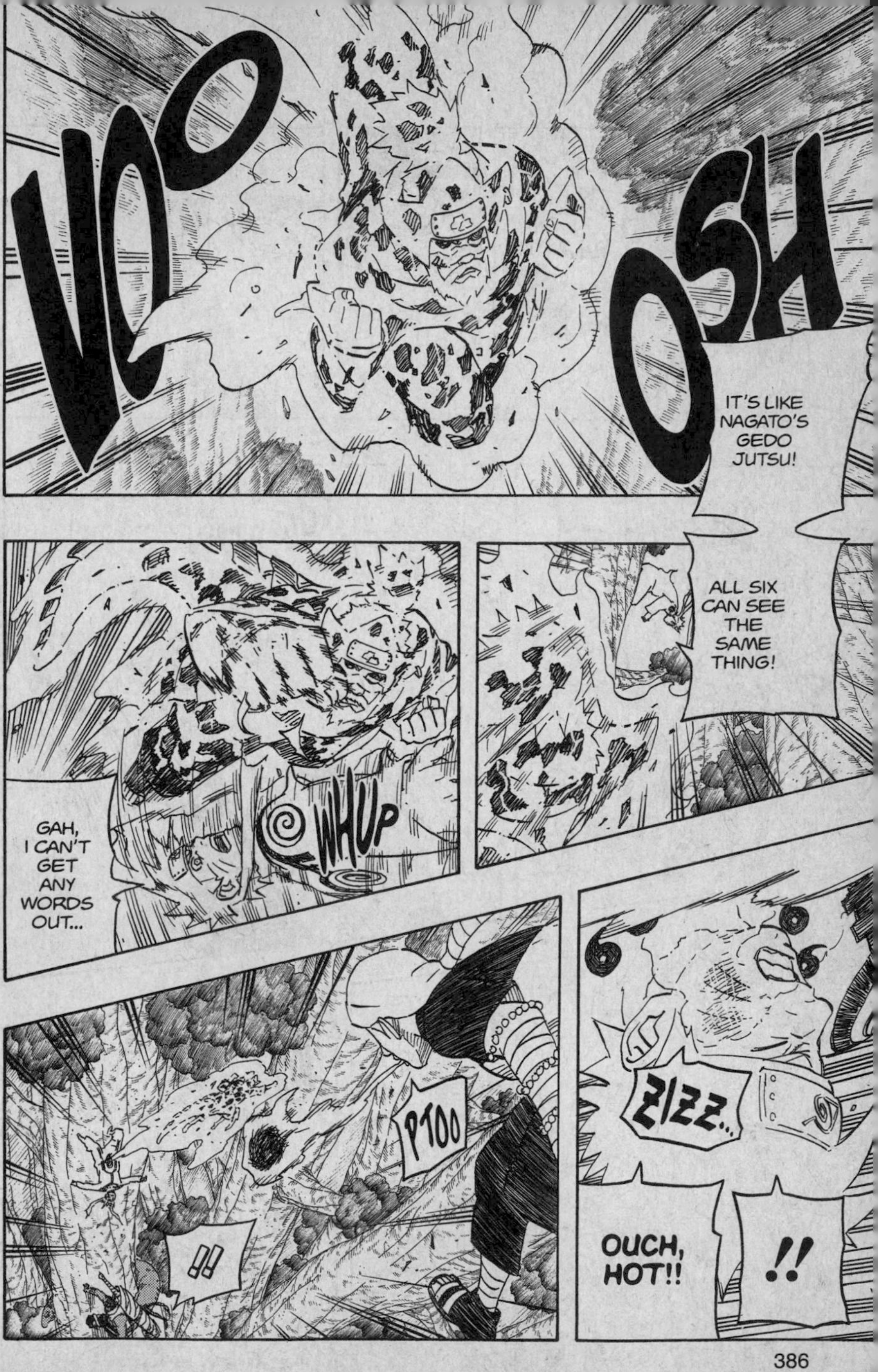
VOOOSH
IT'S LIKE NAGATO'S GEDO JUTSU!
ALL SIX CAN SEE THE SAME THING!
WHUP
GAH, I CAN'T GET ANY WORDS OUT...
ZIZZ...
OUCH, HOT!!
!!
PTOO
!!

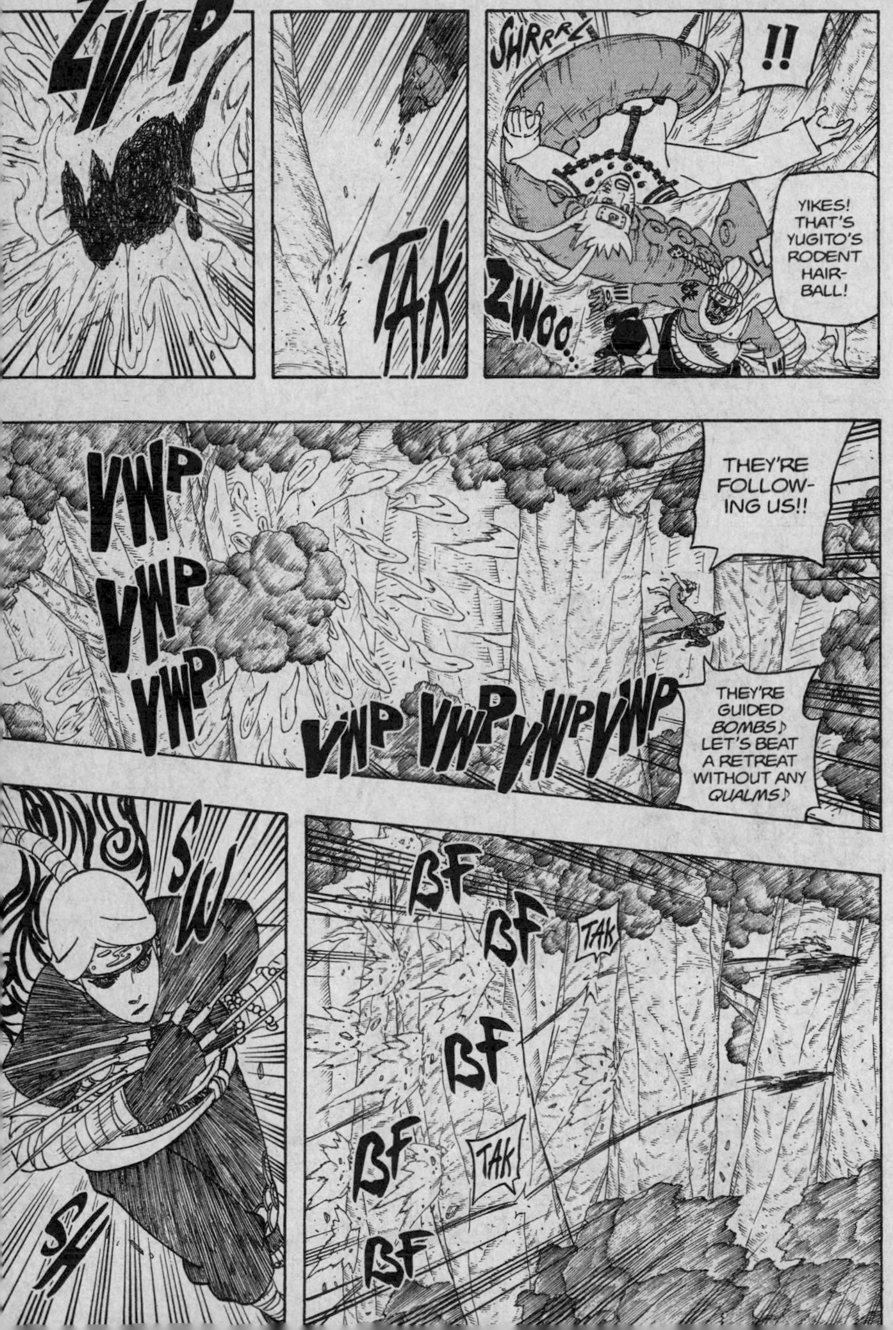
SHRRRL
!!
YIKES! THAT'S YUGITO'S RODENT HAIR-BALL!
ZWOO...
TAK
ZWIP
THEY'RE FOLLOW-ING US!!
THEY'RE GUIDED *BOMBS*♪ LET'S BEAT A RETREAT WITHOUT ANY *QUALMS*♪
VWP VWP VWP VWP VWP VWP VWP
VWP VWP VWP
BF
BF
TAK
BF
BF
TAK
BF
SW
SH

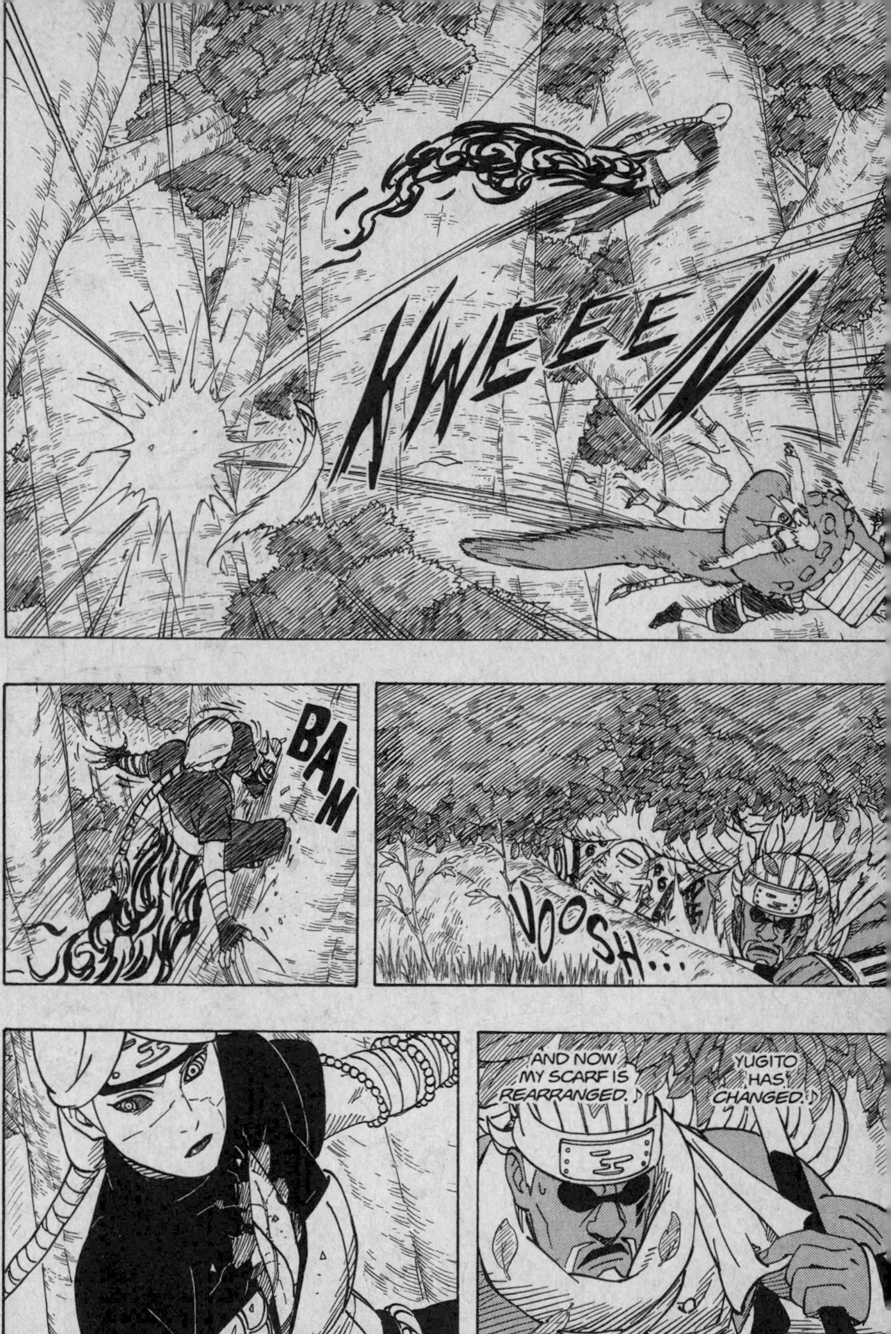
KWEEEN
VOOSH...
BAM
YUGITO HAS CHANGED.♪
AND NOW MY SCARF IS REARRANGED.♪

READ THIS WAY

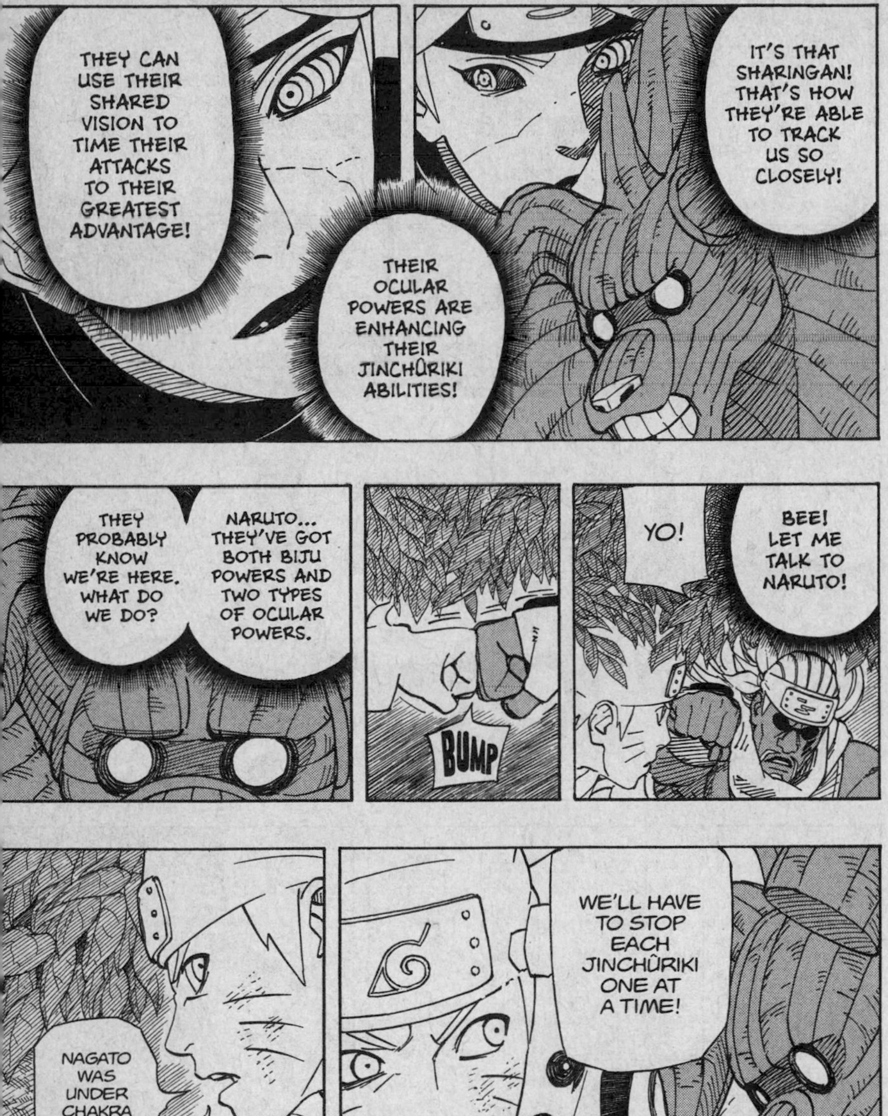
IT'S THAT SHARINGAN! THAT'S HOW THEY'RE ABLE TO TRACK US SO CLOSELY!
THEIR OCULAR POWERS ARE ENHANCING THEIR JINCHÛRIKI ABILITIES!
THEY CAN USE THEIR SHARED VISION TO TIME THEIR ATTACKS TO THEIR GREATEST ADVANTAGE!
BEE! LET ME TALK TO NARUTO!
YO!
BUMP
NARUTO... THEY'VE GOT BOTH BIJU POWERS AND TWO TYPES OF OCULAR POWERS.
THEY PROBABLY KNOW WE'RE HERE. WHAT DO WE DO?
WE'LL HAVE TO STOP EACH JINCHÛRIKI ONE AT A TIME!
NAGATO WAS UNDER CHAKRA CONTROL! THIS MUST BE THE SAME!

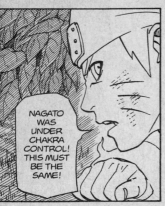

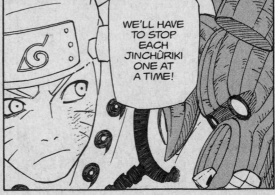

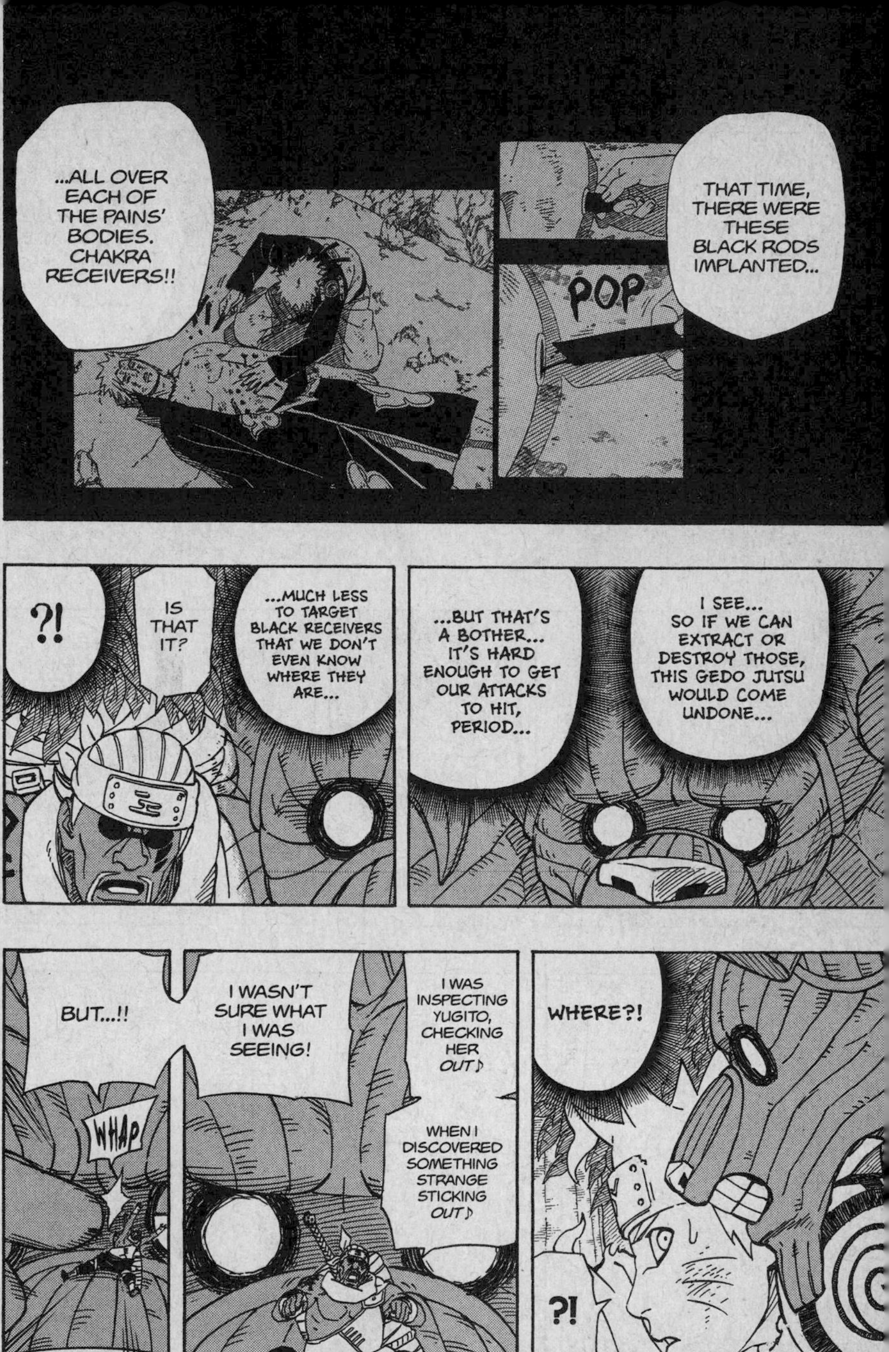
THAT TIME, THERE WERE THESE BLACK RODS IMPLANTED...
POP
...ALL OVER EACH OF THE PAINS' BODIES. CHAKRA RECEIVERS!!
I SEE... SO IF WE CAN EXTRACT OR DESTROY THOSE, THIS GEDO JUTSU WOULD COME UNDONE...
...BUT THAT'S A BOTHER... IT'S HARD ENOUGH TO GET OUR ATTACKS TO HIT, PERIOD...
...MUCH LESS TO TARGET BLACK RECEIVERS THAT WE DON'T EVEN KNOW WHERE THEY ARE...
IS THAT IT?
?!
WHERE?!
?!
I WAS INSPECTING YUGITO, CHECKING HER OUT♪
WHEN I DISCOVERED SOMETHING STRANGE STICKING OUT♪
I WASN'T SURE WHAT I WAS SEEING!
BUT...!!
WHAP

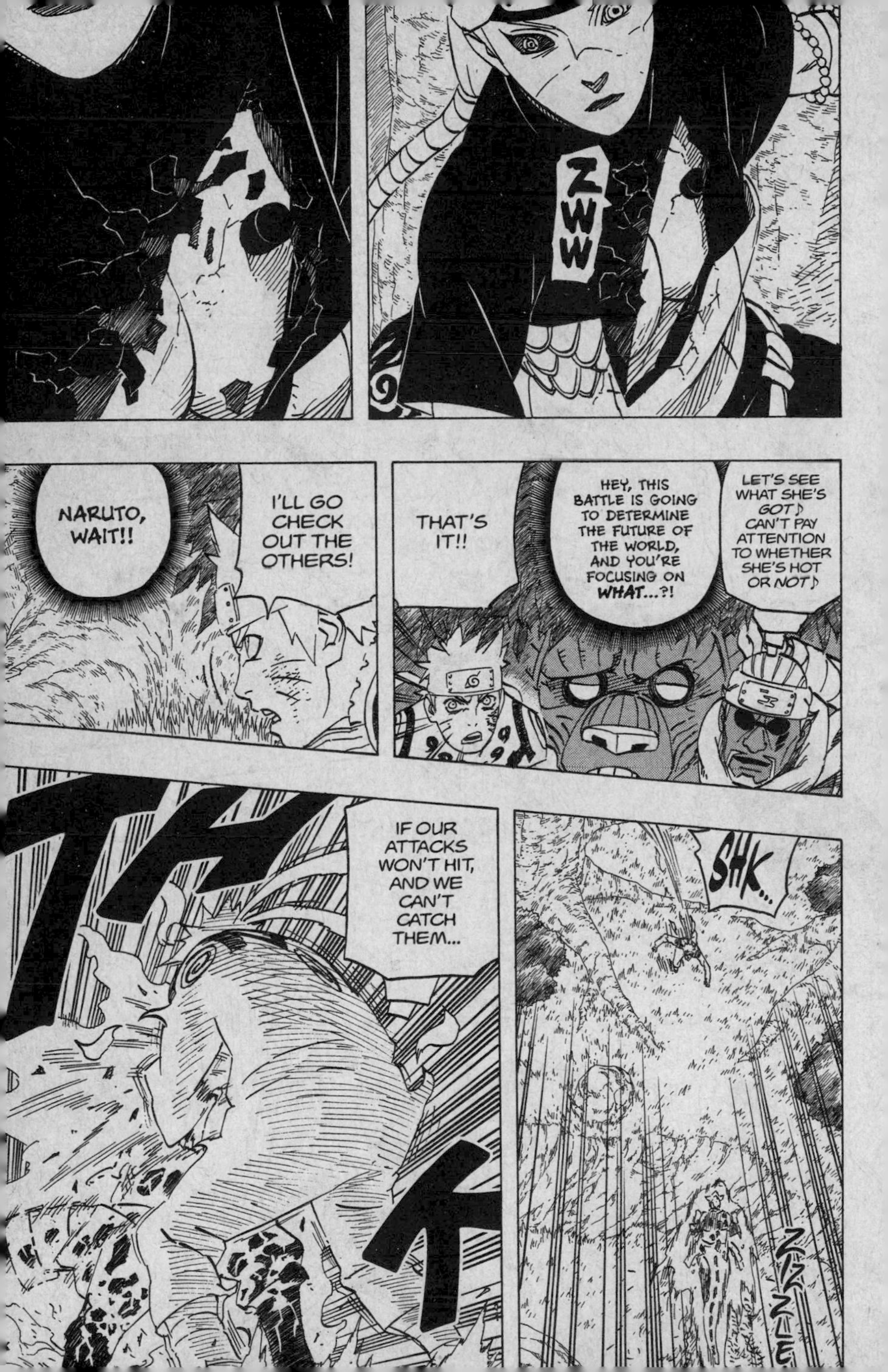
ZWW
LET'S SEE WHAT SHE'S GOT♪ CAN'T PAY ATTENTION TO WHETHER SHE'S HOT OR NOT♪
HEY, THIS BATTLE IS GOING TO DETERMINE THE FUTURE OF THE WORLD, AND YOU'RE FOCUSING ON WHAT...?!
THAT'S IT!!
I'LL GO CHECK OUT THE OTHERS!
NARUTO, WAIT!!
SHK...
ZIZZLE
IF OUR ATTACKS WON'T HIT, AND WE CAN'T CATCH THEM...

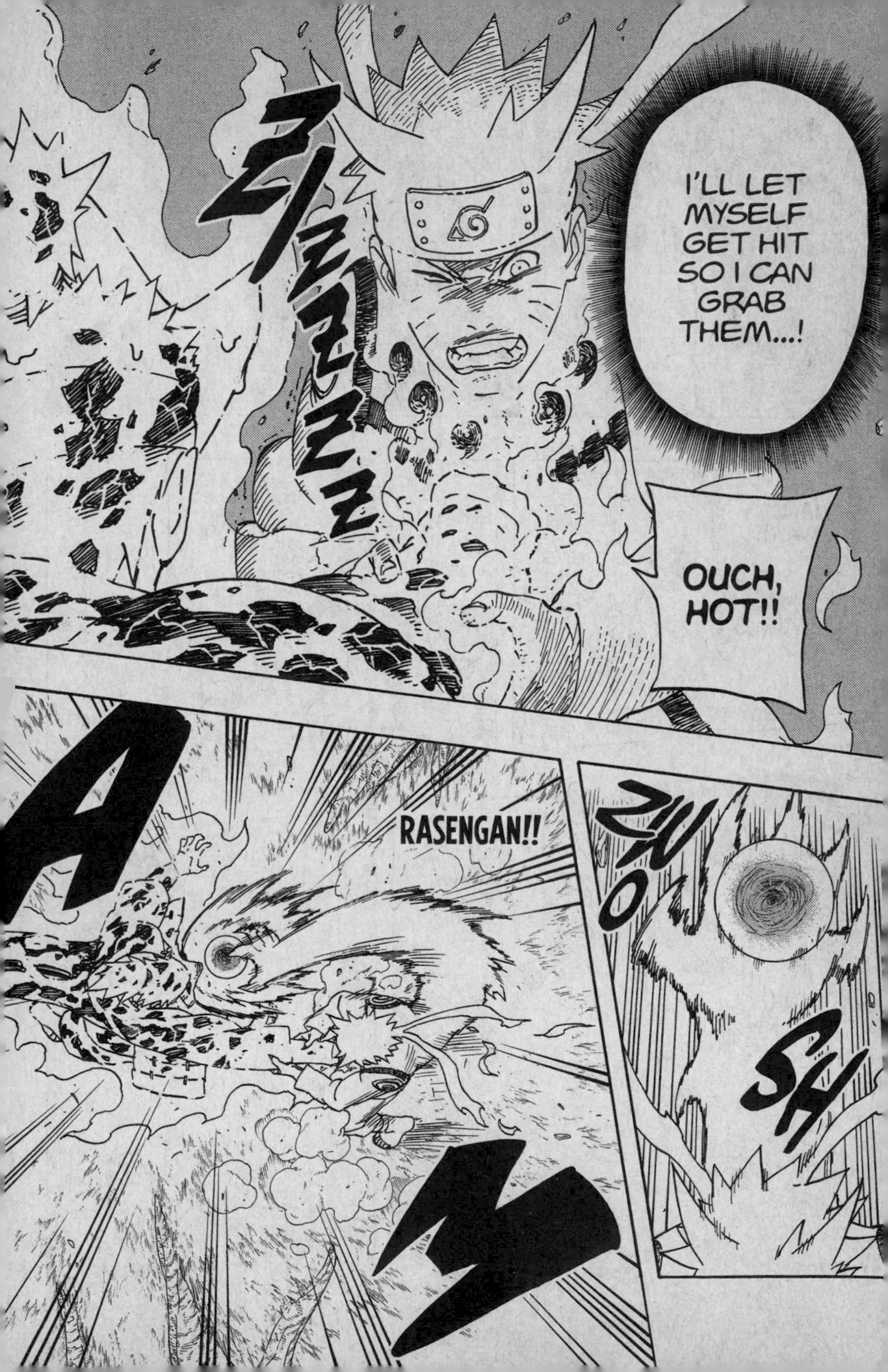
I'LL LET MYSELF GET HIT SO I CAN GRAB THEM...!
OUCH, HOT!!
RASENGAN!!

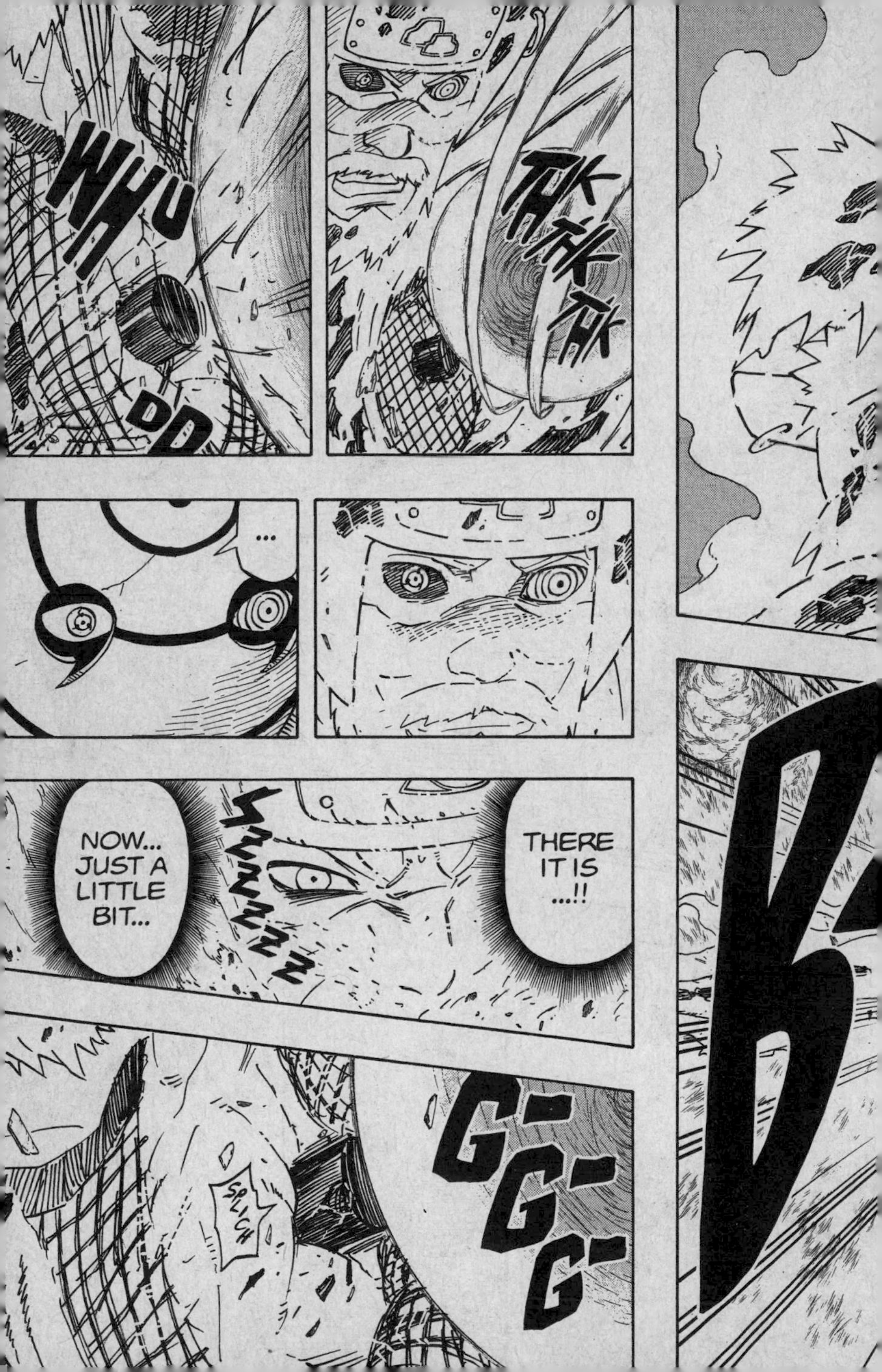
TAK TAK TAK
WHUDD
...
THERE IT IS ...!!
SZZZZZZZZ
NOW... JUST A LITTLE BIT...
B
G-G-G-
SPLICH

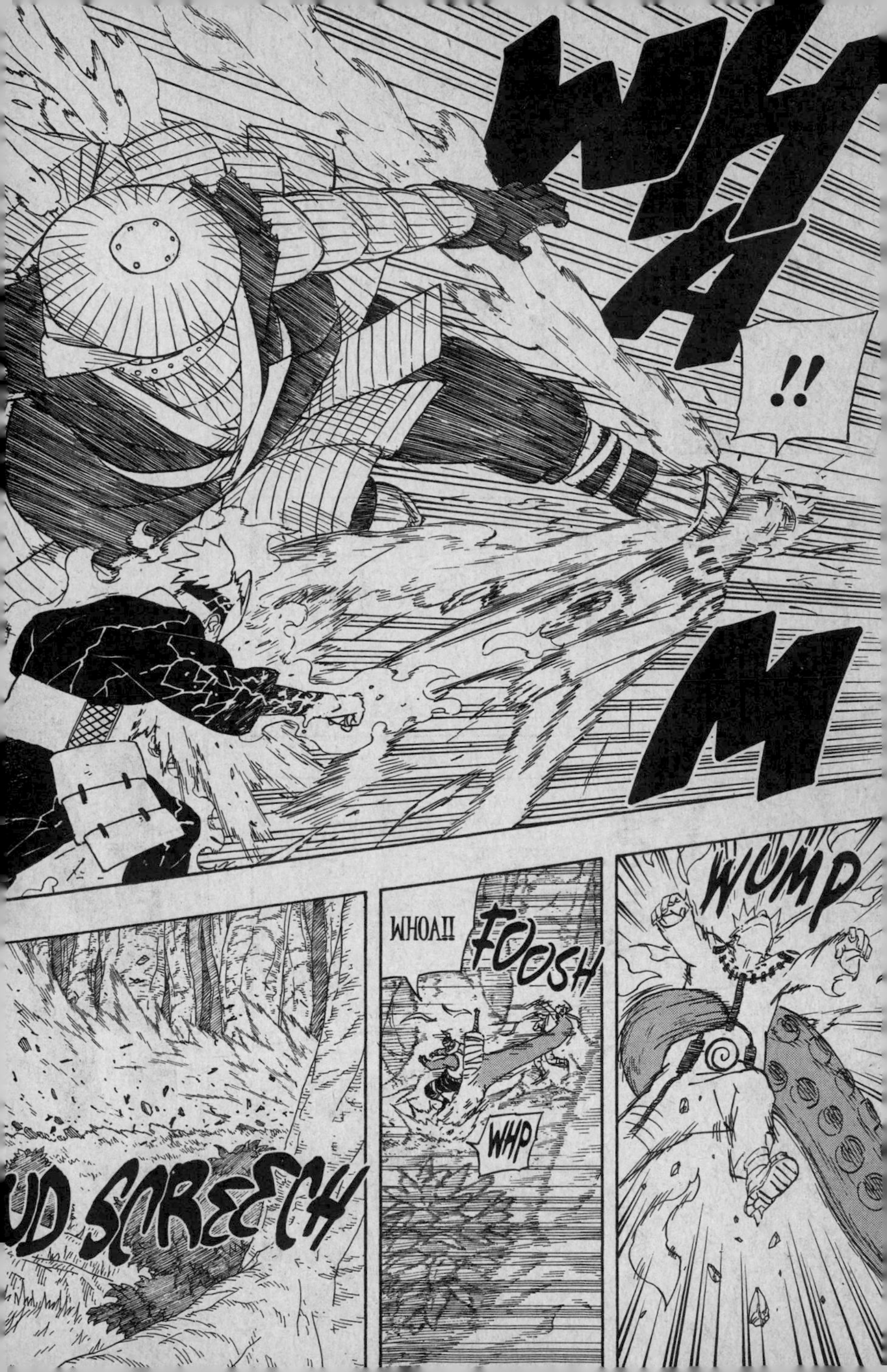
WHAAM
!!
WUMP
WHOA!!
FOOSH
WHP
UD SCREECH

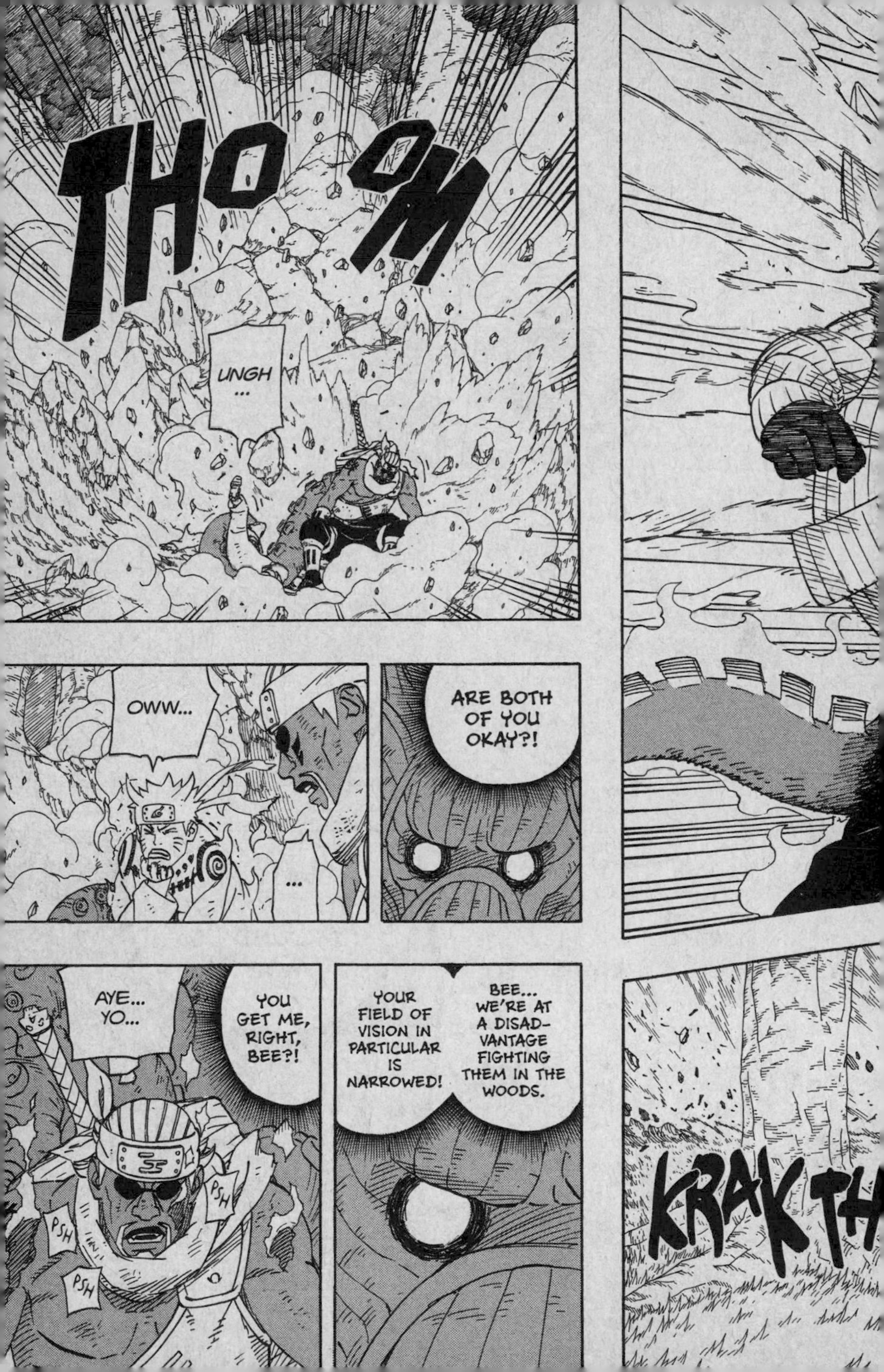
KRAKTH
THOOM
UNGH...
ARE BOTH OF YOU OKAY?!
OWW...
...
BEE... WE'RE AT A DISAD-VANTAGE FIGHTING THEM IN THE WOODS.
YOUR FIELD OF VISION IN PARTICULAR IS NARROWED!
YOU GET ME, RIGHT, BEE?!
AYE... YO...
PSH
PSH
PSH

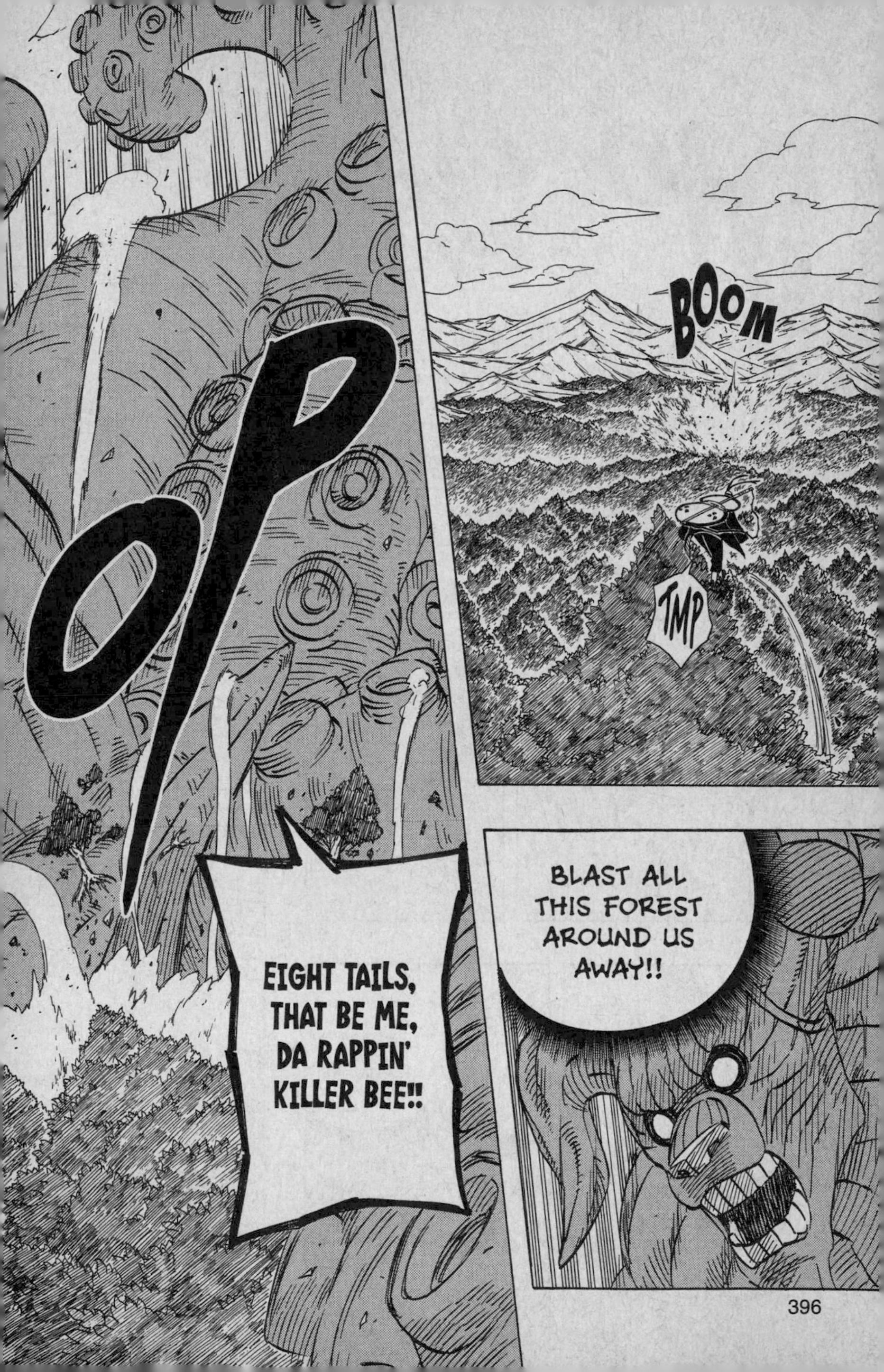
BOOM
TMP
BLAST ALL THIS FOREST AROUND US AWAY!!
OP
EIGHT TAILS, THAT BE ME, DA RAPPIN' KILLER BEE!!

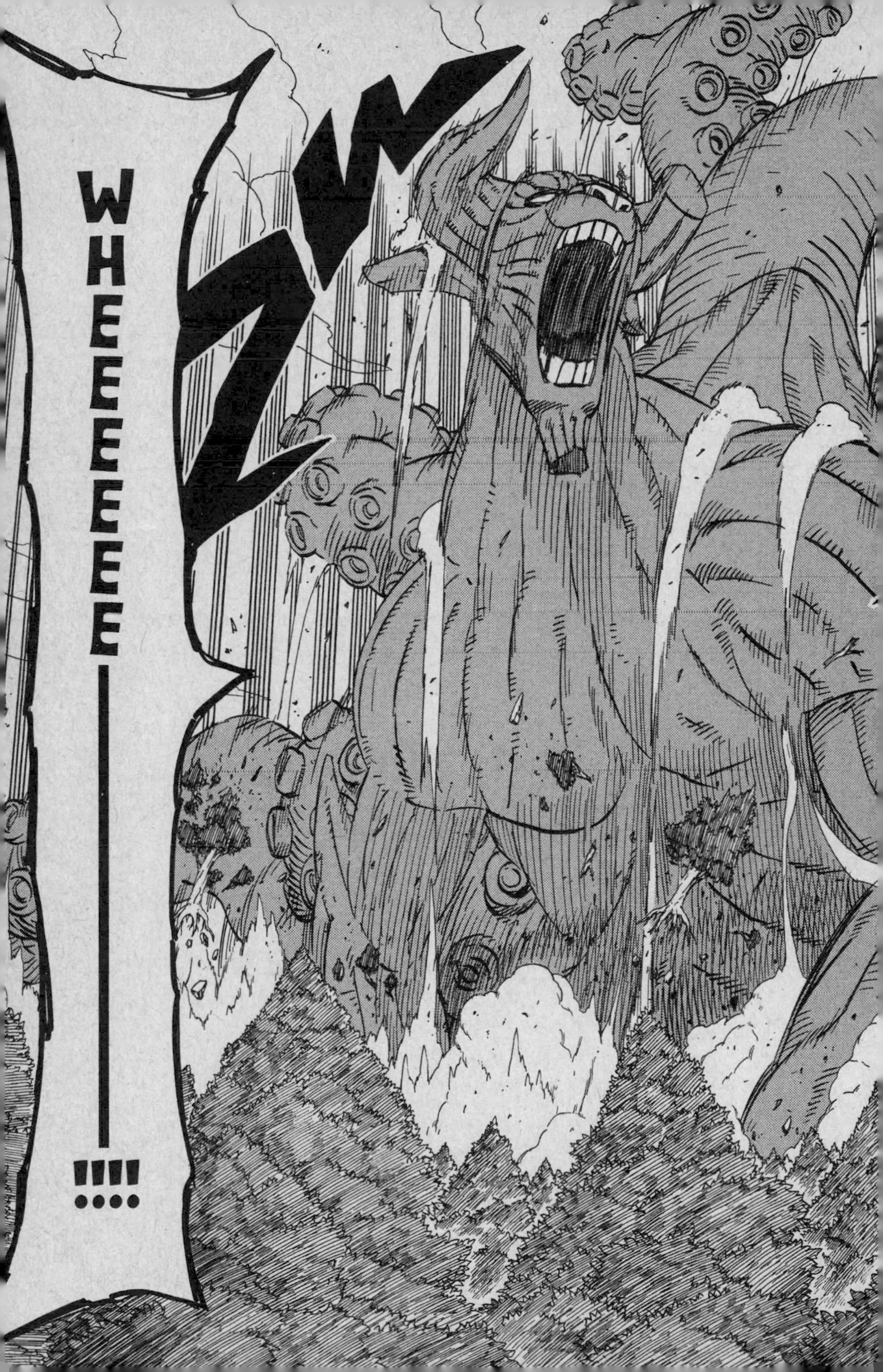
WHEEEEEE——!!!!

NARUTO

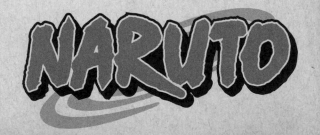

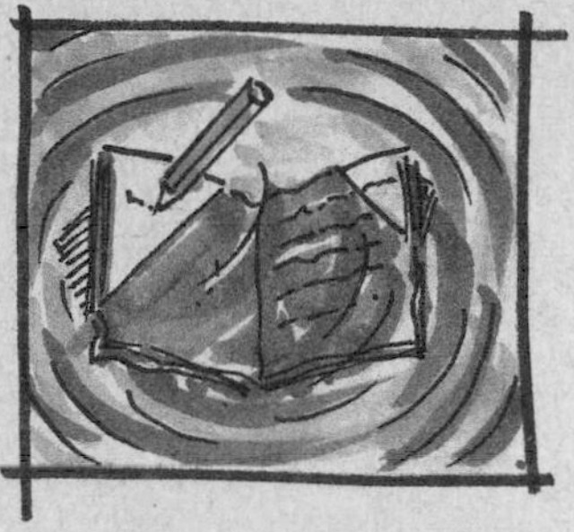

岸本斉史

For quite some time now, there have been occasions when I think of ideas while in the tub. It's because the blood flow to my head improves and makes it easier for ideas to spring forth. However, I cannot take notes in the tub... And after I get out of the tub, before I realize it, I've ended up forgetting what those ideas inside my head were. Both my mind and body have been washed clean.

—Masashi Kishimoto, 2012

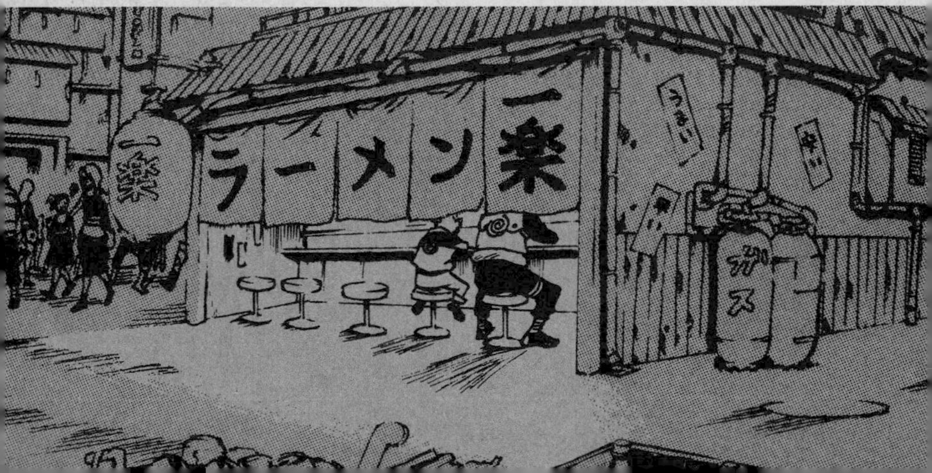
一楽
ラーメン一楽

NARUTO

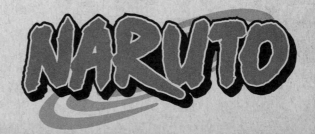

SHONEN JUMP MANGA EDITION

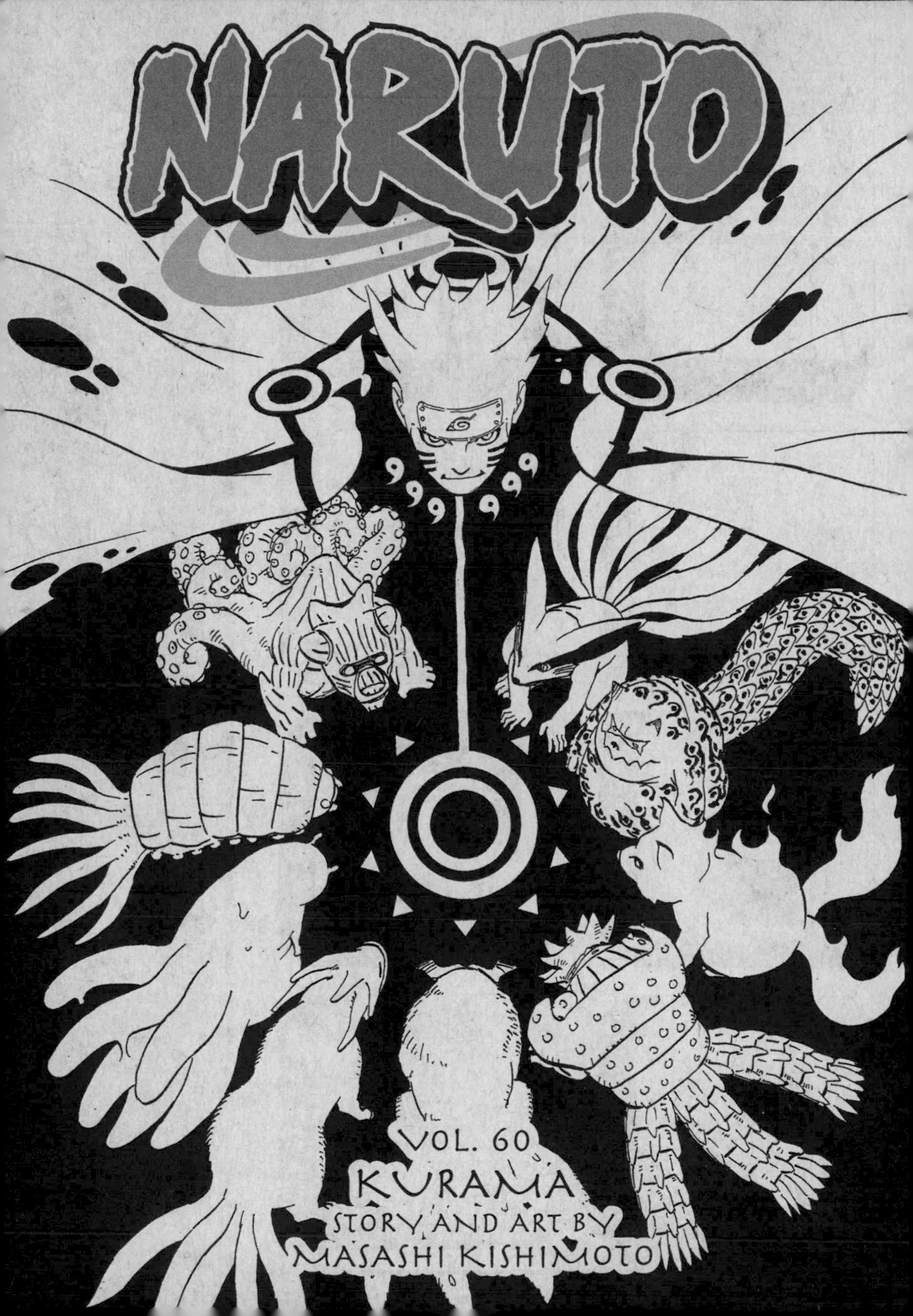

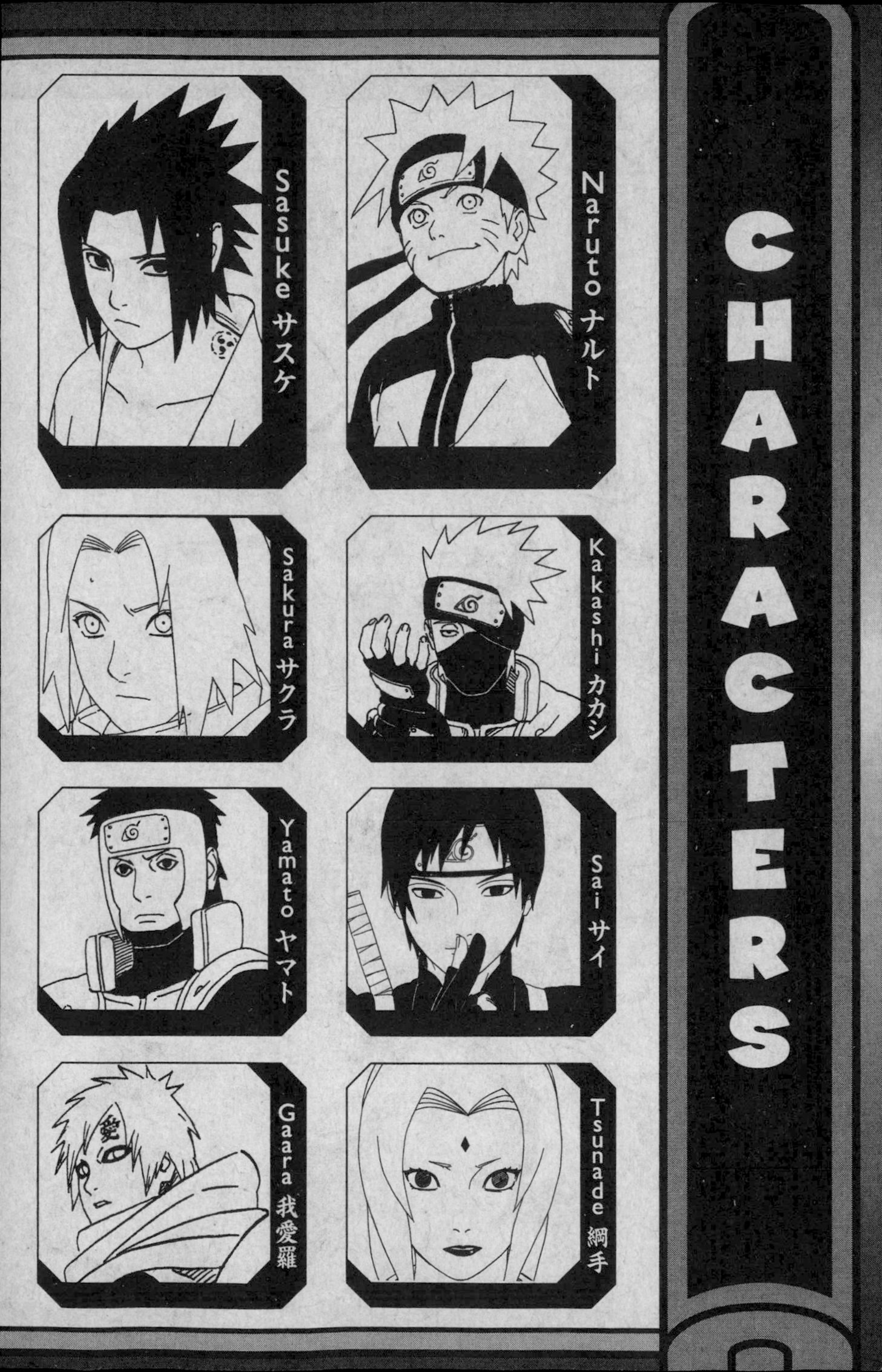
CHARACTERS
Naruto ナルト
Sasuke サスケ
Kakashi カカシ
Sakura サクラ
Sai サイ
Yamato ヤマト
Tsunade 綱手
Gaara 我愛羅

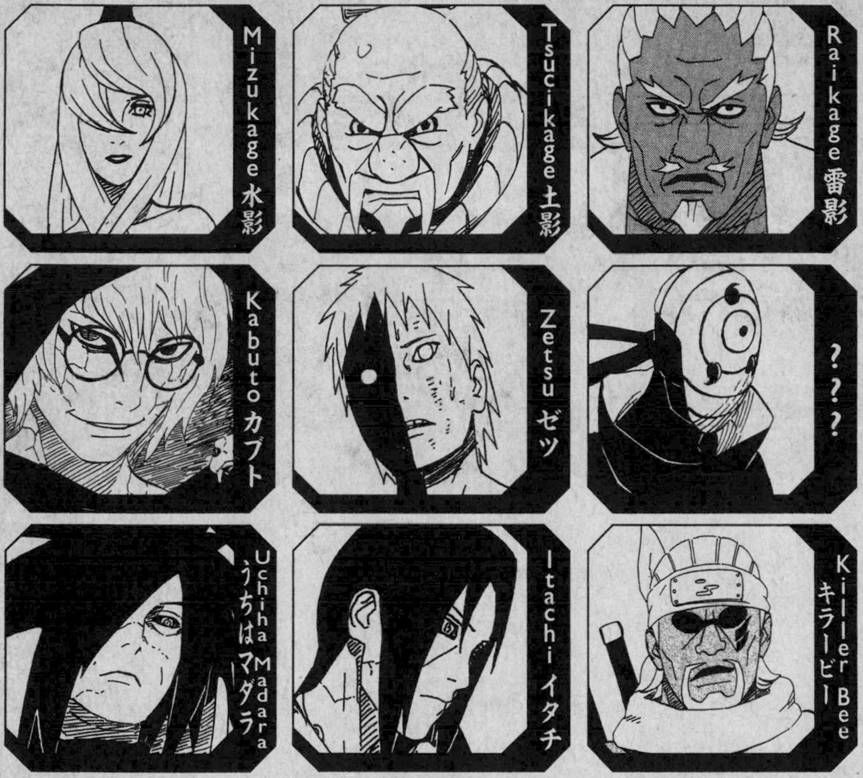
Raikage 雷影
Tsucikage 土影
Mizukage 水影
???
Zetsu ゼツ
Kabuto カブト
Killer Bee キラービー
Itachi イタチ
Uchiha Madara うちはマダラ

THE STORY SO FAR...

Naruto, the biggest troublemaker at the Ninja Academy in the Village of Konohagakure, finally becomes a ninja along with his classmates Sasuke and Sakura. They grow and mature through countless trials and battles. However, Sasuke, unable to give up his quest for vengeance, leaves Konohagakure to seek Orochimaru and his power.

Two years pass. Naruto grows up and engages in fierce battles against the Tailed Beast-targeting Akatsuki. Elsewhere, after winning the heroic battle against Itachi and learning his older brother's true intentions, Sasuke allies with the Akatsuki and sets out to destroy Konoha.

The Fourth Great Ninja War against the Akatsuki begins. After a series of unfavorable battles early on, the Allied Shinobi Forces begin to rally and make a comeback. However, the war situation deteriorates once again thanks to Uchiha Madara, who has been summoned back to life by Kabuto, and the Five Shadows finally assemble upon the battlefield! Meanwhile, Naruto and Bee violently clash with six jinchûriki manipulated by the masked Madara!!

NARUTO

VOL. 60
KURAMA

CONTENTS

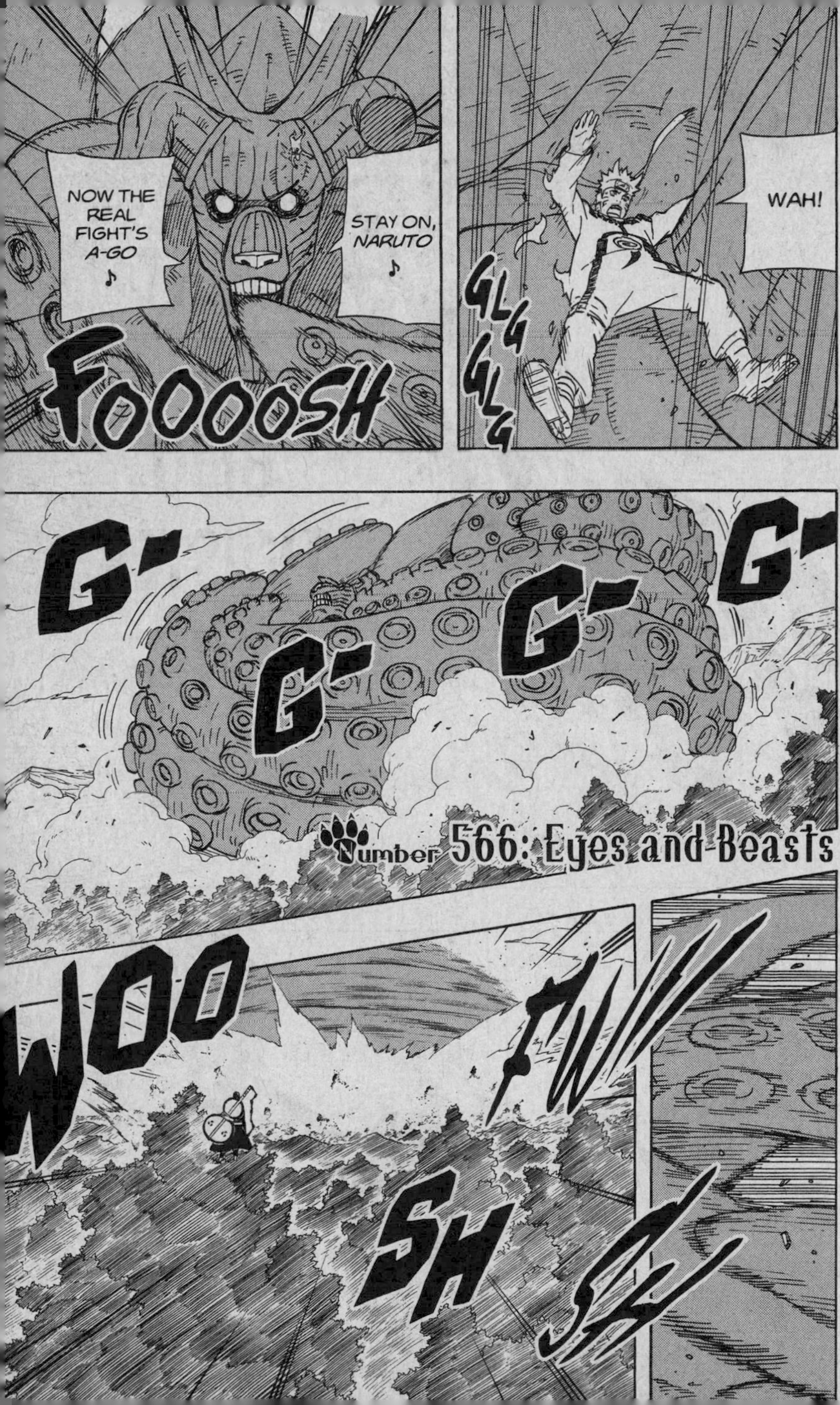
WAH!
GLG GLG
STAY ON, NARUTO ♪
NOW THE REAL FIGHT'S A-GO ♪
FOOOOSH
G- G- G- G- G-
Number 566: Eyes and Beasts
WOO
FW
SH

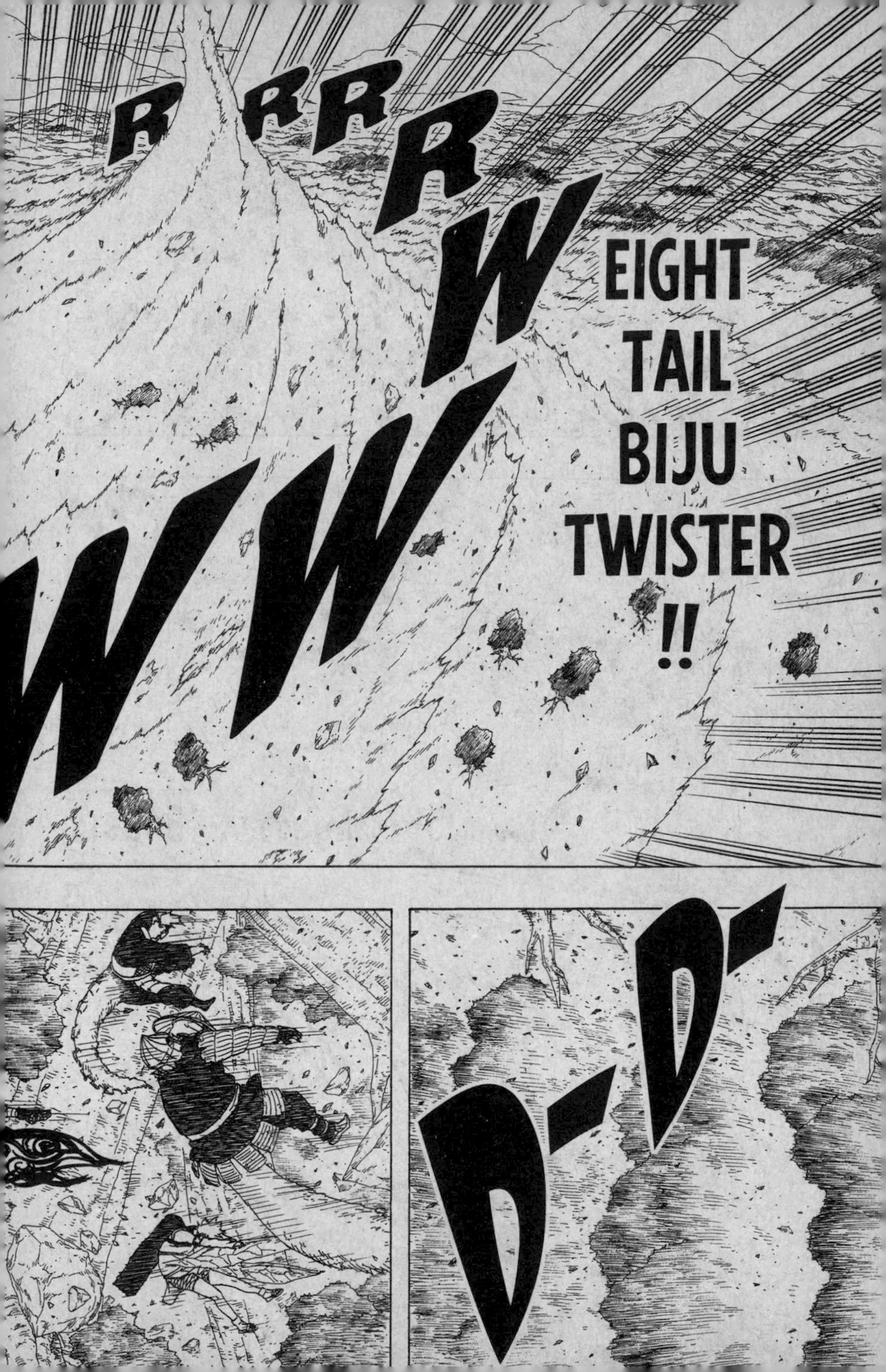
RRRRWWWW
EIGHT TAIL BIJU TWISTER!!
D-D

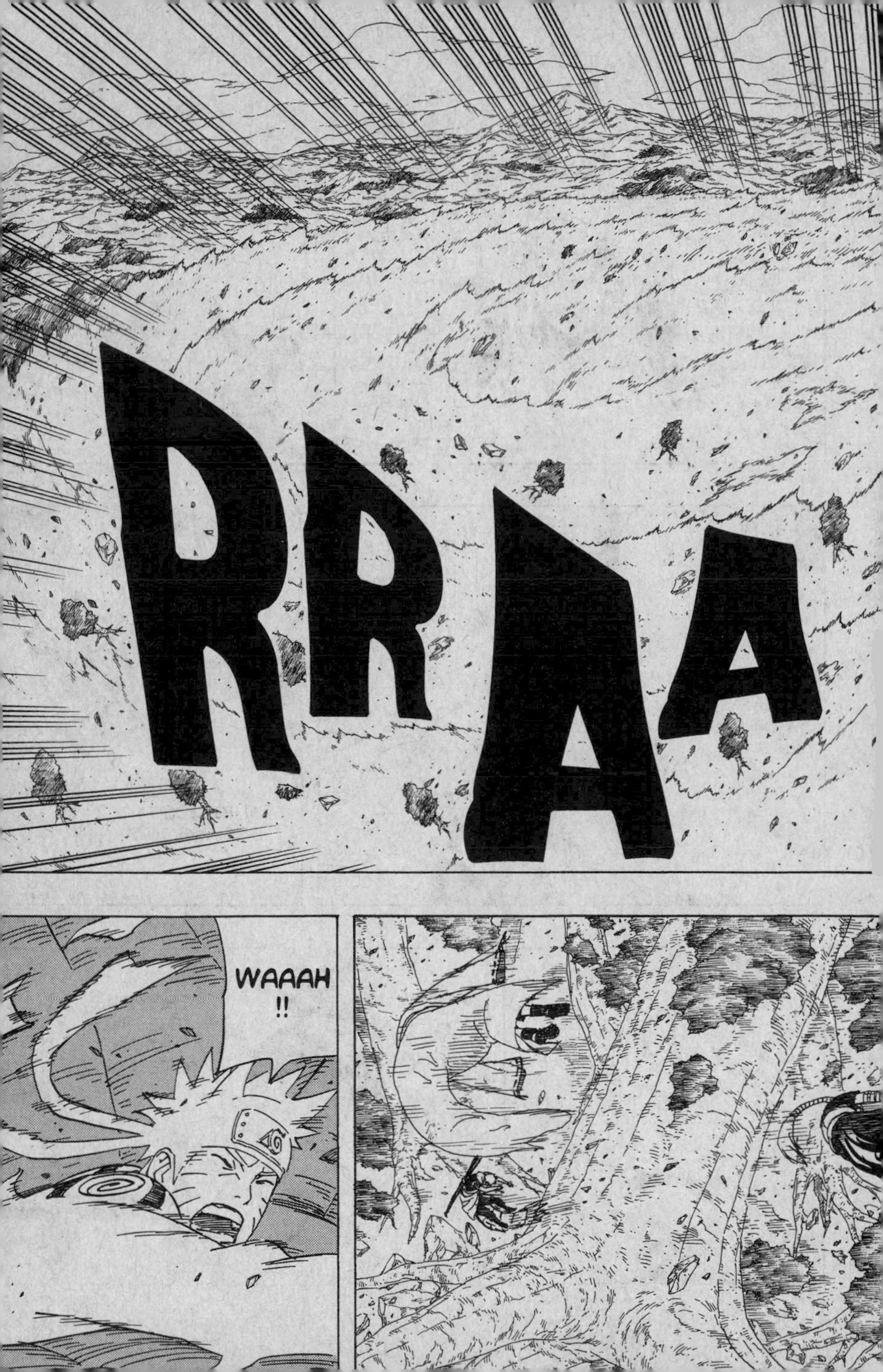
RRAA
WAAAH !!

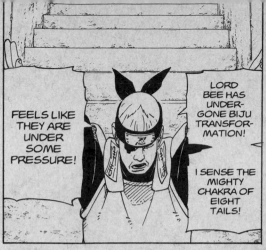

PLIP
PLIP
LORD BEE HAS UNDERGONE BIJU TRANSFORMATION!
I SENSE THE MIGHTY CHAKRA OF EIGHT TAILS!
FEELS LIKE THEY ARE UNDER SOME PRESSURE!
THIS DOESN'T SEEM GOOD...
BUT THE FIVE KAGE ARE HOLDING THEIR OWN AGAINST MADARA!
ALL'S OKAY SO FAR!
THEY ARE THE FIVE KAGE AFTER ALL!
WHAT ABOUT THE COMPANIES?!
FIRST AND SECOND COMPANIES ARE JUST ABOUT DONE ANNIHILATING THE ENEMY!

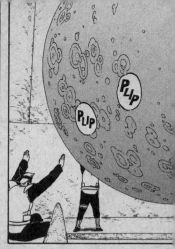

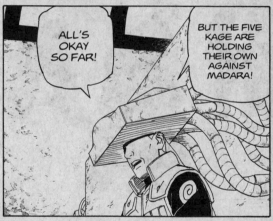

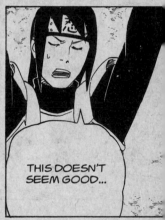

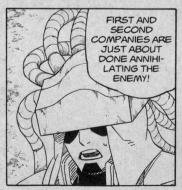

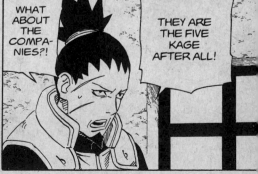

READ THIS WAY

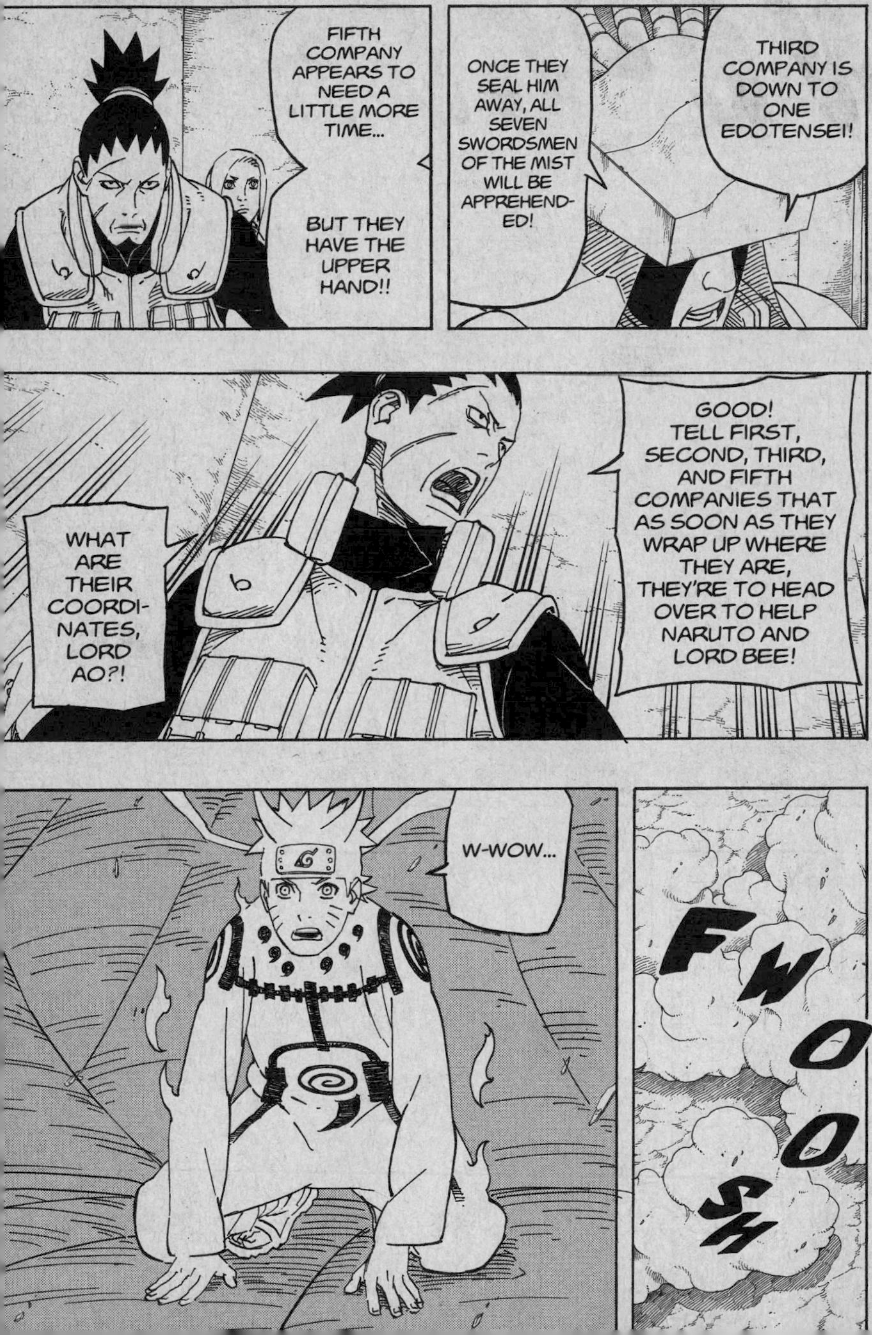
THIRD COMPANY IS DOWN TO ONE EDOTENSEI!
ONCE THEY SEAL HIM AWAY, ALL SEVEN SWORDSMEN OF THE MIST WILL BE APPREHENDED!
FIFTH COMPANY APPEARS TO NEED A LITTLE MORE TIME...
BUT THEY HAVE THE UPPER HAND!!
GOOD! TELL FIRST, SECOND, THIRD, AND FIFTH COMPANIES THAT AS SOON AS THEY WRAP UP WHERE THEY ARE, THEY'RE TO HEAD OVER TO HELP NARUTO AND LORD BEE!
WHAT ARE THEIR COORDINATES, LORD AO?!
FWOOSH
W-WOW...

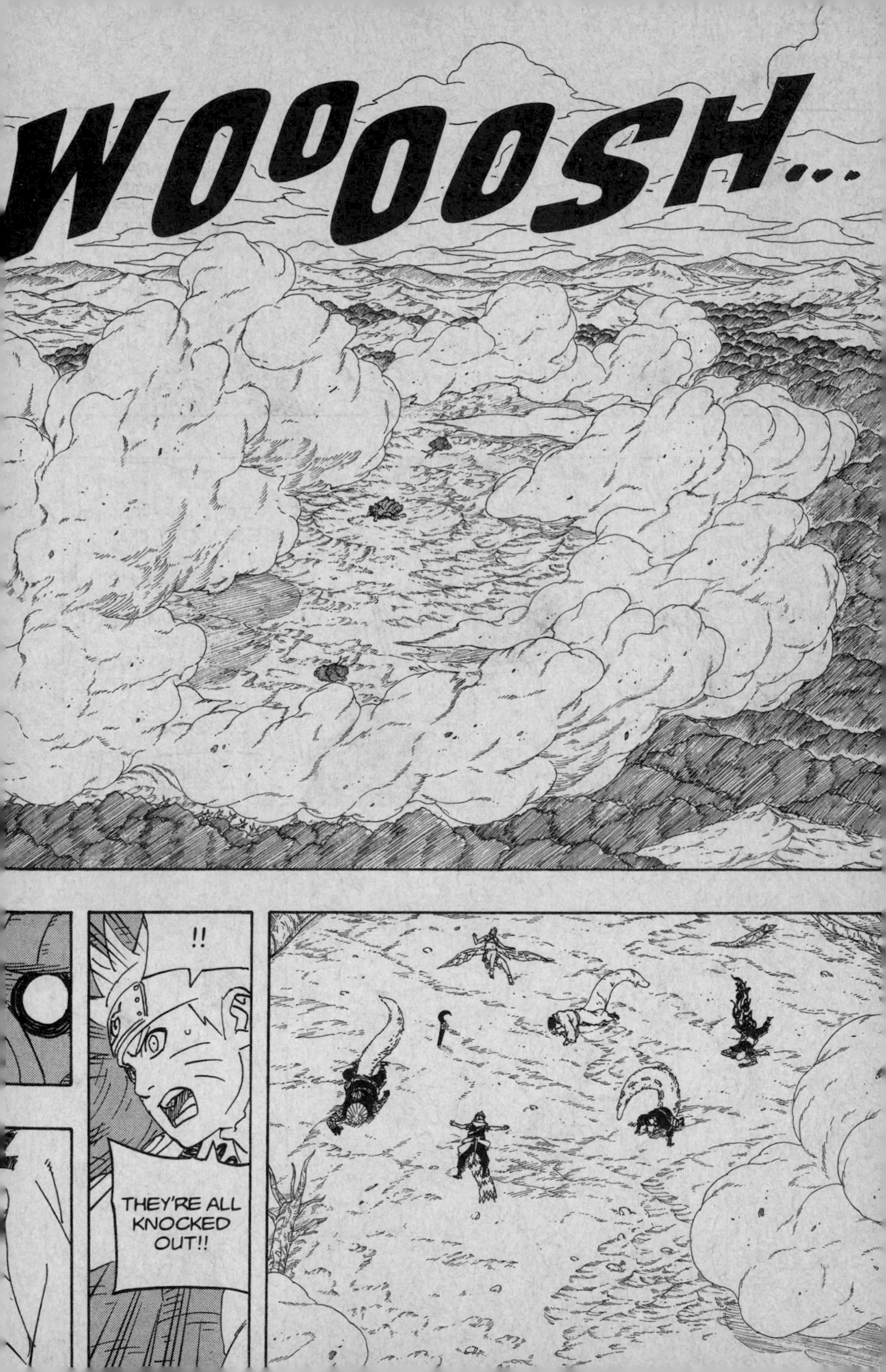
WOOOOSH...
!!
THEY'RE ALL KNOCKED OUT!!

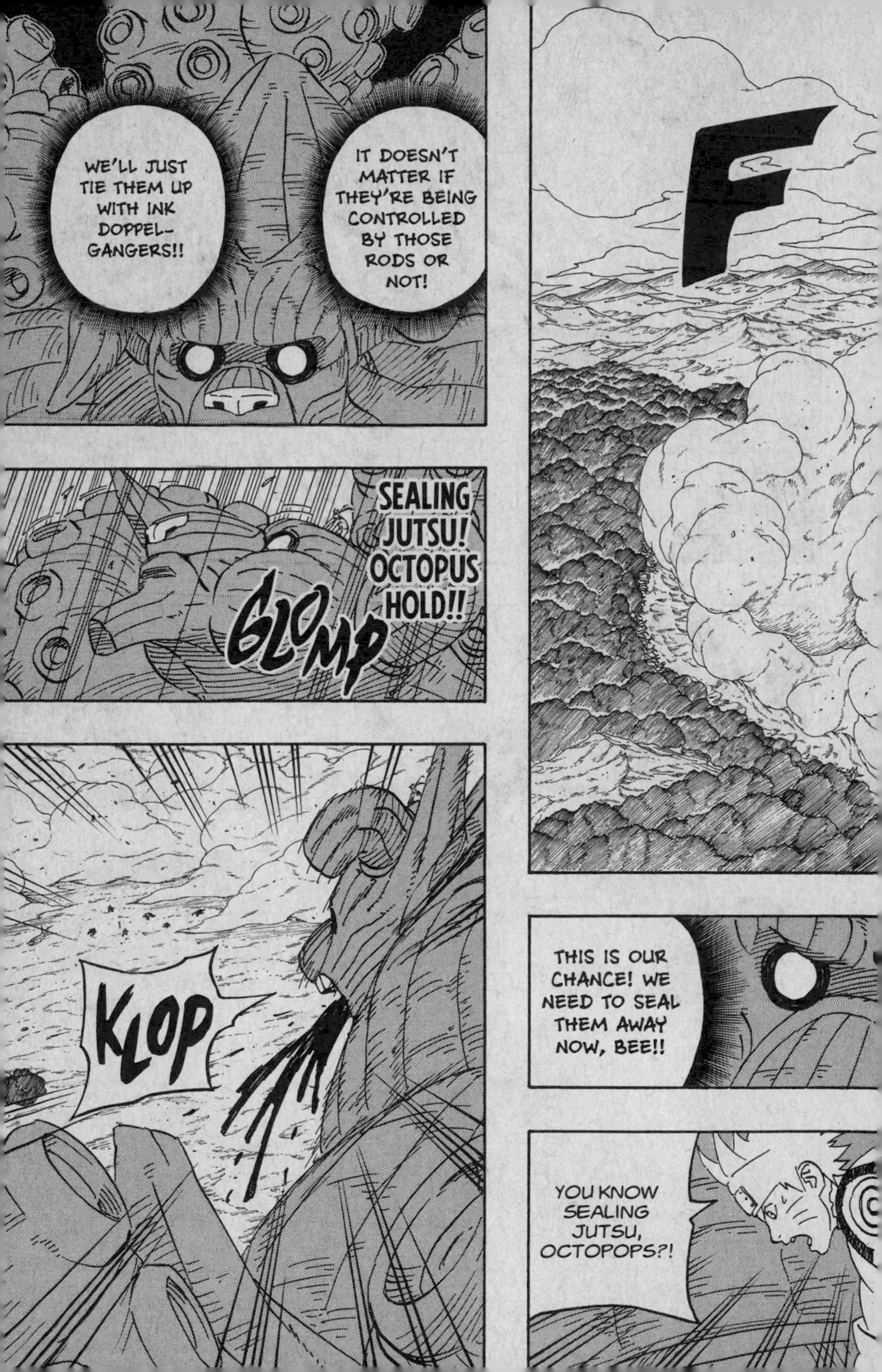
F
THIS IS OUR CHANCE! WE NEED TO SEAL THEM AWAY NOW, BEE!!
YOU KNOW SEALING JUTSU, OCTOPOPS?!
IT DOESN'T MATTER IF THEY'RE BEING CONTROLLED BY THOSE RODS OR NOT!
WE'LL JUST TIE THEM UP WITH INK DOPPEL-GANGERS!!
SEALING JUTSU! OCTOPUS HOLD!!
GLOMP
KLOP

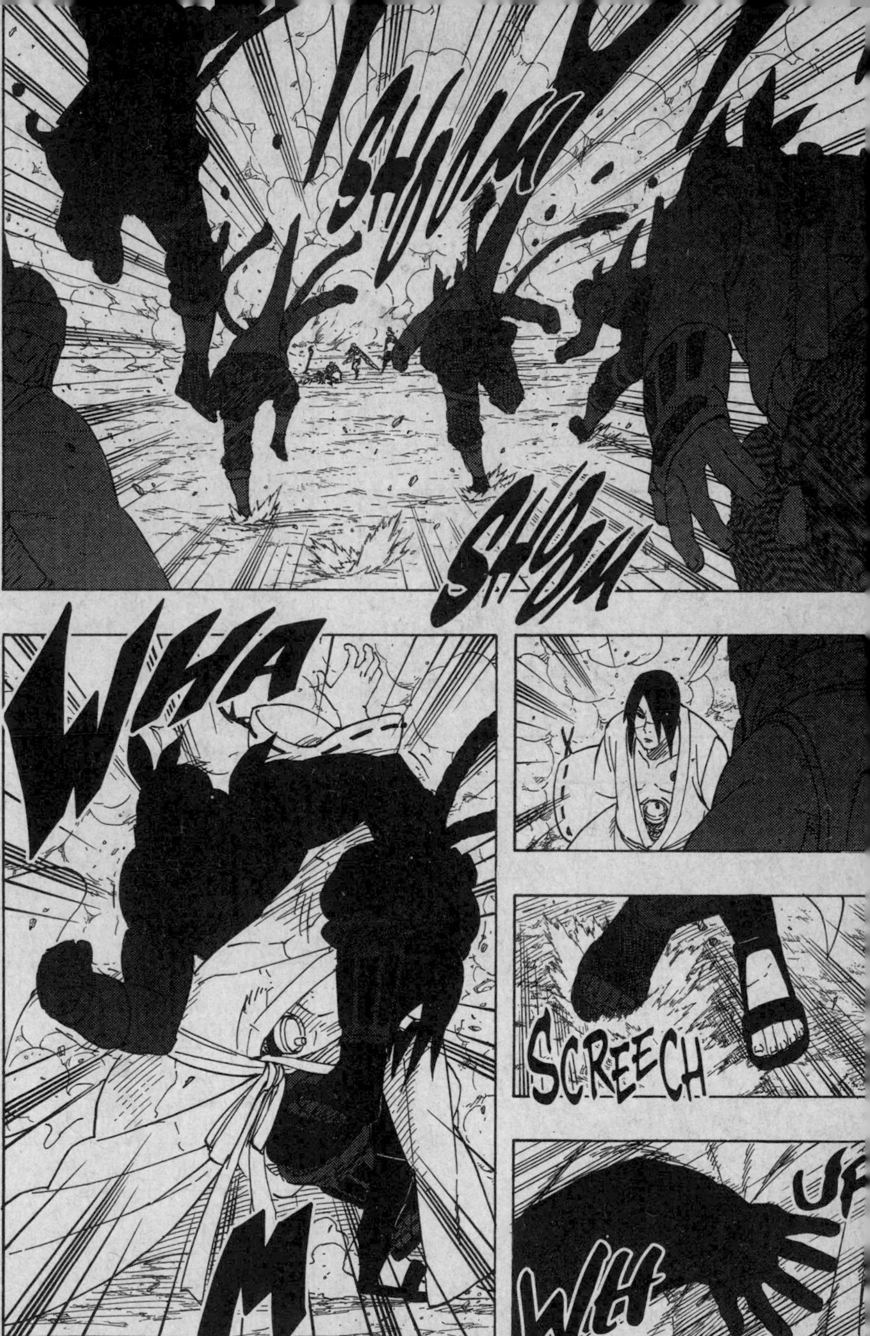
SCREECH
WHAM

READ THIS WAY

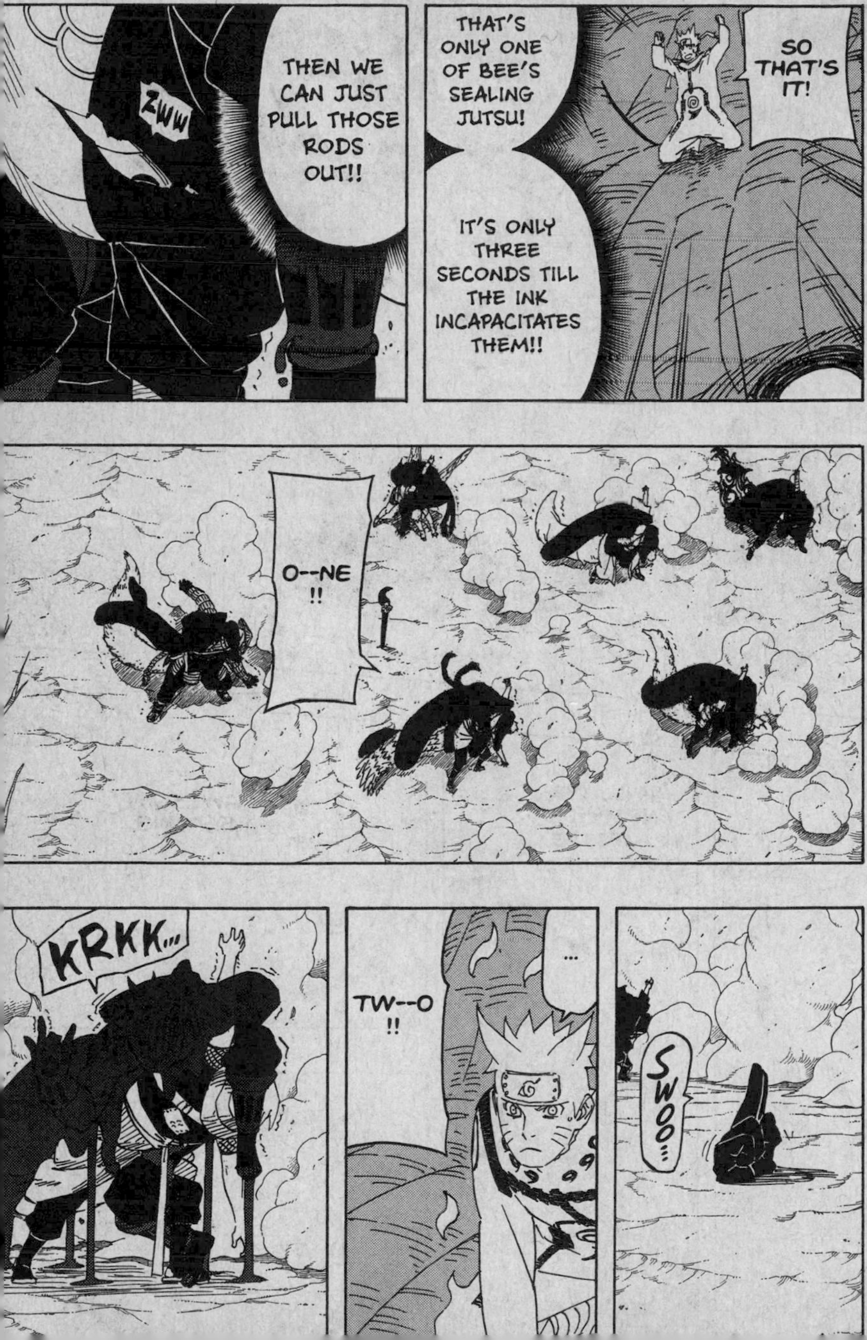
SO THAT'S IT!
THAT'S ONLY ONE OF BEE'S SEALING JUTSU!
IT'S ONLY THREE SECONDS TILL THE INK INCAPACITATES THEM!!
THEN WE CAN JUST PULL THOSE RODS OUT!!
ZWW
O--NE !!
SWOO...
...
TW--O !!
KRKK...

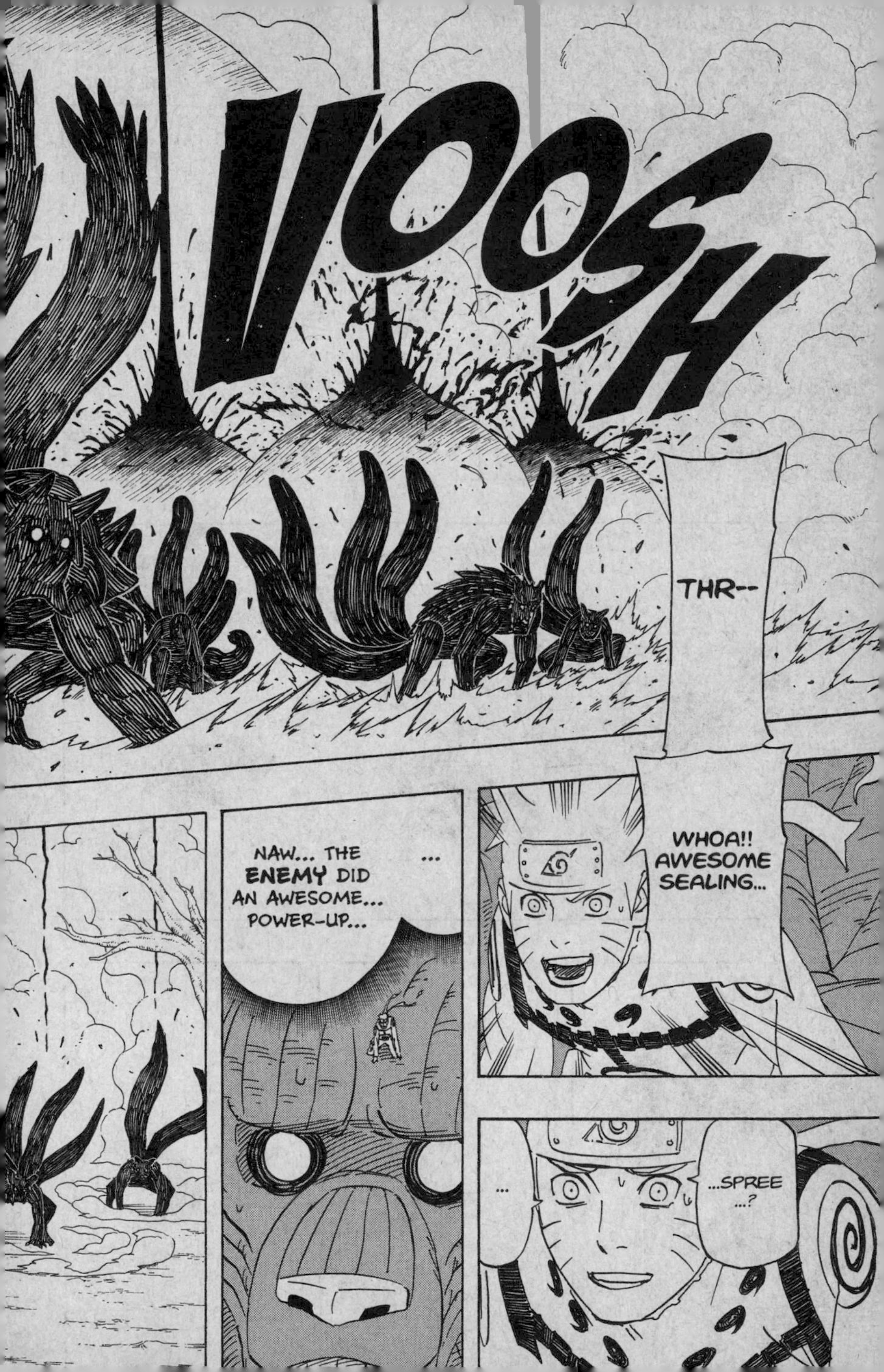
VOOSH
THR--
WHOA!! AWESOME SEALING...
...
NAW... THE ENEMY DID AN AWESOME... POWER-UP...
...SPREE ...?
...

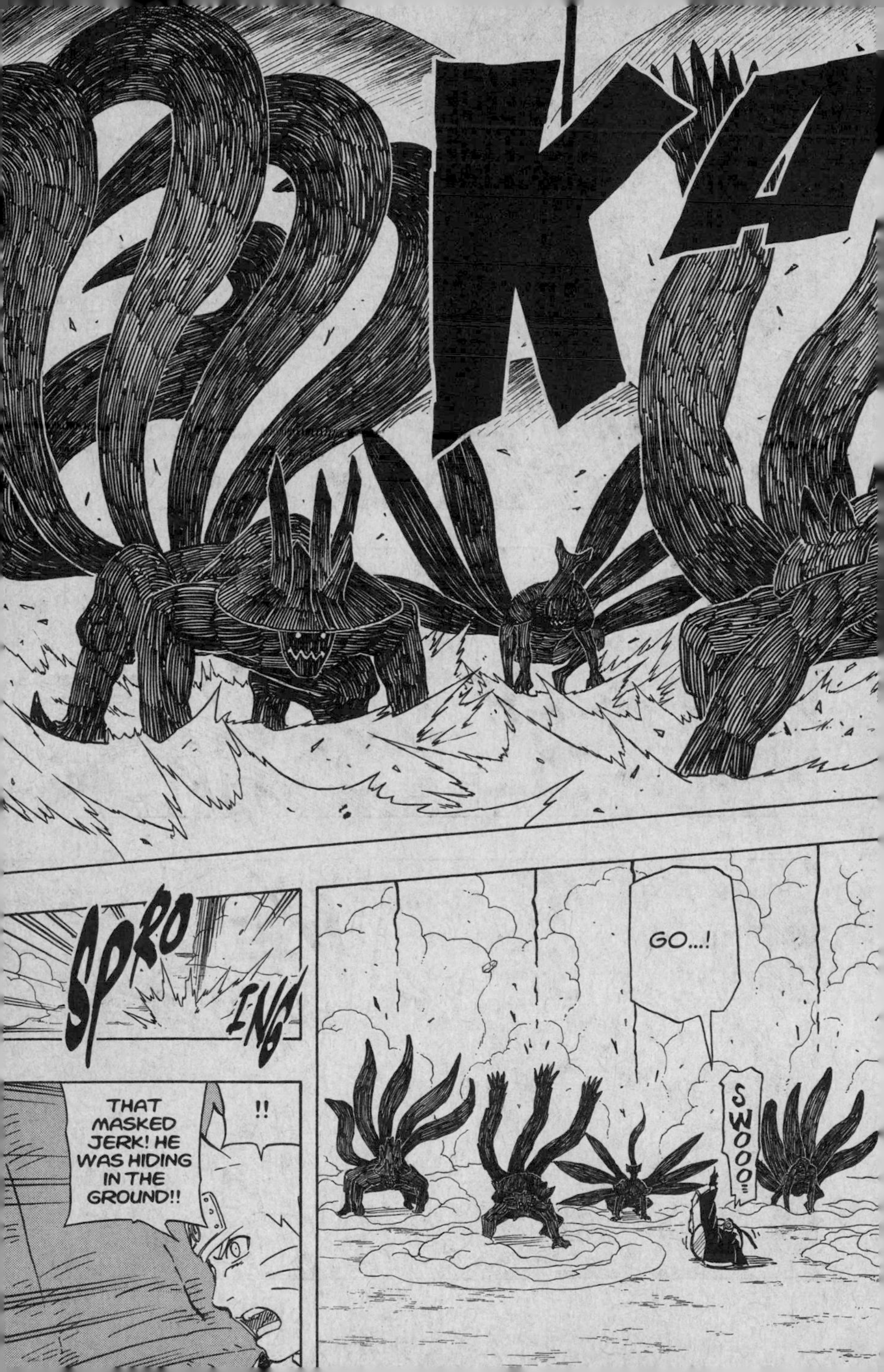
KA
GO...!
SWOOO!!
SPROING
!!
THAT MASKED JERK! HE WAS HIDING IN THE GROUND!!

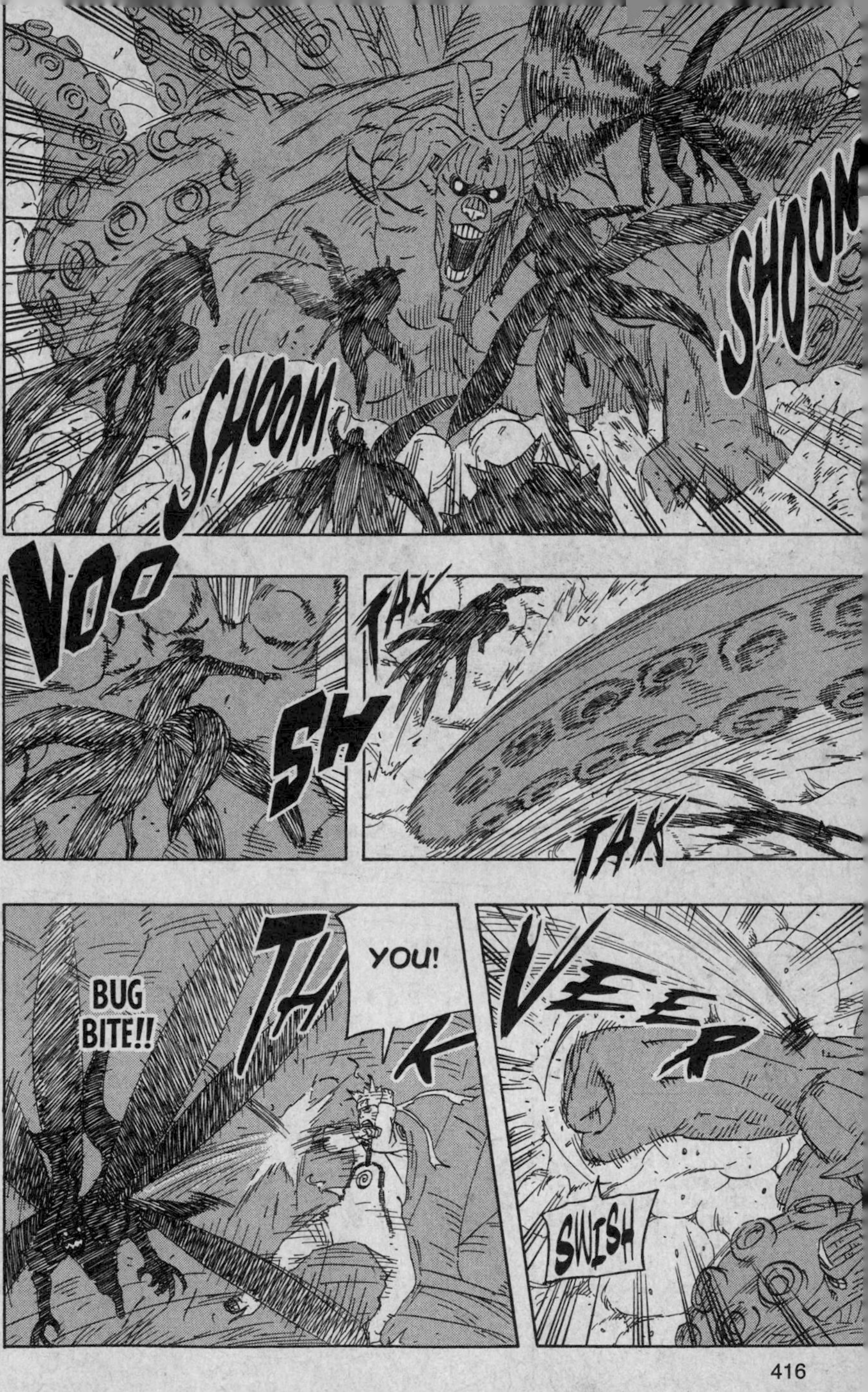
SHOOM
SHOOM
TAK
SH
TAK
VOO
VEEP
SWISH
YOU!
THK
BUG BITE!!

READ THIS WAY

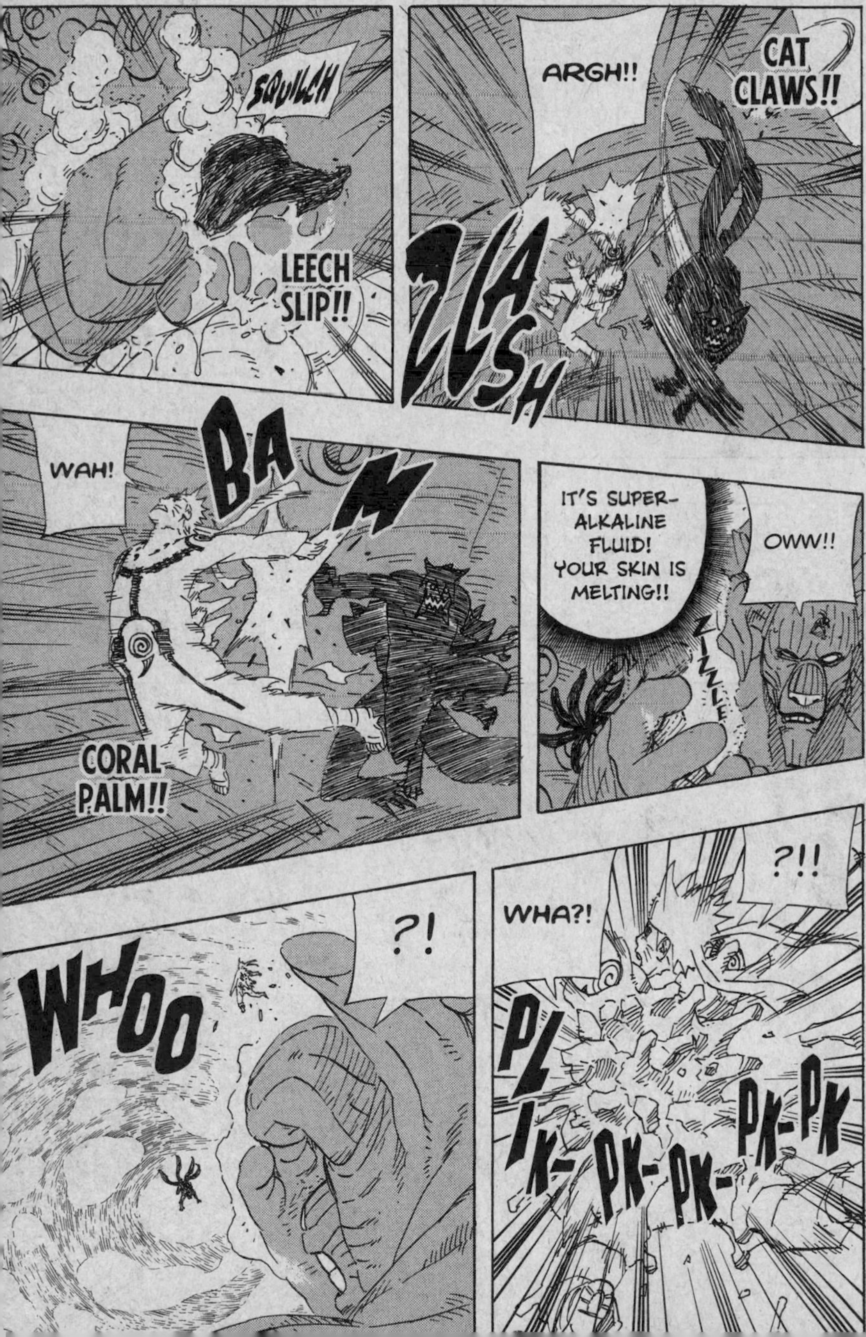

ARGH!!
CAT CLAWS!!
ZLASH
SQUILCH
LEECH SLIP!!
OWW!!
IT'S SUPER-ALKALINE FLUID! YOUR SKIN IS MELTING!!
ZIZZLE
WAH!
BAM
CORAL PALM!!
?!!
WHA?!
PLIK-PK-PK-PK-PK
?!
WHOO

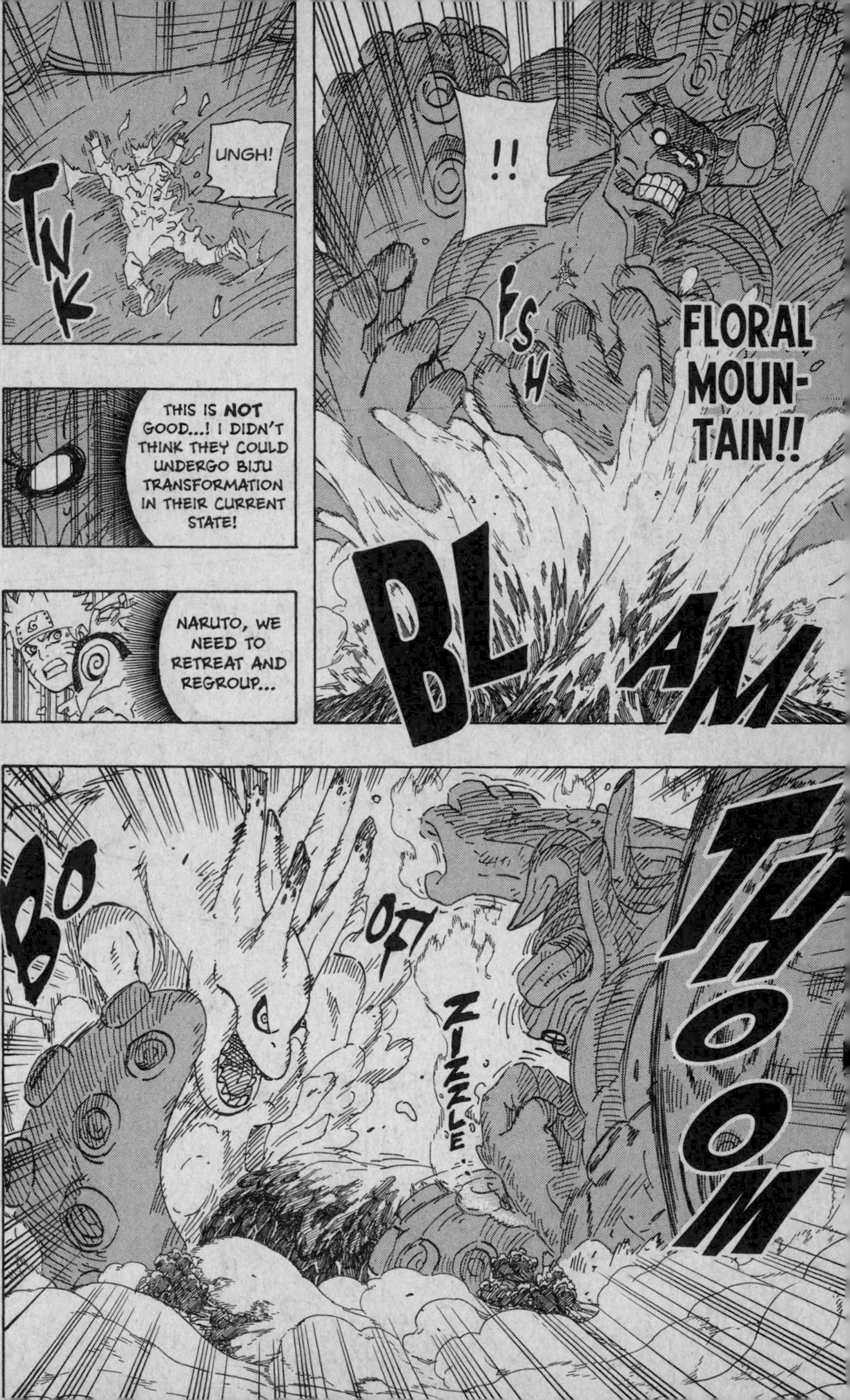
!!
FSH
FLORAL MOUNTAIN!!
BLAM
TNK
UNGH!
THIS IS **NOT** GOOD...! I DIDN'T THINK THEY COULD UNDERGO BIJU TRANSFORMATION IN THEIR CURRENT STATE!
NARUTO, WE NEED TO RETREAT AND REGROUP...
THOOM
ZIZZLE
OFF
BO

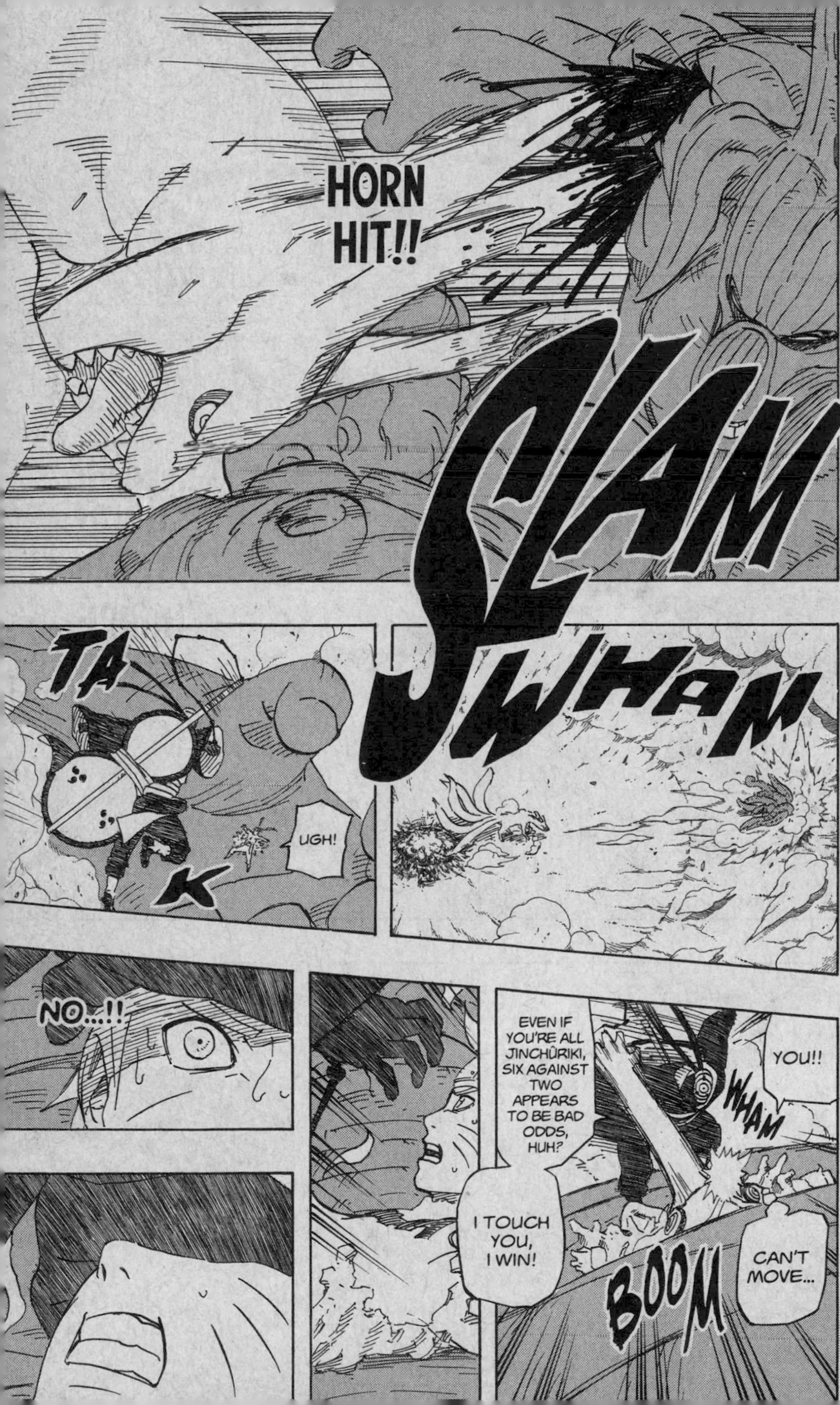
HORN HIT!!
SLAM
SWHAM
TA
UGH!
K
YOU!!
WHAM
EVEN IF YOU'RE ALL JINCHŪRIKI, SIX AGAINST TWO APPEARS TO BE BAD ODDS, HUH?
CAN'T MOVE...
I TOUCH YOU, I WIN!
BOOM
NO...!!

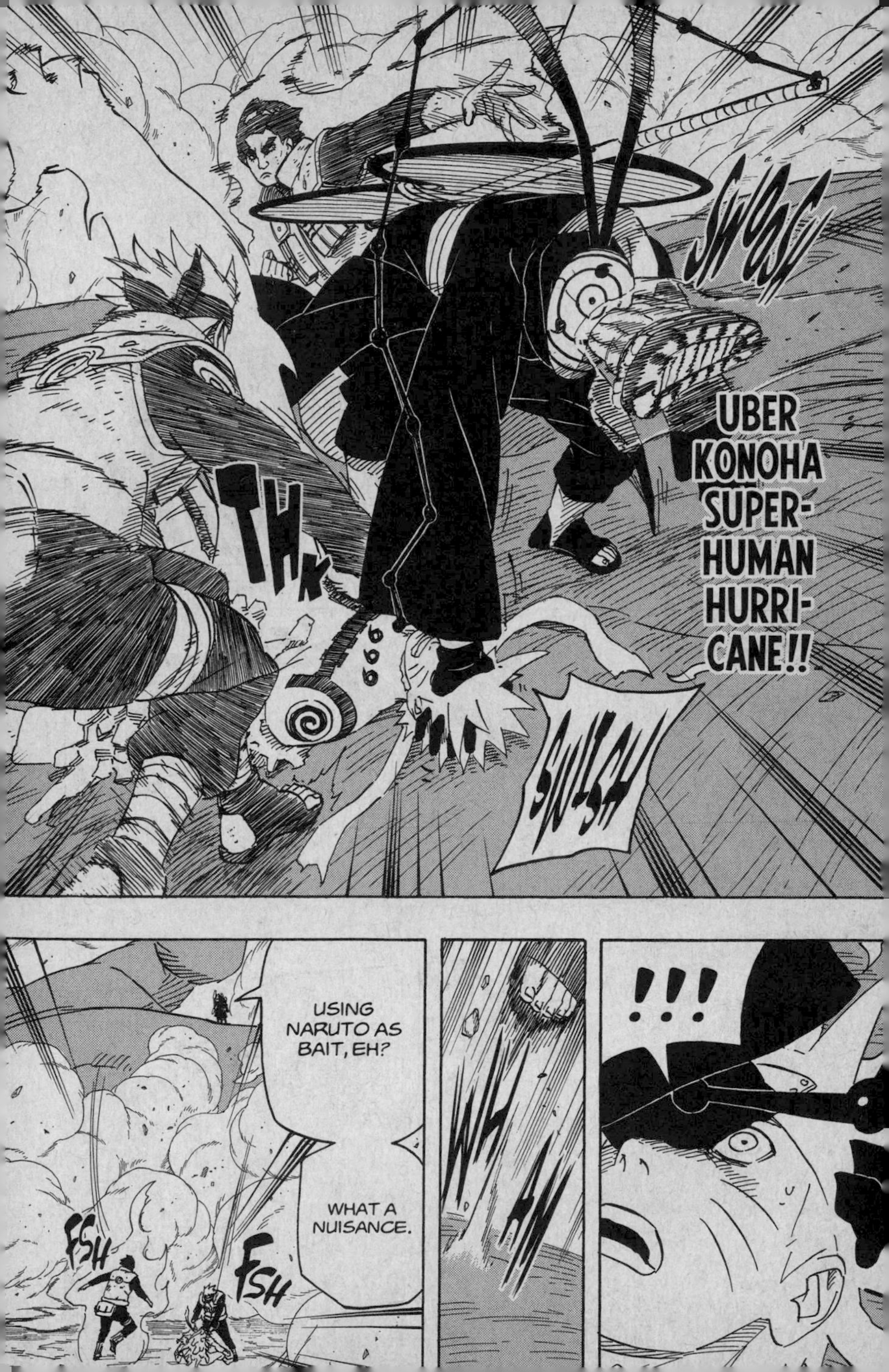
SWOSH
UBER KONOHA SUPER-HUMAN HURRICANE!!
THK
!!!
WHAM
USING NARUTO AS BAIT, EH?
WHAT A NUISANCE.
FSH
FSH

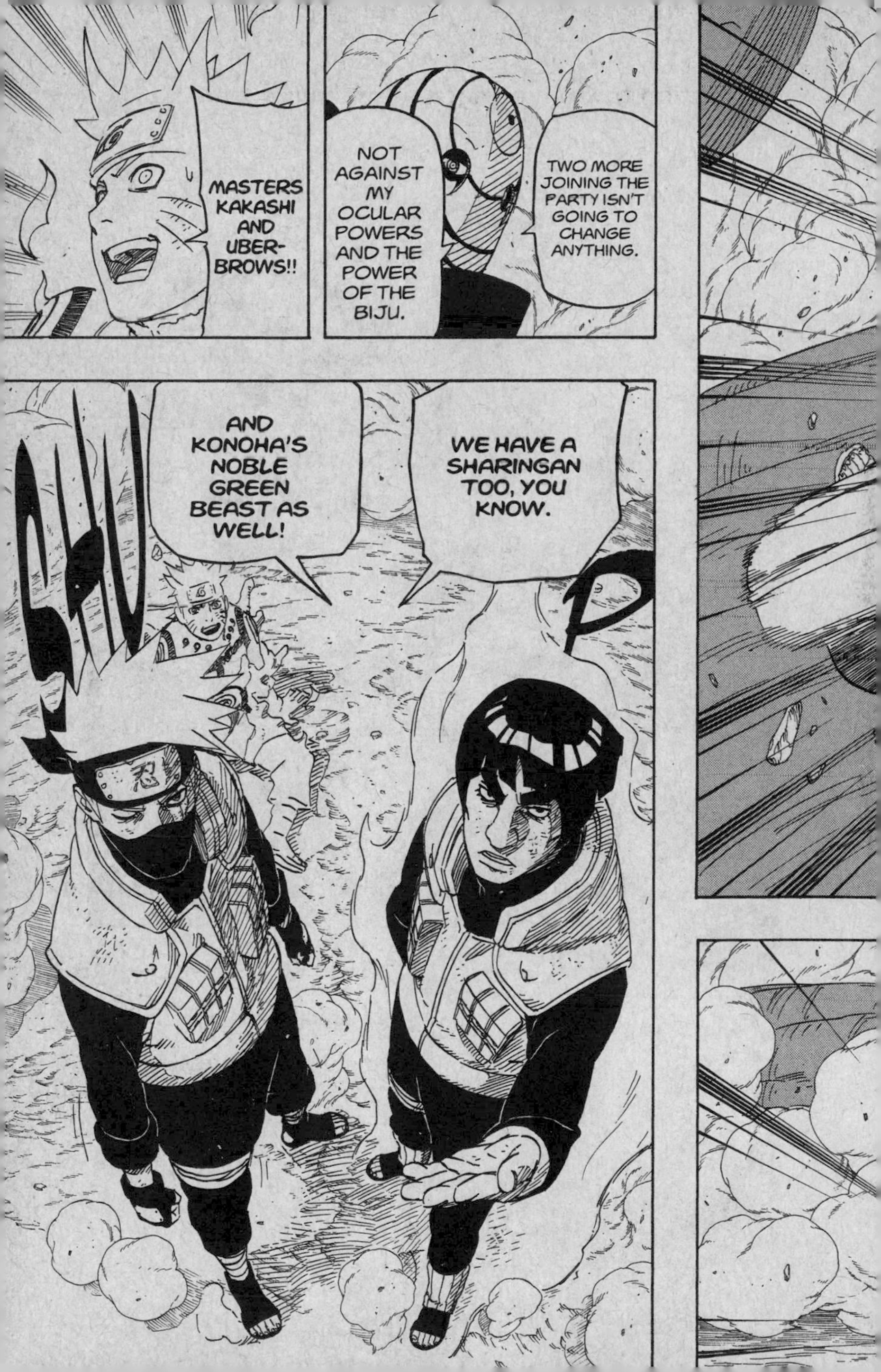
TWO MORE JOINING THE PARTY ISN'T GOING TO CHANGE ANYTHING.
NOT AGAINST MY OCULAR POWERS AND THE POWER OF THE BIJU.
MASTERS KAKASHI AND UBER-BROWS!!
WE HAVE A SHARINGAN TOO, YOU KNOW.
AND KONOHA'S NOBLE GREEN BEAST AS WELL!

Illustration to Commemorate Reaching Volume 60 [1]

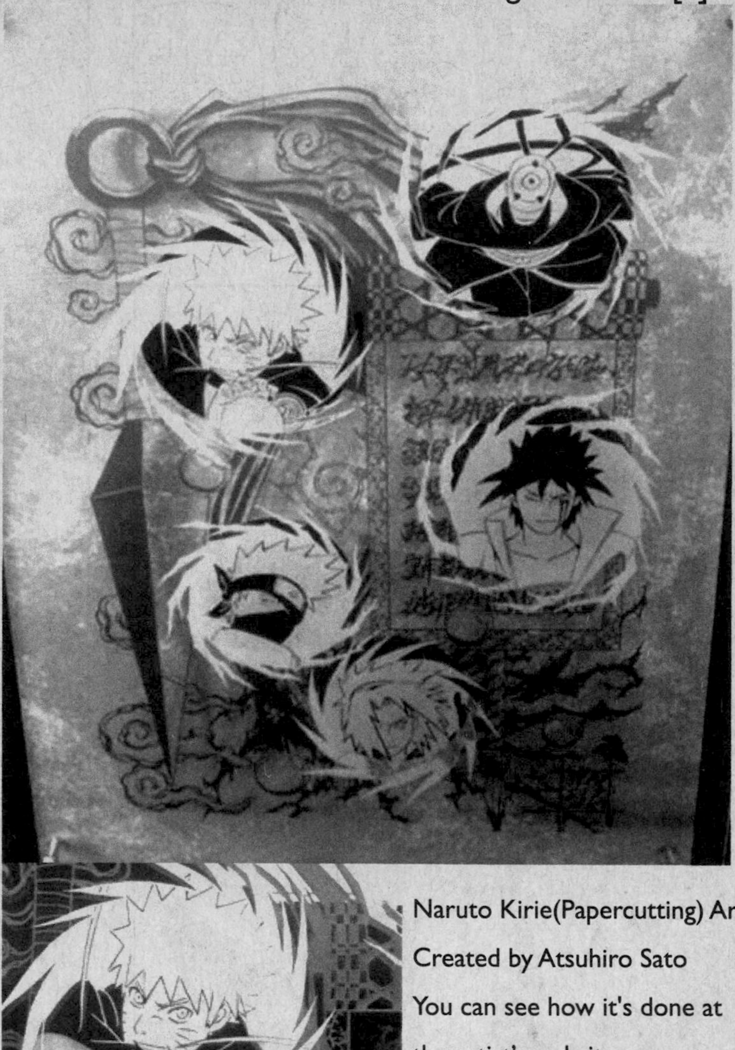

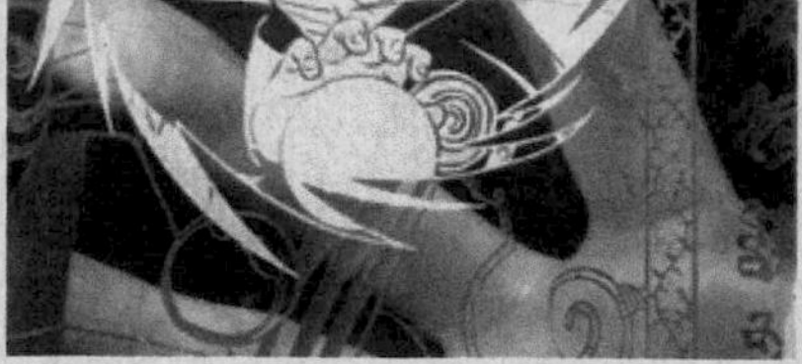

Naruto Kirie(Papercutting) Art

Created by Atsuhiro Sato

You can see how it's done at the artist's website:

http://Kirieatsu.blog.fc2.com/

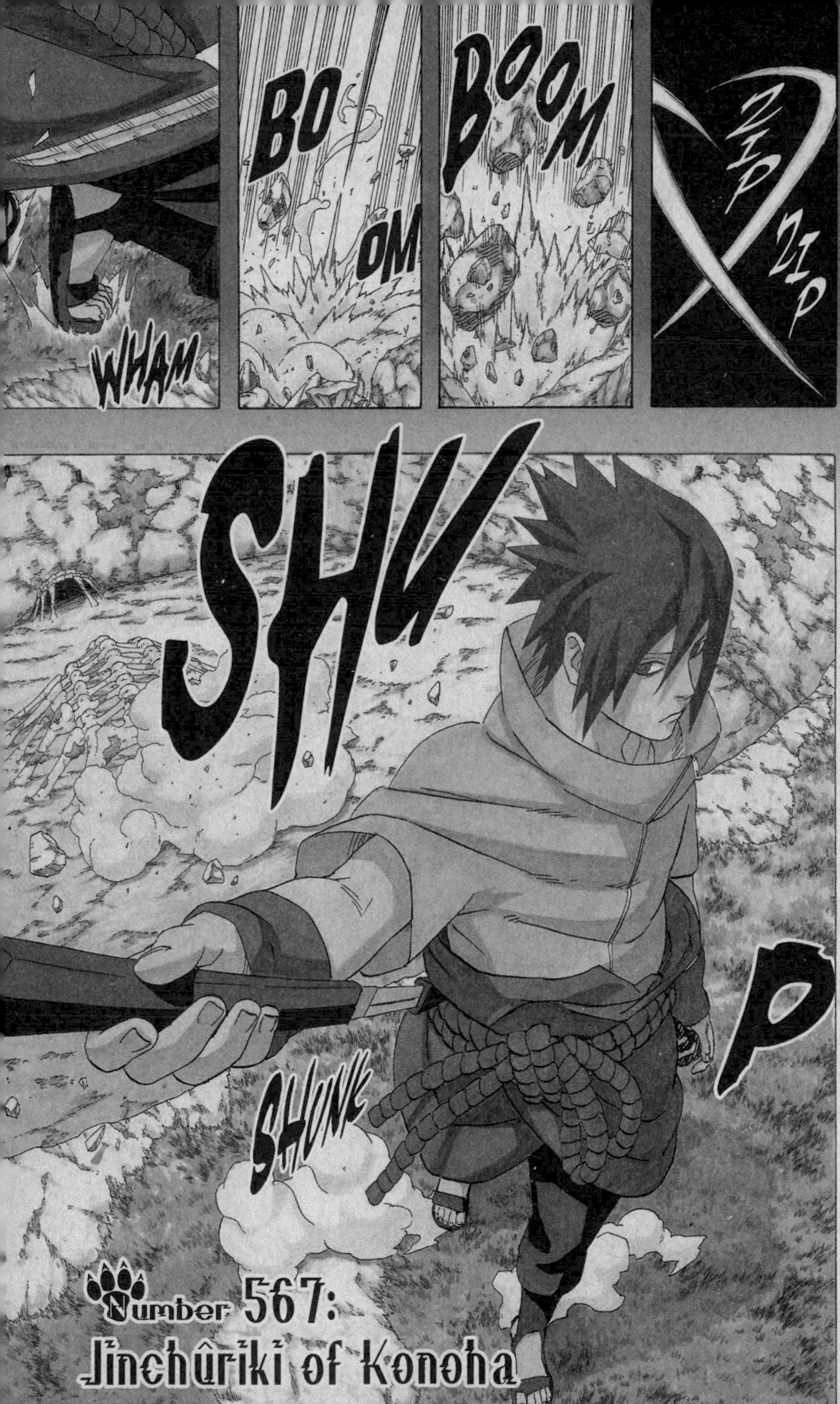
ZIP
ZIP
BOOM
BO
OM
WHAM
SHU
P
SHUNK
Number 567:
Jinchûriki of Konoha

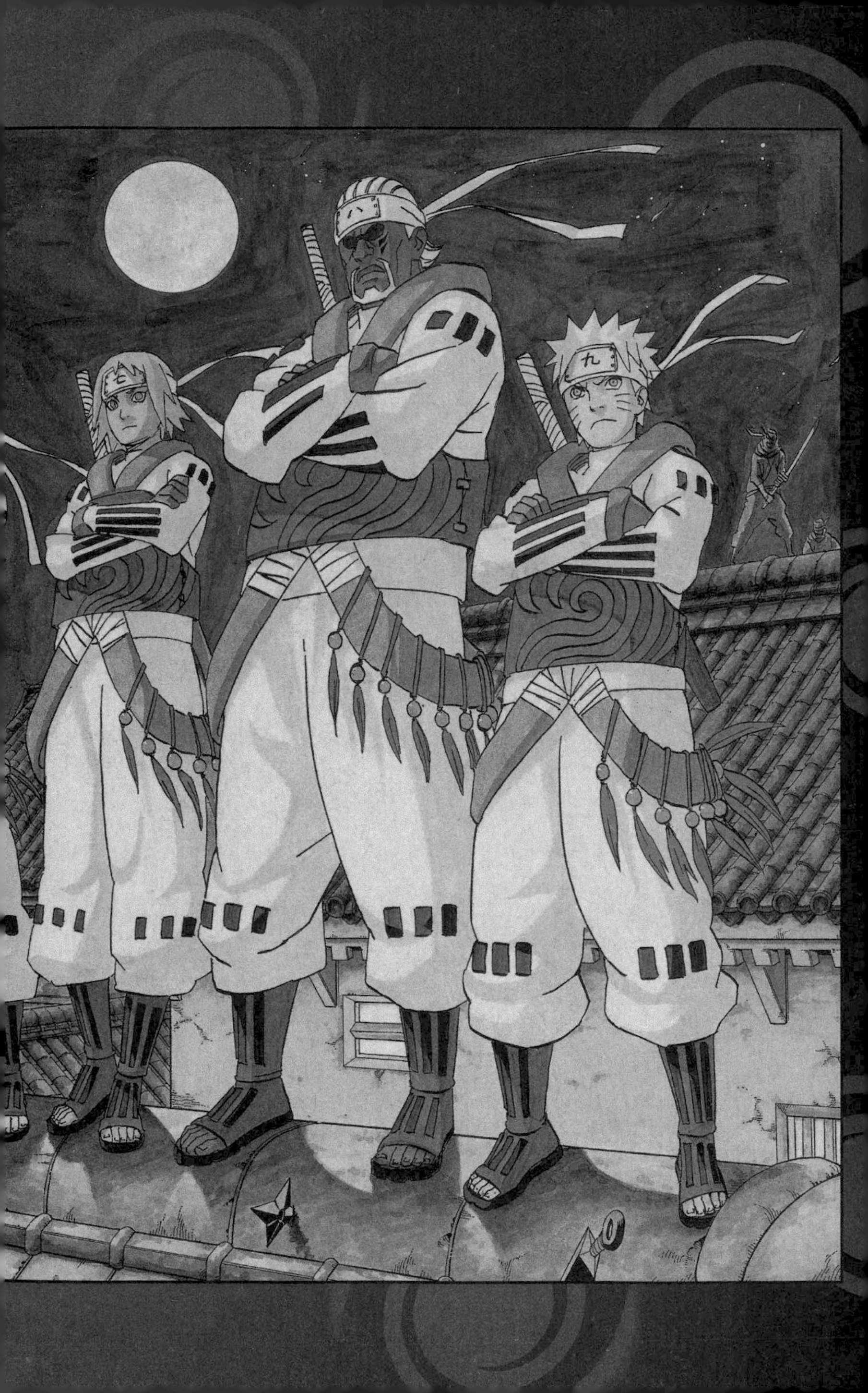

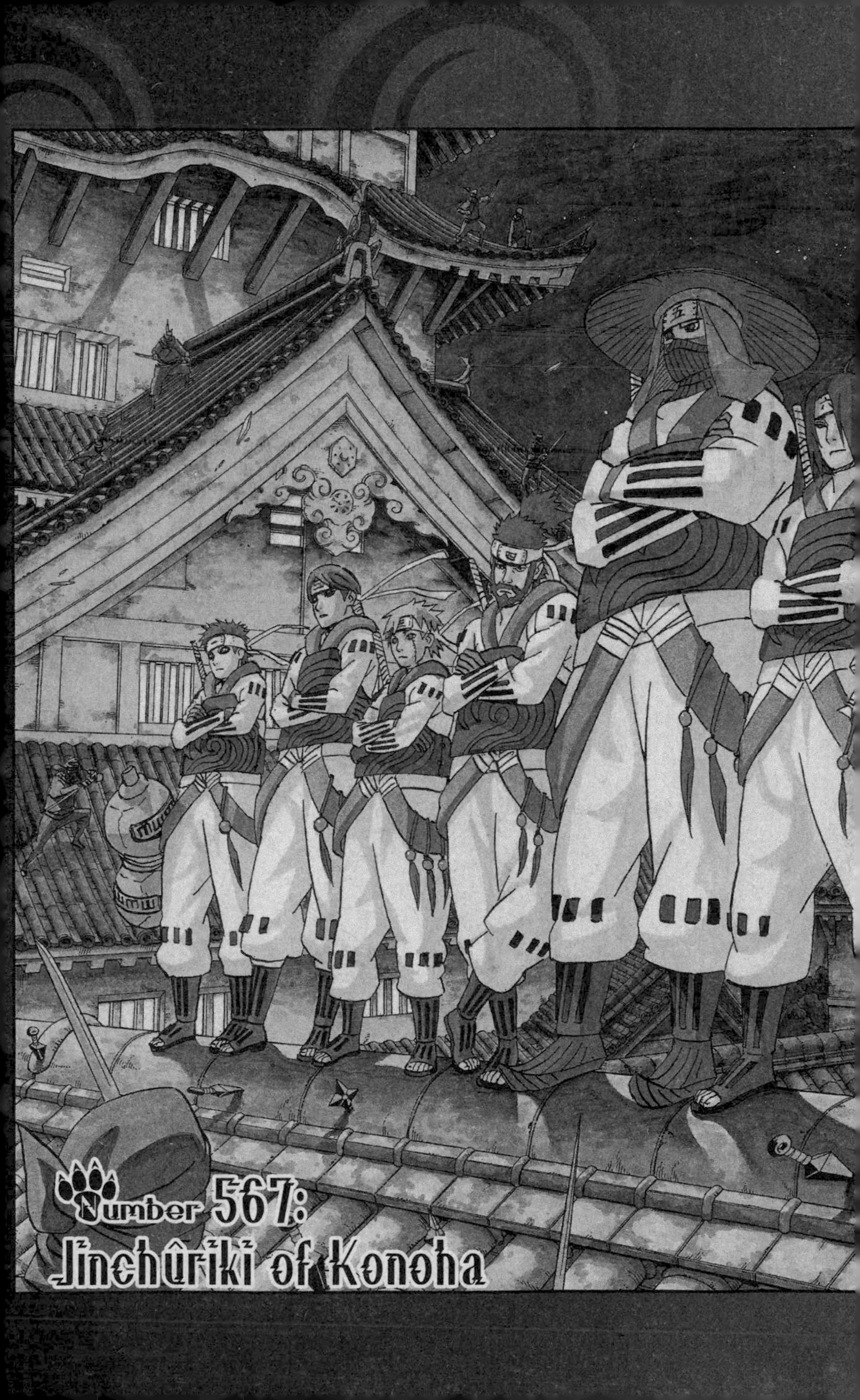
Number 567:
Jinchûriki of Konoha

Illustration to Commemorate Reaching Volume 60 [2]

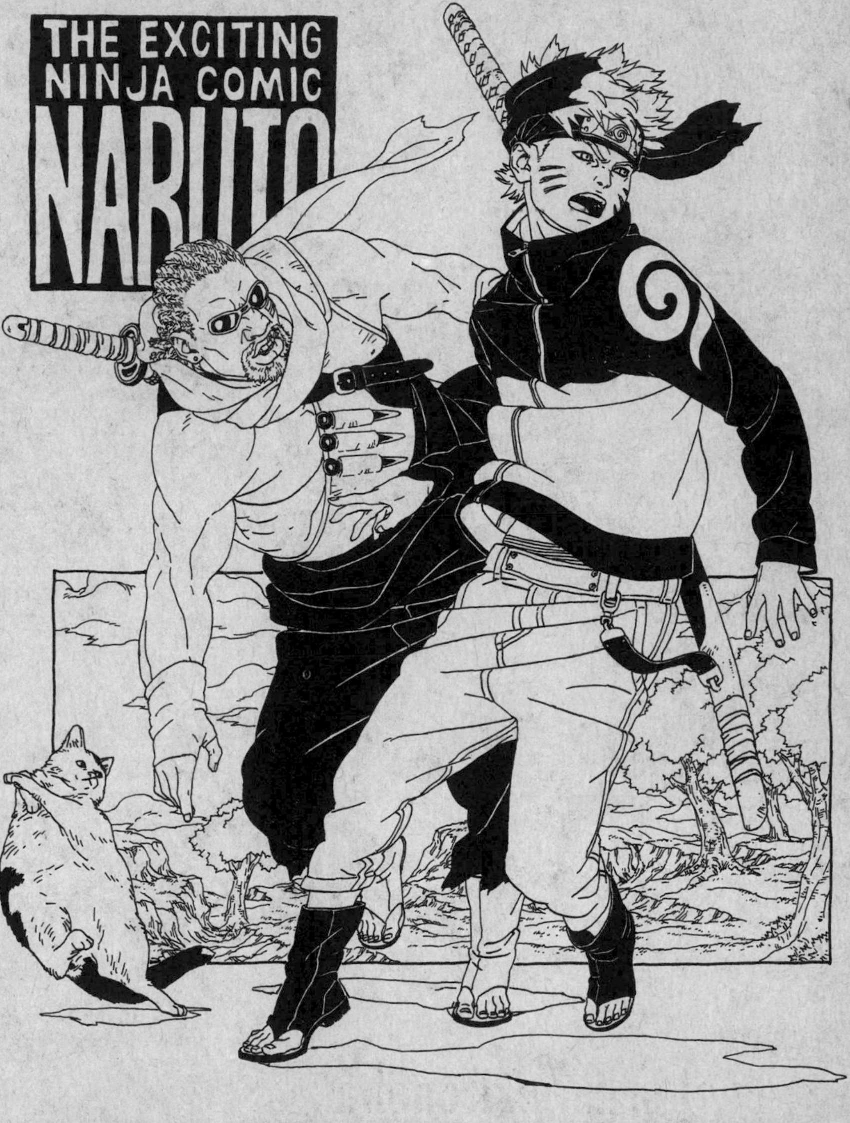
THE EXCITING
NINJA COMIC
NARUTO

Mikio Ikemoto

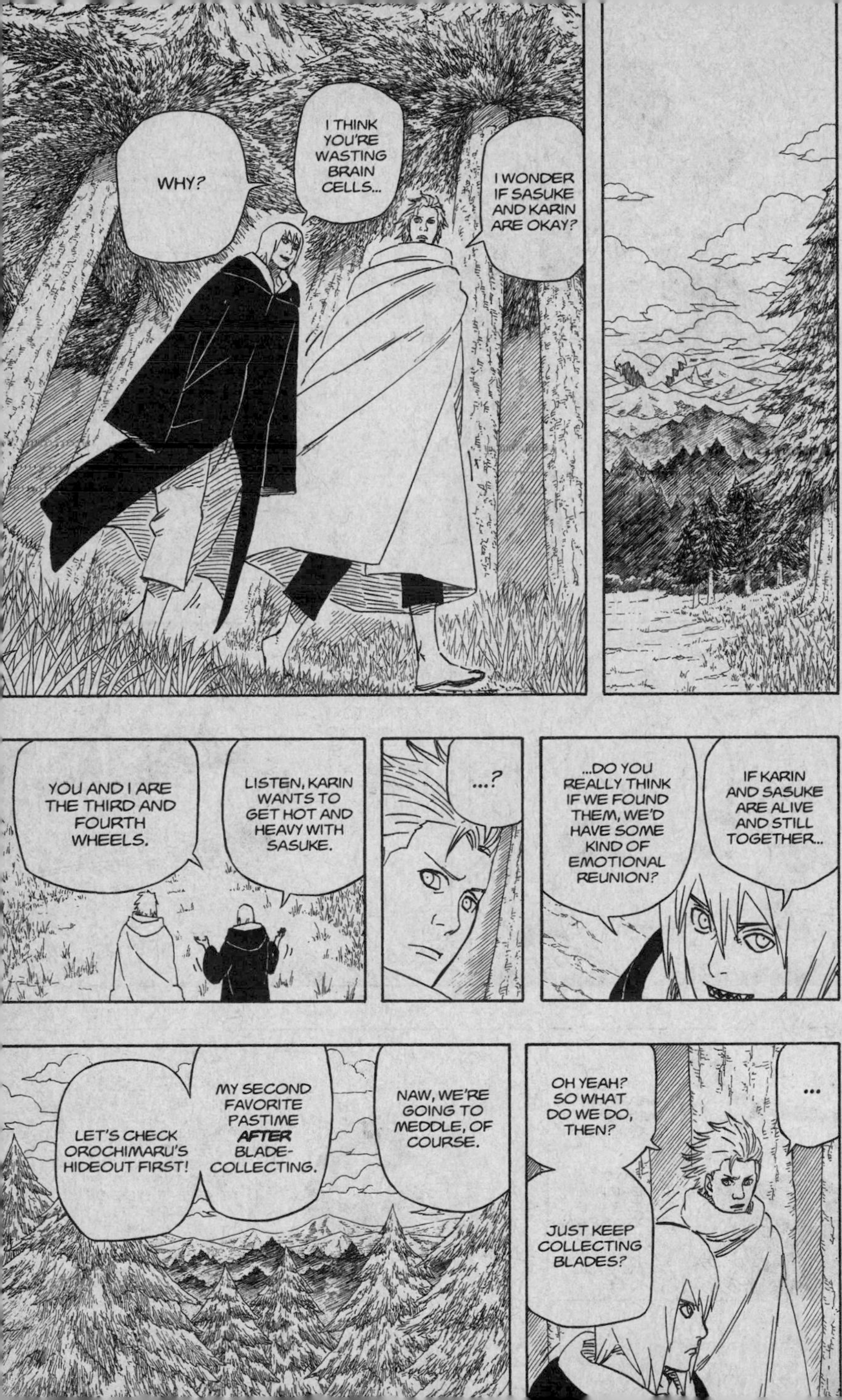
I WONDER IF SASUKE AND KARIN ARE OKAY?
I THINK YOU'RE WASTING BRAIN CELLS...
WHY?
IF KARIN AND SASUKE ARE ALIVE AND STILL TOGETHER...
...DO YOU REALLY THINK IF WE FOUND THEM, WE'D HAVE SOME KIND OF EMOTIONAL REUNION?
...?
LISTEN, KARIN WANTS TO GET HOT AND HEAVY WITH SASUKE.
YOU AND I ARE THE THIRD AND FOURTH WHEELS.
...
OH YEAH? SO WHAT DO WE DO, THEN?
JUST KEEP COLLECTING BLADES?
NAW, WE'RE GOING TO MEDDLE, OF COURSE.
MY SECOND FAVORITE PASTIME **AFTER** BLADE-COLLECTING.
LET'S CHECK OROCHIMARU'S HIDEOUT FIRST!

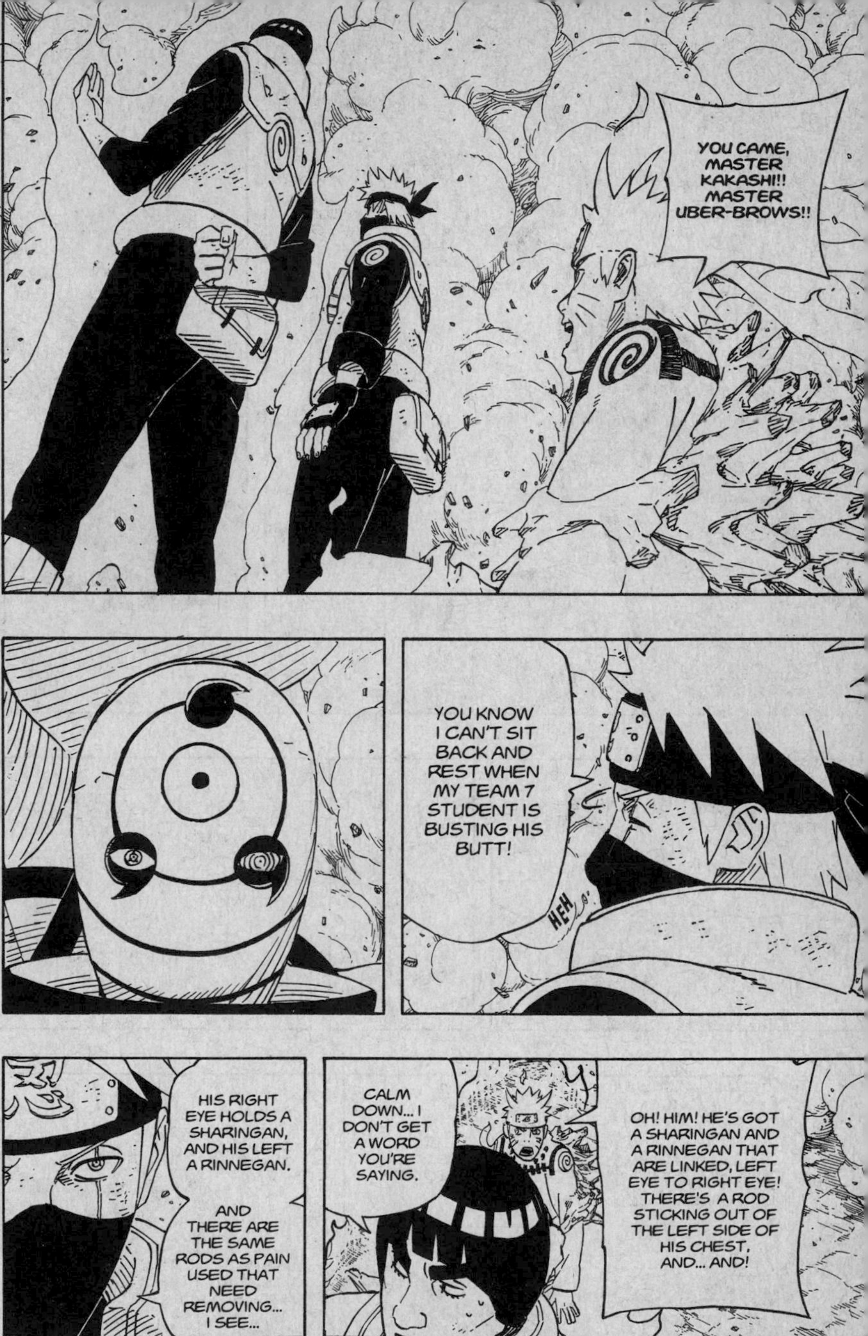
YOU CAME, MASTER KAKASHI!! MASTER UBER-BROWS!!
YOU KNOW I CAN'T SIT BACK AND REST WHEN MY TEAM 7 STUDENT IS BUSTING HIS BUTT!
HEH
OH! HIM! HE'S GOT A SHARINGAN AND A RINNEGAN THAT ARE LINKED, LEFT EYE TO RIGHT EYE! THERE'S A ROD STICKING OUT OF THE LEFT SIDE OF HIS CHEST, AND... AND!
CALM DOWN... I DON'T GET A WORD YOU'RE SAYING.
HIS RIGHT EYE HOLDS A SHARINGAN, AND HIS LEFT A RINNEGAN.
AND THERE ARE THE SAME RODS AS PAIN USED THAT NEED REMOVING... I SEE...

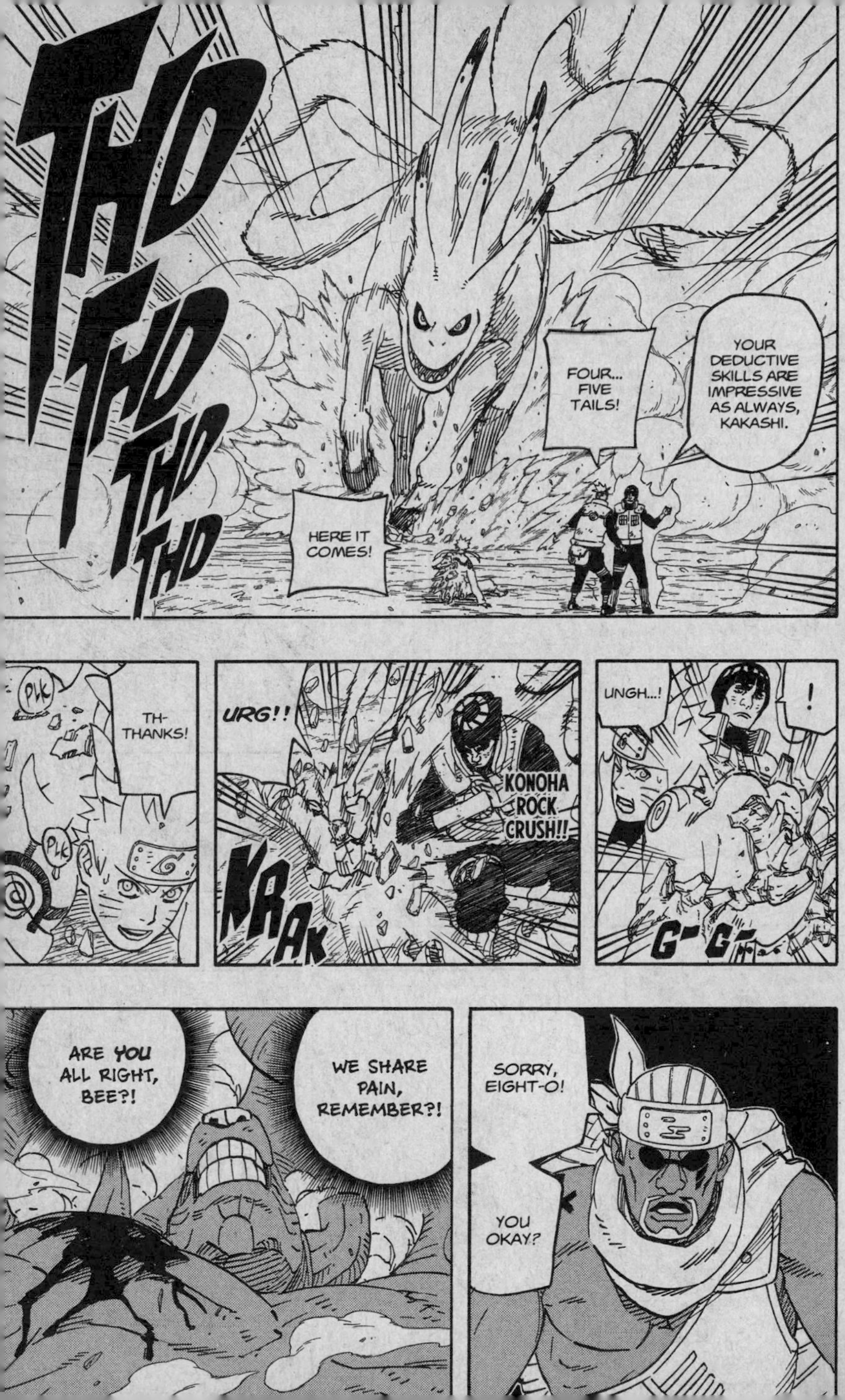
YOUR DEDUCTIVE SKILLS ARE IMPRESSIVE AS ALWAYS, KAKASHI.
FOUR... FIVE TAILS!
HERE IT COMES!
THD THD THD THD
!
UNGH...!
G-G-
URG!!
KONOHA ROCK CRUSH!!
KRAK
TH-THANKS!
PLK
PLK
SORRY, EIGHT-O!
YOU OKAY?
WE SHARE PAIN, REMEMBER?!
ARE YOU ALL RIGHT, BEE?!

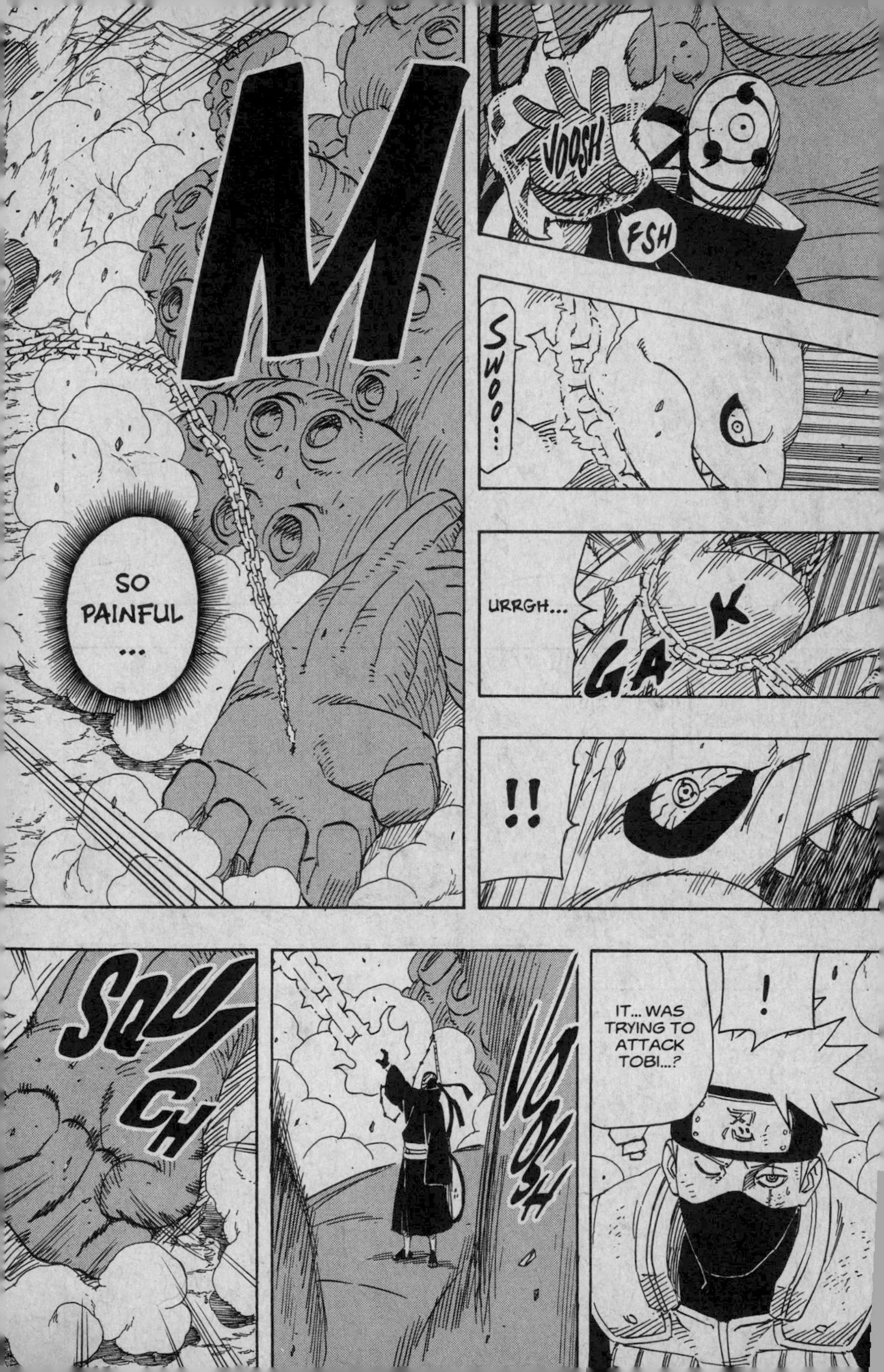
JOOSH
FSH
SWOOO...
URRGH...
GAK
!!
M
SO PAINFUL ...
!
IT... WAS TRYING TO ATTACK TOBI...?
VOOSH
SQUCH

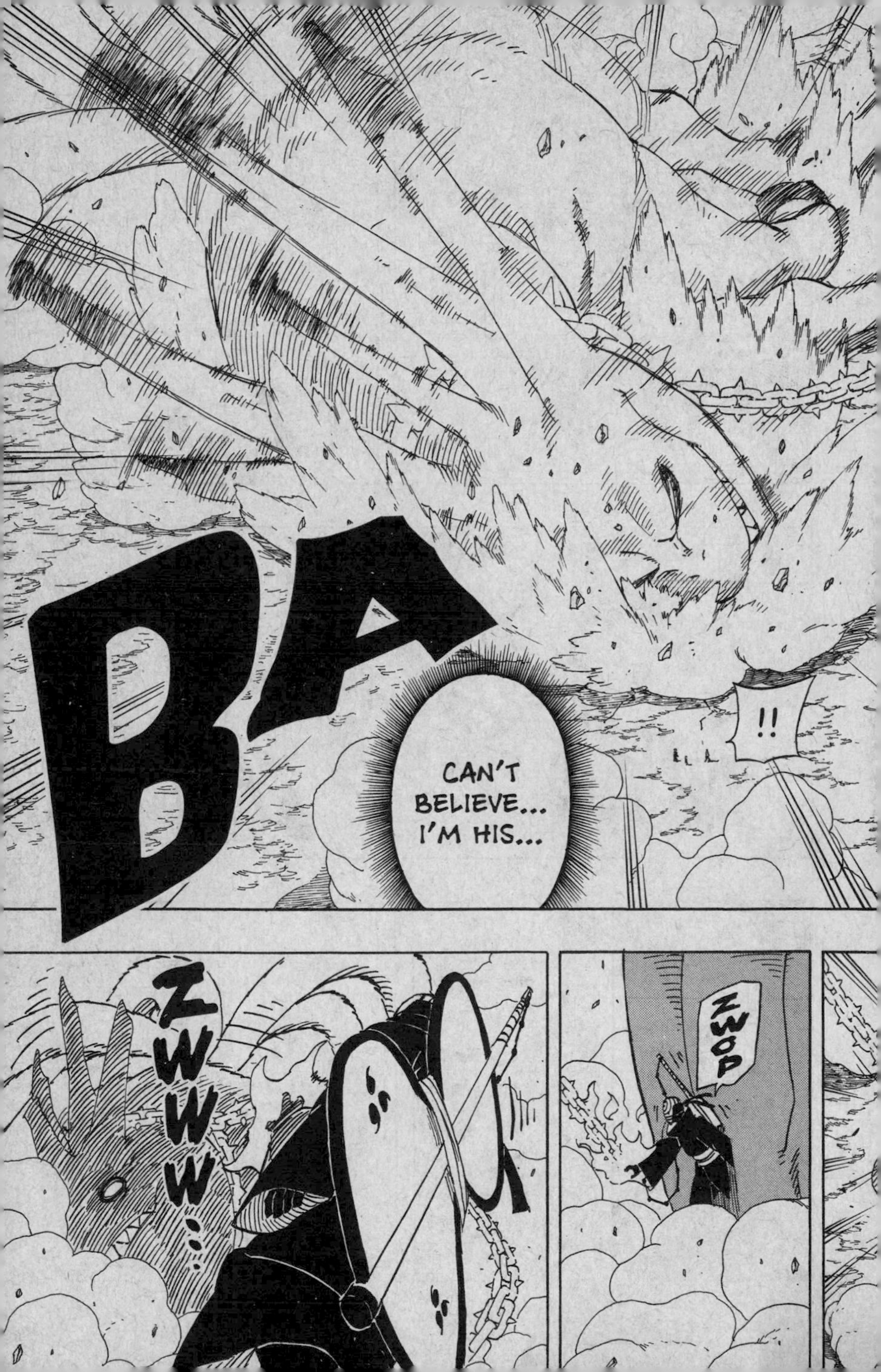
!!
CAN'T BELIEVE... I'M HIS...
BA
ZWOP
ZWWW...

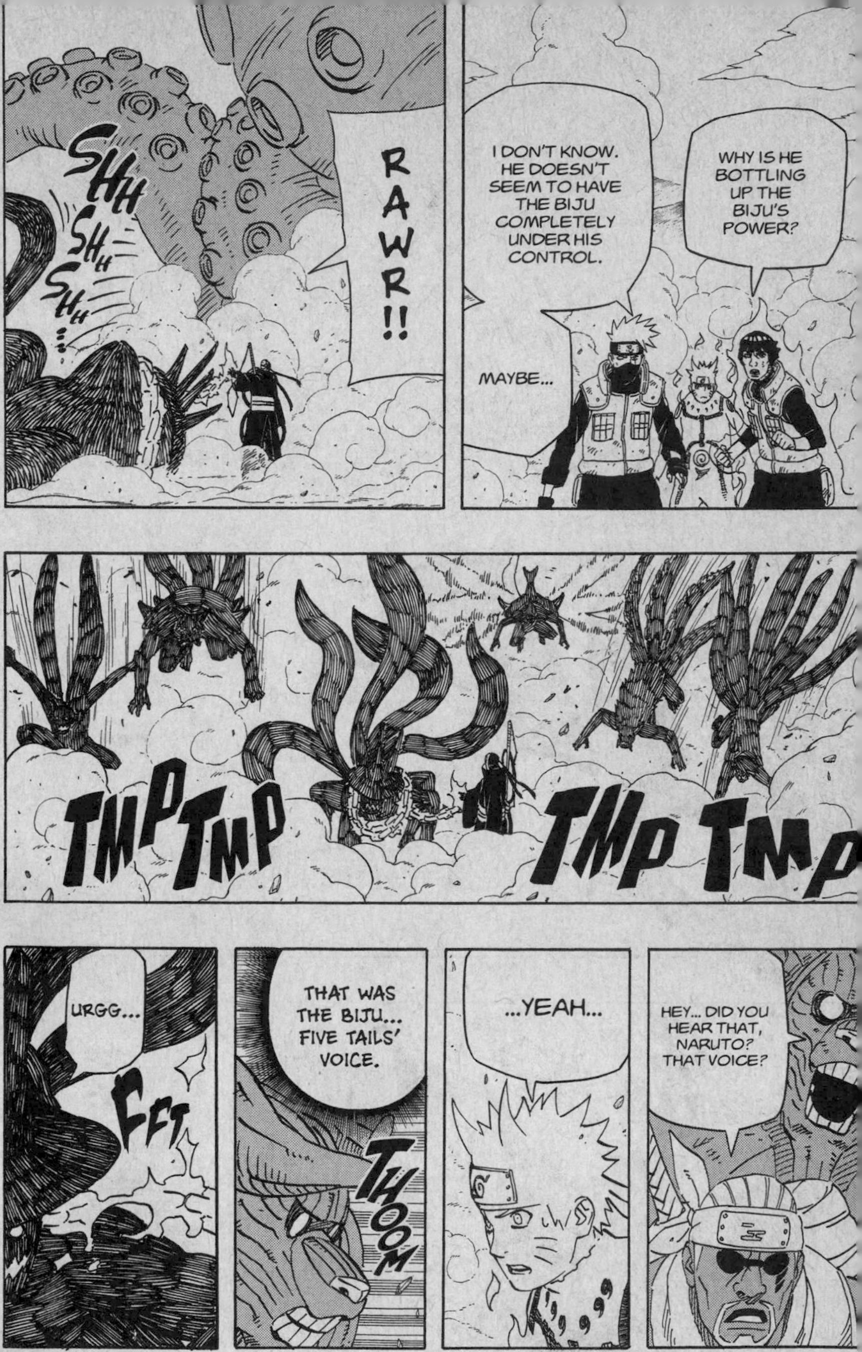
WHY IS HE BOTTLING UP THE BIJU'S POWER?
I DON'T KNOW. HE DOESN'T SEEM TO HAVE THE BIJU COMPLETELY UNDER HIS CONTROL.
MAYBE...
RAWR!!
SHH SHH SHH
TMP TMP
TMP TMP
HEY... DID YOU HEAR THAT, NARUTO? THAT VOICE?
...YEAH...
THAT WAS THE BIJU... FIVE TAILS' VOICE.
THOOM
URGG...
FFT

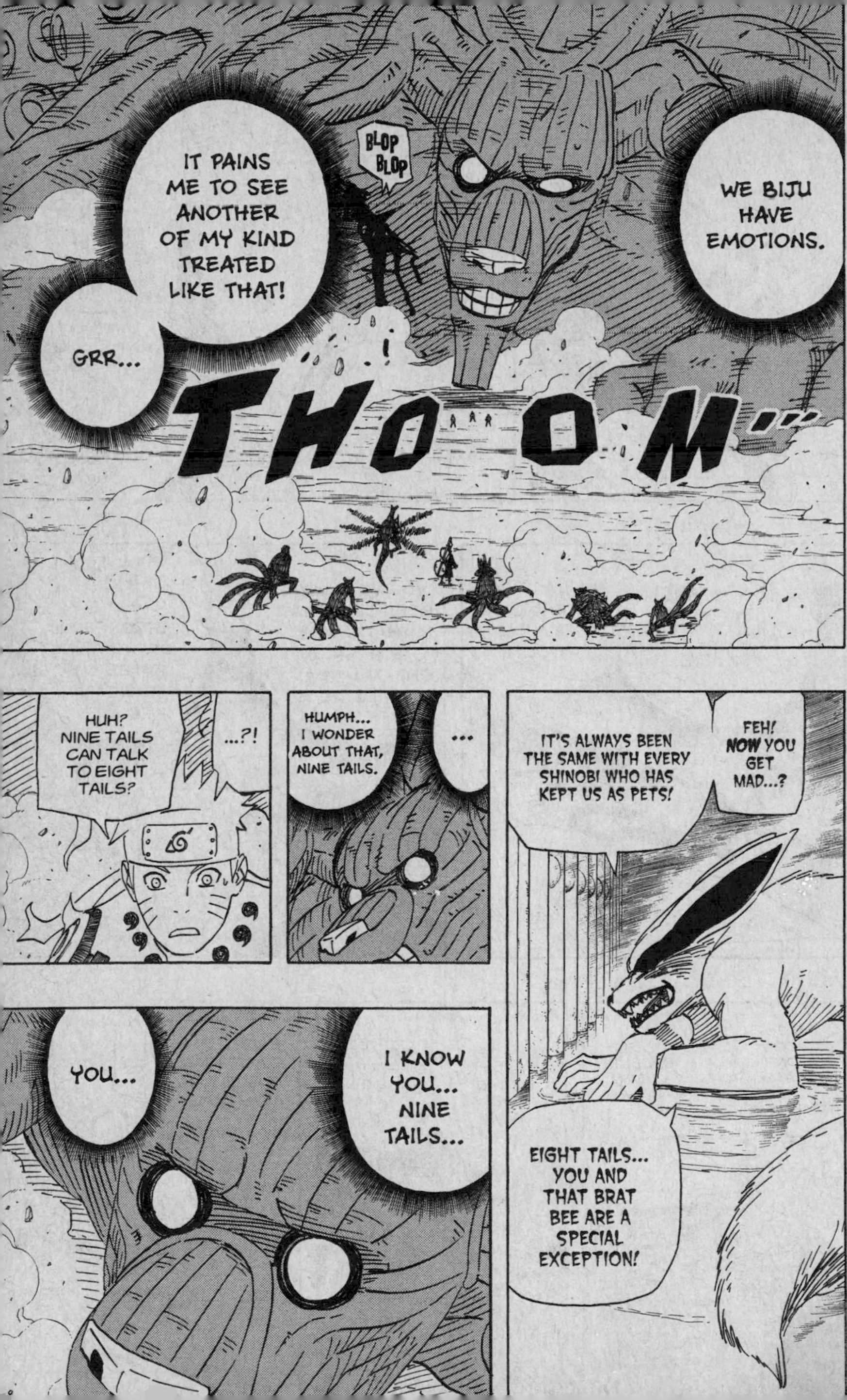

WE BIJU HAVE EMOTIONS.
BLOP BLOP
IT PAINS ME TO SEE ANOTHER OF MY KIND TREATED LIKE THAT!
GRR...
THOOM
FEH! **NOW** YOU GET MAD...?
IT'S ALWAYS BEEN THE SAME WITH EVERY SHINOBI WHO HAS KEPT US AS PETS!
EIGHT TAILS... YOU AND THAT BRAT BEE ARE A SPECIAL EXCEPTION!
...
HUMPH... I WONDER ABOUT THAT, NINE TAILS.
...?!
HUH? NINE TAILS CAN TALK TO EIGHT TAILS?
I KNOW YOU... NINE TAILS...
YOU...

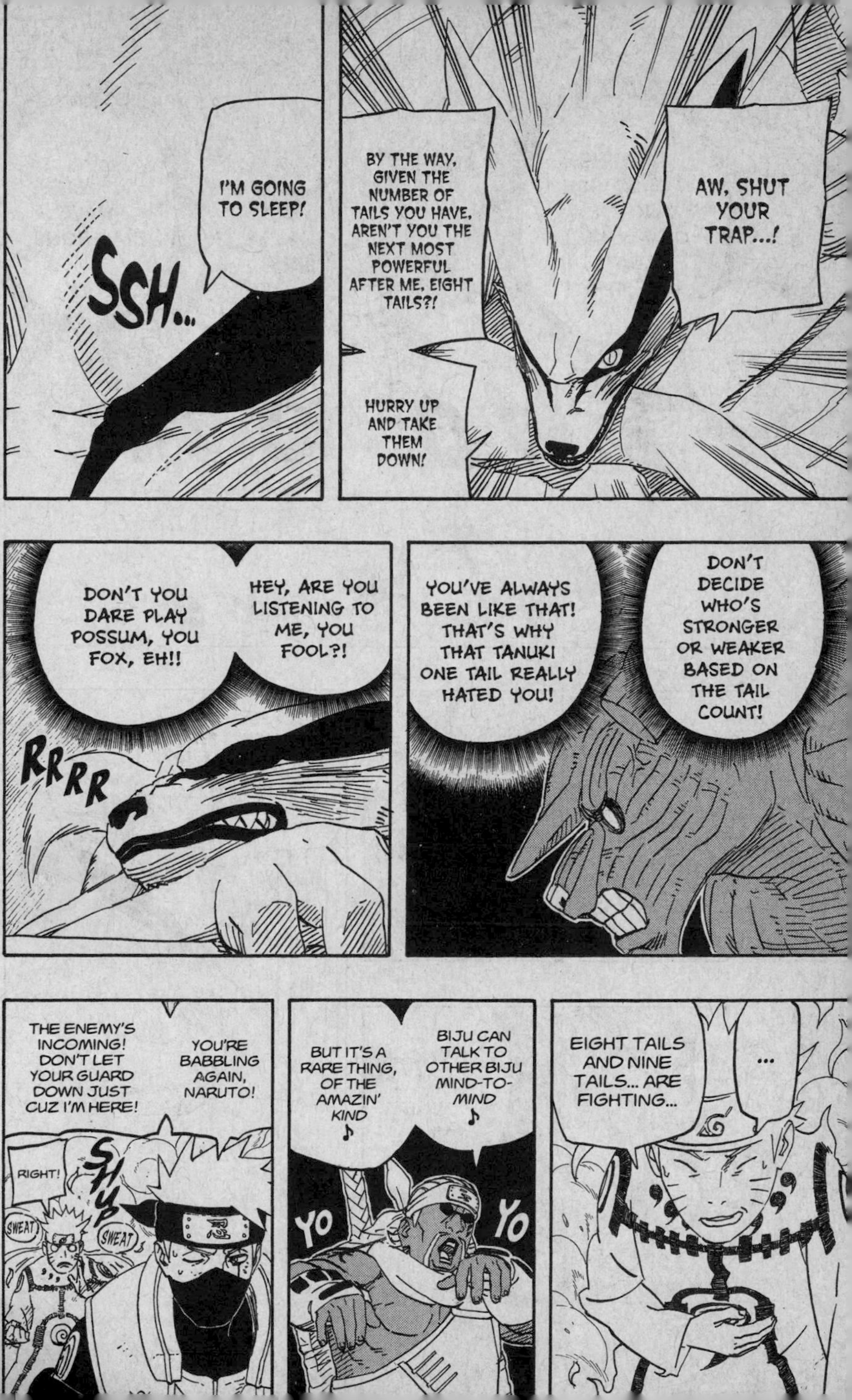
AW, SHUT YOUR TRAP...!
BY THE WAY, GIVEN THE NUMBER OF TAILS YOU HAVE, AREN'T YOU THE NEXT MOST POWERFUL AFTER ME, EIGHT TAILS?!
HURRY UP AND TAKE THEM DOWN!
I'M GOING TO SLEEP!
SSH...
DON'T DECIDE WHO'S STRONGER OR WEAKER BASED ON THE TAIL COUNT!
YOU'VE ALWAYS BEEN LIKE THAT! THAT'S WHY THAT TANUKI ONE TAIL REALLY HATED YOU!
HEY, ARE YOU LISTENING TO ME, YOU FOOL?!
DON'T YOU DARE PLAY POSSUM, YOU FOX, EH!!
RRRR
...
EIGHT TAILS AND NINE TAILS... ARE FIGHTING...
BIJU CAN TALK TO OTHER BIJU MIND-TO-MIND ♪
BUT IT'S A RARE THING, OF THE AMAZIN' KIND ♪
YO
YO
YOU'RE BABBLING AGAIN, NARUTO!
THE ENEMY'S INCOMING! DON'T LET YOUR GUARD DOWN JUST CUZ I'M HERE!
SHUP
RIGHT!
SWEAT
SWEAT

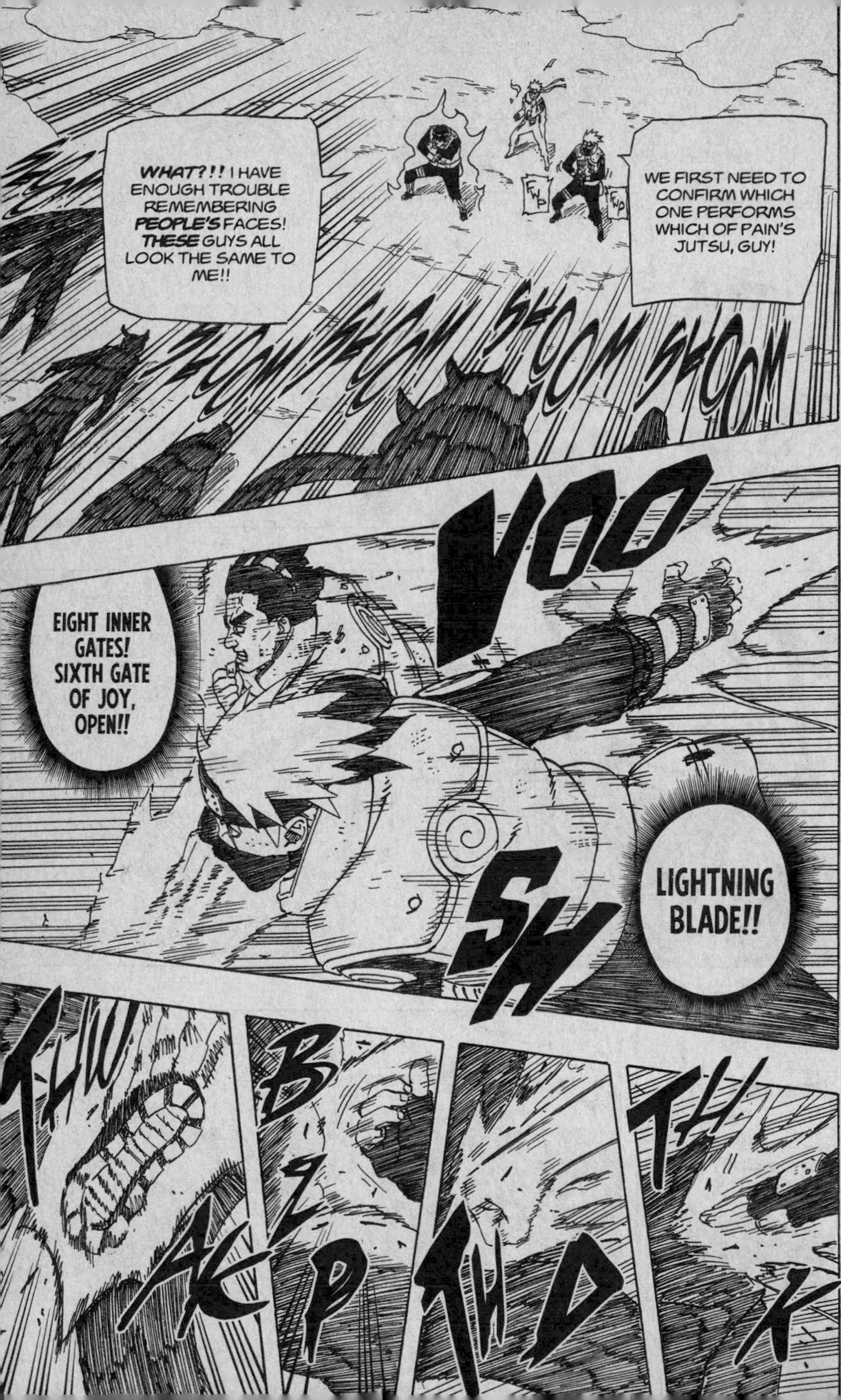

WE FIRST NEED TO CONFIRM WHICH ONE PERFORMS WHICH OF PAIN'S JUTSU, GUY!
FWP
FWP
WHAT?!! I HAVE ENOUGH TROUBLE REMEMBERING PEOPLE'S FACES! THESE GUYS ALL LOOK THE SAME TO ME!!
SHOOM SHOOM SHOOM SHOOM SHOOM
VOO
EIGHT INNER GATES! SIXTH GATE OF JOY, OPEN!!
SH
LIGHTNING BLADE!!
THK
THD
THWAK

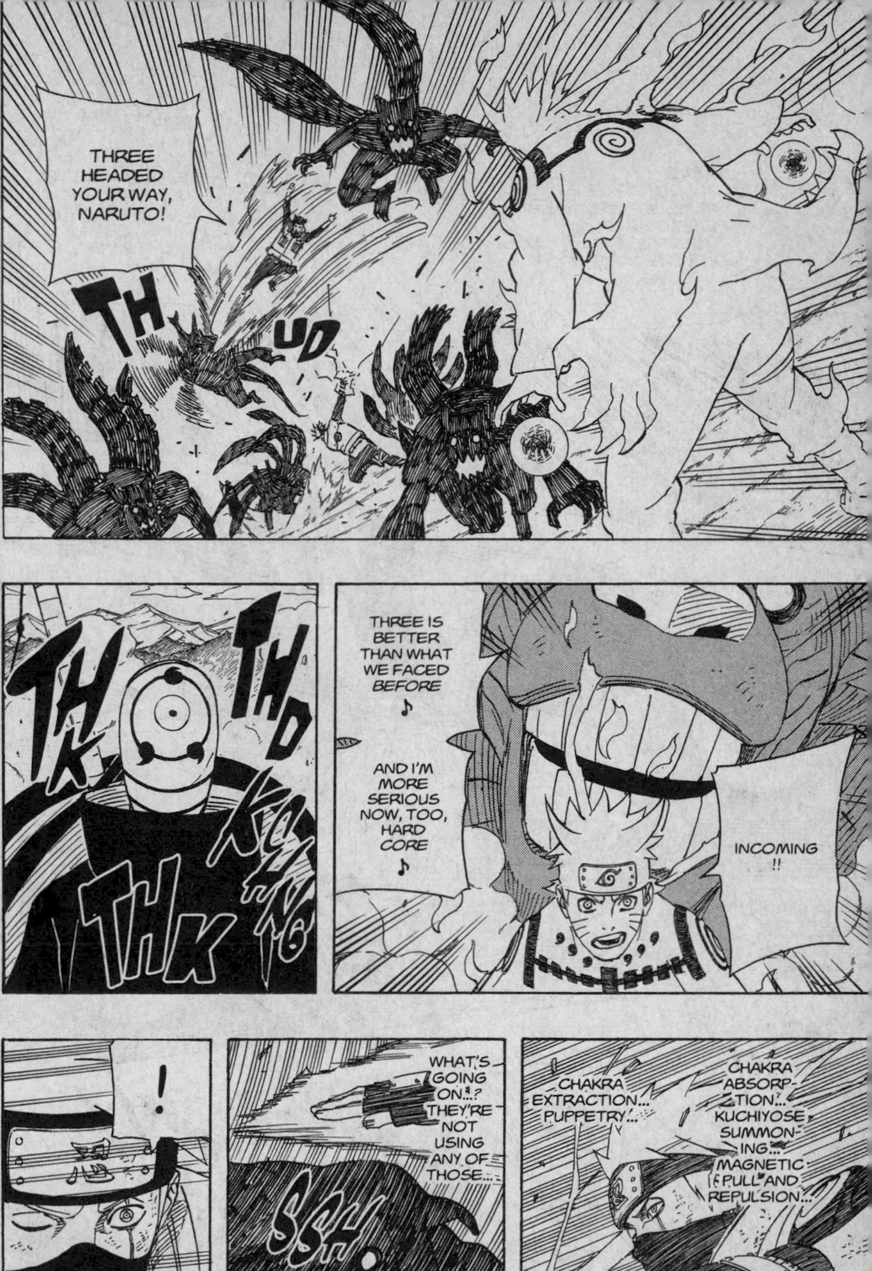
THREE HEADED YOUR WAY, NARUTO!
THUD
INCOMING!!
THREE IS BETTER THAN WHAT WE FACED BEFORE ♪
AND I'M MORE SERIOUS NOW, TOO, HARD CORE ♪
THK
THD
THK
CHAKRA ABSORPTION... KUCHIYOSE SUMMONING... MAGNETIC PULL AND REPULSION...
CHAKRA EXTRACTION... PUPPETRY...
WHAT'S GOING ON...? THEY'RE NOT USING ANY OF THOSE...
!

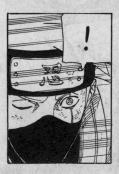

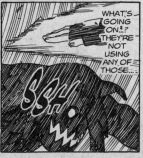

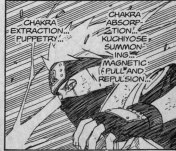

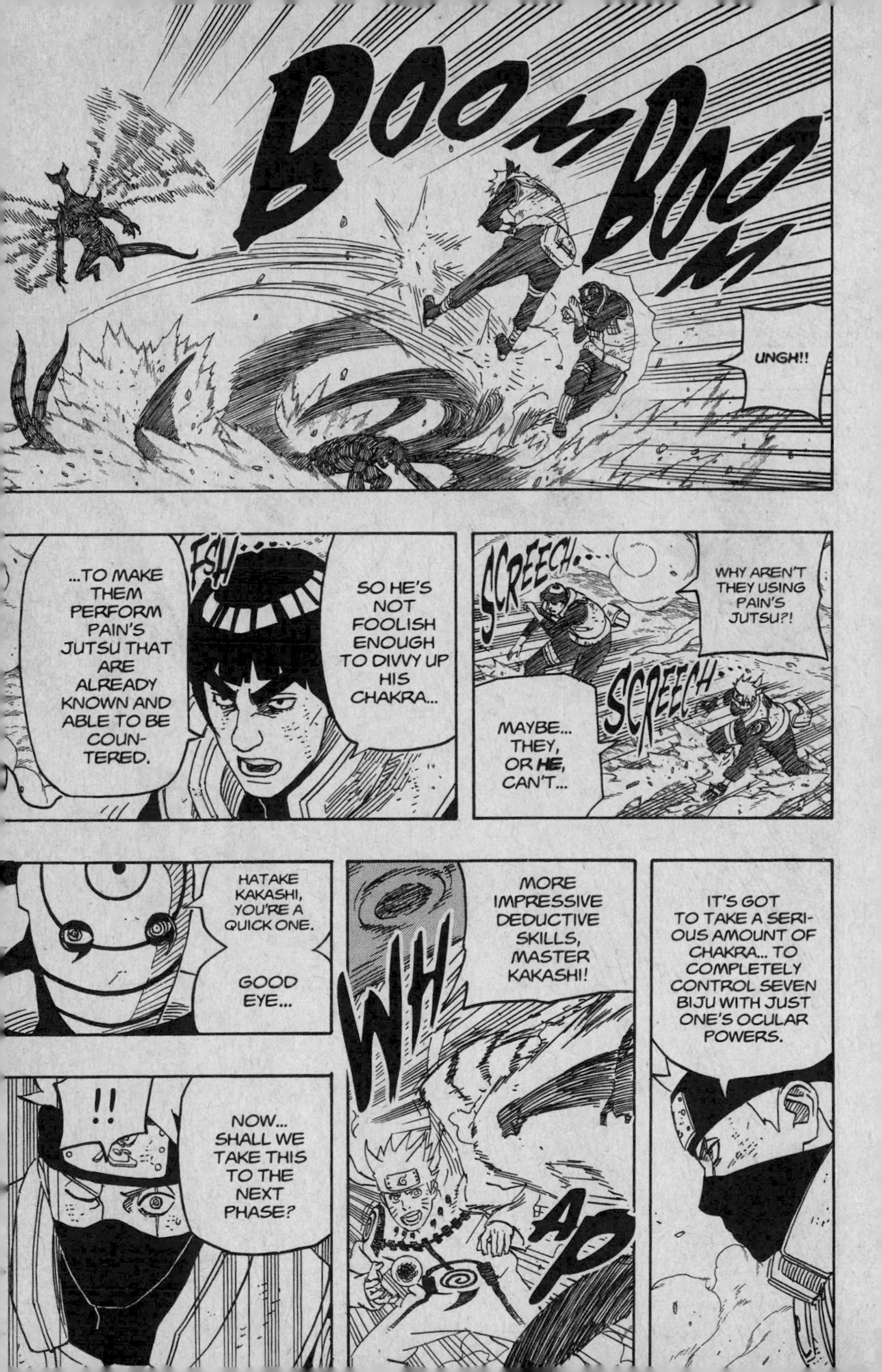
BOOM BOOM
UNGH!!
SCREECH
WHY AREN'T THEY USING PAIN'S JUTSU?!
SCREECH
MAYBE... THEY, OR **HE**, CAN'T...
FSH
SO HE'S NOT FOOLISH ENOUGH TO DIVVY UP HIS CHAKRA...
...TO MAKE THEM PERFORM PAIN'S JUTSU THAT ARE ALREADY KNOWN AND ABLE TO BE COUNTERED.
IT'S GOT TO TAKE A SERIOUS AMOUNT OF CHAKRA... TO COMPLETELY CONTROL SEVEN BIJU WITH JUST ONE'S OCULAR POWERS.
MORE IMPRESSIVE DEDUCTIVE SKILLS, MASTER KAKASHI!
WH
AP
HATAKE KAKASHI, YOU'RE A QUICK ONE.
GOOD EYE...
!!
NOW... SHALL WE TAKE THIS TO THE NEXT PHASE?

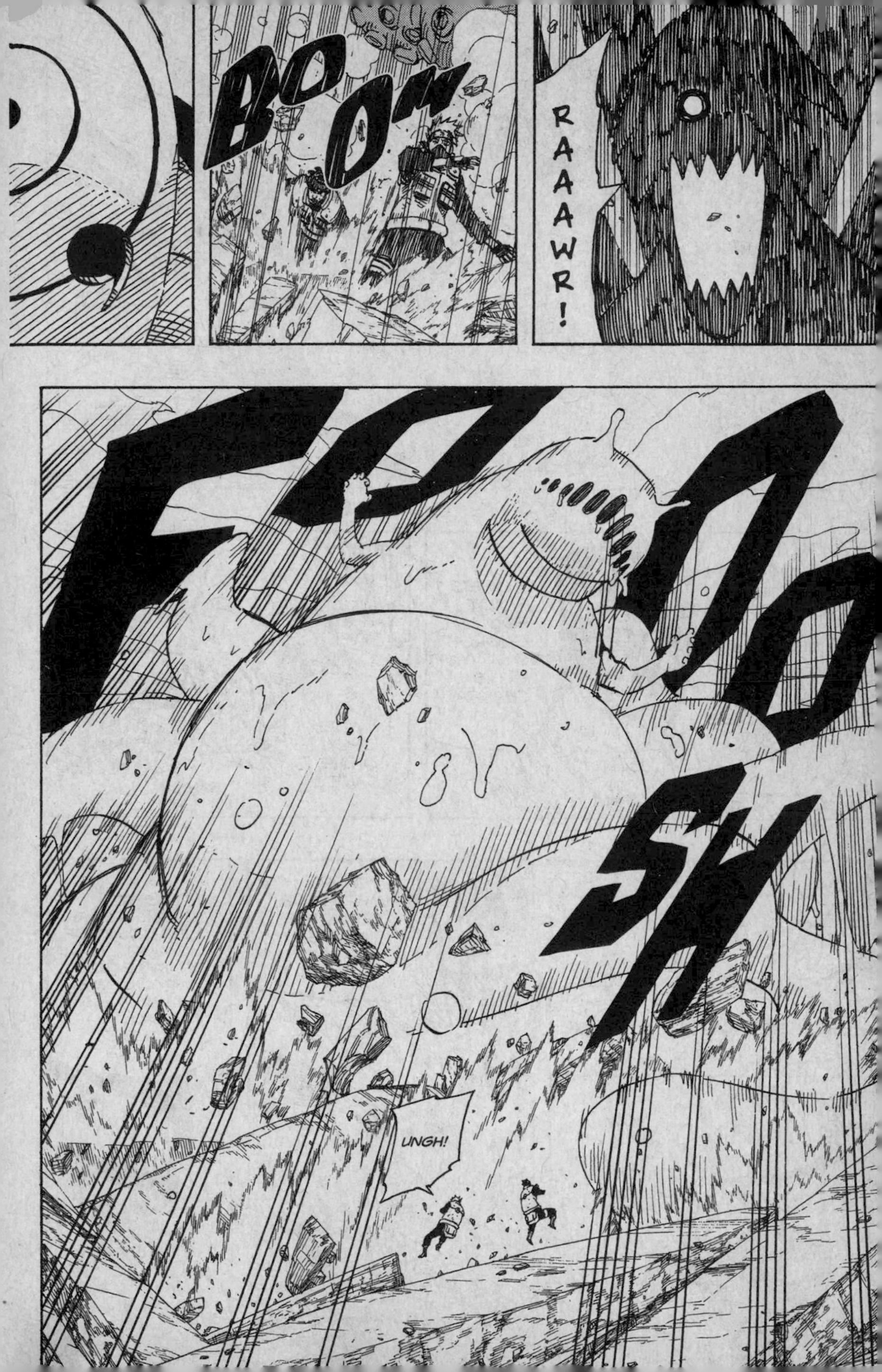
RAAAAWR!
BOOM
UNGH!

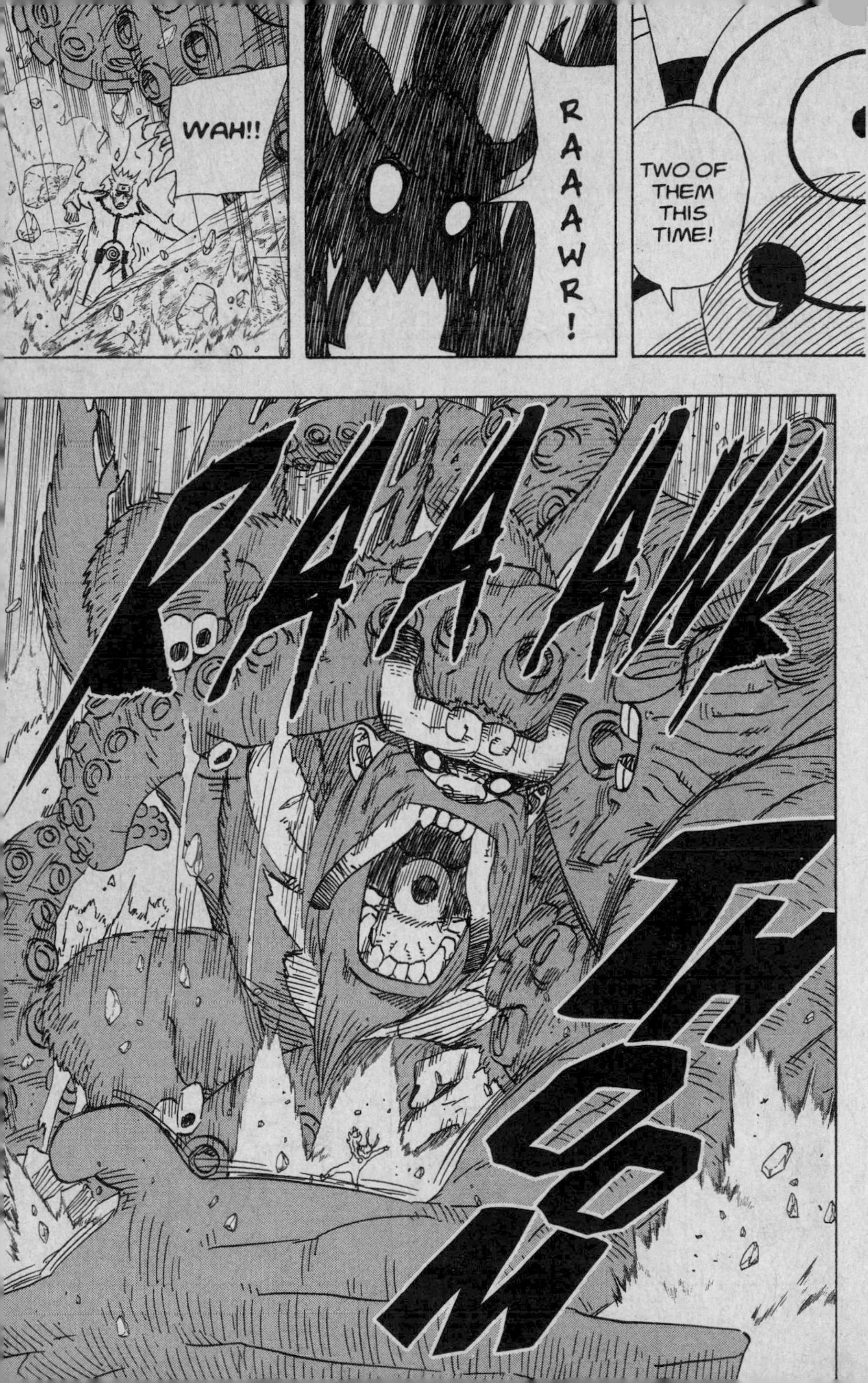
TWO OF THEM THIS TIME!
RAAAAWR!
WAH!!

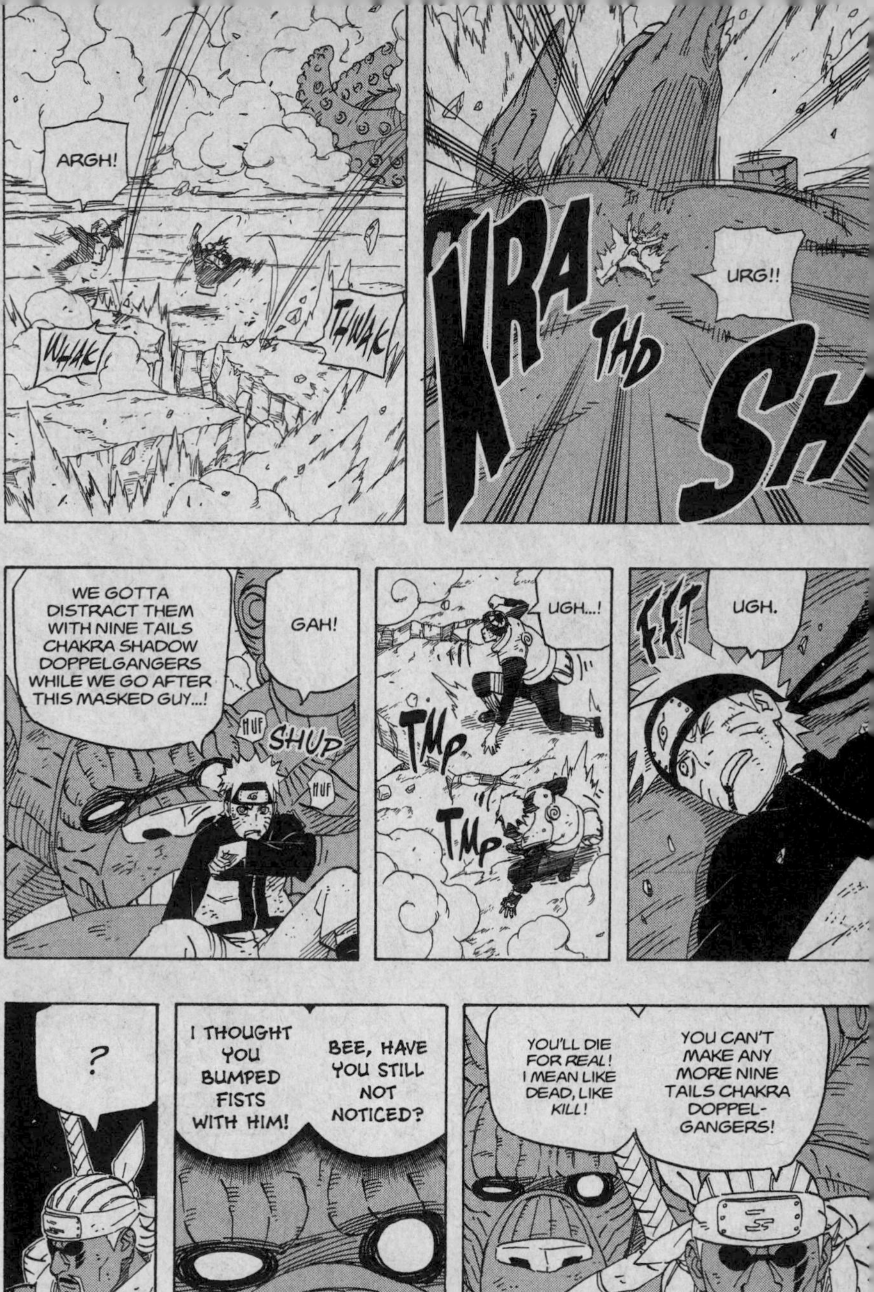
URG!!
KRA
THD
SH
ARGH!
THWAK
WHAK
UGH.
FFT
UGH...!
TMP
TMP
GAH!
WE GOTTA DISTRACT THEM WITH NINE TAILS CHAKRA SHADOW DOPPELGANGERS WHILE WE GO AFTER THIS MASKED GUY...!
SHUP
HUF
HUF
YOU CAN'T MAKE ANY MORE NINE TAILS CHAKRA DOPPEL-GANGERS!
YOU'LL DIE FOR REAL! I MEAN LIKE DEAD, LIKE KILL!
BEE, HAVE YOU STILL NOT NOTICED?
I THOUGHT YOU BUMPED FISTS WITH HIM!
?

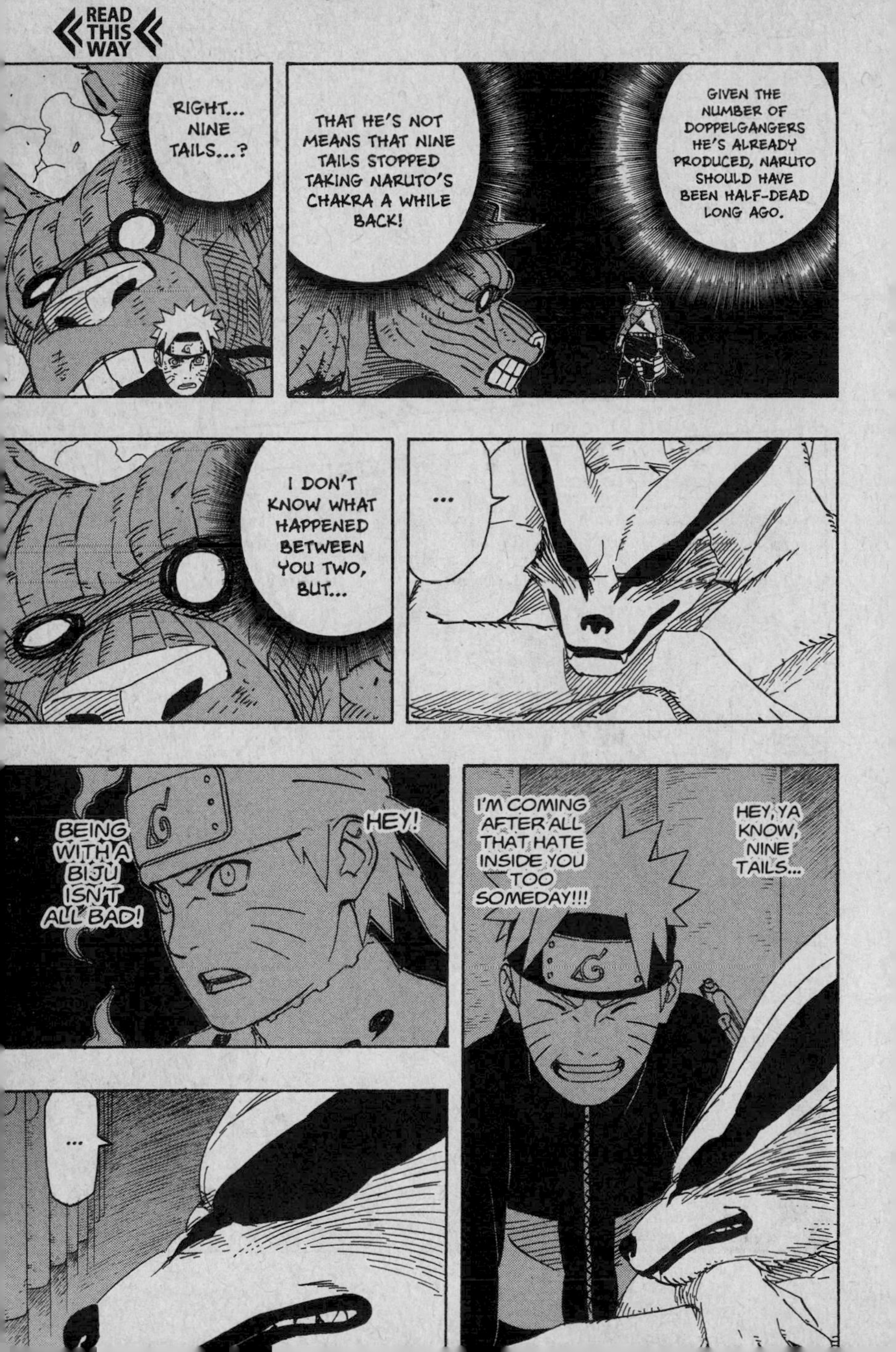
READ THIS WAY
GIVEN THE NUMBER OF DOPPELGANGERS HE'S ALREADY PRODUCED, NARUTO SHOULD HAVE BEEN HALF-DEAD LONG AGO.
THAT HE'S NOT MEANS THAT NINE TAILS STOPPED TAKING NARUTO'S CHAKRA A WHILE BACK!
RIGHT... NINE TAILS...?
...
I DON'T KNOW WHAT HAPPENED BETWEEN YOU TWO, BUT...
HEY, YA KNOW, NINE TAILS...
I'M COMING AFTER ALL THAT HATE INSIDE YOU TOO SOMEDAY!!!
HEY!
BEING WITH A BIJU ISN'T ALL BAD!
...

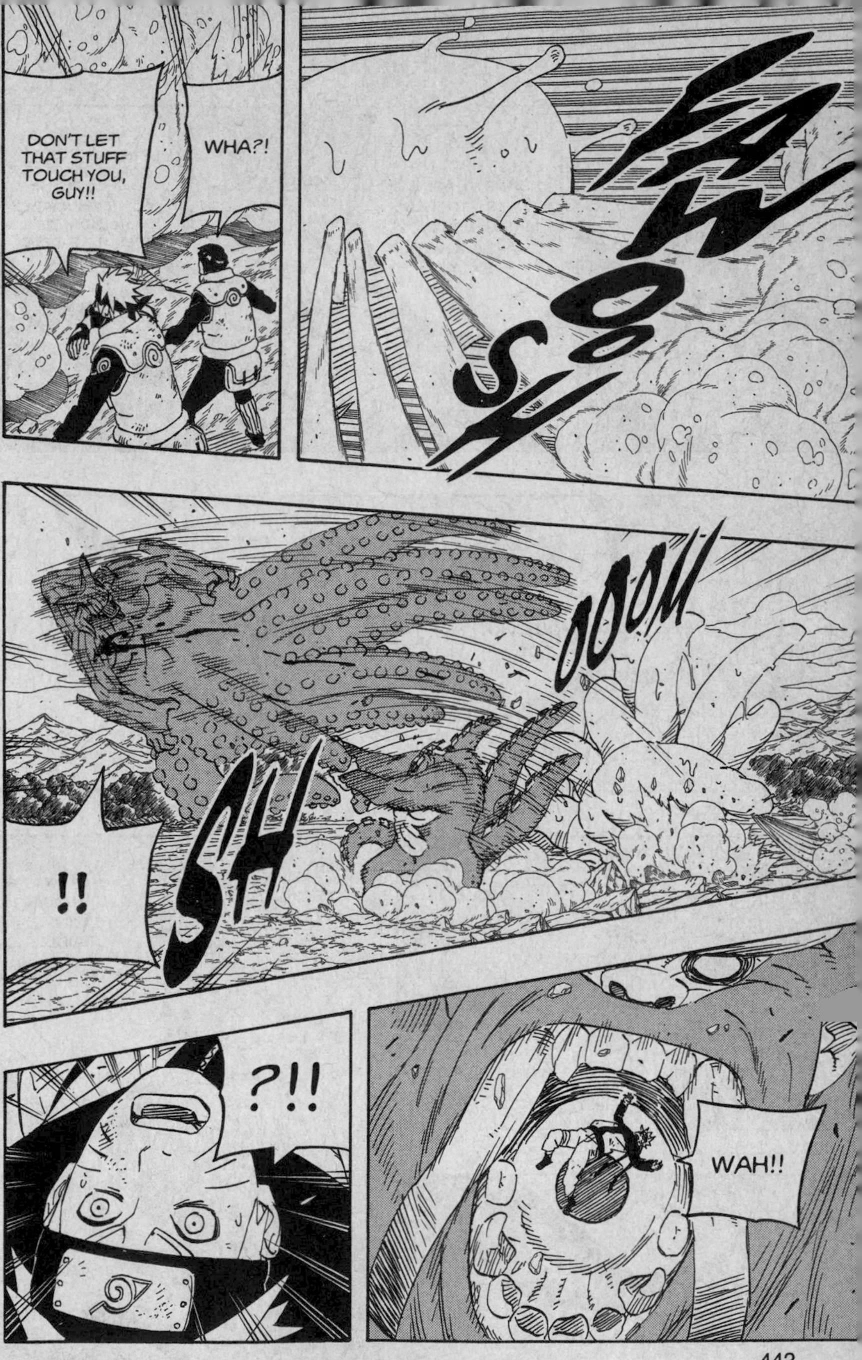
FAWOOSH
WHA?!
DON'T LET THAT STUFF TOUCH YOU, GUY!!
OOOM
SH
!!
WAH!!
?!!

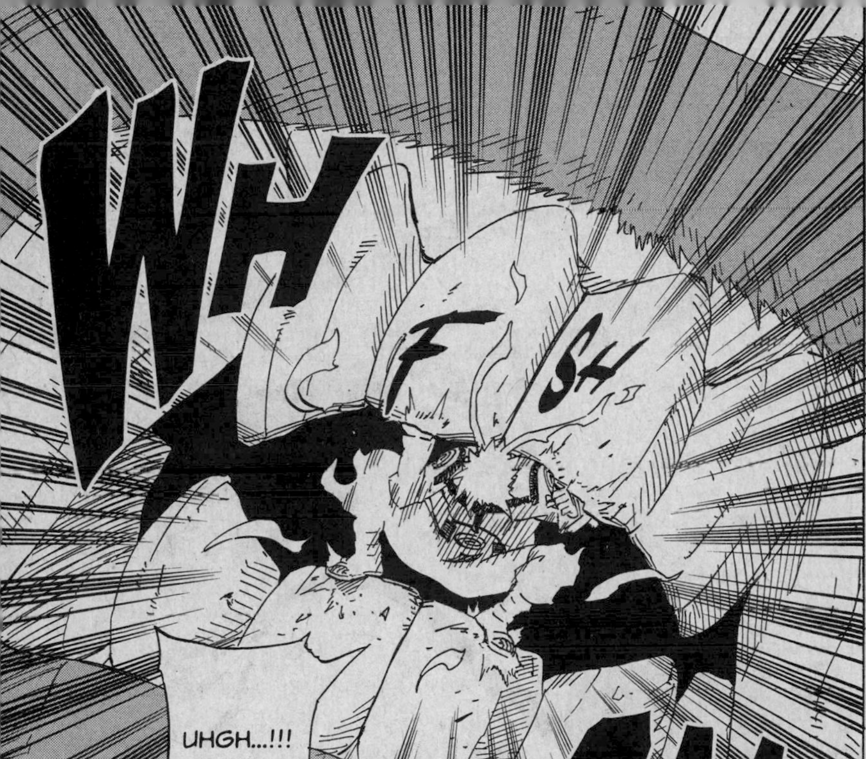
FSH
WHAM
UHGH...!!!
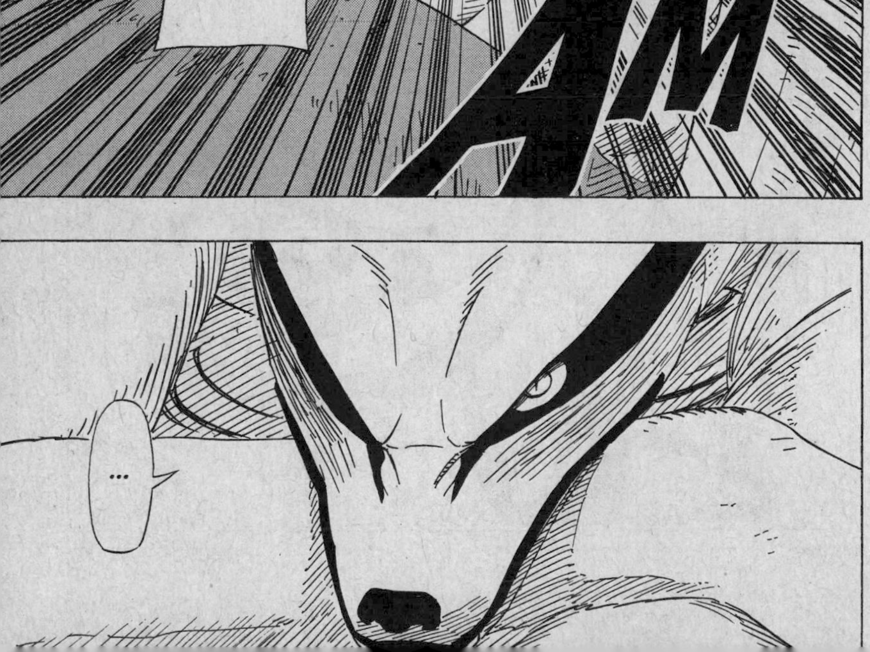
...

Illustration to Commemorate Reaching Volume 60 [3]

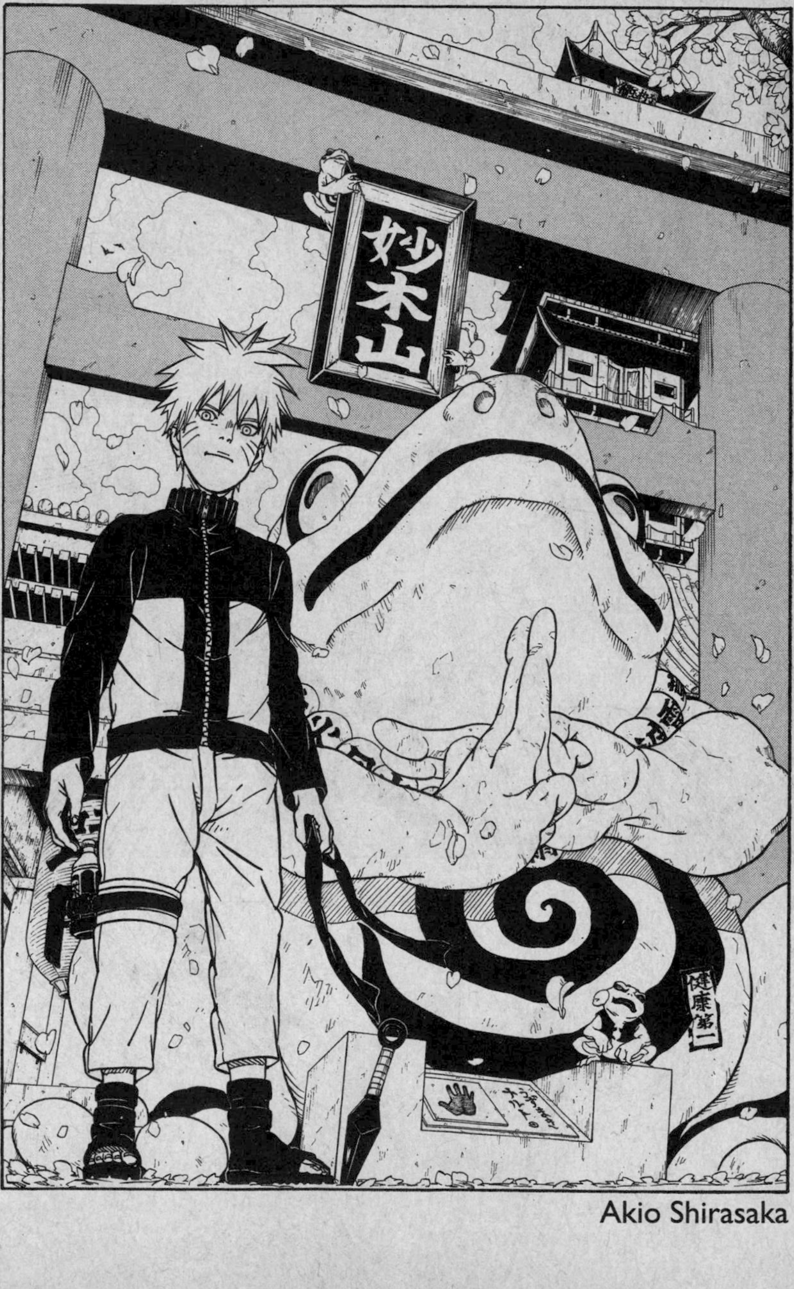
妙木山
健康第一

Akio Shirasaka

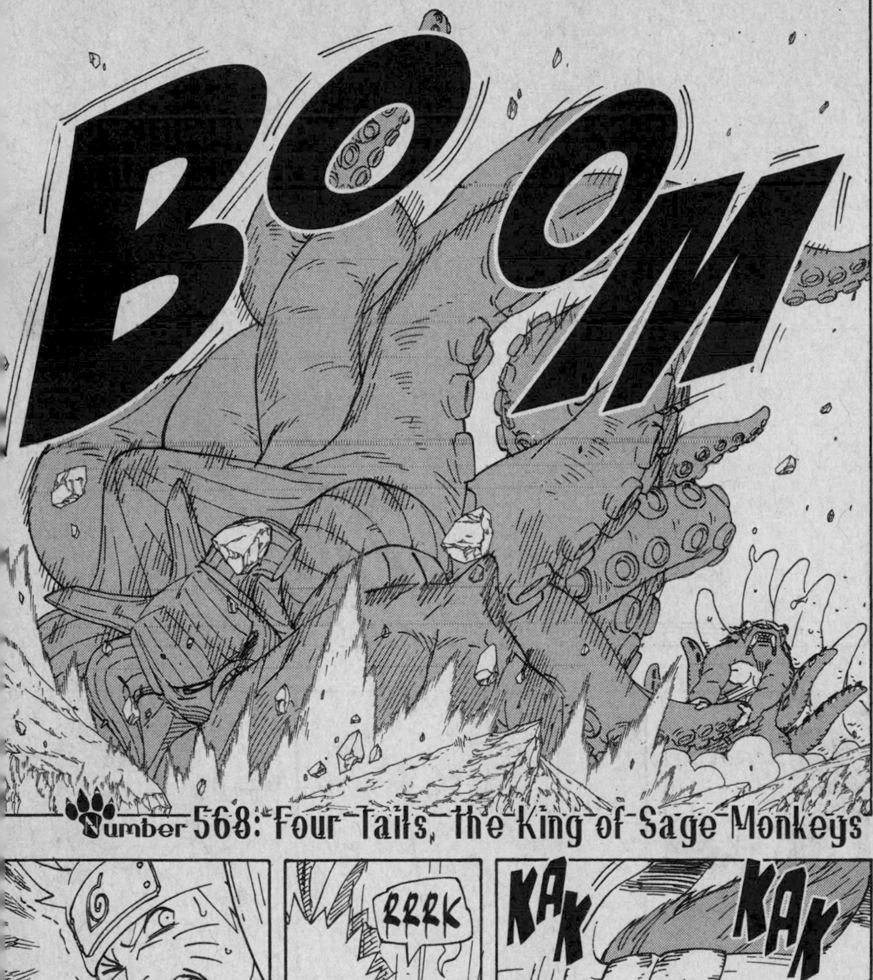
BOOM

Number 568: Four Tails, the King of Sage Monkeys

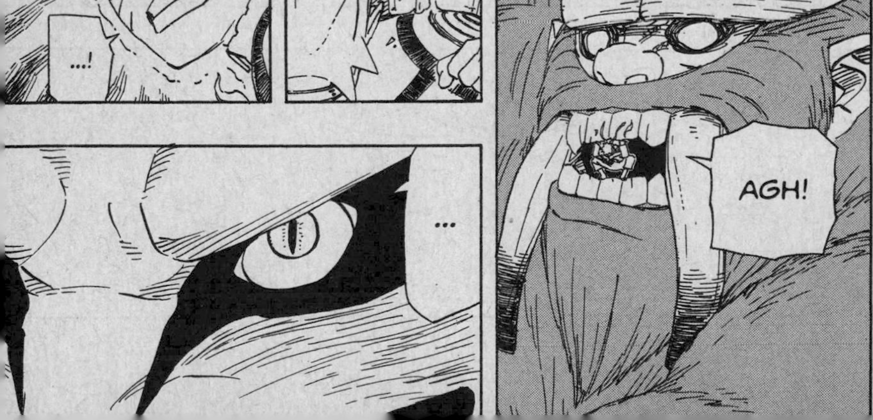
KAK
KAK
AGH!
RRRK
...!
...

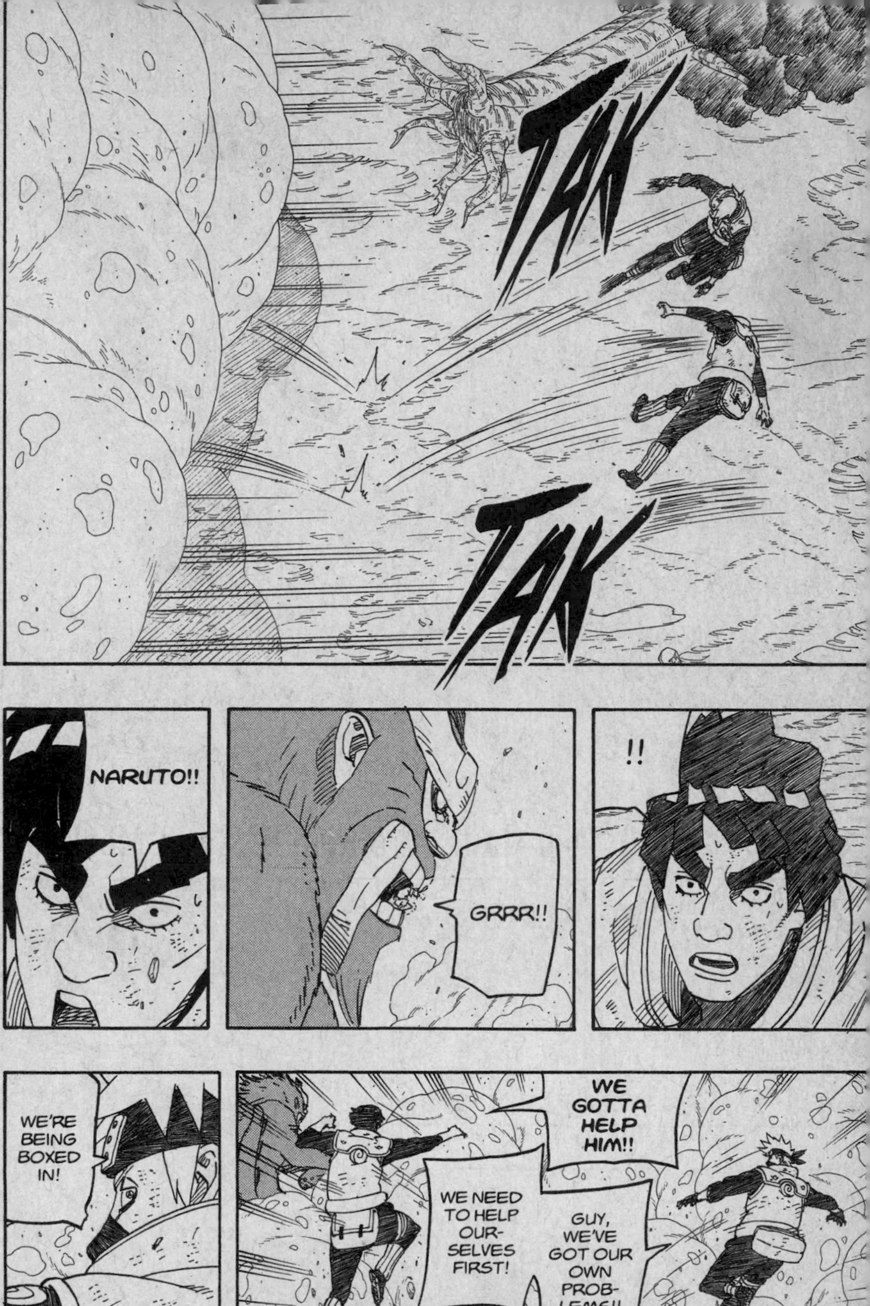

TAK
TAK
!!
GRRR!!
NARUTO!!
WE GOTTA HELP HIM!!
GUY, WE'VE GOT OUR OWN PROBLEMS!!
WE NEED TO HELP OURSELVES FIRST!
WE'RE BEING BOXED IN!

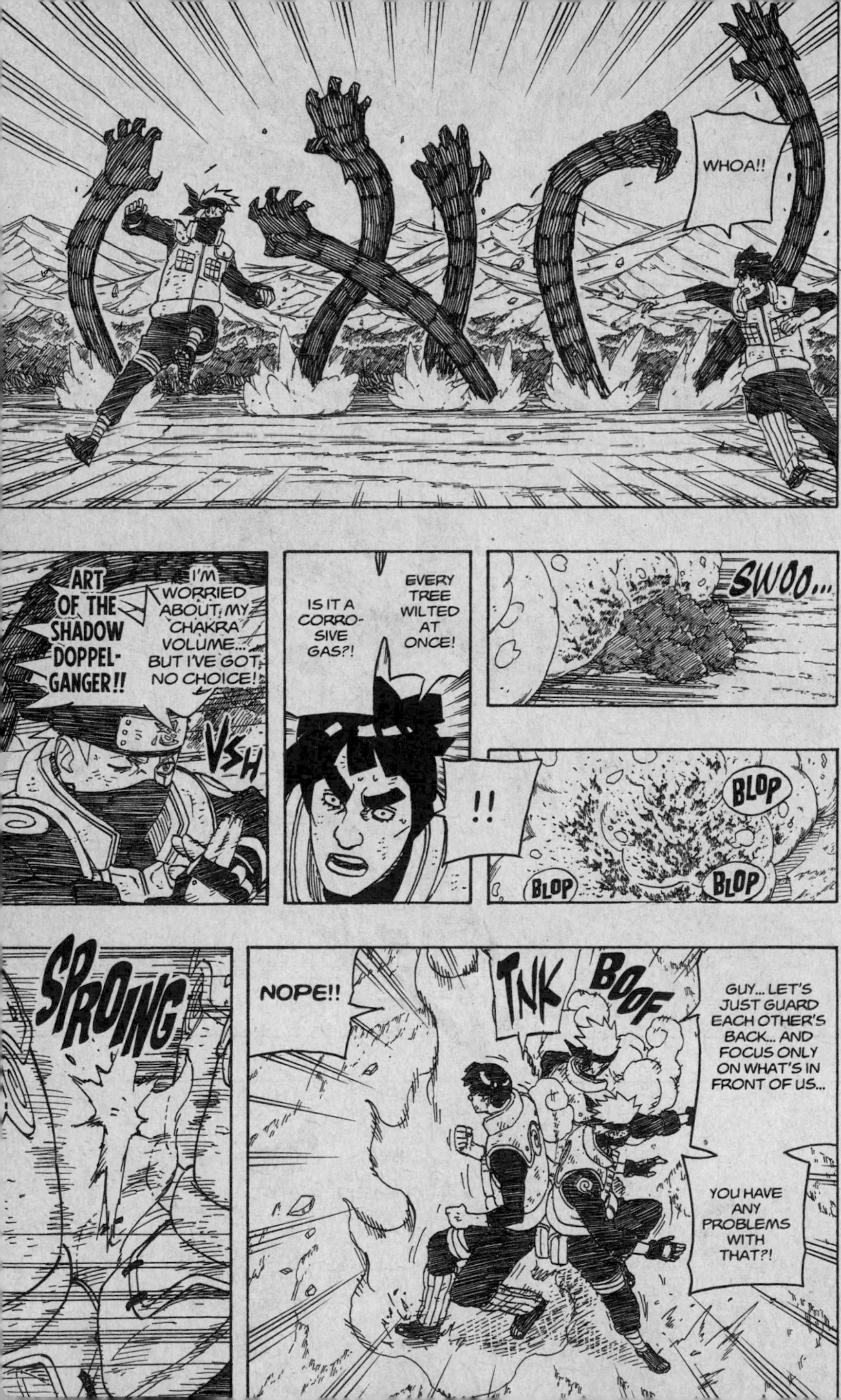
WHOA!!
SWOO...
BLOP
BLOP
BLOP
EVERY TREE WILTED AT ONCE!
IS IT A CORRO-SIVE GAS?!
!!
I'M WORRIED ABOUT MY CHAKRA VOLUME... BUT I'VE GOT NO CHOICE!
ART OF THE SHADOW DOPPEL-GANGER!!
VSH
GUY... LET'S JUST GUARD EACH OTHER'S BACK... AND FOCUS ONLY ON WHAT'S IN FRONT OF US...
YOU HAVE ANY PROBLEMS WITH THAT?!
BOOF
TNK
NOPE!!
SPROING

LIGHTNING CABLE!!

BZZZZZZZZZT

Z-Z-Z-ZLASH

HERE COMES THE NEXT WAVE.

THUD

SHF

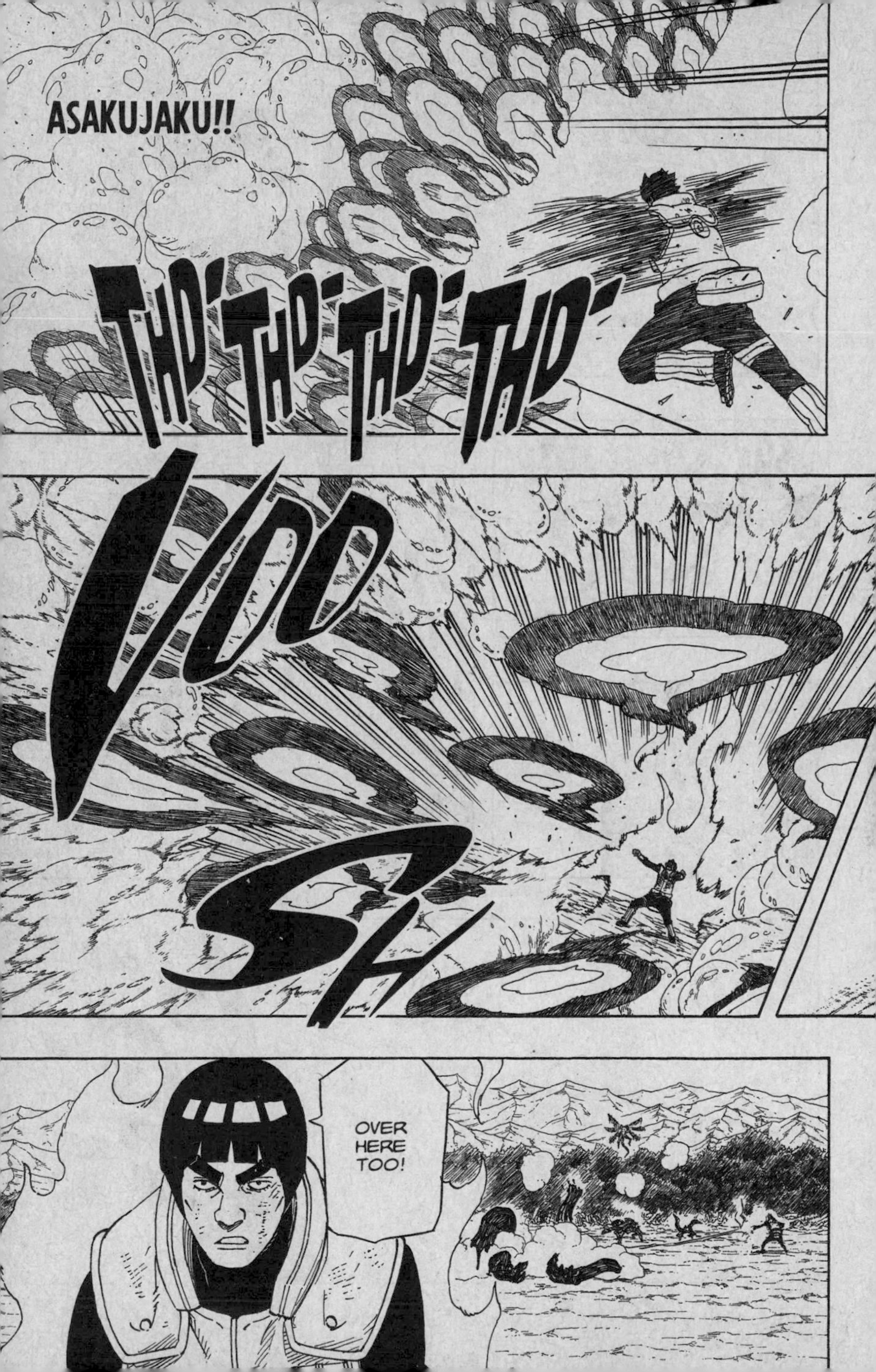
ASAKUJAKU!!
THD' THD' THD' THD'
VOOSH
OVER HERE TOO!

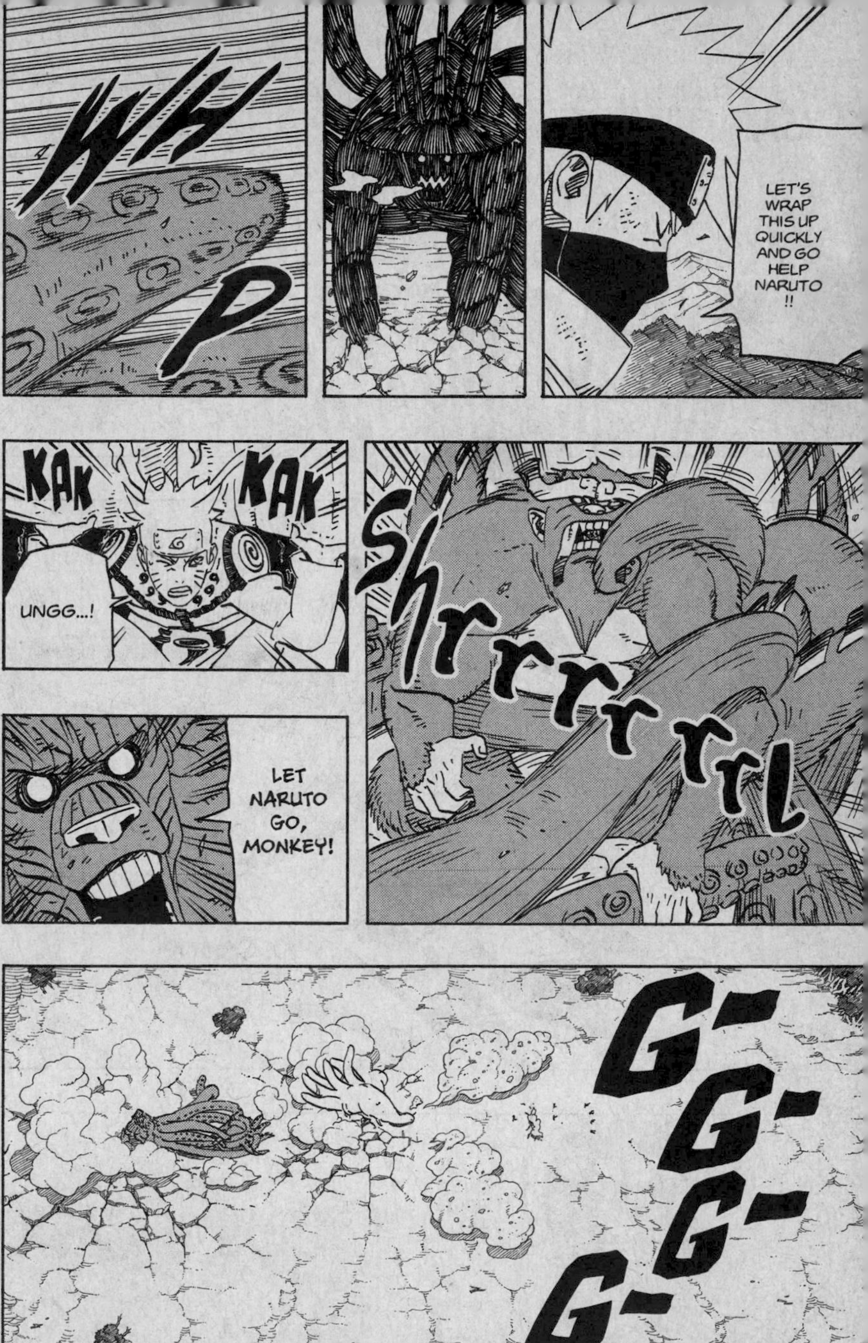
LET'S WRAP THIS UP QUICKLY AND GO HELP NARUTO!!
WHP
Shrrrrrrrl
KAK KAK
UNGG...!
LET NARUTO GO, MONKEY!
G-G-G-G-

READ THIS WAY

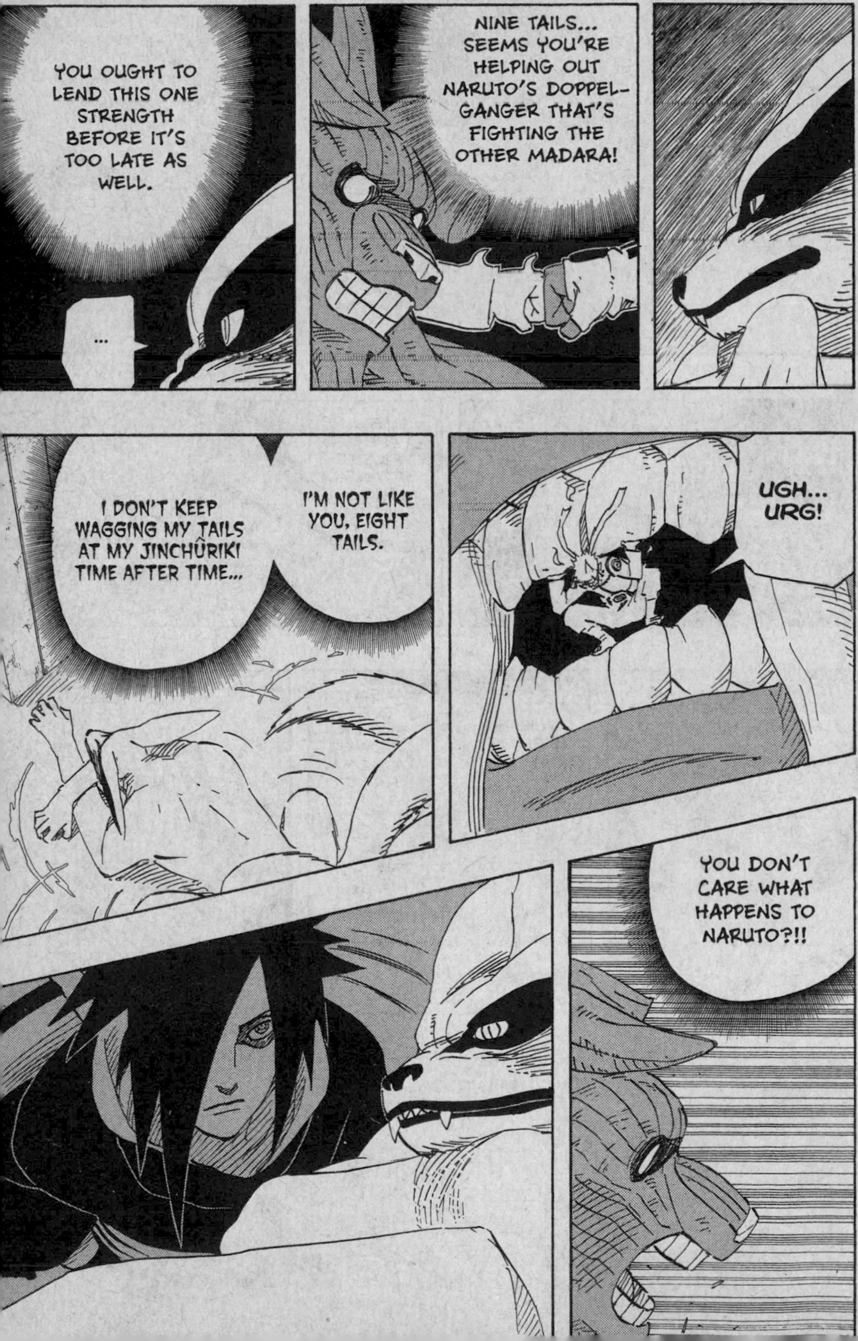
NINE TAILS... SEEMS YOU'RE HELPING OUT NARUTO'S DOPPEL-GANGER THAT'S FIGHTING THE OTHER MADARA!
YOU OUGHT TO LEND THIS ONE STRENGTH BEFORE IT'S TOO LATE AS WELL.
...
UGH... URG!
I'M NOT LIKE YOU, EIGHT TAILS.
I DON'T KEEP WAGGING MY TAILS AT MY JINCHŪRIKI TIME AFTER TIME...
YOU DON'T CARE WHAT HAPPENS TO NARUTO?!!

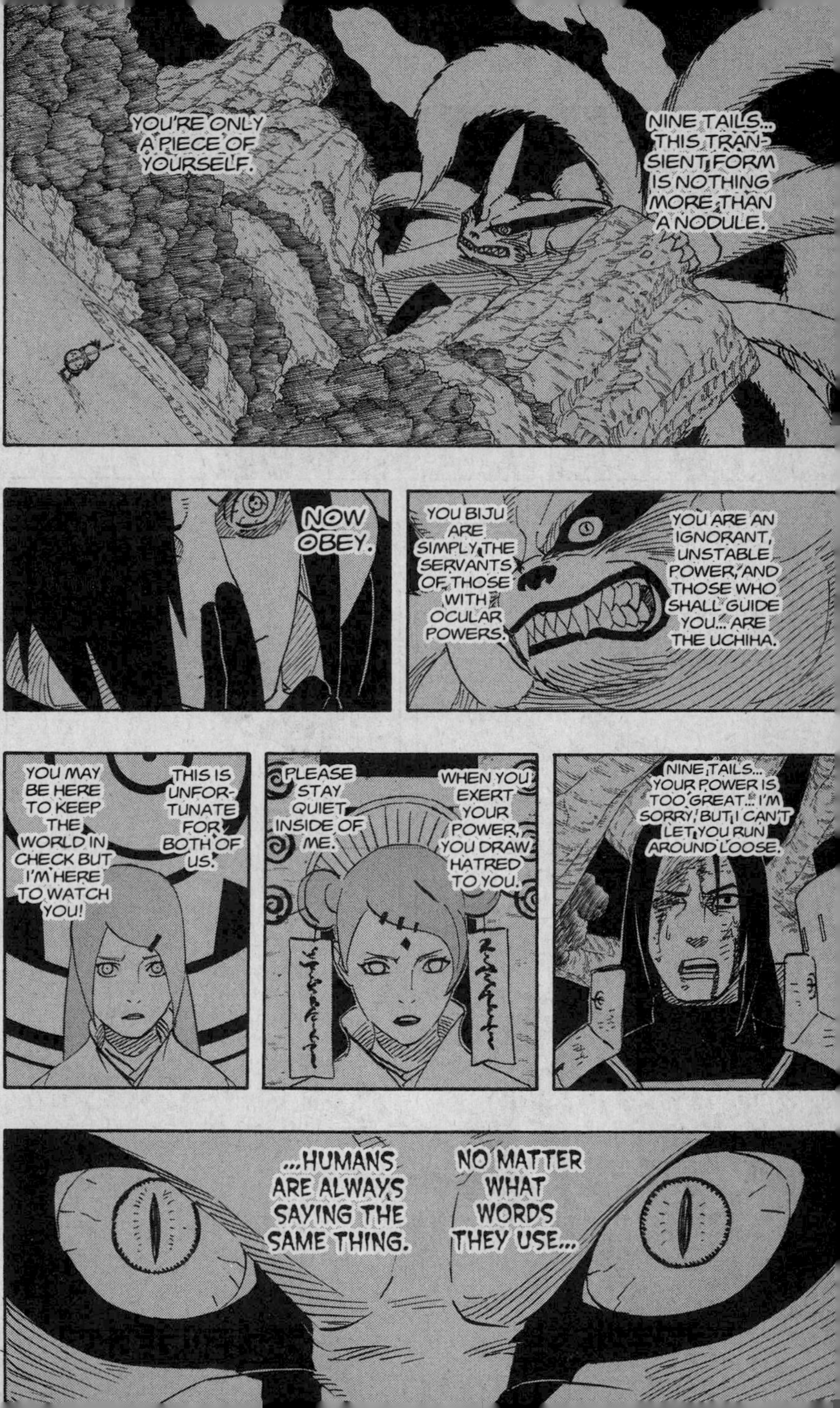
NINE TAILS... THIS TRANSIENT FORM IS NOTHING MORE THAN A NODULE.
YOU'RE ONLY A PIECE OF YOURSELF.
YOU ARE AN IGNORANT, UNSTABLE POWER, AND THOSE WHO SHALL GUIDE YOU... ARE THE UCHIHA.
YOU BIJU ARE SIMPLY THE SERVANTS OF THOSE WITH OCULAR POWERS.
NOW OBEY.
NINE TAILS... YOUR POWER IS TOO GREAT... I'M SORRY, BUT I CAN'T LET YOU RUN AROUND LOOSE.
WHEN YOU EXERT YOUR POWER, YOU DRAW HATRED TO YOU.
PLEASE STAY QUIET INSIDE OF ME.
THIS IS UNFORTUNATE FOR BOTH OF US.
YOU MAY BE HERE TO KEEP THE WORLD IN CHECK BUT I'M HERE TO WATCH YOU!
NO MATTER WHAT WORDS THEY USE...
...HUMANS ARE ALWAYS SAYING THE SAME THING.

READ THIS WAY

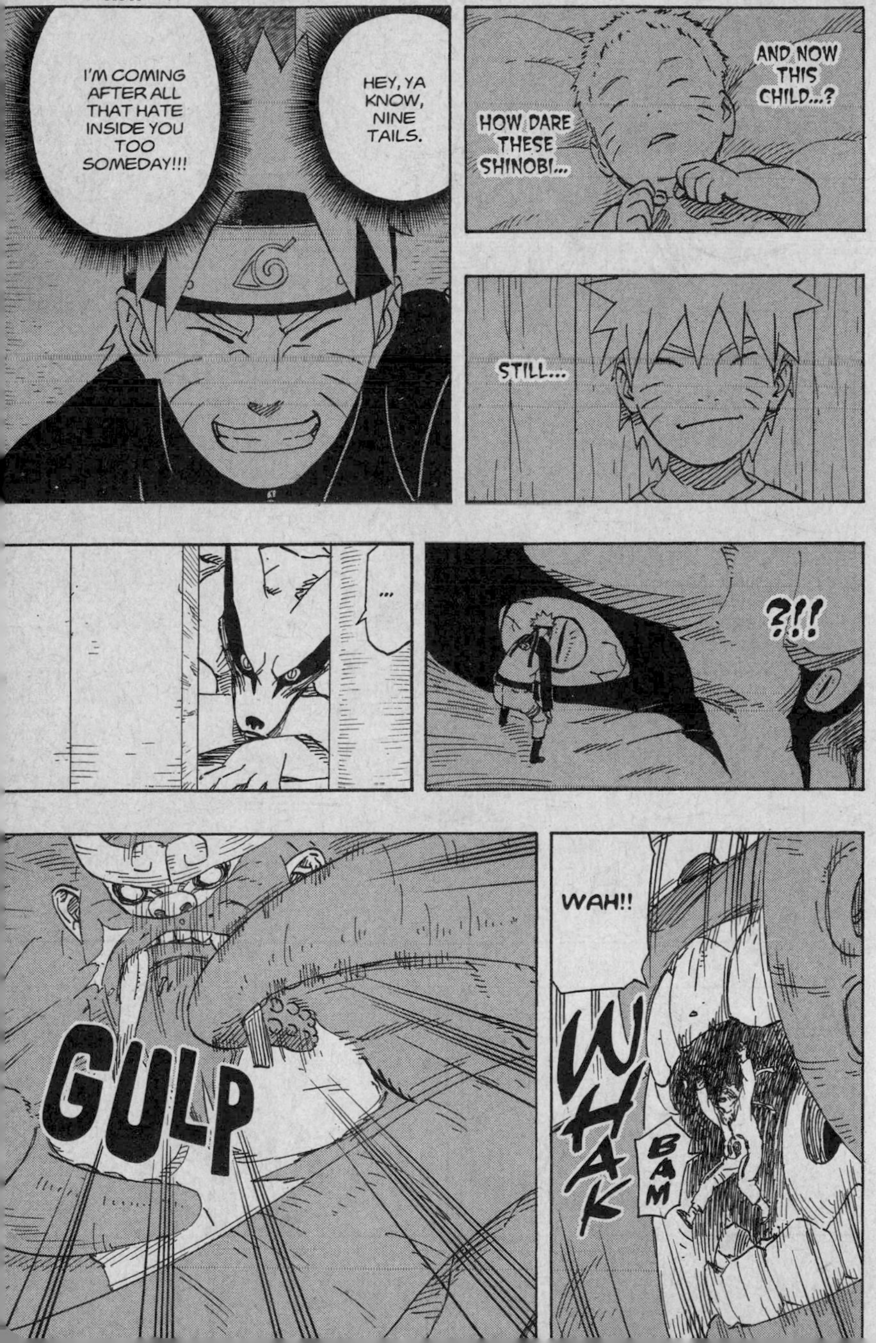
AND NOW THIS CHILD...?
HOW DARE THESE SHINOBI...
STILL...
HEY, YA KNOW, NINE TAILS.
I'M COMING AFTER ALL THAT HATE INSIDE YOU TOO SOMEDAY!!!
?!!
...
WAH!!
WHAK
BAM
GULP

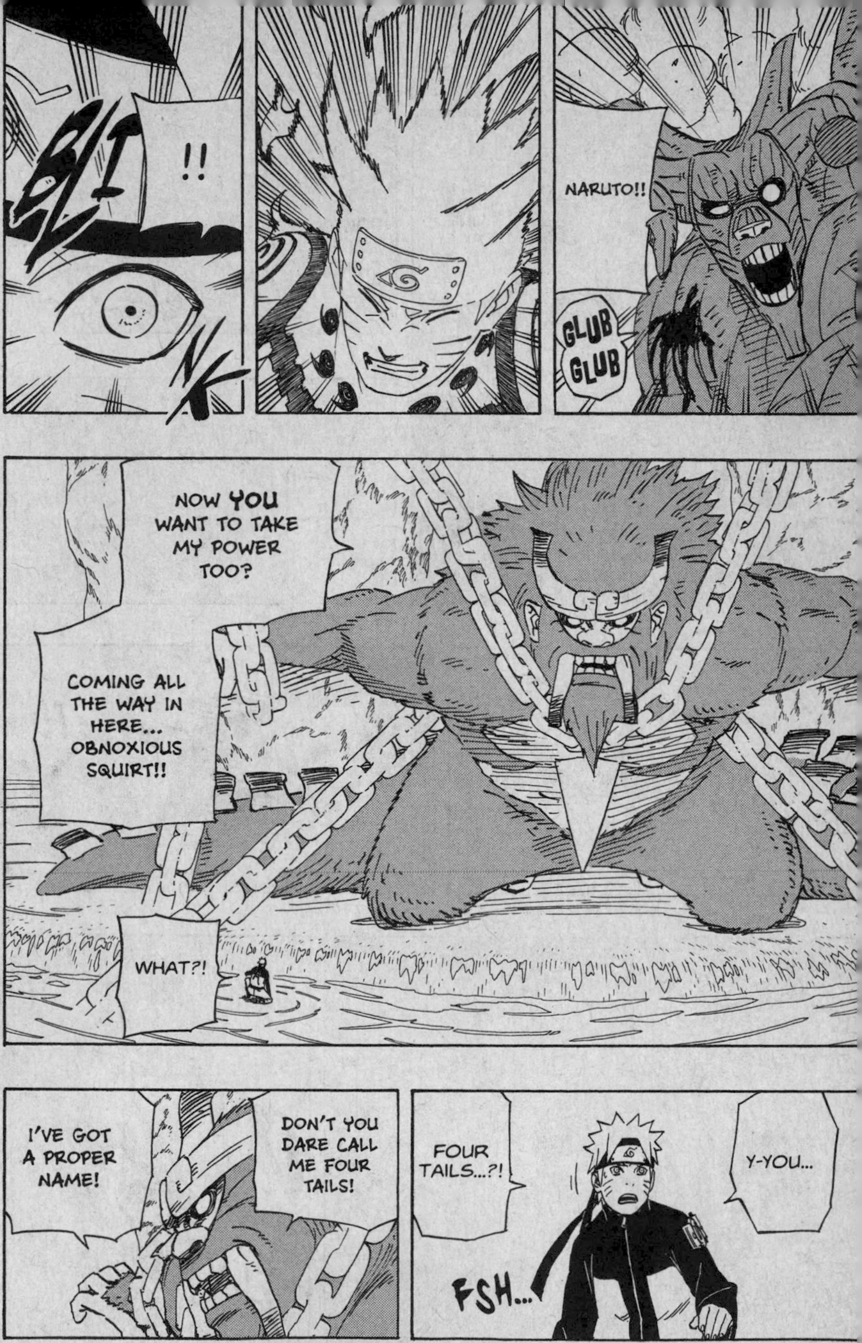
NARUTO!!
GLUB GLUB
!!
BLINK
NOW YOU WANT TO TAKE MY POWER TOO?
COMING ALL THE WAY IN HERE... OBNOXIOUS SQUIRT!!
WHAT?!
Y-YOU...
FOUR TAILS...?!
FSH...
DON'T YOU DARE CALL ME FOUR TAILS!
I'VE GOT A PROPER NAME!

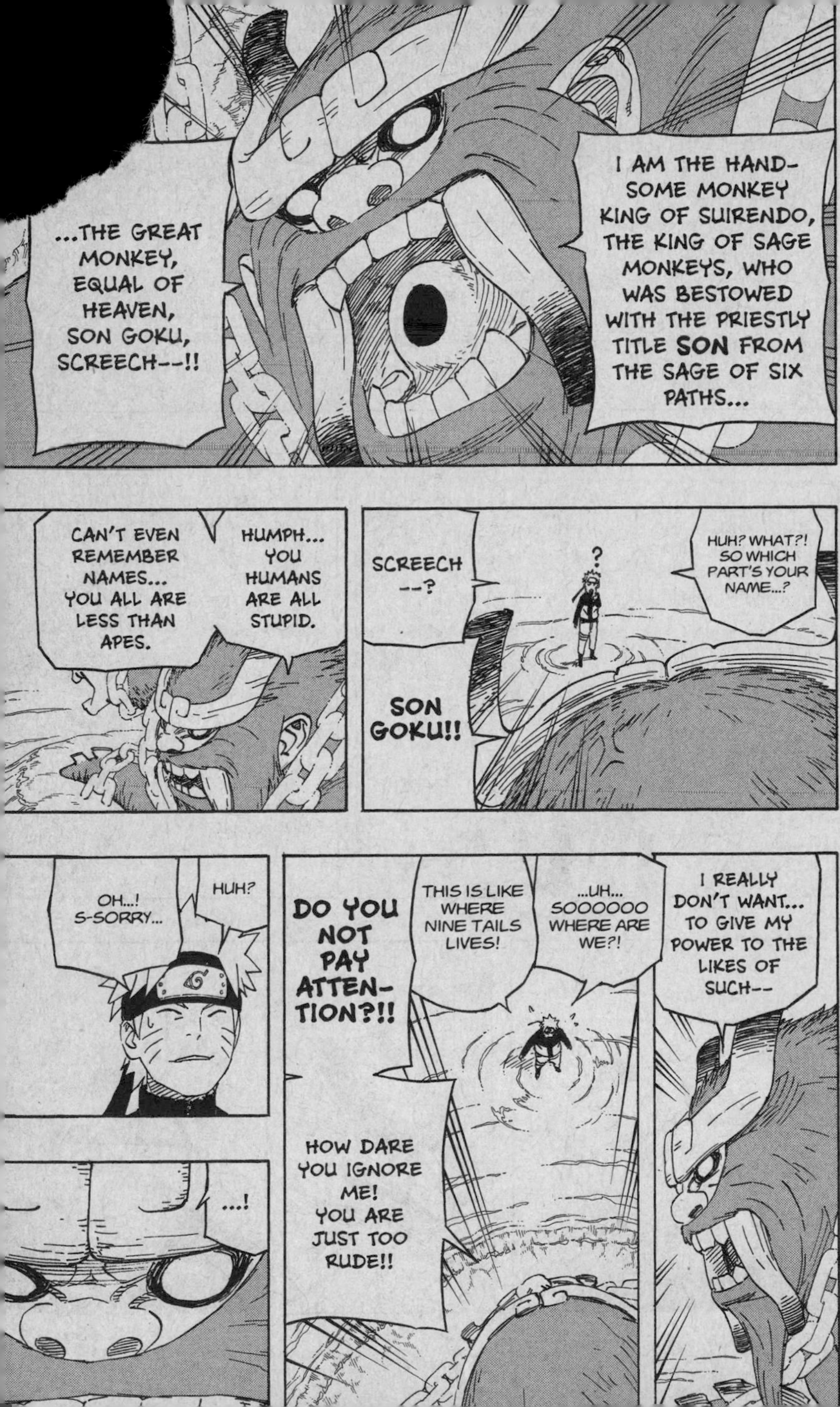

I AM THE HAND-SOME MONKEY KING OF SUIRENDO, THE KING OF SAGE MONKEYS, WHO WAS BESTOWED WITH THE PRIESTLY TITLE SON FROM THE SAGE OF SIX PATHS...
...THE GREAT MONKEY, EQUAL OF HEAVEN, SON GOKU, SCREECH--!!
HUH? WHAT?! SO WHICH PART'S YOUR NAME...?
SCREECH --?
SON GOKU!!
HUMPH... YOU HUMANS ARE ALL STUPID.
CAN'T EVEN REMEMBER NAMES... YOU ALL ARE LESS THAN APES.
I REALLY DON'T WANT... TO GIVE MY POWER TO THE LIKES OF SUCH--
...UH... SOOOOOO WHERE ARE WE?!
THIS IS LIKE WHERE NINE TAILS LIVES!
DO YOU NOT PAY ATTEN-TION?!!
HOW DARE YOU IGNORE ME! YOU ARE JUST TOO RUDE!!
HUH?
OH...! S-SORRY...
...!

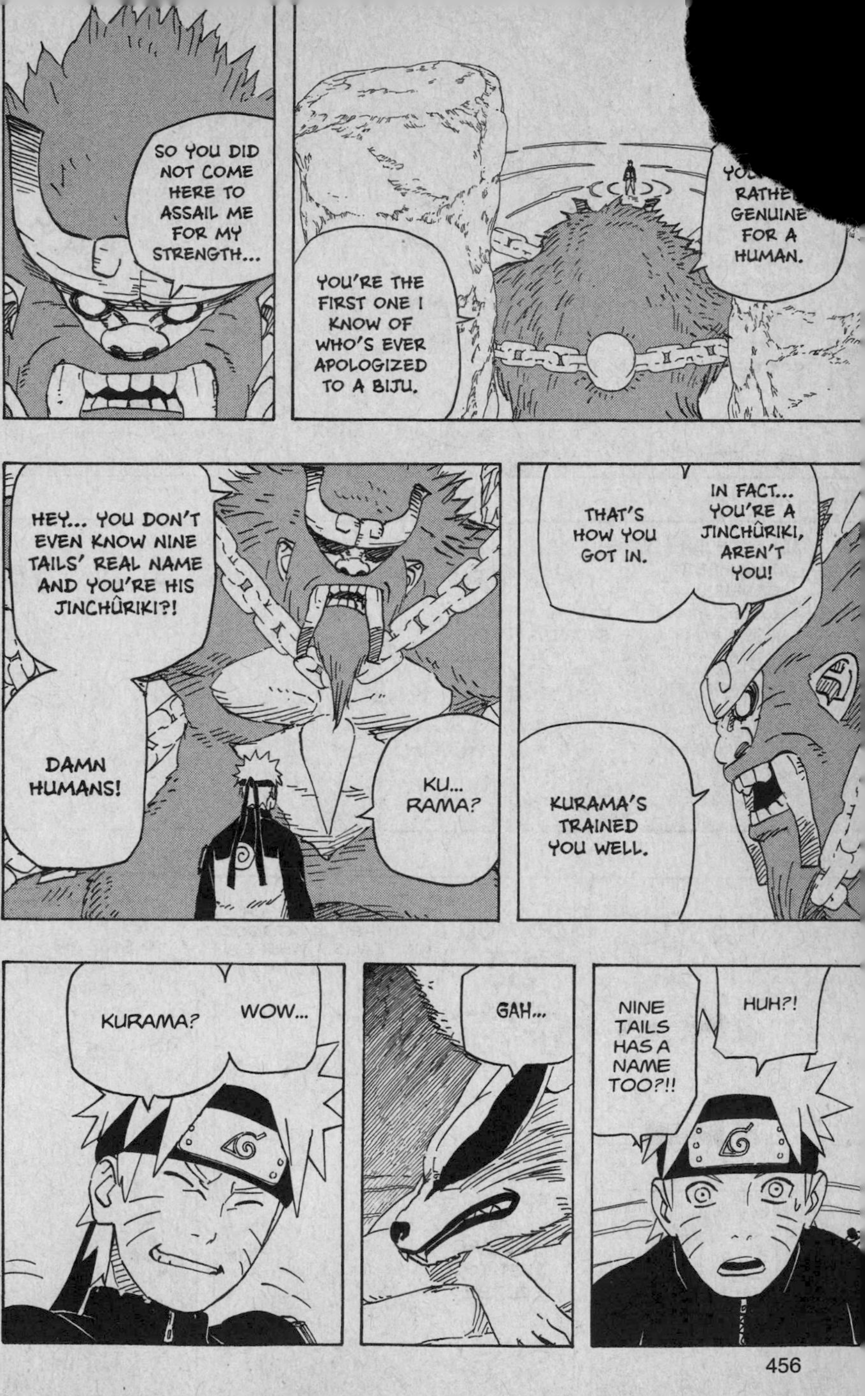

RATHE GENUINE FOR A HUMAN.
YOU'RE THE FIRST ONE I KNOW OF WHO'S EVER APOLOGIZED TO A BIJU.
SO YOU DID NOT COME HERE TO ASSAIL ME FOR MY STRENGTH...
IN FACT... YOU'RE A JINCHÛRIKI, AREN'T YOU!
THAT'S HOW YOU GOT IN.
KURAMA'S TRAINED YOU WELL.
HEY... YOU DON'T EVEN KNOW NINE TAILS' REAL NAME AND YOU'RE HIS JINCHÛRIKI?!
KU... RAMA?
DAMN HUMANS!
HUH?!
NINE TAILS HAS A NAME TOO?!!
GAH...
WOW...
KURAMA?

READ THIS WAY

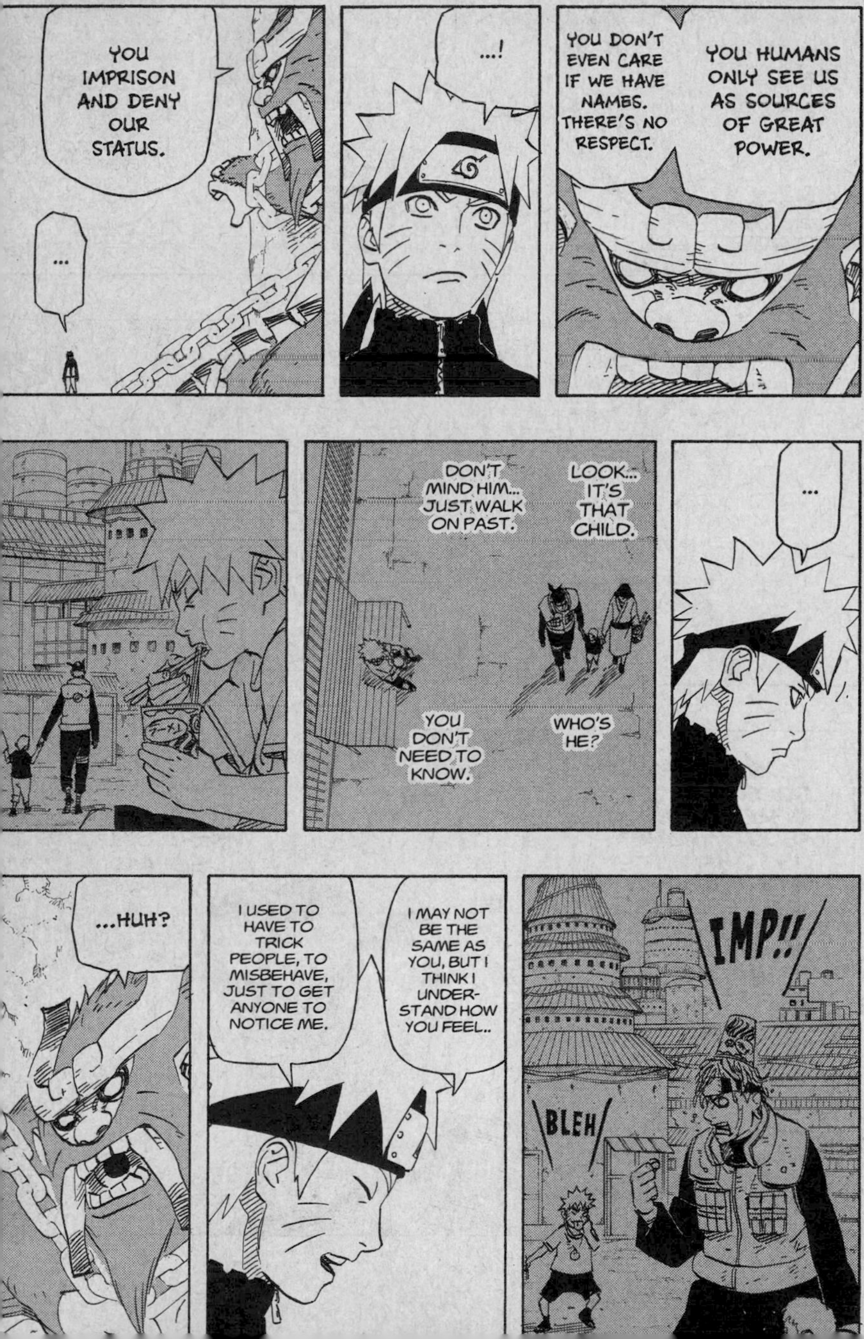
YOU HUMANS ONLY SEE US AS SOURCES OF GREAT POWER.
YOU DON'T EVEN CARE IF WE HAVE NAMES. THERE'S NO RESPECT.
...!
YOU IMPRISON AND DENY OUR STATUS.
...
...
LOOK... IT'S THAT CHILD.
DON'T MIND HIM... JUST WALK ON PAST.
WHO'S HE?
YOU DON'T NEED TO KNOW.
IMP!!
BLEH
I MAY NOT BE THE SAME AS YOU, BUT I THINK I UNDER-STAND HOW YOU FEEL..
I USED TO HAVE TO TRICK PEOPLE, TO MISBEHAVE, JUST TO GET ANYONE TO NOTICE ME.
...HUH?

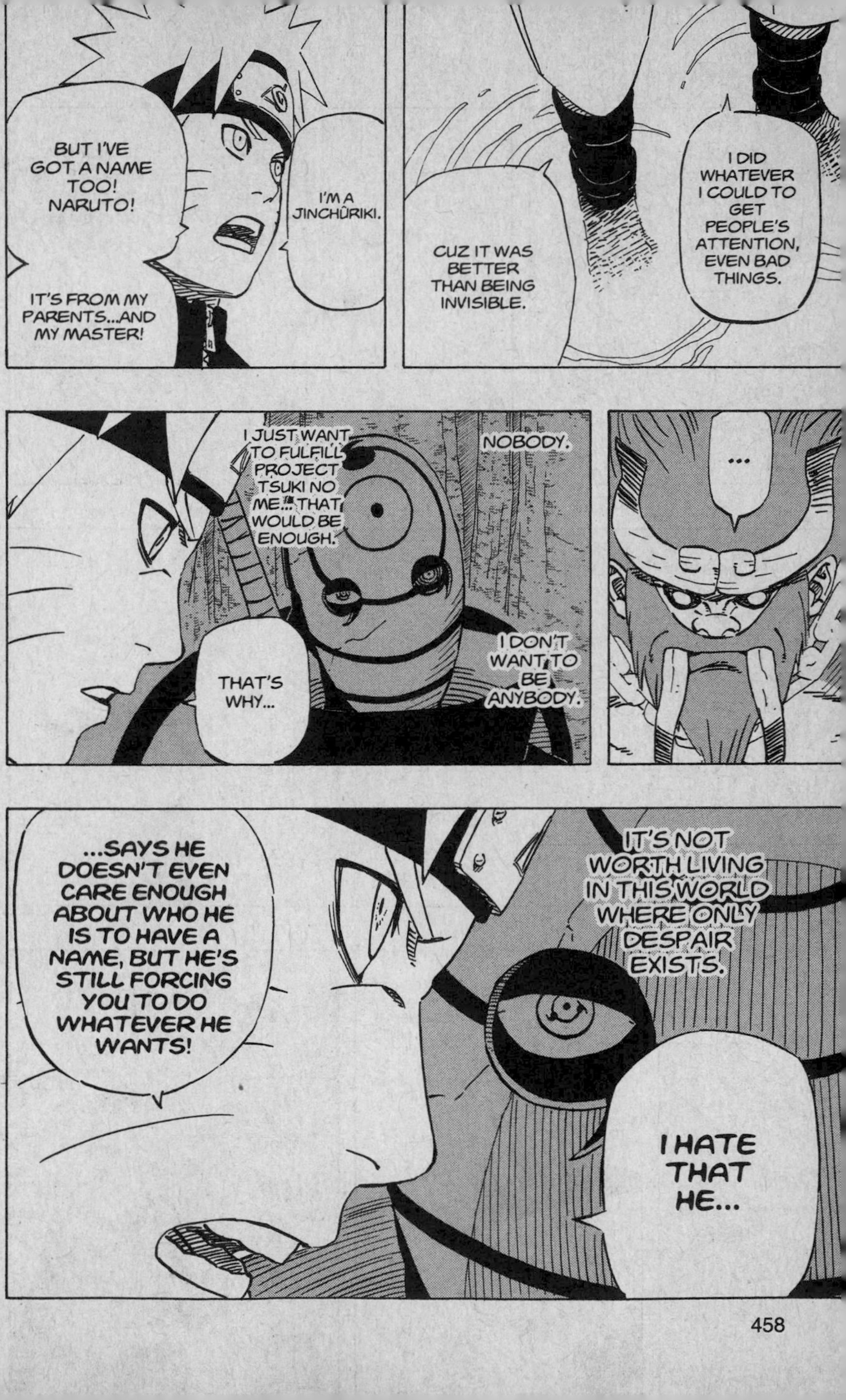
I DID WHATEVER I COULD TO GET PEOPLE'S ATTENTION, EVEN BAD THINGS.
CUZ IT WAS BETTER THAN BEING INVISIBLE.
I'M A JINCHŪRIKI.
BUT I'VE GOT A NAME TOO! NARUTO!
IT'S FROM MY PARENTS...AND MY MASTER!
...
NOBODY.
I JUST WANT TO FULFILL PROJECT TSUKI NO ME... THAT WOULD BE ENOUGH.
I DON'T WANT TO BE ANYBODY.
THAT'S WHY...
IT'S NOT WORTH LIVING IN THIS WORLD WHERE ONLY DESPAIR EXISTS.
I HATE THAT HE...
...SAYS HE DOESN'T EVEN CARE ENOUGH ABOUT WHO HE IS TO HAVE A NAME, BUT HE'S STILL FORCING YOU TO DO WHATEVER HE WANTS!

READ THIS WAY

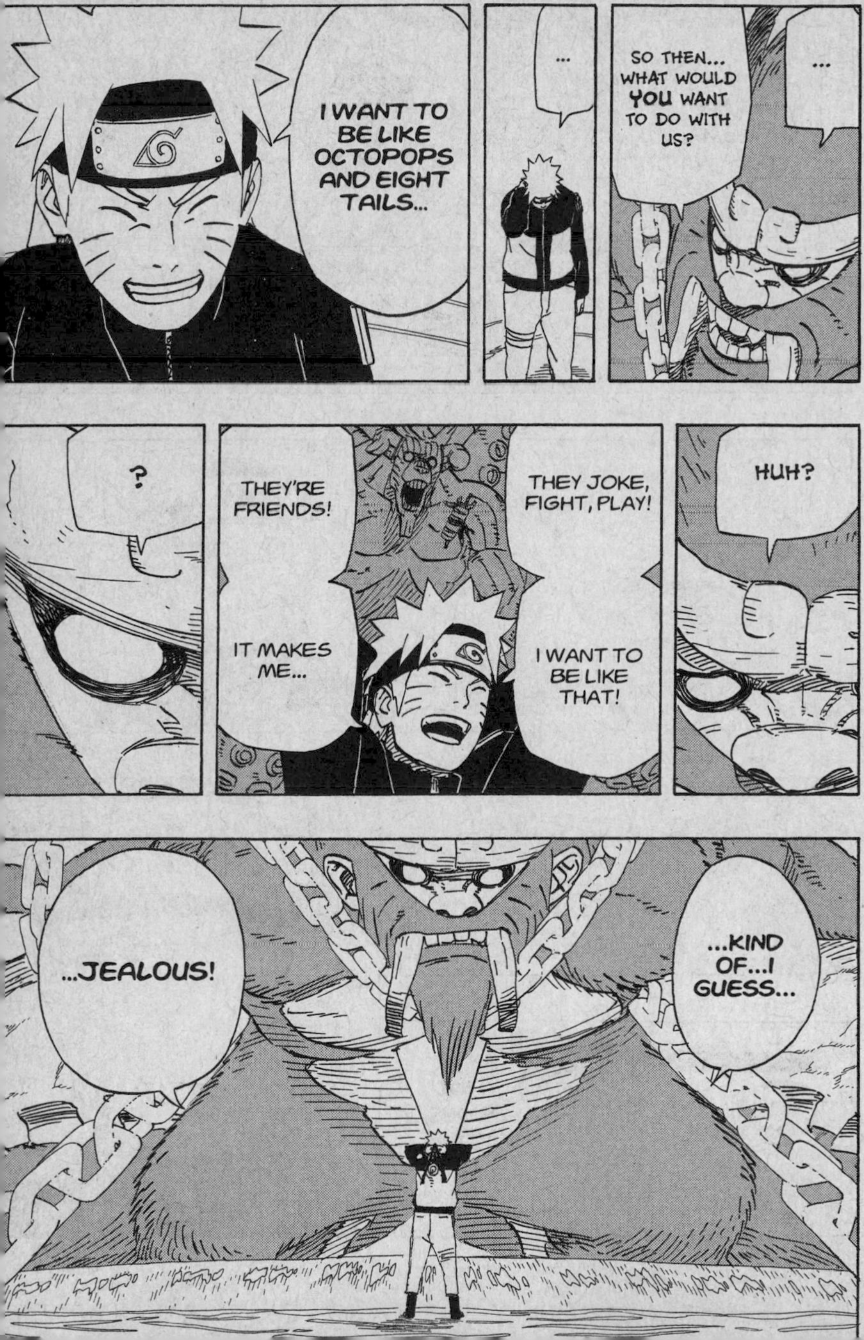
...
SO THEN... WHAT WOULD YOU WANT TO DO WITH US?
...
I WANT TO BE LIKE OCTOPOPS AND EIGHT TAILS...
HUH?
THEY JOKE, FIGHT, PLAY!
THEY'RE FRIENDS!
I WANT TO BE LIKE THAT!
IT MAKES ME...
?
...KIND OF...I GUESS...
...JEALOUS!

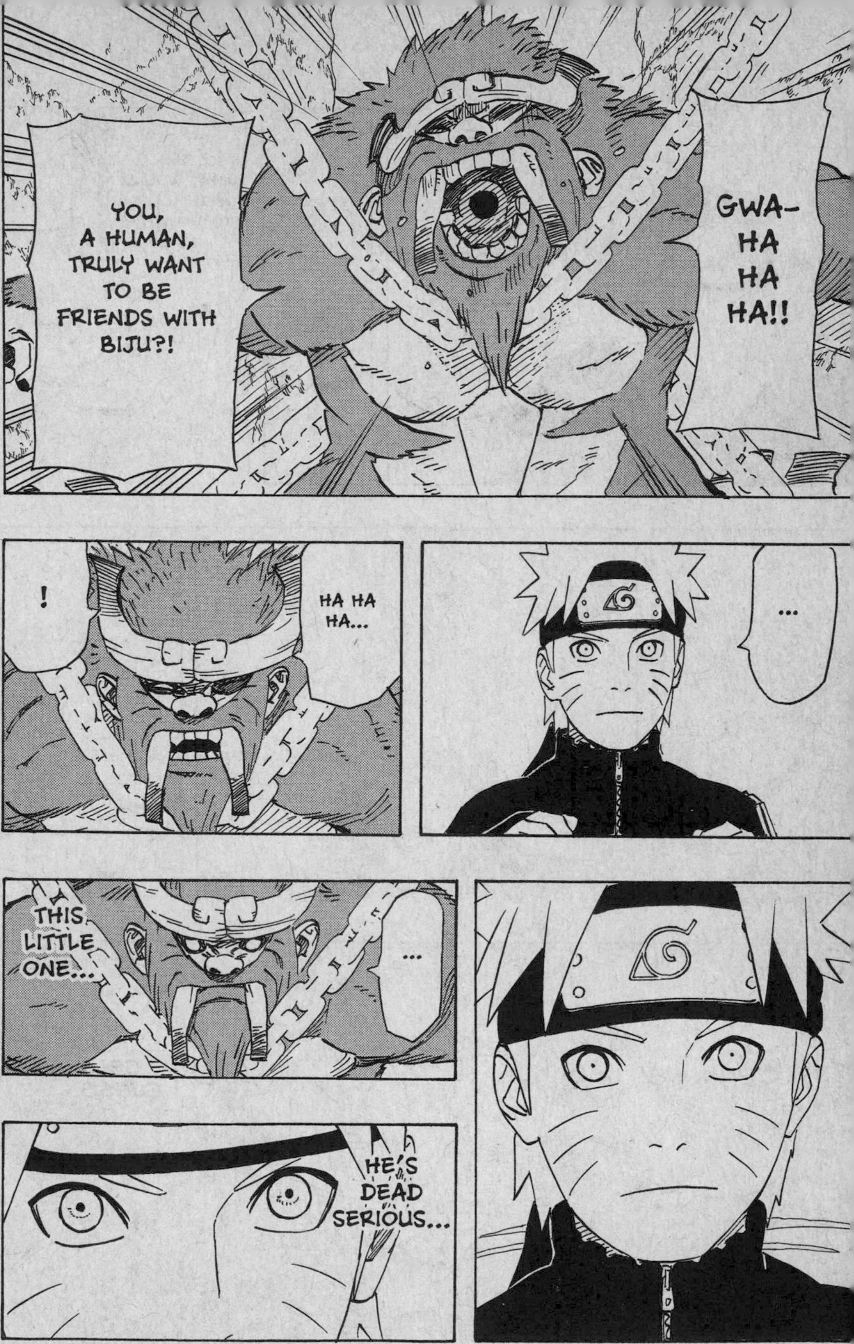
GWA-HA HA HA!!
YOU, A HUMAN, TRULY WANT TO BE FRIENDS WITH BIJU?!
...
HA HA HA...
!
...
THIS LITTLE ONE...
HE'S DEAD SERIOUS...

READ THIS WAY

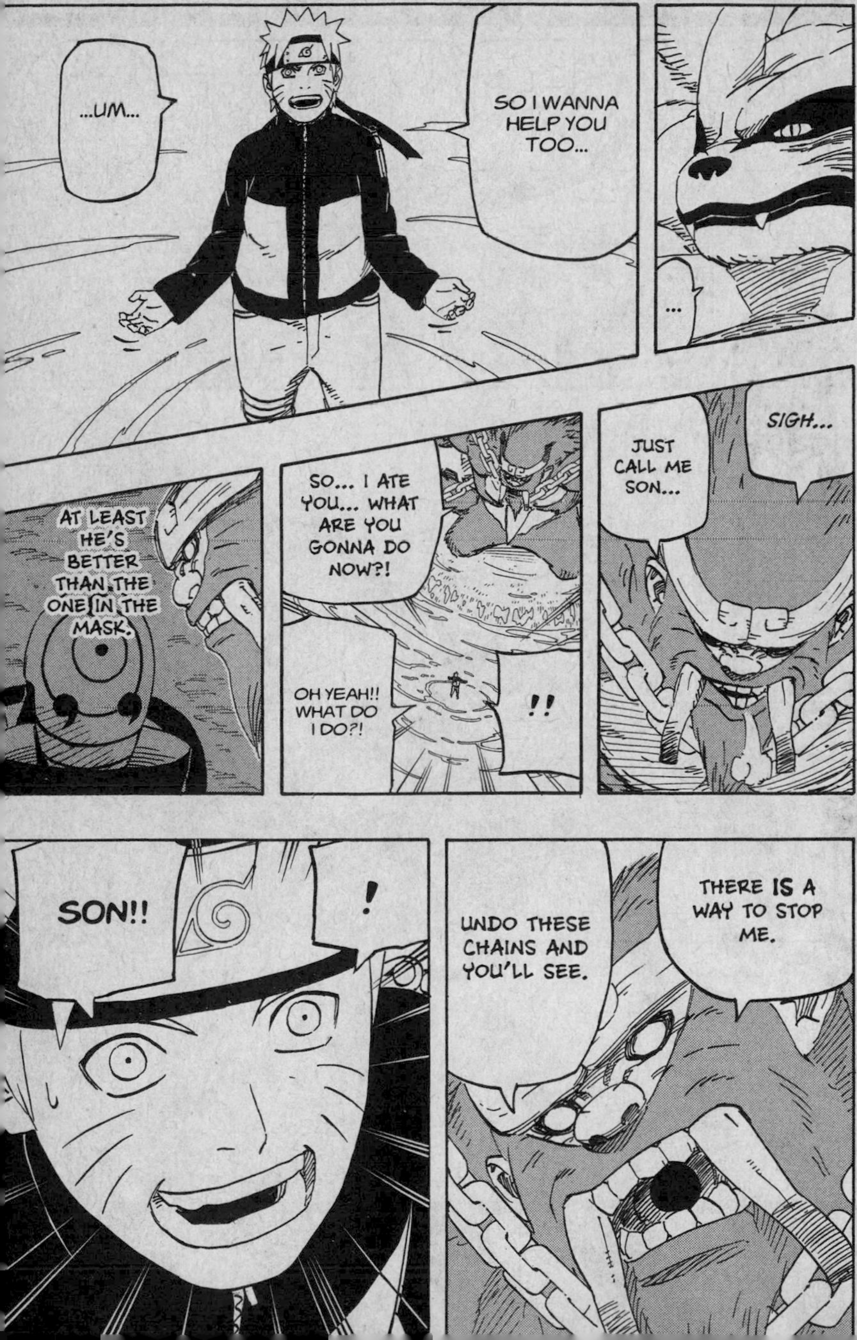
...
SO I WANNA HELP YOU TOO...
...UM...
SIGH...
JUST CALL ME SON...
SO... I ATE YOU... WHAT ARE YOU GONNA DO NOW?!
!!
OH YEAH!! WHAT DO I DO?!
AT LEAST HE'S BETTER THAN THE ONE IN THE MASK.
THERE IS A WAY TO STOP ME.
UNDO THESE CHAINS AND YOU'LL SEE.
!
SON!!

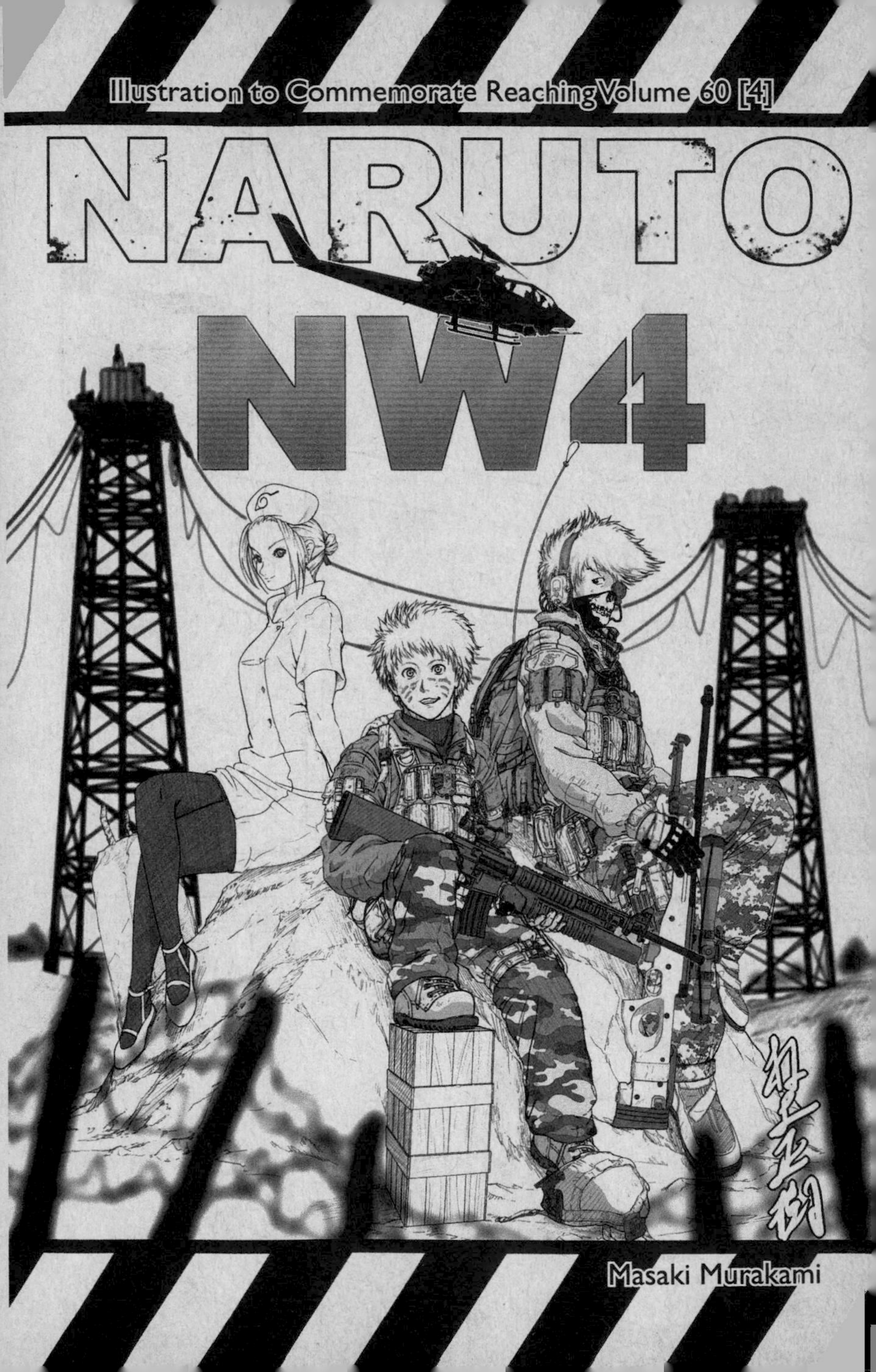
Illustration to Commemorate Reaching Volume 60 [4]
NARUTO
NW4
Masaki Murakami

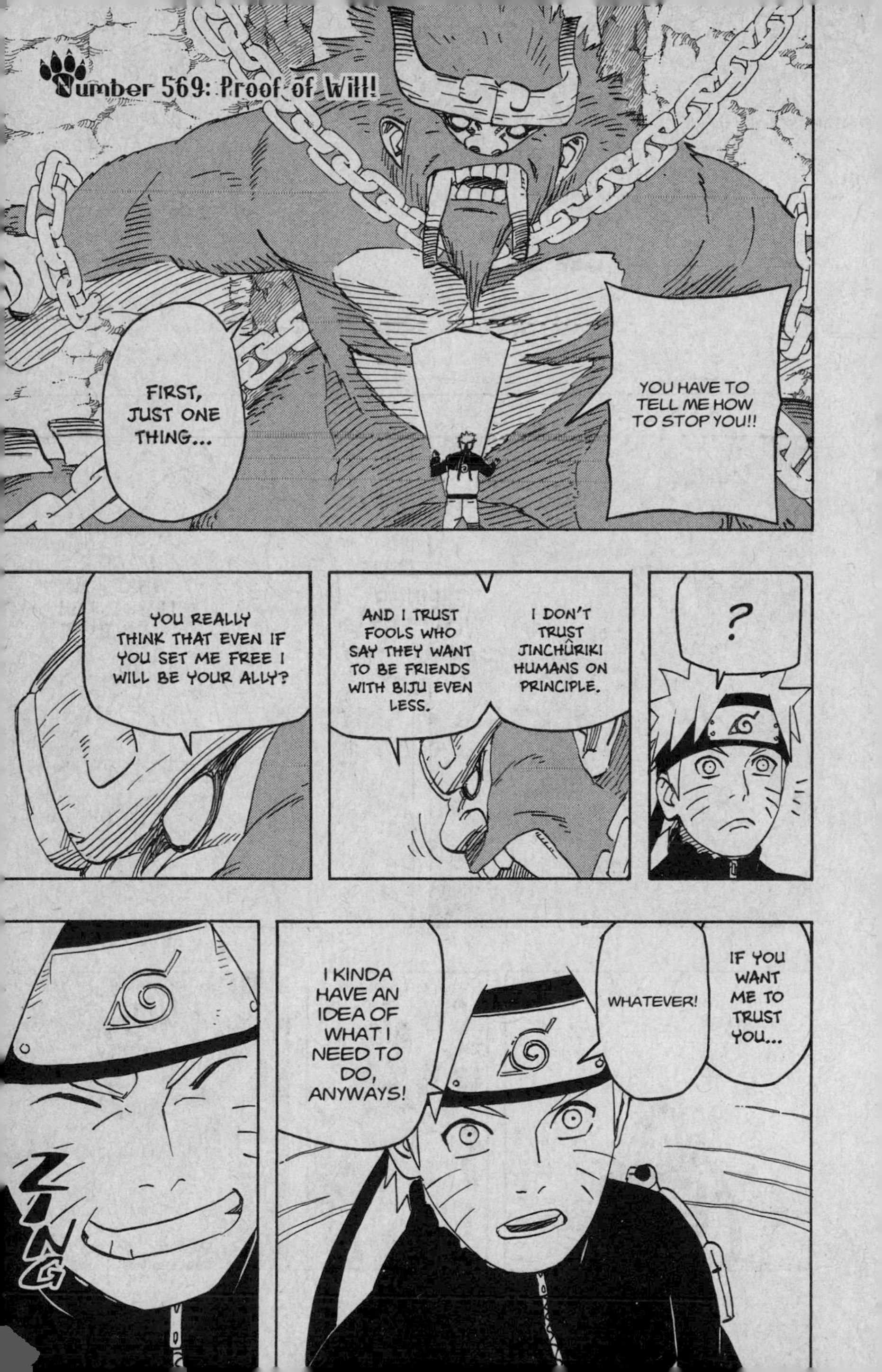
Number 569: Proof of Will!
YOU HAVE TO TELL ME HOW TO STOP YOU!!
FIRST, JUST ONE THING...
?
I DON'T TRUST JINCHŪRIKI HUMANS ON PRINCIPLE.
AND I TRUST FOOLS WHO SAY THEY WANT TO BE FRIENDS WITH BIJU EVEN LESS.
YOU REALLY THINK THAT EVEN IF YOU SET ME FREE I WILL BE YOUR ALLY?
IF YOU WANT ME TO TRUST YOU...
WHATEVER!
I KINDA HAVE AN IDEA OF WHAT I NEED TO DO, ANYWAYS!
ZING

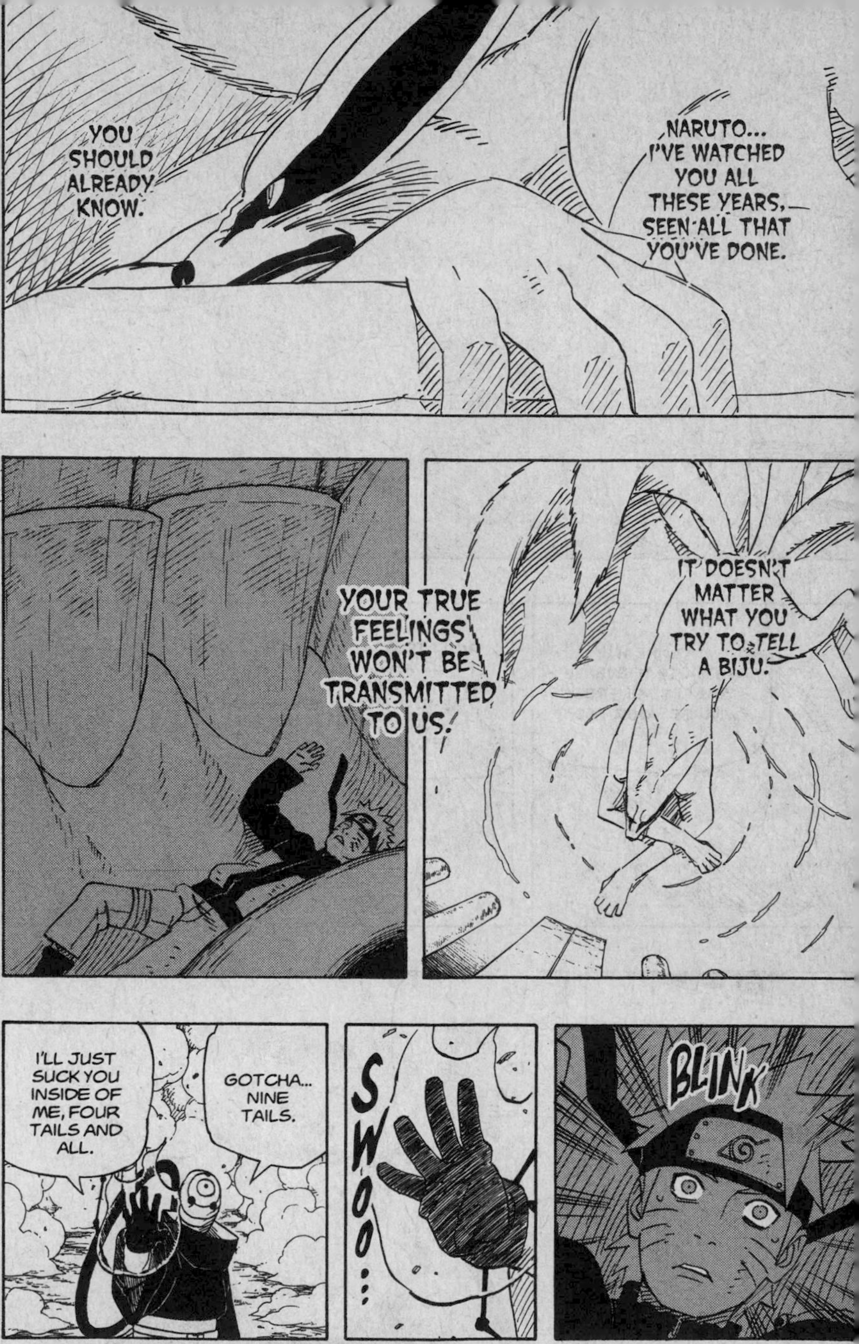
NARUTO... I'VE WATCHED YOU ALL THESE YEARS, SEEN ALL THAT YOU'VE DONE.
YOU SHOULD ALREADY KNOW.
IT DOESN'T MATTER WHAT YOU TRY TO TELL A BIJU.
YOUR TRUE FEELINGS WON'T BE TRANSMITTED TO US.
BLINK
SWOO...
GOTCHA... NINE TAILS.
I'LL JUST SUCK YOU INSIDE OF ME, FOUR TAILS AND ALL.

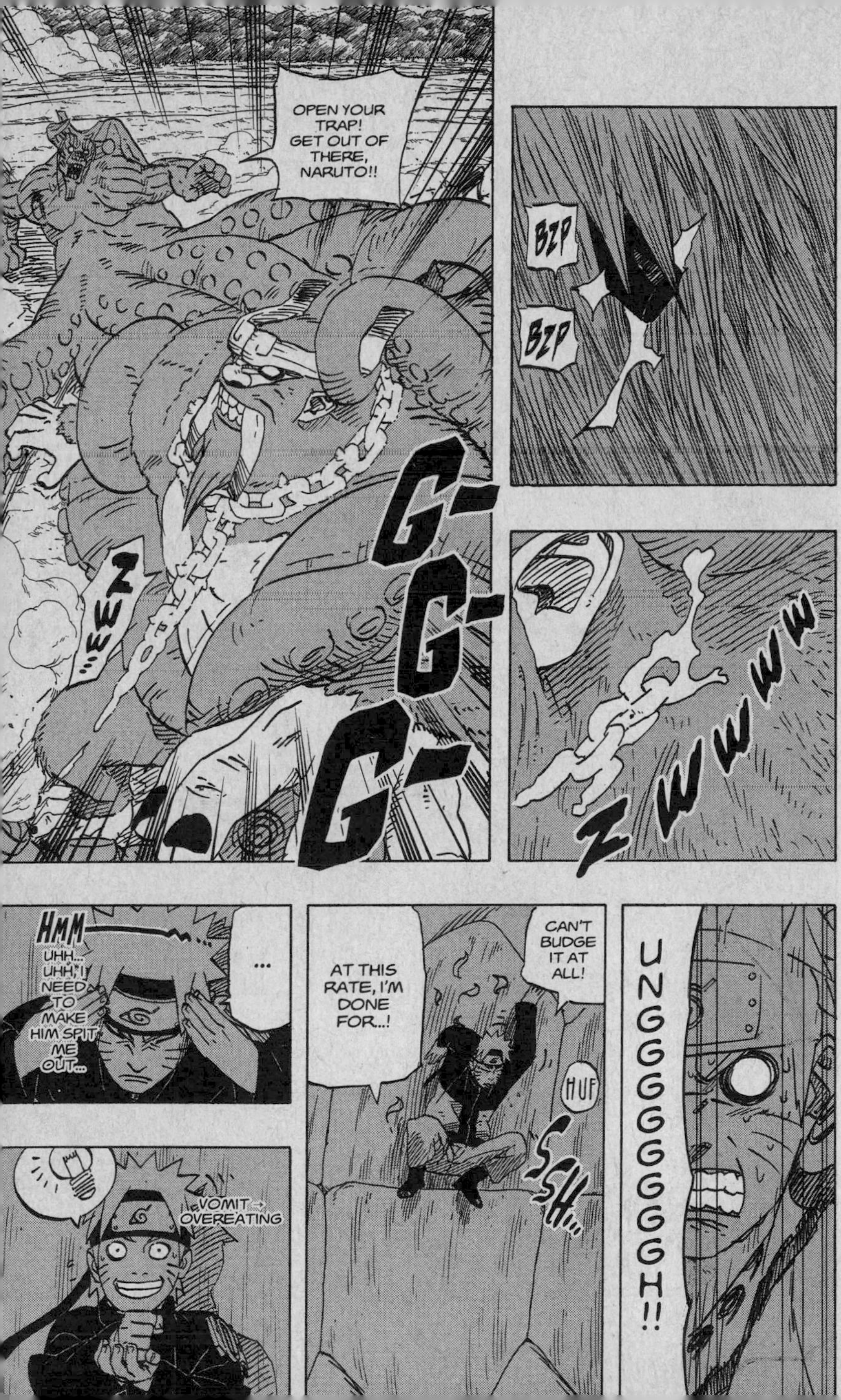
BZP
BZP
ZWWWWW
OPEN YOUR TRAP! GET OUT OF THERE, NARUTO!!
G-G-G-
ZWWW...
UNGGGGGGGGGH!!
CAN'T BUDGE IT AT ALL!
AT THIS RATE, I'M DONE FOR...!
HUF
SSH...
...
HMM...
UHH... UHH, I NEED TO MAKE HIM SPIT ME OUT...
VOMIT → OVEREATING

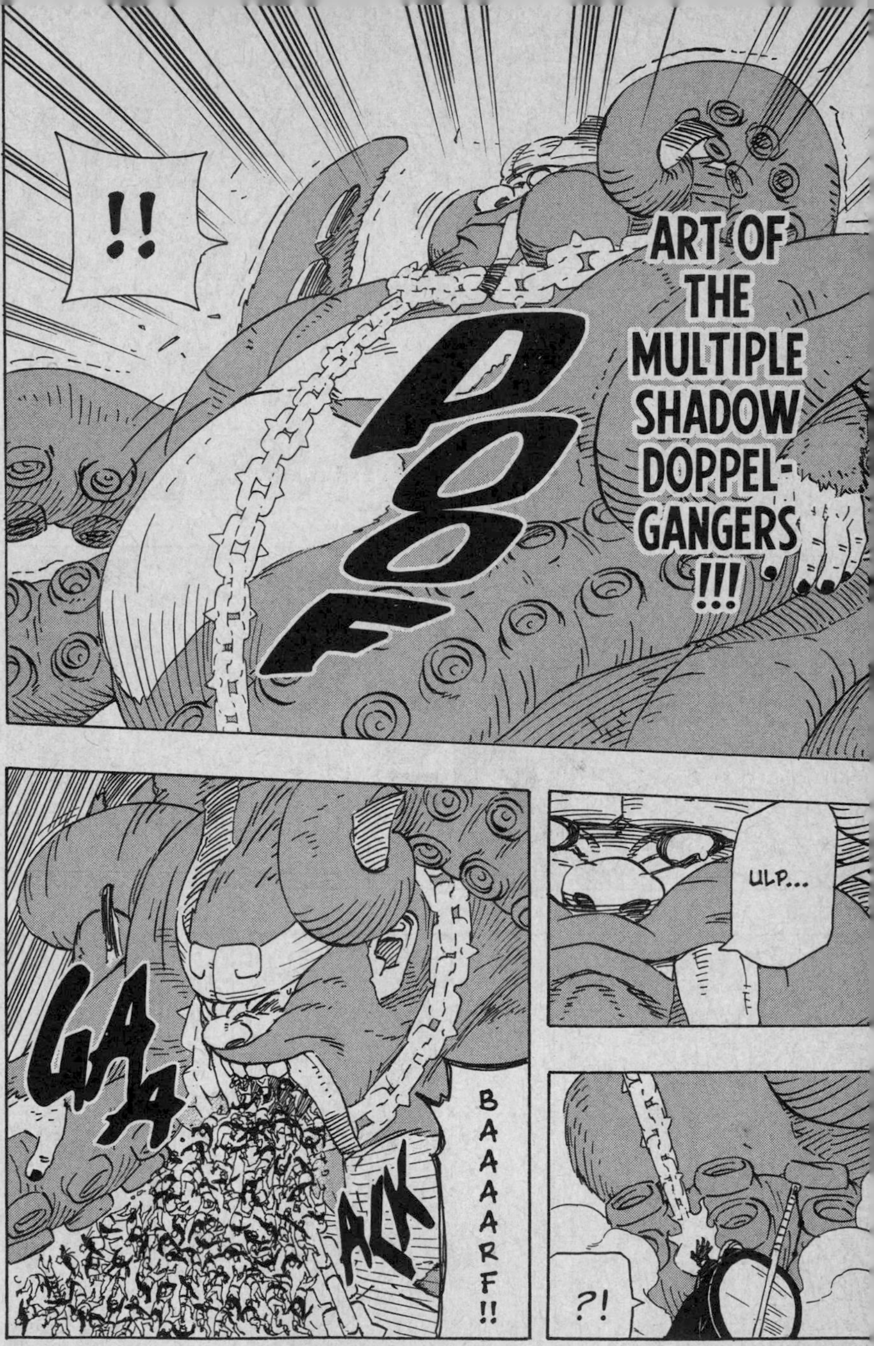
ART OF THE MULTIPLE SHADOW DOPPEL-GANGERS!!!
!!
POOF
ULP...
?!
BAAAARF!!
GAA
ALK

READ THIS WAY

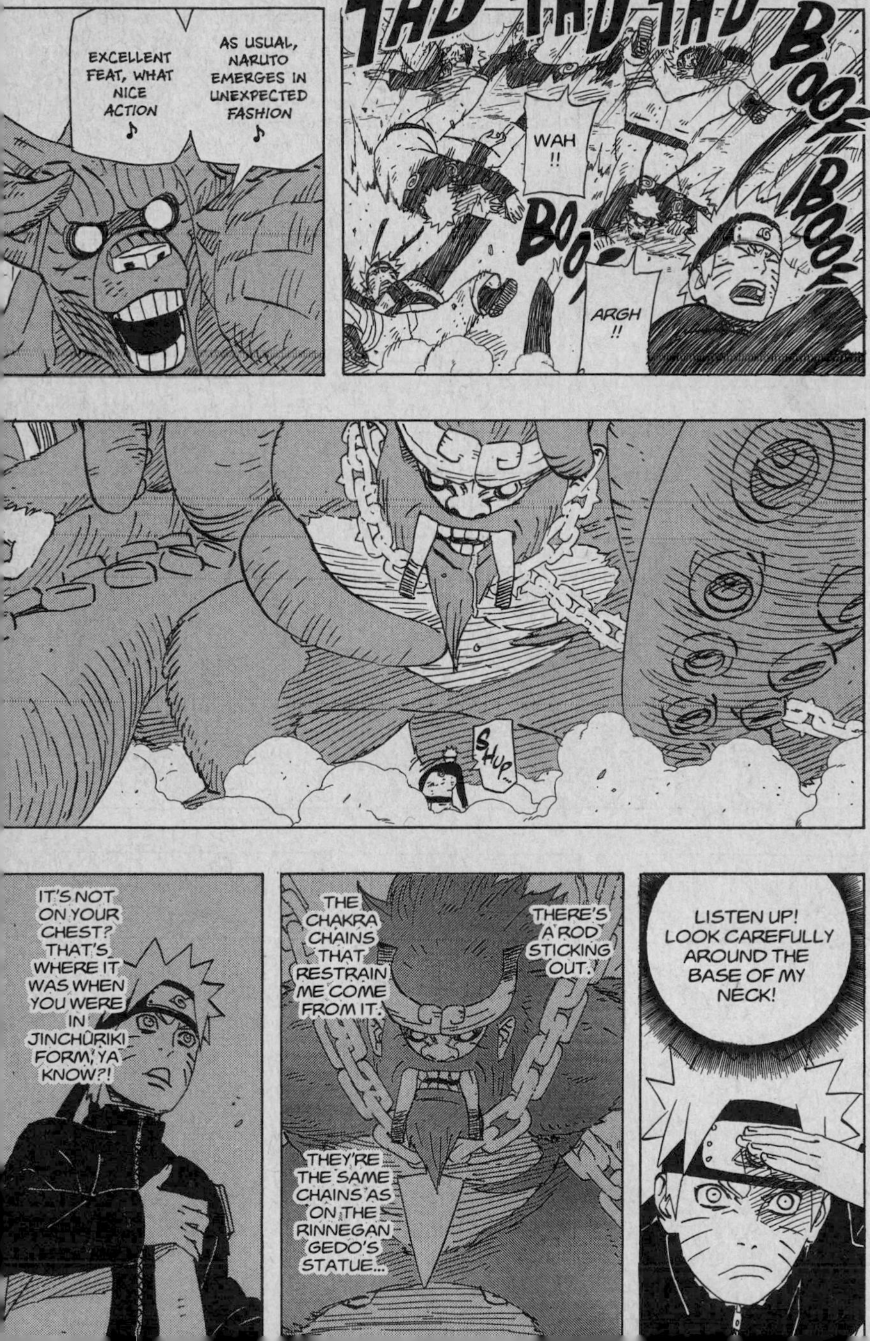
THD THD THD
BOOF
BOOF
WAH !!
BOO
ARGH !!
AS USUAL, NARUTO EMERGES IN UNEXPECTED FASHION ♪
EXCELLENT FEAT, WHAT NICE ACTION ♪
SHUP...
LISTEN UP! LOOK CAREFULLY AROUND THE BASE OF MY NECK!
THERE'S A ROD STICKING OUT.
THE CHAKRA CHAINS THAT RESTRAIN ME COME FROM IT.
THEY'RE THE SAME CHAINS AS ON THE RINNEGAN GEDO'S STATUE...
IT'S NOT ON YOUR CHEST? THAT'S WHERE IT WAS WHEN YOU WERE IN JINCHÛRIKI FORM, YA KNOW?!

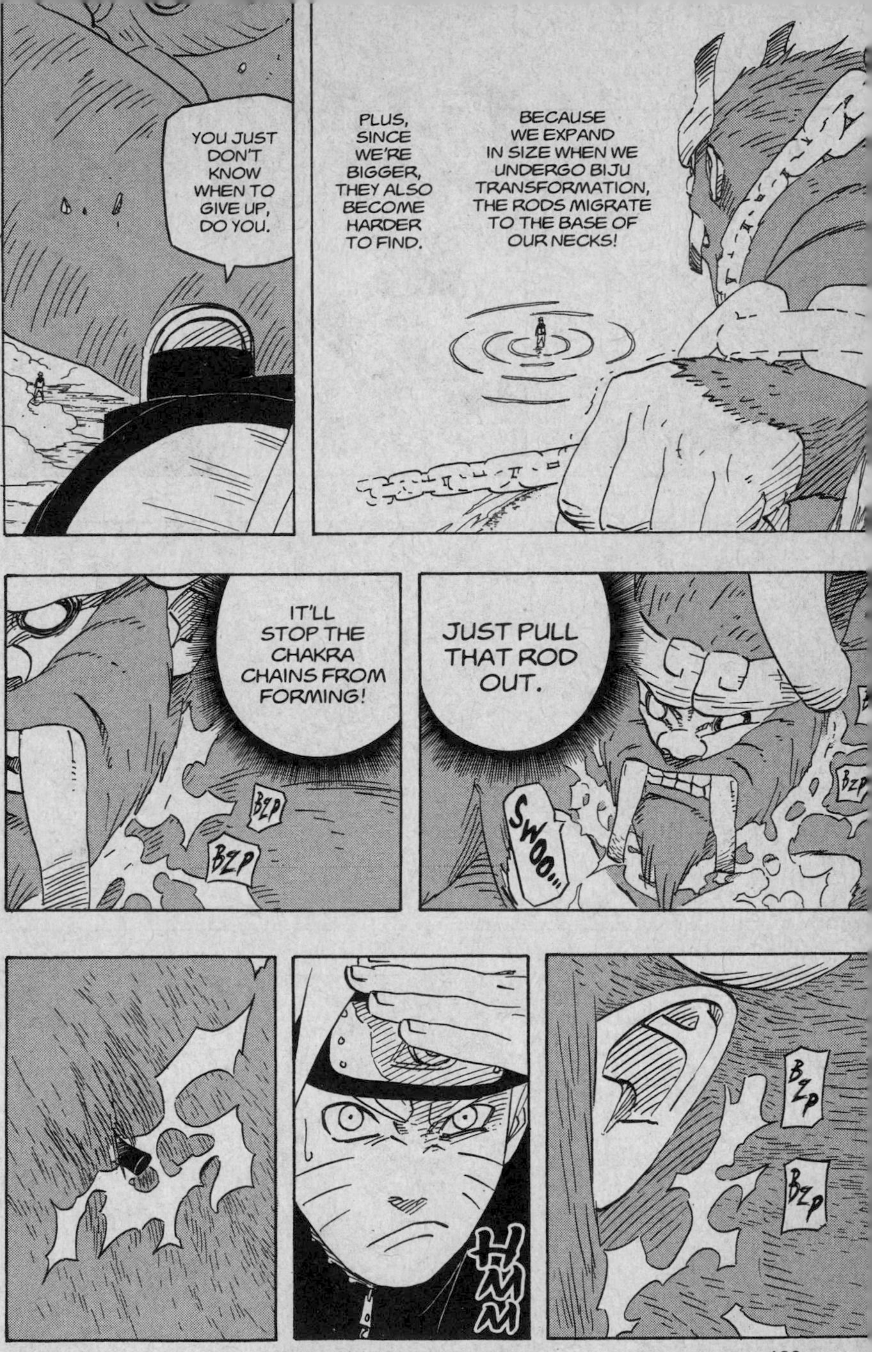
BECAUSE WE EXPAND IN SIZE WHEN WE UNDERGO BIJU TRANSFORMATION, THE RODS MIGRATE TO THE BASE OF OUR NECKS!
PLUS, SINCE WE'RE BIGGER, THEY ALSO BECOME HARDER TO FIND.
YOU JUST DON'T KNOW WHEN TO GIVE UP, DO YOU.
JUST PULL THAT ROD OUT.
BZP
SWOO...
IT'LL STOP THE CHAKRA CHAINS FROM FORMING!
BZP
BZP
BZP
BZP
HMM

READ THIS WAY

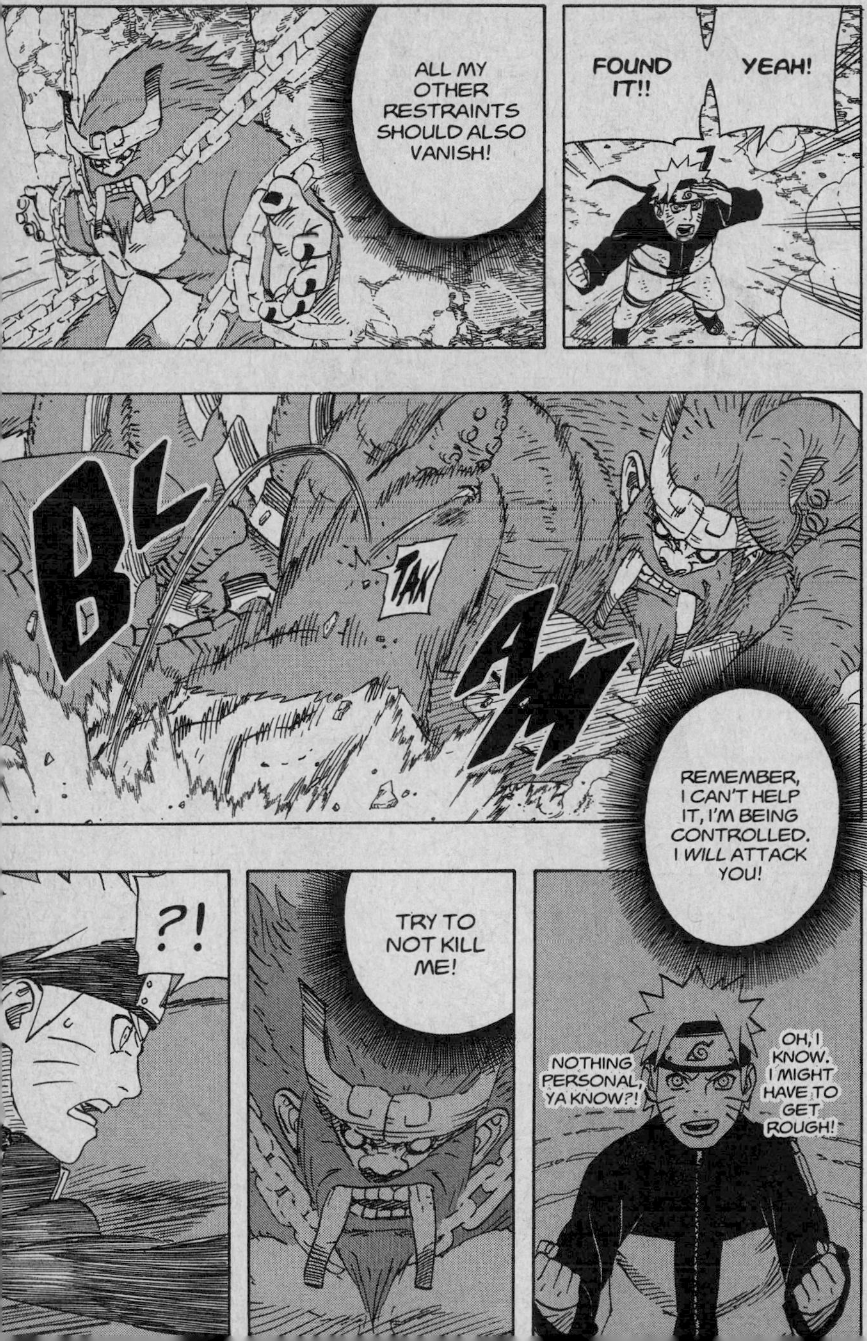
YEAH!
FOUND IT!!
ALL MY OTHER RESTRAINTS SHOULD ALSO VANISH!
TAK
BLAM
REMEMBER, I CAN'T HELP IT, I'M BEING CONTROLLED. I WILL ATTACK YOU!
OH, I KNOW. I MIGHT HAVE TO GET ROUGH!
NOTHING PERSONAL, YA KNOW?!
TRY TO NOT KILL ME!
?!

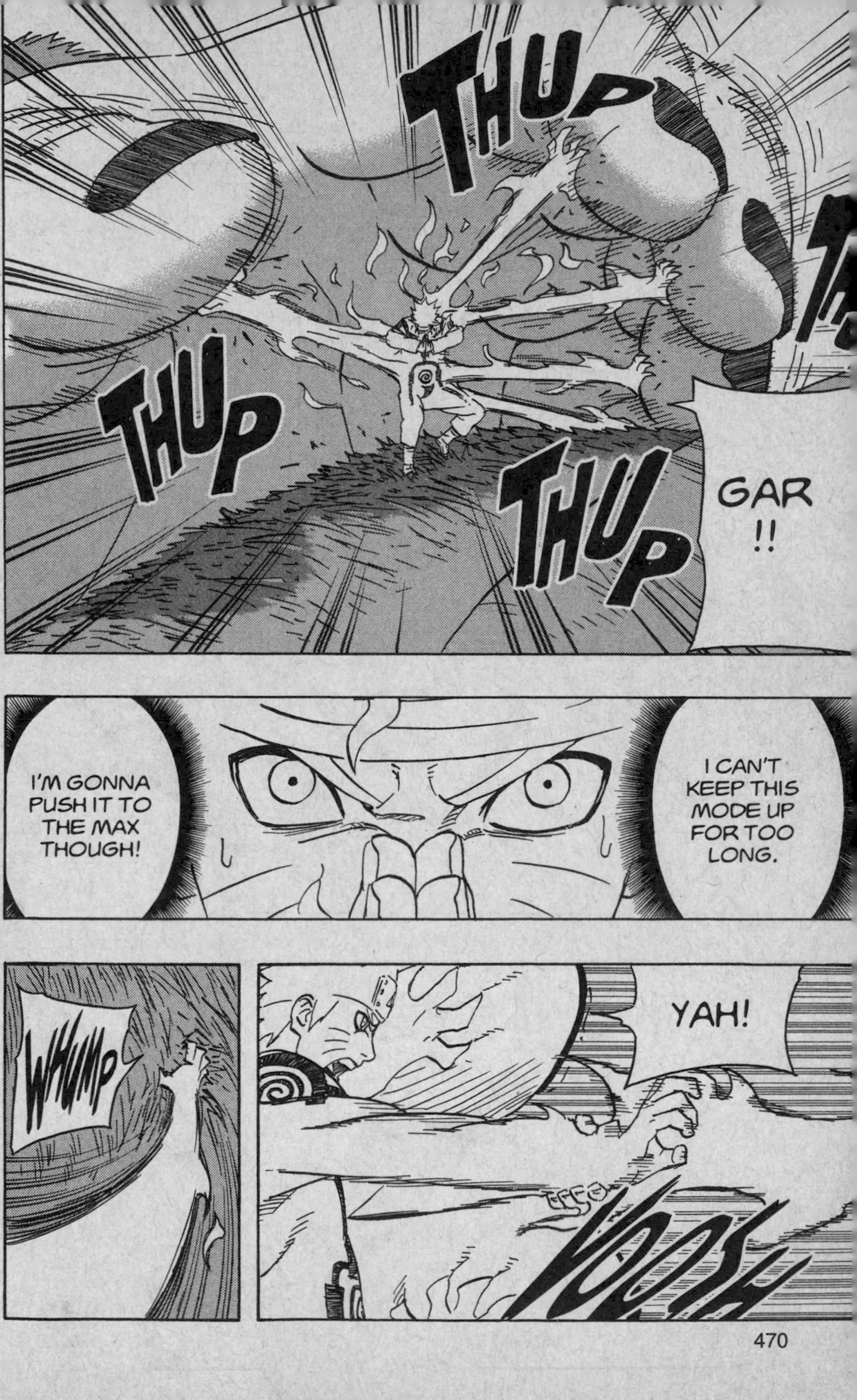
THUP
GAR !!
THUP
THUP
I CAN'T KEEP THIS MODE UP FOR TOO LONG.
I'M GONNA PUSH IT TO THE MAX THOUGH!
YAH!
VOOSH
WHUMP

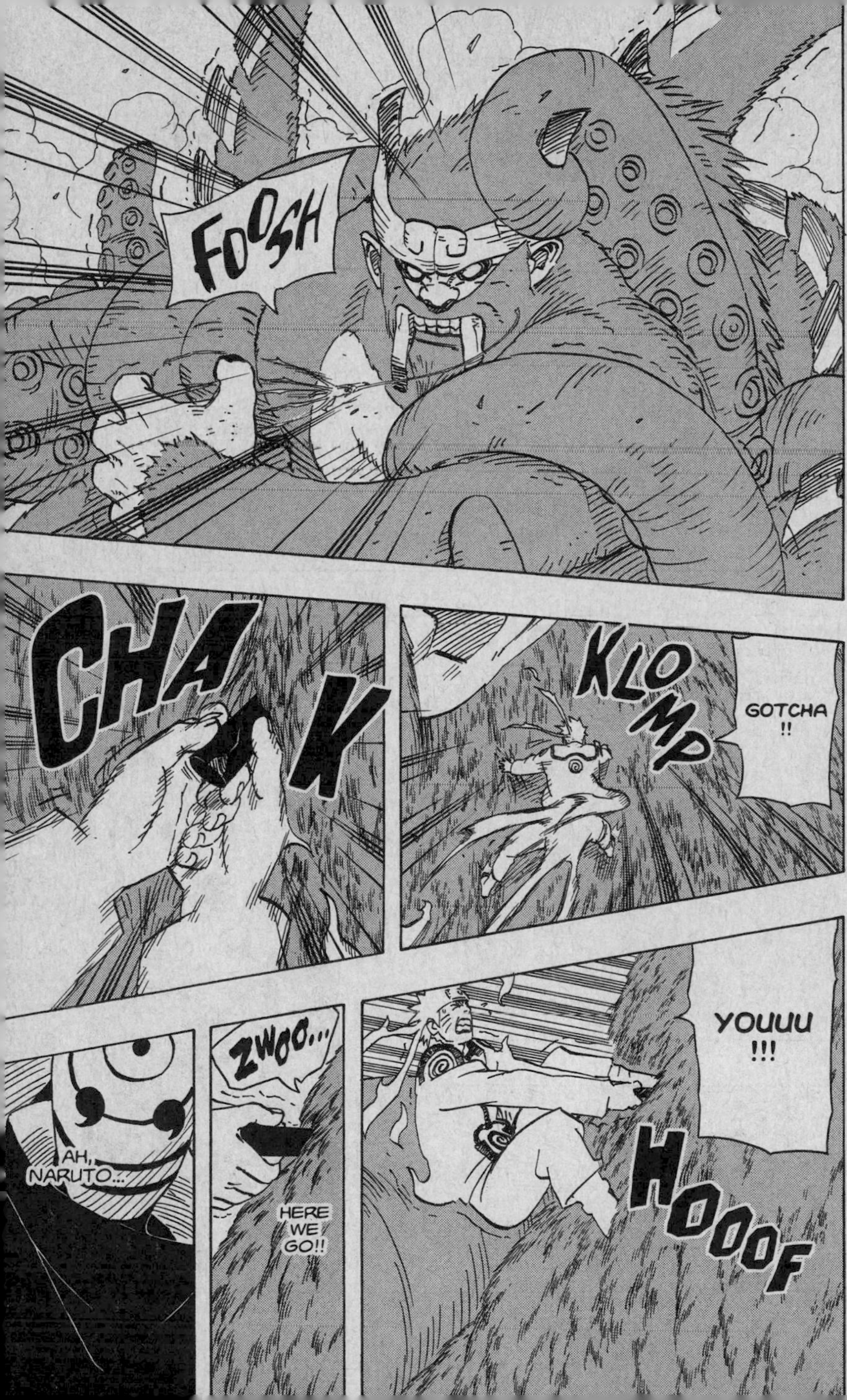
FOOSH
KLOMP
GOTCHA !!
CHAK
YOUUU !!!
HOOOF
ZWOO...
HERE WE GO!!
AH, NARUTO...

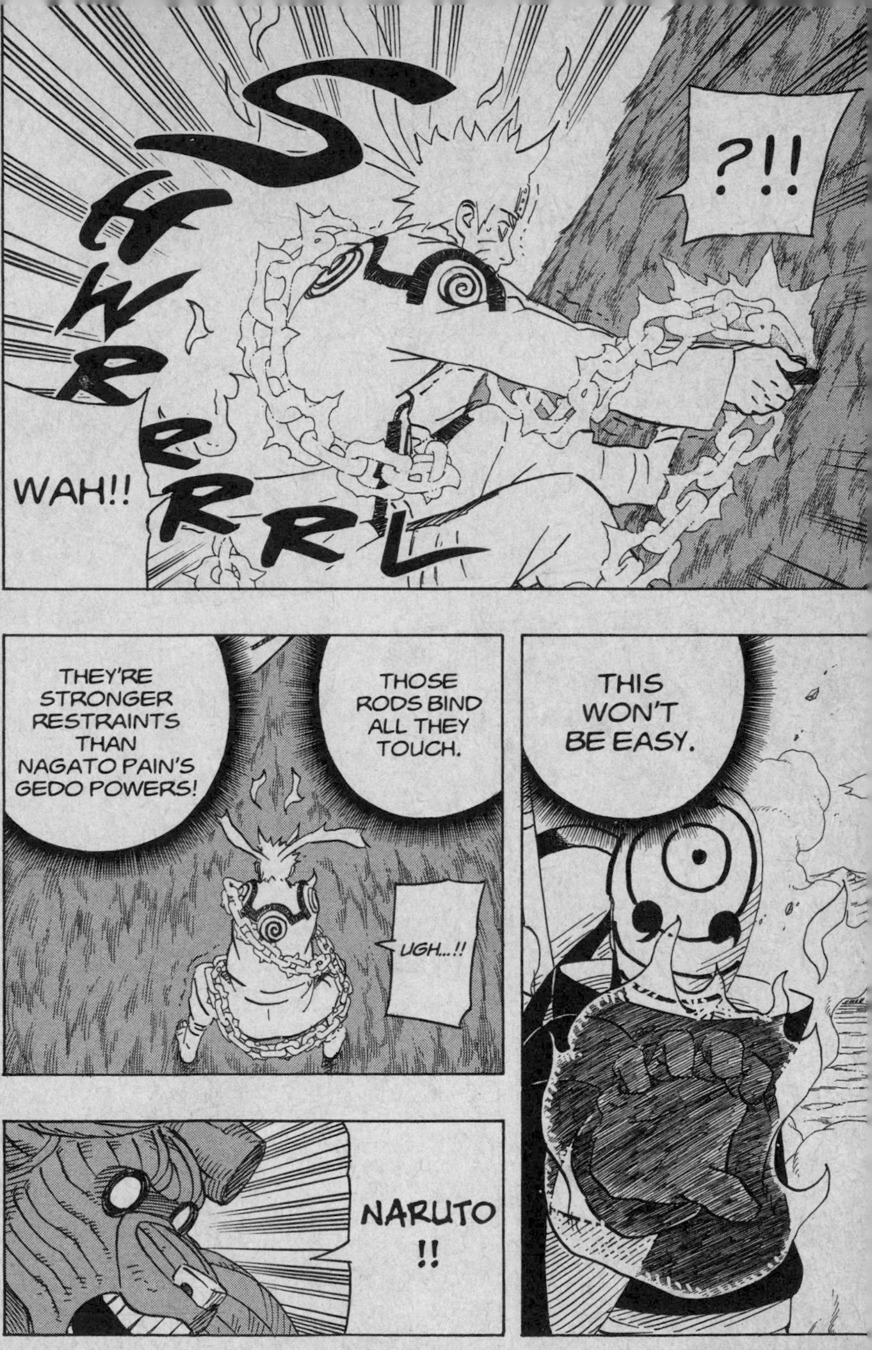
?!!
SHWRRRL
WAH!!
THIS WON'T BE EASY.
THOSE RODS BIND ALL THEY TOUCH.
THEY'RE STRONGER RESTRAINTS THAN NAGATO PAIN'S GEDO POWERS!
UGH...!!
NARUTO !!

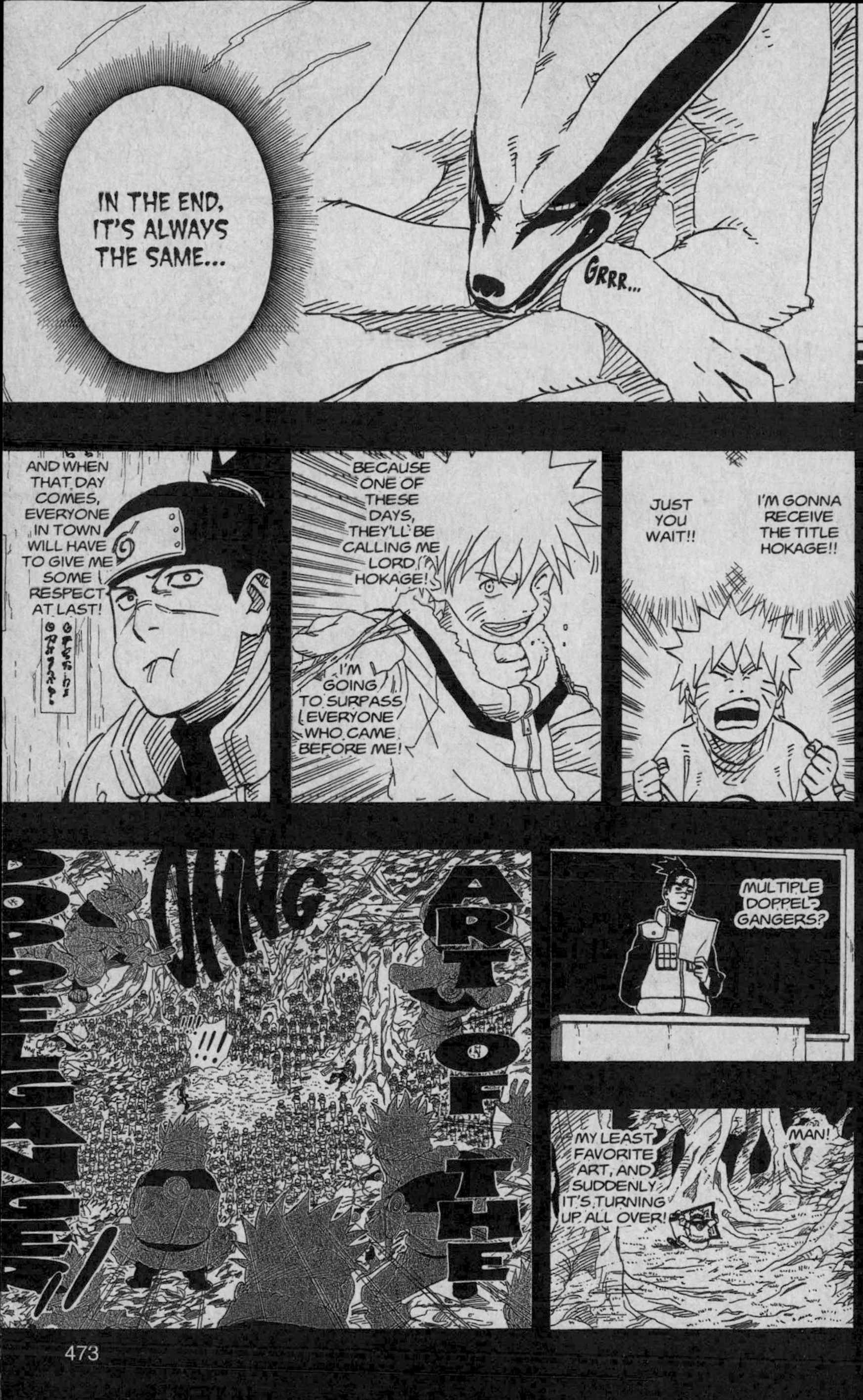
IN THE END, IT'S ALWAYS THE SAME...
GRRR...
I'M GONNA RECEIVE THE TITLE HOKAGE!!
JUST YOU WAIT!!
BECAUSE ONE OF THESE DAYS, THEY'LL BE CALLING ME LORD HOKAGE!
I'M GOING TO SURPASS EVERYONE WHO CAME BEFORE ME!
AND WHEN THAT DAY COMES, EVERYONE IN TOWN WILL HAVE TO GIVE ME SOME RESPECT AT LAST!
MULTIPLE DOPPEL-GANGERS?
MAN!
MY LEAST FAVORITE ART, AND SUDDENLY IT'S TURNING UP ALL OVER!
ART OF THE
!!!

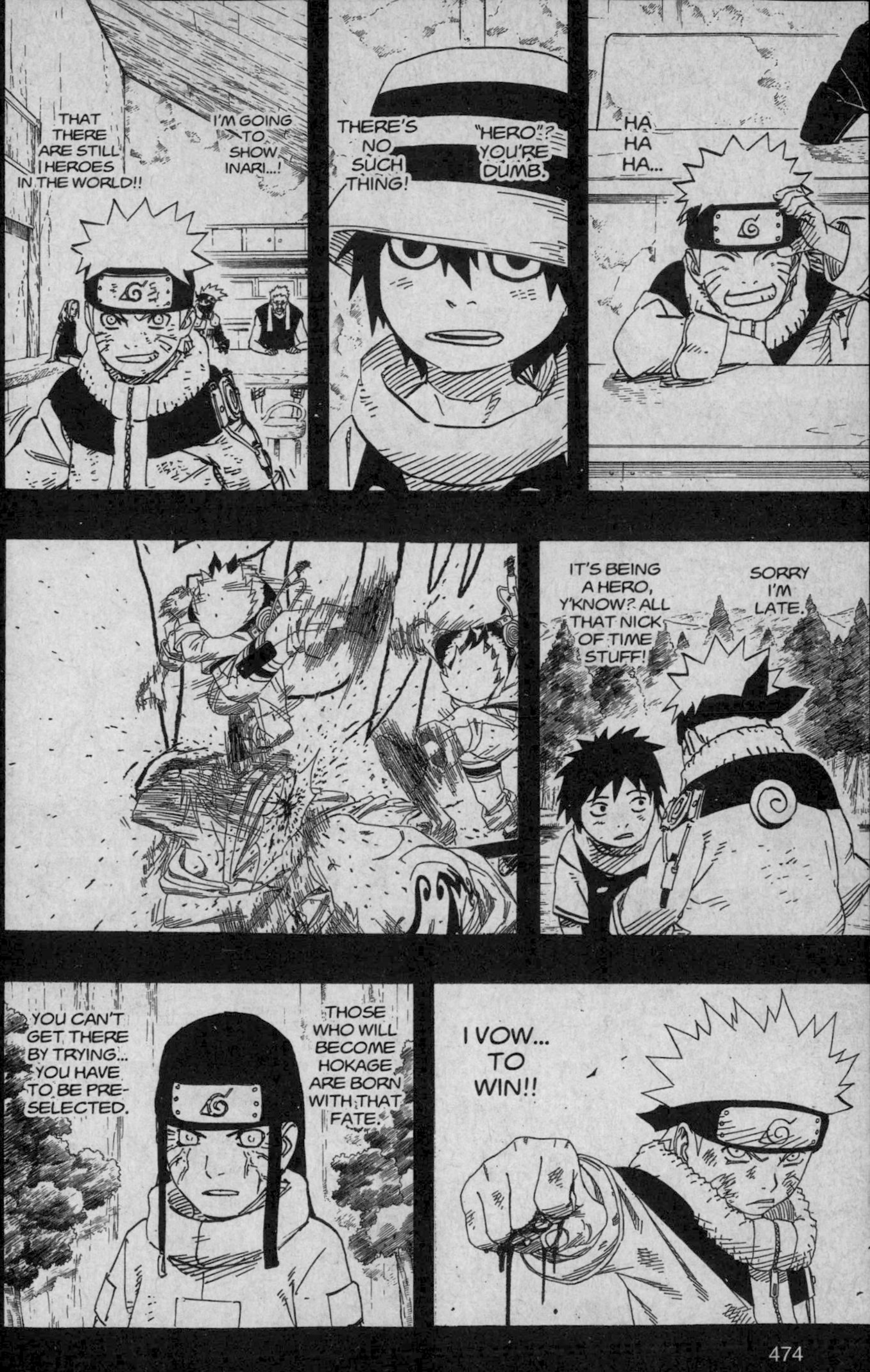
HA HA HA...
"HERO"? YOU'RE DUMB.
THERE'S NO SUCH THING!
I'M GOING TO SHOW INARI...!
THAT THERE ARE STILL HEROES IN THE WORLD!!
SORRY I'M LATE.
IT'S BEING A HERO, Y'KNOW? ALL THAT NICK OF TIME STUFF!
I VOW... TO WIN!!
THOSE WHO WILL BECOME HOKAGE ARE BORN WITH THAT FATE.
YOU CAN'T GET THERE BY TRYING... YOU HAVE TO BE PRE-SELECTED.

READ THIS WAY

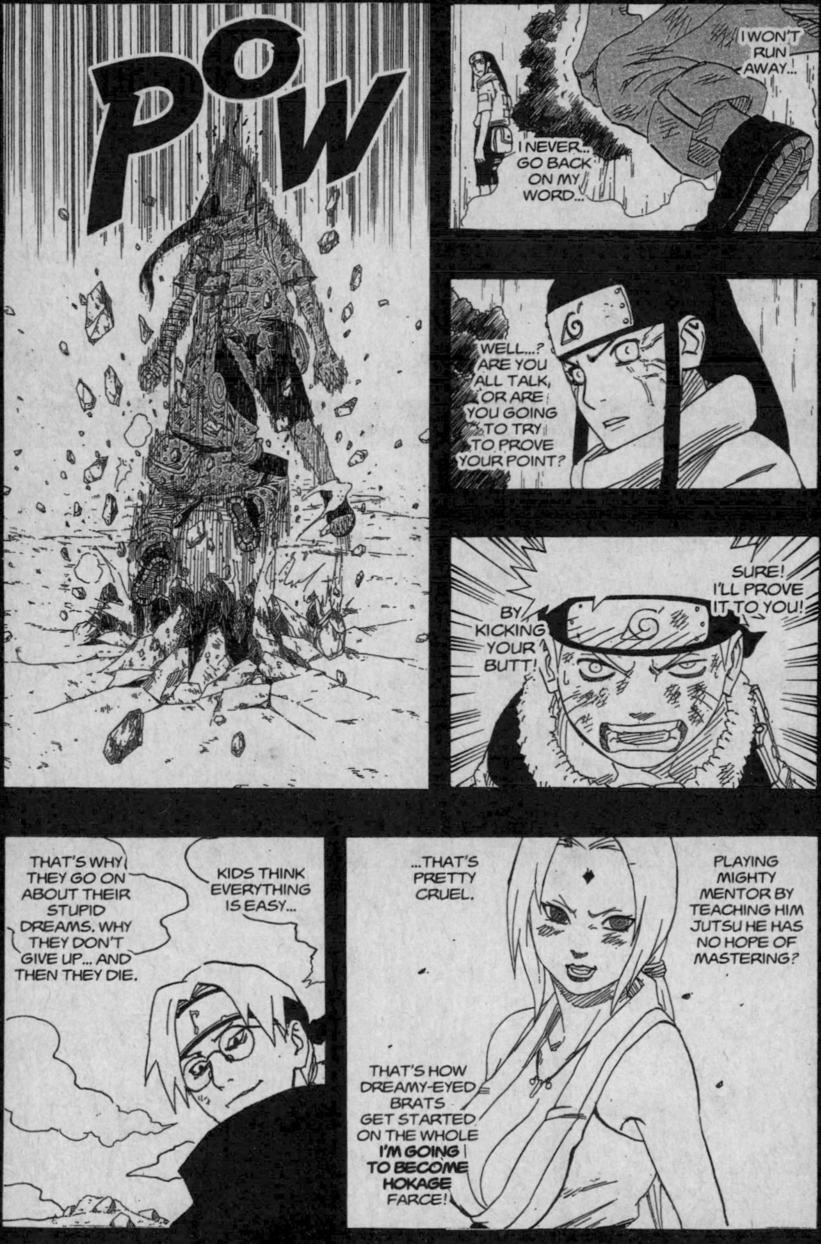
I WON'T RUN AWAY...
I NEVER.. GO BACK ON MY WORD...
WELL...? ARE YOU ALL TALK, OR ARE YOU GOING TO TRY TO PROVE YOUR POINT?
SURE! I'LL PROVE IT TO YOU!
BY KICKING YOUR BUTT!
POW
PLAYING MIGHTY MENTOR BY TEACHING HIM JUTSU HE HAS NO HOPE OF MASTERING?
...THAT'S PRETTY CRUEL.
THAT'S HOW DREAMY-EYED BRATS GET STARTED ON THE WHOLE **I'M GOING TO BECOME HOKAGE** FARCE!
KIDS THINK EVERYTHING IS EASY...
THAT'S WHY THEY GO ON ABOUT THEIR STUPID DREAMS. WHY THEY DON'T GIVE UP... AND THEN THEY DIE.

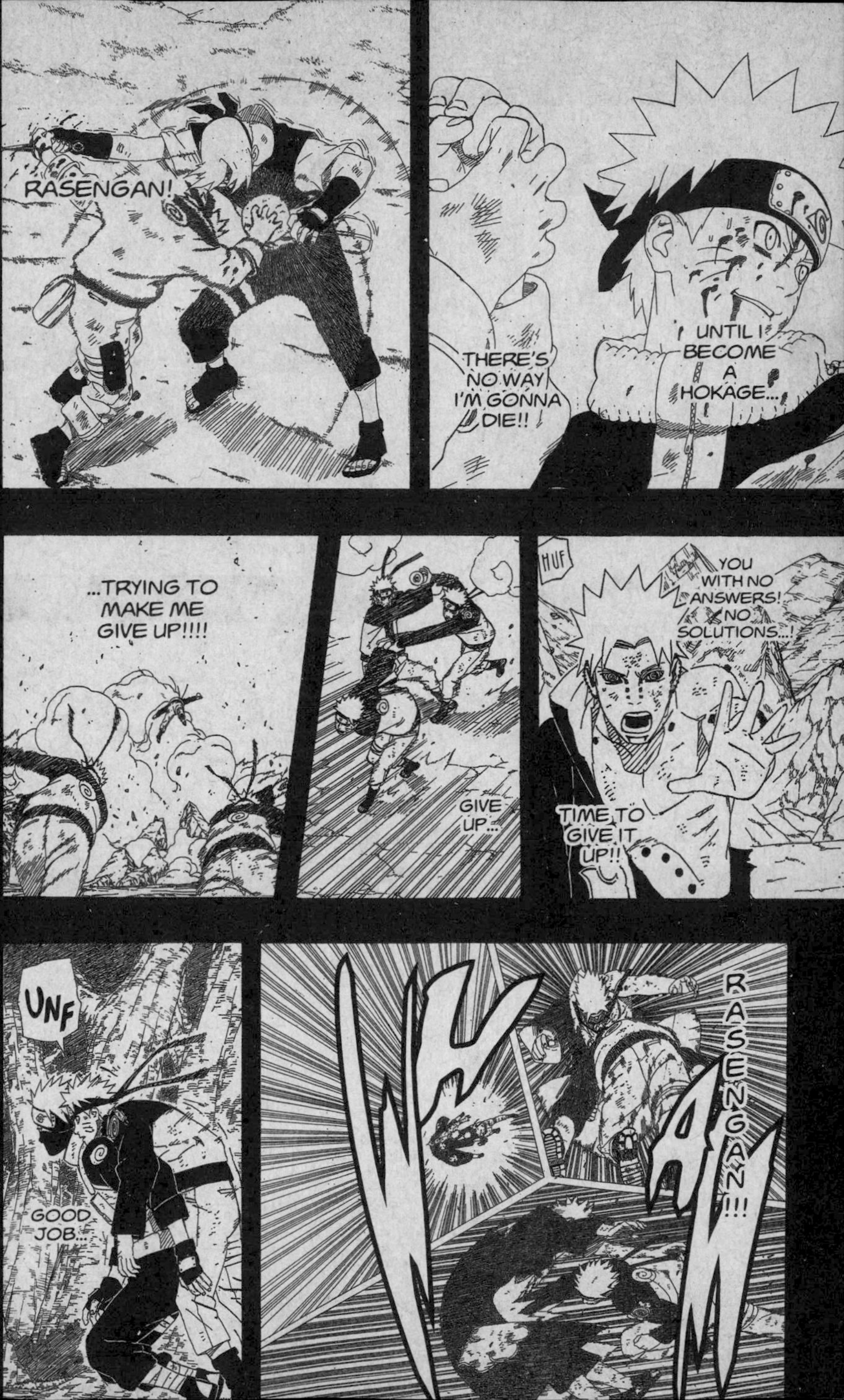
UNTIL I BECOME A HOKAGE...
THERE'S NO WAY I'M GONNA DIE!!
RASENGAN!
HUF
YOU WITH NO ANSWERS! NO SOLUTIONS...!
TIME TO GIVE IT UP!!
GIVE UP...
...TRYING TO MAKE ME GIVE UP!!!!
WHAM
RASENGAN!!!
UNF
GOOD JOB...

READ THIS WAY

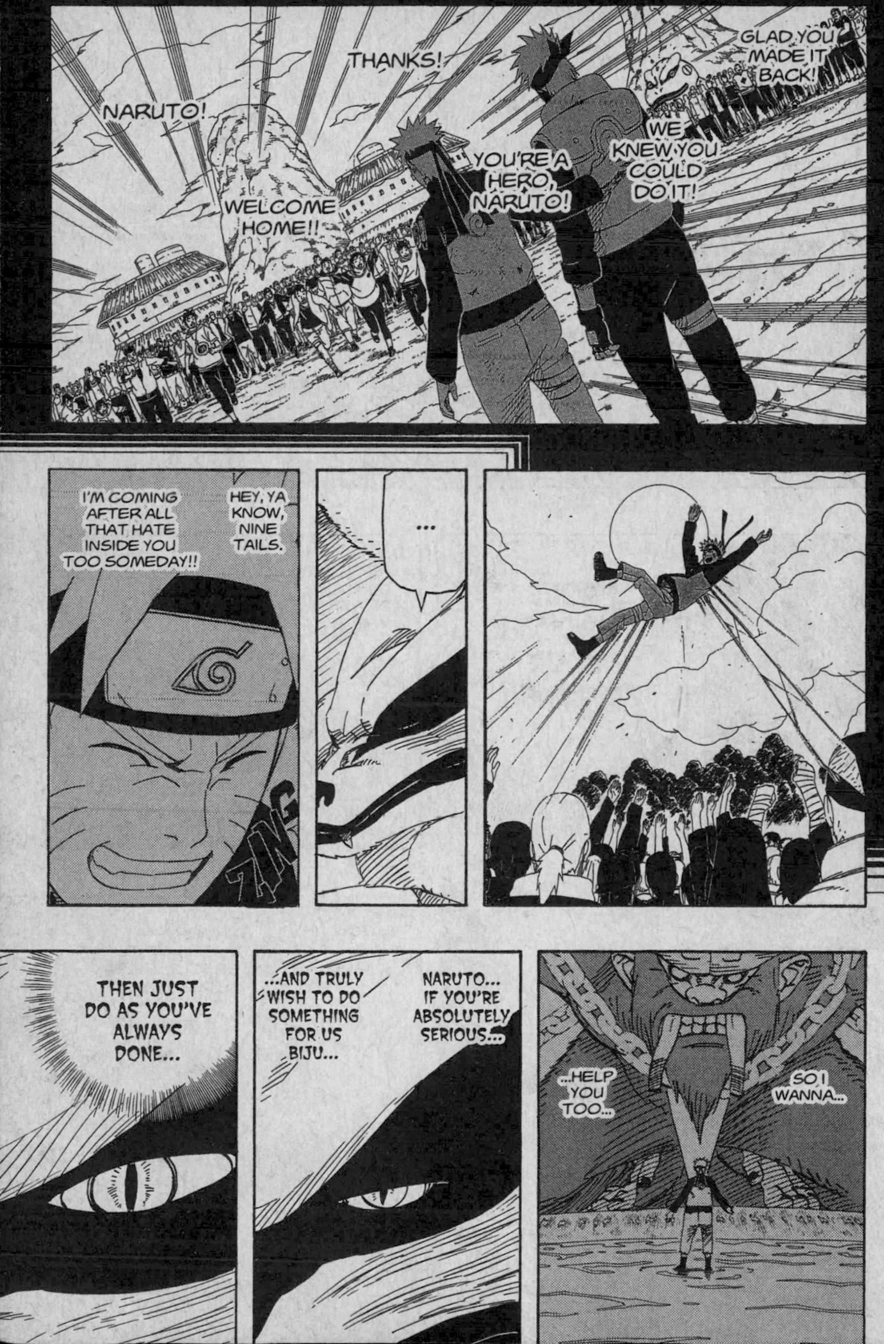
GLAD YOU MADE IT BACK!
WE KNEW YOU COULD DO IT!
THANKS!
YOU'RE A HERO, NARUTO!
NARUTO!
WELCOME HOME!!
...
HEY, YA KNOW, NINE TAILS.
I'M COMING AFTER ALL THAT HATE INSIDE YOU TOO SOMEDAY!!
ZING
SO I WANNA...
...HELP YOU TOO...
NARUTO... IF YOU'RE ABSOLUTELY SERIOUS...
...AND TRULY WISH TO DO SOMETHING FOR US BIJU...
THEN JUST DO AS YOU'VE ALWAYS DONE...

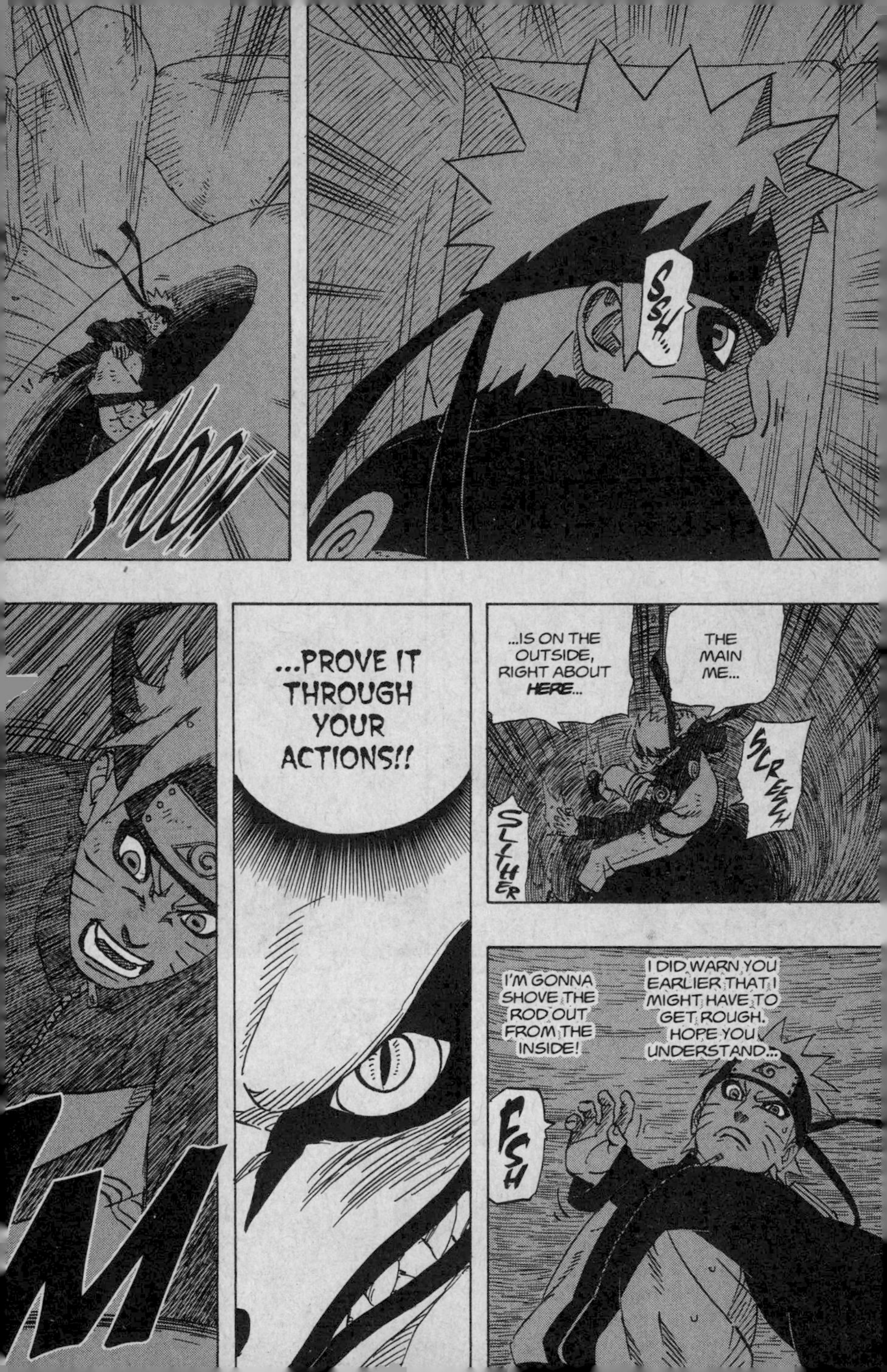
SSH...
THE MAIN ME...
...IS ON THE OUTSIDE, RIGHT ABOUT *HERE*...
SCREECH
SLITHER
I DID WARN YOU EARLIER THAT I MIGHT HAVE TO GET ROUGH. HOPE YOU UNDERSTAND...
I'M GONNA SHOVE THE ROD OUT FROM THE INSIDE!
FSH
...PROVE IT THROUGH YOUR ACTIONS!!

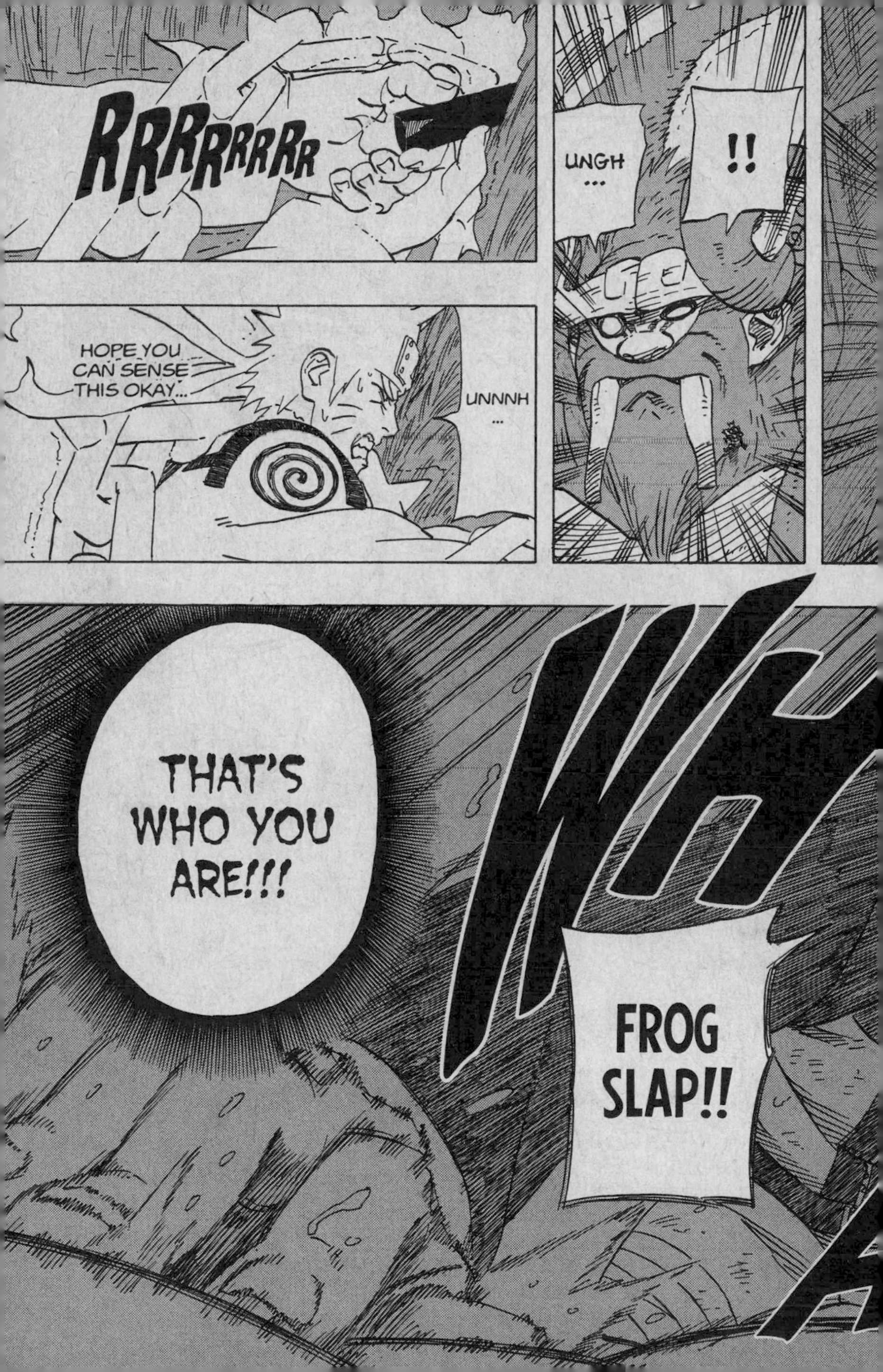
!!
UNGH...
RRRRRRRR
UNNNH...
HOPE YOU CAN SENSE THIS OKAY...
THAT'S WHO YOU ARE!!!
FROG SLAP!!

Illustration to Commemorate Reaching Volume 60 [5]

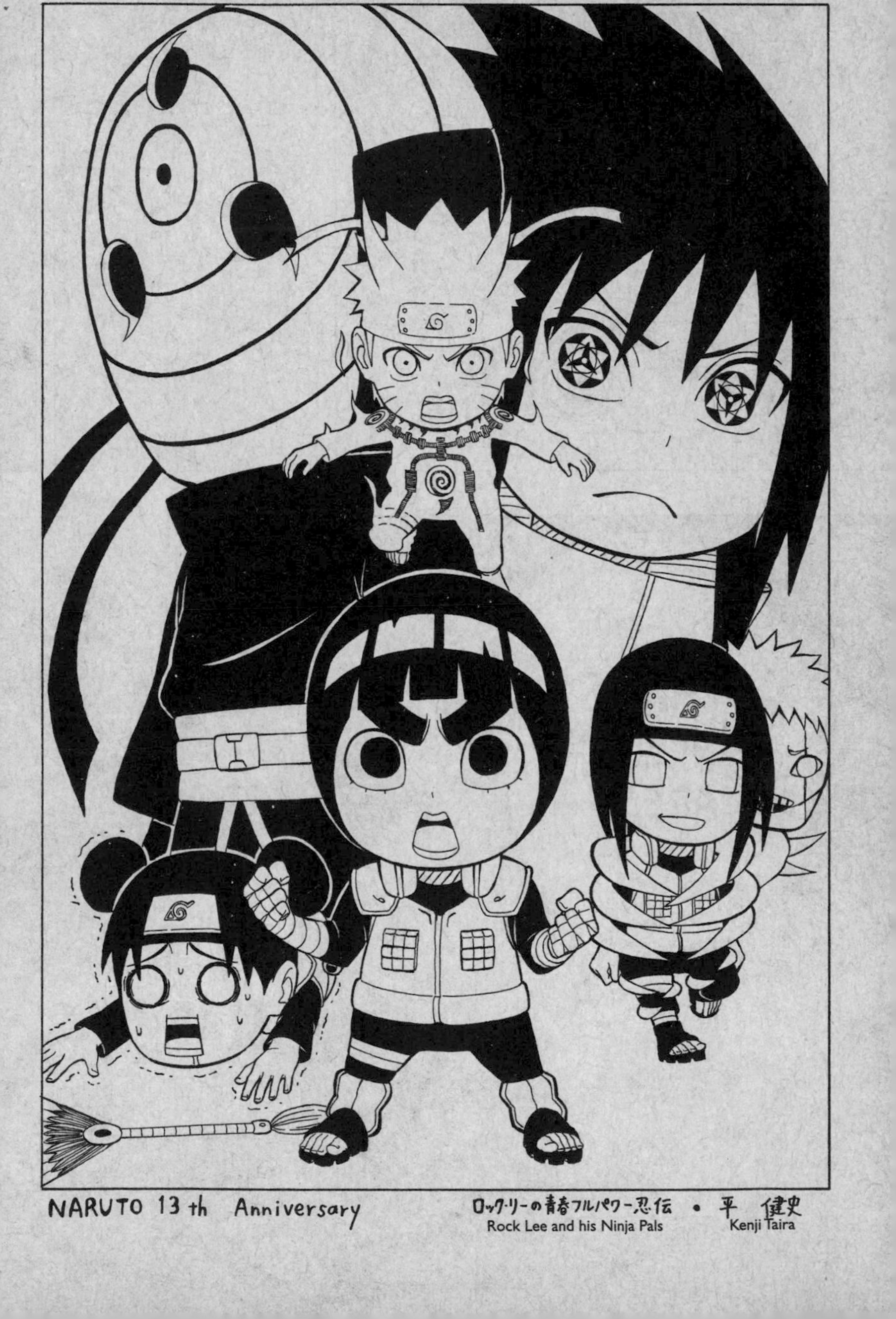

NARUTO 13 th Anniversary

ロック・リーの青春フルパワー忍伝 • 平 健史

Rock Lee and his Ninja Pals Kenji Taira

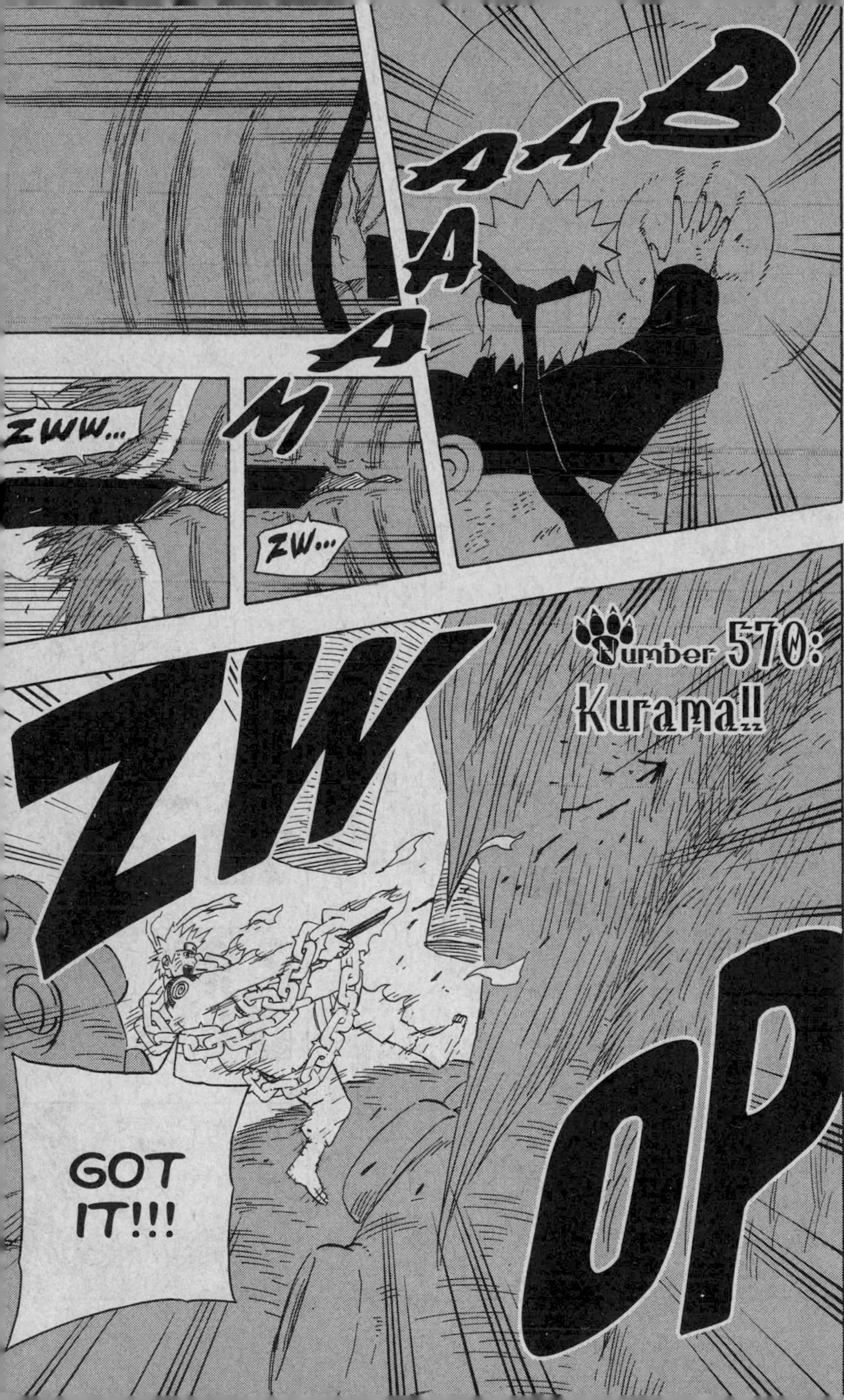
BAAAAAM
ZW...
ZWW...
Number 570: Kurama!!
ZWOOP
GOT IT!!!

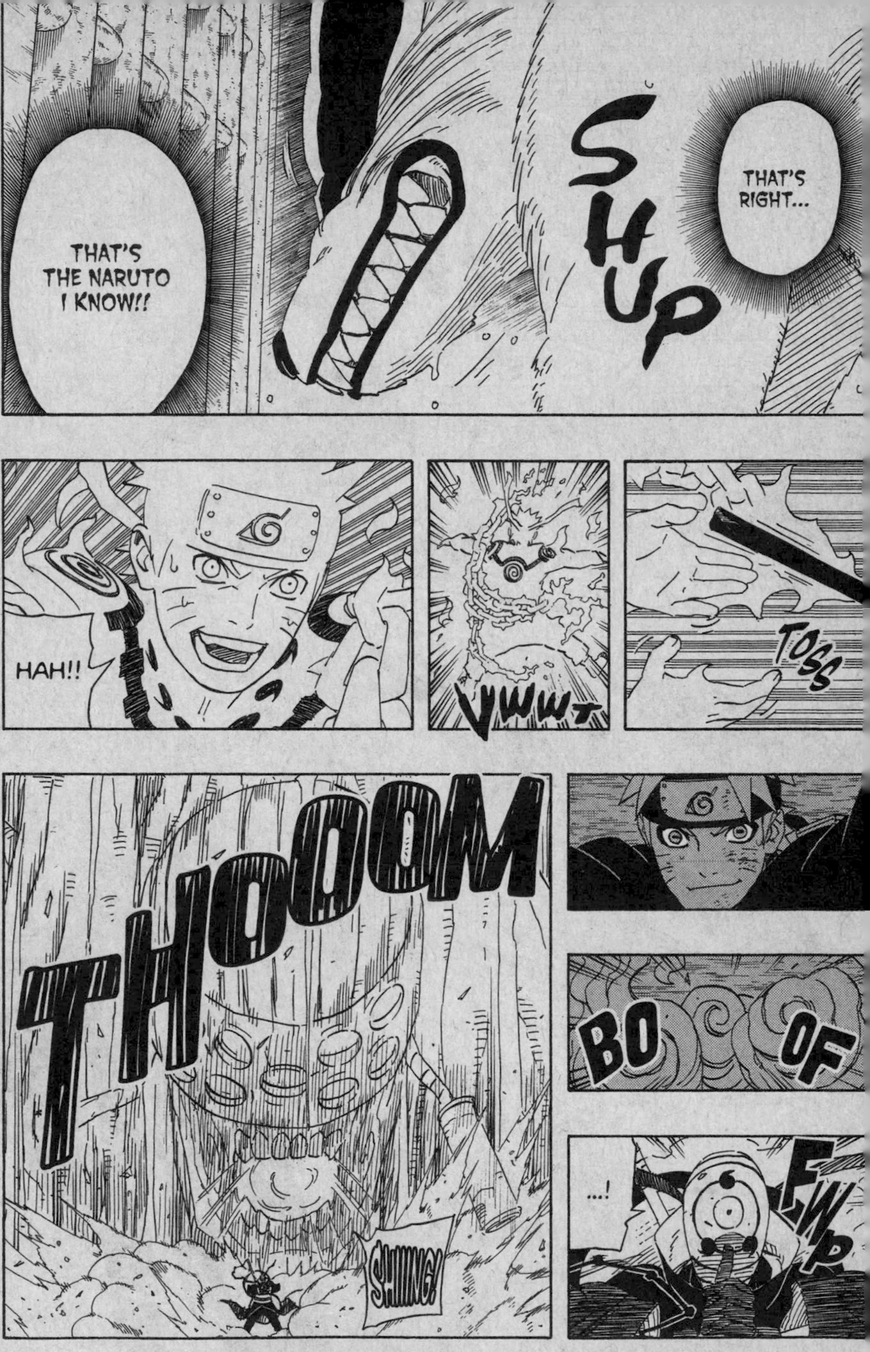
THAT'S RIGHT...
SHUP
THAT'S THE NARUTO I KNOW!!
TOSS
VWWT
HAH!!
BOOF
...!
FWP
THOOOM
SHIIING!

READ THIS WAY

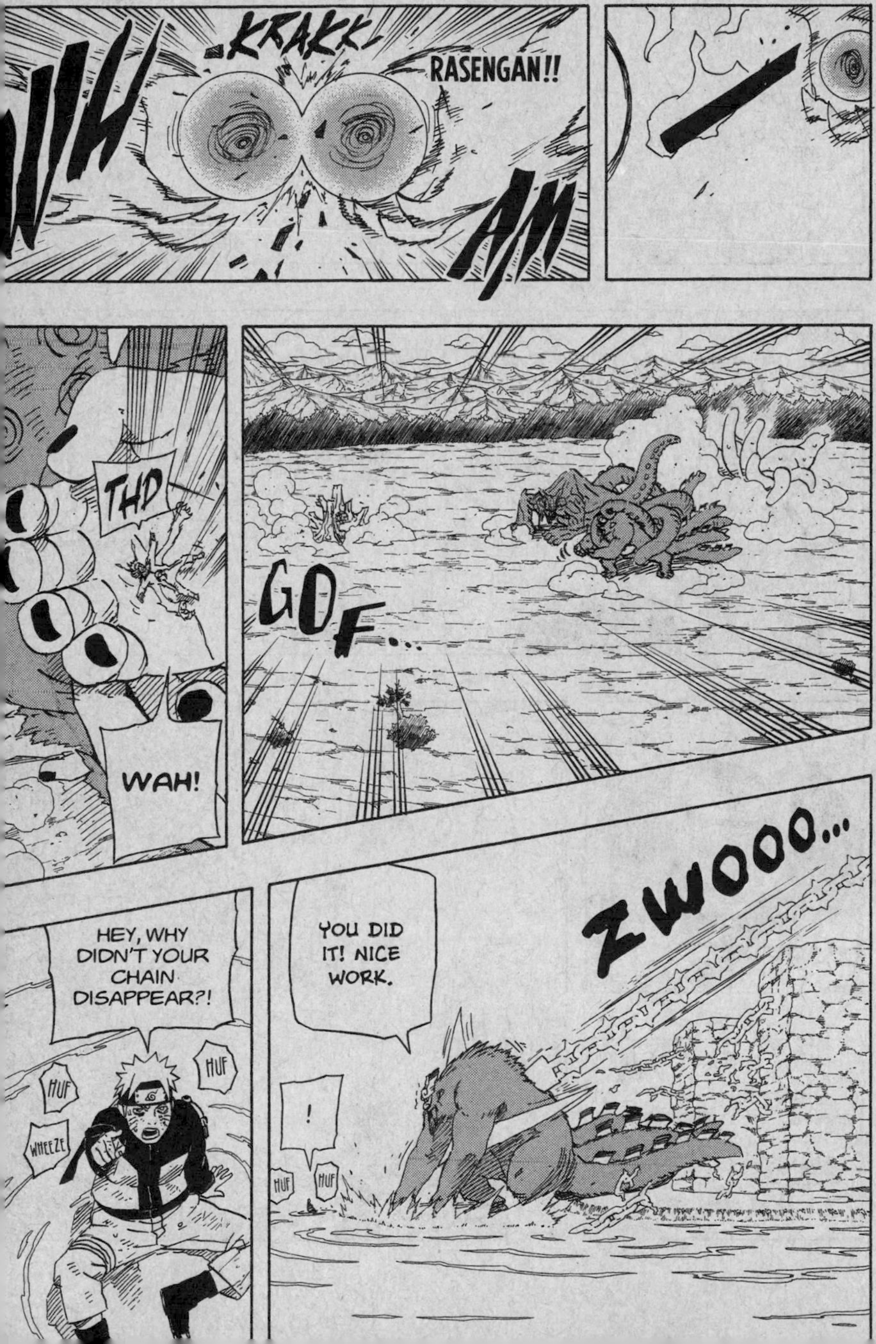
KRAKK
RASENGAN!!
WH
AM
GOF...
THD
WAH!
ZWOOO...
YOU DID IT! NICE WORK.
!
HUF
HUF
HEY, WHY DIDN'T YOUR CHAIN DISAPPEAR?!
HUF
HUF
WHEEZE

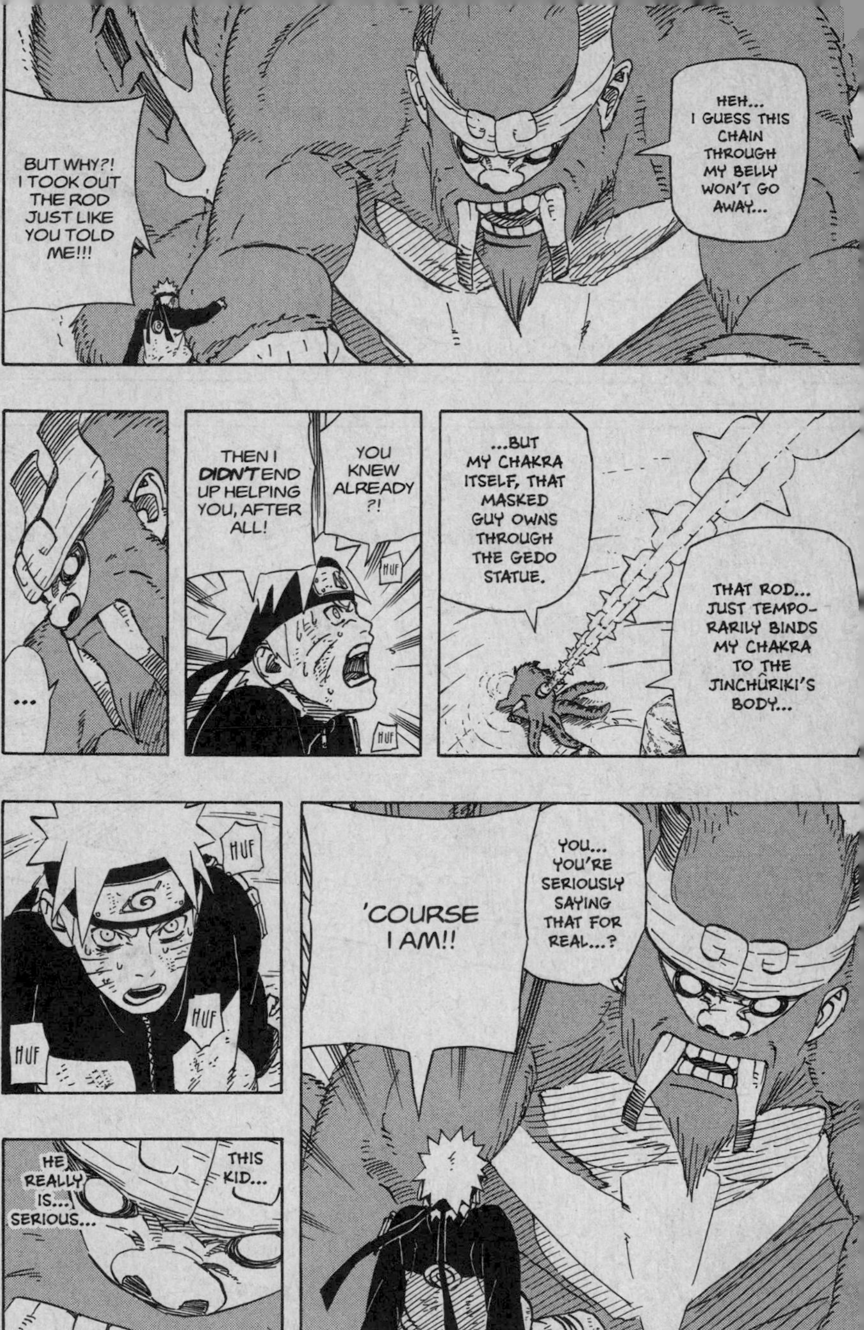
HEH... I GUESS THIS CHAIN THROUGH MY BELLY WON'T GO AWAY...
BUT WHY?! I TOOK OUT THE ROD JUST LIKE YOU TOLD ME!!!
THAT ROD... JUST TEMPORARILY BINDS MY CHAKRA TO THE JINCHÛRIKI'S BODY...
...BUT MY CHAKRA ITSELF, THAT MASKED GUY OWNS THROUGH THE GEDO STATUE.
YOU KNEW ALREADY?!
THEN I DIDN'T END UP HELPING YOU, AFTER ALL!
HUF
HUF
...
YOU... YOU'RE SERIOUSLY SAYING THAT FOR REAL...?
'COURSE I AM!!
HUF
HUF
HUF
THIS KID...
HE REALLY IS... SERIOUS...

READ THIS WAY

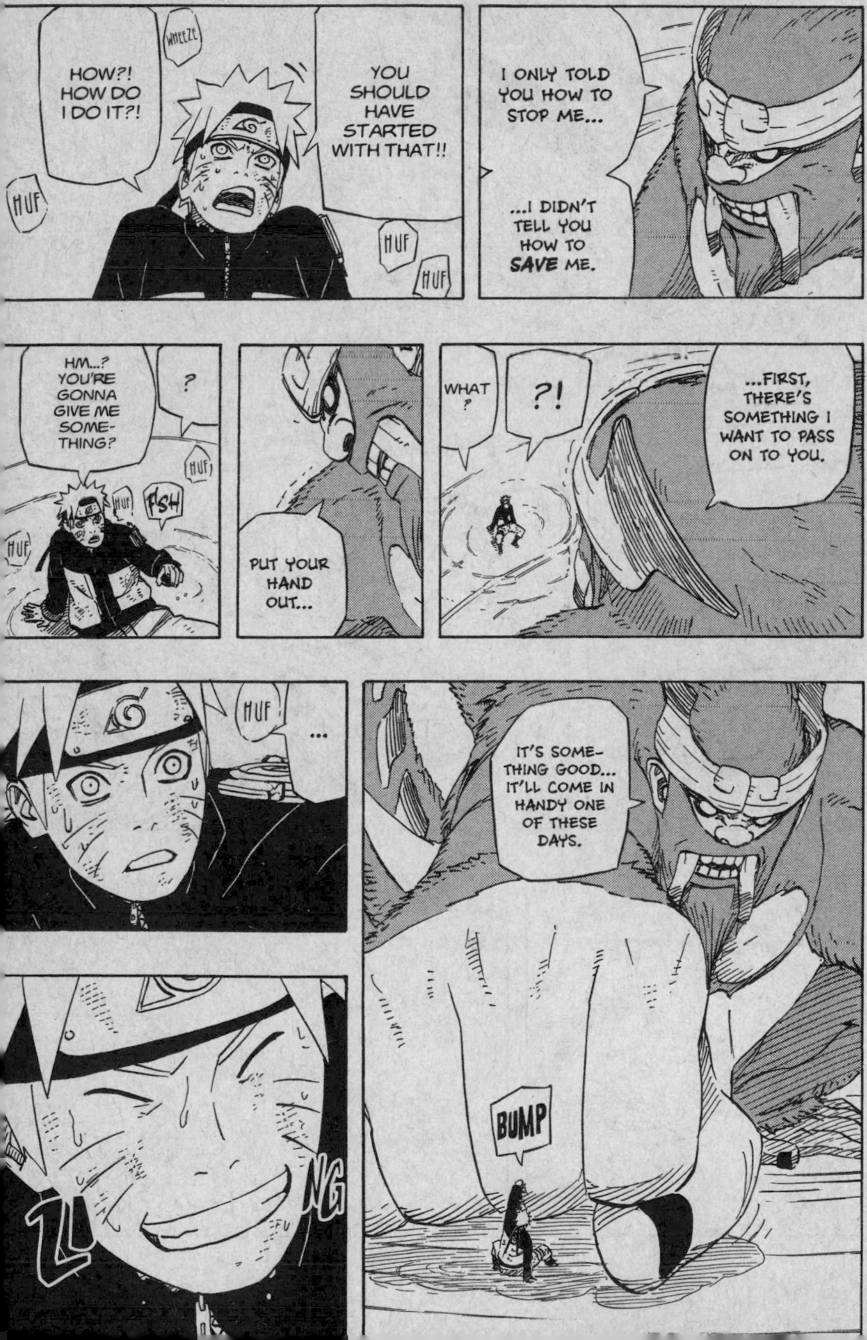
I ONLY TOLD YOU HOW TO STOP ME...
...I DIDN'T TELL YOU HOW TO SAVE ME.
YOU SHOULD HAVE STARTED WITH THAT!!
HUF
HUF
WHEEZE
HOW?! HOW DO I DO IT?!
HUF
...FIRST, THERE'S SOMETHING I WANT TO PASS ON TO YOU.
?!
WHAT?
PUT YOUR HAND OUT...
?
HM...? YOU'RE GONNA GIVE ME SOME-THING?
HUF
FSH
HUF
HUF
IT'S SOME-THING GOOD... IT'LL COME IN HANDY ONE OF THESE DAYS.
BUMP
...
HUF
FU

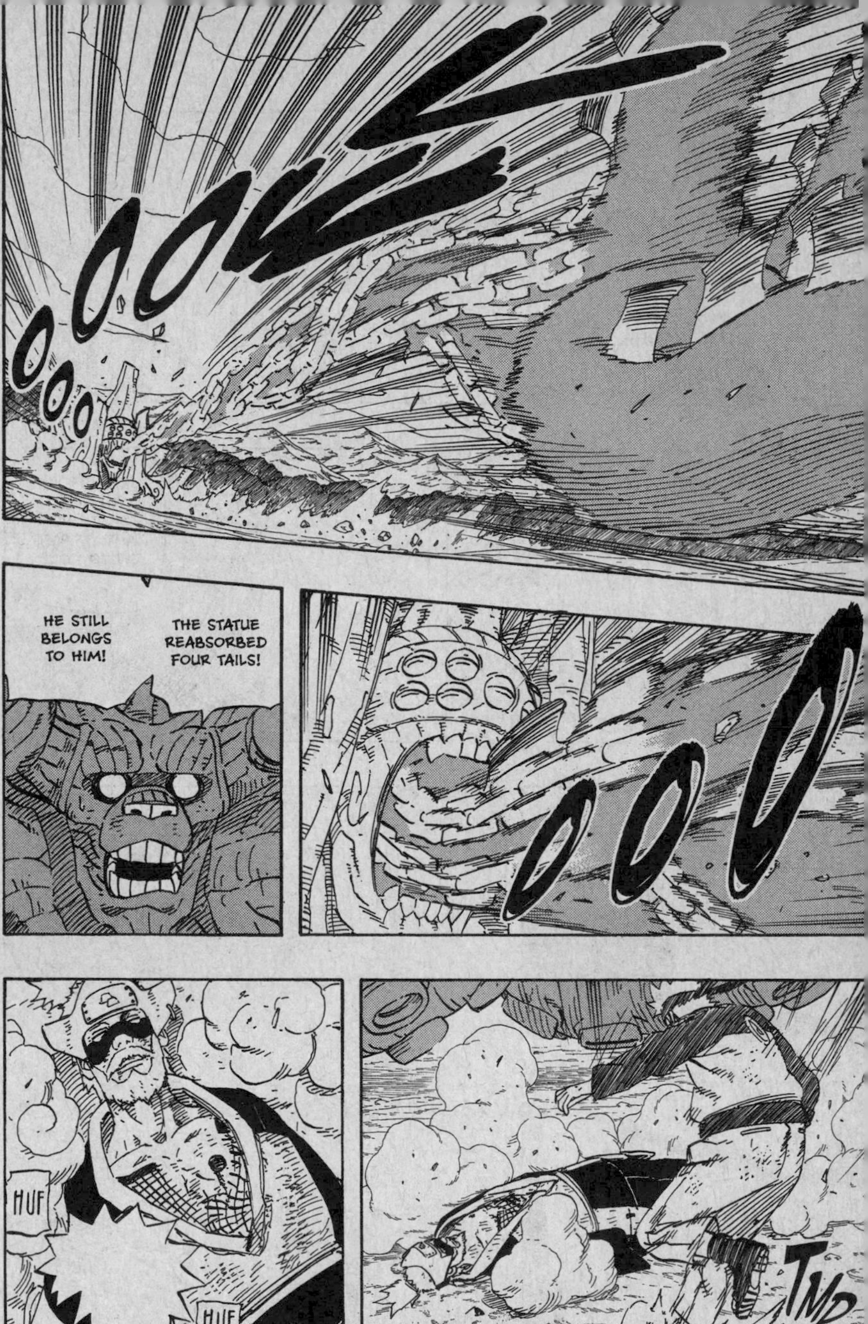
THE STATUE REABSORBED FOUR TAILS!
HE STILL BELONGS TO HIM!
TMP
HUF
HUF

READ THIS WAY

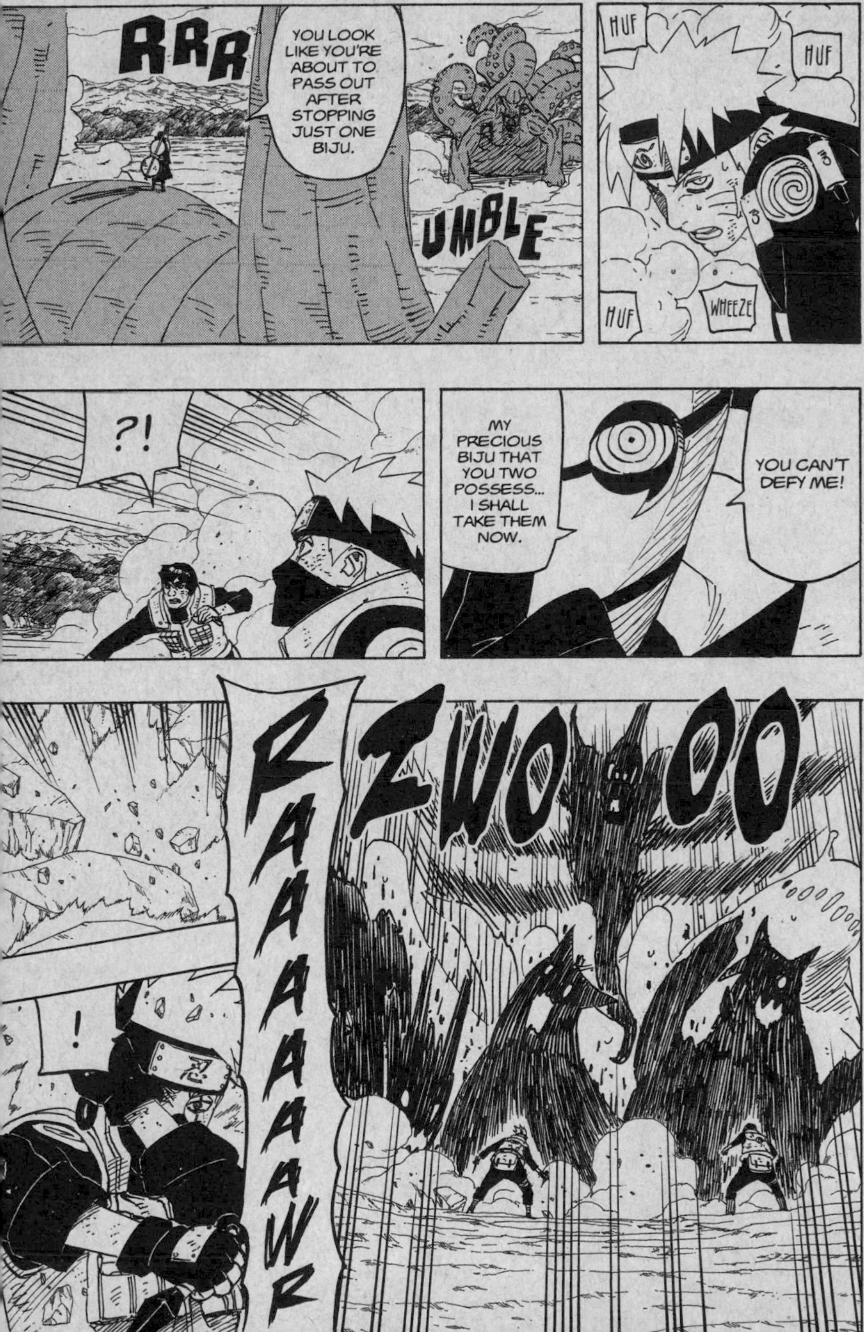
HUF
HUF
HUF
WHEEZE
YOU LOOK LIKE YOU'RE ABOUT TO PASS OUT AFTER STOPPING JUST ONE BIJU.
RRR
UMBLE
YOU CAN'T DEFY ME!
MY PRECIOUS BIJU THAT YOU TWO POSSESS... I SHALL TAKE THEM NOW.
?!
ZWOOOO
RAAAAAAAAAWR
!

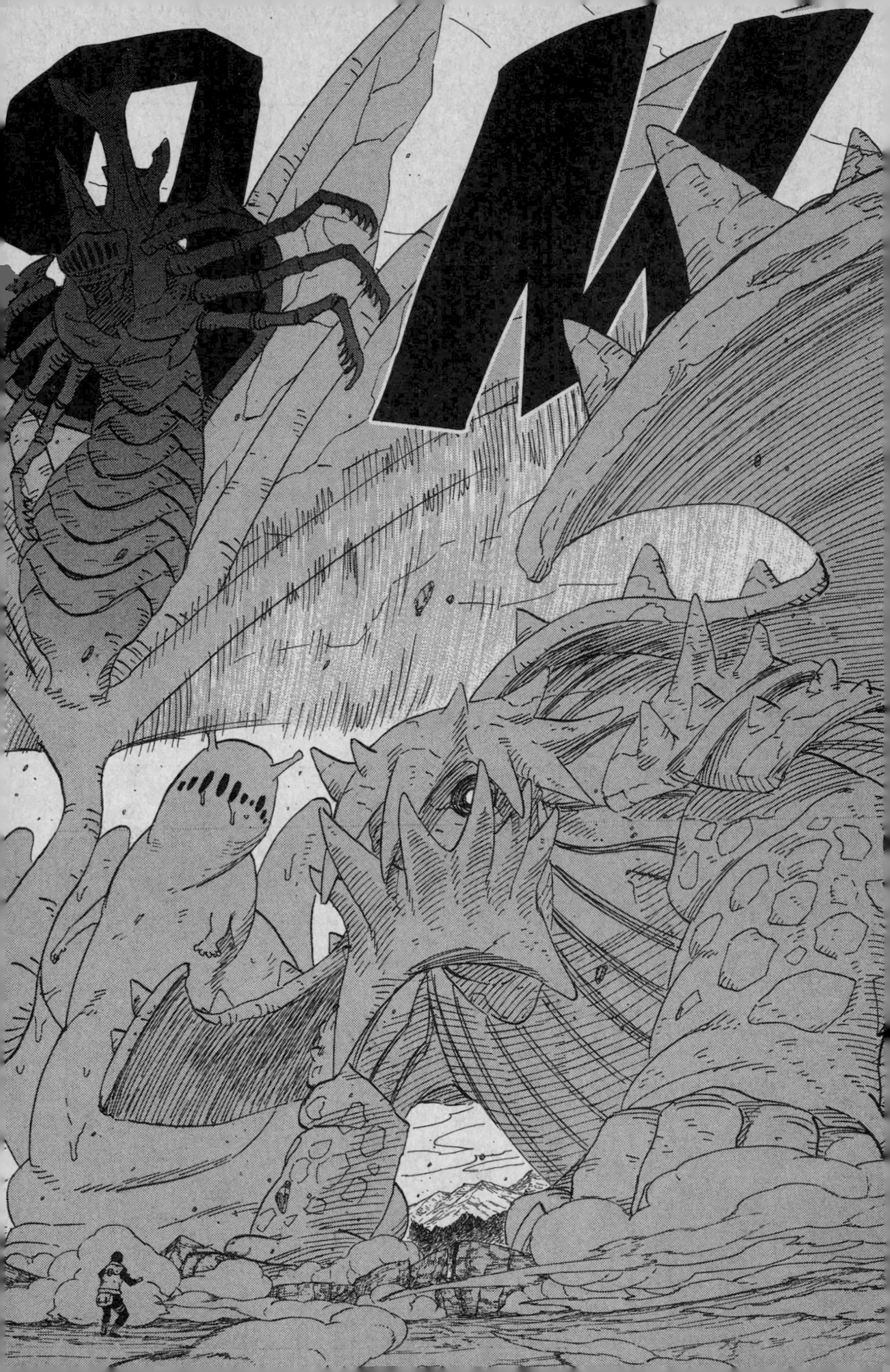

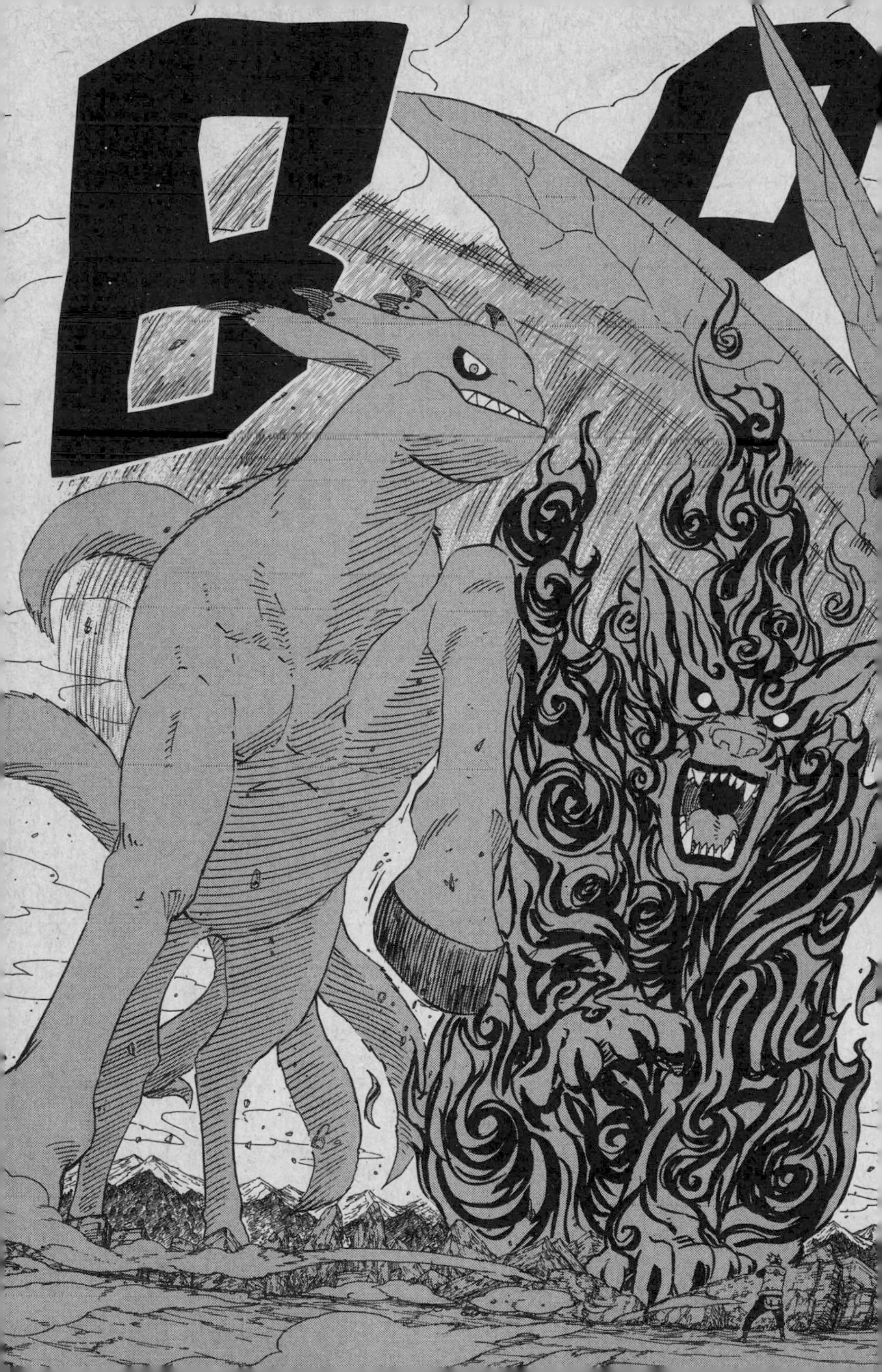

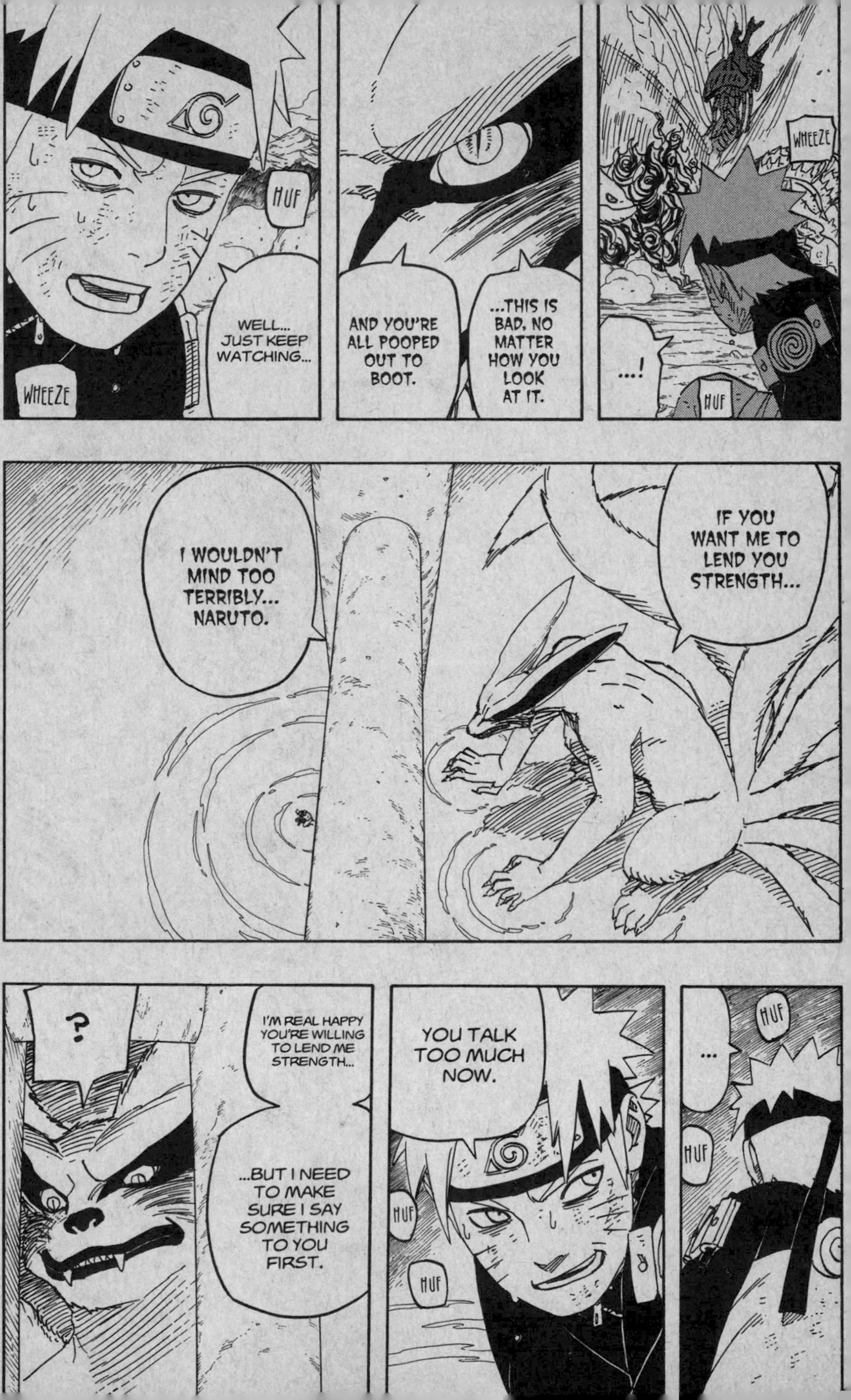
WHEEZE
...!
HUF
...THIS IS BAD, NO MATTER HOW YOU LOOK AT IT.
AND YOU'RE ALL POOPED OUT TO BOOT.
HUF
WELL... JUST KEEP WATCHING...
WHEEZE
IF YOU WANT ME TO LEND YOU STRENGTH...
I WOULDN'T MIND TOO TERRIBLY... NARUTO.
HUF
...
HUF
YOU TALK TOO MUCH NOW.
HUF
HUF
I'M REAL HAPPY YOU'RE WILLING TO LEND ME STRENGTH...
...BUT I NEED TO MAKE SURE I SAY SOMETHING TO YOU FIRST.
?

READ THIS WAY

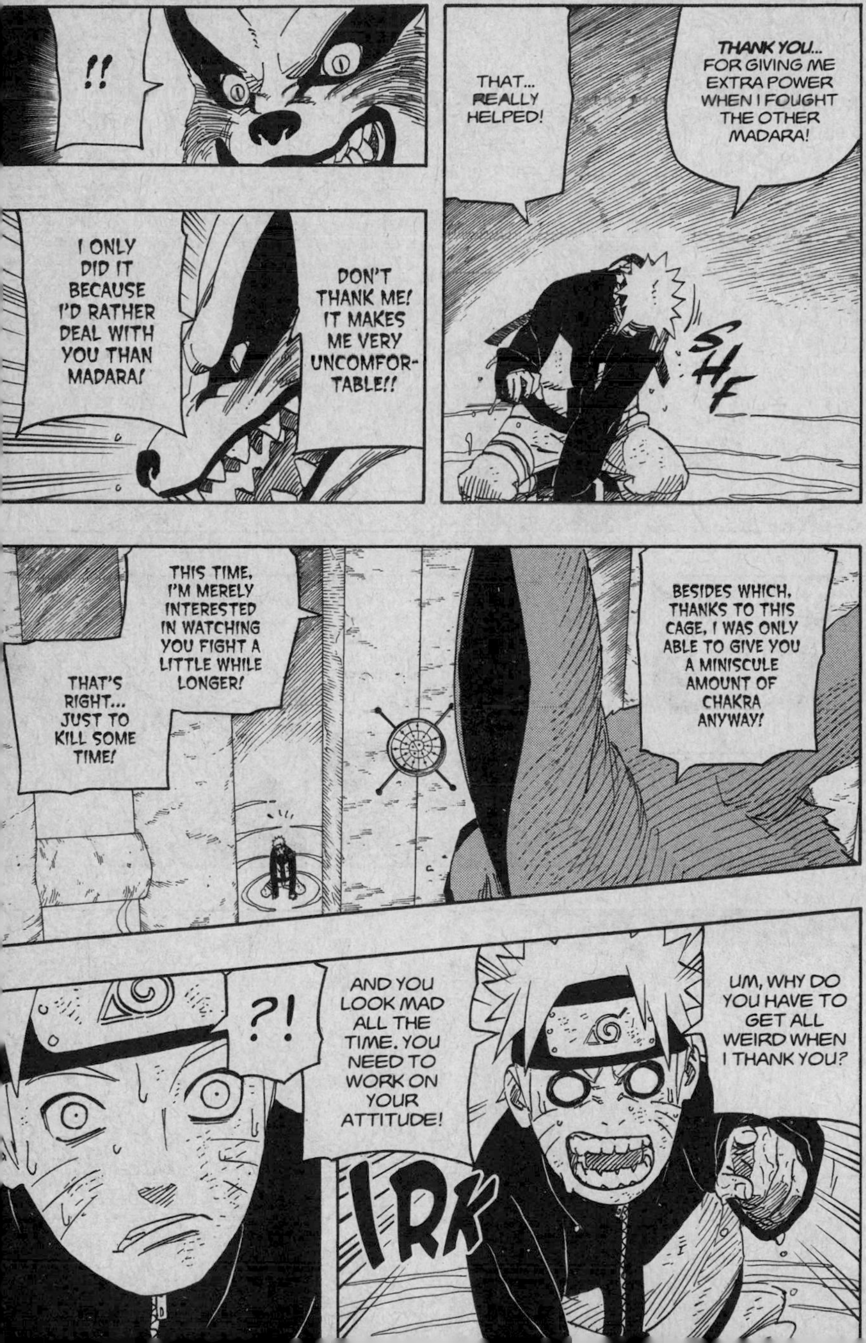
THANK YOU... FOR GIVING ME EXTRA POWER WHEN I FOUGHT THE OTHER MADARA!
THAT... REALLY HELPED!
SHF
!!
DON'T THANK ME! IT MAKES ME VERY UNCOMFORTABLE!!
I ONLY DID IT BECAUSE I'D RATHER DEAL WITH YOU THAN MADARA!
BESIDES WHICH, THANKS TO THIS CAGE, I WAS ONLY ABLE TO GIVE YOU A MINISCULE AMOUNT OF CHAKRA ANYWAY!
THIS TIME, I'M MERELY INTERESTED IN WATCHING YOU FIGHT A LITTLE WHILE LONGER!
THAT'S RIGHT... JUST TO KILL SOME TIME!
UM, WHY DO YOU HAVE TO GET ALL WEIRD WHEN I THANK YOU?
AND YOU LOOK MAD ALL THE TIME. YOU NEED TO WORK ON YOUR ATTITUDE!
IRK
?!

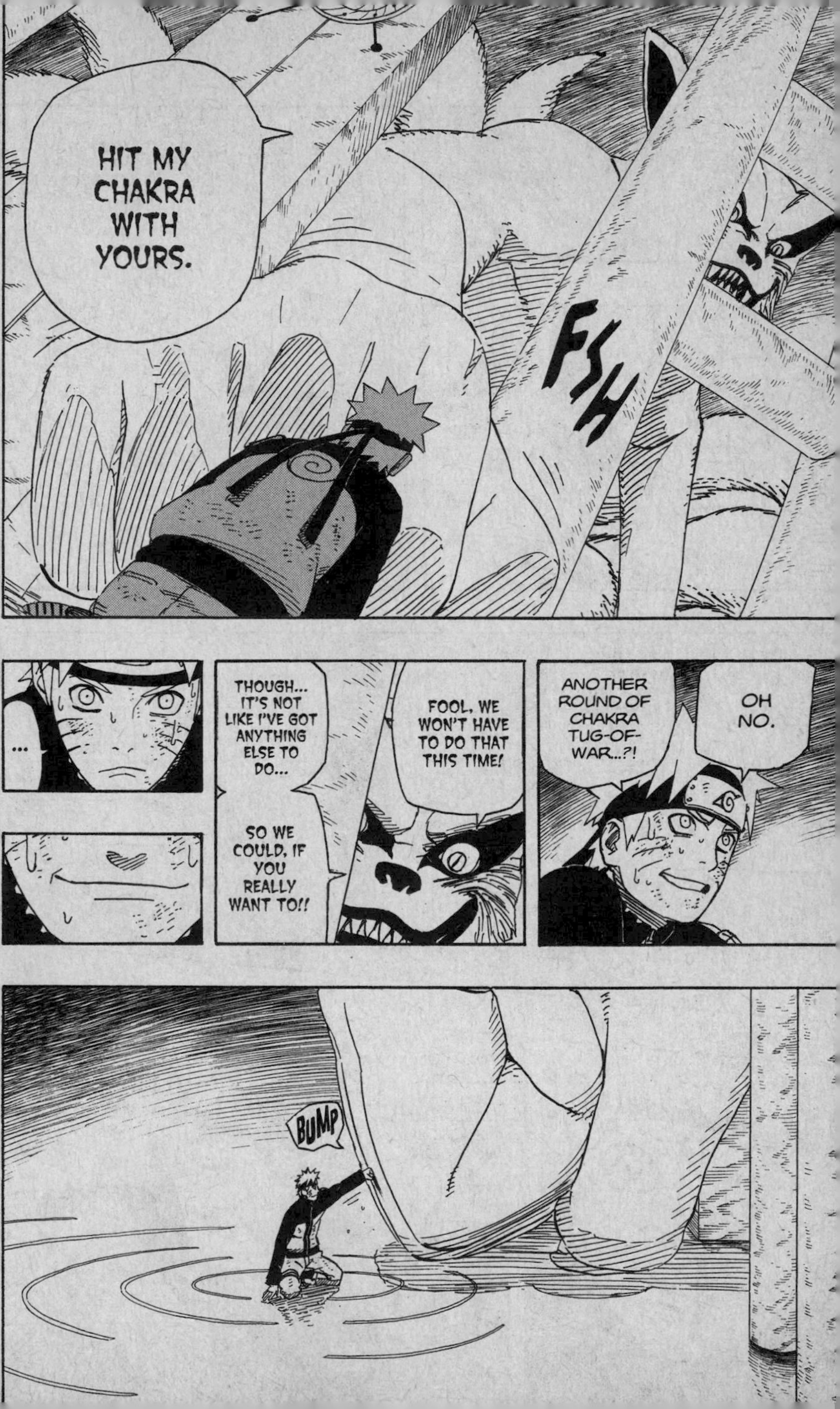
HIT MY CHAKRA WITH YOURS.
FSH
OH NO.
ANOTHER ROUND OF CHAKRA TUG-OF-WAR...?!
FOOL, WE WON'T HAVE TO DO THAT THIS TIME!
THOUGH... IT'S NOT LIKE I'VE GOT ANYTHING ELSE TO DO...
SO WE COULD, IF YOU REALLY WANT TO!!
...
BUMP

READ THIS WAY

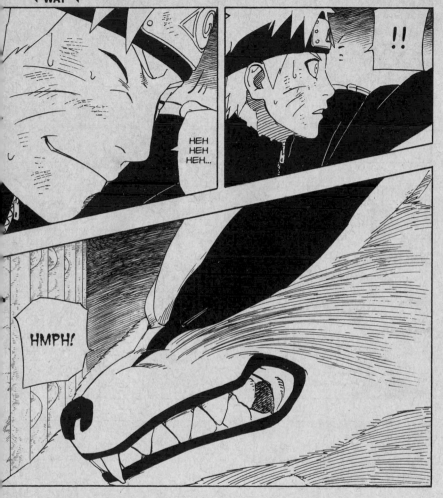

!!
HEH HEH HEH...
HMPH!
BLINK...

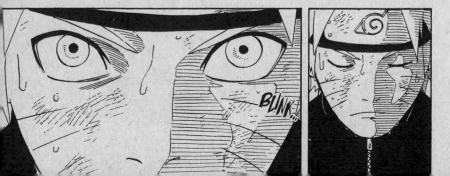

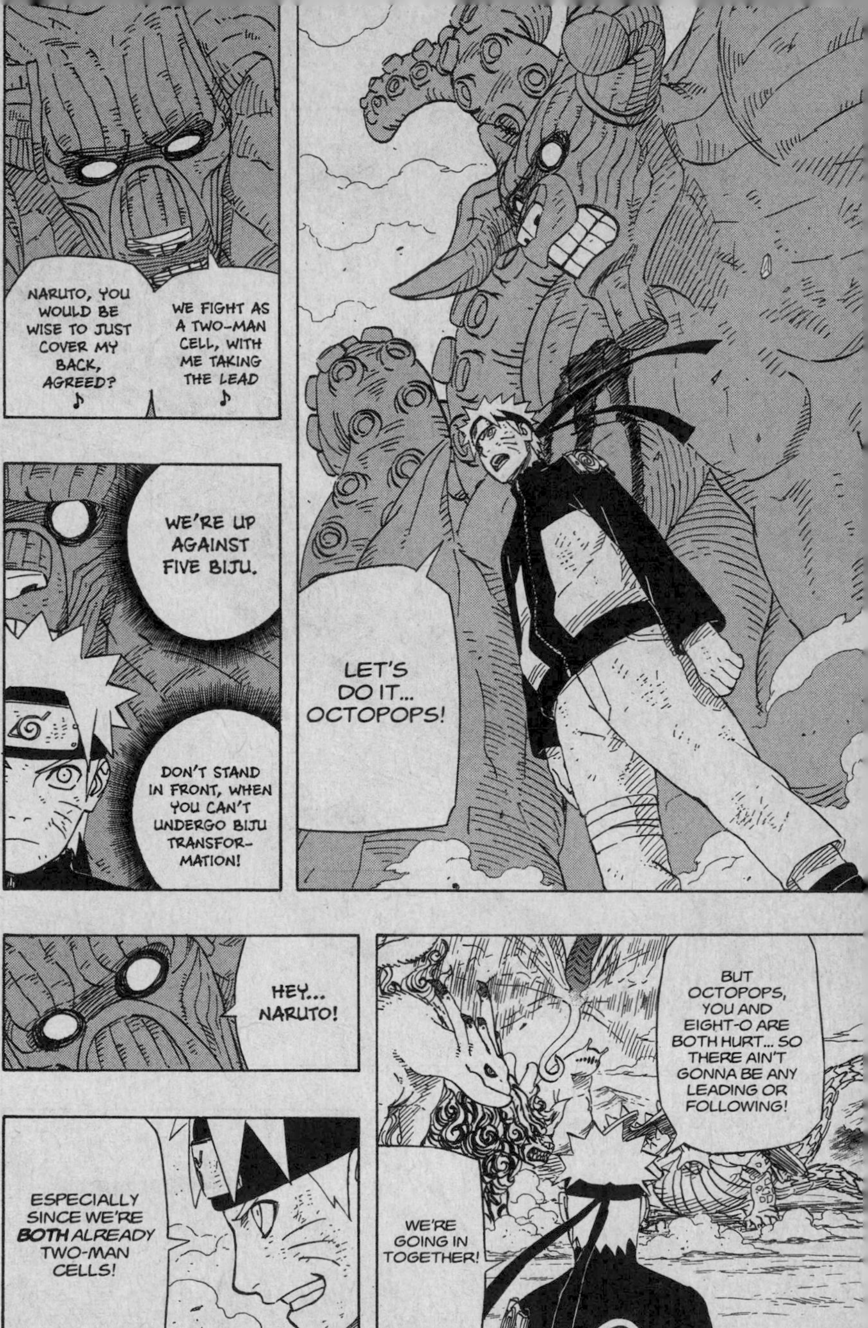
LET'S DO IT... OCTOPOPS!
WE FIGHT AS A TWO-MAN CELL, WITH ME TAKING THE LEAD ♪
NARUTO, YOU WOULD BE WISE TO JUST COVER MY BACK, AGREED? ♪
WE'RE UP AGAINST FIVE BIJU.
DON'T STAND IN FRONT, WHEN YOU CAN'T UNDERGO BIJU TRANSFORMATION!
BUT OCTOPOPS, YOU AND EIGHT-O ARE BOTH HURT... SO THERE AIN'T GONNA BE ANY LEADING OR FOLLOWING!
WE'RE GOING IN TOGETHER!
HEY... NARUTO!
ESPECIALLY SINCE WE'RE **BOTH** ALREADY TWO-MAN CELLS!

READ THIS WAY

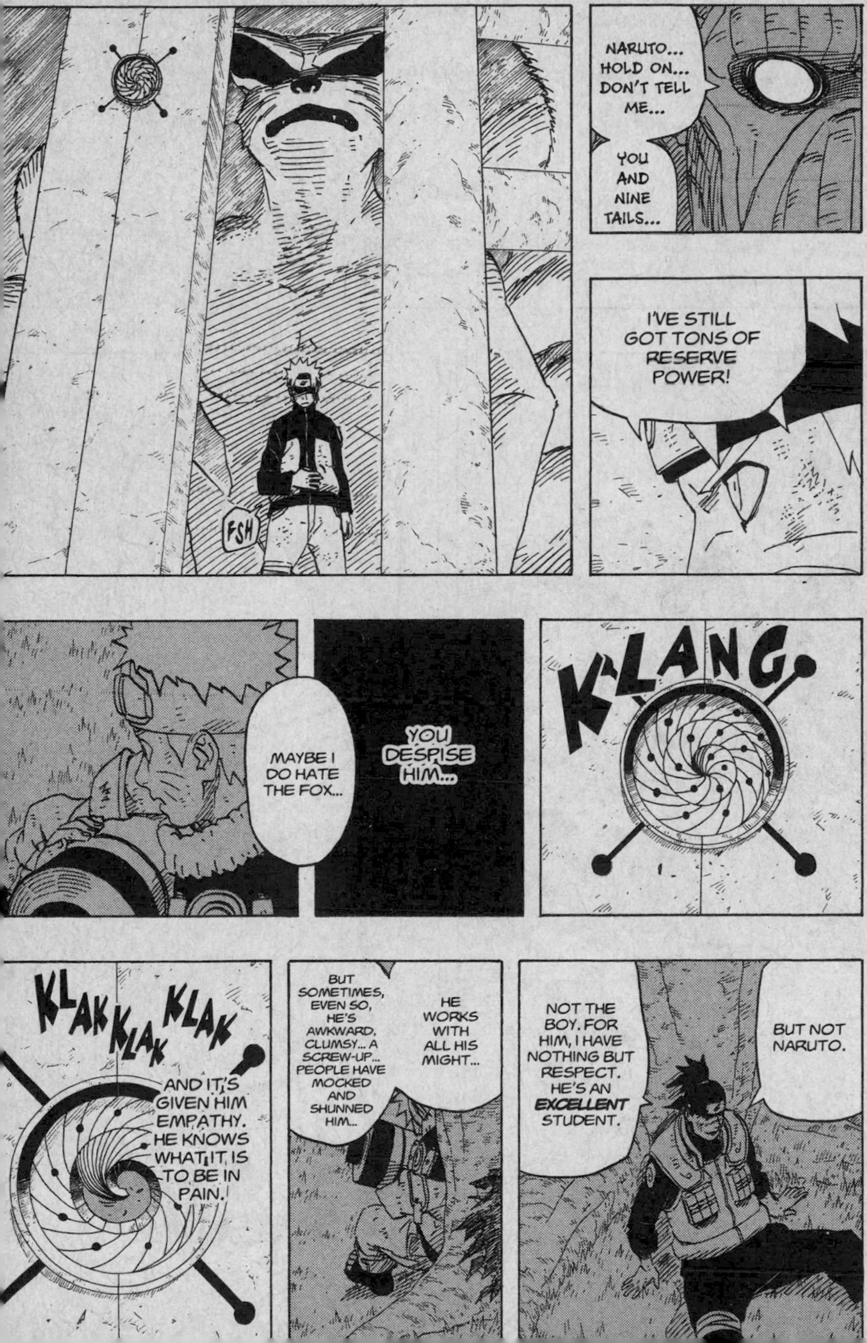

NARUTO... HOLD ON... DON'T TELL ME...
YOU AND NINE TAILS...
I'VE STILL GOT TONS OF RESERVE POWER!
FSH
K'LANG
YOU DESPISE HIM...
MAYBE I DO HATE THE FOX...
BUT NOT NARUTO.
NOT THE BOY. FOR HIM, I HAVE NOTHING BUT RESPECT. HE'S AN ***EXCELLENT*** STUDENT.
HE WORKS WITH ALL HIS MIGHT...
BUT SOMETIMES, EVEN SO, HE'S AWKWARD, CLUMSY... A SCREW-UP... PEOPLE HAVE MOCKED AND SHUNNED HIM...
KLAK KLAK KLAK
AND IT'S GIVEN HIM EMPATHY. HE KNOWS WHAT IT IS TO BE IN PAIN.

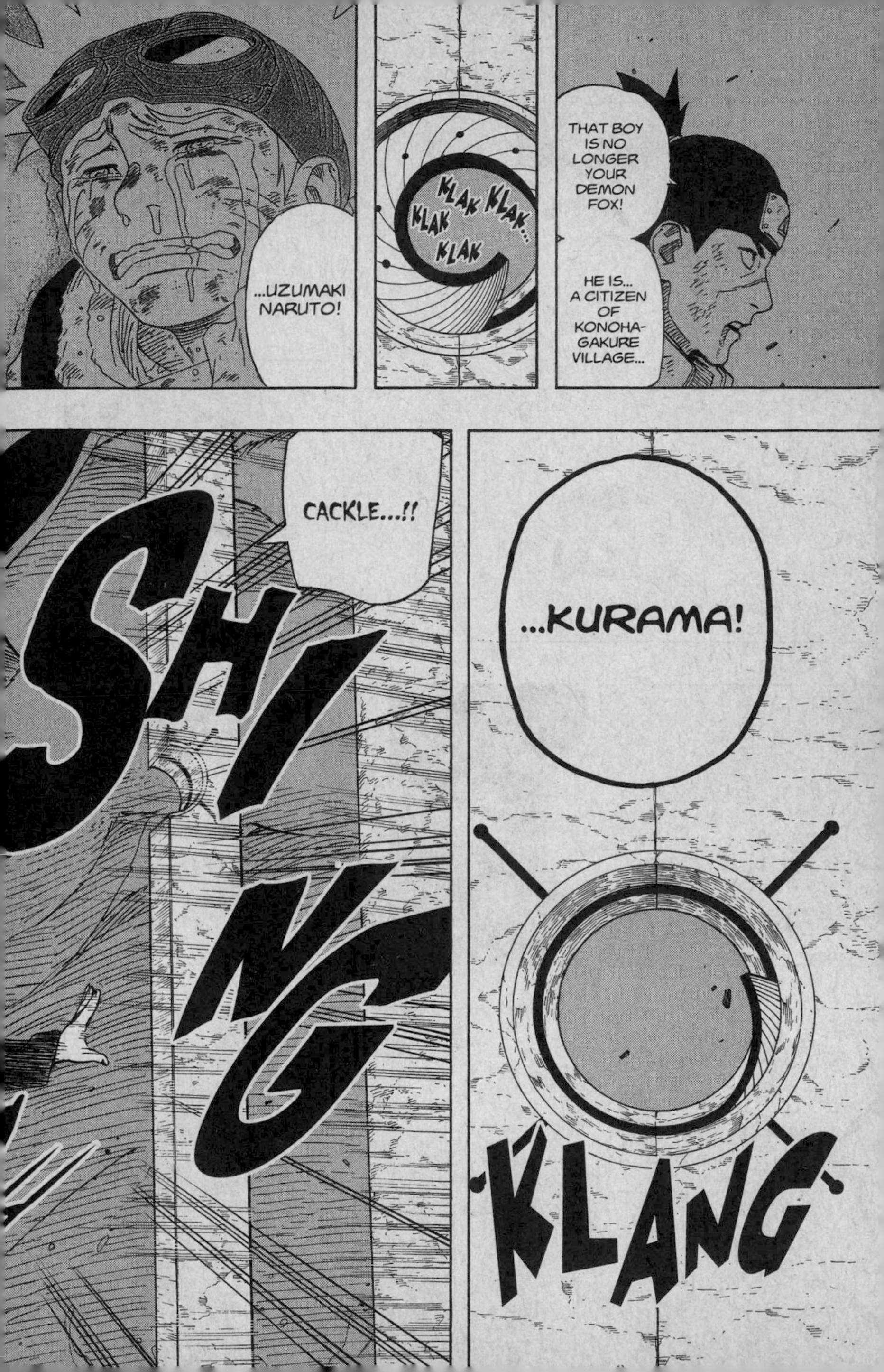
THAT BOY IS NO LONGER YOUR DEMON FOX!
HE IS... A CITIZEN OF KONOHA-GAKURE VILLAGE...
KLAK KLAK KLAK... KLAK
...UZUMAKI NARUTO!
...KURAMA!
KLANG
CACKLE...!!
SHING

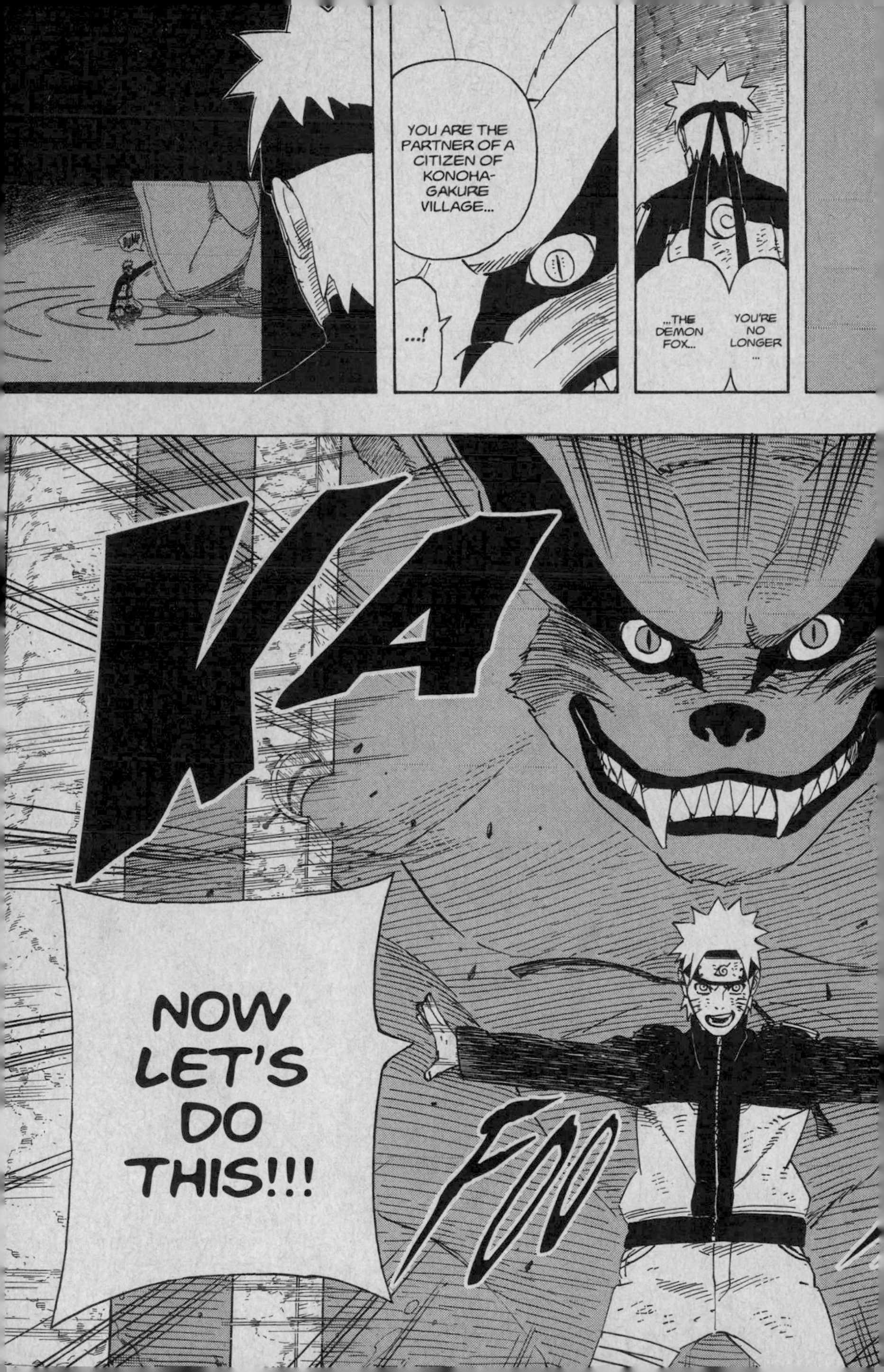
YOU'RE NO LONGER ...
...THE DEMON FOX...
YOU ARE THE PARTNER OF A CITIZEN OF KONOHA-GAKURE VILLAGE...
...!
KA
NOW LET'S DO THIS!!!
FOO

Illustration to Commemorate Reaching Volume 60 [6]

Yuichi Itakura

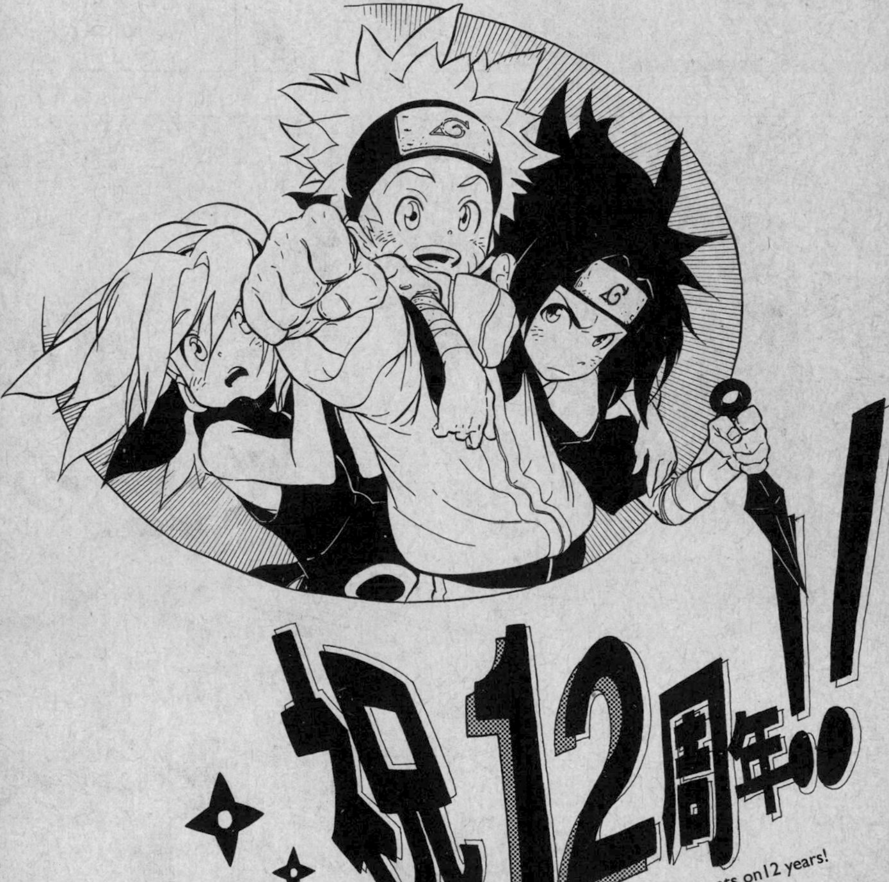
祝12周年!!

Congrats on12 years!

体に気をつけて頑張って下さい!

Take care and keep up the great work!

Number 571: Biju Mode!!

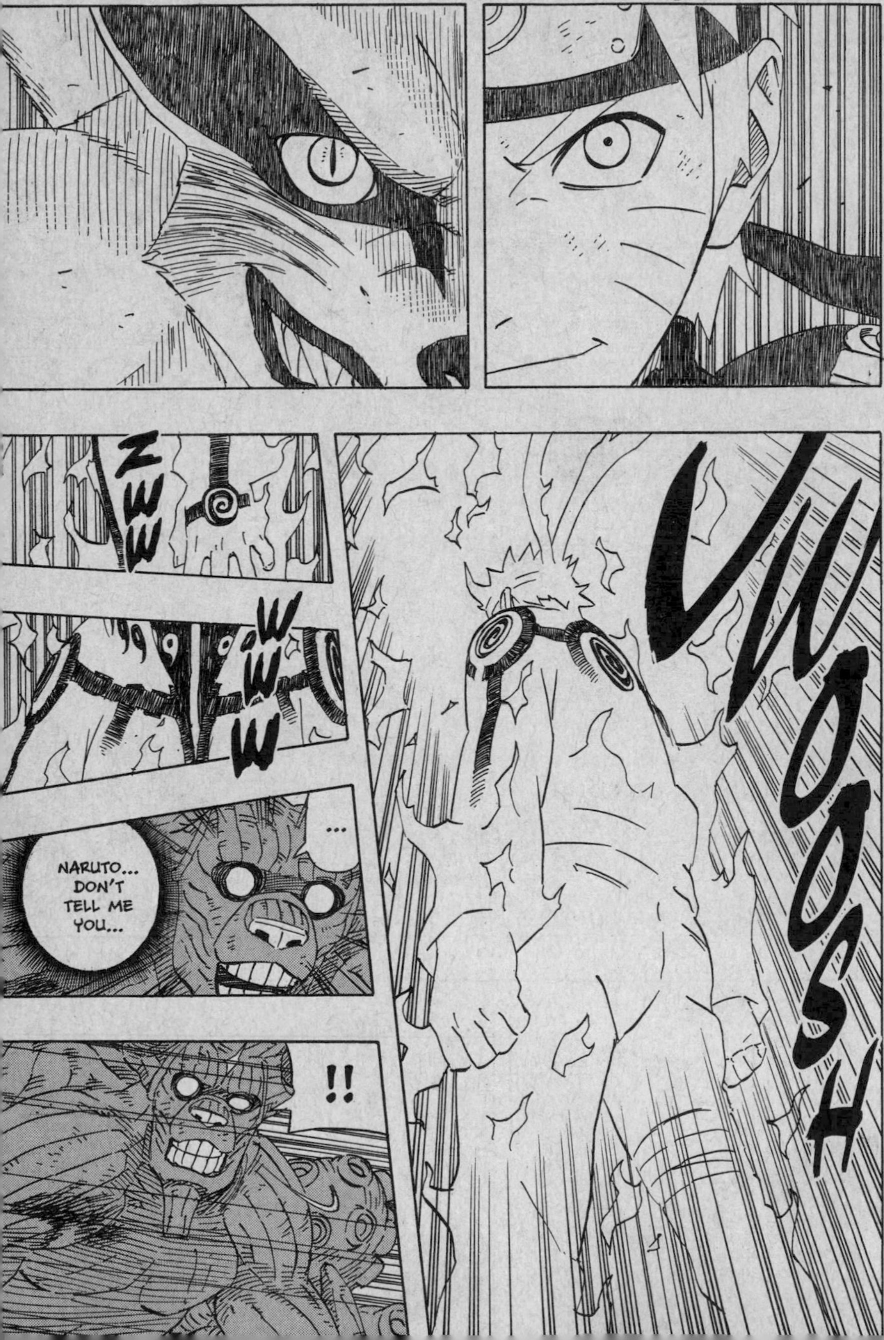
WHOOSH
ZWWW
WWWW
...
NARUTO... DON'T TELL ME YOU...
!!

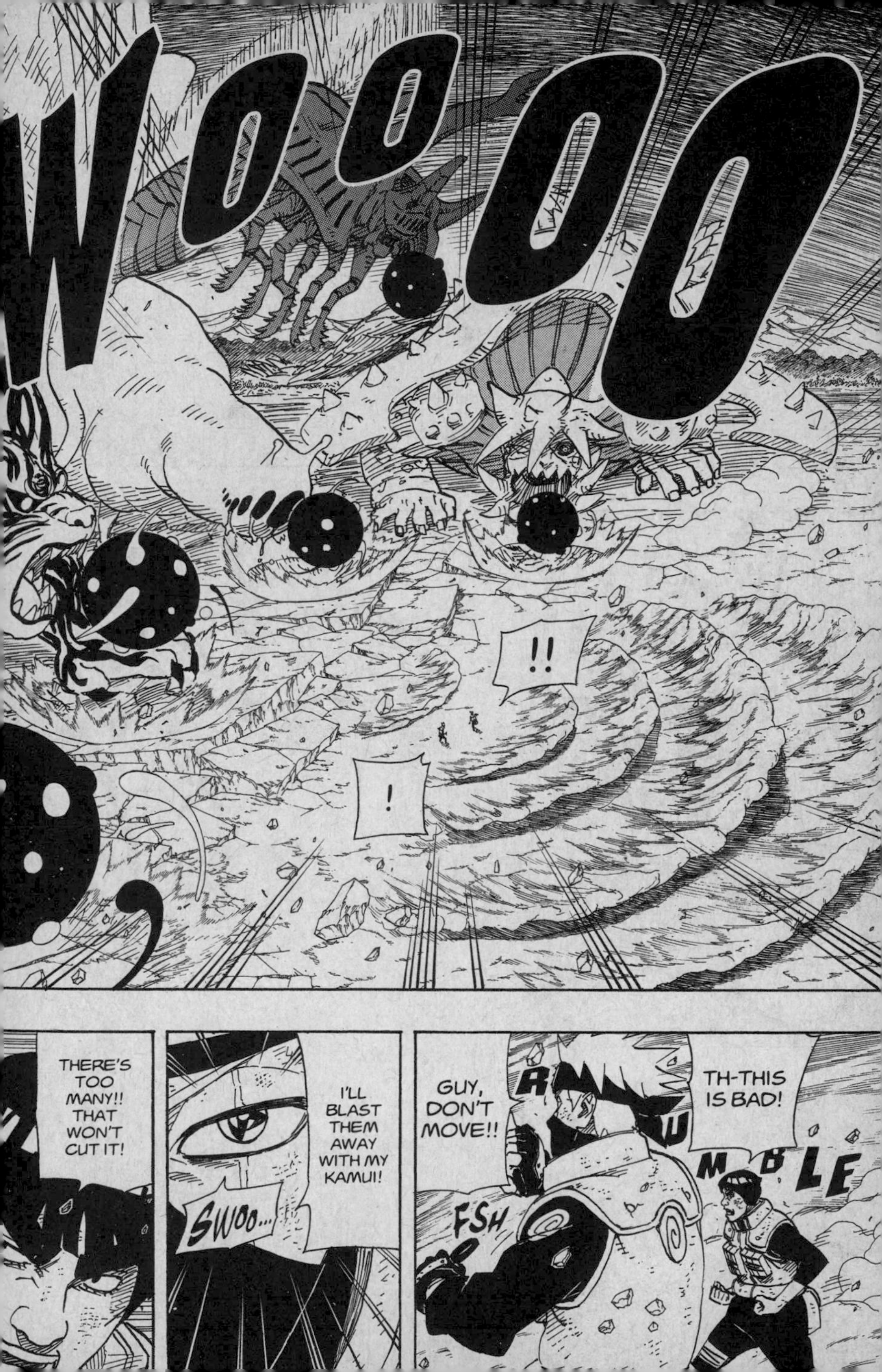
WOOOO
!!
!
TH-THIS IS BAD!
RUMBLE
GUY, DON'T MOVE!!
FSH
I'LL BLAST THEM AWAY WITH MY KAMUI!
SWOO...
THERE'S TOO MANY!! THAT WON'T CUT IT!

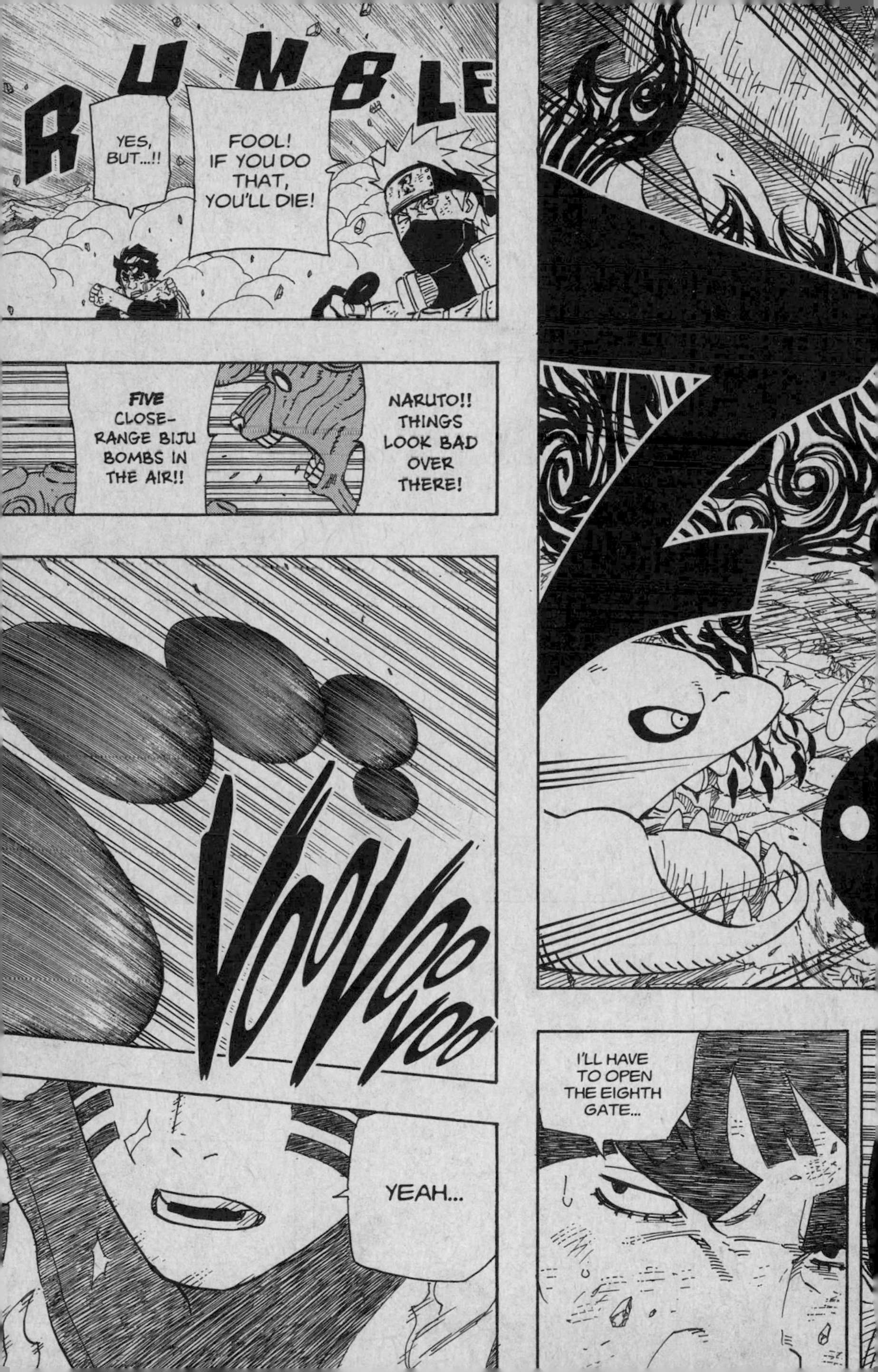
I'LL HAVE TO OPEN THE EIGHTH GATE...
RUMBLE
FOOL! IF YOU DO THAT, YOU'LL DIE!
YES, BUT...!!
NARUTO!! THINGS LOOK BAD OVER THERE!
FIVE CLOSE-RANGE BIJU BOMBS IN THE AIR!!
VOOOOO
YEAH...

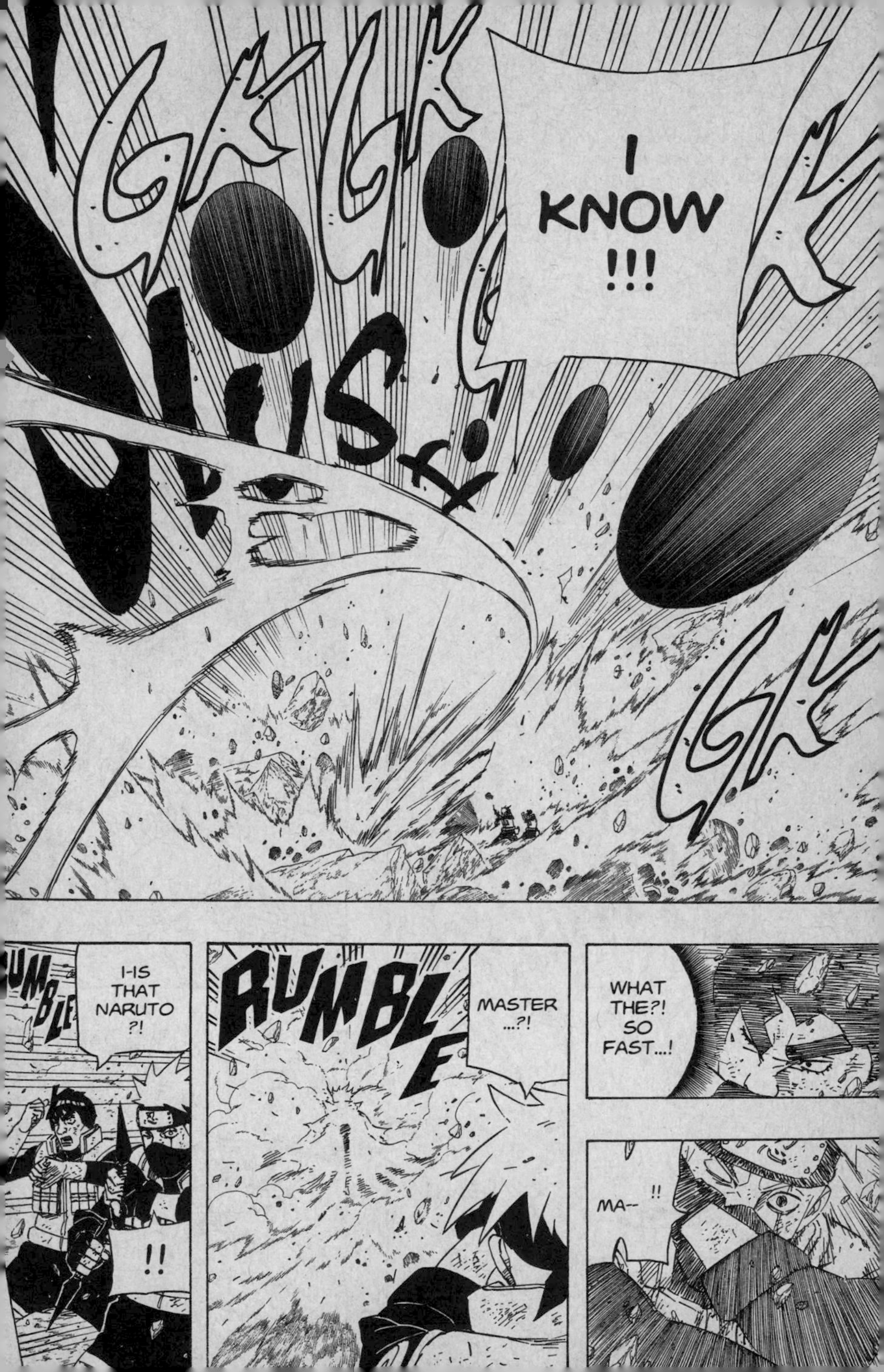
I KNOW !!!
GK
WHAT THE?! SO FAST...!
!!
MA--
RUMBLE
MASTER ...?!
I-IS THAT NARUTO ?!
!!

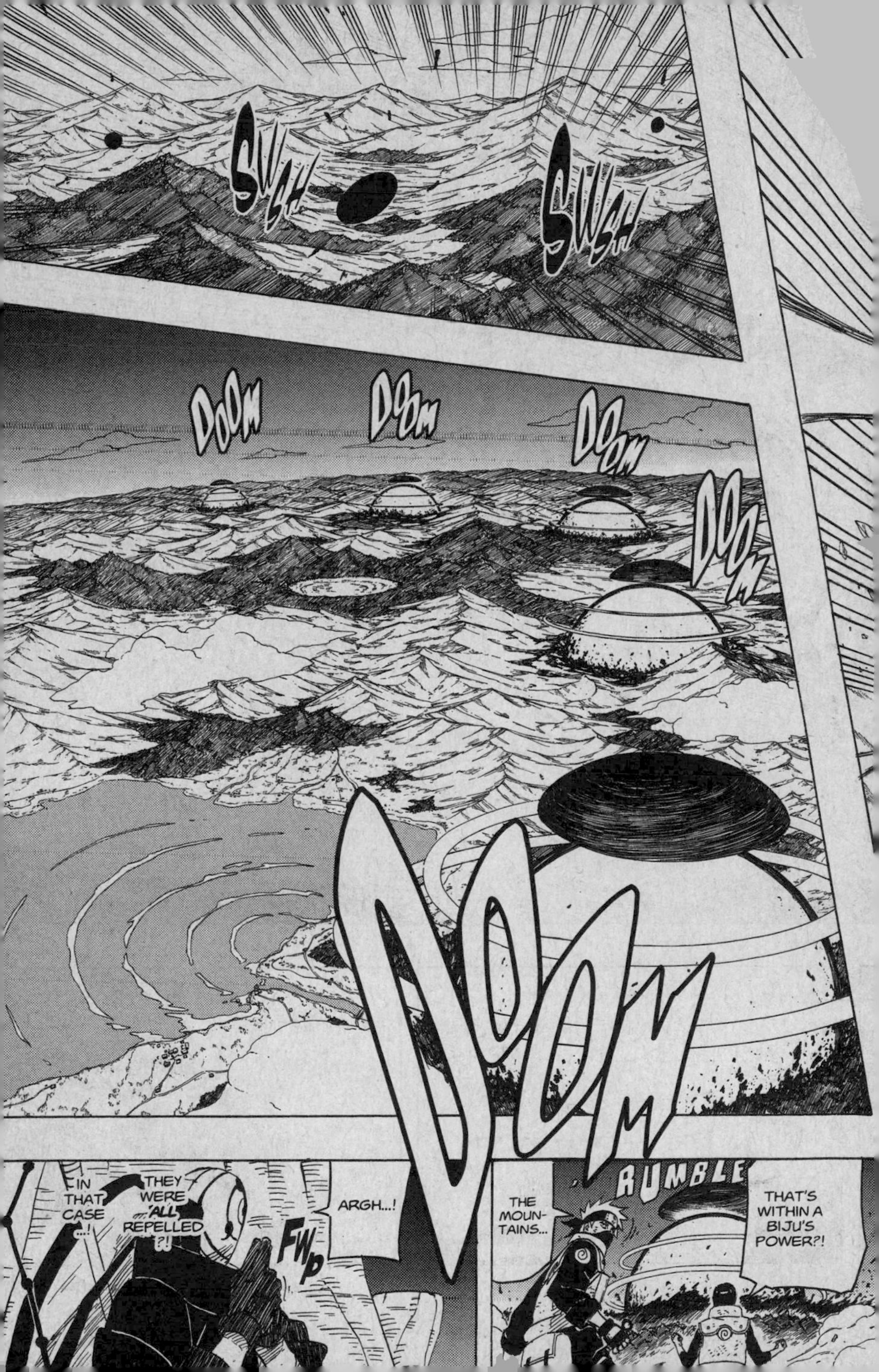
SWSH
SWSH
DOOM
DOOM
DOOM
DOOM
DOOM
RUMBLE
THAT'S WITHIN A BIJU'S POWER?!
THE MOUN-TAINS...
ARGH...!
FWP
THEY WERE ALL REPELLED?!
IN THAT CASE...!

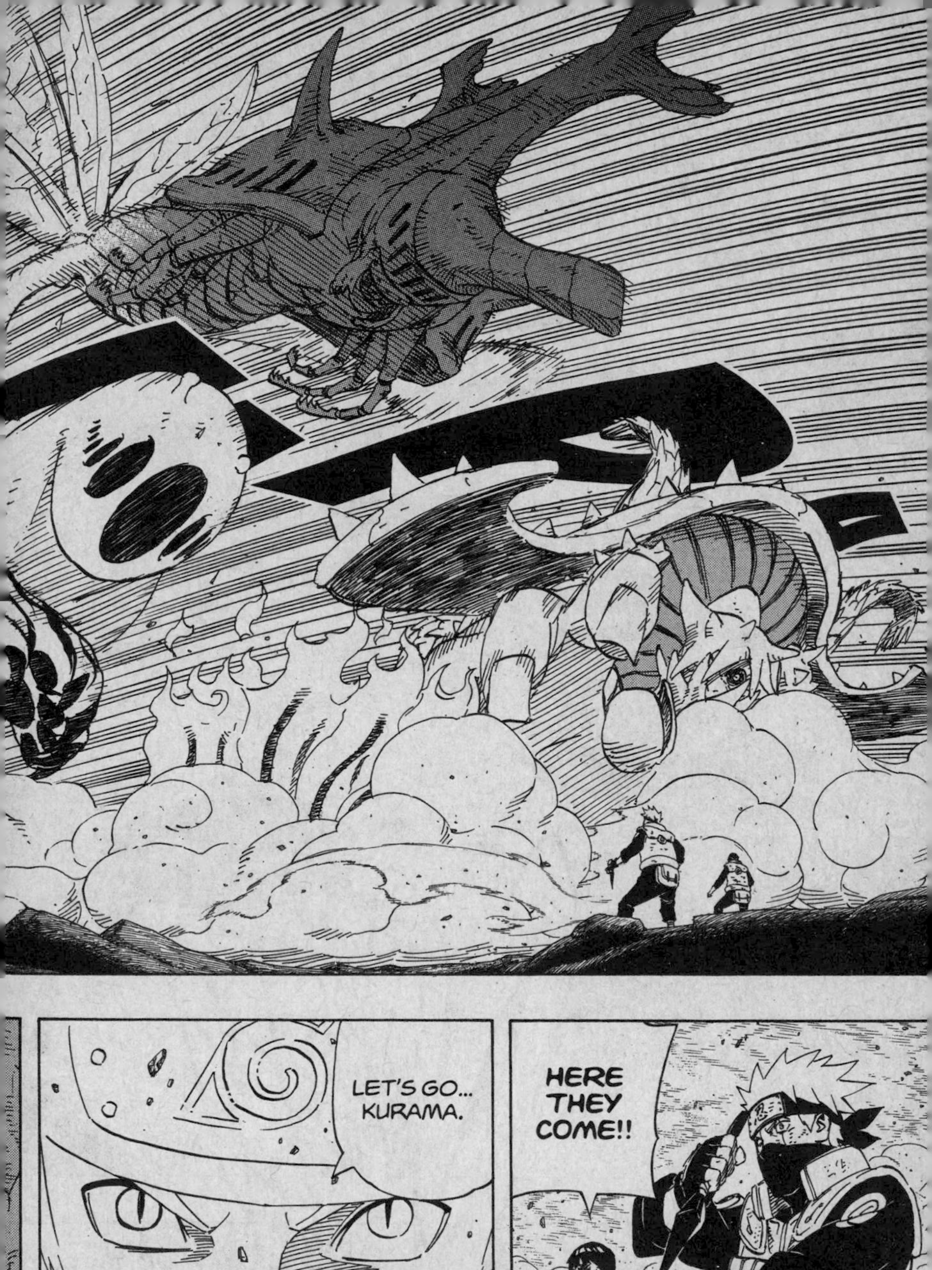
HERE THEY COME!!
LET'S GO... KURAMA.

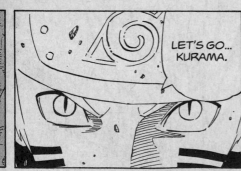

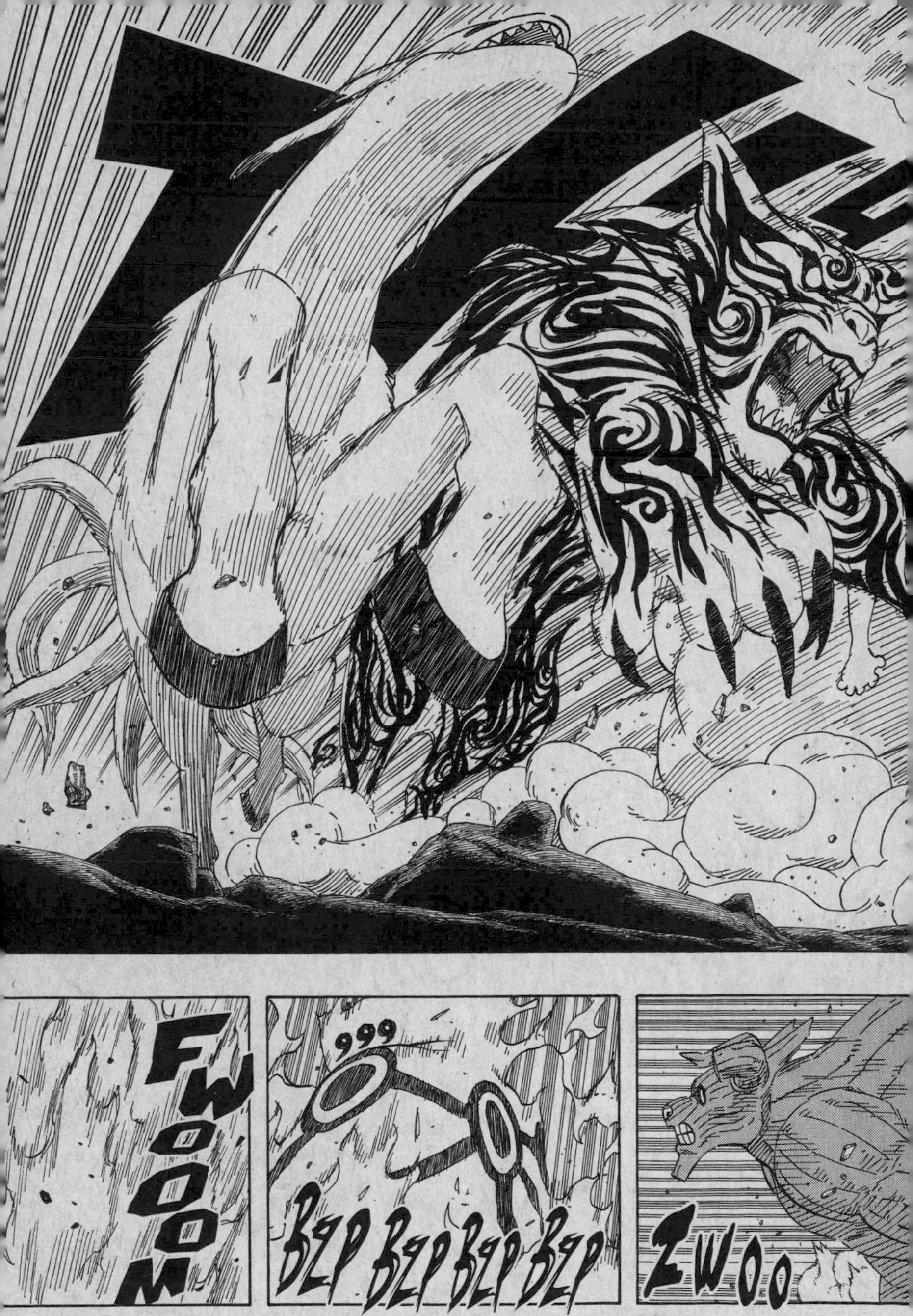
ZWOO
BZP BZP BZP BZP
FWOOOOM

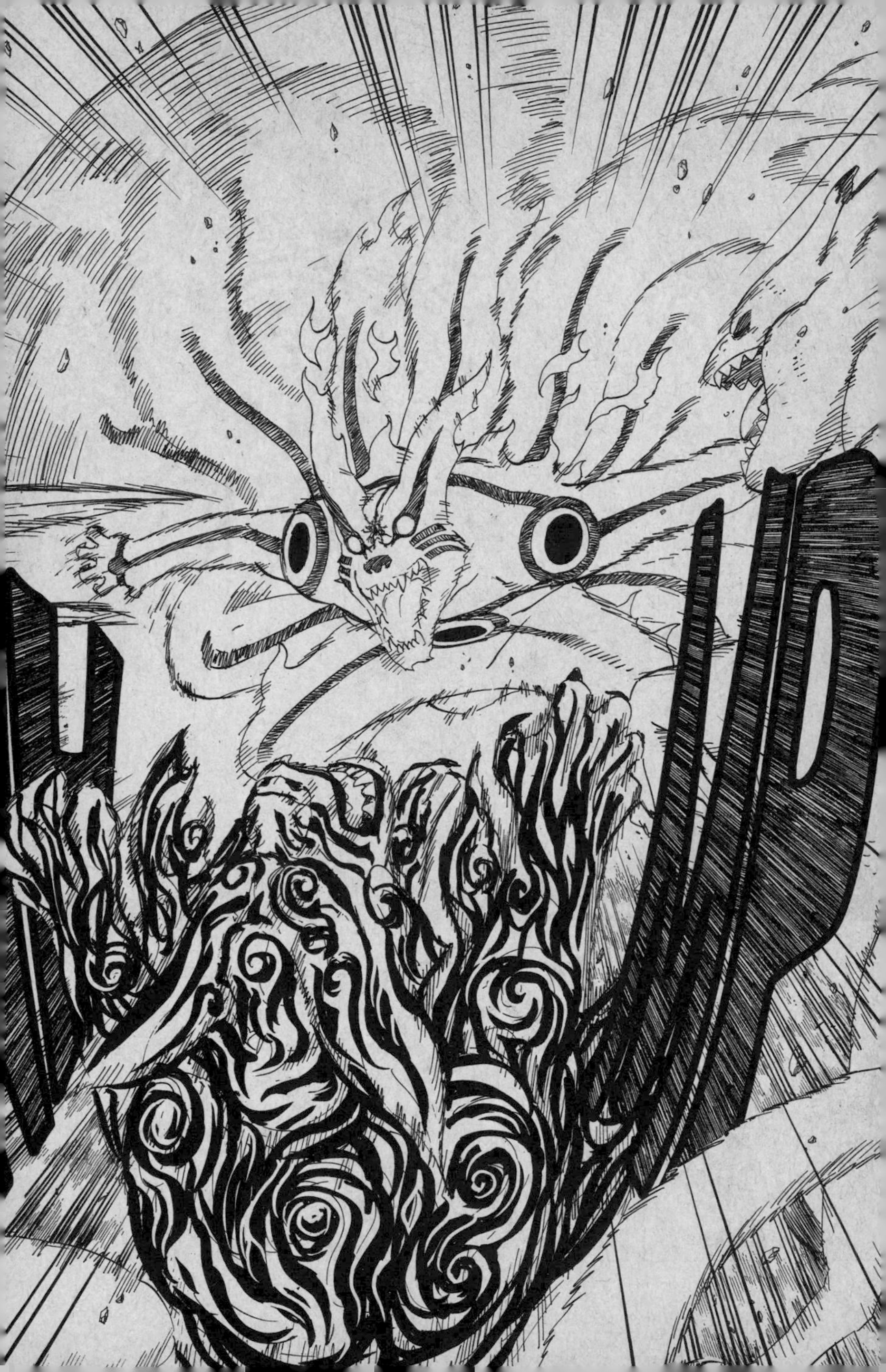

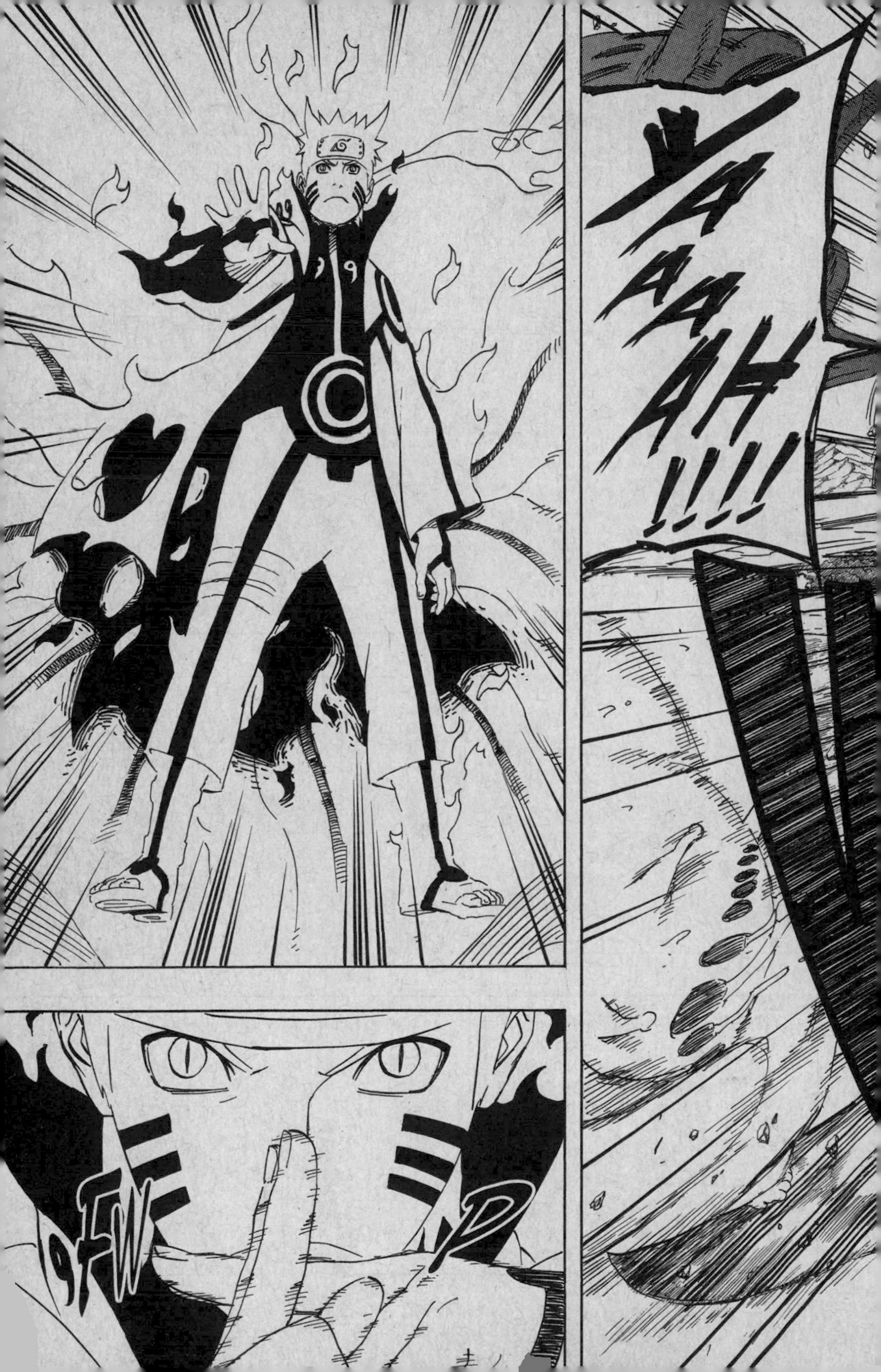
YAAAAH!!!!
FWD

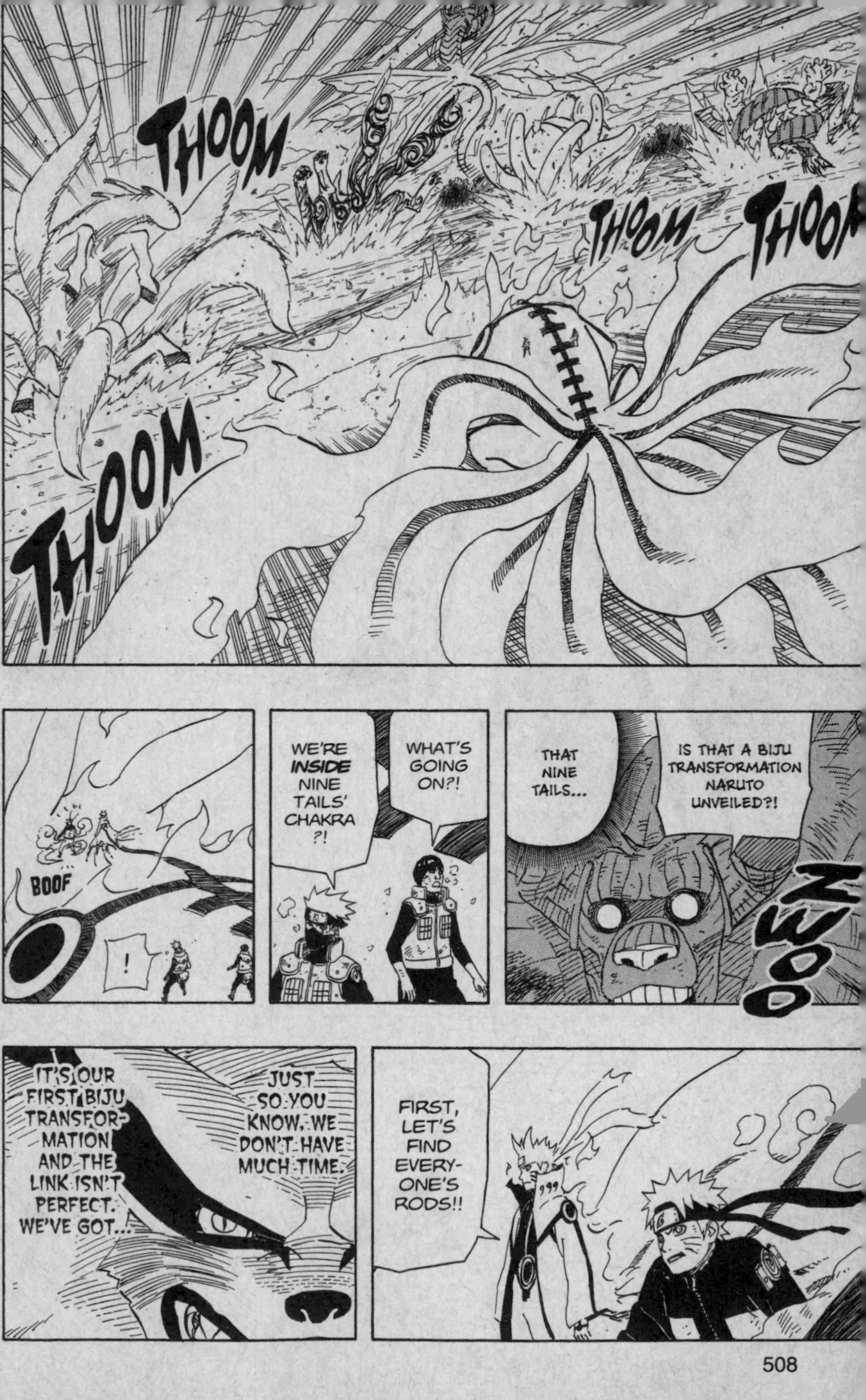
THOOM
THOOM
THOOM
THOOM
IS THAT A BIJU TRANSFORMATION NARUTO UNVEILED?!
THAT NINE TAILS...
ZWOO
WHAT'S GOING ON?!
WE'RE **INSIDE** NINE TAILS' CHAKRA ?!
BOOF
!
FIRST, LET'S FIND EVERY-ONE'S RODS!!
JUST SO YOU KNOW, WE DON'T HAVE MUCH TIME.
IT'S OUR FIRST BIJU TRANSFOR-MATION AND THE LINK ISN'T PERFECT. WE'VE GOT...

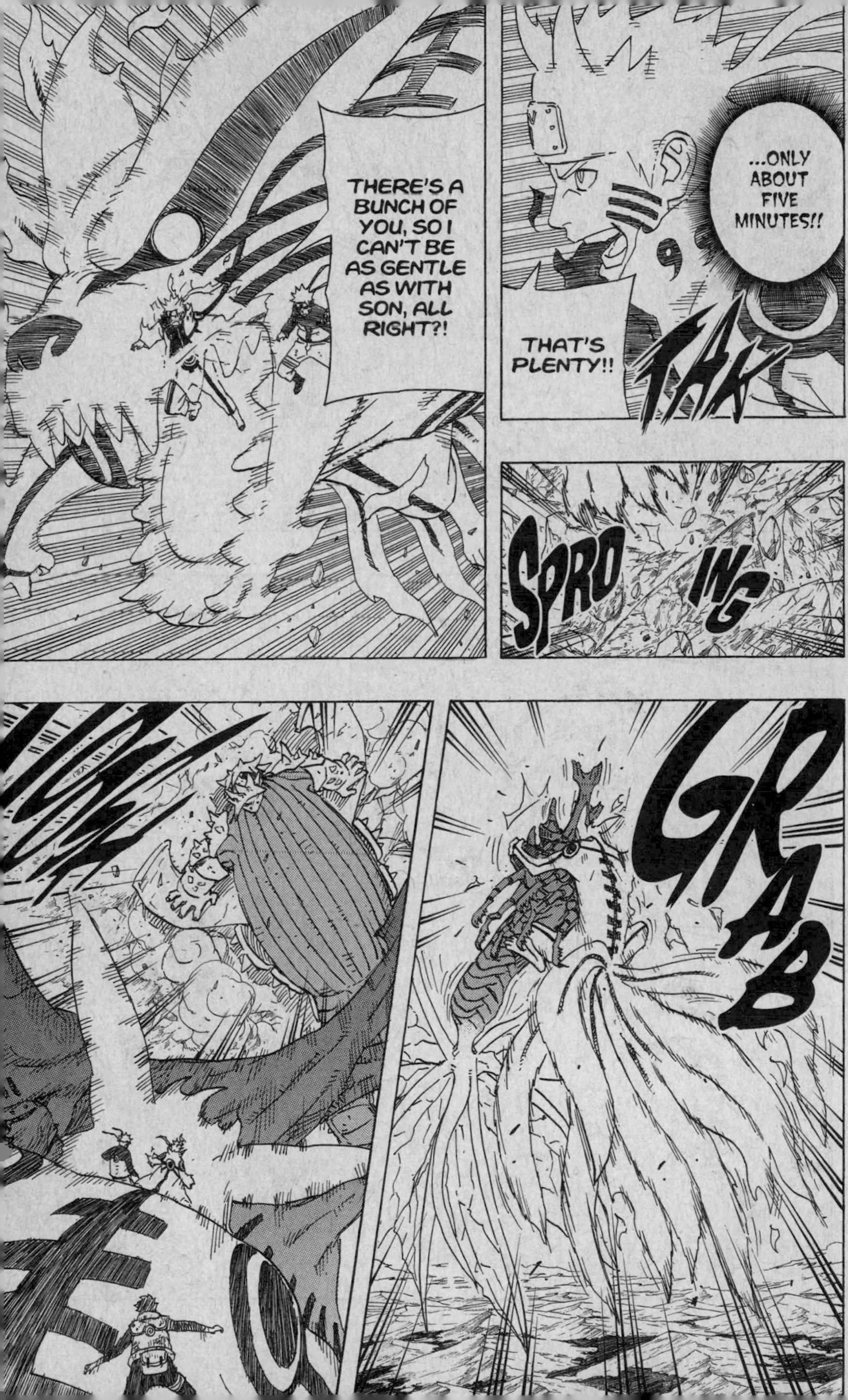
...ONLY ABOUT FIVE MINUTES!!
THAT'S PLENTY!!
TAK
SPROING
THERE'S A BUNCH OF YOU, SO I CAN'T BE AS GENTLE AS WITH SON, ALL RIGHT?!
GRAB

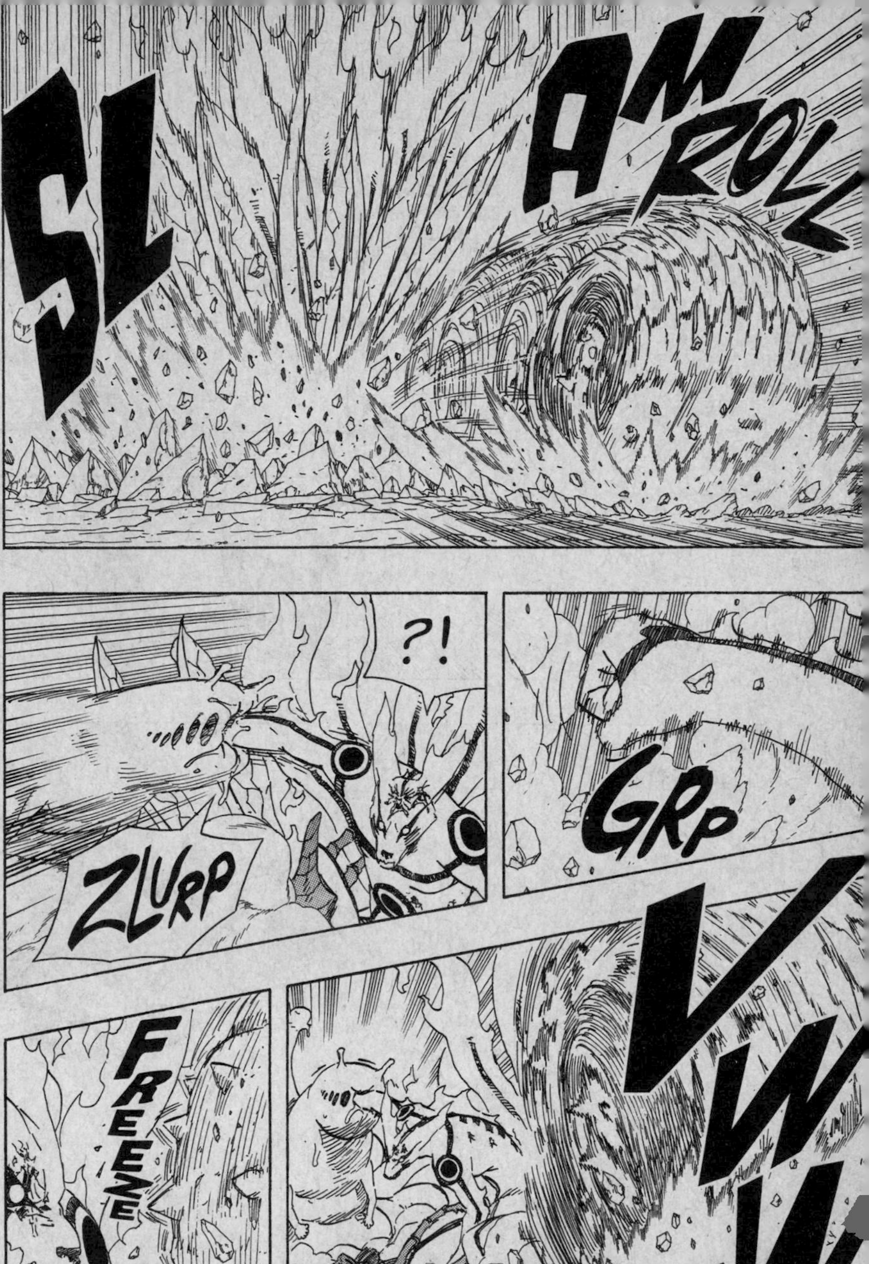
SLAM
ROLL
GRP
?!
ZLURP
VWW
FREEZE

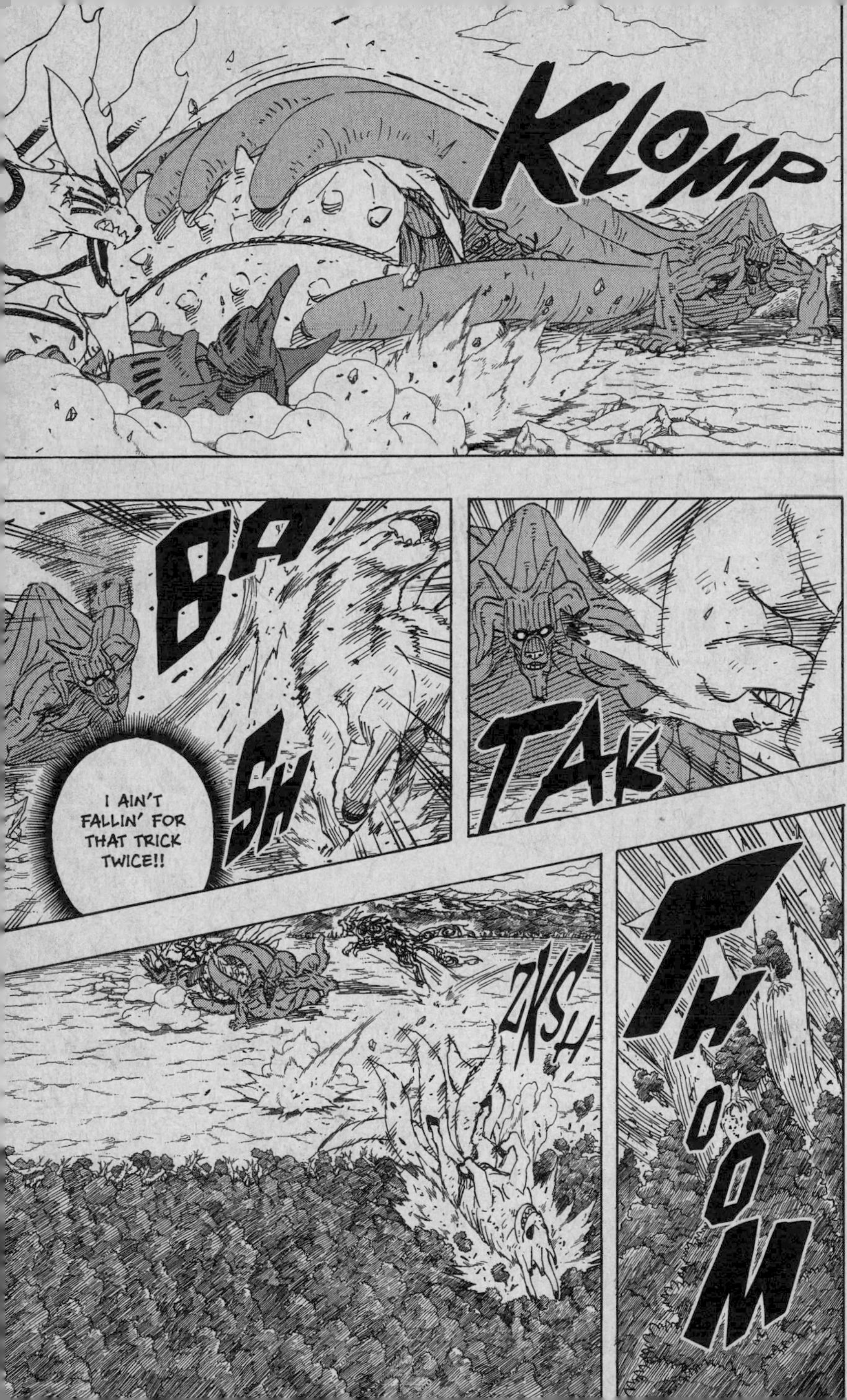
KLOMP
TAK
BASH
I AIN'T FALLIN' FOR THAT TRICK TWICE!!
THOOOM
ZKSH

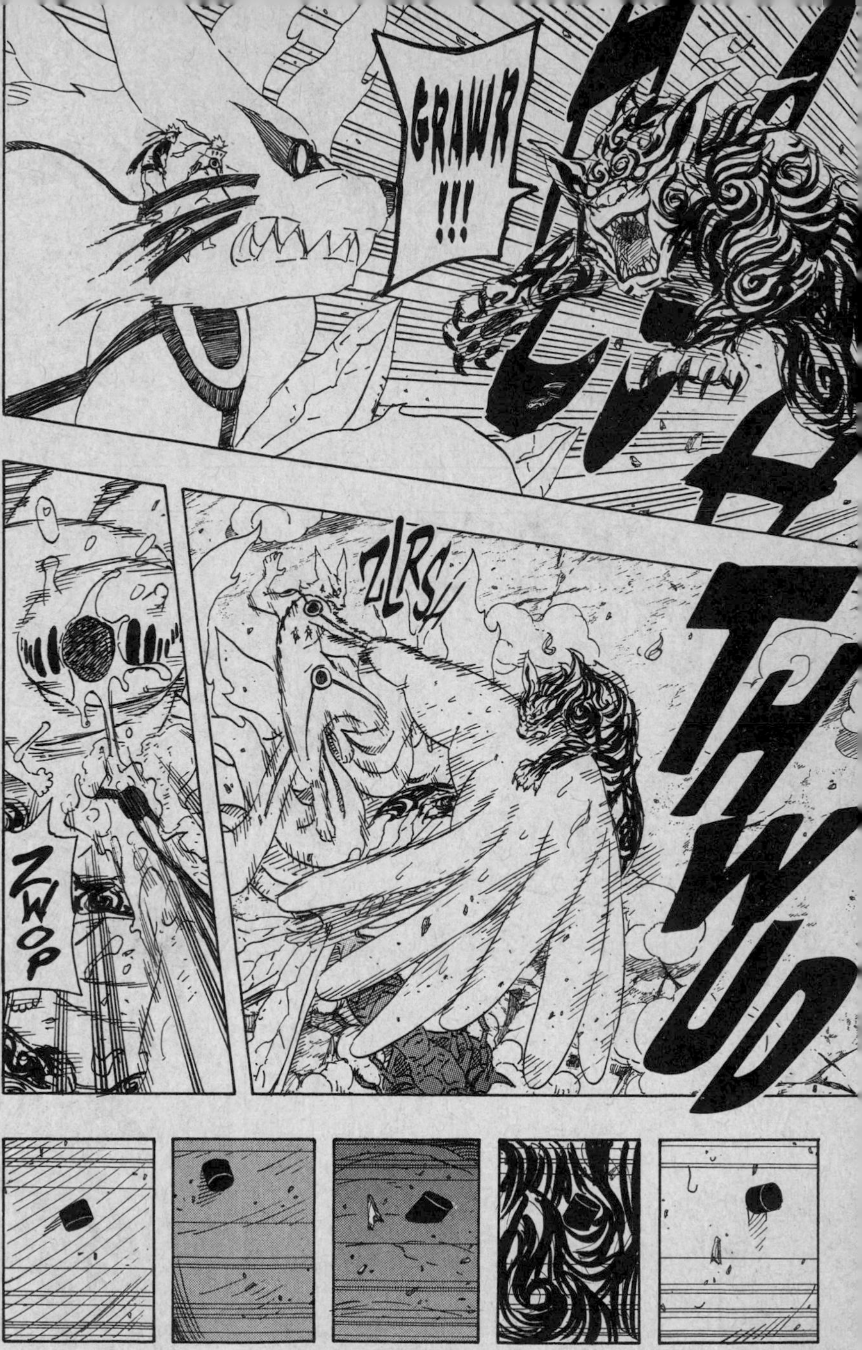
GRAWR !!!
THWUD
ZLRSH
ZWOP

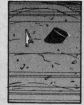

READ THIS WAY

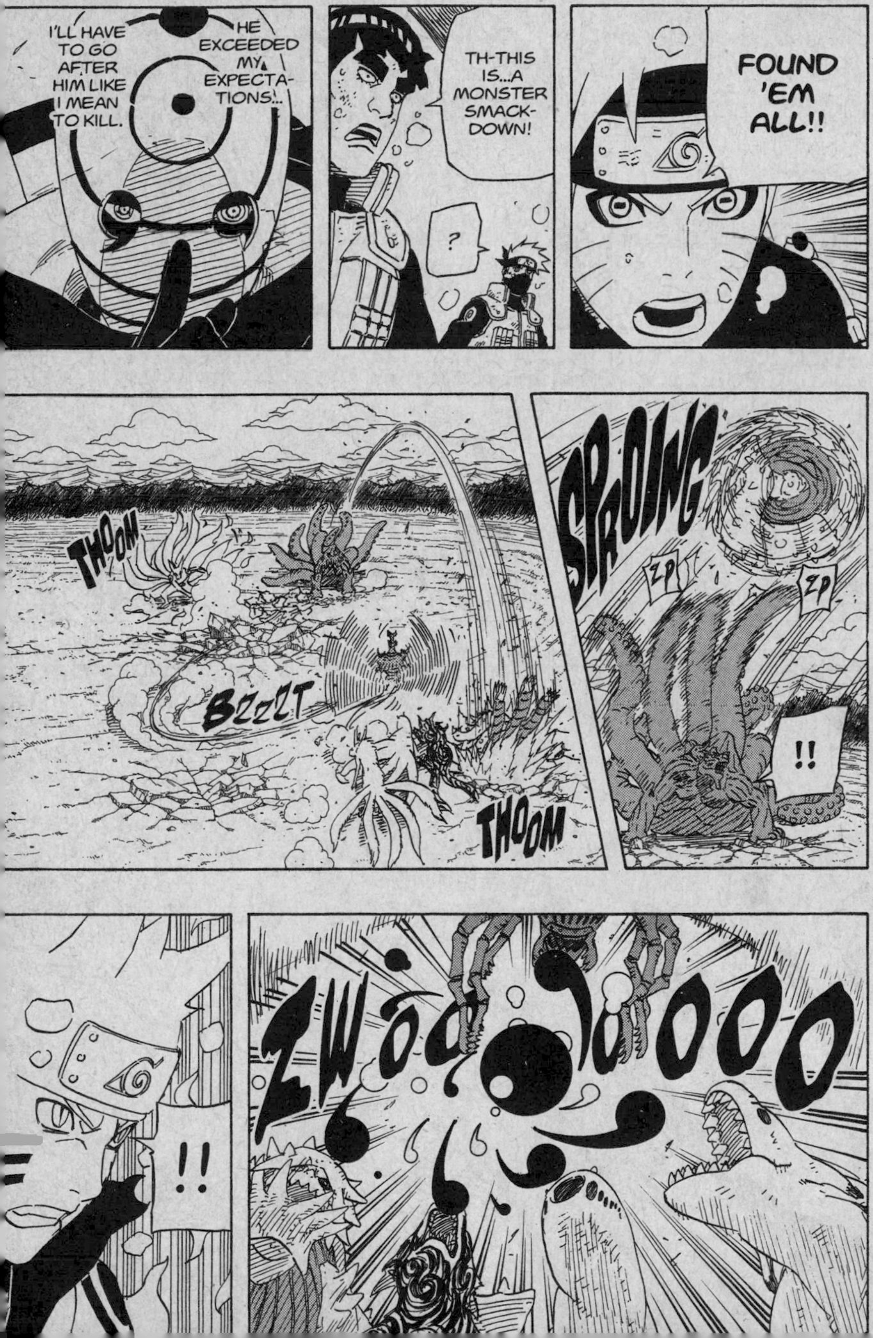
FOUND 'EM ALL!!
TH-THIS IS...A MONSTER SMACK-DOWN!
?
HE EXCEEDED MY EXPECTATIONS...
I'LL HAVE TO GO AFTER HIM LIKE I MEAN TO KILL.
SPROING
ZP
ZP
!!
THOOM
BZZZT
THOOM
ZWOOOOOOO
!!

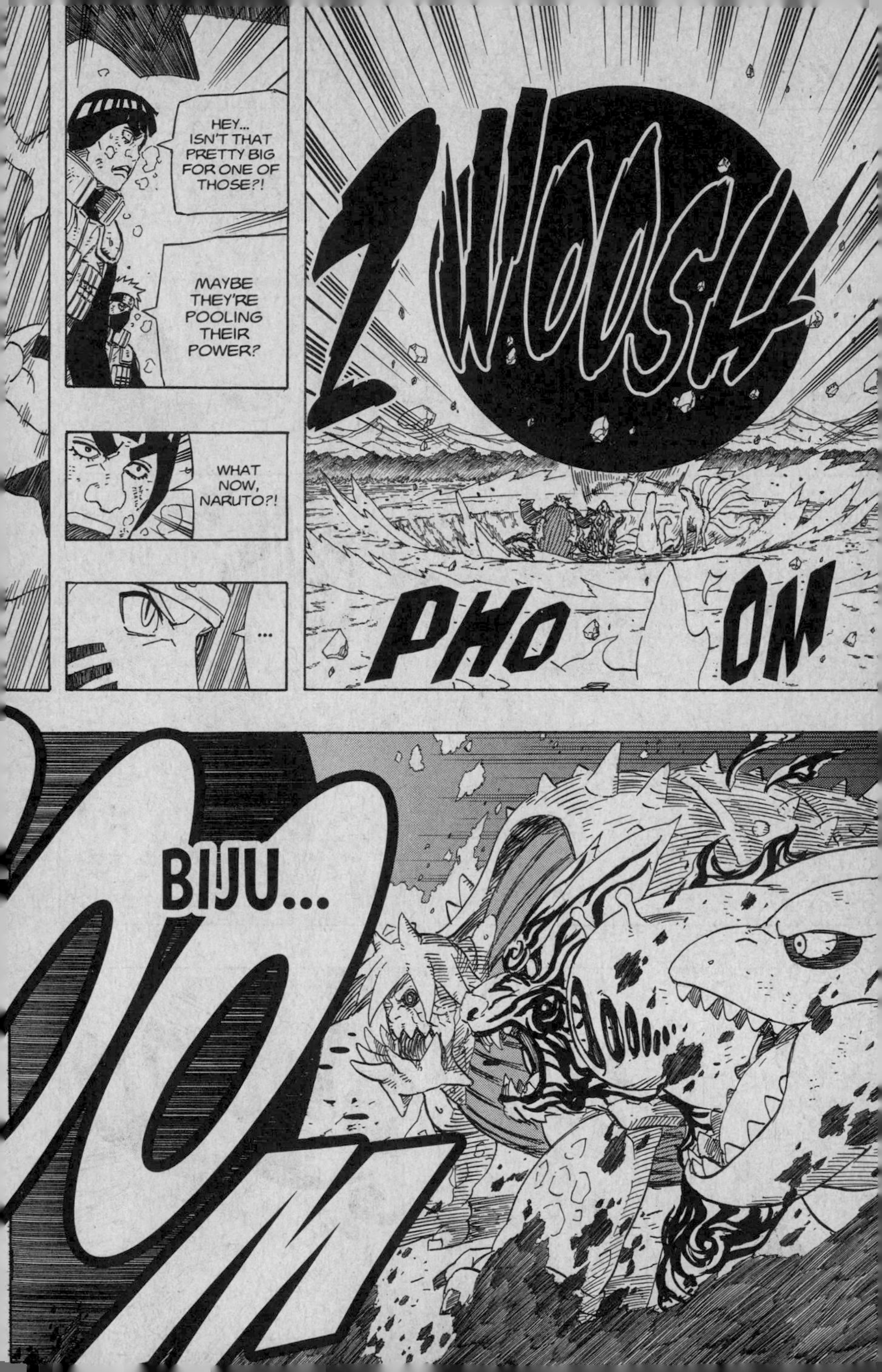
ZWOOSH
PHO OM
HEY... ISN'T THAT PRETTY BIG FOR ONE OF THOSE?!
MAYBE THEY'RE POOLING THEIR POWER?
WHAT NOW, NARUTO?!
...
BIJU...

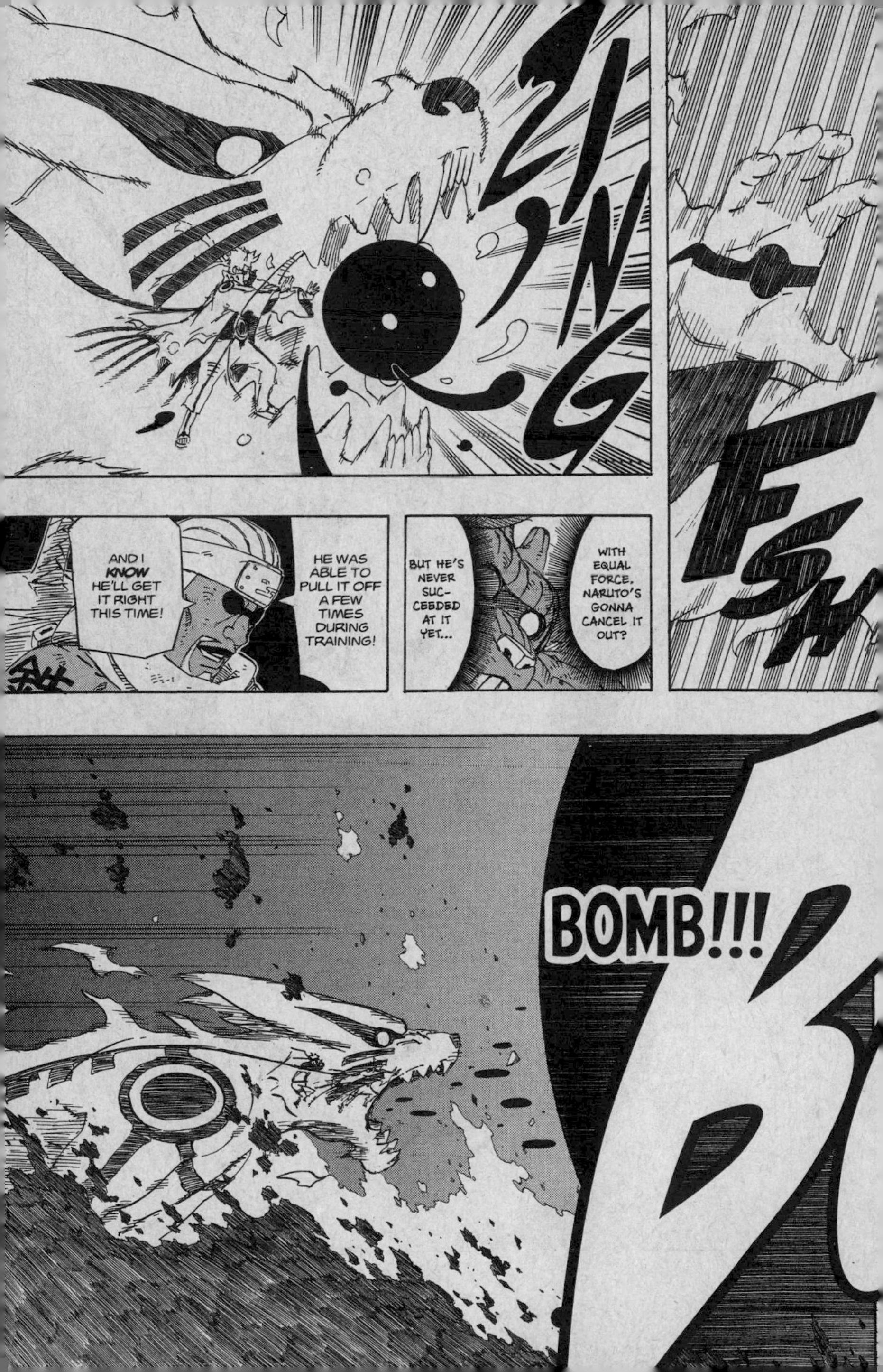
FSH
ZING
WITH EQUAL FORCE, NARUTO'S GONNA CANCEL IT OUT?
BUT HE'S NEVER SUC-CEEDED AT IT YET...
HE WAS ABLE TO PULL IT OFF A FEW TIMES DURING TRAINING!
AND I **KNOW** HE'LL GET IT RIGHT THIS TIME!
BOMB!!!

Illustration to Commemorate Reaching Volume 60 [7]

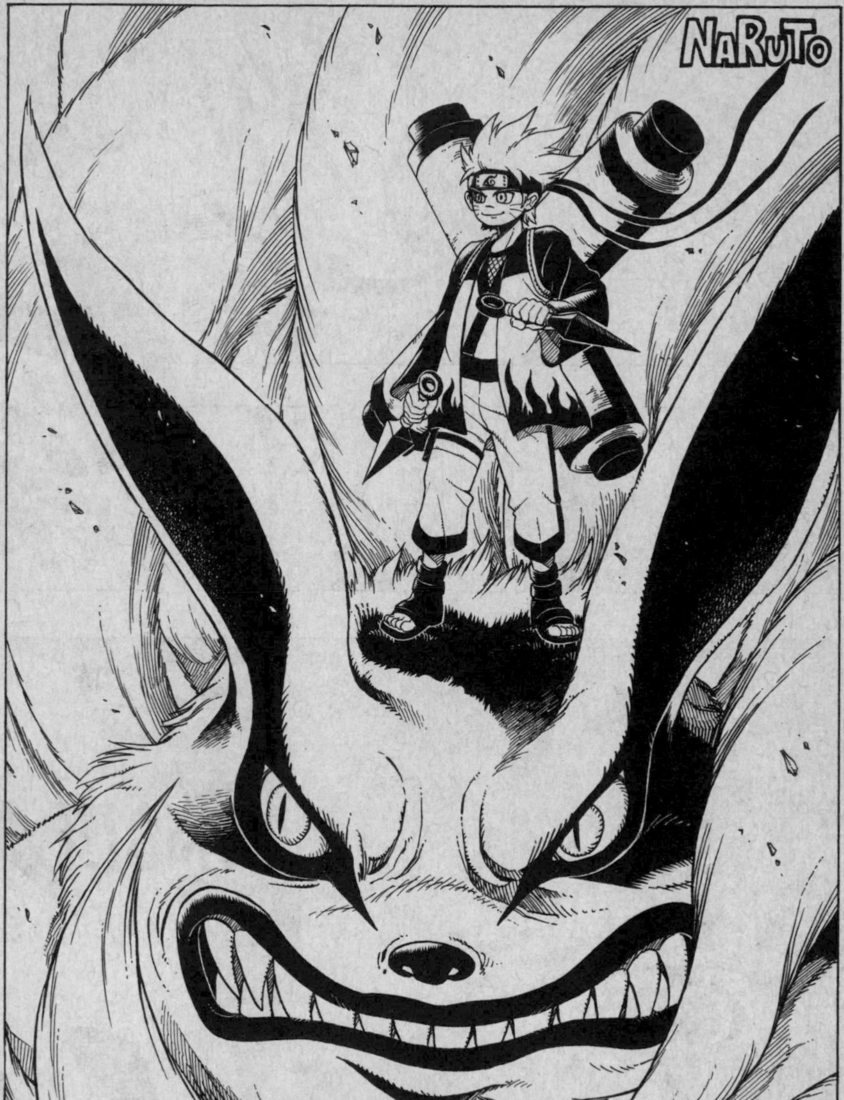
NARUTO

Takahiro Hiraishi

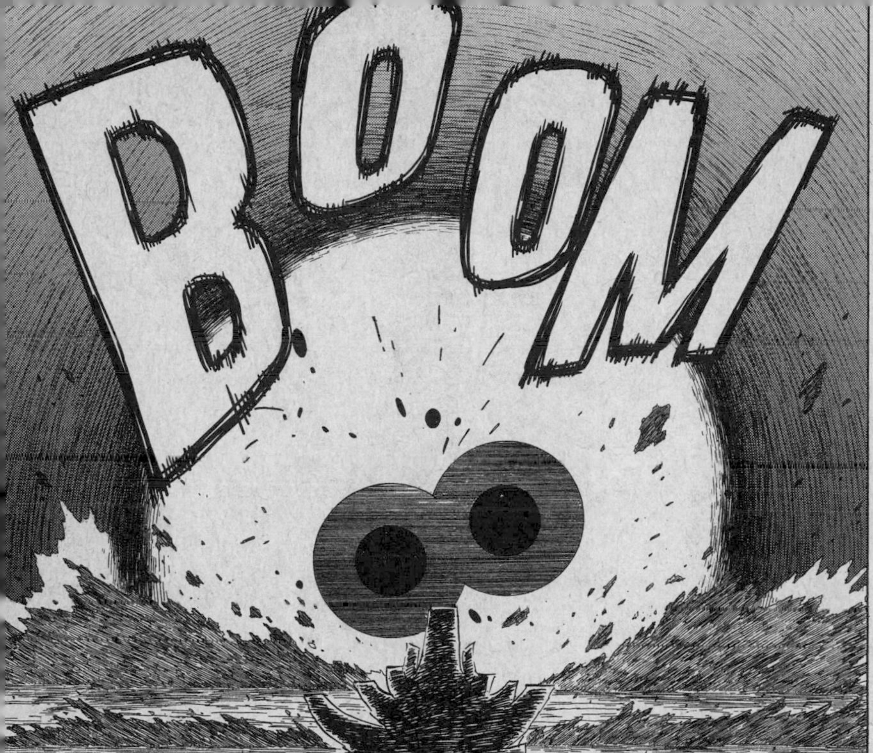
BOOM

Number 572: Nine Names

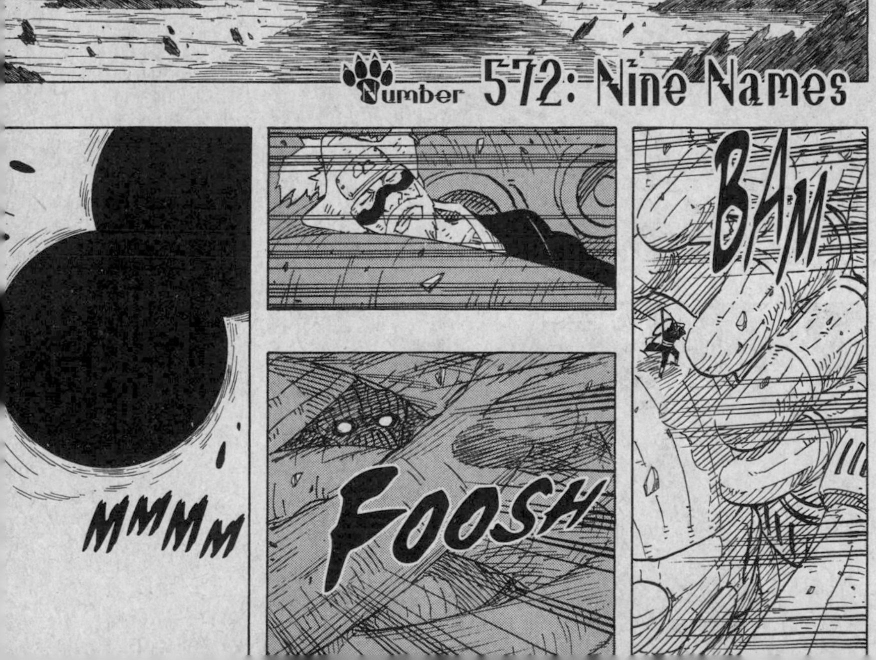
BAM
FOOSH
MMMM

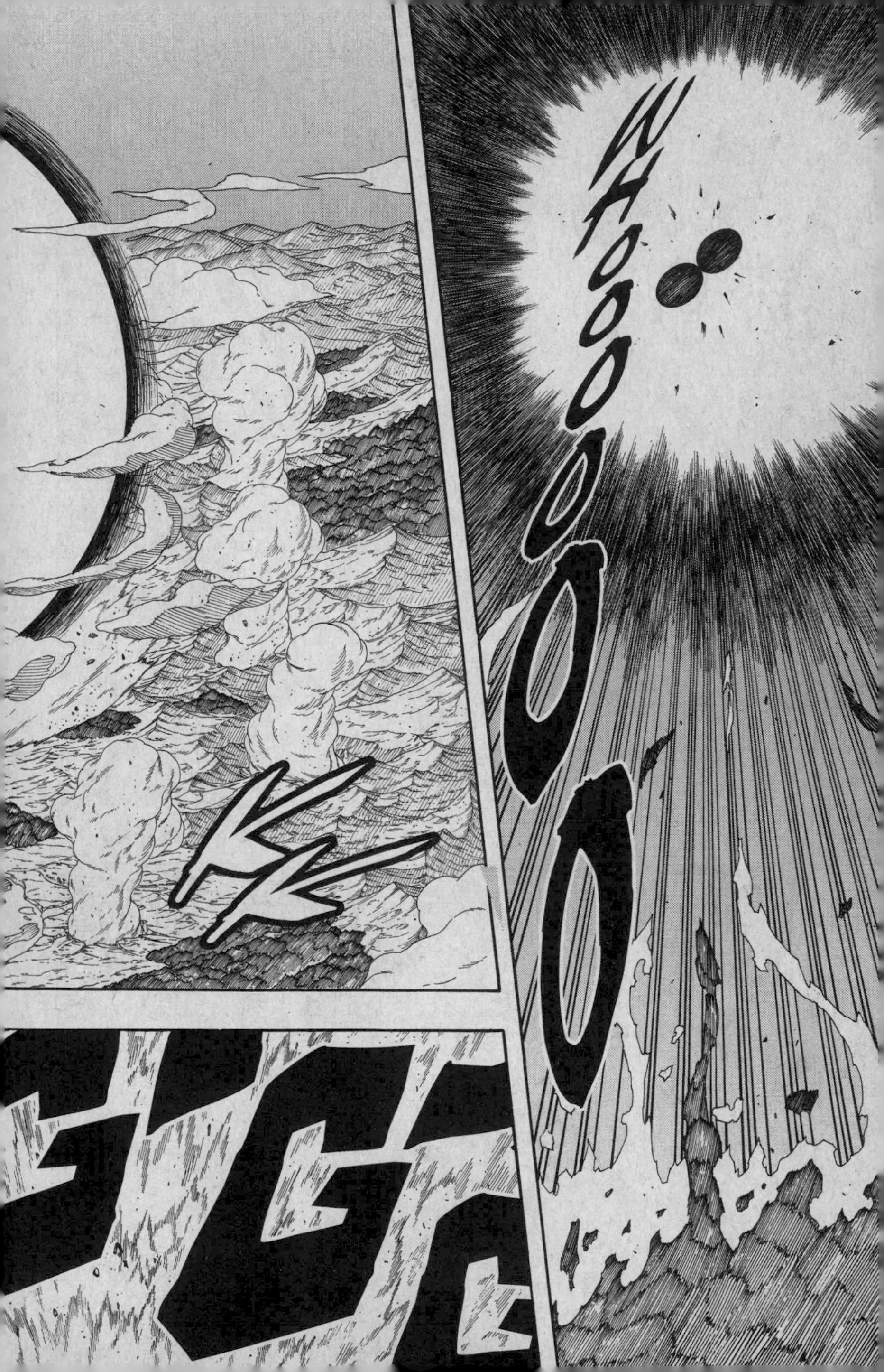
WHOOOOOO

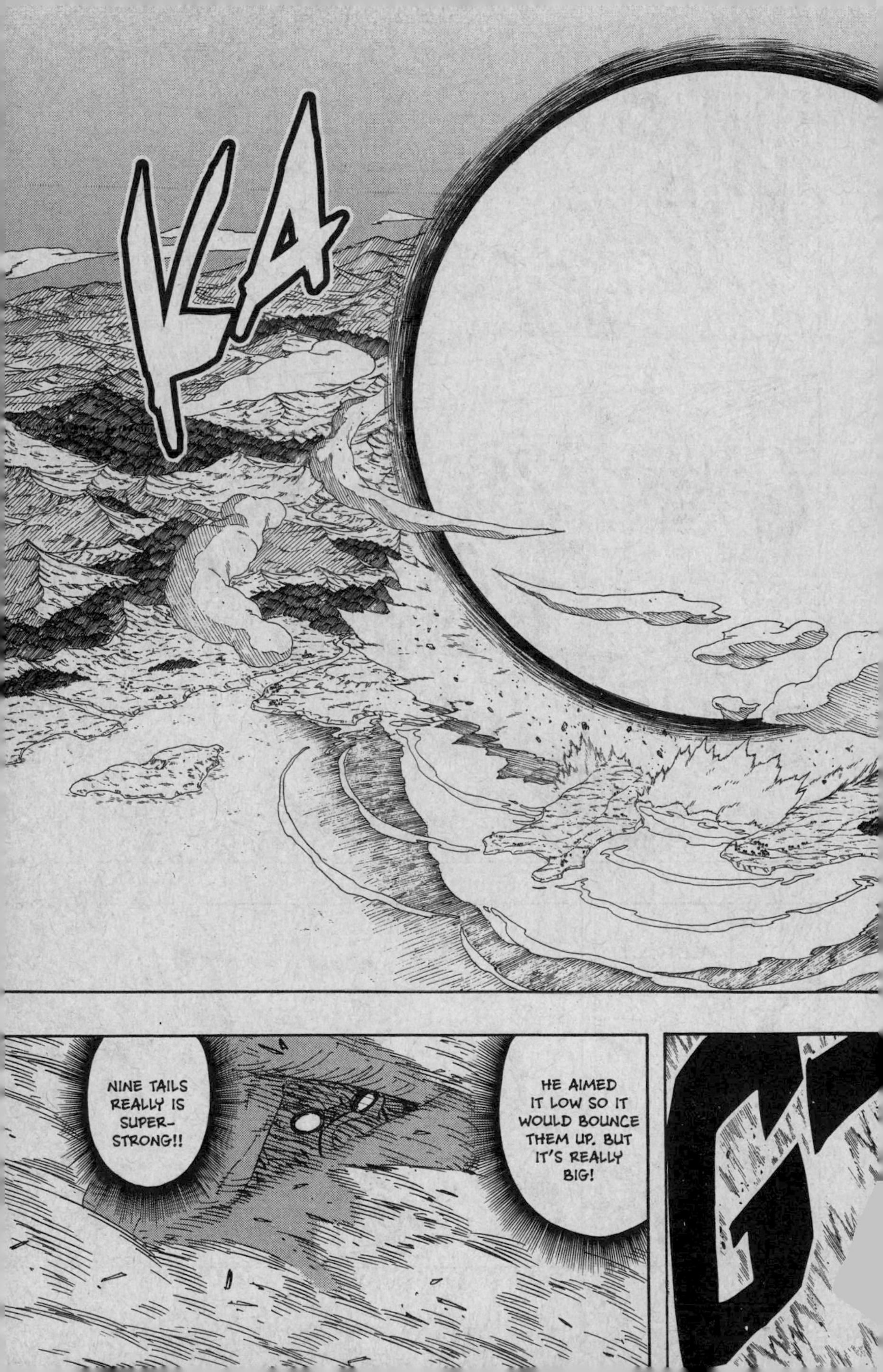
VA
HE AIMED IT LOW SO IT WOULD BOUNCE THEM UP. BUT IT'S REALLY BIG!
NINE TAILS REALLY IS SUPER-STRONG!!

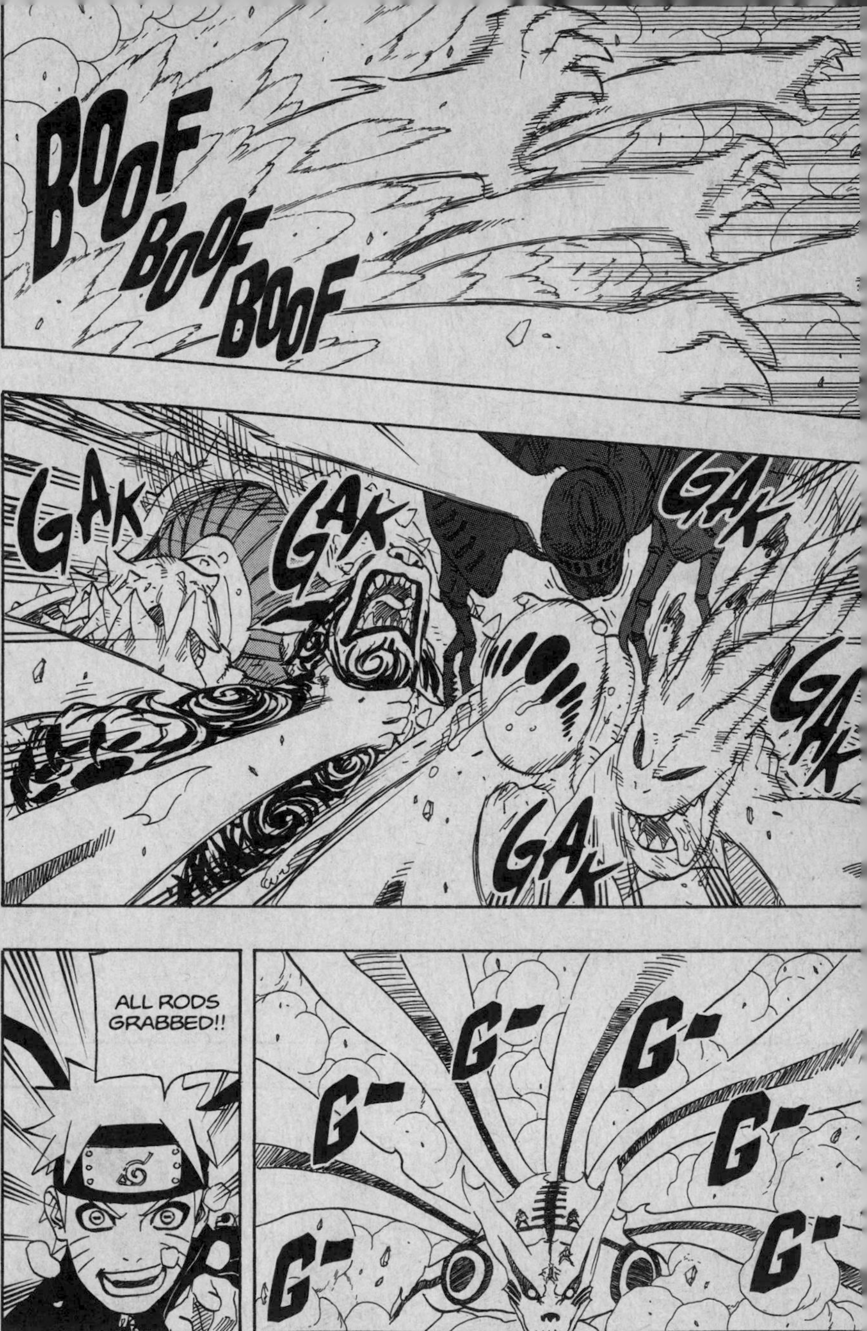
BOOF BOOF BOOF
GAK
GAK
GAK
GAK
GAK
G- G- G- G- G- G- G-
ALL RODS GRABBED!!

READ THIS WAY

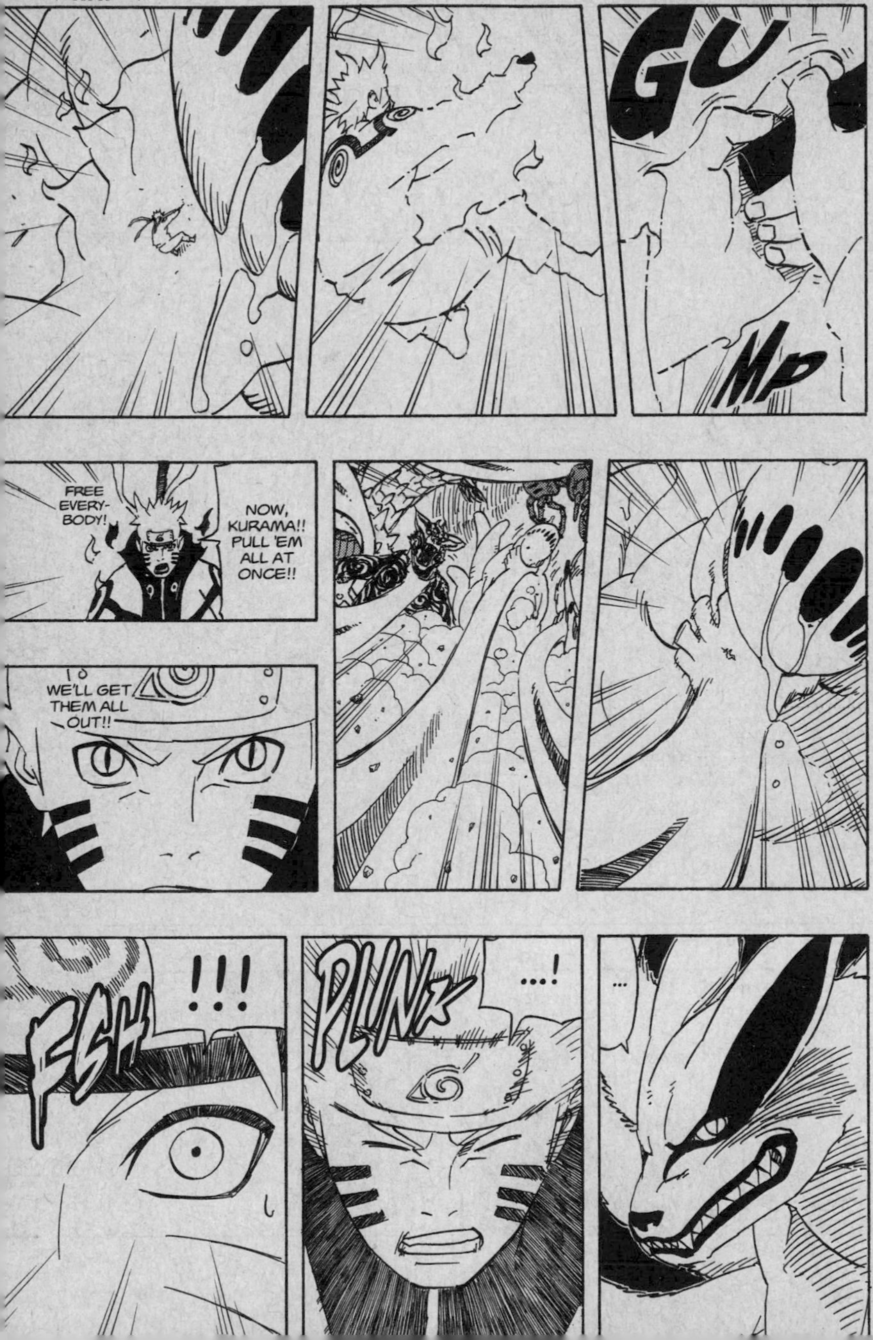
GU
MP
NOW, KURAMA!! PULL 'EM ALL AT ONCE!!
FREE EVERY-BODY!
WE'LL GET THEM ALL OUT!!
...
...!
PLINK
!!!
FSH

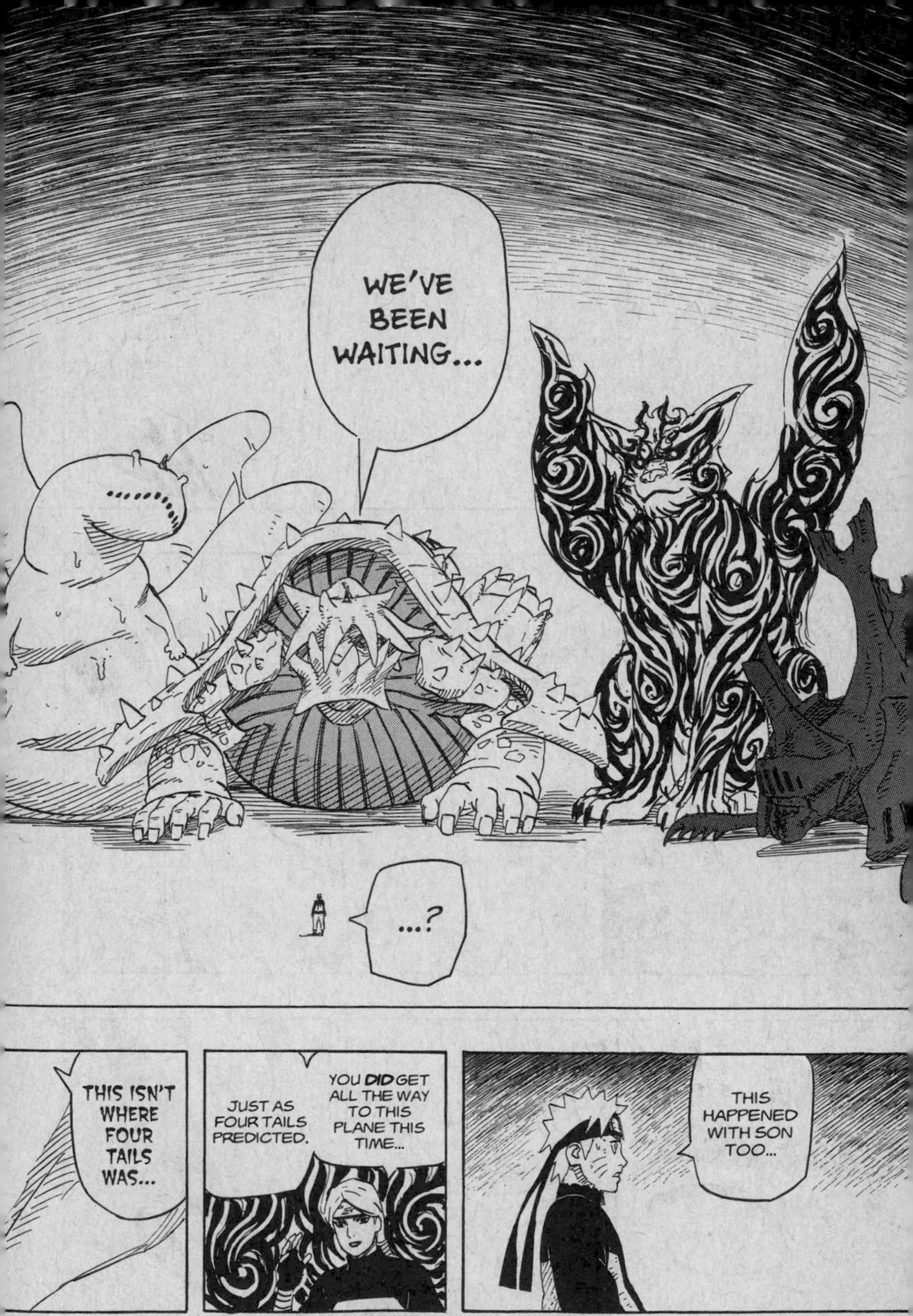
WE'VE BEEN WAITING...
...?
THIS HAPPENED WITH SON TOO...
YOU **DID** GET ALL THE WAY TO THIS PLANE THIS TIME...
JUST AS FOUR TAILS PREDICTED.
THIS ISN'T WHERE FOUR TAILS WAS...

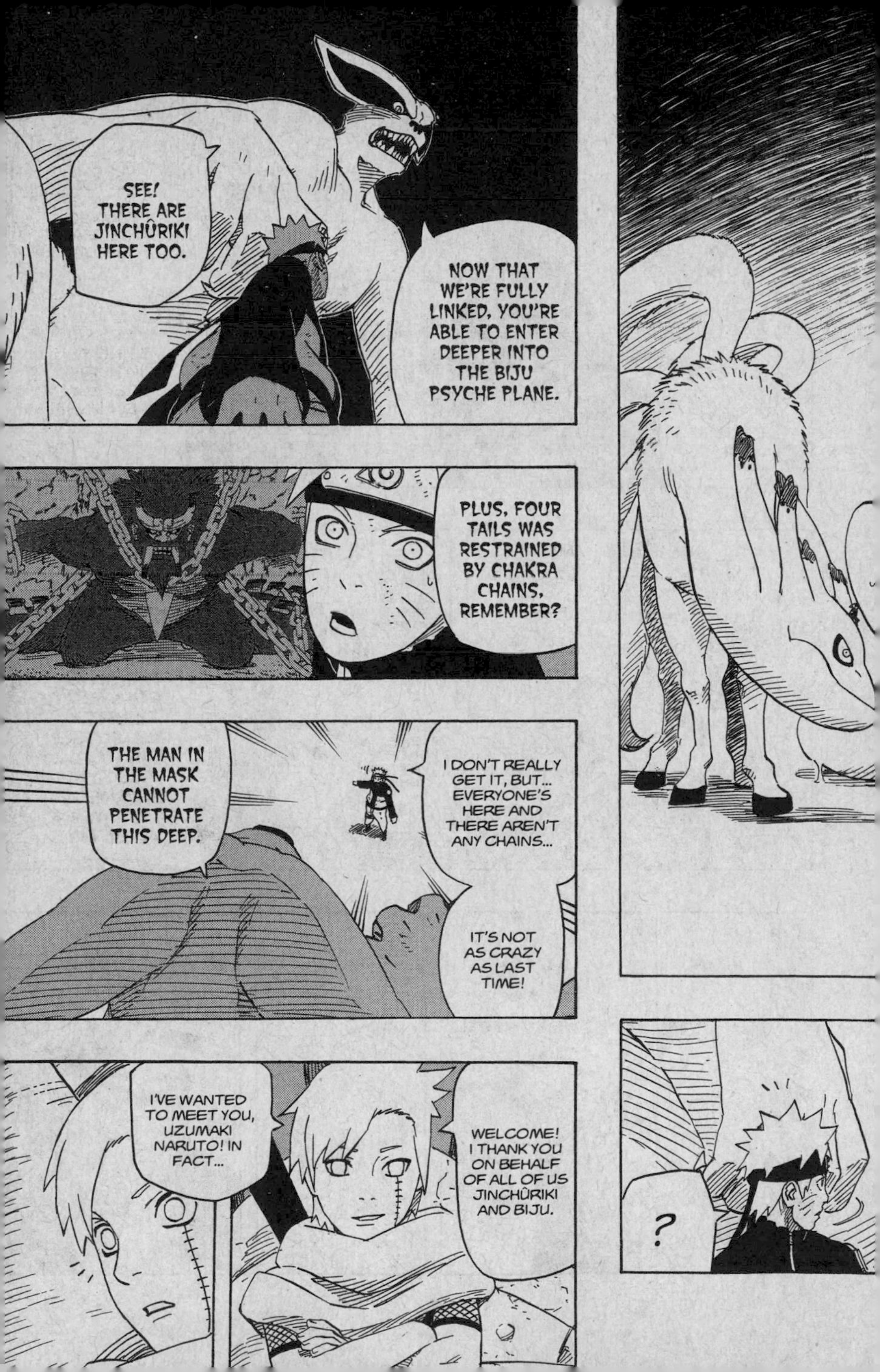
SEE! THERE ARE JINCHÛRIKI HERE TOO.
NOW THAT WE'RE FULLY LINKED, YOU'RE ABLE TO ENTER DEEPER INTO THE BIJU PSYCHE PLANE.
PLUS, FOUR TAILS WAS RESTRAINED BY CHAKRA CHAINS, REMEMBER?
I DON'T REALLY GET IT, BUT... EVERYONE'S HERE AND THERE AREN'T ANY CHAINS...
IT'S NOT AS CRAZY AS LAST TIME!
THE MAN IN THE MASK CANNOT PENETRATE THIS DEEP.
?
WELCOME! I THANK YOU ON BEHALF OF ALL OF US JINCHÛRIKI AND BIJU.
I'VE WANTED TO MEET YOU, UZUMAKI NARUTO! IN FACT...

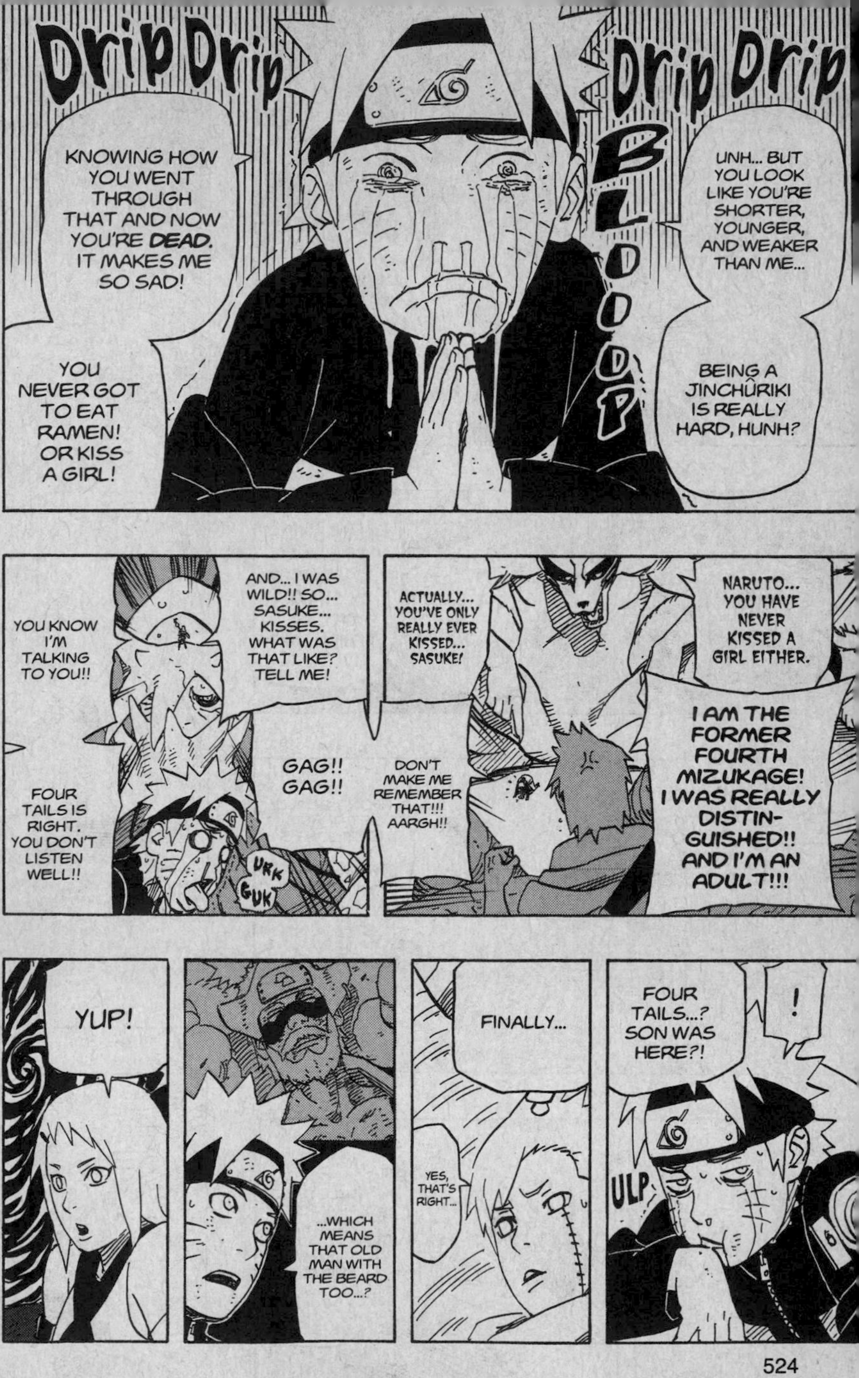
Drip Drip
UNH... BUT YOU LOOK LIKE YOU'RE SHORTER, YOUNGER, AND WEAKER THAN ME...
BEING A JINCHÛRIKI IS REALLY HARD, HUNH?
BLOOOOP
Drip Drip
KNOWING HOW YOU WENT THROUGH THAT AND NOW YOU'RE **DEAD.** IT MAKES ME SO SAD!
YOU NEVER GOT TO EAT RAMEN! OR KISS A GIRL!
NARUTO... YOU HAVE NEVER KISSED A GIRL EITHER.
I AM THE FORMER FOURTH MIZUKAGE! I WAS REALLY DISTIN-GUISHED!! AND I'M AN ADULT!!!
ACTUALLY... YOU'VE ONLY REALLY EVER KISSED... SASUKE!
DON'T MAKE ME REMEMBER THAT!!! AARGH!!
AND... I WAS WILD!! SO... SASUKE... KISSES. WHAT WAS THAT LIKE? TELL ME!
YOU KNOW I'M TALKING TO YOU!!
GAG!! GAG!!
FOUR TAILS IS RIGHT. YOU DON'T LISTEN WELL!!
URK
GUK
!
FOUR TAILS...? SON WAS HERE?!
ULP
FINALLY...
YES, THAT'S RIGHT...
...WHICH MEANS THAT OLD MAN WITH THE BEARD TOO...?
YUP!

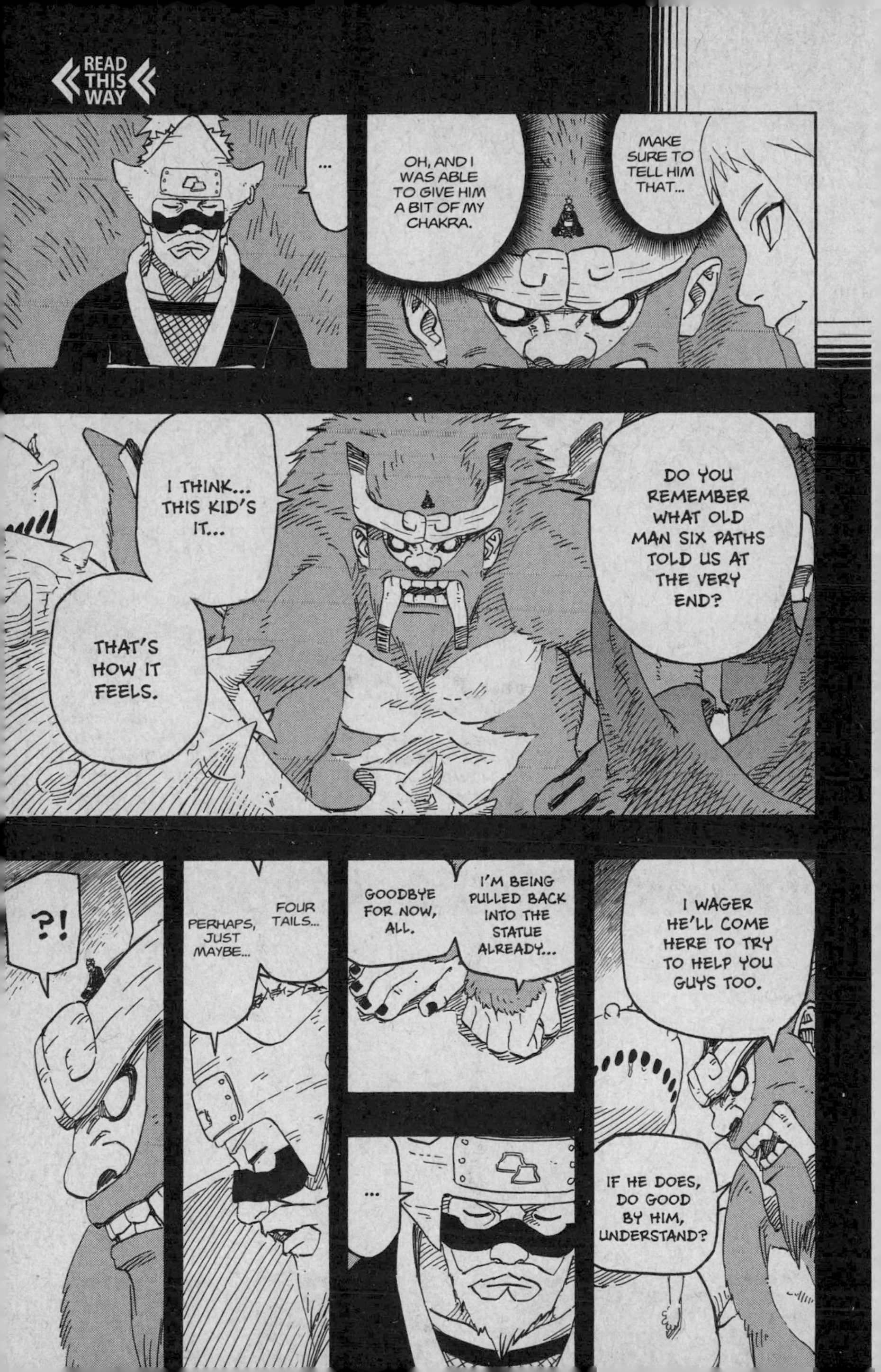
READ THIS WAY
MAKE SURE TO TELL HIM THAT...
OH, AND I WAS ABLE TO GIVE HIM A BIT OF MY CHAKRA.
...
DO YOU REMEMBER WHAT OLD MAN SIX PATHS TOLD US AT THE VERY END?
I THINK... THIS KID'S IT...
THAT'S HOW IT FEELS.
I WAGER HE'LL COME HERE TO TRY TO HELP YOU GUYS TOO.
IF HE DOES, DO GOOD BY HIM, UNDERSTAND?
I'M BEING PULLED BACK INTO THE STATUE ALREADY...
GOODBYE FOR NOW, ALL.
...
FOUR TAILS...
PERHAPS, JUST MAYBE...
?!

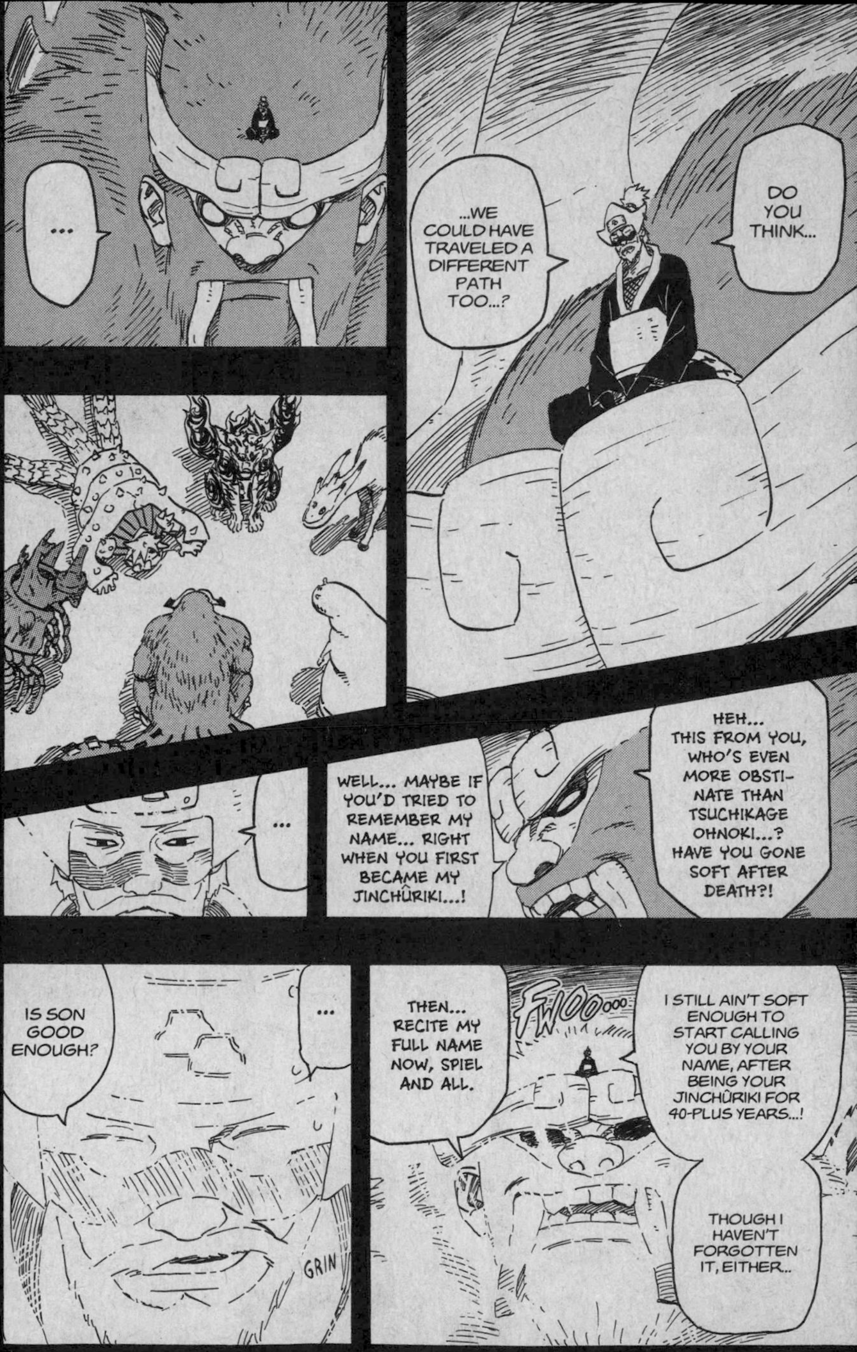
DO YOU THINK...
...WE COULD HAVE TRAVELED A DIFFERENT PATH TOO...?
...
HEH... THIS FROM YOU, WHO'S EVEN MORE OBSTI-NATE THAN TSUCHIKAGE OHNOKI...? HAVE YOU GONE SOFT AFTER DEATH?!
WELL... MAYBE IF YOU'D TRIED TO REMEMBER MY NAME... RIGHT WHEN YOU FIRST BECAME MY JINCHÛRIKI...!
...
I STILL AIN'T SOFT ENOUGH TO START CALLING YOU BY YOUR NAME, AFTER BEING YOUR JINCHÛRIKI FOR 40-PLUS YEARS...!
THOUGH I HAVEN'T FORGOTTEN IT, EITHER..
FWOOooo
THEN... RECITE MY FULL NAME NOW, SPIEL AND ALL.
...
IS SON GOOD ENOUGH?
GRIN

READ THIS WAY

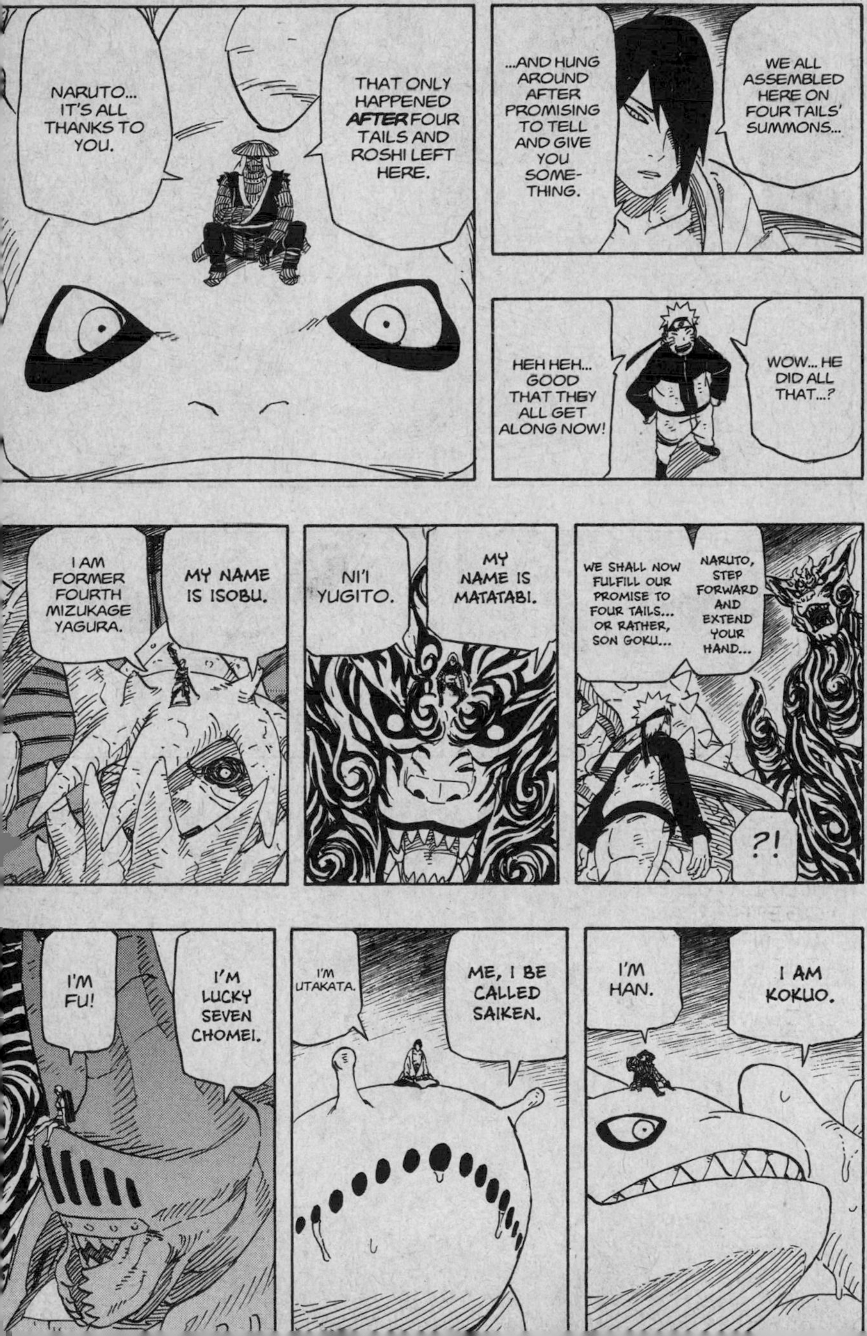
WE ALL ASSEMBLED HERE ON FOUR TAILS' SUMMONS...
...AND HUNG AROUND AFTER PROMISING TO TELL AND GIVE YOU SOME-THING.
WOW... HE DID ALL THAT...?
HEH HEH... GOOD THAT THEY ALL GET ALONG NOW!
THAT ONLY HAPPENED **AFTER** FOUR TAILS AND ROSHI LEFT HERE.
NARUTO... IT'S ALL THANKS TO YOU.
NARUTO, STEP FORWARD AND EXTEND YOUR HAND...
WE SHALL NOW FULFILL OUR PROMISE TO FOUR TAILS... OR RATHER, SON GOKU...
?!
MY NAME IS MATATABI.
NI'I YUGITO.
MY NAME IS ISOBU.
I AM FORMER FOURTH MIZUKAGE YAGURA.
I AM KOKUO.
I'M HAN.
ME, I BE CALLED SAIKEN.
I'M UTAKATA.
I'M LUCKY SEVEN CHOMEI.
I'M FU!

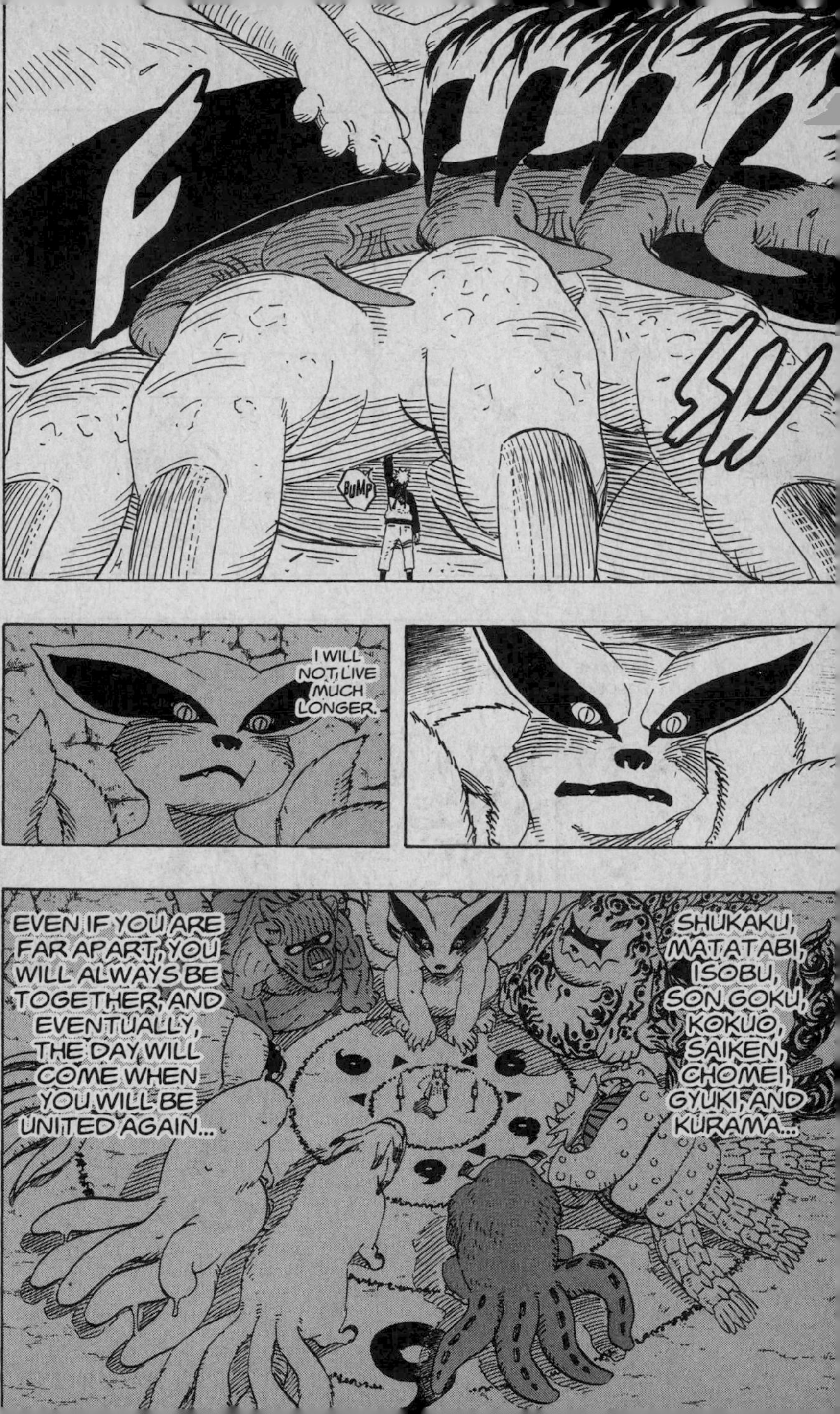
BUMP
I WILL NOT LIVE MUCH LONGER.
SHUKAKU, MATATABI, ISOBU, SON GOKU, KOKUO, SAIKEN, CHOMEI, GYUKI, AND KURAMA...
EVEN IF YOU ARE FAR APART, YOU WILL ALWAYS BE TOGETHER, AND EVENTUALLY, THE DAY WILL COME WHEN YOU WILL BE UNITED AGAIN...

READ THIS WAY

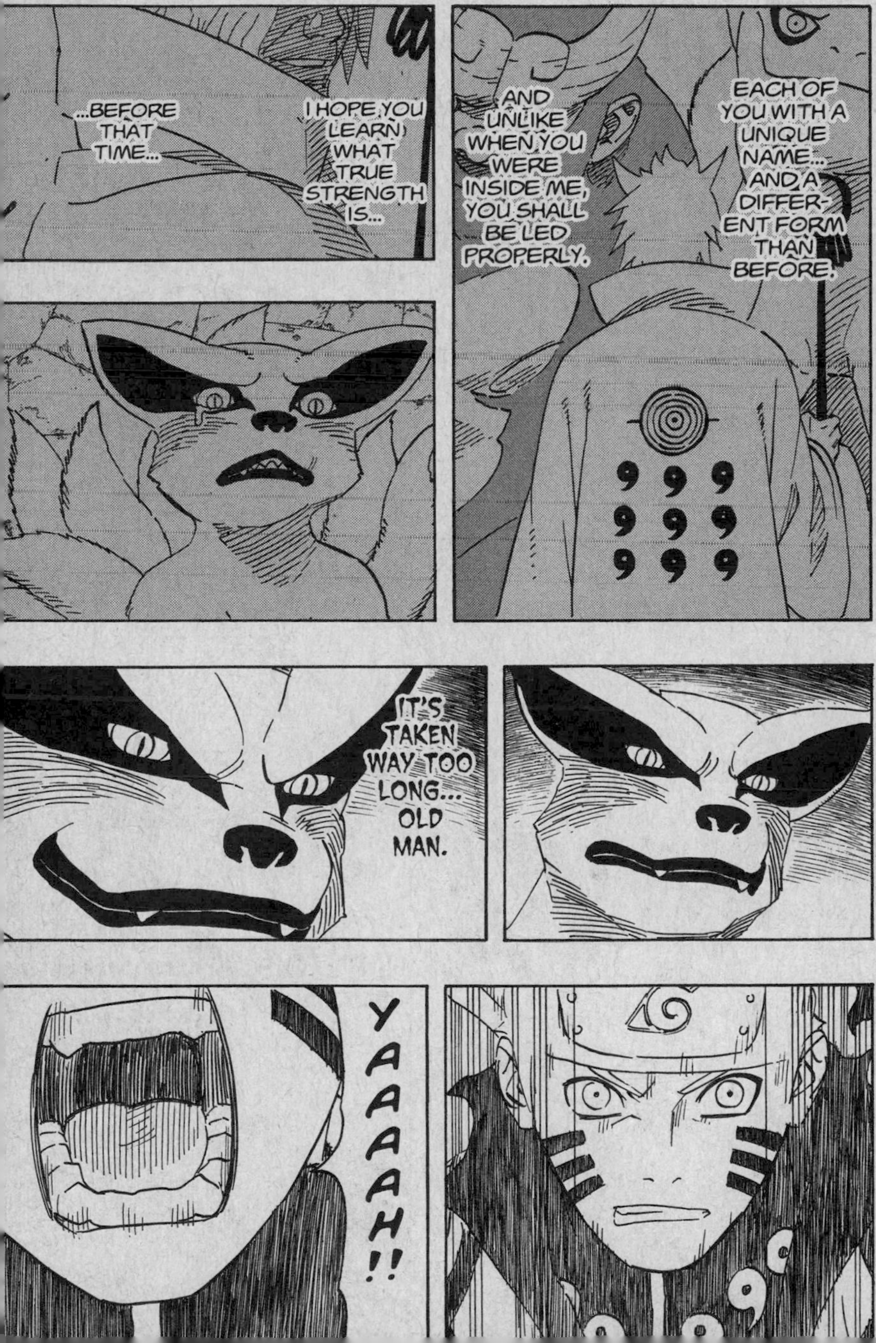

EACH OF YOU WITH A UNIQUE NAME... AND A DIFFER-ENT FORM THAN BEFORE.
AND UNLIKE WHEN YOU WERE INSIDE ME, YOU SHALL BE LED PROPERLY.
I HOPE YOU LEARN WHAT TRUE STRENGTH IS...
...BEFORE THAT TIME...
IT'S TAKEN WAY TOO LONG... OLD MAN.
YAAAAAH!!

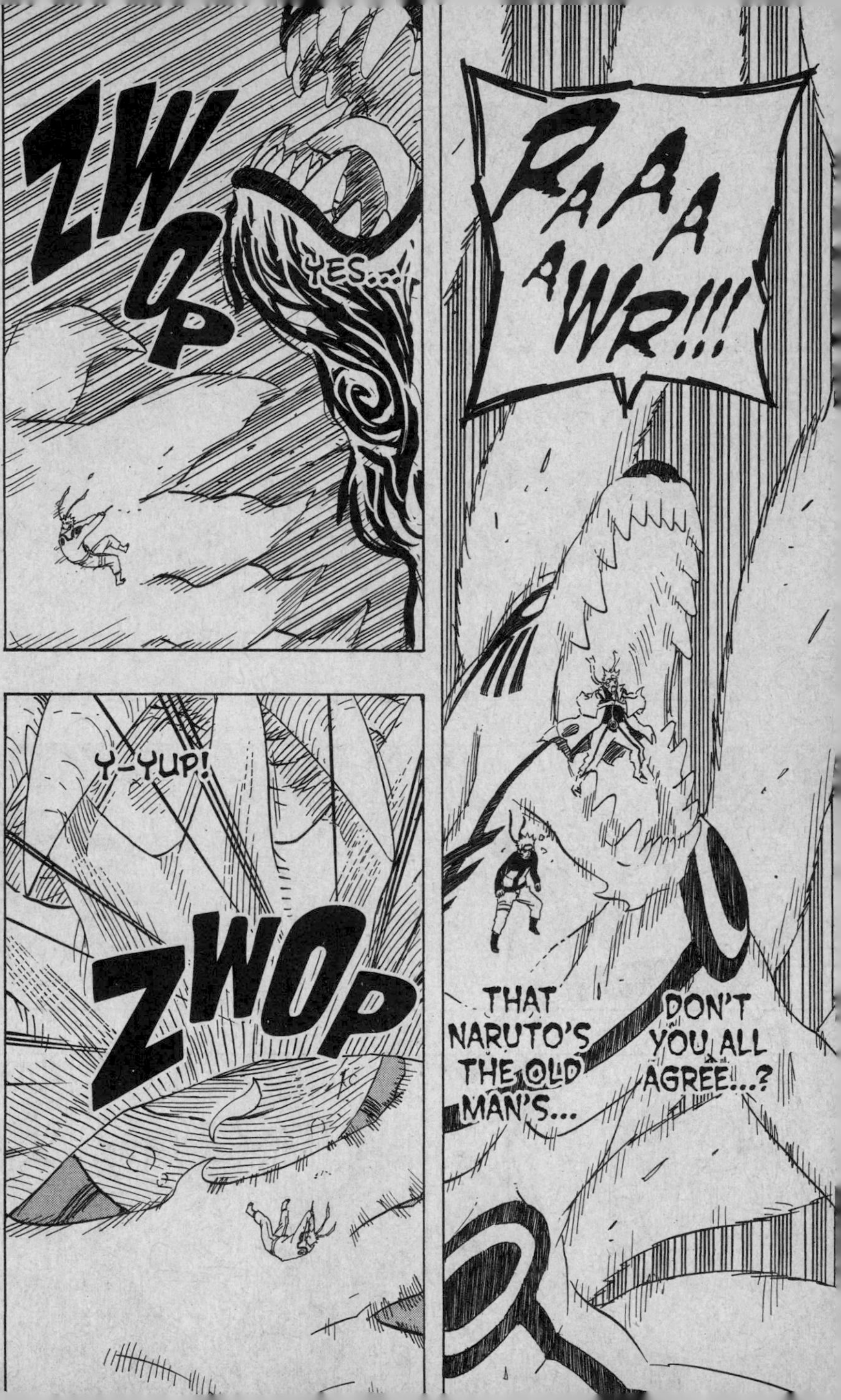
PAAAAAWR!!!
DON'T YOU ALL AGREE...?
THAT NARUTO'S THE OLD MAN'S...
YES...
ZWOP
Y-YUP!
ZWOP

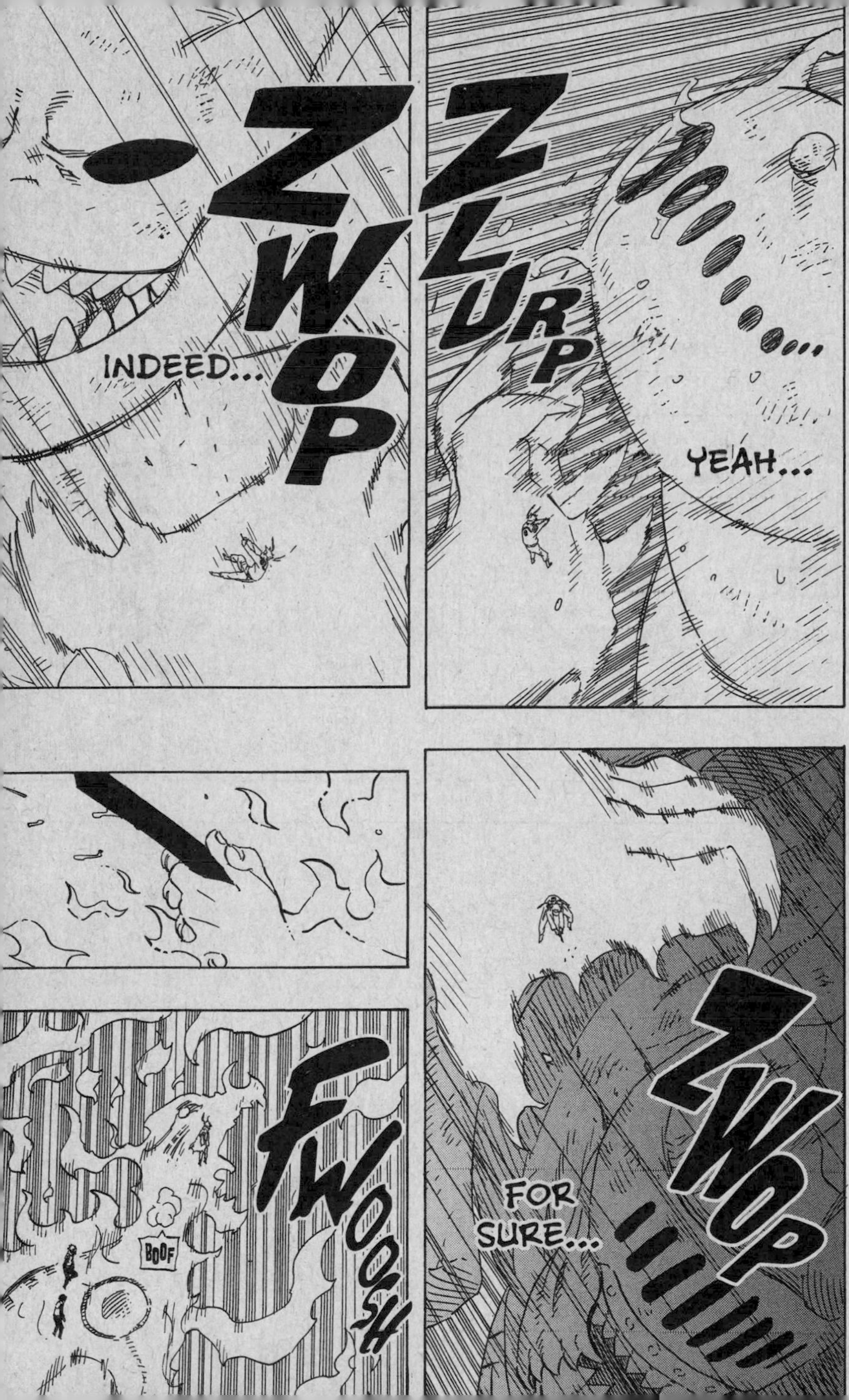
ZLURP
YEAH...
ZWOP
INDEED...
ZWOP
FOR SURE...
FWOOOSH
BOOF

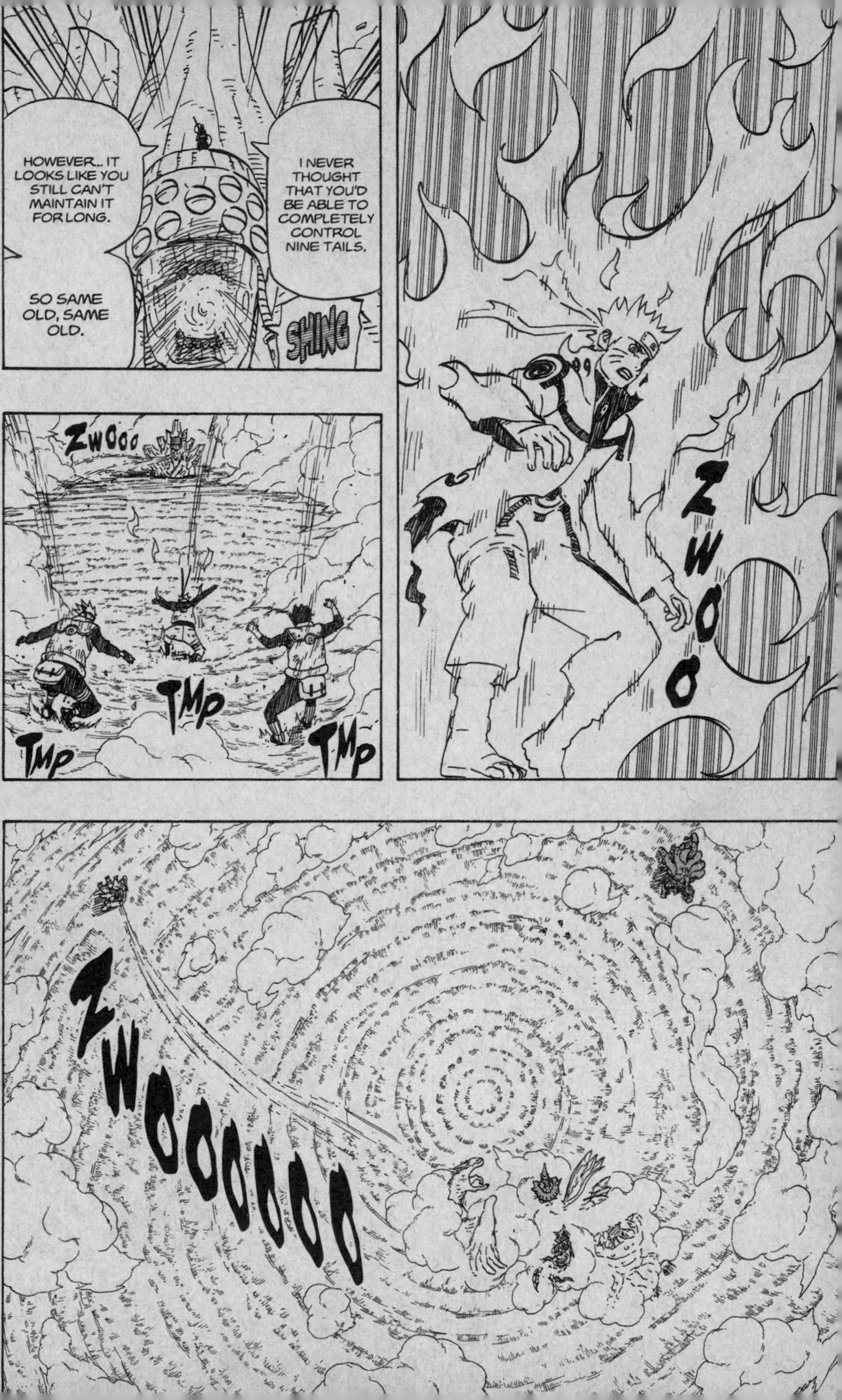
ZWOOO
I NEVER THOUGHT THAT YOU'D BE ABLE TO COMPLETELY CONTROL NINE TAILS.
HOWEVER... IT LOOKS LIKE YOU STILL CAN'T MAINTAIN IT FOR LONG.
SHING
SO SAME OLD, SAME OLD.
ZWOOO
TMP
TMP
TMP
ZWOOOOOOO

READ THIS WAY

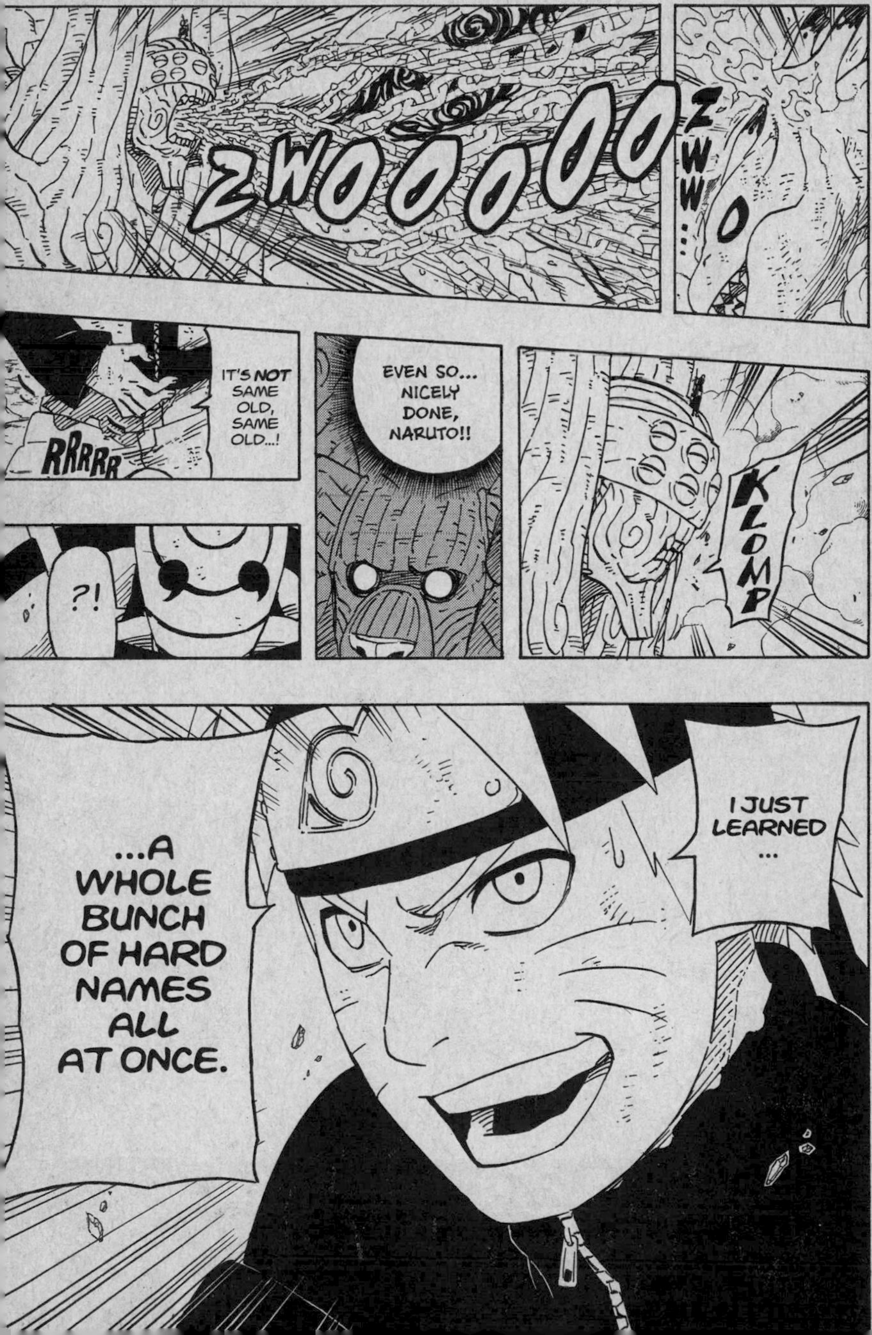
ZWW...O
ZWOOOOOO
KLOMP
EVEN SO... NICELY DONE, NARUTO!!
IT'S NOT SAME OLD, SAME OLD...!
RRRRR
?!
I JUST LEARNED ...
...A WHOLE BUNCH OF HARD NAMES ALL AT ONCE.

Illustration to Commemorate Reaching Volume 60 [8]

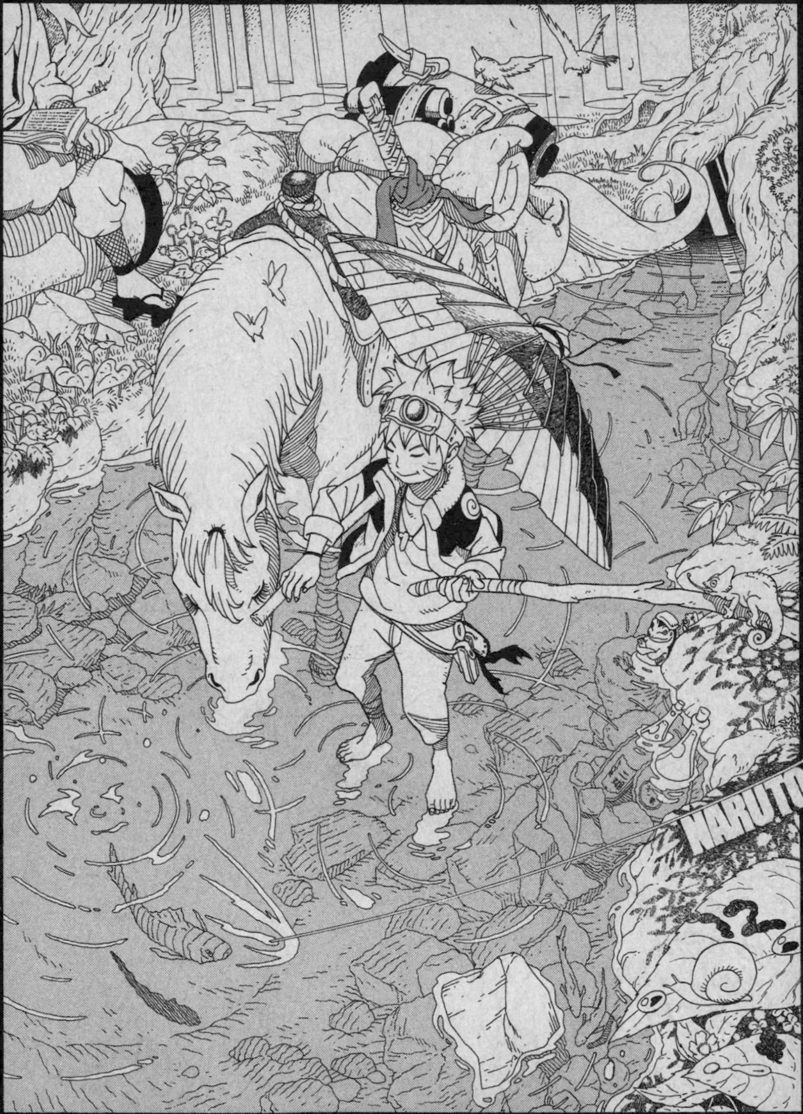
NARUTO

オオクボ アキラ
Akira Okubo

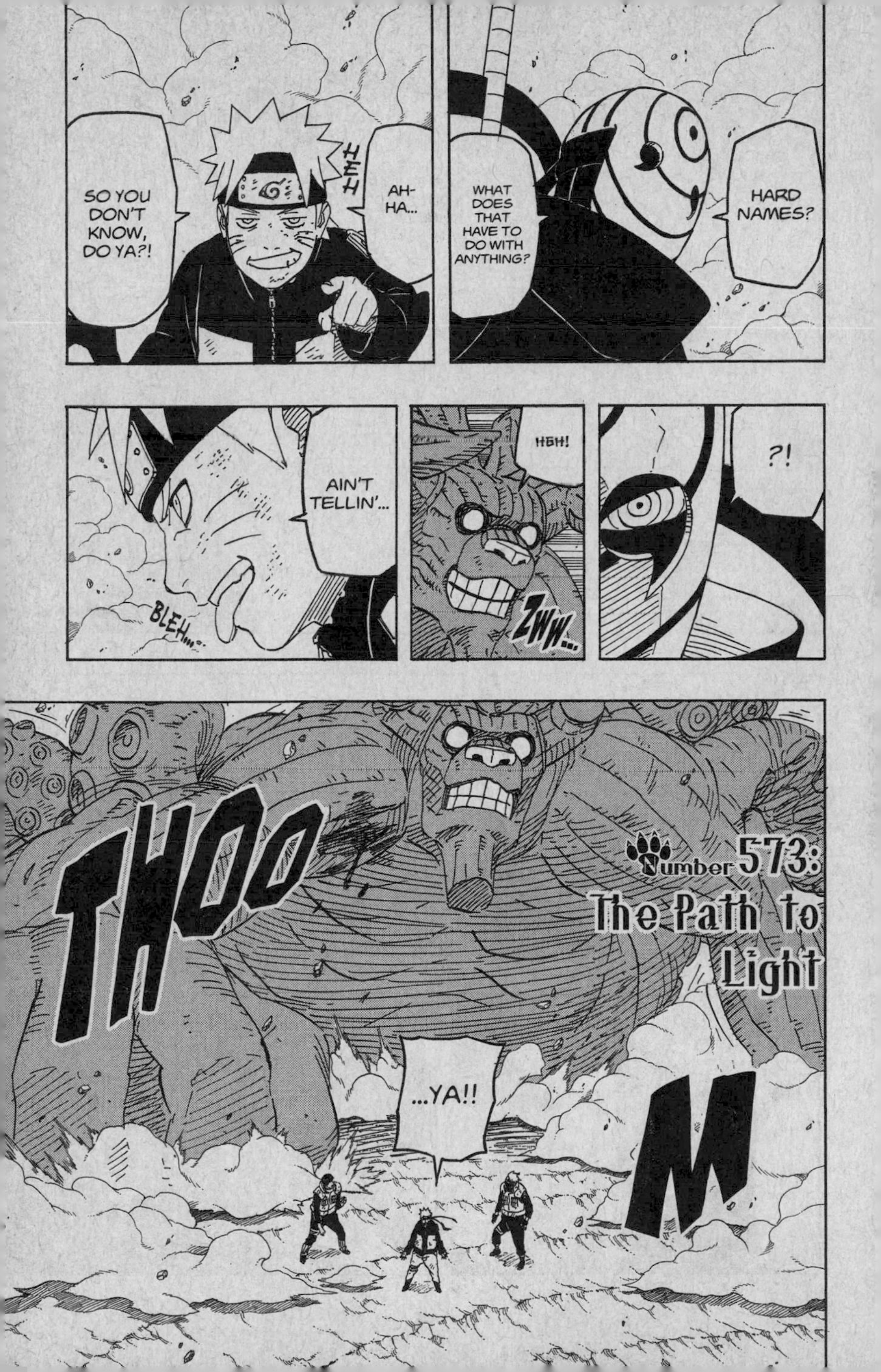
HARD NAMES?
WHAT DOES THAT HAVE TO DO WITH ANYTHING?
HEH
AH-HA...
SO YOU DON'T KNOW, DO YA?!
?!
HEH!
ZWW...
AIN'T TELLIN'...
BLEH...
Number 573: The Path to Light
THOOM
...YA!!

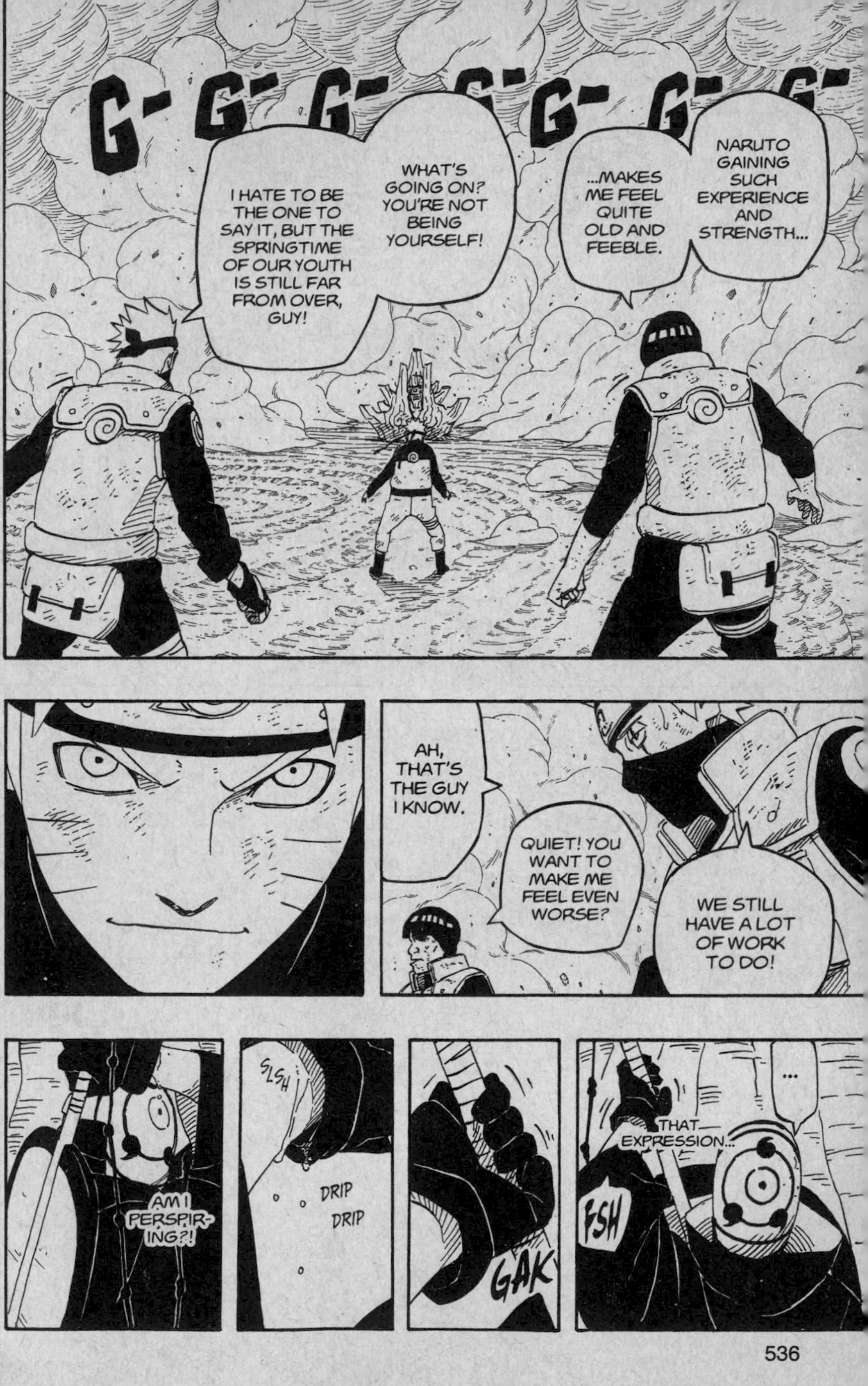
G- G- G- G- G- G- G-
NARUTO GAINING SUCH EXPERIENCE AND STRENGTH...
...MAKES ME FEEL QUITE OLD AND FEEBLE.
WHAT'S GOING ON? YOU'RE NOT BEING YOURSELF!
I HATE TO BE THE ONE TO SAY IT, BUT THE SPRINGTIME OF OUR YOUTH IS STILL FAR FROM OVER, GUY!
AH, THAT'S THE GUY I KNOW.
QUIET! YOU WANT TO MAKE ME FEEL EVEN WORSE?
WE STILL HAVE A LOT OF WORK TO DO!
...
THAT EXPRESSION...
FSH
GAK
SLSH
DRIP DRIP
AM I PERSPIRING?!

READ THIS WAY

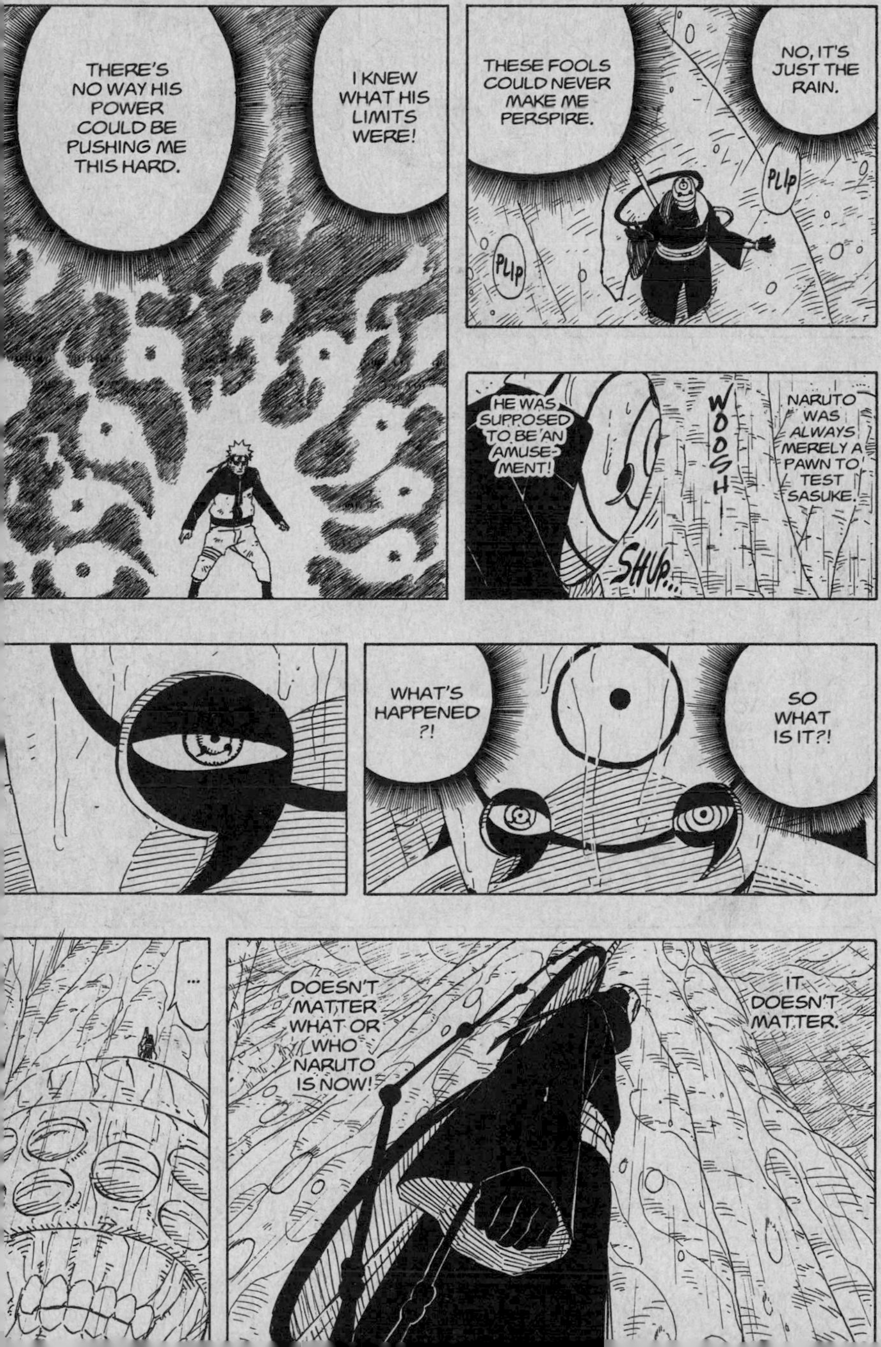
NO, IT'S JUST THE RAIN.
THESE FOOLS COULD NEVER MAKE ME PERSPIRE.
PLIP
PLIP
NARUTO WAS ALWAYS MERELY A PAWN TO TEST SASUKE.
WOOSH
HE WAS SUPPOSED TO BE AN AMUSE-MENT!
SHUP...
I KNEW WHAT HIS LIMITS WERE!
THERE'S NO WAY HIS POWER COULD BE PUSHING ME THIS HARD.
SO WHAT IS IT?!
WHAT'S HAPPENED?!
IT DOESN'T MATTER.
DOESN'T MATTER WHAT OR WHO NARUTO IS NOW!
...

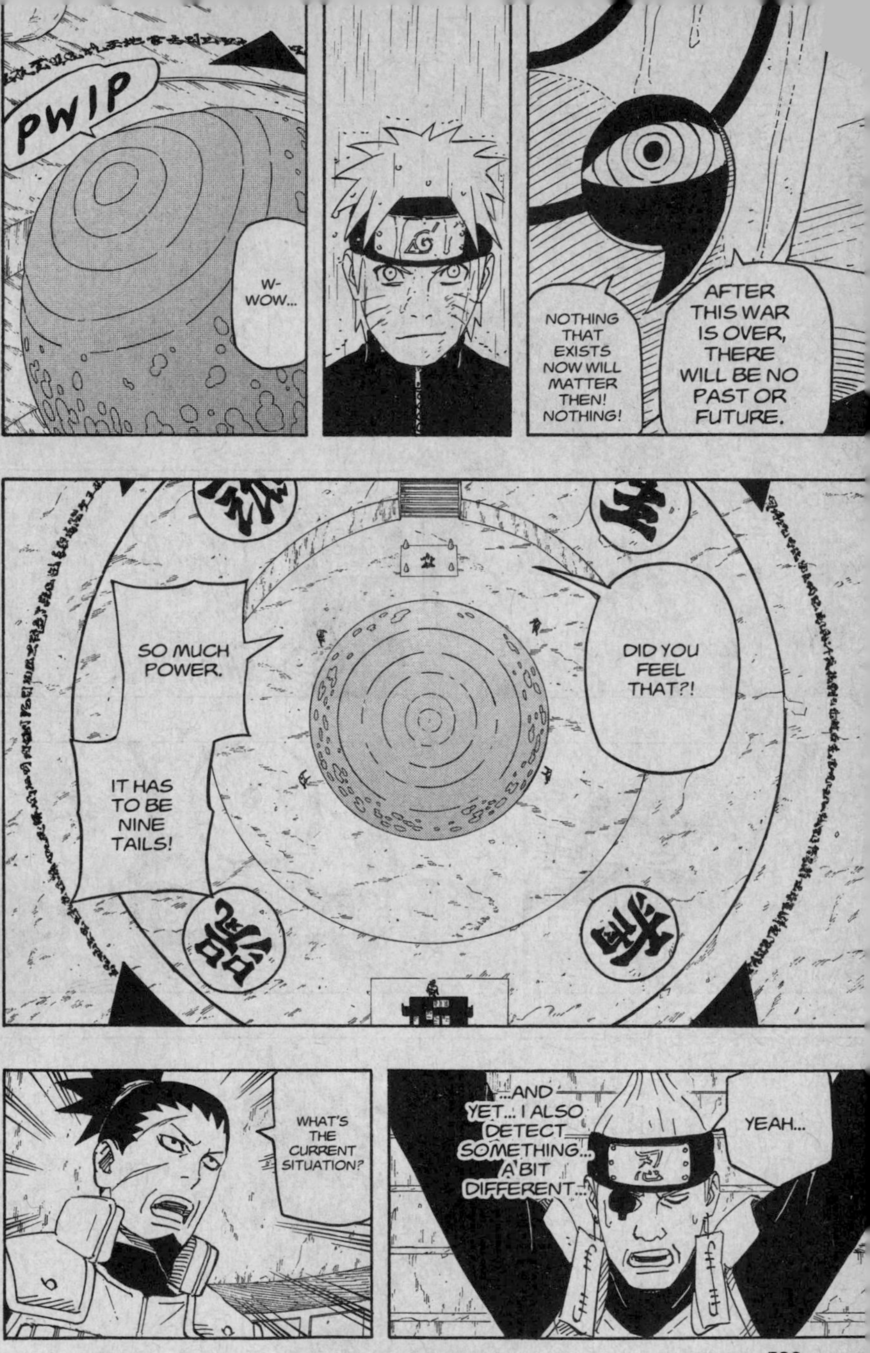
AFTER THIS WAR IS OVER, THERE WILL BE NO PAST OR FUTURE.
NOTHING THAT EXISTS NOW WILL MATTER THEN! NOTHING!
PWIP
W-WOW...
DID YOU FEEL THAT?!
SO MUCH POWER.
IT HAS TO BE NINE TAILS!
YEAH...
...AND YET... I ALSO DETECT SOMETHING... A BIT DIFFERENT...
WHAT'S THE CURRENT SITUATION?

READ THIS WAY

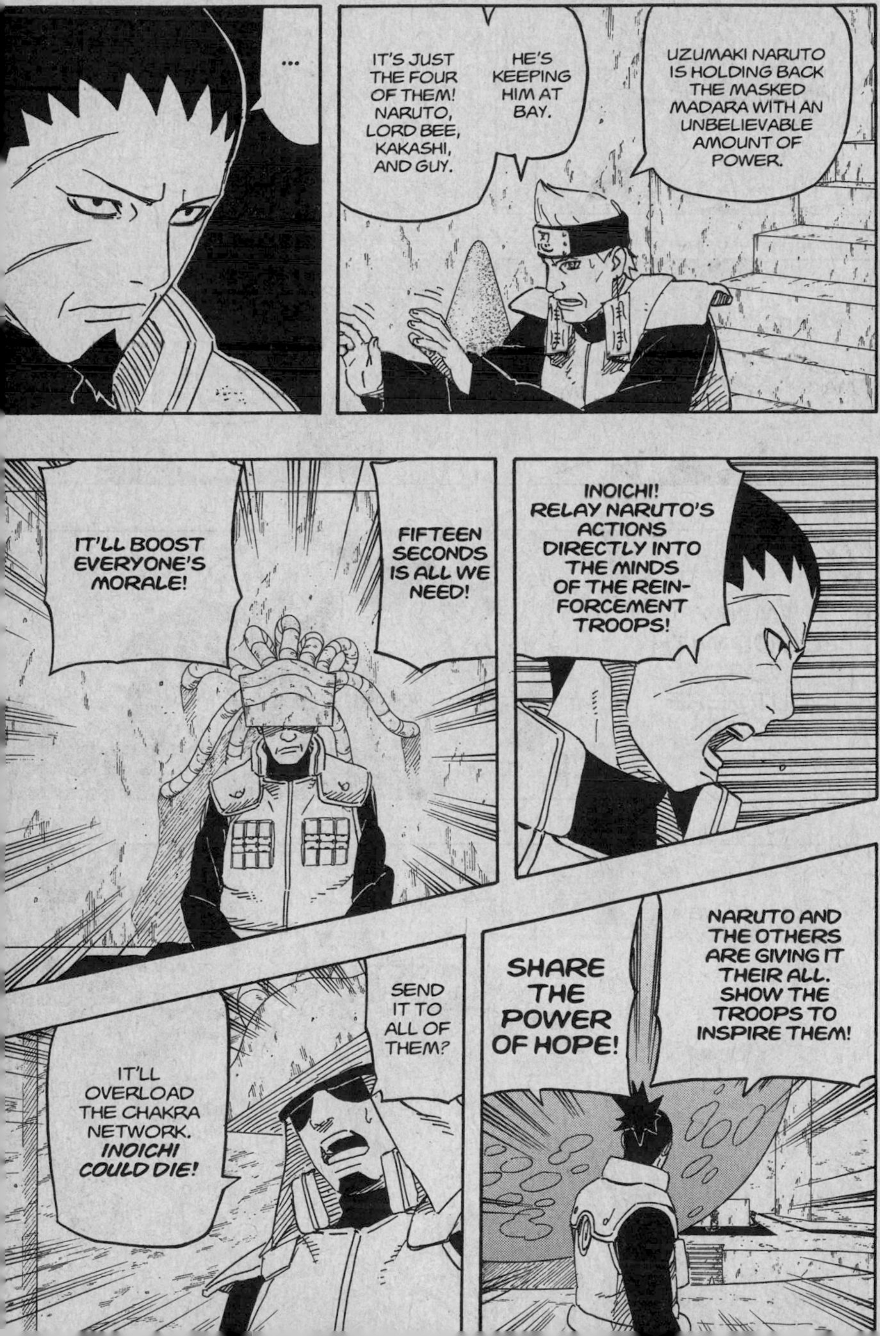

UZUMAKI NARUTO IS HOLDING BACK THE MASKED MADARA WITH AN UNBELIEVABLE AMOUNT OF POWER.
HE'S KEEPING HIM AT BAY.
IT'S JUST THE FOUR OF THEM! NARUTO, LORD BEE, KAKASHI, AND GUY.
...
INOICHI! RELAY NARUTO'S ACTIONS DIRECTLY INTO THE MINDS OF THE REIN-FORCEMENT TROOPS!
FIFTEEN SECONDS IS ALL WE NEED!
IT'LL BOOST EVERYONE'S MORALE!
NARUTO AND THE OTHERS ARE GIVING IT THEIR ALL. SHOW THE TROOPS TO INSPIRE THEM!
SHARE THE POWER OF HOPE!
SEND IT TO ALL OF THEM?
IT'LL OVERLOAD THE CHAKRA NETWORK. INOICHI COULD DIE!

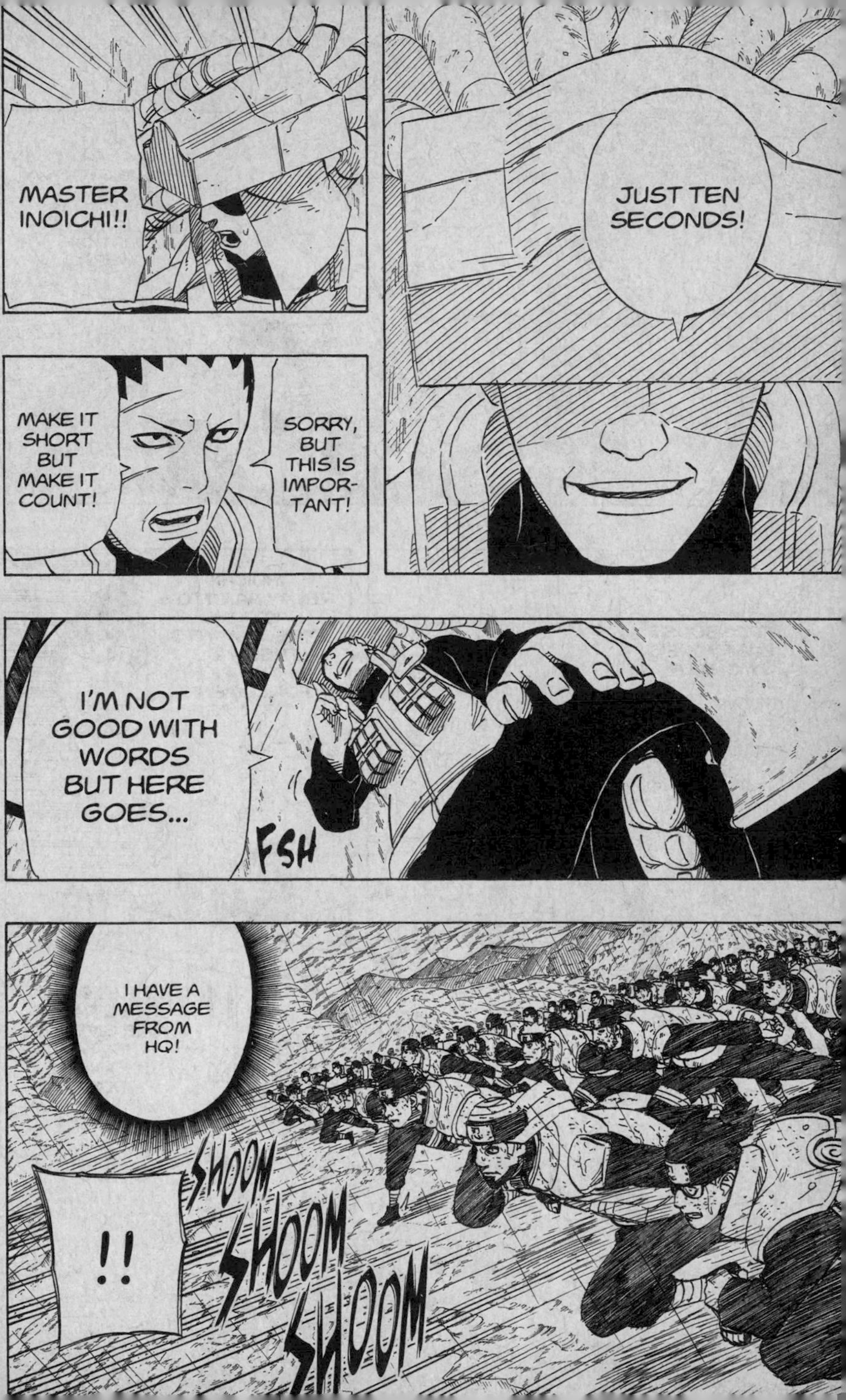

JUST TEN SECONDS!
MASTER INOICHI!!
SORRY, BUT THIS IS IMPORTANT!
MAKE IT SHORT BUT MAKE IT COUNT!
I'M NOT GOOD WITH WORDS BUT HERE GOES...
FSH
I HAVE A MESSAGE FROM HQ!
SHOOM SHOOM SHOOM
!!

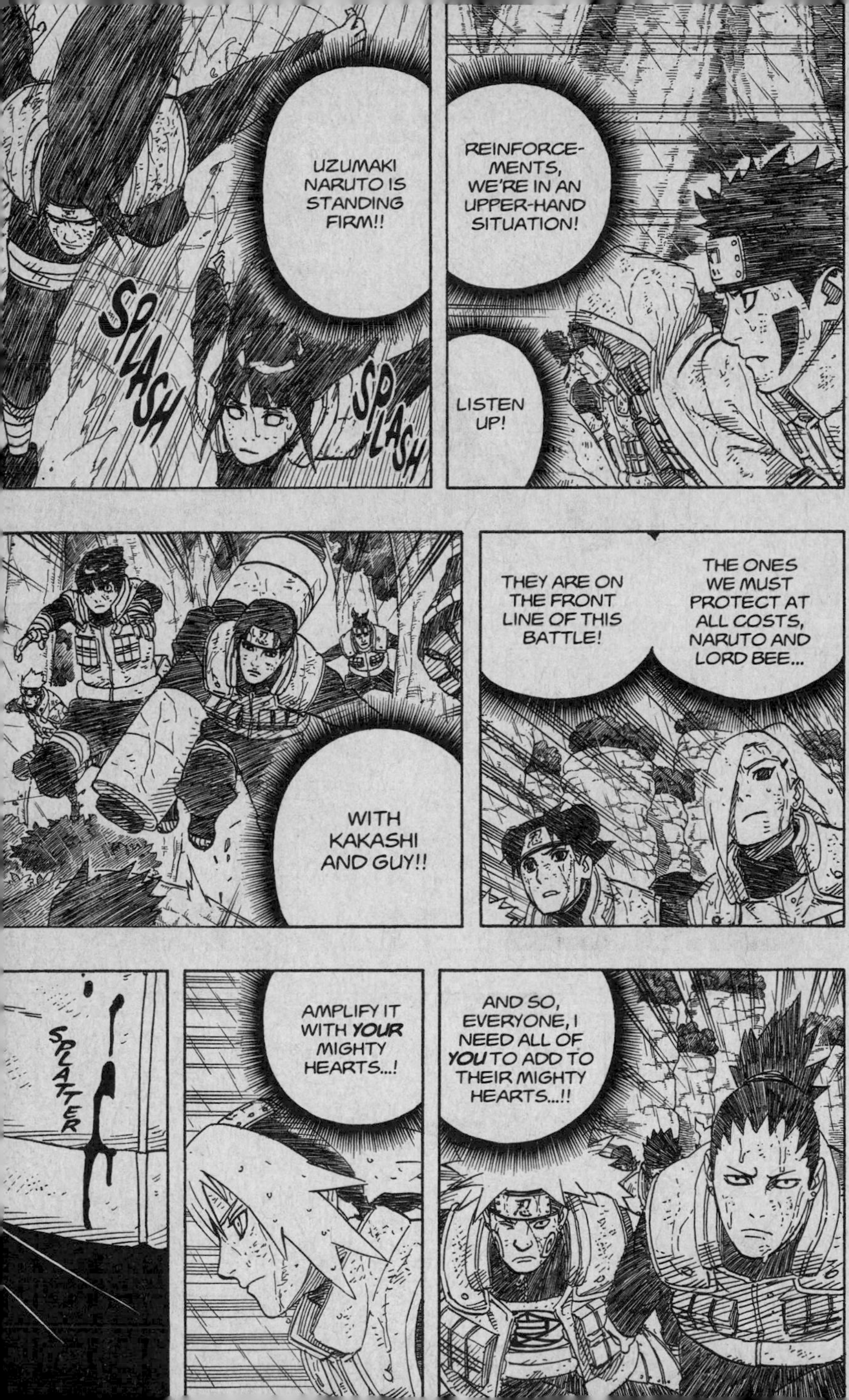
REINFORCE-MENTS, WE'RE IN AN UPPER-HAND SITUATION!
LISTEN UP!
UZUMAKI NARUTO IS STANDING FIRM!!
SPLASH
SPLASH
THE ONES WE MUST PROTECT AT ALL COSTS, NARUTO AND LORD BEE...
THEY ARE ON THE FRONT LINE OF THIS BATTLE!
WITH KAKASHI AND GUY!!
AND SO, EVERYONE, I NEED ALL OF YOU TO ADD TO THEIR MIGHTY HEARTS...!!
AMPLIFY IT WITH YOUR MIGHTY HEARTS...!
SPLATTER

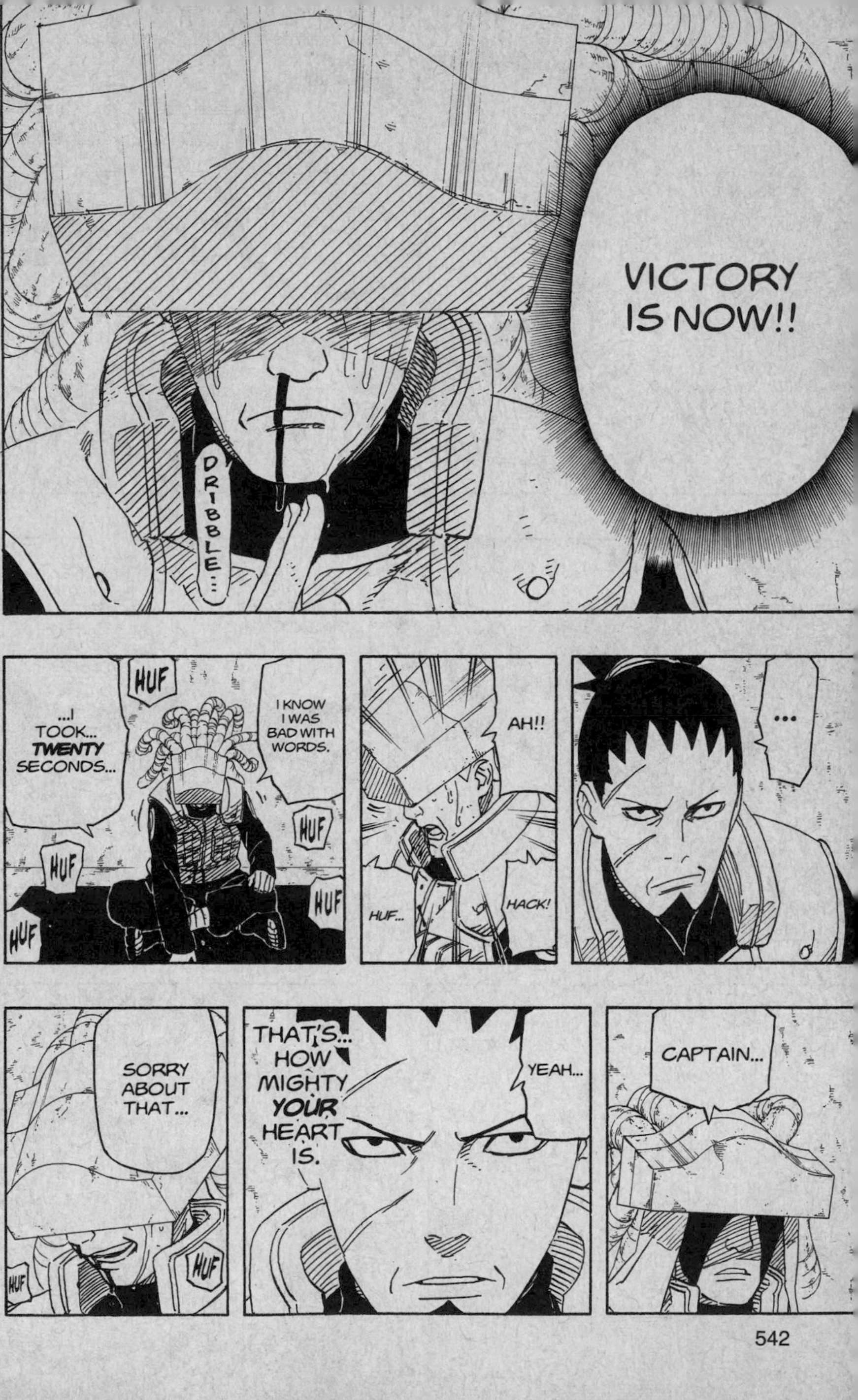
VICTORY IS NOW!!
DRIBBLE...
...
AH!!
HUF...
HACK!
I KNOW I WAS BAD WITH WORDS.
HUF
...I TOOK... TWENTY SECONDS...
HUF
HUF
HUF
HUF
CAPTAIN...
YEAH...
THAT'S... HOW MIGHTY YOUR HEART IS.
SORRY ABOUT THAT...
HUF
HUF

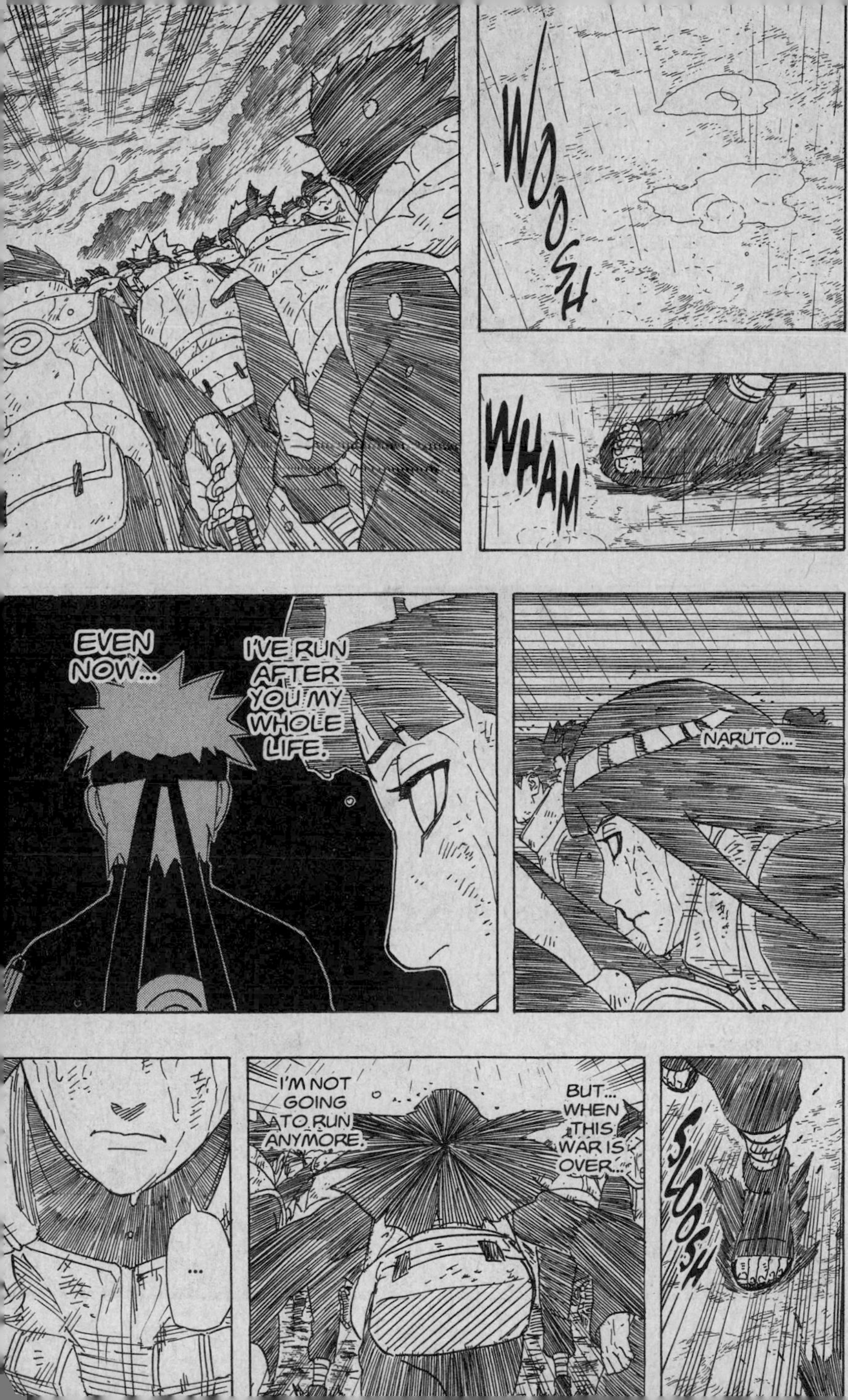
WOOSH
WHAM
NARUTO...
I'VE RUN AFTER YOU MY WHOLE LIFE.
EVEN NOW...
SLOOSH
BUT... WHEN THIS WAR IS OVER...
I'M NOT GOING TO RUN ANYMORE.
...

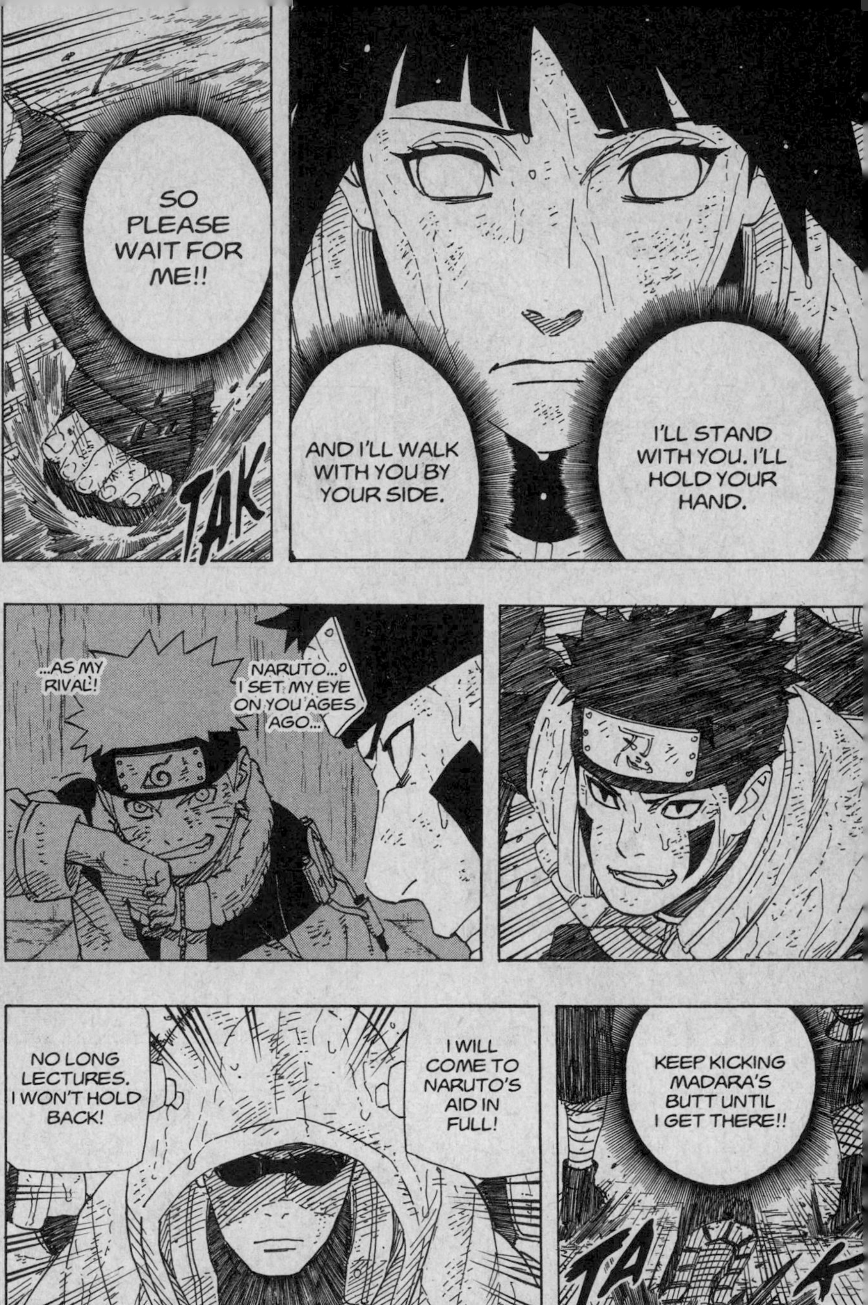
I'LL STAND WITH YOU. I'LL HOLD YOUR HAND.
AND I'LL WALK WITH YOU BY YOUR SIDE.
SO PLEASE WAIT FOR ME!!
TAK
NARUTO... I SET MY EYE ON YOU AGES AGO...
...AS MY RIVAL!
KEEP KICKING MADARA'S BUTT UNTIL I GET THERE!!
I WILL COME TO NARUTO'S AID IN FULL!
NO LONG LECTURES. I WON'T HOLD BACK!

READ THIS WAY

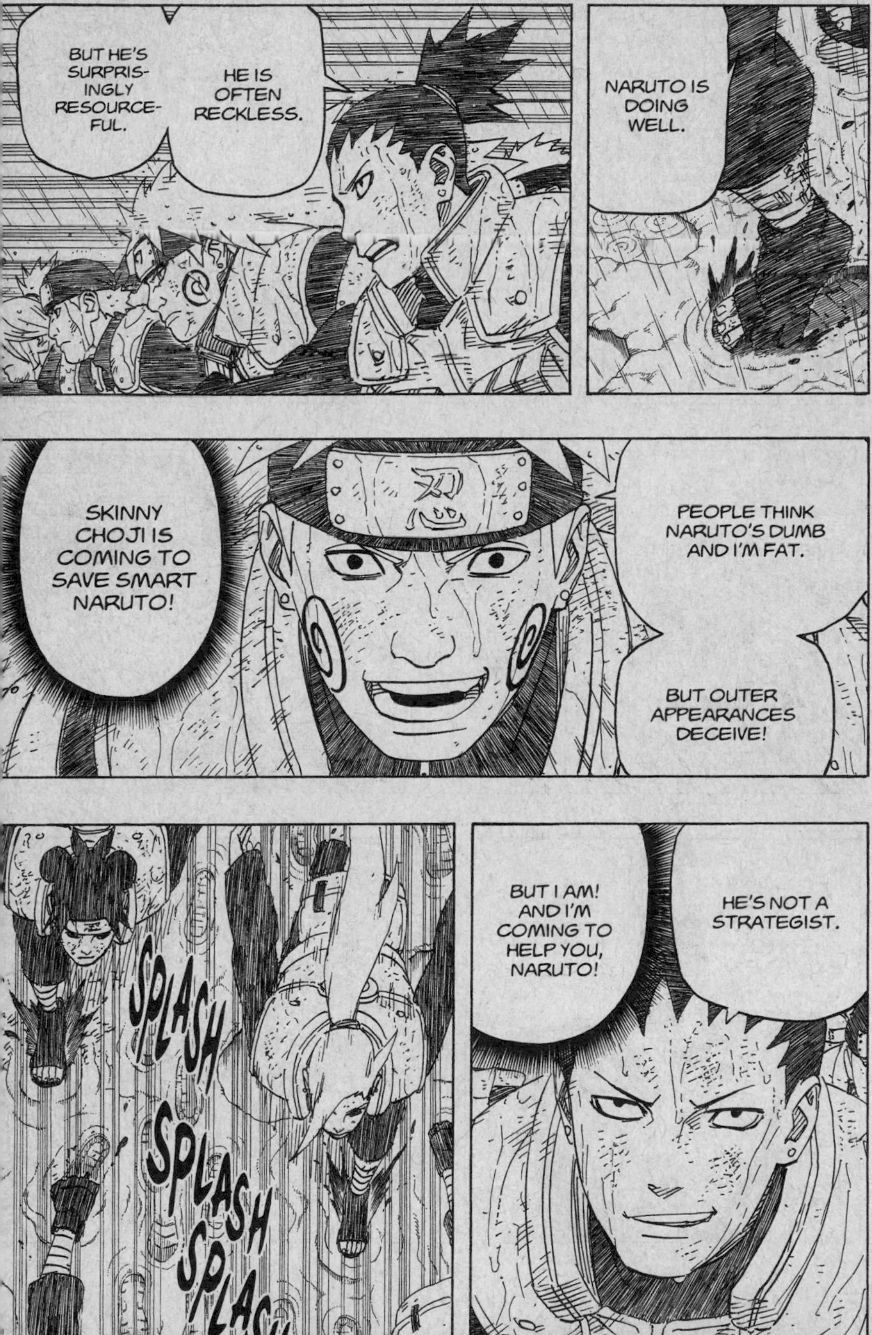
NARUTO IS DOING WELL.
HE IS OFTEN RECKLESS.
BUT HE'S SURPRISINGLY RESOURCEFUL.
PEOPLE THINK NARUTO'S DUMB AND I'M FAT.
BUT OUTER APPEARANCES DECEIVE!
SKINNY CHOJI IS COMING TO SAVE SMART NARUTO!
HE'S NOT A STRATEGIST.
BUT I AM! AND I'M COMING TO HELP YOU, NARUTO!
SPLASH
SPLASH
SPLASH

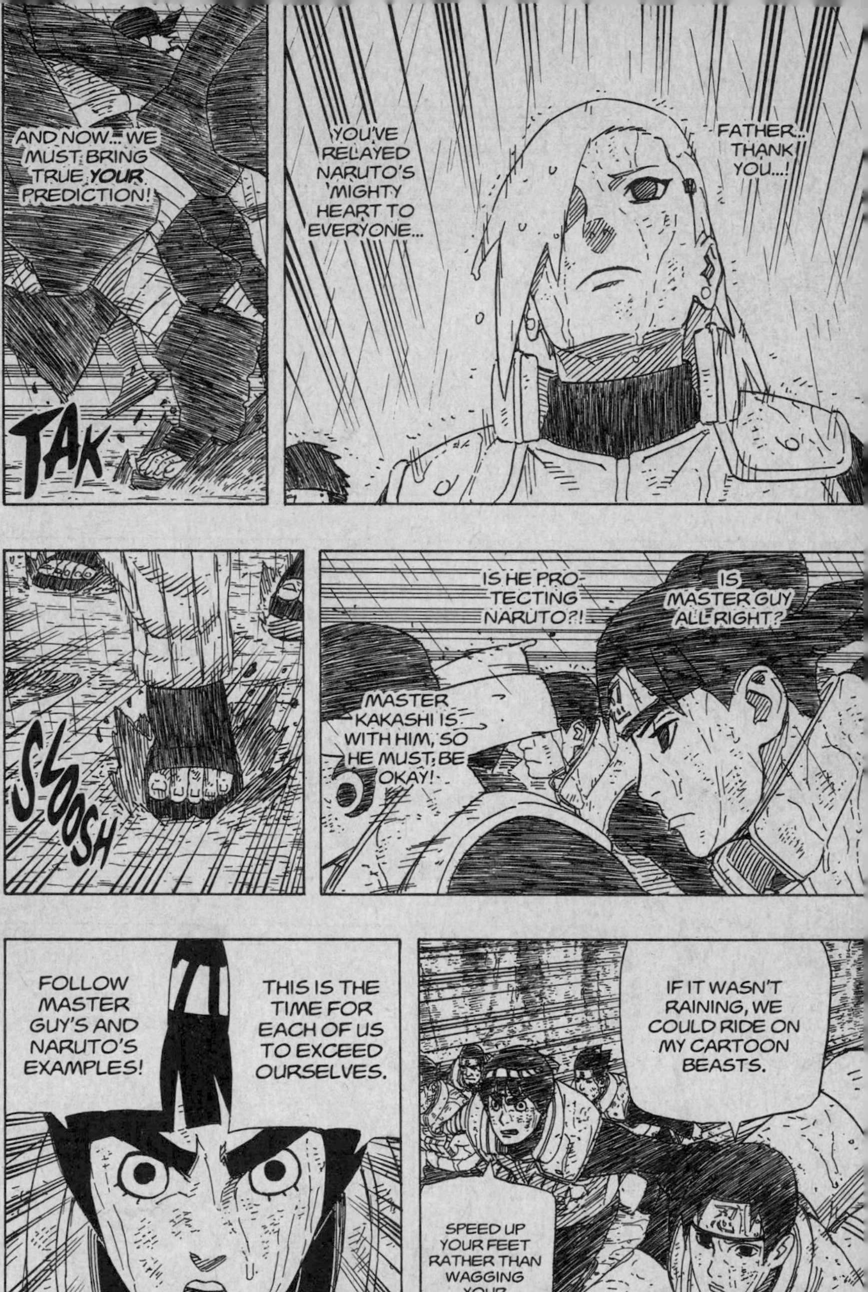
FATHER... THANK YOU...!
YOU'VE RELAYED NARUTO'S MIGHTY HEART TO EVERYONE...
AND NOW... WE MUST BRING TRUE *YOUR* PREDICTION!
TAK
IS MASTER GUY ALL RIGHT?
IS HE PROTECTING NARUTO?!
MASTER KAKASHI IS WITH HIM, SO HE MUST BE OKAY!
SWOOSH
IF IT WASN'T RAINING, WE COULD RIDE ON MY CARTOON BEASTS.
SPEED UP YOUR FEET RATHER THAN WAGGING YOUR TONGUE, SAI!!
THIS IS THE TIME FOR EACH OF US TO EXCEED OURSELVES.
FOLLOW MASTER GUY'S AND NARUTO'S EXAMPLES!

READ THIS WAY

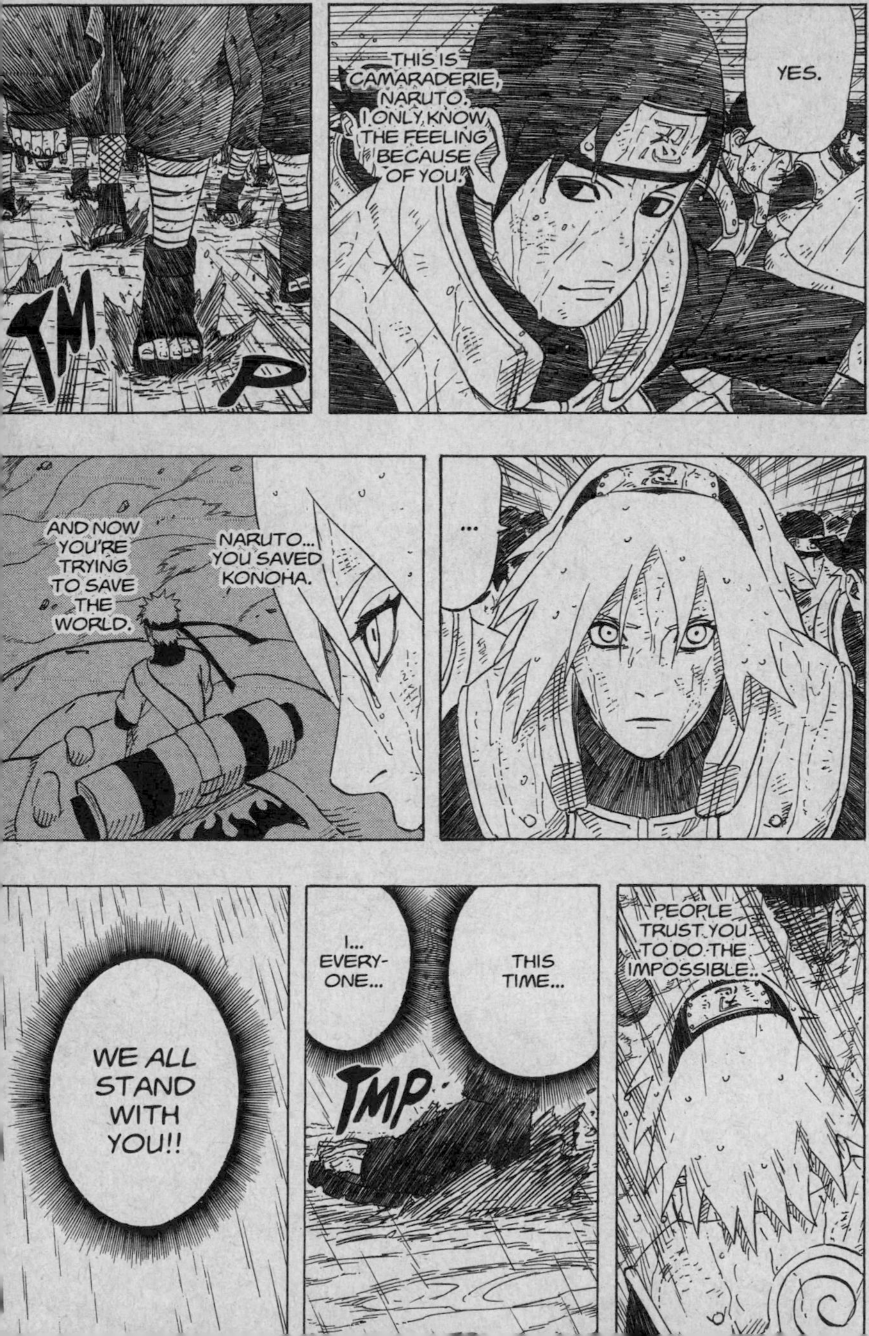
YES.
THIS IS CAMARADERIE, NARUTO. I ONLY KNOW THE FEELING BECAUSE OF YOU.
TMP
...
NARUTO... YOU SAVED KONOHA.
AND NOW YOU'RE TRYING TO SAVE THE WORLD.
PEOPLE TRUST YOU TO DO THE IMPOSSIBLE...
THIS TIME...
I... EVERY-ONE...
TMP
WE ALL STAND WITH YOU!!

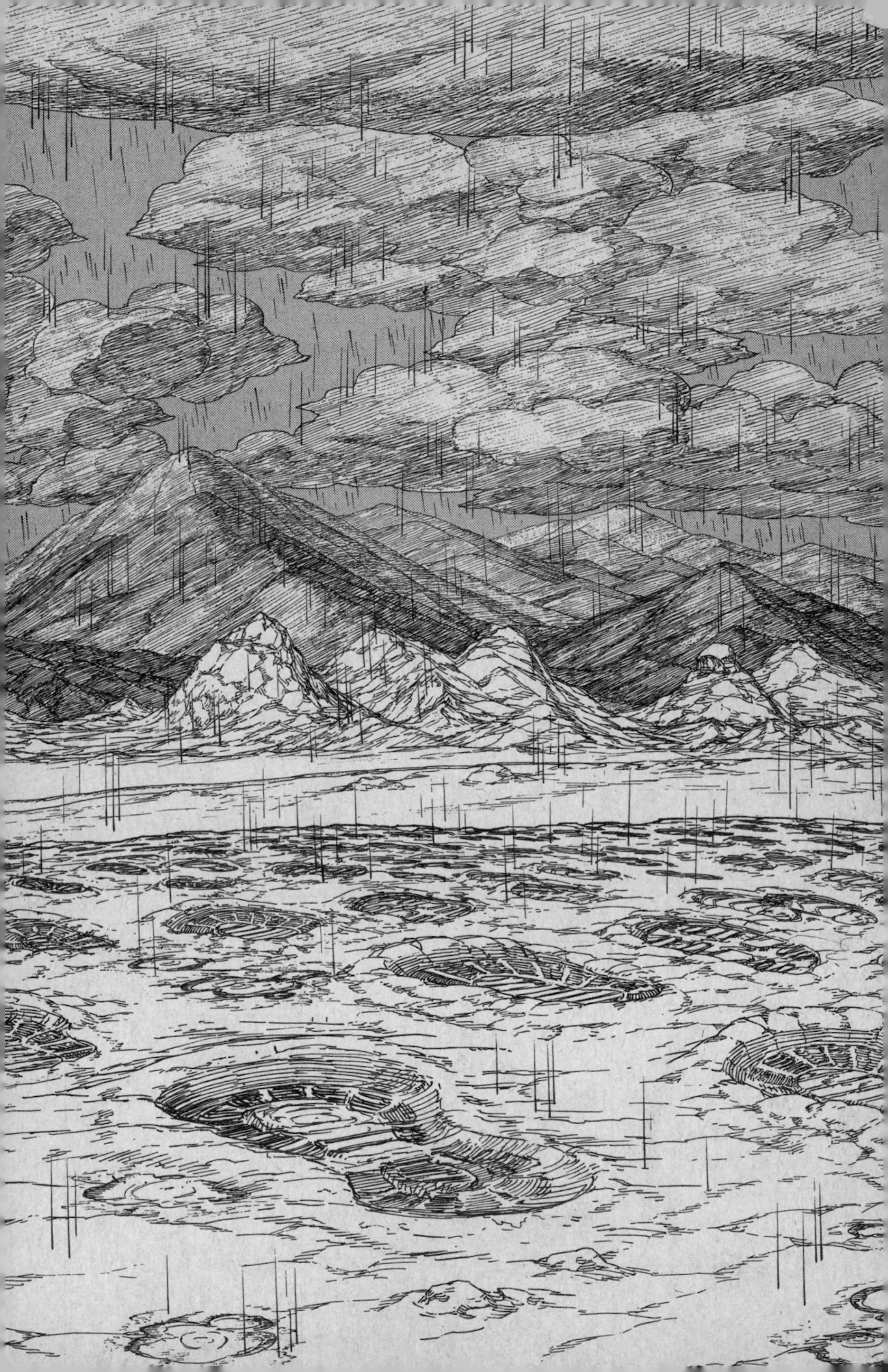

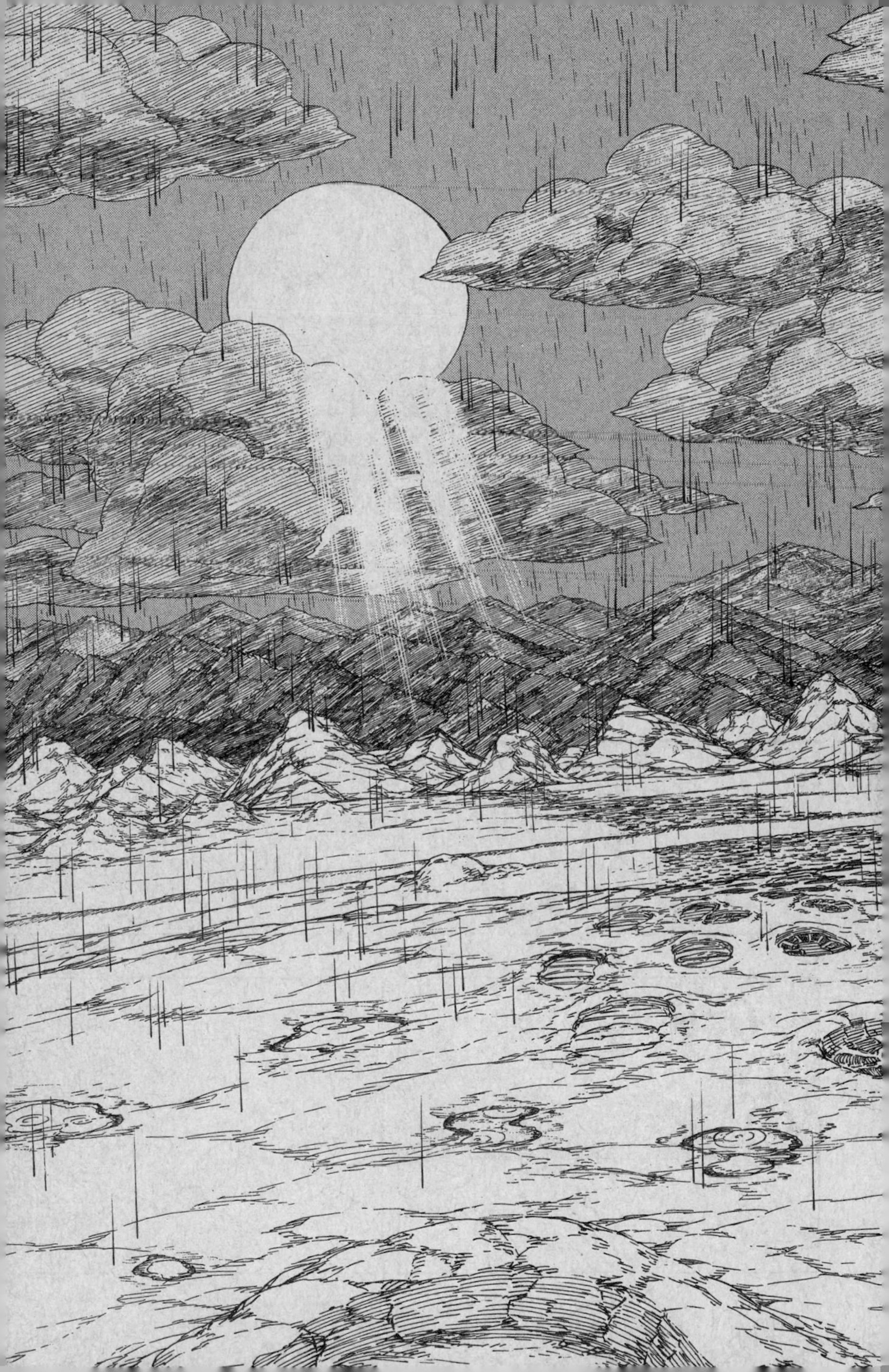

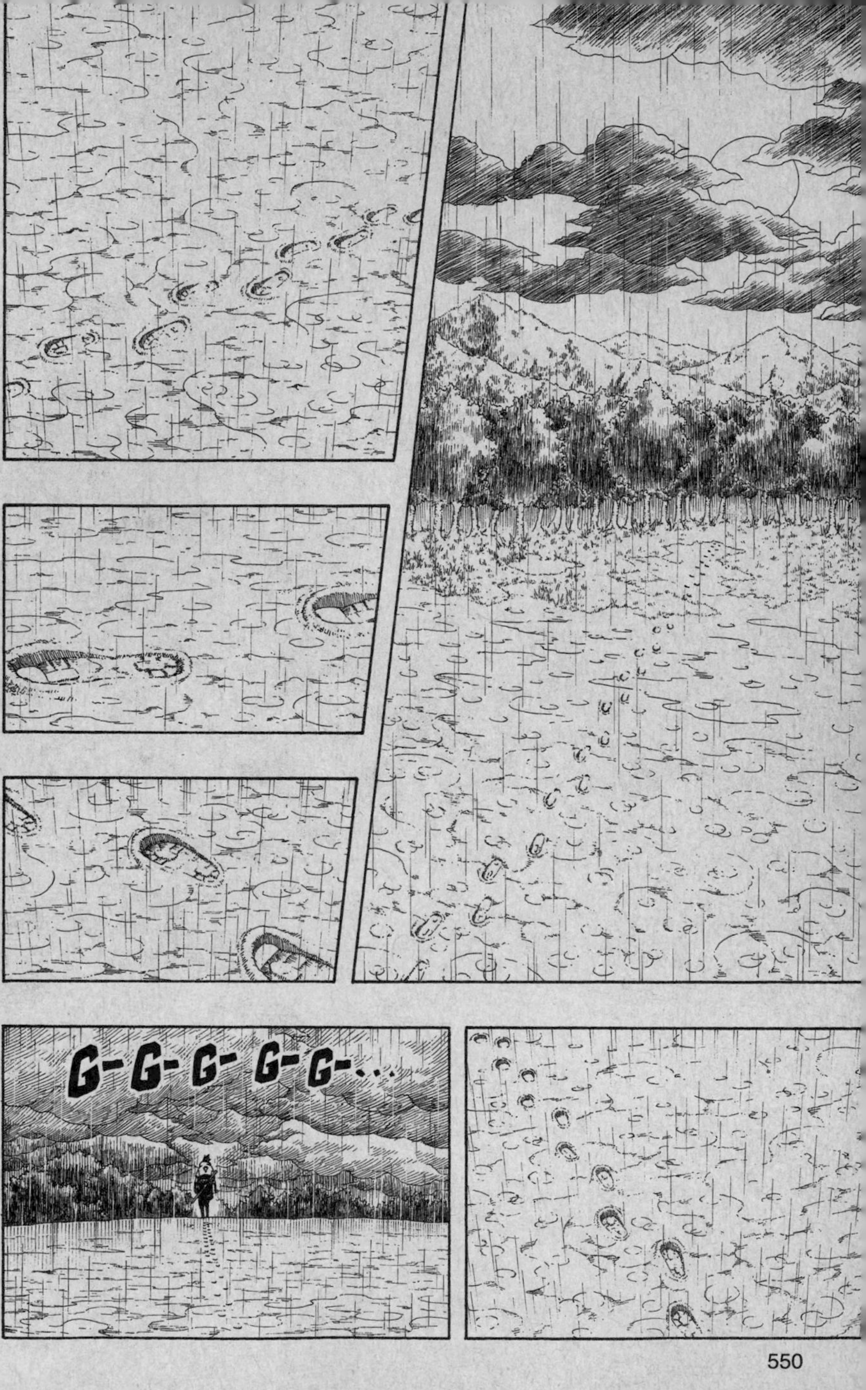
G-G-G-G-G-...

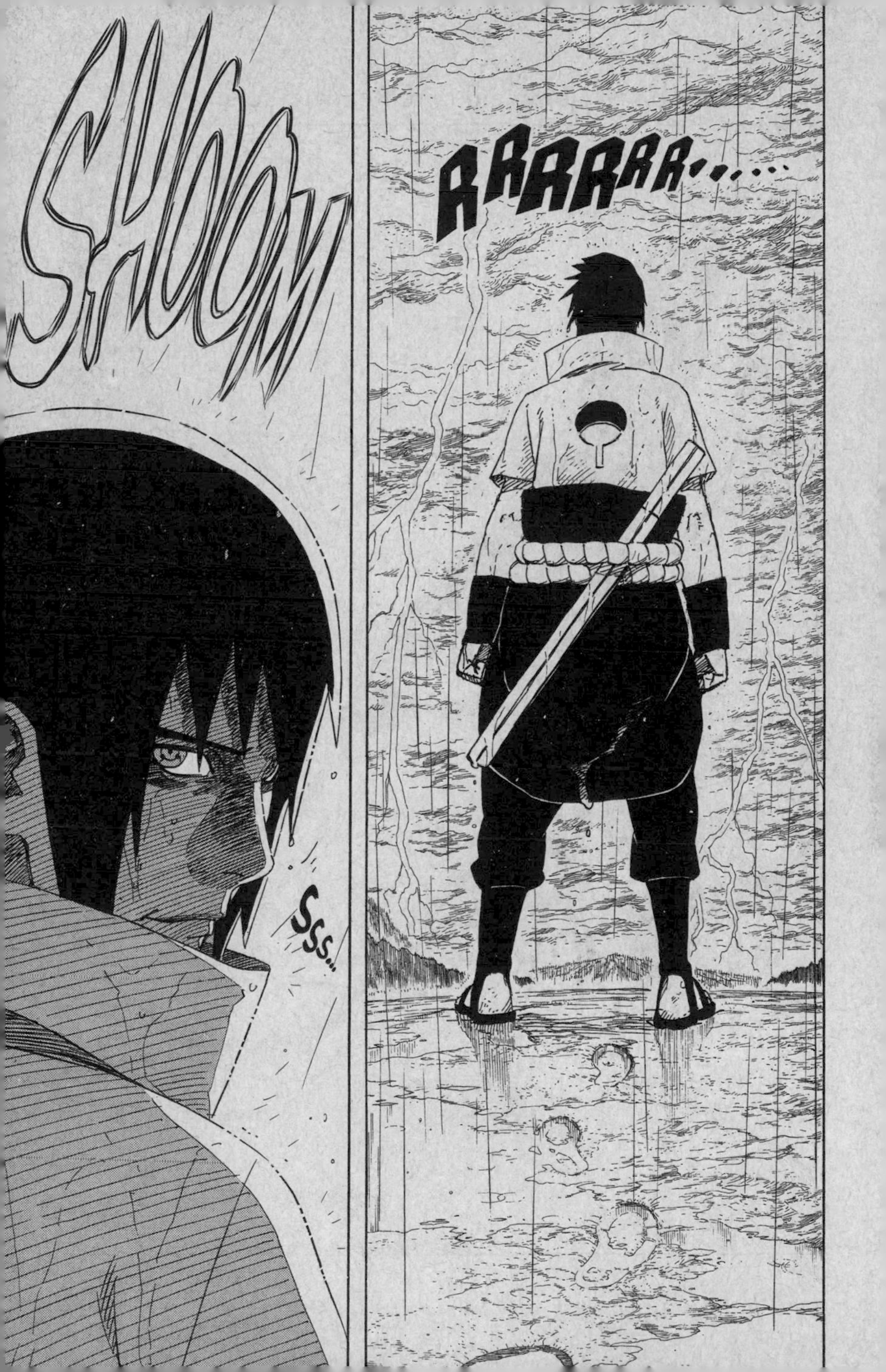
RRRRRR.....
SHOOM
SSS...

Illustration to Commemorate Reaching Volume 60 [9]

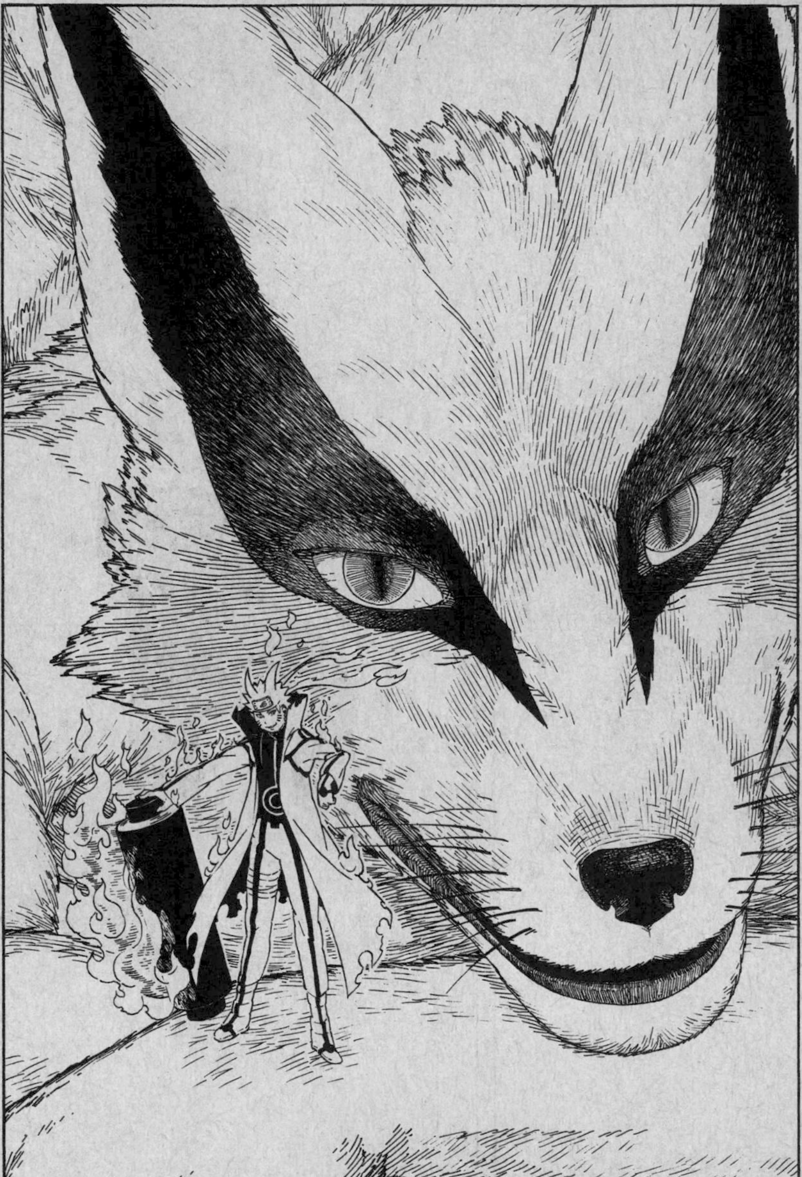

Koichi Nishiya

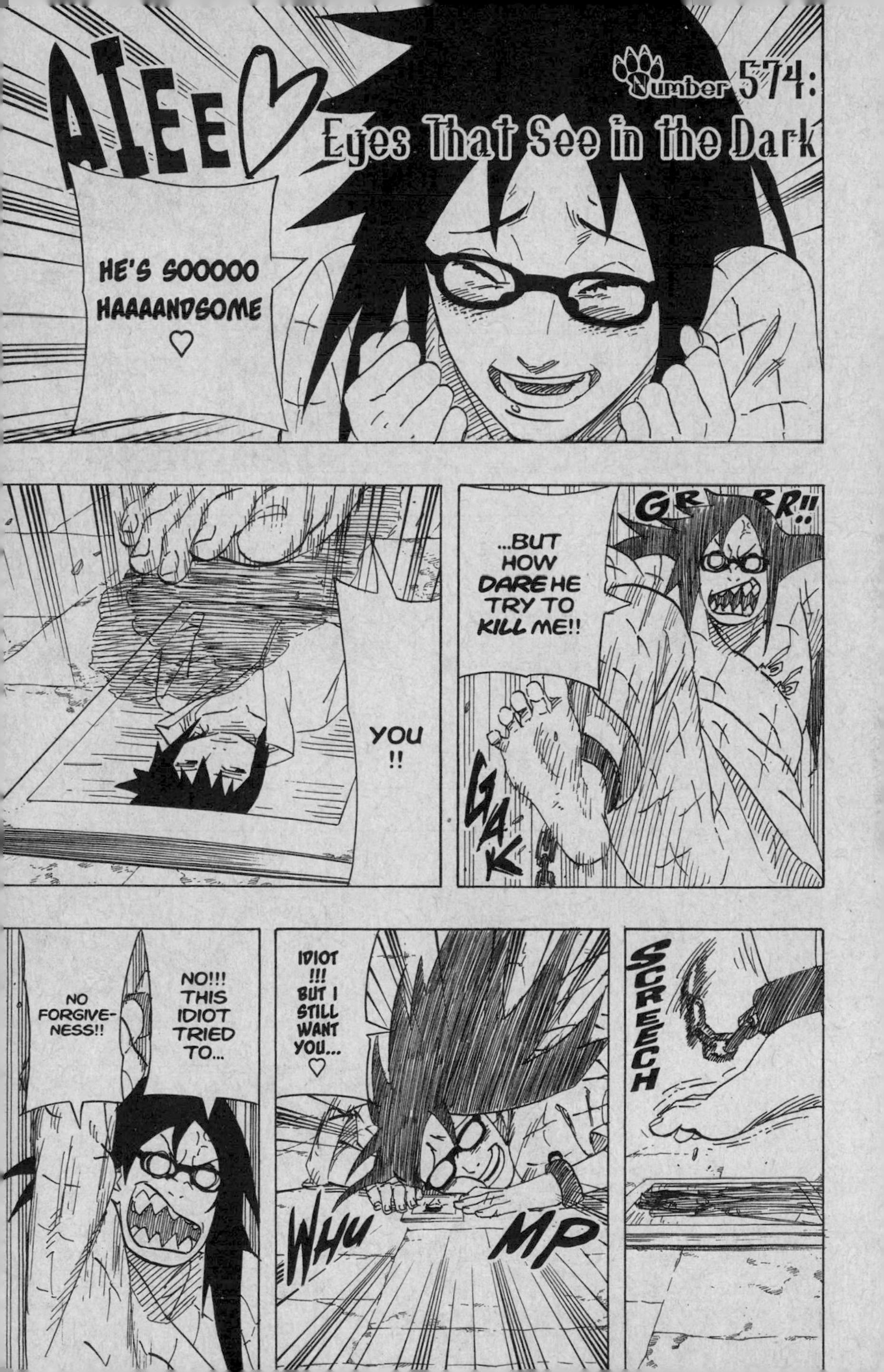
Number 574:
Eyes That See in the Dark
AIEE ♡
HE'S SOOOOO HAAAANDSOME ♡
GRRR!!
...BUT HOW DARE HE TRY TO KILL ME!!
GAK
YOU !!
SCREECH
IDIOT !!! BUT I STILL WANT YOU... ♡
WHUMP
NO!!! THIS IDIOT TRIED TO...
NO FORGIVE-NESS!!

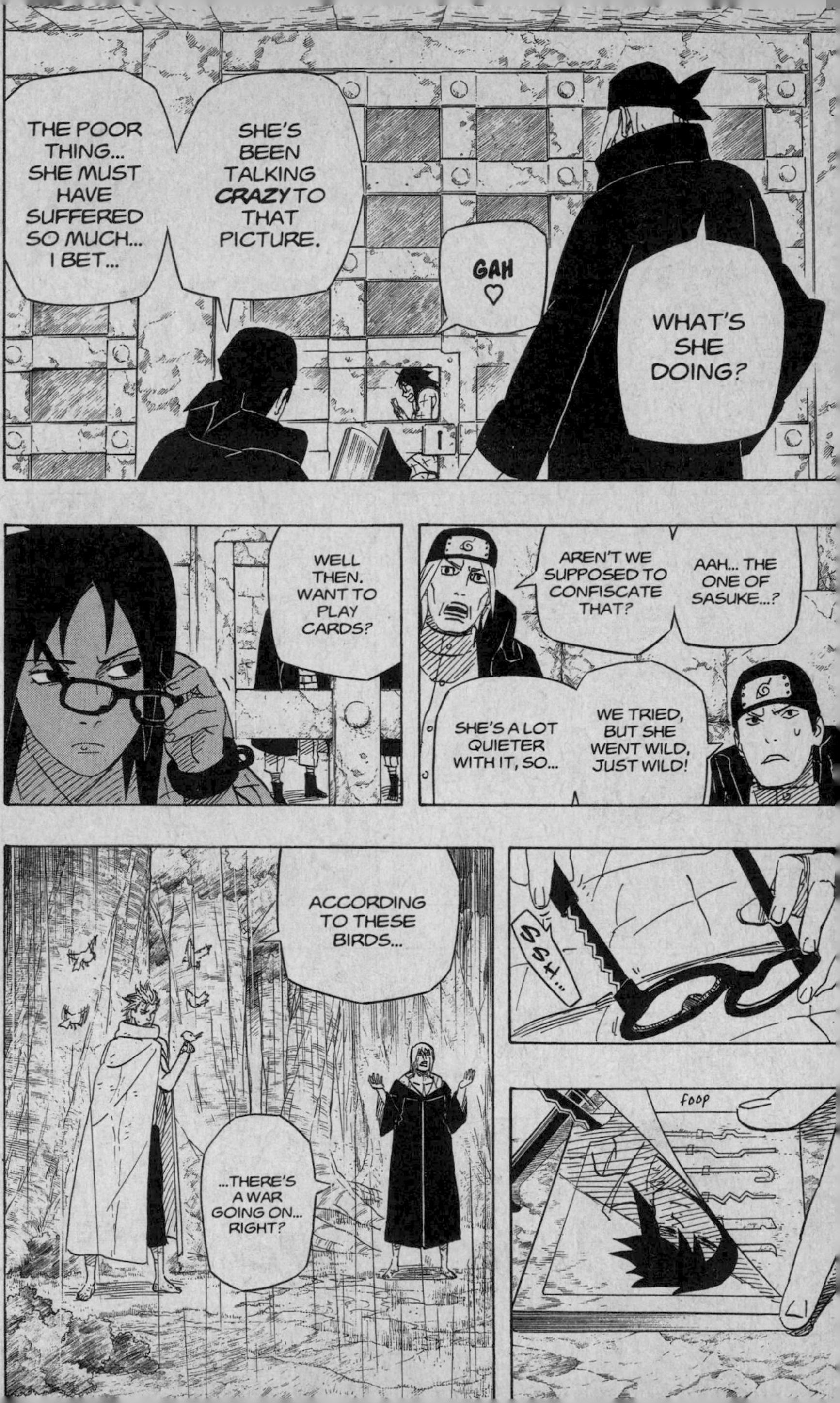
WHAT'S SHE DOING?
GAH ♥
SHE'S BEEN TALKING CRAZY TO THAT PICTURE.
THE POOR THING... SHE MUST HAVE SUFFERED SO MUCH... I BET...
AAH... THE ONE OF SASUKE...?
AREN'T WE SUPPOSED TO CONFISCATE THAT?
WE TRIED, BUT SHE WENT WILD, JUST WILD!
SHE'S A LOT QUIETER WITH IT, SO...
WELL THEN. WANT TO PLAY CARDS?
SSH...
foop
ACCORDING TO THESE BIRDS...
...THERE'S A WAR GOING ON... RIGHT?

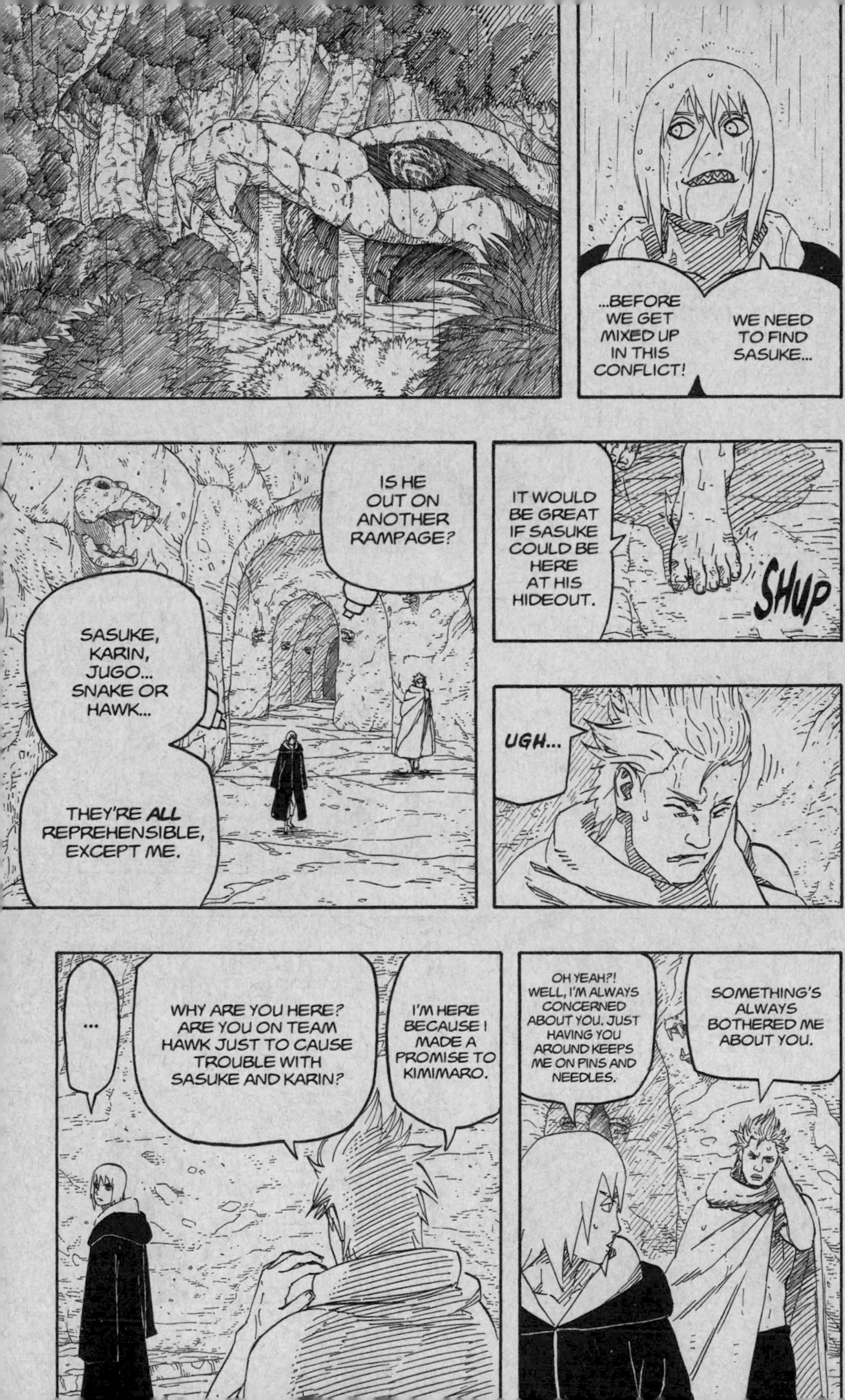
WE NEED TO FIND SASUKE...
...BEFORE WE GET MIXED UP IN THIS CONFLICT!
IT WOULD BE GREAT IF SASUKE COULD BE HERE AT HIS HIDEOUT.
SHUP
UGH...
IS HE OUT ON ANOTHER RAMPAGE?
SASUKE, KARIN, JUGO... SNAKE OR HAWK...
THEY'RE **ALL** REPREHENSIBLE, EXCEPT ME.
SOMETHING'S ALWAYS BOTHERED ME ABOUT YOU.
OH YEAH?! WELL, I'M ALWAYS CONCERNED ABOUT YOU. JUST HAVING YOU AROUND KEEPS ME ON PINS AND NEEDLES.
WHY ARE YOU HERE? ARE YOU ON TEAM HAWK JUST TO CAUSE TROUBLE WITH SASUKE AND KARIN?
I'M HERE BECAUSE I MADE A PROMISE TO KIMIMARO.
...

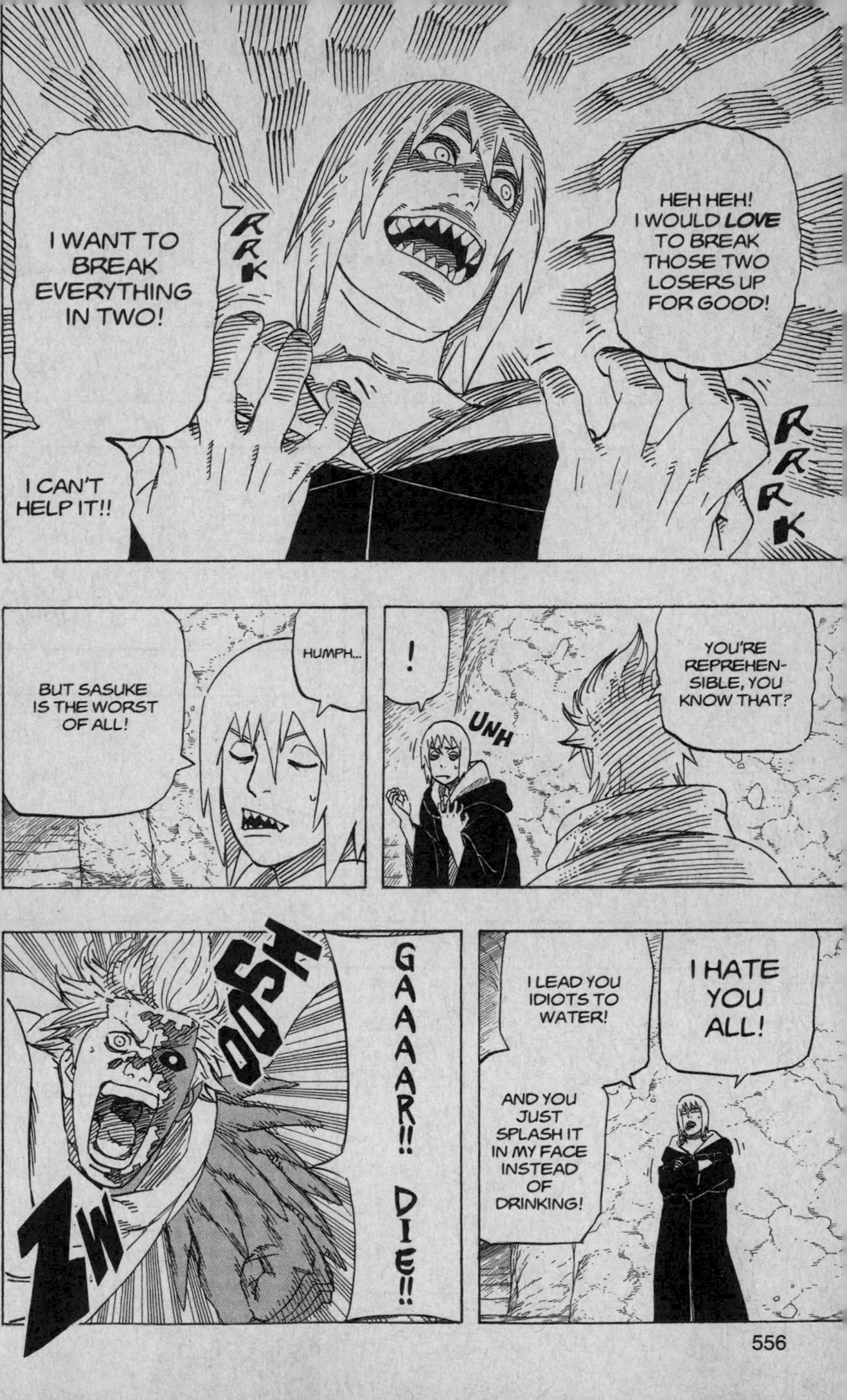
HEH HEH! I WOULD LOVE TO BREAK THOSE TWO LOSERS UP FOR GOOD!
I WANT TO BREAK EVERYTHING IN TWO!
RRK
RRRK
I CAN'T HELP IT!!
YOU'RE REPREHEN-SIBLE, YOU KNOW THAT?
!
UNH
HUMPH...
BUT SASUKE IS THE WORST OF ALL!
I HATE YOU ALL!
I LEAD YOU IDIOTS TO WATER!
AND YOU JUST SPLASH IT IN MY FACE INSTEAD OF DRINKING!
GAAAAR!! DIE!!
OOSH
Z-W

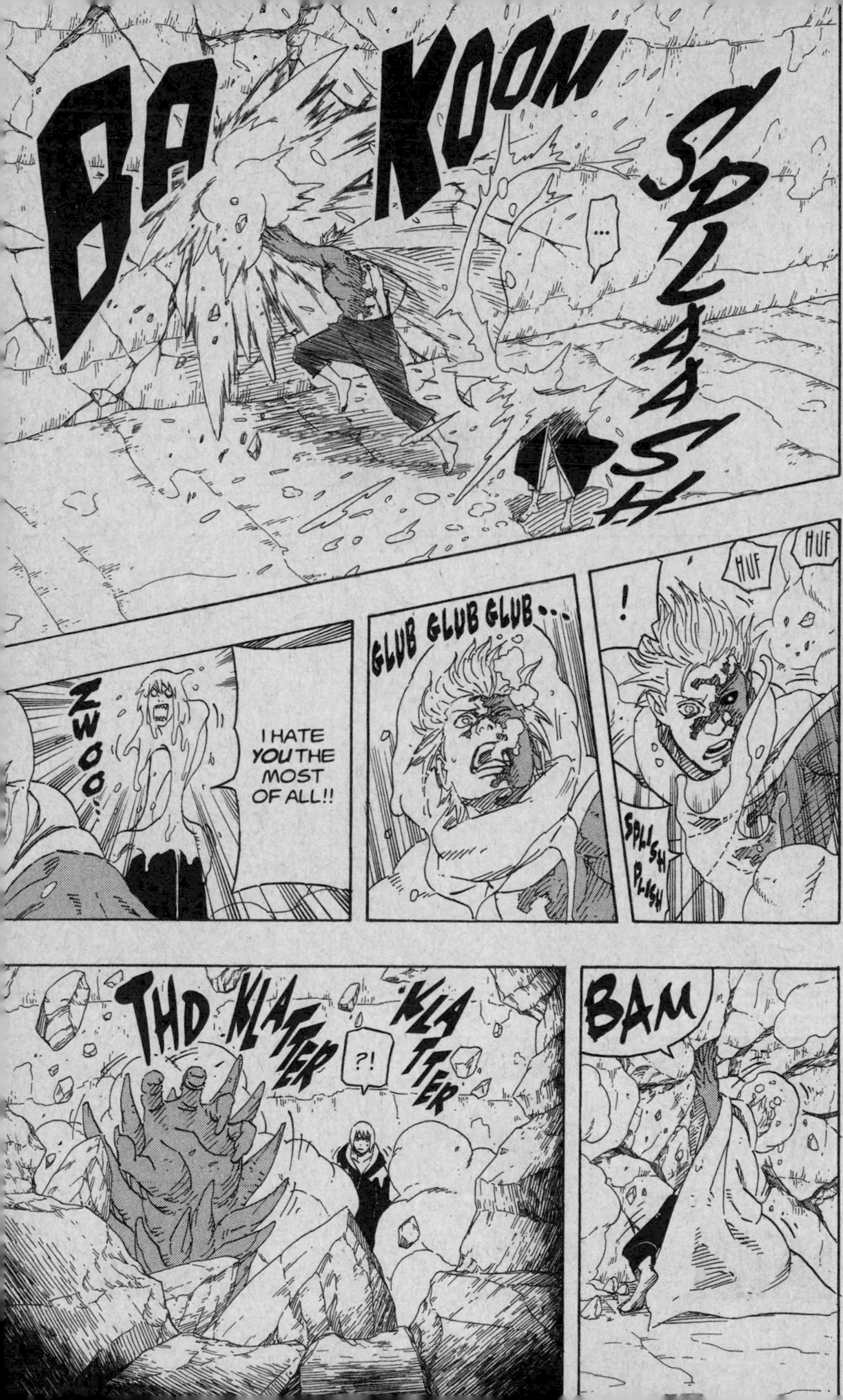
SPLAASH
BA-KOOM
...
HUF
HUF
!
SPLISH PLISH
GLUB GLUB GLUB...
ZWOOO...
I HATE YOU THE MOST OF ALL!!
BAM
KLATTER
?!
KLATTER
THD

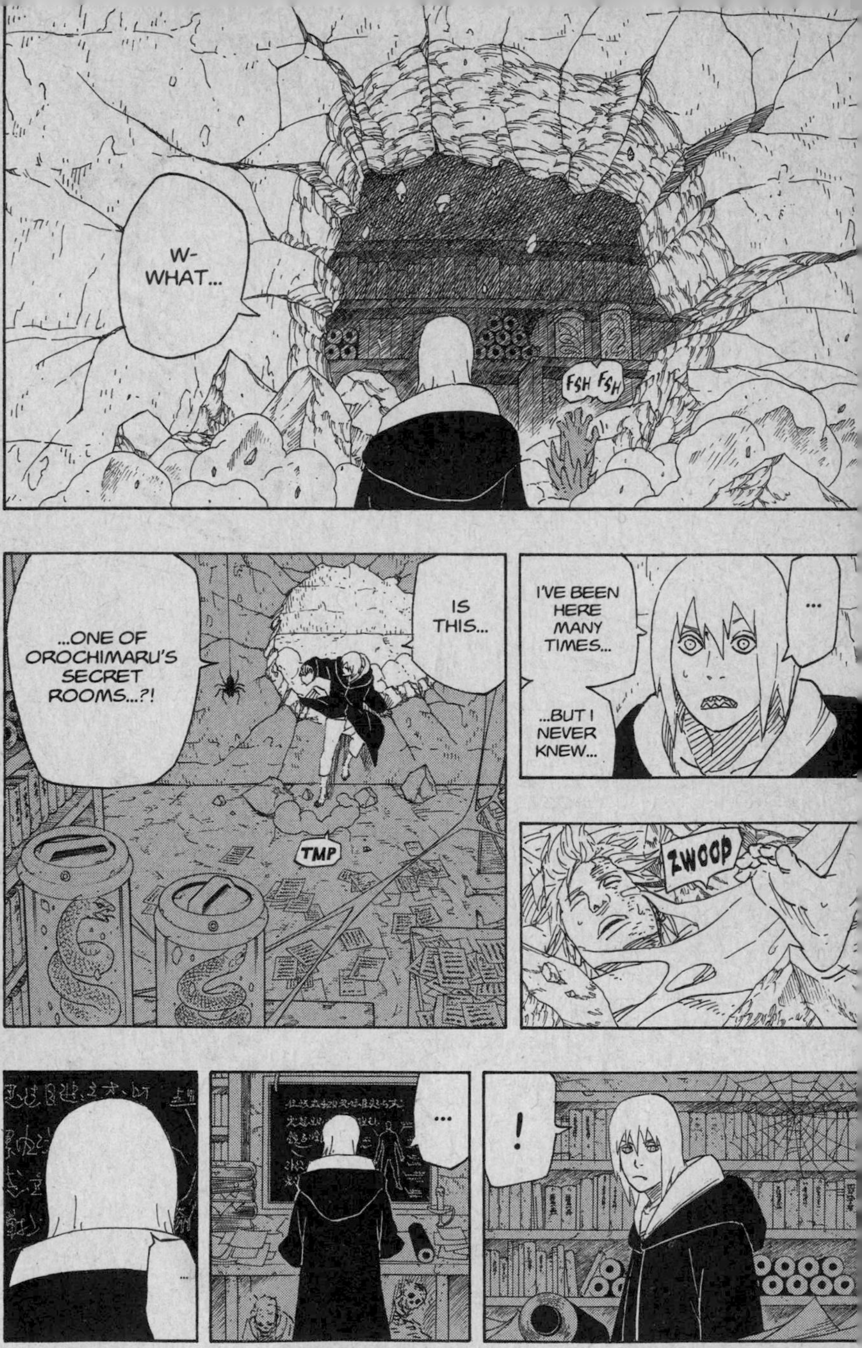
W-
WHAT...
FSH FSH
...
I'VE BEEN HERE MANY TIMES...
...BUT I NEVER KNEW...
ZWOOP
IS THIS...
...ONE OF OROCHIMARU'S SECRET ROOMS...?!
TMP
!
...
...

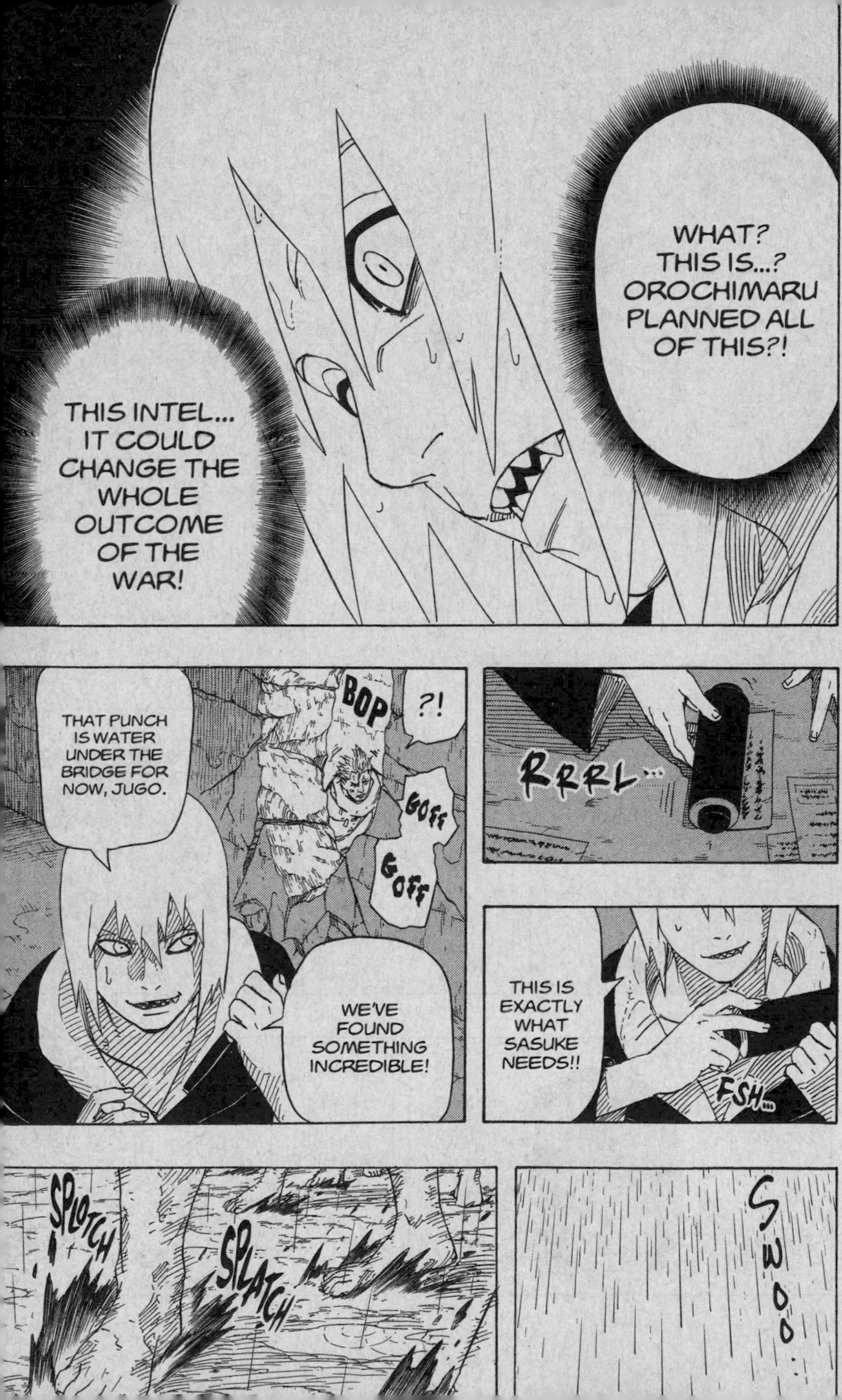
WHAT? THIS IS...? OROCHIMARU PLANNED ALL OF THIS?!
THIS INTEL... IT COULD CHANGE THE WHOLE OUTCOME OF THE WAR!
RRRL...
THIS IS EXACTLY WHAT SASUKE NEEDS!!
FSH...
?!
BOP
GOFF
GOFF
THAT PUNCH IS WATER UNDER THE BRIDGE FOR NOW, JUGO.
WE'VE FOUND SOMETHING INCREDIBLE!
SWOO...
SPLATCH
SPLOTCH

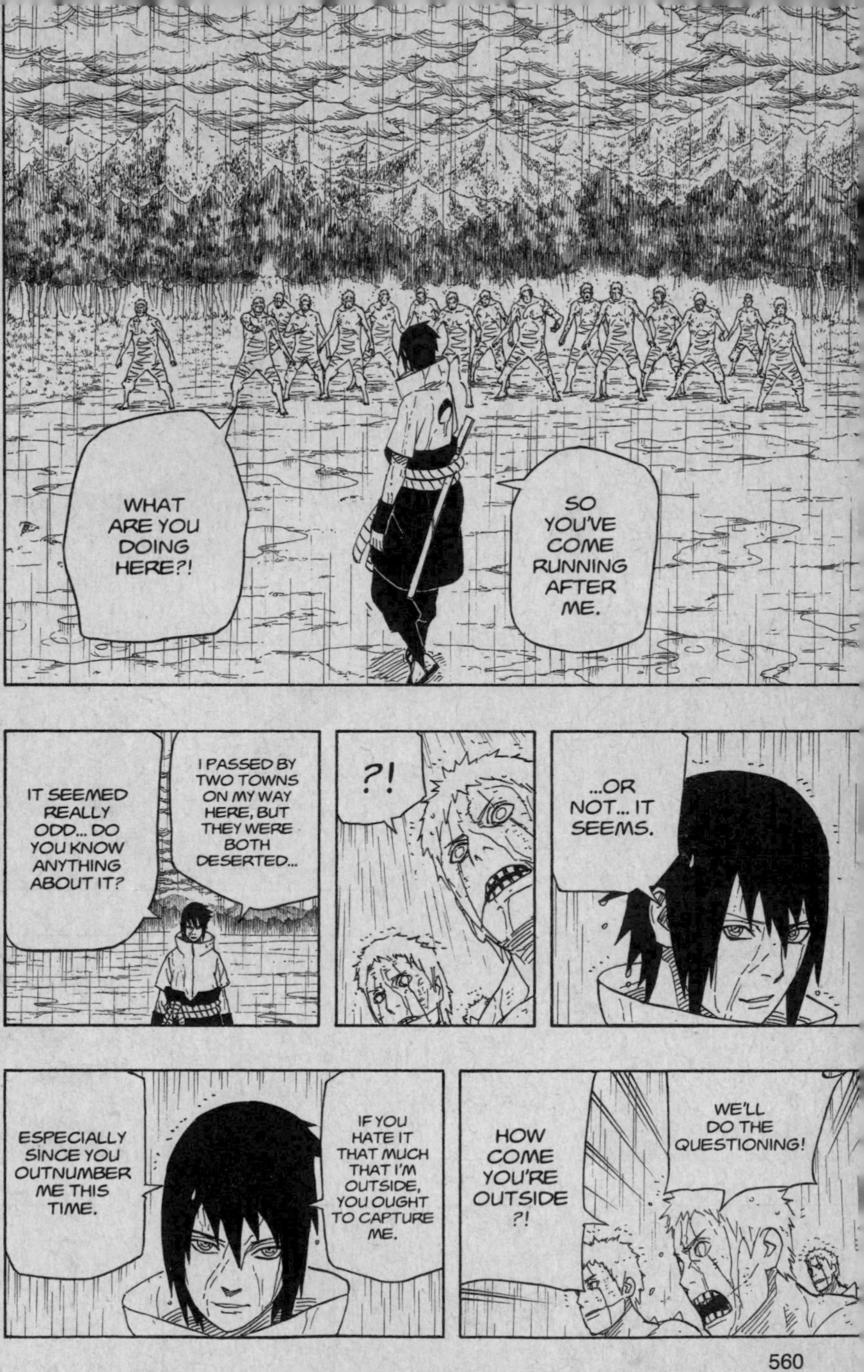
SO YOU'VE COME RUNNING AFTER ME.
WHAT ARE YOU DOING HERE?!
...OR NOT... IT SEEMS.
?!
I PASSED BY TWO TOWNS ON MY WAY HERE, BUT THEY WERE BOTH DESERTED...
IT SEEMED REALLY ODD... DO YOU KNOW ANYTHING ABOUT IT?
WE'LL DO THE QUESTIONING!
HOW COME YOU'RE OUTSIDE ?!
IF YOU HATE IT THAT MUCH THAT I'M OUTSIDE, YOU OUGHT TO CAPTURE ME.
ESPECIALLY SINCE YOU OUTNUMBER ME THIS TIME.

READ THIS WAY

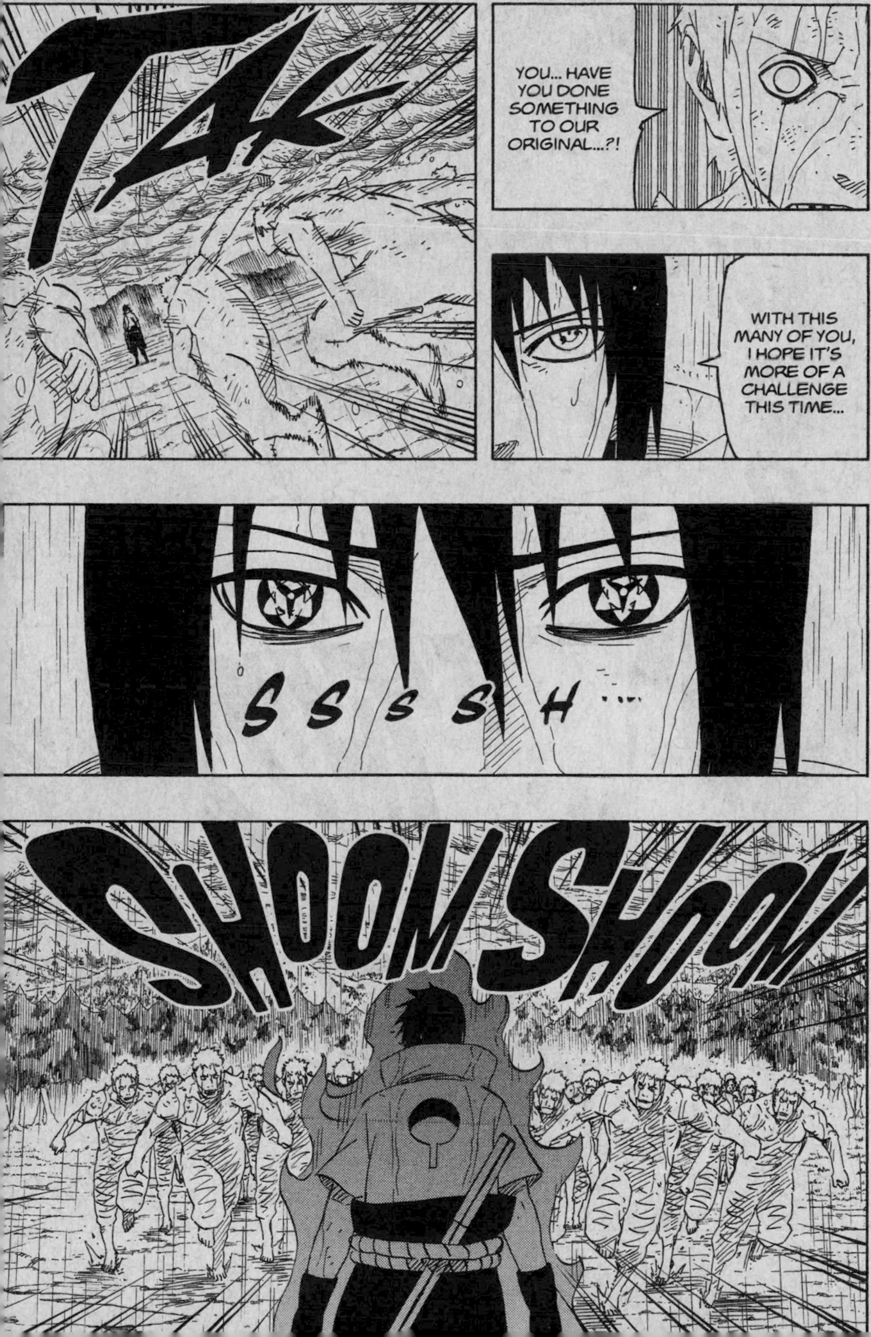
YOU... HAVE YOU DONE SOMETHING TO OUR ORIGINAL...?!
WITH THIS MANY OF YOU, I HOPE IT'S MORE OF A CHALLENGE THIS TIME...
TAK
SSSSH...
SHOOM SHOOM

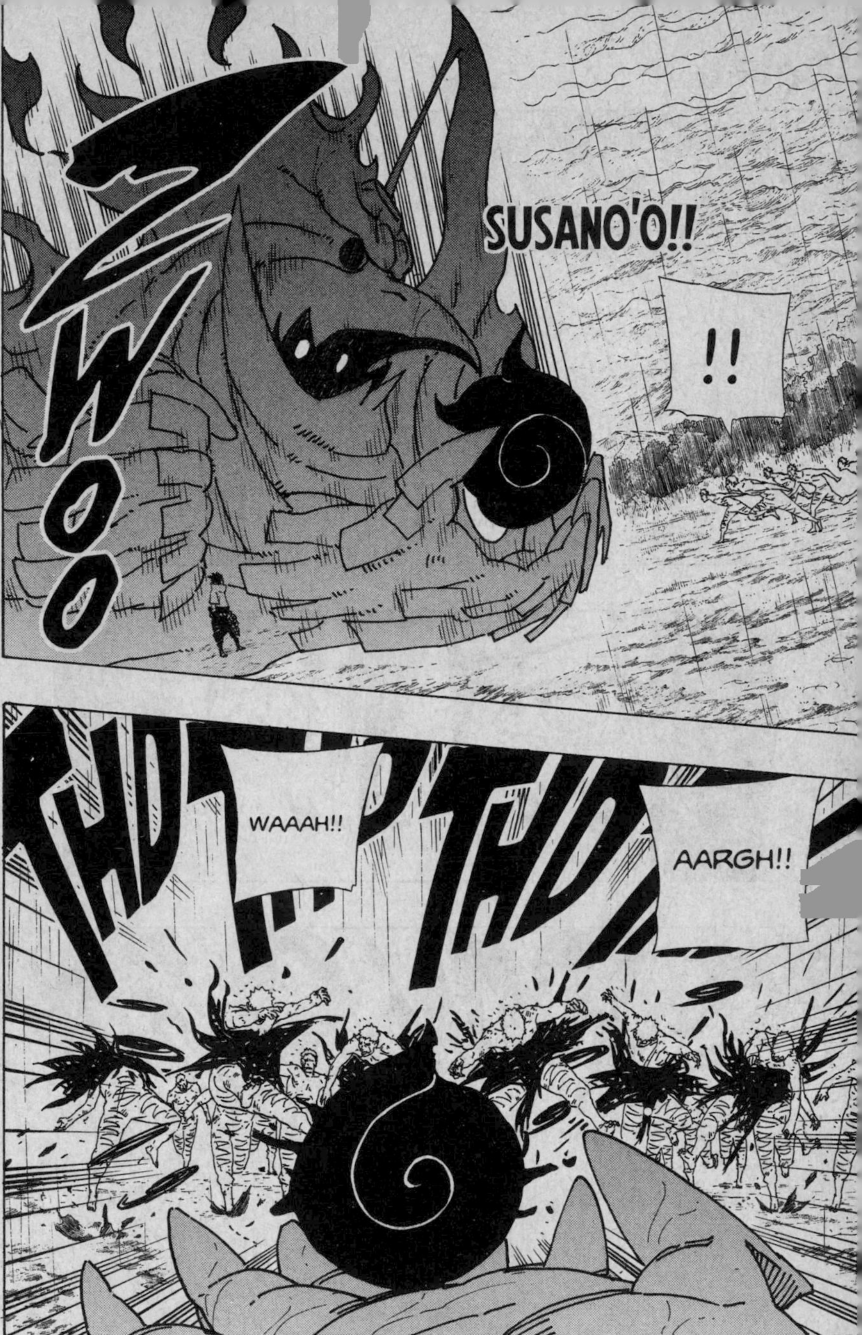
SUSANO'O!!
!!
WOOO
AARGH!!
WAAAH!!

READ THIS WAY

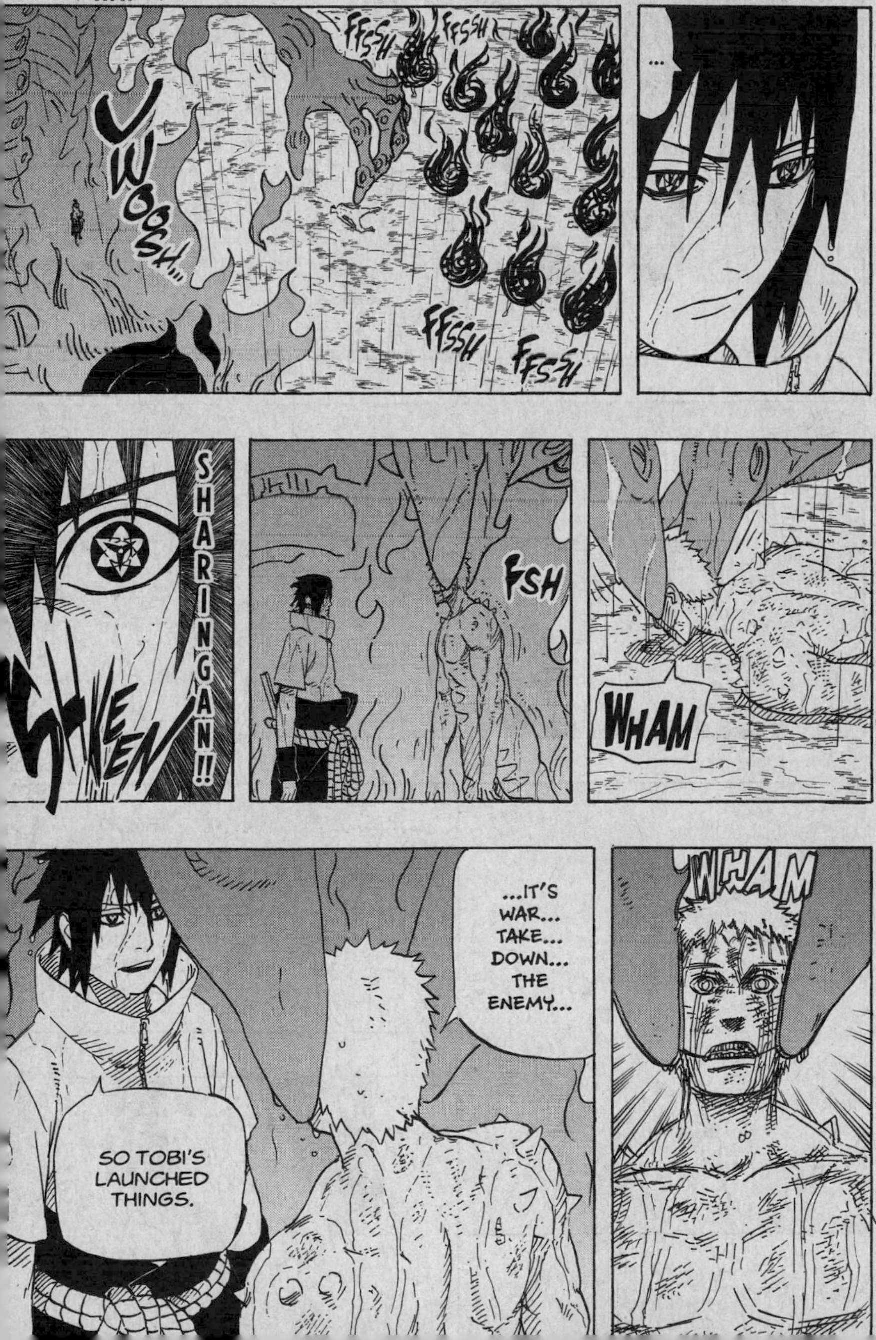
...
JWOOSH...
FFSSH
FFSSH
FFSSH
FFSSH
WHAM
FSH
SHARINGAN!!
SHAKEN
WHAM
...IT'S WAR... TAKE... DOWN... THE ENEMY...
SO TOBI'S LAUNCHED THINGS.

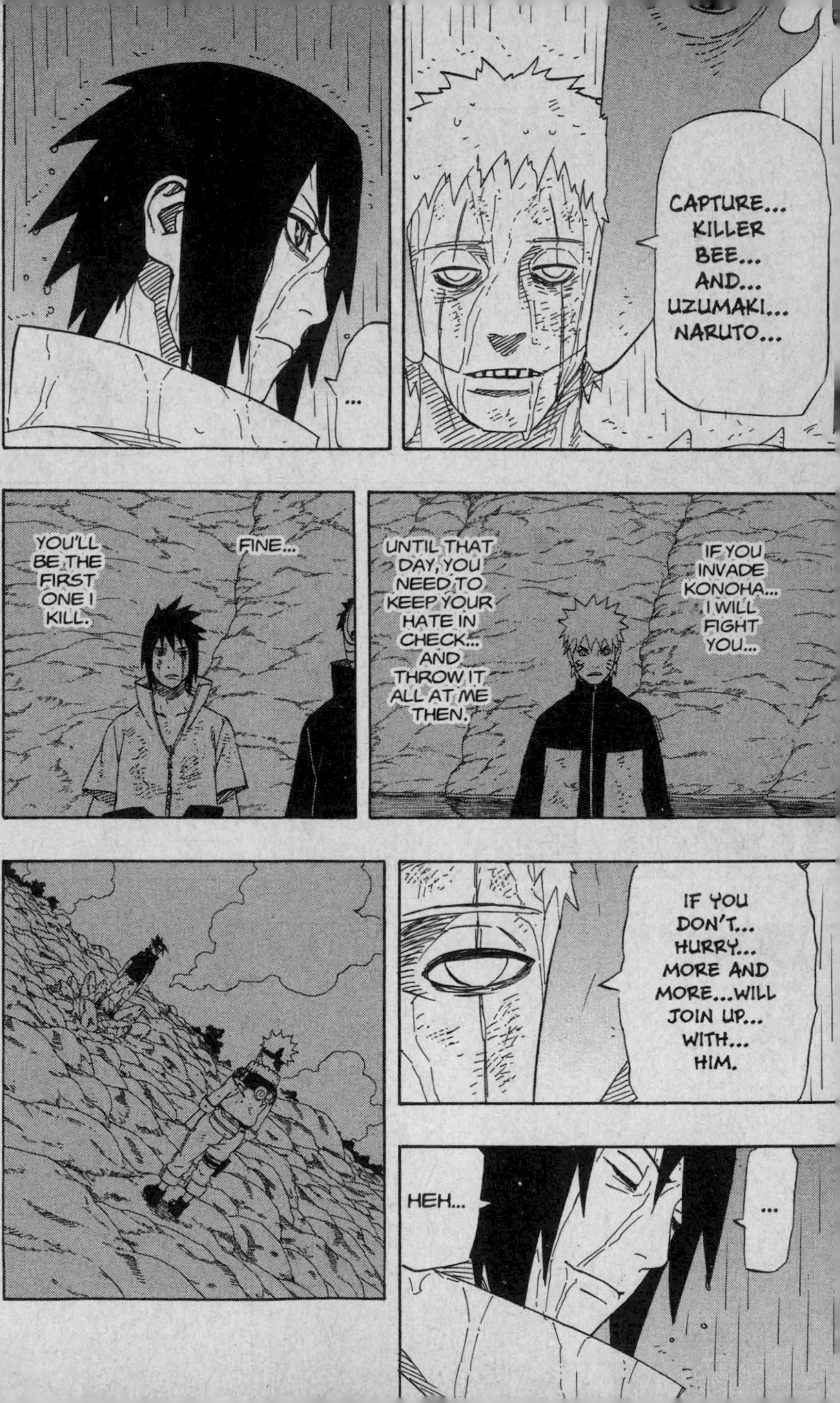
CAPTURE... KILLER BEE... AND... UZUMAKI... NARUTO...
...
IF YOU INVADE KONOHA... I WILL FIGHT YOU...
UNTIL THAT DAY, YOU NEED TO KEEP YOUR HATE IN CHECK... AND THROW IT ALL AT ME THEN.
FINE...
YOU'LL BE THE FIRST ONE I KILL.
IF YOU DON'T... HURRY... MORE AND MORE...WILL JOIN UP... WITH... HIM.
...
HEH...

READ THIS WAY

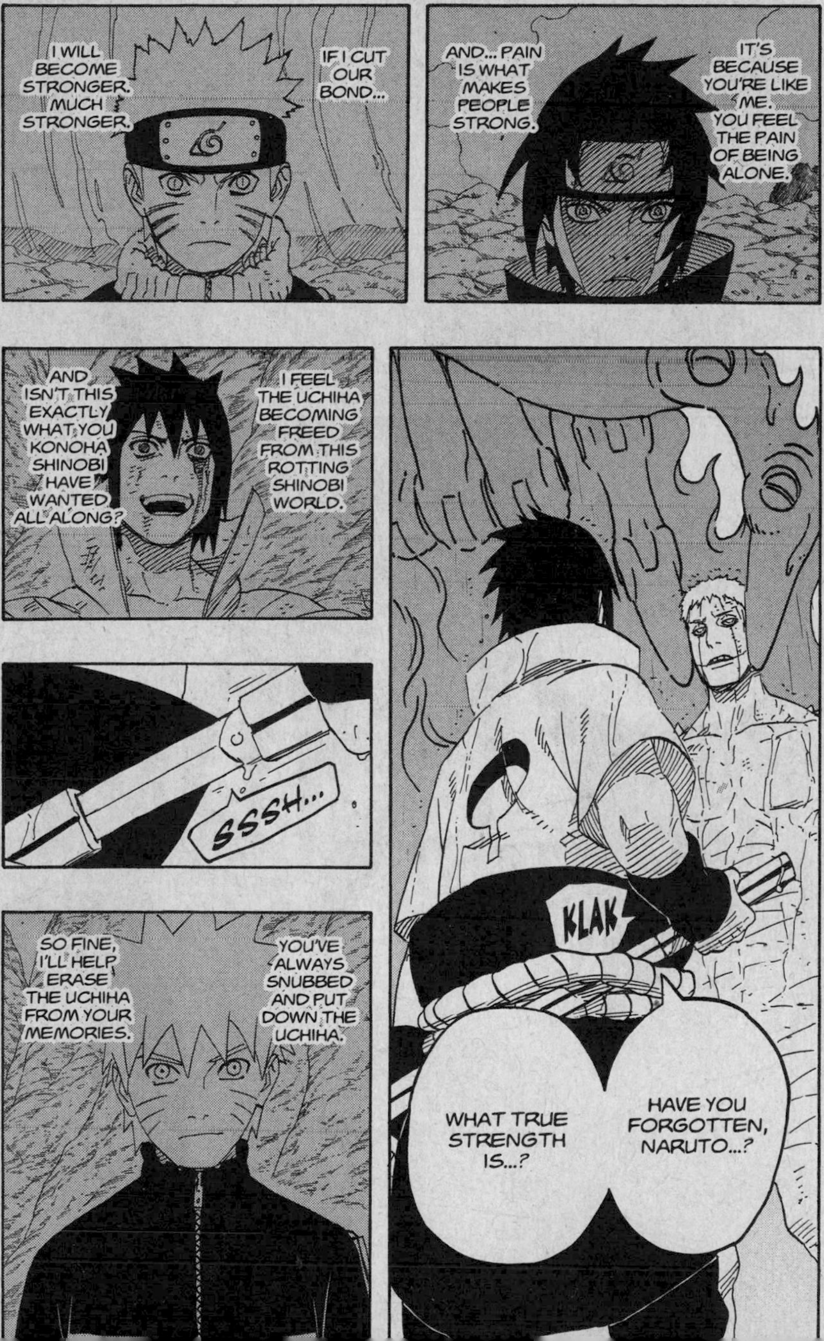
IT'S BECAUSE YOU'RE LIKE ME. YOU FEEL THE PAIN OF BEING ALONE.
AND... PAIN IS WHAT MAKES PEOPLE STRONG.
IF I CUT OUR BOND...
I WILL BECOME STRONGER. MUCH STRONGER.
KLAK
HAVE YOU FORGOTTEN, NARUTO...?
WHAT TRUE STRENGTH IS...?
I FEEL THE UCHIHA BECOMING FREED FROM THIS ROTTING SHINOBI WORLD.
AND ISN'T THIS EXACTLY WHAT YOU KONOHA SHINOBI HAVE WANTED ALL ALONG?
SSSH...
YOU'VE ALWAYS SNUBBED AND PUT DOWN THE UCHIHA.
SO FINE, I'LL HELP ERASE THE UCHIHA FROM YOUR MEMORIES.

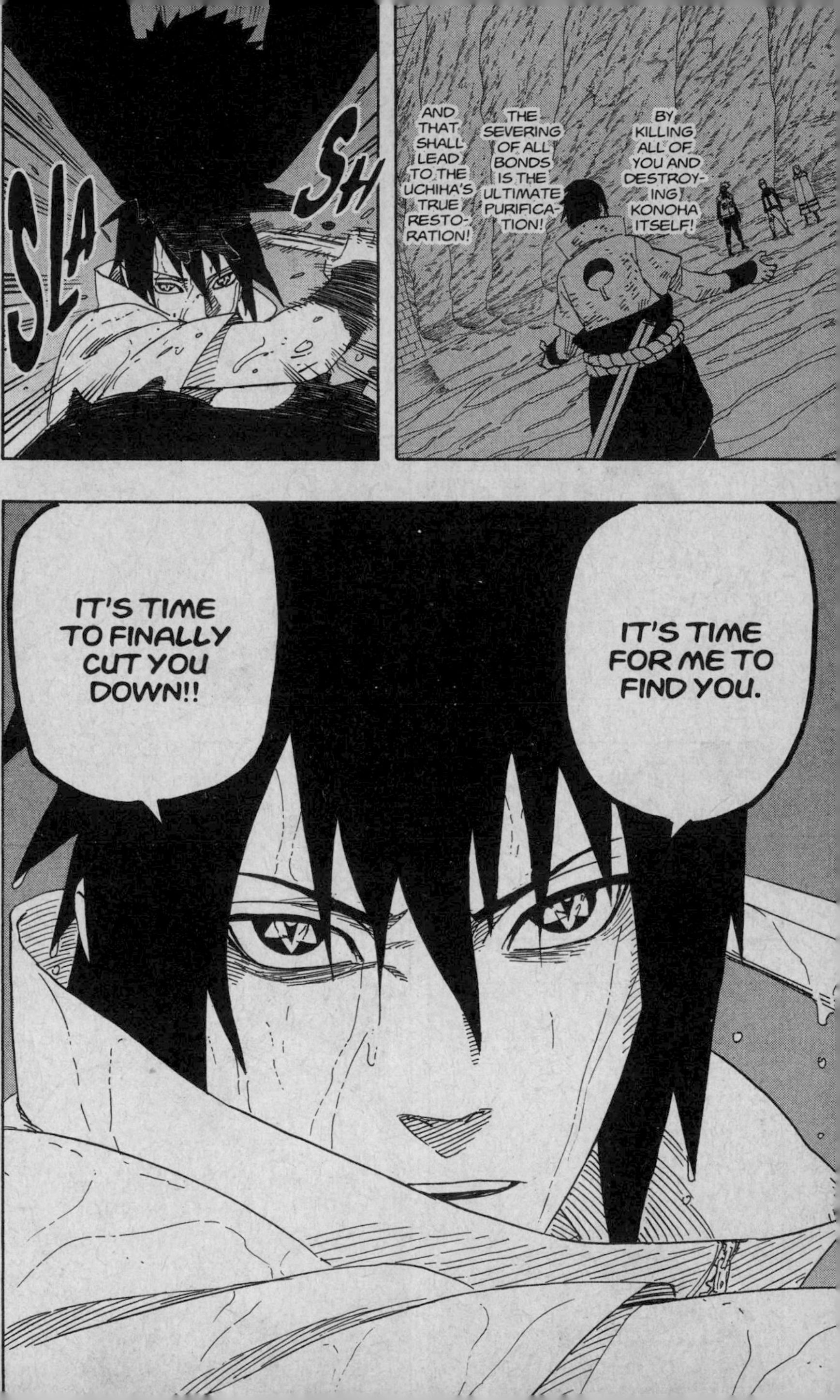
BY KILLING ALL OF YOU AND DESTROYING KONOHA ITSELF!
THE SEVERING OF ALL BONDS IS THE ULTIMATE PURIFICATION!
AND THAT SHALL LEAD TO THE UCHIHA'S TRUE RESTORATION!
SLA
SH
IT'S TIME FOR ME TO FIND YOU.
IT'S TIME TO FINALLY CUT YOU DOWN!!

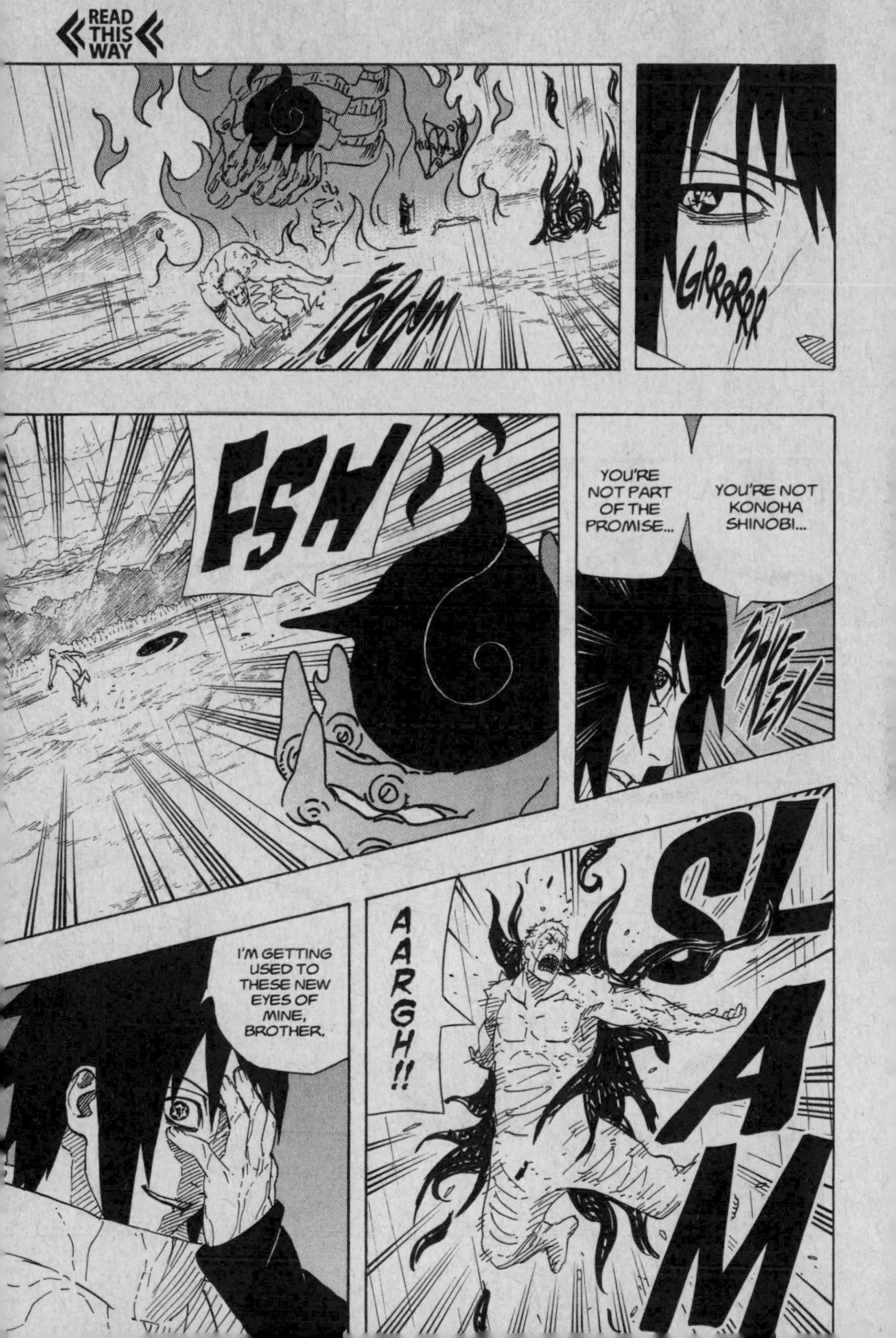
READ THIS WAY
GRRRRRR
FOOOOM
YOU'RE NOT KONOHA SHINOBI...
YOU'RE NOT PART OF THE PROMISE...
SHWEEN
FSH
SLAM
AARGH!!
I'M GETTING USED TO THESE NEW EYES OF MINE, BROTHER.

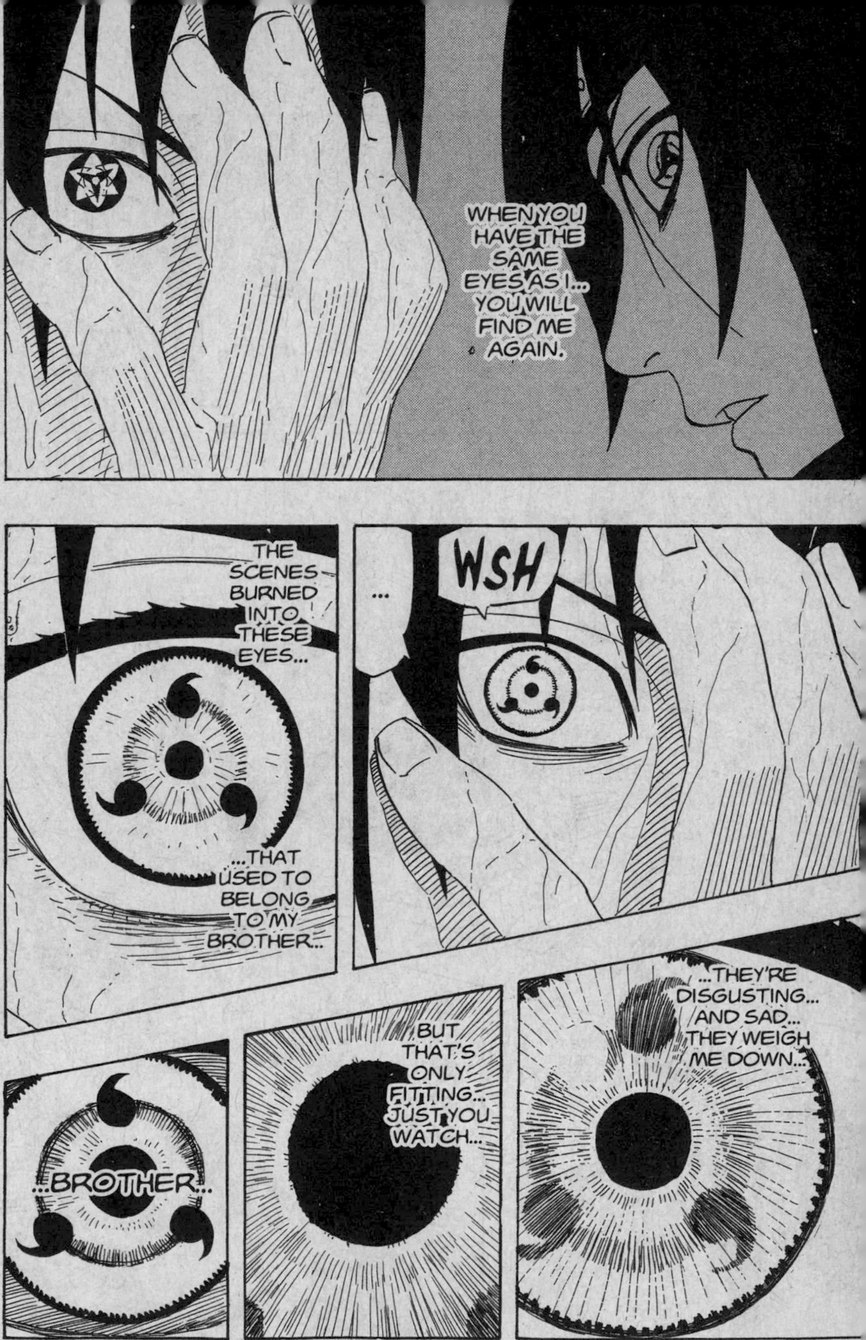
WHEN YOU HAVE THE SAME EYES AS I... YOU WILL FIND ME AGAIN.
WSH
...
THE SCENES BURNED INTO THESE EYES...
...THAT USED TO BELONG TO MY BROTHER...
...THEY'RE DISGUSTING... AND SAD... THEY WEIGH ME DOWN...
BUT THAT'S ONLY FITTING... JUST YOU WATCH...
...BROTHER...

READ THIS WAY

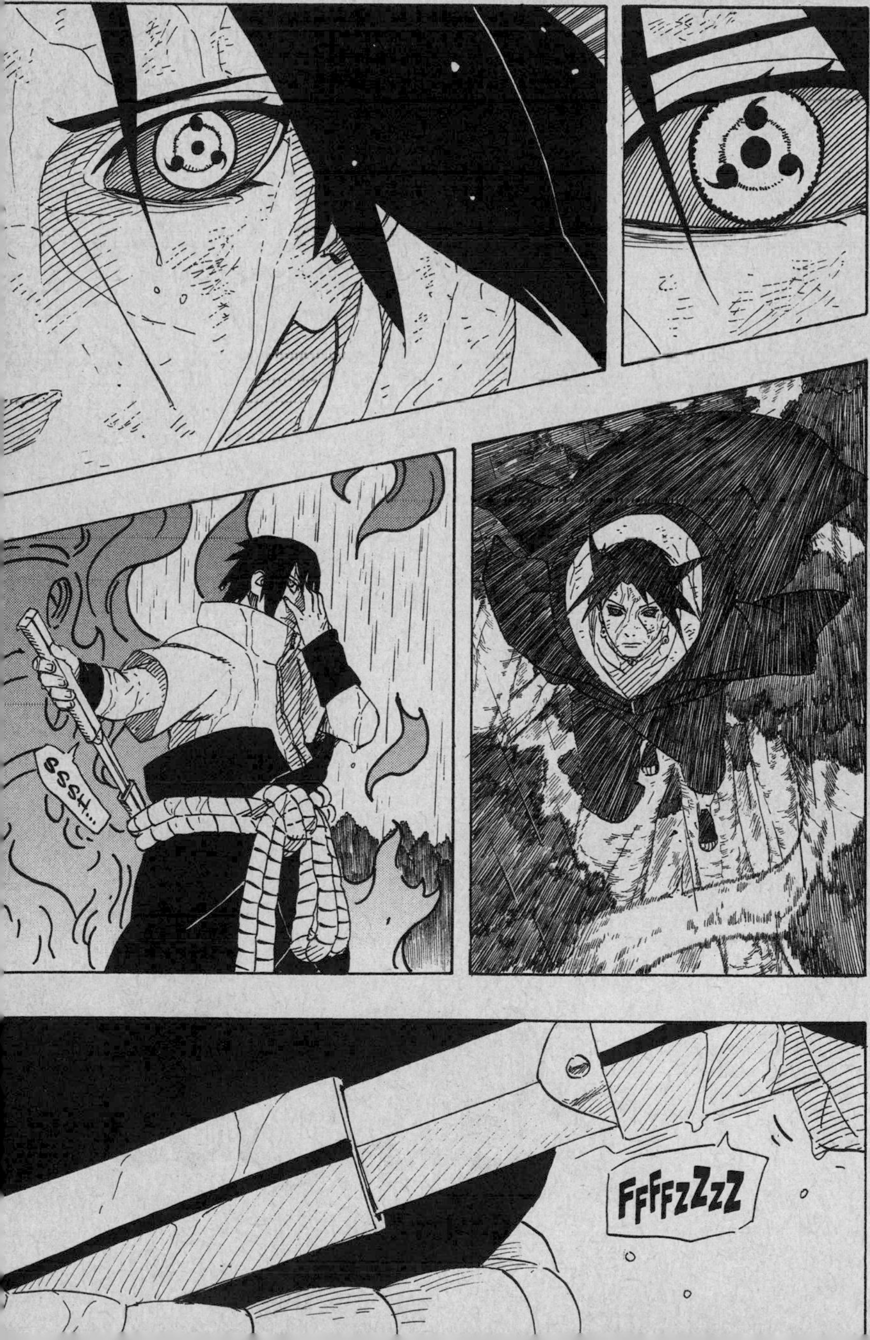
SSSH...
FFFFZZZZ

NARUTO

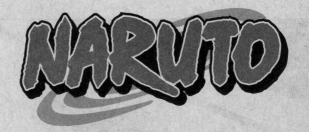

Number 575: A Will of Stone

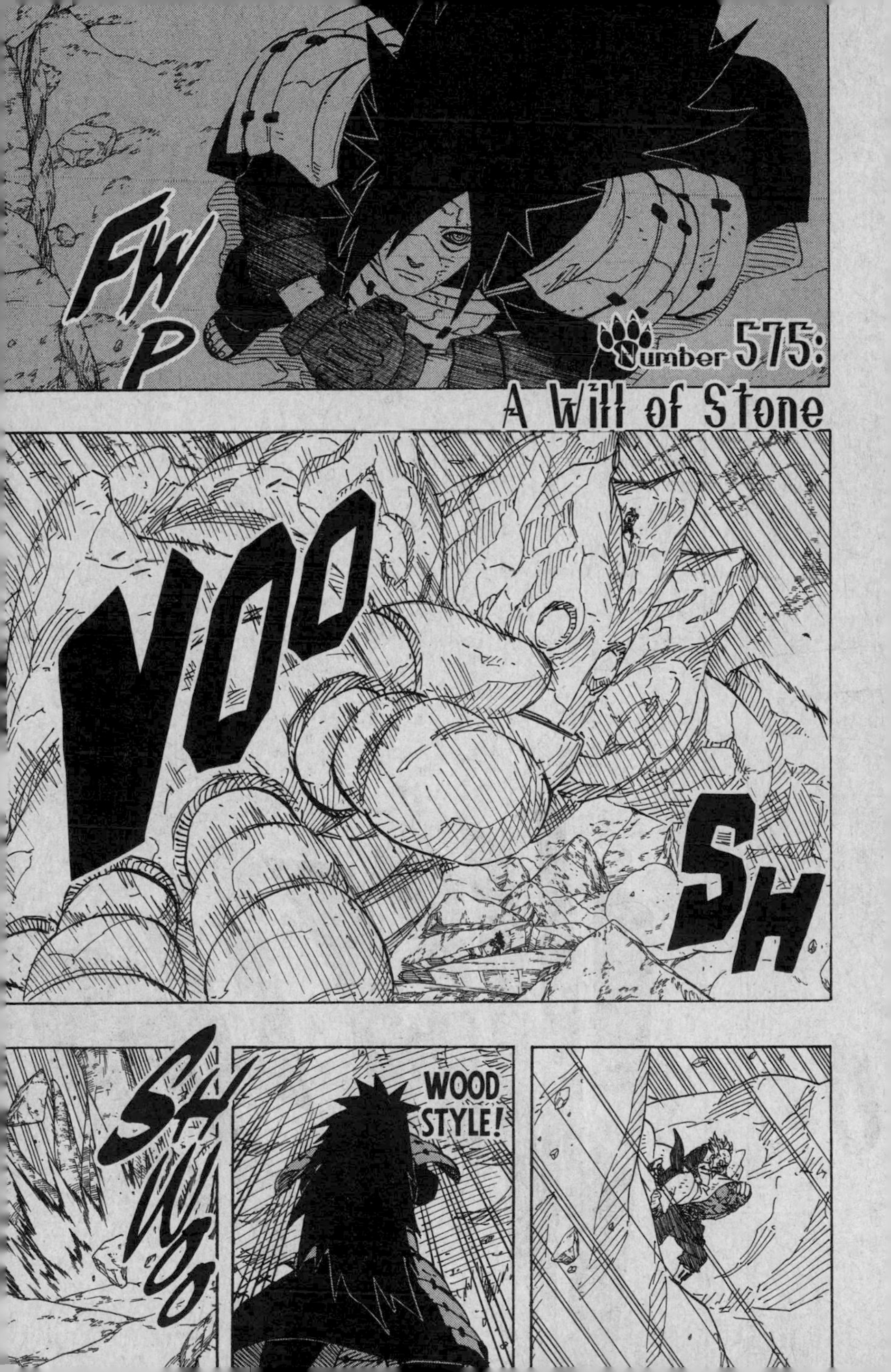
FWP
VOOSH
WOOD STYLE!
SHWOO

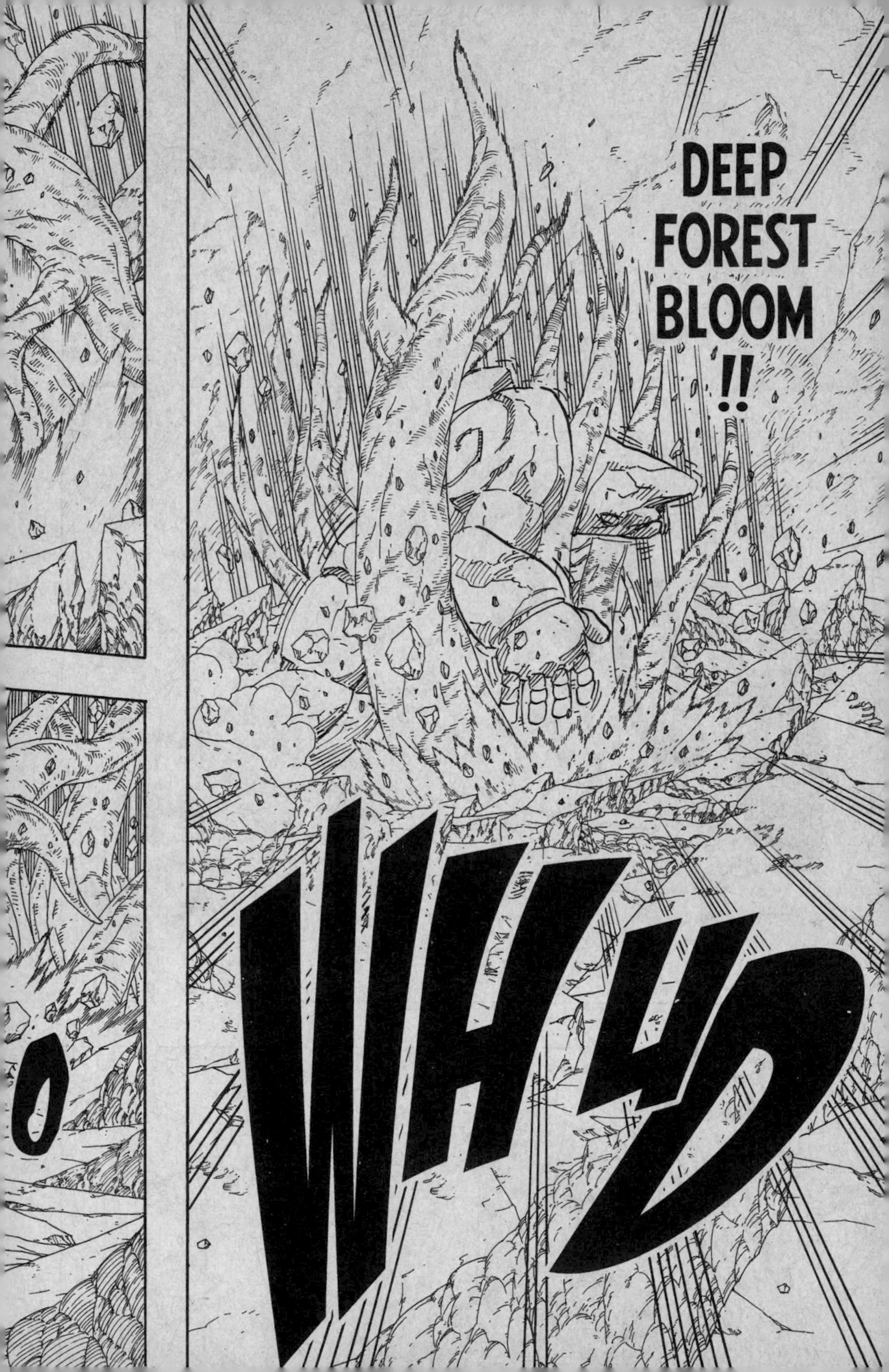
DEEP FOREST BLOOM!!

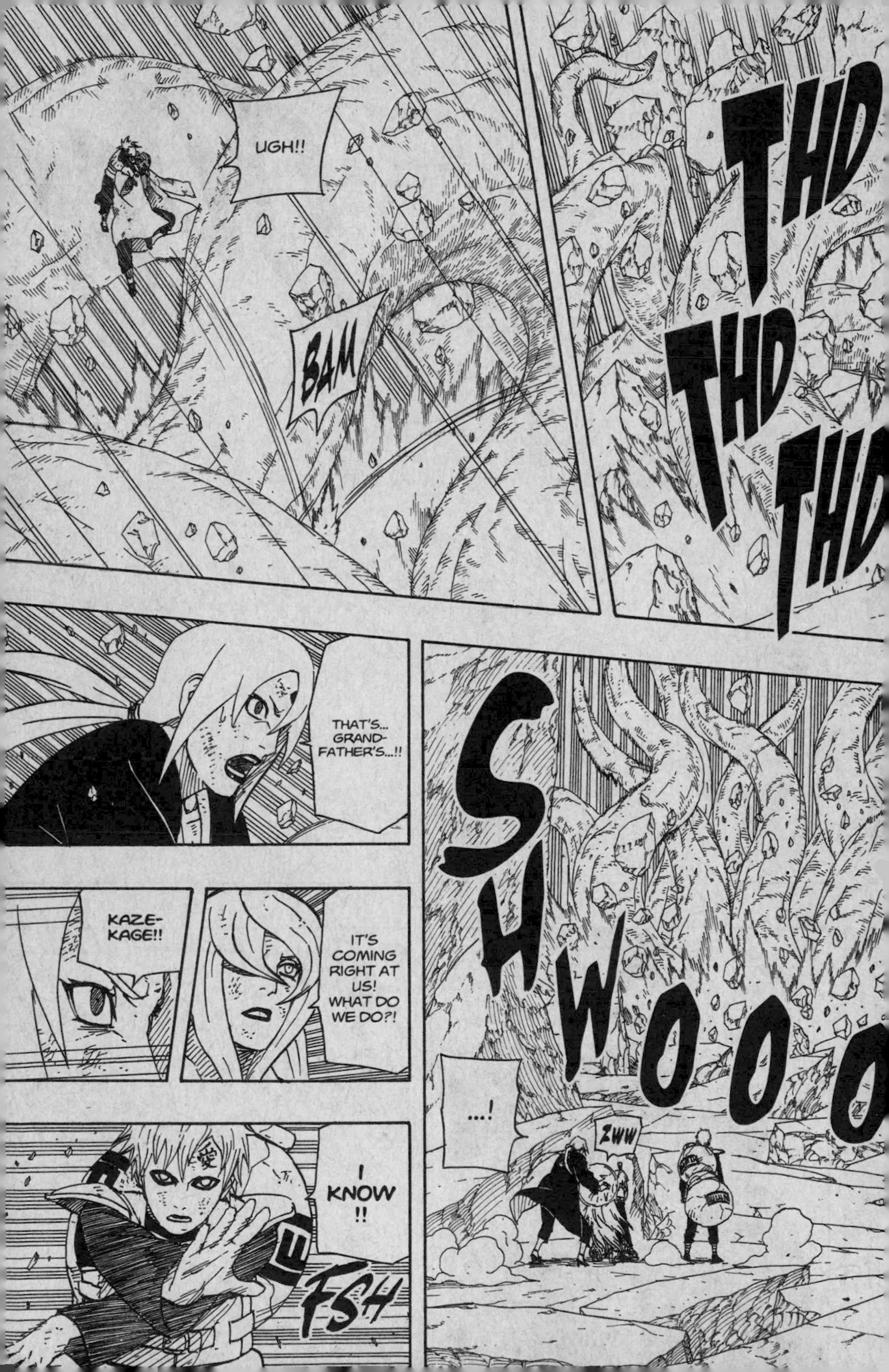
THD
THD
THD
UGH!!
BAM
SHWOOOO
...!
ZWW
THAT'S... GRAND-FATHER'S...!!
IT'S COMING RIGHT AT US! WHAT DO WE DO?!
KAZE-KAGE!!
I KNOW!!
FSH

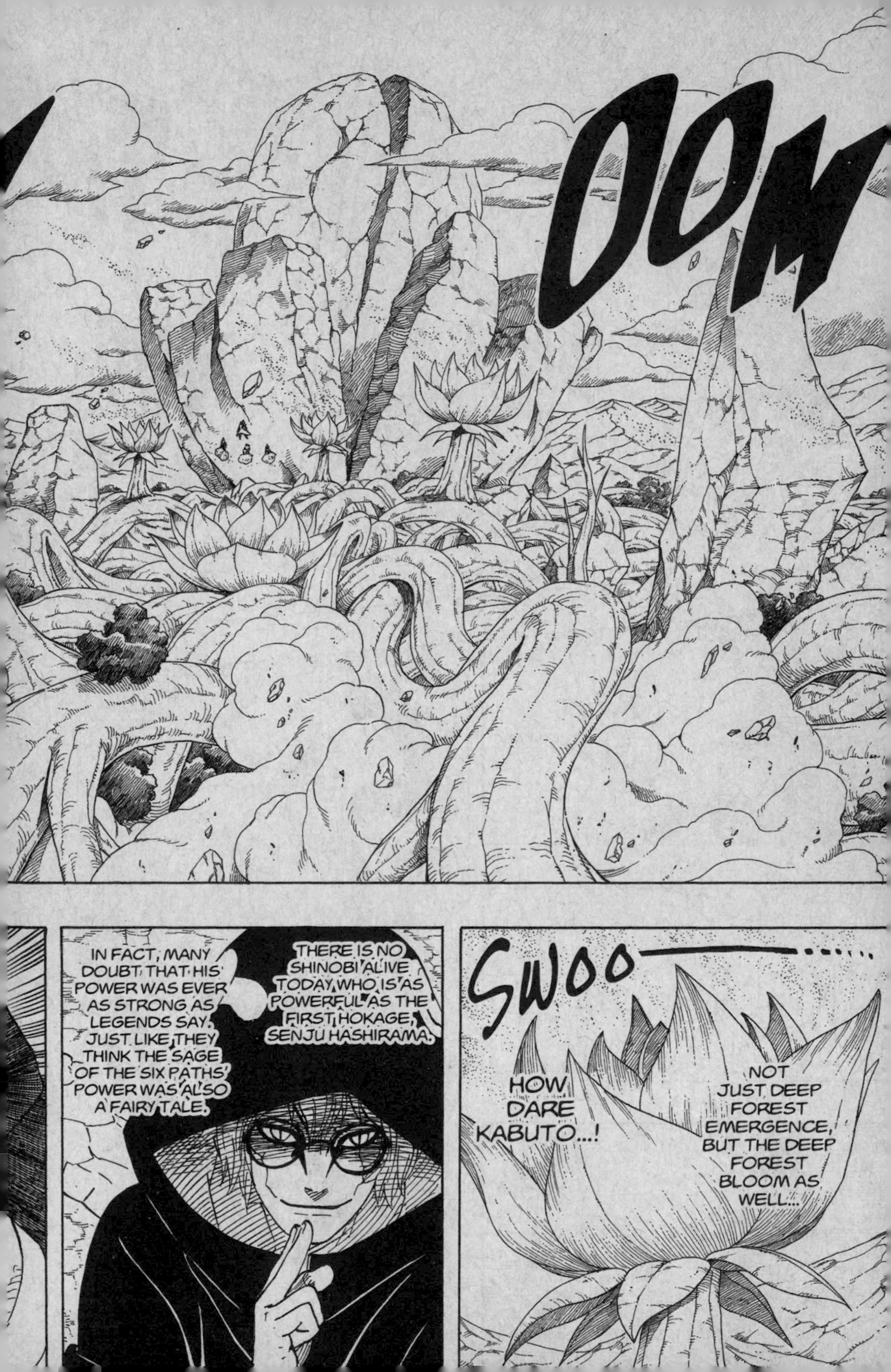
OOM
SWOO——......
NOT JUST DEEP FOREST EMERGENCE, BUT THE DEEP FOREST BLOOM AS WELL...
HOW DARE KABUTO...!
THERE IS NO SHINOBI ALIVE TODAY WHO IS AS POWERFUL AS THE FIRST HOKAGE, SENJU HASHIRAMA.
IN FACT, MANY DOUBT THAT HIS POWER WAS EVER AS STRONG AS LEGENDS SAY. JUST LIKE THEY THINK THE SAGE OF THE SIX PATHS' POWER WAS ALSO A FAIRY TALE.

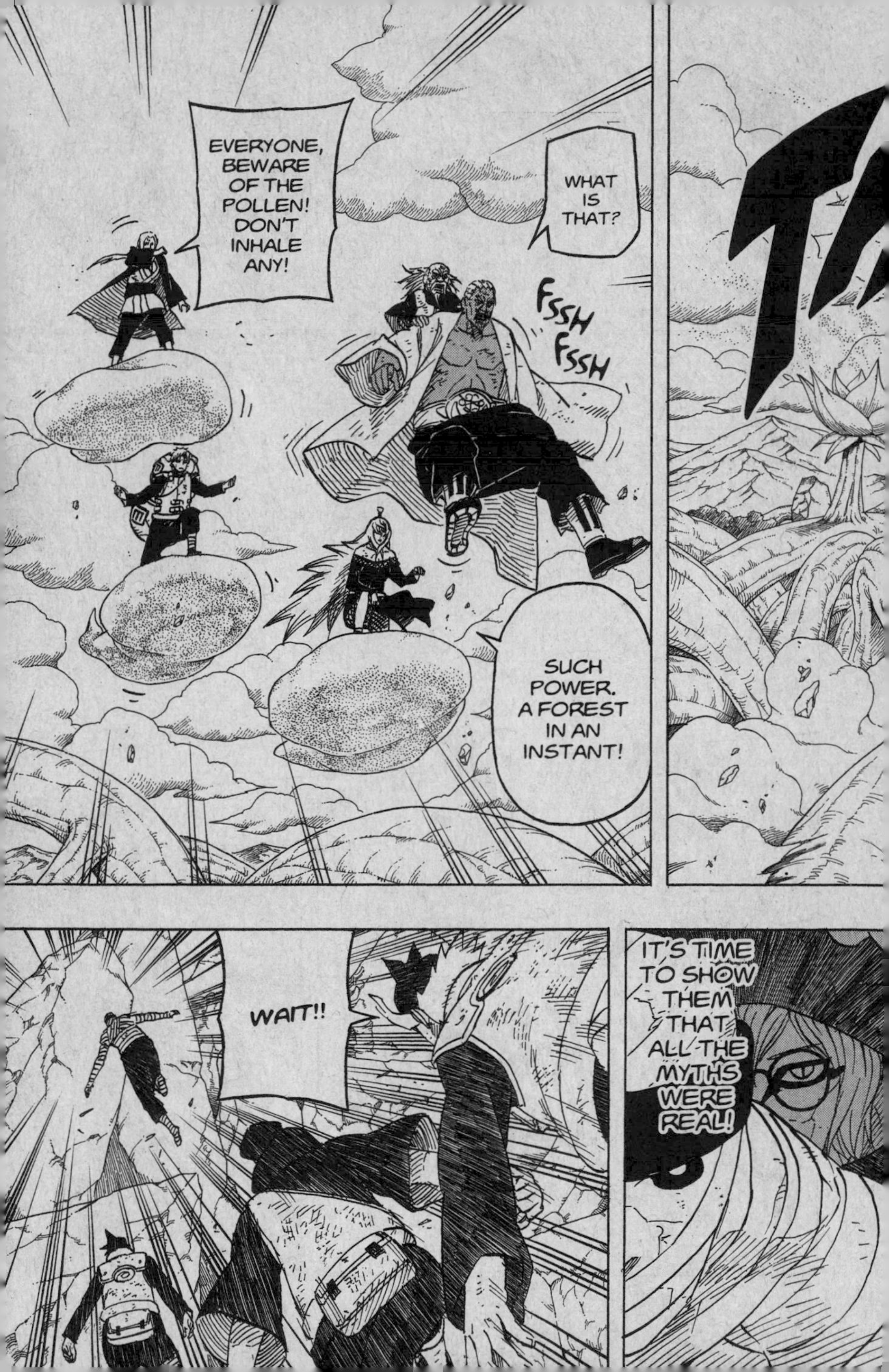
WHAT IS THAT?
EVERYONE, BEWARE OF THE POLLEN! DON'T INHALE ANY!
FSSH FSSH
SUCH POWER. A FOREST IN AN INSTANT!
IT'S TIME TO SHOW THEM THAT ALL THE MYTHS WERE REAL!
WAIT!!

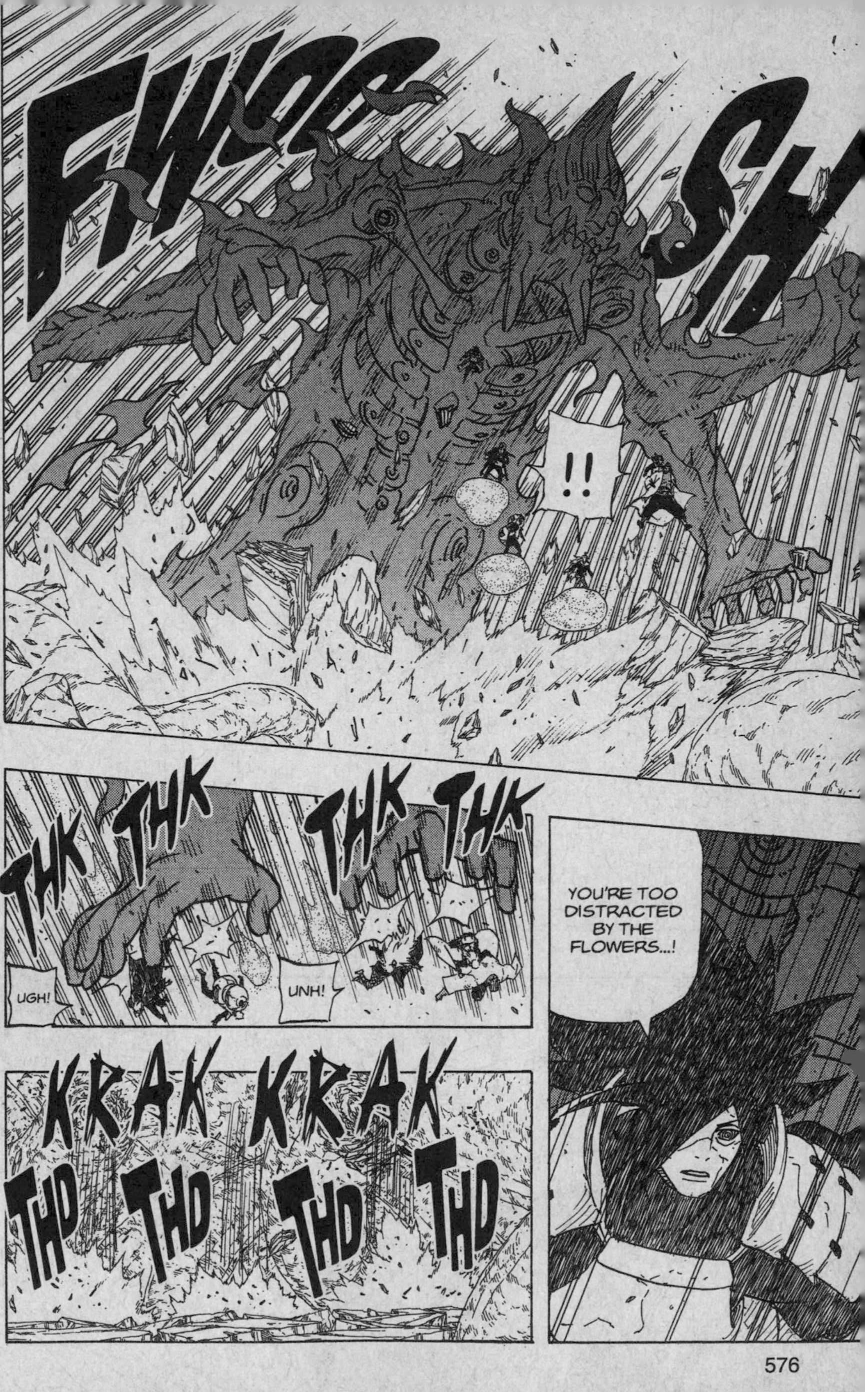
FWOOSH
!!
YOU'RE TOO DISTRACTED BY THE FLOWERS...!
THK THK THK THK
UGH!
UNH!
KRAK KRAK
THD THD THD THD

READ THIS WAY

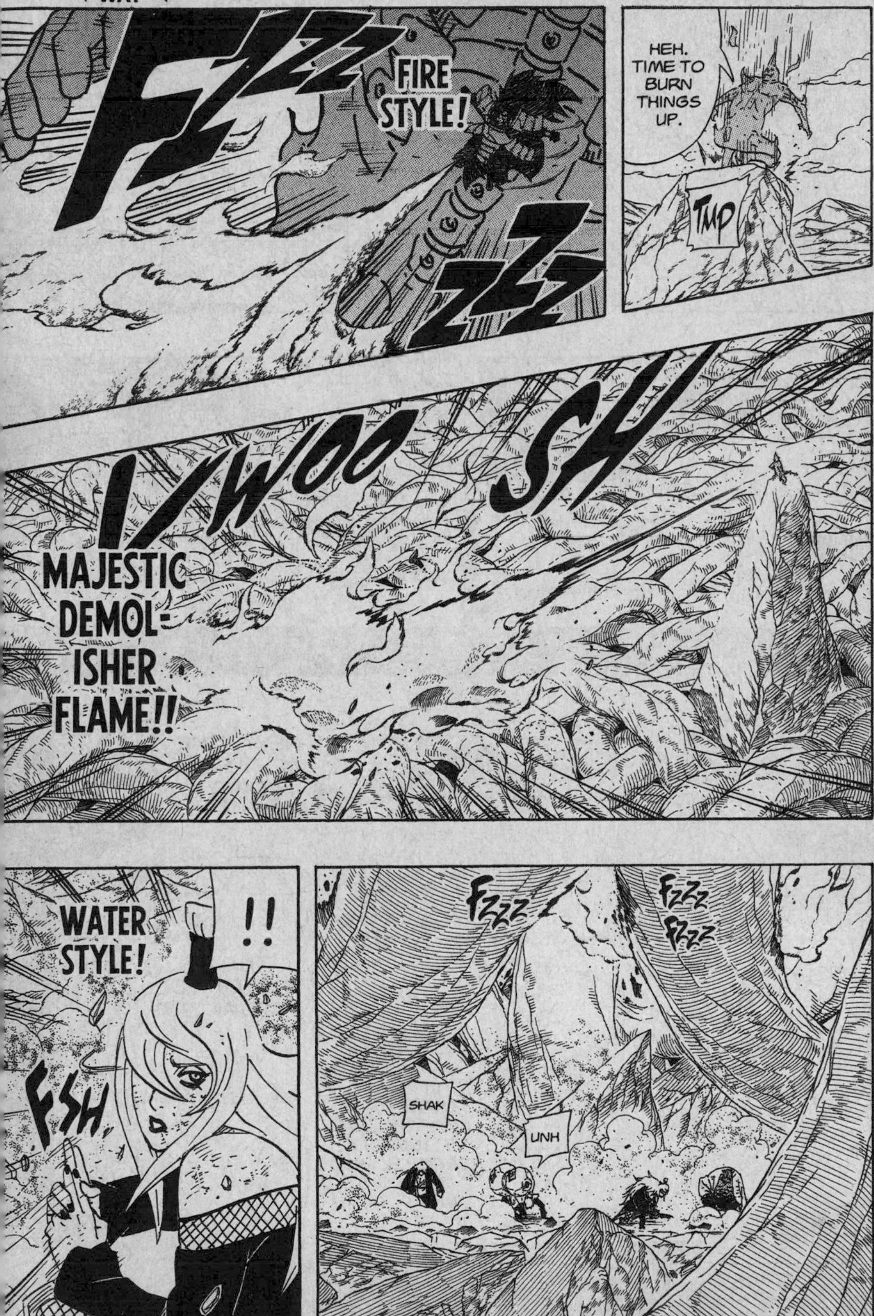
HEH. TIME TO BURN THINGS UP.
TMP
FZZZ
FIRE STYLE!
ZZZ
VWOOSH
MAJESTIC DEMOL-ISHER FLAME!!
FZZZ
FZZZ FZZZ
SHAK
UNH
!!
WATER STYLE!
FSH

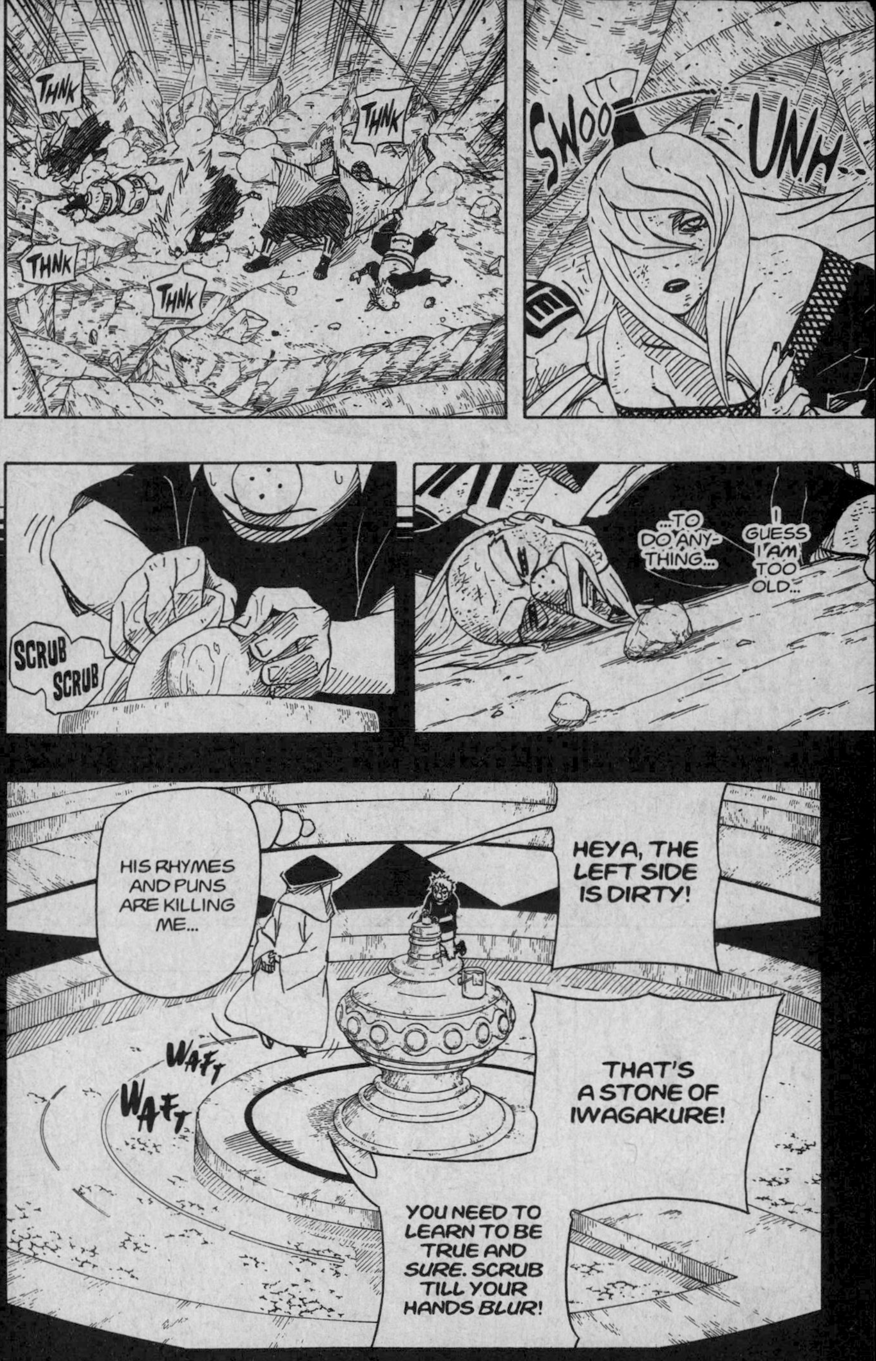
SWOO
UNH...
THNK
THNK
THNK
THNK
I GUESS I AM TOO OLD...
...TO DO ANYTHING...
SCRUB SCRUB
HEYA, THE LEFT SIDE IS DIRTY!
HIS RHYMES AND PUNS ARE KILLING ME...
THAT'S A STONE OF IWAGAKURE!
WAFT WAFT
YOU NEED TO LEARN TO BE TRUE AND SURE. SCRUB TILL YOUR HANDS BLUR!

READ THIS WAY

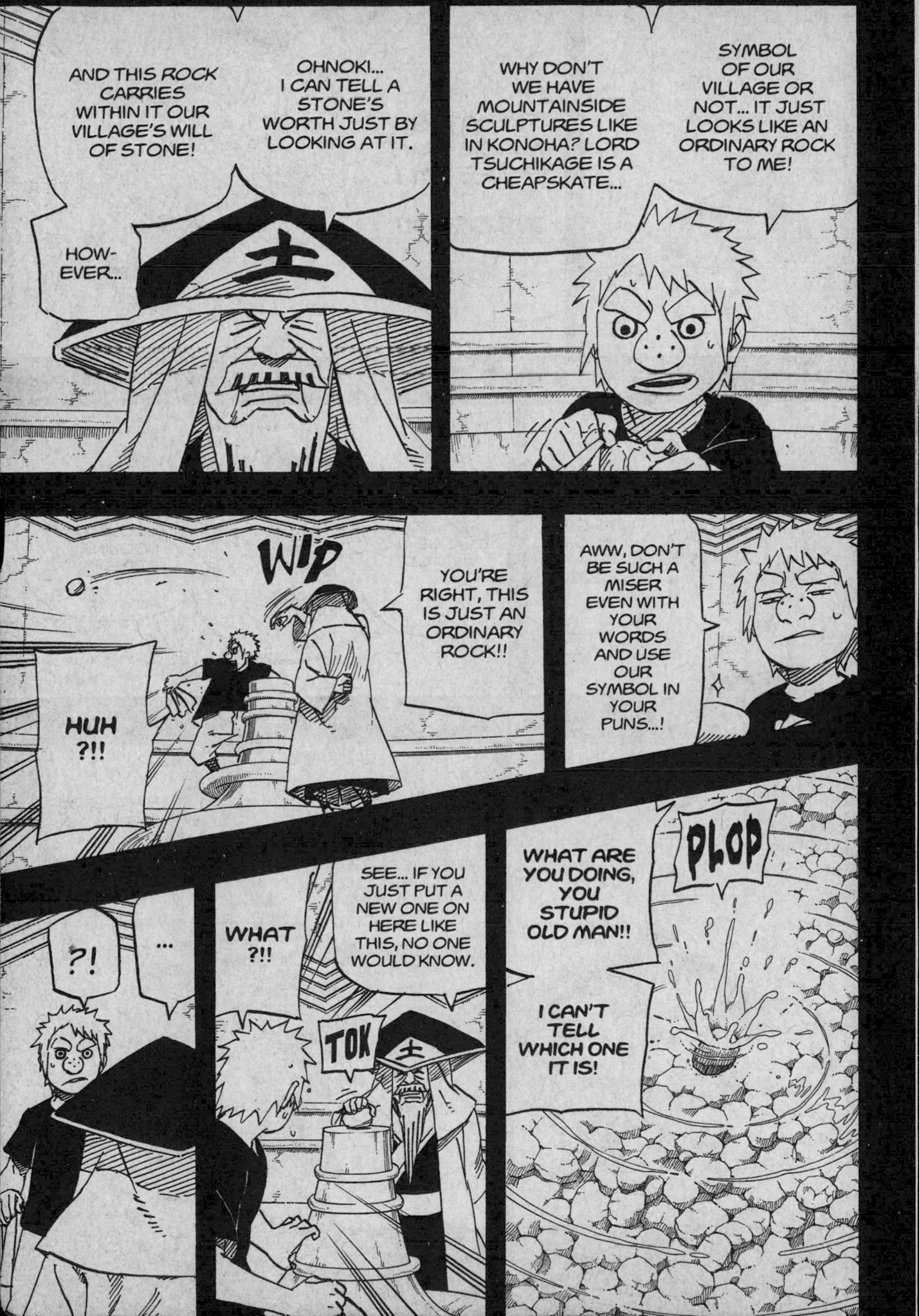
SYMBOL OF OUR VILLAGE OR NOT... IT JUST LOOKS LIKE AN ORDINARY ROCK TO ME!
WHY DON'T WE HAVE MOUNTAINSIDE SCULPTURES LIKE IN KONOHA? LORD TSUCHIKAGE IS A CHEAPSKATE...
OHNOKI... I CAN TELL A STONE'S WORTH JUST BY LOOKING AT IT.
AND THIS ROCK CARRIES WITHIN IT OUR VILLAGE'S WILL OF STONE!
HOW-EVER..
AWW, DON'T BE SUCH A MISER EVEN WITH YOUR WORDS AND USE OUR SYMBOL IN YOUR PUNS...!
WIP
YOU'RE RIGHT, THIS IS JUST AN ORDINARY ROCK!!
HUH ?!!
PLOP
WHAT ARE YOU DOING, YOU STUPID OLD MAN!!
I CAN'T TELL WHICH ONE IT IS!
SEE... IF YOU JUST PUT A NEW ONE ON HERE LIKE THIS, NO ONE WOULD KNOW.
WHAT ?!!
TOK
...
?!

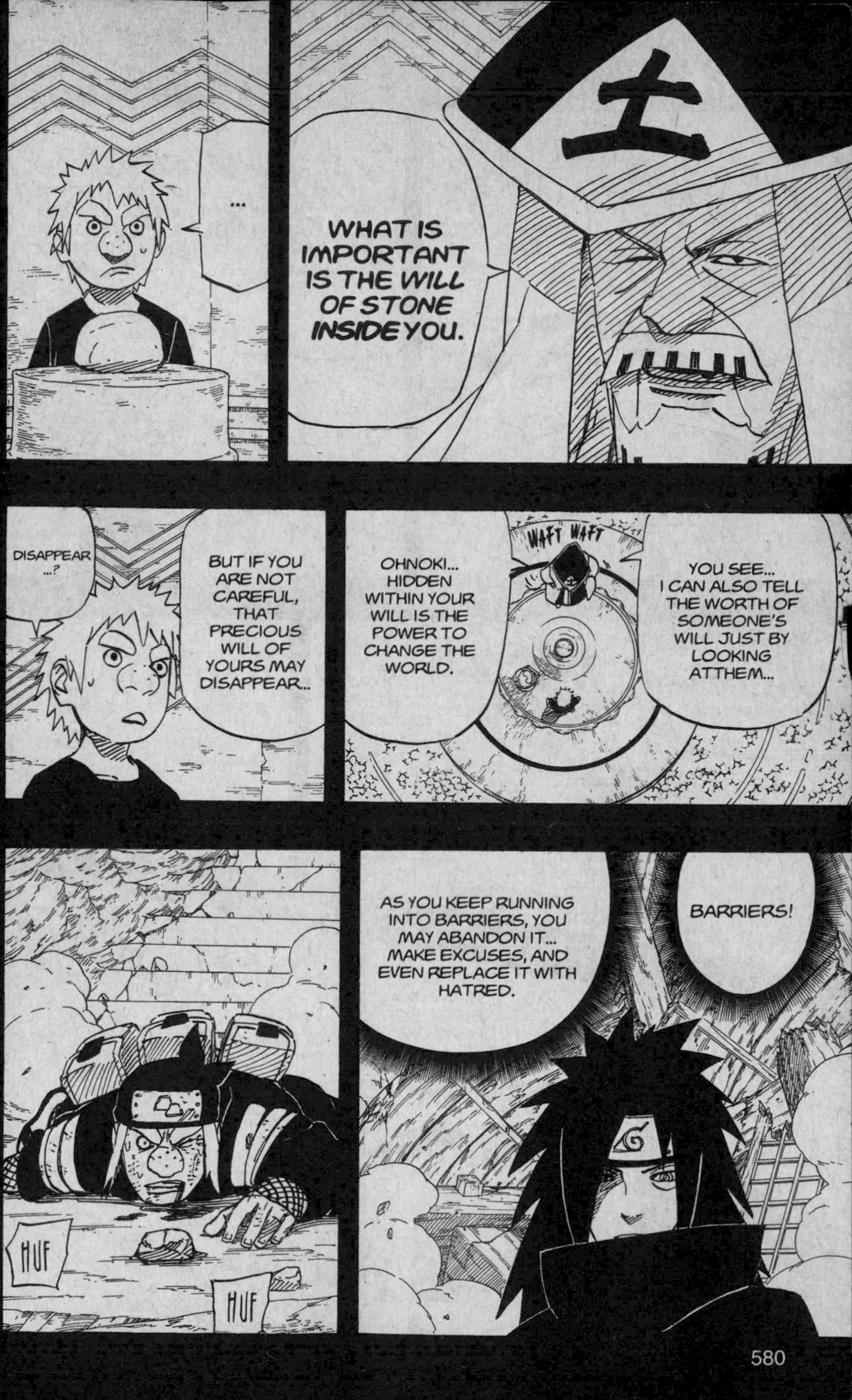
WHAT IS IMPORTANT IS THE WILL OF STONE INSIDE YOU.
...
YOU SEE... I CAN ALSO TELL THE WORTH OF SOMEONE'S WILL JUST BY LOOKING ATTHEM...
WAFT WAFT
OHNOKI... HIDDEN WITHIN YOUR WILL IS THE POWER TO CHANGE THE WORLD.
BUT IF YOU ARE NOT CAREFUL, THAT PRECIOUS WILL OF YOURS MAY DISAPPEAR..
DISAPPEAR ...?
BARRIERS!
AS YOU KEEP RUNNING INTO BARRIERS, YOU MAY ABANDON IT... MAKE EXCUSES, AND EVEN REPLACE IT WITH HATRED.
HUF
HUF

READ THIS WAY

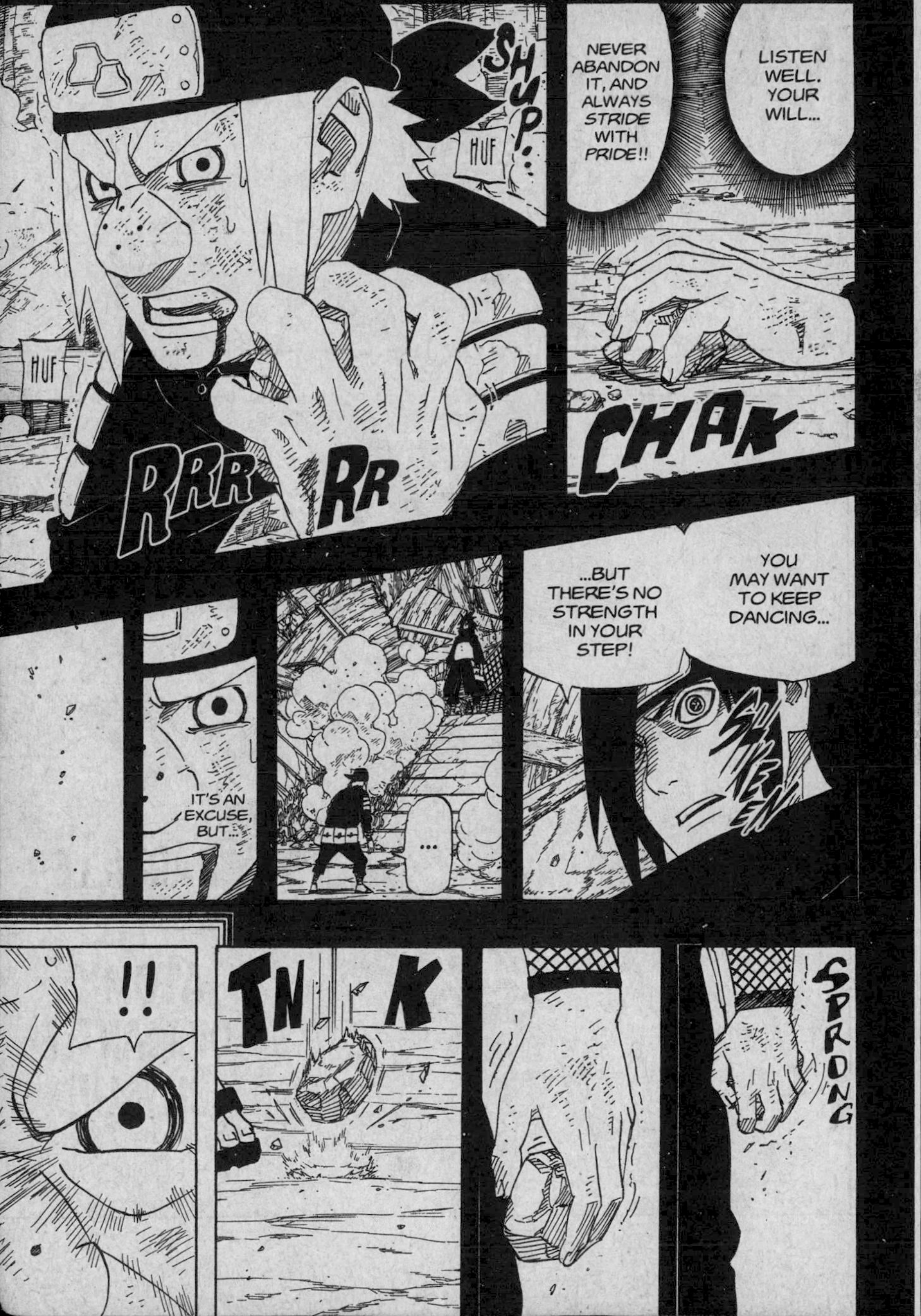
LISTEN WELL. YOUR WILL...
NEVER ABANDON IT, AND ALWAYS STRIDE WITH PRIDE!!
CHAN
SHUP...
HUF
HUF
RRR
RR
YOU MAY WANT TO KEEP DANCING...
...BUT THERE'S NO STRENGTH IN YOUR STEP!
...
IT'S AN EXCUSE, BUT...
SPRONG
TNK
!!

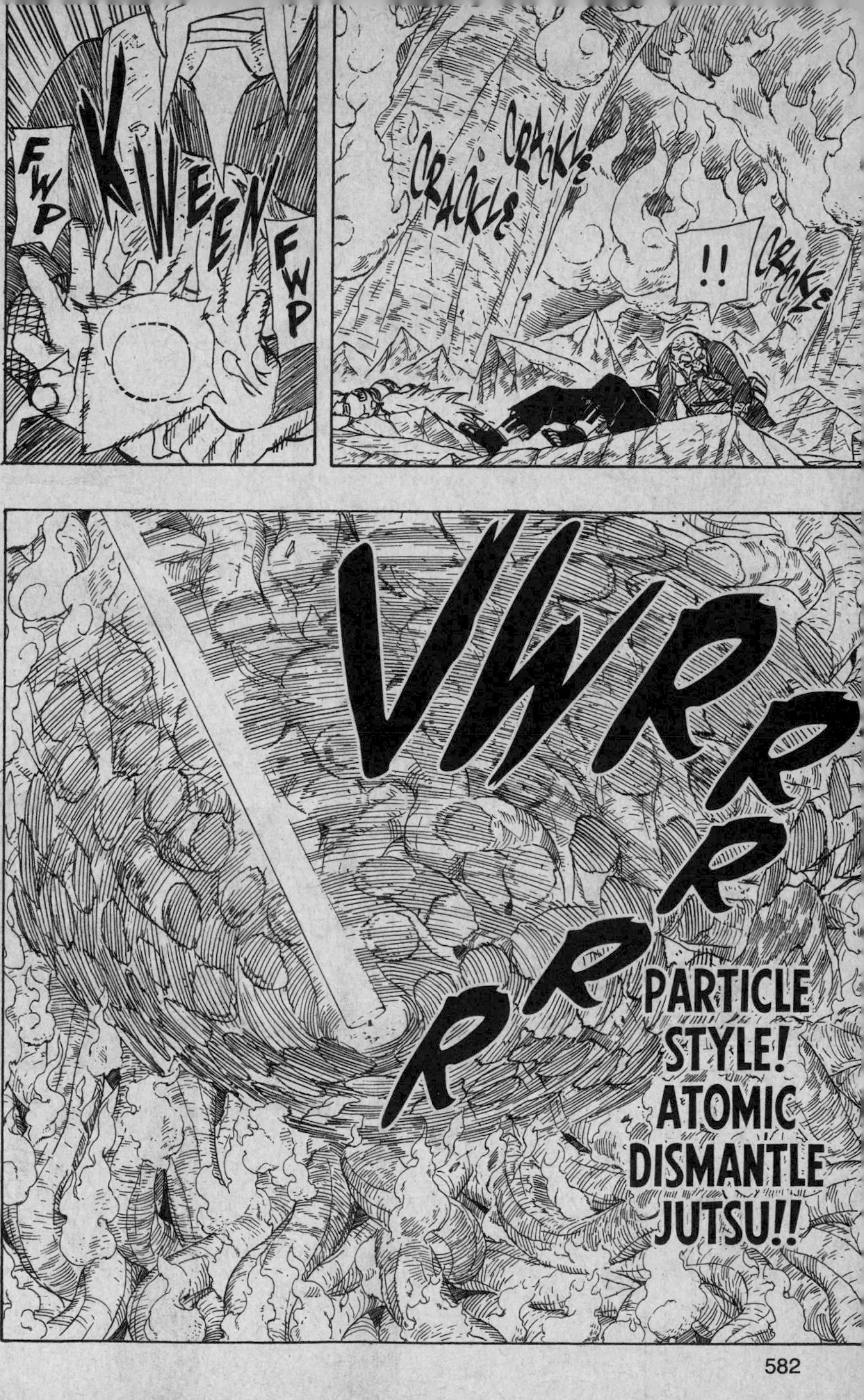
CRACKLE
CRACKLE
!!
CRACKLE
FWP
KWEEN
FWP
VWRRRRR
PARTICLE STYLE! ATOMIC DISMANTLE JUTSU!!

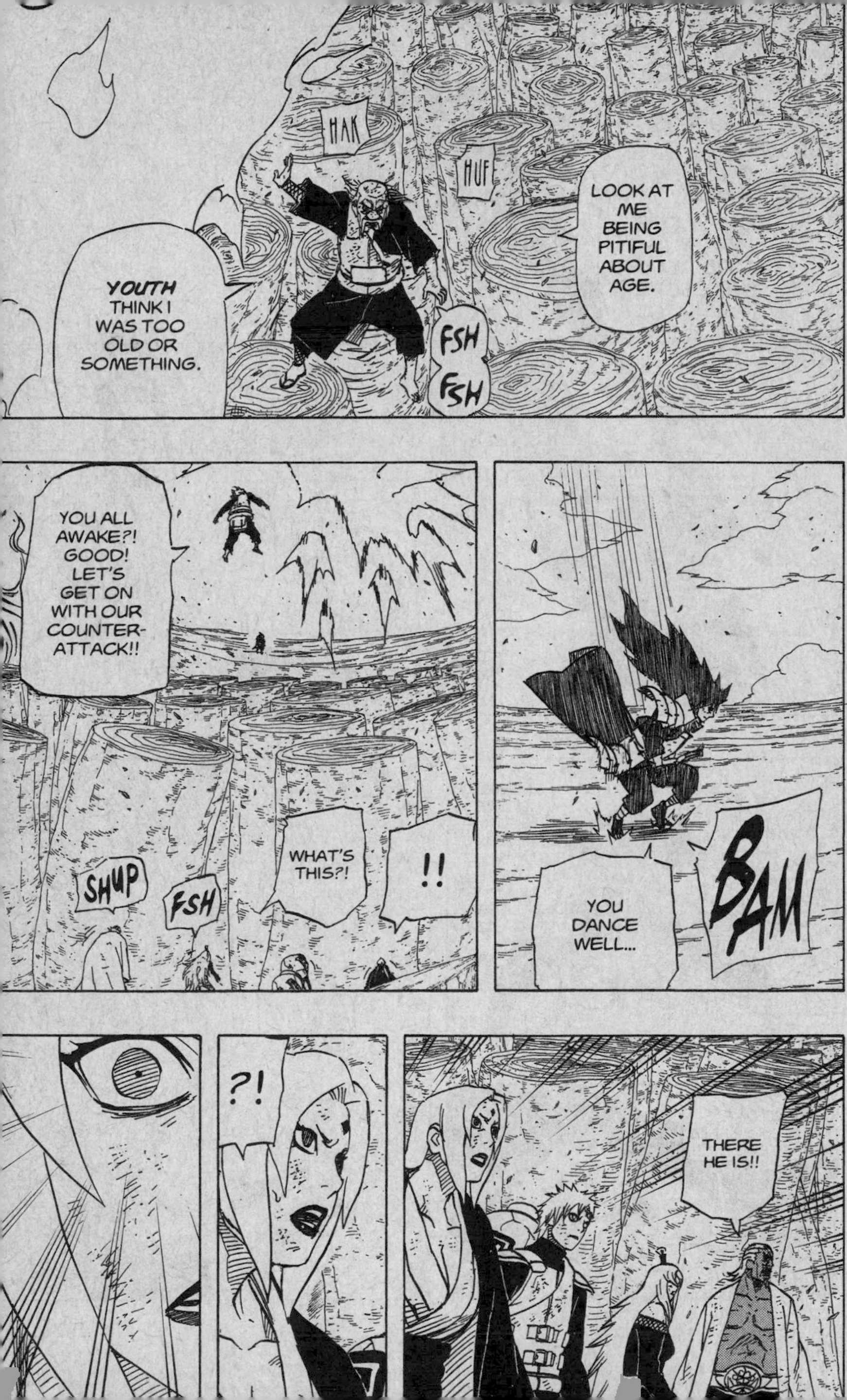
LOOK AT ME BEING PITIFUL ABOUT AGE.
HUF
HAK
FSH
FSH
YOUTH THINK I WAS TOO OLD OR SOMETHING.
BAM
YOU DANCE WELL...
YOU ALL AWAKE?! GOOD! LET'S GET ON WITH OUR COUNTER-ATTACK!!
!!
WHAT'S THIS?!
FSH
SHUP
THERE HE IS!!
?!

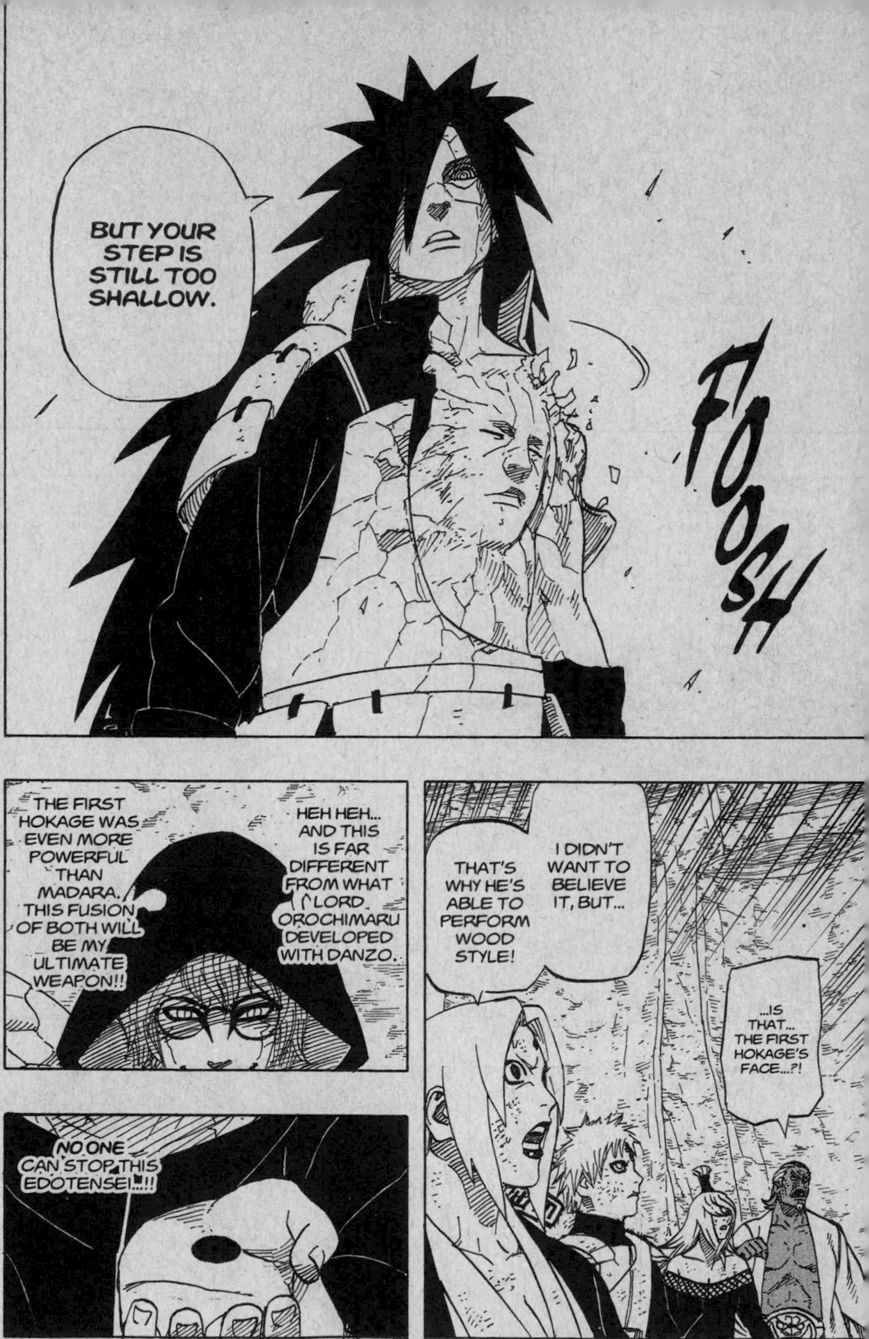
BUT YOUR STEP IS STILL TOO SHALLOW.
FOOSH
...IS THAT... THE FIRST HOKAGE'S FACE...?!
I DIDN'T WANT TO BELIEVE IT, BUT...
THAT'S WHY HE'S ABLE TO PERFORM WOOD STYLE!
HEH HEH... AND THIS IS FAR DIFFERENT FROM WHAT LORD OROCHIMARU DEVELOPED WITH DANZO.
THE FIRST HOKAGE WAS EVEN MORE POWERFUL THAN MADARA. THIS FUSION OF BOTH WILL BE MY ULTIMATE WEAPON!!
NO ONE CAN STOP THIS EDOTENSEI...!!!

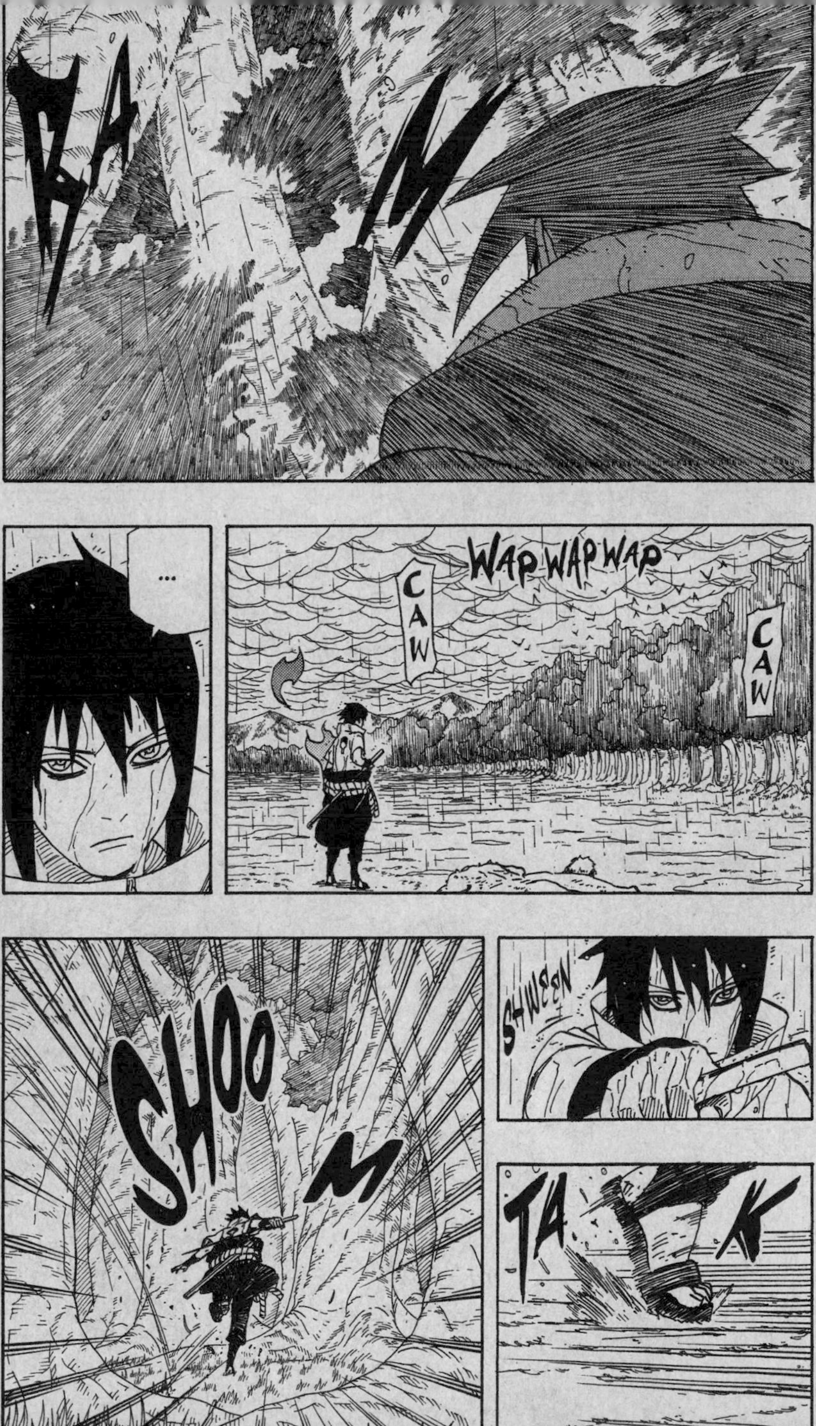
BAM
WAP WAP WAP
CAW
CAW
...
SHWEEN
TAK
SHOOM

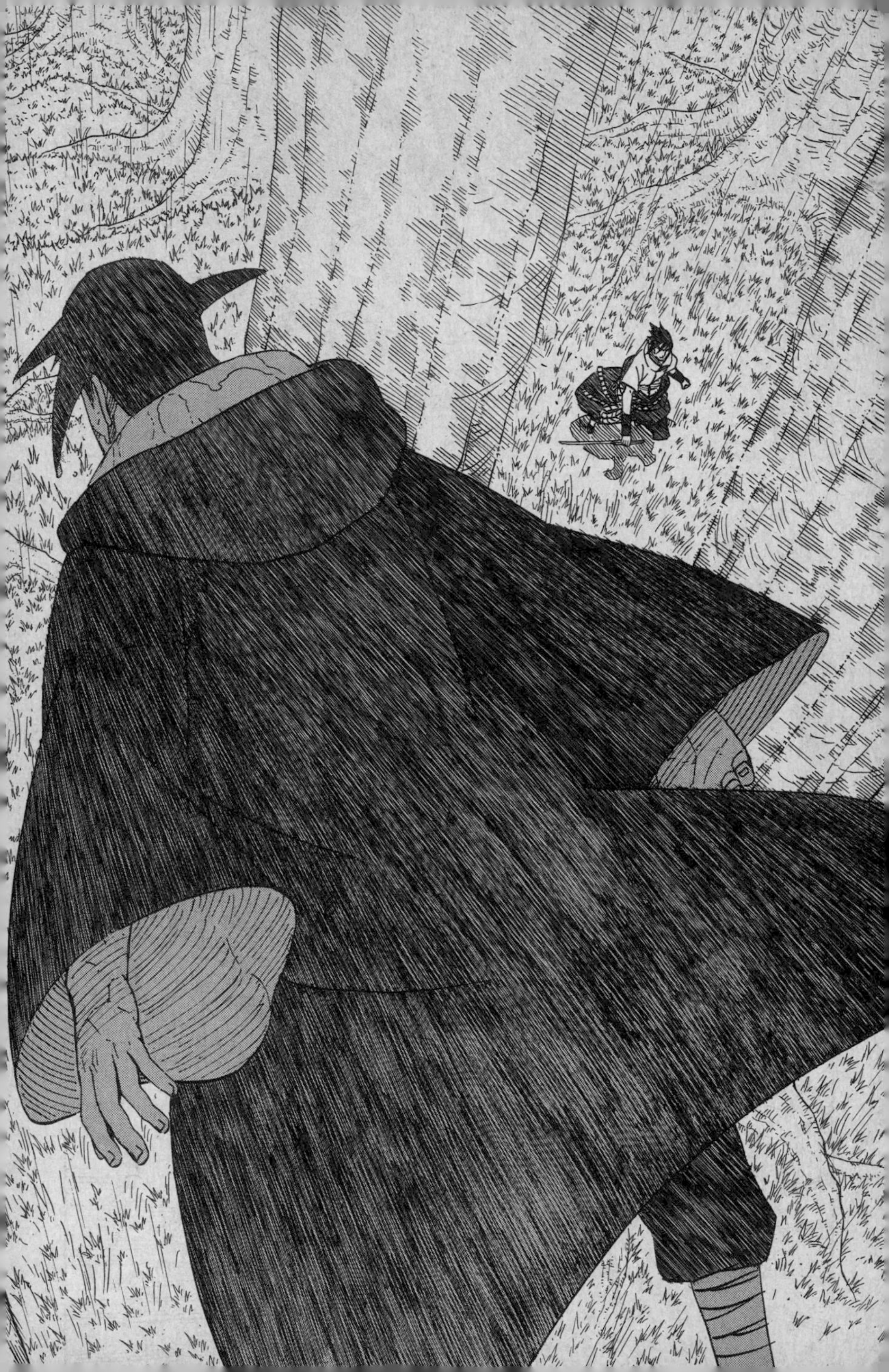

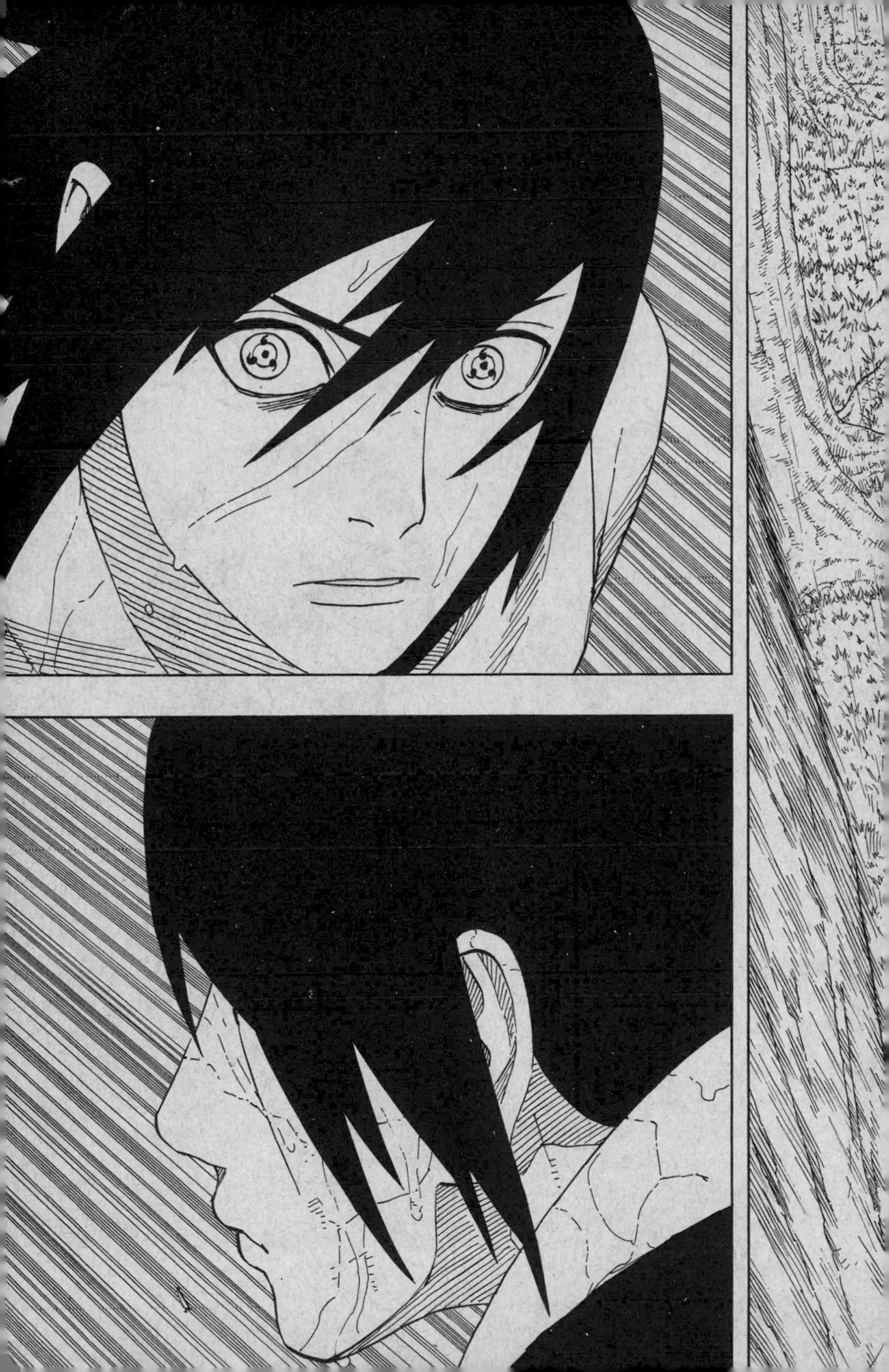

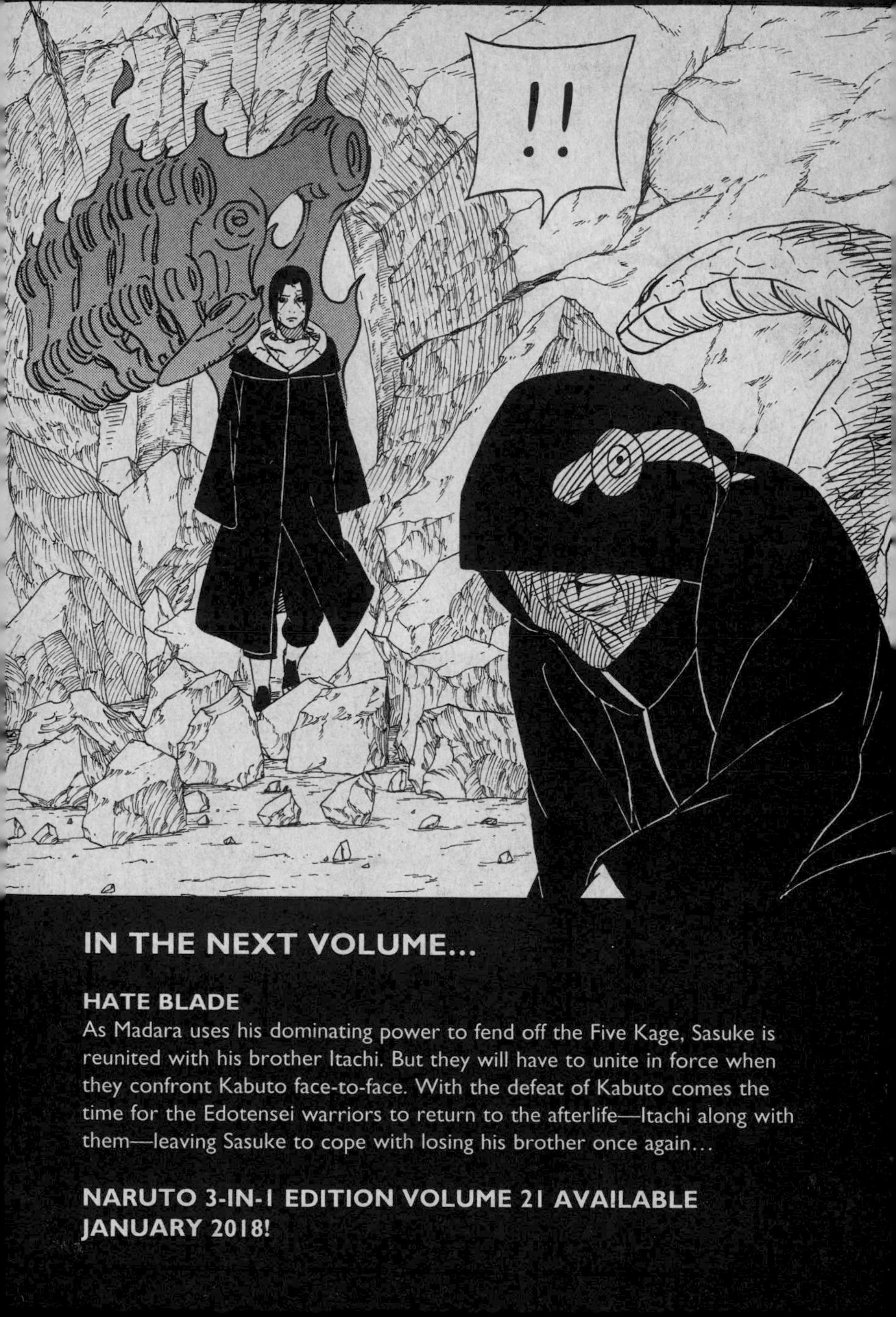
!!

IN THE NEXT VOLUME...

HATE BLADE

As Madara uses his dominating power to fend off the Five Kage, Sasuke is reunited with his brother Itachi. But they will have to unite in force when they confront Kabuto face-to-face. With the defeat of Kabuto comes the time for the Edotensei warriors to return to the afterlife—Itachi along with them—leaving Sasuke to cope with losing his brother once again...

NARUTO 3-IN-1 EDITION VOLUME 21 AVAILABLE JANUARY 2018!

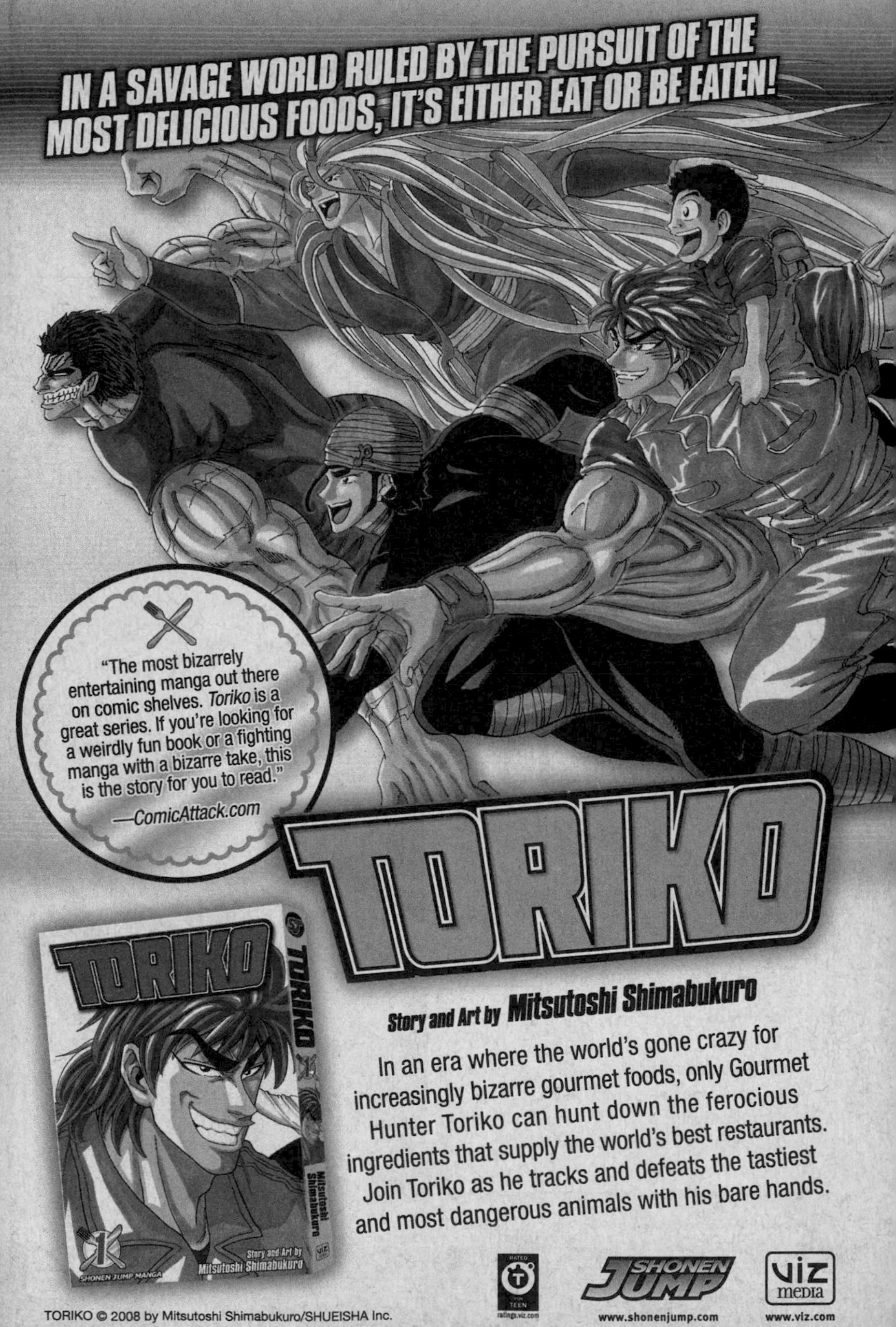
IN A SAVAGE WORLD RULED BY THE PURSUIT OF THE MOST DELICIOUS FOODS, IT'S EITHER EAT OR BE EATEN!
"The most bizarrely entertaining manga out there on comic shelves. *Toriko* is a great series. If you're looking for a weirdly fun book or a fighting manga with a bizarre take, this is the story for you to read."
—ComicAttack.com
TORIKO
TORIKO
1
SHONEN JUMP MANGA
Story and Art by Mitsutoshi Shimabukuro
Story and Art by Mitsutoshi Shimabukuro
In an era where the world's gone crazy for increasingly bizarre gourmet foods, only Gourmet Hunter Toriko can hunt down the ferocious ingredients that supply the world's best restaurants. Join Toriko as he tracks and defeats the tastiest and most dangerous animals with his bare hands.
RATED T FOR TEEN
ratings.viz.com
SHONEN JUMP
www.shonenjump.com
VIZ media
www.viz.com
TORIKO © 2008 by Mitsutoshi Shimabukuro/SHUEISHA Inc.

Black ✽ Clover

STORY & ART BY YUKI TABATA

Asta is a young boy who dreams of becoming the greatest mage in the kingdom. Only one problem—he can't use any magic! Luckily for Asta, he receives the incredibly rare five-leaf clover grimoire that gives him the power of anti-magic. Can someone who can't use magic really become the Wizard King? One thing's for sure—Asta will never give up!

www.viz.com

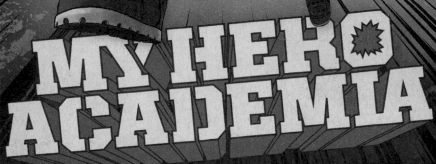

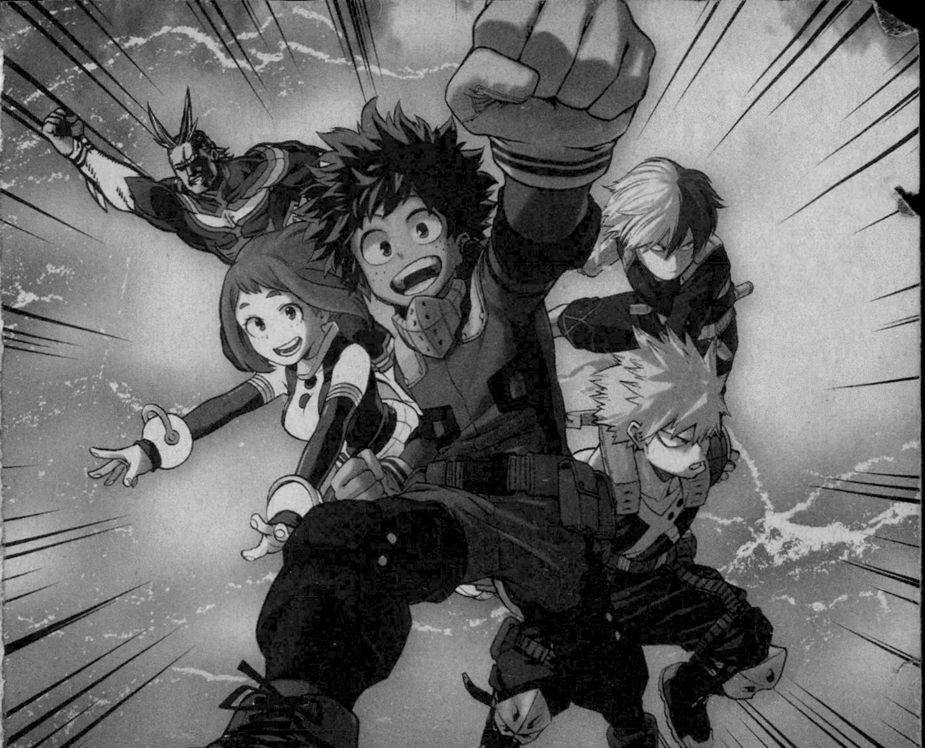
MY HERO ACADEMIA

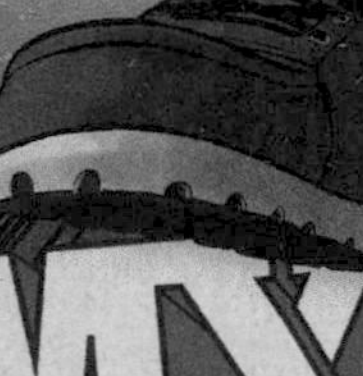
MY HERO ACADEMIA
KOHEI HORIKOSHI

IZUKU MIDORIYA WANTS TO BE A HERO MORE THAN ANYTHING, BUT HE HASN'T GOT AN OUNCE OF POWER IN HIM. WITH NO CHANCE OF GETTING INTO THE U.A. HIGH SCHOOL FOR HEROES, HIS LIFE IS LOOKING LIKE A DEAD END. THEN AN ENCOUNTER WITH ALL MIGHT, THE GREATEST HERO OF ... HIM A CHANCE TO CHANGE HIS DESTINY...

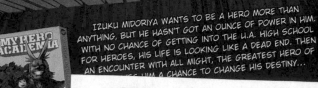